RENEWALS 458-4574

DATE DUE

FEB 2 3			
MAR 2 1			
OCT 2 5			
FEB 1 0			

GAYLORD

PRINTED IN U.S.A.

Hitler

ALSO BY JOACHIM C. FEST

The Face of the Third Reich

JOACHIM C. FEST

Hitler

Translated from the German

by Richard and Clara Winston

A Helen and Kurt Wolff Book

Harcourt Brace Jovanovich, Inc., New York

Library of Congress Cataloging in Publication Data

Fest, Joachim C   1926–
    Hitler.

    "A Helen and Kurt Wolff book."
    1.   Hitler, Adolf, 1889–1945.
DD247.H5F4713   943.086′092′4 [B]   73–18154
ISBN 0–15–141650–8

B C D E

Contents

Prologue   Hitler and Historical Greatness   1

I   AN AIMLESS LIFE
1   Background and Departure   13
2   The Shattered Dream   24
3   The Granite Foundation   36
4   The Flight to Munich   58
5   Redemption by War   67

Interpolation I   The Great Dread   87

II THE ROAD TO POLITICS
1   A Part of the German Future   109
2   Local Triumphs   125
3   Challenging the Powers that Be   160
4   The Putsch   182

III THE LONG WAIT
1   The Vision   199
2   Crises and Resistances   221
3   Deployment for Battle   238

IV   THE TIME OF STRUGGLE

1   From Provincial to National Politics   259
2   The Landslide   287
3   At the Gates of Power   314
4   At the Goal   345

Interpolation II   German Catastrophe or
                   German Consistency?   371

V   SEIZURE OF POWER

1   Legal Revolution   387
2   On the Way to the Führer State   417
3   The Röhm Affair   449

VI   THE YEARS OF PREPARATION

1   The Age of *Faits Accomplis*   483
2   View of an Unperson   511
3   The "Greatest German in History"   539
4   Unleashing the War   574

Interpolation III   The Wrong War   605

VII   VICTORS AND VANQUISHED

1   The Generalissimo   625
2   The Third World War   648
3   Lost Reality   667

VIII CATASTROPHE
   1 Oppositions   697
   2 Götterdämmerung   725

Conclusion   The Dead End   753

Notes   767

Bibliography   817

Index   831

Illustrations

Key to sources, page xii

Between pages 144 and 145

The father, Alois Hitler (StB)
The mother, Klara Pölzl Hitler (StB)
Adolf Hitler as an infant (U)
Hitler at sixteen: drawing by a fellow pupil (HH)
Georg Ritter von Schönerer (HH)
Count Gobineau (SD)
Karl Lueger (HH)
Richard Wagner (SD)
Houston Stewart Chamberlain (SD)
Viennese Jews, 1915 (ÖNB)
The Minorite Church in Vienna, 1909 (F)
Hitler in his dugout (U)
Hitler at a Social Democrat meeting, 1919 (IB)
Prime Minister Kurt Eisner, 1919 (HH)
Eugen Leviné-Nissen (StB)
Members of the Red Army (SD)
Propaganda poster (IFR)
Meeting of the German Workers' Party, January, 1920 (StB)
Gottfried Feder (SD)
Anton Drexler (HH)
Hitler at time of entry into party (U)
Hitler speaks (HH)
Hitler with Alfred Rosenberg and Christian Weber (HH)

ILLUSTRATIONS

Ernst Röhm with friends (StB)
Hermann Esser (HH)
Ernst Pöhner (HH)
Dietrich Eckart (HH)
Julius Streicher (IFR)
Streicher speaks in Munich, 1923 (HH)
Occupation of War Ministry 1923 (SD)
Arrest of mayor of Munich, 1923 (StB)
Hitler and Ludendorff, 1924 (StB)
Hitler with Emil Maurice and Lieutenant Colonel Kriebel (StB)
Sketches by Hitler, 1925 (S)
Gregor Strasser and Joseph Goebbels (StB)
Hitler and Pfeffer von Salomon (HH)

Between pages 304 and 305

Party demonstration, 1925 (HH)
Christmas party, 1925 (SD)
Hitler in the Brown House (HH)
Brown House (HH)
Hitler with Geli Raubal (EPA)
Nuremberg party rally, 1927 (HH)
Hitler at Berlin Sportpalast, 1930 (SD)
Breadlines, 1931 (U)
Goebbels haranguing (HH)
Berlin backyard, 1931 (LB)
Oratorical poses (BAK)
Hitler at Harzburg, 1931 (SD)
Hitler in Brunswick (HH)
Hitler with Franz von Papen and General von Blomberg, 1933 (U)
Hitler with Hindenburg, 1933 (BAK)
Hitler, October, 1934 (SD)
Reichsparteitag, Nuremberg (SD)
Hitler in Breslau (SD)
Hitler greeted by Sudeten women (IFR)
Heinrich and Thomas Mann (SD)
Albert Einstein (StB)

Gerhart Hauptmann (StB)

Gottfried Benn (SD)

Book burning (Sp)

Anti-Semitic outbreaks (HH)

Mass arrests, 1933 (F)

Strength-Through-Joy entertainment (StB)

Hitler inaugurating building of autobahnen (U)

The autobahn near Rosenheim, 1937 (StB)

Hitler at harvest thanksgiving celebration (U)

Hitler with photographer Heinrich Hoffmann (HH)

Between pages 464 and 465

Hitler and Winifred Wagner (HH)

Hitler steering a motorboat (HH)

Hitler sledding (HH)

Hitler with Goebbels (SD)

Hitler in Nuremberg (U)

Hitler and Röhm, 1934 (U)

Hitler at Nuremberg party rally, 1936 (HH)

Vaults of light (IB)

Memorial service in Nuremberg (U & LB)

Memorial procession, Munich, 1935 (U)

Angelika Raubal (HH)

Hitler and Eva Braun at Obersalzberg (StB)

Hitler with his dog (U)

Plan for the rebuilding of Berlin (S)

Hitler sketches, 1925 (S)

Hitler at the Hofburg, Vienna (SD, HH)

SS forcing Viennese Jews to clean sidewalks (F)

Hitler visiting Mussolini in Florence, 1938 (SD)

Chamberlain at Obersalzberg, 1938 (HH)

German troops entering Prague, 1939 (CTK)

Hitler at the window of the Hradschin (SD)

Ribbentrop reporting to Hitler, August, 1939 (HH)

Hitler and Ribbentrop in Poland, 1939 (StB)

Hitler and staff members inspecting West Wall (U)

ILLUSTRATIONS

Between pages 592 and 593

German tanks entering Poland (U)

Warsaw, SS operation (StB)

Hitler looking at burning Warsaw (SD)

Warsaw in flames (HH)

Polish cavalry attack (St)

Hitler's reaction to French armistice, June, 1940 (SD)

Hitler in Paris, 1940 (HH)

German advance in the East, 1943 (StB)

Sketch for Memorial Pyramid (UA)

Heinrich Himmler (SD)

Ribbentrop, Hitler, Bormann (HH)

Pogroms and liquidations, 1942 (StB, StB, HP)

Digging dugouts near Vitebsk (U)

Interrogation of German generals and officers in Russia (U)

Dead German soldiers at Stalingrad (U)

Hitler with heads of Wehrmacht listening to Keitel (U)

Hitler and Dr. Morell (HH)

Dining room in Wolf's Lair (HH)

Stauffenberg at headquarters (SD)

Von Hase and von Witzleben (BAK)

Julius Leber (U)

General Stieff (U)

Major General von Moltke (StB)

Carl Goerdeler (StB)

Hitler, Mussolini, Bormann, Göring, and Ribbentrop (HH)

Werner von Haeften (U)

Ludwig Beck (U)

York von Wartenburg (U)

Von Tresckow (U)

Admiral Canaris (U)

Von Oster (U)

Hitler, July 20, 1944 (HH)

Hitler at the Berghof (HH)

Hitler at headquarters (HH)

Hitler's bunker (KE, HH)

Hitler and Hitler Youths, 1945 (U)
Last photograph of Hitler (SD)
Soviet soldiers in Berlin (Sp)

KEY TO SOURCES

BAK (Bundesarchiv Koblenz)
CTK (Ceskosloveneska Tiskova, Kancelar, Prague)
EPA (European Press Photo Association, Munich)
F (Joachim C. Fest, Hamburg)
HH (Zeitgeschichtliches Bildarchiv Heinrich Hoffmann, Munich)
HP (Heinrich Posener, Hamburg)
IB (Illustrierter Beobachter, Institut für Zeitgeschichte, Munich)
IFR (Interfoto Friedrich Rauch, Munich)
KE (Klaus Eschen, Berlin)
LB (Landesbildstelle Berlin)
ÖNB (Bildarchiv der Österreichischen Nationalbibliothek, Vienna)
S (Albert Speer, Heidelberg)
SD (Bilderdienst Süddeutscher Verlag, Munich)
Sp (Spiegel-Bildarchiv, Hamburg)
St (Stern-Bildarchiv, Hamburg)
StB (Staatsbibliothek Preussischer Kulturbesitz, Bildarchiv, Berlin)
StV (August Kubizek, *Adolf Hitler, Mein Jugendfreund,* Leopold Stocker
    Verlag, Graz 1953)
U (Ullstein GmbH Bilderdienst, Berlin)
UA (Ullstein Archiv, Berlin)
U.-P. (Universal-Photo, Paris)

Hitler and Historical Greatness

> Neither blindness nor ignorance corrupts people and
> governments. They soon realize where the path they
> have taken is leading them. But there is an impulse
> within them, favored by their natures and reinforced
> by their habits, which they do not resist; it continues
> to propel them forward as long as they have a rem-
> nant of strength. He who overcomes himself is divine.
> Most see their ruin before their eyes; but they go on
> into it.[1]
>
> Leopold von Ranke

History records no phenomenon like him. Ought we to call him "great"? No one evoked so much rejoicing, hysteria, and expectation of salvation as he; no one so much hate. No one else produced, in a solitary course lasting only a few years, such incredible accelerations in the pace of history. No one else so changed the state of the world and left behind such a wake of ruins as he did. It took a coalition of almost all the world powers to wipe him from the face of the earth in a war lasting nearly six years, to kill him—to quote an army officer of the German resistance—"like a mad dog."

Hitler's peculiar greatness is essentially linked to the quality of excess. It was a tremendous eruption of energy that shattered all existing standards. Granted, gigantic scale is not necessarily equivalent to historic greatness; there is power in triviality also. But he was not only gigantic and not only trivial. The eruption he unleashed was stamped throughout almost every one of its stages, down to the weeks of final collapse, by his guiding will. In many speeches, he recalled, with a distinctly rapturous note, the period of his beginnings, when he had "nothing at all to back (him), nothing, no name, no fortune, no press, nothing at all, nothing whatsoever," and how, entirely by his own efforts, he had risen from "poor devil" to rule over Germany and soon over part of the world as well. "That has been almost miraculous!"[2] In fact, to a virtually unprecedented degree, he created everything out of himself and was himself everything at once: his own teacher, organizer of a party and author of its ideology, tactician and demagogic savior, leader, statesman, and for a decade the "axis" of the world. He refuted the dictum that all revolutions devour their children; for

3

he was, as has been said, "the Rousseau, the Mirabeau, the Robespierre and the Napoleon of his revolution; he was its Marx, its Lenin, its Trotsky and its Stalin. By character and nature he may have been far inferior to most of these, but he nevertheless managed to achieve what all of them could not: he dominated his revolution in every phase, even in the moment of defeat. That argues a considerable understanding of the forces he evoked."[3]

He also had an amazing instinct for what forces could be mobilized at all and did not allow prevailing trends to deceive him. The period of his entry into politics was wholly dominated by the liberal bourgeois system. But he grasped the latent oppositions to it and by bold and wayward combinations seized upon these factors and incorporated them into his program. His conduct seemed foolish to political minds, and for years the arrogant *Zeitgeist* did not take him seriously. The mockery he earned was justified by his appearance, his rhetorical flights, and the theatrical atmosphere he deliberately created. Yet in a manner difficult to describe he always stood above his banal and dull-witted aspects. One particular source of his strength lay in his ability to build castles in the air with an intrepid and acute rationality.

In 1925, Hitler had been sitting in a furnished room in Munich, a failed Bavarian local politician, drawing his sketches of imaginary arches of triumph and domed halls. In spite of the collapse of all his hopes after the attempted putsch of November, 1923, he did not take back a single one of his words, did not mute his battle cry, and refused to modify any of his plans for domination of the world. In those days, he later remarked, everyone had branded him a visionary. "They always said I was crazy." But only a few years later everything he had wanted was reality, or at any rate a realizable project, and those institutions that had recently seemed to be permanent and unchallenged were on their way out: democracy and political-party government, unions, international workers' solidarity, the European system of alliances, and the League of Nations. "Who was right?" Hitler triumphantly demanded. "The visionary or the others?—I was right."[4]

In this ability to uncover the deeper spirit and tendencies of the age, and to represent those tendencies, there certainly is an element of historic greatness. "It appears to be the destiny of greatness," Jacob Burckhardt wrote in his famous essay on historical greatness, in *Reflections on History,* "that it executes a will going beyond individual desires." Burckhardt speaks of "the mysterious coincidence between the egoism of the individual and the communal will." In general terms and at times in specific details, Hitler's career seems like a classic illustration of this tenet. The following chapters contain a wealth of evidence of that. The same is true for the other elements that in Burckhardt's view constitute historical greatness. Irreplaceability is one; "he leads a people from one stage of cultivation to

4

another." He "stands not only for the program and the fury of a party, but for a more general aim." He manifests the ability "to jump boldly across the abyss"; he has the capacity of simplification, the gift of distinguishing between real and illusory powers, and finally the exceptional will power that creates an atmosphere of fascination. "Contest at close quarters becomes utterly impossible. Anyone desiring to oppose him must live outside of the reach of the man, with his enemies, and can meet him only on the battlefield."[5]

And yet we hesitate to call Hitler "great." Perhaps what gives us pause is not so much the criminal features in this man's psychopathic face. For world history is not played out in the area that is "the true site of morality," and Burckhardt has also spoken of the "strange exemption from the ordinary moral code" which we tend to grant in our minds to great individuals.[6] We may surely ask whether the absolute crime of mass extermination planned and committed by Hitler is not of an utterly different nature, overstepping the bounds of the moral context recognized by both Hegel and Burckhardt. Our doubts of Hitler's historic greatness also spring from another factor. The phenomenon of the great man is primarily aesthetic, very rarely moral in nature; and even if we were prepared to make allowances in the latter realm, in the former we could not. An ancient tenet of aesthetics holds that one who for all his remarkable traits is a repulsive human being, is unfit to be a hero. It may be—and evidence will be offered—that this description fits Hitler very well. His many opaque, instinctual traits, his intolerance and vindictiveness, his lack of generosity, his banal and naked materialism—power was the only motive he would recognize, and he repeatedly forced his table companions to join him in his scorn of anything else as "bosh"—and in general his unmistakably vulgar characteristics give his image a cast of repugnant ordinariness that simply will not square with the traditional concept of greatness. "Impressiveness in this world," wrote Bismarck in a letter, "is always akin to the fallen angel who is beautiful but without peace, great in his plans and efforts, but without success, proud and sad." If this is true greatness, Hitler's distance from it is immeasurable.

It may be that the concept of greatness has become problematical. In one of the pessimistically toned political essays Thomas Mann wrote in exile, he used the terms "greatness" and "genius" in regard to a then triumphant Hitler, but he spoke of "botched greatness" and of a debased stage of genius.[7] In such contradictions a concept takes leave of itself. Perhaps this idea of greatness also springs from the historical consciousness of a past era, which placed almost all its weight on the actors and ideas of the historical process and almost none on the extensive network of forces.

Today this tendency is reversed, and we ascribe little importance to personality compared with the interests, relationships, and material conflicts within the society. This approach has also been applied to Hitler. Thus he has been portrayed as the "hireling" or "sword arm" of capitalism, who organized the class struggle from above and in 1933 subjugated the masses, who had been pressing for political and social self-determination. Later, by unleashing the war, he carried out the expansionist aims of his employers. In this story, which has been presented in a great many variants, Hitler appears as totally interchangeable, "the most vulgar of tin soldiers," as one of the leftist analysts of Fascism wrote as early as 1929. For the proponents of this theory he was, at any rate, merely one factor among others, not a determining cause.

Fundamentally, the argument is directed at the very possibility of arriving at historical knowledge by way of a biographical study. No single person, it runs, can ever make manifest the historical process in all its complexities and contradictions, upon all its many, forever shifting areas of tension. Strictly speaking, the argument continues, the biographical approach merely continues the old tradition of court and adulatory writing, and after 1945 went right along employing basically the same methodology, with merely a change of sign: Hitler remained the all-moving, irresistible force and "merely changed his quality; the savior became the diabolic seducer."[8] Ultimately, the argument continues, every biographical account willy-nilly serves the needs for justification felt by the millions of onetime followers who can easily see themselves as the victims of so much "greatness" or who at any rate can place all responsibility for what happened upon the pathological whims of a diabolic and imperious leader. In short, biography amounts to a surreptitious maneuver in the course of a broad campaign of exculpation.

This argument is strengthened by the fact that the personality of Hitler scarcely arouses our interest. Over the years it remains oddly pallid and expressionless, acquiring tension and fascination only in contact with the age. In Hitler there is a great deal of what Walter Benjamin called "social character." That is, he incorporated all the anxieties, protests, and hopes of the age in his own self to a remarkable degree. But in him all emotions were enormously exaggerated, distorted, and infiltrated with weird features, though never unrelated or incongruent to the historical background. Consequently, Hitler's life would hardly deserve the telling if it were not that extrapersonal tendencies or conditions came to light in it; his biography is essentially part of the biography of the age. And because his life was inextricably linked to his time, it is worth the telling.

Necessarily, then, the background comes more prominently into the fore than is customary in biographies. Hitler must be shown against a dense pattern of objective factors that conditioned, promoted, impelled, and sometimes braked him. The romantic German notion of politics and the peculiarly morose grayness of the Weimar Republic belong equally in this background. So also do the declassing of the nation by the Treaty of Versailles and the secondary social declassing of large sections of the population by the inflation and the world-wide Depression; the weakness of the democratic tradition in Germany; fears of the miscalculations of conservatives who had lost their grip; finally, the widespread fears aroused by the transition from a familiar system to one new and still uncertain. All this was overlaid by the craving to find simple formulas to account for the opaque, intricately involved causes of moroseness, and to flee from all the vexations the age provided into the shelter of an imperious authority.

Hitler as the point of convergence for so many nostalgias, anxieties, and resentments became a historical figure. It is no longer possible to conceive the second quarter of the twentieth century without him. In him an individual once again demonstrated the stupendous power of a solitary person over the historical process. Our account will show to what virulence and potency the many intersecting moods of an age can be brought when demagogic genius, an extraordinary gift for political tactics, and the capacity for that "mysterious coincidence" Burckhardt spoke of, meet in a single person. "History tends at times to become suddenly concentrated in one man, who is then obeyed by the world."[9] It cannot be too strongly emphasized that Hitler's rise was made possible only by the unique conjunction of individual with general prerequisites, by the barely decipherable correspondence that the man entered into with the age and the age with the man.

This close connection tends to refute that school of thought which attributes superhuman abilities to Hitler. His career depended not so much on his demonic traits as on his typical, "normal" characteristics. The course of his life reveals the weaknesses and ideological bias of all the theories that represent Hitler as a fundamental antithesis to the age and its people. He was not so much the great contradiction of the age as its mirror image. We will constantly be encountering traces of that correlation.

The signal importance of objective preconditions (which this book attempts to deal with in a series of special "interpolations") also raises the question of how Hitler particularly affected the course of events. There is no doubt that a movement gathering together all the racist-nationalistic tendencies would have formed during the twenties without the intervention of Hitler's influence and following. But it would very likely have been only one more political grouping within the context of the system. What Hitler conferred upon it was that unique mixture of fantastic vision and consistency which, as we shall see, to a large extent expressed his nature. The radicalism of Gregor Strasser or Goebbels never amounted to more than an infraction of the existing rules of the political game, which underlined the validity of those rules by the very act of challenging them. Hitler's radicalism, on the other hand, annulled all existing assumptions and introduced a novel element into the game. To be sure, the numerous emergencies of the period would have led to crises, but without Hitler they would never have

7

come to those intensifications and explosions that we shall witness. From the first party battle in the summer of 1921 to the last few days of April, 1945, when he expelled Göring and Himmler, Hitler held a wholly unchallenged position; he would not even allow any principle, any doctrine, to hold sway, but only his own dictates. He made history with a highhandedness that even in his own days seemed anachronistic. It is unimaginable that history will ever again be made in quite the same fashion—a succession of private inspirations, filled with surprising coups and veerings, breathtaking perfidies, ideological self-betrayals, but with a tenaciously pursued vision in the background. Something of his singular character, of the subjective element he imposed upon the course of history, emerges in the phrase "Hitler Fascism" favored by Marxist theoreticians in the thirties. In this sense National Socialism has quite rightly been defined as Hitlerism.

But the question remains whether Hitler was not the last politician who could so largely ignore the weight of conditions and interests; whether the coercion of objective factors has not grown visibly stronger, and whether with this the historical possibility of a great doer has not grown ever smaller. For, unquestionably, historical rank is dependent upon the freedom that the person who acts maintains in the face of circumstances. In a secret speech delivered in the early summer of 1939, Hitler declared: "There must be no acceptance of the principle of evading the solution to problems by adjustment to circumstances. Rather, the task is to adjust circumstances to requirements."[10] Following this motto, he, the "visionary," practiced an *imitatio* of the great man; the attempt was boldly carried to the utmost extreme, and ultimately failed. It would appear that such attempts ended with him—just as so much else ended with him.

If men do not make history in the way that traditional hero-worshiping literature assumed, or do so to a far smaller extent, Hitler certainly made much more history than many others. But at the same time history made him, to an altogether extraordinary degree. Nothing entered into this "unperson," as he is defined in one of the following chapters, that was not already present; but whatever did enter acquired a tremendous dynamic. Hitler's biography is the story of an incessant, intensive process of interchange.

We are still asking, however, whether historical greatness can be associated with a hollow individuality. It is challenging to imagine what Hitler's fate would have been had history not produced the circumstances that first awakened him and made him the mouthpiece of millions of defense complexes. It is easy to picture his ignored existence on the fringes of society, to see him embittered and misanthropic, longing for a great destiny and unable to forgive life for having refused him the heroic role he craved. "For the oppressive thing was . . . the complete lack of attention we found

8

in those days from which I suffered most," Hitler wrote concerning the period of his entry into politics.[11] The collapse of order, the age's anxieties and climate of change, played into his hands by giving him the chance to emerge from the shadow of anonymity. Great men, in Burckhardt's judgment, are needed specifically in times of terror.[12]

The phenomenon of Hitler demonstrates, to an extent surpassing all previous experience, that historical greatness can be linked with paltriness on the part of the individual concerned. For considerable periods his personality seemed disintegrated, as if it had evaporated into unreality; and it was this seemingly fictitious character of the man that misled so many conservative politicians and Marxist historians—in curious agreement—to regard Hitler as the instrument for the ends of others. Far from possessing any greatness and any political, let alone historical, stature, he seemed to embody the very type of the "agent," one who acts for others. But both the conservatives and the Marxists were deceiving themselves. It was actually an ingredient in Hitler's recipe for tactical success that he made political capital out of this mistake, in which class resentment against the petty bourgeois was then, and still is, expressed. His biography includes, among other things, the story of a gradual disillusionment. In his day he excited a good deal of ironic contempt, and that attitude persists, though kept in check by the memory of the toll of lives he took. But it was, and still is, a misreading of his character.

The course of this life, and the pattern of events themselves, will throw light upon the whole matter. Yet here we may well ask ourselves a few pertinent questions. If Hitler had succumbed to an assassination or an accident at the end of 1938, few would hesitate to call him one of the greatest of German statesmen, the consummator of Germany's history. The aggressive speeches and *Mein Kampf,* the anti-Semitism and the design for world dominion, would presumably have fallen into oblivion, dismissed as the man's youthful fantasies, and only occasionally would critics remind an irritated nation of them. Six and one-half years separated Hitler from such renown. Granted, only premature death could have given him that, for by nature he was headed toward destruction and did not make an exception of himself. Can we call him great?

BOOK I

An Aimless Life

Chapter 1

The need to magnify themselves, to
bestir themselves, is characteristic
of all illegitimates.

Jacob Burckhardt

BACKGROUND AND
DEPARTURE

All through his life he made the strongest efforts to conceal as well as to
glorify his own personality. Hardly any other prominent figure in history so
covered his tracks, as far as his personal life was concerned. With a carefulness verging on pedantry, he stylized his persona. The concept he had of
himself was more like a monument than like a man. From the start he
endeavored to hide behind it. Rigid in expression, early conscious of his
calling, at the age of thirty-five he had already withdrawn into the concentrated, frozen inapproachability of the Great Leader. In obscurity legends
form; in obscurity the aura of being one of the elect can grow. But that
obscurity which cloaks the early history of his life also accounted for the
anxieties, the secrecy, and the curiously histrionic character of his existence.

Even as leader of the struggling young NSDAP (National Socialist
Workers' Party) he regarded interest in his private life as insulting. As
Chancellor he forbade all publicity about it.[1] The statements of all those
who knew him more than casually, from a friend of his youth to the
members of his intimate dinner circle, stress how he liked to keep his
distance and preserve his privacy. "Throughout his life he had an indescribable aloofness about him."[2] He spent several years in a "home for
men"; but of all the many people who met him there, few could recall him
later. He moved about among them as a permanent stranger, attracting no
attention. At the beginning of his political career he jealously took care
that no pictures of him were published. Some have explained this obsession
as the strategy of a born propagandist; it has been argued that as a man of
mystery he deliberately aroused interest in himself.

13

But even if this is so, his efforts at concealment did not spring entirely from the desire to introduce a note of allure into his portrait. Rather, we have here the anxieties of a constricted nature overwhelmed by a sense of its own ambiguousness. He was forever bent on muddying still further the opaque background of his origins and family. When, in 1942, he was informed that a plaque had been set up for him in the village of Spital, he flew into one of his violent rages. He transformed his ancestors into "poor cottagers." He falsified his father's occupation, changing him from a customs official to a postal official. He curtly repulsed the relatives who tried to approach him. For a time his younger sister Paula ran his household at Obersalzberg, but he made her take another name. After the invasion of Austria he forbade Jörg Lanz von Liebenfels to publish; he owed some vague, early suggestions to this man, the eccentric exponent of a racist philosophy. Reinhold Hanisch was his onetime chum from his days in the home for men; he had Hanisch murdered. He insisted that he was no one's disciple. All knowledge had come to him from his own inspiration, by the grace of Providence and out of his dialogues with the Spirit. Similarly, he would be no one's son. The picture of his parents emerges in the dimmest of outlines from the autobiographical chapters of his book, *Mein Kampf,* and only to the extent that it supported the legend of his life.

His efforts to muddy the waters were favored by the fact that he came from across the border. Like many of the revolutionaries and conquerors of history, from Alexander to Napoleon to Stalin, he was a foreigner among his countrymen. There is surely a psychological link between this sense of being an outsider and the readiness to employ a whole nation as material for wild and expansive projects, even to the point of destroying the nation. At the turning point of the war, during one of the bloody battles of attrition, when his attention was called to the tremendous losses among newly commissioned officers, he replied with surprised incomprehension: "But that's what the young men are there for."

But foreignness did not sufficiently conceal him. His feeling for order, rules, and respectability was always at variance with his rather unsavory family history, and evidently he never lost a sense of the distance between his origins and his claims on the world. His own past always stirred his anxieties. In 1930, when rumors arose that his enemies were preparing to throw light on his family background, Hitler appeared very upset: "These people must not be allowed to find out who I am. They must not know where I come from and who my family is."

On both his father's and his mother's side, his family came from a remote and poverty-stricken area in the Dual Monarchy, the Waldviertel between the Danube and the Bohemian border. A wholly peasant population, with involved kinship ties resulting from generations of inbreeding, occupied the villages whose names repeatedly recur in Hitler's ancestral history: Döllersheim, Strones, Weitra, Spital, Walterschlag. These are all small, scattered settlements in a rather wretched, heavily wooded land-scape. The name Hitler, Hiedler, or Hüttler is probably of Czech origin (Hidlar, Hidlarcek); it first crops up in one of its many variants in the 1430's. Through the generations, however, it remained the name of small farmers; none of them broke out of the pre-existing social framework.

At House No. 13 in Strones, the home of Johann Trummelschlager, an unmarried servant girl by the name of Maria Anna Schicklgruber gave birth to a child on June 7, 1837. That same day the child was baptized Alois. In the registry of births in Döllersheim parish the space for the name of the child's father was left blank. Nor was this changed five years later when the mother married the unemployed journeyman miller Johann Georg Hiedler. That same year she turned her son over to her husband's brother, Johann Nepomuk Hüttler, a Spital farmer—presumably because she thought she could not raise the child properly. At any rate the Hiedlers, the story has it, were so impoverished that "ultimately they did not even have a bed left and slept in a cattle trough."

These two brothers are two of the presumptive fathers of Alois Schickl-gruber. The third possibility, according to a rather wild story that neverthe-less comes from one of Hitler's closer associates, is a Graz Jew named Frankenberger in whose household Maria Anna Schicklgruber is said to have been working when she became pregnant. Such, at any rate, is the testimony of Hans Frank, for many years Hitler's lawyer, later Governor General of Poland. In the course of his trial at Nuremberg Frank reported that in 1930 Hitler had received a letter from a son of his half-brother Alois. Possibly the intention of the letter was blackmail. It indulged in dark hints about "very odd circumstances in our family history." Frank was assigned to look into the matter confidentially. He found some indications to support the idea that Frankenberger had been Hitler's grandfather. The lack of hard evidence, however, makes this thesis appear exceedingly dubious—for all that we may also wonder what had prompted Frank at Nuremberg to ascribe a Jewish ancestor to Hitler. Recent researches have further shaken the credibility of his statement, so that the whole notion can scarcely stand serious investigation. In any case, its real significance is independent of its being true or false. What is psychologically of crucial importance is the fact that Frank's findings forced Hitler to doubt his own descent. A renewed investigation undertaken in August, 1942, by the Gestapo, on orders from Heinrich Himmler, produced no tangible results. All the other theories about Hitler's grandfather are also full of holes, although some ambitious combinational ingenuity has gone into the version that traces Alois Schicklgruber's paternity "with a degree of probability bordering on absolute certainty" to Johann Nepomuk Hüttler.[3] Both arguments peter out in the obscurity of confused relationships marked by meanness, dullness, and rustic bigotry. The long and short of it is that Adolf Hitler did not know who his grandfather was.

Twenty-nine years later, after Maria Anna Schicklgruber had died of "consumption in consequence of thoracic dropsy" in Klein-Motten near Strones, and nineteen years after the death of her husband, the brother Johann Nepomuk Hüttler appeared before parish priest Zahnschirm in Döllersheim, accompanied by three acquaintances. He asked for the legitimation of his "foster son," the customs official Alois Schicklgruber, now nearly forty years of age. Not he himself but his deceased brother Johann Georg was the father, he said; Johann had avowed this, and his companions could witness the facts.

The parish priest allowed himself to be deceived or persuaded. In the old registry, under the entry of June 7, 1837, he altered the item "illegitimate" to "legitimate," filled in the space for the name of the father as requested, and inserted a false marginal note: "The undersigned confirm that Georg Hitler, registered as the father, who is well known to the undersigned witnesses, admits to being the father of the child Alois as stated by the child's mother, Anna Schicklgruber, and has requested the entry of his name in the present baptismal register. XXX Josef Romeder, witness; XXX Johann Breiteneder, witness; XXX Engelbert Paukh." Since the three witnesses could not write, they signed with three crosses, and the priest put in their names. But he neglected to insert the date. His own signature was also missing, as well as that of the (long-since deceased) parents. Though scarcely legal, the legitimation took effect: from January, 1877, on Alois Schicklgruber called himself Alois Hitler.

This rustic intrigue may very well have been set in motion by Alois himself. For he was an enterprising man who in the interval had made quite a career for himself. He may therefore have felt the need to provide himself with security and a firm footing by obtaining an "honorable" name. At the age of thirteen he had been apprenticed to a shoemaker in Vienna. But, by and by, he decided against being an artisan and instead entered the Austrian Finance Office. He advanced rapidly as a customs official and was ultimately promoted to the highest civil service rank open to a man of his education. He was fond of appearing as the representative of constituted authority on public occasions and made a point of being addressed by his correct title. One of his associates in the customs office called him "strict, precise, even pedantic," and he himself told a relation who asked his advice about a son's choice of occupation that working for the treasury demanded absolute obedience and sense of duty, and that it was not for "drinkers, borrowers, card players, and other people who go in for immoral conduct." The photographs that he usually had made on the occasion of his promotions show a portly man with the wary face of an official. Underneath that official mask, bourgeois competence and bourgeois pleasure in public display can be discerned. He presents himself to the viewer with considerable dignity and complacency, his uniform aglitter with buttons.

But this respectability overlaid an obviously unstable temperament marked by a propensity for impulsive decisions. Among other things, his frequent changes of residence suggest a restiveness that the sober practical work of the customs service could not satisfy. He moved at least eleven times in barely twenty-five years—although some of these moves were connected with his job. He also married three times. While his first wife was still alive, his subsequent second wife expected a child by him, and the same was true for the subsequent third during the life of the second. His first wife, Anna Glassl, was fourteen years his senior; his last, Klara Pölzl, twenty-three years younger. She had first entered his household as a maid. Like the Hiedlers or Hüttlers, she came from Spital; and after his change of name she was his niece, at least legally, so that a dispensation from the church had to be obtained for them to marry. The question of whether she was indeed related to him by blood remains as unanswerable as the question of who Alois Hitler's father was. She quietly and conscientiously carried out her domestic tasks, regularly attended church—in accordance with her husband's wishes—and was never quite able to rise above the status of housemaid and bedmate. For many years she had difficulty in regarding herself as the customs official's wife, and used to address her husband as "Uncle Alois." Her picture shows the face of a modest village girl, earnest, impassive, with a trace of despondency.

Adolf Hitler, born April 20, 1889, in Braunau am Inn, in the suburban house numbered 219, was the fourth child of this marriage. Three older children, born 1885, 1886, and 1887, had died in infancy; of the two younger, only the sister, Paula, survived. The family also included the children of Alois's second marriage, Alois and Angela. The small border town had no influence on Adolf's development, for the following year his father was transferred to Gross-Schönau in Lower Austria. Adolf was three years old when the family moved again to Passau, and five when his father was transferred to Linz. In 1895 his father bought a farm of nearly ten acres in the vicinity of Lambach, site of a famous old Benedictine monastery where the six-year-old boy served as choir boy and acolyte. There, according to his own account, he often had the opportunity "to intoxicate myself with the solemn splendor of the brilliant church festivals."[4] But his father soon sold the farm again. That same year he retired on pension, at the age of only fifty-eight. Soon afterward he bought a house in Leonding, a small community just outside Linz, and settled down to his retirement years.

In spite of obvious signs of nervous instability, the dominant feature of this picture is one of respectable solidity and instinct for security. But the cloak of legend Hitler threw over this background (later, with the beginnings of the Hitler personality cult, to be embellished by melodramatic touches and sentimental embroidery) contrasts strongly with the reality. The legend suggests deep poverty and domestic hardship, with the chosen boy triumphing over these dire conditions and over the tyrannical efforts of an obtuse father to break the son's spirit. In order to introduce a few

17

effective touches of black into the picture, the son actually made Alois a drunkard. Hitler tells of scolding and pleading with his father in scenes "of abominable shame," tugging and pulling him out of "reeking, smoky taverns" to bring him home.

Hitler portrays himself as invariably victorious in battles on the village common and in the vicinity of the old fortress tower—nothing else would be in keeping with the precocity of genius. According to his story, the other boys accepted him as a born leader, and he was always ready with masterful plans for knightly adventures and exploration projects. Through these innocent games young Adolf developed an interest in warfare and the soldier's trade that pointed toward the future. In retrospect the author of *Mein Kampf* discovered "two outstanding facts as particularly significant" about the "boy of barely eleven": that he had become a nationalist and had learned "to understand and grasp the meaning of history."[5] The whole fable is brought to a neat and affecting conclusion with the father's sudden death, the privations, illness, and death of the beloved mother, and the departure of the poor orphaned boy "who at the age of seventeen had to go far from home and earn his bread."

In reality Adolf Hitler was a wide-awake, lively, and obviously able pupil whose gifts were undermined by an incapacity for regular work. This pattern appeared quite early. He had a distinct tendency to laziness, coupled with an obstinate nature, and was thus more and more inclined to follow his own bent. Aesthetic matters gave him extraordinary pleasure. However, the reports of the various grammar schools he attended show him to have been a good student. On the basis of this, evidently, his parents sent him to the *Realschule,* the secondary school specializing in modern as opposed to classical subjects, in Linz. Here, surprisingly, he proved a total failure. Twice he had to repeat a grade, and a third time he was promoted only after passing a special examination. In diligence his report cards regularly gave him the mark Four ("unsatisfactory"); only in conduct, drawing, and gymnastics did he receive marks of satisfactory or better; in all other subjects he scarcely ever received marks higher than "inadequate" or "adequate." His report card of September, 1905, noted "unsatisfactory" in German, mathematics, and stenography. Even in geography and history, which he himself called his favorite subjects and maintained that he "led the class,"[6] he received only failing grades. On the whole, his record was so poor that he left the school.

This debacle is unquestionably due to a complex of reasons. One significant factor must have been humiliation. If we are to believe Hitler's story that in the peasant village of Leonding he was the uncontested leader of his playmates—not altogether improbable for the son of a civil servant, given the self-esteem of officialdom in Imperial Austria—his sense of status must have suffered a blow in urban Linz. For here he found himself a rough-hewn rustic, a despised outsider among the sons of academics, businessmen, and persons of quality. It is true that at the turn of the century Linz, in spite of its 50,000 inhabitants, was still pretty much of a provincial town with all the dreariness and somnolence the term connotes. Nevertheless, the city certainly impressed upon Hitler a sense of class distinctions. He made "no friends and pals" at the *Realschule*. Nor was the situation any better at the home of ugly old Frau Sekira, where for a time he boarded with five other schoolmates his age during the school week. He remained stiff, aloof, a stranger. One of the former boarders recalls: "None of the five other boys made friends with him. Whereas we schoolmates naturally called one another *du,* he addressed us as *Sie,* and we also said *Sie* to him and did not even think there was anything odd about it." Significantly, Hitler himself at this time first began making those assertions about coming from a good family which in the future unmistakably stamped his style and his manner. The adolescent fop in Linz, as well as the subsequent proletarian in Vienna, would seem to have acquired a tenacious "class consciousness" and a determination to succeed.

Hitler later represented his failure at secondary school as a way of defying his father, who wanted to steer him into the civil service where the father himself had had so successful a career. In after years Hitler told a vivid story about being taken to the main customs office in Linz; his father hoped the visit would fill him with enthusiasm for the profession, while he himself was filled with "repugnance and hatred" and could see the place only as a "government cage" in which "the old men sat crouching on top of one another, as close as monkeys." But the description of the allegedly prolonged conflict, which Hitler dramatized as a grim struggle between two men of iron will, has since been exposed as pure fantasy.

In fact, we must rather assume that his father paid little attention to his son's vocational future. Certainly he did not insist upon any one course. That is apparent if only because attendance at the *Gymanasium* would have been much more to the point for a civil service career, given the structure of the Austrian school system. But what Hitler does describe accurately is the mood of persistent tension that sprang partly from the difference in temperament between father and son, partly from the father's realizing his long-cherished dream of early retirement—a dream that we may see curiously recurring in the son. When, in the summer of 1895, Alois Hitler retired and was liberated at last from the stringent duties of his vocation, he began living for his leisure and his inclinations. For young Adolf his father's retirement meant an abrupt reduction in his freedom of movement. Suddenly he was continually running into the powerful figure of his father, who insisted on respect and discipline, and who translated his pride in his own achievement into inflexible demands for obedience. The reasons for the conflict are evidently to be sought in this general situation, rather than in any specific differences of opinion over the son's uncertain future.

Moreover, the father saw only the beginning of Adolf's years in the *Realschule*. For, in January, 1903, he took a first sip from a glass of wine in the Wiesinger tavern in Leonding and fell over to one side. He was carried into an adjoining room, where he died immediately, before a doctor and a priest could be sent for. The liberal Linz *Tagespost* gave him a lengthy obituary, referring to his progressive ideas, his sturdy cheerfulness, and his energetic civic sense. It praised him as a "friend of song," an authority on beekeeping, and a temperate family man. By the time his son gave up school out of disgust and capriciousness, Alois Hitler had already been dead for two and a half years. Nor could Adolf's sickly mother have tried to force the boy into a civil servant's career.

Although she seems to have held out for a while against her son's demand that he be allowed to leave school, she soon could find nothing to pit against his self-willed temperament. After losing so many children, her anxiety about the two who remained constantly manifested itself as weakness and indulgence, which her son had quickly learned to exploit. When, in September, 1904, he was promoted only on condition that he leave school, his mother made one last attempt. She sent him to the *Realschule* in Steyr. But there, too, his work continued to be unsatisfactory. His first report card was so bad that Hitler, as he himself relates, got drunk and used the document for toilet paper; he then had to request a duplicate. When his report for the autumn of 1905 likewise showed no improvement, his mother at last gave in and allowed him to leave school. However, the decision was not entirely her own. For, as Hitler involuntarily confessed in *Mein Kampf,* he was "aided by a sudden illness."[7] There is, however, no evidence for such an illness; the principal reason seems to have been that he had again not been promoted.

Hitler left the school "with an elemental hatred," and in spite of all his efforts to explain away his failure by references to his artistic vocation, he never entirely recovered from the smart. Free from the demands of schooling, he was now determined to dedicate his life "wholly to art." He wanted to be a painter. This choice was prompted equally by his talent for sketching and the rather florid notion an official's son from the provinces must have had of the free and untrammeled artist's life. Quite early he showed a bent for attitudinizing. A onetime boarder in his mother's house later described the way the young Adolf would sometimes abruptly begin to draw at meals and with seeming obsessiveness dash down sketches of buildings, archways, or pillars. To be sure, such behavior can be explained as a legitimate way of using art to escape the coercions and confinements of the bourgeois world, and soar instead into realms of the ideal. It is only the manic fervor with which he threw himself into his painting exercises, or into music and dreams, forgetting and rejecting everything else, that casts a disturbing light on this passion. Arrogantly, the young Adolf declared that

20

he would have none of any definite work, any sordid vocation for the sake of a livelihood.

It would seem that he sought elevation through art in a social sense as well. Behind all the whims and decisions of his formative years lay the overpowering desire to be or to become something "higher." His eccentric passion for art was tangibly related to his notion that art was a pursuit of the "better class of society." After his father's death his mother had sold the house in Leonding and moved into an apartment in Linz. Here the sixteen-year-old boy sat idly around. Thanks to his mother's adequate pension, he was in a position to suspend all plans for the future and to assume that appearance of privileged leisure which counted very heavily in his mind. He would take a daily stroll on the promenade. He regularly attended the local theater, joined the musical club, and became a member of the library run by the Association for Popular Education. An awakening interest in sexual questions impelled him, as he related later, to visit the adult section of a wax museum. And around the same time he saw his first film in a small movie house near the Südbahnhof. According to the descriptions we have, he was lanky, pallid, shy, and always dressed with extreme care. Usually he sported an ivory-tipped black cane and tried to look like a university student. His father had been driven by social ambition but had achieved what the son regarded as a paltry career. His own goals were pitched far higher. In the dream world that he set up for himself, he cultivated the expectations and the egotism of a genius.

He visibly retreated into this fantasy world after he had for the first time failed to meet a challenge. In his own world he compensated for his early experiences of helplessness vis-à-vis his father and his teachers. There he celebrated his solitary triumphs over defenseless antagonists; and from this secret realm he hurled his first bolts of anathema against the ill-wishers he believed surrounded him. Everyone who knew him at this time later recalled his low-keyed, withdrawn, "anxious" nature. Unoccupied as he was, everything preoccupied him. The world, he decided, must be "changed thoroughly and in all its parts." Until the late hours of the night, he sat feverishly over clumsy projects for the total rebuilding of the city of Linz. He drew sketches for theaters, mansions, museums, or for that bridge over the Danube which he triumphantly ordered built thirty-five years later on the basis of his own adolescent plans.

He was still incapable of any systematic work. Constantly, he sought new occupations, new stimuli, new goals. For a short while he took piano lessons; then boredom set in and he abandoned them. For a while he had a single boyhood friend, August Kubizek, the son of a Linz decorator, with whom he shared a sentimental passion for music. On August's birthday he made a present to his friend of a villa in the Italian Renaissance style: a gift out of his large stock of delusions. "It made no difference whether he was talking about something finished or something planned."[8] When he

21

bought a lottery ticket, he was at once transported into a future where he occupied the third floor of a fine house on the bank of the Danube. He spent weeks deciding on the *décor,* choosing furniture and fabrics, making sketches, and unfolding to his friend his plans for a life of leisure and devotion to art. The household would be managed by an "elderly, already somewhat gray-haired but extremely elegant lady." He could already see her receiving "their guests on the festively illuminated landing," guests who belonged "to the choice, spirited circle of friends." The daydream seemed to him already a fact, and when the lottery drawing shattered that dream, he flew into a fit of rage. Significantly, it was not only his own bad luck at which he stormed; he denounced human credulity, the state lottery organization, and finally condemned the cheating government itself.

Quite accurately, he described himself as he was during this period as a "loner." In a concentrated and obstinate manner, he lived only for himself. Aside from his mother and "Gustl," who naïvely admired him and served him as an audience, not another human soul occupies the scene during the most important years of his boyhood. In leaving school, he had effectively left society also. On his daily stroll through the center of the city, he would regularly meet a girl accompanied by her mother, who would be passing the Schmiedtoreck at the same time he was going by. He conceived an interest in this girl, whose name was Stefanie, which quickly developed into an intense romantic feeling that lasted for years. At the same time, he consistently refused to speak to her. There is reason to think that his refusal was based not on normal shyness but on a desire to protect his imaginary relationship from the breath of insipid reality. If we may believe the account of his friend, Hitler wrote "innumerable love poems" to this girl. In one of them she appeared "as a damsel of high degree, dressed in a dark-blue, flowing velvet robe and riding upon a white palfrey over flower-strewn meadows, her loose tresses falling over her shoulders like a golden flood. A bright spring sky overhung the scene. All was pure, radiant happiness."[9]

He also succumbed to the music of Richard Wagner and often went to the opera night after night. The charged emotionality of this music seemed to have served him as a means for self-hypnosis, while he found in its lush air of bourgeois luxury the necessary ingredients for escapist fantasy. Significantly, at this period he loved the kind of painting that corresponded to this music: the luscious pomp of Rubens and, among the moderns, Hans Makart. Kubizek has described Hitler's powerful reaction to a performance of Wagner's *Rienzi,* which they attended together. Overwhelmed by the resplendent, dramatic musicality of the work, Hitler was also stirred by the fate of the late medieval rebel and tribune of the people, Cola di Rienzi, alienated from his fellow men and destroyed by their incomprehension. After the opera the two young men went on the Freinberg. There, with nocturnal Linz lying in darkness below them, Hitler began to orate. "Words burst from him like a backed-up flood breaking through crumbling dams. In grandiose, compelling images, he sketched for me his future and that of his people." When these boyhood friends met again thirty years later in Bayreuth, Hitler remarked: "It began at that hour!"[10]

In May, 1905, Adolf Hitler went to Vienna for the first time. He stayed two weeks and was dazzled by the brilliance of the capital, by the splendor of Ringstrasse, which affected him "like magic from the Arabian Nights," by the museums and, as he wrote on a postcard, by the "mighty majesty" of the Opera. He went to the Burgtheater and attended performances of *Tristan* and *The Flying Dutchman*. "When the mighty waves of sound flooded through the room and the whine of the wind gave way before the fearful rush of billows of music, one feels sublimity," he wrote to Kubizek.

It is unclear, however, why after his return to Linz he waited for a year and a half before once more setting out for the city to apply for a place in the Academy of Fine Arts. His mother's qualms may have played a part, but there would also have been his own unwillingness to take a step that would end his existence of ideal drifting and once again subject him to the routines of schooling. In fact, Hitler repeatedly called the years in Linz the happiest time of his life, "a lovely dream." Only the memory of his failure at school somewhat darkened its brightness.

In *Mein Kampf* Hitler described how his father once set out for the city vowing "not to return to his beloved native village until he had made something of himself."[11] With a similar resolve, Hitler left Linz in September, 1907. And however far he diverged from his youthful fantasies, the central craving remained alive: to see the city lying at his feet in fear, shame, and admiration, to transform the "lovely dream" of the past into present reality. During the war he frequently spoke, wearily and impatiently, of his plan to retire to Linz in his old age, to build a museum there, listen to music, read, write, pursue his thoughts. All this was nothing but the ancient daydream of the lordly house with the "extremely elegant lady" and the "spirited circle of friends," still capable of stirring him after all the intervening years. In March, 1945, when the Red Army was at the gates of Berlin, he had the plans for the rebuilding of Linz brought to him in the bunker under the chancellory and for a long time stood dreamily over them.[12]

Chapter 2

You idiot! If I had never in my life
been a visionary, where would you
be, where would we all be today?

Adolf Hitler

THE SHATTERED DREAM

Vienna at the turn of the century was the metropolis of a European empire, the scintillating imperial city embodying the glory and heritage of centuries. Brilliant, self-assured, prosperous, it governed an empire that extended into what is now Russia and deep into the Balkans. Fifty million people, members of more than ten different nations and races, were ruled from Vienna and held together as a unit: Germans, Magyars, Poles, Jews, Slovenes, Croats, Serbs, Italians, Czechs, Slovaks, Rumanians, and Ruthenians. Such was the "genius of this city" that it was able to modulate all the discords of the far-flung empire, to balance its tensions and make them fruitful.

At that point, the empire still seemed destined for permanence. Emperor Franz Joseph, who had celebrated the fiftieth anniversary of his reign in 1898, had become virtually a symbol of the state itself, of its dignity, its continuity, and its anachronisms. The position of the high nobility likewise seemed unshakable. Skeptical, haughty, and weighed down by traditions, it dominated the country politically and socially. The bourgeoisie had attained wealth but no significant influence. Universal suffrage did not yet exist. But industry and commerce were expanding feverishly, and the petty bourgeoisie and working class were being increasingly courted by parties and demagogues.

Nevertheless, for all its contemporaneity and show, Vienna was already a "world of yesterday"—full of scruples, decrepitude, and deep-seated doubts about itself. As the twentieth century began, the brilliance displayed in its theaters, its bourgeois mansions and green boulevards was overhung by this eschatological mood. Amid all the lavish festivals the city celebrated in fact and fiction there was palpable awareness that the age had lost its vital force, that only a lovely semblance still survived. Weariness, defeats, anxieties, the more and more embittered quarrels among the nations of the empire, and the shortsightedness of the ruling groups were eroding the unwieldy structure. Nowhere else in old Europe was the atmosphere of termination and exhaustion so palpable. The end of the bourgeois era was nowhere experienced so resplendently and so elegantly as in Vienna.

By the end of the nineteenth century the inner contradictions of the multinational state were emerging with increasing sharpness. For generations that state had been ruled with highhanded indolence. Problems were evaded, crises ignored. The point was to keep all the nationalities "in equal, well-tempered dissatisfaction." That was how the onetime Premier Count Eduard Taafe ironically defined the art of rule in Austria, and on the whole it was not unsuccessful.

But the precarious equilibrium of the empire had been visibly shaken after 1867, when Hungary wrested special rights for herself in the famous *Ausgleich*. Soon it was being said that the Dual Monarchy was nothing but a pot cracked in many places and held together by a piece of old wire. For the Czechs demanded that their language be given equal status with German. Conflicts erupted in Croatia and Slovenia. And in the year of Hitler's birth Crown Prince Rudolf escaped from a net of political and personal entanglements by his suicide in Mayerling. In Lemberg (Lvov), at the beginning of the century, the Governor of Galicia was assassinated in the street. The number of military draft evaders rose from year to year. At Vienna University there were student demonstrations by national minorities. Columns of workers staged enormous parades down the Ring under bedraggled red banners. From all these symptoms of unrest and weakness it was easy to predict that Austria was on the point of falling apart. It could be expected that the denouement would come when the old Emperor died. In 1905 it was rumored in the German and Russian newspapers that there had been feelers between Berlin and St. Petersburg concerning the future of the Dual Monarchy. Supposedly, inquiries had been made whether it would not be well to agree beforehand on what parts of territory neighbors and other interested parties might count when the empire collapsed. The rumors became so rife that on November 29, 1905, the Foreign Office in Berlin felt compelled to arrange a special meeting with the Austrian ambassador and reassure him.

Naturally, the currents of the period—nationalism and racial consciousness, socialism and parliamentarism—made themselves felt with particular force in this precariously balanced political entity. For a long time it had been impossible to pass a law in the country's Parliament unless the government made outright concessions to various groups in the virtually inextricable tangle of crisscrossing interests. The Germans, approximately a quarter of the population, were ahead of all the other peoples of the empire in education, prosperity, and general development; but their influence was disproportionately smaller. The policy of makeshift concessions worked against them precisely because they were expected to be loyal, whereas efforts had to be made to satisfy the unreliable nationalities.

In addition, the surging nationalism of the various peoples of the empire was no longer countered by the traditional calmness of a self-assured German leadership. Rather, the epidemic spread of nationalism had seized the ruling class of Germans with special intensity from the time that Austria was excluded from German politics in 1866. The Battle of Königgrätz had turned Austria's face away from Germany toward the Balkans and forced the Germans into the role of a minority within their "own" state. They felt themselves being swamped by alien races and began to grumble at the monarchy for ignoring that danger. They themselves compensated by a more and more immoderate glorification of their own breed. "German" became a word with a virtually moralistic cast, carrying strong missionary overtones. It developed into a concept imperiously and pretentiously opposed to everything foreign.

The anxiety underlying such reactions can be fully understood only against the broader background of a general crisis. In the course of a creeping revolution "old, cosmopolitan, feudal and peasant Europe"—which had anachronistically survived in the territory of the Dual Monarchy—was going down to destruction. No class was spared the shocks and conflicts connected with its death. The bourgeois and petty bourgeois in particular felt threatened on all sides by progress, by the abnormal growth of the cities, by technology, mass production, and economic concentration. The future, which for so long had been imagined in hopeful terms, in the form of pleasant private or societal utopias, became associated for greater and greater numbers of people with uneasiness and dread. In Vienna alone, in the thirty years after the abolition of guild regulations in 1859, some 40,000 artisans' shops went bankrupt.

Such troubles naturally gave rise to many contrary movements that reflected the increasing craving for an escape from reality. These were chiefly defensive ideologies with nationalistic and racist overtones, offered by their advocates as panaceas for a threatened world. Such doctrines gave concrete form to vague anxieties, expressing these in familiar, hence manageable, images. One of the most extreme of these complexes was anti-Semitism, which drew together a variety of rival parties and leagues, from the Pan-Germans under the leadership of Georg Ritter von Schönerer to the Christian Socialists under Karl Lueger. There had been an outbreak of anti-Jewish feeling at the time of the depression at the beginning of the 1870's. This emerged afresh when the stream of immigrants from Galicia, Hungary, and Bukovina increased. In the temperate atmosphere of the Hapsburg metropolis, Jews had made considerable progress toward emancipation. But for that very reason the Jews in the East flocked in greater numbers to the more liberal zones of the West. In the interval from 1857 to 1910 their proportion of the population of Vienna rose from 2 per cent to more than 8.5 per cent, higher than in any other city of Central Europe. There were some districts of Vienna where Jews formed about a third of the population. The new immigrants retained both their customs and their style of dress. In long black caftans, tall hats on their heads, their odd and alien-seeming presence strikingly affected the street scene in the capital.

Historical circumstances had confined the Jews to specific roles and specific economic activities. These same circumstances had also bred in them a freedom from bias, an uncommon flexibility and mobility. Representatives of the old bourgeois Europe were still caught up in their traditions, their sentiments and their despairs, and hence were far more apprehensive about the future. The type of personality the Jews had developed corresponded better to the urban, rationalistic style of the age. That, as much as the fact that they had thronged into the academic professions in disproportionate numbers, exerted a dominant influence upon the press, and controlled virtually all the major banks in Vienna and a considerable portion of local industry[13]—produced in the Germans a sense of danger and of being overwhelmed. Generalized anxiety condensed into the charge that the Jews were rootless, seditious, revolutionary, that nothing was sacred to them, that their "cold" intellectuality was opposed to German "inwardness" and German sentiment. In support of this idea anti-Semites could point to the many Jewish intellectuals prominent in the working-class movement. It is characteristic of a minority outcast for generations that it will incline toward rebellion and dreaming of utopias. Thus Jewish intellectuals had indeed flung themselves into the socialist movement and become its leaders. Thus there arose that fateful picture of a grand conspiracy with parts carefully assigned, some to work within capitalism, some within the coming revolution. The small tradesman confusedly feared that both his business and his bourgeois status were being menaced by the Jews in a kind of two-pronged attack. And his racial uniqueness was under assault as well. In the 1890's one Hermann Ahlwardt wrote a book with the significant title, *Der Verzweiflungskampf der arischen Völker mit dem Judentum* ("The Desperate Struggle of the Aryan Peoples with Jewry"). Ahlwardt drew the materials for its "documentation" from events and conditions in Germany. Yet, in the Berlin of the nineties, despite all the fashionable currents of anti-Semitism, this book sounded like the crotchet of a pathological crank. In Vienna, however, it caught the imagination of wide strata of the population.

In this city of Vienna, against this background, Adolf Hitler spent his next six years. He had come to Vienna full of high hopes, craving rich impressions and intending to continue his pampered life style in a more

27

brilliant, more urban setting, thanks to his mother's financial support. Nor did he have any doubts of his artistic vocation. He was, as he himself wrote, full of "confident self-assurance."[14] In October, 1907, he applied for the drawing examination at the Academy. The classification list contains the entry: "The following gentlemen submitted unsatisfactory drawings or were not admitted to the examination: . . . . Adolf Hitler, Braunau a. Inn, April 20, 1889, German, Catholic, Father civil servant, upper rank, four grades of Realschule. Few heads. Sample drawing unsatisfactory."

It was a cruel shock. In his consternation, Hitler called on the director of the Academy, who suggested that the young man study architecture, at the same time repeating that the drawings "incontrovertibly showed my unfitness for painting." Hitler later described this experience as an "abrupt blow," a "glaring flash of lightning."[15] Now he was being punished for having quit secondary school, for he would have needed to have passed the final examination in order to enroll in a school of architecture. But his aversion for school and for all regular study was so great that it did not even occur to him to try to make up for this omission by working toward the examination. Even as a grown man he called this requirement of completing his preliminary education "incredibly difficult" and remarked tersely: "By all reasonable judgment, then, fulfillment of my dream of being an artist was no longer possible."[16]

It is probable that after such a failure he shied away from the humiliation of going home to Linz, and above all of returning to his former school, the scene of his previous defeat. In perplexity, he stayed in Vienna for the present and evidently did not write a word home about his not being accepted. Even when his mother fell severely ill and lay dying, he did not venture to return. He did not go back to Linz until after his mother's death on December 21, 1907. The family doctor who had treated his mother in her last illness declared that he had "never seen a young man so crushed by anguish and filled with grief." According to his own testimony, he wept. For not only were his own hopes shattered, but he had now to face alone, without help, the shock of disenchantment. The experience intensified his already pronounced tendency to keep to himself and to indulge in self-pity. With the death of his mother whatever affection he had ever had for any human being came to an end—except one later emotional tie, again linked to a close relative.

Possibly his mother's death reinforced his intention to return to Vienna. The eighteen-year-old boy's decision to go back to the city that had rejected him, to try again to find his way and his opportunities there, testifies equally to his determination and to his desire to escape into anonymity from the inquiring looks and admonitions of his relatives in Linz. Moreover, in order to qualify for his orphan's pension he had to give the impression that he was engaged on a formal course of studies. Consequently, as soon as the formalities and legal questions were settled, he called on his guardian, Mayor Mayrhofer, and declared—"almost defiantly," as the mayor afterward reported—"Sir, I am going to Vienna." A few days later, in the middle of February, 1908, he left Linz for good.

A letter of recommendation gave him new hope. Magdalena Hanisch, the owner of the house in which his mother had lived until her death, had connections with Alfred Roller, one of the best-known stage designers of the period, who worked at the Hofoper and also taught at the Vienna Academy of Arts and Crafts. In a letter dated February 4, 1908, she asked her mother, who was living in Vienna, to arrange for Hitler to meet Roller. "He is an earnest, aspiring young man," she wrote, "nineteen years old, more mature and sedate than his years warrant, pleasant and steady, from a very honorable family. . . . He has the firm intention of learning something substantial. As far as I know him now, he will not 'loaf,' since he has in mind a serious goal. I trust you will not be interceding for someone unworthy. And you may well be doing a good deed."

Only a few days later the answer came that Roller was prepared to receive Hitler, and the Linz landlady thanked her mother in a second letter: "You would be rewarded for your pains if you could have seen the young man's happy face when I had him summoned here. . . . I gave him your card and let him read Director Roller's letter! Slowly, word for word, as though he wanted to learn the letter by heart, as if in reverence, with a happy smile on his face, he read the letter quietly to himself. Then, with fervent gratitude, he laid it down in front of me. He asked me whether he might write you to express his thanks."

Hitler's own letter, dated two days later, has also been preserved. It is composed in labored imitation of the elaborate style of Imperial Austrian bureaucrats:

Herewith, esteemed and gracious lady, I wish to express my sincerest gratitude for your efforts in obtaining access for me to the great master of stage decoration, Prof. Roller. It was no doubt somewhat overbold of me, Madam, to make such excessive demands upon your kindness, since you after all had to act in behalf of a perfect stranger. All the more, therefore, must I ask you to accept my sincerest thanks for your undertakings, which were accompanied by such success, as well as for the card which you so kindly placed at my disposal. I shall at once make use of this fortunate opportunity. Once again my deepest gratitude. I respectfully kiss your hand.

Sincerely yours,
Adolf Hitler.[17]

The recommendation seemed to open the way for him to enter his dream world: the free life of an artist; music and painting combined in the grand pseudo-world of opera. But there is no indication of how the meeting with Roller came out. The sources are silent. Hitler himself never said a word about it. It seems most likely that the famous man advised him to work, to

29

learn, and in the autumn to apply once more for admission to the Academy.

Hitler afterward called the following five years the worst of his life. In some respects they were also the most important. For the crisis of those years formed his character and provided him with those formulas for mastering fate to which he clung forever after. They became, in fact, so calcified within his mind that they account for the impression his life gives, despite his mania for mobility, of utmost rigidity.

Among the persisting elements of the legend that Hitler himself constructed over the carefully obscured trail of his life is the allegation that "necessity and harsh reality" formed the great and unforgettable experience of those years in Vienna: "For me the name of this Phaeacian city represents five years of hardship and misery. Five years in which I was forced to earn a living, first as a day laborer, then as a small painter; a truly meager living which never sufficed to appease even my daily hunger. Hunger was then my faithful bodyguard; he never left me for a moment. . . ."[18] However, careful calculation of his income has since shown that during the first period of his stay in Vienna, thanks to his share in his father's inheritance, his mother's legacy, the orphan pension, and without counting any earnings of his own, he had at his disposal between eighty and one hundred crowns a month.[19] This was the monthly earnings of a junior magistrate at that time.

In the latter half of February August Kubizek came to Vienna, on Hitler's urging, to study at the Conservatory of Music. Thereafter the two friends lived together in the rear wing of Stumpergasse 29, occupying a "dreary and wretched" room let to them by an old Polish woman named Maria Zakreys. But while Kubizek pursued his studies, Hitler continued the aimless idler's life he had already become accustomed to. He was master of his own time, as he cockily stressed. Usually it was almost noon before he got up, sauntered in the streets or in the park at Schönbrunn, visited the museums, and at night went to the opera. There, during those years alone, he blissfully heard *Tristan und Isolde* thirty to forty times, as he afterward averred. Then again he would bury himself in public libraries, where, with the indiscriminateness of the self-educated, he read whatever his mood and the whim of the moment suggested. Or else he would stand in front of the pompous buildings on Ringstrasse and dream of even more monumental structures he himself would erect some day.

He gave himself up to such fantasies with almost maniacal passion. Until the small hours of the morning he would sit over projects to which he brought equal measures of practical incompetence, intolerance, and priggish conceit. "He could not let anything alone," we are told. Because bricks, he decided, were "an unsolid material for monumental buildings," he planned to tear down and rebuild the Hofburg. He sketched theaters, castles, exhibition halls; he developed a scheme for a nonalcoholic drink;

30

he looked for substitutes for smoking or drew up plans for the reform of schools. He composed theses attacking landlords and officials, outlines for a "German ideal state," all of which expressed his grievances, his resentments, and his pedantic visions. Although he had learned nothing and achieved nothing, he rejected all advice and hated instruction. Knowing nothing of composition, he took up an idea Richard Wagner had dropped, and began writing an opera about Wieland the Smith, full of bloody and incestuous nonsense. Despite his uncertain spelling he tried his hand as a dramatist, using themes from Germanic sagas. Occasionally, too, he painted; but the small water colors filled with finicky detail betrayed nothing of the forces raging in him. Incessantly, he talked, planned, raved, possessed by the urge to justify himself, to prove that he had genius. He concealed from his roommate his failure to pass the entrance examination at the Academy. When Kubizek occasionally asked him what he was doing so intensively day after day, he replied, "I am working on a solution to the wretched housing conditions in Vienna and carrying on certain studies to that end."[20]

In this behavior, despite all the elements of bizarre overstrain and sheer fantasizing—in fact, partly because of those elements—the later Hitler is already recognizable. He himself later remarked upon the connection between his seemingly confused reformist zeal and his subsequent rise. Similarly, the peculiar combination of lethargy and tension, of phlegmatic calm and wild activity, points to the future pattern. With some uneasiness Kubizek noted the abrupt fits of fury and despair, the variety and intensity of Hitler's aggressions, and his seemingly unlimited capacity for hate. In Vienna his friend had been "completely out of balance," he remarked unhappily. States of exaltation alternated frequently with moods of deep depression in which he saw "nothing but injustice, hatred, hostility" and "solitary and alone [railed] against the whole of humanity, which did not understand him, would not accept him, which he felt persecuted and cheated him" and had everywhere set "snares" for him for the sole purpose of preventing his rise.

In September, 1908, Hitler once more made an attempt to enter the painting class at the Academy. The candidates' list noted that this time he was "not admitted to the test"; the paintings he had submitted did not meet the preliminary requirements for the examination.

This new rejection, even more definite and offensive in its tone, seems to have been one of those "awakening" experiences that determined Hitler's future. How deeply wounded he was is indicated by his lifelong hatred for schools and academies. He was fond of pointing out that they had misjudged "Bismarck and Wagner also" and rejected Anselm Feuerbach. They were attended only by "pipsqueaks" and aimed at "killing every genius." At his headquarters thirty-five years later, leader and warlord of the German people, he would launch into furious tirades against his wretched

31

village teachers with their "dirty" appearance, their "filthy collars, un-
kempt beards and so on."[21] Humiliated and evidently keenly embarrassed,
he withdrew from all human contact. Soon his married half-sister, Angela,
who lived in Vienna, heard no more from him. His guardian, too, received
only a last curt postcard, and at the same time his friendship with Kubizek
broke up. At any rate, he utilized Kubizek's temporary absence from
Vienna to move abruptly out of their shared apartment, without leaving so
much as a word of explanation. He disappeared into the darkness of flop-
houses and homes for men. Thirty years passed before Kubizek saw him
again.

First, he rented an apartment in the Fifteenth District, Felberstrasse 22,
Entrance 16. It was here that he was introduced to the ideas and notions
that decisively influenced his future course. He had long explained his
failures in terms of his singular character, of precocious genius uncompre-
hended by the world. By now he needed more specific explanations and
more tangible adversaries.

His spontaneous emotions turned against the bourgeois world that had
rejected him, although he felt he belonged to it by inclination and origins.
The embitterment he harbored toward it henceforth is among the paradoxes of his existence. That bitterness was both nourished and limited by
his fear of social upheaval, by the terrors of proletarianization. In *Mein
Kampf* he describes with surprising frankness the deep-seated "hostility" of
the petty bourgeois for the working class, a hostility he too was imbued
with. The reason for it, he declares, is the fear "that it will sink back into
the old, despised class, or at least become identified with it."[22] He still had
some money left from his parental legacy, and he continued to receive his
monthly allowance, but the uncertainty of his personal future nevertheless
depressed him. He dressed carefully, still went to the opera, the theater, and
the coffeehouses of the city; and, as he himself remarks, he continued, by
careful speech and restrained bearing, to keep up his sense of bourgeois
superiority to the working class. If we are to believe a somewhat dubious
source on those years, he always carried with him an envelope of photographs showing his father in parade uniform and would smugly inform
people that his late father had "retired as a higher official in his Imperial
Majesty's Customs Service."[23]

In spite of the occasional rebellious gestures, such behavior reveals the
young Hitler's intrinsic craving for approval and for a sense of belonging,
which is basic to the bourgeois personality. It is in this light that we must
evaluate his remark that from early on he was a "revolutionary" in both
artistic and political matters. In fact, the twenty-year-old Hitler never
questioned the bourgeois world and its values. Rather, he moved toward it
with undisguised respect, dazzled by its brilliance and its wealth. He
remained a civil servant's son from Linz, full of sentimental admiration for

the bourgeois world. He craved a share in it. His response to his rejection by the bourgeois world was an intensified longing for acceptance and recognition—and this, perhaps, is one of the more remarkable aspects of a youth unusual in many other respects. Europe, after all, had been ringing with denunciations of bourgeois sham for nearly twenty years, so that he could easily have picked up arguments enough to rationalize his own humiliation, and exonerate himself by passing judgment on the age. Instead, worsted and submissive, he held silently aloof from any of that. The rage for total unmasking had no appeal for him. Indeed, all the artistic excitement and clash of ideas so characteristic of the era were lost on him—as well as its intellectual daring.

Vienna in those years shortly after the turn of the century was one of the centers of ferment, but Hitler, astonishingly, remained unaware of this. A sensitive young man with many reasons for protest, for whom music had been among the great liberating experiences of his youth, knew nothing about Schönberg. No reverberations of the "greatest uproar . . . in Vienna's concert halls in the memory of man," which Schönberg and his pupils, Anton von Webern and Alban Berg, had unleashed at that very time seemed to have reached his ears. Nor did he pay any attention to Gustav Mahler or Richard Strauss, whose work seemed to a contemporary critic in 1907 the "hurricane center of the musical world." Instead, the young man from Linz relived in Wagner and Bruckner the raptures of his parents' generation. Kubizek had reported that names like Rilke, whose *Book of Hours* had been published in 1905, or Hofmannsthal, had "never reached" either of them. And although Hitler had applied to the Academy of Fine Arts, he took no part in the affairs of the Secessionists and was in no way stirred by the sensations that Gustav Klimt, Egon Schiele or Oskar Kokoschka were provoking. Instead, he battened on the works of the mid-nineteenth century, venerating Anselm Feuerbach, Ferdinand Waldmüller, Karl Rottmann or Rudolf von Alt. And this future architect with his soaring visions stood enthralled before the classicistic façades of the Ringstrasse, unaware of the proximity of the revolutionary leaders of a new architecture: Otto Wagner, Josef Hoffman, and Adolf Loos. In 1911 a heated controversy had flared over the flat unornamented façade of Loos's commercial building on Michaeler Platz, directly opposite one of the baroque portals of the Hofburg. Moreover, Loos had written an article maintaining that there was an inner link between "ornament and crime"—a scandalous thing to say. But Hitler consistently directed his naïve enthusiasm toward the fulsome style accepted by Viennese salons and respectable society. Here, too, he proved himself reactionary. In everything new he seemed to sense a tendency toward the debasement of sublimity, the emergence of something alien and unknown. And with his bourgeois instincts he shrank back from anything of that sort.

His first brush with political reality took a similar course. Once again, despite his feelings of alienation, revolutionary ideas had no attraction for him. Instead he once again revealed himself a partisan of the establishment, paradoxically defending a reality that he simultaneously repudiated. Rejected himself, he seemingly canceled the humiliation by taking over the cause of the society that had rejected him. Beneath this psychological mechanism was concealed one of the lines of fracture in Hitler's character. He himself has related how as a construction worker he would go off to one side during the noon lunch break to drink his bottle of milk and eat his piece of bread. And whatever we may or may not believe in this story, his "extremely" irritated reaction to the attitude of his fellow workers was consonant with a basic element in his personality: "They rejected everything: the nation as an invention of the 'capitalistic' . . . classes; the Fatherland as an instrument of the bourgeoisie for the exploitation of the working class; the authority of the law as a means for the repression of the proletariat; school as an institution for breeding slave material, but also for training the slavedrivers; religion as a means for stupefying the people intended for exploitation; morality as a sign of stupid, sheeplike patience, etc. There was absolutely nothing at all that was not dragged through the mire of horrible depths."[24]

Significantly, the series of ideas that he defended against the construction workers—nation, fatherland, authority of the law, school, religion, and morality—contains virtually the complete catalogue of standards for bourgeois society, against which he himself was at this time conceiving his first resentments. It is precisely this divided relationship that will come to the fore repeatedly on the most diverse planes throughout his life. It will reappear in the political tactics of constantly seeking alliances with the despised bourgeois, and in the ritualistic formality—verging on the ridiculous—that prompted him to greet his secretaries by kissing their hands, or at the afternoon teas in the Führer's headquarters to serve them personally their cream cake. In all vulgarity he cultivated the airs of a "gentleman of the old school." His manners were his way of demonstrating that he had achieved a desired social affinity; and if there is anything in the picture of young Hitler that betrays specifically Austrian traits, it must be this special status consciousness with which he defended the privilege of being bourgeois. In a society whose craze for titles tended to assign a social ranking to every activity, he wanted at least to be a *Herr,* a gentleman. It did not matter that his life was narrow and gloomy as long as he could claim this distinction. This was why he stayed away from the artistic and political oppositions of the period. Much of his outward behavior, his language and his clothing, and his ideological and aesthetic choices as well can be most plausibly explained as the effort to conform to the bourgeois world, which he admired uncritically, even to its presumptions. Social disdain he felt to be far more painful than social wretchedness; and if he despaired, it was

34

not from the flawed order of the world, but from the insufficient part granted to him to play in it. He was therefore very careful to avoid any dispute with society; he wanted only to be reconciled to it. Staggered by the grandeur and glamour of the metropolis, wistfully standing outside locked gates, he was not revolutionary. He was merely lonely. No one seemed less destined to be a rebel than he.

Chapter 3

D'où vient ce mélange de génie et de stupidité?

Robespierre

THE GRANITE FOUNDATION

Near his room on Felberstrasse there was a tobacco shop that sold periodicals, including one highly popular magazine devoted to racial anthropology. Its title page carried the headlines: "Are you blond? Then you are a creator and preserver of civilization. Are you blond? Then you are threatened by perils. Read the Library for blonds and advocates of Male Rights."* Its editor was a defrocked monk with the arrogated name of Jörg Lanz von Liebenfels. The magazine, which he had named *Ostara* after the Germanic goddess of spring, proclaimed a doctrine, as deranged as it was dangerous, of the struggle between heroic men whom he called Asings or Heldings, and dwarfish, apelike creatures called Äfflings or Schrättlings. Some wealthy industrialist backers had made it possible for Lanz von Liebenfels to buy the castle of Werfenstein in Lower Austria. From this headquarters he directed the formation of a heroic Aryan league that was to form the advance guard of the blond and blue-eyed master race in the coming bloody confrontation with the inferior mixed races. Under the swastika flag, which he had already raised over his castle in 1907, he promised to counter the socialistic class struggle by race struggle "to the hilt of the castration knife." Thus early he called for a systematic program of breeding and extermination: "For the extirpation of the animal-man and the propagation of the higher new man." Along with genetic selection and similar eugenic measures, his platform included sterilization, deportations to the "ape jungle," and liquidations by forced labor or murder. "Offer sacrifices to Frauja, you sons of the gods!" he wrote. "Up, and sacrifice to him the children of the Schrättlings." In order to popularize the Aryan idea, he suggested racial beauty contests.

* *Mannesrechtler*—a coinage based on *Frauenrechtler*. Its present-day equivalent might be "Men's Lib."—TRANS.

Hitler had missed some of the older issues of the magazine, and this gave him a pretext for visiting Lanz several times. He left an impression of youth, pallor, and modesty.[25]

The importance of this rather ludicrous founder of an order does not consist in anything he suggested to or did for Hitler but in the symptomatic place he occupied: he was one of the most eloquent spokesmen of a neurotic mood of the age and contributed a specific coloration to the brooding ideological atmosphere, so rife with fantasies, of Vienna at that time. To say this both describes and delimits his influence upon Hitler. One might say that Hitler did not so much absorb the man's ideology as catch the infection that underlay it.

From this and other influences, such as the newspaper articles and cheap pamphlets that Hitler himself mentioned as early sources of his knowledge, some scholars have concluded that his world view was the product of a perverted subculture opposed to bourgeois culture. And in fact the plebeian hatred for bourgeois mores and bourgeois humanity repeatedly erupts in his ideology. The dilemma, however, consisted in the fact that this culture was in a way permeated by its subculture and had long ago become a blasphemy of everything it was founded on. Or, to put the same thought in a different way, the subculture that Hitler found expressed by Lanz von Liebenfels and others of his ilk in turn-of-the-century Vienna was not the negation of the prevailing system of values but only its rather battered and sordid image. Turn where he might in his craving for ties with the bourgeois world, he came upon the same notions, complexes, and panicky fears that were expressed in the cheap pamphlets, only in a more sublimated and respectable form. He did not have to abandon a single one of the trivial ideas that had helped him to achieve his initial orientation in the world. Everything he had picked up, with reverent astonishment, in the speeches of the most influential politicians of the metropolis, seemed familiar to him. And when he sat in the upper balcony of the Opera House and listened to the works of the most celebrated composer of the era, he encountered only the artistic expression of the familiar vulgarities. Lanz, the *Ostara* pamphlets, and the trashy tracts merely opened for him the rear entrance into the society he wanted to belong to. But, rear or not, it was an entrance.

The need to legitimize and consolidate this affinity also underlay his first groping efforts to give some ideological shape to his resentments. With the morbidly intensified egotism of one who felt threatened by social debasement, he more and more took over the prejudices, slogans, anxieties, and demands of upper-class Viennese society. Among the elements were both anti-Semitism and those master-race theories that reflected the apprehensions of the German populace of the empire. Two other ingredients were a horror of socialism and what were called "social-Darwinist" notions—all founded upon exacerbated nationalism. These were upper-class ideas, and by adopting them he attempted to raise himself to the level of that class.

In later years Hitler always went to considerable lengths to represent his thought as the fruit of personal struggles. He was supposed to have arrived at his ideas by his own penetrating observation and the labors of his intellect. In order to deny all determining influences he even pretended to have been through a period of wild liberalism. For example, he stressed the "repugnance" that "unfavorable remarks" about Jews had aroused in him during his years in Linz. It is more likely, and various persons have attested to this, that his youthful views were marked by the ideological climate of that provincial city.

Linz at the turn of the century swarmed with nationalistic groups and sects. Moreover, a decidedly nationalistic temper prevailed at the secondary school that Hitler attended. The pupils flaunted in their buttonholes the blue cornflower popular among German racist groups. They gave preference to the colors of the German unity movement, black-red-gold; they greeted one another with the Germanic *"Heil!"* and sang the tune of the Hapsburg imperial anthem with the text of "Deutschland über Alles." They felt themselves part of a nationalistic opposition directed chiefly against the Hapsburg dynasty and even put up some youthful resistance to school religious services and Corpus Christi processions—for they identified with the "Protestant" German Reich.

At the Realschule, the spokesman for these trends was Dr. Leopold Pötsch, town councilor and teacher of history. Evidently he had made a deep impression upon young Hitler. His eloquence, and the colored oleos of yesteryear with which he supplemented his lessons, guided the imaginations of his pupils in the desired direction. The pages his pupil devoted to him in *Mein Kampf* contain a measure of hindsighted exaggeration. But the border dweller's sense of being menaced, the hatred for the Danube monarchy's mixture of nations and races, and Hitler's fundamental anti-Semitic attitudes undoubtedly came to him through his old schoolmaster. It is also probable that Hitler read the largely satiric magazine of the Schönerer movement, *Der Scherer, Illustrierte Tiroler Monatsschrift für Politik und Laune in Kunst und Leben* ("Illustrated Tyrolean Monthly for Politics and Entertainment in Art and Life") which was published in Linz during those years. It had a good deal to say about the decline of morals and the evils of alcoholism, but it specialized in attacks on the Jews, the "papists," the suffragettes and members of Parliament. As early as the first issue of May, 1899, it carried a picture of the swastika, which was being taken up as the symbol of Germanic, *völkisch,* (*i.e.,* racial and nationalistic) attitudes. In the magazine, however, it was still described as the "fire whisk" which, according to Germanic myth, had twirled the primal substance at the creation of the universe. Hitler also seems to have read—both during his schooldays and in the following aimless years—the Pan-German and aggressively anti-Semitic sheet *Linzer Fliegende Blätter.* For it was not only in Vienna that anti-Semitism formed a component of political and social ideology—as the author of *Mein Kampf* would have had his readers believe. It was just as strong in the provinces.

In *Mein Kampf* Hitler speaks of an "inner struggle" lasting two years, in the course of which his emotions resisted the inexorable commands of his reason "a thousand times" before he completed his metamorphosis from "a weak-kneed cosmopolitan" to a "fanatical anti-Semite." In fact, what he calls his "greatest spiritual upheaval" was merely development from a groundless and almost elusive dislike to fixed hostility, from mere mood to ideology. The anti-Semitism of Linz had been of a dreamy sort, tending toward neighborly compromises; now it took on the sharpness of principle. It focused on a well-defined enemy. At the beginning of his stay in Vienna Hitler had sent "respectfully grateful" regards to Dr. Eduard Bloch, his parents' Jewish family doctor. Dr. Josef Feingold, the lawyer, and Morgenstern, the picture framer, had encouraged the would-be artist by buying his small water colors. Toward Neumann, his Jewish companion at the home for men, Hitler had felt an exaggerated sense of obligation. Now, during the process of change that continued for several years, all these marginal figures of his youth started to recede into the background. Their place was taken by a vision that steadily acquired an almost mythological power, the "apparition in a long caftan and black hair locks" which once struck him "as I was strolling through the Inner City." He forcefully described how this chance impression "twisted" in his brain and gradually began to become an obsession that dominated all his thinking:

Since I had begun to concern myself with this question and to take cognizance of the Jews, Vienna appeared to me in a different light than before. Wherever I went, I began to see Jews, and the more I saw the more sharply they became distinguished in my eyes from the rest of humanity. Particularly the Inner City and the districts north of the Danube Canal swarmed with a people which even outwardly had lost all resemblance to Germans. . . . All this could scarcely be called very attractive, but it became positively repulsive when, in addition to their physical uncleanliness, you discovered the moral stains on this "chosen people." . . . Was there any form of filth or profligacy, particularly in cultural life, without at least one Jew involved in it? If you cut even cautiously into such an abscess, you found, like a maggot in a rotting body, often dazzled by the sudden light—a kike! . . . Gradually I began to hate them.[26]

We can probably no longer plumb the real cause of this ever-growing hatred, which lasted literally to the last hour of Hitler's life. One of his dubious cronies of those years attributed the hatred to sexual envy on the part of a dropout from the middle class. This crony has described an incident involving a model, the essence of Germanic femininity, a half-Jewish rival, and an attempt on Hitler's part to rape the girl while she was posing. The story is as grotesque as it is stupidly plausible.[27] The theory that Hitler's anti-Semitism was connected with pathological sexual fixations

39

is supported by the whole uneven pattern of Hitler's ideas about sexual relations, which from his boyhood oscillated remarkably between strained idealism and obscure anxiety feelings. It is supported likewise by the language and argumentation of his own account wherever the figure of a Jew enters the story. The scent of obscenity, which can be detected in all the pages of *Mein Kampf* in which he attempts to deal with his repugnance for Jews, is surely not an accidental and superficial characteristic. Nor is it merely an echo of the trashy pamphlets and periodicals to which he owed the unforgotten "illuminations" of his youth. Rather, in that obscenity his own personality and the inner nature of his resentment is revealed.

After the war a member of the dictator's entourage published an extensive list of the women in Adolf Hitler's life. Characteristically, the beautiful Jewish girl from a wealthy family figures in the list. It is far more likely that he had no "actual encounter with the girl," either in Linz or in Vienna. Or, if so, the affair would have been lacking the kind of passion that might have liberated the young man from his theatrical egocentrism.

Contrasting with this lack is a significant dream, the—in his own words—"nightmare vision of the seduction of hundreds and thousands of girls by repulsive, bandy-legged Jew bastards." Lanz, too, had been tormented by the recurrent bugbear of blonde noblewomen in the arms of dark, hairy seducers. His race theory was permeated by sexual-envy complexes and deep-seated antifemale emotions; woman, he maintained, had brought sin into the world, and her susceptibility to the lecherous wiles of bestial submen was the chief cause for the infection of Nordic blood. The same obsession, expressing the toils of a delayed and inhibited masculinity, emerges in a similar vision of Hitler's: "With satanic joy in his face, the black-haired Jewish youth lurks in wait for the unsuspecting girl whom he defiles with his blood, thus stealing her from her people." In both cases we have the fetid, insipid imagery of the sex-starved daydreamer; and it may well be that the peculiarly nasty vapors that rise from large tracts of National Socialist ideology derive from the phenomenon of repressed sexuality within the bourgeois world.[28]

Kubizek, Hitler's boyhood friend, and other companions from the dim twilight of underground Vienna, have pointed out that Hitler had early on fallen out with everybody, that his hatred lashed out in all directions. It is conceivable, therefore, that his anti-Semitism was merely the concentrated form of his hitherto general and undirected hatred, which finally found its object in the Jews. In *Mein Kampf* Hitler argued that the masses must never be shown more than one enemy, because to be aware of several enemies would only arouse doubts. This principle, a number of writers have pointed out, applied to him even more than to the masses. He always concentrated his feelings with undivided intensity upon a single phenomenon as the presumptive cause of the evils in the world. And that phenomenon was always a specifically imaginable figure, never any elusive cluster of causes.

Perhaps we may never be able to trace Hitler's overwhelming Jewish phobia down to its roots. But on the whole we may say that an ambitious and desperate loner was finding a formula for politicizing his personal problems. For he saw himself bit by bit going downhill and was forced to fend off his terror of being declassed. The apparition of the Jew helped to support his self-esteem; he could draw the conclusion that he had the laws of history and of nature on his side. Hitler's own account, incidentally, sustains the view that he became a full-fledged anti-Semite at the time he had used up his inheritance. Although he never suffered the utter destitution he later described, he was under some financial pressure, and at any rate had socially fallen much lower than he could bear, given his dreams of being an artist, a genius, the object of public adulation.

Vienna, the German bourgeois Vienna of the turn of the century, may be regarded as under the aegis of three men. Politically, it was the city of Georg Ritter von Schönerer and Karl Lueger. But in that peculiarly iridescent area where politics and art meet—that border region that so significantly determined Hitler's career—the overwhelmingly dominant figure was Richard Wagner. Ideologically, these three were the key personalities of his formative years.

We are told that in Vienna Hitler appeared as a disciple of Georg von Schönerer, that he had framed mottos by this man hanging over his bed: *Ohne Juda, ohne Rom/ wird gebaut Germaniens Dom. Heil!** And: *Wir schauen frei und offen, wir schauen unverwandt,/ wir schauen froh hinüber ins deutsche Vaterland. Heil!*†

These rhymed maxims gave the gist of von Schönerer's program. His Pan-German movement, unlike the association of the same name in Germany, did not pursue expansionist imperialistic goals but worked instead for the union of all Germans in one national state. In marked contrast to the Pan-German Association of Germany, it was for giving up the non-German lands of the Danube Monarchy. In general it opposed the existence of the multinational state. The founder and leader of this movement, Georg von Schönerer was a landowner of the frontier Waldviertel, which was also the native soil of Hitler's family. He had begun his career as a radical democrat, but subsequently more and more subordinated ideas of political and social reform to extreme nationalism. Obsessed by fears of drowning in a sea of foreignness, he saw deadly threats to his Germanism all around him: from the Jews and equally from Roman Catholicism, from Slavs and Socialists, from the Hapsburg monarchy and every type of internationalism. He signed his letters "with German greetings"; he launched all sorts of proposals for reviving ancient Germanic customs; he recommended that German chronology begin with 113 B.C., date of the Battle of Noreia

---

* We will build Germania's cathedral without the Jews and without Rome. *Heil!*

† We gaze frank and freely, we gaze steadily, we gaze cheerfully across the border into the German Fatherland. *Heil!*

41

at which the Cimbri and the Teutons won a decisive victory over the Roman legions.

Schönerer was a difficult personality, deeply embittered, rigid in his principles. He organized the Away-from-Rome Movement, incurring the hostility of the Catholic Church. He was the first to give European hatred for the Jews, hitherto mostly religious and economic in its motivations, the twist that turned it into formal anti-Semitism with a political, social, and above all, biological basis. A demagogue with a keen sense for the effectiveness of primitive emotions, he led a general fight against the trend toward Jewish assimilation. "Religion's only a disguise, in the blood the foulness lies," ran one of his slogans. In the monomania with which he regarded the Jews as agents of all the evils and troubles of the world, and in the radicality of his declaration of war on them, he can be recognized as Hitler's forerunner. Within the tepid and tolerant atmosphere of old Austria, he was the first to demonstrate the possibilities inherent in organizing racial and national fears. Anxiously, he saw the day coming when the German minority would be overwhelmed and "slaughtered." To ward off that day, he demanded special anti-Jewish laws. His followers wore on their watch chains the insigne of the anti-Semite: a hanged Jew. There were some who spoke up in the Parliament at Vienna, calling for bounties to be awarded for every murdered Jew, either as a set payment or a portion of the victim's property.

Dr. Karl Lueger, the other spokesman for petty bourgeois anti-Semitism, evidently made an even more lasting impression upon Hitler. Lueger was the mayor of Vienna and the eloquent leader of the Christian Social Party. In *Mein Kampf* Hitler expressed his unequivocal admiration for Lueger, hailing him as "truly gifted," "the greatest German mayor of all times," and "the last great German to be born in . . . the Ostmark."[29] It is true that Hitler sharply criticized his program, especially his casual and opportunistic anti-Semitism and his faith in the multinational state. But Lueger's demagogic talent impressed him all the more, as did the mayor's adeptness at making use, for his own purposes, of the prevailing socialistic, Christian, and anti-Jewish impulses of the people.

Unlike Schönerer, whose arrogance and fixation aroused strong opposition and thus condemned him to ineffectiveness, Lueger was conciliatory, skillful, and popular. He merely exploited ideologies; privately, he despised them. His thinking was tactical and pragmatic; accomplishment meant more to him than ideas. In his fifteen years in office the transportation network of Vienna was modernized, the educational system extended, social welfare improved, green belts laid out, and almost a million jobs created. Lueger based his power on the Catholic working class and the petty bourgeoisie: white-collar workers and lower-rank government officials, small shopkeepers, the concierges and lower clergy, all of whom industrialization and changing times threatened with social downgrading or

42

poverty. He, too—in this resembing Schönerer—profited by the widespread feelings of anxiety, but he exploited these feelings only against select and defeatable opponents. Moreover, he did not arouse more anxiety by painting the future in gloomy colors. Instead, he won support with infallibly effective humanitarian platitudes, vividly expressed in his recurrent phrase: "We must do something for the little man!"

But Hitler admired Lueger for more than his Machiavellian qualities. He believed he had discovered a deeper concord between the mayor and himself. Certainly Lueger had things to teach him; but beyond that, Hitler regarded the man as a kindred soul. Like himself the son of simple folk, Lueger had made his way against all obstacles, all slurs and social disparagement. He had prevailed over even the objections of the Emperor, who three times refused to confirm him as mayor, and had won that recognition from society which Hitler, too, was bent on having. While Schönerer scotched his chances by making enemies, Lueger had worked his way up by continuously seeking and cementing alliances with the ruling groups. He had known how—as Hitler in his homage described the well-remembered lesson—"to make use of all existing implements of power, to incline mighty existing institutions in his favor, drawing from these old sources of power the greatest possible profit for his own movement."

The mass party Lueger formed with the aid of emotional slogans was living proof that anxiety was—as happiness had been a century before—a new idea in Europe, powerful enough to bridge even class interests. For the time being, the idea of a nationalistic socialism took much the same course. The Bohemian and Moravian regions of the Danube Monarchy were rapidly becoming industrialized. In 1904 a congress in Trautenau founded the German Workers' Party (DAP—Deutsche Arbeiterpartei). Its aim was to defend the interests of the German workers against cheap Czech labor pouring into the factories from the countryside and frequently acting as strikebreakers. This action was one step—there would be others throughout Europe under the most varied auspices—toward meeting a key weakness of Marxist socialism: its inability to overcome national antagonisms and to give concrete reality to its humanitarian slogans. For there was no room within the theory of class struggle for the German worker's sense of a separate national existence. In fact, the adherents of the new German Workers' Party were recruited largely from among former members of the Social Democratic Party. They had turned away from their previous political convictions out of concern that the policy of proletarian solidarity would favor only the Czech majority in the region. That policy, as the program of the DAP formulated it, was "misguided and immeasurably harmful to the Germans of Central Europe."

To these Germans the inseparability of their national and social interests seemed to be an obvious and universal truth, which they opposed to the high-flown and imprecise internationalism of the Marxists. They thought

43

they would find the reconciliation of socialism and nationalism in the idea of a "national community"—*Volksgemeinschaft*. The program of their party united, in somewhat contradictory fashion, whatever ideas answered their craving for self-defense and self-assertion. The goals of the party were predominantly anticapitalistic, revolutionary-libertarian, and democratic; but from the beginning this was mingled with authoritarian and irrational notions, along with fierce antipathies toward Czechs, Jews, and other so-called "foreign elements." The early followers of the party were workers from small mines, from the textile industry; there were also some railroad workmen and artisans. They regarded themselves as closer to the German bourgeois types, the pharmacist, the industrialist, the high official, or the businessman than to the unskilled Czech workers. Soon they took to calling themselves National Socialists.

In later life Hitler did not like to recall these forerunners, although his ties with them, especially in the immediate aftermath of the First World War, were for a time very close. The existence of these predecessors obviously cast doubt upon his claim, as leader of the National Socialist German Workers' Party (NSDAP), to sole authorship of the idea that was to determine the fate of the century. In *Mein Kampf* he attempted to derive this idea from his comparison between Lueger and Schönerer, and to represent it as his personal synthesis:

If, in addition to its enlightened knowledge of the broad masses the Christian Social Party had had a correct idea of the importance of the racial question, such as the Pan-German movement had achieved; and if, finally, it had itself been nationalistic, or if the Pan-German movement, in addition to its correct knowledge of the aim of the Jewish question, had adopted the practical shrewdness of the Christian Social Party, especially in its attitude toward socialism, there would have resulted a movement which even then in my opinion might have successfully intervened in German destiny.[30]

Hitler would have it that he refrained from joining either of these parties because of these objections. But it would be more accurate to say that for most of his Vienna years he had no independently thought-out political line. Rather, he was filled with inchoate emotions of hatred and defensiveness of the sort to which Schönerer appealed. Alongside these were vague, upwelling prejudices against Jews and other minorities and an aching desire to be influential in some way. He grasped what was happening in the world around him more by instinct than by reason. So excessively subjective was his interest in public affairs at this time that he cannot really be called political. Rather, he was still being "politicalized." He himself admitted that at the time he was so filled with his artistic aspirations that he was only "incidentally" interested in politics; it took the "fist of fate" to open his eyes. Proof of this is the tale he tells of himself as a young building worker deeply disliked by his fellows. The anecdote later found its way into all German schoolbooks as a staple item of the Hitler legend. But, for us, the significant detail is this: that when asked to join the union he refused, giving as his reason that he "did not understand the matter." It would seem that for a long time politics represented to him principally a means for unburdening himself, a way to blame his misfortunes on the world, to explain his own fate as due to a faulty social system, and finally, also, to find specific scapegoats. Significantly, the only organization he joined was the League of Anti-Semites.[31]

Hitler soon gave up the apartment on Felberstrasse that he had taken after parting from Kubizek. Up to November, 1909, he changed his residence several times. Once he listed his occupation as "writer." There is some indication that he wanted to avoid registering for military service and hoped by moving around to throw the authorities off his track. But it may also be that this constant moving reflected both his heritage from his father and the neurasthenia and aimlessness of his life. Those who knew him during this period have described him as pale, with sunken cheeks, hair brushed low over his forehead, his movements jerky. He himself later declared that at that stage of his life he had been extremely shy and would not have ventured to approach a great man or to speak out in the presence of five persons.

He lived on his orphan's pension, which he continued to draw by fraudulently asserting that he was attending the Academy. His inheritance from his father, however, as well as his share in the sale of his parents' home—which for so long had provided him with the means for a carefree and untrammeled existence—appear to have been used up by the end of 1909. At any rate, he gave up the room on Simon Denk Gasse which he had sublet from September to November. Konrad Heiden, the author of the first important biography of Hitler, relates that at this time Hitler "sank into bitterest misery" and spent a few nights without shelter, sleeping on park benches and in cafés, until the advanced season forced him to seek shelter. November, 1908, was unusually cold; there was much rain, often mixed with snow.[32] Sometime during this month Hitler queued up in front of the home for men in Meidling, a Vienna suburb. Here he met a vagabond named Reinhold Hanisch, who in an account he wrote in later years described how "after long wanderings on the roads of Germany and Austria I came to the Refuge for the Homeless in Meidling. On the wire cot to my left was a gaunt young man whose feet were quite sore from tramping the streets. Since I still had some bread that peasants had given me, I shared it with him. At that time I spoke a heavy Berlin dialect; he was enthusiastic about Germany. I had passed through his home town of Braunau on the Inn, so I could easily follow his stories."

For about seven months, until the summer of 1910, Hitler and Hanisch spent their time together in close friendship and joint business affairs. To be sure, this witness is not much more credible than all the others from this

45

early phase of Hitler's life. Nevertheless, there are bits of Hanisch's story which ring true: that Hitler had the tendency to sit idly brooding, and that nothing would persuade him to go job hunting with his pal Hanisch. The contradiction between Hitler's longing for middle-class respectability and his real situation certainly never appeared more plainly than during those weeks in the flophouse, surrounded by broken-down derelicts, befriended by no one but the crudely cunning Reinhold Hanisch. In 1938, when he could do so, he had Hanisch tracked down and killed. At the height of his career, still needing to drown out the humiliating memory of those years, he insisted: "But in imagination I lived in palaces!"

The enterprising Hanisch, wise in the ways of the world, familiar with all the miseries and shifts open to his class, one day asked Hitler his occupation. Hitler replied that he was a painter. Assuming that Hitler meant a house painter, Hanisch said that he certainly should be able to earn money at such a trade. And, despite all our suspicions of Hanisch's reliability, we cannot help recognizing the young Hitler in the phrases that follow: "He was insulted and replied that he was not that kind of painter, but an academician and an artist." The two men eventually went into partnership—the idea seems to have come from Hanisch. Shortly before Christmas they moved into a kind of hostel, the home for men on Meldemann Strasse, in the Twentieth District of Vienna. By day, when regulations forbade staying in the tiny bedrooms, Hitler sat in the reading room perusing the newspapers or popular-science journals, or else copying postcards and lithographs of Viennese scenes. Hanisch sold these careful water colors to picture dealers, framers, and sometimes to upholsterers who, in the fashion of the day, "worked them into the high backs of easy chairs or sofas." The proceeds were shared on a fifty-fifty basis. Hitler himself felt that he would not be able to sell his works since he "could not be seen in his bedraggled clothes." Hanisch, however, maintains that he managed "sometimes to get a very good order, so that we could live fairly well."

The inhabitants of the home for men came from all classes; the largest group consisted of young workers, both blue- and white-collar, with jobs in nearby factories and shops. In addition there were some solid, industrious small craftsmen. Hanisch mentions music copyists, sign painters, and monogram carvers. But more characteristic of the place and the neighborhood were the shipwrecked of various kinds, adventurers, bankrupt businessmen, gamblers, beggars, moneylenders, discharged army officers—flotsam and jetsam from all provinces of the multinational state. There were also the Jews from the eastern regions of the monarchy who, as door-to-door salesmen, peddlers, or knitware dealers were trying to rise. What linked them all was common wretchedness; what separated them was the desperate determination to escape from that world, to scramble out even at the expense of all others. "The lack of solidarity is the supreme characteristic of the great class of the declassed."[33]

Again, in the home for men Hitler had no friends aside from Hanisch. Those who knew him there remembered him as a fanatic; on the other hand, he himself spoke of his dislike for the Viennese personality, which he felt to be "obnoxious." Possibly he avoided friendships; intimacies of any kind irritated and exhausted him. What he became acquainted with, on the other hand, was that sort of cameraderie among ordinary people which simultaneously affords contact and anonymity, and offers a kind of loyalty that can be canceled at any time. This was an experience he was never to forget, and in the following years he repeatedly renewed it on the most varied social planes, with virtually unchanging personnel: in the trenches during the war; in the midst of his orderlies and chauffeurs, whose company he preferred as a party leader and later as Chancellor; and finally in the underground bunker of the Führer's headquarters. He always seemed to be repeating the life style of the home for men, which provided only distant forms of social life and in general neatly fitted into his concept of human relations. The management of the home considered him difficult, a political troublemaker. "Tempers often rose," Hanisch later recalled. "The exchanges of hostile looks made the atmosphere distinctly uncomfortable."

Hitler evidently argued his views sharply and consistently. During the Vienna years he was in a constant state of perturbation, in strong contrast to the famous lightheartedness of the city but in fact far more in keeping with the temper of the times. He was obsessed by fears of Jews and Slavs, hated the House of Hapsburg and the Social Democratic Party, and envisioned the doom of Germanism. His fellows in the home for men did not share his paranoid emotions.

Radical alternatives, wild exaggerations formed the pattern of his thinking. His hate-filled mind pushed everything to extremes, magnified events of minor importance into metaphysical catastrophes. From early on only grandiose themes had attracted him. This tendency was one of the reasons for his naïve and reactionary leaning toward the heroic, the nobly decorative, the idealizing elements in art. Gods and heroes, gigantic aspirations, or horrendous superlatives stimulated him and helped to mask the banality of his circumstances. "In music Richard Wagner brought him to bright flames," Hanisch writes clumsily but vividly. Hitler himself later claimed that as far back as this he began sketching his first plans for the reconstruction of Berlin. His bent for grandiose projects fits into this context. A job in the office of a construction company instantly awoke his old dreams of being an architect; and after a few experiments with model planes he already saw himself as the owner of a great airplane factory and "rich, very rich."

Meanwhile, reputedly through Greiner's mediation, he produced a poster advertising a hair tonic, another poster for a bed-feathers shop, another for an antiperspirant sold under the brand name "Teddy." A copy of this last poster, with Hitler's signature in a corner, has been found. It shows two rather stiff, clumsily drawn figures of letter carriers; one has sat down in exhaustion wringing heavy blue drops of sweat out of his sock; the other is informing his "dear brother" that 10,000 steps a day are "a pleasure with Teddy powder." In another poster that has come down to us the tower of St. Stephan's cathedral rises majestically above a mountain of soap. What Hitler himself considered noteworthy about this period of his life was that he was at last master of his own time. During the long hours he spent over the newspapers in cheap little cafés, he read by preference the anti-Semitic *Deutsches Volksblatt.*

If we were to define the characteristic quality of that period in the life of this eccentric, solitary twenty-year-old (Hitler, too, spoke of himself as having been "eccentric" at this time),[34] we should have to stress the essentially unpolitical nature of his interests. Richard Wagner was his idol during those years, not only "in music." In fact, Hitler saw Wagner's early disappointments, lack of recognition, and obstinate faith in his own vocation, a "life flowing into the glory of world fame,"[35] as a prototype of his own destiny. Hitler was not the only victim to be seduced by that romantic concept of genius whose merits and failings Richard Wagner embodied. Because of Wagner a whole generation was confused, misguided, and alienated from the bourgeois world.

The boy who fled the disciplines of school and then fell prey to the delusive promises of the big city found his idol in the Master of Bayreuth. Many young men of his generation followed the same course, and with similarly exalted expectations. It was a way with great appeal to gifted "outsiders" who otherwise would have no choice but to sink into mediocrity. It may surprise us to find that this unprepossessing son of a Linz customs official represents so typical a phenomenon. With the turn of the century legions of these sons of the nineteenth-century middle class made their appearance. In 1906 Hermann Hesse, in *Under the Wheel,* vividly described the sufferings of one such youth under contemporary conditions and gave a dismal forecast of his future. Robert Musil, in *Young Törless,* and Frank Wedekind, in *The Awakening of Spring,* were among the many writers who dealt with the same theme. Whether these heroes sought escape from the toils of the world or went down to destruction, all of them opposed to the bourgeois world a wild enthusiasm for the arts. They despised their fathers' mean accomplishments and felt only contempt for their values. By contrast, an artist's existence was noble, precisely because it was socially unfruitful. Everything that stood for order, duty, endurance, they dismissed as "bourgeois." The bourgeois mentality, they maintained, promoted efficiency but did not tolerate the extraordinary. The tremendous intensifications of true culture, on the other hand, the glories of the "spirit," could be achieved only in isolation, in extreme human and social aloofness. The artist, the genius, the complex personality in general, was bound to be utterly out of place in the bourgeois world. His true locale was far out on the fringes of society, where the morgue for suicides and the pantheon for immortals were both situated—as Henri Murger, the first analyst of this type bathetically observed. Though the lodginghouses to which Hitler betook himself were squalid, though his notion of being an artist was ridiculously highflown; though no one so far had acknowledged his talent; though his actual life in the home for men was marked by deceit, parasitism, and asociality—all this could be secretly justified in terms of the prevailing concept of genius. And Richard Wagner was the supreme example of the validity of that concept.

Hitler himself, in fact, later declared that with the exception of Richard Wagner he had "no forerunners," and by Wagner he meant not only the composer, but Wagner the personality, "the greatest prophetic figure the German people has had." One of his favorite ideas, to which he returned frequently, concerned Wagner's towering importance "for the development of German man." He admired the courage and energy with which Wagner exerted political influence "without really wishing to be political," and on one occasion admitted that a "literally hysterical excitement" overcame him when he recognized his own psychological kinship with this great man.[36]

The parallels are, in fact, not at all hard to detect. The points of contact between the two temperaments—all the more marked because the young postcard painter consciously modeled himself after his hero—produce a curious sense of family resemblance, which Thomas Mann first pointed out in his disturbing essay *Brother Hitler*. In 1938, when Hitler was at the height of his peacetime triumphs, Mann wrote:

Must we not, even against our will, recognize in this phenomenon an aspect of the artist's character? We are ashamed to admit it, but the whole pattern is there: the recalcitrance, sluggishness and miserable indefiniteness of his youth; the dimness of purpose, the what-do-you-really-want-to-be, the vegetating like a semi-idiot in the lowest social and psychological bohemianism, the arrogant rejection of any sensible and honorable occupation because of the basic feeling that he is too good for that sort of thing. On what is this feeling based? On a vague sense of being reserved for something entirely indefinable. To name it, if it could be named, would make people burst out laughing. Along with that, the uneasy conscience, the sense of guilt, the rage at the world, the revolutionary instinct, the subconscious storing up of explosive cravings for compensation, the churning determination to justify oneself, to prove oneself. . . . It is a thoroughly embarrassing kinship. Still and all, I would not want to close my eyes to it.[37]

But there are other striking parallels between Hitler and Wagner: the uncertainty about ancestry, the failure at school, the flight from military service, the morbid hatred of Jews, even the vegetarianism, which in Wagner ultimately developed into the ludicrous delusion that humanity must be saved by vegetarian diet. Also common to both was the violent

49

quality of their moods: the abrupt alternation of depressions and exaltations, triumphs and disasters. In many of Richard Wagner's operas the theme is the classic conflict between the outsider, subject only to his own laws, and a rigid social order governed by tradition. In Rienzi or Lohengrin or Tannhäuser, Hitler, the rejected Academy candidate sitting over his water colors in the reading room of the home for men, recognized magnified aspects of his own confrontation with the world. Both Wagner and Hitler, moreover, possessed a furious will to power, a basically despotic tendency. All of Richard Wagner's art has never been able to conceal to what extent its underlying urge was the boundless need to dominate. From this impulse sprang the taste for massive effects, for pomposity, for overwhelming hugeness. Wagner's first major composition after *Rienzi* was a choral work for 1,200 male voices and an orchestra of one hundred. This blatant reliance on mass effects, employed to cover up basic weaknesses, this medley of pagan, ritual and music-hall elements anticipated the era of mass hypnosis. The style of public ceremonies in the Third Reich is inconceivable without this operatic tradition, without the essentially demagogical art of Richard Wagner.

Another point in common was a kind of cunning knowledge of the popular mind along with a remarkable insensitivity to banality. This combination resulted in an air of plebeian pretentiousness in which again they were remarkably similar. Gottfried Keller once called the composer a "barber and charlatan"; similarly, a contemporary observer described Hitler, with the acuteness born of hatred, as having "the aura of a head-waiter"; another spoke of him as a speechmaking sex murderer.[38] The element of vulgarity and unsavoriness that phrases of this sort tried to catch was present in both Hitler and Wagner. They were masters of the art of brilliant fraudulence, of inspired swindling. And just as Richard Wagner could call himself a revolutionary yet pride himself on his friendship with a king ("Wagner, the government bandleader," Karl Marx said scornfully), so Hitler, in his vague dreams of mounting the social ladder, reconciled his hatred of society with his opportunistic instincts. Wagner dismissed the patent contradictions in his views by declaring that art was the goal of life and that the artist made the ultimate decisions. It was the artist who would intervene to save the situation wherever "the statesman despairs, the politician gives up, the socialist vexes himself with fruitless systems, and even the philosopher can only interpret but cannot prophesy." His doctrine then was that of the aesthetician who would subordinate life entirely to the dictates of the artist. The state was to be raised to the heights of a work of art; politics would be renewed and perfected by the spirit inherent in art. Elements of this program are clearly visible in the theatricalization of public life in the Third Reich, the regime's passion for histrionics, the staginess of its practical politics—a staginess that often appeared to be the sole end of the politics.

There are still other parallels. The innate tendency toward "dilettant-ism," which Friedrich Nietzsche noted even while Wagner was still his admired friend, was likewise a trait of Hitler's. In both men there was the same striking need to intervene officiously in all sorts of spheres; both had to be forever proving themselves, dazzling the world with their many talents. Yesterday's glory rapidly turned stale for both of them; they had constantly to be surpassing themselves. In both cases we find an outrageous pettiness side by side with far-ranging inspiration; this very conjunction seems to have defined their peculiar mentality.

Hitler, to be sure, entirely lacked the self-discipline and the artist's capacity for taking pains that distinguished Wagner. Hitler's lethargy, his almost narcoticized dullness, are his alone. But at bottom we find in both men a horror of proletarianization, which they are determined to fend off at any cost. Their struggle to raise themselves to the level for which they felt themselves destined represents a remarkable achievement of the will. That sense of destiny was crucial: they were sustained by their premoni-tions that some time in the future everything would change for them, and all the humiliations they had endured, all the wretchedness of years in the lower depths, would be fearfully avenged.

Hitler's theatrical, essentially unpolitical relationship to the world, in the vein of Richard Wagner, emerges from an anecdote he himself relates. Once, after days of "musing and brooding," he came upon a mass demon-stration of Viennese workers. His description of the experience, recollected fifteen years later, still vibrates with the impression that those "endless columns four abreast" made upon him. For nearly two hours, he says, he stood "watching with bated breath the gigantic human dragon slowly wind-ing by," before he turned away "in oppressed anxiety" and went home. What had chiefly moved him, to all appearances, was the theatrical effect of the parade. At any rate, he writes not a word about the background or the political motivations for the demonstration. Evidently these concerned him much less than the question of how to achieve such effects upon masses of human beings. He brooded on theatrical problems; as he saw it, the chief concerns of the politician were matters of staging. Kubizek had in fact been struck by the importance his friend, in his occasional attempts at drama, attributed to "the most magnificent possible staging." Although this naïve early admirer of Hitler could not recall afterward the contents of Hitler's plays, he never forgot the "enormous pomp" Hitler went in for, which put anything Richard Wagner had ever demanded for the stage "completely in the shade."[39]

In retrospect, Hitler laid claim to an intense intellectual development. During the approximately five years he spent in Vienna, he maintained, he read "enormously and thoroughly." Aside from architecture and visiting the opera, he wrote, he "had but one pleasure: books." But it would

51

probably be more accurate to say that the real influences of this phase of his life stemmed not so much from the intellectual realm as from that of demagogy and political tactics. As a construction worker, a declassed bourgeois filled equally with his sense of superiority and fear of intimacy, he kept carefully to one side while the other men had their lunch. Nevertheless, he eventually was drawn into political wrangles. When his fellows threatened, according to his story, to throw him off the scaffolding, he learned something from the clash. As he later put it, with an undertone of admiration, he discovered that a very simple method existed to deal with arguments: "bashing in the head of anybody who dared to oppose." The pages of *Mein Kampf* that deal with his political awakening are extremely scanty on theory; they do not suggest that grappling with the ideas of the time which he claims to have engaged in. Rather, he uncritically followed the existing, widespread ideology of the German bourgeoisie. On the other hand, questions of the manipulation of ideas, of their power over the masses, aroused his eager interest and produced his first flashes of insight.

In the Vienna period we can already see those themes emerging which haunt many of his later utterances: the persistent search for "those who are behind it," the "secret wirepuller" who makes a dupe of the masses. Hanisch tells how one day Hitler emerged "altogether overwhelmed" from a movie based on the novel *The Tunnel* (*Der Tunnel*), by Bernhard Kellermann, in which one of the chief characters was a popular orator. "Henceforth there were eloquent speeches in the Home for Men," Hanisch reports. And Josef Greiner tells of having once referred Hitler to a woman named Anna Csillag who sold a hair-growing lotion by means of false testimonials. For almost an hour, Greiner's story goes, Hitler waxed enthusiastic about the woman's skill and the vast potentialities of psychological persuasion. "Propaganda, propaganda!" he is supposed to have raved. "You must keep it up until it creates a faith and people no longer know what is imagination and what reality." Propaganda, he is quoted as saying, is "the fundamental essence of every religion . . . whether of heaven or hair tonic."

These accounts are dubious. We are on firmer ground when we read what Hitler himself had to say about his study of Social Democratic practice: its propaganda, its demonstrations, and its speeches. The lessons he derived were to shape his own approach:

> The psyche of the great masses is not receptive to anything that is half-hearted or weak.
> Like a woman, whose psychic state is determined less by grounds of abstract reason than by an indefinable emotional longing for a force which will complement her nature, and who, consequently, would rather bow to a strong man than dominate a weakling, likewise the masses love a commander more than a petitioner and feel inwardly more satisfied by a doctrine tolerating no other beside itself than by the granting of liberalistic freedom with which, as a rule,

they can do little, and are prone to feel that they have been abandoned. They are equally unaware of their shameless spiritual terrorization and the hidden abuse of their human freedom, for they absolutely fail to suspect the inner insanity of the whole doctrine. All they see is the ruthless force and brutality of its calculated manifestations, to which they always submit in the end. . . . I achieved an equal understanding of the importance of physical terror toward the individual and the masses.

Here, too, the psychological effect can be calculated with precision.

Terror at the place of employment, in the factory, in the meeting hall, and on the occasion of mass demonstrations will always be successful unless opposed by equal terror.[40]

At the beginning of August Hitler and Hanisch quarreled. Hitler had spent several days painting a view of the Vienna Parliament, a building in the style of a classical temple, which he had called "a Hellenic masterpiece on German soil." His admiration evidently led him to outdo himself. At any rate, he thought the picture was worth fifty crowns, but Hanisch claimed he had sold it for only ten. They quarreled, and when his partner then stayed away for some time, Hitler abruptly had him arrested and instituted legal proceedings. At the trial, on August 11, 1910, Hanisch was sentenced to seven days in jail. He subsequently asserted that the court was prejudiced against him because he was registered at the home for men under the false name of Fritz Walter. The buyer's widow subsequently declared that her husband had indeed paid only about ten crowns for the picture; but Hanisch did not call him as a witness.

Subsequently, a Jewish companion named Neumann, who also lived in the home for men hawked Hitler's pictures, and on occasion even Hitler himself conquered his embarrassment and went after his customers himself.

Hitler spent three and a half of his formative years in this setting. We can well understand how repellent it would all have been to an artistically inclined young man full of highflown ambitions. Even years later, by his own testimony, he shuddered with horror at the memory of the "sordid scenes of garbage, repulsive filth, and worse." Characteristically, he felt no compassion.

His experiences and circumstances during this phase of his life helped Hitler arrive at that philosophy of struggle that became the central core of his view of the world, its "granite foundation," as he stressed, which he had no need of ever again changing. The views he formed from his contacts with the inmates in the home for men came to the fore again and again in later years, whenever he professed his belief in brutal struggle, in harshness, cruelty, destruction, the rights of the stronger—as he did in countless speeches and discussions, in the pages of his book, and in his table talk at the Führer's headquarters during the war. He never forgot the lessons he had learned in that school for meanness in Vienna.

Nevertheless, the component of Social Darwinism in Hitler's thought cannot be attributed solely to his personal experiences in the home for men. He was really reflecting the tendency of the age. Science had become the one truly unchallenged authority. As the laws of evolution and selection put forth by Charles Darwin and Herbert Spencer were popularized in numerous pseudoscientific publications, the average man soon came to know that the "struggle for existence" was the fundamental principle of life, the "survival of the fittest" the basic law governing the societal conduct of individuals and nations. The so-called "Social Darwinist" theory served, for a while at least, all camps, factions, and parties in the second half of the nineteenth century. It became a component of leftist populist education before the Right took up the creed for its own purposes, and argued the unnaturalness of democratic or humanitarian ideas by appealing to Darwinist principles.

The initial concept was that just as in untrammeled nature, social processes and the destinies of nations are determined by biological premises. Only a rigorous process of selection, involving both extermination and deliberate breeding, can prevent faulty lines of evolution and assure one nation superiority over others. Writers like Georges Vacher de Lapouge, Madison Grant, Ludwig Gumplowicz, and Otto Ammon took up the theme and were popularized in their turn by lesser journalists. They had already hit on the whole sinister program: the annihilation of unworthy organisms, the techniques of deliberate population policy, the forcible institutionalization and sterilization of the unfit, the determination of genetic superiority by the size of the head, the shape of the ears or the length of the nose. Often these views were accompanied by a frank rejection of Christian morality, tolerance, and humanitarian progress—all of which, it was argued, favored the weak and were therefore counterselective. To be sure, Social Darwinism was never elaborated into a comprehensive system, and some of its advocates later retracted their views. But this did not diminish its widespread popularity. On the whole, Social Darwinism was one of the classical ideologies of the bourgeois age. The imperialistic practices and robust capitalistic aggrandizement of the period could be justified as part and parcel of inescapable natural law.

The close link between the ideas of Social Darwinism and the antidemocratic tendencies of the period led to the condemnation of liberalism, parliamentarism, egalitarianism, and internationalism as violations of natural law and symptoms of degeneracy due to racial mixture. Count Arthur de Gobineau, the first important racial ideologist (*Essai sur l'inégalité des races humaines,* 1853), became the spokesman for pronounced aristocratic conservatism. He denounced democracy, revolution from below, and everything that he contemptuously called the "community spirit."

Even more influential, as far as the German middle class was concerned, was an Englishman who subsequently became a German citizen. This was

Houston Stewart Chamberlain, scion of a noted family of military men. Highly educated, but of feeble, nervous constitution, Chamberlain devoted himself to study, writing, and the work of Richard Wagner. In the year of Hitler's birth he came to Vienna, and instead of the intended casual visit remained in the city for twenty years. At once fascinated and repelled by it, he derived many of the ideas that underlay his racial theory of history from the Hapsburg multinational state. In his best known work, *Foundations of the Nineteenth Century* (1899), he interpreted European history—in a series of bold hypotheses—as the history of racial struggle. He regarded the decline of the Roman Empire as the classical model of historical decadence resulting from contamination of blood lines. Like declining Rome, he posited, the Dual Monarchy was being swamped by the admixture of Oriental races; the "disease" was advancing at a furious pace. In both cases "not one specific nation, not just one people or one race" was causing disintegration, but "a motley agglomeration" of races who in their turn were the consequence of multiple mixings. "Easy talents, and also, peculiar beauty, what the French call *un charme troublant,* is frequently characteristic of bastards. Nowadays this can daily be observed in cities where, as in Vienna, a wide variety of races meet. But at the same time one can also perceive the peculiar spinelessness, the low resistance, the lack of character, in short, the moral degeneration of such people."[41]

Chamberlain carried the parallel even further, comparing the Teutons thronging to the gates of Rome with the noble race of Prussians who had rightly been victorious in their clash with the racially chaotic Austro-Hungarian monarchy. But the mood of this elitist individualist was far from being cocky, was rather one of anxiety and defensiveness. In recurrent pessimistic visions he saw the Teutons "on the brink of the racial abyss," engaged "in a mute life-and-death struggle." He was tormented by fantasies of bastardization: "It is still morning, but again and again the powers of darkness stretch out their octopus arms, fasten their sucking cups on us in a hundred places and try to draw us back into the darkness."

Hitler's Social Darwinist views, therefore, were not simply the "philosophy of the doss-house."[42] Rather, they show him once again in harmony with the bourgeois age, whose product and destroyer he was. He merely picked up the kind of ideas current in the newspapers he found in cheap cafés, in the books and pamphlets on newsstands, in operas, and in the speechifying of cynical politicians. His experiences in the home for men were reflected only in the whiff of corruption that rises like a penetrating stench from his theories. Of similar origin was the ugly vocabulary that came to his lips, even when he was a statesman and master of a continent, so that he would speak of the "filthy trash from the East," the "swinish pack of parsons," the "crippled dung art," or would characterize Churchill as a "hopeless square-snout," and the Jews as "this vilest sow's brood that ought to be beaten to a pulp."[43]

Hitler absorbed the complex notions that gave his period its mood and peculiar coloration, absorbed them with that heightened sensitivity which was in fact the only quality he shared with the artist. Along with anti-Semitism and Social Darwinism, the age passed on to him the nationalistic missionary faith that was the obverse of pessimistic anxiety dreams. His views, highly confused and haphazardly arranged, also contained scraps drawn from the broader intellectual fads of the turn of the century: skepticism about reason and humanity, romantic glorification of blood and instinct. Oversimplified interpretations of Nietzsche's sermons about the strength and radiant amorality of the superman also formed part of this stock of ideas. It is worth noting, however, that it was Nietzsche who remarked that the nineteenth century took over from Schopenhauer not his desire for clarity and rationality, or his doctrine of the intellectual nature of intuition, but—"determined to be barbarously fascinated and seduced"— his unprovable doctrine of the will, his denial of the individual, his ravings about genius, his hatred of the Jews, and his hostility to science.

Once again Richard Wagner enters the picture—Nietzsche used the example of Wagner to illustrate this misunderstanding of Schopenhauer. For the Master of Bayreuth was not only Hitler's great exemplar; he was also the young man's ideological mentor. Wagner's political writings were Hitler's favorite reading, and the sprawling pomposity of his style unmistakably influenced Hitler's own grammar and syntax. Those political writings, together with the operas, form the entire framework for Hitler's ideology: Darwinism and anti-Semitism ("I hold the Jewish race to be the born enemy of pure humanity and everything noble in man"), the adoration of barbarism and Germanic might, the mystique of blood purification expressed in *Parzifal,* and the general histrionic view in which good and evil, purity and corruption, rulers and the ruled, stand opposed in black and white contrasts. The curse of gold, the inferior race grubbing underground, the conflict between Siegfried and Hagen, the tragic genius of Wotan—this strange brew compounded of bloody vapors, dragon slaying, mania for domination, treachery, sexuality, elitism, paganism, and ultimately salvation and tolling bells on a theatrical Good Friday were the perfect ideological match for Hitler's anxieties and needs. Here he found the "granite foundations" for his view of the world.

Hitler called the Vienna years "the hardest, though most thorough school of my life"; when he left it, he declared, he had "grown quiet and serious." He hated the city ever after for the rejection and insults he had suffered there—in this, too, resembling his model, Richard Wagner, who never overcame his grudge against Paris for the disappointments of his youth and had visions of the city going down to destruction in smoke and flames.[44] It is not far-fetched to suspect that Hitler's subsequent plans for turning Linz into a cultural metropolis on the Danube were inspired by resentment toward Vienna. Although he may not have gone so far as to wish the city burned to the ground, the fact is that in December, 1944, he refused a request for additional antiaircraft units for the city, remarking that Vienna might just as well find out what bomb warfare was like.

His uncertainty about his future increasingly depressed him. At the end of 1910 and the beginning of 1911 he appears to have received a considerable sum of money from his aunt, Johanna Pölzl. But these additional funds produced in him no initiative, no effort to make a serious new beginning. He continued to drift aimlessly: "So the weeks passed by." He still pretended that he was a student, painter, or writer. He went on cherishing vague hopes of a career in architecture. But he did nothing to make a reality of any of these pretensions. Only his dreams were ambitious, directed toward a great destiny. The persistence with which he continued to dream in the face of the actual conditions of his life, confers upon this period a striking note of inner consistency. He avoided being pinned down by anything, persisted in keeping all his relationships tentative. His refusal to enter the union saved him from being identified as a member of the proletariat and allowed him to hang on to his claim to middle-class status. Similarly, as long as he remained in the home for men and did nothing in particular, he could believe his own promise of genius and future fame.

His principal fear was that the circumstances of the times might block his dream. He was afraid of an uneventful era. Even as a boy, he later declared, he had "indulged in angry thoughts concerning my earthly pilgrimage, which . . . had begun too late" and had "regarded the period 'of law and order' ahead . . . as a mean and undeserved trick of fate."[45] This much he sensed: that only a chaotic future and social upheaval could close the gap that separated him from reality. Wedded to his dreams, he was one of those who would prefer a life of disaster to a life of disillusionment.

Chapter 4

I had to get out into the great Reich,
the land of my dreams and my longing.

Adolf Hitler

THE FLIGHT TO MUNICH

On May 24, 1913, Hitler left Vienna and moved to Munich. He was twenty-four years old, a despondent young man who gazed out upon an uncomprehending world with a mixture of yearning and bitterness. The disappointments of the preceding years had reinforced the brooding, withdrawn strain in his nature. He left no friends behind. In keeping with his antirealistic temperament, he tended to feel closest to those who were beyond reach: Richard Wagner, Ritter von Schönerer, Lueger. That "foundation" of his "personal views," acquired "under the pressure of fate," consisted of an assortment of prejudices which from time to time, after periods of vague brooding, were discharged in passionate outbursts. He left Vienna, as he later remarked, "a confirmed anti-Semite, a deadly foe of the whole Marxist world outlook, and pan-German."

Like all such self-descriptions, this one has plainly been tailored so that Hitler can pretend to early judgment in political matters. He practiced the same kind of tailoring in writing *Mein Kampf*. In fact, his moving to Munich, rather than Berlin, the capital of the Reich, is rather plain proof of his continuing unpolitical disposition. Or perhaps we should say that he was guided by romantic and artistic impulses far more than political motives. For prewar Munich had the reputation of being a city of the Muses, a charming, humanely sensual, lighthearted center of art and science. The "life style of the painter was regarded here as the most legitimate of all."[46] This picture of the city stemmed precisely from the contrast it made to noisily modern, proletarian Berlin. The latter city was a Babylon, in which social questions took precedence over aesthetics, ideologies over culture—or, in sum, politics over art. The atmosphere of Munich was more like that of Vienna, which again suggests that Hitler was drawn there by a general feeling rather than by any specific reasons that would have made him choose it in preference to Berlin—if, indeed, he felt confronted with any choice at all. In the *Reich Handbook of German Society* (a kind of *Who's Who*) for 1931 he explained that he had moved to Munich to find "a wider field for political activity." He would have found, however, better conditions in the capital of the Reich.

The same torpor and friendlessness that had marked the years in Vienna continued in Munich. It rather seems as if he spent his youth in a great hollow space. He made no contacts with parties or political factions; and ideologically, too, he remained solitary. Munich was an intellectually restive city, whose whole aura favored human relationships. Here even obsessions were highly thought of, for they betokened originality. Yet even here the young Hitler formed ties with nobody. He could have found his way to those who shared his racist notions, for even the most bizarre variants of *völkisch* ideas had their place in the city. Anti-Semitism also flourished, especially in the economically dislocated petty bourgeoisie. There were also radical leftist movements of widely differing character. It is true that all these tendencies were softened by the climate of Munich and usually expressed in sociable, rhetorical, neighborly forms. In the then suburb of Schwabing anarchists, bohemians, reformers, artists, and various apostles of new principles mingled easily. Pale young geniuses dreamed of an elitist renewal of the world, of redemptions, cataclysmic purgations, and barbarous rejuvenation cures for degenerate mankind.

At the center of one of the most important of those circles that formed at café tables around individuals or ideas was the poet Stefan George. He had gathered around him a band of highly talented disciples who imitated him in his contempt for bourgeois morality, glorification of youth and of instinct, faith in the superman, and an austere ideal of life as art and the life of the artist. One of his disciples, Alfred Schuler, had rediscovered the forgotten swastika. Ludwig Klages, who for a time was close to George, proclaimed "mind as the antagonist of the soul."

Oswald Spengler, at that period, was setting out to proclaim the decline of the West and announcing a line of new Caesars who would, for a time, stem the tide. Lenin had lived at 106 Schleissheimer Strasse, and at number 34 on the same street, only a few blocks away, Adolf Hitler now took a room as a tenant in the apartment of a tailor named Popp.

The intellectual ferment, like the artistic experimentation of the period, passed Hitler by in Munich as it had in Vienna. Vassily Kandinsky, Franz Marc, or Paul Klee, who also lived in the Schwabing neighborhood and were opening new dimensions in painting, meant nothing to Hitler. Throughout all the months he lived in Munich he remained the modest postcard copyist who had his visions, his nightmares, and his anxieties, but did not know how to translate them into art. The pedantic brushwork with which he rendered every blade of grass, every stone in a wall, and every roofing tile, shows his intimate craving for wholeness and idealized beauty.

59

But the phantom world of his complexes and aggressions remained completely unexpressed.

The more conscious he became, deep within himself, of his insufficient abilities as an artist and of his general failure, the more he had to find reasons for asserting his own superiority. He thought himself highly developed because he could recognize the "often infinitely primitive views" of his fellow men. It served a similar purpose that he saw all around him only the basest instincts at work: corruption, the scheming for power, ruthlessness, envy, hatred. It was essential for him to blame his tribulations on the world. His racial identification also helped to raise him in his own eyes. It meant that he was different and better than all proletarians, tramps, Jews, and Czechs who had crossed his path.

But fear weighed upon him as oppressively as ever, the fear of sinking to the point of being indistinguishable from the down-and-outs, the antisocial, the proletarians. The "school of life" had taught him to think in terms of catastrophe. Fear was the overwhelming experience of his formative years, and ultimately, as will be seen, the impulse behind the fierce dynamism of his whole life. His apparently consistent views of the world and of people, his harshness and inhumanity, were preponderantly gestures of defense and a compensation for that "frightened manner" which the few witnesses of his early years observed in him. Wherever he looked he saw nothing but symptoms of exhaustion, dissolution, loss and contamination; signs of blood-poisoning, racial submergence, ruin and catastrophe. In this, it is true, he shared the fundamentally pessimistic attitude that was one of the deeper strains of the nineteenth century and cast its shadow over the faith in progress and science which was another aspect of the age. But in the radical extremes to which he carried this feeling, in the thoroughness with which he yielded to these fears, he made them unmistakably his own.

This state of anxiety shows through his explanation of why, after years of drift and daydreaming, he finally left Vienna. His reasons are a strange mélange of Pan-Germanism and sentimentality, but he leads off by expressing his hatred for the city:

I was repelled by the conglomeration of races which the capital showed me, repelled by this whole mixture of Czechs, Poles, Hungarians, Ruthenians, Serbs, and Croats, and everywhere, the eternal parasitic fungi of humanity—Jews and more Jews.

To me the giant city seemed the embodiment of racial desecration. . . .

For all these reasons a longing rose stronger and stronger in me, to go at last whither since my childhood secret desires and secret love had drawn me.

I hoped some day to make a name for myself as an architect and thus, on the large or small scale which Fate would allot me, to dedicate my sincere services to the nation.

But finally I wanted to enjoy the happiness of living and working in the place which some day would inevitably bring about the fulfillment of my most ardent and heartfelt wish: the union of my beloved homeland with the common fatherland, the German Reich.[47]

It is possible that he did have some such yearnings. Other factors of greater or lesser weight conceivably contributed to the decision. He himself later confessed that he had never been able "to learn the Viennese jargon." He had also decided that the city and Austria as a whole "in the field of cultural and artistic matters . . . showed all symptoms of degeneration." Thus there were no opportunities for him as an aspiring architect, and he was simply wasting his time. "The new architecture could achieve no special successes in Austria, if for no other reason because since the completion of the Ring its tasks, in Vienna at least, had become insignificant. . . ."[48]

But all these reasons were not the decisive ones. What actuated him was once again his repugnance toward normality, his horror of the rules and obligations to which everyone else was subject. In the 1950's the military records pertaining to Adolf Hitler came to light again; in March, 1938, immediately after the invasion of Austria, he had ordered a feverish search for these papers. The documents make it plain beyond a doubt that in moving to Munich he was determined to escape his military obligations. In order to conceal the facts, he registered with the police in Munich as stateless. In *Mein Kampf* he also falsified the date of his departure from Vienna. Actually he left the city not in the spring of 1912, as he maintained, but in May of the following year.

For a time the Austrian authorities searched for him fruitlessly. On August 22, 1913, a Constable Zauner of Linz, who was conducting the investigation, noted: "Adolf Hietler [sic] appears to be registered with the police neither in this city nor in Urfahr, nor can he be located in other places." Hitler's former guardian, Josef Mayrhofer, could provide no information about his whereabouts; and the two sisters, Angela and Paula, when queried about their brother, declared that they had "known nothing about him since 1908." Inquiries in Vienna, however, disclosed that he had moved to Munich and was registered there at 34 Schleissheimer Strasse. On the afternoon of January 18, 1914, an official of the criminal police suddenly turned up at this address, arrested the wanted man, and the following day took him to the Austrian consulate.

The charge he faced was serious, and Hitler, after having imagined himself quite safe, was in imminent danger of a prison sentence. This was one of those prosaic incidents which, like so many later ones, might have changed the whole direction of his career. For with the disgrace of draft dodging on his record it was scarcely likely that Hitler could have mobilized a following of millions and created his paramilitary forces.

But again, as was to happen repeatedly, chance came to his aid. The Linz authorities had given him so little time to report that it was impossible for him to obey the summons. A postponement afforded him the opportunity to draw up a carefully calculated written statement. In a letter of several pages to the Linz Magistracy, Section II—the most voluminous and important document of his youth—he attempted to justify his conduct. The letter shows that his spelling and command of German were still deficient. Beyond that, it reveals that his life in Munich had remained as irregular and aimless as it was during his Vienna years.

In the summons I am called an artist. Although I am rightly accorded this title, it is nevertheless only conditionally correct. It is true that I earn my living as a free-lance painter, but only, since I am entirely without property (my father was a government official), in order to further my education. I am able to devote only a fraction of my time to earning a living, since I am still training myself as an architectural painter. Therefore my income is a very modest one, just large enough for me to get along.

I submit as evidence of this my tax statement and request you kindly to return this document to me. My income is estimated as 1200 marks, rather too much than too little, and does not mean that I make exactly 100 marks a month. Oh no. My monthly income is extremely variable, but certainly very bad right now, since the art trade sort of goes into its winter sleep around this time in Munich . . .

The explanation he offered for his conduct was extremely flimsy. He had missed his first notice to report but shortly afterward had reported of his own accord, only to have his documents lost in the bureaucratic channels. In lachrymose accents, full of self-pity and a servile cunning, he attempted to excuse the omission on the grounds of his desperate circumstances during his years in Vienna:

As far as my sin of omission in the autumn of 1909 is concerned, this was a terribly bitter time for me. I was an inexperienced young man, without any financial aid and also too proud to accept any from anyone, let alone to ask for it. Without any support, dependent on myself alone, the few crowns or often coppers I earned from my works were scarcely sufficient to provide me with a bed. For two years I had no other friend but care and need, no other companion but eternally gnawing hunger. I never knew the beautiful word youth. Today, even after five years, I have the mementos in the form of chilblain sores on my fingers, hands and feet. And yet I cannot recall this period without a certain rejoicing, now that I am after all over the worst. In spite of the greatest misery, in the midst of often more than dubious surroundings, I have always preserved my name unsullied, am altogether blameless before the law, and pure before my own conscience. . . .

Some two weeks later, on February 5, 1914, Hitler appeared before the draft board in Salzburg. The record of his physical examination, which the candidate had to sign, and which bears his signature, read: "Unfit for military and auxiliary service; too weak. Incapable of bearing arms."[49] He immediately returned to Munich.

By all indications, Hitler was not altogether unhappy in Munich. He later spoke of the "heartfelt love" this city had inspired in him from his first moment there. This was a phrase that did not normally occur in his vocabulary. He applied it above all to "the wonderful marriage of rustic strength and fine artistic mood, this unique line from the Hofbräuhaus to the Odeon, from the October Fest to the Pinakothek." Significantly, he does not adduce any political motive to explain his affection. He continued to be solitary, holing up on Schleissheimer Strasse; but he seems to have been as unaware as ever of his lack of human relationships. Actually, he did form a rather tenuous connection with his landlord, the tailor Popp, and with the latter's neighbors and friends, and engaged in a certain amount of socializing and political discussion with them. For the rest, he evidently found in the Schwabing taverns—where origins and status counted for nothing and everyone was socially acceptable—the kind of human contact that was the only kind he could stand because it afforded him closeness and strangeness simultaneously: the loose, chance acquaintanceships over a glass of beer, easily formed and easily lost. These were those "small circles" he later spoke of, where he was considered "educated." Here, for the first time, he apparently encountered more agreement than disagreement when he expatiated on the shakiness of the Dual Monarchy, the dire potentialities of the German-Austrian Alliance, the anti-German, pro-Slavic policy of the Hapsburgs, the Jews, or the salvation of the nation. In a milieu that favored outsiders and assumed that eccentric opinions and manners were a sign of genius, such views did not seem peculiar. If a question excited him, he frequently began to shout; but what he said, no matter how excessively he behaved, struck his listeners as consistent. He also liked to predict political developments in prophetic tones.

Later, he declared that by this time he had given up all plans to become a painter and that he painted only enough to earn a living so that he would be able to pursue his studies. For hours he sat over the newspapers in cafés or in the Hofbräuhaus, brooding, sallow, easily irritated. Sometimes, amid the fumes of beer, he dashed down vignettes of the scene around him, or a rendering of an interior in the sketch pad he carried with him. Josef Greiner claims to have met him in Munich at that time and to have asked what he had in mind to do in the future. Hitler answered, Greiner says, "that there would be a war shortly in any case so that it did not matter whether or not he had a profession beforehand, because in the army a corporation director was no more important than a dog barber."

Hitler's premonition—if Greiner has reported it accurately—was not mistaken. In *Mein Kampf* Hitler has impressively described the earthquake atmosphere of the prewar years, the intangible, almost unendurable feeling of tension on the verge of discharge. It is surely not accidental that these sentences stand out as among the most successful passages in the book, as writing:

As early as my Vienna period, the Balkans were immersed in that livid sultriness which customarily announces the hurricane, and from time to time a beam
of brighter light flared up, only to vanish again in the spectral darkness. But
then came the Balkan War and with it the first gust of wind swept across a
Europe grown nervous. The time which now followed lay on the chests of men
like a heavy nightmare, sultry as feverish tropic heat, so that due to constant
anxiety the sense of the approaching catastrophe turned at last to longing: let
Heaven at last give free rein to the fate which could no longer be thwarted. And
then the first mighty lightning flash struck the earth; the storm was unleashed
and with the thunder of Heaven there mingled the roar of the World War
batteries.[50]

By chance a photograph has been preserved in which Adolf Hitler can
be seen in the cheering crowd on the Odeonsplatz in Munich when the state
of war was proclaimed on August 1, 1914. His face is plainly recognizable:
the half-open mouth, the burning eyes, which at last have a goal and see a
future. For this day liberated him from all the embarrassments, the perplexities, and the loneliness of failure. Describing his own emotions in
Mein Kampf, he wrote:

To me those hours seemed like a release from the painful feelings of my
youth. Even today I am not ashamed to say that, overpowered by stormy
enthusiasm, I fell down on my knees and thanked Heaven from an overflowing
heart.

Virtually the whole era shared this emotion; seldom had Europe seemed
more unified than it was in the martial frenzy of those August days in
1914. One did not have to be an artistic wastrel with no prospects to
regard the day on which the war "broke out and swept away the 'peace'
. . ." as "beautiful for a sacred moment" and even to feel that it satisfied
an "ethical yearning."[51] The whole European world, including Germany,
was suffering from profound ennui. The war seemed an opportunity to
escape from the miseries of normality. Here again we may see Hitler's
intense attunement to his time. He shared its needs and longings, but more
sharply, more radically; whereas his contemporaries felt mere discontent,
he felt desperation. He hoped that the war would overturn all relationships,
all starting points. And wherever the resort to arms was cheered, people
sensed, at bottom, that an age was at last coming to its end and a new one
was in the making. *Fin de siècle*—that was the formula in which the
bourgeois age, with more than a touch of melancholy complacency, summed
up this mood of farewell. In keeping with the romanticizing tendencies of
the age, the war was viewed as a purification process, the great hope of
liberation from mediocrity, weariness with life, and self-disgust. And so the
war was hailed in "sacred hymns"; it was described as "the orgasm of universal life," creating chaos and fructifying it so that the new might be
born.[52] When Sir Edward Grey, the British Foreign Minister, declared at

the outbreak of the war that the lights were going out all over Europe, he was sorrowing at the end of civilization as he knew it. But there were many who exulted at this end.

Photographs taken during those early days of August, 1914, have preserved the hectic air of festivity, the gay expectancy, with which Europe entered the phase of its decline: mobilizing soldiers pelted with flowers, cheering crowds on the sidewalks, ladies in bright summer dresses on the balconies. It was as though fate were mixing the cards afresh in a game that had grown monotonous. The nations of Europe hailed victories they would never win.

In Germany those days brought an unparalleled sense of community experience, almost religious in its nature. The expression of it, struck up spontaneously in the streets and squares, was the song "Deutschland, Deutschland über Alles," which had been written by a long-controversial, liberal revolutionary of 1848 and only now became the real national anthem. On the evening of August 1 Kaiser Wilhelm II proclaimed to tens of thousands assembled in the palace square in Berlin that he no longer recognized "parties or denominations" but "only German brothers." Those were undoubtedly the most popular words he ever spoke. In a traditionally deeply divided nation that statement swept away, for one unforgettable moment, a multitude of barriers. German unity, attained barely fifty years before, seemed only now to have become a reality.

This feeling of unity was an illusion. The old contradictions survived behind the image of a nation reconciled. A welter of motives underlay the surge of rejoicing: personal and patriotic wishful thinking, revolutionary impulses, antisocial rebellions, dreams of hegemony, and, always, the yearning of adventurous spirits to break out of the routine of the bourgeois order. But for that one sublime moment it all combined into a storm of self-sacrifice on behalf of the threatened fatherland.

Hitler's own feelings had their quota of spurious elements: "Thus my heart, like that of a million others, overflowed with proud joy. . . ." he wrote and attributed his enthusiasm to the fact that he would now have a chance to prove by deeds the strength of his nationalistic convictions. On August 3 he addressed a petition directly to the King of Bavaria requesting permission, in spite of his Austrian citizenship, to volunteer for a Bavarian regiment. The contradiction between his draft evasion and this step is not a real one. For peacetime military service would have subjected him to a coercion he regarded as pointless. The war, on the other hand, meant liberation from the conflicts and miseries of his chaotic emotions, from the aimless emptiness of his life. In his boyhood two popular books about the Franco-Prussian War of 1870–71 had fired his enthusiasm for the powerful German army. Now he was entering that army with its nimbus of childhood reading. The past few days had vouchsafed him these feelings of belonging and union with his fellow men that he had lacked for so long.

65

Now, for the first time in his life, he saw his chance to share in the prestige of a great and feared institution.

The very day after he had submitted the petition, the answer arrived. "With trembling hands I opened the document," he relates. It summoned him to report to the 16th Bavarian Reserve Infantry Regiment, also known by its commander's name as the List Regiment. There now began for Hitler "the greatest and most unforgettable time of my earthly existence."[53]

Chapter 5

Without the army we would all not
be here; all of us once came out of
that school.

Adolf Hitler

REDEMPTION BY WAR

In the second half of October, after a training period of barely ten weeks, the List Regiment was sent to the Western front. Hitler had waited impatiently for shipment; he was afraid the war might be over before he saw action. But what was then called the baptism of fire—on October 29, in the first battle of Ypres, one of the bloodiest clashes of the first phase of the war—made him aware of the realities. The British units on this section doggedly and at last successfully opposed the massive German efforts to break through to the Channel coast. The German General Staff regarded this breakthrough as vital to its war plans. For four days the fighting raged. Hitler himself, in a letter to his Munich landlord, reported that in this battle the regiment was reduced by half, from 3,500 to about 1,700 men. Shortly afterward, near the village of Becelaere, it lost its commander; it acquired, partly as the result of stupid orders, a "mournful popularity."

The description given by Hitler of his first war experience in *Mein Kampf* will not stand close examination of the details. But the unusual care he devoted to the literary shaping of this passage, his efforts at poetic elevation, show how much the experience meant to him:

And then came a damp, cold night in Flanders, through which we marched in silence, and when the day began to emerge from the mists, suddenly an iron greeting came whizzing at us over our heads, and with a sharp report sent the little pellets flying between our ranks, ripping up the wet ground; but even before the little cloud had passed, from two hundred throats the first hurrah rose to meet the first messenger of death. Then a crackling and a roaring, a singing and a howling began, and with feverish eyes each one of us was drawn forward, faster and faster, until suddenly past turnip fields and hedges the fight began, the fight of man against man. And from the distance the strains of a song reached our ears, coming closer and closer, leaping from company to company, and just as Death plunged a busy hand into our ranks, the song

67

reached us too and we passed it along: *Deutschland, Deutschland über Alles, über Alles in der Welt!*[54]

Throughout the war Hitler served as a courier between the regimental staff and the advanced positions. This mission, in which he was dependent on no one but himself, suited his solitary temperament. One of his superiors remembered him as a "quiet, rather unmilitary looking man who appeared to differ in no way from his fellows." He was reliable, obedient, and according to the same source, of rather sober disposition. Even in the army he was considered eccentric; the members of his company almost all agreed in calling him a "pipe-dreamer." He often sat "helmet on his head, in a corner, lost in thought, and none of us were able to get him out of his slump." Although impressions of Hitler the soldier are fairly plentiful and date from different periods in nearly four years, they all sound much the same. None of them really brings him to life; but their colorlessness evidently is in keeping with the subject.

Even the eccentric qualities he displayed have an oddly impersonal character. There would be times when he would break out of his broodings into wild monologue. But this would not be the normal soldier's griping, revolving around all the bothers of a soldier's life. Rather, he would express his fears that victory would be lost, his suspicions of betrayal, his anxieties over invisible foes. Not a single episode brings him out as an individual. The only anecdote that was told about him—one that later found its way into German school readers—is in fact nothing but a school-reader anecdote. While carrying dispatches, the story goes, Hitler came upon a squad of fifteen Frenchmen in a trench near Montdidier. Due to his presence of mind, his courage, and his skillful surprise tactics, he succeeded in overpowering the enemy soldiers and leading them captive back to his commander.

His exemplary zeal concealed the man behind a picture cut out of a patriotic calendar; it was another way of escaping from the world, escaping into clichés. On a patrol, enemy machine guns suddenly began to fire; Hitler swept his commander out of the way, took up "a protective position in front of him," and begged the officer "to preserve the regiment from losing its commander twice in so short a time."

Without a doubt, he was a brave soldier; the charges of cowardice raised later were politically motivated. As early as December, 1914, he received the Iron Cross Second Class; in May, 1918, he was awarded a regimental certificate for bravery in the face of the enemy; and on August 4 of the same year he received the Iron Cross First Class, seldom awarded to enlisted men.

However, to this day it has been impossible to discover the specific grounds for these decorations. Hitler himself gives no clues, possibly because he had been proposed for the decorations by the Jewish regimental adjutant Hugo Gutmann. The history of the regiment does not mention them; the accounts that exist differ sharply. They report, apparently on the basis of the above-mentioned anecdote, that Hitler took a fifteen-man English patrol captive, or they describe the dramatic capture of ten, twelve, and even twenty Frenchmen. Some of the stories even endow Hitler with a knowledge of French that he did not have. Still another account claims that he fought his way through the heaviest fire to an artillery unit and in this way prevented the threatening shelling of his regiment's position. But whatever he won them for, those wartime decorations proved of inestimable value for Hitler's future. They gave him, although an Austrian, a kind of spiritual claim to citizenship in Germany. Thus they provided a prerequisite for the beginning of his career. They lent a degree of legitimacy to his claim to participate in German politics and to his demand for loyalty from his followers.

In the field, however, among his fellow soldiers, his exalted sense of responsibility, his anxiety over the total military picture were not appreciated. "We all used to yell at him," one of his fellows later recalled. Others said, "That fellow is bucking for stripes." Others noted that he always looked under some sort of strain. Yet he was, apparently, not distinctly unpopular. Rather, he merely let them see the distance that separated him from them. In contrast to the others, he had no family; he scarcely received or wrote letters, and he did not share in their commonplace worries, amusements, and laughter. "I hated nothing so much as that trash," he later recalled. Instead, he said, he meditated a great deal on the problems of life, and read Homer, the Gospels, and Schopenhauer. The war did for him what thirty years at the university might have done, he alleged. He thought he alone knew what the war was about, and from his isolation he derived a sense of being specially elect. Strictly speaking, what he was defending was not his homeland but the country he was proud of. The photographs taken of Hitler as a soldier suggest something of his peculiarly alienated relationship toward his fellows. Hitler sits beside them with a fixed expression, obviously sharing not at all in their viewpoint.

This complex incapacity for human relationships may be the reason why in four years at the front he never won promotion beyond the rank of private, first class. At the Nuremberg trial the adjutant of the List Regiment recounted that the question of promoting Hitler to the rank of noncommissioned officer had occasionally arisen but had always been decided in the negative "because we could discover no leadership qualities in him." Moreover, the adjutant added, Hitler himself had not wanted to be proposed for promotion.

What Hitler found in the billets and dugouts of wartime was the kind of human relationship that suited his nature. In its impersonality it was the life style of the home for men, but with the difference that the army satisfied his cravings for prestige, his inner restiveness, and his sense of solemnity. Here was the social framework that corresponded both to his misanthropic withdrawnness and his longing for contact. On the battlefield Hitler found the native land he did not possess. In no man's land he felt at home.

One of his former superiors has said this very thing and in much the same language: "For Pfc. Hitler the List Regiment was his homeland." When we understand this, we need no longer be puzzled by the contradiction between his determined desire for subordination in wartime and his lone-wolf asociality in the preceding years. Not since his mother's death had he felt as much at home anywhere, and never afterward was his simultaneous need for adventurousness and order, for unconstraint and discipline fulfilled as it was in the command headquarters, the trenches, and the dugouts at the front. In contrast to the humiliations of the preceding years, the war was Adolf Hitler's great affirmative educational experience, the one to which he exuberantly applied such phrases as "mighty impression," "overwhelming," "so happy."

Hitler himself declared that the war had transformed him. It hardened this touchy and sentimental young man and gave him a sense of his own worth. Caught up in the machinery of war, he learned toughness, the uses of solidarity, and self-discipline. He acquired that belief in fate which was one component of his generation's high-flown irrationality. The coolness with which he moved in the fiercest fire earned him, among his fellows, a reputation for invulnerability. If Hitler was around, they told one another, "nothing will happen." His luck seems to have made the deepest impression on Hitler himself and to have reinforced his faith in his special mission. Through all the years of failure and misery he had clung and continued obstinately to cling to that faith.

But the war also magnified Hitler's tendency to brooding. Like many of his fellow soldiers, he became convinced that the old leadership of society had failed, that the very social order he had marched to war to defend was perishing of internal exhaustion. "I would make the leaders responsible for these men who have fallen," he once declared to an astonished comrade. Hitler's generation, obsessed with its own idiosyncrasies and wrestling with its problems in a literary output of vast dimensions, was searching for a new meaning to life. Basically, this signified, it was searching for a meaningful social order. Hitler himself decided that he wanted "to know nothing about politics at that time." But his need to communicate, his unquenchable craving for speculative thinking, ran counter to such resolves. Soon he was attracting attention by "philosophizing about political and ideological questions in the crude manner of ordinary folk." From the early phase of the war we have a twelve-page letter of his to a Munich acquaintance which bears this out. After giving a detailed description of a frontal attack in which he participated, Hitler concludes the letter:[55]

I think about Munich so often, and each of us has only this one wish, that the final settlement with that gang will soon come, that we'll be able to go at them, no matter what the cost, and that those of us who have the good fortune to see our homeland again will find it purer and more purified of foreignism, so that by the sacrifices and sufferings which so many hundreds of thousands of us are undergoing daily, by the torrent of blood which is pouring out here day after day against an international world of enemies, not only Germany's enemies outside will be shattered, but also our inner internationalism. That would be worth more than all territorial gains. With Austria it will turn out as I have always said.

Politically, this letter carries on the ideological obsessions of Hitler's Vienna years: the fear of overwhelming foreign elements in the nation, together with a defensive reaction against a world of enemies. There were borrowings, also, from the Pan-German teachings, which later led to his thesis of the primacy of domestic over foreign affairs. National and racial unity took precedence over territorial expansion. Greater Germany was first to be German and only subsequently great.

At the beginning of October, 1916, at Le Barqué, Hitler was lightly wounded in the left thigh and sent to Beelitz Hospital near Berlin. He stayed in Germany until March, 1917, and it would appear that this was when there arose in him the first, still unclear signs of that "awakening" which two years later prompted him to enter politics.

August, 1914, and his experiences at the front had above all impressed upon him the inner unity of the nation. For two years he had basked in this new-found sense of togetherness, which he was sure nothing could affect. Having no family, no home address, no destination whatsoever, he had renounced his right to furloughs. His superzeal untroubled, he stayed on in his unreal world. "It was still the front of the old, glorious army of heroes," he later nostalgically recalled.[56] The shock was all the harsher when, in Beelitz and during a first visit to Berlin, he encountered the political, social, and national contradictions of the past. With deep distress he realized that the enthusiasm of the early phase of the war had drained away. Parties and factionalism had replaced that exalted sense of sharing a common destiny. It may be that his future resentment toward the city of Berlin had its origins in this experience. He saw discontent, hunger, and resignation. He was outraged at meeting slackers who boasted of their shrewdness; he noted hypocrisy, egotism, war profiteering, and, faithful to the obsession that dated back to his days in Vienna, he decided that behind all these manifestations was the work of the Jew.

It was the same when, nearly cured, he was sent to a reserve battalion in Munich. "I thought I could no longer recognize the city." He turned his resentment against those who had robbed him of his illusions and destroyed the lovely dream of German unity—the first positive social experience he had had since the days of his childhood. He was filled with fury against the "Hebrew corruptors of the people" on the one hand—12,000 or 15,000 of them should be held "under poison gas"—and against the politicians and journalists on the other hand. "Jabberers," "vermin," "perjuring criminals of the Revolution," they deserved nothing but annihilation. "All the implements of military power should have been ruthlessly used for the extermination of this pestilence."[57] He still longed hysterically for victory; no prophetic sense or strategic instinct told him that defeat would serve him far better as a basis for his rise from namelessness.

Returning to the front in the spring of 1917, he felt once more exalted and still more alienated from the civilian world to which he had never been able to adjust. Military documents indicate that he participated in the positional battles in French Flanders, in the spring Battle of Arras, and in the fierce autumnal conflict of Chemin des Dames. Apprehensively he noted the "senseless letters of thoughtless females" which helped infect that front with the mood of resignation that prevailed back home. At this time he frequently discussed his prospects for a future vocation with a fellow soldier, the painter Ernst Schmidt. Schmidt related that even then Hitler had begun to consider whether he ought not to try politics, but that he had never really decided. There are other indications that he still believed he could make a career as an artist. When he came to Berlin, the political heart of the country, in October, 1917—shortly after the Reichstag's controversial peace resolution and shortly before the German military triumph in the East—Hitler wrote in a postcard to Schmidt: "Now at last have opportunity to study the museums somewhat better." Later he declared that in those days he used to tell a small circle of his friends that when the war was over he meant to be active politically in addition to taking up his profession as an architect. According to his own account, he also knew what form that activity was going to take: he wanted to become a political speaker.

Such an aspiration sprang from the notion he had cherished since his Vienna days, that all modes of human reactions are the calculable result of guidance and background influences. The idea of hidden wirepullers, so disturbing and at the same time so fascinating to him, took on new and seductive colors as soon as he imagined himself as some day being one of the wirepullers. His view of humanity excluded all spontaneity. Everything could be produced by manipulation—"tremendous, almost incomprehensible results," as he noted with a touch of astonishment—if only the right players moved the right members at the right moment. He preposterously considered the movements of history, the rise and decline of nations, classes, or parties largely as the consequence of differing propagandistic abilities. In the famous sixth chapter of *Mein Kampf* he expatiated upon this view, illustrating his points by the difference between German and Allied propaganda.

According to his argument, Germany lost the war because "the form was inadequate, the substance was psychologically wrong: a careful examination of German war propaganda can lead to no other diagnosis." Because Germany's leaders did not recognize the true power of this weapon, they were incapable of creating propaganda worthy of the name. Instead, Germany produced only "insipid pacifistic bilge" that could never "fire men's spirits till they were willing to die." Although "the most brilliant psychologists would have been none too good" for this task, the Germans employed aesthetes and half-hearted failures, with the result that the country derived no advantage and sometimes actual harm from its propaganda.

The enemy, Hitler argued, had done it differently. Their atrocity propaganda, "as ruthless as it was brilliant," had made a deep impression upon Hitler, and he repeatedly extolled its psychological acumen and boldness. He admired the "rabid, impudent bias" and "indefatigable persistence" of the enemy lies,[58] and said that he "learned enormously" from them. In general, Hitler tended to illustrate his own ideas by pointing to what the enemy had done. There is no doubt that he drew his belief in the effectiveness of psychological influence from the example of enemy propaganda of the World War. It must be recognized, however, that a large part of the German public was convinced of the enemy's superiority in psychological warfare. This was actually just one more of those legends with which a nation proud of its military strength attempted to explain on nonmilitary grounds what otherwise seemed inexplicable: that after so many victories on all the battlefields and after so many efforts and sacrifices Germany had nevertheless lost the war. But Hitler, with that characteristic mixture of insight and vapidity that made him wise in his mistakes, used this transparent rationalization as the starting point for his views on the nature and power of propaganda. Propaganda must above all be popular, he argued; it must not be aimed toward the intelligentsia but "always and exclusively to the masses," and its level "must be adjusted to the most limited intelligence among those it is addressed to." Furthermore, effective propaganda must concentrate on a few plausible points and hammer away at these in the form of slogans. It must always appeal to the emotions, never to the intellect, and must eschew any attempt at objectivity. Not even the shadow of a doubt in the rightness of one's own cause is permissible; propaganda must present "love or hate, right or wrong, truth or lie, never half this way and half that way." Again these were not original ideas. But the energy with which Hitler framed them and the frankness with which he viewed the masses—without contempt but recognizing their limitations, their apathy and resistance to change—would soon put him far ahead of every rival for the favor of those same masses.

Even now he began to have intimations of this superiority. For he regarded his experiences in this late phase of the war as confirmation of the opinion he had formed during his Vienna years: that without the masses, without knowledge of their weaknesses, virtues and sensitivities, politics was no longer possible. In his mind the great democratic demagogues, Lloyd George and Clemenceau, joined his idol Karl Lueger. Later he added to these President Wilson—even though the American President was sicklied over by the pale cast of thought. One of the principal reasons for the ever more obvious German inferiority was, Hitler believed, that there was no convincing opponent in the Reich to these Allied populist leaders. Isolated from the common people and incapable of recognizing their growing importance, the German ruling class remained frozen in stubborn conservatism. Arrogant and unimaginative, it clung to its traditional positions. Recognition of its failures was one of the major perceptions Hitler drew from this period in German history. Free of those class prejudices and the self-centeredness that was the characteristic sign of weakness in an abdicating ruling class, Hitler thought only in terms of effects. Hence he admired the stale fables of enemy propaganda when it portrayed German soldiers as butchers hacking off the hands of children or slitting the bellies of pregnant women. For such images exploited the special spell of fear, the mechanism by which atrocities are magnified in the fantasies of the masses.

Again he was deeply struck by the mobilizing power of ideas. He appreciated the crusading formulas with which the Allies decked their cause and made it seem that they were defending the world and its most sacred values against the onslaught of barbarism. The German side had scarcely anything to oppose to this missionary *élan*. The Allied line proved to be all the more telling because the Germans, in the pride of their early military successes, had abandoned the thesis that they were fighting a purely defensive war. More and more boldly they had been announcing the aim of a peace with victory and wholesale annexations—failing to realize that the world might look askance on such ambitions. Some better reason would have had to be found than what Germany offered: that she had come too late to the distribution of the world's lands and so had to make up for it now by territorial aggrandizement. Meanwhile, at the end of 1917, defeated Russia in the fervor of social redemptionism was calling for a "just and democratic peace without annexations based on the right of self-determination of peoples, such as the exhausted and tormented classes of the workers and laborers of all countries long for." And, on the other side, Woodrow Wilson, at the beginning of 1918, presented to the Congress a comprehensive draft of a peace that was to refashion the world on new and better lines. He held out the promise of an order based on justice, of political and moral self-determination, of a world without force and aggression. It was inevitable that these proposals, contrasting with the assertion of sheer might by the Reich, should have had a strong effect upon the exhausted country. A significant anecdote of the autumn of 1918 tells of a German General Staff officer who in a moment of sudden insight clapped his hand to his brow and exclaimed, "To think that there are ideas we have to fight against and that we are losing the war because we didn't know anything about these ideas!"

To this extent, then, there is something to the thesis of extramilitary causes for the German defeat. It cannot be laid solely to the Siegfried complex of a nation that preferred to think it had been defeated by cunning and treachery than in open battle. That thesis, in endless variations, later became a staple item in the repertory of the Right. But it contained a kernel of truth. For in fact Germany had also been defeated on fields other than the battlefields, although in a sense the nationalistic spokesmen did not mean. An outmoded, anachronistic political system had proved itself inferior to a democratic order more in keeping with the needs of the age. For Hitler's part, he was for the first time seized by the thought that an idea can never be successfully combatted by sheer force but only with the aid of another and more suggestive idea. "Any attempt to combat a philosophy with methods of violence will fail in the end, unless the fight takes the form of attack for a new spiritual attitude. Only in the struggle between two philosophies can the weapon of brutal force, persistently and ruthlessly applied, lead to a decision for the sake of the side it supports."[59] It may very well be that these reflections, set down in *Mein Kampf,* were still vague in Hitler's mind at the time of the war. But, even so, they represent his lasting profit from the war years.

In the summer of 1918, however, a German victory seemed once more within grasp. A few months earlier the Reich had won a resounding success, not just one more of those temporary victories in battles that were bleeding it to death. Early in March Germany had imposed upon Russia the peace of Brest-Litovsk, and a month or so later had demonstrated to Rumania, in the Treaty of Bucharest, that its power was still formidable. The two-front war had come to an end, and the German army of the West, with 200 divisions and approximately 3.5 million men had been brought up to the manpower of the Allied armies. In equipment and arms, however, it remained distinctly inferior; to the enemy's 18,000 artillery pieces the Germans had only 14,000. But the High Command, supported by a new although not entirely wholehearted feeling of public confidence, had at the end of March launched the first of five offensives intended to force a decision before American troops could arrive. Now the German people had only the choice between victory or doom, Ludendorff declared in a statement that rang with the same passion for a great gamble that in later years possessed Hitler.

Throwing their last remaining forces into the fight, determined after so many fruitless successes and vain exertions to win victory at last by breaking through on a broad front, the German units went over to the attack. Hitler participated in these battles as a soldier in the List Regiment; he was in the pursuit after the breakthrough at Montdidier-Nyons and later took part in the battles of Soissons and Reims. During the early part of the summer the German formations actually succeeded in throwing the British and French armies back to within nearly forty miles of Paris.

But then the offensive ground to a halt. Once again the German armies had displayed that fatefully limited power which enabled them to win only sham victories. The toll of lives that their gains had cost, the desperate shortage of reserves, the effectiveness of the enemy in stabilizing the front after each of the German breakthroughs—all this was in part concealed from the German public, in part repressed by that public as it exulted over the good news from the front. The German operations came to a standstill, and the Allies passed over to counterattack on a broad front. Yet Hindenburg and Ludendorff continued their policy of systematic deception. A Privy Council meeting was held at army headquarters on August 14, long after the German lines had broken. The army leaders presented such an illusory picture of the military situation to Chancellor Hertling and Foreign Minister Hintze that both men went away completely unaware of the gravity of the military collapse. To be sure, Hertling himself was largely responsible for the policy of bowing to the military authorities. But since the High Command itself had staked everything on the radical alternative of victory or defeat, it was obliged by its own premise to admit defeat, since victory had not been won. Instead, it continued its deceptions into September—purportedly in order not to dishearten the people. It took into account the obvious hopelessness of the situation only by sounding its claims of German invulnerability in a somewhat more muted key.

The consequence was that the German public regarded victory and the longed-for end of the war as closer than ever before—in this summer of 1918 when the country was on the verge of defeat. This state of affairs completely refutes Hitler's arguments about the weakness of German propaganda—although he drew accurate conclusions from his inaccurate premises. Even responsible politicians, even high army officers with a broad view of conditions, were prone to the most amazing delusions. Very few among those who should have known better were able to find their way in the fog of misguided hopes.

The majority were therefore all the more stunned by the sudden plunge into reality. On September 29, 1918, Ludendorff hastily summoned the political leaders and demanded that they immediately ask for an armistice. His nerves were at breaking point; he would not hear of any tactical safeguards. Significantly, in spite of his talk about victory or doom he had launched the new offensive without giving any thought to the possible consequences of its failure. He does not seem to have even developed a clear strategic goal. At any rate, when the Crown Prince questioned him on that, he replied, with characteristic irritability: "We're going to chop a hole. Then we'll see what comes next." And when the new Chancellor, Prince Max von Baden, wanted to know what would happen in case of failure, Ludendorff snarled: "Then Germany is done for, that's all."

As things stood, the last card had actually been played with the great offensive in the spring of 1918. The increasingly vigorous Allied counterattack had had a daunting effect on German troops everywhere. The men were exhausted, "dull and apathetic," as an army commander reported.

For the operations of the spring months, with their heavy casualties, had used up the soldiers' last physical strength. Failure had consumed their remaining psychological reserves. There is much truth in Winston Churchill's remark that it was the Germans' own offensive, not that of the Allies, that devoured the forces of the army on the Western front. Ludendorff, that is, not Joffre or Haig, brought defeat to the Germans. Nevertheless, the troops held their ground on the whole in an amazing fashion. The defensive battles of that final phase were, in both military and human terms, among the most impressive achievements of the war, and paradoxically they added to the myth of the German army. Once again Ludendorff, who had daily expected a vast catastrophic breakthrough by the Allies, found that he was mistaken.

Unprepared politically and psychologically, the nation, which in a contemporary phrase had believed in the superiority of its arms "as in a gospel," was plunged into an abyss. An illuminating although almost unbelievable remark of Hindenburg's shows how hard the national illusion died. Immediately after Ludendorff's admission that the war was lost, old Hindenburg in all seriousness asked the Foreign Minister to do everything possible in the impending negotiations to obtain annexation of the mines of Lorraine. Here was a first example of that peculiar trick of denying reality to which growing numbers of Germans resorted throughout the postwar years to help them through the misery of the times. They continued to do so right up to the intoxicating days of Spring, 1933. The shock effect of this alternation "from the fanfare of victory to the dirge of defeat" strongly colored the history of the period—so much so that we may say the period can scarcely be understood without taking that disenchantment into consideration.

It was a particular shock to the brooding, overtense private, first class of the List Regiment who had surveyed the war in the sweeping terms of a general. His regiment had been thrown into the defensive battle in Flanders in October, 1918. On the night of October 13, south of Ypres, the British launched a gas attack. On a hill near Wervick, Hitler came into several hours of drumfire with gas shells. Toward morning he felt violent pain, and when he arrived at the regimental command post around seven o'clock, he could barely see. A few hours later he went blind: "My eyes had turned into glowing coals," he afterward wrote. He was shipped back to the Pasewalk hospital in Pomerania.[60]

In the hospital a curious excitement prevailed. Confusing rumors went the rounds—that the monarchy was about to fall, that the war would soon be over. Hitler—characteristically as if he bore larger responsibilities—feared local unrest, strikes, insubordination, even though these rumors seemed to him "more the product of the imagination of individual scoundrels"; strangely, he noticed nothing of the discontent and exhaustion so widespread among the people. At the beginning of November the condition

77

of his eyes began to improve, but he still could not read newspapers and expressed his fears to fellow patients that he would never be able to draw again. The revolution came, for him, "suddenly and unexpectedly"; it was led, he thought, by "a few Jewish youths" who had "not been at the front" but had come "by way of a so-called 'clap hospital' and 'raised the red rag.' " Hitler believed that what he was seeing was "a more or less local affair."[61]

On November 10, 1918, however, the truth was brought home to him, "the most terrible certainty of my life." Summoned to a meeting by the hospital pastor, the patients learned that a revolution had broken out, that the House of Hohenzollern had fallen and a republic had been proclaimed in Germany. Sobbing gently to himself—thus Hitler described the "old gentleman"—the pastor recalled the merits of the ruling house, and "not an eye was able to restrain its tears." But when the pastor began to tell them that the war was now lost and that the Reich was throwing itself unconditionally upon the mercy of its previous enemies—"I could stand it no longer. It became impossible for me to sit still one minute more. Again everything went black before my eyes; I tottered and groped my way back to the dormitory, threw myself on my bunk, and dug my burning head into my blanket and pillow. Since the day I had stood at my mother's grave, I had not wept. . . . But now I could not help it."[62]

To Hitler the disillusionment was as sudden and incomprehensible as had been his failure to win acceptance into the Academy. He magnified it into a legend and made it one of the basic themes of his career. Later he ascribed his resolve to enter politics to this moment. In virtually every major speech Hitler would ritualistically refer to the November revolution. He would speak of it as if his whole life dated from that event. This obsession has led some analysts to suggest that the revolution triggered the great political awakening of his life. It has also been suggested that his going blind in October, 1918, was to some extent a hysterical symptom, precipitated by the shock he felt at the abrupt change in the course of the war. Hitler himself occasionally furnished some support for such theories. In a speech to army officers and officer candidates in February, 1942, for example, he referred to the danger he had faced of going completely blind, and declared that eyesight meant nothing if all one could see was a world in which the nation was enslaved. "In that case what can I see worth seeing?" And at the end of 1944, faced with approaching defeat, he gloomily told Albert Speer that he had reason to fear that once again, as toward the end of the First World War, he would go blind.[63]

Similarly, there is a passage in *Mein Kampf* confirming the idea that Hitler had been roused from his inconspicuous existence by an inexorable summons resounding in his ears:

In daily life the so-called genius requires a special cause, indeed, often a positive impetus, to make him shine. . . . In the monotony of everyday life even significant men often seem insignificant, hardly rising above the average of their environment; as soon, however, as they are approached by a situation in which others lose hope or go astray, the genius rises manifestly from the inconspicuous average child, not seldom to the amazement of all those who had hitherto seen him in the pettiness of bourgeois life. . . . If this hour of trial had not come, hardly anyone would ever have guessed that a young hero was hidden in this beardless boy. . . . The hammer-stroke of Fate which throws one man to the ground suddenly strikes steel in another.[64]

We may assume, however, that such remarks were merely meant to explain the transition between the preceding years of bohemianism, apathy, and vague reveries and the phase of revealed genius. In reality, the November days had numbed him and left him in a quandary. "I knew that everything was lost." The requirements imposed by the hated bourgeois world, those requirements that four years of war had set aside, were confronting him once more. He was no further along in meeting the problems of vocation and earning his livelihood. He had no training, no work, no goal, no place to stay, no friends. In that outburst of despair, when he wept into his pillow at the news of the defeat and the revolution, he was expressing more of a personal than a national sense of loss.

For the end of the war deprived the sergeant Hitler of a role he had found at the front, and he lost his homeland at the moment he was dismissed for home. In shocked surprise he noted that at the home front the much-vaunted discipline of the German army collapsed as if on cue. Increasing numbers of soldiers had only one remaining desire: to throw off the suddenly unbearable burden of four years, to make an end of it and go home. They could no longer conceal the fears and humiliations of existence at the front behind patriotic formulas or warrior poses. An overwhelming sense of the vanity of it all became the general sentiment: "And so it had all been in vain. In vain all the sacrifices and privations; in vain the hunger and thirst of months which were often endless; in vain the hours in which, with mortal fear clutching at our hearts, we nevertheless did our duty; and in vain the death of two millions who died."[65]

It was the defeat rather than the revolutionary events that so deeply affected him, for his attachment to the ruling house was as slight as his respect for the leadership of the Reich.

The force of this unrevolutionary revolution was spent chiefly in gestures that suggest a curiously helpless perplexity. From the early days of November on, deserters marched through the streets all over Germany, hunting down officers. Groups of enlisted men lay in wait for the officers, seized them, and with scornful and insulting comments ripped off their decorations, epaulets, and cockades. This was an act of revolt after the fact against the overthrown regime and was as pointless as it was understandable. In the case of the officers, it bred a permanent ire that was to have far-

79

reaching consequences, a deep-seated antipathy for the revolution and hence for the regime which had begun under such circumstances. That antipathy was shared by all the advocates of law and order.

The whim of history had robbed the revolution of that emotional verve which might otherwise have made it memorable in the mind of the nation. As early as October, 1918, the Chancellor, Prince Max von Baden, had met the demands both of President Wilson and his own public by instituting a number of domestic political reforms. Germany was given a parliamentary government. Finally, on the morning of November 9, the Chancellor, acting to a considerable extent on his own initiative, had announced the Kaiser's abdication. The revolution had reached its goal before it had even broken out; it had at any rate missed the chance to define itself by any concrete act. Abruptly, it had been cheated of its storming of the Bastille and its Boston Tea Party.

Given these discouraging circumstances, there was only one way the quasi revolution might have become a real one—by exploiting the attraction of novelty. But the new holders of power, Friedrich Ebert and the Social Democrats, were hard-working, sobersided men. They thought they had done pretty well to eliminate right at the start a whole slew of honorary titles, decorations, and medals. The peculiar pedantry and lack of psychological flair that marked all their behavior explain why they could not fire the masses or draft any major social changes. Theirs was "a revolution entirely lacking in ideas," as one man who lived through it recognized.[66] Certainly they had no answer to the emotional needs of a defeated and disillusioned nation. The Constitution, which was discussed during the first half of 1919 and went into force in Weimar on August 11, fell far short of what was needed. It was intended, strictly speaking, merely as a technical instrument for installing a democratic power system, but it revealed scarcely any understanding of the ends of power.

Indecision and lack of courage early sapped the strength of the new regime. The new men could of course point to the exhaustion of the nation and to the fear of what had happened in Russia. Faced with the multitudinous needs of a defeated country, they might well cite many reasons for restraining the desire for political innovation that was spontaneously springing up on the workers' and soldiers' councils. But the events had prepared the nation for the abandonment of traditional attitudes. That readiness was not exploited. The revolution was hailed even on the right, and "socialism" as well as "socialization" constituted one of the magic formulas for solving the situation even among conservative intellectuals. But in fact its sole program was the restoration of law and order, and the new leaders thought they could accomplish this only in alliance with the traditional powers. Not even a timid approach toward socialization was attempted. The great feudal landholders remained untouched; the civil servants were prematurely guaranteed their positions. With the exception

80

of the ducal and royal houses, the social groups that had hitherto wielded decisive influence emerged from the transition to a new form of government virtually without loss of power. With some cogency Hitler could later ask scornfully who had prevented the men of November from setting up a socialist state, since they had the power to do it.[67]

In the confusion and perplexity of those weeks, only the radical Left was capable of drafting a revolutionary program for the future. But it had neither a following nor, in Max Weber's phrase, the spark of "Catilinarian energy." On January 6, 1919, a crowd numbering tens of thousands of persons in a revolutionary mood gathered in the Siegesallee in Berlin and waited in vain until evening for some sign from the endlessly debating revolutionary committee. Finally, freezing, weary, and disappointed, the crowd dispersed. The gap between thought and deed was as insurmountable as ever. Nevertheless, the revolutionary Left, especially up to the assassination of its two outstanding leaders, Rosa Luxemburg and Karl Liebknecht, engaged in sufficiently violent struggles with counterrevolutionary soldiery to produce turmoil and internecine conflicts. What remained historically unsuccessful was not without its consequences.

For the bedeviled and directionless public soon blamed the battles and controversies of that period on the republic, which was only defending itself. Everything was equated with "the revolution," and the political form that finally emerged from these troubled times was in the common mind obscurely connected with mutiny, defeat, national humiliation, street battles, chaos, and public disorder. Nothing so damaged the prospects of the republic as the fact that the public associated its very beginnings with a "dirty" revolution. Much of the population, including even the political moderates, remembered the inception of the republic with shame, sorrow, and disgust.

The terms of the Versailles peace treaty increased the resentment. The public statements of President Wilson had fostered the illusion that overthrow of the monarchy and the adoption of Western constitutional principles would soften the wrath of the victors and cause them to adopt a milder tone toward men who, after all, were only acting as executors of the legacy of a deceased regime. Many Germans also believed that the "order of world peace," for which the discussions at Versailles were ostensibly laying the groundwork, excluded punishment, injustices, and any kind of coercion. This period of understandable but unrealistic hopes has been called "the dreamland of the Armistice period." The country's reaction at the beginning of May, 1919, when the peace terms were presented to it, was all the more dumfounded. There was a great outcry. The public consternation was expressed politically by the resignations of Chancellor Philipp Scheidemann and of Foreign Minister Count Ulrich von Brockdorff-Rantzau.

One thing is certain: the victorious powers arranged the surrounding circumstances with deliberate desire to harass and insult the Germans. They had opened the peace conference on January 18, 1919, the anniversary of the day the German Empire had been proclaimed barely fifty years before; and they chose as the place for signing the treaty the same Hall of Mirrors in which that proclamation had been issued. Perhaps that could be borne with. But their choosing for the signing date June 28, the fifth anniversary of the assassination of Austrian Archduke Francis Ferdinand at Sarajevo, stood in what was felt to be cynical contrast to the altruism of Wilsonian pledges.

In general, the psychological affronts rather than the material exactions were what produced the extraordinarily traumatic effects of the Treaty of Versailles, so that from Right to Left, running across all factions and parties, it produced a sense of unforgettable humiliation. The territorial demands, the requirements for compensation and reparations, which at first dominated public discussion, certainly did not have that "Carthaginian harshness" which was so much talked about. The terms in fact could stand comparison with the conditions Germany had imposed on Russia in the Treaty of Brest-Litovsk and on Rumania in the Treaty of Bucharest. But certain clauses seemed intolerably insulting and soon figured in rightist agitation as the "disgrace" of Versailles. These were the clauses that struck at German honor: above all Article 228, which provided for the handing over of certain German officers for judgment by Allied military tribunals, and the celebrated Article 231, which placed sole moral guilt for the outbreak of the war upon Germany.

The contradictions and hypocrisies in the 440 articles of the treaty were all too evident. The victors assumed the pose of judges and insisted on the Germans' confessing their sins, where in fact their interests were purely material. The pointless vengeful moralism was what awoke so much hatred and ridicule. Even in the Allied countries there was strong criticism of this hypocritical tone. The right of self-determination, for example, which in President Wilson's proclamations had been raised to the height of a sacred principle, was quietly dropped whenever it might have worked to the advantage of the Germans. There was no question of the German remnant of the shattered Hapsburg monarchy becoming part of the Reich. Supranational states were destroyed and nationalism triumphantly confirmed; but, paradoxically, the League of Nations was created, whose essence was the denial of nationalism.

The treaty solved scarcely any of the problems that had led to the recent hostilities. Instead, it all but destroyed the sense of European solidarity and common tradition that had survived so long, despite the wars and angry passions of centuries. The new order imposed by the peace treaty did little to restore this sense. For all intents and purposes, Germany remained excluded, seemingly forever, from the European community. This discrimination turned the Germans decisively against European co-operation.

In challenging the victors, Hitler was able to build on this feeling. Actually, a large part of Hitler's early successes in foreign affairs were gained by his posing as a firm adherent of Woodrow Wilson's principles and the maxims posited by the Versailles Peace Treaty with regard to the self-determination of national and ethnic groups. "A terrible time is dawning for Europe," wrote one clear-sighted observer on the day the peace treaty was ratified in Paris, "a sultriness before the storm which will probably end in an even more terrible explosion than the World War."[68]

Within Germany, the bitterness over the terms of the peace treaty increased the resentment against the republic, for it had proved incapable of sparing the country the distresses and privations of this "shameful dictated peace." How unwanted the republic really had been now became evident. It had been merely the product of embarrassment, chance, craving for peace, and weariness. Its impotence in domestic affairs had already lost it much credit. To this bad record was now added its weakness in foreign affairs. To a growing number of Germans the very term "republic" seemed synonymous with disgrace, dishonor, and powerlessness. The feeling persisted that the republic had been imposed on the Germans by deception and coercion, that it was something altogether alien to their nature. It is true that in spite of all its drawbacks it held a certain promise; but even in its few fortunate years it was "unable to arouse either the loyalty or the political imagination of the people."[69]

These developments led to a surge of political consciousness. Large segments of the population, who previously had lived in a political limbo, abruptly and violently found themselves caught up in events that aroused in them political passions, hopes, and despairs.

Adolf Hitler, now some thirty years old, was seized by this general mood in the hospital at Pasewalk. A vague but furious sense of misfortune and betrayal swept over him. It brought him a step closer to politics, but his decision to go actively into politics, which in *Mein Kampf* is linked to the events of November, 1918, actually was made a year later, when he discovered his oratorical gifts. The overwhelming moment came to him in the haze of a small meeting; in a burst of rapture he suddenly saw a way out of a hopelessly blocked life and found that he had prospects for a future.

Certainly his behavior during the following months suggests this interpretation. For when he was discharged from Pasewalk hospital at the end of November, he went to Munich and reported to the reserve battalion of his regiment. Munich had played an important part in the November events and had led the way in the overthrow of the German ruling houses. But although the city was vibrating with political excitement, Hitler remained indifferent. In spite of his alleged decision to go into politics, he neither joined nor opposed the political currents. Rather tersely, he comments that Red rule was repugnant to him. But since by his own contention the "Reds" were in power basically throughout the period of the republic, such an observation scarcely justifies the meager interest he took in politics at this period.

At the beginning of February, craving something to do, he volunteered for guard duty in a prisoner-of-war camp at Traunstein, near the Austrian border. But about a month later the few hundred French and Russian soldiers were released, and both camp and guard detail were dissolved. Once more, Hitler was left at loose ends. He returned to Munich.

Since he did not know where else to go, he took up quarters in the barracks in Oberwiesenfeld. Presumably, the decision did not come easily to him, for it meant he had to subordinate himself to the dominant Red Army and don its red armband. Nevertheless, he put up with taking orders from the revolutionary Left at a time when he might have joined units of the Right, a fact revelatory of his underdeveloped political instincts and lack of discrimination at the time. Later, the mere mention of the word "Bolshevism" would drive him wild. But all subsequent revision of the facts to the contrary, at this stage his political indolence was obviously stronger than any horror he might have had at being counted a soldier of the world revolution.

It is true that he also had no choice. The army was the only social framework in which he could feel sheltered. To leave it meant returning to the realm of the shipwrecked. Hitler was distinctly aware of the hopelessness of his personal predicament: "At that time endless plans chased one another through my head. For days I wondered what could be done, but the end of every meditation was the sober realization that I, nameless as I was, did not possess the least basis for any useful action."[70] Plainly, he was as far as ever from thinking of a job, of earning a living, and achieving bourgeois status. Instead, he was agonizingly aware of his insignificance. According to his story, his political activity at that time had incurred "the disapproval of the Central Council" of the new soviet government in Munich, so that at the end of April they came to arrest him. "Faced with my leveled carbine, the scoundrels lacked the necessary courage and marched off as they had come." But in reality the Central Council was no longer in existence at the time he gives.

It is much more likely that his behavior at this time was a mixture of embarrassment, passivity, and opportunistic adjustment. He took no noticeable part even in the turbulent events of early May, when the troops of Colonel von Epp's Free Corps, a paramilitary organization, together with other formations, overthrew the soviet government in Munich. Otto Strasser, who for a time was one of his followers, later asked publicly: "Where was Hitler on that day? In what corner of Munich was the soldier hiding who ought to have fought in our ranks?" In fact Red Army man Adolf Hitler was arrested and questioned by the invading troops; some officers who knew him intervened, and he was released again. Possibly the story of the attempted arrest by the Central Council is the retouched version of this incident.

Afterward, a commission was set up to look into events during the soviet rule, and there has been much speculation on the role Hitler may have played in conjunction with these investigations. All that is certain, however, is that he offered his services to the board of inquiry established by the Second Infantry Regiment. He supplied information for the tribunals, which often handed down very harsh sentences reflecting the bitterness of the recent struggle. He located fellow soldiers who had taken part in the soviet regime, and seems to have carried out his assignment so well that he was soon sent to a training course in "civic thinking."

Now for the first time he was beginning to attract attention, to emerge from the anonymity that had so long concealed and depressed him. He himself called his work for the investigating commission his "first more or less purely political activity."[71] He was still letting himself drift; but the direction in which he now floated rapidly brought him to the end of his formative years, which were compounded of asocial apathy and a messianic sense of vocation.

Looking back over this period, it is astonishing to see that Adolf Hitler, who was to become the century's political phenomenon, did not feel tempted by politics until his thirtieth year. At a comparable age, Napoleon was already First Consul, Lenin in exile after years of persecution, Mussolini editor in chief of the socialist paper *Avanti*. Hitler, however, had not been impelled to take a single step in behalf of any of those ideas that would soon send him forth on a mission of world conquest. He had not entered a single party, had not joined any of the numerous associations of the period, with the exception of the Viennese League of Anti-Semites. There is nothing betokening any impulse toward political action, no sign of anything more than a stammering participation in the platitudes of the era.

On November 23, 1939, when his faith in his own power was at its height, he himself made the astonishing remark to his military commanders that in 1919 he had entered politics only after a long struggle with himself. That had been, he said, "the most difficult decision of all." And although this was said to emphasize that beginnings are always the hardest part of a venture, it also reveals his strong inner reservations about a political career. One element may have been the traditional German contempt for politics as something by nature lower than creative activity. He would have thought a political career demeaning by comparison with his unattainable youthful dream of becoming "one of the foremost architects of Germany, if not the foremost architect." Even at the climax of the war he remarked that he would far sooner have gone to Italy as an "unknown painter" and that only the deadly menace to his own race had forced him on to the road of politics, which was fundamentally alien to him.

If this was so, we can understand why not even the revolution drove him to enter the fray on one side or the other. The November events, the collapse of all authority, the downfall of the dynasties and the prevailing chaos had certainly challenged his conservative instincts. But even these violent changes did not rouse him to active protest. Even stronger than his contempt for political affairs was his repugnance for riot and rebellion. Bourgeois that he was, he was not one to go into the streets. Even twenty-five years later, he told his dinner companions, referring to his experiences at the time of the November revolution, that rebels were no more or less than criminals. He could see in them nothing but an "asocial lot"; the best thing to do with them was to kill them.

Only when he discovered his own oratorical powers did he overcome his qualms against the political life and his fear of odium as a disturber of public order. Even so, when he leaped on the stage as a revolutionary personality, he became, as he justified himself four years later in his trial before the Munich People's Court, a revolutionary against the revolution. But was he any the less an unsociable, easily depressed artist personality whom the peculiar circumstances of the times, together with a monstrous special gift, had propelled into a realm for which he was never intended? The question will arise repeatedly in the course of this biography, and repeatedly we will be tempted to ask whether politics ever meant more to him than the means he employed to practice it: rhetorical overpowering of his enemies, for example; the histrionics of processions, parades, and Party Days; the spectacle of military force applied in war.

There is no denying that the collapse of the old order opened the way for him to enter politics. As long as the bourgeois world persisted and politics was a bourgeois career, he had few prospects of winning a name in it. The formal strictures of that sphere would all have operated against him.

The year 1918 brought down the barriers. "I could not help but laugh at the thought of my own future which only a short time ago had given me such bitter concern," Hitler wrote.[72]

And so he set foot on the political stage.

INTERPOLATION I

The Great Dread

At the end of the First World War the victory of the democratic idea seemed beyond question. Whatever its weaknesses might be, it rose above the turmoil of the times, the uprisings, the dislocations, and the continual quarrels among nations as the unifying principle of the new age. For the war had not only decided a claim to power. It had at the same time altered a conception of government. After the collapse of virtually all the governmental structures of Central and Eastern Europe many new political entities had emerged out of turmoil and revolution. And these for the most part were organized on democratic principles. In 1914 there had been only three republics alongside of seventeen monarchies in Europe. Four years later there were as many republics as monarchies. The spirit of the age seemed to be pointing unequivocally toward various forms of popular rule.

Only Germany seemed to be opposing this mood of the times, after having been temporarily gripped and carried along by it. Those who would not acknowledge the reality created by the war organized into a fantastic swarm of *völkisch* [racist-nationalist] parties, clubs, and free corps. To these groups the revolution had been an act of treason; parliamentary democracy was something foreign and imposed from without, merely a synonym for "everything contrary to the German political will," or else an "institution for pillaging created by Allied capitalism."[1]

Germany's former enemies regarded the multifarious symptoms of nationalistic protest as the response of an inveterately authoritarian people to democracy and civic responsibility. To be sure, the Germans were staggering beneath terrible political and psychological burdens: there was the shock of defeat, the moral censure of the Versailles Treaty, the loss of territory and the demand for reparations, the impoverishment and spiritual undermining of much of the population. Nevertheless, the conviction remained that a great moral gap existed between the Germans and most of their neighbors. Full of resentment, refusing to learn a lesson, this incomprehensible country had withdrawn into its reactionary doctrines, made of them a special virtue, adjured Western rationality and humanity, and in general set itself against the universal trend of the age. For decades this picture of Germany dominated the discussion on the reasons for the rise of National Socialism.

But the image of democracy victorious was also deceptive. The moment in which democracy seemed to be achieving historic fulfillment simultaneously marked the beginning of its crisis. Only a few years later the idea of democracy was challenged in principle as it had never been before. Only a few years after it had celebrated its triumph it was overwhelmed or at least direly threatened by a new movement that had sprung to life in almost all European countries.

This movement recorded its most lasting successes in countries in which the war had aroused considerable discontent or made it conscious of existing discontent, and especially in countries in which the war had been followed by leftist revolutionary uprisings. In some places these movements were conservative, harking back to better times when men were more honorable, the valleys more peaceable, and money had more worth; in others these movements were revolutionary and vied with one another in their contempt for the existing order of things. Some attracted chiefly the petty bourgeois elements, others the peasants, others portions of the working class. Whatever their strange compound of classes, interests, and principles, all seemed to be drawing their dynamic force from the less conscious and more vital lower strata of society. National Socialism was merely one variant of this widespread European movement of protest and opposition aimed at overturning the general order of things.

National Socialism rose from provincial beginnings, from philistine clubs, as Hitler scornfully described them, which met in Munich bars over a few rounds of beer to talk over national and family troubles. No one would have dreamed that they could ever challenge, let alone outdo, the powerful, highly organized Marxist parties. But the following years proved that in these clubs of nationalistic beer drinkers, soon swelled by disillusioned homecoming soldiers and proletarianized members of the middle class, a tremendous force was waiting to be awakened, consolidated, and applied.

In Munich alone there existed, in 1919, nearly fifty more or less political associations, whose membership consisted chiefly of confused remnants of the prewar parties that had been broken up by war and revolution.

They had such names as New Fatherland, Council of Intellectual Work, Siegfried Ring, Universal League, Nova Vaconia, League of Socialist Women, Free Union of Socialist Pupils, and Ostara League. The German Workers' Party was one such group. What united them all and drew them together theoretically and in reality was nothing but an overwhelming feeling of anxiety.

First of all, and most immediate, there was the fear of revolution, that *grande peur* which after the French Revolution had haunted the European bourgeoisie throughout the nineteenth century. The notion that revolutions were like forces of nature, elemental mechanisms operating without reference to the will of the actors in them, following their own logic and leading perforce to reigns of terror, destruction, killing, and chaos—that notion was seared into the public mind. That was the unforgettable experience, not Kant's belief that the French Revolution had also shown the potentiality for betterment inherent in human nature. For generations, particularly in Germany, this fear stood in the way of any practical revolutionary strivings and produced a mania for keeping things quiet, with the result that every revolutionary proclamation up to 1918 was countered by the standard appeal to law and order.

This old fear was revived by the pseudorevolutionary events in Germany and by the menace of the October Revolution in Russia. Diabolical traits were ascribed to the Reds. The refugees pouring into Munich described bloodthirsty barbarians on a rampage of killing. Such imagery had instant appeal to the nationalists. The following article from one of Munich's racist newspapers is a fair example of the fears of the period and the way these were expressed:

Dreadful times in which Christian-hating, circumcised Asiatics everywhere are raising their bloodstained hands to strangle us in droves! The butcheries of Christians by the Jew Issachar Zederblum, alias Lenin, would have made even a Genghis Khan blush. In Hungary his pupil Cohn, alias Béla Kun, marched through the unhappy land with a band of Jewish terrorists schooled in murder and robbery, to set up, among brutal gallows, a mobile machine gallows and execute middle-class citizens and peasants on it. A splendidly equipped harem served him, in his stolen royal train, to rape and defile honorable Christian virgins by the dozen. His lieutenant Samuely has had sixty priests cruelly butchered in a single underground room. Their bellies are ripped open, their corpses mutilated, after they have been plundered to their blood-drenched skin. In the case of eight murdered priests it has been established that they were first crucified on the doors of their own churches! The very same atrocious scenes are . . . now reported from Munich.[2]

Yet the horrifying reports of atrocities in the East were not unfounded and were confirmed by credible witnesses. One of the chiefs of the Cheka, the Latvian M. Latsis, at the end of 1918 established the principle that sentences were not to be determined by guilt or innocence but social class. "We are engaged in exterminating the bourgeoisie as a class. You need not prove that this or that man acted against the interests of Soviet power. The first thing you have to ask an arrested person is: To what class does he belong, where does he come from, what kind of education did he have, what is his occupation? These questions are to decide the fate of the accused. That is the quintessence of the Red Terror."[3]

In what may have been a direct rejoinder to this, National Socialist Party headquarters issued the following proclamation: "Will you wait until you see thousands of people hanging from the lamp posts in every city? Will you wait until, as in Russia, a Bolshevistic murder commission sets to work in every city . . . ? Will you wait until you stumble over the corpses of your wives and children?" The threat of revolution no longer had to be pictured as emanating from a few lonely, harried conspirators. It could now be seen coming from great, uncanny Russia, the "brutal power colossus," as Hitler called it.[4] Moreover, Bolshevik propaganda heralded the imminent conquest of Germany by the united strength of the international proletariat; this would be the decisive step on the road to world revolution. The obscure activities of Soviet agents, the continual unrest, the soviet revolution in Bavaria, the Ruhr uprising of 1920, the revolts in Central Germany during the following year, the risings in Hamburg and later in Saxony and Thuringia, were all too consistent with the Soviet regime's threat of permanent revolution.

This threat dominated Hitler's speeches of the early years. In garish colors he depicted the ravages of the "Red squads of butchers," the "murderous communists," the "bloody morass of Bolshevism." In Russia, he told his audiences, more than thirty million persons had been murdered, "partly on the scaffold, partly by machine guns and similar means, partly in veritable slaughterhouses, partly, millions upon millions, by hunger; and we all know that this wave of hunger is creeping on . . . and see that this scourge is approaching, that it is also coming upon Germany." The intelligentsia of the Soviet Union, he declared, had been exterminated by mass murder, the economy utterly smashed. Thousands of German prisoners-of-war had been drowned in the Neva or sold as slaves. Meanwhile, in Germany the enemy was boring away at the foundations of society "in unremitting, ever unchanging undermining work." The fate of Russia, he said again and again, would soon be ours![5] And years later, when he was already in power, he spoke again of "the horror of the Communist international hate dictatorship" that had preyed on his mind at the beginning of his career: "I tremble at the thought of what would become of our old, overcrowded continent if the chaos of the Bolshevistic revolution were to be successful."

National Socialism owed a considerable part of its emotional appeal, its militancy, and its cohesion to this defensive attitude toward the threat of Marxist revolution. The aim of the National Socialist Party, Hitler repeatedly declared, "is very brief: Annihilation and extermination of the Marxist world view." This was to be accomplished by an "incomparable, brilliantly orchestrated propaganda and information organization" side by side with a movement "of the most ruthless force and most brutal resolution, prepared to oppose all terrorism on the part of the Marxists with tenfold greater terrorism." At about the same time, for similar reasons, Mussolini was founding his Fasci di combattimento. Henceforth, the new movements were to be identified by the general name of "Fascism."

But the fear of revolution would not have been enough to endow the movement with that fierce energy, which for a time seemed to stem the universal trend toward democracy. After all, for many people revolution

92

meant hope. A stronger and more elemental motivation had to be added. And in fact Marxism was feared as the precursor of a far more comprehensive assault upon all traditional ideas. It was viewed as the contemporary political aspect of a metaphysical upheaval, as a "declaration of war upon the European . . . idea of culture." Marxism itself was only the metaphor for something dreaded that escaped definition.

Anxiety was the permanent emotion of the time. It sprang from the intuition that the end of the war meant not only the end of familiar prewar Europe with its grandeur and its urge to world domination, its monarchies, and gilt-edged securities, but also the end of an era. Along with the old forms of government, the accustomed framework of life was being destroyed. The unrest, the radicalism of the politicized masses, the disorders of revolution were interpreted as the afterpains of the war and simultaneously as harbingers of a new, strange, and chaotic age. "That is why the foundations of life quake beneath our feet."[6]

Rarely has any age been so aware of its own transitional state. In accelerating the process, the war also created a general consciousness of it. For the first time Europe had a glimpse of what awaited it. Pessimism, so long the basic attitude of an elite minority, abruptly became the mood of the whole period.

The war had led to gigantic new forms of organization, which helped the capitalistic system attain its full development. Rationalization and the assembly line, trusts and tycoons pitilessly exposed the structural inferiority of smaller economic units.

The trend to bigness was also expressed in the extraordinary increase in cartels—from several hundred to approximately twenty-five hundred—so that in industry "only a few outsiders" remained unattached to some cartel. The number of independent businesses in the major cities had diminished by half in the thirty years before the World War. Now that war and inflation had destroyed their material base, their number dwindled more rapidly. The cruelty of the corporation, which absorbed, consumed, and dropped the individual, was felt more keenly than ever before. Fear of individual economic disaster became generalized. A considerable literature grew up around the theme that the individual's function was disappearing, that man was becoming a cog in a machine he could not understand. "In general, life seems full of dread."[7]

This fear of a standardized, termitelike existence was expressed in the hostility to increasing urbanization, to the canyon streets and grayness of the cities, and in lamentations over the factory chimneys cropping up in quiet valleys. In the face of a ruthlessly practiced "transformation of the planet into a single factory for the exploitation of its materials and energies," belief in progress for the first time underwent a reversal. The cry arose that civilization was destroying the world, that the earth was being made into "a Chicago with a sprinkling of agriculture."

The early issues of the *Völkische Beobachter* give shrill voice to this panic. "How large must our cities still grow before a retroactive movement sets in, before the tenements are torn down, the accumulations of stone shattered, the caves ventilated and . . . gardens planted among the walls so that men can catch their breath again?" Prefabricated housing, Le Corbusier's machines for living, the Bauhaus style, tubular steel furniture—the "technical matter-of-factness" on which such creations plumed themselves were a further threat to the traditionbound, who spoke of all this as "jailhouse style." The romantic hostility to the modern world also gave rise to a large back-to-the-country movement in the twenties. The Artaman Leagues contrasted the earthbound happiness of the simple life to the woes of "asphalt civilization" and hailed the comfort of natural ties against the alienation of the urban world.

The abrupt and challenging breach with previous standards of morality touched people at their most sensitive point. Marriage, as a book titled *Sexual Ethics of Communism* (by E. Friedländer) stated, was nothing but the "evil spawn of capitalism"; the revolution would do away with it along with any prohibition against abortion, homosexuality, bigamy, or incest. But many of the members of the respectable middle classes still felt themselves guardians of time-honored morality and took such attacks as personal threats. In their minds marriage as a mere matter of civil registration, as it was understood in the Soviet Union, was just as intolerable as the "glass of water theory" that sexual desire, like thirst, was a natural appetite and should be satisfied without fuss. The fox trot and brief skirts; pleasure seeking in "Berlin, the national sewer"; the "swinish pictures" of Magnus Hirschfeld, the scientific explorer of sexual pathology; or the prototype of the stylish young man about town ("the rubber cavalier with sleeked-back hair, crepe-soled shoes and Charleston trousers") aroused a shocked resentment in the popular consciousness, which in hindsight is hard to grasp and requires some effort on the historian's part. The theater during the twenties staged celebrated provocations, treating of parricide, incest, and crime. There was a strong streak of self-mockery, typified by the final scene of the Brecht-Weill opera *Mahagonny,* where the actors step up to the footlights and raise placards reading "Up with the chaotic state of our cities," "Up with love for hire," "Up with honor for assassins," or "Up with the immortality of vulgarity."[8]

In the visual arts the revolutionary breakthrough had already come about before the First World War, though, as we have remarked, both in Vienna and Munich Hitler had paid scant attention to this development. Before the war the new art could be considered the quirk of a handful of visionaries. But against the background images of upheaval, revolution, and disintegration it took on the cast of an assault upon the traditional European conception of humanity. The Fauves, the Blaue Reiter, the Brücke, or Dada seemed to be as great a menace as the revolution, and in fact were branded by the popular phrase "cultural Bolshevism." The defensive reaction was therefore just as furious; again what was feared was anarchy, arbitrariness, and formlessness. Modern art was "chaotic hack work"; that was the general opinion.

The fashionable pessimism of the time found a formula for all this: "the decline of the West." It was feared the day would come when all these resentments would fuse and lead to exasperated counteraction. For the Germans, with their conservative temperament, reacted violently to these blithe inroads on familiar social and cultural forms. More than elsewhere, their quickly rising opposition could link up with attitudes and arguments of the end of the nineteenth century. The process of technical and economic modernization had been late in coming to Germany, but for that very reason struck with unusual speed and force. In the abruptness, thoroughness, and extent of her industrial revolution, Germany was unexampled among Western nations, as Thorstein Veblen had noted.[9] The pace of change consequently stirred violent anxieties and reactions. Yet in contrast to the usual cliché, the Germany that united achievement with neglect, feudal elements with highly progressive measures, authoritarianism with state socialism, in a unique and variegated pattern, must be considered as probably the most modern industrial state in Europe on the eve of the First World War. In the previous twenty-five years it had more than doubled its gross national product. The proportion of the population earning the minimum income subject to taxation had risen from 30 to 60 per cent. Steel production, for example, which had amounted to only half of British production in 1887, had attained nearly double the British production. Colonies had been conquered, cities built, industrial empires created. The number of corporations had risen from 2,143 to 5,340, and the tonnage handled in the port of Hamburg had moved up to third place in the world, still behind New York and Amsterdam, but ahead of London. Along with this, the country was governed soberly and frugally. Despite certain areas of autocracy, it provided a high degree of domestic freedom, administrative justice, and social security.

There were anachronistic features in the total picture of imperial Germany, but these came from a quarter other than the economic or social reality. Over this hard-working country, seemingly so sure of its future, with rapidly growing metropolises and industrial areas, there arched a peculiarly romantic sky whose darkness was populated by mythic figures, antiquated giants, and ancient deities. Germany's backwardness was chiefly ideological in nature. A good deal of professorial obscurantism and Teutonic folklorism was involved. So also was the desire for self-improvement on the part of a middle class that longed for "the higher things" even as it so dynamically pursued material goals. Underlying these tendencies on the part of the cultivated middle class was an antagonism to the very modern world it was creating so energetically and successfully. This opposition

95

produced defensive gestures against the new, antipoetic reality, gestures springing not from skepticism but from romantic pessimism. An impulse for counterrevolutionary protest could be detected in these ambivalent attitudes.

Such writers as Paul de Lagarde, Julius Langbehn, and Eugen Dühring became spokesman for a widespread mood hostile to modern civilization. This mood was not confined to Germany. Elsewhere, too, there was a reaction against the unimaginative, life-affirming optimism of the age, and the present was fiercely condemned both from the right and from the left. Around the turn of the century this note was sounded in the United States as well as in the France of the Dreyfus case. It inspired the formation of the Action Française and the manifestos of Maurras and Barrès. Gabriele d'Annunzio, Enrico Corradini, Miguel de Unamuno, Dmitri Merezhkovski and Vladimir Soloviëv, Knut Hamsun, Jacob Burckhardt and D. H. Lawrence, for all their individual differences, became spokesmen for similar fears and antagonisms. But the sharpness of the change in Germany, which shot the country so abruptly from Biedermeier to modernity, with all the painful breaches and partings that such precipitation involves, gave to the protest an especially hysterical high pitch in which anxiety and disgust with modern reality mingled with romantic yearnings for a vanished Arcadia.

This tradition, too, went far back. Such pangs at the onslaughts of civilization could be traced back to Rousseau or to Goethe's *Wilhelm Meister,* whose hero had already sensed the mighty force approaching "like a thunderstorm, slowly, slowly, but . . . it will come and strike." In Germany the spokesmen for this attitude despised progress and professed themselves, with a good measure of pride, unworldly reactionaries; they preferred to be, in Nietzsche's phrase, untimely onlookers who, as Lagarde charged, longed for a Germany that had never existed and perhaps never would exist. They treated the facts that were held up to them with haughty contempt and roundly ridiculed "one-eyed reason." With no regard for logic but with flashes of considerable shrewdness, they opposed the stock exchange and urbanization, compulsory vaccination, the global economy and positivistic science, "communistic" movements and the first attempts at heavier-than-air flight. In brief, they were against the whole concept of modern improvement, and summed up all efforts in that direction as a disastrous "decline of the soul." As "prophets of enraged tradition," they invoked the day when the mad whirl would be checked and "the old gods would once more rise out of the waves."

The values they opposed to the utilitarian ones of the modern age included the sacredness of nature, the loftiness of art, the value of the earthy. They extolled the past, aristocracy, the beauty of death, and the claims of the strong, Caesarean personality. They lamented the decay of German culture while at the same time they were filled with an imperialistic missionary fervor: fear was translated into aggression, and despair sought comfort in the idea of greatness. The most famous book expressive of this trend, Julius Langbehn's *Rembrandt als Erzieher* ("Rembrandt as Educator") had a spectacular success when it was published in 1890 and went through forty printings within two years. The widespread approval for this curious document, approval deriving from panic, antimodernity, and nationalistic missionary delusions suggests that the book itself was an expression of the crisis it so furiously deplored.

The alliance between these anticivilizational sentiments and nationalism was to have grave consequences. Nearly as portentous was the link between those sentiments and antidemocratic ideas. In opposition to democracy, the anticivilization people joined hands with the theoreticians of Social Darwinism and racism. For both groups saw no good in the liberal Western society which traced its beginnings to the principles of the Enlightenment and the French Revolution. This antidemocratic current was present, again, in all of Europe but was especially strong in France and Italy. In those countries, as Julien Benda later wrote, the writers around 1890 "realized with astonishing astuteness that the doctrines of arbitrary authority, discipline, tradition, contempt for the spirit of liberty, association of the morality of war and slavery were opportunities for haughty and rigid poses infinitely more likely to strike the imagination of simple souls than the sentimentalities of Liberalism and Humanitarianism."[10] And although all literary successes not withstanding, unhappiness with modernity remained the affair of a sensitive intellectual minority, these attitudes—to revert to Germany—gradually produced a lasting effect. The youth movement particularly was identified with them and gave them a pure and ardent expression. Friedrich Nietzsche described the tendency as follows: "The whole great tendency of the Germans ran counter to the Enlightenment, and to the revolution of society, which, by a crude misunderstanding, was considered its consequence: piety toward everything still in existence sought to transform itself into piety toward everything that has ever existed, only to make heart and spirit full once again and to leave no room for future goals and innovations. The cult of feeling was erected in place of the cult of reason."[11]

Finally, the anticivilizational mood of the period struck up an alliance with anti-Semitism. "German anti-Semitism is reactionary," wrote Hermann Bahr, the Austrian journalist, in 1894, after intensive study of the question. "It is a revolt of the petty bourgeois against industrial development."[12] In fact, the equating of Judaism and modernity, like the thesis that Jews had a special talent for the capitalistic free-enterprise economy, was not unfounded. And modernity and capitalistic competition were the very things on which anxiety about the future centered. Werner Sombart, the noted economist, actually spoke of "a Jewish mission to promote the transition to capitalism . . . and to clear away the still preserved remnants of pre-capitalistic organization."[13] Against the background of this economic development, the old hatred of Jews, which had had a religious basis, evolved

97

during the second half of the nineteenth century into an anti-Semitism built on biological and social prejudices. In Germany the philosopher Eugen Dühring and the failed journalist Wilhelm Marr popularized these attitudes. (The latter wrote a pamphlet significantly titled, "The Victory of Judaism over Germanism, Regarded from a Non-denominational Point of View. *Vae Victis!*") Anti-Semitism in Germany seemed hardly more intense than in France, let alone in Russia and Austro-Hungary. The anti-Semitic publications of the period repeatedly complained that their ideas, despite their wide dissemination, were not being taken seriously enough. But while irrational nostalgias were skulking about "like masterless dogs," anti-Semitism served as the vehicle for widespread discontent, precisely because of the half-truths contained in it. With the numerous current theories of a conspiracy of dark powers, or a malignant world-wide disease, the figure of the "Wandering Jew" had a curious credibility. In fact, it was still another embodiment of generalized anxiety. And, on another plane, there were the music dramas of Richard Wagner, which restated the problems of the age in mythic terms. The misgivings about the future, the awareness of the dawning age of gold, racial fears, antimaterialistic impulses, horror of an era of plebeian freedom and leveling, and premonitions of impending doom —all this expressed in highly sensuous art spoke to the cultivated middle classes struggling in the toils of their malaise.

The war unleashed and radicalized these manifold hostilities of the bourgeois age toward itself. Life seemed bogged down in the banalities of civilization. Now once again great exaltations were possible; the war sanctified violence and wrought glories of destruction. As Ernst Jünger wrote, its flame throwers accomplished a "great cleansing by Nothingness." War was the perfect negation to the liberal and humanitarian ideal of civilization. The tremendous impact of the war experience, felt throughout Europe and recorded by an extensive European literature, came from this liberating sense of renewal by destruction. Those who considered themselves children of the war had learned the worth of swift, solitary decisions, absolute obedience, and the power of large numbers united by a single idea. The compromising temper of parliamentary systems, their feeble capacity for decision making and frequent self-imposed paralysis invalidated them to a generation that had come away from the war with the myth of a perfect military machine operating at peak performance.

This complex of attitudes helps explain the stubborn resistance of the Germans to their newly established democratic republic and the roles which had been assigned it within the Versailles peace-keeping system. Still haunted by their anticivilizational philosophies, they could not see the republic and the Versailles Treaty as mere aspects of an altered political situation. To them all this was a fall from grace, an act of metaphysical treason and profound unfaithfulness to true selfhood. Only treachery could have delivered Germany, romantic, pensive, unpolitical Germany, into servitude to that idea of Western civilization which threatened her very essence. Significantly, the *Völkische Beobachter* called the Treaty of Versailles a "syphilitic peace," which, like the disease "born of brief, forbidden lust, beginning with a small hard sore, gradually attacks all the limbs and joints, even all the flesh, down to the heart and brain of the sinner."[14] The passionate opposition to "the system" sprang directly from the refusal to participate in the hated "imperium of civilization" with its blabber about human rights, its progressivistic demagoguery, its craze for enlightenment, its superficiality, its corruption, and its vulgar worship of prosperity. The stern German ideals of loyalty, divine rights, love of country, were, as one of the many pamphlets of the time put it, "extinguished mercilessly in the storms of the revolutionary and postrevolutionary period." In their place had come "democracy, the nudist movement, arrant naturalism, and companionate marriage."

Throughout the years of the republic the intellectual Right, which continued to hold to the anticivilizational views of the Wilhelmine era, showed a notable tendency toward alliance with the Soviet Union. Or rather, with Russia, regarded as maternal soil, heartland, the "fourth dimension," the object of indefinite expectations. While Oswald Spengler was calling for struggle against "the England within us," Ernst Niekisch, another defendant of the nation's psychological identity, was writing: "To turn our eyes toward the East is already a sign of Germany's awakening. . . . The movement toward the West was in itself Germany's descent; veering to the East will once again be an ascent to German greatness."

To "shallow liberalism" Niekisch opposed "the Prusso-Slavic principle"; as against Geneva, headquarters of the League of Nations, he proposed "the Potsdam-Moscow axis." To the conservative, nationalistic camp, fear that Germanism would be overwhelmed by the materialistic, demythologized threat to world domination. One might speak of this group as national-conservative Bolshevists.

This first phase of the postwar era was characterized both by fear of revolution and anticivilizational resentments; these together, curiously intertwined and reciprocally stimulating each other, produced a syndrome of extraordinary force. Into the brew went the hate and defense complexes of a society shaken to its foundations. German society had lost its imperial glory, its civil order, its national confidence, its prosperity, and its familiar authorities. The whole system had been turned topsy-turvy, and now many Germans blindly and bitterly wanted back what they thought had been unjustly taken from them. These general feelings of unhappiness were intensified and further radicalized by a variety of unsatisfied group interests. The class of white-color workers, continuing to grow apace, proved especially susceptible to the grand gesture of total criticism. For the industrial revolution had just begun to affect office workers and was reducing the former "non-commissioned officers of capitalism" to the status of last victims of "modern slavery." It was all the worse for them because unlike the proletarians they had never developed a class pride of their own or imagined that the breakdown of the existing order was going to lead to their own apotheosis. Small businessmen were equally susceptible because of their fear of being crushed by corporations, department stores, and rationalized competition. Another unhappy group consisted of farmers who, slow to change and lacking capital, were fettered to backward modes of production. Another group were the academics and formerly solid bourgeois who felt themselves caught in the tremendous suction of proletarianization. Without outside support you found yourself "at once despised, declassed; to be unemployed is the same as being a communist," one victim stated in a questionnaire of the period. No statistics, no figures on rates of inflation, bankruptcies, and suicides can describe the feelings of those threatened by unemployment or poverty, or can express the anxieties of those others who still possessed some property and feared the consequences of so much accumulated discontent. Public institutions in their persistent weakness offered no bulwark against the seething collective emotions. It was all the worse because the widespread anxiety no longer, as in the time of Lagarde and Langbehn, was limited to cries of woe and impotent prophecies. The war had given arms to the fearful.

The vigilante groups and the free corps that were being organized in great numbers, partly on private initiative, partly with covert government support, chiefly to meet the threat of Communist revolution, formed centers of bewildered but determined resistance to the *status quo*. The members of these paramilitary groups were vaguely looking around for someone to lead them into a new system. At first there was another reservoir of militant energies alongside the paramilitary groups: the mass of homecoming soldiers. Many of these stayed in the barracks dragging out a pointless military life, baffled and unable to say good-bye to the warrior dreams of their recent youth. In the front-line trenches they had glimpsed the outlines of a new meaning to life; in the sluggishly resuming normality of the postwar period they tried in vain to find that meaning again. They had not fought and suffered for years for the sake of this weakend regime with its borrowed ideals which, as they saw it, could be pushed around by the most contemptible of their former enemies. And they also feared, after the exalting sense of life the war had given them, the ignobility of the commonplace bourgeois world.

It remained for Hitler to bring together these feelings and to appoint himself their spearhead. Indeed, Hitler regarded as a phenomenon seems like the synthetic product of all the anxiety, pessimism, nostalgia, and defensiveness we have discussed. For him, too, the war had been education and liberation. If there is a "Fascistic" type, it was embodied in him. More than any of his followers he expressed the underlying psychological, social, and ideological motives of the movement. He was never just its leader; he was also its exponent.

His early years had contributed their share to that experience of over-whelming anxiety which dominated his intellectual and emotional constitution. That lurking anxiety can be seen at the root of almost all his statements and reactions. It had everyday as well as cosmic dimensions. Many who knew him in his youth have described his pallid, "timorous" nature, which provided the fertile soil for his lush fantasies. His "constant fear" of contact with strangers was another aspect of that anxiety, as was his extreme distrust and his compulsion to wash frequently, which became more and more pronounced in later life. The same complex is apparent in his oft-expressed fear of venereal disease and his fear of contagion in general. He knew that "microbes are rushing at me."[15] He was ridden by the Austrian Pan-German's fear of being overwhelmed by alien races, by fear of the "locust-like immigration of Russian and Polish Jews," by fear of "the niggerizing of the Germans," by fear of the Germans' "expulsion from Germany," and finally by fear that the Germans would be "exterminated." He had the *Völkische Beobachter* print an alleged French soldier's song whose refrain was: "Germans, we will possess your daughters!" Among his phobias were American technology, the birth rate of the Slavs, big cities, "industrialization as unrestricted as it is harmful," the "economization of the nation," corporations, the "morass of metropolitan amusement culture," and modern art, which sought "to kill the soul of the people" by painting meadows blue and skies green. Wherever he looked he discovered the "signs of decay of a slowly ebbing world." Not an element of pessimistic anticivilizational criticism was missing from his imagination.[16]

What linked Hitler with the leading Fascists of other countries was the resolve to halt this process of degeneration. What set him apart from them, however, was the manic single-mindedness with which he traced all the anxieties he had ever felt back to a single source. For at the heart of the towering structure of anxiety, black and hairy, stood the figure of the Jew: evil-smelling, smacking his lips, lusting after blonde girls, eternal contaminator of the blood, but "racially harder" than the Aryan, as Hitler uneasily declared as late as the summer of 1942.[17] A prey to his psychosis, he saw Germany as the object of a world-wide conspiracy, pressed on all sides by Bolshevists, Freemasons, capitalists, Jesuits, all hand in glove with each other and directed in their nefarious projects by the "bloodthirsty and avaricious Jewish tyrant." *The* Jew had 75 per cent of world capital at his disposal. He dominated the stock exchanges and the Marxist parties, the Gold and Red Internationals. He was the "advocate of birth control and the idea of emigration." He undermined governments, bastardized races, glorified fratricide, fomented civil war, justified baseness, and poisoned nobility: "the wirepuller of the destinies of mankind."[18] The whole world was in danger, Hitler cried imploringly; it had fallen "into the embrace of this octopus." He groped for images in which to make his horror tangible, saw "creeping venom," "belly-worms," and "adders devouring the nation's body." In formulating his anxiety he might equally hit on the maddest and most ludicrous phrases as on impressive or at least memorable ones. Thus he invented the "Jewification of our spiritual life," "the mammonization of our mating instinct," and "the resulting syphilization of our people." He could prophesy: "If, with the help of his Marxist creed, the Jew is victorious over the other peoples of the world, his crown will be the funeral wreath of humanity and this planet will, as it did millions of years ago, move through the ether devoid of men."[19]

The appearance of Hitler signaled a union of those forces that in crisis conditions had great political potential. The Fascistic movements all centered on the charismatic appeal of a unique leader. The leader was to be the resolute voice of order controlling chaos. He would have looked further and thought deeper, would know the despairs but also the means of salvation. This looming giant had already been given established form in a prophetic literature that went back to German folklore. Like the mythology of many other nations unfortunate in their history, that of the Germans has its sleeping leaders dreaming away the centuries in the bowels of a mountain, but destined some day to return to rally their people and punish the guilty world. Into the twenties pessimistic literature repeatedly called up these longings, which were most effectively expressed in the famous lines of Stefan George:

> He shatters fetters, sweeps the rubble heaps
> Back into order, scourges stragglers home
> Back to eternal justice where grandeur once more is grand,
> Lord once more lord. Rule once more rule. He pins
> The true insigne to the race's banner.
> Through the storms and dreadful trumpet blasts
> Of reddening dawn he leads his band of liegemen
> To daylight's work of founding the New Reich.[20]

Around the same time, Max Weber also sketched a picture of the towering personality of the leader with what he termed "plebiscitary legitimacy" and the claim to "blind" obedience. But Weber saw such a leader as a counterforce to the inhuman bureaucratic organizational structures of the future. We would have to probe more deeply than is possible within the present context if we were to examine all the many sources from which the idea of the leader took support.

It is clear, however, that within the Fascistic movements the idea was again heavily influenced by the war. For those movements did not think of themselves as political parties in the traditional sense, but as militant ideological groups, as "parties above the parties." And the struggle they took up with their sinister symbols and resolute miens was nothing but the prolongation of the war into politics with virtually unchanged means. "At the moment we are in the continuation of the war," Hitler repeatedly proclaimed. The leader cult, viewed in terms of the "fiction of permanent warfare," was in one sense the translation of the principles of military hierarchy to political organization. The leader was the army officer lifted to superhuman heights and endowed with supernal powers. Those powers were conferred by the craving to believe and the yearning to surrender self. The tramp of marching feet on all the pavements of Europe attested to the belief in militaristic models as offering a solution to the problems of society. It was the future-minded youth in particular who were drawn to these models, having learned through war, revolution, and chaos to prize "geometrical" systems.

The same factors underlay the paramilitary aspects of the Fascistic movements, the uniforms, the rituals of saluting, reporting, standing at attention. The insigne of the movements all came down to a few basic motifs—various forms of crosses (such as the St. Olaf's cross of the Norwegian Nasjonal Samling and the red St. Andrew's cross of Portugal's National Syndicalists), also arrows, bundles of fasces, scythes. These symbols were constantly displayed on flags, badges, standards, or armbands. To some extent they were meant as defiance of the boring old bourgeois business of tailcoats and stiff collars. But primarily they seemed more in keeping with the brisk technological spirit of the age. Then, too, uniforms and military trappings could conceal social differences and bring some dash to the dullness and emotional barrenness of ordinary civilian life.

The combination of petty bourgeois and military elements gave the National Socialist Party (NSDAP) a peculiar dual character from the very start. This duality was apparent in the organizational division between the Storm Troops (SA) and the Political Organization (PO). It was apparent also in the confusing disparate character of the membership. For the party was made up of idealists as well as of social outcasts, of semicriminals as well as of opportunists. The oddly equivocal conservatism of most Fascistic organizations can also be traced to this initial dualism. For although these organizations were officially bent on preserving the troubled and violated world order, they nevertheless manifested—wherever they had the power —a desire for change without regard to tradition. An odd mixture of medievalism and modernity was typical of them all: they considered themselves a vanguard but stood with their backs to the future; they would plant their folkloristic villages on the asphalt pavements of a coercive totalitarian state. Once again, they dreamed the faded dreams of their forefathers and hailed a past in whose mists they saw glimmerings of a glorious future of territorial expansion: a new Roman Empire, a Spain of Catholic majesty, a Greater Belgium, Greater Hungary, Greater Finland. Hitler's fling at hegemony, carefully planned, cold-blooded, and realistic as it was, and dependent on the most modern weaponry, was justified in the name of a quaint and vanished Germanism. The world was to be conquered for the sake of thatched roofs and an upright peasantry, for folk dances, celebrations of the winter solstice, and swastikas. Thomas Mann spoke of an "explosion of antiquarianism."

But behind it there was always more than muddled reactionary impulses. Hitler was by no means interested in bringing back the good old days. The sentimental reactionaries who in persistent blindness supported him thought he would reinstitute the old feudal social structure. Hitler had no such ideas. What he proposed to overcome was the sum of human alienation caused by the development of civilization.

He was not counting on doing so by economic or social means, which he despised. Like Marinetti, one of the spokesmen of Italian Fascism, he regarded European socialism as a "despicable fuss over the rights of the belly." Instead, he aimed at inner renewal out of the blood and the dark realms of the soul. What was wanted was not politics but the restoration of instinct. In its aims and slogans Fascism was not a class revolution but a cultural revolution; it claimed to serve not the emancipation but the redemption of mankind. One reason for its considerable appeal may well have been that it sought utopia where all paradises are located by the natural inclination of the human mind: in mythic, primordial states of the past. The prevailing fear of the future only strengthened the tendency to shift all apotheoses backward. In Fascistic conservatism, at any rate, the desire was to reverse historical development and to return once more to the starting point, to those better, more nature-oriented, harmonious times before the human race began to go astray. In a 1941 letter to Mussolini, Hitler wrote that the last 1,500 years had been nothing but an interruption, that history was on the point of "returning to the ways of yore." Without attempting, perhaps, to restore the conditions of the past, it craved the past's system of values, the style, the austerity, the morality, as a defense against the forces of dissolution thrusting from all sides. "At last a bulwark against approaching chaos!" as Hitler exclaimed.

In spite of all its revolutionary rhetoric, National Socialism could never conceal its basically defensive attitude, which contrasted perceptibly with the brash gladiatorial poses its advocates loved to adopt. Konrad Heiden called the Fascistic ideologies "boasts while in flight"; they were, he said, "fear of ascent, of new winds and unknown stars, a protest by the flesh, craving its rest, against the restless spirit." And Hitler himself, soon after the beginning of the war against the Soviet Union, remarked that he now understood how the Chinese had come to surround themselves with a wall. He, too, was tempted "to wish for a gigantic wall to shield the new East against the Central Asiatic masses. In spite of all history, which teaches that a people's vigor slackens off in a bulwarked area."

The success of Fascism in contrast to many of its rivals was in large part due to its perceiving the essence of the crisis, of which it was itself the symptom. All the other parties affirmed the process of industrialization and emancipation, whereas the Fascists, evidently sharing the universal anxiety, tried to deal with it by translating it into violent action and histrionics. They also managed to leaven boring, prosaic everyday life by romantic rituals: torchlight processions, standards, death's heads, battle cries, and shouts of *Heil,* by the "new marriage of life with danger," and the idea of "glorious death." They presented men with modern tasks disguised in the costumery of the past. They deprecated material concerns and treated "politics as an area of self-denial and sacrifice of the individual for an idea." In taking this line they were addressing themselves to deeper needs than those who promised the masses higher wages. Ahead of all their rivals, the Fascists appeared to have recognized that the Marxist or liberal conception of man as guided only by reason and material interests was a monstrous abstraction.

Thus Fascism served the craving of the period for a general upheaval more effectively than its antagonists. It alone seemed to be articulating the feeling that everything had gone wrong, that the world had been led into an impasse. That Communism made fewer converts was not due solely to its stigma of being a class party and the agency of a foreign power. Rather, Communism suffered from a vague feeling that it represented part of the wrong turn the world had taken and part of the disease it pretended it could cure. Communism seemed not the negation of bourgeois materialism but merely its obverse, not the superseding of an unjust and inadequate system, but its mirror image turned upside down.

Hitler's unshakable confidence, which often seemed sheer madness, was based on the conviction that he was the only real revolutionary, that he had broken free of the existing system by reinstating the rights of human instincts. In alliance with these interests, he believed, he was invincible, for the instincts always won out in the end "against economic motivation, against the pressure of public opinion, even against reason." No doubt the appeal to instinct brought out a good deal of human baseness. No doubt what Fascism wanted to restore was often a grotesque parody of the tradition they purported to honor, and the order they hailed was a hollow sham. But when Trotsky contemptuously dismissed the adherents of Fascistic movements as "human dust," he was only revealing the Left's characteristic ineptness in dealing with people's needs and impulses. That ineptness led to a multitude of clever errors of judgment by those who purported to understand the spirit of the age better than anyone else.

Fascism satisfied more than romantic needs. Sprung from the anxieties of the age, it was an elemental uprising in favor of authority, a revolt on behalf of order. Such paradox was its very essence. It was rebellion and subordination, a break with tradition and the sanctification of tradition, a "people's community" and strictest hierarchy, private property and social justice. But whatever the slogans it appropriated, the imperious authority of a strong state was always implied. "More than ever the peoples today have a desire for authority, guidance and order," Mussolini declared.

Mussolini spoke of the "more or less decayed corpse of the goddess

Liberty." He argued that liberalism was about to "close the portals of its temple, which the peoples have deserted" because "all the political experiences of the present are antiliberal." And in fact throughout Europe, especially in the countries that had gone over to a liberal parliamentary system only after the end of the World War, there had been growing doubts of adequacy of the parliamentarism. These doubts became all the stronger the more these countries moved into the present age. There would be the feeling that the country lacked the means to meet the challenges of the transition: that the available leadership was not equal to the crisis. Witnessing the endless parliamentary disputes, the bitterness and bargaining of partisan politics, people began to long for earlier days, when rule was by decree and no one had to exercise a choice. With the exception of Czechoslovakia, the parliamentary system collapsed throughout the newly created nations of eastern and central Europe and in many of the countries of southern Europe: in Lithuania, Latvia, Estonia, Poland, Hungary, Rumania, Austria, Italy, Greece, Turkey, Spain, Portugal, and finally in Germany. By 1939 there were only nine countries with parliamentary regimes. And many of the nine, like the French Third Republic, had stabilized in a *drôle d'état,* others in a monarchy. "A fascist Europe was already a possibility."[21]

Thus it was not the case of a single aggrieved and aggressive nation trying to impose a totalitarian pattern on Europe. The liberal age was reaching its twilight in a widespread mood of disgust and the mood manifested itself under all kinds of auspices, reactionary and progressive, ambitious and altruistic. From 1921 on, Germany had lacked a Reichstag majority that professed faith in the parliamentary system with any conviction. The ideas of liberalism had scarcely any advocates but many potential adversaries; they needed only an impetus, the stirring slogans of a leader.

BOOK II

The Road to
Politics

Chapter 1

I would have burst out laughing if anyone had predicted to me that this was the
beginning of a new era in history.

Konrad Heiden, looking back on
his student years in Munich

A PART OF THE
GERMAN FUTURE

No other city in Germany had been so shaken by the events and emotions
of the revolution and the first postwar weeks as excitable Munich. On
November 7, 1918—two days before anything happened in Berlin—the
zeal of a few leftists had toppled the thousand-year-old Wittelsbach
dynasty. To their own surprise the insurgents found themselves in power.
Under the leadership of Kurt Eisner, a bearded bohemian and theater critic
of the *Münchener Post*, they had tried—in all too complete faith in
Woodrow Wilson's statements—"to prepare Germany for the League of
Nations" by a revolutionary change of conditions and "to obtain a peace
which will save the country from the worst."

But whatever chances Eisner may have had were nullified by the weakness and inconsistency of the American President and by the hatred of the
rightists. Their vilification of the "foreign, racially alien vagabond" and
"Schwabing Bolshevist" has lived on to this day.[1] In fact neither he nor a
single one of the other new leaders was Bavarian by birth; they were
conspicuous types of the antibourgeois and often Jewish intellectual. And
in racially conscious Bavaria that sealed the fate of the revolutionary
government. Moreover, the barrage of naïve spectacle with which Eisner
treated the populace, the incessant demonstrations, public concerts,
parades of flags, and inspiring speeches about the "realm of light, beauty
and reason" did little to consolidate his position. The way he carried out
his office evoked as much ridicule as bitterness. Eisner certainly did not
win the affection he had hoped for from his "government by kindness." His

109

utopian promises expressed in broad philosophical terms, which seemed so good on paper, proved hollow at the first puff of reality.

Though he took issue with the extremist leaders of the Spartacists and other such agents of world revolution as Lewien, Eugen Leviné, and Axelrod, though he repudiated the anarchistic ravings of the writer Erich Mühsam, and made at least verbal concessions to the separatist sentiments so widespread in Bavaria, none of these moves to the middle could improve his situation. At a socialist conference in Berne he was so impolitic that he spoke of German guilt for the outbreak of the war, and at once found himself the target of an organized campaign. There were loud cries for his elimination and dark threats to the effect that time was running out for him. A staggering electoral defeat shortly afterward forced him to resign. On February 21, as he was on his way to the Landtag to declare his resignation, he was shot in the back and killed by a twenty-two-year-old count, Anton von Arco-Valley.

It was a senseless, superfluous, and disastrous crime. Only a few hours later, during a memorial service for the victim, a radical leftist butcher and waiter named Alois Lindner forced his way into the Landtag and, firing wildly, shot down three persons, including a government minister. The horrified assemblage scattered in panic. But public opinion now took a great swing to the left. Coming so soon after the assassinations of Rosa Luxemburg and Karl Liebknecht, the murder of Eisner appeared to be the act of reactionary conspirators bent on regaining their lost power. A state of emergency was imposed on Bavaria, and a general strike proclaimed. When part of the student body hailed Arco-Valley as a hero, the university was closed. Large numbers of hostages were taken, a rigorous censorship introduced, banks and public buildings occupied by Red Army men. Armored cars drove through the streets, swarming with soldiers who blared through bullhorns "Revenge for Eisner!"

For a month executive power was wielded by a Central Council (*i.e.,* soviet) under Ernst Niekisch. Then a parliamentary government was formed. But at the beginning of April news came from Hungary that Béla Kun had seized power and proclaimed the dictatorship of the proletariat. Here was evidence that revolution could succeed outside Russia. Once more the uneasy stability of Bavaria was shaken. A minority of radical leftist enthusiasts, without a mass basis and against the clear will, traditions, and feelings of the public, cried, "Germany is next!" and proclaimed a soviet republic. The poets Ernst Toller and Erich Mühsam, in a decree all too revealing of their romanticism, unworldliness, and weakness as leaders, announced the transformation of the world "into a meadow full of flowers in which each man can pick his share." Work, subordination, and legalistic thinking were to be abolished. The newspapers were to print poems by Hölderlin or Schiller on the front page alongside the latest revolutionary decrees. The government retreated to Bamberg; Ernst

Niekisch and most of the ministers resigned; and the leaderless state was left to the muddled gospel of the poets, who soon found themselves supplanted by a group of hard-boiled professional revolutionaries. Chaos and terrorizing of the citizenry followed.

It was an experience that could not be forgotten. The arbitrary confiscations, the practice of seizing hostages, the curbs on the bourgeoisie, revolutionary whim, and increasing hunger accorded all too well with recent horror stories of the October Revolution in Russia and made so deep an imprint on the popular mind that the bloody atrocities committed by the units of the Reichswehr and Free Corps, which advanced on Munich at the beginning of May, faded into oblivion by contrast. The rightists murdered fifty released Russian prisoners of war near Puchheim, slaughtered a medical column of the soviet army near Starnberg, arrested twenty-one innocent members of a Catholic club in their Munich clubroom, took them to the jail on Karolinenplatz and shot them all down, likewise lined up and shot twelve innocent workmen from Perlach. In addition, there were the leaders of the soviet experiment who were beaten to death or shot: Kurt Eglhofer, Gustav Landauer, Eugen Leviné. About these victims little was ever said. On the other hand, eight hostages—members of the conspiratorial radical rightist Thule Society—had been held in the cellar of the Luitpold Gymnasium. A minor functionary, reacting to the crimes of the rightist troops, had them liquidated. For years their memory was repeatedly invoked as an example of the horrors of the Red regime. Wherever the Reichswehr and Free Corps troops appeared, a contemporary diary notes, "the people wave cloths, applaud; everyone looks out the windows; the enthusiasm could not be greater. . . . Everyone is cheering."[2] Bavaria, the land of revolution, now became the land of counter-revolution.

For certain bourgeois groups the experiences of the early postwar months brought a new sense of confidence. For the short-lived revolution revealed the impotence and want of ideas of the German Left, which obviously had more revolutionary enthusiasm than revolutionary courage. The Left as represented by the Social Democrats had proved a force for order; but the leftists who attempted to introduce soviet rule in Bavaria proved to be visionaries who knew nothing about power and nothing about the people. During those months the bourgeoisie, or at any rate the calmer portion of it, for the first time realized that its fears were unjustified, that it could well hold its own beside the supposedly invincible but really naïve German working class.

The army officers of middle rank, action-hungry captains and majors, led the way in infusing new spirit into the bourgeoisie. They had enjoyed the war like a wine and were still intoxicated. Although they had often faced superior forces, they did not feel themselves defeated. Called to the aid of the government, they had tamed rebels and refractory soldiers' councils and crushed the Bavarian soviets. On the unsecured eastern border of Germany they had stood guard against the Poles and Czechs. Then, as they saw it, the Versailles Treaty cutting the army down to 100,000 men had cheated them of their future, reduced their social status, and disgraced their nation. A combination of self-assurance and haplessness sent them into politics. Many of them clung to the glorious freedom of the soldier's life or hated to give up the profession of arms and the company of males. With their knowledge of organization and the planned application of violence, they now set about combatting the revolution— which had long since been destroyed by the nation's fears and craving for order.

The private military bands that appeared everywhere soon transformed the country into a bivouac of brutish soldiery who wore the nimbus of political militancy and patriotism. Secure in the possession of machine guns, hand grenades, and cannon kept in an extensive network of secret arms depots, they profited by the impotence of the political institutions and claimed for themselves a considerable share of power—although the size of the share differed in the various regions. In Bavaria, in reaction to the traumatic experiences of the soviet period, they were able to pursue their ends almost unhindered. During the rule of the soviets, the Social Democratic government had called for "organizing the counterrevolution by all possible means." With such official encouragement, the paramilitary movements sprang up alongside the Reichswehr, intertwined with it in various obscure ways. Colonel (later General) von Epp organized the free corps called the Einwohnerwehr (militia). There were also the Bund Oberland (Oberland League), the officers' association Eiserne Faust (Iron Fist), the Escherich Organization, the Deutschvölkische Schutz-und Trutzbund (Defense and Defiance League of the German Race), the Verband Altreichsflagge (Flag of the Old Reich Association), the Bayreuth, Würzburg, and Wolf Free Corps, and a variety of other organizations. Taken together, they represented an ambitious politico-military autonomous power averse to any return to normality.

In addition to the support of the administration and the government bureaucracy, these associations also enjoyed the favor of much of the population. In a society with a military tradition, cross-grained individuals acquire enormous credibility on moral and national issues as soon as they appear in uniform and march in step. Given the chaotic background, the military association appeared to be an exemplary counterpoise, representing a concept of life and order dear to everyone's heart. Sternly erect, faultlessly in step, the units of Epp's Free Corps had paraded down Ludwigstrasse, along with units of the Ehrhardt Brigade. The latter had brought back from its battles in the Baltic regions an emblem loudly proclaimed in the unit's marching song: "With swastika on steel helmet."

These military groups appealed to the imagination of the public; they embodied something of the glory and security of previous times that were now only nostalgic memories. Bavarian Group Command IV was only expressing prevailing opinion when it issued a directive in June, 1919, referring to the Reichswehr as the "cornerstone" of any "meaningful re-establishment of all domestic affairs." The parties of the Left made the naïve mistake of thinking that the soldiers who had borne the brunt of the suffering shared their own hatred for war. The Right, however, began working on the soldiers' injured pride and disappointed expectations. They launched a vigorous campaign to this effect.

Among the various activities organized by the propaganda department of the Group Command under bustling Captain Mayr was that course in "civic thinking" which Hitler had been sent to after he had done so well as an informant for the military tribunal. The classes were held at the university and were conducted by reliable nationalists. The object was to indoctrinate a select group of participants with certain historical, economic, and political theories.

In his consistent effort to deny or underplay any influences upon his thinking, Hitler would later imply that this course was important for him not so much for the information it provided as for the contacts he made. "For me the value of the whole affair was that I now obtained an opportunity of meeting a few like-minded comrades with whom I could thoroughly discuss the situation of the moment." But he admits that in the field of economic theory he learned something new. He attended the lectures of Gottfried Feder, a rightist engineer, and "for the first time in my life I heard a principled discussion of international stock exchange and loan capital."[3]

In the strict sense, however, the real importance of the lecture course lay in the effect Hitler made with his vehemence and his particular cast of mind. Up to now his audience had consisted only of ignorant chance listeners. One of the teachers, the historian Karl Alexander von Müller, has described how at the end of the lecture, while the hall was emptying, he found his way blocked by a group that "stood fascinated around a man in their midst who was addressing them without pause and with growing passion in a strangely guttural voice. I had the strange feeling that the man was feeding on the excitement which he himself had whipped up. I saw a pale, thin face beneath a drooping, unsoldierly strand of hair, with close-cropped mustache and strikingly large, light blue eyes coldly glistening with fanaticism." Called up to the platform after the next lecture, the man came up "obediently, with awkward movements, in a kind of defiant embarrassment, so it seemed to me." But "the dialogue remained unfruitful."

Here we already have a picture of the two faces of Hitler: powerfully convincing when carried away by his own rhetoric, bumbling and insignificant in personal confrontation. According to his own story, he had his first, never-to-be-forgotten oratorical triumph when "one of the participants felt obliged to break a lance for the Jews." Müller had already called Captain Mayr's attention to the natural orator he had discovered among his students. Now Hitler found himself detailed to a Munich regiment as the "liaison man" of District Command. Shortly afterward, his name appeared on a list of appointees for an "enlightenment squad" attached to the Lechfeld camp for returning soldiers. The squad was there to exert influence on the men, indoctrinating them with nationalistic, anti-Marxist ideas. In addition, the assignment was meant as a "practical course in speaking and agitation" for the squad members.[4]

In the barracks of Camp Lechfeld Hitler developed his gift for oratory and practical psychology. Here he learned to apply his ideological obsessions to current events so that the principles seemed to be irrefutably confirmed and the incidents of the day swelled to a portentous vastness. Some of the opportunistic features that later became incorporated into National Socialist ideology can be traced to this stage of Hitler's career. As a beginner he was somewhat insecure and had to try out his various obsessions, discovering those that would strike a public response. He soon found what was most effective. "This theme kindled particular interest among the participants; that could be read in their faces," a camp report on one of Hitler's talks states. Hitler shared the powerful sense of disillusionment among the returning soldiers, who after years of war saw themselves cheated of everything that had lent greatness and importance to their young lives. They were now seeking explanations for so much wasted heroism, so many squandered victories, so much betrayed confidence. And Hitler offered them a concrete image of the mysterious enemy. His speaking style, we learn from other reports, was marked by "a popular manner," an "easily comprehensible presentation," and a passionate "fanaticism." At the heart of these early speeches were attacks on the group whom he later, in a phrase that was to become a byword, called "the November criminals." There were bitter denunciations of the "shame of Versailles" and corrupt "internationalism." Linking it all up was the thesis that a "Jewish-Marxist world conspiracy" was operating in the background.

His aptitude for stringing together bits of ideas from things he had read and half digested and for presenting the result as his own without the slightest intellectual embarrassment, proved its value. One of his talks in Lechfeld repeated "in a very fine, clear and rousing" manner things which he had only recently learned from the class with Gottfried Feder on the relationships between capitalism and Jewry. His intellectual appropriations were as violent as they were lasting. From this period dates Hitler's first written statement on a specific political question that has come down to us. The subject, significantly, was "the danger Jewry constitutes to our people today." A former "liaison man" of Munich District Headquarters, Adolf Gemlich, had asked Captain Mayr for a position paper on the subject, and

114

Mayr passed the latter on to his subordinate for reply—addressing him as "My Dear Herr Hitler," an unusual salutation from a captain to a corporal. Hitler went into the subject at length, beginning with a condemnation of that emotional anti-Semitism which could be based only on chance personal impressions. The kind of anti-Semitism that aspired to become a political movement, he wrote, presupposed "knowledge of facts."

And the facts are: First, Jewry is unequivocally a race and not a religious community. By thousands of years of inbreeding, frequently undertaken in the narrowest circles, the Jew in general has preserved his race and its peculiarity more keenly than many of the peoples among whom he lives. And thus results the fact that among us a non-German, alien race lives, not willing and also not able to sacrifice its racial peculiarities, to deny its own way of feeling, thinking and striving, and which nevertheless possesses all the political rights we do ourselves. If the Jew's feelings move in purely material realms, even more so does his thinking and striving. . . . Everything that prompts man to strive for higher things, whether religion, socialism, democracy, all that is to him only a means to the end of satisfying his craving for money and dominance. The consequences of his activity become the racial tuberculosis of nations.

And from this the following results: Anti-Semitism on purely emotional grounds will find its ultimate expression in the form of pogroms. The anti-Semitism of reason, however, must lead to the planned judicial opposition to and elimination of the privileges of the Jews. . . . Its ultimate goal, however, must absolutely be the removal of the Jews altogether. Only a government of national power and never a government of national impotence will be capable of both.[5]

Four days after receiving this statement, on September 12, 1919, Captain Mayr ordered Hitler to visit one of the small parties among the bewildering array of radical associations and cliques that formed and fell apart with great rapidity, only to coalesce in new groupings. Here was a vast, unused reservoir of response for one seeking a following. The often weird doctrines of these groups showed the blind readiness of the petit bourgeois masses to seize on anything that let them vent their hatreds and promised some way out of social crisis.

A key center of conspiratorial and propagandistic activities, as well as a meeting ground for right extremists, was the Thule Society. Its headquarters was the luxury hotel Vier Jahreszeiten, and it had connections throughout Bavarian society. At times it counted some 1,500 influential members, and it, too, used the swastika as its symbol. Moreover, it controlled its own newspaper, the *Münchener Beobachter*. Its head was a political adventurer with a rather unsavory past and the sonorous name of Baron Rudolf von Sebottendorf, which he had acquired through adoption by an Austrian nobleman stranded in the Orient. Early in his life Sebottendorf had come under the influence of radical ideologues such as Theodor Fritsch and Lanz von Liebenfels, whose racist mania had also affected

115

young Hitler. His Thule Society, founded in Munich at the beginning of 1918, was a successor to the racist anti-Semitic leagues of the prewar period and followed many of their traditions. Its name, in fact, went back to the Teutonic Thule Sect established in Leipzig in 1912, whose members had to be of "Aryan blood." That group, rather like a lodge in its procedures, required candidates for admission to answer questions on the hirsuteness of various parts of their body. Candidates also had to present a footprint as evidence of their racial purity.

Sebottendorf's new Thule Society began its life by launching into violent anti-Semitic propaganda denouncing the Jews as the "mortal foe of the German people." This was in January, 1918, while the war was still in progress. Later the Society could claim that the bloody and chaotic events of the soviet period were proof of its thesis. Its extravagant slogans contributed greatly to creating that atmosphere of obscene hatred in which racist radicalism could flourish. As early as October, 1918, groups within the Thule Society had forged plans for a rightist uprising. It instigated various assassination attempts against Kurt Eisner, and on April 13, 1918, attempted a putsch against the soviet regime. The Society also maintained connections with the Russian *émigré* circles that had made Munich their headquarters. A young Baltic student of architecture named Alfred Rosenberg, who had been profoundly affected by the trauma of the Russian Revolution, acted as liaison man. Almost all the actors who were to dominate the Bavarian scene in the following years belonged to the Society, including people who were to be prominent within Hitler's party. In various connections we encounter the names of Dietrich Eckart, Gottfried Feder, Hans Frank, Rudolf Hess, and Karl Harrer.

At the behest of the Thule Society, Karl Harrer, a sports journalist, together with a machinist named Anton Drexler, had, in October 1918, founded a "Political Workers Circle." The group described itself as "an association of select persons for the purpose of discussing and studying political affairs." In fact, it was intended as a bridge between the masses and the nationalistic Right. For a while the membership was limited to a very few of Drexler's fellow workers. He himself was a quiet, square-set, rather strange man, employed at the Munich workshops of the Federal Railways. As early as March, 1918, this sober, bespectacled machinist had on his own initiative organized a "Free Workers Committee for a Good Peace," whose program called for fighting usury and rallying the working class behind the war. He had turned against Marxist socialism for its failure to resolve the "national question" either in practice or theory. This, at any rate, was the theme of an article he published titled, "The Failure of the Proletarian International and the Shipwreck of the Idea of Fraternization." The enthusiasm with which the socialists on both sides had supported the war in August, 1914, had certainly exposed this flaw. A similar perception had led to the founding, in 1904, of the German Workers' Party (Deutsche Arbeiterpartei—DAP) by German-Bohemian workers in

Trautenau. Now Anton Drexler revived that name and founded a party of his own. Its charter members were workmen from his own shop, and its first meeting took place on January 5, 1919, in the Fürstenfelder Hof. A few days later, on the initiative of the Thule Society, another meeting was held in the Hotel Vier Jahreszeiten, and a national organization for the party was created. Karl Harrer appointed himself "National Chairman." It was an ambitious title.

Actually, the new party, which hereafter met once a week in the Sternecker beer hall, was very small potatoes. Drexler did occasionally manage to procure a few prominent racists or nationalists as speakers—such as Gottfried Feder or the writer Dietrich Eckart. But the tone of the group remained at a dreary, beer-drinking level. Significantly, it did not address itself to the public at all. It was less a political party in the proper sense than a combination, typical for the Munich of those years, of secret society and locals gathering at the pub for their evening pint. A dull and embittered craving for exchange of opinions had brought them together. The lists of participants mention between ten and forty persons. Germany's shame, the trauma of the lost war, anti-Semitic grumblings, complaints concerning the downfall of order, justice, and morals—these were the themes of the meetings. The "directives" Drexler had read at the initial meeting reveal heartfelt if awkwardly worded resentments toward the rich, the proletarians and Jews, the price gougers and the rabble-rousers. The program called for annual profits being limited to 10,000 marks, for parity representation of the different states in the German Foreign Office, and the right of "skilled workers with a legal residence . . . to be counted in the middle class." For happiness lay not "in talk and empty phrases in meetings, demonstrations and elections, but in good work, a full cookpot and a fair chance for the children."

However philistine and intellectually confused the character of the party as a whole must appear, the first sentence of the "directives" contains an idea that embodied historical experience and a widespread need among the people. It shows that clumsy, crotchety Anton Drexler had grasped the spirit of the age. For the DAP defined itself as a classless "socialist organization led only by German leaders." Drexler's "inspired idea" was to reconcile nationalism and socialism. He was neither the only man, nor even the first, to attempt this, and his concern about children and cookpots was a simplistic notion that certainly could not compete with the impressive Marxist systems of historical interpretation. But the moment in which Drexler seized on the idea—in the midst of the emotional crisis of a defeated, insulted country challenged by revolution—and the fact that he happened to meet Adolf Hitler, placed both the idea and the backroom political party which espoused it squarely on the stage of world history.

At the meeting of September 12, 1919, Gottfried Feder addressed the group on the subject: "How and by what means can capitalism be elimi-

117

nated?" Among the forty-odd persons in the audience was Adolf Hitler, who was there on Captain Mayr's instructions. While Feder was expatiating on his familiar theses, the guest noted that here was one more of those newly founded groups "like so many others" stifling "in their absurd philistinism." Accordingly, "when Feder finally stopped talking, I was happy. I had seen enough."

Nevertheless, Hitler waited for the discussion period, and when one of the visitors urged the separation of Bavaria from the Reich and her union with Austria, he rose in indignation: "I could not help demanding the floor." He attacked the speaker so passionately that Drexler whispered to the locomotive engineer Lotter, who was sitting beside him: "Man, he has a big mouth; we could use him." When Hitler, immediately after talking, turned to leave this "dull club," Drexler hurried after him and asked him to come back soon. He pressed upon Hitler a pamphlet he had written titled *My Political Awakening*. Hitler has described how, lying in his bunk at the barracks early the following morning and watching the mice go after some crusts of bread he had thrown down for them, he began to read the pamphlet. In Drexler's accounts of his life he recognized elements in his own experience: exclusion from jobs by union terrorism; earning a wretched living by semiartistic work (in Drexler's case playing the zither in a night club); and, finally, the great illumination accompanied by feelings of intense anxiety—recognition of the role of the Jewish race as corrupters of the world. These parallels aroused Hitler's interest, even though the person involved was a worker, as Hitler constantly reiterates.[6]

A few days later he received in the mail an unsolicited membership card bearing the number 555. Partly amused, partly annoyed, partly not knowing quite how to react, he decided to accept the invitation to attend a committee meeting. At the Altes Rosenbad tavern in the Herrenstrasse, "a very rundown place," he found at a table in the back room "in the dim light of a broken-down gas lamp" several young people. While the tavernkeeper and his wife and one or two guests sat gloomily around in the other room, the group read the minutes "like the presiding committee of a *Skat* club." They counted the club treasury (cash on hand: seven marks and fifty pfennigs). They approved the reports and drafted letters to similar associations in North Germany. All in all, "this was club life of the worst manner and sort."

For two days Hitler pondered, and as always when he reminisced about decisive situations in his life, he spoke of the strain of the decision and emphasized the "hard," "difficult," or "bitter" mental effort it cost him. It ended with his entering the German Workers' Party as board member number 7, responsible for recruitment and propaganda. "After two days of agonized pondering and reflection, I finally came to the conviction that I had to take this step. It was the most decisive resolve of my life. From here there was and could be no turning back."[7]

118

On the one hand, this is an example of Hitler's trick of throwing a bit of dramatic lighting on turning points in his own career that only later became apparent as such. If the moment lacked any outward drama, he could at least portray the decision as the product of solitary, painful struggle. On the other hand, all available sources show him consistently, up to the very end, displaying a singular indecisiveness, a deep-seated fear of fixing on any one course. His later associates describe him as going through a wearing process of vacillation and changes of mind on many questions until he was so exhausted that he finally left things to chance and a toss of a coin. His cult of fate and Providence was a device to rationalize his indecisiveness. It might be said that all his personal and even some of his political decisions were nothing more than evasions, ways to escape alternatives he felt to be threatening. In any case, throughout his life, from his leaving school, his moves to Vienna and Munich, and his volunteering for the army, up to his step into politics, it is not hard to detect the escape motivation. The same is true for much of his behavior during the following years, right down to the hapless postponements of the very end.

The desire to evade the oppressive demands of duty and order in the respectable world, to put off the feared discharge into civilian life dictated all his actions as a returned soldier and gradually led him into the wings of the Bavarian political stage. He looked upon politics as the vocation of one who was without a vocation and wanted to remain so. Now at last he had a field of action that demanded no qualifications other than those he possessed: passion, imagination, organizational talent, and demagogic gifts. In the barracks he wrote and typed away indefatigably at invitations to meetings, which he then delivered personally. He asked for lists of names and addresses and spoke with the persons mentioned. He sought out connections, support, new members.

The results were meager at first. Every unfamiliar face that turned up at meetings was eagerly noted. Hitler's success was due in considerable part to his being the only one in the organization with unlimited time at his disposal. His prestige rapidly increased in the seven-man party committee, which met once a week at a corner table in the Café Gasteig—later the object of worshipful veneration. The fact was that he had more ideas, was more adept and more energetic than the others in the executive committee.

The other members had been at home in their small-time situation and were perfectly content to remain there. They were stunned when Hitler began pushing the "dull club" into the public view. October 16, 1919, proved a decisive day both for the German Workers' Party and the new man on its executive committee. At the first public meeting, with 111 persons present, Hitler took the floor as the second speaker of the evening. For thirty minutes, in an ever more furious stream of verbiage, he poured out the hatreds that ever since his days in the home for men had been stored up within him or discharged only in fruitless monologues. As if

119

bursting through the silence and human barriers of many years, the sentences, the delusions, the accusations came tumbling out. And at the end "the people in the small room were electrified." He had found "what before I had simply felt within me, without in any way knowing it." Jubilantly, he made the overwhelming discovery: "I could speak!"[8]

That moment signified—if any specific moment did—the breakthrough to himself, the "hammer-stroke of fate" that shattered the "shell of everyday life." His sense of release is palpable in the ecstatic tone of his memories of that evening. To be sure, he had tested his oratorical powers repeatedly in the past several weeks, and had become acquainted with his own ability to persuade and convert. But this was the first time he experienced the subjective force of his oratory, the triumphant self-abandonment to the point of sweating and reeling with exhaustion. And as everything with him turned to excess—his fears, his self-confidence, or even his rapture at hearing *Tristan* for the hundredth time—he henceforth fell into a veritable oratorical fury. Aside from or alongside of all political passions, from now on it was this newly awakened craving for vindication on the part of the "poor devil," as he calls himself in his recollections of the period,[9] that drove him again and again to the speaker's platform.

Soon after his entrance into the DAP Hitler set about transforming the timid, static group of club members into a noisy publicity-conscious party of struggle. He met opposition chiefly from Karl Harrer, who was wedded to the secret-society notions inherited from the Thule Society and would have liked to continue running the DAP as a little discussion circle. From the start Hitler thought in terms of a mass party. Partly, he could not think otherwise, because he had never been able to accept reduced circumstances, but partly also because he understood why the old conservative parties had failed. Harrer's views were a survival, on an absurd scale, of that tendency to exclusiveness which had been the weakness of the bourgeois parties of notables during the Wilhelmine era. By now such an attitude had alienated the masses of the petty bourgeosie, and the working class as well, from the conservative position.

Even before the end of 1919 the German Workers' Party, at Hitler's insistence, set up its headquarters in a dark, vaultlike cellar room in the Sternecker beer hall. The rent was fifty marks; in co-signing the lease Hitler again gave his occupation as "painter." A table and a few borrowed chairs were placed in the room, a telephone installed, and a safe obtained for the membership cards and the party treasury. Soon an old typewriter was added, and a rubber stamp to go with it: when Harrer noticed these beginnings of a veritable bureaucracy, he called Hitler a "megalomaniac." At the same time Hitler had the executive committee expanded to, first, ten, later, twelve and more members. He brought in a number of followers personally devoted to him; quite often these were fellow soldiers whom he had won over in the barracks. Soon he was able to replace the party's humble handwritten notes by printed invitations. At the same time the party began advertising in the *Münchener Beobachter*. Recruiting pamphlets and leaflets were left in the taverns where the party met. And Hitler in his propaganda tactics now began displaying that entirely unfounded self-assurance, all the more challenging because backed by no reality at all, which would frequently produce his successes in the future. He ventured something totally unusual—he began charging admission to the public meetings of this tiny, unknown party.

His growing reputation as a speaker solidified his position inside the party. By the beginning of the next year he had succeeded in making the refractory chairman, Harrer, resign. Soon afterward, the executive committee, though skeptical and worried about making itself ridiculous, followed the biddings of its ambitious propaganda chief and appealed to the masses. The party issued a call for its first mass meeting, to be held in the Festsaal of the Hofbräuhaus on February 24, 1920.

The bright red poster announcing the meeting did not even mention Hitler's name. The principal speaker of the evening was a true-blue nationalist spokesman, Dr. Johannes Dingfelder, a physician, who wrote in racist publications under the pseudonym of Germanus Agricola. He had developed an economic theory whose twistings bizarrely reflected the shortages of the postwar period. Nature would be going on a production strike, he pessimistically predicted; her yields would diminish, vermin would consume the remainder. Consequently, humanity was on the verge of doom. There was only one way out, a return to racial and national principles. That evening he conjured up this hope again, "quite objectively and often imbued with a profound religious spirit." Thus the report of the Munich Political Intelligence Service.[10]

Then Hitler spoke. To take advantage of this unique opportunity of publicizing the ideas of the German Workers' Party to a large audience, he had insisted that a program be worked up. He began by inveighing against the Versailles Treaty and the cowardice of the government, then against the general craving for amusement, the Jews, and the "leeches," namely profiteers and usurers. Then, interrupted frequently by applause or catcalls, he read the program aloud. At the end "some heckler shouted something. This was followed by great commotion. Everyone standing on chairs and tables. Tremendous tumult. Shouts of 'Get out!'" The meeting ended in a general uproar. Some members of the radical Left subsequently tramped, loudly cheering the International and the Soviet Republic, from the Hofbräuhaus to the Rathaustor. "Otherwise no disturbance," the police report stated.

Apparently such turbulence was commonplace, for even the nationalist-racist press took scarcely any notice of the meeting. Only recent finds of source material have made it possible to reconstruct the course of the

121

meeting. Hitler's own myth-making account turned it into a dramatic occasion beginning with a brawl and ending with wild acclaim and mass conversion: "Unanimously and again unanimously" each point of the program was accepted, "and when the last thesis had found its way to the heart of the masses, there stood before me a hall full of people united by a new conviction, a new faith, a new will." Typically, Hitler reverted to his memory of operatic performances and proclaimed that "a fire was kindled from whose flame one day the sword must come which would regain freedom for the Germanic Siegfried." He could already hear striding forth "the goddess of inexorable vengeance for the perjured deed of November 9, 1919." Meanwhile, the nationalist *Münchener Beobachter* merely noted that after Dr. Dingfelder's speech Hitler had "set forth some pointed political ideas" and then announced the program of the DAP.

Nevertheless, in a higher sense the author of *Mein Kampf* was right. For with that mass meeting there began the evolution of Drexler's beer-drinking racist club into Adolf Hitler's mass party. To be sure, he himself had once again had to play a subordinate role. Nevertheless, there had been almost 2,000 persons present, filling the great hall of the Hofbräuhaus. The crowd had been exposed to Hitler's political doctrines, and many had accepted them. Henceforth, more and more, it was his will, his style, his direction that propelled the party and decided its success or failure. Party legend later compared the meeting of February 24, 1920, to Martin Luther's nailing his theses to the door of the church in Wittenberg. In both cases tradition has had to paint its own historically quite dubious picture, because true history tends to scant man's craving for drama and sentimental recollection. But there was some justification for hailing the meeting as the true birthday of the movement, even though no such momentous act had been planned.

The program Hitler offered that evening had been drafted by Anton Drexler, probably with some assistance from Gottfried Feder, and then submitted to the executive committee for revision. Hitler's exact part in the framing can no longer be determined, but the sloganlike compactness of several articles shows his editorial influence. The program consisted of twenty-five points and combined in rather arbitrary fashion elements of the older racist ideology with immediate grievances and the national need to deny reality. The consistent factor throughout was strong emotional appeal. Negatives predominated; the program was anticapitalist, anti-Marxist, antiparliamentarian, anti-Semitic, and most decidedly against the way the war had ended. The positive aims, on the other hand—such as the various demands for the protection of the middle class—were mostly vague and tended to add fuel to the anxieties and desires of the little man. For example, all income not earned by work was to be confiscated (Point 11), as well as all war profits (Point 12), and a profit-sharing plan for large industries was to be introduced (Point 14). Another point called for large department stores to be turned over to the communities and rented out "at cheap prices" to small tradesmen (Point 16). Land reform was also demanded, and a ban on speculation in land (Point 17).

Despite all its opportunistic features this program was not so empty as has sometimes been represented. At any rate, there was a good deal more to it than clever demogogery. It included, at least in the germ, all the essential features of what was to be National Socialist doctrine: the living-space thesis (Point 3), anti-Semitism (Points 4, 5, 6, 7, 8, 24), the harmless-sounding and widely acceptable platitudes (Points 10, 18, 24) that could ultimately be made the basis for a totalitarian state—as, for example, the maxim that the common good takes precedence over the good of the individual.[11] Much was made of the determination to eliminate the abuses of capitalism, to overcome the false class-struggle confrontations of Marxism, and to bring about the reconciliation of all groups in a powerfully integrated racial community.

It would seem that all this possessed a special allure in a country suffering so profoundly from national and social irritations. The idea or formula of "nationalistic socialism," linking as it did the two paramount concepts of the nineteenth century, could be found at the root of many political programs and drafts for social systems of the time. It turned up in Anton Drexler's simple autobiographical account of his "political awakening" and in the Berlin lectures of Eduard Stadtler, who as early as 1918 had founded an Anti-Bolshevist League, with the support of industry. It was the subject of one of those enlightenment courses run by the Munich District Command of the Reichswehr and even entered the thinking of Oswald Spengler, whose essay *Prussianism and Socialism* treated most persuasively of the same theme. Even within Social Democracy the idea had its followers. The disappointment over the failure of the Second International at the outbreak of the war had led a number of independent minds to turn toward a combination of nationalistic and social revolutionary schemes. *National Socialism, Its Growth and Its Aims* was the title of a bulky theoretical work published in 1919 by one of the founders of the German-Socialist Workers' Party, a railroad engineer named Rudolf Jung. That work hailed nationalist socialism as *the* epoch-making political concept that would succeed in checking Marxist socialism. To emphasize their separation from internationalist movements, Jung and his Austrian followers changed the party's name in May, 1918, to German National Socialist Workers' Party.

A week after the meeting in the Hofbräuhaus the DAP also changed its name. Borrowing from the related German and Austrian groups, it called itself National Socialist German Workers' Party (Nationalsozialistische Deutsche Arbeiterpartei—NSDAP) and simultaneously adopted the battle symbol of its Austrian counterparts, the swastika. Dr. Walter Riehl, chairman of the Austrian national socialists, had shortly before set up an "international secretariat" that was to serve as a liaison office for all national socialist parties. There already existed active contacts with various other such groups espousing racial-socialist programs, above all the German Socialist Party of Alfred Brunner, a Düsseldorf engineer. This party tried to be extremely leftish and boasted, "Our demands are more radical than those of the Bolshevists." It had units in many of the larger cities. The one in Nuremberg was headed by a schoolteacher named Julius Streicher.

On April 1, 1920, Hitler finally left the army, for he at last had an alternative. He was determined to devote himself henceforth entirely to political work, to seize the leadership of the NSDAP, and to build the party according to his own ideas. He rented a room at 41 Thierschstrasse, near the Isar River. Although he spent most of his days in the cellar headquarters of the party he avoided being listed as a party employee. What he lived on was something of a mystery, and enemies within the party soon raised this question. His landlady thought the somber young man monosyllabic and seemingly very busy, a "real bohemian."

His self-confidence grew, based on his talent for oratory, his coldness, and his readiness to take risks. He had nothing to lose. Ideas as such mattered little to him. In general he was less interested in a concept than in its potential uses, in whether, as he once remarked, it could yield a "powerful slogan." His total lack of comprehension for thinking without politically malleable substance came out in his outbursts of "detestation" and "profoundest disgust" for the "antiquated folkish theoreticians," the "bigmouths," and "idea thieves." Similarly, he took the floor for his earliest rhetorical displays only when he had something to strike back at polemically. For him it was not evidence that made an idea persuasive but handiness, not truth but the idea's aptness as a weapon. "Every idea, even the best," he noted, "becomes a danger if it parades as a purpose in itself, being in reality only a means to one." Elsewhere he emphasized that in the political struggle force always needs the support of an idea—significantly, he did not put it the other way round. He regarded National Socialism, too, as chiefly a means to his own ambitious ends. It was merely a romantic, attractively vague cue with which he stepped on the stage. The idea of reconciliation implicit in the phrase seemed more modern, closer to the needs of the age, then the slogans of class struggle. The conservative writer Arthur Moeller van den Bruck, who in the early years of the century had promulgated the idea of nationalistic socialism, now declared that it was "certainly a part of the German future." Its potentiality was above all apparent to the cool politicians who had axes to grind. There were many such men, all competing in the same game. But before long Hitler knew that he himself would be that part of the German future.

124

Chapter 2

This Hitler will some day be our greatest!
Rudolf Jung, 1920

LOCAL TRIUMPHS

In those arduous and intoxicated days of his entrance into politics, in the spring of 1920, Hitler was not much more than a local Munich agitator. Night after night he made his way through boisterous smoke-filled taverns to win frequently hostile or scoffing audiences over to his doctrines. His reputation increased steadily. The temper of the city was susceptible to his theatrical style and favored his success as much as the more tangible historical factors.

In the rapture of those first oratorical triumphs, he was capable of extraordinary feats.

His "talent for combination" seized upon the most disparate elements and fitted them together into compact formulas. He learned more from his opponents than from his models or comrades; he always admitted this frankly. He had learned a great deal from the opposite camp; only fools or weaklings feared that in adopting ideas from others they would lose their own. And so he put together Richard Wagner and Lenin, Gobineau, Nietzsche and Le Bon, Ludendorff, Lord Northcliffe, Schopenhauer and Karl Lueger, and formed a composite. The system was arbitrary, queer, full of half-educated rashness, but it had a certain coherence. Mussolini and Italian Fascism also fitted into it, and their importance was to grow. Hitler even took lessons from the so-called Wise Men of Zion; though by now it had been conclusively proved that the "Protocols" were forgeries,[12] that did not lessen the power of their Machiavellian theses.

But Hitler learned his most lasting lessons from Marxism. The energy he devoted to the development of a National Socialist ideology, in spite of his essential indifference to such matters, testifies to the effects of the Marxist model upon him. One of the starting points for his political activity was the insight that the traditional bourgeois type of party could no longer match the force of the leftist mass organizations. Only a similarly organized but even more resolute ideological party would be able to combat Marxism.[13]

125

Tactically, he learned most from the experiences of the revolutionary period. The Bolshevik take-over and the soviet rule in Bavaria had shown how a handful of determined men could seize power. From Lenin one could learn how to heighten a revolutionary impulse, from German socialists like Friedrich Ebert and Philipp Scheidemann how such an impulse could be wasted. Hitler later declared:

I have learned a great deal from Marxism. I admit that without hesitation. Not from that boring social theory and materialist conception of history, not at all from that absurd nonsense. . . . But I've learned from their methods. Only I seriously went about doing what these little tradesmen and secretary minds timidly started. The whole of National Socialism is implicit in that. Just examine it closely. . . . These new methods of political struggle do go back to the Marxists in their essentials. I needed only to take over these methods and develop them, and in essentials I had what we needed. I needed only to pursue consistently what the Social Democrats interrupted ten times over, because they wanted to carry out their revolution within the framework of a democracy. National Socialism is what Marxism could have been had it freed itself from the absurd, artificial link with a democratic system.[14]

He not only applied everything he took over consistently; he also went much further than his model. In his nature there was an infantile fondness for the grand, surpassing gesture, a craving to impress. He dreamed of superlatives and was bent on having the most radical ideology, just as later on he was bent on having the biggest building or the heaviest tank. He picked up his tactics and his aims, as he later observed, "from all the bushes alongside the road of life." He himself contributed the harshness and consistency with which he applied everything, the characteristic boldness about taking the last step.

At the beginning he went at things according to a sensible plan. His first task was a personal one, to break out of anonymity, to emerge from the welter of small-time nationalist-racist parties with an unmistakable image. When he recounted party history in his later speeches he would always allude to his unimportant beginnings—evidence of the pain of those days when he had known the pangs of repressed ambition and unrecognized greatness. With a total lack of scruple, which was the real novelty of his public life and which once and for all proclaimed his refusal to abide by any rules or conventions, he now set about making a name for himself—by unceasing activity, by brawls, scandals, and riots, even by terrorism if that would bring him to the forefront. "Whether they represent us as clowns or criminals, the main thing is that they mention us, that they concern themselves with us again and again."[15]

This intention shaped the style and methods of all he did. The garish red of the party's banners was chosen not only for its psychological effect but also because it provocatively usurped the traditional color of the Left. The posters also would often be a blatant red. They would have a slogan for headlines and offer a pithy editorial in gigantic format. To further the impression of bigness and forcefulness the NSDAP repeatedly organized street processions. Its leaflet distributors and poster squads went about tirelessly. In acknowledged imitation of leftist propaganda techniques, Hitler had trucks loaded with men ride through the streets. But instead of the fist-swinging, Moscow-oriented proletarians who had spread terror and hatred in bourgeois residential districts, these trucks were manned by disciplined former soldiers who now, after armistice and demobilization, were fighting on in a different fashion under the battle standard of the National Socialist Party. These self-controlled radicals lent the demonstrations an intimidating, paramilitary tone. Soon Hitler was holding these demonstrations in the form of a series of meetings that passed like a wave over Munich, and then over other cities.

Gradually, these soldiers began changing the sociological face of the party. The contemplative groups of beer-drinking workers and small tradesmen were infiltrated by tough types of regular army men accustomed to violence. The earliest membership list of the party registers all of twenty-two professional soldiers among 193 names. Directly affected by the terms of the Versailles Treaty, with its check on the size of the army, they had abruptly found themselves confronting the dreary perils of civilian life. Here was a new party that offered a haven from perplexity and the terrors of being declassed. Within its framework they could satisfy their craving for new forms of comradeship and continue to express the contempt for life as well as death that they had absorbed on the battlefield.

With the aid of these military converts accustomed to strict subordination, discipline, and devotion, Hitler gradually succeeded in providing the party with a firm inner structure. Many of the new men were sent to him by the Munich District Command of the Reichswehr. Later, Hitler would repeatedly assert that he had stood alone, nameless and poor, relying on no one but himself, against a world of enemies. That was far from the truth. From the beginning he received protection from the Reichswehr and the paramilitary organizations. They were what made his rise possible.

Ernst Röhm did more for the NSDAP than anyone else. He held the rank of captain as a political adviser on the staff of Colonel Epp and was the real brain of the disguised military regime in Bavaria. Röhm provided the young National Socialist Party with followers, arms, and funds. His efforts were supported in large measure by the officers of the Allied Supervisory Commission, who favored such illegal activities for various reasons. Partly, they had an interest in maintaining conditions approaching civil war in Germany; partly, they wished to strengthen the military power against the obstreperous Left. Chivalric feelings also played their part: they wanted to oblige their former foes, fellow soldiers who had fought honorably against them.

Röhm was a man who from childhood on had had "only one thought and one wish, to become a soldier." Toward the end of the war he had served on the General Staff and was an outstanding organizer, but by temperament he belonged in the front lines, though he scarcely looked it. This stocky little fellow with his rather florid, marred face—he had been wounded many times during the war—was a wild daredevil. He divided the human race into soldiers and civilians, friends and foes; he was frank, unsubtle, rough and tough, a straightforward old campaigner with no conscience to speak of. One of his comrades from those days of illegal activity once remarked that Röhm "livened things up" wherever he appeared. But perhaps the converse was just as often true. Certainly no ideological sophistries complicated his old-fashioned Bavarian bluntness. Ceaselessly active, he had a single goal: to magnify the power of the military within the government. With that in mind, he had organized the General Staff department for propaganda and secret partnership with political groups—the department on whose behalf liaison man Adolf Hitler had first attended a meeting of the German Workers' Party. Impressed, as was almost everyone else, by the oratorical talent of the young agitator, Röhm provided Hitler with his first valuable contacts to politicians and military men. He himself entered the party early, receiving the membership number 623.

The commando element that Röhm's men had brought into the party was colorfully garnished by the liberal use of symbols and emblems. In *Mein Kampf* Hitler pretended that the swastika flag was his invention. In fact, one of the party members, the dentist Friedrich Krohn, had designed it for the founding meeting of the Starnberg *Ortsgruppe* (local party group) in May of 1920. As early as the previous year, in a memorandum, he had recommended using the swastika as "the symbol of national socialist parties." Once again, Hitler's own contribution consisted, not of the original idea, but of his instant perception of the symbol's psychological magic. He therefore raised it to the status of a party emblem and made it obligatory.

Later he would do the same with the "standards," which he took over from Italian Fascism and conferred upon the storm troops. He introduced *"Heil"* as a greeting, made a point of military correctness in ranks and uniforms, and in general stressed all formalities: the setting of scenes, the decorative details, the increasingly solemn ceremonials of dedicating flags, reviews, and parades, all the way up to the mass spectacles of the party rallies, where he directed great blocs of human beings against mighty stone backdrops and reveled in the exercise of his demitalents as actor and architect. He spent many hours hunting through old art magazines and the heraldic department of the Munich State Library to find a model for the eagle to be used on the official rubber stamp of the party. His first circular letter as chairman of the NSDAP, dated September 17, 1921, was largely concerned with party symbolism, which he prescribed in loving detail. He instructed the heads of the local groups "to energetically promote the wearing of the party badge. The members are to be continually reminded to go about everywhere and at all times with the party emblem. Jews who take offense at it are to be dealt with at once."

These two aspects, one ceremonial, the other terroristic, had marked the party from its wretched early beginnings and proved to be an inspired approach on Hitler's part. The references to brute force by no means repelled; rather, they added a note of strong earnestness to the party program and seemed to fit the historic hour better than the false amiability of traditional party procedures.

Another asset of the NSDAP was its egalitarian character. Nationalist parties of the past had appropriated true patriotic principles for the upper classes, as if only men of property and education had a fatherland. The NSDAP was at once nationalistic and plebeian; rude and ready to brawl, it brought together the idea of nationalism and the gutter. Hitherto, the bourgeoisie had looked upon the masses as a danger against which they had always to be on their guard. The NSDAP seemed to be offering itself as a vanguard of the masses on the side of the bourgeoisie. "We need force to win our battle," Hitler declared again and again. "Let the others . . . stretch out in their easy chairs; we are ready to climb on the beer table." One might not want to follow him oneself; yet here was a fellow who clearly knew how to tame the masses and harness their energies for the right cause.

His own energy seemed inexhaustible. None of his rivals was remotely a match for him. His principle was: a mass meeting every week. And he was not only the organizer of these but the speaker. Of forty-eight meetings held between November, 1919, and November, 1920, he was the speaker at thirty-one. The increasingly rapid tempo of his appearances reflects the growing intensity of his affair with the masses. "Herr Hitler . . . flew into a fury and screamed so that not much could be understood at the back," one report records. A poster of May, 1920, announcing his appearance termed him a "brilliant speaker" and promised the visitor "a highly stimulating evening." Reports from this time on speak of rising attendance figures. Often he talked to 3,000 persons or more. Repeatedly, the recording secretaries noted that when he stepped on the platform in his blue uniform he was "stormily cheered." The very clumsiness of the summaries reveals the almost hypnotic power the speaker seemed to have over his audience.

The meeting began at 7:30 and ended at 10:45 P.M. The lecturer delivered an address on Judaism. The lecturer pointed out that everywhere one looks there are Jews. All Germany is ruled by Jews. It is a shame that German labor, brain workers and manual laborers both, let themselves be so hounded by the Jews. Naturally because the Jew has the money. The Jew sits in the government and schemes and smuggles. When he has his pockets full again he again hounds the workers back and forth so that again and again he comes out on top and we

129

poor Germans put up with it all. He went on to talk about Russia also. . . . And who arranged all that? Only the Jew. Therefore Germans be united and fight against the JEWS. For they'll eat our last crust from under our noses. . . . The speaker's concluding words: Let us wage the struggle until the last Jew is removed from the German Reich and even though it comes to a coup and even more to another revolution. . . . The lecturer received great applause. He also denounced the press . . . since at the last meeting one of those dirty journalists wrote everything down.

Another account, of a speech given on August 28, 1920, in the Hofbräuhaus, reads:

The lecturer Hitler explained how things stood for us before the war and how they are now. On usurers and profiteers, that they all belong on the gallows. Further on the mercenary army. He said it probably wouldn't harm the young fellows any if they had to enlist again, for that hadn't harmed anybody, for nobody knows any more that the young ought to keep their mouths shut in the presence of elders, for everywhere the young lack discipline. . . . Then he went through all the points in the program, at which he received a lot of applause. The hall was very full. A man who called Herr Hitler an idiot was calmly kicked out.[16]

With growing self-assurance the party began touting itself as a supporter of "order" by breaking up meetings of the Left, shouting down speakers, administering "reminders" in the form of beatings, and once forcing a piece of sculpture to be removed from a public exhibition on the grounds that it offended public taste. At the beginning of January, 1921, Hitler assured his audience in the Kindl-Keller "that henceforth the National Socialist movement in Munich will ruthlessly prevent all meetings and lectures—if necessary, by force—which are designed to seditiously affect our already sick folk-comrades."

The party found such gestures all the easier because now, in addition to the protection it enjoyed from the Munich District Army Command, it had become the "spoiled darling" of the Bavarian state government. In the middle of March, rightist circles in Berlin, headed by the hitherto nameless Dr. Kapp and supported by the Ehrhardt Brigade, had attempted a coup. The attempt had collapsed, partly because of its amateur nature, partly because it was instantly countered by a general strike. A simultaneous attempt of the same sort by the Reichswehr and the Free Corps bands in Bavaria met with more success. On the night of March 13 the bourgeois Social Democratic regime was overthrown by the military and paramilitary forces and replaced by a rightist government under the "strong man" Gustav von Kahr.

The Left retaliated with its classic weapon: a general strike. The radical leftists saw a chance to exploit the situation for their own revolutionary ends and asserted leadership over the strike, principally in central Germany and the Ruhr. Their call for arming the proletariat was greeted enthusiastically. Soon, in a well-co-ordinated way that spoke of careful planning, masses of workers were organized in regular military formations. Between the Rhein and the Ruhr alone a "Red Army" of more than 50,000 men was set up. Within a few days it took over almost the entire industrial area. The weak Reichswehr and police units that opposed its advance were crushed; in places veritable battles were fought. A wave of killing, looting, and arson passed over the country, briefly bringing to light how much class hatred was present, repressed by the half-measures of a semirevolution. Soon, however, the military launched a bloody counterattack. The summary arrests, the shootings, and other acts of vengeance again revealed deep-seated feuds and unresolved conflicts. The country, so often divided and torn by contradictions in the course of its history, more and more desperately craved order and reconciliation. Instead, it found itself sinking ever more helplessly into a morass of hatred, distrust, and anarchy.

Because of the shift in power relationships, Bavaria became the natural center for radical rightist plots—even more than it had previously been. The Allies had repeatedly demanded that the paramilitary bands be dissolved. The Kahr government in Bavaria resisted, for these bands were its strongest support. Gradually, all those irreconcilable enemies of the republic who could ill stand the climate in other parts of Germany poured into the Bavarian militias and private armies, which already numbered more than 300,000 men. Among them were followers of Kapp who had fled Berlin, determined remnants from the dissolved Free Corps of the eastern regions of the Reich, the "National Warlord" Ludendorff, vigilante killers, adventurers, nationalist revolutionaries of various ideological shades. But all were united in their desire to overthrow the hated "Jews' Republic." They were able to exploit the traditional Old Bavarian separatism; the Bavarians had a long history of intense dislike for Prussian, Protestant Berlin. They flattered their Bavarian hosts with the slogan *Ordnungszelle Bayern* ("Bavaria as the mainstay of public order"). With more and more open support from the state government, these paramilitary groups began setting up arms depots, converting castles and monasteries into secret military bases, and plotting assassinations and coups. The conspiratorial whisperings went on constantly; all the groups were engaged in treasonous projects and often worked at cross-purposes.

These developments proved highly important to the rising National Socialist Party. The military, the paramilitary, and the civilian holders of power all looked upon it with favor, the more so as the party proved itself increasingly successful. After Hitler had been received by Prime Minister von Kahr, one of Hitler's student followers, Rudolf Hess, addressed a letter to the head of state: "The central point is that H. is convinced that a recovery is possible only if it proves possible to lead the masses, particularly the workers, back to the nationalist cause. . . . I know Herr Hitler very well personally and am quite close to him. He has a rarely honorable,

131

pure character, full of profound kindness, is religious, a good Catholic. His one goal is the welfare of his country. For this he is sacrificing himself in the most selfless fashion."

The day of public acceptance had come: The Prime Minister finally mentioned Hitler, in terms of praise, in the Landtag. Pöhner, the police commissioner of Munich, let Hitler do pretty much as he pleased. Roles in the forthcoming drama had been assigned. It became possible to discern the shape of that political constellation which has been called typical of Fascist conquests of power. Henceforth, Hitler was leagued with the conservative power of the Establishment, pledged to it as the advance guard in the fight against the common Marxist enemy. The conservatives thought they would make use of the energies and hypnotic arts of this unruly agitator and, at the proper moment, outmaneuver him by their own intellectual, economic, and political superiority. He, meanwhile, intended to march the battalions he had built up under the benevolent gaze of the ruling powers over the body of the enemy and against his partners in order to seize all the power. Hitler was playing that peculiar game, whose moves were marked by illusions, treacheries, and perjuries, with which he subsequently won almost all his victories and outwitted successively Kahr and Hugenberg, Papen and Chamberlain. On the other hand, his blunders, down to the ultimate failure in the war, were partly due to actions of impatience, petulance, or overconfidence.

The progress of the party was greatly furthered by the purchase of the *Völkische Beobachter* in December, 1920. Apparently Dietrich Eckart and Ernst Röhm raised the 60,000 reichsmarks that represented the down payment for the financially troubled racist-nationalist semiweekly.[17] Among the donors were many members of respectable Munich society, to which Hitler now found an entry. For this, too, he was indebted to Dietrich Eckart, a man of many connections. A roughhewn and comical figure, with his thick round head, his partiality for good wine and crude talk, Eckart had missed the great success he hoped for as a poet and dramatist. (His best known work was the German version of Ibsen's *Peer Gynt*). In compensation he had thrown himself into that bohemian group which indulged in politics. He had founded a political club called the German Citizens Society, but that, too, had come to nought. Another failure was the periodical *Auf gut Deutsch* ("Plain Speaking"), which, in corrosive language, and with displays of pseudoerudition propounded the familiar anti-Semitic theses. Along with Gottfried Feder, Eckart preached a revolution against "interest slavery" and for "true socialism." Influenced by Lanz von Liebenfels, he called for a ban on racially mixed marriages and demanded protection for pure German blood. He referred to Soviet Russia as "the Christian-kosher-butchering dictatorship of the Jewish world savior Lenin" and said that what he wanted most was "to load all Jews into a railroad train and drive into the Red Sea with it."[18]

Eckart had met Hitler early. In March, 1920, during the Kapp putsch, both were sent by their nationalist backers to survey the scene in Berlin. Well read and a shrewd psychologist who possessed extensive knowledge consonant with his prejudices, Eckart exerted great influence upon the awkward and provincial Hitler. With his bluff and uncomplicated manner, he was the first cultivated person whom Hitler was able to endure without an upsurge of his deep-seated complexes. Eckart recommended books to Hitler and lent him some, schooled his manners, corrected his language, and opened many doors to him. For a time they were an inseparable pair on the Munich social scene. As early as 1919 Eckart had prophesied the rise of a national savior, "a fellow who can stand the rattle of a machine gun. The rabble has to be scared shitless. I can't use an officer; the people no longer have any respect for them. Best of all would be a worker who's got his mouth in the right place. . . . He doesn't need much intelligence; politics is the stupidest business in the world." As far as he was concerned, someone who always had "a tough reply" to the Reds was far to be preferred to "a dozen learned professors who sit trembling on the wet pants seat of facts." Last but not least: "He must be a bachelor! Then we'll get the women." Hitler seemed to him the embodiment of this model, and as early as August, 1921, in an article in the *Völkische Beobachter* he for the first time hailed him as the Leader. One of the early battle songs of the NSDAP, "Storm, Storm, Storm!" was written by Eckart, and the refrain of every stanza became a party slogan: "Germany, awake!" Hitler repaid Eckart by declaring that he had written "poems as beautiful as Goethe's." He publicly called the poet his "fatherly friend" and described himself as a disciple of Eckart. Along with Rosenberg, Eckart seems to have wielded the most lasting ideological influence upon Hitler during that early period. Evidently he also made Hitler aware of his own stature. The second volume of *Mein Kampf* ends with the poet's name printed in italics.

The welcome Hitler received in the Munich society to which Dietrich Eckart introduced him was scarcely of a political nature. One of the first ladies to open her salon to him was an American by birth, Catherine Hanfstaengl, mother of a young man named Ernst ("Putzi") Hanfstaengl, who had fallen under Hitler's oratorical spell. She herself was by no means nationalistic. Liberals were intrigued by this phenomenon of a young popular orator with Neanderthal views and unpolished manners. His sometimes shocking public behavior made him the more interesting. He had the aura of a prestidigitator, the acrid odor of both the circus and of tragic embitterment, the sharp glitter of a "famous monster." The common topic of conversation was frequently Richard Wagner; Hitler would rhapsodize at length about Wagner in staccato phrases. The descriptions we have all convey a mixture of eccentricity and clumsiness. With people of importance Hitler was inhibited, brooding, and to some extent servile. During a conversation with Ludendorff at this time he kept raising his backside slightly

133

after each of the general's sentences, "with a half bow uttering a most respectful, 'Very well, your Excellency!' or 'Quite so, your Excellency!' "

His insecurity, the painful sense of being an outsider in bourgeois society, remained with him for a long time. If we are to believe the available accounts, he was eternally bent upon making an impression. He came late; his bouquets of flowers were bigger than others, his bows lower. Intervals of saying nothing alternated abruptly with choleric outbursts. His voice was rough; he made even casual remarks with passion. Once, according to an eyewitness, he had sat silent and weary for about an hour when his hostess happened to drop a friendly remark about the Jews. Only then "did he begin to speak and he spoke without ceasing. After a while he thrust back his chair and stood up, still speaking, or rather yelling, in such a powerful penetrating voice as I have never heard from anyone else. In the next room a child woke up and began to cry. After he had for more than half an hour delivered a quite witty but very one-sided oration on the Jews, he suddenly broke off, went up to his hostess, begged to be excused and kissed her hand as he took his leave."[19]

His social awkwardness reflected his irreparably distorted relationship to bourgeois society. The reek of the home for men clung to his clothing for a long time. When Pfeffer von Salomon—later to become his chief storm troop leader—met him for the first time, Hitler was wearing an old tail-coat, tan shoes, and carrying a knapsack on his back. The Free Corps leader was so unpleasantly impressed that he did not wish to be introduced to this person. Ernst Hanfstaengl recalled that Hitler wore with his blue suit a purple shirt, brown vest and crimson tie; the holster of his revolver made a conspicuous bulge at his hip. Hitler was quite slow in learning to stylize his appearance and to do justice to his conception of himself as grand tribune of the people down to his weird uniform. Even then, the picture he presented betrayed deep insecurity. It combined elements from his long-ago dreams of being a Rienzi with touches of Al Capone and General Ludendorff; the result was something preposterous. But even this effect could be interpreted in a number of ways. Some observers thought Hitler was trying to exploit his insecurity and was using his very awkwardness as a means of self-dramatization. At any rate, he seemed concerned less with making his appearance attractive than with making it memorable.

How he struck others at this time can be seen in the following thumbnail sketch by the historian Karl Alexander von Müller, who met Hitler at a coffee hour at Erna Hanfstaengl's, Ernst's sister. Also present was Abbot Alban Schachleiter, who was curious to meet the rising politician. "My wife and I provided part of the decor. The four of us were already sitting at the polished mahogany table by the window when the bell rang. Through the open door I could see him in the narrow hallway politely and almost servilely greeting our hostess, laying aside riding whip, velour hat and trench coat, finally unbuckling his cartridge belt with revolver attached and likewise hanging it on the clothes hook. It all looked very odd, reminiscent of Karl May's American Indian novels.* As yet we did not know how precisely each of these trivialities in clothing and behavior was even then calculated for effect, as were the strikingly close-cropped mustache, which was narrower than the unpleasantly wide-nostriled nose. . . . The look in his eyes already expressed a consciousness of public success; but something curiously awkward still clung to him, and one had the uneasy feeling that he sensed it and resented anyone's noticing it. His face, too, was still thin and pale, with something like an expression of suffering. But the protruding watery-blue eyes sometimes stared with inflexible hardness, and above the base of his nose, between the curve of the thick eyebrows, a clotted bulge bespoke a fanatical will. This time, too, he spoke very little; most of the time he listened with marked attentiveness."[20]

Now that he was attracting attention, women began to take an interest in him. Most of them were aging ladies who sensed problems behind the inhibitions and complexes of the magnetic young orator, tensions that knowledgeable ministrations could release. Hitler himself later commented on the jealousies among those women who thronged so eagerly and maternally around him. He knew one, he remarked, "whose voice grew hoarse from agitation whenever I exchanged so much as a few words with another woman." One of them, Carola Hoffmann, widow of a secondary-school teacher, who lived in the Munich suburb of Solln, made a sort of home for him and earned herself the title of *"Hitler-Mutti"*—Hitler's Mom. Frau Bruckmann, wife of the publisher of Houston Stewart Chamberlain and a lady descended from an ancient noble line, also took him under her wing. So did the wife of Bechstein, the piano manufacturer. "I wished he were my son," she said, and later, in order to be allowed to visit him in prison, she alleged that she was his adoptive mother. All of them taken together, their houses, their parties, widened the area around him and helped to make his name known.

Within the party, on the other hand, he continued to remain within a circle comprising middle-class philistines and semicriminal bullies who answered his need for aggression and physical violence. Among his rare close friends were Emil Maurice, a typical barroom and meeting-hall brawler, and Christian Weber, a hulking, paunchy former horse dealer who had worked as a bouncer in a notorious taproom and regularly carried a riding whip, as Hitler did. Ulrich Graf, a butcher's apprentice, also belonged to his immediate following, which served as a kind of bodyguard. So also did Max Amann, Hitler's former sergeant, a blunt, capable businessman, who became business manager for the party and the party's publishing house. Noisy and sedulously attentive, these men surrounded Hitler all the time. Evenings after meetings the troop of them would drop in at the

* Karl May, 1848–1912, author of adventure stories highly popular among young readers, many set in the American West or in the Orient.—TRANS.

Osteria Bavaria or the Bratwurstglöckl near the Frauenkirche, or talk for hours over coffee and cake at the Café Heck on Galeriestrasse, where a table was permanently reserved for Hitler in the dusky back of the room, from which he could watch what went on in the restaurant without being observed himself. He was already beginning to find solitude painful; he constantly needed people around him—audience, guards, servants, drivers, but also entertainers, art lovers and storytellers like the photographer Heinrich Hoffmann or Ernst Hanfstaengl. These were the people who gave to his "court" its special coloration compounded of "the bohemian world and the condottiere style." He was not averse to having himself referred to as the "King of Munich." It would be the small hours of the morning before he would return to his furnished room on Thierschstrasse.

The dominant figure in the entourage that formed so early around Hitler was young Hermann Esser. He had done some newspaper work and been a press secretary for the Reichswehr District Headquarters. Aside from Hitler, he was the only person in the party at that time with a talent for demagogy. He was "a noisemaker who is almost better at that business than Hitler . . . a demon speechmaker, though from a lower circle of hell." He was intelligent, cunning, with a knack for vivid and popular phrases. As a yellow journalist he could invent endless stories about Jews and profiteers. The decent petty bourgeois members of the party were soon objecting to the "swineherd tone" of his publicity campaigns. But he clung to his simple-minded radicalism; while still a schoolboy in Kempten, he had demanded that the soldiers' soviet there "string up" a number of citizens. Along with Dietrich Eckart, he was one of the earliest and most zealous authors of the Hitler myth. Hitler himself at times seemed worried about Esser; possibly Esser's intellectual gangsterism rubbed him the wrong way. If the sources are accurate, he repeatedly declared that he knew Esser was "a scoundrel" and was keeping him only as long as he needed him.

In a good many respects Esser resembled Julius Streicher, the Nuremberg schoolmaster, who was making a reputation as the spokesman for a scurrilous kind of pornographic anti-Semitism. Streicher seemed obsessed by wild fantasies of ritual murders, Jewish lust, world conspiracy, miscegenation, and lascivious black-haired devils panting after the innocent flesh of Aryan women. It is true that Streicher was more stupid and limited than Esser, but locally he could rival even Hitler, whom he had at first violently opposed.

Hitler, on the other hand, went to considerable trouble to win over Streicher. He wanted, of course, to make use of Streicher's popularity for his own ends. But he probably also felt a common bond with the man, for did they not share the same complexes and obsessions? Up to the last, Hitler remained loyal to Julius Streicher, despite the revulsion the man aroused. During the war he once remarked that Dietrich Eckart had called

136

Streicher a fool, but that he himself could not share the objections to Streicher's paper, *Der Stürmer*. Actually, he said, "Streicher idealized the Jews."[21]

Cohorts such as these gave the party a narrow character, in spite of all its mass activities, and locked it within a shallow and philistine sphere. By contrast, Air Captain Hermann Göring, the last commander of the legendary Richthofen fighter squadron, gave a gentlemanly tone to Hitler's entourage. A sturdy, jovial man with a booming voice, he was free of those twisted psychopathic traits that characterized the average member of Hitler's following. Göring had joined the party because it promised to satisfy his need for action and comradeship, not, as he stressed, because of the "ideological junk." He was traveled, widely connected, and, when he appeared with his attractive Swedish wife, he seemed to awaken the astonished party members to the fact that human beings also existed outside of Bavaria.

Göring shared certain larcenous tendencies with Max Erwin von Scheubner-Richter, an adventurer with a checkered past and a knack for lucrative undercover political deals. Especially in the early years Hitler owed to Scheubner-Richter's talent for raising funds much of the financial basis for his activities. According to a note in an official file, Scheubner-Richter succeeded in digging up "enormous sums of money." He hovered in the background, surrounded by mystery; but at the same time he had vast social assurance, was a great talker, and maintained connections with many industrialists, with the House of Wittelsbach, with Grand Duke Kyrill, and with high prelates. His influence on Hitler was considerable; he was the only one of those killed at the Feldherrnhalle on November 9, 1923, whom Hitler held to be irreplaceable.

Scheubner-Richter was another of the many Baltic Germans who, together with a group of radical rightist Russian emigrants, played a large part in the early history of the NSDAP. Later, Hitler jokingly remarked that the *Völkische Beobachter* in those years should have been subheaded "Baltic Edition." Alfred Rosenberg had originally met Scheubner-Richter in Riga. At that time Rosenberg was an unpolitical student deeply concerned with Schopenhauer, Richard Wagner, architectural matters and the philosophical doctrines of India. It took the Russian Revolution to shape his ideology, a mixture of anti-Bolshevist and anti-Semitic elements in about equal proportions. The picture of the horrors of Judaism and Bolshevism that Hitler painted derived partly from Rosenberg, even down to its metaphors, and Rosenberg was always considered the party's expert on Russia. Generally speaking, however, too much has been made of his being "chief ideologist of the NSDAP." His principal contribution was the thesis that Communism and world Judaism were identical. He may also have led Hitler to abandon his initial demand for a return of the German colonies and to look instead to the expanses of Russia for *Lebensraum*.

137

But then their ways parted. For Hitler remained a pragmatist, for whom ideology was only a tool. Rosenberg, on the other hand, was a mono-maniac who held these doctrines with almost religious fervor and continued to build them into intellectual systems of majestic absurdity.

Within a year after proclamation of the program the party could look back upon some impressive success. It had held more than forty meetings in Munich and almost as many again in the surrounding countryside. Local party groups had been founded in Starnberg, Rosenheim, Landshut, Pforzheim and Stuttgart. The membership had multiplied more than ten-fold. What an impression this made on the nationalist-racist movement as a whole is evident from a letter written by a "Brother Dietrich" of the Munich Order of Teutons to a likeminded friend in Kiel in February, 1921. "Show me a place," he wrote, "in which your party has held 45 mass meetings in the course of a year. The Munich Local Group now counts more than 2,500 members and some 45,000 followers. Can any of your local groups boast of nearly as many?" He added that he had corresponded with brothers of the order in Cologne, Wilhelmshaven, and Bremen, and "all took the view . . . that the Hitler party is the party of the future."

This growth took place against the backdrop of the Versailles Treaty, whose provisions came into force step by step, each new step striking the Germans as a fresh insult. Along with this came the wild inflation and growing economic distress. In January, 1921, an Allied reparations confer-ence decided to exact a total of 216 billion gold marks from Germany, to be paid over a period of forty-two years. During that period Germany would also be required to turn over to the Allies 12 per cent of her exports. In Munich a crowd of 20,000 assembled on the Odeonsplatz for a protest demonstration, under the sponsorship of the patriotic associations, the Free Corps and the NSDAP. When the organizers refused to let Hitler speak, he promptly announced a mass demonstration of his own for the following night. To the cautious-minded Drexler and Feder this seemed almost insane. But Hitler sent beflagged trucks through the city carrying groups bellowing slogans, and had posters drawn up advertising a mass meeting at the Krone Circus on February 30. "Herr Adolf Hitler," the announcement read, "will speak on 'Future or Doom!'" These were the very terms in which he had cast the problem at the time he decided he must enter politics. When he entered the huge tent, it was jammed with 6,500 persons who cheered him wildly and after his speech broke into the national anthem.

Since that occasion Hitler had been waiting for the opportunity to make himself master of the party, which owed so much to him. The party leader-ship, to be sure, was not too pleased with its propaganda chief's impetuos-ity, and an entry in the party log dated February 22, 1921, noted: "Request Herr Hitler to restrain his activity." But when Gottfried Feder grumbled at Hitler's increasing arrogance, Anton Drexler told him that "every revolutionary movement must have a dictatorial head and I consider our Hitler to be the one person most suitable for that post in our movement, though I myself would not be prepared for that reason to be pushed into the background." Five months later that very thing was to happen. Both circumstances and his opponents played into Hitler's hands, for throughout his career enemies would be Hitler's most effective allies. With a mixture of coldbloodedness, cunning, and resolution, with that readiness to take great risks even for small goals, which he was to exhibit time and again in critical situations, he succeeded in gaining control of the NSDAP while strengthening his claim to leadership of the entire nationalist-racist movement.

The summer crisis of 1921 started with negotiations between the NSDAP and rival *völkisch* parties, especially the German Socialist Party. These negotiations, aiming at closer co-operation, had been going on for months. But Hitler's intransigence blocked all efforts at alliance. He demanded nothing less than the total submission of the other parties and would not even concede them the right of corporate entry into the National Socialist Party. He insisted instead that the other groups must dissolve and their members enter his party on an individual basis. Drexler could not understand Hitler's obstinacy; therein lay the whole difference between the instinct for unconditional power and the conciliatory temperament of a club founder. Hitler must have counted on his enemies in the party leadership using his absence for an ill-considered step when, in the early part of the summer, he went to Berlin for six weeks. Hermann Esser and Dietrich Eckart remained behind as his accomplices and kept him continually informed. Urged on by certain members of the party who wanted to cut the "fanatical would-be big shot" down to size, well-meaning Drexler used this period of Hitler's absence to resume negotiations on the union, or at least the collaboration, of all the socialist rightist parties.

In Berlin, meanwhile, Hitler spoke at the Nationalist Club and established ties with conservative and radical rightists. He met Ludendorff and Count Reventlow, whose French wife, the former Baroness d'Allemont, introduced him to the former Free Corps leader Walter Stennes—describing Hitler as the "coming Messiah." The hectic madness of Berlin, which was then entering its famous, or notorious, twenties, only heightened Hitler's dislike for the city. He despised its greed and its frivolity, comparing conditions there with those of declining Rome in the Late Empire. There, too, he said, "racially alien Christianity" had taken advantage of the city's weakness, as Bolshevism today was battening on the moral decay of Germany. The speeches of those early years are full of attacks upon metropolitan vice, corruption, and excess, as he had observed them on the glittering pavements of Friedrichstrasse or the Kurfürstendamm. "They amuse themselves and dance to make us forget our misery," he cried on one

139

occasion. "It is no accident that new amusements are constantly being invented. They want to artificially enervate us." As if he were once again seventeen years old and arriving in Vienna, he stood baffled and alienated by the phenomenon of the big city, lost in so much noise, turbulence, and miscegenation. He really felt at home only in provincial circumstances and was, despite all his sense of being an outsider, permanently fixated upon provincial moral rectitude. Urban night life could only be an invention of the racial archfoe, a systematic attempt "to turn upside down the most natural hygienic rules of a race. The Jew makes night into day; he stages the notorious night life and knows quite well that it will slowly but surely . . . destroy one man physically, another mentally, and place hatred in the heart of a third because he must look on while others revel." The theaters, he continued, "those halls which a Richard Wagner once wanted darkened in order to call forth the ultimate degree of sanctity and solemnity" and "liberate the individual from grief and misery"—those theaters had become "hotbeds of vice and shamelessness." He saw the city populated by white slavers, and love, "which for millions of others means supreme happiness or the greatest unhappiness," perverted to a commodity, "nothing more than a deal." In the city everything was being undermined and debased; he deplored the mockery of family life, the decay of religion. "One who has lost both these in this age of basest treachery and fraud has only two remaining possibilities: either he despairs and hangs himself, or he becomes a scoundrel."[22]

As soon as word came of Drexler's independent action, Hitler returned to Munich. And when the party executive committee, which had gained some self-assurance in the interval, called upon him to justify his behavior, Hitler responded with a sweeping gesture. On July 11 he declared his resignation from the party. In a lengthy statement three days later he heaped violent reproaches upon the other members of the committee, then stated as an ultimatum his conditions for returning to the party. Among other things he demanded the immediate resignation of the executive committee, the "post of First Chairman with dictatorial powers" for himself, and "the party to be purged of the alien elements that have lately intruded into it." He also insisted that neither the name nor the program of the party could be changed; the absolute precedence of the Munich branch of the party must be preserved; there could be no union with other parties, only the annexation of other parties. And with that stubbornness which presaged the later Hitler he stated: "Concessions on our part are totally out of the question."[23]

The degree of prestige and power that Hitler had already attained is evident from the immediate reply of the party executive committee, which was dated the following day. Instead of risking a showdown, it pleaded guilty to Hitler's charges with timid reminders of its former services, bowed completely, and was even ready to sacrifice the incumbent First Chairman,

Anton Drexler, to Hitler's wrath. The key passage in the document, in which for the first time the Byzantine tones of subsequent homage sounded, read: "The committee is prepared, in acknowledgment of your tremendous knowledge, your singular dedication and selfless service to the Movement, and your rare oratorical gift, to concede to you dictatorial powers, and will be most delighted if after your re-entry you will take over the position of First Chairman, which Drexler long ago and repeatedly offered to you. Drexler will then remain as your coadjutor in the executive committee and, if you approve, in the same position in the action committee. If you should consider it desirable to have him completely excluded from the Movement, the next annual meeting would have to be consulted on that matter."

The affair is a good illustration of Hitler's skill at guiding and mastering crises. Its conclusion also shows his characteristic tendency to ruin a triumph by going a step too far. As soon as the party committee had submitted, he called an extraordinary membership meeting on his own initiative, in order to savor his victory to the full. At this point the good-natured Drexler would take no more. On July 25 he went to the Munich police and stated that the signers of the call for the meeting did not belong to the party and therefore had no right to convoke a membership meeting. He also pointed out that Hitler was aiming at revolution and violence, whereas he himself strove to carry out the party aims by legal, parliamentary procedures. The police, however, said they had no authority to intervene. Meanwhile, Hitler found himself under attack from other quarters. An anonymous leaflet appeared, accusing him of having brought "disunion and dissension into our ranks through power madness and personal ambition." He was thus "doing the business of the Jews and their henchmen." His aim was "to use the party as a springboard for dirty ends"; undoubtedly he was acting as the tool of obscure backers. There must be a reason why he was so anxious to keep his private life as well as his origins a mystery. "When asked by members what he lives on and what his former occupation was, he always became agitated and flew into a rage . . . so his conscience cannot be clear, especially since his excess in relations with women, to whom he has often referred to himself as 'King of Munich,' costs a great deal of money." A poster that the police would not allow to be displayed repeated these accusations and ended with the battle cry: "The tyrant must be overthrown."

The dispute was finally smoothed over by the mediation of Dietrich Eckart. At a membership meeting held on July 29, 1921, the crisis was laid to rest. Once again Hitler could not refrain from vaunting his victory. Although Drexler had pounced on the chance afforded by Hitler's resignation to purge Hermann Esser from the party, Hitler insisted that the membership meeting be chaired by Esser, his satellite. Greeted by "applause that would not cease," Hitler gave so skilled a version of the dispute that almost everyone swung over to his side. Drexler was given the consolation prize of honorary chairmanship, and the bylaws were revised as Hitler wished. His own followers moved into the executive committee; he himself was granted the dictatorial powers he demanded. The NSDAP was in his hand.

That same evening, at the Krone Circus, Hermann Esser hailed Hitler as "our Leader"—*unser Führer*. It was Esser, too, who henceforth held forth with cynical sentimentality in restaurants and taverns as the most zealous preacher of the Führer myth. Simultaneously, Dietrich Eckart in the *Völkische Beobachter* began a well-orchestrated campaign to purvey the same myth. On August 4 he sketched a profile of Hitler as a "selfless, self-sacrificing, devoted and sincere" man, forever "purposeful and alert." A few days later came another account, this written by Rudolf Hess, which further spiritualized the manly picture. It glorified Hitler's "purest intent," his strength, his oratory, his admirable fund of knowledge, and clear intellect. The fantastic growth of the Hitler cult is evidenced by another essay, written by Hess a year later, in connection with a contest on the subject: "What will be the nature of the man who will lead Germany back to the summit?" Hess's piece took first prize and contained thoughts such as the following:

Profound knowledge in all areas of political life and history, the capacity to draw the right lessons from this knowledge, belief in the purity of his own cause and in ultimate victory, and enormous power of will give him the power of thrilling oratory which evokes joyful enthusiasm from the masses. Where the salvation of the nation is in question, he does not disdain utilizing the weapons of the adversary, demagogy, slogans, processions, etc. He himself has nothing in common with the masses; he is all personality, like every great man.

If necessity commands it, he does not shrink from shedding blood. Great questions are always decided by blood and iron. . . . He is concerned solely with the attainment of his goal, even if that calls for trampling over closest friends. . . .

Thus we have the portrait of the dictator; keen of mind, clear and true, passionate and then again controlled, cold and bold, scrupulous in decision, fearless in rapid execution of his acts, ruthless toward himself and others, mercilessly hard and then again soft in his love for his people, tireless in work, with a steel fist in a velvet glove, capable ultimately of overcoming even himself.

We still do not know when he will intervene to save us—this "man." But millions feel that he is coming.[24]

On August 3, 1921, immediately after Hitler's taking full control of the party, the SA was founded. The initials originally meant Sports Division; only later did they come to stand for *Sturmabteilung* or storm troop. The party opposition had earlier objected to Hitler's surrounding himself with a paid bodyguard of former Free Corps soldiers; they demanded that the group be dissolved "because they want to steal and pillage." But the SA was not chiefly an organization of discharged soldiers seeking an outlet for their violent instincts. Nor was it principally an instrument of self-defense on the part of the Right, to be pitted against similar terrorist troops maintained by the enemy. It is true that the troops may originally have been intended for some such purpose. For militant fighting forces of the Left did exist—for example, the Social Democratic Erhard Auer Guard. There is a good deal of confirmation for the stories of deliberate riots launched against the NSDAP by the Left. "The Marxist world, which owes more to terrorism for its survival than any other contemporary phenomenon, also resorted to this method in its struggle against our movement," Hitler once declared in explaining the reasons for creating the SA.

Nevertheless, the SA had a more far-reaching function. From the start it was conceived as an instrument of attack and conquest. According to its founding proclamation, it was to be the "battering-ram" of the movement. Its members were to be trained to obedience and to an unspecified "revolutionary will." One of Hitler's pet ideas was that the weakness of the bourgeois order vis-à-vis Marxism lay in its principled separation of mind and violence, ideology and terror. The bourgeois politician, he argued, was limited to exclusively intellectual weapons, while the soldier was strictly excluded from politics. The Marxists, on the other hand, "united mind and brutal violence harmoniously." The SA was to imitate them. In the first issue of the SA's official gazette he called the organization "not only an instrument for the protection of the movement, but also . . . primarily the training school for the coming struggle for freedom on the domestic front." Similarly, the *Völkische Beobachter* hailed the SA's "ready-for-action spirit."

One motive for its creation was the disbanding of the paramilitary "citizen's militias in June 1921 and, a month later, the dissolution of the Oberland Free Corps, just home from Upper Silesia. Many members of these organizations, who at one blow found themselves deprived of the comradeship and glamour of the soldier's life and felt that life had lost its meaning, joined up with the adventure-hungry juveniles who had already become members of the NSDAP. Almost all of the SA members came from the numerically strong petty bourgeoisie that had long been prevented from rising socially and had attained to positions of some leadership only during the war, because of the heavy casualties in the officers' corps. Robust and eager for action, they had expected glorious careers in the postwar period. The terms of the Versailles Treaty, quite aside from all national humiliations, had thrown them back socially. They had ended up teaching in grammar schools, standing behind store counters, at the grilled windows in government offices. Such lives seemed to them narrow, wretched, and utterly unworthy of them. The same impulse to evade normality that had led Hitler to politics now brought them to Hitler.

Hitler himself regarded these recruits, so like him in type, as ideal material for his militant advance guard. In thinking out the tactics of achieving

143

power, he included in his reckoning the resentments, the energy, and the incipient violence of these men. It was one of his psychological adages that uniformed men showing intent of violence had an attractive as well as an intimidating effect. Terrorism could exert a special magnetism. "Cruelty impresses" was the way he once phrased this insight. "People need a good scare. They want to be afraid of something. They want someone to make them afraid, someone to whom they can submit with a shudder. Haven't you noticed, after a brawl at a meeting, that the ones who get beaten up are the first to apply for membership in the party? What is this rot you talk about violence and how shocked you are about torture? The masses want that. They need something to dread."[25] With growing assurance, then, Hitler made brute force figure in the party's image. It brought in members who would perhaps not be fetched by propaganda and the appeal of ceremony.

Hitler may have had this principle in mind when he instigated the so-called Battle in the Hofbräuhaus of November 4, 1921, in which the "myth of the SA" was created. Sizable Social Democratic heckler squads had turned up at an NSDAP demonstration. Hitler later said there were as many as 700 to 800 of the enemy. It happened that the party business office was moving on this day, so that only fifty of the SA men were present at the meeting. Hitler himself has described how he whipped up the nervous little unit by a passionate address. Today was the day of decision, he declared; they must not leave the hall unless they were carried out dead. He would personally strip cowards of their armbands and badges; the best defense was a good attack. In Hitler's own description:

The answer was a threefold *Heil* that sounded rougher and hoarser than usual.

Then I went into the hall and surveyed the situation with my own eyes. They were sitting in there, tight-packed, and tried to stab me with their very eyes. Innumerable faces were turned toward me with sullen hatred, while again others, with mocking grimaces, let out cries capable of no two interpretations. Today they would "make an end of us," we should look out for our guts. . . .

In spite of the disruptive forces, however, Hitler managed to talk for an hour and a half and had begun to think he was master of the situation, when suddenly a man jumped up on a chair and shouted the Social Democratic slogan: *"Freiheit!"* ("Freedom").

In a few seconds the whole hall was filled with a roaring, screaming crowd, over which, like howitzer shells, flew innumerable beer mugs, and in between the cracking of chair legs, the crashing of the mugs, bawling, howling and screaming.

It was an idiotic spectacle. . . .

The fracas had not yet begun when my storm troopers—for so they were called from this day on—attacked. Like wolves they flung themselves in packs of eight or ten again and again on their enemies, and little by little actually

144

The father, Alois Hitler
The mother,
Klara Pölzl Hitler
Adolf Hitler as an infant

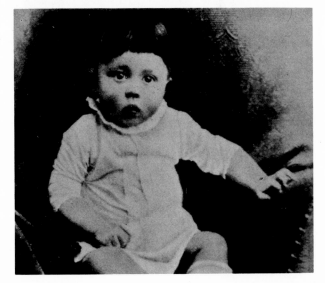

Hitler at sixteen; drawing by a fellow pupil

Hitler's ideological mentors
Top: George Ritter von Schönerer,
Count Gobineau
Left: Karl Lueger, Richard Wagner, Houston Stewart
Chamberlain
Right: Viennese Jews, 1915

Hitler made architectural drawings and copied
postcards, chiefly of Viennese subjects
The Minorite Church in Vienna (1909)

Top: Hitler in his dugout
Center and bottom: Hitler at a Social Democratic
meeting in the winter of 1919. "I have learned
a great deal from Marxism. Not from that boring
social doctrine . . . but from the methods."

Die Reaktion marschiert!
Hoch das Rätesystem

MOSAKODNAK!

Top: Prime Minister Kurt Eisner at a demonstration in
Munich, February, 1919
Bottom, left to right: Eugen Leviné-Nissen; members of
the Red Army; propaganda poster opposing Bolshevism

Top: Meeting of the German Workers' Party, January, 1920
Bottom: Gottfried Feder, one of the early party
ideologues; party founder Anton Drexler; Hitler at the
time of his entry into the party

Series of photos of Hitler as a speaker, in the
melodramatic style of the period

Top: Hitler with Alfred
Rosenberg (left) and
Christian Weber (right) at
a racist nationalist meeting
in Munich
Bottom left: Captain Ernst
Röhm (second from left)
with army officer friends

Row on right: Followers and supporters of the early years: Hermann Esser, Ernst Pöhner, Dietrich Eckart, Julius Streicher

The putsch of November 9, 1923
Top left: Streicher speaks on the Marienplatz in Munich
Top right: Occupation of the War Ministry, with Himmler
as flag bearer
Bottom right: SA storm troopers arrest the mayor of
Munich

Hitler trial in Munich, 1924
Top: Hitler and Ludendorff
during a recess
Bottom: Hitler with his
friends Emil Maurice and
Lieutenant Colonel Kriebel
in his cell in Landsberg

Sketches by Hitler from the year 1925

Top: New men around
Hitler: Gregor Strasser
(center) and Joseph
Goebbels
Bottom: Hitler and Pfeffer
von Salomon, the new chief
of the SA

began to thrash them out of the hall. After only five minutes I saw hardly a one of them who was not covered with blood. . . . Then suddenly two shots were fired from the hall entrance toward the platform, and wild shooting started. Your heart almost rejoiced at such a revival of old war experiences. . . .

About twenty-five minutes had passed; the hall looked almost as if a shell had struck it. Many of my supporters were being bandaged; others had to be driven away, but we had remained masters of the situation. Hermann Esser, who had assumed the chair this evening, declared: *"The meeting goes on. The speaker has the floor."*[26]

In fact, from that day on Hitler had the floor in Munich in a much broader sense. According to his own statement, the streets henceforth belonged to the NSDAP, and with the beginning of the following year the SA carried its successes deeper and deeper into the rest of Bavaria. On weekends it undertook propaganda drives through the countryside. It organized noisy marches, at first marked only by the armband, then in gray windbreakers, carrying knobby walking sticks, parading through villages and booming out the SA's special songs. According to one of Hitler's early followers, they deliberately made themselves look "as savage and martial as possible." They pasted slogans on the walls of houses and factories, brawled with their opponents, tore down black, red, and gold flags, or organized commando strikes against black marketeers or capitalist profiteers. Their songs and slogans had a bloodthirsty ring. At a meeting in the Bürgerbräu they passed around a collection box marked: "Donate for the massacres of Jews." As so-called peacemakers, they broke up meetings or concerts that displeased them. "We're brawling our way to greatness," was the SA's whimsical slogan. And it became apparent that the unspeakably rowdy conduct of the storm troopers was no hindrance to the growth of the party—just as Hitler had thought. Violence did not undercut the attractiveness of the movement even among the solid, honest petty bourgeoisie. The breakdown of standards caused by war and revolution is not the only explanation for this phenomenon. Hitler's party could also count on a certain characteristically Bavarian coarseness; it became the political embodiment of that coarseness. The meeting-hall battles with their flailing chair legs and whirling beer mugs, the "massacres," the murderous songs, the large-scale brawls—it was all a *Gaudi* (great fun). Significantly, it was just at this period that the term "Nazi" came into being. Although actually an abbreviation of National Socialist, in Bavarian ears it sounded like the nickname for Ignaz; thus it had a homey, familiar quality and showed that the party had won a place for itself in the public mind.

The generation of soldiers who had fought in the war and had formed the initial core of the SA was soon followed by younger groups. The combination of promised violence, elitist association of men, and conspiratorial ideology always exerted a strong allure. "There are two things that

145

can unite men," Hitler declared in a public speech at this time: "common ideals, common scoundrelism."[27] The SA offered both, inextricably entwined. In the course of 1922 the SA, organized in groups of 100 men, grew by such leaps and bounds that by autumn the eleventh group, consisting entirely of students, was set up under the leadership of Rudolf Hess. That same year a group from the former Rossbach Free Corps, under Lieutenant Edmund Heines, joined the SA as a separate unit. With all these special formations, the storm troop took on an increasingly military aspect. Rossbach himself set up a bicyclists' section. There was an intelligence unit, a motorized squad, an artillery section, and a cavalry corps.

Except for a generalized nationalistic belligerence, the SA did not develop any distinctive ideology (contrary to what many participants have said in their reminiscences). When it paraded through the streets under waving banners, it was certainly not marching toward a new social order. It had no utopian ideas, merely an enormous restiveness; no goal but dynamic energy, which often ran out of control. Strictly speaking, most of those who joined its columns were not even political soldiers. Rather, their temper was that of mercenaries, and the high-sounding political phrases were only a cloak for their nihilism, their restlessness, and their craving for something to which they could subordinate themselves. Their ideology was action at all costs. In keeping with the spirit of male comradeship and homosexuality that permeated the SA, the average storm trooper gave his allegiance not to a program, but to an individual, "a leader personality." Hitler, in fact, wanted it so. In a proclamation he had stipulated: "Let only those apply who wish to be obedient to the leaders and are prepared, if need be, to meet death."

Nevertheless, this indifference toward ideology made the SA into a hard conspiratorial core free from any factionalism and ready for any order or commitment whatsoever. Here was a source of strength that the traditional bourgeois parties lacked, and which gave a monolithic cast to the party as a whole. The party could thus take in a wide variety of elements actuated by many disparate resentments and complexes. The more disciplined and reliable the storm trooper core was, the more Hitler could broaden his appeals to virtually all groups in the population.

This factor accounts in large part for the curiously heterogeneous sociological basis of the NSDAP. It appeared to have no real class character. Certainly the petty bourgeois groups gave the party many of its characteristic features, and in spite of the name "Workers' Party," several points in Hitler's original program formulated the anxieties and panic of the lower middle class, its fears of being overwhelmed economically by large concerns and department stores, and the little man's resentment of easily acquired wealth, of profiteers and the owners of capital. The party's strident propaganda was also pointedly aimed at the lower middle class. Alfred Rosenberg, for example, hailed this class as the only group that "still opposed the world-wide betrayal." Hitler had not forgotten the lessons he had learned in Vienna from Karl Lueger. Lueger, as Hitler wrote, had mobilized the "middle class menaced with destruction, and thereby assured himself a following that was difficult to shake, whose spirit of sacrifice was as great as its fighting power."[28]

But the various membership lists of that early period in the party's history reveal a rather different picture. Government officials or white-collar workers made up about 30 per cent of the membership. There was an almost equal percentage of skilled and unskilled workers, 16 per cent tradesmen, a good many of them proprietors of small and middle-sized independent businesses, who hoped the NSDAP would shield them from the pressure of the unions. The remainder consisted of soldiers, students, and professionals. The leadership consisted largely of representatives of urban bohemianism. A party directive of 1922 required every local group to reflect the sociological distribution of its region, and the local leadership was to contain no more than one third academics.

The significant fact is that the party attracted people of every origin, every sociological coloration, and developed its dynamism as a movement unifying antagonistic groups, interests, and feelings. In August, 1921, the National Socialists of the German-language area held an international meeting in Linz, Austria, at which they described themselves as a "class party." But this was done in Hitler's absence. He had always regarded the NSDAP as strictly opposed to class conflict; his point was that racial conflict was to replace class antinomies. "Along with members of the middle class and the bourgeoisie, very many workers have also followed the National Socialist banner," a police report of December, 1922, stated. "The old socialist parties view the NSDAP as a grave danger to their continued existence." What provided a common denominator for the many contradictions and antagonisms within the party was its embittered defensiveness toward the proletariat and toward the bourgeoisie, toward capitalism as well as Marxism. "For a class-conscious worker there is no room in the NSDAP, any more than there is for a status-conscious bourgeois," Hitler declared.

On the whole, it was a mentality rather than a class which marked the convert to National Socialism in those early days: it was an ostensibly nonpolitical but actually proauthoritarian and leadership-hungry state of mind, and one which could be found in all classes and subgroups. Under the changed conditions of the republic people of this sort found themselves in a sad plight. Their anxiety complexes were reinforced because the new political form established no authority that could claim their attachment and future loyalty. These people had always owed part of their sense of personal value to identification with the political order. But this present state meant nothing to them. Their stern ideal of order and respect, which they had doggedly preserved through all the chaos of the times, seemed to

147

them challenged by the very constitution of the republic, by democracy and freedom of the press, the clash of opinions and the horse trading among parties. The world had become incomprehensible to them. In their dismay they hit on the National Socialist Party, which was in fact the political incarnation of their own perplexities tricked out with an air of resolution. It was, of course, a paradox that they should have felt their craving for order, morality, and faith best answered by the spokesmen of the Hitler party, so many of whom came from obscure and irregular backgrounds. Yet Hitler understood them. One summary of an early Hitler speech runs: "He compared prewar Germany, in which order, cleanliness and rectitude prevailed, with the present-day Germany of the revolution." The nation had a deeply rooted instinct for rules and discipline; it wanted the world orderly or it did not want the world at all. To this instinct the rising demagogue appealed, and he met with growing approval when he called the republic a negation of German history and the German character. This republic, he said, was the business, the career, the cause of a minority; the majority wanted "peace but no pigsty."

The inflation gave Hitler endless material for slogans. Devaluation of the mark had not yet reached the grotesque extremes of the summer of 1923, but it had already led to the virtual expropriation of a large part of the middle class. As early as the beginning of 1920, the mark had fallen to a tenth of its prewar value; two years later it was worth only a hundredth of that value and was referred to as the "pfennig mark." In this way the state, which since the war had accumulated debts of 150 billion marks and saw new tolls approaching in the still pending reparations negotiations, escaped its obligations. So did all other debtors. Borrowers, tradesmen, and industrialists, above all, the virtually tax-free firms producing for export and paying extremely low wages profited from the inflation. They had a stake in a continuing decline in the value of the currency, and at the very least did nothing to check it. Borrowing cheap money, which with the advancing devaluation they could pay back even more cheaply, they speculated brazenly against their own currency. Clever speculators made fortunes within a few months. Almost out of nothing they created vast economic empires. The sight of such expansion was all the more outrageous because these successes went hand in hand with the impoverishment and proletarianization of whole social groups, the holders of debt certificates, pensioners, and small savers.

The dimly sensed connection between the fantastic careers of some capitalists and the mass impoverishment sowed a feeling among the victims of having been mocked by society. That feeling turned into lasting bitterness. Just as lasting was the belief that the state had ceased to be an unselfish, just, and honest institution. That had been the traditional picture of the state; but now it was seen to have gone into fraudulent bankruptcy by means of the inflation, thus cheating its citizens. Among the little people

148

with a firm faith in the ethics of orderliness, this realization was perhaps even more devastating than the loss of their modest savings. Under the succession of blows, the world in which they had lived austerely, contentedly, and soberly vanished irrevocably. The protracted crisis sent them in search of a figure in whom they could again believe and a will they could obey. The republic could not satisfy this need: that was in fact its problem. Hitler's success as an agitator was due only partly to his oratorical skill. More important was his attunement to the moods of neurotically agitated philistines and his sense of what they wanted from him. He himself regarded this faculty as the true secret of the great orator: "He will always let himself be borne along by the great masses in such a way that instinctively the very words come to his lips that he needs to speak to the hearts of his audience."[29]

What the nation at the moment was experiencing for the first time—the succession of disenchantment, decline, and declassing, together with the search for scapegoats on whom to heap the blame—Hitler had long ago gone through. Ever since he had been turned down at the Academy he had known the anguish of a reality that ran counter to his longings and his expectations. Now he could translate his own complexes and discontents to a superindividual plane. Were it not for this congruence between the personal and the social-pathological situation, Hitler could never have wielded such hypnotic power over his fellow citizens. But he had long ago memorized all their reasons and pretexts; he knew the formulas, had long ago discovered the villain. No wonder his hearers were electrified by his words. What captivated them was not the logic of his arguments nor the pithiness of his slogans and images, but the sense of shared experiences, shared sufferings and hopes. The failed bourgeois Adolf Hitler could communicate with them on the level of a common distress. Their aggressions brought them together. To a great extent his special charisma, a mixture of obsessiveness, passionate banality, and vulgarity derived from his sharing. He proved the truth of Jacob Burckhardt's saying that history sometimes loves to concentrate itself in a single human being, whom the world thereupon obeys; time and the man enter into a great, mysterious covenant.

The "mysteriousness" that Hitler cultivated was, however—like all his alleged instinctual reactions—amply supplemented by rational factors. Though he early discovered his mediumistic powers, he continued to improve his techniques. A series of photos show him posing in the stagey style of the period. Ludicrous though the pictures are, they nevertheless reveal how much of his demagogic magic he acquired by careful practice.

Thus he early began to develop a special style for his public appearances. From start to finish he stressed the theatrical element. Blaring sound trucks and screaming posters would announce a "great public giant demonstration." Elements of spectacle borrowed from circus and grand opera

149

were cleverly combined with edifying ceremonial reminiscent of church ritual. Parades of banners, march music, welcoming slogans, communal singing, and repeated cries of *"Heil"* formed the framework for the Führer's speech. All these histrionic elements built up the suspense and made the speech seem a kind of annunciation. The party guidelines for meetings were constantly improved and handed down in courses for speakers and written directives until no detail was left to chance. Hitler himself would check the acoustics of all the important meeting halls in Munich, to determine whether the Hackerbräu, say, called for a louder voice than the Hofbräuhaus or the Kindl-Keller. He noted the atmosphere, the ventilation, and the tactical arrangement of the rooms. The official guidelines mentioned that a hall should always be too small and that at least a third of the audience should consist of the party's own followers. To ward off the impression of being a petty bourgeois movement and to win the trust of the workers, Hitler occasionally waged a "struggle against the trousers crease" among his followers, and sent them to the demonstrations without ties and collars. Some party members were ordered to attend his opponents' training courses and learn what the enemy was up to.[30]

From 1922 on he began holding series of eight, ten, or twelve rallies on a single evening, at each of which he would appear as the principal speaker. This procedure suited his quantity complex as well as his passion for repetition. An eyewitness of one such serial demonstration at the Munich Löwenbräu has given the following description of it:

How many political meetings had I already attended in this hall. But neither during the war nor during the Revolution had I ever felt such a white-hot wave of mass excitement blast in my face the moment I entered. "Their own songs of struggle, their own flags, their own symbols, their own salute," I noted. "Semi-military monitors, a forest of glaring red banners with a black swastika on a white ground, the strangest mixture of soldierly and revolutionary, nationalist and socialist elements. In the audience too: mostly strata of the middle class on the skids—is this where it will find rebirth? For hours continual, booming march music; for hours short speeches by subordinates; when will he come? Has anything happened to hold him up? Impossible to describe the state of suspense, building up within this atmosphere. Suddenly movement at the entrance to the hall. Shouted commands. The speaker on the platform breaks off in the middle of a sentence. Everyone leaps to his feet shouting *Heil!* And right between the howling masses and the howling banners he comes with his retinue, he for whom all have been waiting. He strides rapidly to the platform, right hand raised rigidly. He passed quite close by me, and I saw that this was a different person from the man I had met now and then in private houses.[31]

The structure of his speeches scarcely varied. First came denunciations of the present period, intended to tune up the audience and establish initial contact with it. "Bitterness has become general; people are beginning to notice that what was promised in 1918 has not turned into anything of dignity and beauty." Thus he opened a speech in September, 1922. There followed historical reviews, a spelling out of the party program, and attacks on Jews, November criminals, or lying politicians. The cheering of the audience or of an official claque would send him into a mounting state of excitement that would last until he reached those exultant appeals for unity with which he always ended. In between, he would tuck in whatever the heat of the moment, the applause, the vapors of beer, or the general atmosphere suggested. With each successive meeting he grasped more surely and translated more accurately the vibrations of that atmosphere: The fatherland's humiliation, the sins of imperialism, the envy of neighbors, the "communalization of the German woman," the smearing of Germany's past, the shallow, commercialized, and debauched West from which had come the republic, the disgraceful dictated peace of Versailles, the Allied control commissions, nigger music, bobbed hair, and modern art, but neither work, security, nor bread. "Germany is starving on democracy!" he cried. For he could coin memorable phrases. In addition, his obscure metaphors, his great use of mythic allusion gave his rantings an air of profundity. Out of trifling local incidents he could construct dramas of universal import. Thus he could prophesy: "What is beginning today will be greater than the World War. It will be fought out on German soil for the entire world. There are only two possibilities: We will be the sacrificial lamb or victors!"

In the past sober Anton Drexler would have been there and would sometimes hear such rhapsodic outbursts and to Hitler's annoyance put in a final word to bring things into perspective. But now there was no longer anyone around to remonstrate when a wildly gesticulating Hitler vowed to tear the peace treaty to shreds if he took power, or let it be known that he would not shrink from another war with France, or conjured up the vision of a mighty German Reich stretching "from Königsberg to Strassburg and from Hamburg to Vienna." His ever-larger audiences proved that what people wanted to hear was precisely such wild challenges. "The thing is not to renounce or to accept, but to venture what is seemingly impossible." The general view of Hitler as an unprincipled opportunist does not do justice either to his daring or his originality. His courage in voicing "forbidden" opinions was extraordinary. Precisely that gave him the aura of manliness, fierceness, and sovereign contempt, which befitted the image of the Great Leader.

The role in which he soon cast himself was that of the outsider; in times of public discontent such a role had great potential. Once, when the *Münchener Post* termed him "the wiliest agitator making mischief in Munich today," Hitler replied with: "Yes, we want to work people up, we're agitators all right!" In the beginning he may well have been pained by the plebeian, quarrelsome features of his public career. But once he realized that certain crudenesses made him more popular in the circus tent

151

and more interesting in the salons, he identified with those qualities without apology. When he was criticized for the dubious company he kept, he replied that he would rather be a German tramp than a French count. "They say we're a bunch of anti-Semitic rowdies. So we are, we want to stir up a storm! We don't want people to sleep, but to know a thunderstorm is brewing. We won't let our Germany be crucified. Call us brutes if you want to. But if we save Germany, we'll have carried out the greatest deed in the world."

The frequency of religious metaphors and motifs in his rhetoric reflects childhood emotions: recollections of his experience as acolyte in Lambach monastery, when he was stirred to the depths by images of suffering and despair against a background of triumphant belief in salvation. He admired the Catholic Church for its genius in devising such combinations, and he learned what he could from it. Without the least scruple or any consciousness of blasphemy he took over "my Lord and Saviour" for his anti-Semitic tirades: "As a Christian and a man I read, in boundless love, through the passage which relates how the Lord at last rallied his strength and reached for the whip to drive the usurers, the brood of adders and otters, out of the temple! Profoundly moved, today, after two thousand years, I recognize the tremendous import of his fight to save the world from the Jewish poison—I see it most powerfully shown by the fact that because of it he had to bleed to death on the cross."

The narrow range of the emotions he played upon corresponded to the monotony of structure in his speeches. There is no saying how much of this was deliberate, how much due to personal fixation. When we read some of these addresses—although they have been considerably revised—we are struck by their repetitiveness. From the multitude of resentments that filled him he extracted always the same meanings, the same accusations, and vows of revenge. "There is only defiance and hate, hate and again hate!" he once cried out. The word was obsessive with him. He would, for instance, cry out for the enemy's hatred; he longed to have the enemy's hate fall upon him, he declared. Or: "To achieve freedom takes pride, will, defiance, hate and again hate!"

With his compulsion to magnify everything, he saw gigantic corruption at work in the most ordinary affairs, detected a comprehensive strategy of treason. Behind every Allied note, every speech in the French Chamber of Deputies, he saw the machinations of the enemy of mankind. Head thrown back, outstretched arm before him, index finger pointing at the ground and twitching up and down—in this characteristic pose Adolf Hitler, still no more than a local Bavarian curiosity, orated himself into a state of frenzy in which he pitted himself against the government, against conditions in Germany, and in fact against the condition of the entire world: "No, we forgive nothing; we demand revenge!"[32]

He had no sense of the ridiculous and despised ridicule's reputedly fatal effects. He had not yet adopted the imperious attitudes of later years; and since he felt that as an artist he was alienated from the masses, he often made deliberate efforts at popular behavior. At such times he would wave a beer mug at his audience or try to check the uproar he was kindling by a clumsy "Sh . . . , sh . . ." Apparently his large audiences were there more for the excitement than for political reasons; at any rate, in contrast to the tens of thousands who came to mass meetings, there were still only 6,000 registered members of the party at the beginning of 1922. But he was listened to. People sat motionless, eyes riveted upon him. After his first few words the thump of the beer mugs generally stopped. Often he spoke into a breathless silence, which from time to time was explosively shattered as if thousands of pebbles suddenly came rattling down on a drum, as one observer described it. Naïvely, with all the hunger for acclaim of the novice, Hitler enjoyed the stir he caused, enjoyed being the center of attention. "When you go through ten halls," he admitted to his entourage, "and everywhere people shout their enthusiasm for you—it is an uplifting feeling, you know." Quite often he would end his performance with an oath of loyalty that he would have the audience repeat after him, or with his eyes fixed upon the ceiling of the hall, his voice hoarse and breaking with emotion, he would cry, "Germany! Germany!"—repeating the word until the crowd fell in with it and the chanting moved on to one of the party's battle or pogrom songs. Often they would pour out of the hall to march singing through the nocturnal streets. Hitler admitted that after each of his speeches he himself would be "soaking wet and would have lost four to six pounds." At every meeting his uniform "dyed his underwear blue."[33]

According to his own testimony, it took him two years to learn to handle all the methods of propagandistic domination, so that he felt himself "master in this art." It has been suggested that he was the first to apply the techniques of American advertising to political struggle. Perhaps the great Barnum was indeed one of his teachers, as *Die Weltbühne* later asserted. But the tone of amusement with which the magazine announced this discovery revealed its own blindness. Many supercilious contemporaries from left to right made the same mistake: confusing Hitler's techniques with his aims and concluding that the aims were laughable because the methods were. He himself never swerved in his determination to overthrow a world and put another in its place; to him there was no incongruity between the techniques of the circus barker and the universal conflagrations and apocalypses he had in mind.

The important figure in the background, the symbol of union throughout the *völkisch* camp, remained—in spite of Hitler's oratorical success—General von Ludendorff. With a respectful eye partly cocked toward the general, Hitler was still regarding himself as something of a forerunner preparing the way for someone greater than himself. He, Hitler, playing the role that John the Baptist played for Christ—"a very small sort of St. John," he called himself—would create a racially united people and a sword for that greater one. But the masses seemed to realize sooner than he himself that he was the one they were waiting for. They streamed to him "as to a Saviour," a contemporary account notes. There are stories in plenty of "awakenings" and conversions—totalitarian movements are often characterized by such pseudoreligious events. For example, Ernst Hanfstaengl first heard Hitler at this time. He had many objections; nevertheless, he felt that "a new period of life" was beginning for him. The businessman Kurt Luedecke, who for a time was counted among the leading members of Hitler's entourage and who later was imprisoned in the Oranienburg concentration camp, after his escape abroad described the spell cast on him and innumerable others by Hitler the orator:

> Presently my critical faculty was swept away. . . . I do not know how to describe the emotions that swept over me as I heard this man. His words were like a scourge. When he spoke of the disgrace of Germany, I felt ready to spring on any enemy. His appeal to German manhood was like a call to arms, the gospel he preached a sacred truth. He seemed another Luther. I forgot everything but the man; then, glancing round, I saw that his magnetism was holding these thousands as one.
>
> Of course I was ripe for this experience. I was a man of thirty-two, weary of disgust and disillusionment, a wanderer seeking a cause; a patriot without a channel for his patriotism, a yearner after the heroic without a hero. The intense will of the man, the passion of his sincerity seemed to flow from him into me. I experienced an exaltation that could be likened only to religious conversion.[34]

From the spring of 1922 on the membership figures began climbing by leaps and bounds. By summer the party had some fifty local groups, and at the beginning of 1923 the Munich business office had to be closed temporarily because it was unable to cope with the mass of applications. Part of this increase was due to an order requiring every "party comrade" to bring in three new members and one subscriber to the *Völkische Beobachter* every three months. But much of it was surely due to Hitler's growing skill as an orator and organizer.

In order to meet the needs of disoriented people, the NSDAP tried to create close links between the party and the personal lives of the members. In this respect it was once more drawing on the tested practices of socialist parties. But the rite of the weekly evening talkfests, at which attendance was obligatory, the joint outings, concerts, or solstice festivals, the singing, the cookouts, and saluting, in addition to the various forms of bland sociability that developed in party headquarters and storm troop barracks—all this went far beyond the model and appealed more directly to the human craving for solidarity. The movement's greatest task, Hitler declared, was to provide "these seeking and erring masses" with the opportunity "at least somewhere once more to find a place where their hearts can rest."

At first Hitler's policy had been to enlarge the party at all costs. But after a while he took another line, establishing new local groups only when a capable leader in whom he personally had confidence could be found, one who could satisfy the craving for authority so obviously crying out for fulfillment.

For the party aimed at being more than an organization for specific political purposes. It never forgot, in its concern with the affairs of the day, that in addition to giving the members a deeply serious interpretation of the world it must also provide them with a touch of that banal contentment so conspicuously missing in the misery and isolation of everyday living. In its effort to be all at once homeland, center of existence, and source of knowledge the party was already manifesting its later claims to totality.

Within a year the NSDAP thus developed into "the strongest power factor in South German nationalism," as one observer wrote. The North German party groups, too, showed such marked growth, inheriting membership from the disintegrating German Socialist Party. When, in June, 1922, the Foreign Minister, Walter Rathenau, was assassinated by nationalist conspirators, some German states, such as Prussia, Baden, and Thuringia, decided to ban Hitler's party. In Bavaria, however, the experiences of the soviet period had not been forgotten; the NSDAP, as the most radical anti-Communist party, was not molested. In fact, many of Hitler's followers held top positions in the Munich police force, including Police Commissioner Pöhner and *Oberamtmann* (Chief Bailiff) Frick, his specialist in political affairs. These two men quashed any protests against the NSDAP, kept the party informed of planned actions against it, and if the police had after all to intervene, took care that such actions came to nothing. Frick later admitted that the police could easily have suppressed the party at this time, but that "we held our protecting hand over the NSDAP and Herr Hitler." And Hitler himself remarked that without the assistance of Frick he would "never have been out of the clink."[35]

Hitler found himself imperiled only once, when Bavarian Interior Minister Schweyer raised the question of having the troublesome alien agitator deported to Austria. A conference in 1922 among the leaders of all the government parties had agreed that the rowdy bands in the streets of Munich, the brawls, the constant molesting of the citizenry, were becoming intolerable. But Erhard Auer, the leader of the Social Democrats, opposed deportation on the grounds that it would be a violation of "democratic and libertarian principles." So Hitler was allowed to go on denouncing the republic as a "sanctuary for foreign swindlers," threatening the administration that when he came to power "may God have mercy on you!" and proclaiming that there could be "only one punishment: the rope" for the treasonous leaders of the Social Democratic Party. Whipped up by his demagogy, the city of Munich became an enclave of antirepublicanism, buzzing with rumors of coups, civil war, and restoration of the monarchy. When Reich President Friedrich Ebert visited Munich in the summer of 1922, he was met at the railroad station with boos, jeers, and the display of red bathing trunks. (The President had been so unwise as to let himself be photographed, along with Noske, his Defense Minister, in a bathing suit. In the authoritarian-minded German nation, the loss of dignity was catastrophic.) Chancellor Wirth's advisors warned him to cancel a planned trip to Munich. At the same time, Hindenburg was being greeted with ovations, and transportation of the body of Ludwig III, the last Wittelsbach monarch, who had died in exile, brought the whole city out into the streets, awash in tears of mourning and nostalgia.

His successes within Munich encouraged Hitler to undertake his first bold stroke outside the city. In mid-October, 1922, the patriotic societies of Coburg organized a demonstration, to which they invited Hitler. It was suggested that he come with "some companions." Hitler interpreted this phrase in his customary brazen manner. Intending to take over and dominate the demonstration, he set out in a special train with some 800 men, a display of standards, and a sizable contingent of band musicians. On arrival he was asked not to march into the city in a solid formation. According to his own report, he "flatly refused" the request and ordered his men to march in formation "with bands playing." Growing hostile crowds formed along both sides of the street. But since the expected mass riot did not begin, they had no sooner reached the meeting hall when Hitler ordered his units to march back the way they had come. Moreover, he added a theatrical touch that brought the tension to an intolerable height: the bands stopped playing and the men marched only to throbbing drumrolls. This time the predictable street battle erupted. It dragged on in a series of small skirmishes all through the day and into the night, and ultimately the National Socialists emerged as the victors.

This was the first of those challenges to the political authorities that were to dominate the following years. Significantly, Coburg became one of the most reliable NSDAP bases. The participants in the trip were honored by a special medal struck as a memorial to the occasion. The braggadocio of Hitler's men during the following weeks repeatedly led to rumors of coups. Finally, Interior Minister Schweyer sent for Hitler and issued a grave warning. If there were any resort to force, Schweyer said, he would order the police to shoot. But Hitler assured him he would "never as long as I live make a putsch." He gave the minister his word of honor.

Such incidents as this, however, encouraged him to think that he could call the next move. All these bans, summonses, and warnings were evidence of how far he had come, starting from nothing. In his emotional states he envisioned a historic role for himself. For confirmation there were

156

Mustafa Kemal Pasha's seizure of power in Ankara and Mussolini's recent march on Rome. All keyed up, he listened to an informant describe how the black shirts, thanks to their enthusiasm, resolution, and the benevolent passivity of the army, had marched tempestuously to victory, snatching one city after the other from the "Reds." Later Hitler spoke of the enormous impetus this "turning point in history" had given him. Very much as in his boyhood, he let himself be carried away on the wings of imagination. At such times he would vividly see the swastika banner "fluttering over the Schloss in Berlin as over the peasant's hut." Or during some quiet coffee break he would casually remark, returning from some distant dream world, that in the next war "the first order of business would be to seize the grain-growing areas of Poland and the Ukraine."

Coburg had given him fresh confidence. "From now on I will go my way alone," he declared. Only a short time before he had still thought of himself as a harbinger and dreamed that "one day someone will come along, with an iron cranium and possibly with filthy boots, but with a pure conscience and strong fist, who will put an end to the blabber of these armchair heroes and give the nation deeds." Now, tentatively at first, he began to think of himself as the coming man and actually ended by comparing himself to Napoleon. His army superiors during the war would not promote him to a noncom on the ground that he would be incapable of arousing respect. Now, by his extraordinary and ultimately devastating capacity to evoke loyalty, he demonstrated his talent for leadership. For it was solely for his sake that his followers went to the lengths they did; it was only with eyes on him that they were ready to stake their lives, trample over their own compunctions, and from the very beginning to commit crimes. He liked to be called "Wolf" in his intimate circle; the name, he decided, was the primitive Germanic form of Adolf. It accorded, moreover, with his jungle image of the world and suggested the qualities of strength, aggressiveness, and solitariness. He also used "Wolf" as a pseudonym occasionally and later gave it to the sister who ran his household. And when it was decided to establish the Volkswagen plant, Robert Ley declared: "We shall name the town Wolfsburg, after you, my Führer."[36]

He early developed a sense that all his actions were taking place under the eyes of the "goddess of history." Though his real party membership number was 555, he invariably claimed to be member number 7. This not only raised his status as an early member but gave him the nimbus of a magic number. Along with this he began blotting out his private life. He made a principle of not inviting even the most intimate members of his entourage to his home. He tried as far as possible to keep them apart from one another. Meeting one of his early acquaintances in Munich at this time, he urgently begged him "never to give information to anyone, not even his closest party comrades, about his youth in Vienna and Munich." He tried out poses, attitudes, posturings; at the start he often made rather a botch of

157

them and showed the strain of trying to be what he was not. But even in the later years close study will separate out the strands, show the constant alternation between rehearsed self-control and attacks of literally senseless rage, between Caesaristic postures and lax stupefaction, between his artificial and his natural existence. In this early phase of the process of stylization he seemed unable to hold to his image consistently. He had only begun to sketch it, and the various elements were hardly congruous. An Italian Fascist at the time saw him as "a Julius Caesar with Tyrolean hat."

Still and all, he had very nearly attained the dream of his youth. He was living unattached, without the bother of an occupation, subject only to his own whims; he was "master of his time" and, moreover, his drama, explosive effects, glitter and applause. It was an artist's life, more or less. He drove fast cars, cut something of a figure at various salons, and was at home in the "great world" among aristocrats, captains of industry, notables, and scientists. There were moments when he thought of settling for bourgeois security within the present framework. He would not ask much, he commented at such times: "All I desire is for the movement to keep going and for me to make a living as chief of the *Völkische Beobachter*."

But those were moods. Such modesty did not really suit his nature. He had no sense of proportion; some demon was constantly driving him to the edge of the possible and beyond. "Everything in him urged him on to radical and total solutions," the friend of his youth had concluded. Now another observer tersely called him a fanatic, "with a streak of craziness in him. Now that he is being pampered, he is altogether out of control."

Certainly the period of painful obscurity was over, and in hindsight Hitler had come an amazingly long way. Even the neutral onlooker must be astounded at the personal progress he had made in the past three years. He was quite a different person from the pallid and inconsequential drifter he had been at thirty. His life seemed to be made out of two wholly separate pieces. With extraordinary boldness and coldness, he had emerged from his condition as underling. All he needed now was to become a little more polished, to get used to his new part. Everything else suggested that he was on the point of entering a new and larger sphere of action to which he was entirely equal. At any rate Hitler had proved able to cope with whatever came his way, taking in at a glance people, motivations, forces, ideas, and bending everything to his own aim—the enlarging of his power.

Not unreasonably, his biographers have tended to look for a particular "breakthrough experience." They have spoken of incubation periods, the disappearance of some block or other, and even demonic powers. But perhaps he was now no different from what he had been, except that he had found some key to himself and been able to reshuffle the unchanged existing elements of his personality into a new arrangement, so that the oddball was transformed into a magnetic demagogue, the "dreamer" into the man of action. He was the catalyst of the masses; without contributing anything

158

new, he set in motion enormous accelerations and crises. But the masses in turn catalyzed him; they were his creation and he, simultaneously, was their creature. "I know," he said to his public in phrases of almost Biblical ring, "that everything you are, you are through me, and everything I am, I am through you alone."

In that lies the explanation for the peculiar rigidity which was present almost from the start. In fact Hitler's world view had not changed since his days in Vienna, as he himself was wont to declare. For the elements remained the same; all that the masses' grand cry of reveille did was to charge that world view with enormous tension. But the emotions themselves, the fears and obsessions, were fixed. Hitler's taste in art also, and even his personal preferences, remained what they had been in the days of his boyhood and youth: Tristan and starchy foods, neoclassicism, anti-Semitism, Karl Spitzweg, and a weakness for cream cake. Though he later declared that while in Vienna he had been "in respect to thinking a babe-in-arms," in a sense he had always remained so. If we compare the drawings and painstaking water colors of the twenty-year-old postcard painter with those of the First World War soldier or with those of the Chancellor twenty years later, their quality hardly differs. No personal experience, no process of development is reflected in these tight little sketches. As if petrified, Hitler remained what he had been.

Yet it may be that these immature features were essential for Hitler's successes. From the summer of 1923 on, the nation reeled from one crisis and emergency to the next. Under such circumstances, fortune favored only the man who despised circumstances, who instead of engaging in politics challenged fate, and who promised not to improve conditions but to overturn them radically and thoroughly. "I guarantee you," Hitler phrased it, "that the impossible always succeeds. What is unlikeliest is surest."

Chapter 3

For me and for all of us, setbacks have been only the whiplash which drove us onward with more determination than before.

Adolf Hitler

CHALLENGING THE POWERS THAT BE

Hitler had planned a party rally in Munich for the end of January, 1923. He meant to turn it into an intimidating demonstration of his own power. Five thousand SA men had been summoned to Munich from all over Bavaria. They would parade before their Führer on the Marsfeld, or Field of Mars, on the outskirts of town, forming the honor guard for the first solemn dedication of the standards. Concurrently, mass meetings were to be held in no fewer than twelve halls in the city. To increase the popular appeal, the party had hired bands, folk-dance ensembles, and the comedian Weiss Ferdl. The sheer size of the affair, combined with the rumors of a Nazi putsch that had been circulating for weeks, underlined Hitler's mounting importance as a political figure.

The way the Bavarian authorities reacted to Hitler's defiant and challenging proclamations revealed their growing perplexity vis-à-vis the Nazi party. The party's rise had been so rapid that the exact nature of it as a force on the political scene remained undefined. On the one hand, it did assume a nationalist stance and manifested laudable energy in its antagonism to the Left. Yet, at the same time, it had no respect for authorities and was constantly violating the public order that it claimed to desire above all else. In 1922 the authorities sentenced Hitler to three months' imprisonment—partly because they were determined to show him that there were limits which they would not allow him to breach. He and his followers had disrupted a meeting of the Bayernbund (Bavarian League) and given its leader, the engineer Otto Ballerstedt, a severe beating. Hitler served only four weeks of the sentence. When he made his first public

160

appearance after his release, he was "carried to the podium amidst applause which seemed as if it would never end." The *Völkische Beobachter* called him "the most popular and most hated man in Munich." The situation involved risks that even Hitler must have found difficult to calculate. The year 1923 was characterized by his repeated efforts to clarify his relationship to the power structure. He tested it from a number of angles, at times taking a wooing tone, at times a threatening one.

The authorities did not know how to deal with this man who was at once somewhat suspect and gratifyingly nationalistic. They finally struck a compromise with their own ambivalence: they issued a ban against the outdoor ceremony of dedicating the standards and forbade half the mass meetings already announced by Hitler. Conversely, they also banned the rally that the Social Democrats had called for the preceding day. Yet Eduard Nortz, who had replaced the Nazi sympathizer Ernst Pöhner as police commissioner, remained unmoved when Hitler pleaded that the ban would be worse than a heavy blow to the nationalist movement, that it would be a disaster for the entire fatherland. Nortz, gray-haired and cool, answered that even patriots had to bow to the government's decrees. Hitler flew into a rage and began to shout that he would hold the SA march anyway, that he was not afraid of the police, that he himself would march at the head of the column and let himself be shot. But the commissioner did not give way. Instead, he hastily convened a session of the Council of Ministers, which proclaimed a state of emergency. That automatically banned all the activities planned for the party rally. The time had come to remind the leader of the National Socialists of the rules of the political game.

Hitler was in despair. It seemed to him that his whole political future was at stake. For one of the rules as he understood them was that he might challenge the government with impunity, since his demands were only a radical extension of the government's own wishes.

At this point the Reichswehr, which had stood by the party since Drexler's time, entered the picture. Röhm and Ritter von Epp had finally succeeded in persuading the Bavarian Reichswehr commander, General von Lossow, to meet with Hitler. By now nervous and unsure of himself, Hitler was prepared to make considerable concessions. He promised Lossow that he would "report to his Excellency" on January 28, immediately after the party rally. Lossow, who had been rather put off by Hitler's eccentric manner, finally agreed to inform the government that he would consider "the suppression of the nationalist organizations unfortunate for security reasons." The ban was then in fact lifted. To save face, however, Nortz requested the leader of the NSDAP at a second meeting to reduce the number of meetings to six and to stage the dedication of the standards not on the Marsfeld, but inside the nearby Krone Circus. Hitler, realizing that he had won this match, vaguely indicated compliance. Then, under the slogan of *Deutschland erwache!* ("Germany, awake!"), he held all twelve mass meetings. The dedication of the standards, which he himself had designed, took place on the Marsfeld after all, in the presence of 5,000 storm troopers. There was a driving snowstorm. "Either the National Socialist German Workers' Party is the coming movement in Germany," Hitler thundered, "in which case not even the devil can stop it, or it is not, and deserves to be destroyed." Battalions of exuberant SA men marched past walls and kiosks covered with proclamations of the state of emergency. With them marched several military bands, and the storm troopers roared out their songs defaming the "Jew Republic." When they reached Schwan-thalerstrasse, Hitler reviewed the units, most of whom now wore uniforms.

It was a telling triumph over governmental authority, and it prepared the ground for the conflicts of the following months. Many observers saw these events as proof that Hitler's rhetorical gifts were matched by his political adroitness. Moreover, his nerves seemed tougher than those of his adversaries. For a long time people had merely smiled at his furious intensity. Now they began to be impressed, and the party's ranks, so long made up of the resentful and the naïve, began to be swelled by people with a keen instinct for the wave of the future. Between February and November, 1923, the National Socialist Party enrolled a good 35,000 new members, while the SA grew to nearly 15,000. The party now had assets of 173,000 gold marks.[37] An intensive program of propaganda and activities covering all of Bavaria was developed. From February 8 on, the *Völkische Beobachter* began appearing as a daily. The name of Dietrich Eckart, who was overworked and ill, remained on the masthead for a few more months, but by the beginning of March the real editor of the newspaper was Alfred Rosenberg.

Hitler had found both the civil and military authorities all too accommodating. Their attitude may be traced in part to the troubles that had recently gripped the country. In the first half of January, France, still full of hatred and suspicion for her neighbor, had insisted on claiming its rights under the Treaty of Versailles and had occupied the Rhineland. Germany was at once plunged into full-scale economic crisis, which had been threatening the country since 1918. The unrest of the early postwar period, the heavy burden of reparations, the general flight of capital, and especially the lack of any reserves, had made it extremely difficult for the economy to recover from the war. To make matters worse, the behavior of the radical rightists and leftists had repeatedly undermined what little confidence other countries might have had in Germany's stability. It was no coincidence that the mark took its first dramatic plunge in June, 1922, after Walther Rathenau, the German Foreign Minister, was assassinated. But now the French occupation set off that mad inflationary spiral that made life so grotesque and destroyed everyone's surviving faith in the social order. People grew used to living in an "atmosphere of the impossible." The inflation meant the collapse of an entire world, with all its assumptions, its norms, and its morality. The consequences were incalculable.

For the moment, however, public interest centered primarily on the attempt at national self-assertion. The paper money, whose value was ultimately to be measured by mere weight, seemed only a fantastic under-scoring of events in the Rhineland. On January 11 the government issued a call for passive resistance. German government employees were instructed not to obey orders from the occupation authorities. French troops advancing into the Ruhr encountered huge crowds of Germans grimly singing "Die Wacht am Rhein." The French answered the challenge with a series of well-chosen humiliations. Occupation courts meted out Draconian punishments for acts of defiance. Many clashes heightened the anger on both sides. At the end of March French troops fired into a crowd of workers demonstrating on the grounds of the Krupp plant in Essen. Thirteen demonstrators were killed and over thirty wounded. Almost half a million persons joined in the funeral for the victims. A French military tribunal tried and convicted the head of the firm and eight of his principal subordinates and imposed prison sentences of fifteen to twenty years.

Episodes of this sort produced a sense of common purpose such as had not been felt in Germany since 1914. But beneath the cloak of national unity the divergent forces attempted to turn the situation to their own advantage. The outlawed paramilitary organizations seized the opportunity to come out into the open and supplement the program of passive resistance with direct action. The radical Left made a strong bid to regain the positions it had lost in Saxony and Central Germany, while the Right fortified its power base in Bavaria. These were the times in which armed proletarian companies faced units of the Ehrhardt Free Corps with leveled weapons on the borders of Bavaria. In many of the larger cities food demonstrations took on the character of riots. In the meantime the French and Belgians were exploiting the disarray in the west to encourage a separatist movement which, however, soon collapsed for want of a clear rationale. The republic, created only four years earlier under adverse circumstances and never more than precariously maintained, seemed on the point of breakdown.

Hitler expressed his new self-confidence in a bold and provocative gesture: he withdrew the NSDAP from the front for national unity and warned his bewildered followers that anyone who took active part in the resistance against France would be expelled from the party. Some such expulsions were actually carried out. To members who objected he gave this explanation: "If they haven't caught on that this idiocy about a common front is fatal for us, they're beyond help." Although he was aware of some of the questionable aspects of this stand, his particular perspective and his sense of tactics told him that he must not line up with the others. The Nazi party could not make common cause with members of the bourgeoisie, Marxists, and Jews; it could not afford to be submerged in the anonymity of the national resistance movement. Hitler feared that the struggle for the Ruhr would unite the people behind the government and strengthen the regime. But he could also hope that his obstructionist tactics would sow confusion and thus further his long-range ambitions for a take-over: "As long as a nation does not drive out the murderers within its own borders," he wrote in the *Völkische Beobachter,* "success in its dealings with other countries remains impossible. While spoken and written protests are hurled against the French, the real enemy of the German people lurks within its gates." With remarkable inflexibility, considering the popular mood, and even in the face of Ludendorff's overwhelming authority, he went on insisting that Germany had first to come to grips with the enemy within. Early in March the army chief of staff, General von Seeckt, inquired whether Hitler would be willing to attach his forces to the Reichswehr if a policy of active resistance were adopted. Hitler replied curtly that first the government would have to be overthrown. Two weeks later he made the same point to a representative of German Chancellor Cuno: "Not down with France, but down with the traitors to the Fatherland, down with the November criminals; that must be our slogan!"

It has become standard to see Hitler's behavior as totally unscrupulous and unprincipled. But here is an instance in which he stood steadfastly by his principles, even though this meant exposing himself to unpopularity and misunderstanding. He himself saw this stand as one of the crucial decisions of his career. His allies and backers—people of prestige and staunch conservatives—always looked upon him as one of their own, as nationalist and conservative as themselves. But in his very first political decision of any magnitude Hitler brushed away all the false alliances, from Kahr to Papen, and showed that when the chips were down he would act like a true revolutionary. Without hesitation he took a revolutionary posture rather than a nationalistic one. Indeed, in later years he never reacted any differently. As late as 1930 he asserted that if the Poles invaded Germany, he would give up East Prussia and Silesia temporarily rather than aid the existing regime by helping to defend German territory. To be sure, he also asserted that he would despise himself if "the moment a conflict broke out he were not first and foremost a German." But in actual fact he differed from his adherents in that he remained cool and consistent and did not allow his own patriotic tirades to shape his strategy. He turned his scorn against the passive resistance movement which, he said, proposed to "kill the French by loafing." He also ridiculed those who thought France could be overcome by sabotage: "What would France be today," he shouted, "if there were no internationalists in Germany, but only National Socialists? What if we had no weapons but our fists? If sixty million people were as one in passionately loving their Fatherland—those fists would sprout guns."

Hitler was certainly no less incensed against the French than the other forces and parties in Germany. What he objected to was not the resistance per se but the fact that it was only passive and therefore a halfway measure. There were also the other political factors already mentioned that determined his refusal to go along with the other nationalist parties. Underlying his stand was the conviction that no consistent and successful foreign policy could be pursued unless a united and revolutionary nation stood behind it. This view reversed the whole political tradition of the Germans, for it asserted the primacy of domestic rather than foreign policy. When the passive resistance began to crumble, Hitler made a passionate speech describing what a true resistance campaign would have been like. The drastic tone of his suggestions anticipates the kind of orders he was to give in March, 1945, for "Operation Scorched Earth":

What matter that in the present catastrophe industrial plants are destroyed? Blast furnaces can explode, coal mines be flooded, houses burn to the ground— if in their place there arises a resurrected people: strong, unshakable, committed to the utmost. For when the German people is resurrected, everything else will be resurrected as well. But if the buildings all remained standing and the people perished of its own inner rottenness, chimneys, industrial plants and seas of houses would be but the tombstones of this people. The Ruhr district should have become the German Moscow. We should have proved to the world that the German people of 1923 is not the German people of 1918. . . . The people of dishonor and shame would once again have become a race of heroes. Against the background of the burning Ruhr district, such a people would have organized a life-or-death resistance. If this had been its course, France would not have dared to take one more step. . . . Furnace after furnace, bridge after bridge blown up. Germany awakes! Not even the lash could have driven France's army into such a universal conflagration. By God, things would be very different for us today![38]

Few of Hitler's contemporaries understood his decision not to participate in the struggle over the Ruhr. The decision lent plausibility to the rumor that French funds were behind the NSDAP's conspicuous expansion of its organization. For it was obvious to everyone that the party was increasing its propaganda and outfitting its members with new uniforms and arms. But no concrete proof of such French backing has ever been found—and, in fact, it is still hard to specify which political or economic interests were trying to exert influence over the growing party. Nevertheless, the party's lavish expenditures, especially after Hitler took over the leadership, were so conspicuously out of all proportion to its numbers that there was every reason to look around for financial backers. Suspicions of this sort are not merely traceable to the "devil theory" of the Left, which could explain its defeat by "counter-historical National Socialism" only by positing a grim conspiracy of monopoly capitalism.

The National Socialists themselves lent encouragement to the most

165

fantastic theories by practicing a psychotic form of secrecy concerning their financial resources. Throughout the Weimar years there was a series of libel cases springing from various charges; after 1933 the records of these cases were spirited away or destroyed. From the very beginning it was an unwritten law of the party that no records should be kept of contributions. Financial transactions were rarely noted in the journal of the party business office; when they were, there would usually be a note: "To be handled by Drexler personally." In October, 1920, Hitler, presiding over a meeting in the Münchener Kindl-Keller, issued strict orders against anyone's making notes on the details of a transaction he had just described.[39]

There is no doubt that the party's basic income derived from membership dues, small donations, the sale of tickets for Hitler's speeches, or collections made at rallies, which might often amount to several thousand marks. Some of the early party members, like Oskar Körner, owner of a small toy store, who was killed in front of the Feldherrnhalle on November 9, 1923, all but ruined themselves in the interest of the party. Shop owners offered special discounts to the party, while others made gifts of jewelry or works of art. Spinster ladies who attended evening rallies were sometimes so emotionally shaken by the personality of Hitler that they made the National Socialist Party the beneficiary under their wills. Prosperous well-wishers like the Bechsteins, the Bruckmanns, or Ernst Hanfstaengl sometimes came forth with sizable gifts. The party also found ways to coax more funds out of its membership than just the regular dues. It floated interest-free loan certificates that the members were supposed to buy and sell to others. According to police records, no fewer than 40,000 loan certificates, each for ten marks, were issued in the first half of 1921 alone.[40]

Nevertheless, the party suffered from a chronic shortage of funds during the early years. Even as late as the middle of 1921 it could not afford to hire a treasurer. According to the story of an early member, the poster brigades could not even buy the necessary paste. In the fall of 1921 Hitler had to cancel plans for a major rally in the Krone Circus for lack of funds. The financial predicament began to improve in the summer of 1922, when the party's feverish activity brought it more into the forefront. Henceforth the party could count on a wide circle of financial benefactors and supporters, not party adherents in the strict sense, but rather representatives of the wealthy middle class, which felt vulnerable to the threat of Communist revolution. These people were ready to support any anti-Communist group, from the Free Corps and nationalist leagues on the right to the crank causes that proliferated within protest journalism. It would probably be correct to say that they were less interested in giving Hitler a boost than in promoting the most vigorous antirevolutionary force they could find.

Hitler owed his connections with the influential and monied segments of Bavarian society to Dietrich Eckart and Max Erwin von Scheubner-Richter. Another such sponsor was probably Ludendorff, who himself received considerable sums from industrialists and large landowners and doled this money out among the militant nationalist-racist organizations as he saw fit. While Ernst Röhm was mobilizing funds, weapons, and equipment for the Reichswehr, Dr. Emil Gansser, a friend of Dietrich Eckart's, put Hitler in touch with a group of big businessmen and bankers belonging to the Nationalist Club (*Nationalklub*). In 1922 Hitler had his first chance to present his plans to them. Among the principal contributors to the party's funds were the locomotive manufacturer Borsig, Fritz Thyssen of Consolidated Steel (Vereinigte Stahlwerke), Privy Councilor Kirdorf, and executives of the Daimler Company and the Bavarian Industrialists Association (Bayrischer Industriellenverband). Support from Czechoslovak, Scandinavian, and Swiss sources was also forthcoming for this dynamic party that was attracting so much attention. In the fall of 1923 Hitler went to Zurich and allegedly returned "with a steamer trunk stuffed with Swiss francs and American dollars."[41] The mysterious and ingenious Kurt W. Luedecke obtained considerable sums from as yet undetermined sources, and among other things set up his "own" SA company consisting of fifty men. Cash flowed in from persons in Hungary as well as from Russian and Baltic-German *émigrés*. During the inflation some party functionaries were paid in foreign currencies. Among these were Julius Schreck, the SA staff sergeant who was later to be Hitler's chauffeur, and the SA Chief of Staff Lieutenant Commander Hoffmann. Even a bordello on Berlin's Tauentzienstrasse did its bit for the nationalist cause. At the urging of Scheubner-Richter, it had been set up by a former army officer; the profits went to swell the party till in Munich.[42]

The motives behind these contributions were highly diverse. It is true that without this support Hitler could not have launched his expensive spectacles after the summer of 1922. But it is also true that he made no binding commitments to any of his backers. The aggrieved leftists never believed in the anticapitalist stance of the National Socialists. It was all too inarticulate and irrational. And, in fact, Nazi anticapitalist ranting against usurers, speculators, and department stores never went beyond the perspective of superintendents and shopkeepers. Nevertheless, the Nazis' sense of outrage was all the more convincing because of their lack of any impressive system. They objected to the morality rather than the material possessions of the propertied classes. This passage from one of the early party speechifiers indicates the psychological effectiveness of the irrational anticapitalist appeal to the desperate masses: "Be patient just a little longer. But then, when we sound the call for action, spare the savings banks, for they are where we working people have put our pennies. Storm the commercial banks! Take all the money you find there and throw it into the streets and set fire to the huge heaps of it! Then use the crossbars of the streetcar lines to string up the black and the white Jews!"

Hitler made similar speeches, similarly emotion-laden, against the grim

167

background of mass suffering caused by the inflation. Again and again, he inveighed against the lies of capitalism, even while his funds were coming from big business. Max Amann, the party's business manager, was interrogated by the Munich police shortly after the putsch attempt of November, 1923. He insisted, not without pride, that Hitler had given his backers "only the party platform" in return for their contributions. This may seem hard to credit; nevertheless, there is reason to think that the only agreements he made were on tactical lines. For the concept of corruption seems strangely alien to this man; it does not accord with his rigidity, his mounting self-confidence, and the force of his delusions.

The National Socialists had emerged victorious from their showdown with the government at the beginning of January. They found themselves top dog among the radical rightist groups in Bavaria and celebrated by a wave of meetings, demonstrations, and marches even rowdier and more aggressive than those of the past. The air was thick with rumors of coups and uprisings. With impassioned slogans Hitler fed a general expectation of some great change impending. At the end of April he gave a speech urging the "workers of the head and the workers of the fist" to close ranks in order to create "the new man . . . of the coming Third Reich." Anticipating the imminent test of strength, the NSDAP had struck up an alliance in early February with a number of militant nationalist organizations. The new partners included the Reichsflagge (Reich Banner), led by Captain Heiss; the Bund Oberland (Oberland League); the Vaterländischer Verein München (Munich Patriotic Club); and the Kampfverb and Niederbayern (Lower Bavarian League of Struggle). Joint authority was vested in a committee known as the Arbeitsgemeinschaft der vaterländischen Kampfverbände (Provisional Committee of the Patriotic Leagues of Struggle), with Lieutenant Colonel Hermann Kriebel in charge of military co-ordination. The arrangements had been worked out by Ernst Röhm.

The National Socialists had thus created a counterpoise to the existing coalition of nationalist groups known as the VVV, Vereinigte Vaterländische Verbände Bayerns (Union of Bavarian Patriotic Associations). Under the leadership of former Prime Minister von Kahr and the *Gymnasium* Professor Bauer, the VVV united the most disparate elements: Bavarian separatists, Pan-Germans, and various brands of racists. On the other hand, the black-white-red Kampfbund (League of Struggle) led by Kriebel represented a more militant, more radical, more "Fascist" group, which took its inspiration and its goals from Mussolini or Kemal Pasha Atatürk. However, Hitler was soon to learn how dubious it was to gain outside support at the price of what had been absolute personal control. The lesson came on May 1 when, impatient and drunk with his latest success, Hitler attempted another showdown with the government.

His attempt to impose a program on the Kampfbund had already met with failure because his partners' slow-moving soldier mentality could not follow his wild flights of fancy. In the course of the spring he had been forced to look on as Kriebel, Röhm, and the Reichswehr pried the SA away from him. He had created the SA as a revolutionary army directly responsible to him, but now Kriebel and Röhm were trying to turn the SA into a secret reserve for the so-called Hundred Thousand Man Army (the Treaty of Versailles limited the official German army to 100,000 men). They were drilling the standards (as the three regiment-sized units were called) and staging night maneuvers or parades. Hitler appeared at these affairs only as an ordinary civilian, sometimes giving a speech, but virtually unable to assert leadership. He noted with annoyance that the storm troops were being stripped of their ideological cast and downgraded to mere military reserve units. A few months later, in order to regain authority, Hitler instructed his old fellow soldier, former Lieutenant Josef Berchtold, to organize a kind of staff guard to be named *Stosstrupp* (Shock Troop) Hitler. This was the origin of the SS.

At the end of April Hitler and the Kampfbund decided that the annual May 1 rallies by the leftist parties were to be taken as a provocation and should be stopped by any and all methods. They themselves would organize their own mass demonstrations for that day, and celebrate the fourth anniversary of the crushing of the Munich soviet republic. The vacillating Bavarian government under von Knilling would seem to have learned nothing from its experience in January. It half yielded to the Kampfbund's demand. The Left would be allowed to hold a mass meeting on the Theresienwiese but forbidden all street processions. Hitler therefore staged one of his tried-and-true fits of rage and, repeating his ruse of January, tried to play off the military authorities against the civilian government. By April 30 the situation had become almost unbearably tense. Kriebel, Bauer, and the newly appointed leader of the SA, Hermann Göring, lodged a vigorous protest with the government and demanded that a state of emergency be declared in the face of leftist agitation. Meanwhile Hitler and Röhm once more went to General von Lossow and insisted not only that the Reichswehr intervene but also that, as prearranged, weapons belonging to the patriotic associations be distributed to them. (These weapons were now stored in the government armories.) To Hitler's astonishment, the general curtly refused both requests. He knew his duty to the security of the state, he declared stiffly. Anyone stirring up disorder would be shot. Colonel Seisser, the head of the Bavarian Landespolizei (state police) took a similar line.

Hitler had once more worked himself into an almost hopeless position. His only choice seemed to be to back down on the whole issue. But, true to his character, he refused to concede defeat. Instead, he doubled his stake. He had already warned Lossow that the "Red rallies" would take place only if the demonstrators marched "over his dead body." Some of this was histrionics, but there was always a measure of dead earnest in Hitler's

169

statements. He was ready to cut off his escape routes and face up to the alternatives of all or nothing.

At any rate, Hitler had the preparations intensified. Weapons, munitions, and vehicles were collected feverishly. Finally, the Reichswehr was tricked by a sudden coup. In direct defiance of Lossow's orders, Hitler sent Röhm and a small group of SA men to the barracks. Explaining that the government feared leftist disorders on May 1, they helped themselves to carbines and machine guns. Such open preparations for a putsch sowed alarm among some of Hitler's nationalist allies. There were open clashes within the Kampfbund, but in the meantime events had caught up with the actors. Obeying Hitler's announcement of an emergency, party stalwarts from Nuremberg, Augsburg, and Freising had arrived in Munich. Many of them were armed. A group from Bad Tölz came with an old field cannon hitched to their truck. The units from Landshut, led by Gregor Strasser and Heinrich Himmler, brought along several light machine guns. All these groups were acting in anticipation of the revolutionary uprising they had been dreaming of for years and which Hitler had repeatedly promised them. They were expecting a "wiping out of the November disgrace," as the grim slogan had it. When Police Commissioner Nortz issued a warning to Kriebel, the answer was: "I can no longer turn back; it is too late . . . whether or not blood flows."

Before dawn on May 1, the patriotic leagues were gathering in Munich at the Oberwiesenfeld, at the Maximilianeum, and at several other key locations throughout the city to quell the socialist coup that was allegedly brewing. Hitler arrived at the Oberwiesenfeld a little later. The place had the look of a military encampment. Hitler, too, looked martial; he was wearing a helmet and his Iron Cross, First Class. His entourage included Göring, Streicher, Rudolf Hess, Gregor Strasser, and Gerhard Rossbach, who was in command of the Munich SA. While the storm troopers began drilling in preparation for orders to launch real attacks, the leaders conferred. Confusion reigned; there was considerable dissension, growing nervousness and dismay, because the expected signal from Röhm had failed to come.

In the meantime, the trade unions and parties of the Left were celebrating their May Day rites on the Theresienwiese. Their slogans were the time-honored revolutionary ones, but the general temper was harmonious and public-spirited. Since the police had cordoned off the side of the Oberwiesenfeld facing the city, the expected clashes did not take place. But Röhm himself was at this moment standing at attention before his commander, General von Lossow, who had learned of the trickery at the barracks and was greatly enraged. Shortly after noon, Captain Röhm, escorted by Reichswehr and police contingents, appeared at the Oberwiesenfeld. He transmitted Lossow's orders: the stolen weapons were to be surrendered on the spot. Strasser and Kriebel urged an immediate attack, reasoning that a civil war situation would bring the Reichswehr over to their side. But Hitler gave in. He found a way to save face by arranging to have his men return the weapons to the barracks. But the defeat was unmistakable, and even the flamboyant language with which he addressed his followers that evening in the Krone Circus could not blot it out.

This would seem to have been the first personal crisis in Hitler's rise to power. True, he had a certain justification for blaming his defeat on the attitude of some of his allies, particularly the squeamish and stiff-necked nationalist organizations. But he must have recognized that the behavior of his partners had also exposed certain weaknesses and mistakes of his own. Above all, he had misread the situation. The Reichswehr, whose might had made him strong and whose co-operation he had counted on, had suddenly turned into an enemy.

It was the first painful reverse after years of steady progress, and Hitler disappeared from public view for several weeks. He took refuge with Dietrich Eckart in Berchtesgaden. Plagued by self-doubt, he only occasionally appeared to give a speech. Once or twice he went to Munich for a bit of distraction. Up to this point he had acted largely instinctively, by hit and miss and imitation. Now, in the light of that disastrous May 1, he conceived the outlines of a consistent strategy: the concept of a "fascist revolution" that takes place not in conflict but in concert with government power—what has been aptly described as "revolution by permission of His Excellency the President."[43] He put some of his thoughts down on paper. These ruminations were later incorporated into *Mein Kampf*.

He had also to contend with the reaction of the public. "It is generally recognized that Hitler and his men have made fools of themselves," one report put it. Even an "assassination plot" against "the great Adolf" (as the *Münchener Post* had ironically dubbed him), a plot uncovered by Hermann Esser at the beginning of July and described with great fanfare in the *Völkische Beobachter,* could do little to revive Hitler's popularity— especially since similar revelations had been published in April and had subsequently been exposed as fabrications by the National Socialists. "Hitler no longer captures the imagination of the German people," wrote a correspondent for the New York German-language newspaper *Staatszeitung.* Another shrewd observer noted early in May that Hitler's star seemed "to be waning."

Currents of this sort cannot have been lost on Hitler, brooding in the solitude of Berchtesgaden. This would help explain his extraordinary retreat, his refusal to try to re-establish contact with Lossow or to inject a new spirit into the leaderless party and the Kampfbund. Gottfried Feder, Oskar Körner, and a few other long-time followers attempted to rouse him, above all urging him to break with "Putzi" Hanfstaengl, who had introduced the virtuous Hitler to "lovely ladies" who went about "in silk underwear" calling for more and more "champagne parties." But Hitler hardly heard what they were saying. He let himself sink into his old state of lethargy and disgust. Yet he took some interest in the court case growing out of the events of May 1 and now pending before the Munich Land-gericht (superior court). If the judgment went against him, Hitler would have to serve the two-month sentence he had received for the Ballerstedt affair. What was worse, Minister of the Interior Schweyer would undoubt-edly rule that Hitler had broken his parole and would have him expelled from Bavaria.

Hitler bestirred himself enough to send a petition to the state prosecutor. He knew that he had friends within the power structure. It was to them that he appealed. "For weeks now I have been the victim of savage vilification in the press and the Landtag," he wrote. "But because of the respect I owe my Fatherland I have not attempted to defend myself publicly. Therefore I can only be grateful to Providence for this chance to defend myself fully and freely in the courtroom." He menacingly indicated, moreover, that he was going to hand his petition over to the press.

The implications were clear enough, and the state prosecutor quickly passed the petition on, with an anxious note appended, to Minister of Justice Gürtner. The latter was a strong nationalist who had not forgotten certain old pacts and promises made to the National Socialists. Had he not even referred to them as "flesh of our flesh"? The nation's plight was worsening from day to day, with galloping inflation, general strikes, the battle of the Ruhr, hunger riots, and mounting agitation by the Left. In view of all this, there seemed good reason to show leniency toward a leader of national stature, even if said leader was part of the problem. Without informing the Minister of the Interior, who had several times inquired about the case, Gürtner let the state prosecutor know that he considered it advisable to have the case postponed "until a calmer period." On August 1, 1923, the investigation was temporarily suspended, and on May 22 of the following year the charges were dropped.

Nevertheless, Hitler's loss of prestige was not easily rectified. That became apparent in early September, when the patriotic organizations cele-brated one of their "German Days," this one on the anniversary of the victory at Sedan, which had ended the Franco-Prussian War. A great parade was held in Nuremberg, complete with flags, wreaths, and retired generals. The attendance ran into the hundreds of thousands, all tempo-rarily ecstatic with the feeling of having overcome national humiliation. The police report of the incident had a highly unbureaucratic, emotional ring: "Roaring cries of 'Heil!' swirled around the guests of honor and their entourage. Countless arms with waving handkerchiefs reached out for them; flowers and bouquets rained on them from all sides. It was like the jubilant outcry of hundreds of thousands of despairing, beaten, down-trodden human beings suddenly glimpsing a ray of hope, a way out of their bondage and distress. Many, men and women both, stood and wept. . . ."

172

According to this report, the National Socialists formed one of the largest contingents among the 100,000 marchers. But at the center of the cheering stood General Ludendorff. Hitler, caught in the sway of the mass demonstration but also aware of the ground he had lost in the recent past, declared himself ready for a new alliance. He joined with the Reichsflagge group under Captain Heiss, and the Bund Oberland under Friedrich Weber, to form the Deutscher Kampfbund—a new version of the older league of nationalist parties. This time, however, there was no longer any question of Hitler's assuming the principal role. What had damaged his status was not so much the defeat of May 1 as his withdrawal from Munich afterward. For as soon as he was no longer on the scene to cause a sensation, his name, his authority, his demagogic powers all faded away. The indefatigable Röhm had to campaign for three weeks before he was able to persuade the leaders of the Kampfbund to relinquish the leadership in political affairs to Hitler.

The turning point came when the national government decided that the struggle at the Ruhr was draining the country's energies to no avail. On September 24, six weeks after becoming Chancellor, Gustav Stresemann called off the passive resistance movement and resumed reparations payments to France. During all the preceding months Hitler had spoken out against the passive resistance, but his revolutionary aims now required him to brand the administration's unpopular step a piece of cowardly, despicable treason and to exploit the situation to the full for the purpose of undermining the government. On the very next day he met with the leaders of the Kampfbund: Kriebel, Heiss, Weber, Göring, and Röhm. In a stormy two-and-a-half hour speech he unfolded his plans and visions, ending with the plea that he be given the leadership of the Deutscher Kampfbund. As Röhm later reported, Heiss was in tears as he extended his hand to Hitler. Weber, too, was moved, while Röhm himself wept and trembled, as he says, from the depth of his emotion. Convinced that matters were moving toward a climax, he resigned from the Reichswehr the very next day and threw his lot in entirely with Hitler.

Hitler's plan apparently was to make such a show of decisiveness as to overwhelm all skepticism. He immediately ordered his 15,000 SA men on emergency alert. To enhance the prestige of his own organization, all members of the NSDAP were to resign from whatever other nationalist groups they might belong to. He launched a program of hectic activity. As with all his moves, however, the real aim of all the plans, tactics, and commands seemed to be a veritable explosion of propaganda, a turbulent spectacle. He projected no fewer than fourteen simultaneous mass meetings for September 27, with himself making a personal appearance at all fourteen to whip emotions to fever pitch. Certainly the ultimate aims of the Kampfbund were plain enough: liberation "from bondage and shame," a march on Berlin, establishment of a nationalist dictatorship, and eradication of the "accursed enemies within." Hitler had flung down the challenge to the government three weeks earlier in his speech of September 5, when he said: "Either Berlin will march and end up in Munich, or Munich will march and end up in Berlin. A Bolshevist North Germany cannot exist side by side with a nationalist Bavaria." But whether he was planning a putsch at that point or was merely carried away by his own rhetoric has never been clear. There is reason to believe that he intended to take his cue from the effect that he had on the crowds. With his characteristic overestimation of propaganda methods, he must have counted on the government's being swayed by the passion of the masses. "Out of the endless battles of words," he declared, "the new Germany will be born." In any case, members of the Kampfbund received secret orders not to leave Munich and were issued the password to be used if a real coup were attempted.

But the Munich government acted before Hitler could. Some specifically Bavarian grievances and separatist tendencies had combined with rumors of an impending putsch and distrust of the "Marxist" national government to produce, for the Bavarian government, an intolerable situation. On September 26 Prime Minister von Knilling declared a state of emergency and appointed Gustav von Kahr as state commissioner with dictatorial powers. Von Kahr, an instrument of the Reichswehr, had briefly headed a right-wing government in Bavaria in 1920. He now declared that he welcomed the co-operation of the Kampfbund but warned Hitler against what he called "private initiatives." The fourteen rallies could not be permitted. Hitler was beside himself with rage. As head of the Kampfbund, the most powerful paramilitary organization on the scene, Hitler had begun to think himself the equal and partner of the government. With one stroke Kahr had reduced him to a public nuisance. In one of those tantrums later to become so famous, ranting and raving until he almost blacked out, Hitler threatened revolution. That would have meant breaking his own ground rules, which called for moving in concert with the power of the state. Only in the course of an all-night session were Röhm, Pöhner, and Scheubner-Richter able to dissuade him from a *coup d'état*.

In any case, events had long since caught up with Hitler's intentions. For in the meantime the cabinet in Berlin, headed by President Ebert, a socialist, had met to discuss the situation. Kahr had been closely identified with the separatist and monarchist trends. He had emphasized the "Bavarian mission of saving the Fatherland," which would involve the overthrow of the republic, the establishment of a conservative, authoritarian regime, and so much Bavarian autonomy that Bavaria would once more be ruled by a king. Thus it was understandable that the national government should feel considerable concern when Kahr was named state commissioner. With the country in desperate straits, with Communism raising its head in Saxony and Hamburg while separatism gained influence in the west, the harassed government might well see the events in Munich as the signal for total collapse.

In this tense and murky situation, the future of the country depended on the Reichswehr. Its commander, General von Seeckt, was himself often mentioned in rightist circles as a possible dictator. With the composure of one who knows the ultimate power rests with him, he made a late entrance to the cabinet meeting. Asked by Ebert where the Reichswehr stood at this moment, he replied: "The Reichswehr, Mr. President, stands behind me." For one brief moment the real power relationships were blindingly illuminated. Nevertheless, at this point he displayed loyalty to the political authorities. A nationwide state of emergency was declared, and executive power throughout the Reich was given to Seeckt. In the weeks to come he proved capable of even-handed dealing with the disruptive forces of both Right and Left.

On September 29 there was a rising of the "Black Reichswehr," the illegal reserve of the regular army. Threatened with suppression since the end of the struggle for the Ruhr, the Black Reichswehr now tried to stage a coup which would trigger an action by the entire Right, including the legal Reichswehr. The operation was hasty and poorly co-ordinated, and Seeckt quickly put an end to the rebellion. With that threat out of the way, Seeckt took resolute steps to stamp out leftist unrest in Saxony, Thuringia, and Hamburg. Then he turned to the test of strength with Bavaria.

In Bavaria, meanwhile, Hitler had after all managed to bring Kahr nearly over to his side. Seeckt had demanded that the *Völkische Beobachter* be banned for publishing an incendiary and libelous article. But neither Kahr nor Lossow made the slightest move against the newspaper. Nor did they obey an order to arrest Rossbach, Captain Heiss, and Naval Captain Ehrhardt. Lossow was thereupon stripped of his office; but in open defiance of the Constitution, State Commissioner von Kahr promptly named him regional commander of the Bavarian Reichswehr. Kahr went on to sharpen the challenge and bring the strife between Bavaria and the central government to a head. A warrant for the arrest of Captain Ehrhardt, the former Free Corps leader, had been issued by the Reichsgericht (federal court). Not only was he not arrested, but Kahr summoned him from his Salzburg hiding place and directed him to accelerate preparations for a march on Berlin. The date set was November 15.

These provocative gestures were accompanied by strong words. Kahr himself denounced the Weimar Constitution for being totally un-German and described the administration as a "colossus with feet of clay." He represented himself as the embodiment of the nationalist cause in the decisive battle with the internationalist-Marxist-Judaic front. The situation played directly into Hitler's hands, for now the power holders in Bavaria had aligned themselves on the side of the extremist they had tried to curb. When Seeckt demanded Lossow's resignation, all the nationalist organizations placed themselves at Hitler's disposal for the final reckoning with the government in Berlin.

175

Hitler saw himself presented with great and unexpected opportunities. In an interview with the *Corriere d'Italia* he predicted that the winter would bring a decision. He went several times in rapid succession to see General von Lossow, with whom he now could take an easy tone; they had common interests and common enemies, he happily declared, while Lossow in his turn assured the rabble-rouser that he "agreed completely with Hitler on nine out of ten points." Somewhat against his will, the commander of the Bavarian Reichswehr found himself caught up in a conspiracy. As an unpolitical soldier, he was unhappy in this role. Hitler, who soon had to propel the general the way he wanted him to go, could perceive the dilemma: "A military leader with such far-reaching powers who disobeys his commander-in-chief must be ready either to face the ultimate consequences or to remain a common mutineer and rebel," he later declared.

Coming to an agreement with Kahr proved more difficult. Hitler could not forget the injury he had received from the state commissioner on September 26, whereas Kahr was aware that he had been appointed partly to bring this hothead "to blue-and-white [*i.e.,* Bavarian loyalist] reason." Indeed, throughout his dealings with Hitler he remained on the lookout for the proper moment to issue the talented troublemaker "orders to withdraw from politics."

Despite the tensions on both sides, the confrontation with the federal government brought the two men together. When they disagreed, it was over the question of leadership and the timing of the attack. Kahr, who soon joined Lossow and Hans von Seisser, chief of the Bavarian state police, in a "triumvirate" of legal power holders, tended to be cautious in spite of his bold words. But Hitler was pressing for action. "The German people are asking only one question: 'When do we strike?' " he raved, and went on to describe the coming action in almost apocalyptic terms:

> Then the day will have come for which this movement was created. The hour for which we have fought all these years. The moment in which the National Socialist movement will launch its triumphal march for the salvation of Germany. Not for an election were we founded, but to leap into the breach in time of greatest need, when this people in fear and trembling sees the red monster advancing upon it. . . . Our movement alone holds the key to salvation—that is already perceived by millions. That has become almost a new article of faith.[44]

Both factions devoted the month of October to preparing for the fray. The atmosphere was heavy with secrecy, intrigue, and deep mutual distrust. Councils of war were held almost continuously, plans of action forged, passwords coined. In a more serious vein, weapons were collected and military exercises staged. By the beginning of October the rumors of a Hitler putsch had become so persistent that Lieutenant Colonel Kriebel, the military commander of the Kampfbund, felt it necessary to address a letter to Bavarian Prime Minister von Knilling denying any intentions of overthrowing the national government. Walls bloomed with slogans and counterslogans, and "the march to Berlin" became a magic formula that seemed to promise an end to all problems. Hitler fanned the flames with his own brand of rhetoric: "This November Republic is nearing its end. We begin to hear the soft rustling which heralds a storm. And this storm will break, and in it this Republic will experience a transformation one way or another. The time is ripe."[45]

Hitler seemed fairly sure that Kahr could be relied on. But he suspected the triumvirate of intending to launch the operation without him or of meaning to replace his revolutionary slogan of "On to Berlin!" with the Bavarian separatist cry of "Away from Berlin!" At times he must have feared that there might be no action at all. There is some evidence that he started thinking early in October of ways to force his partners to attack and have himself put in command of the assault. But he never doubted that the people would follow him rather than Kahr once the fight was on. He despised the members of the so-called ruling class, their bland assumption of superiority, their inability to move the masses, whom he could so masterfully sway. In an interview he referred to Kahr as a "feeble prewar bureaucrat." True, the triumvirate officially held power, but he, Hitler, had on his side the "national commander" Ludendorff, "the army corps on two legs," whose political obtuseness Hitler had quickly recognized and learned to exploit. By now his self-confidence tended to go beyond all bounds. He compared himself to the French statesman Gambetta and Mussolini; it did not matter that his partners treated him as a laughable figure or that Kriebel explained to a visitor that of course Hitler could not be considered for a leadership position, since he had nothing in his head but his own propaganda. Hitler, on the other hand, told one of the high officers close to Lossow that he felt himself called to save Germany, although he would need Ludendorff to win over the Reichswehr. "In politics he will not interfere with me in the slightest. . . . Did you know that Napoleon also surrounded himself with insignificant men when he was setting himself up as consul?"

By the second half of October the plans for a march on Berlin began to take more definite shape. On October 16 Kriebel signed an order for strengthening the border guard to the north; this was represented as a security measure in response to the disturbances in Thuringia. The actual directive, however, was cast in military terminology: there are references to "deployment areas" and "opening of hostilities," "offensive morale," "spirit of pursuit," and "annihilation of the enemy forces." The directive in fact was tantamount to a mobilization order. The volunteers meanwhile were using a map of Berlin as the basis of their war games. Speaking to the cadets of the Infantry Academy, Hitler told them: "Your highest obligation under your oath to the flag, gentlemen, is to break that oath." The speech received thunderous applause. To put further pressure on their partners, the National Socialists called upon members of the state police to join the SA. Hitler later noted that from sixty to eighty mortars, howitzers, and heavy artillery pieces had come out of hiding and been added to the common arsenal. At a debate at the Kampfbund on October 23 Göring presented details for the "Offensive Against Berlin," and recommended, among other things, that blacklists be drawn up: "The most vigorous forms of terror must be employed; anyone who creates the slightest obstruction must be shot. It is essential that the leaders decide now which individuals must be eliminated. As soon as the decree is issued at least one person must be shot immediately as an example."

On October 24 Lossow summoned representatives of the Reichswehr, the state police, and the patriotic organizations to a meeting at District Headquarters, so that he could present the Reichswehr's plans of mobilization for the march on Berlin. The code name of the operation was Sunrise. He had also invited Hermann Kriebel, the military leader of the Kampfbund, but Hitler had been omitted, along with the leadership of the SA. In response, Hitler promptly staged a "grand military review," of which we have a contemporary description: "All over the city the beat of drums and peals of band music could be heard from early in the morning. As the day wore on, one saw uniformed men everywhere with Hitler's swastika on their collars. . . ." Kahr must have understood the implications, for he issued an announcement "in order to put down the many rumors in circulation" that he totally refused to enter into any negotiations with the present national government.

The only question seemed to be who would strike first and thus receive "the victor's laurel at the Brandenburg Gate" from the redeemed nation. Even while the excitement mounted, a certain regional quality gave the whole thing a comic cast, a dash of cowboy-and-Indian gamesmanship. Seemingly forgetful of issues, the protagonists blustered that the time had come "to march and finally solve certain problems in the manner of Bismarck." Others hailed the *Ordnungszelle Bayern* ("Bavaria as the mainstay of public order") or the "Bavarian fist" that would have to "clean up that Berlin pigsty." The image of Berlin as a great Babylon was often invoked; it had a cozily familiar ring, and many a speaker won the hearts of his listeners by promising the "sturdy Bavarians a punitive expedition to Berlin, conquest of the apocalyptic Great Whore, and perhaps a bit of a fling with her." A reliable informant from the Hamburg area let Hitler know that "on the day of reckoning millions of North Germans" would be on his side. There was widespread confidence that once Munich had led the way, all of Germany's tribes and regions would join in and that a "springlike uprising of the German people like that of 1813" was just around the corner. On October 30 Hitler withdrew his pledge to Kahr not to press forward on his own.

Even now Kahr could not make up his mind to act. Perhaps he had never meant, any more than Lossow, to attempt to overthrow the government by force. It seems far more likely that the triumvirate encouraged the bellicose preparations in order to prod Seeckt and the conservative nationalist "gentlemen from the North" into imposing their own dictatorship. If the venture went well, the Bavarians would then join in and see to it that Bavarian interests were given their due. Early in November Kahr and Lossow sent Colonel Seisser to Berlin to feel out the situation. His report, however, proved disappointing: no action was to be hoped for, and Seeckt especially had responded very coolly.

Thereupon the triumvirate called in the leaders of the patriotic organizations on November 6 and peremptorily informed them that they, the heads of government, were directing the forthcoming operation and would smash any private initiatives. This was their final attempt to regain control. Hitler was excluded from this meeting as well. That same evening the Kampfbund resolved to seize the next opportunity for striking, thus bringing the triumvirate and as many of the undecided as possible to join in a contagious rush on Berlin.

This decision is often cited as proof of Hitler's theatrical, overwrought, megalomaniac temperament. There is a tendency to make the operation seem ridiculous by the use of such terms as "Beer-hall Putsch," "Political *Fasching,*" and so on. To be sure, the undertaking had its comic aspect. Nevertheless, it also reveals Hitler's knack for sizing up a situation, his courage, and his tactical consistency.

In actual fact Hitler no longer had a choice on the evening of November 6. Since the defeat of May 1, from which he had barely recovered, the call to act was almost unavoidable. Otherwise he would jeopardize the very quality that made him unique among the profusion of parties and politicians: the radical, almost existential seriousness of his sense of outrage. It was his unyieldingness and refusal to compromise that made him impressive and credible. As leader of the Kampfbund he had acquired command over a striking force whose will to act was no longer fragmented by collective leadership. And finally, the storm troopers themselves were impatiently pressing for action.

Their restlessness had various causes. They were professional soldiers, who after weeks of conspiratorial preparations were all keyed up for action. Some of the paramilitary organizations, which had been on battle alert for weeks, had taken part in the "fall maneuvers" of the Reichswehr, but now all their funds had been used up. Hitler's treasury was also exhausted, and the men were going hungry.

The pressures on Hitler become the more apparent from the statement made by Wilhelm Brückner, the commander of the Munich SA regiment, at a secret session of the subsequent trial:

I had the impression that the Reichswehr officers were dissatisfied too, because the march on Berlin was being held up. They were saying: Hitler is a fraud just like the rest of them. You are not attacking. It makes no difference to

179

us who strikes first; we are going along. And I myself told Hitler: one of these days I will not be able to hold the men back. Unless something happens now, the men will take off on you. We had many unemployed in the ranks, fellows who had sacrificed their last pair of shoes, their last suit of clothing, their last penny for their training and who thought: soon things will get under way and we'll be taken into the Reichswehr and be out of this mess.[46]

In a discussion with Seisser at the beginning of November, Hitler himself said that something had to be done immediately or the troops of the Kampfbund would be driven by economic necessity into the Communist camp.

Hitler had not only to worry about the morale of his troops; the mere passage of time also had its dangers. The revolutionary discontent threatened to evaporate; it had been strained far too long. Meanwhile, the end of the struggle for the Ruhr and the defeat of the Left had brought a turn toward normality. Even the inflation seemed about to be checked, and the spirit of revolution seemed to be vanishing along with the crisis. There was no question that Hitler's effectiveness was entirely bound up with national distress. So to hesitate now would be fatal, even if certain pledges he had made stood in his way. These did not trouble him so much as a flaw in the plan: contrary to his principles he would have to venture on the revolution without the approval of the Prime Minister of Bavaria.

Nevertheless, he hoped that sufficient boldness on his part would extort this approval, and even the Prime Minister's participation. "We were convinced that action would only come if desire were backed up by will," Hitler later told the court. The sum total of significant reasons for action was thus counterweighed only by the risk that the coup might fail to ignite the courage of the triumvirate. It would seem that Hitler gave little thought to this danger, for he felt that he would only be forcing the triumvirate into something it had been planning in any case. In the end the entire undertaking foundered on this one point. The episode showed up the weakness of Hitler's sense of reality. He himself, to be sure, never accepted this charge; on the contrary, he was always somewhat proud of his disdain for reality. He quoted Lossow's statement that he would take part in a coup d'état only if the odds were 51 to 49 for a successful outcome as an example of hopeless enslavement to reality.

Yet there were other reasons besides the calculable ones that spoke in favor of action; in fact, the course of history has shown Hitler to have been right in a broader sense. For the undertaking that ended in debacle nevertheless turned out to be the decisive breakthrough on Hitler's way to power.

At the end of September, in the midst of all the hectic preparations and maneuverings for position, Hitler had staged a "German Day" in Bayreuth and used the occasion to present himself at Wahnfried, the home of the

Wagners. Deeply moved, he had gone through the rooms, sought out the Master's study, and stood a long time before the grave in the garden. Then he was introduced to Houston Stewart Chamberlain, who had married one of Richard Wagner's daughters and through his books had been a formative influence on Hitler. It was a poor sort of interview with the partially paralyzed, speechless old man; yet Chamberlain sensed the quality of the visitor. Writing to him a week later, on October 7, he lauded Hitler not as the precursor for someone greater, but as the savior himself, the key figure of the German counterrevolution. He had expected to meet a fanatic, he wrote, but now his instinct told him that Hitler was of a higher order, more creative and, despite his palpable force of will, not a man of violence. The meeting, Chamberlain added, had set his soul at rest, for "the fact that in the hour of her greatest need Germany should produce a Hitler is a sign that she is yet alive."[47]

To the demagogue at that very moment facing a crucial decision, those words came as the answer to his doubts, as a benediction from the Bayreuth Master himself.

Chapter 4

And then a voice shouted, "There
they come, Heil Hitler!"

Eyewitness account,
November 9, 1923

THE PUTSCH

The two days leading up to November 8 were filled with nervous activity.
Everyone negotiated with everyone else, Munich reverberated with warlike
preparations and rumors. The Kampfbund's original plan called for staging
a major night maneuver north of Munich on November 10; the next
morning they would march into the city, still pretending to be an ordinary
parade, and on reaching the center would proclaim the nationalist dictatorship, thus forcing Kahr, Lossow, and Seisser to commit themselves. While
consultations were still going on, it was learned that Kahr was planning to
deliver an important address on the evening of November 8 in the Bürgerbräukeller; the cabinet, Lossow, Seisser, the heads of all the government
agencies, industrial leaders and directors of the patriotic organizations were
invited. Fearing that Kahr might get the jump on him, Hitler revised all his
plans at the last moment and decided to act the following day. The SA and
the Kampfbund units were mobilized in great haste, and the stage was
set.

The meeting was to begin at 8:15 P.M. Dressed in a black dress suit,
wearing his Iron Cross, Hitler drove to the Bürgerbräukeller. Next to him
in the recently acquired red Mercedes sat Alfred Rosenberg and Ulrich
Graf, as well as the unsuspecting Anton Drexler, for whom this was to be
the last appearance with Hitler's coterie. For reasons of secrecy he had
been told that the group was driving out to the country for a meeting.
When Hitler now revealed that he was going to strike at 8:30, Drexler
replied shortly and testily that he wished Hitler luck in his undertaking but
he himself would have nothing to do with it.

A large crowd was milling about in front of the Bürgerbräukeller, so
large that Hitler feared he might be unable to storm the meeting, which was
already under way. Hitler summarily ordered the police officer on duty to
clear the area. Kahr was well into his speech, evoking the image of the

"new man" as the "moral justification for dictatorship," when Hitler appeared in the door of the beer hall. According to eyewitness accounts, he was extremely agitated. In a moment some trucks full of SA men roared up, and the troops swarmed out to cordon off the building in good warlike style. With his typical love for the theatrical gesture, Hitler held up a beer stein, and as a heavy machine gun made its appearance at his side, he took a dramatic swallow, then dashed the stein to the floor, and with a pistol in his raised hand stormed into the middle of the hall at the head of an armed squad. As steins crashed onto the floor and chairs toppled, Hitler leaped up on a table, fired his famous shot into the ceiling to catch the crowd's attention, and forced his way through the dumfounded throng to the podium. "The national revolution has begun," he cried. "The hall is surrounded by 600 heavily armed men. No one may leave the premises. Unless quiet is restored immediately, I shall have a machine gun placed in the gallery. The Bavarian government and the national government have been overthrown, and a provisional national government is being formed. The barracks of the Reichswehr and the state police have been occupied; the Reichswehr and the state police are already approaching under the swastika flag." He then told Kahr, Lossow, and Seisser "in a harsh tone of command," the account goes, to follow him into the next room. The crowd inside the hall began calming down, only spluttering now and then, "Playacting!" or "South America!" The SA, however, suppressed such remarks in its own special fashion. Meanwhile, Hitler, in a bizarre scene, attempted to win the reluctant representatives of state power over to his side.

Despite the contradictions and obscurities, the basic outlines of events are fairly plain. Gesturing wildly with his pistol, Hitler first threatened the three men that not one of them would leave the room alive, then excused himself with considerable formality for having had to create a *fait accompli* in such an unusual manner. He had only wanted to make it easier for the gentlemen to assume their new posts. To be sure, their only choice was to co-operate: Pöhner had been named the Bavarian Prime Minister with dictatorial powers; Kahr was to be state administrator; he himself was taking over the presidency of the new national government. Ludendorff was to command the national army in its march on Berlin, and Seisser had been appointed minister of police. In mounting excitement he exclaimed, "I know that you gentlemen find this step difficult, but the step must be taken. I shall have to make it easier for you to get set for the leap. Each of you must assume his allotted position; whoever fails to do so has forfeited his right to exist. You must fight with me, triumph with me—or die with me. If things go wrong I have four bullets in this pistol: three for my collaborators should they desert me, and the last bullet for myself." To emphasize his point he theatrically pressed the pistol against his forehead and swore: "If I am not victorious by tomorrow afternoon, I am a dead man."

To Hitler's astonishment his three prisoners hardly seemed impressed.

183

Kahr especially proved equal to the situation. With visible distaste for this whole melodrama, he replied, "Herr Hitler, you can have me shot, you can shoot me yourself. But whether or not I die is of no consequence to me." Seisser upbraided Hitler for having broken his word of honor. Lossow said nothing. Meanwhile, Hitler's henchmen stood at all the doors and windows and occasionally gestured menacingly with their rifles.

For a moment it seemed as though the calm indifference of the three might spell the doom of the entire operation. Meanwhile, Scheubner-Richter had dashed off in the Mercedes to fetch Ludendorff, who had not been let in on the secret. Hitler now hoped that Ludendorff, with his authority, would turn the trick. Nervous and somewhat shaken by his failure to convince Kahr and the other two, Hitler returned to the crowd, where he felt surer of himself. The historian Karl Alexander von Müller was present and has described the indignation of the prominent people in the audience at being trapped in the hall and bullied by the crude SA men. And now the leader was forcing his way through to the podium, a pretentious young man of obscure origins who seemed somewhat cracked and yet had some sort of appeal for the common man. There he stood, ludicrous in his tail coat, looking much like a waiter by contrast with the urbane, complacent notables in the audience—and in a masterly speech he turned "the mood of the meeting completely inside out . . . like a glove, with just a few words. I have seldom experienced anything of the kind. When he stepped up to the podium, the noise was so great that he could not be heard. He fired a shot. I can still see the gesture. He took the Browning out of his rear pocket. . . . He had actually come in to apologize for taking so long, for he had promised that people would be free to go in ten minutes." But no sooner was he standing before the crowd and noting how the faces all turned his way, expecting something from him, and the voices subsided, than he regained his self-confidence.

In actual fact he did not have much to tell the gathering. In a peremptory tone he simply announced what up to then had been largely his own fantasy: the new names, the new offices, and a series of proposals. "The task of the provisional German national government is to muster the entire might of this province and the additional help of all the German states for the march on that sinful Babylon, Berlin, for the German people must be saved. I will now put the question before you: out there are three men, Kahr, Lossow, and Seisser. The decision to act has cost them severe inner struggle. Are you in agreement with this solution of the German question? You can see that what guides us is not self-interest, not egotism. Rather, we wish to take up the cudgels for our German fatherland, at the eleventh hour. We want to rebuild Germany as a federation in which Bavaria shall receive her rightful due. Tomorrow morning will either find Germany with a German nationalist government—or us dead!" Hitler's persuasiveness as well as his clever trick of implying that Kahr, Lossow, and Seisser were

184

already won over created what the eyewitness calls a complete turnabout; Hitler left the hall "with the authorization of the gathering to tell Kahr that the whole assembly would stand behind him if he joined in."

In the meantime, Ludendorff had arrived, testy at Hitler's elaborate secrecy as well as at not having been consulted when posts were assigned, so that he had received only command of the army. Without preliminaries, he launched into speech, urging the three men to shake hands on the coup; he himself had also been taken by surprise, but a great historical event hung in the balance. Only now, under the personal sway of the legendary national figure did the men begin to give in, one by one. Lossow, like a good soldier, took Ludendorff's recommendation as a command; Seisser followed his lead; and only Kahr stubbornly refused. When Hitler offered Kahr, as the supreme inducement, the promise that "the people will kneel down before you," Kahr replied dryly that such a thing meant nothing to him. This little exchange between the two men points up all the difference between Hitler's hunger for stagy triumphs and the experienced politician with his sober grasp of power relationships.

But in the end Kahr yielded to the pressures from all around him and submitted. The five returned to the hall to put on a show of brotherhood. The semblance of unity was enough to fire the audience. As the spectators climbed up on chairs and applauded tumultuously, the actors shook hands. Ludendorff and Kahr appeared pale and stiff, while Hitler seemed to be "glowing with joy," as the report tells us, "blissful . . . that he had succeeded in persuading Kahr to co-operate." For a short, precious moment the thing he had long dreamed of seemed achieved. He had come so far! Here he stood, the focal point of cheers, flanked by dignitaries whose approval gave him such satisfaction after all he had suffered in Vienna. At his side stood Kahr and the other most powerful men in the country, as well as the great General Ludendorff. And he, as the national dictator designate, towered above them all—he, Hitler, the man without a profession, the failure. "It will seem like a fairy tale to later ages," he was fond of saying, amazed himself at the bold upturn in his fortunes. In fact he could rightly say that no matter how this putsch gamble turned out, he would no longer be performing on provincial stages; he had stepped out on the great national stage. With great emotion, he concluded, "Now I am going to carry out what I swore to myself five years ago today when I lay blind and crippled in the army hospital: neither to rest nor to sleep until the November criminals have been hurled to the ground, until on the ruins of the present pitiful Germany has been raised a Germany of power and greatness, of freedom and glory. Amen!" And as the crowd shouted and applauded, the others, too, had each to give a short speech. Kahr muttered a few vague phrases of allegiance to the monarchy, the Bavarian homeland, and the German fatherland. Ludendorff spoke of a turning point in history and, though still infuriated by Hitler's behavior, assured the assemblage:

"Deeply moved by the majesty of this moment and taken by surprise, I place myself of my own accord at the disposal of the German national government."

As the meeting broke up, Prime Minister von Knilling, the ministers present, and the police commissioner were arrested. The leader of the SA student company, Rudolf Hess, took charge of transferring the prisoners to the villa of the rightist publisher Julius Lehmann. Meanwhile, Hitler was called away to deal with some minor crisis outside the barracks of the engineers. As soon as he left the room, at about 10:30 P.M., Lossow, Kahr, and Seisser said comradely good-byes to Ludendorff and disappeared. When Scheubner-Richter and Hitler returned, they immediately expressed suspicion. But Ludendorff snapped that he forbade them to doubt a German officer's word of honor. Some two hours earlier, Seisser had protested that Hitler in launching the putsch had broken his word of honor. Honor was certainly a fetish with these people. They were crippled by their high principles, while Hitler, the new man, respected nothing but the pragmatics of power. For years he had been piously using these bourgeois principles and platitudes of honor, solemnly invoking rules that he despised, at the same time recognizing their erosion. This gave him a great advantage vis-à-vis a class unable to free itself from principles in which it no longer believed. But on this night Hitler had run into "opponents who answered breach of faith with breach of faith, and won the game."[48]

All the same, it was a great night for Hitler, rich in the elements he loved best: drama, cheering, defiance, the euphoria of action, and the supreme ecstasy that comes of half-realized dreams, an ecstasy that no reality can yield. In the anniversary ceremony he was to stage in later years, he would attempt to recapture the momentousness of this evening. "Now better times are coming," he said extravagantly to Röhm as he embraced him. "We shall all work day and night on the great task of rescuing Germany from shame and suffering." He issued a proclamation to the German people and two decrees establishing a special tribunal to try political crimes, and declaring "the scoundrels who engineered the betrayal of November 9, 1918," outlaws from this day: it was every citizen's duty "to deliver them dead or alive into the hands of the *völkisch* national government."

In the meantime countermeasures were already under way. Lossow had met with his officers. They greeted him with the rather menacing remark that they assumed the show of solidarity with Hitler had been sheer bluff. Whatever the vacillating general's real position may have been, in the face of his outraged officers he abandoned any thoughts he may have had of really undertaking a putsch. Shortly afterward, Kahr issued a proclamation rescinding his statements in the Bürgerbräukeller; they had been wrung from him at gunpoint, he claimed. He declared the National Socialist Party as well as the Kampfbund dissolved. Hitler, all unsuspecting and reveling

186

in his role, was mobilizing his forces for the great march on Berlin. The state commissioner general had already given orders that no Hitler followers should be allowed to enter Munich. One SA shock troop, carried away by revolutionary fervor, smashed the premises of the *Münchener Post,* the Social Democratic newspaper. Other units were rampaging, taking hostages, and looting a bit at random, while Röhm seized control of the District Army Command headquarters on Schönfeldstrasse. Once that was done, no one quite knew what to do next. A light, wet snow began to fall. Midnight came, and still Hitler had no word from Kahr and Lossow. He began to grow uneasy. Messengers were sent out but failed to return. Frick seemed to have been arrested, and somewhat later Pöhner could not be found. Hitler began to realize that he had been tricked.

As always, when he found himself blocked or disappointed, Hitler's sensitive nervous system gave way. With the collapse of this one project, all his projects collapsed. In the wee hours of the morning Streicher turned up at the Bürgerbräukeller and urged Hitler to address an impassioned appeal to the masses and thus seize the initiative again. According to Streicher's story, Hitler stared at him wide-eyed and then scrawled a statement handing "the entire organization" over to Streicher, as if he had completely given up.[49] He then went through a strange alternation of moods, first apathy, then violent despair, histrionics that anticipated the convulsions and rages of later years. Finally he let himself be persuaded to order a demonstration the following day. "If it comes off, all's well, if not, we'll hang ourselves," he declared, and this statement, too, anticipated those of later years, when he swung from one extreme to another, from total victory to downfall, from conquest of the world to suicide. However, a group he had dispatched to sound out the general mood returned with a favorable report, and Hitler instantly regained hope, exuberance, and faith in the power of agitation: "Propaganda, propaganda," he exclaimed, "now it all depends on propaganda!" He promptly slated fourteen mass meetings for the coming evening, at each of which he would appear as the principal speaker. The day after that, an enormous rally would be held on the Königsplatz, where tens of thousands would celebrate the national uprising. As dawn broke, he was giving instructions for posters to be printed for these events.

This last-ditch effort was not merely a typical Hitler reaction; it represented the only avenue still left to him. Most historians have concluded that Hitler failed as a revolutionary at the decisive moment. Such criticism, however, ignores Hitler's basic assumptions and goals.[50] True, his nerves gave way, but it would not have been consistent with his policy for him to try to occupy telegraph offices and ministries, railroad stations and barracks. He had never planned a revolutionary take-over in Munich; rather, he had intended to march against Berlin, with Munich's might behind him. His resigned attitude, after this one night, was more realistic than his critics would have us believe. For he saw that the loss of his partners rendered the entire undertaking impossible. He apparently did not hope for any turn-about as a result of the demonstration and the planned wave of propaganda; all he counted on was that a massive show of support would serve to protect the erstwhile conspirators from reprisals. Now and then, during one of the wild shifts of mood he went through that night, Hitler must have dreamed of sweeping the masses along and heading for Berlin after all, leaving Munich aside. Drunk with such visions, Hitler conceived the plan of sending patrols through the streets shouting, "Show the flag!" "Then we'll see if we don't whip up some enthusiasm!"

And in fact the prospects for a "March on Berlin" were by no means unfavorable. As became clear the next morning, public sentiment was clearly on the side of Hitler and the Kampfbund. From numerous apart-ment house windows and even from City Hall and public buildings the swastika flag fluttered, and the newspaper accounts of the events in the Bürgerbräukeller had an approving tone. Many people came to the cam-paign headquarters the Kampfbund had set up in various parts of the city, while in the barracks the lower rank officers and the enlisted men frankly expressed their sympathy with Hitler's plans for the march. The speakers whom Streicher had sent around were met with hearty applause in the strangely feverish atmosphere of that bleak November morning.

But during these hours Hitler was isolated from the public, cut off from the impetus and encouragement he might have received from the crowds. Thus, as the day wore on, he began to have second thoughts; even at this early stage in his career he appeared to be entirely dependent on the masses for increasing or diminishing his assurance, energy, and courage. Early in the morning he had sent the Kampfbund's communications director, Lieu-tenant Neunzert, to Crown Prince Rupprecht in Berchtesgaden to ask him to act as intermediary. Now he was waiting inactively for Neunzert's return. He also feared that a demonstration might lead to a clash with armed soldiers and police and thus repeat the debacle of May 1 in a far more fatal manner. Ludendorff finally put an end to Hitler's temporizing with an energetic, "We shall march!" Toward noon several thousand persons lined up behind the standard bearers. The leaders and officers were sent to the head of the line: Ludendorff appeared in civilian clothes; Hitler had thrown a trench coat over his tail coat of the previous evening. Beside him stood Ulrich Graf and Scheubner-Richter; then came Dr. Weber, Kriebel, and Göring. "We set out convinced that this was the end, one way or another," Hitler later remarked. "I remember someone who said to me as we were coming down the steps, 'this finishes it!' Everyone had that same conviction." They set out singing.

On the Isar bridge the procession was met by a strong detachment of state police, but Göring intimidated the policemen with the threat that if a single shot was fired, all the hostages would be killed instantly. As the policemen wavered, they found themselves being pushed aside by the columns of sixteen men abreast, surrounded, disarmed, spat upon, and cuffed by the crowd. In front of the Munich City Hall Streicher was just delivering a speech from the top of a staircase; the crowd was large. How grave a juncture this was for Hitler can be measured from the fact that he, to whom the masses had rushed as "to a savior," marched silently on this day. He had taken Scheubner-Richter's arm as if he needed support; this, too, was an odd gesture, scarcely according with his image of a Führer. Amidst the cheering of the crowd the procession swung haphazardly into the narrow streets of the Old City; when it neared the Residenzstrasse the lead party began to sing "O Deutschland hoch in Ehren" ("Oh, Germany high in honor"). At the Odeonsplatz the procession again encountered a police cordon.

What happened next is not exactly clear. From the confusion of accounts, some fanciful, some in the nature of apologies, agreement prevails on only one point: a single shot rang out, provoking a steady exchange of fire that lasted only about sixty seconds. The first to fall was Scheubner-Richter, fatally wounded. In his fall, he pulled Hitler with him, wrenching his arm out of joint. Oskar Körner, the former vice-chairman of the party, was hit, as was Chief Magistrate von der Pfordten. When it was all over, fourteen members of the procession and three policemen lay dead or dying on the street, and many others, including Hermann Göring, had been wounded. Amidst the hail of bullets, while all were dropping to the ground or scurrying for cover, Ludendorff stalked upright, trembling with rage, through the police cordon. The day might possibly have ended differently had a small band of determined men followed him; but no one did. It was certainly not cowardice that forced many to the ground; it was the rightists' respect for the legitimate representatives of government authority. With grandiose arrogance the general stood waiting for the commanding officer and allowed himself to be arrested. Brückner, Frick, Drexler, and Dr. Weber also submitted to arrest. Rossbach fled to Salzburg, Hermann Esser to Czechoslovakia. In the course of the afternoon Ernst Röhm also capitulated; earlier he had occupied army headquarters, after a short exchange of gunfire that had cost two members of the Kampfbund their lives. His standard bearer on this particular day was a young man with a somewhat girlish face and wearing glasses, the son of a respected Munich *gymnasium* headmaster. The young man's name was Heinrich Himmler. In a farewell march, the company paraded silently through the streets, unarmed, the men carrying their dead on their shoulders. Then it disbanded. Röhm himself was arrested.

Ludendorff's heroic bearing had cast an unflattering light on Hitler, whose nerves had again failed him. The reports of his followers are contradictory only in small details: they agree that even while the situation was still fluid, he scrambled up from the pavement and took to his heels, leaving behind him the dead and wounded. His later excuse that in the confusion he had thought Ludendorff had been killed was hardly impressive, for in that event there would have been even more reason for him to stay. In the midst of the general chaos he managed to escape with the help of an ambulance. A few years later he concocted the legend that he had carried a child out of the firing line to safety; he even produced the child. But the Ludendorff circle demolished this legend before Hitler himself abandoned it. He reached Uffing on the Staffelsee, about thirty-five miles from Munich, where he took refuge in Ernst Hanfstaengl's country house and nursed the painful sprained shoulder he had suffered in the course of the battle. Broken in spirit, he kept repeating that the time had come to put an end to things and shoot himself, but the Hanfstaengls managed to dissuade him. Two days later he was arrested and taken off to the fortress of Landsberg am Lech. "His face was pale and hunted, with a wild lock of hair falling into it." Concerned with his image even in the depths of defeat, he had the officer of the arrest party pin the Iron Cross First Class to his lapel before he was led off.

Once behind bars he remained in a state of total despondency. At first he believed "that he was going to be shot." In the following days Amann, Streicher, Dietrich Eckart, and Drexler were also brought in. Scattered about in various Munich jails were Dr. Weber, Pöhner, Dr. Frick, Röhm, and others. The government had not dared to arrest Ludendorff. Hitler himself apparently felt he was in the wrong simply because he had survived. In any case, he considered his cause lost. For a few days he considered—how seriously it is impossible to say—cheating the firing squad by starving himself to death in a hunger strike. Anton Drexler later claimed credit for talking him out of this plan. The widow of his slain friend, Frau von Scheubner-Richter, also helped him come through the depression of this period. For the shots fired in front of the Feldherrnhalle meant not only the sudden end of three years of progress that had verged on the miraculous; it also meant a terrible collision with reality. Hitler's whole system of tactics had been demolished.

Characteristically enough, he regained his spirits when it became apparent that an ordinary court trial was in the offing. He instantly saw his chance for playing a dramatic role. Later he referred to the defeat of November 9, 1923, as "perhaps the greatest stroke of luck in my life." As part of the good fortune he must have included the opportunity offered by this trial, which shook him out of his despondency and cast him in his favorite role, that of gambler. Once more he could stake everything on a single card. The disaster of the bungled putsch could be converted into a demogogic triumph.

The trial for high treason opened on February 24, 1924, in the former Infantry School on Blutenburgstrasse. Throughout the proceedings, all parties were tacitly agreed "on no account to bring up the 'central facts' of the events under discussion." The defendants were Hitler, Ludendorff, Röhm, Frick, Pöhner, Kriebel, and four other participants, while Kahr, Lossow, and Seisser appeared as witnesses. Hitler made maximum capital of this strange confrontation, which corresponded so little to the complicated alliances of the recent past. He did not want to follow the example of the perpetrators of the Kapp putsch, who had all pleaded innocent: "Thereupon every man raised his hand to swear that he had known nothing. He had had no plans and no intentions. This was what destroyed the bourgeois world: the fact that they did not have the courage to affirm their deed, to stand before the judge and say, 'Yes, this is what we did, we wanted to overthrow this state.' " Hitler, on the contrary, openly acknowledged his intentions, but rejected the charge of high treason:

I cannot declare myself guilty. True, I confess to the deed, but I do not confess to the crime of high treason. There can be no question of treason in an action which aims to undo the betrayal of this country in 1918. Besides, by no definition can the deed of November 8 and 9 be called treason; the word can at most apply to the alliances and activities of the previous weeks and months. And if we *were* committing treason, I am surprised that those who at the time had the same aims as I are not sitting beside me now. At any event, I must reject the charge until I am joined by those gentlemen who wanted the same action as we, who discussed it with us and helped prepare it down to the smallest details. I consider myself not a traitor but a German, who desired what was best for his people.[51]

None of those under attack knew how to answer these arguments. Hitler managed not only to turn the trial into a "political carnival," in the phrase of one journalist, but also to reverse the roles of accuser and accused, so that the state prosecutor found himself forced to defend the former triumvirate. The presiding judge did not seem exactly displeased at these developments. He did not object to any of the denunciations and challenges hurled at the "November criminals," and only when the applause from the audience became too stormy did he issue a mild rebuke. Even when Pöhner referred to Germany's President as "Ebert Fritze" and maintained that he was in no way bound by the laws of the Weimar Republic, the judge did not demur. As one of the Bavarian ministers stated at the cabinet meeting of March 4, the court had "never yet shown itself to be on any side but that of the defendants."[52]

Under these circumstances Kahr and Seisser soon lost hope. The former state commissioner looked fixedly before him and ascribed the responsibility for everything to Hitler. He kept falling into contradictions and did not seem to realize that he was playing into Hitler's hands. Only Lossow resisted energetically. Time and again he accused his antagonist of lying: "No matter how often Herr Hitler says so, it is not true." Speaking with the full arrogance of his class he described the Führer of the NSDAP as "tactless, limited, boring, sometimes brutal, sometimes sentimental, and unquestionably inferior." He had a psychiatrist certify that Hitler "considers himself the German Mussolini, the German Gambetta, and his following, which has inherited the Byzantine manners of the monarchy, speaks of him as the German messiah." Hitler occasionally shouted Seisser down. For this he received no "penalty for contempt of court," which, the presiding judge declared, would have only "slight practical value." Instead, he was simply asked to control himself. Even the chief prosecutor interspersed his charges with tributes to Hitler, remarking on his "unique gifts as an orator," and holding that it would be "unjust to describe him as a demagogue." Benevolently the prosecutor stated: "He has always kept his private life impeccable, something which merits particular note, given the temptations to which he, as the celebrated leader of the party, was naturally subject. . . . Hitler is a highly gifted man, who has risen from humble beginnings to achieve a respected position in public life, the result of much hard work and dedication. He has devoted himself to the ideas he cherishes, to the point of self-sacrifice. As a soldier he did his duty to the utmost. He cannot be accused of having used the position he created for himself in any self-serving way."

All of this helped Hitler turn the trial to his own purposes. Still, one should not fail to mark the boldness with which Hitler faced the proceedings, even after so recent a defeat. He assumed responsibility for the whole sorry operation and thus contrived to justify his actions in the name of higher patriotic and historic duty. Unquestionably, this was one of his "most impressive political accomplishments." In his concluding speech, which is of a piece with his self-confident tone throughout the trial, he referred to a remark by Lossow, who described him as a mad "propagandist and rabble-rouser":

In what small terms small minds think! I want you to come away from here with the clear understanding that I do not covet the post of a minister. I consider it unworthy of a great man to want to make his name go down in history by becoming a minister. . . . What I had in mind from the very first day was a thousand times more important than becoming a minister. I wanted to become the destroyer of Marxism. I shall carry through this task, and when I do, the title of minister would be utterly ridiculous. When I first stood at Wagner's grave, my heart overflowed with pride that here was a man who had forbidden his family to write on his stone, "Here lies Privy-councillor, Music Director, his Excellency Baron Richard von Wagner." I was proud that this man and so many men in German history have been content to transmit their *names* to posterity, not their titles. It was not out of modesty that I wanted to be a "drummer" [*i.e.*, rabble-rouser]; that is what counts, and everything else is a mere triviality.

The assumption being, of course, that he had every right to call himself a great man. Such unabashed self-aggrandizement did not fail to have its effect, and made Hitler from the very outset the central figure of the trial. True, the official transcript followed the "proper" order of rank to the bitter end, listing Ludendorff before Hitler; but the desire of all parties to avert any blame from the distinguished general again redounded to Hitler's advantage. He was quick to recognize this. With his claim to sole responsibility he thrust himself past Ludendorff into the vacant position of leader of the entire *völkisch* movement. And as the trial went on, he managed to wipe out the desperado character of the undertaking. Similarly, he was unable to gloss over his own passive and confused behavior on the morning of the demonstration. More and more the events took on the semblance of a cleverly planned and daringly executed masterstroke. "The operation of November 8 did not fail," he told the court, thus laying the ground for the future legend. As he came to the end of his statement, he prophesied his ultimate victory in politics and history in visionary terms:

The army we have trained is growing from day to day, from hour to hour. At this very time I hold to the proud hope that the hour will come when these wild bands will be formed into battalions, the battalions into regiments, the regiments into divisions, that the old cockade will be rescued from the mud, that the old banners will wave on ahead, that reconciliation will be achieved before the eternal judgment seat of God which we are ready to face. Then from our bones and our graves will speak the voice of that court which alone is empowered to sit in judgment upon us all. For not you, gentlemen, will deliver judgment on us; that judgment will be pronounced by the eternal court of history, which will arbitrate the charge that has been made against us. I already know what verdict you will hand down. But that other court will not ask us: did you or did you not commit high treason? That court will judge us, will judge the Quartermaster-general of the former army, will judge his officers and soldiers, as Germans who wanted the best for their people and their Fatherland, who were willing to fight and to die. May you declare us guilty a thousand times; the goddess of the Eternal Court will smile and gently tear in two the brief of the State Prosecutor and the verdict of the court; for she acquits us.

The verdict handed down by the Munich Volksgericht was not so far removed from the verdict of "the eternal court of history" that Hitler had invoked. The presiding judge had a hard time cajoling the three lay judges into passing any guilty verdict at all; he had to assure them that Hitler would certainly be pardoned before serving his full sentence. The reading of the verdict was a real event for Munich society. The courtroom was crowded with spectators ready to applaud this troublemaker with so many friends in high places. The verdict once more laid stress on the "pure patriotic motives and honorable intentions" of the defendant, but sentenced him to a minimum of five years in prison. However, he would become eligible for parole after six months. Ludendorff was acquitted. The law called for the deportation of any troublesome foreigner, but the court decided to waive this in the case of a man "who thinks and feels in such German terms as Hitler." This decision called forth a storm of approving

193

bravos from the audience. When the judges had filed out, Brückner raised the cry: "It's up to us now!" Hitler appeared at a window of the court building to show himself to the cheering crowd. Bouquets of flowers were piling up in the room behind him. The state had once again lost the match.

Nevertheless, it seemed as though Hitler's period of ascent was over. To be sure, immediately after November 9, there had been mass demonstrations in Munich in his favor. The elections to the Bavarian Landtag as well as to the Reichstag brought sizable gains for the *völkisch* forces. Yet the party, or the front that had taken its place after it was banned, began to show the effects of Hitler's absence. It would seem that only his personal magic and Machiavellian gifts held it together. It broke down into jealous, bitterly hostile factions of little significance. Drexler was already accusing Hitler of "destroying the party for good with his insane putsch." The party had drawn its strength principally from general discontent; toward the end of 1923 this element was in somewhat shorter supply. Conditions in the country began to stabilize. The inflation was overcome, and the "happy years" of the so far ill-fated republic commenced. The events of November 9, though local in character, in a way represented the turning point in the larger drama of the Weimar Republic; they marked the end of the postwar period. The shots fired in front of the Feldherrnhalle seemed to introduce a new sobriety and draw the gaze of the nation away from dreams and delusions and back to reality.

For Hitler himself and the history of his party the debacle also proved a turning point, for the tactical and personal lessons he drew from it were to guide his entire future course. Later on, he would stage a memorial procession year after year, marching to the Königsplatz, where he called on the victims of that grim November day to rise from their bronze caskets and come to the last reveille. This may be explained not merely in terms of his love for theater, his penchant for turning historical event into political spectacle. It may also be seen as the act of a successful politician paying tribute to one of his most instructive experiences, indeed to "perhaps the greatest stroke of good luck" in his life, the "real birthday" of the party. For the first time the name of Hitler reached far beyond the boundaries of Bavaria. The party acquired martyrs, a legend, the romantic aura of persecuted loyalty, and the nimbus of stern resolve. "Let there be no mistake about it," Hitler would stress in a later memorial address, "had we not acted then, I would never have been able . . . to found a revolutionary movement. People would have justifiably told me: you talk like all the others and you act as little as they."

At the same time, Hitler's dropping to the ground before the guns of the police at the Feldherrnhalle had clarified once and for all his relationship to government. The events of November 23 taught him that it was hopeless to attempt to conquer a modern state by violent means. His struggle for power would succeed only if he based it on the Constitution, he concluded.

Of course, this did not mean any real deference to the Constitution on Hitler's part; rather, it meant cloaking his illegal acts in the guise of legality. In subsequent years he left no doubt that all his protestations of loyalty to the Constitution were valid only for this interim period; he spoke openly of the time of reckoning that would follow. As early as September 24, 1923, Scheubner-Richter had stated in a memorandum: "The nationalist revolution must not precede the acquisition of political power; rather, control over the nation's police constitutes the prerequisite to the nationalist revolution." Hitler transformed himself into a man of strict law and order. Thus he won the good opinion of dignitaries and powerful institutions, and veiled his revolutionary intentions with untiring protestations of how well he was determined to behave and how dearly he cherished tradition. He muted his earlier aggressive tone, only now and then dropping into it for the shock effect. For he purported to seek not the defeat but the co-operation of the state. This pose deceived many observers and interpreters, and continued to deceive them. "Adolphe Légalité," as some of his witty contemporaries dubbed him, could well be taken for a boring, reactionary petty bourgeois.

Hitler's new strategy called for a changed relationship to the Reichswehr. He attributed his defeat on November 9 in no small part to his inability to win over the leaders of the army and the police. In his concluding words before the Munich court he already intimates the goal of his future tactics: "The hour will come," he cried to the courtroom, "when the Reichswehr will be on our side." With this goal in mind, he firmly consigned his own party army to a secondary role. But at the same time he freed his storm troops from their dependency on the army; the SA was to be neither a part nor a rival of the Reichswehr.

Hitler emerged from the defeat at the Feldherrnhalle, therefore, with a good deal more than a clearly formulated tactical recipe. His relationship to politics in general had changed. Up to this time he had distinguished himself by his categorical refusal to compromise, by his radical alternatives. He had behaved "like a force of nature," had thought of politics— drawing his model from the battle fronts—as storming the enemy positions, breaking through the lines, fighting at close quarters, and coming out in the end either victorious or dead. Only now did Hitler seem to grasp the meaning and the opportunities of the political game, the tactical dodges, the sham compromises and maneuvers by which one played for time. Only now did he progress beyond his emotionally overcharged, naïvely demagogic, "artistic" relationship to politics. The image of the agitator carried away by events and by his own impulsive reactions was replaced by that of the cool and methodical technician of power. The unsuccessful putsch of November 9 marks an important caesura: it concludes Hitler's political apprenticeship. In fact, strictly speaking, it marks Hitler's first real entry into politics.

Hans Frank, Hitler's lawyer, and later governor of Poland, remarked at the Nuremberg trials that Hitler's "entire historical life," the "substance of his whole personality" were revealed in the course of the November putsch. The most striking qualities are the jumble of contradictory states of mind and the whipping up of his own emotions, which are so in character with the hysterical daydreaming and egotistic fantasies of the adolescent city planner, composer, and inventor—as are the sudden collapse, the desperate gambler's grandiose gesture of abdication, the headlong plunge into apathy. In September he had told his entourage: "Do you know Roman history? I am Marius and Kahr is Sulla; I am the leader of the people, but he represents the ruling class. This time, however, Marius will win." But with the first signs of difficulty he had dropped everything. He was not the man of action but its herald. He could set himself great tasks, that was clear, but his nerves were not equal to his lust for action. He had predicted a "battle of the Titans" and then disgracefully taken to his heels, "not wanting to have anything more to do with this mendacious world," as he explained in court. He had once more played for highest stakes—and lost.

Yet he saved himself through rhetoric. His version of the incident revealed how little he understood reality and how well he understood how to present reality, color it, mold it to his propagandistic purposes. The elements of the gambler and the knight-errant were always present, as well as his propensity for the hopeless situation, the lost cause. In every critical juncture during 1923 Hitler had shown a pathological tendency not to leave himself any tactical options. He seemed always to be seeking out a wall to have at his back. He was always doubling his stakes, which were already too high for him. One might well consider this a suicidal mentality. Then again, he would always pour scorn on other politicians who tried to follow a prudent course, calling them "political Tom Thumbs." He had nothing but contempt for those who "never expose themselves to extreme strain." Bismarck's description of politics as the art of the possible Hitler considered "a cheap excuse." We can see a consistency, too, in the fact that from 1905 on he repeatedly threatened to take his own life. But he kept postponing the act until the very last moment, until the alternatives of world power or downfall ceased to exist, and nothing remained but a sofa in the shelter under the Berlin chancellery. Certainly much of his behavior continued to seem overwrought and verged on grandiose farce. But are we only projecting from later experience when we see the high-strung actor of that early phase already surrounded by an aura of catastrophe?

On that ambiguous noon of November 9, 1923, when the procession of demonstrators neared the Odeonsplatz, a passer-by had asked whether the man at the head of the marching column was "really that fellow from the street corner." Now "that fellow" had entered history.

BOOK III

The Long Wait

Chapter 1

They had better realize that we see events
in terms of a historical vision.

Adolf Hitler

THE VISION

The laurel wreath Hitler hung on his wall in the Landsberg fortress-prison
was more than a token that his spirit was unbroken. The forced isolation
from political activity was of benefit to him politically and personally. For
one thing, it permitted him to escape the aftermath of the disaster of
November 9. He could follow the wrangles of his embittered and scattered
adherents from the sidelines, while remaining the untarnished martyr of the
nationalist cause. It also gave him time for introspection after years of
almost mindless unrest and excitement. He recovered his faith in himself
and in his mission. And, as his turbulent emotions died down, he felt
himself strengthened in his role as leader of the *völkisch* right wing. He had
at first claimed this role hesitantly, but in the course of the trial he became
more confident, and finally he boldly came forth as the divinely appointed
one and only Führer. Filled with this consciousness, Hitler managed to
impress this image of himself upon his fellow prisoners. From this time on,
the sense of mission never left him. It froze his features in that mask which
no smile, no altruistic gesture, no moment of spontaneity ever softened.
Even before the November putsch Dietrich Eckart had complained of
Hitler's delusions of grandeur, his "messiah complex." Now Hitler hardened more and more into the monument that corresponded to his notions
of what a great man and a Führer would be like.

Thus his imprisonment in no way hampered the process of self-styliza-
tion. In a subsequent trial some forty more participants in the putsch were
convicted and sent to Landsberg. They included members of the "Hitler
shock troop," Berchtold, Haug, Maurice, Amann, Hess, Heines, Schreck,
and the student Walter Hewel. Hitler now had what amounted to an
entourage. The prison authorities were highly accommodating to the
special requirements of their prisoner. When he took his meals in the large
common room, at a special table with his followers, he was allowed to sit
at the head of the table under a swastika banner. Fellow prisoners were

assigned the task of cleaning and tidying his room. He himself was not required to participate in the work program or the prison athletics. It was taken for granted that his followers, on arrival at the prison, were to "report to the Führer without delay." Every morning at ten o'clock, moreover, they came in for the daily "conference with the Chief." Hitler devoted much of his time to his extensive correspondence. One adulatory letter he received came from a recent Ph.D. in philology named Joseph Goebbels, who commented on Hitler's closing address at the trial: "What you stated there is the catechism of a new political creed coming to birth in the midst of a collapsing, secularized world. . . . To you a god has given the tongue with which to express our sufferings.* You formulated our agony in words that promise salvation." He also received a letter from Houston Stewart Chamberlain.

Hitler often took walks in the fortress garden. He was still having his old trouble arriving at a consistent style, for he combined his airs of a Caesar with *Lederhosen,* a Bavarian peasant jacket, and often a hat. When he spoke at the so-called comradeship evenings, we are told, "all the officials of the fortress gathered silently in the stairwell outside and listened." As if wound up by his defeat, he continued to elaborate his legends and visions and to work out practical plans for the state, whose dictator he still expected to be. Supposedly the idea for the building of the autobahns and the creation of the Volkswagen dated from this period. Although visiting hours were officially restricted to six hours weekly, Hitler received visitors for up to six hours a day—adherents, petitioners, and friendly politicians, all of whom made the pilgrimage to Landsberg. The visitors included many women, for which reason the prison had been jokingly referred to as the "first Brown House."[1] On Hitler's thirty-fifth birthday, with the trial not far behind him, the flowers and packages for the famous prisoner filled several rooms.

But principally he used his time for taking stock. He attempted to give some rational form to his jumble of emotions and to combine all the scattered pieces of earlier readings and half-baked ideas with his most recent literary gleanings into an organized ideological system. "This period gave me a chance to obtain clarity on certain concepts which I had previously understood only instinctively."[2]

We know about Hitler's reading matter only through what others have reported, for he himself very seldom spoke of books or favorite writers; like so many self-educated people, he was afraid of being considered derivative in his ideas. The only writer he mentioned fairly often and in various connections was Schopenhauer, whose works he claimed to have taken to the front with him, and from whom he could quote longish passages. He also referred to Nietzsche, Schiller, and Lessing. In an autobiographical sketch written in 1921 he maintains that in his youth he

---

* A famous quotation from Goethe's *Torquato Tasso.*—TRANS.

"thoroughly studied economic theory, as well as the entire anti-Semitic literature available at the time," and he comments: "From my twenty-second year on, I threw myself with special eagerness upon writings on military and political matters, and I never ceased my probing preoccupation with general world history." Yet he does not name a specific work in these fields. It was part of his character always to try to create the impression that he had mastered whole areas of knowledge. Similarly, he goes on to speak of his deep study of art history, cultural history, the history of architecture, and "political problems." Yet it seems all too probable that up to the time of his imprisonment Hitler had acquired his knowledge of those areas only from second- or third-hand digests. Hans Frank mentions Hitler's reading Nietzsche, Chamberlain, Ranke, Treitschke, Marx, and Bismarck, as well as war memoirs of German and Allied statesmen—all this during the period in Landsberg. Yet he went on extracting the elements of his world view from pseudoscientific secondary works: tracts on race theory, anti-Semitic pamphlets, treatises on the Teutons, on racial mysticism and eugenics, as well as popular treatments of Darwinism and the philosophy of history.

In all that various witnesses have said about Hitler's reading, the one detail that rings true is the description of his intensity, his hunger for material. Kubizek reports that back in Linz the young Hitler had cards at three separate libraries and never appeared before his mind's eye other than surrounded by books. Indeed, Hitler's vocabulary reflects extensive reading. Yet his speeches and writings, right up to the table talk, as well as the memoirs of his entourage, show him to have been remarkably indifferent to intellectual and literary questions; in the good 200 monologues that make up his table talk, the names of two or three German classics turn up casually; *Mein Kampf* refers to Goethe and to Schopenhauer only once, and that in a somewhat tasteless anti-Semitic connection. In actual fact, knowledge meant nothing to Hitler; he was not acquainted with the pleasure or the struggle that go with its acquisition; to him it was merely useful, and the "art of correct reading" of which he spoke was nothing more than the hunt for formulations to borrow and authorities to cite in support of his own preconceptions: "correctly coordinated within the somehow existing picture."[3]

At the beginning of July Hitler plunged into the writing of *Mein Kampf* in the same immoderate spirit he had shown in his reading. He finished the first part in three and a half months. He later commented that he had had "to write in order to get everything off my chest." "The typewriter rattled late into the night, and he could be heard in his little room dictating to his friend Hess. On Saturday evenings he usually read . . . the finished passages to his fellow prisoners, who sat around him like disciples." The book was originally conceived as an account and evaluation of "four and

201

one half years of struggle." But it more and more developed into a mixture of autobiography, ideological tract, and theory of tactics; it also helped complete the Führer legend. In Hitler's mythologizing self-portrait, the unhappy and vacant years before his entrance into politics are boldly filled out with elements of want, asceticism, and solitude to represent a phase of inner growth and preparation, a sojourn, so to speak, in the desert. Max Amann, the book's publisher, had apparently expected a memoir of quite another sort, full of political revelations. He was at first terribly disappointed by the stiff, long-winded, and boring manuscript.

Konrad Heiden, Hitler's biographer, believed that Hitler had made a pact with the authorities not to divulge too much about the recent conspiracy. That may or may not be so. But in any case, it seems certain that Hitler's ambition aimed higher than the kind of recital that Amann envisaged. Hitler saw his chance to give a deeper rationale to his recently developed claim to leadership and to show himself as that compound of politician and theoretician that he had invoked as the only possible savior for the country. Here, in an inconspicuous spot midway in the first part, is a passage that reveals his true aims:

For if the art of the politician is really the art of the possible, the theoretician is one of those of whom it can be said that they are pleasing to the gods only if they demand and want the impossible. . . . In long periods of humanity, it may happen once that the politician is wedded to the theoretician. The more profound this fusion, however, the greater are the obstacles opposing the work of the politician. He no longer works for necessities which will be understood by any shopkeeper, but for aims which only the fewest comprehend. Therefore, his life is torn by love and hate. . . .

The rarer [is] success. If, however, once in centuries success does come to a man, perhaps in his latter days a faint beam of his coming glory may shine upon him. To be sure, these great men are only the Marathon runners of history; the laurel wreath of the present touches only the brow of the dying hero.[4]

The book constantly reinforces the insinuation that Hitler is in fact this prodigy. The image of the dying hero can be construed as an attempt to give a cast of tragic nobility to the recent defeats. Hitler went at the job with an application that was rare for him. Here was his chance to prove that despite his lack of schooling, despite his failure to be admitted to the Academy, despite his humiliating past in the home for men, he had reached the lofty heights of bourgeois culture. It may have seemed that he was doing nothing, but all through the years he had thought long and hard and could offer not only an interpretation of the present but also an outline for the future. Such were the pretensions that went into the making of *Mein Kampf*.

Behind the front of bold words lurks the anxiety of the half-educated author that his readers may question his intellectual competence. He tries to make his language imposing by stringing together long series of nouns, many of them formed from adjectives or verbs, so that they sound empty and artificial. Taken as a whole, it is a language that lacks all natural ease; it can scarcely move or breathe:

I again immersed myself in the theoretical literature of this new world, attempting to achieve clarity concerning its possible effects, and then compared it with the actual phenomena and events it brings about in political, cultural and economic life. . . . Gradually I obtained a positively granite foundation for my own convictions, so that since that time I have never been forced to undertake a shift in my own inner view on this question.*[5]

Several of Hitler's followers put in long hard hours editing the book, but they could not weed out the stylistic slips and infelicities that were part and parcel of Hitler's verbose, pseudoeducated manner. Thus we find the text studded with such phrases as "the rats that politically poison our nation" gnawing the meager education "from the heart and memory of the broad masses," or "the flag of the Reich" springing "from the womb of war." Rudolf Olden has pointed out the numerous absurdities of Hitler's over-wrought style. The following, for instance, is a typical Hitlerian metaphor. He is speaking of privation: "He who has not himself been gripped in the clutches of this strangulating viper will never come to know its poisoned fangs." Olden comments: "That one sentence contains more mistakes than one could correct in an entire essay. A viper has no clutches, and a snake which can coil itself around a human being has no poison fangs. Moreover, if a person is strangled by a snake, he never comes to know its fangs."[6]

Yet, along with all the pretentious and disordered thoughts, the book contains some deep insights, born directly of Hitler's profound irrationality, as well as many sharp formulations and striking images. Hitler's stiffness and doggedness make a strange contrast with his longing for the flowing period, as does his search for stylization with his lack of self-control. His attempts at logic are at variance with his dull repetitiousness, and the one element in the book that nothing counteracts is the monotonous, manic egocentricity. This corresponds only too well with the lack of human feeling and human beings in its many pages. The book may be tedious and hard to read. Yet it does convey a remarkably faithful portrait of its author, who in his constant fear of being unmasked actually unmasks himself.

* The original German even more drastically illustrates the point: "Indem ich neuerdings mich in die theoretische Literatur dieser neuen Welt vertiefte und mir deren mögliche Auswirkungen klarzumachen versuchte, verglich ich diese dann mit den tatsächlichen Erscheinungen und Ereignissen ihrer Wirksamkeit im politischen, kulturellen und wirtschaftlichen Leben . . . Allmählich erhielt ich dann eine für meine eigene Überzeugung allerdings geradezu granitene Grundlage, so dass ich seit dieser Zeit eine Umstellung meiner inneren Anschauung in dieser Frage niemals mehr vorzunehmen gezwungen wurde."

Probably realizing that the book betrayed him, Hitler later tried to disassociate himself from it, describing it as a stylistically unfortunate collection of editorials for the *Völkische Beobachter* and dismissing it as "fantasies behind bars." "This much I know, that if I had suspected in 1924 that I was to become Reichskanzler, I would not have written the book." But at the same time he implied that his reservations were purely tactical or stylistic in nature: "As to the substance, there is nothing I would want to change."

The book's convoluted style militated against it; the almost 10 million copies ultimately distributed suffered the same fate as all works bought out of duty or to show political orthodoxy. It remained unread. Another discouraging element may have been the grim, compulsive quality of Hitler's mind. As a speaker, amidst the fanfare of carefully prepared appearances, Hitler was apparently able to cover this up. But a curiously nasty, obscene odor emanates from the pages of *Mein Kampf*. It is strongest in the incredible and revealing chapter on syphilis, but it also rises out of the grubby jargon, the stale images, and the poor-mouth attitudes that represent his stylistic stance. The mixed-up young man, who throughout the war and the frenzied activity of the following years never managed to find more than motherly woman friends, and who, according to someone close to him, "was terrified of even chatting with a woman," projects his own starvations and repressions onto the world. Stamped on his concepts of history, politics, nature, or human life, are the anxieties and lusts of the former inmate of the home for men. He is haunted by the images of puberty: copulation, sodomy, perversion, rape, contamination of the blood.

The final Jewish goal is denationalization, is sowing confusion by the bastardization of other nations, lowering the racial level of the highest, and dominating this racial stew by exterminating the folkish intelligentsias and replacing them by members of his own race. . . . Just as he himself [the Jew] systematically ruins women and girls, he does not shrink back from pulling down the blood barriers for others, even on a large scale. It was and is Jews who bring the Negroes into the Rhineland, always with the same secret thought and clear aim of ruining the hated white race by the necessarily resulting bastardization of other nations, lowering the racial level of the highest, and himself rising to be its master. . . . If physical beauty were today not forced entirely into the background by our foppish fashions, the seduction of hundreds of thousands of girls by bow-legged, repulsive Jewish bastards would not be possible. . . . Systematically these black parasites of the nation defile our inexperienced young blond girls and thereby destroy something which can no longer be replaced in this world. . . . The folkish ideology must at last succeed in bringing about that nobler age in which men will no longer see it as their concern to breed superior dogs, horses and cats, but in the raising of man himself. . . .[7]

The book's peculiarly neurotic aura, its queerness, its fragmentary and disorganized quality, help account for the disdain so long accorded to the doctrines of National Socialists. "No one took it seriously, could take it seriously, or even understand this style at all," wrote Hermann Rauschning.* He asserted, on the basis of his intimate background knowledge: "Hitler's real goals . . . are not to be found in *Mein Kampf*."[8] With a good deal of persuasive brilliance Rauschning formulated a theory that widely influenced later historians, the theory that National Socialism was a "Revolution of Nihilism." Rauschning maintained that Hitler and the movements he led had no ideas, no systematic ideology; the Nazis merely exploited existing moods and trends that would help to swell their membership rolls. A joke current in the 1930's made a similar point: National Socialist ideology was referred to as "the World as Will without Idea."† Rauschning felt that all the tenets of Nazism, nationalism, anticapitalism, the cult of ritual, foreign-policy goals, even racial theory and anti-Semitism were the sport of Hitler's completely unprincipled opportunism. Hitler the opportunist, Rauschning argues, respected nothing, feared nothing, believed in nothing, and broke the most solemn oaths with never a qualm. To Rauschning, the perfidy of National Socialism was literally boundless. All its ideology was merely sound and fury to mesmerize the masses. Central to it was a will to power that craved for nothing but power itself and regarded every success merely as a step to new and ever bolder adventures—without meaning, without goals, without the possibility of satisfaction. "This movement is totally without ideals and lacks even the semblance of a program. Its commitment is entirely to action; its crack troops are instinctively geared for mindless action; the leaders choose action on a cold, calculating and cunning basis. For National Socialists there was and is no aim which they would not take up or drop at a moment's notice, their only criterion being the strengthening of the movement."

Rauschning was right in recognizing that as a movement National Socialism always manifested a great willingness to adapt and that Hitler himself was remarkably indifferent to programmatic and ideological issues. He admitted that he adhered to his twenty-five points, even when they were obsolete, only for tactical reasons. Any change, he had observed, breeds confusion in the popular mind, and it really did not matter what one's program was supposed to be. Of Alfred Rosenberg's magnum opus *The Myth of the Twentieth Century*, widely considered one of the basic works of National Socialism, he openly stated that he had "read only a small part of it since it is . . . written in a style too hard to understand." But even if National Socialism did not develop a true party line and was content to accept certain gestures and formulas as sufficient proof of orthodoxy, it was not entirely ruled by cynical considerations of success and power.

* President of the Danzig Senate 1933–34. A former Nazi, Rauschning fled to England and then to the United States in 1940, where he later became a naturalized citizen. He wrote extensively about Germany and Nazism.

† An allusion to Schopenhauer's *The World as Will and Idea.*—TRANS.

National Socialism combined the practice of total control with the doctrine thereof; the two elements were continually intertwined, and even as Hitler and his cohorts confessed on occasion to the simplest and most unscrupulous power mania, they always revealed themselves the prisoners of their own prejudices and baleful utopias. Hitler's astonishing career can be seen as the triumph of his tactical genius. Time and again he owed his salvation to some inspired tactical move. Yet his success in a deeper sense emanated from the entire complex of national anxieties, hopes, and visions that Hitler shared, even as he manipulated it. Nor can we overlook the compelling force he managed to impart to his thoughts on certain basic questions of history and politics, power and human existence.

Inadequate and clumsy *Mein Kampf* may have been. But it set forth, although in fragmentary and unorganized form, all the elements of National Socialist ideology. Here Hitler spelled out his aims, although his contemporaries failed to recognize them. As one begins to arrange the scattered sections and grasp their inner logic, one comes upon "a scheme of thought so consistent as to take one's breath away." In the following years Hitler did tinker somewhat with the text, rounding it off and making it more systematic, but on the whole the book evolved no further after his imprisonment at Landsberg. The phenomenon of early ossification, which stamps so much of this man's life, is nowhere so evident as in the field of ideology, where ideas espoused in youth persist, down to their very phraseology, throughout the rise to power and the years of dictatorship, and even when the end is in sight retain their crippling hold. Nationalism, anti-Bolshevism, and anti-Semitism, linked by a Darwinistic theory of struggle, formed the pillars of his world view and shaped his utterances from the very first to the very last.

Hitler's world view did not contain any new vistas or a new concept of social well-being. Rather, it was a synthesis of all that Hitler's "spongelike memory" had soaked up in his early years of voracious reading. The material appears, however, in startling permutations and relationships. Hitler's originality manifested itself precisely in his ability to force heterogeneous elements together and to impose solidity and structure on the patchwork creed. His mind, one might say, hardly produced thoughts, but it did produce energy. It concentrated and shaped the variegated ideas, pressing them into a glacial mass that from the very beginning clearly portended conquest, enslavement, mass murder. Hugh Trevor-Roper has described the cold insanity of this world in a telling image: "imposing indeed in its granite harshness and yet infinitely squalid with miscellaneous cumber—like some huge barbarian monolith, the expression of giant strength and savage genius, surrounded by a festering heap of refuse—old tins and dead vermin, ashes and eggshells and ordure,—the intellectual *detritus* of centuries."[9]

Of special significance was Hitler's way of perceiving everything from the angle of power. In contrast to the spokesmen of the *völkisch* movement, whose failure was in no small part due to their love for ideological subtleties, Hitler regarded ideas in themselves as "mere theory" and only took up those that lent themselves to useful practical application. When he spoke of "thinking in party terms," he was describing his own habit of casting all ideas, trends, and beliefs into a form that fitted the needs of power, and was political in the true sense.

In fact he was formulating a last-ditch ideology for a bourgeoisie long on the defensive; he took its beliefs, diluted and coarsened them, and overlaid them with an aggressive and purposeful theory of action. His philosophy was a compound of all the nightmares and intellectual fads of the bourgeois age: the fear of revolution from the Left, a threat that had haunted Europe since 1789 and had actually been realized recently in Russia and, briefly, in Germany. Then there was the German Austrian's psychosis about being overrun by foreigners; this emerged as an obsession with racial and biological questions. Then came the fear of the *völkisch* group, expressed in any number of ways, that awkward, dreamy Germany would be the loser in the contest of nations; this emerged as nationalist feeling. And finally there was the historical angst of the bourgeoisie who felt their period of greatness coming to an end and whose sense of security was eroding. "Nothing is anchored any longer," Hitler declaimed. "Nothing is rooted within us any longer. Everything is superficial, flies away from us. The thinking of our people is becoming restless and hasty. All of life is being torn asunder. . . ."[10]

Hitler himself had soaked up this basic mood of angst, and with his disposition to drive things to extremes, to see periods in terms of eons, he felt that the fate of mankind was at stake. "This world is at an end!" He was obsessed by the notion of a world-wide disease, by viruses, termites, and the tumors of humanity. He later turned to Hörbiger's world ice theory, which held that fire and ice had always struggled for supremacy in the universe, and his imagination was caught by the idea that the history of the planet and the evolution of man could be traced back to massive cosmic cataclysms. With deep fascination he anticipated the fall of nations and civilizations, and this cataclysmic view of history came to be coupled with his belief in messianic figures and his sense of his own great destiny. Students of the period have marveled at the determination with which he pursued his program for destroying the Jews right up to the last possible moment during the war, without regard for military necessities. This determination cannot be explained as mere obstinacy. Rather, Hitler was convinced that he was in the midst of a titanic struggle whose importance outweighed any events of the moment. He felt himself to be that "other force" which hurls evil "back to Lucifer" in order to save the universe.[11]

The concept of a cosmic struggle runs all through *Mein Kampf.* How-

ever absurd or fantastical this may appear in retrospect, we cannot deny
the metaphysical earnestness of Hitler's thinking. "We may perish, perhaps. But we shall take a world with us. Muspilli, universal conflagration,"
he once said in one of his apocalyptic moods. There are many passages in
Mein Kampf that soar into universal dimensions. "The Jewish doctrine of
Marxism," he asserts, ". . . as a foundation of the universe . . . would
bring about the end of any order intellectually conceivable to man." The
very illogic of such a thesis, which raises an ideology to the level of a
principle of order in the universe, demonstrates Hitler's urge to think in
cosmic terms. It was necessary for "the stars," "the planets," "the world
ether," and the "light years" to take part in his personal struggle, for which
"creation," the "planet Earth," and the "Kingdom of Heaven" served as
backdrop.

These terms could readily be combined with the principle of the struggle
for life and of the survival of the fittest, resulting in a sort of eschatological
Darwinism. "The earth," Hitler was fond of saying, "is like a chalice
passed from hand to hand, which explains the efforts to always get it into
the hand of the strongest. For tens of thousands of years . . ." He discerned a sort of fundamental law of the universe in the perpetual and
deadly conflict of all against all:

Nature . . . puts living creatures on this globe and watches the free play of
forces. She then confers the master's right on her favorite child, the strongest in
courage and industry. . . . Only the born weakling can view this as cruel, but
he after all is only a weak and limited man; for if this law did not prevail, any
conceivable higher development of organic living beings would be unthinkable.
. . . In the end, only the urge for self-preservation can conquer. Beneath it so-
called humanity, the expression of a mixture of stupidity, cowardice, and know-
it-all conceit, will melt like snow in the March sun. Mankind has grown great in
eternal struggle, and only in eternal peace does it perish.

This "iron law of nature" represented the beginning and end of all his
lucubrations. From it he drew such lessons as that "all imaginable means"
were permissible in the struggle for survival of nations: "persuasion,
cunning, cleverness, persistence, kindness, wiliness, and brutality," or that
there was basically no contradiction between war and politics, rather that
"the ultimate goal of politics" was war. The idea of such an iron law
pervades Hitler's concepts of justice and morality, which he tried to pattern
on what happened in nature. It also underlies his belief in the Führer
principle as well as his concern with nationalistic and openly bellicose
racial selection. He boasted of his intention of marching over Europe in
great "blood-based fishing expeditions" to help blond, pale-skinned human
material "spread its blood" and thereby win dominance. Within this
philosophy of total struggle, obedience ranked far higher than intelligence,
readiness for action far higher than insight, while fanatical blindness
became the highest virtue. "Woe unto him who lacks faith!" Hitler some-

times cried. Even marriage was seen as a union for purposes of self-perpetuation, while the home was defined as a "fortress from which the battle of life is waged." Using rough analogies between the animal world and human society, Hitler pronounced the superiority of the ruthless over delicately structured organisms, of strength over mind. The apes, he claimed, trampled every outsider to death as an enemy of the community, "and what was right for apes must be even more applicable to men. . . ."[12]

One might suspect a trace of irony in such statements, but that is belied by the earnest tone of conviction with which Hitler cites the eating habits of apes as confirmation of his own vegetarianism; the apes showed the way. And, he continued, a glance at nature reveals that the bicycle, for instance, is correctly conceived, whereas the airship is "totally insane." Man has no choice but to look to the laws of nature and follow them; there can be "no better system" than the merciless principles of selection prevailing among wild animals. Nature is not immoral: "Who is at fault when the cat eats the mouse?" he asks scornfully. Man's so-called humanity is only "a tool of his weakness and thus in actuality the most cruel destroyer of his existence." Struggle, conquest, destruction are immutable. "One being drinks the blood of another. By dying, the one furnishes food for the other. We should not blather about humanity."

Hitler's complete blindness to the rights of others and others' claim to happiness, his utter amorality, are nowhere revealed so clearly as in this "unconditional reverence for the . . . divine laws of existence." There is surely an element of late-bourgeois ideology here, which tried to compensate for the decadence and feebleness of the age by glorifying mindlessness and equating brutality and primitiveness with the natural and primeval state of things. It would also seem that such a creed provided Hitler with a lofty justification for his personal coldness and lack of feeling. He could better deal with his aggressive impulses by converting struggle, murder, and "blood sacrifice" into acts of obedience to a divine command. "By defending myself against the Jew, I am fighting for the work of the Lord," he wrote in *Mein Kampf,* and almost twenty years later, in the midst of war and extermination, he asserted with considerable complacency: "I have always had a clear conscience."

War and destruction were essential to restore the shaky balance of the world: that was the morality and the metaphysics of his policies. Pursuing his favorite game of letting the epochs of history unreel before his eyes in broad vague outline, mulling over the reasons for the decline of peoples and cultures, he always discovered the cause of their downfall in their failure to obey their instincts. The crumbling of mighty systems of power could be traced to a flouting of Nature, especially to miscegenation. For although all creatures adhere strictly to the instinct for racial purity, and the "titmouse seeks the titmouse, the finch the finch, the stork the stork, the field mouse the field mouse," man is prone to act contrary to the laws of nature and to commit biological adultery. Impotence and the death of nations from old age were simply the revenge taken by Nature for the denial of her primal order: "Blood mixture and the resultant drop in the racial level is the sole cause of the dying out of old cultures; for men do not perish as a result of lost wars, but by the loss of that force of resistance which is contained only in pure blood. All who are not of good race in this world are chaff."[13]

Behind this stood the doctrine of creative racial nuclei: since primeval times small Aryan elites have prevailed over the dull, slumbering masses of historyless inferior peoples, using them to further those abilities that are the mark of the Aryan genius. Aryans are the Promethean bearers of light. They alone are capable of establishing states and founding cultures, "forever kindling anew that fire of knowledge which illumined the night of silent mysteries and thus called man to climb the path to mastery over the other beings of this earth." Only when the Aryan nucleus began mingling with the subject people did decline and downfall follow. For "human culture and civilization on this continent are inseparably bound up with the presence of the Aryan. If he dies out or declines, the dark veils of an age without culture will again descend on this globe."[14]

This was the very peril mankind was once again confronting. Unlike the times of demise of the great empires of antiquity, what was now threatening was not just the extinction of a culture but the end of all higher humanness. The decay of the Aryan nuclear substance had gone further than ever before. "Germanic blood on this earth is gradually approaching exhaustion," Hitler warned. He saw the forces of darkness pressing in from all sides, as if aware of impending victory. "I tremble for Europe!" he exclaimed in one speech and conjured up a vision of the old continent "sinking into a sea of blood and grief." Once again, "cowardly know-it-alls and critics of Nature" were undermining Nature's elemental laws. These scoundrels were agents of an "all-embracing general offensive" that appeared under numerous guises: Communism, pacifism, the League of Nations, all international movements and institutions in general. Similarly, the Judaeo-Christian morality of pity and its verbose cosmopolitan variants tried to persuade man that he could overcome Nature, raise himself up to be master of his instincts, and achieve eternal peace. But the truth was that no one could "rebel against a firmament." The indubitable will of Nature determined the existence of nations, their clashes in war, the division of mankind into masters and slaves, the brutal preservation of the species.

It is not difficult to discern the mark of Arthur de Gobineau upon this system. In his doctrine of the inequality of races Gobineau had first formulated the anxiety connected with the modern age's racial conglomerations. The downfall of all cultures could be traced to promiscuous racial mixing, he had argued. This French aristocrat's race complex, his aversion for the "corrupt blood of the rabble" clearly sprang from the resentments of an abdicating ruling class. Nevertheless, his doctrine was taken up by certain literary sects of the period and spawned a whole literature along similar lines. Significantly, Hitler simplified Gobineau's elaborate doctrine until it became demagogically usable and offered a set of plausible explanations for all the discontents, anxieties, and crises of the contemporary scene. Versailles and the excesses of the Bavarian soviet republic, the evils of the capitalistic system, and the outrages of modern art, night life and syphilis —all became aspects of that age-old struggle whereby the lower races attempted to destroy the noble Aryan. And hidden behind it all, instigator, mastermind and power-greedy archfoe, a bugbear of mythological dimensions, stood the Eternal Jew.

He was an infernal, crazily grimacing phantom, "a growth spreading across the whole earth," the "lord of the antiworld," a complex product of obsessions and clever psychology. In keeping with his theory of focusing upon a single opponent, Hitler made the figure of the Jew the incarnation of all imaginable vices and dreads, the cause and its opposite, the thesis and the antithesis, literally "to blame for everything," for the tyranny of the stock market and for Bolshevism, for humanitarian ideology and for 30 million victims tortured to death in the Soviet Union "in veritable slaughterhouses." In a conversation with Dietrich Eckart, published after Eckart's death but while Hitler was still in Landsberg prison, Hitler expounded the identity of Judaism, Christianity, and Bolshevism by references to Isaiah 19:2-3 and Exodus 12:38.[15] He showed that the Jews had been expelled from Egypt because they had tried to produce a revolutionary mood by inciting the rabble with humanitarian phrases ("just as they do here"). From this it followed that Moses was the first leader of Bolshevism. And just as Paul virtually invented Christianity in order to undermine the Roman Empire, so Lenin employed the doctrine of Marxism to bring about the end of the present system. Thus, Hitler argued, the Old Testament already provided the pattern of the Jewish assault upon the superior, creative race, a pattern repeated again and again down the ages.

To be sure, Hitler never lost sight of the propaganda value of his anti-Semitism. He was highly aware of that aspect of things. If the Jew did not exist, he remarked, "we would have had to invent him. A visible enemy, not just an invisible one, is what is needed." But at the same time the Jew was the focus of his emotions, a pathological mania; the form the Jew took in Hitler's own mind did not differ greatly from the diabolical propaganda image he had created. The Jew was the grotesque projection of everything Hitler hated and craved. Certainly the thesis that the Jews were striving for world domination made good propaganda; but over and beyond such Machiavellian considerations he really believed this thesis, saw it as the key to all sorts of phenomena. He clung more and more to this "redeeming formula," convinced that through it he understood the nature of the great crisis of the age that he alone could cure. Toward the end of July, 1924, a Nazi from Czechoslovakia, who had come to Landsberg for an interview with the Führer, asked Hitler whether his attitude toward Judaism had changed since his imprisonment. He replied: "Yes, yes, it's quite right that I have changed my mind about the way to fight Judaism. I have realized that hitherto I have been much too mild. In the course of working out my book I have come to realize that in the future the most stringent methods of struggle must be employed if we are to fight through successfully. I am convinced that this is a vital question not only for our people, but for all peoples. For the Jews are the pestilence of the world."[16]

Though he pretended that these more relentless views had come to him during his imprisonment in Landsberg, in fact this aggravation of his hate complex had already taken place. As early as May, 1923, during a speech in the Krone Circus, Hitler had cried out: "The Jews are undoubtedly a race, but not human. They cannot be human in the sense of being an image of God, the Eternal. The Jews are the image of the devil. Jewry means the racial tuberculosis of the nations." But when he began organizing his many scraps of ideas and feelings into something resembling a coherent system, they took on a different cast. Henceforth, when he denied that the Jews were human, it was not just the ranting of the demagogue but deadly earnest and fanatical belief. He borrowed his rhetoric from the language of parasitology: the laws of nature themselves demanded that measures be taken against the "parasites," the "eternal leeches" and "vampires upon other peoples." Such measures would have their own irrevocable morality. Once he had cast the problem in such terms, annihilation and mass murder came to seem the extreme triumph of this morality. To the last Hitler insisted that his services to mankind lay in his recognition of the "true role" of the Jews and his courage in pushing that recognition to its consequences. It wasn't as if he had merely sought the glory of a conqueror like Napoleon, who after all had been "only a human being, not a worldshaking event."[17] At the end of February, 1942, shortly after the Wannsee conference at which the "final solution" was ordained, he declared to his table companions: "The discovery of the Jewish virus is one of the greatest revolutions which has been undertaken in the world. The struggle we are waging is of the same kind as, in the past century, that of Pasteur and Koch. How many diseases can be traced back to the Jewish virus! We shall regain our health only when we exterminate the Jews." With the directness and determination of one who had thought more deeply and seen more clearly than all others, he had recognized his true mission, his "cyclopean task."[18]

For that was the other key correction he made in Gobineau. He not only personalized the process of racial and cultural death in the figure of the Jew as the prime mover of all decline; he also restored utopianism to history by transforming Gobineau's "melancholic and fatalistic pessimism into aggressive optimism." In contrast to the French aristocrat, he held that racial decadence was not inevitable. Of course, the Jewish world conspiracy would see Aryan hegemony in Germany as the crucial enemy. In no other country was biological contamination or the interplay of capitalistic and Bolshevistic machinations carried out so systematically with such dire results. But for this very reason Hitler could appeal to the redeeming will: Germany was the world's battlefield on which the future of the globe would be decided.

And now it became obvious to what extent his anti-Semitism went beyond the traditional European brand; his fantasies about the Jews have a manic dynamism far surpassing all his visions of national grandeur. "If our people and our state become the victim of these bloodthirsty and avaricious Jewish tyrants of nations, the whole earth will sink into the snares of this octopus; if Germany frees herself from this embrace, this greatest of dangers to man may be regarded as broken for the whole world." And with that operation out of the way, he already saw dawning the Millennial Kingdom, the Thousand-Year Reich, which he was impatiently hailing when he had taken only a small step toward it. Then order would once again arise out of chaos, unity would be achieved, masters and slaves would hold their proper places, and the wisely led "nucleus peoples of the world" would respect one another and live in peace, since the root of the world's ills would at last have been eliminated.

It was this ideology, well developed though never spelled out as a coherent system, that gave his career what he himself was fond of calling its "somnambulistic sureness." Things might look fairly sanguine at the moment, but he would not allow this to alter his picture of the state of the world and his sense of being engaged in a life-and-death struggle. This interpretation and this feeling were what gave his politics such savage consistency. His indecisiveness, which almost all his associates report, always involved tactical alternatives; he was never in doubt on questions of principle. And in spite of his bent for postponements and temporizings, he pushed dauntlessly toward the great final confrontation. In trying to explain away many of the inhumanities of the regime, common folk would naïvely say, "If only the Führer knew!" But there they showed how utterly they misunderstood their ruler. In fact, he knew far more than anyone suspected, in a way far more than actually happened. As one of his close followers commented, Hitler himself was "the most radical Nazi of all."

These theories particularly shaped his thoughts on foreign policy, which he expounded in *Mein Kampf* and was to pursue right to the end. But no one realized that the seemingly fantastic goals he set forth in his book were meant as a concrete political program. It all revolved around the premise that the plight of Germany was caused by racial factors and that its salvation would come only when it had restored its racial integrity. He argued:

"If the German people in its historical development had possessed that herd unity which other peoples have enjoyed, the German Reich today would doubtless be mistress of the globe." He took the traditional nationalistic phrase *Volk ohne Raum* ("people without space") and turned it around into *Raum ohne Volk*. The pressing domestic mission of the National Socialist Party was, he considered, "to establish a nation in the empty space between the Meuse and the Memel." For "what we see there today are Marxist human herds, but no longer a German nation."

The concept of revolution that he had dimly in mind also had a strongly elitist, biological cast. He thought of revolution as aiming not only at new forms of rule and new institutions but also at a new type of man. In many of his speeches and proclamations he hailed the emergence of that new type as the dawn of a "vertitable golden age." One of his oft-repeated statements was: "Anyone who understands National Socialism only as a political movement knows virtually nothing about it. It is even more than religion; it is the will to a new creation of man." Thus one of the most pressing tasks of the new state would be to bring to a halt "further bastardization," to "lift marriage from the level of continual miscegenation," and enable it once more "to beget images of the Lord and not abortions midway between man and ape." The pure Aryan type could be recovered by breeding back in a series of "regression crossings." By such biological and pedagogical procedures, the German people could once more be restored to its pristine purity. In a secret speech to the 1938 officer class he spoke of a development continuing for a hundred years, at the end of which a majority would possess those select characteristics that would enable it to conquer and rule the world.

The living space that he continually called for was not intended merely to provide food for a surplus population, to insure against "starvation and misery," and to receive a peasantry threatened by industry and trade. Rather, these territorial demands were a prelude to a program for world conquest. Every ambitious nation needed a certain amount of territory, enough to make it independent of alliances and the political alignments of a given period. Historical greatness was intimately connected with geographic extension. To this idea Hitler clung to the very last. Brooding in the bunker shortly before the end, he complained that fate had forced him into premature conquests because a nation without great space could not even set itself great goals.

He early saw four ways to meet the future threat of overpopulation. Three of these—restriction of births, internal colonization, overseas colonialism—he rejected as timid dreams or "unworthy tasks." With explicit reference to the United States, he then argued that the only acceptable course was a continental war of conquest. "What is refused to amicable methods must be taken by force," he wrote in Landsberg and made no secret of what he had in mind: "If land was desired in Europe, it could be obtained by and large only at the expense of Russia, and this meant that

214

the new Reich must again set itself on the march along the road of the Teutonic Knights of old."[19]

Underlying such pronunciamentos was, once again, the concept of a great turning point in the history of the world. A new age was beginning; history was once more setting the mighty wheel in motion and apportioning lots anew. An end was coming to the era of sea powers who conquered distant lands with their navies, heaped up riches, established bases, and dominated the world. In the pretechnical age the sea had been the road to expansion. But under modern conditions that had totally changed. Colonial greatness was anachronistic and slated for destruction. Present-day technical capacities, the possibility of pushing roads and railways into vast, still unopened areas and linking these by a network of strongpoints, meant that the old order was being reversed. The empire of the future, Hitler held, would be a land power, a compact, integrally organized military giant. The age was already moving in that direction. Undoubtedly Hitler's way of conducting foreign policy in later years—as a succession of surprise blows—sprang from his inward restlessness. But he was also waging a desperate battle against time, against what he regarded as the course of history. He was forever seized by fear that Germany might for the second time arrive too late at the distribution of the world's goods. When he considered the powers who might compete with Germany for future mastery, his thoughts repeatedly returned to Russia. Racial, political, geographic, and historical indications coincided: everything pointed to the East.[20]

In line with prevailing sentiment, Hitler had begun as a revisionist, demanding annulment of the Versailles Treaty, restoration of the borders of 1914, by force if necessary, and the joining of all Germans in one mighty great power. To this school of thought the main enemy was France, and Germany's best hopes lay in exploiting the difficulties France was in increasing measure having with Italy and England. But Hitler did not keep to this view. True to his bent for thinking in larger terms, he was soon contemplating the Continent as a whole, and replacing border politics with area politics.

The core of his thesis was that Germany, in her militarily, politically, and geographically threatened middle position, could survive "only by ruthlessly placing power politics in the foreground." In an earlier discussion of Germany's foreign policy in the age of Kaiser Wilhelm, Hitler had held that Germany should either have renounced sea trade and colonies in order to join England against Russia or, alternatively, if she sought sea power and world trade, she should have joined Russia against England. In the early twenties Hitler favored the second course. He viewed England as one of the "principal" opponents of the Reich, and on this basis developed a marked pro-Russian bias. Under the influence of the *emigré* circle around Scheubner-Richter and Rosenberg, he looked toward an alliance with a "nationalistic" Russia, one "restored to health" and freed from the "Jewish-

215

Bolshevik yoke." Teamed with this new Russia, Germany would confront the West. Neither the concept of *Lebensraum* nor the inferiority of the Slavic race—which later was to be the basis for his expansionist Eastern policy—seems to have entered his head at this time. It was not until the beginning of 1923, probably in view of the stabilization of the Soviet regime, that he began to think of taking the opposite course and forming a pact with England against Russia. The sources seem to suggest that Hitler weighed this idea for more than a year, considered its ramifications, its consequences, and its chances of being realized. The fruit of this thinking appears in the famous fourth chapter of *Mein Kampf,* where he speaks of a war for living space fought against Russia.

In presenting this program, Hitler certainly had not abandoned the idea of a war against France. That remained one of the primary points of his foreign policy right down to the last monologues in the bunker. But it now assumed another character. Just as Italy was to be placated by Germany's renouncing the South Tyrol and England was to be wooed into an alliance by Germany's dropping all colonial demands, war with France became simply another step that would allow Germany a free hand in the East. By the time he was writing the second volume of *Mein Kampf* in the course of 1925, Hitler forcefully assailed the revisionist approach; it aimed, he argued, at the restoration of wholly illogical, accidental, far too constricted borders, which, moreover, made no sense in terms of military geography. Worse still, such demands would stir up all of Germany's former wartime foes and lead them to revive their crumbling alliance. *"The demand for restoration of the frontiers of 1914 is a political absurdity of such proportions and consequences as to make it seem a crime,"* Hitler declared in italics. National Socialism, on the contrary, aimed at securing land and soil for the German people. "This action is the only one which, before God and our German posterity, would make any sacrifice of blood seem justified." Such broad gains would "some day acquit the responsible statesmen of blood-guilt and sacrifice of the people."[21]

Henceforth, the idea of attacking Russia, of a mighty Teutonic expedition to establish a vast continental empire in the old "German area of command in the East," became the central tenet of Hitler's foreign policy. He assigned it epoch-making importance:

And so we National Socialists consciously draw a line beneath the foreign policy tendency of our pre-War period. We take up where we broke off six hundred years ago. We stop the endless German movement to the south and west, and turn our gaze toward the land in the east. At long last we break off the colonial and commercial policy of the pre-War period and shift to the soil policy of the future.[22]

How he arrived at this concept, as logical as it was monstrous, really does not matter. Some of it was original, some of it an extension of current theories. The notion of living space seems to have been a borrowing from Rudolf Hess. Thanks to his adulation of "the man," as he called Hitler, Hess had gradually won himself an important place among the group at the Landsberg prison. In particular, he replaced Emil Maurice in the position of Hitler's secretary. Hess also brought Hitler into personal contact with his teacher, Karl Haushofer, who had taken the highly suggestive subject of political geography, the "geopolitics" expounded by Sir Halford Mackinder, and shaped it into a philosophy of imperialistic expansion.

Mackinder had already drawn attention to the basic strength of what he called "the heartland": Eastern Europe and European Russia, protected by huge land masses, were destined to be the "citadel of world rule." The founder of geopolitics had decreed: "Whoever rules the heartland rules the world." As we have seen, such pseudoscientific formulas had a special appeal to Hitler's mind. But with all due credit to outside influences, Hitler's version of these ideas was distinctively his own. Seldom had his "combinative talent" operated so brilliantly, for he drew the outlines of a foreign policy that not only guided Germany's relations with the various great powers of Europe but satisfied her craving for revenge upon France, her desire for expansion and conquest, and his own miscellaneous ideological fixations, including his sense that a new age was dawning. To give this scheme the final fillip, it was made to fit into a pattern of "racial" history.

Here Fate itself seems desirous of giving us a sign. By handing Russia to Bolshevism, it robbed the Russian nation of that intelligentsia which previously brought about and guaranteed its existence as a state. For the organization of a Russian state was not the result of the political abilities of the Slavs in Russia, but only a wonderful example of the state-forming efficacy of the German element in an inferior race. . . . For centuries Russia drew nourishment from this Germanic nucleus of its upper leading strata. Today it can be regarded as almost totally exterminated and extinguished. It has been replaced by the Jew. Impossible as it is for the Russian by himself to shake off the yoke of the Jew by his own resources, it is equally impossible for the Jew to maintain the mighty empire forever. He himself is no element of organization, but a ferment of decomposition. The giant empire in the east is ripe for collapse. And the end of Jewish rule in Russia will also be the end of Russia as a state. We have been chosen by fate as witnesses of a catastrophe which will be the mightiest confirmation of the soundness of the folkish theory.[23]

Out of theories of this sort Hitler had formed, by the mid-twenties, the essentials of the foreign policy he later put into practice: the early attempts at alliance with England and the Rome-Berlin Axis, the campaign against France and the vast war of annihilation in the East to conquer and take possession of the world's "heartland." Moral considerations played no part in these plans. "An alliance whose aim does not embrace a plan for war is senseless and worthless," he declared in *Mein Kampf*. "State boundaries are made by man and changed by man." They seem unalterable "only to the thoughtless idiot"; the conqueror's might adequately demonstrates his right; "he who has, has." Such were his maxims. And however extravagant the program he patched together out of his nightmares, his theories of history, his distorted view of biology and his situation analyses, in its hyperactive radicality it held greater promise of success than the temperate revisionist demands for the return of West Prussia or South Tyrol. Unlike his nationalist partners, Hitler had realized that Germany had no chances within the existing world political system. His profound emotional bias against normality served him well when he set out to challenge the normal ideas of foreign policy from the very roots. The game could be won only by refusing to play it. By turning in another direction, against the Soviet Union, which was felt as a threat by other respectable nations, he made these nations his confederates and rendered Germany "potentially so strong . . . that the conquest of an empire was in a very precise sense easier than the isolated recovery of Bromberg or Königshütte."[24] He had a better chance to seize Moscow than Strassburg or Bozen.

Along with the goal, Hitler recognized and accepted the risk. It is astonishing to see how directly, in 1933, he began to put his program into effect. The alternative for him was never anything but world power or doom in the most literal sense. "Every being strives for expansion," he told the professors and students of Erlangen in a 1930 speech, "and every nation strives for world dominion." That proposition derived, he thought, straight from the aristocratic principle of Nature, which everywhere desired the victory of the stronger and the annihilation or unconditional subjugation of the weak. From this point of view he was entirely consistent at the end, when he saw the whole game lost and doom impending, and remarked to Albert Speer, who found the sentiment profoundly shocking: "If the war is lost, the people will be lost also. It is not necessary to worry about what the German people will need for elemental survival. . . . For the nation has proved to be the weaker, and the future belongs solely to the stronger eastern nation."[25] Germany had lost far more than a war; he was entirely without hope. For the last time he bowed to the law of Nature, "this cruel queen of all wisdom," which had imperiously ruled his life and thought.

Toward the closing days of 1924, after approximately a year, the imprisonment that Hitler ironically called his "university at state expense" approached its end. At the request of the state prosecutor, prison warden Leybold on September 15, 1924, drew up a report that made the granting of parole a virtual certainty. "Hitler has shown himself a man of order," the report states, "of discipline not only in respect to himself, but also in respect to his fellow inmates. He is easily content, modest and desirous to please. Makes no demands, is quiet and sensible, serious and quite without aggressiveness, and tries painstakingly to abide by prison rules. He is a man without personal vanity, is satisfied with the institution's food, does not smoke and drink, and though comradely, is able to exert a certain authority over his fellow inmates. . . . Hitler will attempt to revitalize the nationalist movement according to his own principles, but no longer, as in the past by violent methods which if necessary(!) may be directed against the government; instead, he will work in league with the concerned governmental bureaus."

Such model behavior and political change of heart were the conditions for parole, the court having held out some prospect for this after Hitler had served a mere six months of his five-year-sentence. We may well wonder how the Nazi leader who had already violated one parole, had escaped another prosecution by the intercession of a government minister, had for years instigated riots and meeting-hall rows, who had deposed the national government, arrested cabinet ministers and been responsible for killings, could possibly be granted so early a release. And in fact a complaint from the office of the state prosecutor had for the time being delayed the court's action. But the state authority was inclined to pardon the lawbreaker for sharing its own bent. Consequently, it put very little pressure behind the obligatory deportation of Hitler. In a letter to the Ministry of the Interior dated September 22, 1924, the Munich police commissioner's office had referred to this deportation as "essential," and Prime Minister Held, the new Bavarian governmental chief, had even sent out feelers to discover whether the Austrians would be willing to take Hitler if he were deported. But nothing further had been done. Hitler himself was extremely worried; he tried in every conceivable way to prove his docility. He was angry when Gregor Strasser arose in the Landtag to denounce the continued imprisonment of Hitler as a disgrace for Bavaria and splutter that the country was being ruled by a "gang of swine, a mean, disgusting gang of swine." He was also displeased by Röhm's underground activity.

Once more, circumstances were working in his favor. In the Reichstag elections held on December 7, the *völkisch* movement was able to garner only 3 per cent of the votes. It had previously had thirty-three deputies in the Reichstag; of these, only fourteen returned after the election. The results seemed to indicate that the radical Right had passed its peak. Apparently the Bavarian supreme court saw it that way, too, for it supported the lower court's decision to grant Hitler parole, despite the protest of the state prosecutor. On December 20, while the inmates in Landsberg were already preparing to celebrate Christmas there, a telegram from Munich ordered the immediate release of Hitler and Kriebel.

A few friends and followers, who had been informed beforehand, appeared with a car outside the prison gate. They were a disappointingly tiny group. The movement had fallen apart, its members scattered or at odds. Hermann Esser and Julius Streicher were waiting at Hitler's Munich apartment. There was no grand scene, no triumph. Hitler, who had put on weight, seemed restive and tense. That very evening he went to see Ernst

219

Hanfstaengl and at once asked him: "Play the *Liebestod* for me." Even while in Landsberg, such sorrowful moods had taken hold of him. *Die Weltbühne* carried an ironic obituary reporting the early demise of Adolf Hitler and adding that the Germanic gods had no doubt loved him too well.

Chapter 2

Hitler will run out of gas!

Karl Stützel, Bavarian Minister
of the Interior, in 1925

CRISES AND RESISTANCES

It was in fact a depressingly changed scene to which Hitler returned from
Landsberg. The turn of events could be traced to the stabilization of the
currency. On the one hand, people could again feel that society had a
reliable foundation. On the other hand, the end of the inflation worked
hardship on the professional promoters of turmoil—for the Free Corps and
the paramilitary associations had depended for support on foreign currency, trivial sums of which could go a long way under inflationary conditions. Gradually, the government acquired solidity and authority. By the
end of February, 1924, it rescinded the state of emergency proclaimed on
the night of November 9. In the course of the same year Foreign Minister
Stresemann's policy of reconciliation began to show results. These were not
so much a matter of specifics as an improvement in the psychological
climate within Germany. Gradually, the anachronistic hatreds and resentments of wartime began to dissolve. The Dawes Plan offered a prospect of
solving the reparations problem. The French gave signs of willingness to
evacuate the Ruhr. Security treaties were being discussed and even the
question of Germany's entry into the League of Nations. With the influx of
American capital, the economy began to recover. Unemployment, which
had created such scenes of misery on street corners and at bread lines and
welfare offices, was tangibly receding. These changes for the better were
reflected in the election results. In May, 1924, the radical forces still had
one more success, but by the December elections of the same year they had
been markedly thrown back. In Bavaria alone the racist-nationalist groups
lost nearly 70 per cent of their following. Although this shift was not
instantly reflected in a strengthening of the democratic centrist parties, it
did appear as though Germany, after years of crisis, depressions, and
threats of upheaval, was beginning to return to normality.

221

Like many others among the brand-new class of unemployed professional politicians, Hitler himself seemed to have reached the end of a ten-year phase of irregular living and to be faced once again with the law and order, the "domestic tranquillity," that had horrified him as an adolescent. Viewed in sober terms his situation was hopeless. Though he had covered himself with glory during his trial, he had since been reduced to the sorry role of the failed and half-forgotten politician. The National Socialist Party and all its organizations had been banned, as had the *Völkische Beobachter*. The Reichswehr and most of the private patrons of the movement had withdrawn their support; after all the excitement and playing at civil war, they had turned back to the routine of everyday life. In retrospect, many people dismissed the year 1923 with an irritated shrug. It had been a crazy time, a bad time. Dietrich Eckart and Scheubner-Richter were dead, Göring living in exile, Kriebel on the way to exile. Most of Hitler's closer followers were either in jail or had quarreled with one another and dispersed. Immediately before his arrest, Hitler had managed to send a scribbled note to Alfred Rosenberg: "Dear Rosenberg, from now on you will lead the movement." Adopting the pseudonym Rolf Eidhalt (Ralph Oath-keeper), an anagram of Adolf Hitler, Rosenberg tried to hold the remnants of Hitler's former following together under the guise of a Grossdeutsche Volksgemeinschaft (GVG) (Greater German People's Community). The SA was continued under the guise of various sports clubs, glee clubs, and marksmen's clubs. But Rosenberg had no talent as a leader; the movement soon broke up into feuding cliques. In Bamberg Streicher founded a Völkischer Block Bayern (Bavarian Racial-Nationalist Bloc), which claimed a measure of independence. Finally, Esser, Streicher, and a Dr. Artur Dinter from Thuringia, author of some wild racist maunderings in the form of novels, seized the leadership of the GVG, while Ludendorff, together with von Graefe and Gregor Strasser (soon joined by Ernst Röhm) organized the National Socialist Freedom Party as a kind of united front for the nationalist and racist groups. Thus various would-be leaders tried to make use of Hitler's absence as a means of rising in the nationalist movement or even dislodging Hitler from the star position he had won during the trial and forcing him back into the role of "drummer."

Hitler, however, was not discouraged by the situation. Rather, he saw it as rich in promise. Rosenberg later admitted that he had been greatly surprised at being appointed interim leader of the movement and suspected that Hitler had chosen him for some secret reason of his own. Perhaps Hitler was quite ready to let the movement fall apart, if that would reinforce his own claim to leadership. Nor was this reprehensible, in view of the sort of claim Hitler was by now making. For the summons he had received from fate could not be delegated. In religion, too, there is no such person as the vice-savior.

With curious dispassion, Hitler had watched the squabbles among

Rosenberg, Streicher, Esser, Pöhner, Röhm, Amann, Strasser, and Ludendorff, and, as one of his followers commented, "did not even lift his little finger." While still in prison, he had tried as far as possible to keep any decision from being taken, any power center formed or claim to leadership established. For similar reasons he opposed nationalist participation in the parliamentary elections, although such participation was in keeping with the new strategy of seeking the legal conquest of power. The point was that every party member who acquired parliamentary immunity and a legislator's salary thereby gained some independence of his authority. He was not at all pleased to learn that the National Socialist Freedom Party had won 32 of 472 seats in the Reichstag elections of May, 1924. Shortly afterward, in an open letter, Hitler resigned the leadership of the NSDAP, withdrew the appointments he had made to various offices, and refused to receive politically motivated visits. With a touch of smugness Rudolf Hess, writing from Landsberg, commented on the "stupidity" of the party followers. As for Hitler's gamble, it proved to be a clever one. When he came out of prison, he found nothing but the ruins of the party; but on the other hand he no longer had any serious rival. He appeared on the scene as the longed-for rescuer of a nationalist-racist movement that had been, with some assistance from him, sinking into the swamp. On this basis, Hitler was able to assert an authority that soon could no longer be challenged. He later frankly admitted: "Otherwise it would not have been possible. At that time [after his release from prison] I was able to say to everyone in the party: Now we are going to fight the way I want to and no differently."

Nevertheless, upon his release he found himself confronting soaring hopes and the most contradictory expectations and demands from his disunited followers. His political future would be dependent upon whether he succeeded in freeing himself from all the splinter groups and, within the densely inhabited sphere of the Right, giving his party an unmistakable profile—which, however, had also to be vague enough to hold the divergent aspirations together. Many rightists were expecting him to join Ludendorff in organizing a racist-nationalist unity movement. But he realized that only a towering leader, a supreme personality standing alone upon a kind of supernatural pinnacle, could serve as the cohesive force his concept required. At the moment, therefore, he was not interested in concluding hasty alliances but in marking out dividing lines and in establishing his personal claim to absolutism. His behavior during the following weeks was determined by these considerations.

Only a few days after his release, Hitler, on Pöhner's advice, asked Held, the new Bavarian Prime Minister, for an interview. Held, chairman of the Bavarian People's Party, was strictly Catholic and resolutely federalistic; Hitler and his associates had been violently hostile to him. To play down the significance of the meeting, Hitler pretended that his sole purpose was to ask for the release of those of his comrades still imprisoned in Landsberg.

Critics within the *völkisch* camp accused him of making his "peace with Rome." In reality he was trying to make peace with the government. Unlike Ludendorff, he remarked, he could not afford to inform his opponents beforehand that he wanted to kill them.

His personal fate as well as the future of the movement depended on the success of this maneuver. His ambition was unchanged: to seize power. For this he must build up an autocratic, military party; but he must also regain the lost trust of powerful groups and institutions. That is, he had to appear simultaneously as revolutionary and as defender of existing conditions, radical and moderate at once. He must both threaten the system and play the part of its preserver; he must violate the law and establish credibility as its defender. It is not certain whether Hitler ever consciously spelled out this paradoxical strategy; but almost everything he did in practice aimed at the tactical realization of these paradoxes. In his talk with Held he assured the Prime Minister of his loyalty. In the future, he promised, he would work only by legal means; the putsch of November 9 had been a mistake. He had since recognized, he continued, that the authority of the state must be respected; he himself, as a bourgeois patriot, was ready to contribute to the best of his ability to that end. Above all, he was at the disposal of the government in the struggle against the seditious forces of Marxism. But, of course, if he were to be effective, he needed his party and the *Völkische Beobachter*. Asked how he intended to reconcile this order with the anti-Catholic bias of the nationalist-racist groups, Hitler replied that this hostility to the Catholics sprang from an idiosyncrasy of Ludendorff's, that he himself took a skeptical attitude toward the general and would have nothing to do with it; he had always been against denominational bickerings; but, after all, the true-blue nationalist forces had to stick together.

Held listened to this tommyrot with a reserved air. He was glad to hear, he said, that Hitler was at last inclined to respect government authority, but it was a matter of indifference whether he did or did not respect it. As Prime Minister, he, Held, would maintain this authority against anyone. He would not stand for conditions such as had prevailed in Bavaria before November 9.

Nevertheless, at the suasion of his personal friend, Dr. Gürtner, who was one of Hitler's patrons, Held finally agreed to lift the ban on the National Socialist Party and its newspaper. For, as he summed up his impression of the talk with Hitler, "the beast has been tamed."

A few days later, Hitler turned up at a meeting of the nationalist faction in the Landtag, the Bavarian state legislature. And, as if the nationalist movement were not in bad enough shape, he opened a new breach in its ranks. Sporting the leather whip that was by now one of his regular props, he entered the Landtag building, where the deputies, in a solemn mood, had gathered to welcome him. But after only the briefest of preliminaries, he began assailing them for their lack of leadership and ideas. He was particularly angry at their having refused participation in the government, which Prime Minister Held had offered. Totally dismayed, the group protested that there were principles an honorable man could not abandon; one could not first come out against a rival party for betraying the German people and then go ahead and form a government in collaboration with it. As the wrangle went on, one of the faction members suggested that Hitler's one reason for wanting the coalition had been to buy his release from prison on parole. Hitler answered witheringly that his release was a thousand times more important to the movement than all the principles of two dozen nationalist deputies.

His idea seems to have been to make so bold a claim to leadership that those who were not willing to submit to him would be driven out of his camp. He had spoken ironically of the "inflationary gains" of the party in 1923, seeing its too rapid growth as the reason for its lack of fiber during the crisis. He was now separating the chaff from the wheat. The leaders of the other nationalist groups were soon complaining bitterly that Hitler would not co-operate with them. They kept referring to the blood that all had shed together at the Feldherrnhalle. But mystical sentimentalities of this sort had little effect on Hitler. Instead, he remembered how dependent he had been in 1923, how he had had to defer to all these fellow nationalists. He had learned a lesson from that: every partnership was a form of imprisonment. So now he would pretend to be pliable as far as the government and the power holders were concerned. But within the movement he imperiously enforced his will. He was quite willing to accept the consequences: that of the twenty-four conservative deputies, only six stood the test. The remainder went over to other parties.

Nor was this battle the last. Impatiently, he started fresh quarrels and blasted more pieces away from the margins of the shrinking movement. He made much of the differences between himself and the flock of other racist, nationalist, and radical rightist groups, and refused to collaborate with any of them. By now he had alienated all but four of the deputies in the Reichstag. Even those showed resistance and wanted him to break with such ambiguous and unsavory followers as Hermann Esser and Julius Streicher. The wrangles went on for months. But since Hitler realized far more clearly than his opponents that what was at stake was not the purity of the party, but control of it, he did not yield an inch.

Meanwhile, he was preparing for the break with Ludendorff. The general had become something of a burden, especially in South Germany, where he had involved himself in endless bickerings. He feuded with the Catholic Church; he provoked an unnecessary tiff with the Bavarian crown prince over questions of honor; he quarreled with the officers' corps. Ludendorff was growing more and more unreasonable, under the influence of his second wife, Dr. Mathilde von Kemnitz. He was increasingly preoccupied with the pseudoreligious obscurities of a sectarian ideology, a mélange of psychotic fears, Germanic religion and anticivilizational pessimism. Such tendencies reminded Hitler of the teachings of Lanz von Liebenfels and the Thule Society that had dominated his early years. He had long since freed himself from such things, and in *Mein Kampf* had expressed biting scorn for the kind of *völkisch* romanticism that nevertheless lingered on in his imagination. His attitude toward Ludendorff was also colored by jealousy. He was all too aware of the disabilities suffered by a former private first class vis-à-vis a general—especially in so military-minded a country. Finally, Hitler took it as a personal affront that Ludendorff by a military order had detached his personal adjutant, Ulrich Graf, from him. In his first conversation with the general after his release Hitler made a big issue of this. At the same time, as if driven by a demon of quarrelsomeness, he took up arms against the leaders of the North German National Socialist Freedom Movement. These men, Albrecht von Graefe and Count Ernst von Reventlow, had publicly declared that Hitler must not be allowed to regain his former position of power, that he was a talented agitator but not a politician. Hitler now answered Graefe in a letter that not only threw down the gauntlet but was in itself a token of his new self-assurance. In the past, Hitler said, he had been the "drummer" and would be again, but only for Germany and never again for Graefe and his ilk, "so help me God!"

On February 26, 1925, the first issue of the *Völkische Beobachter* since the putsch appeared. It announced that next day at the Bürgerbräukeller, the site of the unsuccessful coup, the National Socialist German Workers' Party would be founded anew. In his editorial "A New Beginning" and in an article, "Fundamental Directives" for the organization of the party, Hitler upheld his claim to leadership. He refused to make any concessions. With a side glance at the allegations against Esser and Streicher, he declared that the leadership of the party had nothing to do with the morality of its followers, any more than it did with doctrinaire squabbles. Its business was to practice politics. Those who were sniping at him he called "political children." This strong line proved to be just what was wanted; declarations of loyalty poured in from all over the country.

Strategically, his appearance next day had been carefully thought out. In order to give greater force to his appeal, Hitler had not spoken in public for two months. This had raised to an extraordinary degree the expectations of his adherents and the nervousness of his rivals. He had received no visitors, even rebuffed foreign delegations, and had let it be known that he was throwing all political letters "into the wastebasket unread." Although the meeting was not to begin until eight o'clock, the first of the audience—admission one mark—arrived by early afternoon. At six o'clock the police had to close the hall; some 4,000 followers had crowded into it.

Many of those present had been battling with each other. But when

Hitler entered the hall, he was greeted with that wildly excessive homage that was later to become so common. People climbed on the tables, cheered, waved beer mugs, or joyfully embraced one another. Max Amann chaired the meeting, since Anton Drexler had refused to participate unless Esser and Streicher were expelled from the party. Gregor Strasser, Röhm, and Rosenberg were also among the missing. Hitler addressed all of them, the faltering, the skeptical or the obstinate partisans, in an extremely effective two-hour speech. He began with generalities, hailed the achievements of the Aryan as a creator of culture, discussed foreign policy, held forth on the theme that the peace treaty could be broken, the reparations agreement disavowed, but even so Germany would ultimately die of Jewish blood poisoning. Prey to his old obsession, he impressed his listeners with the fact that on Berlin's Friedrichstrasse every Jew had a blonde German girl on his arm. Nevertheless Marxism could "be overthrown as soon as it is confronted by a doctrine of superior truthfulness but the same brutality in execution." He went on to criticize Ludendorff for making enemies everywhere and not realizing that it is possible to speak of one enemy and mean another. Finally he came to the heart of his argument:

If anyone comes and wants to set me conditions, I tell him: My friend, wait awhile until you hear the conditions I am setting you. I'm not wooing the masses, you know. After a year has passed, you be the judges, my party comrades. If I have not acted rightly, then I shall return my office to your hands. But until then this is the rule: I and I alone shall lead the movement, and no one sets me conditions as long as I personally bear the responsibility. And I on the other hand bear all the responsibility for everything that happens in the movement.[26]

At the end, face flushed with excitement, he called upon the members of the audience to bury their enmities, forget the past, and put an end to the conflicts within the movement. He did not ask for obedience, did not offer any bargains; he simply demanded submission or withdrawal from the movement. The ecstatic cheering at the end confirmed his resolve to shape the NSDAP into a tightly organized party under his sole command. In the midst of this display of enthusiasm Max Amann stepped forward and called out to the crowd: "The quarreling must stop. Everyone for Hitler!" Suddenly all the old foes thronged to the platform: Streicher, Esser, Feder, Frick, the Thuringian gauleiter Dinter, the Bavarian faction leader Buttmann. In a spectacular scene, before thousands of people shouting and waving and climbing on tables and chairs, they ostentatiously shook hands with one another. Streicher stammered something about a "godsend," and Buttmann—who only recently had taken sharp issue with Hitler at a meeting of the Landtag faction—testified that all the doubts he had felt when he arrived "melted away inside me when the Führer spoke." What the dominant figure of Ludendorff had been unable to accomplish, what Graefe, Strasser, Rosenberg, and Röhm individually or in conjunction with one another had failed to do, Hitler accomplished with a few strokes. The experience strengthened his self-confidence as well as his authority. Buttmann's phrase had been used occasionally before, though it had been applied also to Ludendorff and other competitors for leadership. From this day on, however, Hitler was the only one indisputably known as "the Führer."

As soon as Hitler had asserted his control over the party, he set about accomplishing his second goal: organizing the Nazi party into a pliable and vigorous instrument for his tactical aims. While still in Landsberg he had, in a cynical mood, commented to one of his followers: "When I resume active work, it will be necessary to pursue a new policy. Instead of working to achieve power by an armed coup, we shall have to hold our noses and enter the Reichstag against the Catholic and Marxist deputies. If out-voting them takes longer than out-shooting them, at least the results will be guaranteed by their own Constitution! Any lawful process is slow."[27]

The business was far slower and more toilsome than Hitler had imagined, and was accompanied by repeated setbacks, obstacles, and conflicts. As luck would have it, he himself was to blame for the first severe setback. The Bavarian government had taken note of his remark that one could speak of one enemy and mean another and had interpreted it—just as it was meant—as proof of his inveterate hostility to the Constitution. It also resented his remark that either the enemy would pass over his dead body or he over the enemy's. "It is my wish," he had continued, "that the swastika flag shall be my shroud if next time the struggle lays me low." This sort of talk cast such question on his pledge to be law-abiding that the authorities in Bavaria, and soon afterward in most of the other German states, simply forbade him to make public speeches. In conjunction with his parole, with the ever-present threat of deportation, and with the changes in the general situation, this ban seemed to put an end to all his prospects. It came as a surprise and a terrible reversal, for it seemed to scotch his idea of working with the government.

Nevertheless, Hitler seemed totally unperturbed. A year and a half before, in the summer of 1923, a setback would have thrown him off balance, would have thrust him back into the lethargy and weaknesses of his youth. Now he remained unaffected. He did not even seem to mind the personal consequences of the ban on public speaking: the loss of his chief source of income. He depended instead on fees for the editorials he was now writing for the party press. In addition, he frequently addressed groups of from forty to sixty guests at the home of his friends, the Bruckmanns, where the small audience and the absence of intoxicants produced a new atmosphere that called for another style of propaganda. Contemporary observers all report the changes Hitler seems to have undergone during his imprisonment, the sterner, more rigorous expression that gave a new stamp

228

to his countenance. "The thin, pale, sickly, often seemingly empty face was more forcefully composed; the strong bony structure from brow to chin emerged more distinctly; what formerly might have given the effect of sentimentality had yielded to an unmistakable note of hardness."

He had also acquired that arrogant tenacity which would serve him well through all misfortunes, enabling him to keep going throughout the period of stagnation and persist until the march to victory began at the outset of the thirties. In the summer of 1925, when his hopes were at their nadir, a meeting of party leaders discussed a motion to appoint a deputy for him; he would not hear of it, on the infuriating ground that the movement would stand or fall with him alone.

Undoubtedly, anyone observing his immediate entourage would have had to concede that he was right. After the deliberate clashes and schisms of the preceding months, it was in the nature of things that most of the followers who remained with him were the mediocrities. His retinue had shrunk again to that cohort of cattle dealers, chauffeurs, bouncers, and onetime professional soldiers with whom he had formed, ever since the murky beginnings of the party, a curiously sentimental and almost human relationship. The unsavory reputation of most of these satellites bothered him no more than did their rowdy manners. His keeping such company above all showed how far he had come from the bourgeois aesthete he had once been. In answer to occasional reprimands, he would say, with a trace of embarrassment, that he too could make a wrong choice; it was human nature to be "not infallible." And yet, right on into his years as Chancellor such types remained his preferred associates; they were always on hand in these long, empty evenings when Hitler, watching movies or engaging in trivial chitchat in the rooms that had once been Bismarck's, unbuttoned his jacket and slumped in the big armchair with his legs stretched out before him. These men without background, without families or professions, all of them with some crack in their characters or their careers, aroused familiar associations in the former inmate of the home for men. Admiration and sincere devotion were all they could offer him, and these they gave without reserve. They listened raptly when he sat with them in the Italian restaurant Osteria Bavaria or the Café Neumaier and embarked on one of his tirades. Perhaps their uncritical devotion served him as a substitute for that mass enthusiasm he needed like a drug and which for the time being he had to do without.

Among the few successes Hitler could tote up during this period of paralysis was the winning over of Gregor Strasser. Until the failure of the November putsch Strasser, a pharmacist from Landshut and the gauleiter of Lower Bavaria, whom "experience at the front" had brought to politics, could hardly have been considered prominent. But he had profited by the absence of Hitler to push forward and had won a considerable following for Nazism in North Germany and the Ruhr. The National Socialist Freedom Movement was his personal vehicle. This hulking but sensitive man who brawled in taverns and read Homer in Greek was of impressive appearance. He was an excellent speaker and had an important ally in his brother Otto, a skillful journalist. It was hard for him to work with the cold, slippery, neurasthenic Hitler; for a man like Gregor Strasser there was something repellent about Hitler's personality. Nor could he stomach Hitler's entourage. All that the two men had in common was allegiance to an as yet shifting, ill-defined concept of "National Socialism." Nevertheless, Strasser admired Hitler's magnetism and his grip over his followers.

Strasser had not taken part in the meeting aimed at refounding the party. In March, 1925, to compensate Strasser for his resignation from the National Socialist Freedom Movement, Hitler offered him the largely independent post of leader of the Nazi party in the entire North German area. Strasser accepted with the proud proviso that he was joining Hitler not as a follower but as a fellow warrior. He still had his moral scruples and his doubts, but felt that the essential cause, the idea promising the birth of the future, must stand above all else. "That is why I have offered Herr Hitler my co-operation."

But this addition to the ranks was balanced out by a major loss. While Strasser applied his vast energy to building up a party organization in North Germany, within a short time establishing seven new gaus between Schleswig-Holstein, Pomerania, and Lower Saxony, Hitler showed how bent he was on imposing his own authority, no matter what the cost. For now he broke with Ernst Röhm. After Röhm's brush with the Munich People's Court (he was pronounced guilty but given no sentence), the former army captain had promptly begun to unite his old comrades of the Free Corps and Kampfbund days in a new association, the *Frontbann* ("the Front-liners"). These "liners," who knew only soldiering and were totally unable to adjust to the increasingly normal conditions, almost to a man were recruited into the new movement.

Even while he was still in Landsberg, Hitler had looked askance at Röhm's activities, since everything Röhm was doing was a threat to his parole, his power within the nationalist movement, and his new tactics. One of the lessons of November had been to have done, once and for all, with the swaggering ways and conspiratorial games of the military leagues. What the NSDAP needed, Hitler had decided, was a party force organized on paramilitary lines and totally subordinate to the political leadership, hence to himself personally. Röhm, on the other hand, was still clinging to the idea of an underground auxiliary army that would enable the Reichswehr to evade the provisions of the Versailles Treaty. He even thought of making the SA completely independent of the party and turning it into a subordinate unit of his Frontbann.

Fundamentally, this was a renewal of the old dispute over the SA's function and command status. In contrast to the slower-minded Röhm,

Hitler had in the interval acquired new insights and resentments. He had not forgiven Lossow and the officers of his staff for their betrayal on November 8 and 9. But at the same time he had learned from the events of that night that the majority of army officers were morally fettered by their oath and their respect for legality.

During the first half of April the quarrel erupted into the open. Röhm had a strong sentimental attachment to Hitler; he was forthright, easygoing, and as doggedly faithful to his friends as he was to his views. Presumably Hitler had not forgotten all he had owed to Röhm since the beginnings of his political career. But he also realized that times had changed. This once-influential person who in the past could be counted on to round up money, machine guns or members at the drop of a hat, had by now turned into a stubborn, difficult friend awkward to fit into the more solid establishment Hitler was trying to create.

Nevertheless, for some time Hitler said neither yes nor no to Röhm's urging. But at last he decided to take a stand. During a conversation in mid-April Röhm once more demanded strict separation between the National Socialist Party and the SA. Moreover, he wanted to lead his units as a nonpolitical private army that would be above all partisan strife and the issues of the day. A heated quarrel ensued. Hitler was particularly incensed, because Röhm's idea would once again degrade him to the "drummer" of the movement. What is more, it would return him to the subordinate role forced on him in the summer of 1923, that of adjunct to aims set by others. Full of hurt feelings, he charged Röhm with betraying their friendship. Röhm thereupon cut the conversation short. The following day he formally resigned in writing his leadership of the SA. Hitler did not answer. At the end of April, after Röhm had also resigned the leadership of the Frontbann, he wrote Hitler once again, closing his letter on the significant note: "I take this opportunity, in memory of the great and the trying times we have been through together, to thank you warmly for your comradeship and to ask you not to deprive me of your personal friendship." But that, too, was not answered. The following day, when he sent a note on his resignation to the nationalist newspapers, the *Völkische Beobachter* printed it without comment.

During this same period an event occurred that showed Hitler how bleak his prospects had become and how wise he had been to separate his political fortunes from those of Ludendorff, though his reasons for the break had been largely personal. At the end of February, 1925, Friedrich Ebert, the Social Democratic President of Germany, died. The nationalist-racist groups put up Ludendorff, while the candidate of the bourgeois rightist parties was a competent but totally unknown person named Dr. Jarres. Despite his fame, the general suffered an annihilating defeat, receiving little more than 1 per cent of the national vote. Hitler noted the result with a measure of grim satisfaction.

A few days after the election, Dr. Pöhner, the only trustworthy and important associate Hitler had left, was killed in an accident. Hitler truly seemed to have reached the end of his political career. In Munich the party had no more than 700 members left. Anton Drexler seceded and despondently founded a party more congenial to his quieter tendencies. But Hitler's bullies made a point of tracking down their erstwhile comrades and beating them up. In this way they smashed the rival enterprise. Other kindred groups suffered a similar fate. Quite often Hitler himself, leather whip in hand, stormed the meetings. Since he was not allowed to speak, he showed himself to the crowds from the platform, merely smiling and waving. Before the second round in the elections for the presidency, he called upon his followers to vote for Field Marshal von Hindenburg, who had meanwhile been nominated. Some writers have seen this choice as a farsighted political speculation. But he really had no ground for such speculation, as things stood; moreover, the few votes he controlled could not change anything. It was important, however, that he was ostentatiously aligning himself with the parties of order and that he was moving closer to the man of legend, the secret "ersatz kaiser" who had or some day would have a key to virtually all the powerful institutions in the country.

The continuing setbacks inevitably sapped Hitler's position within the party. In Thuringia, Saxony, and Württemberg he had to fight for his challenged leadership; in North Germany Gregor Strasser went on building up the party. Strasser was forever on the move. He spent most of his nights on trains or in waiting rooms; by day he visited followers, founded branches, saw functionaries, conferred, or appeared at meetings. During 1925 and 1926 he appeared as principal speaker at nearly one hundred meetings, while Hitler was condemned to silence. This fact, less than any ambitions on Strasser's part to rival Hitler, for a while made it seem as though the party's center of gravity were shifting to the north. Thanks to Strasser's loyalty, Hitler's position as leader was on the whole acknowledged. But the sober Protestant North Germans' suspicions of the flamboyant petty bourgeois bohemian with his alleged "pro-Rome" course came repeatedly to the fore, and many people would join the party only if they were assured considerable independence of Munich headquarters. For quite a while Hitler had to waive his requirement that leaders of local groups in the north be appointed by party headquarters. Until the late autumn of 1925, moreover, the North Rhineland gau had membership cards of its own and would not use the membership booklets provided by Munich headquarters.

The business manager of this North Rhineland gau, with headquarters in Elberfeld, was a young academic who had made a stab at being a journalist, writer, and crier at the stock exchange, before he found a post as secretary to a nationalist-racist politician, made contact with the National Socialists, and met Gregor Strasser. His name was Paul Joseph Goebbels, and what had brought him to Strasser's side was chiefly his intellectual radicalism, which he expounded in various literary works and diary notes, wherein he often marveled at his own personality. "I am the most radical. Of the new type. Man as revolutionary." His style ranged from such incisiveness to rhapsody, which, however, at the time was found quite acceptable. His radicalism was a compound of nationalistic and social-revolutionary ideologies; it seemed a thinner, shriller version of the doctrine of his mentor. For, in contrast to the cold Hitler, who moved in a curiously abstract world of feeling, the more emotional Gregor Strasser had been affected by the misery of the postwar era. His heart went out to the common people. Sooner or later, he believed, the proletariat would embrace National Socialism. For a time Gregor Strasser found in Joseph Goebbels and in his brother Otto Strasser the advocates for an ideological course that no one ever followed. Gregor Strasser's "program" won merely temporary importance as the fleeting expression of a socialist alternative to Hitler's "Fascist" South German National Socialism.

The special temper of the North German Nazis manifested itself in a committee organized in Hagen on September 10, 1925. Goebbels immediately took command of it, along with Gregor Strasser. And although the participants kept saying that they were not opposed to Munich headquarters, they nevertheless spoke of themselves as a "west bloc," and of a "counterattack" against "the calcified big-shots in Munich." They also criticized the party leadership for its meager interest in questions of program. Gregor Strasser deplored the "atrociously low level" of the *Völkische Beobachter*. Significantly, however, none of the reproaches were directed at Hitler in person or at his conduct of his office. In fact, what the critics wanted was to strengthen rather than to diminish his position. They were objecting to the "slovenly, lousy way they run things at headquarters," and once again to the brashness of Esser and Streicher. Totally misconstruing the situation, this circle hoped to free Hitler from the clutches of the "corrupt Munich clique," the "Esser dictatorship," and win him over to their own cause. Here, in these early years, and not for the first time, we find that notion so widespread later on: that the "Führer" was frail and human, surrounded by bad advisers who prevented him from carrying out his honest intentions.

The program of the Strasser group was set forth in a fortnightly review, *Nationalsozialistische Briefe* ("National Socialist Letters"). Unpretentious in format, the magazine was edited by Goebbels and was chiefly concerned with escaping the narrowness of a nostalgic, backward-looking middle-class ideology and turning the movement's face toward the present. Almost everything that "was held sacred in Munich was at some time or other thrown into question or frankly run down" in the magazine. There was constant stress on the difference in social conditions in Bavaria and the north. The magazine's pronouncedly anticapitalist thrust was a response to the urban, proletarian social structure of North Germany. As a letter from a Berlin reader put it, the National Socialist Party should not consist "of radicalized bourgeois" and "be afraid of the words worker and socialist." Thus the magazine announced: "We are socialists; we are enemies, mortal enemies, of the present-day capitalist economic system with its exploitation of the economically weak, with its injustice in wages. . . . We are resolved to annihilate this system despite everything." Looking for formulas which could unite the nationalistic socialists and Communists, Goebbels found a whole catalogue of identical attitudes and convictions. He by no means rejected the theory of class struggle. He contended that the collapse of Russia would "bury forever our dreams of a National Socialist Germany." Moreover, he questioned Hitler's theory of the Jews as the universal enemy, remarking: "It is by no means settled that the capitalist and the Bolshevik Jew are one and the same" and going so far as to say that the Jewish question in general was "more complicated than one imagines."

The Strasser people also held quite different ideas on foreign policy from the Munich leadership. Strasser and his associates had responded to the socialist appeal of the times, but "not as to the call of the proletarian class but of proletarian nations," in the forefront of which stood humiliated, betrayed, and plundered Germany. They saw the world as divided into oppressing and oppressed peoples and supported those very revisionist demands that Hitler in *Mein Kampf* had branded "political nonsense." Where Hitler saw Soviet Russia as a target for conquest, and Rosenberg described her as a "Jewish colony of hangmen," Goebbels spoke with deep respect of the Russian utopian impulse, while Strasser even called for an alliance with Moscow "against the militarism of France, against the imperialism of England, against the capitalism of Wall Street." Even more socialistic was the group's economic program: large landholdings were to be abolished, and all peasants were to be organized into agricultural cooperatives; small businesses were to be grouped in guilds; corporations with more than twenty employees were to be partially socialized. Where enterprises continued in private hands, the personnel were to be entitled to a share of 10 per cent of the profits, the national government to 30 per cent, the county to 6 and the local community to 5 per cent. The group also advocated simplification of legislation, creation of a school system open to all classes, and payment of wages partly in goods. This last was a romantic expression of the popular distrust of money resulting from the inflation.

All this was outlined by Gregor Strasser at a meeting in Hanover on November 22, 1926. Here the rebellious mood of the North and West German party organizations, their antipathy to headquarters and the "pope in Munich"—as Gauleiter Rust put it, to general applause—emerged in public to a startling degree. At another such meeting in the same city at the end of January, this time held in Gauleiter Rust's apartment, Goebbels demanded that the group bluntly show the door to Gottfried Feder, whom Hitler had recently sent as an observer. Nor was this all. If the sources are to be believed, Goebbels followed this up with a motion "that the petty bourgeois Adolf Hitler be expelled from the National Socialist Party."[28]

The challenge to Hitler's authority was to increase. In December, without knowledge of headquarters, Strasser distributed his draft program among the party members. It was meant to replace the twenty-five points so arbitrarily thrown together long ago, and to overturn the image of the party's representing only petty bourgeois interests. Although Hitler was reported to be "furious" over this show of autonomy, no one paid attention to Feder's objections. In fact, the Strasser group refused to allow Feder to vote on any motions. Only one of the twenty-five who took part in the discussion, the gauleiter of Cologne, Robert Ley, "a moron and possibly an intriguer," came out openly for Hitler.

At the moment, the German public was passionately discussing the question of whether the royal and ducal houses should be expropriated or whether their property, confiscated in 1918, should be returned. Hitler found himself impelled by his tactical reasoning to side with the German princes, and in general with the propertied classes. The Strasser group decided, as did the parties of the Left, for expropriation of the former rulers without compensation. They also undertook, without authorization from Munich, to publish a newspaper entitled *Der Nationale Sozialist* ("The Nationalist Socialist") and, with funds Gregor Strasser obtained by mortgaging his drugstore in Landshut, to set up a publishing house called the Kampfverlag. This soon developed into a sizable concern; with its six weekly newspapers it for a while outdid the Eher Verlag, run by Munich headquarters. Moreover, in the judgment of Konrad Heiden, its publications were far superior to those of the Munich firm "in intellectual variety and honesty."

But the most naked challenge to Hitler on the part of the Hanover circle came when Gregor Strasser called upon the party to abandon its timorous pledge of legality and follow a "politics of catastrophe," prepared for the worst contingencies. He declared his resolve to seize power by frontal attack and sanctioned any means that damaged the government and shattered public order: putsch, bombs, strikes, street battles, or brawls. As Goebbels was to express it shortly after: "We will attain everything if we set hunger, despair and sacrifice marching for our aims." The party was "to light the beacon in our people so that nationalist and socialist despair flame in a single great fire."

Hitler had so far remained silent about the group's activities, although it was setting up a power center that threatened to become a secondary governing committee within the party and although in North Germany the name of Gregor Strasser meant "almost more" than his own. "Nobody has faith in Munich any more," Goebbels noted jubilantly in his diary. "Elberfeld is going to become the mecca of German socialism." But Hitler

235

haughtily ignored the plans to kick him upstairs by making him honorary chairman and then unite the disorganized nationalist camp in one great movement. A few scornful pages in *Mein Kampf* were the only notice Hitler ever took of such projects.

Hitler's restraint was partly due to his personal affairs. For in the interval he had rented a country house belonging to a Hamburg businessman on the Obersalzberg, near Berchtesgaden. The situation of the house was extraordinarily beautiful, although the place was otherwise quite modest, consisting of a large living room and a veranda on the ground floor, and three attic rooms. In talking to visitors, Hitler made a point of saying that the house did not belong to him, "so that there could be no question of any corrupt practices, in line with the bad example of other 'party bigwigs.' " He had asked his widowed half-sister, Angela Raubal, to be his housekeeper. She was accompanied by her seventeen-year-old daughter Geli. The affection Hitler felt for this pretty, superficial niece soon developed into a passionate relationship hopelessly burdened by his intolerance, his romantic ideal of womanhood, and avuncular scruples, so that it was finally to end in an act of desperation. Hitler rarely left his rural retreat; when he did, it would be to attend the Munich opera with his niece or to visit friends in the city. These were still the Hanfstaengls, the Bruckmanns, the Essers. He scarcely bothered about the party; even in South Germany criticisms of his indifferent leadership were voiced; but Hitler paid these little attention. The summer of 1925 saw the publication of the first volume of *Mein Kampf,* and although the book was not a success—it sold fewer than 10,000 copies the first year—Hitler promptly set about dictating the second volume. His need to justify himself was as much a motive force as his urge to communicate.

From his mountain hideout he had followed with apparent apathy the program discussions in the North German wing of the party. His silence did not stem entirely from his characteristic reluctance to take steps. It also sprang from the politician's indifference to theory, his contempt for ideas in themselves. Moreover, he might have been secretly hoping to repeat the game he had played so successfully while in Landsberg, when he encouraged rivals, promoted antagonisms, and actually increased his own authority by slackening the reins.

Strasser's "catastrophe politics" abruptly changed the situation. Rather justifiably Hitler saw this as a direct challenge to himself, since, as with Röhm's activities, it threatened his parole and hence his entire political future. Immediately, he went on the offensive and could barely wait for the chance to strike out against the rebels and restore his authority.

In retrospect it would seem as if Hitler's imperious and impatient nature wrecked the party just when it was making such great strides. He was striking out at all his former associates, including Anton Drexler, with

236

whom he was waging a libel suit. In the course of the proceedings, one of Hitler's former followers appeared as witness against him. Calling out in court to Hitler that the National Socialist Party would in the long run fail if it used his methods, the man struck a prophetic chord, "You will come to a very sad end."

Only Hitler himself seemed unmoved by the continuing chain of failures. The certitude that had come to him as he formulated his philosophy in *Mein Kampf,* together with his obstinacy, enabled him to withstand all the crises without a hint of discouragement or resignation. It seemed as if he were once again, and with a measure of satisfaction, letting events take their course toward the highest dramatic pitch. As if untouched by all the bothersome events around him, he busied himself drawing, on postcards or in a sketchbook, baroque public buildings, arches of triumph, ornate domed halls—in short, a backdrop that expressed his unrelinquished plans for world domination and his extravagant millennial expectations.[29]

Chapter 3

If we wish to create a power factor, we need unity, authority, and drill. Our purpose must be not to create an army of politicians but an army of soldiers of the new philosophy.

Adolf Hitler, 1925

DEPLOYMENT FOR BATTLE

Hitler's position would seem to be on the verge of crumbling. He had come back from Landsberg with a certain messianic aura. This had given a degree of sanction to his strange behavior, to his insults, rifts and splitting maneuvers. But after a year that aura had worn off, and it was clear that the party could not survive any more such purges. To regain his lost ground, Hitler would have to smash the opposition while capturing its members for himself. He would have to make the North Germans renounce their socialistic tendencies and abjure their catastrophe policy. He would have to unseat Gregor Strasser, while swinging him around to his own side again, and somehow reconcile him to the plebeian Munich coterie of Streichers, Essers, and Amanns. Hitler's tactical agility, his artistry in handling people, his hypnotic talent, were seldom better revealed than in the way he went about this.

The question of the expropriated property of the princely houses served him as his lever. For the referendum proposed by the socialist parties had aroused a storm throughout the nation, and driven a wedge through fronts and political factions. Working class and middle class alike, the small savers and small property holders, even the most trusty of party members, realized with spontaneous indignation that any reimbursement for the princely families would come out of their own pockets. Yet they could not bear the thought of striking up an alliance with the Marxists against the former rulers of the country and by sanctioning the expropriation partially sanctioning the outrage of the revolution. Caught in this intellectual and emotional dilemma, the people spent themselves in furious argument. In Hanover, too, the matter was passionately debated.

Hitler saw how he could turn this situation to his own advantage. He called a meeting of the leaders of the entire party to be held in Bamberg on February 14, 1926. Bamberg was one of the bailiwicks of Julius Streicher, a fanatical Hitler devotee, and Hitler had recently honored the local party group by participating in their Christmas celebrations. Hitler saw to it that the North German district leaders with their mainly modest organizations would be impressed and possibly also somewhat demoralized by the display of banners, giant posters, and the announcement of massive demonstrations. By giving very short notice and by manipulating the list of participants, he took care that his own following would have a distinct majority. Hitler himself opened the discussion, which went on for the whole day, in a speech lasting nearly five hours. He called the proponents of expropriation deceitful because they spared the property of the Jewish lords of banking and the stock exchange. To be sure, the former rulers should not receive anything they had no right to; nevertheless, what did belong to them should not be taken from them: the National Socialist Party stood for private property and justice. As his South German followers applauded these sentiments, and were joined gradually and hesitantly by a few of the North Germans, he began to tear into the program of the Strasser group, point by point, opposing to it the party program of 1920: this was "the Founding Charter of our religion, our philosophy. To deviate from it would imply a betrayal of those who died for their faith in our ideas." A diary entry by Goebbels reflects the feelings of dismay on the part of the North German rebels: "I feel stunned. What is Hitler? A reactionary? Incredibly clumsy and insecure. Russian question: completely beside the point. Italy and England our natural allies: Horrible! Our task is smashing Bolshevism. Bolshevism is a Jewish plot! We must inherit Russia! 180 million people!!! Pay off the princes! . . . Horrible! Program suffices. Content with it. Feder nods. Ley nods. Streicher nods. Esser nods. It hurts my soul when I see you in this company! Brief discussion. Strasser speaks. Falteringly, tremblingly, clumsily, good, honest Strasser. Oh God, how ill-equipped we are for coping with those swine down there. . . . I cannot say a word! I feel dumbfounded."[30]

Even so, Strasser would not recant. He persisted in calling anti-Bolshevism totally misguided, a prime example of the way the capitalist system sowed confusion among its enemies and tricked the nationalist forces into serving its exploitative interests. Nevertheless, Strasser's defeat was complete. His brother Otto Strasser, to gloss over the humiliation, later pointed out that Hitler had cunningly convoked the meeting for a weekday, thus ensuring the absence of the unpaid North German gauleiters, who had jobs in addition to their party functions. Only Gregor Strasser and Goebbels had been in Bamberg, Otto Strasser alleged.

In fact, February 14, 1926, was a Sunday, and almost all the principal spokesmen of the Strasser coterie were present: Hinrich Lohse of

Schleswig-Holstein, Theodor Vahlen of Pomerania, Rust of Hanover, Klant of Hamburg. None of them, however, stood up to defend the idea of leftist National Socialism. In embarrassment they looked to Joseph Goebbels, the one man in their ranks with a natural gift for oratory; and like him, they felt stunned. Goebbels was cowed by Hitler's magnetic powers, by his brilliantly staged arrival complete with a column of cars, by the organizational ability and display of wealth of the Munich group. Gregor Strasser also succumbed, for the moment at least, to Hitler's talent for seduction. Thus Hitler had just finished fulminating against the "company of traitors" when he suddenly and demonstratively went over to Strasser and put his arm around his shoulders. Although the gesture did not convert Strasser himself, it made an impression upon the leaders at the meeting and forced them to take a conciliatory attitude. The working committee of North and West German gauleiters was in practice dissolved, its draft program not even put up for discussion, and the party took its stand against expropriation of the princely houses. Three weeks later, on March 5, Gregor Strasser sent out a hectographed circular letter to his fellow party leaders asking them to return the draft program "for very particular reasons" and because he had "promised Herr Hitler" that he would "see to the rounding up of every last copy of the draft."

It would seem that Hitler's vigorous intervention was directed not so much against the leftist program as against the leftist mentality of the Strasser following. Goebbels had even imagined, shortly before the Bamberg meeting, that "Hitler could be coaxed over to our terrain." But, in fact, what incensed Hitler most was the kind of Nazi the Strasser brothers were fostering: a National Socialist perpetually engaged in discussions, involved in problems, prone to doubt and needing to square things intellectually. To Hitler's mind, this was a deadly peril to the movement, bringing back the sort of sectarian dissension that had ruined the nationalist movement in the past. For Hitler equated all argument over ideas with sectarianism. Much as he favored and sometimes promoted personal conflicts among his followers, he hated theoretical differences of opinion. These, he thought, merely consumed energies and diminished the force of the movement. One of the secrets of Christianity's success, he was always saying, was the unalterability of its dogmas. Hitler's "Catholic" streak seldom emerges so clearly as in his respect for rigid, immutable formulas. All that really matters is a political creed, he would say; "that is what the whole world revolves around." And he would add that "no matter how idiotic" a program was, "people will believe in it because of the firmness with which it is advocated." In fact, a few weeks later Hitler took occasion to declare the old party program, in spite of its obvious weaknesses, "unalterable." The very outmoded, archaic features of the program transformed it from an object of discussion to one of veneration. Moreover, its purpose was not to answer questions or define aims but to attract attention.

Clarification would mean only division, Hitler declared. Faith was all. Once he had insisted on the identity of Führer and idea, the principle of the infallible, immutable Führer was equally established. One of his adherents put it in a nutshell: "Our program can be expressed in two words: 'Adolf Hitler.' "

The Bamberg meeting and the concomitant humiliation of Gregor Strasser marked the beginning of the end for leftist National Socialism. In spite of the clamorous publicity stirred up at the time, especially by Otto Strasser, the Nazi Left henceforth could only be a troublesome deviation, no longer an effective political alternative. From the time of the meeting, the NSDAP was increasingly molded into a regimented leader-directed party. Thereafter, and until the end, there were no longer any battles over principles, no longer any ideological disputes; what remained was only the struggle for office and favoritism. "Our movement has tremendous powers of assimilation," Hitler stated shortly afterward. Along with this, National Socialism no longer tried to rival the system of the democratic republic by presenting its own plan for a social order. Rather than an idea, it opposed to the republic a committed, disciplined, militant association whose members basked obtusely in the Führer's charisma. Theirs was the "primitive force of one-sidedness" that "arouses such horror precisely in people of the better class," that "male fist which," as Hitler put it in one of his weirder mixed metaphors, "knows that a toxin can only be smashed by an antitoxin. . . . The harder head must decide, the greatest resolution and the greater idealism." Elsewhere he assured the party members: "Such a struggle is not waged with 'intellectual' weapons, but with fanaticism."

It was this ruthlessly instrumental character of the party in the hands of a seemingly unchallenged leader that soon distinguished the National Socialist Party from all other political parties and militant movements. Its discipline surpassed that of the Communists, in whose obedient cadres elements of deviation, skepticism, and intellectual resistance were continually cropping up. There were no such problems within the NSDAP; the abject way in which the anti-Hitler opposition had caved in seemed to inspire a passion for conformity. Many of Strasser's followers now made it their ambition to convert the "movement into a handy, flawlessly functioning tool in the Führer's hand." Henceforth Hitler literally cracked his whip over even the highest-ranking members of the party leadership, insisting on his supremacy. The man to be hailed as "prototype of a good National Socialist," he declared, is one who "would let himself be killed for his Führer at any time." According to the bylaws the general membership meetings had to elect Hitler first chairman of the party; but from now on the motion to this effect would be treated as a humorous formality. As Göring later declared, alongside of Hitler's overwhelming authority "none of us counts more than the stones on which we are standing."[31]

Contrary to his usual inclination to exult over any triumphs, Hitler followed up his victory at Bamberg with conciliatory personal gestures. When Gregor Strasser was injured in an auto accident, Hitler appeared at his bedside "with a gigantic bouquet of flowers" and was, according to a letter of the patient himself, "very nice." He used the same approach with Goebbels, who had the worst reputation at Munich party headquarters as spokesman for the Strasser clique. Goebbels found himself suddenly being wooed. He was asked to be the principal speaker at a meeting in the Munich Bürgerbräu, and at the end of his speech Hitler embraced him with tears in his eyes. "He is embarrassingly good to us," Goebbels noted, deeply moved. At the same time, however, Hitler began to create the party machinery that would safeguard his newly acquired authority.

A general membership meeting held in Munich on May 22, 1926, established new bylaws for the NSDAP that were undisguisedly tailored to Hitler's personal needs. The National Socialist German Workers' Club in Munich was to be the cornerstone of the party; its directors also constituted the directorate of the party throughout Germany. The first chairman would still be elected—that was required by the laws regulating associations—but the electoral college for the entire party was to consist of the few thousand members of the Munich *Ortsgruppe* ("local group"). Thus the rest of the party was completely disenfranchised. Moreover, the Munich group alone had the right to demand an accounting of the first chairman—and the procedure for doing so was extremely complicated. In practice, therefore, Hitler's total control over the party was assured. There would be no majority decisions binding on him. Hereafter, in fact, even the gauleiters would not be elected by local party meetings, and the same was true of the chairmen of committees. Thus factions could not form, not even powerless ones.

In order to bolster this system even further, an investigation and mediation committee (USCHLA) was created, a kind of party tribunal whose sole importance lay in its right to expel individuals or even entire local groups from the NSDAP. Its first chairman, former Lieutenant General Heinemann, misunderstood the purpose of the committee. He thought it was meant to be an instrument for fighting corruption and immorality within the party. Hitler thereupon replaced him by the more docile Major Walter Buch, and as associate magistrates appointed his obedient Ulrich Graf and a young lawyer named Hans Frank.

In early July, six weeks later, Hitler celebrated his victory at a party rally in Weimar, where the new trend was clearly manifest. All critical—or, as Hitler contemptuously phrased it, "ingenious"—notions, all "half-baked and vague ideas" were repressed. The practice that later became standard for party rallies was applied here for the first time: only those motions were admitted which "have received the signature of the First Chairman." Instead of a wrangling party involved in differences over programs, the public image was to be that of "perfectly welded and consolidated leadership." In his "Fundamental Directives" Hitler ruled that the chairmen of the various special sessions were "to feel themselves leaders and not executive organs of the results of voting." In general, there was no voting, and Hitler wanted "endless discussions smothered." For they led people to think that political questions "can be solved by people sitting on their bottoms at a club meeting." Finally, strict bounds were set for speaking time in plenary sessions "so that the whole program cannot be wrecked by a single individual."

After the meeting in the National Theater, Hitler, dressed in a leather belted tunic and puttees, reviewed a parade by 5,000 of his followers and for the first time saluted them with outstretched arm in the fashion of the Italian Fascists. Goebbels, watching the uniformed columns of storm troopers, jubilantly saw the dawning of the Third Reich and the awakening of Germany. But other contemporary observers found the party rally a dull affair lacking in all spontaneity—the more so since Nazism had not yet developed the brilliant theatrical effects of later years that served to cover up its ideological poverty and ideational dreariness. Among the honored guests, it was true, was Theodor Duesterberg, leader of the Stahlhelm (the conservative veterans' organization), and another was the Kaiser's son, Prince August Wilhelm, soon afterward to join the SA. Also present, though in the background, was Gregor Strasser, who was heard muttering gloomily that National Socialism was dead.

As a last element of restlessness and rebellious energy there remained the SA, in whose ranks the radical slogans of the Strasser clique had struck lasting reverberations. Hitler therefore let a year elapse after Röhm's resignation before he appointed a supreme leader for the new SA: onetime Captain Franz Pfeffer von Salomon, who had been involved in various Free Corps and vigilante activities and had most recently been gauleiter of Westphalia. Together with Pfeffer, Hitler tried to settle the traditional problem of the SA's role and to shape it into an organization that would be neither a military auxiliary nor a secret society nor a brutish bodyguard for local party leaders. Rather, it was to become a specialized instrument for propaganda and mass intimidation, under firm control from party headquarters. Hitler wanted the SA to be the translation of the National Socialist idea into fanatical, unadulterated fighting power. To underline the SA's complete and final incorporation into the Nazi party, he arranged a ceremony at the National Theater in Weimar. The new SA units were put through mystical rituals culminating in the "oath of loyalty" and the presentation of standards Hitler had himself designed. "The training of the SA," he decreed in a letter to Pfeffer, "must be guided by party needs rather than by military points of view." The military associations of the past had been powerful but had had no underlying doctrines, he went on to say, and therefore had failed. The secret organizations and terrorist units,

243

on the other hand, had not realized that the enemy operated anonymously in men's brains and souls, so that there was little good in assassinating individual spokesmen. Consequently, the struggle must "be lifted out of the atmosphere of minor acts of revenge and conspiracy, raised to the grandeur of an ideological war of annihilation against Marxism, its structures and its henchmen. . . . The work must be conducted not in secret conventicles, but in huge mass processions. The way can be cleared for the Movement not by dagger and poison or pistol, but by conquering the streets."

In a succession of orders and basic instructions Pfeffer further delineated the special character of the SA. He evidenced a remarkable feeling for the mass psychological effectiveness of strict, drillmasterly arrangements. His orders for meetings and ceremonies reveal the point of view of a theatrical director as much as that of a leader; he regulated every platform appearance, every marching movement, every salute with raised arms or shout of *Heil*. His dictates often sounded like lessons in the techniques of mass psychology. Thus he would state: "The only form in which the SA displays itself to the public must be en masse. This is one of the most powerful forms of propaganda. The sight of a large body of disciplined men, inwardly and outwardly alike, whose militancy can be plainly seen or sensed, makes the most profound impression upon every German and speaks to his heart in a more convincing and persuasive language than writing and oratory and logic ever can. Calm composure and matter-of-factness emphasizes the impression of strength—the strength of marching columns."

But the attempt to transform the SA into an unarmed host of propagandists and to give to it the glamour but not the arrogance of the military remained on the whole a failure. Despite all his efforts, Hitler never really succeeded in shaping it into an obedient instrument for his political aims. The reason was only in part the rough cut-and-thrust temperament, the raw mercenary spirit of these perpetual soldiers. Another explanation lay in the traditions of a country that assigned special moral prerogatives to the military as opposed to the civilian, political authorities. Pfeffer's re-educational slogans could never change the fact that the SA considered itself the "Fighting Movement" in contrast to the Political Organization (PO). It viewed the PO as merely the talking branch of the party, and contemptuously spoke the initials as "P-Nought." In line with this attitude, the SA regarded itself as "the crown of our organization." With a scathing glance at the "parliamentary" parties, the spokesmen for the SA declared: "One thing they can't copy from us is our SA man." On the other hand, those parliamentary parties escaped the permanent difficulties in which the NSDAP was embroiled because of its party army. The trouble was that the World War I officers and soldiers, with their heavy baggage of complexes, could not be expected to execute the delicate balancing acts required of the other servile members of the master race. Only the next generation was able to do that. Soon Hitler began quarreling with Pfeffer, who proved to be as unmanageable as Röhm. In fact, more so, for he did not have Röhm's streak of sentimentality. He was not impressed by Hitler, that "flabby Austrian," as he termed him. Pfeffer was, after all, the son of a Prussian privy councilor.

The style of the Berlin SA was particularly mutinous. Its auxiliary organizations went their own way, frequently marked by criminal tendencies and gangster behavior. The Berlin gauleiter, Dr. Schlange, could do nothing to control the storm troopers. In fact, there were instances of fist fights between the Berlin leaders of the Political Organization and the SA. But the hullabaloo was somewhat out of proportion to the size of the Berlin branch of the Nazi party. Its membership was below 1,000 and only began to attract some attention after the Strasser brothers had started building up their newspaper in the city early in the summer of 1926. "The situation within the party this month has not been a good one," a report noted in October, 1926. "Things have reached such a pass in our district [gau] that complete shattering of the Berlin organization may be imminent. The tragedy of the gau is that it has never had a real leader."

At this juncture Hitler decided to clean up the untenable state of affairs in Berlin. His move was a masterly one, for he made use of the crisis to shake the local party organization free of the influence of Gregor Strasser. He also stole away Strasser's most capable adherent, for he appointed Joseph Goebbels new gauleiter of the capital. As early as July that ambitious rebel, under the impact of a magnanimous invitation to Munich and Berchtesgaden, had developed strong doubts about his radical leftist convictions. In his diary he now described Hitler, whom he had reviled so often, as "a genius . . . the naturally creative instrument of a divine destiny." He confided: "I stand before him deeply moved. This is how he is: like a child, lovable, good, merciful. Like a cat, cunning, prudent and agile; like a lion, roaringly great and gigantic. A hell of a fellow; a man . . . He pampers me like a child. My kindly friend and master!"[32] Yet raptures such as these are still accompanied by compunctions. Opportunist though Goebbels was, he was uneasy about his defection from Strasser, for he went on to say of the latter: "I suppose in the end he cannot follow along with his mind. With his heart, always. Sometimes I love him dearly."

However, Hitler knew how to make Goebbels his man. He gave him special powers that were not only designed to strengthen the new gauleiter's position but to create areas of friction with Strasser. For example, Hitler explicitly withdrew Goebbels from subordination to Strasser, while on the other hand subordinating the SA to Goebbels, although everywhere else the SA was jealously defending its independence from the Gauleiters. In order to placate Strasser, or at any rate to soften his resistance, Hitler promoted him to the post of Reich propaganda leader of the party. But in order to make the conflict between Goebbels and Strasser inevitable and

245

permanent, he made Goebbels autonomous in the field of propaganda also. Goebbels's erstwhile friends and party comrades thereupon charged him with shameful treachery—but in the short or long run all these leftist Nazi factionalists committed exactly the same treachery—unless, like the Strasser brothers, they chose expulsion, exile, or death.

With Goebbels as gauleiter of Berlin, things went from bad to worse for the already shattered power of the Left in northern Germany. The unsuspecting Strasser had supported the appointment of his supposed ally against the opposition of such Munich party dignitaries as Hess and Rosenberg. But Goebbels seemed to have had a keener grasp of Hitler's secret intentions. At any rate, he was soon openly warring with his recent cronies. He staged brawls and started a rival newspaper, *Der Angriff* ["The Attack"], directed against the Strasser brothers. He even spread rumors that they were of Jewish descent and had been bought by finance capital. Gregor Strasser, remembering how he had been taken in by Goebbels, later branded himself "a dopey super-idiot."

Cold-blooded, a master of sophistry and emotional manipulation, Goebbels started a new era in demagoguery, whose potentialities under modern conditions he perceived and exploited with unique success. To gain attention for the little-known Berlin party organization, he set up a ferocious band of toughs, who were continually instigating meeting-hall battles, brawls, and shootouts. These—in the words of a police report on a bloody battle with Communists at the Lichterfelde-Ost railroad station in March, 1927—put "anything seen previously into the shade."[33] By these tactics Goebbels was undoubtedly risking a ban on the Nazi party in Berlin—which came soon enough. But his followers were acquiring a sense of martyrdom and solidarity. At any rate, the Berlin organization emerged from unimportance and in the course of time was able to make considerable breaches in the massive walls of so-called Red Berlin.

Along with these efforts at expansion, Hitler began upon a gradual but consistent strengthening of the internal party organization. He aimed at a coherent, centralized command structure under a single charismatic leader. The hierarchic chain of authority, the strict tone with which all orders and instructions came down from the top, and the growing practice of wearing uniforms underlined the paramilitary character of a party whose leadership had been molded by the war. That leadership, as Goebbels once phrased it, had to be ready to obey "the slightest pressure with all its limbs at the decisive moment." The restrictions and governmental controls to which the party was subject merely furthered these aims—as in general the awareness of the outside world's hostility tautened the apparatus and furthered Hitler's drive for total leadership. It was easy now for Munich headquarters to impose its will on even the lowest branches of the party. In the first editions of *Mein Kampf* Hitler had made some slight concessions to democratic elements; in subsequent editions he revised these passages, laying stress, instead, on "Germanic democracy" and the "principle of unconditional authority of the Führer." In the party, similarly, he now warned local groups against holding "too many membership meetings," which would only constitute "a source of disputes."

Along with the party organization there now grew up a full-fledged bureaucracy, divided into numerous departments. The Nazi party was rapidly sloughing off its small-town club aspect—which it had retained even during its stormy early phase as a putschist party. Though Hitler's personal life and working habits were anything but organized, he was childishly proud of the triple registration system for party members and reported with fervor on the acquisition of modern office equipment, filing cabinets, and the like. In place of the primitive master-sergeant bureaucracy of the early years, an extensive network of new bureaus and subdivisions was established; in one year, 1926, the space in the Munich central party office was expanded three times. Before long, this apparatus surpassed even the fabulous bureaucracy of the Social Democratic Party. Its size was altogether disproportionate to the small number of the NSDAP's membership, which increased quite slowly. For Hitler himself seemed to want to build up the party in the form of a small, tough kernel of specialists in propaganda and violence. He repeatedly stressed that an organization of 10 million people was necessarily peaceable and could not be set in motion of its own accord; only fanatical minorities would be able to move it. Of the 55,000 members the party had had in 1923, it had won back only half by the end of 1925. A year later the membership amounted to somewhat more than 108,000. But the seemingly swollen bureaucracy would be useful for the future mass party in which Hitler continued to believe with absolute confidence. What is more, the great number of party offices provided him with varied possibilities for patronage and for dividing the power of others, thus extending and securing his own.

To this period belong the first efforts toward formation of a shadow government. Soon Gregor Strasser, who had been appointed Reich organization leader, took charge of this operation and pushed it vigorously. In *Mein Kampf* Hitler had already called for a movement geared for the coming overturn, because it would "already contain the future government within itself" and, moreover, would "be able to place the perfected body of its own government at the disposal" of the state. In these terms, the party posts also served as alternatives to the "Weimar mis-State," challenging the republic's authority and legitimacy in the name of the allegedly unrepresented people. The departments of the shadow government were set up to correspond with the state bureaucracy; thus the Nazi party had departments for foreign policy, justice, and defense. Other departments dealt with the favorite themes of Nazi policy: public health and race, propaganda, resettlement, and agrarian policy. They rehearsed their role in a new government with proposals and draft legislation marked to a large extent by bold amateurishness.

From 1926 on, moreover, a host of auxiliary party organizations were

247

set up: National Socialist Leagues of doctors, lawyers, students, teachers, and civil servants. Even gardening and poultry raising had their place in the network of bureaus and subdivisions. In 1927 the creation of a women's SA was briefly considered but then rejected. The following year, however, the Red Swastika, which later became the Nazi women's organization, was formed to receive the growing hordes of sharply politicized women and assign them a place—largely limited to practical works of mercy—in the men's party, which at this time was still heavily homosexual.

Later, in a secret statement made in 1940, Goebbels boasted that when Nazism came to power in 1933, "it had only to transfer its organization, its intellectual and spiritual principles, to the State," for it had already been "a state within the State," which had "prepared everything and considered everything." That was a gross exaggeration. Nevertheless, it is true that the Nazi party was better prepared for its claim to power than any other totalitarian party. The Reichsleiters and the gauleiters put on the airs of cabinet ministers long before 1933. On public occasions the SA usurped the functions of the police without asking anyone's leave. Quite often, Hitler, as leader of the "opposition government" contrived to be represented by a personal observer at international conferences. The same polemical principle underlay the wide display of the party symbols. The swastika was represented as the insignia of the true, honorable Germany. The Horst Wessel song became the anthem of the shadow government, while brown shirts, medals, and badges, as well as the party's memorial days, promoted a sense of togetherness in those irreconcilably opposed to the existing government.

In spite of its mania for bureaucracy, the National Socialist government was highly personal. At crucial moments, administrative rulings and bureaucratic channels had little bearing; subjective factors decided the issue. Positions within the party hierarchy were defined less by actual rank than by the signs of favor the holders enjoyed. Similarly, all standards were subject to arbitrary change, at the mercy of whim. High above all else stood the "will of the Führer"—the basic fact of the constitution, supreme and unassailable. He impulsively followed his inspirations. He installed and dismissed the party's lesser leaders and employees, determined candidatures and electoral lists, regulated the income of underlings and even supervised their private lives.

In principle, there were no restrictions whatsoever upon the absolute power of the Führer. Early in 1928 Albert Krebs, gauleiter of Hamburg, having had differences with others in the district, submitted his resignation. Hitler initially refused to accept the resignation. In a magnificently circumstantial report he made the point that the confidence of the membership could neither grant nor rescind positions of power within the party. These depended solely on the confidence of the Führer. He alone praised merit, reproved failure, mediated, thanked, or forgave. Only after this elaborate exposition did Hitler accept the resignation of Krebs.

By such means Hitler's personality increasingly dominated and determined the structures of the party. In fact, the bureaucracy itself mirrored aspects of his personal history. The bureaucratic passion that expressed itself in the proliferation of departments, the craze for titles, and the meaningless departmental functions hearkened back to the complicated officialdom of Imperial Austria, to which Hitler's father, albeit humbly, belonged. The prevalence of arbitrary subjectivity pointed to Hitler's past in the lawless and freebooting veterans' associations. The megalomaniac tendencies of his youth came to the surface again in the fantastically exaggerated scale of the bureaucracy. So did his craving for inflated display; he invented high-sounding labels for offices that scarcely existed except in his imagination.

Yet this shadow government and swollen party bureaucracy were a form of impatient snatching at the future, efforts to anticipate reality. Endless meetings were held. In 1925 alone, according to a count of Hitler's, the party could boast of almost 2,400 demonstrations. But the public showed only sluggish interest. All the noise, the brawls, the battle for headlines yielded only meager results. During those years of the Weimar Republic's gradual consolidation, when in Goebbels's phrase the Nazi party could not claim even its opponents' hatred, Hitler himself sometimes seemed to doubt ultimate success. At such times he would escape from reality into one of his grand, breathtaking prospects and transfer his faith to the distant future: "Perhaps another twenty or a hundred years may pass before our idea is victorious. Those who believe in the idea today may die—what does any one person amount to in the evolution of the race, of humanity?" In different moods he saw himself leading the great war of the future. Sitting before a plate of pastries in the Café Heck he said to Captain Stennes in a loud voice: "And then, Stennes, after we have won the victory, we'll build a Victory Boulevard, from Döberitz to the Brandenburg Gate, sixty meters wide, lined on the right and the left by trophies and war booty."[34]

The central office, however, complained that some thirty local party groups (there were about 200) had failed to order posters for the August, 1927, party rally, and generally deplored the difficulties it encountered in organizing mass meetings. This contributed to Hitler's decision to hold the 1927 annual party rally for the first time against the backdrop of the ancient imperial city of Nuremberg, where, as in Bamberg, Julius Streicher provided a further attraction. By now Hitler's staging had improved immensely; his touch could be felt in all the proceedings that dramatized with such éclat the movement's coherence and belligerency. After it, one of his followers called him a "wizard in leadership of the masses." With benefit of hindsight we can in fact see in this rally first elements of what later developed into a pompous ritual. The storm troopers and the party units from all the regions of Germany arrived in special trains, with their flags, pennants, and bands. Included, too, were many delegations from foreign countries, and the Hitler Youth, founded the previous year, also marched for the first time. The uniforming of the party, which in Weimar had still been hit and miss, had by now become standardized. Gerhard Rossbach had obtained a supply of brown shirts from old militia stocks and had introduced them into the SA. Hitler thought them exceedingly ugly, but even he now wore one.

The grand demonstration in the Luitpoldhain, on the outskirts of Nuremberg, featured an "address by the Führer." In conclusion, twelve standards were solemnly dedicated. Then, in the market place, Hitler sat in his open car, arm stiffly outstretched, reviewing the marching contingents. The Nazi press spoke of a parade of 30,000; the *Völkische Beobachter* magnified that figure to 100,000; but more sober estimates did not go beyond 15,000 marchers. Some women and girls, who had appeared in fanciful brown costumes, were not allowed to participate in the march past Hitler.

This party rally passed a number of resolutions. It called for a congress on labor-union problems, considered the idea of a "sacrifice circle" to cope with the party's precarious financial situation, and called for the creation of a National Socialist scientific society in order to extend the influence of the party's propaganda to intellectual groups.

Some time later, in Hamburg, Hitler for the first time addressed several thousand farmers from Schleswig-Holstein. Stagnation was forcing the party to seek followers among new, hitherto untapped classes of society.

The government, meanwhile, had successfully continued the stabilization efforts of 1923–24. A new reparations agreement, the Treaty of Locarno, the acceptance of Germany into the League of Nations, the Kellogg Pact, and finally some degree of reconciliation between Germany and France (based initially on the personal factor of the two Foreign Ministers'— Stresemann and Briand—respect for one another, but supported by a growing public mood)—all these factors indicated that the trend of the times was toward relaxation of tensions, a trend to which the strained radicalism of the Nazis was directly opposed. Large American loans had meant an increase in Germany's indebtedness, but at the same time had made possible large investments for the rationalization and modernization of the economy. German production indices between 1923 and 1928 showed rises greater than those of all other European countries in virtually every sector of the economy. What is more, in spite of the losses in territory, production surpassed the prewar achievements of the country. In 1928 national income was some 12 per cent higher than in 1913; improvement in social conditions had been considerable; and unemployment had been reduced to approximately 400,000.

It was obvious that the times were countering the efforts of the Nazis. Hitler himself lived largely in retirement at Obersalzberg, often virtually invisible for weeks. But his withdrawal was proof that he felt himself unassailable within the party. Now and then, at shrewdly calculated intervals, he brought his authority to bear, issuing a reprimand or a threat. Occasionally he went on trips to cultivate contacts or to find contributors. On December 10, 1926, the second volume of *Mein Kampf* came out; but it, too, failed to bring him the smashing success he had expected. In 1925 almost 10,000 copies of the first volume had been sold, and in the following year nearly 7,000. But in 1927 the sale of the entire two-volume work dropped to 5,607, and in 1928 the figure was only 3,015.[35]

At any rate, his publishing income allowed him to buy the property on Obersalzberg. Frau Bechstein helped him with the furnishing; the Wagners in Bayreuth donated linens and china and later sent a set of the Master's collected works, together with a page from the original score of *Lohengrin*. At about the same time Hitler spent 20,000 marks to acquire a six-seater, supercharged open Mercedes that satisfied both his taste for technology and his love of display.

Hitler's tax declarations, found after the war, indicate that these expenditures considerably exceeded his reported income—and that the Treasury was not unaware of this fact. In a letter to the tax collectors reminiscent, in its whimpering slyness, of his appeal to the authorities of Linz after he had been tracked down as a draft dodger, he maintained that he was without funds and insisted on the modesty of his life style: "Nowhere do I possess property or other capital assets that I can call my own. I restrict of necessity my personal wants so far that I am a complete abstainer from alcohol and tobacco, take my meals in most modest restaurants, and aside from my minimal apartment rent make no expenditures that are not chargeable to my expenses as a political writer. . . . Also the automobile is for me but a means to an end. It alone makes it possible for me to accomplish my daily work."[36]

In September, 1926, he declared himself incapable of paying his taxes and spoke repeatedly of his sizable bank debts. Years later, he occasionally recalled this period in which he was constantly strapped for money and said that at times he had lived on nothing but apples. His Munich home on Thierschstrasse, sublet from the widow Reichert, was in fact unostentatious: a small, scantily furnished room whose floor was covered with worn linoleum.

In order to increase his income, Hitler joined with the photographer Heinrich Hoffmann—to whom he had granted virtually exclusive rights to pictures of him—to found a picture magazine, the *Illustrierte Beobachter,* to which he henceforth contributed an article in every issue. In the summer of 1928, in the very middle of this period of waiting, planning, and keeping still, he began writing another book, setting forth the ideas of foreign policy he had been developing. This, however, remained unpublished during his lifetime.

By means of a succession of strained-sounding appeals, he kept the party together in spite of the divergent forces tugging it every which way. He turned a deaf ear to those dissatisfied with the legal course he had chosen. The consolidation of the republic did not mislead him into the shortsighted conclusions many of his followers came to. His instinct for the frangible allowed him to nurse his plans patiently. In characteristic fashion he used the very obstacles the party was encountering, the very hopelessness of its predicament, to bolster his belief in ultimate success: "In this very fact is to be found the absolute, or rather, the mathematically calculable reason for the future victory of our movement," he told his followers. "As long as we are a radical movement, as long as public opinion proscribes us, as long as momentary circumstances in the country are against us—just so long will we continue to gather around us the most valuable human material, even in times when, as people say, rational arguments are against us." At a Christmas party given by a Munich section of the NSDAP he raised morale by comparing the woes of the party with the situation of the early Christians. National Socialism, he went on—sustaining the parallel because he had been carried away by his own bold image and the Christmas mood of the gathering—would "translate the ideals of Christ into deeds." He, Hitler, would complete "the work which Christ had begun but could not finish."

The preceding amateur performance of a skit titled *Redemption* had prepared the way for his appearance by dramatizing the present "misery and bondage." As the *Völkische Beobachter* described the action: "The rising star of Christmas Eve pointed to the Redeemer; the parting curtain now showed the new redeemer who will save the German people from shame and misery—our Leader Adolf Hitler."

To the outside world, such pronouncements added to the aura of dementia surrounding the man. As at the beginning of his career, the reputation of being a queer duck preceded him. It was hard for people to take him seriously; one theory was that his odd traits sprang from the colorful idiosyncrasies of Bavarian politics. The style he cultivated often aroused ridicule. Thus, for example, he made an object of veneration of the flag that had been carried on the march to the Feldherrnhalle; it was called the "Blood Banner" and whenever other standards were consecrated, they were touched with the tip of this Blood Banner. Presumably mystical forces flowed on contact. Party members to whose radically pure pedigree he wanted to pay tribute might find themselves addressed, in letters, as *Euer Deutschgeboren,* a form of address roughly equivalent to "Your German-born Worship." But other activities suggested that the Nazi party was pursuing its goals with seriousness and determination. At the end of 1926 the party set up a speakers' school to give its followers the techniques and information needed for effective public speaking. By the end of 1932 this school had, according to its records, trained some 6,000 speakers.

In the spring of 1927 the governments of Saxony and Bavaria, no longer nervous about the Nazi party, decided to lift the ban on speeches by the party leader. Hitler readily gave the requested assurances that he would not pursue any unlawful goals or use any unlawful means. But speak he would, and glaring red posters announced that at eight o'clock in the evening of March 9 Adolf Hitler would once again, for the first time since the ban, address the people of Munich at the Krone Circus. The police report on the meeting reveals how deep an impression the event made on the informant himself:

The circus is considerably more than half filled by ten minutes past seven. From the stage hangs the red swastika flag. The stage is reserved for prominent party members and the speaker. The seats in the boxes also seem to be reserved for special party members, since they are assigned by brownshirts. A band has assembled on the platform. No other decorations were to be seen.

The people on the benches are excited and filled with anticipation. They talk about Hitler, about his former oratorical triumphs at the Krone Circus. The women, who are present in great numbers, still seem to be enthusiastic about him. . . . There is a craving for sensation in the hot, insipid air. The band plays rousing marches while fresh crowds keep pouring in. The *Völkische Beobachter* is hawked about. At the ticket office each visitor is given a copy of the Program of the National Socialist Workers' Party, and at the entrance a slip is pressed into everyone's hand warning against reacting to provocations and emphasizing the need to maintain order. Small flags are sold: "Welcoming flags, 10 pfennig apiece." They are either black-white-red or entirely red, and show the swastika. The women are the best customers.

Meanwhile the ranks are filling. "We have to make it like the old days!" people are saying. The arena fills. . . . Most of the spectators belong to the lower economic groups, workers, small artisans, small tradesmen. Many youths in windbreakers and knee socks. Few, hardly any, representatives of the radical working class are to be seen. The people are well dressed; some men are even in evening dress. The crowd in the circus, which is nearly entirely filled, is estimated at seven thousand persons.

It is now half past eight. From the entrance come roars of *Heil*. Brownshirts march in, the band plays, the crowd cheers noisily. Hitler appears in a brown raincoat, walks swiftly, accompanied by his retinue, the whole length of the circus and up to the stage. The people gesticulate in happy excitement, wave, continually shout *Heil*, stand on the benches, stamp their feet thunderously. Then comes a trumpet blast, as in the theater. Sudden silence.

Amid roars of welcome from the spectators, the brownshirts now march into the hall in rank and file, led by two rows of drummers and then the flag. The men salute in the manner of the Fascists, with outstretched arms. The audience cheers them. On the stage Hitler has similarly stretched out his arm in salute. The music surges up. Flags move past, glittering standards with swastikas inside the wreath and with eagles, modeled on the ancient Roman military standards. Perhaps about two hundred men file past. They fill the arena and stand at attention while the flag-bearers and standard-bearers people the stage. . . .

Hitler steps swiftly to the front of the stage. He speaks without a manuscript, at first in a slow, emphatic way; later the words come tumbling forth, and in

253

passages spoken with exaggerated emotion his voice becomes thin and high and ceases to be intelligible. He gesticulates with arms and hands, jumps agitatedly about, and is bent on fascinating the thousands in the audience, who listen with close attention. When applause interrupts him, he raises his hands theatrically. This protest, which occurs frequently in the later course of the speech, strikes a histrionic note, and indeed is deliberately overplayed. The oratorical performance in itself . . . did not strike this observer as anything remarkable.[37]

That Hitler could speak again did not remove the difficulties of the party. Yet Hitler himself, it now appeared, had gained rather than lost by the ban. For he had been tided over the period of general amused indifference, when meeting halls would have remained empty and his name and message would have only become a bore. He soon realized this and behaved accordingly. In 1927 he spoke in public fifty-six times; two years later he had reduced his public appearances to twenty-nine. There are indications that at this period he began to see the advantages of living in semidivine remoteness. The moment he returned to the masses, he was competing with the overpowering force of unfavorable circumstances. Failures began to pile up, and with this came criticism from within the party. It was directed equally against his style of leadership and against the stringently maintained policy of legality. Even Goebbels, so embarrassingly subservient to Hitler and one of the prophets of the Führer cult, assailed the strictly legal course in his 1927 pamphlet, *Der Nazi-Sozi*. Answering the question of what the party should do if its efforts to obtain a majority failed, Goebbels broke out with: "What then? Then we'll clench our teeth and get ready. Then we'll march against this government; then we'll dare the last great coup for Germany; then revolutionaries of the word will become revolutionaries of the deed. Then we'll make a revolution!"

Hitler's personal conduct also met with criticism, particularly his arrogance toward tried-and-true party comrades. One old party man objected to "the much-discussed wall around Herr Hitler." There were murmurings about Hitler's negligent conduct of party business and his jealousy complex in regard to his niece. In the early summer of 1928, when his chauffeur Emil Maurice surprised him in Geli Raubal's room, Hitler raised his riding whip in such threatening fury that Maurice saved himself only by leaping out the window. With "unconditional devotion" the chairman of the Investigation and Mediation Committee, Walter Buch finally felt compelled to express his view "that you, Herr Hitler, are gradually falling into a degree of misanthropy that causes me worry."[38]

Faced with these rumblings within the party, Hitler canceled the planned party rally for 1928 and instead convoked a meeting of the leaders in Munich. He forbade all preparatory local meetings, and when he opened the session on August 31 he delivered a highly charged speech in praise of obedience and discipline. Only totally committed elites could constitute a "historic minority," he declared, and thus shape history. To remain operative, the NSDAP must have at most 100,000 members: "That is a number to work with!" All the rest must be followers, rallying around and serving the purposes of the party only in specific cases. Scornfully, he dismissed a motion to elect a "senate" to aid him. He did not think much of advisers, he said. The motion had been offered by Gauleiter Artur Dinter of Thuringia; he had Dinter removed from his post and soon afterward expelled from the party. There had, it is true, been some background to this seemingly arbitrary action. Hitler had previously had a correspondence with Gauleiter Dinter in which he announced that as a politician he "claimed infallibility" and "had the blind faith that he would some day belong among those who make history."

Shortly afterward, a meeting was convoked that had not been organized in the form by then becoming customary: a briefing session in which Hitler simply issued commands. During the discussion Hitler sat silent, with a markedly bored or sardonic expression, gradually creating such a sense of paralysis and futility that the meeting wound to an end in general resignation. One of the participants later conjectured that Hitler had permitted the meeting to be held only in order to show how his indifference could ruin it.

Hitler felt his chance would come as leader of an inconspicuous but rigorously organized party. Personally, he saw no reason for discouragement, for in establishing his hold over the party he had made important progress. Henceforth, the party sometimes referred to itself officially as the "Hitler movement." Without significant support from influential patrons and powerful institutions, the movement was now proving that if it could not win, it could at least survive on its own resources.

On May 20, 1928, a new Reichstag was elected. The NSDAP placed ninth, with 2.6 per cent of the votes, winning twelve seats. Among its deputies were Gregor Strasser, Gottfried Feder, Goebbels, Frick, and Hermann Göring, who in the interval had returned home from Sweden bringing with him a wealthy wife and extensive connections. Hitler himself, being "stateless," had not been a candidate. But with his remarkable capacity for turning his embarrassments and disabilities to advantage, he used this circumstance to reinforce his pose of the unique leader who refused to make any concessions to the despised parliamentary system and stood far above the scramble, the deals and greeds of daily life. If he had decided to let the party participate in the elections—a decision taken only after long vacillation—it had been partly out of the desire to get a share in the privileges of Reichstag deputies. Sure enough, a week after the elections Goebbels wrote an article that cast quite another light on the party's pretense to legalism: "I am not a member of the Reichstag. I am an HOI. A Holder of Immunity. An HORP. A Holder of a Railroad Pass. What do we care about the Reichstag? We have been elected against the Reichstag, and we will exercise our mandate in the interests of our employer. . . . An HOI is allowed to call a dungheap a dungheap and does not have to use such euphemisms as 'government.' " Goebbels concluded this amazing confession with: "This startles you, does it? But don't think we're finished yet. . . . You'll have lots more fun with us before it's over. Just wait till the comedy begins."

Yet such remarks seemed mere rhetorical taunts. The NSDAP remained a splinter party given to *outré* gestures. But Hitler himself, sure of his ground, his cadres ready for action, waited coolly for a new radicalization of the masses. Once conditions had brought that about, he would be able to make the breakthrough and transform his following into a mass party. In spite of all his organizational bustle, he had so far not managed to emerge from the shadow of the republic, which by now was functioning competently, if without any special brilliance. It sometimes seemed as if the nation were at last ready to make its peace with the republic, to accept the gray dullness of Weimar and be reconciled to the ordinariness of history. The Reichstag elections had, it is true, revealed a degree of disintegration going on in the bourgeois center, as manifested by the rise of many splinter parties. The Nazi party, moreover, could now count 150,000 members. But at the beginning of 1929 the Bonn sociologist Joseph A. Schumpeter spoke of the "impressive stability in our social conditions" and concluded: "In no sense, in no area, in no direction, are eruptions, upheavals or disasters probable."

But Hitler understood things much more keenly. In a speech given during this brief happy period in the history of the republic, he remarked on the psychology of the Germans: "We have a third value: our fighting spirit. It is there, only buried under a pile of foreign theories and doctrines. A great and powerful party goes to a lot of trouble to prove the opposite, until suddenly an ordinary military band comes along and plays. Then the straggler comes to, out of his dreamy state; all at once he begins to feel himself a comrade of the marching men, and joins their columns. That's the way it is today. Our people only have to be shown this better course— and you'll see, we'll start marching."[39]

He was waiting for his cue. The question was whether the party could preserve, over the long pull, its dynamism, its hopes, its conception of its aims, and its image of the chosen leader—that whole system of fictions and credulities on which it was founded. In an analysis of the May, 1928, elections Otto Strasser had complained that "National Socialism's tidings of redemption" had not caught the ear of the masses and that the party had failed to make any inroads into proletarian circles. In fact, the party's following consisted chiefly of lower-grade white-collar workers, artisans, some farm groups, and young people inclined to romantic protest—the advance guard of those classes of the German population who were especially susceptible to the rousing music of "an ordinary military band."

Only a few months later, the scene had totally changed.

BOOK IV

The Time of Struggle

Chapter 1

Following our old method, we once more take up the struggle and say: Attack! Attack! Always attack! If someone says we can't possibly have another try, remember that I can attack not just one more time but ten times over.

Adolf Hitler

FROM PROVINCIAL TO NATIONAL POLITICS

Hitler launched his first massive offensive against the consolidated system of the republic in the summer of 1929, and at once his advance carried him a long way. He had long been in search of a slogan that could mobilize the masses. Suddenly, Gustav Stresemann's foreign policy offered a breach into which he could hurl the full weight of his propaganda. The debate over reparations had broken out afresh, and Hitler mustered all his energy to move the NSDAP from its role of isolated sectarian party and propel it into the limelight of national politics. By good luck his campaign coincided in time with the world-wide Depression, and derived its psychological impact from economic conditions. This gave him the opportunity to test his forces, his organization, and his tactics in a kind of prelude. The struggle that raged around the reparations question brought on the crisis that was to grip the republic to the very end, a crisis initiated by Hitler and cleverly fomented until the republic broke down.

Strictly speaking, the point of departure came with the death of Gustav Stresemann at the beginning of October, 1929. The German Foreign Minister had worn himself out trying to put over his subtle foreign policy. Branded as a "compliance policy,"* it actually aimed at gradual abrogation of the Versailles Treaty. Until shortly before his death Stresemann, though with considerable doubts, had backed the reparations arrangements

* *Erfüllungspolitik*, literally fulfillment [of the terms of the Versailles Treaty] policy.—TRANS.

259

drafted by a committee of experts under the chairmanship of Owen D. Young, the American banker. The Young Plan represented a distinct improvement on the existing conditions. Moreover, thanks to Stresemann's obstinacy and diplomatic adroitness, it had been coupled with the promise of the Allied occupying forces evacuating the Rhineland before the date stipulated by treaty.

Nevertheless, the agreement encountered vehement opposition inside Germany. It even disappointed many of those who had a clear view of the Reich's predicament. For there was an element of cruel mockery in having Germany undertake obligations for payments extending over nearly sixty years when she did not even have the first few annual payments at her disposal. Two hundred and twenty notables of economics, science, and politics, among them Carl Duisberg, of I. G. Farben, the theologian Adolf Harnack, the physicist Max Planck, Konrad Adenauer, then mayor of Cologne, and former Chancellor Hans Luther, issued a public statement expressing their great concern. It would appear that the many conciliatory gestures had been a mere front; eleven years after the war, the Young Plan exposed the merciless attitude of the victors toward the vanquished. What was more, the plan once again adverted to the war-guilt clause, Article 231 of the Versailles Treaty, which had earlier inflicted such wounds to the nation's self-esteem. With payments continuing until 1988, the Young Plan was fundamentally unrealistic, and the radical nationalist groups were able to make effective capital out of the phrase *le boche payera tout*. Conceived as a further step in a gradual process of softening the penalties of the war, and thus supposedly serving to stabilize the republic, the Young Plan became just the contrary, the "point of crystallization for fundamental opposition to the Weimar 'system.' "[1]

On July 9, 1929, the radical Right united to form a national committee for a plebiscite to reject the Young Plan. They staged a wild and vehement campaign (joined by the Communists on the extreme Left) that never let up until the agreement was eventually signed nine months later. The issue brought together a strange assortment of associations and interdependencies whose differences were temporarily forgotten in favor of a few hypnotic slogans. These, endlessly repeated, tried to concentrate hatred upon a few sharply etched images of the enemy. The plan was described as the "death penalty on the unborn," the "Golgotha of the German people" whom the executioners were "nailing to the cross with scornful laughter." Along with this the "Nationalist Opposition" demanded annulment of the war-guilt clause, the end of all reparations, immediate evacuation of the occupied territories, and the punishment of all cabinet ministers and members of the government aiding and abetting the "enslavement" of the German people.

The committee was headed by privy councillor Alfred Hugenberg, an ambitious, narrow-minded, and unscrupulous man of sixty-three who had served as settlement commissioner in the East, had been a director of the Krupp Company, and finally had built up an intricate and far-ranging press empire. In addition to an extensive list of newspapers, he controlled a news agency and UFA, the motion picture company. As the political liaison man of heavy industry, he also had sizable sums at his disposal. This money he deliberately committed to undermining the "Socialist Republic," to smashing the unions, and to answering "class struggle from below," as he put it, with "class struggle by the upper class." A short, rotund figure with a mustache and close-cropped hair, he looked like a pensioned-off sergeant posing for a martial photo, not like the proud and embittered patrician he wished to be.

In the fall of 1928 Hugenberg had emerged as a dark horse and assumed leadership of the Deutschnationale Volkspartei (the German Nationalist People's Party). He promptly made himself the spokesman of radical resentment. The Right had been slowly warming toward the republic; but under Hugenberg's control all such signs of rapprochement abruptly came to an end. Both in methods and in some points of its program, the DNVP began copying the Hitler party. It never succeeded in being more than the bourgeois caricature of the Nazis. Still and all, Hugenberg broke all limits in his battle against the hated republic. The first signs of the world-wide Depression were beginning to be felt in Germany; but during the storm over the Young Plan, Hugenberg warned 3,000 American businessmen, in a circular letter, against granting credits to Germany.[2] Under this leader, the German Nationalists quickly lost something like half their membership. But this made little impression on Hugenberg; he declared coolly that he preferred a small block to a large pulp.

The campaign against the Young Plan gave Hugenberg the chance to assert leadership over the scattered forces of the Right, mainly the Stahl-helm (Steel Helmets), the Pan-Germans, the Landbund (Agrarian League), and the Nazis. His larger purpose was to reconquer for the old upper class some of its lost initiative. The misfired revolution of 1918 had not deprived that class of influence, positions of status, money, and prop-erty, but it no longer had any credit with the people. With all the arrogance of one of the "top-drawer people" toward a figure associated with the rabble, Hugenberg thought he could make use of Hitler. Here was someone with a proven gift for agitation, he calculated, the very man to lead the masses back to conservatism. For Hugenberg was intelligent enough to see that the usual spokesmen for the conservative cause were largely isolated by their social vanity. When the time came, he thought, he would know how to put Hitler in his place.

Hitler's own thoughts were far less devious. When Reichstag deputy Hinrich Lohse heard of the alliance, he commented anxiously: "Let's hope the Führer knows how to pull a fast one on Hugenberg." But Hitler was not thinking of deceptions. From the start he came on with an air of unmistakable superiority. He scarcely bothered to hide his contemptuous opinion of Hugenberg, the bourgeois reactionary, and all the "gray, moth-eaten eagles," as Goebbels called them. He said no to the concessions Hugenberg demanded—all the more flatly since the "Left" within the Nazi party was keeping a suspicious watch over the proceedings. What it amounted to was that Hitler alone named the conditions under which he would permit these new backers to help him move forward. At first he proposed marching separately but finally let himself be coaxed into the alliance. However, he demanded complete independence in propaganda and a sizable share of the proffered funds. Then, as if bent on confounding or humiliating his new allies, he appointed the most prominent anticapi-talist in the ranks of the Nazi party, Gregor Strasser, to be his representa-tive on the joint financing committee.

The alliance was his first success in a remarkable series of maneuvers that brought Hitler a long way ahead and finally to his goal. His insight into the true nature of situations, his knack for penetrating the various strata of interests, for spotting weaknesses and setting up temporary coali-tions, in short, his tactical instinct, certainly contributed as much to his rise as his oratorical powers, the backing of the army, industry, and the judi-ciary, and the terrorism of his brown shirts. To insist on the magical, the conspiratorial, or the brutal elements in Hitler's rise to power certainly betrays an inadequate understanding of the course of events. But beyond that, it perpetuates the erroneous notion of the leader of the Nazi party as a mere propagandist or tool. All the facts belie that picture. Hitler was consummately skillful in the field of politics.

With an actor's agility, at first playing hesitant, conducting his negotia-tions in a sometimes provocative, sometimes sulky manner, while at the same time conveying an impression of sincerity, ambition, and drive, Hitler finally lured his partners into such a position that they were furthering and financing his rise even as they were paying for it politically. A factor in this particular success, however, was the leftist element in his own ranks, which kept him from making any significant concessions. While the negotiations were going on, Strasser's militant newspapers carried banner headlines featuring a saying of Hitler's: The greatest danger to the German people is not Marxism but the bourgeois parties.

In evaluating this episode we must not overlook the power-hungry blind-ness of the German nationalist conservatives. By parasitically seizing on the force and vitality of the Nazi movement, by uniting with the secretly despised but also admired upstart Hitler, they were trying to forestall German nationalist conservatism's departure from the stage of history, when that departure had been long since decided. Still, Hitler's success remains remarkable. For four and a half years he had waited, preparing himself and, in keeping with the unforgotten doctrine of Karl Lueger, working toward alliance with the "powerful institutions," the holders of political and social influence. When the offer was finally made to him, he had coolly and firmly named his terms. For years Adolf Hitler had stood at the head of an inconspicuous extremist party, ignored or an object of mockery. Only in the light of that fact can we grasp what is meant to him to team up with Hugenberg. It freed him from the noisome odor of being a crackpot revolutionary and putschist. He could appear in public within a circle of respectable, influential patrons and make their good reputation his own. Once before he had had that chance and thrown it away; now he indicated that he meant to behave much more circumspectly.

After concluding the alliance, the Nazi party for the first time had funds enough to crank up its excellent propaganda apparatus. It at once began showing the public a style of propaganda of unprecedented radicality and impact. Nothing of the kind had ever existed in Germany, Hitler declared in a letter of that period. "We have thoroughly worked over our people as no other party has done." None of the other partners in the nationalist alliance could approach the Nazi party in stridency, sharpness, and psychological cunning. From the start the Nazis made it plain that the Young Plan was only the pretext for the campaign. They broadened their attack to include the whole "system," which they claimed was collapsing from incompetence, treason, and corruption. "The time will come," Hitler cried out in a speech at Hersbruck, near Nuremberg, toward the end of November, "when those responsible for Germany's collapse will laugh out of the other side of their faces. Fear will grip them. Let them know that their judgment is on the way." Fascinated by the demogogic wildness of the Nazis, Hugenberg and the rest of the conservatives in the coalition stared at the tremendous wave they had set in motion. They encouraged it, repeatedly lent impetus to it, and in their smug faith in their natural leadership thought they were riding it when they had long since been swamped by it.

In these circumstances it did not very much matter to Hitler that the campaign was less than a smashing success. The referendum was held; the draft proposal for a "law against the enslavement of the German people" barely received the 10 per cent of the votes required if it were to be submitted to the Reichstag. But in the Reichstag the proposal was accepted by only eighty-two representatives, with 318 votes against it. The third stage in the process, the holding of a plebiscite on December 22, 1929, likewise ended in defeat. The proponents of the draft law won barely 14 per cent of the votes, about a quarter of the number needed—some 5 per cent less than the votes the Nazi party and the Nationalist party had won in the Reichstag elections the previous year.

Nevertheless, this campaign meant for Hitler the final breakthrough into national politics. Thanks to the support provided by the many and variegated publications of the Hugenberg empire, he had made a name for himself nationally and had proved himself the most energetic and purposeful force on the divided and directionless Right. He himself spoke of the "extremely great reversal" in public opinion and marveled at "the way arrogant, snobbish or stupid rejection of the party, which was the rule only a few years ago, has been transformed into expectant hope." On August 3 and 4, 1929, after the opening of the campaign, he convoked a party rally in Nuremberg, probably to show his conservative partners something of the mettle of his movement. By now he knew a great deal about staging such demonstrations. More than thirty special trains brought some 200,000 followers (if the figures are correct) from all over Germany. For several days their uniforms, banners, and bands dominated the scene in the medieval walled city. The majority of the twenty-four new standards, which were consecrated in a highly emotional ceremony, came from Bavaria, Austria, and Schleswig-Holstein. At the grand final muster, some 60,000 SA men, by this time all in uniform and provided with active-service field equipment, paraded past Hitler for three and a half hours. In the euphoria of the day some units threatened to take immediate violent action. A similar mood underlay a motion by the party's radical wing proposing that any participation in government by the NSDAP should be "forbidden now and for ever." With the terse and characteristic remark that any step was justified that might "lead the movement into the possession of political power," Hitler rejected the motion. Nevertheless, his adherence to legality was now threatened anew by the self-assurance of the rapidly growing party army. By the end of the year the SA was the equal of the Reichswehr in manpower.

The alliance with Hugenberg also provided Hitler with many connections among industrialists who by and large had over the years supported Stresemann's foreign policy but who now vigorously opposed the Young Plan. Hitherto, Hitler had received material support only from small factory owners—aside from such notable exceptions as the industrialist Fritz Thyssen. His antisocialist, proproperty attitude on the question of the expropriation of the sovereigns had made him no new friends. Now, suddenly, he could draw on more opulent sources. While still banned from public speaking, he had used his time in systematically traveling through the industrial regions of Germany, primarily the Ruhr, talking at closed meetings often to several hundred largely skeptical businessmen and endeavoring to remove their fears of his form of nationalistic socialism by presenting himself as a staunch defender of private property. True to his belief that success was an index of aristocracy, he hailed the large-scale entrepreneur as the type of a superior race, "destined for leadership." On the whole he tried to convey that what he was "demanding was nothing employers need object to."

Hitler's connections with the Munich salons, in which he continued to be something of a lion, also proved their value once again. Elsa Bruckmann had by now made it her "life task to bring Hitler into contact with the leading men in heavy industry," as she herself put it. In 1927 she arranged for him to meet old Emil Kirdorf, who became extremely important to Hitler—not only as an influential industrialist but also as administrator of a political fund known as the "Ruhr Treasury." Hitler was deeply impressed by this rough old man who had spent his life plotting against those above him and despising those below him. And Kirdorf in turn was fascinated by Hitler; he soon became one of his most valuable supporters, possibly the most valuable. Kirdorf participated as a guest of honor in the party rally in Nuremberg, and subsequently wrote to Hitler that those days had been an overwhelming experience he would never forget.

All this new assistance and new money would be translated into significant successes in the regional elections of 1929. In Saxony and Mecklenburg-Schwerin the Nazis had won nearly 5 per cent of the vote the previous spring. But their progress in the Prussian community elections was more impressive. In Coburg they elected the mayor, and in Thuringia they succeeded in voting into office the first Nazi provincial government minister, Wilhelm Frick. Frick soon made a stir by introducing Nazi prayers into the schools and came into conflict with the national government—although on the whole he tried to demonstrate that his party was quite capable of co-operating in coalitions.

In keeping with his greed for public display, Hitler set about creating a glorious backdrop for his newly won success. The setting, in turn, was to prepare the ground for future successes. Since 1925, the Munich party headquarters had been located in an unostentatious, utilitarian building on Schellingstrasse. Now, with funds supplied largely by Fritz Thyssen, Hitler bought the Barlow Palace on Briennerstrasse in Munich and renovated it to serve as the "Brown House." Together with the architect Paul Ludwig Troost, he spent much of his time planning the interior decoration. It was as if he were returning to his youthful dreams of a fine, aristocratic mansion. He sketched furniture, doors, and designs for marquetry. A grand open stairwell led up to his office, which was furnished with a few outsized pieces, a portrait of Frederick the Great, a bust of Mussolini, and a painting of an attack by the List Regiment in Flanders. Adjoining was the so-called Senate Hall. Here, around a gigantic horseshoe-shaped table, stood sixty armchairs in red morocco, their backs displaying the party eagle. Bronze tablets to either side of the entrance listed the names of the victims of the abortive putsch of November 9, 1923. In the room itself there were busts of Bismarck and Dietrich Eckart. This hall, however, never served its ostensible purpose. It existed solely to satisfy Hitler's theatrical needs, for he had always firmly rejected any thought of placing a senate or any other group of advisers at his side. The canteen in the cellar of the Brown House had a "Führer's seat" reserved for him under a portrait of Dietrich Eckart. Here he would sit for hours in his circle of adjutants and reverent chauffeurs, indulging in the idle chatter beloved by Vienna coffeehouse habitués.

His personal affairs also reflected the improved financial state of the party. In the course of 1929, the interest and amortization payments for his considerably swollen debts abruptly disappear from the documents concerning his personal finances. At the same time he moved into an opulent nine-room apartment at 16 Prinzregentenstrasse in one of the solidly middle-class residential districts of Munich. Frau Reichert, his former landlady from Thierschstrasse, and Frau Anny Winter did the housekeeping for him, while Frau Raubal, his half-sister, continued to run Haus Wachenfeld on the slope of Obersalzberg. His niece Geli, who had picked up her uncle's love for the theater and was now taking singing and acting lessons, soon moved into the apartment. The gossip about this relationship bothered him somewhat, but he also rather enjoyed the aura of bohemian freedom and the suggestion of a grand and fateful passion in this liaison between uncle and niece.

The campaign against the Young Plan had barely come to its end when Hitler once more committed an act of political audacity. He dramatically broke with Hugenberg's conservative associates, on the grounds that their half-heartedness and bourgeois weakness had been responsible for the failure of the plebiscite. The ease with which he made such ruptures, undeterred by any sense of common purpose and common struggles, once more served him well. For this sudden swerve silenced the critics within the party who had been grumbling at his alliance with "the capitalist pig Hugenberg." Moreover, the move enabled him to disavow his own share in the defeat, so that he could once again emerge as the only vigorous force on the antirepublican Right.

Such bold gestures made all the more of an impression because they seemed entirely out of keeping with the numerical strength of the still small party. But Hitler had recognized that it was all important to keep alive that interest in the movement which he had at last succeeded in arousing. Stripping the party for more aggressive tasks, as it were, he undertook a reorganization of headquarters. Gregor Strasser was placed in charge of Organization Section I (Political Organization). Former Colonel Konstantin Hierl became head of Organization Section II (National Socialist State; the shadow government). Goebbels became propaganda chief. In a letter of February 2, 1930, Hitler predicted "with almost clairvoyant certainty" that "the victory of our movement will take place . . . at the most in two and a half to three years."

After the break with Hugenberg he continued without interruption, and with virtually undiminished violence, the campaign against the republic. Only now it was the Nazi party's own campaign. The previous year, instructions from party headquarters, signed by the then director of propaganda Heinrich Himmler, had called for a series of "propaganda operations" that represented a new departure in the art of politicking. An onslaught would be made on a single district, down to its remotest villages. In the course of a week all the party's top speakers would be hurled in to address several hundred meetings. They would be enlisted "to the extreme limit" of their capacities. During this period every city and town would be bombarded with posters, banners, and leaflets—with Hitler himself frequently deciding the designs and slogans. "Recruiting nights" would be staged, when the SA was to show—in the words of the directive—"what it can do out of its own resources, including: athletic events, living tableaus, plays, singing of songs, lectures by SA men, showing of the movie of the Party Rally." In the period preceding the elections for the Landtag (legislature) of Saxony in June, 1930, the party held no fewer than 1,300 such affairs.

Along with these regional actions the party continued its efforts to gain a foothold within specific social groups, and in particular to win over some of the white-color workers and the rural population. In a series of vigorous thrusts the party conquered leading positions in co-operatives, craft unions, and professional organizations. In some rural areas conditions of acute distress prevailed: a peasant protest movement in Schleswig-Holstein, for example, marched under black banners. The party responded with the elusive slogan of "land reform" and by blaming matters on the Jews—tapping the springs of latent peasant anti-Semitism, which, as the party training directive put it, "must be incited to the point of furious rage." A young *Auslandsdeutscher* (German from abroad) named Walter Darré, whom Rudolf Hess had introduced to Hitler, was meanwhile working out an agrarian program that was published early in March, 1930. It combined a generous offer of subsidies with fulsome tributes to the "noblest class in the nation." At the same time, the party took advantage, in its propaganda among white-collar workers, of that general sense of crisis which had been engendered by the outcome of the war, urbanization, and the pressure of changes in the social structure. For the time being the factory workers remained aloof from the party. But the influx of office and agricultural workers that started in 1929 seemed to justify the party's claim to being the "party of all toilers." Throughout the country there sprang into being a host of small cells and bases that prepared the way for the great breakthrough.

Hitler kept whipping the party on; but these successes were not entirely the result of his drive or of his talent for addressing himself to the confused and emotional thinking of the traditionally splintered Right. Rather, the incipient world-wide Depression came to his aid. Signs of crisis became apparent in Germany by the beginning of 1929, when the number of unemployed for the first time passed the 3 million mark. In the course of the spring the number of business failures began to increase alarmingly. By

267

the first five days of November, in Berlin alone, fifty-five bankruptcies were recorded and from 500 to 700 persons daily were taking the debtor's oath that they were unable to satisfy their creditors. These figures partly reflected the economic and psychological consequences of October 24, 1929, the famous Black Friday on which prices on the New York Stock Exchange collapsed.

In Germany, especially, the devastating effects were felt almost immediately. The foreign loans, mostly short-term, that had underwritten the country's economic revival and countenanced a certain recklessness on the part of some municipalities, were withdrawn by the anxious creditors. The abrupt recession in world trade simultaneously destroyed all prospects of making up for the losses, at least temporarily, by increased exports. As world market prices dropped, agriculture was drawn into the crisis; soon farms could be kept going only by subsidies which in turn increased the burden on the general public. One disaster fed the next in a classic chain reaction. In Germany, too, stock prices tumbled, unemployment grew by leaps and bounds, factories closed their doors, and new pawnshops opened theirs. Long columns in the newspapers announced forced auction sales. The political effects soon followed. Ever since the election of 1928 the country had been governed by a broad coalition painfully held together and straining to fly apart. This government was headed by the Social Democratic Chancellor Hermann Müller. When diminished tax receipts forced rigorous belt tightening, a stubborn fight ensued between the capitalistic and the left-wing groups within the government, each trying to make the other assume the burdens of the Depression.

Actually, by this time it was obvious that nobody was going to be spared. The most prominent characteristic of the Depression in Germany was its totality. Although the ancillary economic and social consequences in, say, England—and especially in the United States—were no less far-reaching, they did not lead in those countries to an overwhelming psychological crisis that destroyed all political, moral, and intellectual standards and was felt to be something far greater than its specific causes: a shattering of faith in the existing order of the world. The turn of events in Germany simply cannot be adequately considered in terms of the objective economic conditions. For it was more than an economic slump; it was a psychological shock. Weary of everlasting troubles, their psychic resistance worn thin by war, defeat, and inflation, sick of democratic rhetoric with its constant appeals to reason and sobriety, people let their emotions run rampant.

First reactions, to be sure, were nonpolitical: resignation in the face of the fatefulness and inscrutable character of the disaster. People thought primarily about their own survival, about the daily trek to the employment offices, standing in front of grocery stores or on breadlines. And along with all the trivial daily vexations, there was the terrible idleness of men who had nothing to do but to hang around, apathetically or desperately, in dreary taverns, on street corners or in darkened apartments, feeling life was going to waste. In September, 1930, the number of jobless once again crossed the 3 million mark; a year later it had reached almost 4.5 million, and in September, 1932, more than 5 million—which was an improvement over the beginning of the year, for in January more than 6 million unemployed had been registered, not including temporary workers. Approximately every second family was directly affected, and from 15 million to 20 million persons found themselves dependent on the dole. This "relief" was in a sense sufficient to sustain life since, according to the figures of the American journalist H. R. Knickerbocker, it would take ten years to starve to death on it.

A sense of total discouragement and meaninglessness pervaded everything. Among the most striking concomitants of the Great Depression was an unprecedented wave of suicides. At first the victims were chiefly failed bankers and businessmen, but as the Depression deepened, members of the middle class and the petty bourgeoisie more and more frequently took their own lives. With their keen sense of status, many office workers, owners of small shops, and persons with small private incomes had long regarded poverty as a badge of social degradation. They suffered less from the deprivations than the disgrace. Quite often whole families chose death together. Dropping birth rates and rising death rates led to decreasing populations in at least twenty of Germany's major cities. The combination of public misery and the unfeelingness displayed by a hard-pressed and sickly capitalism led to the sense that everything was doomed to go down to destruction very soon. And, as always, such eschatological moods were accompanied by wild hopes that sprang up like weeds, along with irrational longings for a complete alteration of the world. Charlatans, astrologers, clairvoyants, numerologists, and mediums flourished. These times of distress taught men, if not to pray, pseudoreligious feelings, and turned their eyes willy-nilly to those seemingly elect personalities who saw beyond mere human tasks and promised more than normality, order, and politics as usual—who offered, in fact, to restore to life its lost meaning.

With remarkable instinct, Hitler grasped these cravings and knew how to make himself the object of them. This was his hour in every sense. For the past years he had been given to spells of apathy, had seemed inclined to withdraw into private life. But this was over now. For a long while the factors that could rouse his energies had simply been missing. The Dawes Plan, the vexations imposed by the occupying forces, or Stresemann's foreign policy had hardly lent themselves to his purposes. He must have been aware that the disproportion between these facts and the excitement he tried to whip up over them could all too easily lead to absurd effects. Now, however, he saw emerging that state catastrophe which made the perfect background for his demagogic flights. To be sure the staples of his propaganda remained what they had always been: Versailles and Strese-mann's foreign policy, parliamentarism and the French occupation, capi-talism, Marxism, and above all the Jewish world conspiracy. But now each of these items could easily be linked with the prevailing malaise, with the misery everyone was conscious of.

Hitler surpassed all his rivals in knowing how to give the color of a political decision to the personal wishes and despairs of the masses, and to insinuate his own aims into those who held the most divergent views and expectations. When spokesmen of other parties encountered the populace, their own lack of faith became apparent despite their efforts to win the people. They, too, had no answers and could count only on the solidarity of the powerless in the face of disaster. Hitler, on the other hand, took an optimistic and aggressive tone. He showed confidence in the future and cultivated his animosities. "Never in my life," he declared, "have I been so well disposed and inwardly contented as in these days."[3]

Hitler was also able to ring many changes on his cries of alarm. He appealed to bewildered people terrified by the prospect of being declassed, people who felt threatened equally by the Right and the Left, by capitalism and by Communism, and who blamed the existing system for having failed them. The program Hitler outlined rejected everything: it was anticapital-istic and antiproletarian, revolutionary and restorational; it conjured up its dire visions of the future along with nostalgic pictures of the good old days. It was of a piece with and helped sustain the paradox of a revolutionary attitude that denounced the present state of things and aimed at reinstating the way things used to be. Hitler deliberately cut across all the traditional fronts. But while he took up a radical position far outside the "system," he kept asserting that he was in no way responsible for the prevailing misery, and that those very conditions proved how right he was in condemning the existing state of affairs.

As if to confirm his charges, the parliamentary institutions of the repub-lic failed their first serious test. The coalition government fell apart in the spring of 1930, even before the Depression reached its peak. The end of the coalition was a signal for multitudes to abandon the republic. What precipitated the breakup of the coalition was a long-simmering but essen-tially trivial disagreement among the parties on how the costs of unemploy-ment insurance were to be distributed. But in fact Chancellor Hermann Müller's government was shattered by the general tendency to flee to the extremes, a tendency that manifested itself in all the political camps. The process revealed how thin the underlying support of the republic was, how little loyalty it could command. In the preceding few years the Weimar Republic had made some considerable achievements; but there had been a grayness about its competence, so that even during its best years it had, fundamentally, only bored people. It had remained for Hitler to tap those wellsprings which the republican politicians in their hard-working, com-monplace efficiency had neither recognized nor utilized. Among these were: the craving for utopia and for suprapersonal goals; an idealism that welcomed the appeal to generosity and the spirit of sacrifice; the quest for leaders in whom the opaqueness of modern power processes would be made visible; and the demand for some interpretation of the present misery that would give heroic stature to those who were suffering it.

The slogans that formulated the "spiritual" alternatives did far more than the vague economic pledges to lead the disoriented masses toward the Nazi party. Hitler himself put aside his reservations about a mass party. For the first time the flexibility of the widely ramified party organization proved its worth. The NSDAP could effortlessly absorb the most heterogeneous elements, for it was not restricted to a single class and not hampered by a rigid program. It could offer room to persons of every background, every age, every motivation. Its membership appeared peculiarly structureless; certainly no strict class analysis applied to it. We would be wrong to see it solely as a movement of the reactionary bourgeois and peasant masses, whose impetus came chiefly from the material interests of its following. To take this view would be to miss the decisive factor in its rise.

Small tradesmen, peasants, industrialists and consumers had all become indispensable to the party. The manifold contradictions among these groups stood in the way of the formation of a class movement. Sooner or later every party had come up against this barrier. It seemed insuperable. Certainly in a period of intense economic and social distress it could not be overcome simply by making empty promises to all and sundry. There were too many politicians trying the same dodge; it soon ceased to fool anyone. Those who concerned themselves with material questions could win the masses only by promising higher wages and lower prices, more dividends and fewer taxes, better pensions, higher tariffs, higher prices to the farmers and lower prices to the consumers. But Hitler's great trick was to leap over the economic contradictions and offer instead high-sounding principles. When he spoke of material interests it was chiefly to make an effective contrast between himself and his opponents. "I do not promise happiness and prosperity, like the others," he would occasionally proclaim. "I can only say this one thing: we want to be National Socialists; we want to realize that we cannot rightfully be nationalistic and shout, 'Deutschland, Deutschland über alles' when millions of us have to go on the dole and have nothing to wear." For his key weapon was his understanding that the behavior of human beings is not motivated exclusively by economic forces or interests. He counted instead on their need to have a suprapersonal reason for living and trusted in the power of an "alternative culture" to dissolve class limits. This alternative was a package of slogans—an invocation of national honor, national greatness, oaths of loyalty and readiness for sacrifice. He called for dedication without prospect of advantage: "And you will see—we'll be marching!"

Nevertheless, the party still won influence and members chiefly among

271

those middle-level groups who had clung to the rudiments of their political ideas and who had all along tended to flee from dubious existential situations into the shelter of a stern and uncomplicated system of order. Their wishes, resentments, and interests were not too well represented by the existing spread of parties. The unloved republic had alienated them from politics, but now hunger and anxiety sent them in search of "their" party in a series of aimless vacillations. In their encounter with Hitler they succumbed, to be sure, to his great demagogic powers. But almost equally they were drawn by a similarity of destinies: he, too, unmistakably bourgeois, sharing that overwhelming fear of being declassed, a failure in civilian life until he discovered politics, which had liberated him and lifted him socially. Wouldn't the same magic affect them? Hitler's fate seemed to be the apotheosis of their own.

It was this "sinking middle class" who joined the NSDAP in vast numbers and dominated the sociological picture of the party during those years. Yet it would be wrong to assume a direct link between economic distress and the appeal of the party. Its greatest increment of members came not in the big cities and industrial regions where the slump had struck hardest, but in the small towns and rural areas. For there, against the background of an on the whole still intact order of things, economic crisis was felt as far more elemental and catastrophic than in the big cities, which had always known such ups and downs.[4]

As the Depression went on, however, the Nazi party began winning its first successes among the workers. Gregor Strasser even tried to set up an organization of party cells in every shop to combat what was called "shop Marxism" (Goebbels coined the slogan, "A Nazi cell on top in every shop"). What remained of the Nazi Left was desperately trying to keep its social-revolutionary workers' party from degenerating into a collecton of anti-Semites and petty bourgeois. "Winning a single worker is incomparably more valuable than declarations of adherence by a dozen Excellencies or 'superior' personages in general." By and large, Strasser's efforts failed. But what the Nazi party for a long time could not achieve within the class-conscious proletariat, it did achieve more and more among the growing masses of the unemployed. The SA proved to be an ideal catchment basin. In Hamburg, of 4,500 members of the SA, 2,600 were unemployed—nearly 60 per cent. Party stalwarts would be posted outside relief offices, where the jobless had to report twice a week, to hand out the propaganda sheet, *The Jobless,* which was skillfully slanted toward the problems of this group. They would deliberately start long discussions with the men who were standing around, and thus put across the Nazi message.

Counteraction by the Communists, who saw the Nazis challenging them in their very own domain, led to brawls and street battles. Step by step the numbers involved in these struggles increased, until gradually there developed that "silent civil war" which until January, 1933, left behind it a thin but steadily bleeding trail. Then it came to an abrupt end when the one side seized power.

The battles with the Communists had begun as early as March, 1929, in the area of Dithmarschen (Schlesing-Holstein). During a fierce brawl, two members of the SA (a farmer named Hermann Schmidt and a cabinet-maker named Otto Streibel) had been killed and thirty persons injured, some of them gravely. Hereafter the strife shifted to the big cities whose working-class districts and networks of alleys served as a grim terrain for a form of guerrilla warfare. Corner cafés and basement bistros served as bases for the belligerents; these were the so-called storm pubs; one contemporary described his as a "fortified position in the battle zone." As early as May 1, 1929, hostilities broke out on Berlin's East End between the storm troopers and the Communists' military organization, the Red Front Fighters League. For days whole rows of streets were in the grip of virtual war; the strife resulted in nineteen dead and forty wounded, most of them severely. It took massive intervention by the police, ultimately supported by armored cars, to stop the fighting.

Berlin was now moving more and more into the center of the Nazi strategy for seizing power. The city was traditionally leftist, with the Marxist parties there far outstripping all rivals in strength. For that very reason it was the bastion which had to be taken. And Gauleiter Goebbels had just the temperament to pit his tiny following against the "Reds" right in the heart of their power, where they imagined themselves unassailable. "Adolf Hitler devours Karl Marx!" was one of the slogans with which Goebbels launched his offensive. From the bourgeois suburbs where the Nazi party had led a clubbish existence taken up chiefly with internal squabbles, Goebbels sent the members straight toward the bleak proletarian districts in the northern and eastern parts of the city. For the first time someone was disputing the Left's control of the streets and the shops. Goebbels himself, sallow, looking in need of sleep, wearing a leather jacket, was also often on the scene, and became a well-known figure in the period's gallery of types. The nervousness of the Left—which for too long had fobbed off its shadow play of world revolution on increasingly skeptical masses—was reflected in the slogan issued by the Communist Party district leadership in Berlin in answer to Goebbels' competition: "Drive the Fascists out of the shops! Strike them wherever you meet them!"

Following Hitler's example, Goebbels also developed his tactics by studying his opponent's methods. The slogan squads, the parading bands, the political activity on the job, the system of street cells, the mass demonstrations, the door-to-door canvassing—all this represented techniques of building the party long practiced by the socialists, combined with the "grand Munich style" Hitler had created. Goebbels added a few intellectual and metropolitan trappings to the party's provincial look, thereby making it attractive to more sophisticated strata of the population. He was witty,

273

hard-boiled, and cynical in a way that usually impresses the public. Labeled by his adversaries "chief bandit of Berlin," he adopted this insult as an honorary title.

What distinguished the Nazis from conservatives of the old school was their absence of false pride about the manner of achieving power. They were more than willing to learn from their opponents, and this gave their reactionary notions a cast of modernity. They were far more attentive to the radical leftist press than to the bourgeois papers, and in their own publications they often printed "significant sections" from Communist instructions, applying them to their own following. They tried to throw their opponents off balance by rude behavior—again borrowing from Communist practice—while at the same time pluming themselves on their innocence and idealism. "Heroes with the hearts of big children" and "Christlike socialists" were among the descriptions Goebbels gave to the Nazis in the process of creating a martyr out of the SA leader Horst Wessel. In actuality Wessel had been shot by a Communist rival for the affections of a slut; the killing was at least in part a matter of jealousy.

One of Goebbels' most effective tactics was to exhibit the heavily bandaged victims of street battles on stretchers beside his speaker's platform. The incident in Dithmarschen had confirmed the propagandistic value of the dead and wounded, and the leaders of the party had seen that a few bloody victims were a good investment. According to police reports, the party membership rolls increased by 30 per cent after that affair. The report stated that since the battle "simple old peasant women are wearing the swastika on their blue work smocks. In talking with such old mothers you sensed at once that they knew nothing at all about the aims and intentions of the National Socialist Party. But they are convinced that all honest people in Germany today are being exploited, that the government is incompetent and . . . only the National Socialists can save the country from this alleged misery."

The NSDAP made its most remarkable inroads among the youth. More than any other political party it was able to exploit the state of mind of the younger generation. In the nature of things the generation from eighteen to thirty had been especially hard hit by the Depression. Their ambition and their desire to prove themselves had been thwarted by the prevailing mass unemployment. At once radical and looking for some way to escape reality, the young generation formed a gigantic aggressive potential. They despised their environment, the homes of their parents, their educators and traditional authorities, engaged only in restoring the old bourgeois order. The young people had long ago moved beyond that order. A contemporary poem voiced this mood: "No longer content with faith in the past and yet too sound for mere negation." Germany, it was also said, had lost not only the war but the revolution as well, and she must make up for both.

The republic was held in contempt not only because of its powerlessness but also for pretending that its indecisiveness was a virtue, a democratic willingness to compromise. The young people also rejected the republic's unimaginative welfare-state materialism, its "epicurean ideals"—in which they found no trace of that tragic sense of life they had made their own.

They were equally unattracted to the traditional type of party that in no way satisfied their craving for "organic" forms of community—a craving awakened by the youth movement before the war and strengthened by the war experience itself. They were repelled by "the rule of old men" and bristled at the very thought of the usual party leaders, narrow-minded and self-righteous and all alike.

A good many of the young joined the Communists, although the narrow class-struggle bias of the party was for some a psychological stumbling block. Others tried to buttress their vulnerability by joining one of the many splinter groups among the wilder nationalistic conservatives. But the majority, especially among the students, went over to the National Social-ists. The NSDAP was their natural alternative. In the ideological gamut offered by Nazi propaganda, they heard chiefly the revolutionary notes. They were seeking discipline and heroism and were susceptible to the romantic lure of a movement that operated close to the edge of legality and permitted the wholly committed to step over the edge. The NSDAP seemed less a party than an association of fighters who made demands on the whole man and answered a brittle and crumbling world with the battle cry of a new order.

With the influx of younger members, the Nazi party—especially before the masses began flocking to it—became for a while a new kind of youth movement. In the Hamburg district, for example, some two thirds of the party members were under thirty in 1925; in Halle the figure went as high as 86 per cent; and in the other party districts the percentages were much the same. In 1931, 70 per cent of the Berlin SA men were under thirty; in the party as a whole nearly 40 per cent of the total membership belonged to this age group. The Social Democratic Party had barely half as many young people. Only 10 per cent of the Social Democratic Reichstag deputies were under forty; among the Nazis the figure was 60 per cent. Hitler's enlistment of the young proved to be a canny policy. He also saw the wisdom of entrusting them with high positions. Goebbels became a gauleiter at twenty-eight, Karl Kaufmann at twenty-five. Baldur von Schi-rach was twenty-six when he was appointed Reich youth leader, and Himmler was only two years older when he was promoted to chief of the SS, with the impressive new title of Reichsführer-SS. The dedication and faith of these youthful leaders, their "purely physical energy and mili-tancy," as one of them later recalled, "gave the party a momentum the bourgeois parties could not begin to match."

All these elements had had a place in the party since 1929, even before the sudden large-scale influx of members. But the sociological range of the party remained vague. In fact, it was deliberately obscured by pretentious slogans, behind which Hitler tried to disguise the fact that he had made few conquests among the politically conscious working class and that the National Socialist Party on the whole remained restricted to its original strata of the population. Moreover, the government began again to show displeasure. On June 5, 1930, Bavaria issued a ban on the private wearing of uniforms. A week later Prussia forbade the brown shirt, so that the storm troopers henceforth had to appear in white shirts. Only two weeks later the state of Prussia prohibited membership in the National Socialist or the Communist Party for all civil servants. The new toughness of the Weimar Republic was expressed in the increasing number of court cases against members of both parties. Up to 1933 some 40,000 trials were held, as a consequence of which a total of 14,000 years' imprisonment and nearly 1.5 million marks in fines were imposed.[5]

Such measures, however, did not dispel the impression of weakness that clung to the "system." After the inglorious end of the Great Coalition there was pressure within the government itself for some sort of change in the machinery of rule. Up to this point President von Hindenburg had conducted his office with fidelity to the letter of the Constitution, although he had no particular respect for its spirit. But some members of his entourage began to say that the incompetent parliamentary regime should be replaced by authoritarian presidential rule. It is difficult to judge to what extent the President accepted such counsels; but in any case he for the first time intervened vigorously and decisively in the formation of the new government. His choice of Heinrich Brüning for Chancellor indicated that from now on he would exert influence on the daily business of government. The personality of the new Chancellor combined integrity, austerity, and sense of duty. He seemed ready for those mute self-sacrifices that Hindenburg demanded of his associates. Soon after taking office, with unseemly haste, without exhausting the possibilities for compromise, Brüning risked a vote of confidence and dissolved the Reichstag. The moment was particularly ill chosen; unemployment was increasing sharply, and terror of the Depression was mounting. In vain Interior Minister Wirth implored the antagonists to compromise and not to expand the parliamentary crisis into a crisis of the system, as if democracy were tired of itself. No one yielded, and new elections were set for September, 1930.

Nazi propaganda immediately flared to new heights. Once again the mobil agitation squads made loud and turbulent irruptions into towns and rural areas, organizing an endless succession of open-air concerts, sports festivals, "rallyes," solemn bugling of taps church meetings. Their stock-in-trade was diatribes against their competitors. "Throw the scum out! Tear the masks off their mugs! Take them by the scruff of the neck and kick them in their fat bellies on September 14, and sweep them out of the temple with trumpets and drums!" Goebbels wrote; in this election campaign he was undergoing his first test since his appointment as Reich propaganda chief. The philosopher Ernst Bloch has spoken contemptuously of the Nazis' "stupid enthusiasm." But in fact that was their greatest strength. The Communists, by contrast, in spite of their grandiloquent faith in ultimate victory, seemed colorless and without *élan,* as though they had, not history, but only the daily grind on their side. The 2,000 to 3,000 graduates of the Nazi party speakers' school were now thrown into the fray for marathon sessions. And though their expositions of party doctrine often sounded crude and memorized, and probably won few new adherents, the mere appearance of these hordes of preachers spread the impression of a vast party engaged in tireless and overwhelming activity. Simultaneously, the better-known and experienced party speakers addressed the populace at large-scale meetings. "Meetings attended by between a thousand and five hundred persons are of daily occurrence in the larger cities," a memorandum of the Prussian Interior Ministry noted. "Often, in fact, one or several parallel meetings have to be held because the previously selected halls cannot hold the number of persons wishing to attend."

Heading it all as leader, star performer, and organizer was Hitler himself. He had led off the campaign with a mass meeting in Weimar and continued his tour indefatigably, by car, by train, or by plane. Wherever he turned up, he set the masses into motion, although he had no plan, no theory of the Depression and how to fight it. But he could name those responsible: the Allies, the corrupt politicians of the system, the Marxists, and the Jews. And he had his formula for ending the distress of the people: determination, self-assurance, and recaptured power. His emotional appeals remained in the realm of generalities. Topical concerns be damned, he would declare. The German people had been ruined by wrestling with such petty matters. "Topical concerns blind our eyes to greatness." The crisis of the parliamentary system arose from the very fact that the parties were focusing their attention on the "everyday junk," for which people were not "willing to make sacrifices."

Hitler's effectiveness was due as much to the decisiveness of his manner and the impressive ritual with which he was surrounded as to his oratorical powers. His ideas could easily be translated into slogans; once planted, these sank into the deeper layers of men's mind, took root and grew. During those weeks of the election campaign he acquired, in addition to a vast amount of organizational experience, the refined psychological technique for the larger and stormier campaigns he was to launch two years later.

The paucity of the actual Nazi program, as against the energy and noise level of its agitation, caused many people to underestimate the NSDAP. In the view of intelligent contemporaries, the party was asserting itself as a noisy, bothersome and slightly crazy phenomenon in noisy and slightly crazy times. Thus, the political satirist Kurt Tucholsky made this quip about Hitler: "The man doesn't exist; he is only the noise he makes." Meanwhile, on a more serious plane, little attention was paid to a memorandum from the Reich Interior Ministry disclosing the anti-Constitutional character of the party, so thinly disguised by formal professions of legality.

Instead, those most concerned with defense of the republic trusted to the pent-up explosive forces within the party. It was growing too fast, they thought; surely its inner contradictions would cause it to blow up. And surely it would be destroyed by the intellectual mediocrity, the crudeness and the warring ambitions of its corps of leaders.

Such prognoses seemed confirmed by the upheavals within the National Socialist Party in the summer of 1930. Only in hindsight could these be recognized as purges which tightened party discipline and strengthened its thrust. First of all, Hitler forced the long-delayed confrontation with the party Left, whose position had patently become more contradictory. As long as the NSDAP had been a marginal party, making a considerable uproar but not having to put its ideas into practice in legislatures or administrations, it had been easy to conceal its internal ideological disagreements. But after the recent victories in regional elections, the party was being compelled to take a definite stand. Otto Strasser and his followers obstinately held to their old principles. They advocated aggressive "catastrophe tactics," preached crude anticapitalism, came out for extensive nationalization of industry and an alliance with the Soviet Union, and flouted the party line by supporting local strike movements. This last activity, of course, was bound to strain the party's new and highly profitable entente with industry. In addition their habit of rashly discussing programs caused trouble, for Hitler liked to skirt such questions and keep his options open.

As early as January, 1930, the Führer had asked Otto Strasser to turn over the publishing house to him. Cunningly mixing flattery with threats and attempts at bribery, Hitler promised the refractory comrade the post of press chief at Munich headquarters and offered to pay some 80,000 marks for the publishing organization. He appealed to Strasser as an old soldier and a National Socialist of many years standing. But Strasser, who regarded himself as the repository of true National Socialism, had rejected all such bids. The final showdown came on the night of May 21, 1930, in what was then Hitler's Berlin headquarters, the Hotel Sanssouci on Linkstrasse. Max Amann was present, as well as Rudolf Hess and Otto Strasser's brother Gregor, when the two sides fell into a heated debate that was to go on for seven hours and to expose the full extent of their differences.

In that grandiloquent manner of the self-educated which was later to drive his entourage to distraction, Hitler began by sounding off on the subject of art (there are no revolutionary breaks in art; there is only "eternal art," and whatever deserves the name is art of the Greco-Nordic type; anything else is fraud). He then expatiated on the role of personality, the problems of race, the global economy, Italian Fascism, and finally turned to socialism, which was the "Pilate's question"—that is, the question of the nature of truth. That question, to be sure, had been present from the start. Now Hitler took Strasser to task for placing "the idea"

278

above the Führer and wanting "to give every party comrade the right to decide the nature of the idea, even to decide whether or not the Führer is true to the so-called idea." That, he cried angrily, was the worst kind of democracy, for which there was no place in their movement. "With us the Führer and the idea are one and the same, and every party comrade has to do what the Führer commands, for he embodies the idea and he alone knows its ultimate goal." He was not going to allow the whole party organization, which was built up on the discipline of the members, "to be destroyed by a few megalomaniac scriveners."

Hitler's incapacity to see human relationships in anything but hierarchic terms had seldom shown itself so clearly as in the course of this dispute. Compulsively, he answered every objection, every consideration, by referring back to the question of power: Who was to give the orders and who was the subordinate? Everything was mercilessly reduced to the contrast between master and servants; all that existed was the raw, unshaped mass and the great personality for which that mass was an instrument, material for manipulation. To satisfy the legitimate needs of this mass for protection and welfare was, to his mind, socialism. When Strasser came out with the charge that Hitler was trying to throttle the party's revolutionary socialism in the interests of his new connections with bourgeois reaction, Hitler replied heatedly: "I am a socialist of an entirely different type from, for instance, the high and mighty Count Reventlow [an aristocratic party member]. I started out as a plain workman. To this day I can't bear to have my chauffeur eat less well than myself. But what you mean by socialism is simply crude Marxism. You see, the great mass of the workers don't want anything but bread and circuses. They have no understanding for any kind of ideals and we will never be able to count on winning over the workers to any considerable degree. We want an elite of the new master class who will not be motivated by any morality of pity, but who will realize clearly that they are entitled to rule because of their superior race and who will ruthlessly maintain and secure this rule over the broad masses. . . . Your whole system is a desk product that has nothing to do with real life."

He turned to his publisher: "Herr Amann, would you stand for it if your stenographers suddenly wanted to interfere with your work? The employer who bears the responsibility for production also provides the workers with their livelihood. Our biggest employers in particular are not so much concerned about amassing money, about luxurious living, and so on. What is most important to them is the responsibility and the power. Because of their capability they have worked their way to the top, and because of their selectness, which again only proves their superior race, they have a right to lead."

After more excited discussion Strasser posed what to him was the key question: If the Nazis took power, would the means of production remain unchanged? Hitler replied: "But of course. Do you think I am so mad as to destroy the economy? The state would intervene only if the employers were not acting in the interests of the nation. But for that there would be no need for expropriation or the workers having any voice in the decisions." Actually, he said, only one system existed: "Responsibility toward superiors, authority toward inferiors." So it had been for thousands of years, and no other way was possible.

Obviously, there was no humanitarian impulse or desire for a new form of society in Hitler's version of socialism. He himself declared that his socialism had "nothing at all to do with a mechanical construction of economic life"; rather, it was the complementary concept to the word "nationalism." Socialism meant the responsibility of the whole for the individual, whereas "nationalism" was the devotion of the individual to the whole; thus the two elements could be combined in National Socialism. This prestidigitation allowed all interest groups to have their way and reduced the ideas to mere counters: capitalism found its true and ultimate fulfillment in Hitler's socialism, whereas socialism was only attainable under the capitalistic economic system. This ideology took a leftist label chiefly for tactical reasons. It demanded, within the party and within the state, a powerful system of rule that would exercise unchallenged leadership over the "great mass of the anonymous." And whatever premises the party may have started with, by 1930 Hitler's party was "socialist" only to take advantage of the emotional value of the word, and a "workers' party" in order to lure the most energetic social force. As with Hitler's protestations of belief in tradition, in conservative values, or in Christianity, the socialist slogans were merely movable ideological props to serve as camouflage and confuse the enemy. They could be changed or rearranged, depending on the situation. The leaders, at any rate, were totally cynical about the principles of the program—as one enthusiastic young convert learned from a talk with Goebbels. When the young man remarked that Feder's call for smashing the enslaving system of interest payment did contain an element of socialism, Goebbels replied that what ought to be smashed was anyone who listened to such twaddle.

Nevertheless, Otto Strasser's reasoned attack on the inconsistencies of his position hit Hitler hard. Sulkily, he returned to Munich, and as was his way kept silent for weeks about the whole matter, so that Strasser was left in uncertainty. In fact, Hitler did not strike back until Strasser published a pamphlet entitled "Cushioned Ministerial Seats or Revolution," in which he renewed the controversy and accused the party leader of betraying the socialist heart of their common cause. At this point, Hitler sent a letter to his Berlin gauleiter ordering Strasser and his followers to be expelled from the party.

For months as responsible leader of the National Socialist Party I have been watching attempts to introduce strife, confusion and insubordination into the ranks of the movement. Under the mask of desiring to fight for socialism a policy has been advocated which corresponds totally to the policy of our Jewish-liberal-Marxist opponents. These cliques call for the very things our enemies desire. . . . I now consider it necessary to ruthlessly throw these destructive elements out of the party, every single one of them. *We* have shaped and determined the essential content of our movement; we who founded this movement and fought for it, suffered for it in the prisons, and we who led it back from collapse and up to its present height. Anyone who does not like the essential content of the movement which was established by us, and primarily by me, should not enter the movement or must leave it again. As long as I am leading the National Socialist Party, it will not become a debating club for rootless scribblers or unruly parlor Bolsheviks. It will remain what it is today: a disciplined organization which was not created for the doctrinaire games of political boy scouts, but for the fight for a future Germany in which the concepts of class will have been smashed.[6]

On June 30 Goebbels called a membership meeting of the gau, to assemble at the Hasenheide in Berlin. "Those who do not fit in will be kicked out!" he thundered. Otto Strasser and his followers, who had come to argue their point of view, were forcibly ejected from the hall by the SA. The Strasser group thenceforth talked of "purebred Stalinism" and deliberate "persecution of socialists" on the part of the leadership; however, the Strassers and their followers were put more and more on the defensive. On July 1 Gregor Strasser resigned his editorship of the Kampfverlag newspapers and disassociated himself from his brother's views. Von Reventlow and other prominent members of the party's left wing also abandoned the rebels. Some of them probably did so for economic reasons, since they owed a post, a living, a deputy seat to Hitler. But most of them acted out of that "almost perverse personal loyalty" that Hitler evoked and which persisted despite countless acts of disloyalty on his part. With great assurance Goebbels declared that the party would "sweat out this attempt at sabotage."

Thereupon, on July 4, Otto Strasser's newspapers announced: "The socialists are leaving the NSDAP." But hardly anyone followed Otto Strasser. It turned out that the party had virtually no socialist members and in general very few who cared about the theoretical aspects of their politics. Otto Strasser founded a new party which first called itself the Revolutionary National Socialists and later the Black Front but never escaped the odor of mere dogmatism. Hitler's followers were forbidden to read the publications of the Kampfverlag; but the subjects belabored by these publications soon ceased to attract attention anyhow. Who cared about petty revelations of party secrets when the party was obviously answering the summons of history and valiantly struggling against world-wide disaster. The masses were fixing their hopes of salvation on Hitler, not on his program.

The departure of Otto Strasser ended once and for all the sole conflict

281

over principles within the Nazi party. It also meant a considerable loss in status for Gregor Strasser, who thereafter had no seat of power and no newspaper platform. He continued to be organization leader of the party, resided in Munich, and held many threads in his hand, but he became more and more remote from the members and the public. Only six months earlier the political journal *Weltbühne* had predicted that "one of these days not so far in the future he will overshadow his lord and master Hitler" and himself seize the power in the party. That was now out of the question. His more decisive defeat was to follow two years later, when he roused himself for one last opposition gesture and then, weary and broken, turned his back on the party.

Among the afterpains of the Strasser crisis must be counted the mutiny of the Berlin SA under former Police Captain Walter Stennes. The discontent among the storm troopers had less to do with the wrangle over socialism than with the recurrent rumors about bossism and favoritism, as well as the poor pay for strenuous service during the election campaign. While the storm troopers had to be out on duty night after night until thoroughly exhausted, the Political Organization was making itself comfortable in a luxurious palace. That was the most common charge. Reminded that there was to be a monument in marble and bronze to the SA in the Brown House, the storm troopers responded that such a monument looked more like a mausoleum. "As far as the PO was concerned," one SA Oberführer wrote, "the SA is here just to die." Things were getting more and more out of hand, and Goebbels called for help from Hitler and the SS. Only a few days after his appeal, the dissident Berlin SA men stormed the district party office on Hedemannstrasse, and there was a bloody clash with Himmler's black-shirted elite guards. It speaks well for Hitler's authority that he had only to appear for the rebellion to die down. Significantly, however, he made a point of avoiding a frank discussion with Stennes and instead tried to win over the rank-and-file storm trooper. Accompanied by armed SS men, he went from one beer hall to the next, seeking out the regular tables and guardrooms of the SA. He pleaded with the units, even occasionally broke into tears, spoke of impending victories and the rich rewards that would be due to them, the soldiers of the revolution. For the time being he promised them legal services and better treatment: the funds for these benefits would come from a special levy of twenty pfennig on every party member. As for the SS, he repaid it for its services in this juncture by awarding it the watchword: "Your honor is loyalty!"

The collapse of the rebellion meant the departure of Captain Pfeffer von Salomon. With growing fatalism, the commander of the SA had watched the power of the Political Organization swell while that of the SA had dwindled perceptibly. One reason for this shift was Hitler's own changing psychological requirements. With his sense of mission daily reinforced by mass cheering, he developed a craving for homage that could far more easily be paid by the petty bourgeois functionary type of the Political Organization than by the soldierly leaders of the SA. Consequently, the PO received the lion's share of the party's limited funds and was distinctly favored in the drawing up of deputy lists and other acts of patronage. But there was also the personal incompatibility between Hitler, with his semi-artistic and South German temperament, and the austere, "Prussian"-minded Pfeffer von Salomon.

At the end of August Hitler relieved Pfeffer of his duties and then, as he was to do later on after his conflicts with the army in 1938 and 1941, himself assumed the post of supreme SA leader. Ernst Röhm, who had meanwhile become a military instructor in Bolivia, was called back to take over the day-to-day work of SA leader. By becoming Oberster SA-Führer (OSAF) Hitler finally made himself master of the movement; all the special privileges Pfeffer had obtained or claimed now devolved upon Hitler himself. Only a few days after assuming the post, Hitler issued an order requiring every SA leader to take an "unconditional oath of loyalty" to him personally and subsequently to have every single member of the SA do the same. This reinforced the oath taken by every member on entering the SA: "To carry out all orders fearlessly and conscientiously, since I know that my leaders will require of me nothing illegal."

It was significant that no resistance was offered to the total subordination implicit in such formulas. Institutionally as well as psychologically the movement had at last prepared its members to fit into the totalitarian framework. In June, as a matter of fact, Hitler had revealed his totalitarian vision to a number of chosen party journalists. Speaking to them in the Senators' Hall of the new Brown House, he had sketched a picture of the hierarchy and organization of the Catholic Church. The party, he declared, must build its leadership pyramid after the model of the church, "on a broad pedestal of . . . political parish priests who stand in the midst of the people." The pyramid itself must "rise above the tiers of the Kreisleiter and Gauleiter to the body of Senators and finally to the Leader-Pope."

He did not shy away from the comparison between gauleiters and bishops, and between future senators and cardinals, one of those present reported; and similarly he boldly transferred the concepts of authority, obedience, and faith from the spiritual to the secular realms in a series of bewildering parallels. He concluded by saying, without a trace of irony, that he did not "wish to contest the Holy Father in Rome his claim to mental—or is the word spiritual—infallibility on questions of faith, I don't know much about that. But I think I know a great deal more about politics. Therefore I hope that the Holy Father henceforth will not contest my claim. And herewith I now lay claim, for myself and my successors in the leadership of the National Socialist German Workers' Party, to political infallibility. I hope the world will bow to that as quickly as it has bowed to the Holy Father's claim."[7]

Perhaps even more illuminating than these remarks was the reaction to them. There was no sign of astonishment or demur among the party journalists. Here is proof of the effectiveness of Hitler's policy of subjugating the entire internal life of the Nazi party to himself personally. Many circumstances had aided him. The movement had always viewed itself as a militant community founded upon charismatic leadership and the discipline of faith. This was the source of the dynamic confidence so lacking in the traditional parties with their interests and programs. In addition Hitler had been able to count on the background and experience of the "Old Fighters." Almost all of them had taken part in the World War. They had grown to manhood in a climate of strict orders and obedience. Many of them, moreover, came from homes whose pedagogical patterns were based on the rigid mores of the cadet schools. Altogether, Hitler profited greatly from the peculiarities of an authoritarian educational system. It is surely more than a matter of chance that of his seventy-three gauleiters, no fewer than twenty were drawn from the teaching profession.

Once the two intraparty crises of the summer of 1930 had been mastered with relative ease, there no longer existed any office or authority within the Nazi party that did not emanate directly from Hitler. However slight a danger Otto Strasser, Stennes, or Pfeffer may have been—their names stood for at least a theoretical alternative which set certain limits to any claim to absolute power. Now the South German SA commander August Schneidhuber issued a memorandum giving full credit for the growing might of the movement not to any of its functionaries but entirely to Hitler. With busy propagandists singing his praises in more and more transcendental terms, *"der Führer"* was on his way to becoming a legendary figure, immune from all criticism, standing far above any intraparty voting procedures. One observer commented that the party press at this time contained nothing but deifications of Hitler and attacks on the Jews.

Still, the complaint arose that Hitler was putting himself at too great a remove from his followers. The loyal Schneidhuber described the sense of desertion that filled "almost every SA man." He wrote: "The SA is struggling with the Führer for his soul and does not yet have it. But it must have it." He spoke of the "clamor for the Führer," which remained unanswered.

It was at this period, and not by chance, that the greeting *"Heil Hitler"* became generally established. (It had cropped up occasionally before and had been deliberately introduced into Berlin practice by Goebbels.) At the same time, posters announcing meetings no longer mentioned "Adolf Hitler" as the speaker. Instead, nameless and already with the aloofness of a general concept, he appeared simply as the Führer. If party members thronged around him in hotel lobbies or offices, he reacted with irritation, would take notice of them only reluctantly; he was bothered by so much familiarity. Nor was he happy at having hard-working party members introduced to him; he shunned social occasions with unknown persons.

To be sure, he could also show an engaging side. If he dropped his pose of unapproachability, he might chat charmingly in a group of ladies, might present himself to a group of workers as one of them, with the bluff manner of the common man, or might appear in a fatherly role, gazing benevolently over the heads of blond children. "In solemn handshakes and wide-open eyes he is unmatched," a contemporary noted. But his intimates could not help observing how much deliberate play-acting was involved. He was constantly calculating effects, practicing the touching as well as the grand gesture. He had grasped precisely what makes a celebrity, what laws he must follow, and to what extent he must conform to a specific craving of the age. His delicate health had made him give up smoking some time ago; in the meantime, he had also been compelled to give up alcohol. Both these facts he used to cultivate a reputation for asceticism. With his clear awareness of role-playing, he was certainly the most modern phenomenon in the German politics of the period. At any rate, he knew the secrets of public effectiveness far better than any of his rivals, from Hugenberg to Brüning. These politicians had never even considered their public image, showing again their rootedness in past conditions and their lack of instinct for the mood of the present.

From this point on, there was no one who could be said to exert a significant, demonstrable influence upon Hitler. The days of Dietrich Eckart, even those of Alfred Rosenberg, lay far behind. "I never make a mistake. Every one of my words is historic," he had screamed at Otto Strasser in the course of their quarrel. His intellectual curiosity continued to dwindle the more he fitted himself into the stylized role of "Leader-Pope." Surrounded entirely by sycophants and simple-minded members of his retinue, he gradually slid intellectually also into a state of isolation. His onetime model Karl Lueger, the mayor of Vienna, had impressed him with his pessimistic opinion of mankind. Now he himself scarcely troubled to conceal his own contempt for his followers as well as his opponents. In keeping with his fundamentally conservative instinct, he insisted that man was evil by nature, "stuff running rampant on this earth," as he put it in a letter. And: "The masses are blind and stupid and do not know what they do."

His consumption of people was as great as his contempt for them. He was forever demoting, rebuking, or elevating, juggling people and positions—this habit, in fact, was one of the secrets of his success. But experience had also taught him that followers wanted to be treated ruthlessly. Thus, in connection with the forthcoming election, he made impossible demands of his campaign workers. The nucleus of the party's functionaries and auxiliaries came from the traditionally unpolitical classes of the population. They were brisk, brash, and ready to throw themselves heart and soul into the contest. Their tempestuousness was in marked contrast to the dull, routine way in which the established parties went through the motions of an election campaign. During the two days before the election, in Berlin alone the Nazis held twenty-four major demonstrations. Once more their posters were pasted on every wall and fence, immersing the city in shrieking red. The party newspapers were put out in huge editions and sold to members for a pfennig apiece to be distributed door-to-door or outside factories. Hitler himself regarded these activities of his followers as a kind of process of selection: "Now a magnet is simply being passed over a heap of dung; and afterwards we will see how much iron there was in the dung heap that has clung to the magnet."

The elections were set for September 14, 1930. Hitler hoped for fifty or, in exuberant moods, even sixty to eighty Nazi seats. He was counting on the voters of the crumbling bourgeois center, on the young people who were voting for the first time, and on inveterate nonvoters who by all political logic ought to fall to his party, assuming that they could be persuaded to vote at all.

Chapter 2

At the right moment the right weapon must be employed. One stage is probing the opponent, a second
is preparation, a third is assault.

Adolf Hitler

THE LANDSLIDE

September 14, 1930, became one of the turning points in the history of the
Weimar Republic. It signified the end of the reign of democratic parties,
and announced the initial death throes of the republic. By the time the
election results became available, toward three o'clock in the morning,
everything had changed. With a single step the Nazi party had advanced
into the anteroom of power, and its leader, object of ridicule and idolatry,
the "drummer" Adolf Hitler, had become one of the key figures on the
political scene. The fate of the republic was sealed, the Nazi press exulted.
Now mopping-up operations could begin.

No less than 18 per cent of the voters had responded to the appeals of
the National Socialist German Workers' Party. In the two years since the
last elections the party had succeeded in increasing the number of votes it
received from 810,000 to 6.4 million. Instead of 12 seats in the Reichstag,
it now had 107; after the Social Democratic Party it was the second
strongest in the Reich. No comparable breakthrough can be found in the
history of German political parties. Of the bourgeois parties, only the
Catholic Center Party had been able to maintain its position. All others
had suffered severe losses. The four center parties henceforth held only
seventy-two seats. Hugenberg's rightist Deutschnationale Volkspartei
(German National People's Party) had been cut almost exactly by half;
from 14.3 per cent of the vote it had fallen to 7 per cent. Its alliance with
the more radical Nazis had proved to be suicidal. With only forty-one seats
in the Reichstag it was now blatantly inferior to the Nazi party, and
Hitler's claim to leadership of the Right seemed to be impressively
confirmed. The Social Democrats had also suffered considerable losses.
The Communists were the only other party to have emerged from the

elections with gains, although theirs were considerably more modest than the Nazis'. Their share in the vote had risen from 10.6 to 13.1 per cent. The Communists hailed the results in their usual fashion: "The only victor in the September elections is the Communist Party."

On the whole, most observers recognized the historic importance of what had happened. With varying accents they attributed it to the deep crisis of the party system or saw it as the expression of a spreading lack of faith in the liberal and capitalist systems, coupled with a desire for a fundamental change in all conditions of life. "Most of those who have given their vote to the extremist parties are not at all radical; they have only lost faith in the old way." No less than a third of the people had rejected the existing system in principle without knowing or asking what would follow it. There was talk of the "bitterness vote."

At this point it is pertinent to recall once more the circumstances that had marked the birth of the republic ten years before; it came into being as a state no one had really wanted. Now those origins rebounded against it. It had never won more than the nation's tolerance, and many seem to have considered it merely a transitional phase with "nothing inspiring" about it, which had brought forth "no bold crime," "no memorable slogan" and "no great man," to quote the rhetoric of Oswald Spengler. On both Left and Right visibly growing numbers waited for the state to recall its fundamental meaning and assert its old power. All the repressed doubts of the democratic party system, all the slumbering contempt for "un-German" parliamentarism, came to the fore once more and could not be argued away. Hitler's thesis, repeated thousands of times, that this republic was a sop to Germany's enemies and the worst shackle of the Treaty of Versailles, was widely and eagerly embraced.

Interestingly enough, a good deal of foreign opinion, particularly as expressed in the British and American journals, took a similar tone, interpreting the electoral results as a reaction to the impossible harshness of the peace-treaty provisions and the hypocritical conduct of the victorious powers. On the whole, only France was incensed, although she, too, cherished a secret hope that the extreme rightist tendencies might give her a reason for a more rigorous policy toward her neighbor across the Rhine. Out of the chorus of reactions there arose, for the first time, one of those voices that was to be heard for ten years to come, condoning all of Hitler's excesses and provocation's own purposes. Thus, Lord Rothermere in the *Daily Mail* of September 24, 1930, pointed out that Hitler's victory should not be regarded as a danger; it should be recognized that the man offered all sorts of advantages; that he was building a bulwark against Bolshevism; that he was eliminating the grave danger that the Soviet campaign against European civilization might reach into Germany.[8]

The Nazi party's victory was to a large extent due to its mobilization of the youth and of the nonpolitical elements who ordinarily did not go to the

288

polls. Compared with 1928 the votes cast had increased by more than 4.5 million, to 80.2 per cent of the electorate. The Communists, too, had picked up votes—though considerably fewer—from among the same group; remarkably enough, they had waged their campaign with outspokenly nationalistic slogans. The Nazis were so little ready for their sweep that they had not even put up the required 107 candidates and did not have people immediately available. Hitler himself had not run for office since he still did not hold German citizenship.

The results of this election have often been described as a landslide; its consequences were in fact even more fateful. In the consternation of election night wild rumors arose of Nazi plans for a putsch; the result was massive withdrawal of foreign funds from Germany, which worsened the already catastrophic credit crisis. All at once, everyone was interested in this new party. The adventurers, the fearful, and the opportunists made a quick adjustment to the new situation. This was especially true of the horde of eternally alert journalists who now hastily attempted to ride "the wave of the future," and by their extensive reporting made up for the traditional weakness of the Nazi press. In many quarters it became chic to join the Nazi party. In the spring one of the Kaiser's sons, Prince August Wilhelm ("Auwi"), had become a member, remarking that where a Hitler led anyone could find a place. Now came Hjalmar Schacht, then president of the German Federal Bank (Reichsbank), one of the co-authors of the Young Plan which the Nazis had so viciously attacked. Many others followed. "Nobody likes being a failed politician," Hitler sneered as he watched the flurry. During the two and a half months to the end of the year the membership of the NSDAP rose by almost 100,000, to 389,000. Special interest groups also tried to adjust to the shift in power and to the obvious trend. "Almost automatically the NSDAP now acquired those cross-connections and positions necessary for the further extension and consolidation of the 'movement.' "

"Once the great masses swing over to us shouting hurrah, we are lost," Hitler had declared two years earlier, at the 1928 meeting of the leaders in Munich. And Goebbels now spoke contemptuously of the "Septemberlings." Often, he remarked, he thought back "with nostalgia to the good old days when we were only a small sect throughout the Reich, and National Socialism in the capital had hardly a baker's dozen followers."

What worried them was that the unprincipled masses would swamp the party and corrupt its revolutionary will, only to desert it again at the first setbacks, like the unforgotten "inflation recruits" of 1923. "We must not allow ourselves to be weighted down with the corpses of a ruined bourgeoisie," a memorandum stated five days after the election. But contrary to such fears, the party had little trouble bringing the new members—as Gregor Strasser wrote—"into the great pot of the National Socialist idea" and melting them down. While the adversaries of the movement were still

289

looking for soothing explanations, the party continued its tempestuous advance. Faithful to his maxim that the best time to attack is right after the victory, Hitler staged a wave of party actions after September 14 and garnered new successes for the party. In the Bremen mayoralty election of November 30 the party's percentage of the vote was almost double what it had been in the recent Reichstag election. It won more than 25 per cent of the seats in the city council; all the other parties suffered losses. The results were similar in Danzig, Baden, and Mecklenburg. In the intoxication of such triumphs Hitler at times seemed to believe that the regime could now be "voted to death," without any external aid.

On October 13 the session of the Reichstag began amidst tumultuous scenes. In protest against the persisting Prussian ban on uniforms, the Nazi party deputies had marched through the Reichstag building and entered the chamber in brown shirts, howling and making unmistakable gestures of protest. In a passionate speech Gregor Strasser declared war on "the system of shamelessness, corruption and crime." His party would not cringe from even the ultimate step of civil war, he announced; the Reichstag was not going to frustrate the party's goals. The people were the decisive factor and the people were on his party's side. Outside, meanwhile, brawls with the Communists were being staged, as well as the first pogrom—organized by Goebbels—against Jewish businesses and passersby. Questioned on this matter, Hitler replied that the excesses were the work of rowdies, looters, and Communist provocateurs. The *Völkische Beobachter* proclaimed that in the Third Reich the windows of Jewish stores would be better protected than they were now under the reign of the Marxist police. Simultaneously, more than 100,000 metal workers went on strike, supported by both the Communists and the Nazis. Civil order was visibly disintegrating.

Hitler himself appeared not to waver for a moment in his tactical conduct. What he had learned back in 1923 and not forgotten was that even the shakiest system remained impervious to attacks by street mobs. There were plenty of romantic hotheads in the party who could not imagine a revolution without powder smoke and who immediately after the triumph of September 14 began to rant about marching on Berlin and waging the final struggle. Hitler, however, would not be budged from his policy of legality, although he made no secret of his reasons for it: "We are not in principle a parliamentary party," he declared in Munich, "for that would be a contradiction of our whole outlook; we are a parliamentary party by compulsion, and that compulsion is the Constitution. . . . The victory we have just won is nothing but the winning of a new weapon for our struggle." Göring stated the matter even more cynically: "We are fighting against this State and the present system because we wish to destroy it utterly, but in a legal manner. Before we had the Law for the Protection of the Republic, we said we hated this State; under this law, we say we love it—and still everyone knows what we mean."⁹

Hitler's caution was partly guided by the one eye he kept cocked in the direction of the army. It was on the Reichwehr's account, he later admitted, that he had renounced the idea of a *coup d'état*. For the more patently public order was disintegrating, the more decisive the power and influence of the Reichswehr became. The 1923 putsch, and the subsequent ban on contact between the army and the newly founded SA, had considerably clouded mutual relationships. As early as March, 1929, however, Hitler had made tentative overtures to the representatives of the state's armed might. In a pointed speech he had questioned the concept of the "unpolitical soldier," formulated by General von Seeckt. He drew a picture of a leftist victory, after which the army officers would find themselves serving as "executioners and political commissars." Then he contrasted this dreadful prospect with the radiant aims of his own movement, concerned as it was for the greatness and the military honor of the nation. The speech was a piece of skillful psychology and impressed in particular the younger members of the officer corps.

A few days after the September election three officers of the army garrison at Ulm were placed on trial at the federal high court in Leipzig. They were charged with violating a decree of the Reich Defense Ministry by establishing connections with the NSDAP and proselytizing for the Nazis inside the Reichswehr. At the request of his lawyer, Hans Frank, Hitler was invited to testify. The sensational trial gave him an opportunity for publicly wooing the army and a platform for presenting his political aims effectively. On the third day of the trial, September 25, 1930, Hitler stepped forward to testify with the self-assurance of a recently victorious party leader, confident more than ever of ultimate victory.

Under cross-examination he explained that his convictions were a response to three challenges: the peril of foreign racial influences, or internationalism; the devaluation of personality and the rise of the democratic idea; and the poisoning of the German people with the spirit of pacifism. In 1918, he said, he had entered public life in order to oppose to these disturbing tendencies a party of fanatical Germanism, of absolute authority for the leader, and of uncompromising struggle. But he was by no means an antagonist of the armed power of the state. Whoever sowed sedition in the army was an enemy of the people; the SA was not intended to attack the state or to compete with the army.

He was then questioned about his position on legality and boldly assured the court that the National Socialist Party had no need of violence: "Another two or three elections and the National Socialist movement will have the majority in the Reichstag, and then we will make the national revolution." Asked what he meant by that, Hitler replied:

291

The concept of National Revolution has generally been considered in terms of purely domestic politics, but to National Socialists it means simply a German patriotic uprising. Germany was tied hand and foot by the peace treaties. All German legislation today is nothing but an attempt to impose the terms of the peace treaties on the German people. The National Socialists regard these treaties not as binding law, but as something forced upon us. We do not acknowledge our war guilt, nor will we burden future generations who are entirely guiltless with these fictitious debts. We will proceed against these treaties both on the diplomatic front and by circumventing every one of their provisions. If we fight against them with every means at our disposal, we will be on the way of the Revolution.

This reply, which turned the concept of revolution against the outside world, concealed his plans for domestic policy. When the presiding judge asked whether the revolution directed against the outside world would also make use of illegal methods, Hitler was remarkably frank: "All methods, including those that from the world's viewpoint are illegal." Asked about his many threats against so-called traitors at home, Hitler responded:

I stand here under oath to God Almighty. I tell you that if I come to power legally, in my legal government I will set up state tribunals which will be empowered to pass sentences by law on those responsible for the misfortunes of our nation. Possibly, then, quite a few heads will roll legally.[10]

The applause from the gallery indicated the mood in the courtroom. The counterarguments of the Ministry of the Interior, which came forth with ample proofs of the Nazi party's anti-Constitutional activities, were disregarded. With perfect calm the court heard Hitler's subsequent statement that he felt bound by the Constitution only during the struggle for power; as soon as he possessed constitutional powers he would eliminate or at any rate replace the Constitution. In fact, according to the tenets of the time, this was not so brazen as it seems. The Constitution could be legally abrogated. One of the people's rights was to give up its sovereignty. This was a door through which Hitler could advance unhindered, paralyze all resistance, seize the government and subject the state to his will.

But there was more behind Hitler's pledges of loyalty to the Constitution, more than his frank admission that he was forgoing violence only until he could cloak it with legality. Throughout this period Hitler injected into his professions of legalism a note of disturbing ambiguity. Though he proclaimed that he stood "hard as granite on the ground of legality," he was encouraging his followers to make reckless speeches in which violence appeared chiefly in images and frightening metaphors: "We come as enemies! Like the wolf breaking into the sheepfold, that is how we are coming." Strictly speaking, only the party heads talked the language of legality. Further down, in the backyards of the Berlin Wedding District, a working-class area, in the nocturnal streets of Altona or Essen, murder, manslaughter, and contempt for the law prevailed. Evidence of such conduct was dismissed with a shrug as "excesses of local units." Goebbels gave the game away. Speaking to Lieutenant Scheringer, one of the three young officers at the Leipzig trial (who were ultimately convicted), Goebbels said jokingly: "I regard this oath [of Hitler's] as a brilliant move in the chess game. Now what can they possibly do to us? They were only waiting for the chance to strike. Now we're strictly on the up and up."

The very uncertainty about Hitler's intentions, his continual veering between oaths of loyalty to the Constitution and threats against it, served his cause in many ways—which was precisely what he intended. The general public was reassured, but there was always that edge of uneasiness which produces deserters and renegades. As for those who guarded the doors to power, above all Hindenburg and the army, Hitler was on the one hand making an offer of alliance, on the other hand warning them that they had better meet him halfway. Finally, the ambiguity was directed to those among his followers who were still expecting a march on Berlin. To them he seemed to be winking the message that the Führer would know how to trick every imaginable adversary. From all these angles, then, Hitler's testimony under oath at Leipzig was enormously effective.

Viewed as a whole, however, Hitler's tactics of leaving doors open on all sides reveal something more than clever calculation. They also reveal his character; for such tactics conformed to the deeply rooted indecisiveness of his nature. There are paradoxes here, for such tactics were also extremely risky; they required a keen sense of balance and therefore also satisfied his craving for risks. If he failed, there remained only a premature and all but hopeless attempt at a putsch, or withdrawal from politics.

The SA was a living example of the idea underlying Hitler's tactics and illustrated the risks and difficulties inherent in them. For by Hitler's complicated principle, the party's brown-shirted army was to combine a formal respect for the law with the romanticism of insurgency. The men were supposed to abjure weapons but keep up the spirit of armed conflict. Pfeffer had been unable to slant things along these paradoxical lines. Early in 1931 Ernst Röhm took office as chief of staff of the SA, and immediately shifted the stress back toward the military model. The territory of the Reich was divided into five supergroups (*Obergruppen*) and eighteen groups (*Gruppen*). Standards (*Standarten*)—which corresponded to regiments—were assigned the numbers of former regiments of the imperial army, and a system of special units, such as the air storm troops, the naval, engineering and medical storm troops, further stressed the military structure.

Pfeffer had issued a vast number of isolated orders that added up to a highly complicated system. Röhm now had these summed up in an SA service manual. As if under some mechanical compulsion, all his measures continually reverted to the old idea of an army for civil war. This time,

293

unlike 1925, Hitler gave him the green light. One reason for this was Hitler's greater confidence in his own authority; but more important, Röhm's idea suited his deliberate policy of ambiguity. If we examine the reforms put through after the replacement of Pfeffer, we see all the traits of Hitlerian sham reforms. Instead of a decision made on basic principles, a few of the leading personalities were changed. Oaths of loyalty were taken, and a competing institution was created. For in view of his continuing difficulties with the SA, Hitler began cautiously to expand the SS, which, as a kind of elite and "inner party police," had played a shadowy role and by 1929 numbered only 280 men, and to give it increasing independence of Röhm. Moreover, the whole thing was to end in a manner characteristically Hitler's: the inevitable conflicts arising from contradictory tendencies would be resolved by a bloody and disproportionately violent coup.

Under Röhm the SA began its development into a mass army. Thanks to the new chief of staff's outstanding organizational gifts, by the end of 1932 his army had swollen to more than half a million men. Attracted by the SA homes and the SA kitchens, vast numbers of the out-of-work poured into the brown-shirt formations. The bitterness of the unemployed combined with the hatreds of the adventurous activists into a high charge of aggressiveness.

One of Röhm's first acts was to oust Pfeffer's Frontbann officers and replace them with his own homosexual friends. Behind them, a sizable and notorious company moved in; word went around that Röhm was building a "private army within the private army." Soon there were noisy protests. Hitler replied to these in a message that was to become famous. He rejected the reports on the morally culpable behavior of the supreme SA leadership "fundamentally and with all sharpness." The SA, he declared, was "an association of men for a political purpose . . . not an ethical institution for the education of gentlewomen." What counted was whether or not the individual did his duty. "The men's private lives can be the object of examination only if they run contrary to essential principles of National Socialist ideology."

This message constituted a charter for the lawless elements within the SA. In spite of all the pledges of legality, Hitler's army was soon creating a wave of paralysis and terror which in turn increased the demand for a dictatorship. According to reports of the police, the arms stores of the SA contained all the classic weapons of criminals: blackjacks, brass knuckles and rubber truncheons. In tight situations, they had their "molls" carry the hand guns. Their jargon also had an underworld ring. In Munich a pistol was called a "lighter" and the rubber truncheon an "eraser." The Berlin SA, in the manner of gangs, adopted nicknames that gave the lie to their allegedly revolutionary spirit. One SA "storm" in Wedding called itself the Robber Storm, while many troopers assumed various desperado names— Potshot Müller or Pistol Packer. The typical mixture of assertive proletarianism, love of violence, and threadbare ideology can be seen in the Berlin SA song, which ran:

We are the hungry toilers,
A strong courageous band,
We grip our rifles firmly
In sooty, callused hand.

The Storm Troops stand at ready
The racial fight to lead,
Until the Jews are bleeding
We know we are not freed.

But that was the frightening reverse of the coin, flashes of which appeared only now and then. The other side was marked by the austere regularity of marching columns, by uniforms and sharp cries of command—those military noises so familiar to the nation as symbols of order. Germany, Hitler later commented, thirsted for order during those years of chaos and wanted it restored at any price. More and more often, behind flags and brass bands, the brown columns turned into strangely stilled streets. They paraded with an air of self-assurance, their discipline contrasting in what seemed a significant manner with the dismal gray processions of the Communists. For the latter straggled along in uncertain order behind the provocative nasal sound of a woodwind ensemble, raising clenched fists and intoning the slogan "Hunger!"—a pathetic sight whose effect was to make the poor conscious of their misery but never give them anything to hope for.

Yet these SA rowdies brought a considerable degree of self-sacrifice to their role as guerrilla fighters. This can be seen in a letter to Gregor Strasser from a thirty-four-year-old SA standard leader:

In my work for the NSDAP I have faced a court more than thirty times and have been convicted eight times for assault and battery, resistance to a police officer, and other such misdemeanors that are natural for a Nazi. To this day I am still paying installments on my fines, and in addition have other trials coming up. Furthermore, I have been more or less severely wounded at least twenty times. I have knife scars on the back of my head, on my left shoulder, on my lower lip, on my right cheek, on the left side of my upper lip, and on my right arm. Furthermore, I have never yet claimed or received a penny of party money, but have sacrificed my time to our movement at the expense of the good business I inherited from my father. Today I am facing financial ruin. . . .[11]

Against this kind of dedication the republic could do little. Moreover, once the Hitler movement had made its breakthrough and become a mass party, the republic no longer had the strength to steer a determined course against the Nazis without risking conditions bordering on civil war. The defenders of the republic clung to the hope that they could stem the assault of irrationalism by the power of argument. They trusted in the educational effect of democratic institutions, in what they believed to be the irreversible trend toward more humane social conditions. Some of the old nineteenth-century faith in progress lingered on in these views. But even then, at the beginning of the thirties, it should have been clear that this theory was erroneous because it assumed rationality and the capacity to discriminate, where in fact there was nothing but a tangled web of anxiety, panic, and aggression. That the Nazi propagandists were by and large ignorant fellows, that their answers to the problems of the Depression were inadequate, that they fell back so tediously on their anti-Semitic slogans, discredited them for only a select group. The experts might dismiss them as a pack of dumbbells, but the Nazis continued their rise. By contrast, when Chancellor Brüning went on a tour of East Prussia and Silesia, where unemployment and misery were rife, he was everywhere greeted coolly, if not with hostility. When he spoke to crowds, banners were strung up bearing the words: "Hunger dictator," and he was often booed.

In the Reichstag, meanwhile, the Nazis played with growing mastery their double game as destroyers and judges of the "system." Thanks to the strength of their fraction they were now in a position to paralyze the workings of the legislature and to confirm their reputation as "noise-makers" by putting on displays of undisciplined catcalling. They opposed every serious attempt at stabilization on the grounds that any improvement in conditions would only serve the ends of "compliance politics"—that is, the policy of meeting the terms imposed by the Allies. In that light, they maintained, every sacrifice the government asked of the people was an act of high treason.

In addition to argument, they utilized the devices of sheer obstruction: clamor, debates on points of order, or marching out of the hall in a body as soon as a "Marxist" took the floor. It is a measure of the unruliness of the Nazi faction that, according to a report of the Agenda Committee, some 400 motions of censure had been filed against the 107 Nazi deputies. In February, 1931, a law was passed setting limits on parliamentary immunity. Thereupon, the Nazis, followed by the German Nationalists and for a time by the Communists also, withdrew completely from the Reichstag. They threw their energy more than ever into street demonstrations and public meetings, where they rightly conjectured they had far better prospects for winning followers and projecting a clear and definite image. Goebbels sneered at the deputies who remained in the Reichstag as "backside parties" and pointed out that while they were talking to a powerless legislature he had, in four days, spoken to more than 50,000 persons. For a time the Nazis toyed with the demagogic notion of setting up in Weimar, with the aid of Minister of the Interior Frick of Thuringia, a counter-Reichstag of the nationalist opposition. But they dropped this idea when the federal government threatened sanctions against the state.

296

There was a certain logic to the Nazi exodus from the Reichstag. After all, the Nazis themselves had done everything they could to paralyze the work of the legislature and to reduce its prestige. It was now no longer the site of political decision making. Even before the elections of September, 1930, Chancellor Brüning had sometimes acted without the assent of the dissension-torn Reichstag, invoking the President's emergency powers under Article 48 of the Weimar Constitution. But now that the paths to normal legislative operations by the formation of a majority were blocked, he governed almost exclusively by drawing on the President's exceptional powers. In practice, he was running a semidictatorial administration. Anyone, however, who considers Brüning's action as "the death knell for the Weimar Republic" (as the Marxist historian Arthur Rosenberg did) ought to consider that the shift in power from the legislature to the executive was possible only because it accorded with the tendency of nearly all the parties to dodge political responsibility. To this day, some historians blame the turn to authoritarianism upon the "nonpolitical masses." But, rather than the masses, it was the political parties, from right to left, who at moments of crisis rushed to shift the responsibility to the "Ersatz Kaiser," the President, anxious to be disassociated from the unpopular decisions that crises called for. In leaving the Reichstag, the Nazis were only demonstrating that they were superior in consistency compared with the other political parties; and although they, too, were running from responsibility, running forward not backward. Part of the "secret" of their rise was this lead in consistency.

The vexation with democracy—to understate the case—was intensified by the government's obvious failures in both domestic and foreign affairs. Brüning's austerity policy, which he pursued to the point of masochism, had not succeeded in eliminating either the fiscal problems or the decline of demand, and in no way diminished the vast army of unemployed. Nor did the government win any ground on questions of reparations and disarmament. Above all, France—alarmed by the results of the September elections—refused all concessions and cultivated her hysterias.

The Depression had brought on general economic warfare among governments. Tentative efforts toward trade agreements and a lowering of customs barriers stagnated at the beginning of 1931. Germany and Austria thereupon, on their own initiative, concluded a tariffs treaty that did not infringe on the economic autonomy of both partners and explicitly called upon other countries to join. But France viewed this agreement as undermining a crucial feature of the Treaty of Versailles and concluded that "peace on the old Continent was once again imperiled."[12] French banks in both Germany and Austria promptly called their short-term loans, throwing both countries "into a massive bankruptcy," which compelled them, in the autumn of 1931, abjectly to abandon the plan. Austria had to make considerable economic concessions. In Germany Hitler and the radical

297

Right gloated over the government's loss of prestige and its further enforced efforts at accommodation. When, on June 20, President Hoover proposed a moratorium on reparations payments for one year, "a mood like that at the outbreak of war" prevailed in the Chamber of Deputies in Paris.[13] Subsequently, France, which admittedly would be most affected by this plan, spun out the negotiations until a series of vast collapses in Germany intensified the crisis to a degree far worse than anyone had thought possible. In Berlin, too, a contemporary observer was reminded of the days before the outbreak of the war. But it was more the deserted look of the streets, the silence brooding over the city, and the extreme tension in the atmosphere, that produced this feeling.[14] At the end of 1931 Hitler announced that during the previous year the party had had fifty men killed and about 4,000 wounded.

It was apparent to all that the democratic party system was on its last legs, in theory as well as reality. There were all sorts of proposals for a revised Constitution. They combined contempt for the inadequacies of parliamentary democracy with anxiety over the totalitarian drive of extremists from both Right and Left. Conservative journalists offered foggy plans for a "new state" or a "constitutional dictatorship," that would head off Hitler's more radical alternative by a more moderate option.

Similar intentions inspired the ideas for an authoritarian constitution reestablishing the prerevolutionary state, which in view of the increasing weariness with democratic methods were discussed among the Reich President's entourage. Among the principal advocates of such plans that tended to a gradual restoration of the monarchy were Chancellor Brüning himself; Minister of Defense Groener; Groener's liaison man with the other departments of government, the chief of the newly created Ministerial Bureau, General Kurt von Schleicher, who, thanks to his intimacy with Hindenburg, had become a key figure, albeit a background one, of the political scene.

Schleicher had already made his presence felt in the appointment of Brüning as Chancellor; he had adroitly proceeded in extending his influence to the point that no Chancellor or cabinet minister could be appointed or dismissed without his consent. His preference for background activity and finespun nets of intrigue had earned him the reputation of being a "field-gray eminence." He was cynical, as highly sensitive persons tend to be, impulsive, unprejudiced, and wary. He used the army intelligence service to spy even on friends and neighbors. His peculiar combination of frivolity, sense of responsibility, and bent for intrigue made him a distinctly difficult person to deal with.

Schleicher's reasoning started from the thesis that a broad popular movement like Hitler's could not be quelled by governmental instruments of power. The shock of the revolution, when the officers' corps suddenly found itself pitted against the strange gray hordes of the masses, had convinced the more open-minded members of the Reichswehr leadership that the army must never again be turned against the people. Although

298

Schleicher hardly took the Nazi party leader seriously, describing him as a "visionary and idol of stupidity," he acknowledged and respected the factors that had obtained for Hitler so tremendous a following. Schleicher by no means overlooked the disturbing aspects of the movement, that blend of lawlessness, resentment, and fanaticism that one of Schleicher's fellow officers had called the "Russian character" of the Nazi party. But this made him all the more intent on putting through his plan. As long as Hindenburg was still alive and the army seemed organically sound, Schleicher thought he could "domesticate" Hitler by taking him into the inner circle of political responsibility. The mass army of his following, meanwhile, as long as the curbs of the Versailles Treaty remained in effect, would be used to strengthen Germany's "defense posture." Cautiously, therefore, Schleicher began seeking contact with Hitler by way of Ernst Röhm and Gregor Strasser.

Other conservative leaders were likewise eager to have a hand in polishing the rough diamond who happened to be master of the stadia and meeting halls; among them was Alfred Hugenberg. In the summer of 1931 President Hindenburg complained to Hugenberg about Hitler's "ruffians" and said he did not regard the NSDAP "as a reliable nationalist party." Hugenberg replied that that was all the more reason to strike up an alliance; he believed he had already contributed to the political education of the Nazis, he said. In spite of all previous unpleasant experiences, he added, he, too, was seeking to re-establish the broken connection with Hitler.

These efforts at rapprochement from several sides corresponded to the advances that the vexed Führer of the Nazi party was making at the same time. He was vexed because his success of September still profited him nothing. The outcome of the elections had indeed made him one of the chief actors on the political stage; but as long as his isolation continued he was condemned to play a mute part. "Hitler has lost many months," Carl von Ossietzky wrote. "He has wasted his time in inactivity, and no eternity will ever restore that lost time to him. No power in the world will ever give him back the 15th of September with the defeated parties trembling and officialdom bewildered. At that time the hour for the German Duce had come; who would have asked whether he was acting legally or illegally? But this German Duce is a cowardly, effeminate slugabed, a petty bourgeois rebel who's fast grown fat, who takes it easy and does not realize when fate lays him in a pickling solution along with his laurels. This drummer pounds his tomtom only in rear echelon. . . . Brutus sleeps."

Given a following held together less by political convictions than by volatile emotions, Hitler was actually dependent, far more than the other party leaders, on a train of new, spectacular successes. True, the party continued its victorious march in 1931: at the beginning of May it won 26.9 per cent of the vote in the elections for the Landtag, the provincial legislature, in Schaumburg-Lippe; two weeks later it reached 37.2 per cent in Oldenburg, thus for the first time becoming the strongest party in a Landtag. But these successes were only repeating on the provincial scale what the party had already achieved on the plane of national politics in September. When the Nazis marched through squares or narrow streets roaring in unison, "Hitler at the gates!" it sounded more as though they were trying to get him to the gates, despite their boast that he was already there. Nor could the Nazi party accomplish anything in the legislatures, since it continued to pursue its policy of paralysis. Thus there remained only the stale boasts over the ever-increasing membership figures, the more and more record-breaking meetings, or—these always announced with sanctimonious hypocrisy—more and more martyrs. Dissatisfaction with this state of affairs manifested itself once again in the spring of 1931, when the Berlin SA under Walter Stennes revolted. But before the SA leader could organize this open defection from the party and draw the vacillating Goebbels over to his side, an order arrived from Hitler deposing Stennes. The other conspirators quickly returned to the fold amid renewed assurances on Hitler's part and new vows of loyalty on their own.

Despite his boast that he would bring down the "system" in a succession of election campaigns, Hitler had exerted himself since the spring to gain the confidence and support of influential circles, realizing more keenly than ever before that he would never attain governmental power solely on the basis of his success among the masses. Article 48, which shifted effective power to the President and his immediate entourage, reduced both the power of the Reichstag and the importance of an electoral victory. Not the number of votes but the will of the President determined the holder of the chancellorship. In a sense, therefore, it was more important to commend himself to Hindenburg than to win a majority.

As always, Hitler advanced on several fronts at once. His oath of legality at Leipzig had already contained a hidden offer of good behavior and partnership. At the beginning of 1931 he received a hint from Schleicher: the ban on participation of Nazis in the Frontier Guard was lifted. In return, Hitler instructed the SA to refrain from street fighting. He even had an SA unit in Kassel dissolved because it had obtained weapons contrary to orders. To strengthen the point, Röhm was required to issue a memorandum implying that the storm troop detachments might be dissolved altogether; they "would be superfluous" if Hitler assumed the chancellorship. "Pretty-boy Adolf is dripping with loyalty," General Groener wrote to a friend at this time. Hitler was no longer a problem for the Defense Ministry, he added.

When the Catholic bishops issued a sharp statement warning their flock against the Nazi party, Hitler instantly dispatched his most ingratiating associate, Hermann Göring, to Rome to negotiate. In an interview with the *Daily Express* Hitler expressed himself in favor of strong German-English co-operation to abolish reparations; he took a conciliatory, mature tone and emphasized the elements uniting England and Germany. When Wilhelm Pieck, the Communist deputy, announced that the Red Army stood ready to come to the aid of revolutionary armies of liberation within Germany, Hitler told an American newspaper that the National Socialist Party was the bulwark against advancing world Bolshevism. "He rants much less than he used to," a contemporary account noted. "He no longer has Jews for breakfast" and was evidently doing his best "not to seem monomaniac." His eagerness to be thought respectable extended to outward matters. He left the modest little Hotel Sanssouci, where he had previously stayed on his visits to Berlin, and chose to reside in the prestigious Kaiserhof. There was also deliberate challenge in this; the hotel lay diagonally across the square from the chancellery. Convinced that they had tamed their man, the spokesmen for the Right assured one another that Hitler was at last on the way to being a useful implement of state power.

He also wooed the financiers, who on the whole had remained rather reserved. Frau von Dircksen, who held court in the Kaiserhof and had many influential connections, came to his aid just at the right time—one more of those aging female friends to whose zeal he owed so much. Frau Bechstein also continued to promote his cause. Other contacts were made through Göring, who ran a lavish house, and through the financial journalist Walther Funk. Wilhelm Keppler, a small businessman ruined by the Depression, also brought sympathetic industrialists into the movement. He founded the "Economic Friendship Circle," which was to become notorious through its later connection with Himmler. Otto Dietrich, who had extensive family connections with men in industry, noted: "In Munich in the summer of 1931 the Führer suddenly made the decision to work systematically on leading personalities in business and in the bourgeois Center parties, who were at the heart of the opposition to him." He toured Germany in his supercharged Mercedes, going to confidential conferences. The better to keep them secret, some of these were held "in solitary forest clearings, in the bosom of nature." At Streithof ("Squabble Farm"), the estate of Emil Kirdorf, the Ruhr industrialist, Hitler addressed more than thirty captains of heavy industry.[15] He ostentatiously forced Gregor Strasser and Gottfried Feder to withdraw a motion they had introduced in the Reichstag as a kind of last bow to their abandoned socialist aims, a motion calling for the expropriation of the "bank and stock exchange barons." And when the Communist Party faction, seeing a good joke, proposed the selfsame motion on their own account, Hitler had the Nazi deputies vote against it. Henceforth, his only comments on his economic program were dark allusions. At the same time, he drew away from the somewhat pigheaded Gottfried Feder and occasionally kept Feder from speaking in public.

During the early part of July, 1931, Hitler finally met with Hugenberg in Berlin. Soon thereafter he had a talk with Franz Seldte and Theodor

Duesterberg, leaders of the paramilitary veteran association Stahlhelm ("steel helmet"), who once again wanted to join forces with him. Then he met with General von Schleicher and General von Hammerstein-Equord, chief of the army command. He conferred with Brüning, Groener, and once again with Schleicher. The purpose of all these conversations was to sound out Hitler's intentions, but they were also rapprochements designed to draw Hitler into the system against which he had been battling on principle. The idea was to capture him by tactical alliances and, as General Groener put it, "bind him doubly and triply to the stake of legality." But none of these important persons had any idea of Hitler's toughness and intransigence. They also seemed to discount Hitler's capacity for dissimulation. Consequently, the gains were all on his side—the leader of the Nazi party emerged from his isolation and was raised several ranks in status. The conversations encouraged his followers, confused his antagonists, and impressed the voters. How desperately Hitler had been waiting for this turn of events is evident from his reaction when he was summoned to Berlin for the meeting with Chancellor Brüning. Hess, Rosenberg, and Rosenberg's deputy, Wilhelm Weiss, were with him in Munich when the telegram arrived. He skimmed it hastily, then held it out to the others. "Now I have them in my pocket!" he exclaimed. "They have recognized me as an equal partner in negotiations." The image he was trying to project is reflected in Groener's summary: "Hitler's intentions and aims are good, but [he is an] enthusiast, fervent, many-sided. Likable impression, modest, orderly person and in manner the type of the ambitious, self-educated man." Hereafter, in confidential communications among his distinguished counterparts he would be referred to—with a shade of mockery—as "Adolf." He had made his successful entree.

Only the conversation with Hindenburg—which Schleicher arranged for October 10—ended in a failure. The President's entourage had the strongest reservations; in fact, Oskar, Hindenburg's son, had acidly commented on Hitler's request for an interview: "I suppose he wants a free drink." Hitler came with Göring. He seemed nervous during the meeting; when the President suggested that he support the administration, in view of the predicament of the whole country, Hitler launched into divagations on the aims of his party. On being reprimanded for the increasing acts of violence on the part of his followers, Hitler responded with verbose assurances that obviously did not satisfy the President. From Hindenburg's entourage the remark was subsequently leaked that the President was at most prepared to appoint this "Bohemian corporal" Postmaster General, certainly not Chancellor.[16]

After the interview Hitler went to Bad Harzburg, where next day the Nationalist opposition was celebrating its union by a great demonstration. Once more Hugenberg had gathered together everybody on the Right who had power, money, or prestige: the leaders of the Nazis and of the German

Nationalists, the rightist members of the Reichstag and of the Prussian Landtag, the representatives of the German People's Party (Deutsche Volkspartei), the Economic Party, the Stahlhelm, and the Reichslandbund. In addition, he had assembled many prominent patrons, members of former ruling houses headed by two Hohenzollern princes. Also present were Heinrich Class, leader of the Pan-Germans, and his presiding committee, such retired generals as von Lüttwitz and von Seeckt, and many notables of finance and industry, including Hjalmar Schacht, Fritz Thyssen, Ernst Poensgen of the Vereinigte Stahlwerke (United Steel), Louis Ravene of the Iron Wholesalers' Association, the shipbuilding magnate Blohm of Hamburg, the bankers von Stauss, Regendanz, and Sogemeyer. All the enemies of the republic, with the exception of the Communists, were deployed here: a variegated army of the discontented, united less by a single aim than by a single animosity.

Hitler was in the worst of humors. He had consented to participate only with great reluctance, and the failure of his interview with Hindenburg had increased his sullenness. As in the case of the alliance against the Young Plan, he once more had to expect criticism from his own ranks; and personally he could not help feeling uncomfortable about this liaison with all the bourgeois forces. Shortly before the beginning of the meeting, therefore, he had a closed session of his own following. Frick spoke, justifying the pact with this "bourgeois mishmash" on purely tactical grounds. Mussolini, too, Frick said, had had to win power by the roundabout route of a nationalist coalition.

As soon as Frick had ended his speech, Hitler, with that dramatic surprise technique of his, entered the room with his personal retinue and in a solemn ceremony had everyone there take a pledge to follow his line. Meanwhile, the "Nationalist United Front" was waiting in the Kursaal for Hitler to appear.

For Hugenberg, who had already made all sorts of concessions to the Nazi party leader during the preparatory phases, this delay was not the last humiliation of the meeting. Hitler deliberately trampled on the feelings of his influential partners. He did not bother to appear at the session of the joint editorial committee, declaring its work to be a sheer waste of time. And at the final parade, which was supposed to be the inspiring climax of the meeting, Hitler ostentatiously left the stands as soon as the SA formations had marched past and the Stahlhelm was approaching. Nor would he attend the dinner; he could not feast, he declared, as long as thousands of his followers did their "duty on empty stomachs." Only "concern over the adverse publicity, which none of the participants desired," Hugenberg complained in disappointment, had prevented a "breach right out in the open."

To Hitler, the disharmony at Harzburg was by no means a tactical feint. Nor was it part of his prima-donna pose. Rather, the meeting confronted him again with the crucial question of power. Hugenberg's talk about unity did not disguise the claim to leadership, which as arranger of the festivities he was actually making. With his own peculiar consistency, Hitler realized that any community of action could mean only subordination. At best it would imply that henceforth Germany would have to be looking up to two "saviors"—an absurdity from Hitler's point of view. In order to dispel any such mistaken impression, only a week after the Harzburg meeting, Hitler organized a huge demonstration on the Franzensfeld in Brunswick. More than 100,000 SA men were brought there in special trains. During the hours that the parade lasted, planes with gigantic swastikas streaming behind them circled over the field. And during the dedication of standards Hitler declared that this would be the last such ceremony before the seizure of power. The movement, he said, stood "within a yard of its goal."

At the same time there can be no doubt that Hitler's rudeness at Harzburg expressed some of his hostility toward the bourgeois world, which he was never able to completely quell. The very sight of top hats, tailcoats, and starched shirt fronts irritated him, as did the titles, the decorations, and the conceit they suggested. Here were people who thought morality itself sustained their claims to dominance, who liked to speak of their "historically appointed role." But Hitler sensed the weakness and rot behind the display of composure, the outmodedness of these swarms of mummies with middle-class manners.

Yet this was the very bourgeois world that the young coffeehouse dandy, the lazy disciple of the arts, had longed to join. Though it had rejected him, he had nevertheless uncritically taken over its social, ideological, and aesthetic evaluations and held on to them for a long time. But in the meantime that world had declared its bankruptcy, and Hitler—unlike the representatives of the bourgeois world—never forgot that fact. In Hugenberg he was meeting a replica of the cunning, arrogant, and feeble Bavarian Prime Minister, Herr von Kahr, who had for him become the prototype of bourgeois notables. He now regarded them as a group who claimed to rule, yet had the souls of lackeys. "Cowardly," "stupid," "idiotic," and "rotten," were the adjectives he now attached to the mention of any member of this group. "No class of the population is stupider in political matters than this so-called bourgeoisie," he would often remark. Once he said that he had for a long time deliberately tried, by strident propaganda and improper manners, to keep bourgeois people from joining the party.

In May, 1931, Richard Breiting, editor in chief of the *Leipziger Neueste Nachrichten,* asked Hitler for an interview. Hitler began the conversation by remarking, "You are a representative of the bourgeoisie which we are fighting." He stressed that he had no intention of rescuing the dying bourgeoisie; on the contrary, he would eliminate it and would, at any rate, find it much easier to handle than Marxism. Hitler openly flaunted his present aloofness from bourgeois culture: "If a proletarian brutally tells me what

Top: Party demonstration,
1925
Bottom: Christmas party
with his followers, 1925

Left: Hitler in his role as statesman, at his desk in the Brown House
Right: Brown House, Briennerstrasse, Munich
Bottom: Hitler with his niece, Geli Raubal

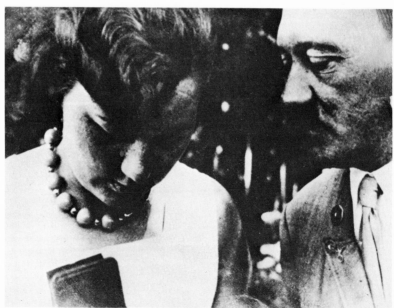

Top: The first Nuremberg party rally, 1927; far left, Julius Streicher
Bottom: Hitler speaks at the Berlin Sportspalast, 1930

The Depression
Top: Breadlines, 1931
Bottom left: Communist and Nazi flags in a Berlin backyard; the slogan reads, "Our children go to the dogs here"
Bottom right: Goebbels haranguing

Oratorical poses

Top: Hitler at the Harzburg
meeting in 1931
Bottom right: Reviewing the
SA parade in Brunswick

The newly appointed Chancellor in conversation with
Franz von Papen and General von Blomberg, January, 1933

Top: Hitler with
Hindenburg, 1933
Bottom: Hitler, October,
1934, shortly before
Hindenburg's death

Mass enthusiasm

"The miracle of German unification"; the nation is divided into desirables and undesirables
Top left: Heinrich and Thomas Mann, Albert Einstein
Top right: Gerhart Hauptmann, Gottfried Benn
Bottom: Book burning and the first anti-Semitic outbreaks by SA units

The dual aspect of the
revolution
Top: Mass arrests in the
spring of 1933
Bottom: Strength-Through-
Joy entertainment

Top: Hitler inaugurating the
building of the autobahn
network; by a succession of
cornerstone layings and
similar ceremonies Hitler
created an atmosphere akin
to mobilization
Bottom: The autobahn near
Rosenheim, July, 1937

Top: At the harvest thanksgiving celebration Hitler is
handed the harvest crown
Bottom: Hitler with his photographer Heinrich Hoffmann

he thinks, I can cherish the hope that some day this brutality can be turned toward the enemy. When a bourgeois indulges in daydreams of culture, civilization and aesthetic joys for the world, I say to him: 'You are lost to the German nation! You belong in Berlin's West End! Go there, dance your nigger dances till you're worn out, and croak!' "

He occasionally referred to himself as a "proletarian," but with an emphasis that made it appear as though he were talking not so much of his social status but of a social renunciation. "I can never be understood in terms of the bourgeoisie," he declared. Even in his hope of winning over the working class—to which he referred occasionally as a class of "true nobility"—he seemed to be agitated not so much by any fondness for the workers than by his abiding hatred of the bourgeoisie, which had rejected him. There was an incestuous element in his hatred of the bourgeoisie, with the resentment of a would-be bourgeois who had been first rejected, then deceived, constantly erupting. The type of low-class bully he preferred for his immediate personal entourage, the crude "chauffeur types" like Schaub, Schreck, Graf, and Maurice, reflected in an extreme fashion this prejudice, which could be overcome only temporarily by a few individuals: by Ernst Hanfstaengl, for example, or by Albert Speer, or by Carl Jacob Burck-hardt, League of Nations commissioner for Danzig, to whom Hitler said "sadly" in 1939: "You come from a world that is foreign to me."[17]

No genuine bond with this foreign world was possible; as the meeting at Harzburg had demonstrated, not even a tenable tactical relationship could be established. Nothing came of the plan for a joint opposition; nothing came of the previously much-discussed shadow cabinet or of agreement on a common candidate for the impending presidential election.

Much has been made of the "Harzburg Front." Those who like to see history in terms of conspiracies and clever wirepulling find Harzburg convenient proof of their thesis that Hitler was nothing but a tool of finance capital. However, a closer look at the incident reveals the very opposite. Far from lending himself to the schemes of his would-be manipulators, Hitler treated these people insultingly and disappointed all their hopes. It might be more correct to say that Harzburg proved Hitler's independence of these interests.

Undeniably, there did exist a network of relationships between the leader of the Nazi party and a number of important businessmen. The party actually obtained considerable funds as well as increased prestige from these connections. But it was only inheriting the contributions that had gone earlier, and in considerably greater sums, to the parties of the Center. Neither the gains in votes of the Nazi party nor the losses of the Center parties can be ascribed to the presence or absence of wealthy patronage. As late as April, 1932, as Hitler was disturbed to learn, the shrunken Deutsche Volkspartei (German People's Party) was receiving

305

larger sums from industry than his own party. And when Walther Funk, toward the end of 1932, went on a begging tour in the Ruhr district, all he came back with was a single contribution of some 20,000 marks. The total of such aid has often been estimated far too high. Some 6 million marks is probably a fairly realistic estimate of industry's gifts to the Nazi party up to January 30, 1933. For those who consider such a figure too low it must be pointed out that even twice that sum could not have financed a party organization of some 10,000 local groups, with a large corps of functionaries, a private army of nearly half a million men, and twelve expensively conducted election campaigns in 1932. In fact, the annual budget of the NSDAP, as Konrad Heiden discovered, amounted at this time to between 70 million and 90 million marks. Conscious that he was dealing in sums of this magnitude, Hitler would sometimes refer to himself jokingly as one of the foremost German captains of industry.[18]

It suits the purposes of pseudoscientific polemic to be broad and imprecise concerning the links between the Nazi party and finance capital. According to this school of thought, Hitler was the "rigorously manipulated and dearly paid political implement" of a capitalistic "Nazi clique" that needed him for "public relations."[19]

But the very categories are misleading here. There were, for instance, clearly divergent interests among capitalists and among various branches of Industry Club on January 26, 1932, was intended specifically to overcome department stores, also the chemical industry and old family enterprises, such as the firms of Krupp, Hoesch, Bosch and Klöckner had great reservations about the Hitler party, at least before 1933. They were usually motivated by economic considerations. In addition, there was the rather significant number of Jewish enterprises. Otto Dietrich, who arranged some of Hitler's contracts with Rhenish-Westphalian industry, noted that the leaders of the economy refused "to believe in Hitler . . . in the period of our hardest struggle." As late as early 1932 there were "strong foci of industrial resistance." And Hitler's famous speech to the Düsseldorf Industry Club on January 26, 1932, was intended specifically to overcome this opposition.[20] After that speech the party was in fact granted larger subsidies, which took care of its most pressing concerns; but the sums were by no means as large as expected. At the end of 1932 Hjalmar Schacht, former president of the Reichsbank, Albert Vögler, general manager of the Vereinigte Stahlwerke (United Steel), and Kurt von Schröder, the banker, drew up a petition to President Hindenburg asking him to appoint Hitler Chancellor. But this move was a failure; the majority of businessmen who were approached refused to give their signatures.

The theory of a close, pragmatic alliance between Hitler and the major capitalists also fails to explain the time lag between the explosive growth of the party and the injection of funds from industry. By the time Hitler delivered his Düsseldorf speech the Nazi party had more than 800,000 members and could command between 6.5 million and 13 million votes. The party's strength depended on these legions of little people, and Hitler had to keep in mind their "enormous anticapitalist nostalgia." All in all, he was more attuned to them than to the proud, pigheaded businessmen. To the industrialists he sacrificed little more than that troublemaker Otto Strasser, for whom he too had no love. When his followers joined in the Berlin metalworkers strike, Hitler explained the situation tersely by telling the employers that striking Nazis were still better than striking Marxists. But the thesis that Hitler's party was in the pay of capitalism is most unsatisfactory in its failure to answer the key question: why this novel mass movement sprung from nothing could so effortlessly outstrip the splendidly organized German Left with its depth of tradition behind it. To call Hitler a tool of capitalism, as Marxist theory does, is merely to fall back on belief in demons. Marxist orthodoxy is prone to such simplifications. Such demonology is, as it were, "the anti-Semitism of the Left."[21]

But it is one thing to speak of an outright plot between industry and Nazism, quite another to speak of the atmosphere of "partiality" or sympathy that surrounded Nazism. Many elements within industry were frankly in favor of Hitler's becoming Chancellor, even though they were not themselves disposed to do anything about it. And many who were not prepared to offer him material support nevertheless regarded his program with some approval. They expected no concrete economic or political gains from it and never entirely lost their distrust for the socialistic, antibourgeois sentiments within the NSDAP. But they had never really accepted bourgeois democracy with its consequent rights of the masses. The republic had never been their state. To many of them Hitler's promise of law and order meant a larger scope for enterprise, tax privileges, and restraints upon the unions. Implicit within the slogan, "salvation from this system," coined by Hjalmar Schacht were vague plans for restoring the old order of things. Petrified remnants of the authoritarian state paradoxically survived more obstinately in the dynamic business world than in almost any other stratum of the German social structure. If we are to blame "capital" for the rise of the Nazi party, it was not so much on the basis of common aims, let alone of some dark plot, but on the basis of the antidemocratic spirit, the rancor against the "system," emanating from big business. It is true that the spokesmen for business were deceived about Hitler. They saw only his mania for order, his rigid cult of authority, his reactionary features. They failed to sense the peculiar vibrations he threw off, the pulse of futurity.

Hitler's above-mentioned address to the Düsseldorf Industry Club was one of the most masterly samples of his oratorical skill. Appearing in a dark pin-striped suit, behaving skillfully and correctly, he expounded the ideological foundations of his policies to an initially reserved group of big businessmen. Every word of the two-and-one-half-hour presentation was carefully adapted to his audience. Not only did he understand how attached these people were to law, order, and authority, but he was able to turn that attachment toward himself.

Early in the speech, Hitler outlined his argument for the primacy of domestic politics. He explicitly disagreed with the view—elevated to a kind of dogma by Chancellor Brüning—that Germany's fate was largely dependent upon her foreign relations. Foreign policy, Hitler maintained, was, on the contrary, "determined by the inner condition" of a people. Any other view would be resignation, surrender of self-determination, or a dodge on the part of bad governments. In Germany the caliber of the nation had been undermined by the leveling influences of democracy:

When the capable minds of a nation, which are always in the minority, are regarded as only of the same value as all the rest, then genius, capacity, the value of personality are slowly rendered subject to the majority, and this process is then falsely named the rule of the people. For this is not rule of the people, but in reality the rule of stupidity, of mediocrity, of half-heartedness, of cowardice, of weakness, and of inadequacy. It is more the rule of the people to let a people be governed and led in all the walks of life by its most capable individuals, those who are born for the task, rather than . . . by a majority who in the very nature of things must always find these realms entirely alien to them.

The democratic principle of equality, he continued, was not an inconsequential idea with merely theroretic bearing. Rather, in the short or long run it would extend into all the aspects of life and could slowly poison a nation. Private property, he told the industrialists, was fundamentally incompatible with the principle of democracy. For the logical and moral rationale for private property was the belief that people are different in nature and achievement. At this point, Hitler came to the heart of his argument:

Once this is admitted, it is madness to say: in the economic sphere there are undoubtedly differences in value, but that is not true in the political sphere. It is absurd to build up economic life on the conception of achievement, of the value of personality, and therefore in practice on the authority of personality, but in the political sphere to deny the authority of personality and to thrust into its place the law of the greater number—democracy. In that case there must slowly arise a gulf between the economic and the political point of view, and to bridge that gulf an attempt will be made to assimilate the former to the latter. . . . In the economic sphere communism is analogous to democracy in the political sphere. We find ourselves today in a period in which these two fundamental principles clash in all areas where they meet. . . .

In the State there is an organization—the army—which cannot in any way be democratized without surrendering its very existence. . . . The army can exist only if it maintains the absolutely undemocratic principle of unconditional authority proceeding downwards and absolute responsibility proceeding upwards. But the result is that in a State in which the whole political life—beginning with the municipality and ending with the Reichstag—is built upon the conception of democracy, the army is bound to gradually become an alien body.

He cited many other examples to demonstrate this structural contradiction, and then described the menacing spread of the democratic, and hence the communistic, idea in Germany. He dwelt at length on the terrors of Bolshevism:

Can't you see that Bolshevism today is not merely a mob storming about in some of our streets in Germany but is a conception of the world which is on the point of subjecting to itself the entire Asiatic Continent, and . . . will gradually shatter the whole world and bring it down in ruins. Bolshevism, if it proceeds unchecked, will transform the world as completely as in times past did Christianity. . . . Thirty or fifty years count for nothing where fundamental ideologies are at issue. Three hundred years after Christ Christianity was only slowly beginning to establish itself throughout all of southern Europe.

Because of Germany's intellectual confusion and psychological disintegration, he continued, Communism had already made greater inroads there than in other countries. Millions of persons had been persuaded that Communism was the "logical theoretical complement of their actual, practical economic situation." It was therefore wrong to seek the causes of the present misery in external factors and to attempt to fight them with external methods. Economic measures or "another twenty emergency decrees" would not be able to halt the disintegration of the nation. The reasons for Germany's decline were political in nature and therefore required political decisions, nothing less than "a fundamental solution":

That solution rests upon the realization that economic systems in collapse have always as their forerunner the collapse of the State and not vice versa—that there can be no flourishing economic life which has not before it and behind it the flourishing powerful State as its protection—that there was no Carthaginian economic life without the fleet of Carthage. . . .

But the power and well-being of states, he added, are a consequence of their internal organization, of the "firmness of common views on certain fundamental questions." Germany is in a state of great internal dissension; approximately half of the people are Bolshevistic, in the broad sense of the word, the other half nationalistic. One half affirm private property; the other half regard it as a kind of theft. One half consider treason a crime, the other half a duty. In order to halt this decomposition and to overcome Germany's impotence, he had created a movement and an ideology:

For here you see before you an organization . . . inspired to the highest degree by nationalist sentiment, built on the concept of the absolute authority of the leadership in all spheres, at every stage—the sole party in whose adherents not only the conception of internationalism but also the idea of democracy has

309

been completely overcome, which in its entire organization acknowledges the principles of Command and Obedience, and which has thus introduced into the political life of Germany a body numbering millions which is built up on the principle of achievement. Here is an organization which is filled with an indomitable aggressive spirit, an organization which when a political opponent says, "We regard your behavior as a provocation," for the first time does not submissively retire from the scene but brutally enforces its own will and hurls against the opponent the retort, We fight today! We fight tomorrow! And if you do not regard our meeting today as a provocation we shall hold another one next week. . . . And when you say, "You must not come into the street," we go into the street nevertheless. And when you say, "We shall kill you," however many sacrifices you force upon us, this young Germany will always continue its marches. . . . And when people cast in our teeth our intolerance, we proudly acknowledge it—yes, we have formed the inexorable decision to destroy Marxism in Germany down to its very last root. And this decision we formed not from any love of brawling; I could easily imagine a pleasanter life than being harried all over Germany. . . .

Today we stand at the turning point of Germany's destiny. If the present course continues, Germany must one day land in Bolshevist chaos, but if this development is broken, then our people must be enrolled in a school of iron discipline. . . . Either we will succeed in once more forging out of this conglomerate of parties, leagues, associations, ideologies, upper-class conceit and lower-class madness an iron-hard national body, or Germany will finally perish because of the lack of this inner consolidation. . . .

People say to me so often: "You are only the drummer of nationalist Germany." And what if I were only the drummer? It would be a far more statesmanlike achievement to drum a new faith into this German people than gradually to squander the only faith they have [cheers from the audience]. . . . I know quite well, gentlemen, that when National Socialists march through the streets and suddenly a tumult and commotion breaks out in the evening, then the bourgeois draws back the window curtain, looks out, and says: "Once more my night's rest disturbed; no more sleep for me." . . . But remember there is sacrifice involved when those many hundred thousands of SA and SS men of the National Socialist movement every day have to climb into their trucks, protect meetings, stage marches, exert themselves night after night and then come back in the gray dawn either to workshop and factory or as unemployed to take the pittance of the dole. . . . If the whole German nation today had the same faith in its vocation as these hundred thousands, if the whole nation possessed this idealism, Germany would stand in the eyes of the world otherwise than she stands now! [Loud applause.][22]

Yet for all the applause, at the end of the meeting only about a third of the audience joined in Fritz Thyssen's cry of *"Heil, Herr Hitler!"* The financial benefits from this appearance were also disappointing. But what it did accomplish was to bring Hitler out of isolation. It was the government, now, which was more and more becoming isolated. From all sides growing armies of opponents besieged the battered positions of the Weimar Republic. In the state of Prussia, still ruled by a coalition under Social Democratic leadership, an attempt was made to dissolve the Landtag by referendum. All the nationalist parties united for a common action and were actually joined by the Communists. And although their united forces represented only 37 per cent of the votes, the impression lingered of a broad front of opponents ready and eager to overthrow the existing government.

The bitter clashes between the paramilitary formations, especially between Communists and Nazis, and between these squadrons and the police, were further symptoms of the shattered authority of the state. General chaos in the streets and a train of bloody outrages on weekends became almost the rule. On the Jewish New Year the Berlin SA under Count Helldorf (who was subsequently to become police chief of Berlin) organized a series of wild riots. At the universities there were sometimes physical assaults on professors whom the Nazis did not like. The court trials of party members became the occasions for unprecedented scenes. There was no actual civil war, but Hitler's remark that some day heads would roll still rang in the nation's ears, and a general impression arose that more was happening in the streets than occasional bloody brawls between rival parties struggling for the favor of the voters and seats in the legislature. Some time before, Hitler had declared:

The goal the bourgeois parties have in mind is not annihilation [of the opponent] but merely an electoral victory. . . . We recognize quite clearly that if Marxism wins, we will be annihilated. Nor would we expect anything else. But if we win, Marxism will be annihilated, and totally. We too know no tolerance. We shall not rest until the last newspaper is crushed, the last organization destroyed, the last educational institution eliminated and the last Marxist converted or exterminated. There is no middle course.[23]

The fighting in the streets amounted to the preliminary skirmishes of a civil war that had been interrupted rather than fought to a decision in 1919 and which would shortly, in the spring of 1933, be carried to its logical conclusion in the torture cellars and concentration camps of the SA.

In this highly charged atmosphere, the authorities were frightened of driving Hitler to extremes. At the end of November, 1931, ten days after the elections to the Landtag of Hesse in which the National Socialist Party won 38.5 per cent of the seats, thus becoming by far the strongest party in this provincial legislature, a Nazi renegade gave the police chief of Frankfurt the Nazi plan of action in case the Communists attempted an uprising. These "Boxheim Papers"—as they were known from the estate at which the Nazi leaders had held their secret meetings—outlined the manner in which the SA and kindred organizations would assume power. The Papers spoke of "ruthless measures" to achieve "sharpest discipline of the populace." Any act of resistance or even of disobedience would incur the death penalty, in certain cases "on the spot without trial." Private property and all interest payments were to be suspended, the population fed communally, and everyone would be required to work. Jews, however, would not be allowed to work or receive food.

The disclosure of the plan created a stir. Hitler, however, disclaimed any part in the affair, though he also took no disciplinary measures against the authors of the project. Again, he seemed not too displeased to have the public given a good scare. Although the plan deviated from his own conception in its details, and especially in its semisocialist elements, its basic assumption was the same as his: that the ideal starting point for the seizure of power would be an attempt at a Communist rising. This would evoke a cry for help on the part of the threatened government and bring him forward with his SA, so that he could take over in the name of justice and with an appearance of righteousness. That was the cry he had vainly tried to force Herr von Kahr to utter on the night of November 8–9, 1923. He had never wanted to be cast merely as one politician among many others. His idea was always to come on the scene as savior from the deadly embrace of Communism, surrounded by his rescuing hosts, and thus take power. This role coincided with both his dramatic and his eschatological temperament, his sense of being always engaged in a global struggle with the powers of darkness. Wagnerian motifs, the image of the White Knight, of Lohengrin, of the Grail and an endangered fair-haired woman vaguely and half-consciously entered into this picture. Later, when circumstances did not produce this constellation, when no Communist putsch seemed in the offing, he tried to create it.

Nothing happened to the authors of the Boxheim Papers. That in itself was indicative of the deterioration of concepts of legality throughout the governmental apparatus. The bureaucracy and the judiciary obviously delayed prosecuting a case of treason. The political authorities, too, dismissed the affair with a resigned shrug, instead of seizing the chance for a strong last-minute effort to save the republic. Hitler could have been arrested and brought to trial on the basis of the clear and damning evidence. Instead, the administration remained conciliatory. Alarmed by his threats, it tried even harder to placate him. Nor was it forgotten that he had been received by Schleicher and Hindenburg and accepted as an equal by influential politicians, businessmen, and notables. In short, he had moved once more "into the vicinity of the President." By now, moreover, one might well ask whether the movement could be curbed by police or judicial measures, or whether any such measures might not produce a most undesirable swing in the Nazis' favor. In any case, in December, 1931, Prussian Minister of the Interior Severing shelved a plan to have Hitler arrested and deported. And around the same time General von Schleicher, urged to take energetic measures against the Nazis, replied: "We are no longer strong enough. Should we try to, we would simply be swept away!"

Suddenly people were no longer so sure that the Hitler party was merely a collection of petty bourgeois vermin and demagogic windbags. A feeling of paralysis spread, rather similar to the apathy felt before a force of nature. "It is the *Jugendbewegung* [youth movement], it can't be stopped," the British military attaché wrote,[24] describing the prevalent attitude in the German officers corps. The story of the rise of the National Socialist Party, which we have been tracing, is equally the story of the corrosion and decline of the republic. For the republic lacked the strength to resist; it also lacked any compelling vision of the future, such as Hitler was able to conjure up in his rhetorical flights. There were few who still believed the republic would long survive.

"Poor system!" Goebbels noted ironically in his diary.

Chapter 3

Vote, vote! Get at the people!
We are all very happy.

Joseph Goebbels

AT THE GATES OF POWER

It was not only Hitler's demagogic gifts, not only his tactical skill and radical verve that sped his fortunes; the force of irrationality itself seemed cunningly at work for him. Thus there were five major elections, held largely by chance in the course of 1932, in which Hitler could employ his special brand of agitation.

The term of the President of the Reich was to expire in the spring. In order to avoid the risks and radicalizing effects of an election campaign, Brüning had earlier proposed that Hindenburg be made President for life by an amendment to the Constitution. Brüning's whole policy was aimed at gaining time. The winter had seen an almost inconceivable worsening of the Depression. In February, 1932, the number of unemployed rose to over 6 million. But with the rigidity of the technical expert who feels that his principles stand far above the base adaptability of the politician, Brüning kept firmly to his course. He was counting on eventual cancellation of reparations, on some success in the disarmament conference, on Germany's being granted equal rights. In the shorter perspective, he was hoping that the spring would bring proof of the efficacy of his austerity policy, rigorous to the point of starvation.

But the common people shared neither his rigor nor his hopes. They were suffering from hunger, cold, and the humiliating side effects of misery. They hated the endless stream of emergency decrees with their stereotyped appeals to the spirit of sacrifice. The government was administering misery instead of relieving it, a bitter joke had it. Certainly Brüning's policy of belt tightening was questionable from the economic point of view; but it proved to be far more questionable politically. For the Chancellor, with his matter-of-fact approach to the problem, did not know how to frame his plea for sacrifice in terms people could respond to. All that he seemed to

314

promise was a program of further austerity stretching on into the dim future.

Brüning's effort to gain time was totally dependent on the support from the President. But to his surprise Hindenburg himself had no desire to stay in office. Hindenburg was by now eighty-four; he had long since grown tired, and he foresaw troublesome discussions in connection with the plan and new attacks upon him from his already disappointed friends on the Right. All that he would consent to was a two-year extension of his term—and even this only after much persuasion. Significantly, what swayed him was a reference to Kaiser Wilhelm I, who at the age of ninety-one had declared that he had no time to be tired. But, in the course of it all, the old President lost confidence in Brüning, whom he recognized as the motive force behind all the urging. In putting across his stratagem, the Chancellor had actually lost what he had hoped to gain.

Brüning had next to deal with the various parties and win them over to the constitutional amendment. At this point, Hitler became a key figure and was wooed and sued accordingly. This certainly helped his prestige, but it also confronted him with a perilous choice. For now he either had to make common cause with the "pillars of the system," and thus help to consolidate Brüning's position and deny his own radicalism, or else he had to wage an electoral campaign against the gray-haired old President, the object of so much reverence, the personification of German loyalty and the nation's surrogate kaiser. To oppose Hindenburg might seriously hurt the movement and, moreover, offend the President personally. Given the decisive powers of the presidency, such a course might have dire consequences for Hitler's access to power.

Gregor Strasser was for accepting Brüning's proposal. Röhm and, above all, Goebbels were strongly against it. "What is involved here is not the President himself," Goebbels noted in his diary. "Herr Brüning is anxious to stabilize his own position and that of his cabinet for the foreseeable future. The Führer has asked for time to consider. The situation must be clarified on all sides. . . . The chess game for power is beginning. Perhaps it will last throughout the year. A game that will be played with drive, prudence, and partly with cunning. The main thing is that we remain strong and make no compromises."

Hitler remained in this quandary for some time. While Hugenberg responded with a prompt and blunt rejection, Hitler kept silent. The answer he finally gave reflected both his doubts and his caution. Each man behaved in character. Hugenberg was aping Hitler's radicalism and breathlessly trying to surpass it but in the process only revealing his poor understanding of tactics. Hitler, on the other hand, employed his radicalism as an instrument, offsetting it with a goodly dash of shrewdness. In the present case he surrounded his rejection with so many ifs and buts that he seemed to be asking for further negotiations. He had sensed the increasing

315

estrangement between Hindenburg and Brüning and did what he could to widen the rift. In a sudden display of pendantry he assumed the role of guardian of the Constitution, and in long-winded arguments that seemed to be scrupulously concerned about the President's being faithful to his oath of office, he advanced all kinds of legalistic objections to the Chancellor's plan.

Basically, this answer meant that Hitler had already decided to run against Hindenburg. But he hesitated for several weeks more before announcing the decision. For his dream had always been to come into power with the President's blessing, not as the President's opponent. He also realized, more keenly than did his satellites, the dangers of challenging the Hindenburg legend. Consequently, he remained impassive while Goebbels and others hammered away at him to announce his candidature. However, he went along with the proposal that German citizenship be obtained for him through the good offices of Minister of the Interior Klagges of Brunswick, who was a member of the Nazi party.[25] Hitler would have to be a citizen in order to run. Here was still another instance of Hitler's curious indecisiveness. He had a fatalistic streak and liked to let things take their course, postponing action until the last moment. For, strictly speaking, the decision had been taken long ago. Goebbel's diary reveals, step by step, Hitler's tortuous, almost bizarre vacillations:

January 9, 1932. Everything in confusion. Much guessing about what the Führer will do. People will be surprised! —January 19, 1932. Discussed the question of the presidency with the Führer. I report my conversations. No decision has been taken yet. I plead strongly for his own candidacy. Actually, there probably is no other course. We draw up calculations with figures. —January 21. In this situation there really is no other choice; we have to put up our own candidate. A difficult and unpleasant struggle, but we must go through with it. —January 25. The party is quivering with militancy. —January 27. The election slogan for or against Hindenburg seems to have become inevitable. Now we must come out with our candidate. —January 29. The Hindenburg Committee is meeting. Now we must show our colors. —January 31. The Führer will make his decisions on Wednesday. There can no longer be any doubts. —February 2. The arguments for the Führer's candidacy are so thoroughly persuasive that anything else is out of the question. . . . At noon had a long discussion with the Führer. He sets forth his view of the presidential election. He decides to run himself. But first the opposition must occupy fixed positions. The Social Democratic Party will be the decisive factor. Then our decision will be communicated to the public. It is a struggle of enormously embarrassing alternatives, but we must go through with it. The Führer makes his moves without the slightest haste and with a clear head. —February 3. The gauleiters are waiting for the announcement of the decision to run for the presidency. They wait in vain. This is a game of chess. You don't tell in advance what moves you are going to make. . . . The party is terribly nervous, tense, but nevertheless everybody is still keeping silent. . . . In his leisure hours the Führer is occupying himself with architectural plans for a new party headquarters as well as for a spectacular rebuilding of Berlin. He has the project all worked out, and I am constantly astonished anew at his expertise in so many fields. At night many loyal old party comrades come to see me. They are depressed because they have not yet heard of any decision. They are worried that the Führer will wait too long. —February 9. Everything is still in suspense. —February 10. Outside a glassy cold winter day. Clear decisions are hovering in the clear air. They cannot be much longer in coming. —February 12. At the Kaiserhof with the Führer I once again go over our computations. It is a gamble, but we must go ahead. The decision has now been taken. . . . The Führer is back in Munich; the public decision postponed for a few days. —February 12. This week we must announce our stand on the presidential question. —February 15. Now we no longer have to hide our decision beneath a bushel. —February 16. I am going ahead as if the election campaign were already in progress. That makes for some difficulties, since the Führer has not yet officially announced his candidacy. —February 19. With the Führer at the Kaiserhof. I talked to him privately for a long time. The decision has been taken. —February 21. This eternal waiting is almost wearing me out.

For the following night Goebbels had scheduled a membership meeting at the Berlin Sportpalast. This was to be his first public appearance since he had been banned from public speaking on January 25. By now the election was only three weeks away, and Hitler was still wavering. In the course of the day Goebbels went to the Kaiserhof to brief Hitler on the contents of his speech. When he once more brought up the question of candidature, he unexpectedly received the permission he had so desperately waited for: to announce Hitler's decision to run. "Thank God," Goebbels noted. He added:

Sportpalast jammed. General membership meeting of the West, East and North regions. Stormy ovations right at the start. After an hour of preamble I publicly announce the Führer's candidacy. A storm of enthusiasm rages for almost ten minutes. Wild demonstrations for the Führer. People stand up cheering and shouting. They raise the roof. An overwhelming sight. This is truly a Movement that must win. An indescribable excitement and rapture prevails. . . . Late at night the Führer telephones. I report to him, and then he comes to our house. He is glad that the proclamation of his candidacy has struck home so effectively. He is and remains our Führer after all.[26]

The last sentence reveals the doubts that had assailed Goebbels during the preceding weeks in the face of Hitler's weak leadership. But the sequel is just as characteristic of Hitler's psychic pattern: the sudden surge of energy with which he threw himself into the battle without a single glance backward, once the decision had been made. On February 26, in a ceremony at the Hotel Kaiserhof, he had himself appointed a Regierungsrat in Brunswick for the period of a week, thus acquiring German citizenship. The following day, at a meeting in the Sportpalast, he cried out to his opponents: "I know your slogan! You say: 'We will stay at any cost.' And I tell you: We will overthrow you in any case! . . . I am overjoyed to be able to fight alongside my comrades, whatever the outcome." He picked up a remark by Police Commissioner Albert Grzesinski of Berlin, who had spoken of driving him out of Germany with a dog whip: "Go ahead and threaten me with the dog whip. We shall see whether at the end of this struggle the whip is still in your hands." At the same time, he tried to disclaim the unwelcome role of opponent to Hindenburg, which Brüning had forced on him. Rather, it was his duty to say to the Field Marshal—whose "name the German people must always hail as that of their leader in the great struggle"—"Dear old man, our veneration for you is too great for us to allow those whom we would destroy to hide behind you. With our deep regret, therefore, you must step aside, for they want to fight us and we want to fight them." Beside himself with delight, Goebbels noted that the Führer was "once more master of the situation."

The extent to which Hitler and the Nazis had come to dominate the political scene became clear right at the outset. For although Hindenburg, the Communist candidate Ernst Thälmann, and the Conservative Theodor Duesterberg were already running, the election campaign did not really begin until Hitler entered the race. Instantly, the Nazis began sweeping everything wildly before them. Their campaign testified both to the improved condition of the party's treasury and to their more effective organization. In February Goebbels had transferred the national propaganda headquarters of the party to Berlin, and in his bombastic style had predicted an election campaign "such as the world has never seen before." The top people of the party's corps of speakers were called upon. Hitler himself traveled by car back and forth across Germany from March 1 to March 11, and if the *Völkische Beobachter* was to be believed, spoke to some 500,000 people. At the side of this "demagogue on the grandest scale" stood, as Hitler had prescribed, that "army of agitators who will whip up the passions of the already tormented people." Their wit and ingenuity—they employed modern technical media for the first time—once more put to shame all their rivals. Fifty thousand copies of a phonograph record were distributed. Sound movies were made, and pressure was exerted on cinema owners to have these shown before the main film. A special illustrated magazine, devoted to the election, was launched and what Goebbels called a "war of posters and banners" unleashed, which overnight would paint whole cities or districts of cities bloody red. For days on end long columns of trucks drove through the streets. SA units stood under waving banners, chin straps drawn down, singing or shouting their "Germany, awake!" The incessant booming of slogans soon engendered within the party an autosuggestive mood of victory that Himmler tried to keep in check by restricting alcohol consumption at victory celebrations.

On the other side stood Brüning, who seemed peculiarly alone. In homage to the President, he was going through this exhausting election campaign. As for the Social Democrats, their posture all too plainly betrayed their real intentions: they were supporting Hindenburg solely in order to defeat Hitler. And their uneasiness was matched by Hindenburg's; in the one radio address the old man made during the campaign he rather mournfully defended himself against the charge that he was the candidate of a "black-and-red [*i.e.,* Catholic-socialist] coalition." Nevertheless, it turned out that the election, which shifted all fronts and split all loyalties, was a match entirely between Hindenburg and Hitler. On the eve of March 13 the Berlin *Angriff* announced confidently: "Tomorrow Hitler will be President of the Reich."

Given such high expectations, the actual result was a severe and shocking blow. Hindenburg, with 49.6 per cent of the votes, won an impressive victory over Hitler (30.1 per cent). Triumphantly, Otto Strasser had posters pasted in the streets showing Hitler in the role of Napoleon retreating from Moscow. The legend read: "The Grand Army is annihilated. His Majesty the Emperor is in good health." Overwhelmingly defeated, with only 6.8 per cent of the voters supporting him, was the Conservative Duesterberg. Thus the rivalry within the nationalist camp was decided once and for all in favor of Hitler. The Communist Thälmann received 13.2 per cent of the votes.

However, Hindenburg had fallen short of the absolute majority, and the election therefore had to be repeated. Once more Hitler faced the situation in a characteristic way. While spirits fell throughout the party and some members saw no point in entering upon a second campaign, Hitler showed no emotion at all. On the very night of March 13 he issued a series of proclamations to the party, the SA, the SS, the Hitler Youth, and the NSKK (Motorized Corps of the National Socialist Party) calling for renewed and increased activity: "The first election campaign has ended; the second has begun today. I shall lead it in person," he announced, and as Goebbels rapturously phrased it, Hitler raised up the party "in a single symphony of the aggressive spirit." But late one night Ernst Hanfstaengl found him in his darkened apartment sunk in apathetic brooding, "the image of a disappointed, discouraged gambler who had wagered beyond his means."

Alfred Rosenberg, meanwhile, was using the *Völkische Beobachter* to give the fainthearted followers a good shaking: "Now the fight goes on with a fierceness, a ruthlessness, such as Germany has never before experienced. . . . The basis of our struggle is hatred for everything that is opposed to us. Now no quarter will be given." A few days later nearly fifty prestigious personages—nobles, generals, Hamburg patricians, and university professors—issued a statement declaring themselves for Hitler. Election day was set for April 10. But with the idea of keeping down the agitation by radicals of the Right and Left, with its eruptions of hatred and threats of civil war, the government declared a mandatory truce until April 3—on the pretext of preserving peace during Easter. This meant that the actual election campaign was limited to about a week. But as always when he found himself with his back to the wall, Hitler turned this obstacle into one of his most effective gestures. To make maximum use of the short time at his disposal, he chartered a plane for himself and his intimates, Schreck, Schaub, Brückner, Hanfstaengl, Otto Dietrich, and the photographer Heinrich Hoffmann. On April 3 he started off on the first day of his subsequently famous flights over Germany, which day after day took him to four or five demonstrations organized with military precision. In all he visited twenty-one cities. And quite apart from the party propaganda that tried to weave a legendary wreath around this undertaking, there is no doubt that the flights created an impression of brilliant inspiration, bold modernity, fighting spirit, and a rather sinister omnipresence. "Hitler over Germany" was the effective slogan for these flights; its double meaning stirred millionfold expectations and millionfold anxieties. Moved by his own daring and the waves of cheering that greeted him, Hitler declared that he thought he was an instrument of God, chosen to liberate Germany.

As predicted, Hindenburg had no difficulty winning the requisite absolute majority, with nearly 20 million votes, 53 per cent of the total. Nevertheless, Hitler chalked up a larger increase in votes than the President; the 13.5 million voters who cast their ballots for him represented a percentage of 36.7. Duesterberg had not run in the second campaign; the Communist Thälmann received little more than 10 per cent of the total.

On the very day of the election, in a mood that mingled exhaustion, feverish excitement, and the intoxication of success, Hitler issued instructions for the elections to the state legislatures in Prussia, Anhalt, Württemberg, Bavaria, and Hamburg, which once more involved the entire country, four-fifths of the population. Goebbels recorded Hitler's orders: "We will not rest for a moment and are already making decisions." Once more Hitler set out on an airplane flight over Germany, speaking in twenty-five cities in eight days. His entourage boasted of a "world record" in personal encounters. But that was precisely what did not happen. Rather, Hitler's individuality seemed to disappear behind the ceaseless activity, as if nothing but a dynamic principle were at work: "Our whole life is now a frantic chase after success and after power."

For long stretches of his life, therefore, the personality of this man, elusive in any case, evaporates, slips from the biographer's grasp. Hitler's entourage tried in vain to give color, individuality, and a human aura to the phenomenon. Even the masters of propaganda, who could command almost any effect, found themselves at a loss here. The diaries and accounts of Goebbels or Otto Dietrich are prime examples of that failure. The anecdotes his publicists endlessly circulated about Hitler the lover of children, the navigator with an infallible sense of direction in the lost airplane, the "dead shot" with a pistol, the hero with remarkable presence of mind in the midst of the "Red rabble"—all these tales sounded strained and added to the impression they were trying to dispel: remoteness from real life. Only the props he had gradually acquired gave him a certain individual outline: the raincoat, the felt hat or leather cap, the snapping whip, the intensely black mustache, and the way his hair was brushed down over his forehead. But because these items always remained the same, they, too, depersonalized him.

Goebbels has vividly described the restiveness that gripped the leading members of the party at this time:

This endless traveling begins again. Work must be taken care of standing, walking, driving and flying. You hold your most important conversations on stairs, in hallways, at the door, or on the drive to the railroad station. You scarcely have time to think. By train, car and plane you're carried back and forth across Germany. You turn up in a city a half hour before your speech is scheduled, sometimes with even less time to spare; you climb to the speaker's platform and speak. . . . By the time you're done you're in a state as if you'd just been pulled out of a hot bath fully dressed. Then you get into the car and drive another two hours. . . .[27]

Only a few times during this year and a half of nonstop electioneering did circumstances jolt Hitler out of his impersonality and for brief moments offer a glimpse of his real character.

On September 18, 1931, just as the frantic chase across Germany was beginning and while he was setting out on an election campaign visit to Hamburg, word reached him that his niece Geli Raubal had committed suicide in the apartment they shared on Prinzregentenstrasse in Munich. According to the accounts, Hitler, stunned and horrified, abruptly turned about; and unless all the indications are deceptive, no other event in his personal life affected him as strongly as did this one. For weeks he seemed close to a nervous breakdown and repeatedly swore to give up politics. In his fits of gloom he spoke of suicide; this was, once again, the mood of total capitulation into which he recurrently fell when misfortune struck. This melancholia testified to the highly charged quality of his life, demanding constant effort of will in order to be the person he wanted to seem to be. The energy that emanated from him was not the exuberance of a vigorous man but the forced product of neurosis. In keeping with his belief that the great man must have no feelings, he hid away for several days in a house on the Tegernsee, in southern Bavaria. According to his intimates, tears would come to his eyes whenever he spoke of his niece in later years; it was an unwritten rule that no one but he might mention her name. Her memory was surrounded with a kind of cult. Her room at the Berghof was kept just as she had left it; a bust of her was set up in the room at Prinzregentenstrasse in Munich, where her body had been found. There, year after year, on the anniversary of her death, Hitler would lock himself in for a meditation that might last for hours.[28]

There was a strangely exaggerated, idolizing quality about all of Hitler's reactions to his niece's death—in strong contrast to his usual coldness and inability to relate to others. We have reason to think that he was not putting on a performance, that in fact the incident was one of the key events in his personal life. It seems to have fixed forever his relationship to the opposite sex, which was curious enough in any case.

If our evidence is to be believed, for some time after his mother's death, women had played only the most peripheral part in his life. The men's home, chance acquaintanceships in Munich beer halls, the dugout, the barracks, the male circles of politics and the party—these had been his world. The realm that complemented them tended to be the brothel, which, however, he found despicable, or light, casual relationships—but these were not easy for him to form, with his stiff unyielding nature. The shy inhibited attitude he had toward women was early expressed in his youthful crush on Stefanie. His fellow soldiers in the field considered him a "woman hater." Though later on he was always involved in close social relationships, always surrounded by a host of people, his biography is eerily empty of other human beings. His fear of all undignified attitudes included, according to a remark by a member of his entourage, constant anxiety about "having his name linked with a woman."

His complexes seemed to loosen up only after Geli Raubal appeared with her sentimental and at first, evidently, half-childish fondness for "Uncle Alf." It may be that he could be more relaxed with someone of his own blood. In fact, his feelings for Geli may have sprung from this very incestuous factor. There is a precedent in his own immediate family. His father had taken a niece into his house when she was sixteen and made her his mistress. Among the many women who crossed Hitler's path—from Jenny Haug, the sister of his first chauffeur, to Helena Hanfstaengl, the first wife of Ernst Hanfstaengl, Leni Riefenstahl, and all those he addressed or referred to in the Austrian intimate style as *"Mein Prinzesschen," "Meine kleine Gräfin," "Tschapperl,"* or *"Flietscherl,"* and up to Eva Braun—none meant as much to him as Geli Raubal. She was, oddly inappropriate though the phrase sounds, his great love, a tabooed love of Tristan moods and tragic sentimentality.

One must wonder at Hitler's obtuseness in regard to Geli, for he could be acute enough psychologically where others were concerned. Did he not see that the situation was becoming impossible for this impulsive and unbalanced girl? It has never been established that she was Hitler's mistress. Some informants claim to know she was, and explain the suicide as a desperate escape from what had become the unendurably oppressive relationship with her uncle. Another story is that certain abnormal acts demanded of her by a perverted Hitler drove the girl to suicide. Still a third version denies that there was any sexual relation between the two, but lays stress on Geli Raubal's promiscuity with the men of Hitler's uniformed staff.[29]

It is fairly certain that she enjoyed her uncle's fame and naïvely participated in his celebrity. But the relationship, which for years had been sustained by joint enthusiasms, by love for the opera and the pleasures of coffeehouses and country outings, had gradually developed oppressive aspects. Hitler's shadow fell heavily upon his niece. He was given to furious jealousy, and to making inordinate demands upon her. Though she had only a moderate gift and scarcely any ambition, he insisted on sending her to famous singing teachers so that she could be trained as a Wagnerian heroine. And his tyranny cut her off from any opportunity to lead a life of her own. Members of his entourage reported that immediately before his departure for Hamburg there had been a loud, violent scene between them, triggered by the girl's wish to go to Vienna for a while. It seems probable that all these complex and seemingly hopeless circumstances finally sent her over the brink. Less plausible is the story popular among his political enemies that the girl shot herself because she was expecting a child by Hitler. Still others held that Hitler himself ordered her murdered, or purported to know that the SS had passed a *Feme* (vigilante) sentence on Geli because she had distracted her uncle from his historic mission. Hitler himself occasionally grumbled that all this "terrible filth" was killing him. He also declared darkly that he would never forgive his enemies for the nasty gossip of those weeks.[30]

As soon as he had recovered his composure, he continued on to Hamburg after all. There, amid the cheers of thousands, he delivered one of his passionate speeches that whipped the audience into a kind of collective orgy, all waiting tensely for the moment of release, the orgasm that manifested itself in a wild outcry. The parallel is too patent to be passed over; it lets us see Hitler's oratorical triumphs as surrogate actions of a churning sexuality unable to find its object. No doubt there was a deeper meaning to Hitler's frequent comparison of the masses to "woman." And we need only look at the corresponding pages in *Mein Kampf,* at the wholly erotic fervor that the idea and the image of the masses aroused in him, to see what he sought and found as he stood on the platform high above the masses filling the arena—his masses. Solitary, unable to make contact, he more and more craved such collective unions. In a revealing turn of phrase (if we may believe the source) he once called the masses his "only bride." His oratorical discharges were largely instinctual, and his audience, unnerved by prolonged distress and reduced to a few elemental needs, reacted on the same instinctual wave length. The sound recordings of the period clearly convey the peculiarly obscene, copulatory character of mass meetings: the

323

silence at the beginning, as of a whole multitude holding its breath; the short, shrill yappings; the minor climaxes and first sounds of liberation on the part of the crowd; finally the frenzy, more climaxes, and then the ecstasies released by the finally unblocked oratorical orgasms. The writer René Schickele once spoke of Hitler's speeches as being "like sex murders." And many other contemporary observers have tried to describe the sensually charged liquescence of these demonstrations in the language of diabolism.

Nevertheless, anyone who thought the entire secret of Hitler's success as an orator lay in this use of speech as a sexual surrogate would be making a serious mistake. Rather, once again it was the curious coupling of delirium and rationality that characterized his oratory. Gesticulating in the glare of spotlights, pale, his voice hoarse as he hurled his charges, tirades, and outbursts of hatred, he remained always the alert master of his emotions. For all his seeming abandon, he never lost control. We are dealing here with the same ambiguity that governed his entire behavior and was one of the basic facts of his character. His oratorical technique was as tangibly marked by it as his tactic of legality and later the methodology of his conquest of power or his maneuvers in foreign policy. The very regime he set up assumed this character and has actually been defined as a "dual state."[31]

In fact, the triumphs of this phase were distinguished from those of earlier years by the greater planning that went into his performances, as well as the elaborated stagecraft. Essentially, Hitler's effectiveness still depended upon his always going to the utmost extreme; but he was now more radical not only in his emotions but also in his calculations. As long ago as August, 1920, he had, in a speech, described his task as "to arouse and whip up and incite . . . the instinctive" on the basis of sober understanding. He had, it would seem, a fairly good grasp of these basic principles right from the start. But only now, under the impact of the worldwide Depression, did he consciously shape his style of agitation to achieve the psychological "capitulation" that he had called the goal of all propaganda. When he planned his campaigns, every detail was, as Goebbels wrote, "organized down to the least item." Nothing was left to chance: the route, the massing of party units, the size of the meetings, the carefully determined proportions of the audiences, the mounting suspense produced by processions with waving banners, march rhythms, and rapturous shouts of *Heil,* while the speaker's appearance was again and again artificially delayed. Then, suddenly, he would step out in a blaze of lighting effects in front of an audience deliberately starved and prepared for frenzy. Ever since Hitler had once, in the early days of the party, arranged a morning meeting and in spite of the full hall had felt "profoundly unhappy at being unable to create any bond, not even the slightest contact" between himself and his audience, he had held his meetings only in the evening hours. Even during his campaign by plane throughout Germany, he kept to this rule as far as possible, although concentrating the already concentrated meetings within a few hours made for many difficulties. Thus it could happen that on a flight to Stralsund he was delayed and did not arrive at the demonstration until half past two in the morning. But 40,000 persons had waited it out nearly seven hours, and by the time he began his speech dawn was breaking.

He assigned a high significance to space as well as time. The "mysterious magic" of the darkened Bayreuth Festspielhaus during a performance of Parsifal and the "artificially created, yet mysterious twilight in Catholic churches" were, he believed, almost perfect examples of places treated for their maximum psychological effect. This was, in his words, what all propaganda aimed at: to achieve "an encroachment upon man's freedom of will."[32]

In that solemn annunciatory tone he reserved for his fundamental insights he declared: "For, in truth, every such meeting represents a wrestling bout between two opposing forces." In accord with his views on the nature of fighting, he approved of any and all means by which the agitator might overwhelm his adversary. His methods were meant for the "elimination of thinking," "paralysis by suggestion," creating a "receptive state of fanatical devotion." Along with the place, the time, the march music, and the play of lights, the mass meeting was itself a form of psychotechnical warfare. Hitler offered the following explanation:

When from his little workshop or big factory, in which he feels very small, [the individual] steps for the first time into a mass meeting and has thousands and thousands of people of the same opinions around him, when, as a seeker, he is swept away by three or four thousand others into the mighty effect of suggestive intoxication and enthusiasm, when the visible success and agreement of thousands confirm to him the rightness of the new doctrine and for the first time arouse doubt in the truth of his previous conviction—then he himself has succumbed to the magic influence of what we designate as "mass suggestion." The will, the longing, and also the power of thousands are accumulated in every individual. The man who enters such a meeting doubting and wavering leaves it inwardly reinforced: he has become a link in the community.[33]

He boasted that an "exact calculation of all human weaknesses" underlay his ideas and demagogic maxims, and this assured them a virtually "mathematical" certainty of success. In the course of his second airplane campaign he discovered the emotional effect the illuminated plane had in the night sky as it circled above tens of thousands of people staring in fascination. He thereupon used this trick again and again. Any invocation of the martyrs of the movement was also, he found, highly effective, though not as much as it might be. After the first defeat in the presidential election he criticized the party press for "dullness, monotony, lack of independence, lukewarm absence of passion." Above all, he wanted to know what the

325

press had done with the deaths of so many SA men. Mismanagement of this matter drove him into a fury. As one person present at the meeting recalled his words, he declared that the party comrades had "been buried with pipes and drums and the party sheet had written a pompous and self-pitying sermon about it. Why hadn't the newspapers displayed the corpses in their own windows, so the people could see the dead men with shattered skulls, their shirts bloody and ripped by knives? Why had these newspapers not preached funeral sermons calling on the people to riot, to rise up against the murderers and their manipulators, instead of bleating out ridiculous political half-truths? The sailors of the battleship *Potemkin* made a revolution out of rotten food, but we could not make a national struggle of liberation out of the deaths of our comrades."[34]

But his thoughts returned again and again to the subject of the mass meetings which "burned into the small, wretched individual the proud conviction that, paltry worm that he was, he was nevertheless a part of a great dragon, beneath whose burning breath the hated bourgeois world would some day go up in fire and flame."[35] The procedure of these meetings followed an unchanging tactical and liturgical order, which he was forever improving, to dramatize his own appearance. While the flags, the marches, and the shouts of expectation sent the audience into a state of restlessness and receptivity, he himself sat nervously, drinking mineral water almost continually, in a hotel room or a party business office. Every few minutes he would check on the mood in the hall. Quite often he issued final instructions or suggested some message to be relayed to the audience. Only when the excitement of the masses threatened to sag would he set out for the meeting.

He had learned that long processions increased the suspense and therefore made a principle of entering the meeting halls only from the rear. He had chosen the "Badenweiler March" for his own entrance music, reserved for him alone. The distant sound of it would hush the murmuring and send the people springing from their seats with raised arms, shouting wildly—overwhelmed in the double sense of being manipulated and ecstatic: now HE was here. Many films of the period have preserved his appearance as he strode down the path of light made by the spotlights between lines of shouting, sobbing people—a *"via triumphalis . . .* of living human bodies," as Goebbels extravagantly wrote. Often women pressed to the front, while he himself remained unapproachable, tight-lipped, in no way lending himself to their hungers. He ruled out introductory speeches or greetings that could only distract the audience from his person. For a few moments he would linger before the platform, mechanically shaking hands, mute, absent-minded, eyes flickering restively, but ready like a medium to be imbued and carried aloft by the strength that was already there, latent, in the shouting of the masses.

The first words were dropped mutedly, gropingly, into the breathless silence; they were often preceded by a pause that seemed to become utterly unbearable, while the speaker collected himself. The beginning was monotonous, trivial, usually lingering on the legend of his rise: "When in 1918 as a nameless soldier at the front I . . ." This formal beginning prolonged the suspense once more, into the very speech itself. But it also allowed him to sense the mood and to adjust to it. A catcall might abruptly inspire him to take a fighting tone until the first eagerly awaited applause surged up. For that was what gave him contact, what intoxicated him, and "after about fifteen minutes," a contemporary observer commented, "there takes place what can only be described in the primitive old figure of speech: The spirit enters into him." With wild, explosive movements, driving his metallicly transformed voice mercilessly to its highest pitch, he would hurl out the words. Quite often, in the furor of his conjuring, he would cover his grimacing face with his clenched fists and close his eyes, surrendering to the spasms of his transposed sexuality.

Although his speeches were carefully prepared and strictly followed the notes he always had in front of him, they nevertheless all sprang from his close communication and immediate exchange with the masses. It seemed to one of his temporary followers that he actually inhaled the feelings of his audience. This remarkable sensitivity of his, which endowed him with an unmistakably feminine aura, made possible those orgiastic unions with his public; it "knew him" in the Biblical sense of the word. To be sure, he was a shrewd psychologist and a superb stage manager. Yet he could not have bewitched the masses if he had not shared their secret emotions and incorporated all their psychoses into his own psyche. When he spoke, the masses met, hailed, and idolized themselves. An exchange of pathologies took place, the union of individual and collective crises in heady festivals of released repression.

It has often been asserted that Hitler told every meeting only what it wanted to hear, that he merely brought its true intentions to the fore and flaunted them for all to see. That, too, is true. Nevertheless, he was not an opportunistic flatterer of the crowd; rather, he was the spokesman for the massed feelings of being victimized, of fear, of hatred. He at once integrated those feelings and transformed them into political dynamics. The American journalist H. R. Knickerbocker noted after a mass meeting in Munich:

In the Circus Krone, Hitler spoke. He was an evangelist speaking to a camp meeting, the Billy Sunday of German politics. His converts moved with him, laughed with him, felt with him. They booed with him the French. They hissed with him the Republic. . . . The 8,000 were an instrument on which Hitler played a symphony of national passion.[36]

At such moments Hitler made "the collective neurosis the echo of his own obsession." He had to have applause to bring out his full oratorical powers. Even a reluctant mood in the hall irritated him, and the SA—which he had had surrounding him at all public appearances right from the beginning—served not so much to keep order as to silence all opposition, all feelings of resistance, and to whip up enthusiasm by sheer menace. There were a number of occasions when Hitler, faced with an unfriendly audience, would abruptly lose the thread, break off his speech, and turning on his heel sulkily leave the room.

His whole being needed the mass acclaim. For this sort of cheering had once aroused him; now it maintained his states of tension and propelled him onward. He himself said that in the midst of the tumult he became "another person." The historian Karl Alexander von Müller had long ago observed that Hitler communicated to his listeners an excitement that in turn provided fresh impetus to his voice. Certainly Hitler was a superior tactician, a capable organizer, a canny psychologist, and, despite all his deficiencies, one of the most remarkable phenomena of the period. But his invincible genius came to him only in the course of mass meetings, when he exalted platitudes into the resounding words of a prophet and seemed truly to transform himself into the leader; for in his everyday state he seemed only to be posing as *der Führer* with considerable effort. His basic condition was lethargy punctuated by "Austrian" spells of weariness. Left to himself, he seemed ready to fall back on dull movies, endless performances of the *Meistersinger,* the Carlton Tearoom's luscious chocolate confections called *Mohrenköpfe,* or going on and on about architecture. He needed hubbub around him to be fired for action. He drew his dynamism from the crowd. Its worship also gave him the stamina to carry out those terribly strenuous campaigns and flights over Germany; it was the drug his strained, driven existence constantly needed. When in October, 1931, he met Brüning for his first private talk with the Chancellor, he launched into a one-hour speech, in the course of which he worked himself up to a frenzy—lashed on by the singing of his SA unit, which he had ordered to march up and down past the windows. Obviously he had done this partly to intimidate Brüning, partly to recharge himself.[37]

It was this deep pathological link with the masses that made Hitler more than an effective demagogue and gave him his undeniable advantage over Goebbels, whose speeches were more pointed and clever. Hitler lifted the crowds out of their apathy and despair to, as he himself called it, "forward-driving hysteria." Goebbels called these demonstrations "the divine services of our political work," and a Hamburg schoolmistress wrote in April, 1932, after an election meeting attended by 120,000 persons, that she had witnessed scenes of "moving faith" which showed Hitler "as the helper, rescuer, redeemer from overwhelming need." Elisabeth Förster-Nietzsche, the philosopher's sister, drew similar conclusions after Hitler paid a visit to her in Weimar. He "struck her as a religious rather than political leader."[38]

In this phase of his career Hitler operated more on the metaphysical than on the ideological plane. His success with the masses was above all a phenomenon of the psychology of religion. He spoke less to people's political convictions than to their spiritual state. Of course Hitler could link up with an extensive system of traditional thought and conduct: with the German bent for authoritarianism and unrealistic intellectual constructs; with profound needs to follow a leader, and with a peculiar disorientation in politics. But, beyond this, agreement for the most part ended. His anti-Jewish slogans derived their force not so much from any especially violent German anti-Semitism as from the old demagogic trick of presenting people with a visible enemy. Nor was it the unique bellicose character of the Germans that Hitler mobilized; rather, he appealed to their long-ignored feelings of self-respect and national pride. The masses were not seduced by his images of land in the Ukraine; rather, they followed Hitler for the sake of their lost dignity, because they wanted once more to be participants in history. While *Mein Kampf* was issued in numerous editions, it was read by hardly anyone; this testifies to the general lack of interest all along in Hitler's specific programs.

Hence, the rise of the National Socialist Party and its coming to power was not—as has often been argued in hindsight—a great conspiracy of the Germans against the world aimed at carrying out imperialistic and anti-Semitic ends. Hitler's speeches during the years he was attracting mass audiences in the greatest numbers contain very little in the way of specific statements of intentions, and even scant his ideological obsessions, anti-Semitism and *Lebensraum*. Their salient characteristic, in fact, is their vague, general subject matter and the frequent resort to philosophical metaphors acceptable to all. As for spelling out aims, they are a far cry from the candor of *Mein Kampf*. A few months before the outbreak of the Second World War, in the midst of one of the crises he had unleashed, Hitler himself admitted that for years he had put on a show of harmlessness. Circumstances, he declared, had forced him to masquerade as peaceable.

With the bravura of a great orator, however, he was freeing himself more and more from specific content and concrete ideas. His continuous triumphs were proof that Nazism was a charismatic rather than an ideological movement, not looking to a progam but looking up to a leader. His personality gave outline and consistency to the loose jumble of ideas in the foreground. What people followed was merely the tone, a hypnotic voice; and although Hitler could draw upon unfulfilled nostalgias and dreams of hegemony, most of those who wildly cheered him were longing to forget, beneath his speaker's platform, their exhaustion and their panic. They were certainly not thinking of Minsk or Kiev, or of Auschwitz, either. They wanted, above all, things to change. Their political faith scarcely went beyond blind negation of the *status quo*.

Hitler recognized what could be done with these negativistic complexes more keenly than did any of his rivals on the Left or the Right. His agitational technique really consisted in defamation and vision, in indicting the present and promising a potent future. All he did was ring the changes on his praise of a strong state, his glorification of the nation, his call for racial and national rebirth and for a free hand on the domestic and the foreign fronts. He appealed to the German longing for unity, decried the nation's "self-laceration," called class struggle the "religion of the inferior," hailed the movement as the "bridge building of the nation," and conjured up the fear that the Germans might once more become the world's "cultural manure."

But his major theme, which he found as harrowing as did the masses, was the "ruin of the Reich." He cited the vast numbers who were reduced to wretchedness, the danger of Marxism, the "unnatural incest of party government," the "tragedy of the small savers," hunger, unemployment, suicides. His descriptions were deliberately generalized, first, because that assured him the maximum following, and secondly because he had recognized that within parties the precise statements of policy led to dissension and the impetus of a movement increased with the vagueness of its goals. Whoever succeeded in combining the most thorough negation of the present with the most indefinite promises for the future would capture the masses and ultimately win power. Thus, in one of his typical dualities of image and counterimage, of damnation and utopia, he demanded: "Is it by any chance German when our people is torn apart into thirty parties, when not one can get along with the others? But I tell all these sorry politicians: 'Germany will become one single party, the party of a heroic great nation!' "

By turning all his propaganda against the *status quo,* he achieved the simplicity that he himself saw as one of the requirements for success. "All propaganda must be popular and its intellectual level must be adjusted to the most limited intelligence among those it is addressed to." To illustrate his approach, here is a passage from a speech of March, 1932, in which he upbraids the government for having had thirteen years to prove its worth yet having produced nothing but a "series of disasters":

Starting with the day of the Revolution up to the epoch of subjugation and enslavement, up to the time of treaties and emergency decrees, we see failure upon failure, collapse upon collapse, misery upon misery. Timidity, lethargy and hopelessness are everywhere the milestones of these disasters. . . . The peasantry today is ground down, industry is collapsing, millions have lost their saved pennies, millions of others are unemployed. Everything that formerly stood firm has changed, everything that formerly seemed great has been overthrown. Only one thing has remained preserved for us: The men and the parties who are responsible for the misfortunes. They are still here to this day.[39]

With such accusatory formulas, varied and repeated a thousand times over, with vague invocations of fatherland, honor, greatness, power, and revenge, he mobilized the masses. He saw to it that their stormy emotions

330

furthered the chaos he so scathingly described. He placed his hope in everything that could destroy existing conditions, or could at least create disturbance, because any movement would have to be movement away from the existing system and would ultimately accrue to his profit. For nobody else was formulating in so credible, decisive, and mass-effective a manner the agonizing craving for change. People in Germany were so desperate, Harold Nicolson noted in his diary during his visit to Berlin at the beginning of 1932, that they would "accept anything that looks like an alternative."[40]

The vagueness of his terms also enabled him to brush aside social conflicts and veil social contradictions in a cloud of verbosity. After one midnight speech by Hitler in the Berlin Friedrichshain district, Goebbels noted: "That is where the very little people are. They are deeply moved after the Führer's speech." But the very big people were no less moved, and those in between as well. A Professor Burmeister proposed Hitler as the "candidate of the German artists" and spoke of the "humanly gripping heartwarming tones of his oratory." After Hitler had given a two-hour talk to leaders of the Agrarian League and the Brandenburg nobility, one of the landowners stood up and "in the name of everyone present" called for omitting the customary discussion: "We would not want our sense of solemn dedication to be disturbed by anything distracting." Hitler continually exacted such an unquestioning response from his audiences on the ground that with skeptics one "of course could not conquer the world; with them one cannot storm either a kingdom of heaven or a State." Out of the curious hodgepodge of his slogans, bits of eclectic philosophy, and cleverly played-on emotions, everyone could take what he had put in. The frightened bourgeoisie could find the promise of order and recovered social status; the revolutionary-minded youth the outline for a new, romantic society; the demoralized workers security and bread; the members of the 100,000-man army the prospect for careers and fine uniforms; the intellectuals a bold and vital creed in line with the fashionable attitude of contempt for reason and idolization of "life." Underneath all this ambiguity was not so much deception as the gift of striking the fundamental note of an unpolitical attitude. Like Napoleon, Hitler could say of himself that everyone had run into his net and that when he came to power there was not a single group which in some way did not place its hopes in him.

On the whole, 1932 was undoubtedly the year of Hitler's greatest oratorical triumphs. To be sure, some members of his entourage would recall that he had spoken more richly and persuasively in earlier years, and in the perfectly ritualized mass meetings of his years as Chancellor he reached larger, almost unbelievably large crowds. But never again did the longing for redemption, consciousness of his charismatic powers, utter concentration upon a goal, and faith in his own chosenness, against the highly emotional background of misery, all enter into such an "alchemical" combination. For Hitler himself that period of his life was one of his key experiences, and the examples he drew from it served again and again to influence his decisions. In the myth of the "time of struggle," this period was glorified as "heroic epic," a "hell fought through," a "titanic battle of character."

Just as the ritual of opening a mass meeting was carefully orchestrated, so was the conclusion. Amid the din and the cheering the band burst out with "Deutschland, Deutschland über Alles," or else one of the party anthems. The music created an impression of closed ranks and high pledges. But it was also intended to hold the audience until Hitler, still dazed and soaked in sweat, had left the room and entered the waiting car. Sometimes he stood for a few moments beside the chauffeur, saluting, mechanically smiling, while the crowd surged up or SA and SS units formed into broad columns for a torchlight parade. He, however, went back to his hotel room, totally drained; and this bears out the erotic quality of these mass meetings. One follower, who came upon Hitler at such a moment, staring silently into space with a glazed look, started toward him but was blocked by his adjutant Brückner, who said: "Leave him be; the man is done in!" And the morning after one speech a gauleiter found him in the remotest room of a hotel suite occupied by him and his retinue. Hitler, "alone, back bent, looking tired and morose, sat at a round table slowly sipping his vegetable soup."

The uproar unleashed by Hitler would, however, never have led to power by itself. The elections to the Prussian Landtag had given the NSDAP 36.3 per cent of the vote and eliminated the preponderance hitherto enjoyed by the coalition of Social Democrats and Center parties. But the hoped-for absolute majority had not been attained, nor was it reached three months later in the Reichstag elections of July 31, 1932. Nevertheless, the party had more than doubled its previous number of seats, to 230, and was by far the strongest party in the Reichstag. There were many indications that Hitler had expanded as far as he could go. True, he had decimated or entirely absorbed the bourgeois parties of the Center and the Right. But he had not been able to make significant inroads on the Social Democratic Party and the Communist Party. All that tremendous propaganda effort, the incessant mass meetings, parades, poster and leaflet distributions, the party speakers pushing their strength to the limit, and even Hitler's third "flight over Germany," in the course of which he spoke in fifty cities within fifteen days—all of it had brought the party an increase of only 1 per cent compared with the vote for the Prussian Landtag. Goebbels remarked on the results: "Now something must happen. We must come to power in the near future. Otherwise we'll drop dead from winning elections."[41]

Alarmingly, the first signs of this sinister prospect began to appear. With the switch to governing purely by emergency decree, and especially since his re-election, Hindenburg had given his office an increasingly personal touch and had more and more obstinately equated his wishes with the welfare of the state. In this opinionated behavior he was supported by a small group of irresponsible advisers. One of these was his son Oskar, whose role in the government, to quote a popular sarcasm, "was not provided for in the Constitution." Others were State Secretary Meissner, General Schleicher, the young conservative deputy Dr. Gereke, Hindenburg's neighboring estate owner, von Oldenburg-Januschau (who had long enjoyed the reputation of being a "reactionary brute" and who, for example, outraged public opinion by asserting that it should always be possible to dissolve Parliament by sending a lieutenant and ten enlisted men to do the job). In addition there were some other Prussian magnates, and later the group was joined by Franz von Papen.

The following months were filled with the background maneuvers of these men. Their various motives and interests are hard to determine. Hitler had appeared on the political scene as a tremendous and troublesome force, and their general intention was to integrate him, to bind him, and also to use him as a threat against the Left. This was the last attempt, springing from the deluded arrogance of a traditional leadership, by old Germany to regain a forfeited role in history.

The first victim of this group was, ironically, Brüning himself. The Chancellor, trusting that he would be backed by the President, had incurred the enmity of some of those "mighty institutions" that his opponent Hitler was trying so persistently and successfully to cultivate. He had too often refused to consider the demands of industry. Now he antagonized Hindenburg's peers in the landowning class. They expected subsidies from the state, but Brüning wanted to make such financial aid conditional on an examination of the profitability of the estate in question. Hopelessly indebted properties were to be used for resettling some of the unemployed upon the land.

The landowners were appalled. Their fierce attacks on the proposal culminated in the charge that the Chancellor had Bolshevistic tendencies. Given the President's age and weak judgment, one cannot say how much he was swayed by such pressure. But there is no doubt that it at least contributed to his decision to drop Brüning. Moreover, Hindenburg bore a grudge against the Chancellor for leading him to fight on the wrong front for re-election. Nor did his entourage let him forget that painful affair. Brüning's hour struck when he lost the confidence of Schleicher, who alleged that he spoke in the name of the army.

The beginning of Brüning's overthrow was marked by what looked like an act of governmental vigor, but actually exposed the hidden contradictions within the leadership of the Reich, thereby hastening the death of the republic. The government banned the SA and the SS. Since the discovery of

333

the Boxheim Papers, fresh evidence had accumulated of the real intentions of the Nazis. The party's army was becoming more impatient and brash than ever. And Hitler kept up his pretense of legality by off and on publicly worrying how long he would be able to keep his brown storm troops in check. Testily, Ludendorff referred to Germany as territory "occupied by the SA."

Two days before the first presidential election, Goebbels had noted in his diary: "Thorough discussion with SA and SS leadership of standards of behavior for the next few days. Everywhere a wild restiveness prevails. The word putsch haunts the scene." For election day, Röhm had decreed a state of emergency readiness and his brown shirts encircled Berlin. While raiding several of the SA's organizational centers, the Prussian police found detailed instructions for violent measures to be taken if Hitler won. Although there was no evidence of any plans for a large-scale uprising, the police did come upon the secret putsch cue familiar from other documents: "Grandmother dead." Orders were also found instructing the storm troopers of the eastern territories to refuse to participate in the country's defense if there were a Polish attack—a discovery that must have made its impression on Hindenburg in particular. Several state governments were urging a Reich ban on the SA and SS. The decision to impose the ban was now taken unanimously; it was an action long weighed and repeatedly postponed before finally being taken.

But a few days before proclamation of the ban, events took a dramatic turn. Schleicher, who had at first agreed to the ban and even boasted of being its author, changed his mind overnight, and when his shift did not meet with instant approval, began intriguing furiously against the ban. Soon he had won over Hindenburg, on grounds that the ban would make the President even more unpopular with his already disappointed followers on the Right. Schleicher himself had decided that it would be better to collaborate with the SA in dissolving all other private defense organizations, such as the Stahlhelm or the loyally Republican Reichsbanner, and to collect them all into a militia or a military sports association subordinated to the army. But his change of heart also sprang from his temperamental love of intrigue. The crude method of a ban was antipathetic to him; he liked subtler procedures. His counterproposal, significantly, was to present Hitler with a number of ultimatums demanding the demilitarization of the SA. The demands would be so impossible to meet that by rejecting them Hitler would be placed in the wrong.

With some scruples, and with anxious side glances at the "old wartime comrades" now serving in the SA and SS, Hindenburg finally signed the decree; and on April 14, in a widespread police action, Hitler's private army was broken up, its headquarters, shelters, schools and depots occupied. This action was the most energetic blow that the government had struck against Nazism since November, 1923. The official statement at last showed a certain mettle on the part of the republic: "It is exclusively the concern of the State to maintain an organized force. As soon as such a force is organized by private parties and the State tolerates this, a danger to law and order already exists. . . . Undoubtedly, in a constitutional state power may be organized by the constitutional organs of the State itself. Any private organized force therefore cannot by its very nature be a legal institution. . . . In the interests of its own preservation, the State must order such forces dissolved."

Backed by the belligerence and strength of his 400,000 men, Röhm at first seemed ready for a trial of strength. But Hitler would not hear of it. Instead, without more ado, he incorporated the SA into the party organization and in this way kept its organization intact. Here was another example of a Fascist movement abandoning the field without a fight at the first show of resistance by the government. Similarly, in 1920 Gabriele d'Annunzio had evacuated the city of Fiume in response to a single cannon shot. Once more Hitler declared himself on the side of legality, and called for strict observance of the ban. He did this not out of fear but because any other measure would have nullified the "Fascist constellation," the alliance between conservative rule and a revolutionary-popular movement.

Hitler's compliance may have come easily to him since by that time he had received information—from Schleicher or people close to Schleicher— about friction within the administration. On the whole he showed an air of confidence. On the eve of the day that was to begin the dismemberment of the Hitler movement, Goebbels noted a conversation with Hitler in the Hotel Kaiserhof: "We discussed personnel questions for the period of taking power just as if we were already the government. I think no movement in the opposition has ever been so sure of its success as ours!"

The very next day a strikingly frosty letter from Hindenburg to Minister of Defense Groener gave the signal for a monumental intrigue. A passionate campaign in the rightist newspapers, joined by a choir of prominent voices of the nationalist camp, went along with it. The Crown Prince thought it "incomprehensible" that the Defense Minister of all persons should help to "shatter the marvelous human material that has been brought together in the SA and SS and is receiving valuable training there." Schleicher advised his Minister, who still regarded him as his "adopted son," to resign, and either circulated spiteful slanders against Groener or did nothing to stem such slanders. Word went round that Groener was ill, or that he was a pacifist, or that he had brought the army into disrepute when his second wife gave birth prematurely. Schleicher wittily told President Hindenburg that in the army the baby was called "Nurmi," after the Finnish runner famous for his speed in the final spurt.

Meanwhile, Schleicher let the leadership of the NSDAP know that he personally was not at all in favor of the ban on the SA. He still clung to the idea of disabling the Nazis by letting them participate in power and "locking them in"—to use the magic formula of the moment—by surrounding them with a cabinet of influential specialists. The example of Mussolini should have shown him that such tricks are useless against tribunes of the people who can call upon a private army.

At the end of April Schleicher met with Hitler for a first discussion. "The conversation went well," Goebbels noted. Soon afterward there was a second meeting, in which State Secretary Meissner, Hindenburg's man of confidence, and Oskar von Hindenburg were included; at this time not only the dismissal of Groener but the fall of the entire Brüning cabinet was discussed. "Everything is going well. . . ." Goebbels noted again. "Delightful feeling that nobody suspects anything, Brüning himself least of all."

After about a month of such intrigues, matters finally came to a head. On May 10 Groener defended in the Reichstag the SA ban against furious attacks from the Right. He was a feeble speaker at best, and his protests against the National Socialist "state within the State" and "state against the State" made little headway against the wild uproar that the Nazis unleashed. The angered, helpless, and no doubt exhausted Minister went down to defeat, and with him the cause he was advocating. Schleicher and General Kurt von Hammerstein, commander in chief of the army, coolly informed the Minister of Defense that he no longer enjoyed the confidence of the army, and must resign. Two days later, after a vain appeal to Hindenburg, Groener handed in his resignation.

That act was, in keeping with the camarilla's plans, only the prelude. On May 12 Hindenburg left Berlin for nearly two weeks, to spend the Whitsun holidays on his estate, Gut Neudeck. Brüning asked to see him, but the President irritably refused. During this period he was obviously under the influence of his fellow Junkers, who were now preparing the assault on Brüning's weakening position. Whatever line of argument they followed, they no doubt brought to the task "that heavy force peculiar to large landowners and old army officers, which dispensed with honesty and concern for principle." When Hindenburg returned to Berlin at the end of the month, he was determined to part with his Chancellor. Brüning thought he was on the verge of great successes in foreign policy, and as late as the morning of May 30, shortly before he set out to see Hindenburg, had heard that there was going to be a significant turn in the matter of disarmament. But as things turned out, he was not given the time to inform the President of this. Only a year before, Hindenburg had assured him that he would be his last Chancellor, that he would not part with him. Now Brüning found himself dismissed in an insultingly brusk interview. He had been allowed only a few minutes on the President's calendar; Hindenburg did not want to miss the parade of the naval guard in commemoration of the Battle of Jutland. A wartime memory and a minor military spectacle took precedence over an act that decided the fate of the republic.[42]

General von Schleicher put forward as Brüning's successor a man who at best could be considered a political dilettante. Franz von Papen came from an aristocratic Westphalian family, had served in a Junker cavalry regiment, and come to wide public notice for the first time—in a characteristic way—during the World War: in 1916 he had been expelled from the United States, where he was serving as military attaché, for sabotage activities; on the crossing to Europe he carelessly let important documents regarding his secret service work fall into the hands of the British authorities. His marriage to the daughter of a leading Saar industrialist had brought him considerable wealth and excellent connections with industry. As a Catholic nobleman he also had connections with the higher clergy, and as a former General Staff officer multiple contacts with the army. It may be that this position of Papen's at the intersection of many interests first attracted Schleicher's attention. The man seemed grotesquely antiquated; in all his long-legged stiffness, haughtiness, and bleating arrogance he was almost a caricature of himself—a figure from *Alice in Wonderland,* as a contemporary observer remarked. He was considered foolish, overhasty; nobody took him quite seriously. "If he succeeds with a thing, he is very pleased; if he fails, he does not worry about it."

Yet it was obviously this cavalier quality of Papen that recommended him to Schleicher. For Schleicher was plainly thinking more and more of doing away with the weakened parliamentary system and replacing it by some kind of "moderate" dictatorship. Papen might be just the man to carry out such plans for him. Schleicher must also have imagined that the inexperienced Papen, a man concerned largely with externals, would find his vanity satisfied with the office and its ceremonial functions, and for the rest would be a docile tool. Schleicher, as ambitious as he was wary of publicity, needed exactly that kind of man. When Schleicher's friends, incredulous at his choice, protested that Papen was a man without a head, Schleicher replied: "I don't need a head, I need a hat."

If, however, Schleicher had considered that Papen, thanks to his extensive connections, would be able to put together a coalition, or at any rate to win parliamentary approval of a cabinet including all parties to the right of the Social Democrats, he soon found that he was mistaken. The new Chancellor had no political base at all. The Center, embittered by the betrayal of Brüning, sharply opposed him. And Hugenberg, who saw himself once more passed over, also proved indignant. From the public, too, Papen encountered hostile rejection. Although he cashed in on Brüning's successful negotiations and came back from the Lausanne Conference with the reparations question settled, he gained no popularity. The fact was that his cabinet could in no way be regarded as a legitimate solution to Germany's problems, neither in terms of democracy nor expertise. It consisted entirely of men of distinguished families who had not been able to resist the President's appeal to their patriotism and who now "surrounded Hindenburg like officers their general." Seven of them were noblemen, two company directors; the roster also included Hitler's protector from his Munich days, Franz Gürtner, and a general. Not a single representative of the middle class or the working class was included in the cabinet. The shadows seemed to be returning. But the mass indignation, the scorn and protest on the part of the populace, had no effect—proof of how thoroughly the members of the former ruling class had lost contact with reality. The "cabinet of barons," as it was soon called, drew its support solely from Hindenburg's authority and the army's power.

The extraordinary unpopularity of the government prompted Hitler to take an attitude of cautious restraint. In his negotiations with Schleicher he had agreed to tolerate the government if new elections were called, the ban against the SA lifted, and the NSDAP allowed full freedom to carry on agitation. A few hours after Brüning's dismissal, he had answered positively when the President asked him whether he agreed to the appointment of Papen. The new Chancellor promptly, on June 4, began his series of fateful concessions by dissolving the Reichstag and indicating that he would shortly lift the ban on the SA. Nevertheless, the Nazis began disentangling themselves. "We must part company as quickly as possible with the bourgeois transitional cabinet," Goebbels noted. "All these are questions of delicately feeling one's way." A few days later he noted: "We had better betake ourselves as swiftly as possible out of the compromising vicinity of these bourgeois adolescents. Otherwise we are lost. In the *Angriff* I am launching a fresh attack on the Papen cabinet." When the SA ban was not dropped in the first few days, as anticipated, Goebbels one evening entered "a large café on Potsdamer Platz with forty or fifty SA leaders in full uniform in spite of the ban, for the sake of provocation. All of us longing to have the police arrest us. . . . Around midnight we stroll very slowly on Potsdamer Platz and Potsdamer Strasse. But nobody lifts a finger. The patrolmen look stumped and then shamefacedly turn their eyes away."

Two days later, on June 16, the ban was lifted; but the period of hesitancy had meanwhile given the impression of a "virtual genuflection by the administration before the coming new power." At the last moment Papen made a transparent effort to trade off his conciliatory gesture for a promise that the Nazis would later help form a government. Tactically, he made his offer too late; but it also revealed a grotesque incomprehension of the urgency of Hitler's hunger for power. Coolly, Hitler put him off; there would be time enough to consider his requests after the Reichstag elections.

Thereupon the conditions of virtual civil war, with wild clashes in the streets, were abruptly revived, and now reached their real climax. In the five weeks up to July 20 there were nearly 500 such clashes in Prussia alone, with a toll of 99 dead and 1,125 wounded. Throughout the Reich seventeen persons were killed on July 10; in many places the army had to intervene in the furious street battles. Ernst Thälmann, the Communist leader, rightly defined the lifting of the ban on the SA as an open invitation to murder, although he did not say whether his own fighting units took an active or a passive part. On July 17 one of the bloodiest conflicts of the summer took place in Hamburg-Altona. A deliberately provocative parade of some 7,000 Nazis through the streets of the Red working-class quarter was answered by the Communists with heavy sniping from roofs and windows, which the Nazis answered in kind. There was a bitter battle over hastily erected barricades. At the end there were seventeen dead and many severely wounded. Of the eighty-six persons who died in political clashes in July, 1932, thirty were on the side of the Communists, thirty-eight on the side of the Nazis.[43] "There is brawling and shooting," Goebbels remarked. "The regime's last show."

Refusing to realize that his concessions were only emboldening the Nazis, Papen went a step further. His idea was to strengthen the prestige of his virtually isolated administration, and simultaneously conciliate Hitler and the Nazis, by some grand gesture of authoritarianism. Accordingly, on the morning of July 20 Papen summoned three members of the Prussian government to the chancellery and abruptly informed them that he had just deposed Prussian Prime Minister Braun and Interior Minister Severing by emergency decree. He himself, he said, would assume the duties of the Prime Minister as Reich Commissioner.

Severing declared that he would yield only to force. Papen—"a cavalier even in a *coup d'état*"—inquired what exactly he meant by that. The Minister retorted that he would move out of his office only under pressure. Meanwhile, using a prepared second emergency decree, Papen imposed a military state of emergency on Berlin and Brandenburg, thus seizing the police powers for himself. In the evening three police officers came to the Ministry of the Interior and requested Severing to leave. He was now yielding to force, Severing replied, and stepped out of his office and into his adjacent apartment. By the following afternoon, similarly without resistance, the leadership of the redoubtable Prussian police had been "overwhelmed." Berlin Police Commissioner Grzesinski, Deputy Commissioner Weiss, and Police Commander Heimannsberg were led across the yard of police headquarters for a brief internment. It is said that some of the policemen called after their chiefs the slogan of the Social Democratic Reichsbanner: *"Freiheit!"* Konrad Heiden has pointedly remarked that this was the last gasp of the crumbling, unwanted and now surrendered freedom of the Weimar Republic.

Widespread resistance had, to be sure, been considered. According to a contemporary observer, Grzesinski and Heimannsberg, in conjunction with Undersecretary Klausener are supposed to have urged Severing to "carry on the fight by every means." In particular they allegedly demanded "immediate action by the Berlin police, proclamation of a general strike, immediate arrest of the Reich government and the President, and declaration of the President's incapacity to perform his duties." But Severing is said to have rejected this proposal. Opposition did not go beyond ineffectual publication of protests and an appeal to the Supreme Court. The Prussian government had at its disposal more than 90,000 well-equipped police troops, the paramilitary Reichsbanner, the adherence of the republican parties, the unions, and all the important key posts. Fear of civil war, respect for the Constitution, doubts of the force of a general strike when so many men were unemployed, and many similar considerations ultimately undermined all ideas of resistance. Papen was able to seize power in the "strongest bulwark of the Republic," with nothing to stop him beyond the looks of anguished resignation in his opponents' eyes.

It is hard to deny a good deal of validity to the arguments of the Prussian politicians. In view of all the circumstances, their decision may well have been a reasonable one. But in the face of history their reasonableness counts for little. No thought was given to a demonstration of defiance, and in no phase of the events did Severing and his unnerved, morally broken fellows consider the possibility that going down to defeat in honor might have made people forget the halfway measures and missed opportunites of the past thirteen years, and have sparked a renewal of confidence in democracy. The real and immense importance of July 20, 1932, lies in its psychological consequences. It discouraged one side and taught the others how little fight the defenders of the republic would be likely to put up.

As a result, Papen's coup only increased the impatience of the Nazis. In the struggle for power three sharply divided camps now faced one another: the nationalist-authoritarian group around Papen, who in parliamentary terms represented barely 10 per cent of the voters but who had the backing of Hindenburg and the army; the exhausted democratic groups, who however could still count on considerable support by the public; and the totalitarian opposition consisting of both Nazis and Communists. Together these last held a negative majority of 53 per cent. But just as the Nazis and Communists could not work together, all the groups blocked and paralyzed one another. The summer and autumn of 1932 were marked by continuous efforts to overcome the current political rigidity by some new tactical maneuver.

On August 5 Hitler met Schleicher in Fürstenberg, Mecklenburg, near Berlin, and for the first time demanded full power: the office of Chancellor for himself, the Ministries of the Interior, Justice, Agriculture, and Air Transport, and a Propaganda Ministry to be newly created. He also insisted, on the basis of the coup of July 20, on the posts of Prussian Prime Minister and Prussian Minister of the Interior. Furthermore, he wanted a law empowering him to rule by decree with unlimited powers. For, as Goebbels remarked, "if we have the power we'll never give it up again unless we're carried out of our offices as corpses."

Hitler left Schleicher convinced that he stood on the verge of power. As they parted, he genially proposed that a plaque be put on the house in Fürstenberg to commemorate their meeting. The storm troopers were already leaving their places of work and preparing for the day of victory with its celebrations, its excesses, and the promise of becoming big shots. To quiet them, as well as lend emphasis to his demands, Hitler had the SA units around Berlin parade within the city, and encircle it in an ever tighter ring. Throughout the Reich, but especially in Silesia and East Prussia, the number of bloody clashes increased. Thereupon, a decree of August 9 threatened the death penalty for anyone who "in the passion of the political struggle undertakes, in rage and hatred, a fatal assault upon his opponent." The very next night five uniformed SA men in Potempa, a village in Upper Silesia, forced their way into the apartment of a Communist worker, pulled him out of bed, and literally trampled him to death before his mother's eyes.

These events obviously contributed to the sudden shift that once again barred the gates of power from the Nazis. But to what degree has not yet been clarified. Schleicher may have abandoned his idea of taming the Nazis by making Hitler Chancellor in a rightist coalition government, thus fettering him with responsibility and undermining his popularity. At any rate this plan now encountered vigorous resistance from the President, who had developed a paternal fondness for the agile and frivolous Papen. Hindenburg certainly did not care to exchange Papen for the Bohemian fanatic and ersatz messiah Hitler, who, moreover, would want to take over the Kaiser role that the President had grown attached to. On August 13 an extended round of negotiations with the National Socialist leadership was held. In conjunction with Papen, Hindenburg rejected all Hitler's claims to assume full powers and instead offered him the post of Vice-Chancellor in the existing cabinet. Furious, in the all-or-nothing mood of those days, Hitler turned down the offer, and stuck to his refusal, even when Papen broadened the terms. He would give his word of honor, he proposed, that after an interlude of "trusting and fruitful collaboration" he would resign the chancellorship in favor of Hitler.

We can be sure that Hitler had already visualized how he would offer to a dumfounded and doomed world the spectacle of his summons to rule. On the way to Berlin he had stopped in a restaurant at Chiemsee and, "while eating a large piece of sponge cake," had described to his lieutenants how he was going to massacre the Marxists. Instead he suddenly found himself made a fool of. And as always in response to setbacks, a dramatic gesture of despair followed hard upon the disappointment. When he was summoned to see Hindenburg that afternoon, he at first wanted to refuse to come. Only an explicit assurance from the presidential palace that nothing had yet been decided gave him hope once more. But Hindenburg merely inquired whether he was prepared to support the present administration. Hitler said no. An appeal to patriotism, such as the old man commonly sprinkled into his personal interviews, left Hitler unaffected. The meeting ended with a few admonishments and an "icy leave-taking." In the hallway Hitler excitedly prophesied the overthrow of the President.

Hitler's bitterness increased when he found himself outmaneuvered by the official communiqué. Hindenburg, it stated, had rejected Hitler's demands "very firmly on the grounds that he could not reconcile with his conscience and his duties to the Fatherland transferring all administrative power exclusively to the National Socialist movement which intends to apply this power onesidedly." There was also an expression of official regret that Hitler did not see fit to support, in keeping with his earlier promises, a nationalist government that enjoyed the President's confidence. In the oblique style of officialese, this was nothing less than charging Hitler with breaking his word; and for Hitler the reproach conjured up figures of the past, Seisser and the hated Herr von Kahr. Only a few months later, however, such spasms of resentment were forgotten.

For the moment, however, the National Socialists threw their whole weight into embittered opposition. When on August 22 the five who had trampled the Communist to death at Potempa were condemned to death on the basis of the new law against political terrorism, the Nazis demonstrated wildly inside the courtroom. The SA leader in Silesia, Edmund Heines, stood up in court in full uniform and shouted threats of vengeance. And Hitler sent a telegram to the five assuring them that "in the face of this monstrous, bloodthirsty sentence" he remained linked to them in "boundless loyalty." He promised that they would soon be released. Now he was throwing off the mask of respectable conduct that he had so carefully maintained for the past two years. Once more, as in wilder early days, he was expressing solidarity with murderers. Such recklessness revealed how badly disappointed he had been—although to some extent he was driven by the need to placate his followers. Once more the SA felt itself thwarted. It was by far the largest paramilitary organization in the country, was raring to fight, and despised the tail-coated von Papen. Toughs of this sort could not comprehend why Hitler would go on accepting humiliations when he could turn loose his loyal warriors and let them take over the streets for that bloody carnival they thought they were entitled to.

At any rate, Hitler was now deploying the SA in a more and more threatening manner. And on September 2, after ten days of disorders, Papen actually backed down and sacrificed the slender remnant of his prestige: he recommended to the President commuting the five men's sentences to life imprisonment—from which they were released a few months later, hailed as glorious fighters. Yet in a speech that Hitler delivered on September 4 the rage and indignation of a man who felt he had been duped rang out:

I know what those gentlemen have in mind. They would like to provide us with a few posts now and silence us. But they won't ride far in that old rattletrap. . . . No, gentlemen, I did not form the party to haggle, to sell it, to barter it away! This isn't a lion's skin that any old sheep can slip into. The party is the party and that's all there is to it! . . . Do you really think you can bait me with a couple of ministerial posts? I don't even want to associate with any of you. Those gentlemen have no idea how little I give a damn about all that. If God had wanted things to be the way they are, we would have come into the world wearing a monocle. Not on your life! They can keep those posts because they don't belong to them at all.[44]

Hitler's fury over the snub from Hindenburg and Papen was so strong that he seemed for the first time tempted to abandon his course of legality and seize power by a bloody insurrection. The affront had not only meant a political setback; it had been a personal insult, a fresh reminder that he could not be part of respectable circles. More and more often the grim formula was uttered in demonstrations: "The hour of reckoning is coming!" He began negotiations with the Center with the aim of overthrowing the Papen government; and once during the discussions the wild proposal arose to form an alliance with the disappointed Left and force the deposing of Hindenburg by decree of the Reichstag; this would then be followed by a referendum. Then again, in the vengeful mood of those weeks, he painted for himself and his entourage the circumstances and the chances for a revolutionary seizure of the key government posts. Once again he dwelt on the bloodbath he would prepare for his Marxist opponents. In any case, the legal course he had been following for years corresponded only to the circumspect, instinctively dependent side of his nature; on the other side were his aggressiveness, his powerful imagination, and the conviction that historical greatness could not be achieved without bloodshed.

This dichotomy was on his mind when Hermann Rauschning, the Nazi President of the Danzig Senate, called upon him at Obersalzberg around this time. Rauschning was astonished at the petty bourgeois life style of the mighty tribune of the people, the cretonne curtains on the windows, the so-called peasant furniture, the chirping songbirds in the draped cage, and the society of stout elderly ladies. Hitler inveighed violently against Papen and called the nationalistic bourgeoisie "the real enemy of Germany." He justified his protest against the Potempa sentences in grandiloquent abstract terms: "We must be cruel. We must recover the capacity to commit cruelties with a clear conscience. Only in this way can we expel our nation's softheartedness and sentimental philistinism, this *Gemütlichkeit* and easygoing evening-beer mood. We have no more time for fine feelings. We must compel our nation to greatness if it is to fulfill its historic task."

And while he was expatiating on the historical challenge he had seen and accepted, and was comparing himself to Bismarck, he abruptly asked whether there was a formal extradition treaty between the Free City of Danzig and the German Reich. When Rauschning indicated that he did not understand the question, Hitler explained that a situation might arise in which he would need a place of refuge.

Then again his mood swung to confidence. Papen's frivolity, foolishness, and weakness, together with the President's softness toward all nationalist elements, not to speak of the old general's age (it made him laugh, Hitler publicly stated)—all these things gave him cause for hope. A few days after he had called the Potempa murderers "comrades" Hitler received a message from Hjalmar Schacht. It assured him of the writer's "unalterable sympathy," and expressed faith that sooner or later power would come to him, one way or another. Schacht advised him for the present not to allow himself to be identified with any specific economic program, and concluded: "Wherever my work may lead me in the near future—even if some day you should see me inside the fortress—you can count on me as your reliable helper."

When an Associated Press correspondent asked Hitler at this time whether he might not after all march on Berlin, as Mussolini had marched on Rome, he answered ambiguously: "Why should I march on Berlin? I'm already there, you know."[45]

Chapter 4

As you see, the Republic, the Senate,
dignity dwelt in none of us.

Cicero to his brother Quintus

AT THE GOAL

Obeying the rules of classical drama, the events of the autumn of 1932 took a turn which seemed to promise that the crisis might be overcome. The elements to which Nazism chiefly owed its rise began to be undermined. For one ironic moment the play seemed to reverse itself on every plane and to expose Hitler's expectations of power as wildly exaggerated—before the scene suddenly collapsed.

Ever since August 13 Papen had obviously made up his mind to make no more concessions to Hitler. Why he took this hard line is something of a mystery, since his own explanations do not ring true. It may be that he belatedly caught on to the trickery of the Nazis, saw through their posture, which Goebbels later accurately described as "sham moderation," and changed his attitude accordingly. He realized also that the National Socialist Party depended heavily on a constant series of successes. Its internal situation was so precarious that it could not long stand up to determined sternness. To be sure, the government had had to give in to Nazi pressure and commute the Potempa sentences. But in the end Hitler had been outmaneuvered; he had become nervous and betrayed himself by his telegram to the murderers. Shortly afterward he once more made a serious mistake.

Papen had convoked the Reichstag for its first working session on September 12. In his drive to take vengeance on Papen, Hitler lost sight of all other considerations. Göring had in the meantime been elected President of the Reichstag, and with his help Hitler dealt the Chancellor the severest defeat in German parliamentary history, a vote of no confidence carried by a vote of 512 to 42. Papen had already obtained an order of dissolution before the session; he carried it in the traditional red portfolio for everyone to see; but Göring deliberately ignored it until the no-confidence vote had been taken. Papen was thus given his comeuppance; but the result was that the newly elected legislature was dissolved after a session lasting approximately one hour. The new elections were set for November 6.

Unless all indications are wrong, Hitler originally wanted to avoid this turn of events, for it obviously ran counter to his interests. "Everyone is dumbfounded," Goebbels noted. "Nobody thought it possible that we would have the courage to bring about this decision. We alone are rejoicing." But this euphoric mood was soon over, giving way to a degree of depression the Nazi leaders had not known for years. Hitler himself was only too keenly aware that the impulse voters to whom the party owed its recent increments could not be depended on. He distinctly sensed that the debacle of August 13, the falling back into the opposition, the Potempa affair and the conflict with Hindenburg were spoiling the image of himself as the destined savior and unequaled leader. Once the trend to success was reversed, the party's attraction was dispelled and it could plunge straight to the bottom.

Hitler had additional worries. After the expensive campaigns of the past year the movement's funds were exhausted. Moreover, it seemed for the present to have reached the limits of its strength. "Our opponents," Goebbels wrote in diary notes that grew increasingly gloomy, "are counting on our losing our nerve in this struggle and being worn out." A month later he noted friction among the party's followers, disputes over money and seats in the Reichstag, and observed that "the organization has of course become very nervous as a result of the many election campaigns. It is overworked like a company that has lain too long in the trenches." He tried to look at the bright side: "Our chances are improving from day to day. Although the prospects are still fairly rotten, they at any rate cannot be compared with our hopeless prospects of a few weeks ago."

Hitler alone seemed once again confident and free of moods, as always after he had made a decision. During the first half of October he set out on his fourth airplane campaign, and with his compulsion to magnify everything constantly, increased the number of his speeches and the miles flown. To Kurt Luedecke, who had accompanied him in the dramatic Mercedes motorcade, surrounded by heavily armed "men from Mars," to the Reich Youth Day functions in Potsdam, he sketched ideas that were a curious mixture of hopes and reality—in which he appeared as Chancellor. Two days later, after an impressive propaganda show with 70,000 members of the Hitler Youth parading by for hours, Luedecke bade good-bye to Hitler at the railroad station. He found him sitting in the corner of his compartment exhausted, capable only of weary and feeble gestures.

Only the exaltation of struggle, the promise of power, the theater of public appearances, homages and collective deliriums kept him going. Three days later he appeared at a Munich meeting of Nazi leaders "in great

346

form," as Goebbels noted, and gave "a fabulous outline of the development and status of our struggle in the very long view. He is indeed the Great Man, above us all. He pulls the party to its feet again out of every despairing mood." The difficulties the party was facing were in fact growing ever more hopeless. The shortage of money tended to paralyze all activity. With their attacks on Papen and his "Cabinet of Reaction," the Nazis inevitably forfeited the sympathy of the wealthy members of the Nationalist opposition, whose contributions now flowed more sparsely than ever before. "Raising money is extraordinarily difficult. The gentlemen of 'property and culture' all stand with the government."

The election campaign, too, was conducted chiefly against the "clique of the nobles," the "bourgeois young bravos," and the "corrupt Junker regime." The party propaganda office issued a host of slogans to be spread by word of mouth and whose intent was to whip up "an outright mood of panic against Papen and his Cabinet." Once again Gregor Strasser and his shrunken following had a period of great although deceptive hopes. "Against reaction!" was the official election slogan given out by Hitler. Nazi speakers passionately denounced the business-oriented economic policies of the administration. Nazi rowdies now took to breaking up nationalist meetings and organizing attacks on Stahlhelm leaders. To be sure, the NSDAP's socialism remained without a program, as it had always been; it was formulated only in the figurative language of a prescientific mentality. Thus Nazi socialism was "the principle of achievement of the Prussian officer, of the incorruptible German civil servant, the walls, the town hall, the cathedral, the hospital of a Free City of the German Reich— all that." It was also the "changeover from working class to labor" (*"von der Arbeiterschaft zum Arbeitertum"*). The very ambiguities of such language made it popular. "An honest living for honest work"—that had a more persuasive ring than any economic theory learned in the evening schools run by workmen's circles. "If the distribution apparatus of today's world economic system does not know how to properly distribute nature's lavish productivity, this system is false and must be changed." That corresponded to a basic popular feeling, and people did not think to ask what this change would consist of. Significantly, it was not the Communists but Gregor Strasser who was able to sum up the broad general dissatisfaction of the period in a phrase that instantly became part of the language. In one of his speeches he spoke of a mood that was passing through the public and was in itself a sign of a great turning point in history—this mood he described as "anticapitalist nostalgia."

A few days before the election, as the campaign was approaching its end—it had been conducted at obvious excess pressure and with failing strength—the party had an opportunity to demonstrate the seriousness of its leftist slogans. At the beginning of November a strike broke out in Berlin among the transportation workers. It had been instigated by the

Communists over the vote of the unions, and contrary to all expectations the Nazis actually supported the strikers. Together, the SA and the Red Front paralyzed public transportation for five days. They tore up streetcar tracks, formed picket lines, beat up scabs, and forcibly stopped the sketchily organized auxiliary transport. This unity of action has always been cited as evidence for the fatal community of leftist and rightist radicalism. But in fact the Nazis at this moment had scarcely any other choice, even though it meant alienating many of their bourgeois voters and finding that their financial contributions dried up almost completely. "The entire press is denouncing us," Goebbels noted. "It calls our action Bolshevism; and yet we really could not do anything else. If we had withdrawn our support for this strike, which involves the most basic rights of the streetcar workers, our firm position among the working people would have been shaken. This way, with the election coming, we can once again show the public that our antireactionary course comes from the heart and is genuine. A great opportunity." And a few days later, on November 5: "Last onslaught. Desperate drive of the party against defeat. At the last minute we manage to scare up another 10,000 marks which we blow on propaganda Saturday afternoon. We have done whatever could be done. Now fate must decide."

Fate decided, for the first time since 1930, emphatically against the National Socialists' claims to power. They lost 2 million votes and thirty-four Reichstag seats. The Social Democratic Party also lost a few seats, while the German Nationalists emerged from the election with eleven additional seats and the Communists with an increase of fourteen. On the whole it seemed as if the steady decline of the bourgeois Center parties, which had been going on for years, had at last come to a halt. It was significant that the NSDAP's losses were evenly distributed throughout the country, and hence could not be considered regional setbacks. They reflected a weariness with Nazi propaganda. Even in predominantly agricultural regions, such as Schleswig-Holstein, Lower Saxony, or Pomerania, which in the preceding elections had contributed the strongest and most reliable support for the NSDAP and thus gave the party quite another cast from the urban petty bourgeois party it had been originally, the Nazis suffered considerable losses.[46] And although party leaders promised they would "sweat and fight until this disgrace is wiped out," the wave continued to ebb in the local elections of the following week. The party's march to victory seemed broken at last, and even though it could still be called a large party, it was no longer a myth. The question was precisely whether it could continue to exist as an ordinary party, or whether its survival depended on its being a myth.

Papen, in particular, was gratified by the outcome of the elections. Conscious of a great personal success, he turned to Hitler with the proposal that they put aside old quarrels and have another try at a union of all nationalistic forces. The Chancellor's self-assured tone made Hitler only too aware of his own weakness; the Führer's response was to stay away from Berlin and remain inaccessible for days on end. On the eve of the elections he had issued a call to the party disdaining all thought of a reconciliation with the government and calling for "adamant continuation of the struggle until this partly overt, partly camouflaged opponent is brought to his knees" and a stop put to the reactionary policies that were driving the country into the arms of Bolshevism. Papen had to dispatch a second official letter to him before, after a deliberate delay of several days, he sent a rejection which he cloaked once again in a series of unfulfillable demands. The Chancellor received similar cold answers from the other nationalist parties.

The government, then, had only two alternatives, neither of which was very popular: either to dissolve the Reichstag once more and thus obtain a political breathing spell, as risky as it was expensive, or else to take the open step against the Constitution that had long been contemplated. This would involve using presidential and military powers to ban the Nazi party, the Communist Party, and possibly other parties. Then the rights of the legislature would be drastically pruned, a new electoral law promulgated, and Hindenburg established as a kind of superauthority in the midst of representatives of the old ruling class whom he would appoint to the seats of power. The argument in Papen's circles went that the parliamentary-democratic "rule of the minorities" had obviously failed. The new state they were planning would ensure the "rule of the best" and thus undercut such wild ideas about dictatorship as the Nazis were advocating. Papen hinted at some of these matters in a speech delivered on October 12. Many of the details remained nebulous and indeed were never worked out. But the concept as a whole had progressed far beyond the stage of mere theory. In his reactionary bluntness Hindenburg's neighbor and confidant, old Oldenburg-Januschau, averred that he and his friends would shortly "brand the German people with a constitution that would make their senses reel."[47]

While Papen was still drawing up blueprints for the sort of state "which will not be pushed around as the plaything of political and social forces, but will stand unshakably above them," he suddenly met with unexpected resistance on the part of Schleicher. The general had originally chosen Papen to serve as a willing and handy instrument for taming the Hitler party within the framework of a broad nationalist coalition. Instead, Papen had become involved in a futile personal dispute with Hitler. As he consolidated his position with Hindenburg, he had also shown less of that docility that would have made him useful to the publicity-shy general. "Well, what do you think of that?" Schleicher would occasionally remark sarcastically to a visitor. "Little Franz has discovered himself." Unlike Papen, Schleicher took a serious view of the problems of a Depression-shaken

349

industrial state. There was more to the question than the proposition that the government must be strong. He therefore had little patience with the Chancellor's plans. Schleicher had no intention of letting the army be used to help put over this scheme. For it would mean virtual civil war, with the troops pitted against Nazis and Communists, who together were almost 18 million strong at the polls and had millions of militant followers at their disposal. But there was another factor in Schleicher's change of front, and probably this was the decisive one. He had meanwhile discov red, or thought he had discovered, how at last to carry out his plan of taming and gradually wearing down the National Socialist Party. All that was needed was a different constellation.

With some mental reservations, therefore, Schleicher advised Papen to resign and let Hindenburg in person negotiate with the party leaders for a "Cabinet of National Concentration." On November 17 Papen followed this recommendation, secretly hoping that the talks would fail and he would once more be summoned to the chancellorship. Two days later Hitler, cheered by a hastily assembled crowd, drove the few yards from the Hotel Kaiserhof to the presidential palace. But two talks with Hindenburg proved fruitless. Hitler obstinately demanded a presidential cabinet with special powers, whereas Hindenburg, directed by Papen in the background, would not hear of this. If the country were still to be governed by special decree, he saw no reason to dismiss Papen. Hitler, the President said, could become Chancellor only if he could put together a parliamentary majority, something the Nazi party leader was clearly in no position to do. Hindenburg's state secretary, Meissner, summed up the matter in a letter dated November 24:

The President thanks you, my dear Herr Hitler, for your willingness to assume the leadership of a presidential cabinet. But he believes he could not justify it to the German people if he were to give his presidential powers to the leader of a party which has always stressed its exclusiveness, and which has taken a predominantly negative attitude toward him personally as well as toward the political and economic measures he has considered necessary. In these circumstances the President must fear that a presidential cabinet led by you would inevitably develop into a party dictatorship, with all the consequences of a drastic intensification of the antagonisms within the German nation that that would involve. The President, in view of his oath and his conscience, could not take the responsibility for this.[48]

This was another and painful rebuff. "Once again the revolution is facing closed doors," Goebbels angrily noted. Nevertheless, this time Hitler succeeded in hiding the defeat by adroit propaganda. In a detailed letter he analyzed with considerable acumen the inherent contradictions of Hindenburg's offer, sketching for the first time the solution finally arrived at on January 30. What attracted particular attention at the presidential palace was his suggestion of a new approach to the process of forming a government. All that was needed was legislation which would free Hindenburg from involvement in the daily business of politics and thus relieve him of onorous responsibilities. This was a proposal whose importance to the further course of events can scarcely be overestimated. Certainly it did a great deal to persuade the President to assent to the claims of the man to whom, a short while back, he had at most been willing to concede the postal ministry.

Although Papen had counted on the negotiations coming to naught and himself returning to the Chancellor's office, things turned out differently. For in the meantime Schleicher had got in touch with the Nazi party through Gregor Strasser and was exploring the possibilities of having the Nazis enter a cabinet under his own leadership. This was basically a maneuver and one typical of Schleicher: he reasoned that a generous offer of a share in the administration would produce an explosive conflict among the members of the Hitler party. The blasting powder lay ready to hand. Gregor Strasser had, in the face of recent setbacks, argued repeatedly that the party should adopt more conciliatory tactics. Göring and especially Goebbels had denounced all "halfway solutions" and insisted on demanding undivided power.

On the evening of December 1, Schleicher was summoned to the presidential palace along with Papen. Where did he stand? Hindenburg asked Papen. Papen outlined his plan for a constitutional reform involving a virtual *coup d'état*. Since the matter had been discussed openly for months, the request for the President's consent was only a formality; but Schleicher broke in before Papen was finished. He called Papen's plan both superfluous and dangerous, pointed out the danger of a civil war, and presented his own suggestion: prying the Strasser wing loose from the NSDAP and uniting all constructive forces from the Stahlhelm and the unions to the Social Democrats in a multipartisan cabinet under his own leadership.

But Hindenburg, scarcely troubling to examine the plan, waved this away. Schleicher persisted, pointing out that his plan would spare the President the unpleasantness of violating his oath of office. But by now the doddering old man could not bear to part with his favorite Chancellor, regardless of constitutional questions.

Schleicher, however, refused to accept defeat. When Papen, later in the evening, asked whether the Reichswehr would be ready to back his actions, Schleicher flatly refused to give any such assurances. To Papen that night, and at a cabinet meeting next day, he spoke of a study made by his ministry, based on a three-day war game. It concluded that the army was incapable of handling a joint uprising by the Nazis and the Communists. Such an emergency could no longer be ruled out, since the two parties had already joined forces during the Berlin transportation strike. In the event of a simultaneous general strike along with Polish attacks on the eastern border, the Reichswehr would be totally helpless. In addition, Schleicher

351

expressed his doubts about employing the nonpartisan instrument of the army to put across a "restoration" such as Papen had in mind—the wild idea of a Chancellor supported by a vanishing minority.

Schleicher's arguments made a strong impression on the cabinet. An indignant Papen went crying to the President that he had been betrayed, and even demanded that Schleicher be replaced by a new and more co-operative army minister. But at this point Hindenburg himself beat a re-treat. Papen has described the emotional scene that followed:

> In a voice that sounded almost tormented . . . he turned to me: "My dear Papen, you will think me a scoundrel for changing my mind now. But I am now too old to accept the responsibility for a civil war. All we can do is to let Herr von Schleicher try his luck."
> Two large tears rolled down his cheeks as this tall, strong man extended his hands to me in parting. Our collaboration was at an end. The degree of spiritual harmony between us . . . may perhaps be seen from the inscription the Field Marshal wrote under the photograph of himself which he gave me a few hours later as a farewell gift: *Ich hatt' einen Kameraden!*[49]

Papen had been as quick to win the President's heart as he had been "to throw away the last chances for a sensible solution to the political crisis." But while he felt worsted, there was some comfort in the thought that his enemy could no longer operate discreetly in the wings but would have to expose himself to the public, while Papen could now assume the well-nigh omnipotent role Schleicher had enjoyed as confidant of the President. Papen might be leaving, but it was not yet a real good-bye. No less signifi-cant than his "spiritual harmony" with Hindenburg was the fact that even out of office Papen continued to occupy his official apartment—with the self-assurance of a person who regarded the state as his own property. Only a garden path separated this apartment from Hindenburg's dwelling. It was like a joint household—which also included State Secretary Meiss-ner and Oskar von Hindenburg. All four together looked spitefully on while the general played his cards, obstructed him when they could, and ultimately had the satisfaction of seeing Schleicher fail—at a high price.

Basically, the moment was favorable for Schleicher's plans. For the crisis Hitler was facing had just reached its height, and the pressures upon him were greater than any he had previously known. The rank and file were seething with impatience and disappointed hopes. Moreover, the party seemed about to be crushed by its burden of debt. Creditors were growing restless—the printers of the party newspapers, the makers of uniforms, the suppliers of equipment, the landlords of business offices, and the innumer-able holders of promissory notes. With flippant logic Hitler later admitted that at the time he had borrowed to the hilt because victory would make repayment easy and defeat would make it superfluous. On all the street corners storm troopers hung about, extending collection boxes to passersby "like discharged soldiers whom the warlord has given, instead of a pension, a permit for begging." "For the wicked Nazis!" they could cry ironically. Konrad Heiden has reported that many desperate SA subleaders were running to opposition parties and newspapers to betray alleged secrets for hard cash. There were other signs of decay. The motley crowd of opportunists that had gathered around the rising movement was gradually beginning to disperse. In the Landtag elections in Thuringia, formerly one of Hitler's bastions, the NSDAP received its most stunning setback. Goebbels's diary entry for December 6 notes: "The situation in the Reich is catastrophic. Since July 31 we have suffered almost 40 per cent losses in Thuringia." Goebbels later admitted publicly that at that time he had sometimes wondered whether the movement would not perish after all. In the offices controlled by Gregor Strasser statements of resignation from the party piled up.

With the skepticism about the party's future Hitler's whole concept came into question. He had repeatedly rejected offers of partial power but had not managed to win total power. The investiture of Schleicher represented one more miscarriage of his policy. To be sure, his stand had its own impressive consistency. But we might ask, as one commentator did at the time, whether Hitler's unyieldingness had not by now become stupidity. At any rate, a sizable band of his followers, headed by Strasser, Frick, and Feder, felt that the opportunity to come to "power" had been allowed to slip by. True, the Depression to which the party owed so much was far from over; the total number of the unemployed, including the "invisible" jobless, had been set at 8.75 million in October, 1932, and the country was heading into a new winter of misery with all its predictable demoralizing and radicalizing effects. But the experts claimed to see signs of a turning point. And in foreign policy also the long-delayed process of equalization was once more on its way. Hitler's all-or-nothing slogan, as the Strasser group recognized, was fundamentally revolutionary in nature and therefore stood in contradiction to the tactics of legality. They were now afraid that Schleicher might once more dissolve the Reichstag and call an election. The party was neither financially nor psychologically able to cope with another campaign.

It can no longer be determined how large a following Strasser commanded and how ready it was to obey him against the Führer. One version has it that Hitler gave way and was on the point of permitting Strasser to enter the cabinet, since such a solution would preserve his own charismatic claim to all or nothing and would at the same time bring the party to power. According to this version, Göring and Goebbels pressed Hitler to return to his unyielding course. According to other informants, he kept to that course throughout. It is likewise uncertain whether Schleicher, in negotiations on the formation of his "cabinet of anticapitalist nostalgia," offered Strasser the posts of Vice-Chancellor and Minister of Labor in return for a promise from Strasser to split the party. Nor is there real proof that Strasser had any thought of outmaneuvering Hitler. He may simply have acted with the self-assurance of the second man in the party, feeling entitled to take up negotiations on his own—perhaps just like Göring, who, according to still another version, proposed himself to Schleicher as Minister of Air Transport. Out of the welter of secret agreements, implied pledges, and presumptuous claims, scarcely a single reliable document has survived. What is thoroughly documented is the confusion of intrigues, the cabals, accusations, and embittered rivalries. This was the other face of the party based entirely on the Führer idea and the principle of loyalty. In the absence of any firm ideology or objective principles, every issue was decided on purely personal grounds. The leadership remained to the last a retinue of mutually feuding satellites around Hitler, with each against each at some time or other.

On December 5, after the costly election in Thuringia, the party leadership held a meeting in the Hotel Kaiserhof. There was a violent dispute, in the course of which Strasser, evidently already abandoned by Frick and vanquished by Hitler's oratory, found himself forced into isolation. Two days later he confronted Hitler once more in the same place. This time he was accused of underhandedness and treachery. Possibly the temper of the meeting had already convinced Strasser of the hopelessness of his efforts. At any rate, in the midst of general furor, he picked up his things and silently left the room, bidding no one good-bye. In his hotel room he wrote Hitler a long letter reviewing their relations over many years. He deplored the influence of Goebbels and Göring upon the party, criticized Hitler's lack of principle, and finally prophesied that he was heading toward "acts of violence and a German rubble heap." He concluded by tendering his resignation from all the posts he held in the party.

The letter threw the party into a panic—all the more so since it contained no indications of what Strasser planned to do next. Strasser's following, such men as Erich Koch, Kube, Kaufmann, Count Reventlow, Feder, Frick, and Stöhr, were obviously waiting for some sign from him. Hitler, too, seemed to have become nervous and prepared to smooth over the quarrel in a public discussion. The uneasiness increased when nobody could locate Strasser. "The Führer spends the evening at our house," Goebbels noted. "Nobody is in a lively mood. We are all greatly depressed, mostly because of the danger of the whole party's falling apart and all our work having been in vain. We are facing the decisive test." Later, back in his hotel room, Hitler abruptly broke his silence to say: "If the party ever falls apart, it won't take me more than three minutes to shoot myself."

But the much-sought and much-feared Strasser, who for one historic moment seemed to hold the fate of the movement in his hands, spent the afternoon drinking beer with a friend and getting the whole thing off his chest in a torrent of words. He then took the train to Munich, where he picked up his family and continued on to Italy for a vacation. The followers he left behind were bewildered. They could not believe that he would totally abandon the field in this way. But Gregor Strasser had remained loyal too long to strike out on his own. The very next day, as soon as Strasser's departure became known, Hitler set about smashing his apparatus. Instantaneously, with feverish sureness, he drew up a flock of decrees and appeals. Following the pattern he had used in the SA crisis, he himself took over Strasser's post as national organization leader and appointed Robert Ley, who had already proved his blind loyalty years earlier in Hanover, as his chief of staff. He installed Rudolf Hess, who had been his private secretary, as chief of a political central secretariat, which was clearly meant to serve as a counterweight to the power hunger of other leaders. In addition, subdivisions that had formerly handled agriculture and education were converted into independent departments and assigned to Darré and Goebbels.

Hitler then called the functionaries and deputies of the NSDAP to a meeting in Hermann Göring's office at the palace of the President of the Reichstag. Political histrionics were in order. Hitler declared that he had always been loyal to Strasser, but that Strasser had repeatedly broken faith and had brought the party, now so close to victory, to the brink of ruin. The story goes that Hitler dropped his head to the table, sobbing and playing out his despair. Goebbels at any rate thought the address had "so intense a personal note that one's heart is altogether healed. . . . Old party comrades who have fought and worked for years unswervingly for the Movement have tears in their eyes from rage, grief and shame. The evening is an enormous success for the unity of the Movement." Hitler insisted on the old Strasser adherents making an act of public submission. "All shake hands with him and promise . . . to continue the struggle and not to deviate from the great cause, whatever may happen, even at the cost of their lives. Strasser is now completely isolated. A dead man."

Hitler once more had mastered one of the great crises of his career and showed his talent for converting breakdown and dissolution into a new source of strength. To be sure, Strasser had made it easy for him, had forced neither a fight nor a compromise, and had conveniently made himself a scapegoat for the failures of the preceding months. But that, too, was one of the concomitants of Hitler's rise; his opponents seemingly never knew how to fight and in the face of his obstinate determination tended to shrug and give up. Brüning capitulated almost as soon as he sensed that Hindenburg was turning away from him. Now it was the turn of Strasser and his followers; later Hugenberg and others would take the same course. All of them threw in the towel and walked out when Hitler flew into one of his rages. Unlike Hitler, they lacked the passion for power. For them a crisis was tantamount to a defeat, whereas for him it was the opportunity for struggle and a springboard for fresh certainties. "Let us not fool our-

355

selves," he once said, acutely analyzing the character of his bourgeois opposition. "They no longer even want to put up resistance against us. Every word from them cries out their need to make a pact with us. They are none of them men who crave power and feel pleasure in the possession of power. They talk only about duty and responsibility, and would be delighted if they could tend their flowers quietly, go fishing, and for the rest spend their time in devout contemplation."[50] The December crisis of 1932 confirmed Hitler's view of his opponents; and deep into the war years he would remember the crisis whenever things looked darkest. Defeats and collapses were only the preludes to victory, Hitler would assure himself, for had he not more than once had to "pass through between two entirely different abysses and confront the alternatives of to be or not to be"?

The expulsion of Strasser by no means meant that the difficulties of the National Socialist Party were over. In the following weeks, Goebbels's diary continued to be full of gloom, and noted "a great deal of griping and dissension." The top leadership of the party, particularly Hitler, Goebbels, Göring, and Ley, made trips to the various party districts every weekend, trying to restore the morale and confidence of their followers. And as he had done during the major election campaigns, Hitler spoke as much as four times a day in widely scattered cities. The financial pressure, too, continued to be calamitous. In the Berlin gau salaries of party officials had to be cut, and the Nazi members of the Prussian Landtag could not afford the usual Christmas tips to the staff of the legislature. On December 23 Goebbels noted affectedly: "The most terrible loneliness descends like mournful inconsolability upon me." At the year's end the *Frankfurter Zeitung* somewhat prematurely celebrated the "disenchantment of the NSDAP," while Harold Laski, one of the leading intellectuals of the English Left, considered that the day the National Socialists represented a real menace was past. Barring accidents, it appeared not improbable that Hitler would end his career as an old man in a Bavarian village, spending his evenings in the *Biergarten* telling his cronies how he once almost overthrew the German Reich.[51] As if in response to that prediction, Goebbels wrote sullenly: "The year 1932 has been one interminable streak of bad luck. Now we must smash it to pieces. . . . All prospects and hopes have completely vanished."

At that moment, to everyone's surprise, there came a sudden turnabout. For although Schleicher's reign as Chancellor had begun auspiciously, he soon found that he was pleasing nobody. He had introduced himself upon taking office as a "social-minded general." But his concessions to labor did not manage to win over the Social Democrats, while antagonizing the employers. The small farmers were embittered by the favor shown to labor, and the large landowners opposed the projected land settlement program with that caste solidarity that had already proved Brüning's undoing.

Schleicher was going at things too abruptly, and the general himself, with his well-known bent for intrigue, did not inspire trust. He may very well have been sincere about his proposals for a planned economy, or his wooing of the unions, or his efforts to reinvigorate the parliamentary system. But whatever he undertook was met with suspicion and resistance. The optimism he nevertheless expressed was based on the thought that his various opponents were in no position to join forces against him. Granted, his stratagem with Gregor Strasser had failed for the present; but the affair had done heavy damage to the demoralized and debt-ridden Nazi party. The result was that Hitler, once considered the key figure in any coalition against the administration, was now hardly a viable partner.

It was none other than Franz von Papen who confounded all Schleicher's reasoning and helped give the National Socialist Party its unexpected chance. In Papen the mutually antagonistic adversaries of Schleicher found a "common broker" after all.[52]

Only two weeks after the general took office as Chancellor, Papen had informed Kurt von Schröder, the Cologne banker, that he would like to meet the leader of the National Socialist Party. As it happened, this overture coincided with the rout of Gregor Strasser. This last development could be taken as a sign to actual or potential patrons in industry that the revolutionary, anticapitalistic tendencies within the party had been, if not overcome, at any rate seriously weakened. Moreover, the Reichstag elections of November had again shown significant gains for the Communists. In view of this, employers who had had reservations toward Hitler might be inclined to see things differently. The NSDAP's propaganda hammered away at this idea with the slogan: If the party breaks up tomorrow, the day after tomorrow Germany will have 10 million more Communists.

As president of the Cologne *Herrenklub,* Schröder had extensive connections throughout heavy industry in the Rhineland. He had actively supported Hitler on various occasions, had sketched plans for Nazi economic policies, and in November, 1932, had signed the petition drawn up by Hjalmar Schacht blatantly backing Hitler's claims to power. At the time, Papen had issued a sharp statement declaring this proposal impermissible. Now, on the contrary, he gladly took up the invitation, conveyed by Schröder, to a meeting with Hitler on January 4, 1933.

The conversation was held under conditions of extreme secrecy. Hitler began with a bitter monologue revolving chiefly around the humiliation of August 13 of the previous year. It was some time before Papen managed to propitiate him by placing the full blame on Schleicher for the President's refusal to appoint Hitler Chancellor. Then Papen proposed a coalition between the German Nationalists and the National Socialists, to be headed jointly by Hitler and himself. Thereupon, Hitler again launched into "a long speech"—so von Schröder testified in Nuremberg—"in which he declared that if he were appointed Chancellor he could not relinquish his

357

demand to stand alone at the head of the government." Nevertheless, Papen's people could enter his government as ministers if they were prepared to collaborate with policies that would change many things. Among the changes he hinted at were the removal of the Social Democrats, Communists, and Jews from leading positions in Germany and the restoration of order in public life. Papen and Hitler came to an agreement in principle. In the course of the conversation Hitler received the extremely valuable information that Schleicher had not been granted an Enabling Decree to dissolve the Reichstag and so the Nazi party need not fear new elections for the present.

With good reason that meeting has been called "the hour of birth of the Third Reich,"[53] for from it a direct chain of cause and effect leads to January 30, 1933, and the realization of the coalition that was first sketched in Cologne. At the same time, the conversation threw some light upon the economic interests that supported Hitler's ambitions. Whether anything was said about the Nazi party's catastrophic financial predicament and whether measures to pay the party's debts were discussed has never been definitely clarified. But undoubtedly the conversation itself restored the party's credit, brought it, in fact, back into the game of politics. As late as January 2 a party tax adviser had stated to a Berlin tax collection office that the party could pay its taxes only by giving up its independence; now Goebbels noted that the financial situation had "improved very suddenly" and that the party as a whole was once again "sitting pretty." Thyssen spoke of a "number of sizable contributions" that "flowed from sources in heavy industry into the treasuries of the NSDAP." Though Hitler vehemently denied that he had made concessions to business—such talk was all "inventions and lies," he said—he did not deny these links with industry.

To the extent to which the Cologne meeting restored the Nazis' self-confidence and hope of victory, it inflicted a probably decisive blow upon Schleicher and his government. Conscious of the rising danger, the Chancellor immediately informed the press and went to Hindenburg to remonstrate against Papen's actions. But when he begged the President to henceforth receive Papen only in his—Schleicher's—presence, he received an evasive answer, which for the first time showed him what he was up against. Hindenburg was again ready to sacrifice the propriety of his office and the very institutions of the state to his fondness for his "young friend" Papen, who had such charming manners and told anecdotes so expertly.

Now Papen was called up on the carpet. Untruthfully, he told the President that Hitler had at last softened and abandoned his demand for exclusive power to govern. Far from reproving Papen for having acted on his own, Hindenburg remarked that he had "thought right away that this account [Schleicher's] could not be correct." He actually ordered Papen to remain in touch with Hitler—personally and in strict confidence. Finally, he instructed his aide, State Secretary Meissner, not to mention Papen's assignment to Schleicher. Thus the President himself was taking part in the plot against his own Chancellor.

Soon afterward, the nascent Papen-Hitler front received significant reinforcement. While Schleicher was still trying, though with failing hopes, to win over Strasser and the unions, a delegation from the Reich Agrarian League called at the presidential palace on January 11 to protest against the administration's laggardness in aiding farming estates, and particularly its lack of protective tariffs. Behind these complaints was anxiety about the resumption of the government's settlement program in the eastern lands— the program started by Brüning. They were also nervous about a parliamentary investigation of the *Osthilfe*—the scandalous subsidies to debt-ridden landowners in the lands east of the Elbe. Many of Hindenburg's peers had enriched themselves on these *Osthilfe* funds, thereby taking their revenge on the hated republic. Members of the cabinet were called in at once for consultation, and in their presence Hindenburg vigorously took the part of the delegation. Schleicher was unwilling to make binding promises on a moment's notice. The owner of Estate Neudeck, thereupon, according to an eyewitness, pounded his fist on the table and delivered an ultimatum: "I request you, Chancellor von Schleicher—and as an old soldier you know such a request is merely the polite form of a command— to hold a cabinet meeting this very night, at which legislation to meet these problems is to be drawn up and presented to me for signature tomorrow morning."

At first Schleicher seemed about to give way. But a few hours later he learned of some machinations by the Agrarian League that made him decide to stand his ground and abruptly break off the discussions. Two days later he refused to give the reactionary Hugenberg the Ministry of Economy and explicitly reaffirmed his "socialistic" platform. Now the Right was up in arms against him. The Social Democrats had from the first withheld their support for this "general in the flesh" and had even forbidden Theodor Leipart, the union leader, to negotiate with Schleicher. In their estimate of Hitler the Social Democrats had fallen back on old platitudes. In their complacency they counted on the mechanical operations of progress. (Their opposites in the conservative camp had similar notions of a "historically sanctioned" special mentality.) Hitler, the Social Democrats had decided, represented at most a brief detour, a dramatic incident before the final triumph of a libertarian system. Certainly Schleicher had compromised his credibility by his innumerable intrigues directed against the very institutions of the state. But this was hardly reason enough to distrust him more than Hitler.

At any rate, the Social Democrats failed to realize that Schleicher was the last remaining alternative to a Hitler who was waiting impatiently outside the gates to power. In the years since the collapse of the Great Coalition the Social Democratic Party had advanced scarcely a single

359

initiative. Now it roused itself just once more—but only in order to spoil the last slim chance of survival that the republic had.

Far sooner than could have been expected, the devious Chancellor found himself facing an impasse. His approach was a promising one, but he was discovering that he was not the man for it. His employment program alienated the employers, his settlement program the agrarians, his origins the Social Democrats, his offer to Strasser the Nazis. His constitutional reform proved as unfeasible as the systems it replaced. For the time being Schleicher was able to remain in office only because his opponents had not yet put together a new cabinet. This question now became the subject of feverish activity conducted in a twilight zone.

Hitler himself, in order to improve his bargaining position and shore up the party's claims to power, concentrated all his forces on the Landtag elections that were to take place on January 15 in the miniature state of Lippe. He conducted one of his most lavish election campaigns. Assembling the best known party speakers in the castle of Baron von Oeynhausen, he sent them out night after night, saturating the little state with the Nazi message. On the first day, Goebbels noted, "I have spoken three times, partly in tiny peasant villages." Hitler himself addressed eighteen demonstrations within a few days. With that sure psychological insight which his critics failed to understand or regarded with disdain he saw that this election offered him an unparalleled opportunity. From the start he hammered away at the theme that this was to be the decisive test in the struggle for power, and he managed to impose this view of the election on the country at large. Thus the German public awaited this marginal event, the decision of some 100,000 voters, as if it were a kind of trial by ordeal that would decide "the political future of a nation of 68 millions."

As a result of his massive commitment, on January 15 Hitler won his first success since the July elections. Even so, the party, with 39.5 per cent of the vote, lagged behind the share of the vote it had won in July. Moreover, the democratic parties, in particular the Social Democratic Party, in toto achieved greater gains than Hitler's party. But compared with the results of the November election, the results in Lippe were good. Instead of reading this success in terms of the excessive effort behind it, the public was persuaded that the Hitler movement had regained its irresistible impetus. Even the heads of the government took this view. And Hitler's own self-confidence mounted.

On January 18 Hitler met with Franz von Papen in the Berlin apartment of Joachim von Ribbentrop, a liquor salesman who had recently joined Hitler's movement. At this meeting Hitler demanded the chancellorship for himself. Papen replied that his influence with the President was not great enough for him to put across such a demand. That refusal nearly blocked the negotiations, and only the sudden inspiration of involving Hindenburg's son started them moving again. The meeting took place a few days later, with extraordinary precautions to insure secrecy. Hitler and his team entered von Ribbentrop's apartment under cover of darkness, from the garden side. Meanwhile, Oskar von Hindenburg and State Secretary Meissner first appeared ostentatiously at the opera. Shortly after the intermission they slipped out of their box. Papen, for his part, was brought to the meeting in Ribbentrop's car.

As soon as everyone was present, Hitler asked the President's son to step into another room with him. Suddenly, Oskar von Hindenburg, who had insisted on being accompanied by Meissner, found himself forced into a man-to-man encounter with Hitler. To this day no one knows what was said during their two-hour private talk. Hitler must have attempted to swing the President's son over to his side by a combination of blackmail and bribery. Among the threats there might well be the charge, repeatedly raised by the Nazis, that Hindenburg had participated in a *coup d'état* against Prussia. Hitler may also have hinted that the Nazis would publicize the tax evasion by the Hindenburgs when Estate Neudeck was transferred to them.[54] In addition, Hitler's magnetic personality must have made an impression upon the President's opportunistic son. In any case, Oskar, who had come to the conference prejudiced against Hitler, remarked to Meissner on his way home that there was no alternative, that Hitler would have to become Chancellor—especially now that Papen had agreed to accept the Vice-Chancellorship.

At this moment Schleicher seems for the first time to have realized what was brewing. On January 23 he called on Hindenburg and admitted that his plan for splitting the Nazi party and providing a parliamentary basis for the cabinet had failed. He then asked the President for powers to dissolve the Reichstag, declare a state of emergency, and issue a general ban on the National Socialist and Communist parties. Hindenburg, however, reminded him of their disagreement of December 2. At that time Papen had proposed a similar solution, but Schleicher had scotched it. The situation had changed, the Chancellor replied. But this reasoning had no effect on the old man; after talking the matter over with Meissner, he denied Schleicher's request.

As might be expected, the camarilla saw to it that the public was immediately informed of Schleicher's wish to dissolve the Reichstag and rule by decree. There was a general outcry. The Nazis made a great fuss over "Primo de Schleicheros' " would-be *coup d'état*. The Communists, too, were understandably indignant. And the Chancellor lost the remnant of the prestige he had enjoyed among the democratic Center parties. This unanimous reaction made its impression on Hindenburg and may have made him look with greater favor on plans for a Hitler cabinet. On January 27, moreover, Göring called on Meissner at the presidential palace and asked him to inform the "revered Field Marshal" that Hitler, unlike Schleicher,

361

had no intention of burdening the President's conscience by violating the law but would practice strict and loyal adherence to the Constitution.

Meanwhile, the tireless Papen was pushing matters forward. His thought was to make the planned cabinet more acceptable to Hindenburg by securing participation of the German Nationalists and of the Stahlhelm leaders, who were close to the President's heart. While Duesterberg vigorously disagreed that there was anything like the so-called compelling necessity for a Hitler cabinet, Seldte and Hugenberg fell in with Papen's plans. Having learned nothing from the experiences of recent years, Hugenberg declared with self-assurance "that nothing much would be able to happen"; Hindenburg would be remaining President and commander in chief of the armed forces, Papen would be Vice-Chancellor, he himself would be taking charge of the entire economy, and Seldte of the Ministry of Labor. "We'll be boxing Hitler in."

Hindenburg himself, tired, confused, and capable of grasping the situation only for brief spells, was at this time evidently still thinking of a Papen cabinet with Hitler as Vice-Chancellor. On the morning of January 26 General von Hammerstein, army commander in chief, called on him to express his concern about the way things were going. Hindenburg was "quick to suppress any attempt to influence him politically, but then said, apparently to reassure me, that he 'had no intention at all of making the Austrian lance corporal Defense Minister or Chancellor.'" But next day Papen called on the President and reported that a Papen cabinet was impossible at the moment. Now Hindenburg stood alone in his resolve not to have Hitler form a government.

The factors that made him change his mind in the course of the following day are almost too complicated to list. Among them were the schemings of the camarilla, the blackmail of the NSDAP, the pressure of his friends from among the large landowner and nationalist groups. The effect of all this counsel was that the name of Schleicher ceased to represent an alternative either to Hindenburg or anyone else. Another significant factor was Papen's promise to the President that the new government would be made up exclusively of members of the Right. For the thing Hindenburg was most set against was what was summed up in his exhausted mind as "rule of the union functionaries." The prospect of a rightist government had been one of the decisive elements in his dismissal of Brüning; now the same promise was being dangled before him if he would get rid of Schleicher.

The party leaders, whom Hindenburg once more consulted, also turned against General Schleicher. But they were not in favor of another try with Papen. Rather, they indicated, the time had come at last to summon Hitler to power, with all appropriate guarantees; let him be exposed to that chastening by responsibility, which they had all undergone. The republic had truly reached the end of its rope.

On the morning of January 28 Schleicher made one last attempt to regain control. He let the public know, through the press, that he would ask Hindenburg for powers to dissolve the Reichstag or offer his resignation. Toward noon he went to the presidential palace. At this time he himself clearly knew nothing about the imminence of Hitler's chancellorship—a measure of his loss of grip. On the contrary, he seems to have counted to the last on Hindenburg's support. He had assumed office with the President pledged to give him the power of dissolution of the Reichstag at any time. But the President tersely turned down his request. Stung to the quick, Schleicher is reported to have said angrily: "I concede your right, Mr. President, to be dissatisfied with the way I have conducted my office, although you assured me of the contrary four weeks ago in writing. I concede your right to depose me. But I do not concede you the right to make alliances with someone else behind the back of the Chancellor you yourself summoned to office. That is a breach of faith." Hindenburg thought for a moment, then answered. He stood with one foot in the grave, he said, and did not know whether or not he might regret his decision in heaven. Schleicher is supposed to have shot back: "After this breach of confidence, Your Excellency, I would not be too sure that you will go to heaven."[55]

Schleicher had scarcely left when Papen, in conjunction with Oskar von Hindenburg and Meissner, began urging the President to appoint Hitler Chancellor. Still vacillating, Hindenburg made a last effort to evade responsibility for this decision. Contrary to custom, he did not personally request Hitler to form a new government, but appointed Papen his *homo regius* with the assignment "to clarify the political situation by negotiations with the parties and to determine the available possibilities."

That afternoon Papen was able to win Hugenberg by promising his party two seats in the cabinet. He then got in touch with Hitler. In the elaborate preliminary talks they had already agreed that Hitler's people should have the Ministry of the Interior and a Ministry for Civil Air Transport, to be newly created especially for Göring. Now Hitler insisted on the posts of Reich Commissioner for Prussia and Prussian Minister of the Interior. These would assure him control of the Prussian police. In addition, he demanded new elections.

Once more everything teetered. On hearing of Hitler's further demands, Hindenburg had a fresh siege of foreboding. He calmed down only after he had received Hitler's assurance—in highly equivocal words—"that these would be the last elections." Finally the President let things take their course. With the exception of the post of Reich Commissioner for Prussia —which was reserved for Papen himself—all of Hitler's demands were met. The decision had been taken.

On the afternoon of January 29 a rumor arose that Schleicher, together with General Hammerstein, had put the Potsdam garrison on alert and was planning to seize the President, proclaim a state of emergency, and with the aid of the army take power. Days later, Oskar von Hindenburg's wife was still exercised over the matter: the plan had called for the President's being removed to Neudeck "in a sealed cattle car." Hitler, who was in Goebbels's apartment on Reichskanzlerplatz when he heard the rumor, reacted with an audacious gesture: he instantly placed the Berlin SA on alert and, in a flamboyant anticipation of the power he expected to receive, ordered six nonexistent police battalions to prepare to occupy the Wilhelmstrasse.

The author of this rumor has never been traced, but the person who profited by it is obvious. None other than Papen used the phantom of a threatening military dictatorship to push forward his plans. General von Blomberg had been summoned from Geneva, and on the morning of January 30 Papen was sworn in as Minister of Defense, before any other members of the cabinet. Evidently this was to prevent any last-minute desperate intervention by Schleicher, who on his own had been making contact with Hitler. Hugenberg, who had obstinately rejected Hitler's demand for new elections, felt blackmailed by the new threat of a military take-over. To avert any possibility that the mysterious reports of an imminent putsch might be clarified, Papen summoned Hugenberg at seven o'clock in the morning on January 30 to beg him—"in greatest excitement"—to change his mind. "Unless a new government has been formed by eleven o'clock this morning," he exclaimed, "the army will march!" But Hugenberg would not be stampeded. More keenly than Papen, he saw through Hitler's scheme. The Nazis wanted to improve on the election results of November 6. With the power and unlimited funds of the state at their disposal, they could unquestonably do so. No new elections, Hugenberg said.

Once again his stubbornness seemed to be imperiling the whole agreement. At fifteen minutes before ten o'clock Papen led the members of the projected government through the snow-covered ministerial gardens to the presidential palace and into Meissner's office. There he formally greeted Hitler as the new Chancellor. Even as he expressed his thanks, Hitler declared that "now the German people must confirm the completed formation of the cabinet." Hugenberg resolutely spoke up against this. A vehement argument broke out. Hitler finally went up to his antagonist and gave him his "solemn word of honor" that the new elections would change nothing in regard to the persons composing the cabinet. He would, he said, "never part with any of those present here." Anxiously, Papen followed this up: "Herr Geheimrat, would you want to undermine the agreement reached with such difficulty? Surely you cannot doubt the solemn word of honor of a German!"

The cheerful notion of boxing Hitler in and taming him thus came to grief at the first test. In purely arithmetic terms, it is true, the conservatives

364

had managed to retain the advantage. There were three National Socialist as against eight conservative ministers, and virtually all the key positions in the government were in the hands of a group of men united on certain basic social and ideological principles. The trouble was that such men as Papen, Neurath, Seldte or Schwerin-Krosigk were not the right persons to box anyone in. For that they would have needed a sense of values and the energy to defend it. Instead they considered themselves summoned merely to preserve traditional privileges. Hitler's readiness to accept such a numerically unfavorable arrangement testifies to his self-assurance and his deadly contempt for his conservative adversaries.

Now his would-be tamers had drawn Hugenberg into a window niche and were pleading with him to co-operate. Hugenberg held out. In the adjoining room, meanwhile, the President sent for State Secretary Meissner and wanted to know the meaning of the delay. "Watch in hand," Meissner returned to the disputants: "Gentlemen, the President set the swearing-in for eleven o'clock. It is eleven-fifteen. You cannot make the President wait any longer." And what could not be accomplished by the arm twisting of Hugenberg's conservative friends, by Hitler's cajolery and by Papen's pleas, was done easily—for the last time, at the hour of the republic's last agony—by the allusion to the legendary figure of the Field Marshal-President. Hugenberg was in the habit of referring to himself, with candid pride, as "a stubborn mule"; as recently as August, 1932, he had told Hindenburg that he had found Hitler "somewhat remiss at keeping agreements." Now, however, knowing full well what was at stake, he yielded to the exigencies of Hindenburg's appointments calendar. A few minutes later the cabinet had been sworn in.

Papen seems actually to have thought that he had put across a political master stroke. He had avenged himself upon Schleicher while at the same time using Schleicher's concept of taming the wicked Nazis. He had satisfied his own ambition, which had swollen to absurd proportions during his brief, unexpected chancellorship, by entering the government once more. And he had made Hitler take a position of responsibility without turning control of the government over to him completely. For the leader of the NSDAP was not even the Chancellor of a presidential cabinet; he would have to maintain a parliamentary majority. Moreover, he did not enjoy Hindenburg's confidence; it was Franz von Papen who continued to have a special relationship with the old President. In the negotiations Papen had insisted—this was one of the results he was proudest of—that he must participate in all conversations between Hitler and the President. Finally, Papen was also Vice-Chancellor and Prime Minister of Prussia. In the cabinet the Nazis held only the Ministry of the Interior, which did not control the federal police, and a Ministry without Portfolio which was intended to satisfy Göring's vanity but not to have any powers. To be sure, Göring was also Prussian Minister of the Interior, and in Prussia this

365

ministry did control the police. But Papen was confident that he would block any independent action on Göring's part. Finally, within the cabinet foreign policy, finance, economics, labor, and agriculture were in the hands of experienced conservatives, and command of the army still remained the prerogative of the President. Papen saw it as a brilliantly conceived, splendid combination, which, moreover, placed that troublesome Herr Hitler at the service of employers and big landowners and of Papen's own plans for an authoritarian new state. His own unfortunate fling at the chancellorship seemed to have taught Papen that a modern industrial nation shaken by crisis could not be openly governed by the dismissed representatives of an outmoded epoch. By harnessing the slightly unsavory manipulator of the masses to his own wagon, Papen seemed to be solving the ancient problem of conservatism: that it did not enjoy the support of the people. In this sense, using the vocabulary of a political impresario, Papen complacently replied to all warnings: "No danger at all. We've hired him for our act."

Hitler himself undoubtedly saw through this strategy from the start. His demand for new elections was intended as a direct counterstroke. By winning an unprecedented electoral triumph he wanted to break out of the box Papen had nailed together and with the sanction of the vote behind him throw off the role of puppet Chancellor. He certainly did not mean to let cheap words of honor stand in his way. Thus the "Cabinet of National Concentration" was already a system of crisscrossing mental reservations even before Hindenburg sent it out into the world with the words: "And now, gentlemen, forward with God!"

The Wilhelmstrasse had meanwhile filled with a silent crowd, assembled there by Goebbels. "Torn between doubt, hope, happiness and discouragement," Hitler's entourage waited in the Hotel Kaiserhof, across the square. Through binoculars Ernst Röhm nervously watched the entrance to the chancellery. Göring emerged first and called out the news to the people waiting. Immediately afterward, Hitler's car came out of the driveway. Standing, Hitler received the plaudits of the crowd. When he joined his followers in the Kaiserhof a few minutes later, he had tears in his eyes, according to one of those present. Sometime before he had publicly vowed that once he possessed power he would never let it be taken from him. On the very afternoon of this January 30 he took a first step to guarantee this matter. Calling an immediate cabinet meeting, he had the cabinet formally decide—against the now impotent objections of Hugenberg—on the dissolution of the Reichstag and new elections. It was Papen himself who cleverly overcame Hindenburg's last scruples by describing Hugenberg's obstructionism as "a matter of party tactics," which the President abhorred.

That evening the Nazis celebrated with a tremendous torchlight parade. All restrictions within the government quarter were lifted; spectators crowded the sidewalks, excited and noisy. "Tonight Berlin is in a really festive mood."[56] And among the spectators, keeping order and intervening in self-important delight, was the huge corps of police deputies. From seven in the evening until after midnight, 25,000 uniformed Hitler followers, together with Stahlhelm units, marched through the Brandenburg Gate and past the chancellery. In one of the illuminated windows the nervous, prancing figure of Hitler could be seen. From time to time the upper part of his body, with raised arm, abruptly leaned forward over the railing. Beside him were Göring, Goebbels, and Hess. A few windows farther along the façade Hindenburg looked out reflectively at the marching formations, abstractedly pounding his cane in time to the music of the bands. Despite the protests of those in charge, Goebbels had insisted that the Reich radio stations broadcast an account of the demonstration. Only the Munich station stuck to its refusal, as Hitler irritably noted. It was past midnight before the last columns had marched through the government quarter. And as Goebbels dismissed the waiting crowd with a shout of *Heil* for Hindenburg and Hitler, "this night of the great miracle ended . . . in an insensate tumult of enthusiasm."

The so-called Seizure of Power by the Nazis was soon being hailed as "miracle" and a "fairytale." The regime's propaganda specialists deliberately chose phrases from the realm of magic to give the event the aura of a supernatural consecration. They could count on striking an echoing chord, because the event itself undeniably had something peculiarly displaced, something scarcely credible about it. On the political plane Hitler had made the unexpected step from a crisis that had nearly destroyed the party into the President's office; and on the individual plane he had taken the leap from dreary beginnings, from lethargy and a tramp's existence, to power. In truth: "Elements of fairy tales are recognizable in it, though badly botched."[57]

The notion of a miracle, invented by Goebbels, has lived on to the present day. It colors all those analyses that postulate a demonic theory of Hitler, that try to view his success as the result of background intrigues by nameless powers, or make much of Papen and his machinations. The central thought, in all these theories, is that the seizure of power was a historical accident.

Undoubtedly Hitler's way could have been blocked up to the very last moment. These opportunities were lost by chance, frivolity, and bad luck. Nevertheless, history was not diverted from its rightful course. A host of powerful trends, partly historical, partly political in nature, pointed toward what happened on January 30. The real miracle would have been a decision to resist Nazism. From the time Brüning was dismissed, all that stood between the republic and Hitler were the whims of a senescent President, Schleicher's faculty for conniving, and the blinded simple-mindedness of Franz von Papen. Thus the background machinations, the schemings of various interest groups, and the high-level intrigues are relatively unimportant. All these influenced the circumstances in which the republic went aground but did not bring about the shipwreck itself.

This is by no means to assert that Hitler would have prevailed over more resolute opponents. Seldom in modern political history has a change of such enormous impact been more strongly determined by personal factors, by the caprices, prejudices, and emotions of a tiny minority. And seldom have the institutions of a state been so invisible at the moment of decision. Hitler in power is scarcely conceivable without the camarilla around the President. And however short a step separated him from power after the summer of 1932, that step was still beyond his own strength. His adversaries were the ones to make it possible: they had shorn the parties and the Reichstag of political power; they set up the series of election campaigns; they created the precedent of undermining the Constitution. Whenever one of them decided to resist the Nazis, another inevitably stood up to frustrate him. On the whole, the forces of the other side were up to the last greater than Hitler's own. But since they turned against one another, they balanced one another out. It was not hard to see that Nazism was the enemy of all: the bourgeois, the Communists and Marxists, the Jews, the republicans. But these groups were all so blind and weak that very few came to the natural conclusion: they must unite against their common foe.

In the apologias of participants, the argument still arises that Hitler's summoning to the chancellorship had become inescapable once the NSDAP rose to the rank of strongest party in Germany. But this argument overlooks a vital fact: throughout all the years of the republic up to a few months before January 30, 1933, the Social Democratic Party held the same preponderance, yet did not take part in most of the cabinets. Also ignored is the fact that Hitler had always been the declared foe of the very Constitution in whose spirit such views are propounded. The Communists might have won far more votes than the Nazis, yet would have encountered massive resistance. The truth was that Hitler's conservative backers thought he could be trusted to carry out their intentions—in a more vulgar manner than they liked, granted, but effectively. They realized too late that he was just as radically (though differently) opposed to them and the world they wanted to preserve as was the Communist leader Thälmann. The nameless Bavarian plain-clothes man who attended a demonstration of the NSDAP in the summer of 1921 and reported to his office that Hitler was "nothing but . . . the leader of a second Red Army" had grasped the essence of the man more keenly than the conservative notables of 1933.[58]

Given all these favoring forces and circumstances, we may be tempted to ask what Hitler's particular feat was during those weeks. The fact is that his real abilities scarcely show up very convincingly during the period just before January 30, 1933. His principal feat was a passive one: he was able to wait in spite of his impatience, was able to control his refractory following, keep his composure during a fiasco, and even at the last moment, in the President's anteroom, play his cards with the icy poise of a great gambler who accepts all risks. A retrospective look at the years since the plebiscite on the Young Plan makes it plain to what extent he had outgrown the riot-and-propaganda phase of his career and had become a politician. At the same time, the experience of those weeks once again confirmed his gambler's instinct. What was most amazing about his life, he declared during this period, was that he was always being saved when he himself had already given up.[59]

That night, after the cheering was over, after the music and the thunder of marching feet had faded, Hitler stayed up until early morning in the small room adjacent to the Chancellor's reception room. Deeply moved, he lost himself in one of his endless rambling monologues. He recalled the morning's swearing-in ceremony, happily went over his triumphs, commented on the consternation of his "Red" adversaries, and reverted to one of his favorite topics: the art of propaganda. He had not looked forward to any election campaign as much as he did to this one, he declared. Some people thought there would be war, he then remarked. His chancellorship, he continued, was inaugurating the final struggle of the white man, the Aryan, for mastery of the earth. The non-Aryans, the colored races, the Mongols, were already striving to seize the mastery for themselves under Bolshevism, but this day marked the beginning of "the greatest Germanic racial revolution in world history." His eschatological visions intersected with architectural projects: the first thing he would do, he said, would be to rebuild the chancellery; it was a "mere cigar box."[60] It was close to dawn before he left the building through a small door in the rear wall and went across to his hotel.

The day had been an overwhelming one, full of satisfactions and vindications. But this was not yet his goal; it was only a stage along the way to it. Though we have no actual text of his protracted monologue of that night, it is clear that his mind was now dwelling on the revolution he had repeatedly proclaimed as imminent. Like every real revolutionary, he believed that with his coming a new day in history had begun.

Significantly, he framed this idea in negative terms. "We are the last who will be making history in Germany," he declared at this time.

INTERPOLATION II

German Catastrophe or German Consistency?

The idea is not so impotent as to amount to no more than an idea.

G. W. F. Hegel

Thought precedes action like lightning thunder. Admittedly the German thunder is also German and not very nimble; it rolls up rather slowly. But it will come, and once you hear it peal, as nothing has ever pealed before in the history of the world, know this: the German thunder has reached its goal.

Heinrich Heine, 1834

The dramatic ceremonial with which Hitler took over the chancellorship, the accompaniment of torchlight parades and mass demonstrations, bore no relationship to the constitutional importance of the event. For, strictly speaking, January 30, 1933, brought nothing more than a change of administrations. Nevertheless, the public sensed that the appointment of Hitler as Chancellor could not be compared with the cabinet reshufflings of former years. Despite all the vaunted intentions of the German Nationalist coalition partners "to keep the frustrated Austrian painter on the leash," the Nazis from the start made ready to seize full power and to apply it in revolutionary ways. All the efforts of Papen and his fellows to play a part in the oratory, the celebrating, or the directing of affairs only gave the impression of breathless running to keep up. Numerical superiority in the cabinet, influence with the President, or in the economy, the army, and the bureaucracy could not conceal the fact that this was their rival's hour.

After January 30 a mass desertion to the Nazi camp began. Once again the axiom was proved that in revolutionary times principles are cheap, and perfidy, calculation, and fear reign supreme. This was true, but not the whole truth. For the massive political turncoatism bespoke not only lack of character and servility. Quite often it represented the spontaneous desire to give up old prejudices, ideologies, and social restrictions and to join with others in making a fresh start. "We were not all opportunists," wrote the poet Gottfried Benn in retrospect, speaking as one of that vast host of people who were carried along by the force of the spreading revolutionary mood.[1] Powerful traditional parties and associations cracked under the

373

propagandistic onslaught; and even before they were forcibly dissolved and banned they left a leaderless following to its own devices. The past—republic, divisiveness, impotence—was over and done with. A rapidly shrinking minority did not succumb to the frenzy. But such holdouts were driven into isolation; they saw themselves excluded from those celebrations of the new sense of community, from those who could reveal in mass oaths in cathedrals of light, in addresses by the Führer, in mountaintop bonfires and choral singing by hundreds of thousands of voices. Even the first signs of the reign of terror could not mute the rejoicing. The public mind interpreted the terror as an expression of a ruthlessly operating energy for which it had looked all too long in vain.

These concomitants of enthusiasm are what have given Hitler's seizure of power its distressing note. For they undermine all the arguments for its having been a historical accident, the product of intrigues or dark conspiracies. Any attempt to explain the events of those years has always had to face the question of how Nazism could so rapidly and effortlessly have conquered the majority, not just attained power, in an ancient and experienced civilized nation. And how could it have thrown that majority into a peculiarly hysterical state compounded of enthusiasm, credulity, and devotion? How could the political, social, and moral checks and balances, which a country belonging to the "nobility of nations"[2] after all possesses, have so glaringly failed? Before Hitler came to power, an observer described what he considered the inevitable course of events: "Dictatorship, abolition of the parliament, crushing of all intellectual liberties, inflation, terror, civil war; for the opposition could not simply be made to disappear. A general strike would be called. The unions would provide a core for the bitterest kind of resistance; they would be joined by the Reichsbanner and by all those concerned about the future. And if Hitler won over even the Army and met the opposition with cannon—he would find millions of resolute antagonists."[3] But there were no millions of resolute antagonists and consequently no need for a bloody coup. On the other hand, Hitler did not come like a thief in the night. With his histrionic verbosity he revealed, more perhaps than any other politician, what he had been aiming for through all the byways and tactical maneuvers: dictatorship, anti-Semitism, conquest of living space.

Understandably enough, the euphoria of those weeks gave many observers the impression that Germany had rediscovered her true self. Although the Constitution and the rules of the political game as played in the republic remained valid for the time being, they nevertheless seemed curiously obsolete, cast off like an alien shell. And for decades this image—of a nation that seemed to have found itself in exuberantly turning away from the European tradition of rationality and humane progress—determined the interpretation of events.

The first attempts at tracing the success of Nazism to a special mentality rooted in German history thus began early in the thirties. The German was pictured as perplexing, full of antitheses, making a principle of his aloofness from civilization and civil conduct. He seemed to take a truculent pride in being the representative of a culturally advanced nation that could so offensively scandalize the world. Reckless pedigrees were constructed extending through Bismarck and Frederick the Great all the way back to Luther or into the Middle Ages, sometimes even as far back as the Teutonic leader Arminius who at the Battle of the Teutoburg Forest A.D. 9 defended German living space from Roman penetration. Such "ancestry" was supposed to prove a tradition of latent Hitlerism long before Hitler. This theory was best expressed in a number of books by the French specialist in Germanic studies, Edmond Vermeil. For a time, subsequently, it dominated British and American efforts at interpretation; William L. Shirer's *The Rise and Fall of the Third Reich,* which has to a large degree formed the world's picture of Germany, made use of it. Vermeil wrote:

At various stages of their history the Germans have believed with a desperate certainty, which sprang either from inner dissension and weakness or, on the contrary, from the notion of their insurpassable and invincible strength, that they had a divine mission to fulfill and that Germany has been chosen by Providence.[4]

The usurpation of the Roman Empire, the Hanseatic League, the Reformation, German mysticism, the rise of Prussia, romanticism—all these were more or less disguised manifestations of this missionary urge. And the sense of mission began to take a more overt turn with Bismarck's blood-and-iron policies and the German Empire's determination to achieve the status of a global power. Seen from this angle, nothing in German history was "innocent." Even in its most idyllic moments, the specters of obedience, militarism, and expansionism were palpably present. The German yearning for the infinite could be seen as an endeavor to exert in the realm of the mind a dominion that Germany still had not the power to achieve in reality. Ultimately everything terminated in Hitler; he was by no means a "German catastrophe," as the title of a well-known book[5] asserted, but a product of German consistency.

Without doubt there were unmistakably German features in National Socialism; but they are of a different and more complex kind than those set forth by Vermeil or Shirer. No genealogy of evil, no single explanation, can do justice to the nature of the phenomenon. Nor should we see its seeds only in the obviously dark and ominous elements in the German past. Many naïve attitudes, or at any rate attitudes that for generations caused no trouble, and even some virtues and commendable values, made the success of Nazism possible. One of the lessons the era has to teach us is that a totalitarian power system need not be built up upon a nation's deviant or even criminal tendencies. A nation cannot decide, like a Richard

III, to become a villain. Historical, psychological, and even social conditions comparable to those in Germany existed in many countries, and frequently only a fine line separated other nations from Fascist rule. The Germans were not the only people to arrive late at the sense of nationhood, or to be behindhand at developing democratic institutions. As for the unbridgeable gulfs between liberal and socialist forces, between the bourgeoisie and the working class, these, too, were not peculiarly German. We may also question whether revanchist yearnings, bellicose ideologies, or dreams of great power status were more pronounced in Germany than in some of her European neighbors. And even anti-Semitism, decisively though it governed Hitler's thinking, was surely not a specifically German phenomenon. In fact, it was rather weaker among the Germans than in most other peoples. Racial emotions did not, at any rate, win the masses over to National Socialism or kindle their enthusiasm. Hitler himself was cognizant of this, as his efforts to play down his anti-Semitism during the final phase of his struggle for power plainly showed.[6]

During the same era many Fascist or Fascist-oriented movements came to power—in Italy, Turkey, Poland, Austria, and Spain, for example. What was peculiarly German about National Socialism emerges most clearly by comparison with the systems in these other countries: it was the most radical, the most absolute manifestation of Fascism.

This fundamental rigor, which came out on the intellectual as well as the administrative plane, was Hitler's personal contribution to the nature of National Socialism. In his way of sharply opposing an idea to reality, of elevating what ought to be above what is, he was truly German. The failed local politician, subletting a room on Thierschstrasse, sketched triumphal arches and domed halls that were to assure his posthumous fame. Ignoring mockery, the Chancellor did not reckon in generations, but in millennia; he wanted to undo not merely the Treaty of Versailles and Germany's impotence but nothing less than the consequences of the great migrations. Whereas Mussolini's ambition aimed at restoring a lost historical grandeur, whereas Maurras called for a return to the *ancien régime* and the *"gloire de la Déesse France,"* whereas all the other Fascisms could do no better than invoke a past golden age, Hitler set himself a goal more grandiose than anything the world had ever seen: an empire stretching from the Atlantic to the Urals and from Narvik to Suez. His pure master race seeking its rightful place would fight for and win this empire. Would other countries oppose him? He would crush them. Were peoples located contrary to his plans? He would resettle them. Did the races fail to correspond to his image? He would select, breed, eliminate until the reality fitted his conception. He was always thinking the unthinkable; in his statements an element of bitter refusal to submit to reality invariably emerged. His personality was not without manic characteristics. "I confront everything with a tremendous, ice-cold lack of bias," he declared. He seemed authentically

376

himself only when he spoke and acted with the utmost radicality. To that extent, National Socialism cannot be conceived apart from Hitler.

Among the things that set Nazism apart from the Fascist movements of other countries is the fact that Hitler always found obedient instruments to carry out his eccentric radicalism. No stirrings of pity mitigated the concentrated and punctilious harshness of the regime. Its barbarous features have often been ascribed to the deliberate application of cruelty by murderers and sadists, and such criminal elements continue to loom large in the popular mind. To this day types of this sort appear in literary works, whip in hand, as the personifications of Nazism. But the regime had quite another picture of itself. No question about its making use of such people, especially in the initial phase; but it quickly realized that lasting rule cannot be founded upon the unleashing of criminal instincts. The radicality that constituted the true nature of National Socialism does not really spring from the license it offered to instinctual gratification. The problem was not one of criminal impulses but of a perverted moral energy.

Those to whom Nazism chiefly appealed were people with a strong but directionless craving for morality. In the SS, National Socialism trained this type and organized it into an elite corps. The "inner values" that were perpetually being preached within this secular monastic order—the theme of many an evening meeting complete with romantic torchlight—included, according to the prescript of Heinrich Himmler, the following virtues: loyalty, honesty, obedience, hardness, decency, poverty, and bravery. But all these virtues were detached from any comprehensive frame of reference and directed entirely toward the purposes of the regime. Under the command of such imperatives a type of person was trained who demanded "cold, in fact, stony attitudes" of himself, as one of them wrote, and had "ceased to have human feelings."[7] Out of his harshness toward himself he derived the justification for harshness toward others. The ability to walk over dead bodies was literally demanded of him; and before that could be developed, his own self had to be deadened. It is this impassive, mechanical quality that strikes the observer as far more extreme than sheer brutality. For the killer who acts out of an overpowering social, intellectual, or human resentment exerts a claim, however small, upon our sympathy.

The moral imperative was supplemented and crowned by the idea of a special mission: the sense of taking part in an apocalyptic confrontation, of obeying a "higher law," of being the agent of an ideal. Images and slogans alike were made to seem like metaphysical commandments, and a special consecration was conferred upon relentlessness. That is how Hitler meant it when he denounced those who cast doubt on his mission as "enemies of the people." This fanaticism, this fixation upon his own deeper insight and his own loftier missionary aims, reflected the traditional German false relationship to politics, and beyond that the nation's peculiarly distorted

377

relationship to reality in general. The real world in which ideas take form and are experienced by people, in which thoughts can be translated into despairs, anxieties, hatreds, and terrors, simply did not exist. All that existed was the program, and the process of putting it across, as Hitler occasionally remarked, involved either positive or negative activity. The lack of humanitarian imagination (which comes to the fore whenever Nazi criminals are brought to trial, from the Nuremberg Trials on) was nothing but the expression of this loss of a sense of reality. That was the characteristically German element in National Socialism, and there is reason to believe that various connecting lines run far back into German history.

According to a paradoxical epigram, the most significant event in modern German history was "the revolution that did not take place."[8] Often this incapacity for revolution has been seen as the expression of a particularly submissive character. For a long time the type of good-natured, dreamy, unwarlike German served as a kind of laughingstock for more self-assured neighbors. But in reality the profound suspicion of revolution was only the reaction of a nation whose historical experiences were largely dominated by the sense of being menaced. Due to her central position geographically Germany early developed defensive and encirclement complexes. These seemed to be all too justified by the horrible, never to be forgotten experiences of the Thirty Years' War, when the country was transformed into an underpopulated wasteland. The most momentous legacy of that war was the traumatic feeling of helplessness and a deep-seated dread of all chaotic conditions. This feeling was perpetuated and used to good advantage by Germany's rulers for generations. Keeping the peace was regarded as a citizen's foremost duty; but peace and order in turn became the citizen's foremost demand upon his government. The role of the authorities was to keep out fear and misery; the Protestant view of governmental authority accorded well with this.

The tendency of the Enlightenment throughout Europe was to challenge existing authorities. But the spokesmen of the Enlightenment in Germany refrained from criticizing the government of princes; some even lauded it—so ingrained were the terrors of the past. The German mind accords unusual respect to the categories of order, discipline, and self-restraint. Idolization of the state as court of last resort and bulwark against evil, and even faith in a leader, have their origin in such historical experiences. Hitler was able to play on such attitudes and use them to further his plans for dominion. Thus he created the cult of obedience to the Führer or staged those militarylike demonstrations whose precise geometry offered protection against the chaos so feared by all and sundry.

The epigram about the German revolution that did not take place contains only half the truth. For the nation whose past is devoid of beheaded kings or victorious popular risings has contributed more than any other to the revolutionary mobilization of the world. It supplied the most provocative insights, the most trenchant revolutionary slogans, for the so-called

Age of Revolutions. It heaved up rocky masses of ideas, out of which future ages built their houses. In intellectual radicalism Germany has had no match; and this, too, is part of a heritage that has conferred greatness and a characteristic bravura upon the better minds in Germany. But this again had little to do with the ability to assume pragmatic attitudes in which thought and life became reconciled and reason turned rational. The German mind had small concern with that; it was asocial in the literal sense of the word and thus basically oriented neither to the right nor the left but, rather, chiefly to the celebrated antithesis to life: uncompromising, always taking the "I can do no other" position, revealing a nearly apocalyptic "tendency toward the intellectual abyss."

The process of alienation from reality was intensified by the many disillusionments the bourgeois mind experienced in the course of its efforts to achieve political emancipation during the nineteenth century. The traces of this process can be seen on almost every plane: in the unreal character of political thought; in the mythologizing of history by Winckelmann and Wagner; and in the German adulation of culture. The superior man was supposed to live in the phantom realm of art and the sublime. The realm of politics was situated off to one side, and finer spirits would not venture there.

The social type in whom these tendencies became concentrated has enjoyed the highest prestige to this day. We recognize him, for his professorial face conforms to those old portraits of withdrawn, thoughtful men, whose features are imprinted with high-minded austerity and adherence to principle, though there could be some strange strains within their depths. They thought in sweeping terms, toppled or erected systems; they gazed toward remote horizons. At the same time, they were surrounded by an atmosphere of intimacy and cozy domesticity and led what would seem happy private lives. Books and dreams, as Paul de Lagarde has remarked, were their element. Their imaginations made up for their distance from reality. They had a good opinion of themselves, feeling themselves ennobled by their intellectual occupation, and were on the whole content with civilization and their own contribution to it.

Contempt for reality corresponded to an increasingly overt belittling of politics. Politics was reality in the bluntest, most obtrusive sense: the "rule of the inferior," as the title of a celebrated book of the twenties put it.[9] Aside from a thin minority that was forever being forced into isolation, the public in Germany did not know what to make of politics. The German world was oriented toward private concepts, aims, virtues. No social goals could match the rewards of the private world: family happiness, the emotions aroused by nature, the quiet passions of the study. Joys such as these made a whole world of intelligible satisfactions, and no one was going to abandon them, exchanging the mystery of the forest for the "din of the market place" and the freedom of dreams for constitutional rights.

This feeling also was driven to an extreme. "A political person is repulsive," Richard Wagner wrote to Franz Liszt. One of his admirers has remarked: "If Wagner was in any way an expression of his nation, if there was anything in which he was German, humanistically German and bourgeois German in the highest and purest sense of those words, he was so in his hatred for politics."[10] The antipolitical bias tended to be dressed up as defense of morality against power, of humanity against socialistic trends, of the intellect against public life. From these pairs of opposites, constantly elaborated by new profundities and polemical ponderings, the favorite themes of bourgeois self-examination developed. The supremely brilliant expression of the general attitude, in the form of a complex confession and profession of faith, was Thomas Mann's *Betrachtungen eines Unpolitischen* ("Reflections of a Nonpolitical Man"), published in 1918. It was intended as a brief on the part of culture-proud Germany against the "enlightened," Western "terrorism of politics."

This attitude was also evident in the way the Germans responded when war and the postwar era confronted them squarely with politics. They reacted to the "dirty" revolution with passionate disdain and made a scramble for the traditional escape route that led into aesthetic or mythological realms. In their inability to make any sense of political facts, they spawned all the conspiracy theories that thickened the air during the Weimar years: the myth of the stab in the back, for example, or the theory of the dual menace by a Red (Communist) and a golden (capitalist) International. Anti-Semitism and the widespread anxiety complexes about Freemasons and Jesuits also sprang from the same source. In short, the Germans' abhorrence of politics drove them into an imaginary world full of the romantic concepts of treason, loneliness, and deceived greatness.

What political thought there was was also marked by nonpolitical images. Ideologies were constructed out of "the war experience" and out of such notions as "young nations," "total mobilization" or "barbaric Caesarism." The vast flood of nationalistic and utopian schemes and catchword philosophies of the so-called Conservative Revolution aimed at dressing up the world in the costume of irrationalism. These ideologies pitted their radical slogans against the toilsome compromises of political reality. They passed judgment on everyday life in the name of grandiose myths. It is true that they exerted little direct influence. But by presenting confusing romantic alternatives they contributed to the process of intellectually starving out the republic. This was all the easier because reality had become so hateful that "disgust with politics" could be aroused far more effectively than ever before. While the advocates of Weimar often seemed like apologists for a corrupt system, the attackers of the Right seemed imaginative, overflowing with projects, as they constructed out of mythology, sentimentality, and concentrated bitterness an anti-image to the republic. Among their most contemptuous slurs aimed at the "system" was that it had nothing to offer to the nation but "domestic bliss," consumption, and petty bourgeois epicureanism. Adventure, tragedy, doom—such words fascinated the age. Among Germany's intellectuals, Carl von Ossietzky found many "altruistic lovers of every catastrophe, gourmets of world-political misfortunes." Meanwhile, a French observer at the beginning of the thirties wondered whether Germany's "present crisis is not too passionately and violently felt."[11] In fact, it was this tendency toward melodrama that gave the crisis its hopeless, desperate cast. This in turn made the craving to escape from reality a mass phenomenon and the idea of a heroic leap into the unknown the most familiar of all thoughts.

The phenomenon of Hitler must be seen against this ideological milieu. Sometimes he actually seems the artificial product of these attitudes and complexes: he illustrates so neatly the combination of mythological and rational thinking, the extreme radicality of the socially alienated intellectual. His speeches contain the stock in trade of antipolitical bias as he pours out his hatred for parties, for the compromises of the "system," for the republic's lack of "grandeur." To him politics was a concept closely related to fate, incapable of producing anything of its own accord, needing to be liberated by the strong man, by art, or by a higher power called "Providence." In one of the key speeches he made during the course of the seizure of power—the speech of March 21, that famous "day" of Potsdam—he dealt with the very question of the relationship between political impotence, surrogate reveries and redemption by art as follows:

The German, at odds with himself, with deep divisions in his mind, likewise in his will and therefore impotent in action, becomes powerless to direct his own life. He dreams of justice in the stars and loses his footing on earth. . . . In the end, then, only the inward road remained open for German men. As a nation of singers, poets and thinkers they dreamed of a world in which the others lived, and only when misery and wretchedness dealt them inhuman blows did there perhaps grow up out of art the longing for a new rising, for a new Reich, and therefore for new life.[12]

Once he had given up his dream of being an artist, he came to regard himself as the savior the nation awaited. He considered politics principally as a means to achieve greatness, allowing him to compensate for his inadequate artistic talent by entering upon another grandiloquent role. For all his bathos about art, "the humanities" left him indifferent. The documents that reveal him at his most spontaneous, his early speeches and the table talk at the Führer's headquarters, are convincing evidence of this. Probably few tributes gratified him so much as the remark of Houston Stewart Chamberlain in a letter of October, 1923, hailing him as "the opposite of a politician." Chamberlain had added: "The ideal of politics would be to have none; but this non-politics would have to be frankly acknowledged and imposed upon the world." In this sense Hitler actually had no politics; what he had, rather, was a large, portentous idea of destiny

381

and the world. And with manic persistence he made it the goal of his life to attain that ideal.

Walter Benjamin called Fascism the "aestheticizing of politics." The German conception of politics had always been infected with aesthetics, and Nazism gave a central place to this quality. One of the reasons for the Weimar Republic's failure was that its representatives did not understand the German psychology and thought of politics solely as politics. It remained for Hitler to endow public affairs with the necessary éclat. This he did by his endless obfuscations, his theatrical scenarios, the storms of ecstasy and idolization. Those vaults created by massed searchlight beams were the fitting symbol for it all: walls of magic and light erected against the dark menace of the outside world. And if the Germans did not share Hitler's hunger for space, his anti-Semitism, his vulgar and brutal qualities, they applauded him and followed him because he had once more restored passion to politics, and overlaid it with a note of dire significance.

In keeping with the theory of the unpolitical "aesthetic state," Hitler regarded his artistic and political ideas as a unity and was fond of repeating that his regime had at last reconciled art and politics. He considered himself a ruler in the mold of Pericles and was wont to draw parallels; Albert Speer recalls that he regarded the Autobahnen as his Parthenon.[13] He declared quite seriously that neither Heinrich Himmler nor Rudolf Hess could succeed him because they were "totally unartistic," whereas Speer rose so high and was for a while actually the intended successor to the Führer chiefly because he ranked in Hitler's mind as an "artistic person," an "artist," a "genius." Characteristically, at the beginning of the war, Hitler exempted the artists from military service, but not the scientists and technicians. Even when being shown new weapons, he seldom overlooked the aesthetic form. He was capable, for example, of praising the "elegance" of the barrel on an artillery piece. There was absolutely nothing that mattered outside of art, he would say; even as a general, only an artistic person could be successful. After the victory over France he preferred to enter Paris not as a conqueror but as a sort of museum visitor. His early yearnings for retirement, which later on he expressed with increasing urgency, also sprang from this basic attitude. "I became a politician against my will," he remarked repeatedly. "For me politics is only a means to an end. There are people who think that I would find it hard someday to be no longer active as I am now. Not at all! It will be the best day of my life when I drop out of political life and leave all the worries, the troubles and the vexation behind me. . . . Wars come and go. What remains are the values of culture alone." Hans Frank regarded such sentiments as expressing the tendency of the age: "To be able to banish everything that is connected with governments, war, politics, etc., and to subordinate these to the high ideal of cultural activity." In this context it is significant that the top Nazi leadership consisted of a disproportionately large number of inchoate, frustrated, or failed semiartists. Aside from Hitler, Dietrich Eckart is a case in point. Goebbels had tried his hand as a novelist. Rosenberg had started out as an architect, von Schirach and Hans Frank as poets. Funk dabbled in music. Speer, too, in his determinedly individualistic and nonpolitical stance, may be counted among them. The same is true for that type of intellectual whose aestheticizing pronunciamentos, at once vague and unqualified, accompanied and furthered the rise of National Socialism.

Hitler's private style also exemplified the lack of grip upon reality characteristic of socially alienated intellectuals. Many of his contemporaries noted his tendency to take off, in conversation, into "higher regions," from which he had constantly to be "pulled down to the solid ground of facts," as one of them wrote. Significantly, Hitler gave himself to his fantasies particularly when he was at home at Obersalzberg, or in the Eagle's Nest, which he had built on the Kehlstein above the Berghof, at an altitude of more than 6,000 feet. Here, in thinner air, against the backdrop of the mountains, he thought over his projects; here, he repeatedly said, he had come to all major decisions. But the fantasies of a vast empire extending to the Urals, the wild geopolitical schemes for partitioning the world, the visions of mass slaughter of whole peoples and races, the superman dreams and phantasmagorias of blood purity and Holy Grail, and finally the elaborate diagrams of runways, military installations, and fortified villages conceived on a continental scale—all this in substance can hardly be called "German." What was German about it was only the intellectual consistency with which he constructed these mental systems. What was German also was the merciless rigor, the shrinking from no logical conclusion. Certainly Hitler's harshness stemmed from a monstrous character structure, while his radicality always had something of the brutality of the gutter. But over and beyond that, this radicality may be attributed to the apolitical attitude, the hostility toward reality, which belongs to the intellectual tradition of the country.

On the other hand, what distinguished him from all his ilk was his capacity for political action. He was the exception, the intellectual with a practical understanding of power. More radical postulates than his can easily be found in the texts of his forerunners. Both Germans and other Europeans came out with even stronger anathemas against the present, showed an even stronger aestheticizing contempt for reality. The Futurist Filippo Marinetti, for example, proclaimed redemption from "infamous reality," and in a 1920 manifesto demanded "all power to the artists." But these and similar pronouncements were merely the bombast of intellectuals who were all too conscious of their impotence. What made Hitler the exception once again was his readiness to take his intellectual fictions literally.

It is certainly true that he did not take the Germans by surprise, as the tyrant Pisistratus did the Athenians while they were at table. Like the rest of the world, the Germans could have been warned, since Hitler always set forth his intentions. He had scarcely any intellectual reserve. But the traditional divorce of conceptual from social reality had long ago persuaded Germany that words were cheap, and none seemed less expensive than his. That is the only way to explain the great misjudgment of him, which was also a misjudgment of the times. Rudolf Breitscheid, chairman of the Social Democratic Party faction in the Reichstag, clapped his hands with pleasure when he heard the news of Hitler's appointment as Chancellor. Now at last the man would ruin himself, he said. Breitscheid ultimately died in the Buchenwald concentration camp. Other parliamentarians added up the votes to prove that Hitler would never be able to achieve the two-thirds majority necessary to alter the Constitution. Julius Leber, another leading Social Democrat, remarked sardonically that he was waiting like everybody else in the hope of at last "finding out the intellectual foundations of this movement."[14]

No one seemed to grasp who Hitler really was. The expected sanctions from abroad were never imposed. Instead, foreign governments, with that same combination of blindness, weakness, and hopes of "taming" the wild man that afflicted Germany prepared for the agreements and pacts of the coming years. There were only a few isolated expressions of forebodings, even these mingled with an odd fascination. A German observer in Paris noted among Frenchmen "a feeling as if a volcano has opened up in their immediate vicinity, the eruption of which may devastate their fields and cities any day. Consequently they are watching its slightest stirrings with astonishment and dread. A natural phenomenon which they confront almost helplessly. Today Germany is again the great international star that appears in every newspaper, in every cinema, fascinating the masses with a mixture of fear, incomprehension, and reluctant admiration, to which a goodly dash of delighted malice has been added. Germany is the great, tragic, uncanny, dangerous adventurer."[15]

Scarcely one of the ideas under whose aegis the country began this adventure belonged to it alone. But the inhuman earnestness with which it embarked on its flight from reality was authentically German. The tendencies and biases described above, reinforced by the exacerbated tension between a revolutionary idea formulated a century ago and the immobility of social conditions, gave this emergence extraordinary force, the fury of a belated reaction. The German thunder had reached its goal at last.

But the rejection of reality in the name of radically idealized concepts cannot be suppressed, linked as it is to the spontaneity of the imagination and the risk-taking of thinking. That this involves hazards in the political sphere is undeniable. In the final analysis, however, the German mind owes a good deal of its glory to this tendency, and, despite what many think, not all its issues necessarily lead to Auschwitz.

BOOK V

Seizure of Power

Chapter 1

So then he reached his goal!

Reinhold Hanisch, 1933

That was no victory, for there were no opponents.

Oswald Spengler

LEGAL REVOLUTION

In a tempestuous process lasting only a few months, Hitler both took power and put across a good part of his far-reaching totalitarian claims. According to the sneering commentaries published at the time of his accession to office, he would not survive as Chancellor for very long. Illusions were the order of the day; from the Center all the way to the Social Democratic and the Communist parties he was widely regarded as a "prisoner" of Hugenberg. Skeptical predictions were legion. He would run afoul of the power of his conservative partners in the coalition of Hindenburg and the army, of the resistance of the masses, of the multiplicity and difficulty of the country's economic problems. Or else there would be foreign intervention. Or his amateurishness would be exposed at last. But Hitler gave all these prophecies the lie in an almost unprecedented process of conquering power. Granted, every detail of his actions was not so minutely calculated in advance as may sometimes appear in historical hindsight. But he never forgot for a moment what he was after, namely, to gather all the threads of power into his own hand by the time the eighty-five-year-old President died. And he knew how to go about it: namely, to continue to use those tactics of legality he had so successfully tested in past years. A dynamic program of surprise assaults enabled him to deliver blow upon blow, smashing open each new position the opponent occupied. The discouraged forces that tried to oppose him were given no opportunity to compose themselves and regroup their ranks. They unwittingly threw all kinds of chances into his path, and with growing cleverness he learned to seize them.

Hitler devoted the cabinet session of February 2, 1933, chiefly to preparations for the new elections, in which Hugenberg had reluctantly acquiesced shortly before the swearing-in on January 30. After the ceremony Hitler had promptly provided a reason for these elections by conducting sham negotiations with the Center and being unable to reach agreement. Here was his chance to repair the defeat of the preceding November. If the elections turned out well for him, and with his control of the machinery of government, such a result was assured, he would be able to shake off the control of his German-nationalist partner. Hitler's old comrade Wilhelm Frick, now Minister of the Interior, proposed that the government set aside a million marks for the election campaign. This suggestion was rejected by Finance Minister von Schwerin-Krosigk. Nevertheless, with the power of the state behind him, Hitler no longer needed such additional help to put across that "masterpiece of agitation" foretold by Goebbels in one of his diary entries.

Characteristically, every tactical move henceforth was slanted toward the elections to be held on March 5. Hitler himself signaled the opening of the campaign with a "Proclamation to the German People," which he read on the radio late in the evening of February 1. He had adapted swiftly to his new role and the pose it demanded. Hjalmar Schacht, president of the Reichsbank, was present at the reading and noted Hitler's agitation; he has described how at times "his whole body quivered and shook." But the document itself, which had been offered to all the cabinet members for their approval, adhered to the moderate tone of most proclamations by statesmen. Since the days of treachery in November, 1918, Hitler began, "the Almighty has withheld his blessing from our people." Partisan dissension, hatred and chaos had converted the unity of the nation into "a confusion of political and personal opinions, economic interests, and ideological differences." Since those days Germany "has presented a picture of heartbreaking disunity." He deplored in general terms the inner decay, misery, hunger, lack of dignity, and the disasters of the recent past. He drew an eschatological picture of the last days of a 2,000-year-old culture faced with "a powerful and insidious attack" by Communism:

This negative, destroying spirit spared nothing of all that is highest and most valuable. Beginning with the family, it has undermined the very foundations of morality and faith and scoffs at culture and business, nation and Fatherland, justice and honor. Fourteen years of Marxism have ruined Germany; one year of Bolshevism would destroy her. The richest and fairest territories of the world would be turned into a smoking heap of ruins. Even the sufferings of the last decade and a half could not be compared to the misery of a Europe in the heart of which the red flag of destruction has been hoisted.

The new government would regard it as its task, he declared, "to revive in the nation the spirit of unity and co-operation." He would be pledged to foster "Christianity as the foundation of our national morality, and the family as the basis of racial and political life." He promised to eliminate class struggle and to restore traditions to honor. The economy would be reconstructed by means of two great Four Year Plans (the principle of which was borrowed from the Marxist enemy). As for foreign policy, Hitler spoke of Germany's right to live, but reassured the foreign powers with placatory formulas of eagerness for reconciliation. His government, he concluded, was "determined to rectify in four years the ills of fourteen years." But before going on to a pious appeal for God's blessing on the work, he made it plain that his administration would not be bound by constitutional checks: "It cannot make the work of reconstruction dependent upon the approval of those who were responsible for the collapse. The Marxist parties and their leaders have had fourteen years to show what they can do. The result is a heap of ruins."

On the whole, this address had demonstrated his capacity for restraint. But only two days later he threw off that restraint when he met with the commanders of the Reichswehr in the official residence of General von Hammerstein, the army commander in chief. Busy as he was, he had been impatient for this encounter. The reason lay not only in the key position he assigned to the military in his concept for the conquest of power. Rather, in the exhilaration of these first days in office he wanted to find others to share his grand perspectives—despite his usual bent for secrecy. In the grip of this feeling, Hitler unveiled his entire plan with remarkable candor to the army commanders.

According to one of the participants, von Hammerstein "somewhat condescendingly and 'benevolently' introduced the 'Chancellor of the Reich'; the phalanx of generals responded with polite coolness; Hitler made modest, awkward bows in all directions and remained embarrassed until the time came for him to make a long after-dinner speech." He assured the army, as the sole bearer of arms, a tranquil period of development and explained right at the outset his idea of the primacy of domestic politics. The most urgent aim of the new government was to recapture political power by the "complete reversal of present conditions in domestic politics," by ruthless extermination of Marxism and pacifism, and by creation of a broadly based state of preparedness for attack and defense. This was to be done by "stringently authoritarian administration." Only this, combined with a shrewd foreign policy, would put the country in a fit position to take up the struggle against the Versailles Treaty. This would be followed by a concentration of power for the "conquest of new living space in the East and its ruthless Germanization."

By now Hitler was no longer content to justify his expansionist aims on grounds of military geography and the need to acquire new sources of food. To these arguments he now added the Depression, whose cause, he claimed to be lack of *Lebensraum* and whose cure lay in conquering *Lebensraum*. As he examined the situation, the only doubtful aspects seemed the coming years of concealed political and military rebuilding; during this period they would all find out whether France possessed statesmen. "If so, she will not allow us time, but will fall upon us (probably with eastern satellites)," one of those present recalled him saying.

This speech is another example of Hitler's tendency to make new combinations out of disparate ideas. The structure of his thinking was such that he understood every phenomenon merely as a further argument for ideas long ago fixed—even if that involved grotesquely misunderstanding the nature of the phenomena, as he was doing with regard to the Depression. And, as always, the only solution he recognized was in the realm of violence. At the same time, the speech also reveals the continuity in Hitler's thought. It gives the lie to those theorists who maintain that responsibility did indeed have a moderating effect upon him, and pretend to see a later change in Hitler's personality—usually ascribed to the year 1938—when he fell back into the old aggressive hate complexes or, according to another version, into a new pathological system of delusions.

Though Hitler freely borrowed the well-tested Bolshevik and Fascist formulas for the *coup d'état,* he was highly original in the methods by which he consolidated his new-won power. He may be credited with inventing the classical method by which democratic institutions are crushed from within and totalitarian rule imposed with the full aid of the pre-existent state.

It was important, first of all, to adapt the terrorist practices of the preceding months to the new situation. Thus, while he continued to send his brown auxiliary troops on revolutionary rampages, he permitted a few of these "excesses" to be punished by legal action. In any particular case it would be difficult to say that justice was being done, but the impression was created that the Nazis were maintaining discipline. A convincing screen of legality concealed the real nature of the regime.

Similarly, many of the old institutional façades were left intact. In their shadow fundamental upheavals in all conditions and relationships could be carried on unhindered, until at last people no longer knew whether the system was acting justly or unjustly and could no longer decide between loyalty and opposition. Thus the paradoxical concept of the legal revolution was a good deal "more than a propagandistic trick." It was basic to Hitler's whole program for entrenching himself. Hitler himself later declared that Germany at that time thirsted for order, so that he was obliged to shun any open use of force. In one of his despairing moods during the last days of January, when he was reviewing all the mistakes and omissions of the past, he roundly condemned the Germans' craving for law and order. Their mania for legalism and profound dislike of chaos had made the revolution of 1918 an indecisive affair, but it had also caused his own failure in the Munich putsch of 1923. He blamed himself along with all other Germans for the halfway measures, the compromises, and the

390

eschewing of a bloody surprise operation: "Had we gone ahead as we should have, thousands would have been eliminated at that time. . . . Only afterwards does one regret having been so good."

At the moment, to be sure, the strategy of encasing a revolution within a legal framework was proving highly successful. Before February was over, three decrees decided the whole future course of events—and yet their legitimacy seemed guaranteed by the bourgeois associates at Hitler's side, by Hindenburg's signature, and by the accompanying fog of nationalistic slogans. As early as February 4 the decree "For the protection of the German people" was issued. It permitted the government on the vaguest grounds to forbid political meetings and ban the newspapers and publications of the rival parties. Almost at once the government moved against deviant political views of all kinds. A congress of leftist intellectuals and artists was banned shortly after it opened, purportedly because of atheistic statements made by some of the delegates. Two days later another emergency measure, a kind of second *coup d'état,* ordered dissolution of the Prussian Landtag; an attempt to dissolve the Prussian legislature by parliamentary means had just failed. Another two days later Hitler, addressing German journalists, justified the emergency decree of February 4 by pointing to certain newspaper criticisms of Richard Wagner; his purpose was "to preserve the present-day press from similar errors." Along with this he threatened harsh measures against all those "who consciously want to harm Germany." Meanwhile, the general public was being fed carefully calculated bulletins to bring out the human side of the new Chancellor. On February 5 the Reich press agency of the National Socialist Party announced that Adolf Hitler, "who personally is also deeply attached to Munich," was keeping his apartment in that city and had resolved not to accept his Chancellor's salary.

With every day that passed the Nazis were penetrating deeper into the administrative apparatus. Hitler's script for legal revolution had assigned a special role to Göring, whose fatness lent a jovial note to outright brutality. According to the new arrangements, von Papen held governmental authority in Prussia; but the real power was in Göring's hands. While the Vice-Chancellor continued to hope that his "educational work in the cabinet" would succeed, Göring was installing a number of so-called honorary commissioners in the Prussian Ministry of the Interior. Such men as SS Oberführer Kurt Daluege at once took hold in this ministry, which constituted the largest administrative apparatus in Germany. By a massive series of personnel shifts, dismissals, and appointments "the System bigwigs are being thrown out one after the other," as a contemporary report put it. "From high-ranking official down to doorkeeper, this ruthless purge is going on."

Göring kept his eye particularly on the police chiefs; within a short time he replaced most of them by high-ranking SA leaders. On February 17 he

391

issued a decree ordering the police to "establish the finest concord with the nationalist associations (SA, SS, and Stahlhelm)," but in dealing with the Left the police were "to make free use of their weapons whenever necessary." In a later speech he explicitly confirmed these instructions: "Every bullet that is now fired from the barrel of a police pistol is my bullet. If that is called murder, then I have committed murder, for I have ordered it all; I take the responsibility for it."

Out of an inconspicuous minor department in Berlin police headquarters, which had been detailed to keep watch on anti-Constitutional activities, Göring began building the Geheime Staatspolizei (Secret State Police), soon to become notorious as the Gestapo. Within four years, its budget had increased forty times. It had 4,000 men in Berlin alone. In order to "relieve the burden on the ordinary police in special cases," on February 22 Göring set up an auxiliary police force approximately 50,000 strong, consisting chiefly of SA and SS men. This amounted to dropping the fiction of police neutrality and openly admitting the link between the party toughs and the forces of law and order. Henceforth, Nazi excesses became governmental action. "My measures," Göring boasted, "will not be sicklied o'er by any legal scruples. My measures will not be sicklied o'er by any bureaucracy. It's not my business to do justice; it's my business to annihilate and exterminate, that's all!"

This challenge was directed chiefly against the Communists. Not only were they the main enemy; they also would hold the balance in the next Reichstag. Three days after the formation of the cabinet, Göring had already banned all Communist meetings in Prussia in response to the Communist Party's call for a general strike and demonstrations. Nevertheless, the muffled civil war continued; in the first few days of February there were clashes costing fifteen lives and ten times that number of wounded. On February 24 the police made a large-scale raid on the Communist Party headquarters, Karl Liebknecht House on Bülow Platz in Berlin. It had long since been abandoned by the Communist Party leadership, but the very next day the press and radio reported sensational finds of "tons of treasonous materials." Subsequently these documents—which were never published—provided Nazi electioneering with atrocity stories of a projected Communist revolution: "The populace is to be terrified and cowed by preliminary measures involving murderous attacks etc. upon leaders of the nation and government, assaults upon vital factories and public buildings, poisoning of entire groups of especially feared persons, the taking of hostages, the kidnapping of wives and children of prominent men," the police report stated. Nevertheless, the Communist Party was not banned, for that might have driven its voters into the arms of the Social Democratic Party.

The Nazis intensified their propaganda to make this campaign the noisiest and wildest of all the electoral battles of recent years. Hitler himself, who again made the greatest impact, had opened the campaign with a major speech in the Berlin Sportpalast. In it he verbosely repeated the old cry of fourteen years of shame and misery, the old denunciations of the November criminals and the parties of the "system," and the old formulas for salvation. He ended on a pseudoreligious note. He had, he cried, the "rock-hard conviction that sooner or later the hour will come in which the millions who hate us today will stand behind us and together with us will hail what we have jointly created, toilsomely struggled for, bitterly paid for: the new German Reich of greatness and honor and power and glory and justice. Amen!"

Once again all technical media were utilized—this time with the prestige and support of the government. The country was inundated with appeals, slogans, parades, displays of banners. Once again Hitler was flying over Germany. Goebbels had hit on a new propaganda tool—radio. "Our opponents did not know what to do with its possibilities," the propaganda chief wrote. "We must learn all the better how to handle it." As Hitler visited city after city, the local radio station was to report on his appearance. "We will have our broadcasts held in the midst of the people and so give the listener a vivid picture of what goes on at our meetings. For each of the Führer's speeches I myself will give an introduction in which I mean to try to convey to the listener the magic and the atmosphere of our mass demonstrations."

A considerable portion of the expenses for the election campaign was obtained at an affair in the palace of the Reichstag President, to which Göring invited a number of leading businessmen on February 20. Among the participants were Hjalmar Schacht, Krupp von Bohlen, Albert Vögler of Vereinigte Stahlwerke (United Steel), Georg von Schnitzler of I. G. Farben, the banker Kurt von Schröder, and other representatives of heavy industry, mining, and banking. In his speech to these notables Hitler once again emphasized the difference between the authoritarian ideology of employers and the democratic Constitution, which he derided as the political expression of weakness and decadence. He hailed the tightly organized ideological state as the sole possible means for combating the Communist menace, and lauded the supreme right of the great individual. He had refused to be merely tolerated by the Center, he continued. Hugenberg and the German Nationalists were only holding him back. To vanquish the enemy once and for all, he must have full control of the state. In language that abandoned even the sham of legality, he called upon his listeners for financial assistance: "We now are facing the last election. Whatever its outcome, there is no going backward. . . . One way or another, if the election does not decide, the decision will have to be taken in another way." Göring followed up the appeal with a few remarks. The contribution, he said, "would surely come all the more easily to industry if it knew that the election on March 5 would surely be the last for ten years, or even for a hundred years." Thereupon Schacht turned to the company, saying, "And now, gentlemen, to the cashier!" He proposed the creation of an "election fund" and promptly collected from the leading industrial firms at least 3 million marks, possibly more.[1]

In his campaign speeches, too, Hitler abandoned a good deal of his restraint. "The period of international babble, the promise of reconciliation among nations, is over and done with; its place will be taken by the German People's Community," he declared in Kassel. In Stuttgart he promised to "burn out the symptoms of rottenness and eliminate the poison." He was determined, he said, "under no circumstances to let Germany fall back into the past regime." He carefully avoided defining his program in detail ("We do not want to lie and we do not want to deceive . . . and give cheap promises"); his only specific statement was his pledge "never, never . . . to depart from the task of exterminating Marxism and everything connected with it" in Germany. The "first point" in his program would be to notify the adversary: "Away with all illusions!" Four years hence he would give the German people another chance to vote for him, but he would give no such opportunity to the parties of disintegration. Then let the German people judge, he exclaimed, falling into that messianic tone to which he was so prone at that period. He would admit no other judge, but "for my part the people may crucify me if they think that I have not done my duty."[2]

One of the stratagems of legal revolution was not to openly crush the adversary, but instead to provoke him to acts of violence so that he himself provided the pretext for legal measures of repression. Goebbels described these tactics in a diary note dated January 31: "For the present we intend to refrain from direct countermeasures [against the Communists]. First the Bolshevist attempt at revolution must flare up. Then we will strike at the proper moment." This was Hitler's old dream: to be called in at the climax of a Communist uprising, and annihilate the great foe in a single dramatic clash. Then he would be hailed by the nation as the restorer of order and granted legitimacy and respect. As early as the first cabinet meeting of January 30, therefore, he had dismissed Hugenberg's proposal that the Communist Party be banned outright, its seats in the Reichstag withdrawn, thus assuring a parliamentary majority by doing away with the need for new elections.

He was worried, however, that the Communists might be in no position for a full-scale, vigorous act of rebellion. At various times he had expressed doubts of their revolutionary impetus—which, incidentally, Goebbels had also done early in 1932 when he said he could no longer see them as a danger. As a matter of fact, Nazi propaganda had to work hard to create the necessary bogey man. The revelations about the tons of seditious material found in Communist Party headquarters served this purpose along with a flock of rumors, obviously inspired by the Nazis themselves from the middle of February on, concerning a plan to assassinate Hitler. Rosa Luxemburg's vain question of 1918, "Where is the German proletariat?" remained unanswered this time as well. To be sure, a few street battles occurred during the early weeks of February, but these were all local clashes. There was no sign of a centrally directed attempt at a major uprising of the sort that could stimulate full-blown anxiety complexes. Partly, the reason for this was the Depression and the depleted energies of the working class. But the principal reason was the grotesque error of the Communist leadership in its estimate of the historical situation. In spite of persecution and torture, the flight of many comrades and the mass defections of their followers, the Communists clung to their doctrine that the real enemy was Social Democracy, that there was nothing to choose between Fascism and parliamentary democracy, and that Hitler was merely a puppet whose installation in power was only bringing the victory of Communism closer. In this stage of history, the Communist leaders preached, patience was the supreme revolutionary virtue.

These tactical errors evidently expressed an underlying shift in the realities of power. One of the strange aspects of the seizure of power was the disappearance of the enemy at the moment of confrontation. For a long time the Communists had provided Nazism with psychological nourishment. The Red menace had been the crucial inspiration, had sparked the growth of National Socialism into a mass movement. Now a Communist following numbering millions, forming a powerful and effective threat, terrifying the bourgeoisie, had evaporated without even token resistance, without dramatic action, without so much as sounding the trumpet blast for "the final conflict." If we accept the principle that we cannot speak of Fascism without mentioning both capitalism and Communism, the historical links to both were snapped at this time. Henceforth Fascism was neither an instrument nor a negation nor a mirror image of anything. During those days of the seizure of power it came into its own. And from then on, right to the end, Communism would not again emerge as a counterforce provoking a Fascist reaction.

The dramatic Reichstag fire of February 28, 1933, must be seen against this background, as well as the years of discussion that followed over the authorship of this deed. The Communists always passionately denied any connection with the fire, and in fact they had no motive whatsoever for it. For this very reason it was possible to paint a convincing picture of Nazi responsibility, since the fire fitted so neatly into the pattern of Hitler's strategy. For a long time the argument that the Nazis themselves were the incendiaries went almost unchallenged, although details remained unclarified.

In the early sixties Fritz Tobias published a study of the Reichstag fire which analyzed the many crude partisan fictions and myths that had grown up around the subject. Tobias came to the conclusion that the Nazis did not set fire to the Reichstag, that the act was in fact committed by the half-naked Dutchman Marinus van der Lubbe who was caught in the burning building, dripping with sweat and triumphantly babbling, "Protest! Protest!" Tobias mustered a good deal of convincing evidence for his thesis. But considerable doubts remain, and the controversy has continued.[3] We need not go into it ourselves, since the question of what individual set the fire is a criminological one, with only small bearing on our understanding of the political currents. By instantly taking advantage of the fire to further their plans for dictatorship, the Nazis made the deed their own and manifested their complicity in a sense that is independent of "whodunit" questions. In Nuremberg Göring admitted that the wave of arrests and persecutions would have been carried out in any case, that the Reichstag fire only accelerated those steps.[4]

The first measures were taken at once, right on the spot. Hitler had been spending the evening of February 27 in Goebbels's apartment on Reichskanzlerplatz. A telephone call from Hanfstaengl informed Goebbels that the Reichstag was in flames. Goebbels at first assumed that this report was a "wild fantasy" and forbore to tell Hitler. But, shortly afterward, the news was confirmed, and he then passed it on. Hitler's spontaneous exclamation, "Now I have them," indicated how he meant to use the event tactically and propagandistically. Immediately afterward, the two raced "at sixty miles an hour" down Charlottenburger Chaussee to the Reichstag. Clambering over fire hoses, they finally reached the grand lobby. Here they met Göring, who had arrived first and was "going great guns." He had already issued the obvious statements about an organized political action by the Communists, statements that immediately prejudiced political, journalistic, and criminological opinion. One of Göring's associates of that period, Rudolf Diels, who later became first chief of the Gestapo, has provided a description of the scene:

When I entered, Göring strode forward to meet me. His voice rang with all the fateful emotions of that dramatic hour: "This is the beginning of the Communist uprising. Now they are going to strike. Not a minute must be lost!"

Göring was unable to continue. Hitler turned to the assemblage. Now I saw that his face was flaming red from excitement and from the heat which had accumulated under the dome. As if he were going to burst, he screamed in an utterly uncontrolled manner such as I had never before witnessed in him: "Now there can be no mercy; whoever gets in our way will be cut down. The German people will not put up with leniency. Every Communist functionary will be shot wherever we find him. The Communist deputies must be hanged this very night. Everyone in alliance with the Communists is to be arrested. We are not going to spare the Social Democrats and members of the Reichsbanner either!

Meanwhile, Göring ordered the entire police force on maximum emergency footing. That night some 4,000 functionaries were arrested; most of

396

them were members of the Communist Party, but included in the bag were some writers, doctors, and lawyers whom the Nazis disliked, among them Carl von Ossietzky, Ludwig Renn, Erich Mühsam, and Egon Erwin Kisch. Several Social Democratic Party headquarters and newspaper offices were occupied. "If resistance is offered," Goebbels threatened, "then clear the streets for the SA." And although most of those arrested had to be fetched out of their beds, and the Reichstag faction leader of the Communist Party, Ernst Torgler, voluntarily surrendered to the police in order to demonstrate the untenability of the charges, the first official account— dated that very February 27!—stated:

The burning of the Reichstag was intended to be the signal for a bloody uprising and civil war. Large-scale pillaging in Berlin was planned for as early as four o'clock in the morning on Tuesday. It has been determined that starting today throughout Germany acts of terrorism were to begin against prominent individuals, against private property, against the lives and safety of the peaceful population, and general civil war was to be unleashed. . . .

Warrants have been issued for the arrest of two leading Communist Reichstag deputies on grounds of urgent suspicion. The other deputies and functionaries of the Communist Party are being taken into protective custody. Communist newspapers, magazines, leaflets and posters are banned for four months throughout Prussia. For two weeks all newspapers, magazines, leaflets and posters of the Social Democratic Party are banned. . . .

Next morning Hitler, accompanied by Papen, called on the President. After giving a highly colored account of the events, he placed a prepared emergency decree before Hindenburg for signature. It utilized the pretext of the fire in truly comprehensive fashion, annulling all important fundamental rights of citizens, considerably extending the list of crimes subject to the death penalty, and providing the Reich government with numerous levers against the states. "People behaved as if stunned," a contemporary noted. The Communist threat was taken very seriously by the ordinary man. Apartment houses organized guards against the feared pillaging. Peasants set up watches at springs and wells for fear of their being poisoned. These fears, further fanned by the whole propaganda apparatus of government and party, made it possible for the moment for Hitler to do almost anything. And with great presence of mind he made the most of the opportunity. Yet it remains incomprehensible that Papen and his conservative fellow "tamers" approved a decree that snatched all power from their hands and enabled the National Socialist revolution to burst through all the dikes.

The decisive factor was that the conservatives made no effort to preserve the rights of habeas corpus. This "fearful gap" meant that henceforth there was no limit to outrages by the state. The police could arbitrarily "arrest and extend the period of detention indefinitely. They could leave relatives without any news concerning the reasons for the arrest and the fate of the person arrested. They could prevent a lawyer or other persons from visiting

him or examining the files on the case. . . . They could crush their
prisoner with work, give him the vilest food and shelter, force him to repeat
hated slogans or sing songs. They could torture him. . . . No court would
ever find the case in its files. No court had the right to interfere, even if a
judge unofficially obtained knowledge of the circumstances."[5]

The emergency decree "for the protection of the people and the state,"
supplemented by another decree "against betrayal of the German people
and treasonous machinations" issued that same day, proved to be the
decisive legal basis for Nazi rule and undoubtedly the most important law
ever laid down in the Third Reich. The decree replaced a constitutional
government by a permanent state of emergency. It has been trenchantly
pointed out that this decree, not the Enabling Act passed a few weeks later,
provided the legal basis for the regime. The decree remained in force until
1945; it provided the sham of a legal basis for persecution, totalitarian
terrorism, and the repression of the German resistance right up to July 20,
1944. At the same time, one of its side effects was that the Nazis' authority
stood or fell on the thesis that the Communists had set the Reichstag fire.
The subsequent trial, which could prove only the guilt of van der Lubbe,
had to be regarded as a grave defeat for the Nazis. In these aspects, not in
the criminological details, the crucial historical importance of the Reichstag fire lies. When Sefton Delmer, the correspondent of the London *Daily
Express,* asked Hitler whether there was any truth to the rumors of an
impending massacre of the domestic opposition, Hitler could reply sarcastically: "My dear Delmer, I need no St. Bartholomew's Night. By the
decrees issued legally we have appointed tribunals which will try enemies
of the State legally, and deal with them legally in a way which will put an
end to these conspiracies." The number of persons arrested in Prussia
alone within two weeks after the decree of February 28 has been estimated
at more than 10,000. Beside himself with delight at the way things were
going, Goebbels commented, "Once again it is a joy to live!"[6]

Goebbels had proclaimed March 5, the date of the election, "the day of
the awakening nation." All mass demonstrations were now directed toward
it. The wild momentum of the Nazis' propaganda activities all but drove
their German Nationalist partners from the scene. The other parties were
hounded and hectored, while the police looked on in silence. By election
day the casualties among the opponents of the Nazis amounted to fifty-one
dead and several hundred injured. The Nazis, for their part, had lost
eighteen dead. The *Völkische Beobachter* quite rightly compared the
NSDAP's agitation and propaganda to "hard hammer blows."

The eve of the election was celebrated with a grandiose spectacle in
Königsberg. Hitler ended his speech with an injunction to the German
people: "Now hold your heads high and proud, once again! Now you are
no longer enslaved and unfree; now you are free again . . . by God's

gracious aid." Whereupon the strains of a hymn rang out, the final stanza sung amid the clangor of bells from Königsberg cathedral. All radio stations had been instructed to broadcast the event live, and, according to a party directive, every station "that has the technical means will transmit the Chancellor's voice to the street." After the broadcast SA columns started marching throughout the country, while on the mountains and along the frontier so-called freedom fires were kindled. "It will be an enormous victory," the organizers exulted.

Their disappointment was all the greater when the results were announced on the evening of March 5. With nearly 89 per cent of the electorate voting, the Nazi party won 288 seats. Their Nationalist coalition partners won 52. The Center retained their 73 seats, the Social Democratic Party held its own with 120, and even the Communists had lost only 19 of their 100 seats. The Nazis achieved real successes only in the South German states of Württemberg and Bavaria, where their representation had hitherto been less than their average for the country. But they missed the majority they had hoped for by nearly 40, winning 43.9 per cent of the votes. In a formal sense at least, therefore, Hitler was still dependent on the support of Papen and Hugenberg, whose share of the vote assured him a scanty majority of 51.9 per cent. In Göring's apartment, where he heard the returns, he had muttered that as long as Hindenburg lived they would not be able to get rid of "that gang," by which he meant his German Nationalist partners in the coalition. Goebbels, however, exclaimed: "What do figures matter now? We're the masters in the Reich and in Prussia." An editorial by Goebbels in *Der Angriff* advised the Reichstag, with astonishing cheek, "to make . . . no difficulties for the administration and let things take their course."

It was part of the whole approach to the seizure of power, and part of Nazi psychology in general, to think only in terms of triumph, to counter all appearances by celebrating even the severest setbacks as victories. In spite of their disappointment the Nazis therefore pretended that the election results were an overwhelming success and made this assumed success the basis for a historic mission—"to execute the verdict that the people have passed upon Marxism." Immediately after the election the Center protested the raising of the swastika flag on public buildings. Göring haughtily replied that "the preponderant part of the German population" had declared its adherence to the swastika flag on March 5. He added: "I am responsible for seeing that the will of the majority of the German people is observed, but not the wishes of a group which apparently has failed to understand the signs of the times."

In the cabinet session of March 7 Hitler brashly claimed that the election had been a "revolution." During the next four days he seized control in the states in the equivalent of a *coup d'état*. The SA everywhere played its customary part of embodying the wrath of a people outraged beyond the

399

point of self-control. Storm troopers marched through the streets, besieged government offices, demanded the deposition of mayors, police commissioners, and finally the state governments themselves. In Hamburg, Bremen, and Lübeck, the Free Cities, and in Hesse, Baden-Württemberg, and Saxony the same procedures forced the governments to resign and thus left the road clear for a "nationalist" cabinet.

Sometimes the careful language of legality cracked, and the real voice of the new masters was heard. "The government will strike down with all brutality anyone who opposes it," Wilhelm Murr, gauleiter of Württemberg, declared after his manipulated election as the new governor of the state. "We do not say: an eye for an eye, a tooth for a tooth. No, if anyone strikes an eye from us, we will chop off his head, and if anyone knocks out one of our teeth, we will smash in his jaw." In Bavaria Gauleiter Adolf Wagner, assisted by Ernst Röhm and Heinrich Himmler, forced Premier Held to resign on March 9 and promptly had the government building occupied. In Munich a few days earlier the state government, in an effort to fend off *Gleichschaltung* (forcible co-ordination), had considered restoring the monarchy under Crown Prince Rupprecht. The Bavarians warned that they would arrest any Reich commissioner who attempted to cross the line of the Main River. But now it turned out that the Reich commissioner had long been inside the country and that his popularity was far greater than that of any ministers of the state government. On March 9 state governmental authority was transferred to General von Epp, the same von Epp who had smashed soviet rule in Bavaria in 1919. Three days later, Hitler came to Munich. That morning he had announced over the radio that the black-red-gold colors of the Weimar Republic were abolished; henceforth the black-white-red flag and the swastika flag would together constitute the colors of the nation. Simultaneously, "to celebrate the victory" of the Nationalist forces, he had ordered a three-day display of flags. Now he declared "the first part of the struggle" ended, and added: "The co-ordination of the political will of the states with the will of the nation has been completed."

The fact was that co-ordination—*Gleichschaltung*—was the peculiar form in which the Nazi revolution was carried to completion. In the preceding years Hitler had repeatedly decried old-fashioned and sentimental revolutionaries who saw in revolution "a spectacle for the masses." "We aren't wild-eyed revolutionaries who are counting on the lumpenproletariat." The revolution Hitler had in mind was not a matter of rioting but of directed confusion, not anarchy but the triumph of orderly violence. He therefore noted with distinct displeasure the acts of terrorism that erupted immediately after the election, committed by SA men additionally inflamed by the noisy slogans of victory. Such acts disturbed him not because they were violent, but because they were undirected. In the Chemnitz district of Saxony five Communists were murdered within two days, and the editor of

400

a Social Democratic newspaper was shot down. In Gleiwitz a hand grenade was thrown through the window of a Center deputy. In Düsseldorf armed storm troopers forced their way into a meeting being held by the mayor and lashed one of the participants with a whip. In Dresden the SA broke up a concert by the conductor Fritz Busch. In Kiel they killed a Social Democratic lawyer. They harassed Jewish businesses, released party members from prison, occupied banks, forced the dismissal of politically unpalatable officials. The number of deaths within the first few months has been reckoned at between 500 and 600; the number of those swept off to the abject concentration camps—the establishment of which was announced by Frick as early as March 8—has been estimated at about 100,000.

As always in Nazi behavior, the motive forces are a tangle of political elements, personal spite, and cold calculation. This is apparent from the names of some of the victims. Alongside the anarchist poet Erich Mühsam, we find, in the list of the murdered, the theatrical agent Rotter and his wife; the former Nazi deputy Schäfer, who had given the Boxheim Papers to the authorities; the professional clairvoyant Hanussen; Major Hunglinger of the Bavarian police, who had opposed Hitler at the Bürgerbräukeller on November 9, 1923; the former SS leader Erhard Heiden; and, finally, one Ali Höhler, who happened to be the killer of Horst Wessel.

Yet Hitler assumed a sharp and injured tone when reproved by his bourgeois partners for the mounting "rule of the streets." He told Papen that in fact he admired "the incredible discipline" of his SA and SS men. "Some day the judgment of history will not spare us a reproach because in a historic hour, ourselves perhaps already sicklied o'er by the weakness and cowardice of our bourgeois world, we proceeded with kid gloves instead of with an iron fist." He would not let anyone deter him from his mission of exterminating Marxism, he said, and therefore "most insistently" requested Papen "henceforth no longer to bring up these complaints."

Nevertheless, on March 10 he told the SA and SS "to see to it that the nationalist revolution of 1933 will never be compared with the revolution of knapsack Spartacists in 1918."[7]

The SA men took such restraints in bad part. They had always assumed that coming to power would entitle them to the open use of force without having to account to anyone. Their brutalities, in fact, were meant in part to "give the revolution its true tone." For years they had been promised that after victory Germany would belong to them. Was this pledge to turn into a mere figure of speech? To their minds, very specific things went with it; they were counting on being made officers and administrative chiefs, on receiving sinecures and pensions. But Hitler's plan merely envisaged—at least in its first phase—sufficient pressure to bring about a complete change of personnel in key positions. As for the great mass of smaller bureaucrats, Hitler counted on their being tricked or frightened into co-operation. But the storm troopers had to be mollified as well. "The hour for smashing the

Communists is coming!" he promised them as early as the beginning of February.

The disappointments of the SA constituted the hopes of the bourgeoisie. That class had looked to the brown pretorians to restore order, not to make things worse by excesses, killings, and the establishment of sinister concentration camps. They were therefore pleased to see that the SA was being set to such harmless activities as going around with collection boxes or marching in a body to church services. The deceptive notion of a moderate Hitler, the guardian of law and order, forever trying to subdue his radical followers—this notion so necessary for his good repute came into being in this early period.

In addition Nazi propaganda had coined a "second magic phrase" that immensely assisted the process of legal revolution. This phrase was the "National Rising." It could serve as camouflage for the most brazen behavior on the part of the Nazis and as a cloak for a good many acts of violence. Moreover, it offered a slogan full of reverberations to a country still suffering from national inferiority feelings. By such creative use of language the Nazis were able to accomplish their aims and paralyze a broad sector of the public, from their conservative colleagues in the cabinet to the ordinary bourgeois citizen. They encountered no resistance. On the contrary, their seizure of power was actually hailed as a "nonpartisan" breakthrough.

Such was the pattern of thought and feeling that was imposed upon the nation and from which there was henceforth no escape. At its center, subject to innumerable and sometimes grotesque variations, stood the propaganda creation known as the *Volkskanzler,* the populist Chancellor remote from partisan disputes and petty selfish interests, concerned only with the law and the good of the nation. Goebbels personally now assumed the task of constructing and cultivating this image. On March 13 Hindenburg had signed the measure installing Goebbels in the post planned for him from the start but so far postponed out of consideration for the other partners in the coalition, the post of Reich Minister for People's Enlightenment and Propaganda. In establishing the Propaganda Ministry Hitler was riding roughshod over his previous pledge that the composition of the cabinet would be unalterable.

The new minister snatched sizable administrative areas from his colleagues. But at the same time he adopted a manner of courteous urbanity that contrasted favorably with the victory-drunk, "slap-in-the-face" tone taken by most of the Nazi leaders. In his first speech to the press, in which he outlined his program, he stated that "in instituting the new Ministry the government is carrying out its plan of no longer neglecting the people. This government is a people's government. . . . The new Ministry will enlighten the people concerning the plans of the administration, with the aim of establishing political coordination [*Gleichschaltung*] between the people and the government."

Hitler had had to justify the establishment of the new ministry to the rest of the cabinet; he did so on the most innocent grounds, though with a good measure of irony. He made a great point, for example, of the need to prepare the people for what was going to be done about the oil and fats problem. And in fact his explanation was accepted without demur. It testifies to Hitler's tact and magnetism that within a few weeks the conservatives had entirely forgotten their intention of "taming" him. Papen showed himself abjectly accommodating; Blomberg had succumbed all too readily when Hitler laid on the charm; Hugenberg muttered a bit under his breath, but that was all. The others scarcely counted. The task for which Goebbels was actually appointed, and into which he flung himself without delay, consisted in preparing the new government's first public function, which was intended to pave the way psychologically for the planned Enabling Act. Of course, Hitler could have put across this law—which was meant as a "death blow" to the parliamentary system—by invoking the Reichstag fire decree and on the basis of that arresting enough deputies of the Left parties until he had attained the requisite two-thirds majority. As a matter of fact, Frick presented this possibility to the cabinet, citing figures, and it was discussed.[8] But Hitler could also choose a formally correct course and attempt to win the consent of the Center parties. It is characteristic of his tactical style that Hitler used both approaches.

While the deputies of the Communist Party and the Social Democratic Party were intimidated, and many of them arrested, Hitler courted the bourgeois parties in the most ostentatious fashion—though not without reminding them, too, of the powers given him by the Reichstag fire emergency decree of February 28. His pronounced nationalistic pose of that period, his evocations of Christian morality, his bows to tradition, and in general the civil, statesmanlike, controlled manner he adopted were a part of the sham. His courtship of the bourgeoisie reached its apogee on the day of Potsdam.

That day was also the first test for the new Propaganda Minister, and he passed it brilliantly. Just as he had declared election day, March 5, the "Day of the Awakening Nation," he now declared March 21, when the first Reichstag session of the Third Reich was to be held, the "Day of the National Rising." A solemn state function in the Potsdam Garrison Church, above the tomb of Frederick the Great, was to mark the opening of the Reichstag. Potsdam, the soberly graceful residence of the Prussian kings, was linked in many ways to the sense of national pride, and so was the date. March 21 was not only the first day of spring but also the day on which Bismarck in 1871 had opened the first German Reichstag, thus celebrating a turning point in history.

Goebbels had directed every phase of the ceremony, and Hitler approved every detail of the script. The scenes that later seemed so overwhelming or so moving—the precise order of the marching columns, the child with a bunch of flowers by the roadside, the guns firing salutes, the sight of white-

bearded veterans of the wars of 1864, 1866, and 1871, the troops presenting arms, the organ music—all this compelling mixture of tight precision
and loose sentimentality was the product of cool planning and a remarkable instinct for theater. Goebbels had gone to have a look at the site
beforehand and had noted: "With such great state ceremonies, the smallest
touches matter."

Significantly, the festive day began with services in the Protestant
Nikolaikirche. Shortly after ten o'clock the first columns of automobiles
arrived from Berlin and made their way slowly through streets jammed
with people. In the cars sat Hindenburg, Göring, Papen, Frick, Reichstag
deputies, SA leaders, generals: the old and the new Germany. Along the
façades of the buildings hung garlands and bright tapestries; everywhere
flags were festooned, the black-white-red alternating with the swastika
flags, in a striking symbol of the new order. Hindenburg in his old field
marshal's uniform—he now more and more preferred it to the civilian
black tailcoat—entered the church. After the service he was driven around
the city. The Center deputies attended the Catholic services at the church
of St. Peter and Paul. Hitler and Goebbels stayed away "because of the
hostile attitude of the Catholic episcopate." But then, among the others
absent from this "people's festival of national unity" were the Communists
and Social Democrats, some of whom—as Frick had boldly announced on
March 14—were detained "by urgent and more useful work . . . in the
concentration camps."

Shortly before twelve o'clock Hindenburg and Hitler met on the steps of
the Garrison Church and exchanged that handshake which was subsequently reproduced a millionfold on postcards and posters. It symbolized
the longing of the nation for reconciliation. Without "the old gentleman's
blessing," Hitler had said, he would not have wanted to take power. Now
the blessing had been bestowed. The choir and gallery of the church were
filled with generals of the imperial army and the present Reichswehr, with
diplomats and dignitaries. Members of the government had taken their
seats in the nave. Behind them, brown-shirted, were the Nazi deputies,
flanked by the representatives of the Center parties. The Kaiser's seat had
been left empty, but behind it the Crown Prince sat in full-dress uniform.
As Hindenburg moved slowly to his seat in the nave, he paused for a
moment before the Kaiser's box and raised his marshal's baton in salute.
Respectfully, in a black cutaway coat, wearing the parvenu's air of embarrassment, Hitler followed the sorrowful-looking old man. Behind them a
sea of uniforms. Then the organ sounded the choral that the entire victorious army of Frederick the Great had sung after the Battle of Leuthen,
which regained Silesia for the Prussians: *Nun danket alle Gott.*

Hindenburg's address was brief. He pointed to the confidence that he
and the people had come to feel in the new regime, so that a "constitu-

tional basis for its work exists." He appealed to the deputies to support the government in its difficult task, and invoked the "old spirit of this shrine" as a bulwark against "selfishness and party strife . . . and a blessing upon a free, proud Germany united within herself." Hitler's speech was pitched on the same note of moderate, deeply felt solemnity. He looked back upon the greatness and downfall of the nation and then declared his faith in the "eternal foundations" of its life, the traditions of its history and culture. After a stirring tribute to Hindenburg, whose "greathearted decision" had made possible this union "between the symbols of old greatness and youthful strength," he asked Providence for "that courage and that perseverance which we feel around us in this room sacred to every German, as men struggling for our nation's freedom and greatness at the feet of the bier of the country's greatest king."

Goebbels noted:

At the end everyone is profoundly moved. I am sitting close to Hindenburg and see tears filling his eyes. All rise from their seats and jubilantly pay homage to the gray-haired Field Marshal who is extending his hand to the young Chancellor. A historic moment. The shield of German honor is once again washed clean. The standards with our eagles rise high. Hindenburg places laurel wreaths on the tombs of the great Prussian kings. Outside, the cannon thunder. Now the trumpets sound; the President of the Reich stands upon a podium, Field Marshal's baton in hand, and salutes the Reichswehr, the SA, SS and Stahlhelm, which march past him. He stands and salutes. . . .

These scenes had an extraordinary effect upon all the participants, upon the deputies, the soldiers, the diplomats, the foreign observers, and the public. That day at Potsdam truly proved to be a turning point in history.

Some time before that Papen had boasted that within a few months he would have Hitler squeezed into such a corner "that he'll squeak." Things were clearly not turning out that way. Nevertheless, the "Potsdam emotional farce" seemed to demonstrate that the wild-eyed Nazi leader had after all fallen into the snares of nationalist conservatism. The picture was of a young, credulous and deferential Hitler bowing to the tradition embodied in the personality of Hindenburg and concentrated in the former capital of the Prussian kings. Only a minority of those present were not entirely duped. And many who had voted against Hitler as recently as March 5 now obviously began to waver in their judgments. To this day it is troubling to realize that many government officials, army officers, lawyers and judges, many members of the nationalistic bourgeoisie who had distrusted Hitler on rational grounds, abandoned their stand the moment the regime let them taste the joys of nationalistic feeling. "Like a tidal wave," a newspaper of the bourgeois Right wrote, "nationalist enthusiasm swept over Germany yesterday and, let us hope, poured over the dikes that a good many of the parties had erected against it, and broke open doors which until now had been defiantly closed to it."[9] Long torchlight parades

405

through the streets of Berlin and a gala performance of *Die Meistersinger* concluded the festival program.

Two days later the regime, and Hitler himself, showed itself in a different aspect. About two o'clock in the afternoon on March 23 the Reichstag met in the Kroll Opera House, its temporary quarters, for the session that had already had its ceremonial prelude in Potsdam. The very setting was unequivocally dominated by the colors and symbols of the National Socialist Party. Units of the SS had taken responsibility for cordoning off the building—this was the first time the SS was assuming an important public function. Inside the opera house stood long lines of brown-shirted SA men. At the back of the stage, where the cabinet and the presiding officers of the Reichstag were seated, hung a huge swastika flag. And Göring opened the session with a speech that rudely ignored the existence of other parties in the Reichstag. Turning to his "comrades," he delivered a totally uncalled-for memorial address on Dietrich Eckart.

Then Hitler, likewise in a brown shirt, after having sported for the past few weeks predominantly civilian clothing, stepped forward on the platform to deliver his first parliamentary speech. Faithful to his unvarying rhetorical pattern, he once again began with a gloomy panorama of the period after November, 1918, of the distress and perils into which the Reich had fallen. Then he sketched in largely general terms the program of the government. He continued:

In order for the government to be in a position to carry out the tasks I have outlined, it has had the two parties, the National Socialists and the German Nationalists, submit the Enabling Act. . . . It would be against the meaning of the National Rising and would hamper the intended purpose if the government were to negotiate with and petition for the Reichstag's approval of its measures from case to case. The government, in making this request, is not impelled by any intention of abolishing the Reichstag as such. On the contrary, it reserves for the future the right to inform it of its measures from time to time. . . . The government intends to make use of this Act only to the extent required to carry out vitally necessary measures. The existence of neither the Reichstag nor the Reichsrat is threatened. The position and the rights of the President are not affected. . . . The existence of the states will not be eliminated. . . .

In spite of all these soothing assurances, each of the five articles of the Enabling Act smashed "an essential part of the German Constitution to smithereens." By Article 1 legislation passed from the Reichstag to the administration; Article 2 gave the government power to make constitutional changes; Article 3 transferred the right to draft laws from the President to the Chancellor; Article 4 extended the application of the Enabling Act to treaties with foreign states; Article 5 limited the validity of the Act to four years and also to the existence of the present administration. With another characteristic change of tone, Hitler concluded his speech with a challenge to battle:

Since the government itself has a clear majority behind it, the number of cases in which there will be any need to resort to such an Act is in itself limited. But the Government of the National Rising insists all the more upon the passing of this bill. This government prefers a clear decision in every case. It offers the parties of the Reichstag the chance for peaceful development in Germany and the reconciliation which will spring from that in the future. But it is resolute and equally prepared to meet any announcement of refusal, and will take that as a statement of opposition. You, the Deputies, must decide for yourselves whether it is to be peace or war.[10]

As if rehearsing for their future role, the deputies, with all too few honorable exceptions, greeted Hitler's speech with an ovation. Then all assembled rose to their feet and sang "Deutschland über Alles." In an atmosphere that resembled a state of siege, thanks to the SA and SS guards drawn up everywhere, the parliamentary factions withdrew for a three-hour recess for consultations. Outside the building Hitler's uniformed men began bellowing: "We want the Enabling Act—or there'll be hell to pay."

Everything depended upon the conduct of the Center Party. Its consent would assure the government the majority it needed to amend the Constitution. In negotiations with Dr. Kaas, the leader of the party, Hitler had given a number of assurances. Above all, he promised a concordat and, "as a return favor for an assenting vote by the Center Party," had indicated that he would write a letter "concerning revocation of those parts of the Reichstag fire decree which prejudiced the civil and political liberties of citizens"; the letter would also stipulate that the decree was to be applied only in specific circumstances. What was more, Hugenberg and Brüning had held a conference on the evening of March 21 and agreed to make consent of the Center dependent on a clause guaranteeing civil and political liberties. The German Nationalist faction, it was decided, would introduce the motion formulated by Brüning.

During the recess, however, Brüning was informed that members of the German Nationalist faction had raised objections to the projected motion and would not sponsor it. Once more indecisive, the Center faction considered what it should do. The majority pleaded for assent; Brüning passionately opposed any such thing. It would be better, he cried, to go down gloriously than to expire wretchedly. But finally it was agreed that they would cast a bloc vote for the opinion of the majority. It could scarcely have been otherwise, given the party's traditional opportunism, the impression made by the day at Potsdam, and the resigned recognition that the party was in no position to prevent passage of the act. After all, in conjunction with the promised letter, would not the Enabling Act bind Hitler to legality more effectively than he was bound at present?

By the time the recess ended, however, Hitler's letter had not arrived. At Brüning's urging, Monsignor Kaas went to see Hitler, and returned with the explanation that the letter was already signed and had been turned over to the Minister of the Interior for transmission to the Reichstag; it would arrive while the measure was being voted on. Kaas added that "if he had ever believed Hitler at all, he would have to do it this time, given the conviction in his tone."

Meanwhile the Social Democratic Party chairman, Otto Wels, had stepped upon the platform in deep silence, during which the distant, menacing chanting of the SA and SS could be heard. In explaining his faction's refusal to vote in favor of the bill, he made a last public profession of faith in democracy. Answering Hitler's earlier statement on foreign policy, he said that the Social Democrats, too, had always been for German equality with other nations and against any attempt to impugn Germany's honor. But to be defenseless, he declared, did not mean to be without honor (a play on the words *wehrlos* and *ehrlos*). That was just as true in domestic as in foreign politics. The elections had given the government parties the majority and therefore granted them the opportunity to govern constitutionally. Since this opportunity existed, it also constituted an obligation. Criticism was salutary; to persecute it would accomplish nothing. He concluded his speech with an appeal to the people's sense of justice and a greeting to his friends and victims of persecution.

This moderate and dignified rejoinder threw Hitler into a fury. Violently thrusting aside Papen, who tried to restrain him, he mounted the platform for the second time. Pointing directly at the Social Democratic leader, he began: "You come late, but still you come!* The pretty theories you have just proclaimed here, Mr. Deputy, are being communicated to world history just a bit too late." In growing agitation, he declared that Social Democracy had no right to claim any common goals in foreign policy, that the Social Democrats had no feeling for national honor, no sense of justice. Then, repeatedly interrupted by stormy applause, he continued with even greater fervor:

You talk about persecutions. I think there are only a few of us here who did not have to suffer persecutions from your side in prison. . . . You seem to have forgotten completely that for years our shirts were ripped off our backs because you did not like the color. . . . We have outgrown your persecutions!

You say furthermore that criticism is salutary. Certainly, those who love Germany may criticize us; but those who worship an International cannot criticize us. Here, too, insight comes to you very late indeed, Mr. Deputy. You should have recognized the salutariness of criticism during the time we were in the opposition. . . . In those days our press was forbidden and forbidden and again forbidden, our meetings were forbidden, and we were forbidden to speak and I was forbidden to speak, for years on end. And now you say: criticism is salutary!

At this point the Social Democrats began to shout loudly in protest. The Reichstag President's bell rang, and Göring called out into the ebbing din: "Stop talking nonsense now and listen to this!" Hitler continued:

* Quotation from Schiller's drama, *Die Piccolomini,* I:1.—TRANS.

You say: "Now they want to shunt aside the Reichstag in order to continue the revolution." Gentlemen, if that had been our purpose we would not have needed . . . to have this bill presented. By God, we would have had the courage to deal with you differently!

You also say that not even we can abolish Social Democracy because it was the first to open these seats here to the common people, to the working men and women, and not just to barons and counts. In all that, Mr. Deputy, you have come too late. Why didn't you, while there was still time, make your principles known to your friend Grzesinski,* or your other friends Braun* and Severing,* who for years kept saying that I was after all only a housepainter! For years you asserted that on your posters. [Interjection by Göring: "Now the Chancellor is settling accounts!"] And finally you even threatened to drive me out of Germany with a dog whip.

From now on we National Socialists will make it possible for the German worker to attain what he is able to demand and insist on. We National Socialists will be his intercessors. You, gentlemen, are no longer needed! . . . And don't confound us with the bourgeois world. You think that your star may rise again. Gentlemen, the star of Germany will rise and yours will sink. . . . In the life of nations, what is rotten, old and feeble passes and does not come again.

With the revealing remark that he was appealing only "on account of justice" and for psychological reasons "to the German Reichstag to grant us what in any case we could have taken," Hitler fired his parting shot. Turning to the Social Democrats, he cried:

My feeling is that you are not voting for this bill because by the very nature of your mentality you cannot comprehend the intentions that animate us in asking for it . . . and I can only tell you: I do not want you to vote for it! Germany shall be free, but not through you!

The minutes noted after these sentences: "Prolonged, stormy shouts of *Heil,* furious applause among the National Socialists and in the galleries. Hand-clapping among the German Nationalists. Stormy applause and shouts of *Heil* starting up repeatedly."

Hitler's reply has generally been considered an outstanding example of his gift for impromptu speaking. Thus it is worth knowing that the preceding speech by Otto Wels had been released to the newspapers beforehand, and evidently Hitler was already acquainted with it. Goebbels saw the enemy's "fur flying" and rejoiced: "Never has anyone been so thrown to the ground and given such a brushing off as was done here." In its bravura crudity and zest for crushing an opponent, the speech recalled that early performance of September, 1919, when a professorial speaker at a discussion first opened the sluices of Hitlerian oratory, to the astonished admiration of sober Anton Drexler. Now it was Hugenberg who at the cabinet meeting on the following day thanked Hitler "in the name of the

* Albert Grzesinski, police commissioner of Berlin; Otto Braun, Premier of Prussia; Carl Severing, Prussian Minister of the Interior; all Social Democrats.

other cabinet members . . . for so brilliantly putting the Marxist leader Wels in his place."

When the storm of applause after Hitler's speech had subsided, the representatives of the other parties took the floor. One after another they gave their reasons for consenting. Kaas, however, spoke with some embarrassment, and only after Frick, in response to another inquiry, had "solemnly assured him that the messenger had already delivered Hitler's letter to his office in the Kroll Opera House." The requisite three readings of the bill took only a few minutes. The result of the vote was 441 to 94; only the Social Democrats stuck to their nays. That was far more than the required two-thirds majority; it would have been sufficient even if the 81 Communist and the 26 Social Democratic deputies who had been detained by arrest, flight, or sickness had likewise voted no. As soon as Göring announced the result, the Nazis rushed to the fore. Arms raised in the Hitler salute, they gathered in front of the government bench and began singing the Horst Wessel song. That same evening the bill passed the already "co-ordinated" Reichsrat by unanimous vote. The promised letter from Hitler never reached any member of the Center.

With the passage of the "Law for the Removal of the Distress of People and Reich," as the Enabling Act was officially called, the Reichstag was eliminated from any active role in German politics, and the administration had won unlimited freedom of action. The infamy lay not in the fact that the parties of the Center capitulated to a stronger opponent and bowed to a more unscrupulous will but that they actually collaborated to bring about their own exclusion from government. To be sure, the bourgeois parties were not altogether wrong when they pointed out that the so-called Reichstag fire decree of February 28 had decisively opened the way to dictatorship and that the Enabling Act was actually only a formality, the seizure of power having taken place already. But even so, the vote offered them a chance to bear witness to their objections by a memorable gesture. Instead, they chose to set the seal of legality upon the revolutionary actions of those weeks. If the decree of February 28 represented the actual downfall of the Weimar Republic, the Enabling Act meant its moral collapse. The act sealed the process of abdication by the political parties, a process that had started in 1930 when the Great Coalition was shattered.

The Enabling Act concluded the first phase of the seizure of power. It made Hitler independent of the alliance with his conservative partners. That in itself thwarted any chance for an organized power struggle against the new regime. The *Völkische Beobachter* was completely right when it commented: "A historic day. The parliamentary system has capitulated to the new Germany. For four years Hitler will be able to do everything he considers necessary: negatively, the extermination of all the corrupting forces of Marxism; positively, the establishment of a new people's community. The great undertaking is begun. The day of the Third Reich has come!"

Actually, Hitler had needed less than three months to outmaneuver his partners and checkmate almost all the opposing forces. To realize the swiftness of the process we must keep in mind that Mussolini in Italy took seven years to accumulate approximately as much power. Hitler's purposefulness and his feeling for the statesmanlike style had made their impression on Hindenburg from the start and soon prompted the President to drop his former reservations. The affirmative vote in the Reichstag now reinforced him in his change of attitude. The cold, self-centered old man ignored the persecutions which, after all, affected a good many of his own former voters. Hindenburg felt that at last he was once more in the right camp. If Hitler was doing away with that "wretched undisciplined party nonsense," wasn't that to his credit?

Only two days after the appointment of Hitler as Chancellor, Ludendorff had written to the aged field marshal reproaching him for having "delivered the country to one of the greatest demagogues of all time." The man who had marched with Hitler in 1923 added: "I solemnly prophesy to you that this damnable man will plunge our Reich into the abyss and bring inconceivable misery down upon our nation. Coming generations will curse you in your grave because of this action."[11] But Hindenburg appeared to be well pleased with his decision. He had "taken the leap over the hurdle and would now have peace for a considerable time." As part of his program for withdrawing personally from the business of government, he had State Secretary Meissner explain, during the cabinet conference on the Enabling Act, that presidential collaboration on the laws issued as a result of this Enabling Act would be "not requisite." He was glad to be relieved of the responsibility that had long been oppressive to him.

Papen's insistence on attending all meetings between the President and the Chancellor was soon dropped. Hindenburg himself asked Papen "not to insult" Hitler, as he put it. And when Prime Minister Held of Bavaria came to the presidential palace to protest against the terrorism and violations of the Constitution committed by the Nazis, the doddering old man told him to speak to Hitler himself. In the cabinet, too, Goebbels noted, "the authority of the Führer has now been wholly established. Votes are no longer taken. The Führer decides. All this is going much faster than we dared to hope."

For the time being the slogans and open challenges of the Nazis were almost all directed against the Marxists, but the thrust was aimed equally at their German Nationalist partner in the government. In their own shortsighted zeal against the Left, Papen, Hugenberg, and their following entirely overlooked the fact that elimination of the Left would leave Hitler in command of the means to liquidate them also. Instead, Carl Goerdeler, the conservative mayor of Leipzig, cheerfully asserted that they would soon be sending Hitler back to his hobby of architecture and resume the conduct of the state themselves. Hitler himself, his old resentments again aroused, called his bourgeois coalition partners "ghosts" and declared: "The reactionaries think they have put me on a leash. They are going to set traps for me, as many as they can. But we will not wait until they act. . . . We are ruthless. I have no bourgeois scruples! They think I am uncultured, a barbarian. Yes, we are barbarians! We want to be. That is an honorable epithet. We are the ones who will rejuvenate the world. This old world is done for. . . ."[12]

But leverage against both the Left and Right was not all of the profit Hitler derived from the Enabling Act. By virtue of the act, the entire apparatus of the government bureaucracy was at Hitler's disposal. This included the judiciary, which was indispensable to his far-reaching plans. The act offered a basis that satisfied both the consciences and the craving for security of the bureaucrats. Most government officials were pleased to note the legal nature of this revolution, which in spite of the many isolated outrages contrasted so favorably with the chaos of 1918. This legality, even more than the antidemocratic traditions of the civil service made them ready to co-operate. Moreover, a special decree had been issued, which made no acquiescent civil servants liable to punishment. What is more, resistance would have equaled illegal action.

There are those who to this day maintain that there was no definite break, that the parliamentary republic glided by degrees into totalitarian dictatorship. But examination of all the facts reveals that within the process of the legal revolution the revolutionary elements far outweighed the legal ones. The public was duped by the brilliant trick of having the change of scene take place on the uncurtained stage, so to speak. But the real drama consisted in a revolutionary seizure of power confirmed by the Enabling Act. As the act itself provided, it was formally extended in 1937, 1941, and once again in 1943. But it remained an emergency measure promulgated in a state of emergency. Nor did the language of the regime attempt to hide its revolutionary intentions. Even in his speech on the Enabling Act Hitler constantly spoke of "national revolution" when he might have used the safer euphemism of "national rising." And two weeks later Göring in a speech explicitly repudiated this formula, replacing it by the concept "national socialist revolution."

There remained only a rounding off of power positions already achieved. Within a few weeks the centralist *Gleichschaltung* of the states had been completed, and in tandem with that action the complete shattering of all political groups and associations. The collapse of the Communists took place almost silently, in an atmosphere ot muffled terrorism. Some members of the Communist Party retreated into the underground; others opportunistically deserted to the National Socialists. The Nazis then turned upon the unions, which had already exposed their dismay and weakness during the early March days. They seemed to think they could buy off the impending doom by a series of placating gestures. Although the harassment and arrests of leading union members were steadily increasing throughout the Reich and the SA was staging a series of raids on local union offices, on March 20 the labor federation's executive committee addressed a kind of declaration of loyalty to Hitler. It spoke of the purely social tasks of the unions, "no matter what the nature of the political regime." When Hitler took over an old demand of the labor movement and declared May 1 a national holiday, the union leadership called upon the rank and file to participate in the demonstrations. Everywhere, thereupon, the unionized blue-collar and white-collar workers marched under alien banners in huge holiday parades. They listened bitterly to the speeches of Nazi functionaries but were nevertheless forced to applaud, and found themselves suddenly lined up in the very ranks they had so recently faced with fierce enmity. This confusing experience contributed more than anything else to shattering the will to resist of a movement numbering millions of workers. And while the labor-union paper, following the line of the union leadership, hailed May 1 as a "day of victory," on May 2 the SA and SS occupied union headquarters throughout Germany. They also took over the businesses and the banks belonging to the labor federation, arrested the leading officials, and shipped a good many of them off to concentration camps. The unions went ingloriously down to destruction.

The end of the Social Democratic Party took place in an equally undramatic fashion. Isolated appeals to resistance on the part of some leaders evoked at best contrary appeals from others, revealing the impotence of a mass party that had petrified in its traditional forms. Ever since January 30 the Social Democratic Party had constantly upheld the Constitution, which had already been undermined by the Nazis, and the Social Democrats kept on pledging that their party would never take the first step away from the solid ground of the law. Literal-minded Marxists that they were, they insisted on seeing Nazism as "the last card of reaction," which by the laws of historical determinism could never win. The party leadership therefore justified its immobility on the grounds of a tactical slogan: "Readiness is all!" This passivity had a profoundly demoralizing effect upon many of the lower branches of the organization, which were urging action.

On May 10, without a sign of resistance, all party headquarters, newspapers, and all the property of the Social Democratic Party and the Reichsbanner were confiscated on orders from Göring. After violent disagreements within the leadership, the advocates of appeasement won out: they thought they could force the government to moderation by conciliatory tactics. Following the same logic, the Social Democratic Reichstag faction decided that they would approve Hitler's major statement on foreign policy of May 17, though they would frame their consent in a special, independent statement. But this position was much too subtle for Hitler, who was already determined to annihilate them. Blackmailed by Frick's threat to kill the Social Democrats imprisoned in concentration camps, the party hurried to vote unconditionally for the government statement. With a mocking glance to the left, Göring could declare at the end of the Reichstag session: "The world has seen that the German people are united where their fate is at stake." The Social Democratic Party had been so crushed and humiliated that no one expected so much as a gesture of resistance when, on June 22, it was at last banned and its seats in the Reichstag invalidated.

All other political groupings were now likewise "co-ordinated"—sucked into the whirlpool of *Gleichschaltung*. Almost every day the newspapers reported liquidations or voluntary dissolutions. The Stahlhelm and the German Nationalist militias led the procession (June 21). There followed all remaining employee and employer organizations (June 22). Then came the German National People's Party, which as a fellow fighter in the national rising had vainly insisted on its right to continue in existence; its members could not see why they now had to run with the hares after they had for so long hunted with the hounds. Then came the dissolution of the State Party (June 28), of the German National Front (June 28), of the Center Association (July 1), of the Young German Order (July 3), of the Bavarian People's Party (July 4), of the German People's Party (July 4), and finally of the Center itself—which was tactically paralyzed by the ongoing negotiations on a concordat and then forced to capitulate (July 5).

Co-ordination of the various industrial, commercial, artisan, and agricultural associations ran parallel to the breakup of the political and paramilitary groups. But in no case was there any act of resistance. Scarcely an incident of more than local importance occurred. On June 27 Hugenberg was forced to resign, and not one of his conservative friends lifted a finger. He had just attended the World Economic Conference in London, where he had tried once more to outbid the Nazis in demagoguery by making excessive demands for a colonial empire and German economic expansion into the Ukraine. But he had succeeded only in providing Hitler with an easy opportunity to stand up for common sense and peace among nations against the Pan-German mischief-maker.

Hugenberg had held cabinet posts in the Reich and in Prussia, which now fell vacant. Two days later Hitler assigned economics to Kurt Schmitt, general manager of the Allianz Insurance Company, and food and agriculture to Walter Darré. At the same time, he ordered the permanent participation of Rudolf Hess, the "Führer's deputy," in cabinet meetings. In April Franz Seldte, the leader of the Veterans' Organization, joined the National Socialist Party; this meant that the proportions of Nazis to German Nationalists in the cabinet had been nearly reversed (eight to five). Since the German Nationalist ministers no longer had the backing of a party, they were essentially demoted to mere technicians without political pull. The regime fastened its grip on what had already been achieved by issuing, on July 14, a whole catalogue of decrees. The chief of these declared the National Socialist Party the sole legal party.

This rapid, unopposed extinction of all political forces from Left to Right remains the most striking feature of the Nazi take-over. If anything could have demonstrated the sapped vitality of the Weimar Republic, it was the ease with which the institutions that had sustained it let themselves be overwhelmed. Even Hitler was astonished. "One would never have thought so miserable a collapse possible," he declared in Dortmund at the beginning of July. Actions that only a short time before would have unleashed riots close to civil war were now met with a shrugging fatalism. The great capitulation of these months cannot be understood in political terms alone. We must consider its intellectual and psychological causes also. For over and above the illegality and violence of those weeks, the capitulation provides a certain historical justification for Hitler. Brüning, as he marched with the deputies to the Garrison Church on the day of Potsdam, felt as if he "were being led to the execution ground"—and that feeling was more prophetic than he himself imagined. One of the keen observers of the period noted that as the unanswered blows "into the face of truth, of freedom" went on, as the elimination of the other parties and of the parliamentary system progressed, there was a growing feeling "that all the things being abolished no longer concerned people very much."

In fact all these inglorious downfalls meant that the nation was inwardly bidding good-bye to the Weimar Republic. From now on the political order of the past was no longer a concept in whose name some hope, let alone opposition, might have gathered. The feeling of a great change, which had affected people vaguely, as a kind of euphoric expectation, when Hitler entered the government, now overcame wider and wider sectors of the population. Hitler had moved rapidly from the status of demagogue to that of a respected statesman. The craving to join the ranks of the victors was spreading like an epidemic, and the shrunken minority of those who resisted the urge were being visibly pushed into isolation. Faced with a defeat apparently imposed "by history itself," they concealed their bitterness and their lonely disgust. The past was dead. The future, it seemed, belonged to the regime, which had more and more followers, which was being hailed everywhere and suddenly had sound reasons on its side. "The only ones who give the impression of resolute refusal to accept it all, although they say nothing, are the servant girls," Robert Musil ironically noted in March, 1933. But he, too, admitted that he lacked any alternative for which to fight; he was unable, he wrote, to imagine the new order being replaced by a return of the old or of a still older state of affairs. "What this feeling probably signifies is that National Socialism has a mission and that its hour has come, that it is no puff of smoke, but a stage of history." Kurt

Tucholsky on the Left implied much the same thing when he wrote, with that brash resignation peculiar to him: "You don't go railing against the ocean."

Such moods of fatalism, of cultural resignation, speeded the success of Nazism. Only a few were able to resist the swelling current of the triumphant cause. Not that the terrorism and the injustices went unnoticed. But in the old European dichotomy *d'être en mauvais ménage avec la conscience ou avec les affaires du siècle,* more and more people swung over to those who seemed to have history and business as well on their side. Now that it had conquered power, the regime set about conquering people.

Chapter 2

I did not become Chancellor in order
to act otherwise than I have preached
for fourteen long years.

Adolf Hitler, November 1, 1933

ON THE WAY TO
THE FÜHRER STATE

There was no pause, no sign of failing grip, in the transition from the first
to the second phase of seizing power. The smashing of the democratic
constitutional and parliamentary state was barely concluded in the summer
of 1933 when its metal began to be smelted into the monolith of the
totalitarian Führer state. "We have the power. Today nobody can offer us
any resistance. But now we must educate German man for this new State.
A gigantic project lies ahead." Thus Hitler outlined the tasks of the future
to the SA on July 9.

For Hitler was never interested in establishing a mere tyranny. Sheer
greed for power will not suffice as explanation for his personality and
energy. Unquestionably, power, the virtually unrestricted use of it, with no
necessity to account to anyone—that kind of power meant a great deal to
him. But he was at no time satisfied with it alone. The restlessness with
which he conquered, extended, and applied that power, and finally used it
up, is evidence of how little he was born to be a mere tyrant. He was
fixated upon his mission of defending Europe and the Aryan race from
deadly menace, and to this end he wanted to create an empire that would
last. The study of history, particularly the history of his own age, had
taught him that material instruments of power alone would not suffice to
guarantee duration. Rather, only a great "revolution comparable to the
Russian Revolution" could develop the tremendous dynamism such a goal
required.

As always, he thought of this task also chiefly in terms of psychology
and propaganda. Never had he felt so dependent upon the masses as he did

417

at this time, and he watched their reactions with anxious concern. He feared their fickleness, not only as the child of a democratic age but because of his personal craving for approval and acclamation. "I am not a dictator and never will be a dictator," he declared, and added rather contemptuously: "As a dictator any clown can govern." He had, he admitted, eliminated the principle of democratic voting, but that by no means meant that he was free; strictly speaking, no such thing as arbitrary rule existed, only various ways of expressing the "general will." He solemnly assured his listeners: "National Socialism is the true realization of democracy, which has degenerated under parliamentarianism. . . . We have cast aside outmoded institutions precisely because they no longer served to keep in fruitful contact with the totality of the nation, because they led to idle chatter, to impudent cheating." Goebbels was saying the same thing when he remarked that in the age of political masses, government could not function "by states of emergency and nine-o'clock curfews." Either the people would have to be given an ideal, an object for their imaginations and their loyalties, or they would go their own ways. The scholars of the period spoke of "democratic Caesarism."

In keeping with this view, the psychological mobilization of the country was not left to chance or whim, certainly not to the operations of dissent. It was the product of consistent, totalitarian penetration of all social structures by means of a close-knit system of supervision, regimentation, and guidance. The object was to "belabor people as long as necessary, until they succumb to us." That meant penetrating the private realm as well as every social area: "We must develop organizations in which an individual's entire life can take place. Then every activity and every need of every individual will be regulated by the collectivity represented by the party. There is no longer any arbitrary will, there are no longer any free realms in which the individual belongs to himself. . . . The time of personal happiness is over."

But the whole of national existence could not be reshaped overnight. Part of Hitler's keen tactical sense was a sure feeling for tempo. More than once during the hectic early summer of 1933 he worried that control of events might slip away from him: "More revolutions have succeeded in the first onslaught than successful ones have been checked and brought to a halt," he told his followers during this period in one of those speeches exhorting them to patience.[13] Unlike them, he was not carried away by the headiness of success. He was prepared at any time to subordinate the emotions of the moment to his further power aims. Thus he vigorously opposed efforts to push on with further seizures of the government apparatus after those first months. His instinct told him to go slow. The departmental chiefs of the shadow government that the party had developed during the years of waiting had to cool their heels a while longer. Only Goebbels, Darré, and to an extent Himmler enjoyed the fruits of victory during this second phase. Rosenberg, for example, whose ambition had been the Foreign Office, was disappointed. So was Ernst Röhm.

Hitler's refusal to turn the government over to the party was based on two considerations. By showing constraint, he would create the sense that he was engaged in healing the nation's wounds and thus entrench himself deeper. With the coolness of the modern revolutionary, whose nature differs fundamentally from that of the fervent barricade builders of the eighteenth and nineteenth centuries, Hitler repeatedly warned his followers in the summer of 1933 "to be prepared for many years and to calculate in very long spans of time." If in doctrinaire haste they went "looking around to see whether there was anything else to revolutionize," they would gain nothing, he told them; rather, they must be "prudent and cautious."[14]

On the other hand, he had begun to regard the government as an instrument with which to keep the party, whose leader he was, in check. The technology of power was involved. Just as he had always encouraged competing institutions and rival subleaders within the party so that he might stand above their dissensions and bickerings and maintain his omnipotence all the more unchallenged, so he now employed the various executive offices of the government as counters in an even more baffling and Machiavellian game by which he strengthened his control. In the course of time he even increased the number of such offices. Two, and after Hindenburg's death three secretariats were at his sole disposal: the Reich secretariat (Reichskanzlei) under Dr. Hans Lammers, the Führer's secretariat under Hess and Bormann, and, finally, the presidential secretariat under State Secretary Meissner, a holdover from the days of Ebert and Hindenburg. Foreign policy, education, the press, art, the economy, were battlegrounds fought over by three or four competing departments, and this guerrilla warfare over territory, the din of which continued down to the last days of the regime, permeated even the lowest branches of the bureaucracy. One official complained about contradictory instructions and conflicts over areas of authority when he was only trying to organize a proper celebration of the solstice. In 1942 there existed fifty-eight Supreme Reich boards as well as a plethora of extragovernmental bureaus whose orders criss-crossed, who wrestled over precedence, insisting on authority they might or might not have. With some justice the Third Reich can be called authoritarian anarchy. Cabinet ministers, commissioners, special emissaries, officials of party affiliates, administrators, governors, many of them with assignments kept deliberately vague, formed an inextricable knot of interlocking authorities, which Hitler alone, with virtually a Hapsburgian grasp of puppet mastery, could supervise, balance, and dominate.

This bureaucratic chaos was also one of the reasons the regime was so extremely bound up with the person of Hitler, so that to the end there were no struggles over ideological questions, only over the Führer's favor. Such squabbles, it must be granted, were as fierce as any conflict over orthodoxies. While it is generally thought that authoritarian systems manifest decisiveness and energy in execution, in fact they are far more rife with chaos than other forms of governmental organization. The to-do about "order" was largely meant to conceal the deliberate confusion. During the war the SS leader Walter Schellenberg complained about the practice of issuing commands twice over and about pointlessly competing bureaus. Hitler defended such duplications in the pseudoscientific terms he loved so well: "People must be allowed friction with one another; friction produces warmth, and warmth is energy." But what Hitler had really discovered was that such friction was useful for consuming energy which might otherwise be a threat to him. When, after 1938, he abolished cabinet meetings, it may have been because there was too much comradely spirit at such sessions. Once State Secretary Dr. Lammers wanted to invite his fellow ministers to an evening of social drinking. Hitler forbade such conviviality. His style of leadership has aptly been described as "institutionalized Darwinism," and the widespread view of his greater efficiency has been called the self-delusion of all authoritarian systems.

The fact that Hitler did not simply turn the government over to the party as part of the loot of victory caused great dissatisfaction among his followers. For, in spite of all the ideological motives, the material impetus that underlay the movement remained of the greatest importance. Six or more million unemployed represented a source of tremendous revolutionary energy: they longed for work, hungered for booty, and hoped for rapid careers. The Nazi victory had carried only a thin stratum of functionaries into the legislatures and the town halls, and washed others up to the desks of dismissed officials. Now the empty-handed, still nourishing the anticapitalistic moods of preceding years, were pressing into the larger and more profitable fields of trade and industry. "Old Fighters"—those who had early joined the Nazi party—wanted to become managers, presidents of chambers of commerce, directors, or simply, by force or blackmail, partners. Their robust conquistadorial ambitions gave a revolutionary complexion to events that otherwise might have passed unnoticed. Kurt W. Luedecke has reported how one of these power-hungry and job-greedy party functionaries, on entering the office he had just taken over, called out happily: "Hi there, Luedecke! Terrific! I'm a big shot!" At the other end of this social spectrum is the desperate outburst reported by Hermann Rauschning on the part of a party member who feared he would miss his chance: "I don't want to fall back down. Maybe you can bide your time. You're not sitting in any fire. But I've been unemployed, do you hear! Before I go through that again I'll turn criminal. I'm staying on top, no matter what. We won't climb up twice."[15]

Hitler was conscious of the need to tame these radical, uncontrolled energies. His three major speeches at the beginning of July were an attempt to apply the brakes to revolutionary *élan,* much as he had done in March, on the occasion of the "SA revolt." Everything depended, he said, on "channeling the released current of revolution into the secure bed of evoluton."[16] Yet he also needed to give the current greater impetus. For a freezing of existing conditions was equally dangerous. Things could too easily come to a standstill because of exaggerated anxiety about revolution or simply because of the unwieldiness of a party of millions suffocating from the constant influx of new members. Thus, while Hitler was still calling on his followers to maintain discipline, he was also worrying about the tendency toward "bourgeoisization." An influx of 1,500,000 new members within three months had made the 850,000 "old comrades" a minority. At this point Hitler ordered a halt to admissions. For show, he had certain members expelled, with a good deal of fanfare, for having permitted themselves unauthorized raids on chambers of commerce and industrial concerns. To set an example, some were sent to concentration camps.

Among his intimates he defended the desire for personal gain as a revolutionary motive force and spoke of "justified corruption." Bourgeois circles were criticizing him for trying former officials for corruption while his own men were lining their pockets, he said. "I have answered these simpletons," he thundered, "could they tell me how I am to meet the legitimate wishes of my party comrades for some kind of compensation for their inhuman years of struggle. I asked them whether they would prefer me to turn the streets over to my SA. I could still do that, I said. I wouldn't mind. And I said it would be healthier for the whole nation if there were a real bloody revolution lasting for a few weeks. Out of consideration for them and their bourgeois comfort I'd refrained from doing that, I said. But I could always make up for lost time! . . . If we make Germany great, we have a right to think of ourselves also."

With this dual goal of keeping the revolution in flux and simultaneously stabilizing it, of reining it in and giving it its head, Hitler was again following his tried and tested maxims on the nature of power. "I can lead the masses only if I can wrench them out of their apathy," he declared. "Only the fanaticized masses are malleable. Masses that are apathetic, dull, are the greatest danger for any society."

This effort to awaken the masses "so that they may be made the instrument of my policy," now moved entirely into the foreground. The whipped-up fear of Communism at the time of the Reichstag fire, the parades, receptions, collections, the new semantic coinages, the leader cult, in short, the whole clever mixture of trickery and terrorism was meant to prime the nation to think and feel according to a single pattern laid down by the government. Significantly, as soon as this experiment seemed to be succeeding, the long repressed ideological fixations emerged once again. With a sharpness reminiscent of the earlier years of struggle, the figure of the Jew—as the principle of evil and ever-present menace—once again took center stage.

421

As early as March, 1933, SA units, acting on orders, committed the first anti-Semitic excesses. So strong was the outcry from abroad that Goebbels and Julius Streicher urged Hitler to muzzle criticism by openly increasing the pressure. They would have liked Hitler to allow his followers to stage a carnival of terror against all Jewish firms, against Jewish employers, lawyers, and officials. Hitler did not assent to this, but he gave instructions for a one-day boycott. On Saturday, April 1, armed SA squads stood guard at the doors of Jewish businesses and offices, calling out to visitors or customers not to enter. Posters urging boycott were pasted to the shop windows: "Germans, do not buy at the Jew's!" Others contained a terse: *"Juden raus!"* But at this point the nation's often ridiculed sense of order turned against the regime. The action seemed highhanded and rather shameful, and the hoped-for effect was not achieved. The populace, a later report on the mood in western Germany stated, "is rather inclined to pity the Jews . . . Sales figures of Jewish firms, especially in the countryside, have in no way declined."[17]

The boycott was therefore not resumed. In a speech redolent of disappointment, Streicher hinted that the regime had retreated under the pressure of world Jewry. Goebbels, however, for the fraction of a second opened the door just enough to permit a glance into the future when he announced that there would be a new blow, such a one "as to annihilate German Jewry. . . . Let no one doubt our resolution." Legal measures, the first of which was issued a few days after the unsuccessful boycott, banished Jews from public life in a quieter fashion, forcing them out of their social and, soon afterward, out of their business positions.

"The wonder of German unification," as the regime phrased it in its jargon of self-praise, involved the constant effort to separate the true nation from the unwanted nation of Marxists and Jews. But even more important was the need to win the nation's applause. The failure of the boycott had taught Hitler that the public could not be swung so easily on this question. But if April 1 had proved a negative experience in community feeling, May 1, which celebrated the workers, and October 1, the day of the farmers, were each a stupendous success.

French Ambassador André François-Poncet has described the concluding ceremonies on May Day evening at Tempelhof Field in Berlin:

At dusk the streets of Berlin were packed with wide columns of men headed for the rally, marching behind banners, with fife and drum units and regimental bands in attendance.

Stands had been set up at one end of the field for the guests of the government, among them the diplomatic corps, compulsory spectators, bidden to be awed into respect and admiration. A forest of glittering banners provided a background for the spectacle; a grandstand, bristling with microphones, cut forward like a prow looming over a sea of human heads. Downstage, Reichswehr units stood at attention with one million civilians assembled behind them; the policing of this stupendous rally was effected by SA and SS troopers. The Nazi leaders appeared in turn as the crowd cheered. Then came Bavarian peasants, miners and fishermen from other parts of Germany, all in professional garb, then delegates from Austria and the Saar and Danzig, the last being guests of honor of the Reich. An atmosphere of good humor and general glee pervaded the assembly, there was never the slightest indication of constraint. . . .

At eight o'clock the crowds backed up as Hitler made his appearance, standing in his car, his arm outstretched, his face stern and drawn. A protracted clamor of powerful acclaim greeted his passage. Night was now fallen; floodlights were turned on, set at spacious gaps, their gentle bluish light allowing for dark interjacent spaces. The perspective of this human sea stretched out to infinity, moving and palpitant, extraordinary when at once sighted in the light and divined in the darkness.

After some introductory remarks by Goebbels, Hitler took the stand. All floodlights were turned off save such as might envelop the Führer in so dazzling a nimbus that he seemed to be looming upon that magical prow over the human tide below. The crowd lapsed into a religious silence as Hitler prepared to speak.[18]

The foreign guests in the stands were not the only ones who carried away from the nocturnal parade of uniforms, from the play of light and the throb of the music, from the flags and the fireworks, the impression of a "really beautiful, a wonderful festival." They were not alone in discovering an "air of reconciliation and unity throughout the Third Reich." Such events made an even greater impression on the Germans. By the morning of May 1, 1,500,000 persons of all classes had lined up for the parade in Berlin: workers, government officials, managers, craftsmen, professors, film stars, clerks. This was the very array Hitler had conjured up the night before when he promised the end of all class differences and proclaimed the people's community of all "workers of the hand and the head." His rallying cry, to be sure, fell into a preacherly tone that approached travesty: "We want to be active, to work and make brotherly peace with one another, to struggle together, so that some day the hour will come when we can step before Him and will have the right to ask Him: Lord, You see, we have changed; the German nation is no longer the nation of dishonor, of shame, of self-laceration, of timidity and little faith; no, Lord, the German nation has once more grown strong in spirit, strong in will, strong in persistence, strong in enduring all sacrifices. Lord, we will not swerve from You; now bless our struggle."

These religious exhortations and indeed the whole liturgical character of the demonstrations did not fail to take effect and restored to many Germans their lost sense of belonging and their feeling of collective camaraderie. The combination of religious service and popular amusement was, precisely because of its apparently unpolitical stamp, of the widest possible appeal. Thus we would be aiming very wide of the mark—which the regime invites because of the monstrous features it later acquired—if we

423

divided the people of the spring of 1933 into victors and vanquished. Rather, as the historian Golo Mann has trenchantly observed, many persons felt at once triumph and uncertainty, fear and shame.[19] They partook both of victory and defeat. Engulfed by the hypnotic power of mass festivals, they thought they felt the touch of history itself. Memories of the long-ago days of August, 1914, flooded back, and again they experienced the intoxication of national brotherhood.

Later, those months would live on in the nation's memory as an almost incomprehensible jumble of euphoria, jingoism, a sense of rebirth, of transformation, though without a national explanation for such feelings. Hitler had the ability, in ways that are hard to analyze, to engender a kind of historical ecstasy. He had many instant conversions to his credit, particularly at this period. Yet his May 1 speech contained neither a concrete program for providing employment nor the expected statement of the principles of nationalist socialism and economic reconstruction. Nevertheless, his words reverberated with a sense of historical momentousness. The concomitant acts of terrorism were psychologically in accord with this mood. For the terror gave the events the quality of extreme, fateful seriousness. Many people felt the scruples that beset them as petty compared with the scale of the historical event.

The prevailing feeling was expressed by one of the prominent intellectuals of the time, who wrote that labor, freed from the curse of proletarian misery, had at last been made the basis of a new sense of community and that "part of the rights of man has been newly proclaimed."[20] But only a day later the surprise action against the unions exposed the other face of Hitler's familiar dual tactics. Similarly, on May 10, while the regime under "artist-statesman Adolf Hitler" was still talking in terms of a new Augustan age, there was a brutal gesture of open hostility to intellect: the burning of the books. With SA and SS bands playing "patriotic melodies," preceded by torchlight parades and so-called fire sermons, nearly 20,000 specimens of "un-German writings" were burned in the public squares of university cities.

The take-over was thus accomplished by a combination of intoxicants and pressures. This compound had a special potency; after twelve years of the parliamentary interregnum people felt again that there was a firm hand at the helm of state. Here, in a new form, was the time-honored political style of the Hohenzollern authoritarian state. The new regime was taking off from there.

Initially, the measures for establishing psychological domination over the nation were often hit-and-miss. But they were soon developed into a system and given an administrative framework. In the covert struggle for power over this arm of the government, victory went to Joseph Goebbels. His Propaganda Ministry, divided into seven departments (propaganda, radio, press, film, theater, music, and fine arts), soon took charge of the entire intellectual and cultural realm. It saw to the establishment of the Reich Chamber of Culture (Reichskulturkammer), which in turn had seven separate divisions and embraced all persons engaged in artistic or publicist activities. Architects and art dealers, painters, stage designers, lighting technicians and newsstand operators—one and all, Goebbels declared with cynical candor, would be rescued by the new state from their "feeling of desolate emptiness." These cultural organizations were meant both to politicize and supervise their members. Nonadmittance or expulsion meant that a person was debarred from his profession or occupation. Soon the police were following up a host of denunciations, tracking down the works of outlawed artists, or checking to make certain that the blacklist was not being violated. In December, 1933, a total of more than a thousand books and complete works of some writers, had been banned by no fewer than twenty-one bureaus, some of them in competition with one another. By the next year more than 4,000 publications had been forbidden. The revolution bowed before nothing, Goebbels declared in one of his "fundamental speeches" on culture; what mattered was "that in place of the individual person and his deification we now have the racial nation and its deification. The racial nation is the center of things. . . . The artist undeniably has the right to call himself non-political in a period when politics consists of nothing but shouting matches between parliamentary parties. But at this moment when politics is writing a national drama, when a world is being overthrown—in such a moment the artist cannot say: 'That doesn't concern me.' It concerns him a great deal." In his capacity as Reich propaganda chief of the NSDAP, Goebbels simultaneously spread a dense network of propaganda offices over the country—forty-one in all. A few years later these were raised to the status of federal bureaus.

By the spring of 1933 *Gleischschaltung* of radio broadcasting was largely completed; both staff and subject matter had been "co-ordinated." The press followed. There had been approximately 3,000 newspapers in Germany. A large number of these, chiefly local papers, were eliminated by economic pressure backed by all the powers of the state. Others were confiscated. Only a few of the major newspapers, whose prestige might make them useful tools, were allowed to survive. Some of these, such as the *Frankfurter Zeitung,* continued on into the war years. But drastic restrictions were placed upon them even in the initial phase of the seizure of power. A shower of instructions and "language rules," usually handed down at the daily Reich press conference, established political regimentation and banished freedom of the press to whatever small space it could find between the lines. At the same time, however, Goebbels looked kindly upon all differences in form and style. In general he tried to conceal the governmental monopoly of opinion by stressing journalistic variety. He put it in a pithy slogan: the press, like culture in general, was to be "monoform in will, polyform in the outward trappings of that will."

If we survey the whole scene, we must grant that in the cultural realm as well, "co-ordination" proceeded without a protest, without a sign of effective opposition. Only the Protestant Church was able to resist the open seizure of power in its ranks, although at the price of fission. The Catholic bishops had hitherto attacked Nazism in a series of strongly militant statements and had officially condemned it. But their will to resist was undermined by the negotiations for a concordat, already begun during the Weimar years and eagerly resumed by Hitler. Nazi promises and sham concessions knocked the ground from under their feet. Belatedly, they would find their way back to opposition, but by then they did not see clearly how to proceed. In the universities, too, what feeble resistance came to the fore was soon subdued by the tried-and-true combination of "spontaneous expressions of the people's will" from below followed by an administrative act from above.

The point has often been made that the corps of high-ranking military officers or big business proved to be the weakest spot in the country's defenses against Nazism. But that thesis becomes somewhat questionable when we consider how swiftly and easily the regime succeeded in overwhelming the intellectuals, the professors, the artists and writers, the universities and academies. There were only scattered acts of rebellion here and there. During the early months, when the regime was courting recognition and decorative names, testimonials of loyalty rained down upon it unrequested. As early as the beginning of March, and again in May, several hundred university teachers of all political persuasions publicly declared their adherence to Hitler and the new regime. A "pledge of loyalty by German writers to the People's Chancellor Adolf Hitler" was signed by such distinguished names as Rudolf Binding, Walter von Molo, and Joseph Ponten; another such document bore the names of noted people like Ferdinand Sauerbruch, the great surgeon, and Martin Heidegger, the philosopher. Alongside these lists of signatures, there was a great deal of applause from individuals. Gerhart Hauptmann, the Nobel prize winner, whom Goebbels had mocked for years as a "unionized Goethe," published an article titled "I Say Yes!" It turned out later that the editors had added the title—which nevertheless accurately summed up the content. Hans Friedrich Blunck, president of the Reichsschrifttumskammer, the writers' organization, described the attitude appropriate to the new era with the formula: "Humility before God, honor to the Reich, flowering of the arts." The critic Ernst Bertram composed a "fire song" for the book burning, in which the works of his friend Thomas Mann were consumed:

> Reject what confuses you
> Outlaw what seduces you,
> What did not spring from a pure will,
> Into the flames with what threatens you!

Even Theodor W. Adorno noticed in the composition of a poetry cycle by Baldur von Schirach "the strongest conceivable effects" of the "romantic realism" proclaimed by Goebbels.

Meanwhile, in the early weeks of the regime, 250 notable writers and professors left the country. Many others were harassed, relieved of their posts, or otherwise made aware of their vulnerability. Soon the spokesmen for a regime with cultural ambitions had to acknowledge that the first "summer of art" in Germany looked more like a battlefield than a field of ripening grain. The Minister of the Interior announced the expatriation of writers and scholars, one after another, among them Lion Feuchtwanger, Alfred Kerr, Heinrich and Thomas Mann, Theodor Plievier, Anna Seghers, and Albert Einstein. But those who remained were not averse to taking the evacuated seats in the academies and at banquets, insensitive to the tragedies of the expelled and the outlawed.

Those who were asked placed themselves at the regime's disposal: the composer Richard Strauss, the conductor Wilhelm Furtwängler, the actors Werner Krauss and Gustaf Gründgens. Such actions surely cannot always be ascribed to weakness or opportunism. A great many were sucked in by the emotional surge of the national rising, wanting to take their place in the ranks and "co-ordinate" themselves. Others felt it their mission to strengthen the affirmative forces within the "great idealistic popular movement" called National Socialism. They meant to take those honest but primitive Nazi ruffians under their wings, to sublimate those unthinking energies, to refine the "well-meant but still clumsy ideas of Adolf Hitler, the 'man of the people,'" and in this way "show the National Socialists what really is contained within their dim strivings and thus make possible a 'better' National Socialism."[21] This was the hope, so frequently found in revolutionary eras, of averting something worse—oddly coupled with the notion that under the banner of the new fraternity idealism could be introduced into "dirty politics." Cowardice and conformism were certainly present and widespread; but in such intellectual illusions can be found the specifically German continuity within Nazism.

But we would still have only a partial understanding of the phenomenon if we failed to consider the dominant feeling of the age. The eternally unsettled question of how the blatantly anti-intellectual Hitler movement could have enjoyed such success among writers, professors, and intellectuals in general may to some extent be answered in terms of the anti-intellectual tendency of the age. Even Max Scheler, the philosopher, gave a certain sanction to the irrationalist movements of the period—although he indicated that he did not subscribe to the modish denigration of the intellect. In a lecture toward the end of the twenties he spoke of a "systematic instinctual revolt in men of the new epoch . . . against the exaggerated intellectuality of our fathers" and called it a "healing process." The victory of the Hitler movement was widely seen as the political form of this healing

427

process. Certainly Nazism embodied, in political terms, all those pseudo-religious tendencies to escapism, that hatred of civilization, and revulsion against the intellect with which the period was rife. This will explain why Nazism exerted a seductive influence upon many intellectuals who, isolated within their disciplines, longed for fraternization with the masses, for sharing in the vitality of the common people, for mental torpor and historical effectiveness. Again, this mood was an all-European phenomenon. Not only Edgar Jung, the nationalist-conservative writer, affirmed his "respect for the primitivity of a popular movement, for the militant vitality of victorious gauleiters and storm troop leaders . . ."; Paul Valéry, too, found it "charming that the Nazis despise the intellect so much."[22] We can find the whole catalogue of motivations—the illusions, the hopes, the self-delusions—spelled out in the famous letter the poet Gottfried Benn sent to Klaus Mann in exile:

> On purely personal grounds I declare myself for the new State, because it is my *Volk* that is making its way now. Who am I to exclude myself; do I know anything better? No! Within the limits of my powers I can try to guide the *Volk* to where I would like to see it; but if I should not succeed, still it would remain my *Volk*. *Volk* is a great deal! My intellectual and economic existence, my language, my life, my human relationships, the entire sum of my brain, I owe primarily to this *Volk*. My ancestors came from it; my children return to it. And since I grew up in the country, and among farm animals, I also still remember what native grounds stand for. Big cities, industrialism, intellectualism—these are all shadows that the age has cast upon my thoughts, all powers of the century, which I have confronted in my writing. There are moments in which this whole tormented life falls away and nothing exists but the plains, expanses, seasons, soil, simple words: *Volk*.[23]

Such statements reveal how irrelevant it was to charge Nazism with ideological poverty. Compared with the ideational systems of the Left, it might seem to offer no more than collective warmth: crowds, heated faces, shouts of approval, marches, arms raised in salute. But that was precisely what made it attractive to a body of intellectuals who had long been in existential despair. They had emerged from the many theoretical disputes of the age with the one insight that one could "no longer approach things with ideas." It was the very craving to escape from ideas, concepts, and systems into some uncomplicated sense of belonging that provided Nazism with so many deserters from other causes.

Nazism tried to satisfy this craving by inventing a multitude of new social arenas; one of Hitler's fundamental insights, acquired in the loneliness of his youth, was that people wanted to belong. It would be a mistake to see nothing but coercion in the multitudinous organizations of the party, the politicized professional associations, the chambers, bureaus and leagues that proliferated throughout the country. Rather, the practice of taking every individual into the fold according to his age, his function, and even his preferences in leisure or entertainment, of leaving people nothing but sleep as their private domain, as Robert Ley remarked on occasion—this practice sprang from a widespread craving for social participation. Hitler was not exaggerating when he asserted, as he regularly did, that he had asked his followers for nothing but sacrifices. In fact he had rediscovered the old truism that most people have a need for fitting into an organized whole, that there is joy in fulfilling a function, and that for the majority of the German people, the demand for selfless service frequently had a far greater appeal than the intellectuals' demand of freedom for the individual.

Hitler succeeded in converting all the diffuse impulses awakened during that first spring after his coming to power into purposeful social energies—that was one of his most remarkable achievements. Challenging the individual to total disinterested effort, he kindled enthusiasm in people nerve-wracked by unemployment, misery, and hunger. He was able to proclaim convincingly: "It is glorious to live in an age that confronts its people with great tasks." He went to unprecedented lengths in travel and speechmaking. By an endless succession of cornerstone layings and ground-breaking ceremonies, he created a mood of general mobilization. In hundreds of let's-get-to-work speeches he initiated labor campaigns which, in the military jargon of the regime, soon developed into labor battles and were triumphantly concluded by a series of victories or by breakthroughs on the agricultural front. The metaphor of warfare that made such formulas effective also sparked a readiness for sacrifice. And all sorts of slogans furthered the mood, though sometimes these slogans verged on the preposterous, as for example: "The German woman is knitting again!"

Like the festivals and parades, these stylistic devices aimed at making the regime popular by concretizing it. Hitler had a remarkable knack for translating into simple images the abstract character of modern political and social functional relationships. Of course, the masses had lost their political autonomy; their rights had been reduced or abolished. But those liberties of the past had hardly profited them—they remembered them with nothing but contempt—whereas Hitler's unrelenting image projection, his eagerness for public display, engendered in the masses a clear feeling that they were participating in the operations of government. After years of gloom it seemed to many people that their work was once again becoming meaningful. The most menial jobs were being raised to praiseworthy importance. As Hitler put it, it was an honor "to clean the streets as a citizen of this Reich." Remarkably enough, he seemed to succeed in generating this state of mind.

This capacity for awakening initiative and self-confidence was all the more amazing in view of the fact that Hitler had no specific program. At the cabinet meeting of March 15 he for the first time admitted his dilemma, saying that it was necessary to employ demonstrations, pomp, and a show of activity "to divert attention to the purely political affairs, because the economic decisions will have to be postponed for a while." And as late as September at the groundbreaking ceremony for the first section of the Frankfurt-Heidelberg autobahn he let slip the revealing statement that it was now essential "by grand, monumental works to set the German economy in motion again at some point." As Hermann Rauschning saw it, Hitler took power with virtually no other guideline than his total confidence in his own ability to deal with things on the primitive but effective maxim: give an order and it will get done, more or less roughly, perhaps, but for a while something will be moving, and meanwhile we'll look around for the next step.

As things stood, however, this conception proved to be a kind of magic, since it overcame the prevailing feeling of discouragement. Although there was no visible improvement in material conditions until 1934, from almost the very first day Hitler's approach generated an enormous "suggestion of consolidation." At the same time, it assured Hitler considerable room for maneuvering, which enabled him to adjust his plans to changing requirements. The style of his rule has rightly been called "permanent improvisation." Even while he insisted on the unalterability of the party program, he was filled with that lively instinct of the born tactician not to commit himself. Thus he forbade the press in the first few months to publish unauthorized quotations from *Mein Kampf*. Even republication of one of the twenty-five points of the party program was banned on the grounds that henceforth what mattered would not be programs but practical work. As a pamphlet of the period put it: "The new Chancellor has so far refused, quite understandably from his standpoint, to set forth a program in detail. ('Party Comrade No. 1 did not answer,' the Berlin joke has it.)" One of the early party functionaries believes that Hitler at no time had a clearly formulated goal, let alone a strategy for attaining his ends. And indeed it does seem as if he had only visions, and an unusual capacity for taking in at a glance changing situations, and rapidly and forcefully seizing the opportunities they offered. The grandiose phantasmagorias, floating in eschatological mists of cosmic dooms and racial twilights, were just as much his element as tenacious, cunning, cold-bloodedly staged rapid-fire events—he was a curious combination of visionary and tactician. But the realm in between, that of soundly planned, patiently practiced politics, the realm of human history, was and remained alien to him.

There could be no doubt, from his actions, that programs did not concern him. He forced the "reactionary" Hugenberg out of the cabinet, even as he compelled Gottfried Feder, now State Secretary in the Ministry of Economics, to modify to the verge of recantation the great idea of his life, his "breaking the bondage of interest." Hitler now dismissed Feder's idea, which had long ago flashed through him like an illumination, as one of a group of "officially approved fantasies." The small shopkeepers, the original members of the party, were already looking over the department stores to find the spots where, according to Point 16 of the party program, they would set up their sales booths in the near future. As late as July, 1933, Rudolf Hess was still allowed to state that the attitude of the party on the question of the department stores was "unchanged in principle." In reality Hitler had discarded that point in the program for good and all.

What had happened to Feder happened to many other old fighters in the party ranks, who, as ideological lone wolves, found themselves more and more openly ridiculed and excluded from the positions of power. As the party embracing all the discontented and resentful, during the period of its rise, the NSDAP had attracted many mini-utopians: people obsessed with an idea, a conception of a new order. They had imagined that their desire for reform was most emphatically represented by the dynamic Hitler party. Now, however, that there was a chance of these ideas being realized, the unreality and in many cases the ludicrous quality of many of these notions came to light, while others held no interest for Hitler, since they offered no promise for increasing his power. The idea of the corporate state, constitutional reforms, rearrangement of the relationships between the states and the Reich, the idea of Germanic law, nationalization of the trusts, land reform, or the idea of the state's feudal tenure of the means of production—nothing ever came of these save for a few isolated projects no one ever followed up. Moreover, the ideas were often so contradictory that their spokesmen turned fiercely upon one another, whereupon Hitler again could leave everything suspended. Complaints about "lack of organization" left him unmoved. This lack allowed his will free scope and made it the real law of the regime.

But although the energies that National Socialism had unleashed were incapable of tracing more than the beginnings of a new order, they were nevertheless strong enough to undermine the old conditions. Even in this early phase the peculiar weakness of the regime was revealed. To be sure, it had with uncanny accuracy exposed the anachronistic structures and empty claims of the old order. But it was never able to legitimize its destructive ingenuity by a constructive sequel; in the larger historical context it assumed solely functions of clearance. It could not even develop rational, purposeful forms in which to clothe its power-political aims; even in establishing the totalitarian state it hardly went beyond initial steps. It was behemoth rather than leviathan, as Franz Neumann put it; a non-state, a manipulated chaos, not the terroristic coercive state that still is a state. Everything was improvised with one purpose or another in view. That was true for the great campaign of conquest that dominated Hitler's imagination so powerfully that it overrode everything else. Certainly, he had no interest in ordering the social and political structures and arranging for their continuance beyond his own life. If he thought and spoke in terms of a millennium, this was vague literary phraseology. Consequently, the Third Reich developed into a peculiarly unfinished makeshift, a field of rubble

431

patterned on contradictory sketches. Façades left over from the past covered newly laid foundations, among which jutted pieces of wall started and abandoned, fragments destroyed or torn down. What alone imposed meaning and consistency upon it all was Hitler's monstrous will to power.

Socialistic notions still survived in the Nazi party, isolated leftovers from the Strasser phase. Hitler's attitude toward these doctrines is interesting, for here again we see how all his decisions were governed by the power factor. As leader of a movement which had profited from the bourgeoisie's dread of revolution, he had to avoid all activities that might move the regime anywhere close to the traditional concept of revolution. In particular, he must avoid the appearance of nationalization or an overplanned economy. But since this was what he really intended, he used the slogan of "national socialism" to proclaim unconditional co-operation by everyone, on all levels, with the state. And since all authority ultimately issued from him, this meant nothing less than the abolition of all private economic life under the fiction of its continuance. As compensation for the state's intrusion into their affairs, the businessmen received imposed labor peace, guaranteed markets, and in the course of time a good many vague hopes of a tremendous expansion of the national economic base. The whole idea was conceived, however, for short-term benefits: it was Hitler's way of providing himself with henchmen. Among his intimates he justified this course with some cynicism and acuteness: he had not the slightest intention, he declared, of killing off the propertied class, as had been done in Russia. Rather, he would force it in every conceivable way to use its abilities to build the economy. Businessmen, that much was sure, would be glad if their lives and property were spared, and in this way they would become true dependents. Why should he change this advantageous relationship when to do so would only mean he would afterward have to thresh everything out with Old Fighters and overzealous party comrades who would be forever reminding him of all they had done for the party? Formal title to means of production was only a question of detail, was it not? How much landed property or how many factories people owned did not matter when they had consented to a master they could no longer overthrow. "The decisive factor is that the State through the party controls them whether they are owners or workers. Do you understand, all this no longer means anything. Our socialism reaches much deeper. It does not change the external order of things, but it orders solely the relationship of man to the State. . . . Then what does property and income count for? Why should we need to socialize the banks and the factories? We are socializing the people."[24]

Hitler's pragmatism was remarkably effective in overcoming mass unemployment. He did not doubt that both the fate of the regime and his personal prestige hung on this question. It was all important that the condition of the suffering population be significantly improved. He had been walking the high wire propagandistically for so long that there was no way to make good his promises except by some such miracle. Moreover, it was also the only way he could pacify the Old Fighters who were grumbling at his many compromises and adjustments, which in their view amounted to a "betrayal of the revolution."

Hitler grasped the psychological aspect of the Depression as none of the Weimar politicians had done. Undoubtedly, the gradual recovery of the world economy also came to his aid. But more important, at least as far as the tempo was concerned, was his perception that gloom, apathy, and slump sprang from deep-seated, pessimistic doubts regarding the world order and that the masses required stimulus just as much as did the economy. His many comments friendly to business and his consistent efforts to keep the economy out of the revolutionary turmoil of the early phase were primarily aimed at generating a mood of confidence. Most of the measures initiated during the early months were introduced less for their economic rationale than for the sake of making a vigorous gesture. In a number of cases Hitler fell back on older plans, such as the "program for the immediate provision of work," which belonged to the Schleicher regime. Other projects that were now spectacularly launched also came out of the Weimar files; democratic red tape, timidity about decisions, or the resignation prevalent during the Weimar years had kept them dormant. For example, the autobahn project, so closely linked with the regime's reputation from the very outset, had been under discussion for years but had never been begun.

When Dr. Hans Luther, president of the Reichsbank, clung to his deflationary tight-credit policy and refused to make large sums available for providing work, Hitler forced him to resign. To the anger of many of his followers, he replaced Luther by the "notorious capitalist" Hjalmar Schacht. With his eagerness for results and his absence of scruples, Hitler cranked up production by a variety of impressive measures. In his May 1 speech he appealed to the "entire German people," declaring that "every individual . . . every entrepreneur, every homeowner, every businessman," had the obligation to provide for work in a sustained community effort. The government, for its part, would take action by means of a program Hitler described as "gigantic"—one of his favorite words. "We will clear all obstacles and begin the task grandly," he promised. Government contracts for housing projects and roads together with a system of public and private stimuli to investment, loans, tax concessions and subsidies, promoted an upswing in the economy. And along with it all went more and more words, slogans, proclamations. They contributed to the success of the effort and gave surprising significance to Hitler's epigram: "Great liars are also great wizards."

The establishment and extension of the initially voluntary Labor Service was also part of the psychology of generating confidence. The Labor

433

Service was useful, to be sure, as a catchment basin for unemployed youth. But in addition it gave vivid expression to the regime's constructive optimism. Reclaiming swamps and wetlands, reforestation, building auto-bahns and regulating streams became visible and inspiring signs of accom-plishment and faith in the future. At the same time, the organization served to overcome class barriers—especially after it became compulsory in 1935—and to improve the status of manual laborers.

All these factors operated together, and by 1934 a shortage of techni-cians was noted, although there were still 3 million unemployed. Two years later full employment was attained.

The initial upswing also opened the way for considerable effective action in the realm of social politics. To be sure, strikes were banned and a single state-controlled union was created, the German Labor Front. But for fear of seeming reactionary, the regime attempted to cover up such manifesta-tions of authoritarianism by ostentatious prolabor activities. Thus vast institutions were created to organize the people, to provide them with vacation travel, sports festivals, art shows, dances, and training courses. These organizations—Kraft durch Freude ("Strength Through Joy") and Schönheit der Arbeit ("Beauty of Work")—served their purpose, and at the same time superintended and placated the masses.

There was labor opposition, to be sure. Some lists giving the results of factory elections held in April, 1935, have been discovered; these reveal that in some plants at this time no more than 30 per cent to 40 per cent of the personnel voted for the Nazi unity list, and thus for the new order. But in 1932 the NSBO, the Nazi factory organization, received on the average only 4 per cent of the votes. Even such a leftist historian as Arthur Rosen-berg had to admit that Nazism realized certain unfulfilled demands of the democratic revolution. In the long run, at any rate, the regime's stubborn, wide-ranging wooing of the workers had its effect, especially since many of them saw the difference between present and past "less in lost rights than in regained employment."[25]

Employment was indeed the key factor for the success of the Third Reich's rigorous social policies. The loss of freedom and of social auton-omy, the strict supervision, the distinctly smaller share of labor in the growing national product—all this did not greatly bother the workers. Ideological slogans persuaded them even less than the bourgeoisie. What really mattered was the feeling of restored social security after traumatic years of anxiety and gloom. This feeling dissolved the initially widespread tendencies toward opposition. It roused the determination to produce and helped enormously to create that image of social contentment to which the new rulers could proudly point: class struggle was not only tabooed and banned; it had also been largely abandoned. The regime insisted that it was not the rule of one social class above all others, and by granting everyone opportunities to rise, it in fact demonstrated class neutrality. What class consciousness remained was stamped out by the political pressures to which businessmen, blue- and white-collar workers, and farmers were subjected.

These measures did indeed break through the old, petrified social structures. They tangibly improved the material condition of much of the population. Yet no really new sociopolitical concepts can be detected underlying these programs. Hitler's only ideas were concerned with the seizure of power; he had no vision of the new state or the new society. Fundamentally he did not want change; he wanted only to put his hand on the wheel. Just as the party had served him as an instrument for conquering Germany, Germany was now to serve him as an instrument "for pushing open the gate to lasting domination of the world." Hitler's domestic policy must be seen as an adjunct to his foreign policy.

In addition to his use of the available social energies, he employed the dynamism of nationalistic motivation to mobilize the masses. The onetime victors in the World War had already conceded German equality in principle, but in reality she had remained the pariah nation. France, above all, deeply disturbed by Hitler's accession to power, was unrelenting, whereas England showed some discomfort at the contradictions into which she was being forced by her former ally. During the first year and a half of his rule Hitler exploited France's fears, England's scruples, and Germany's indignation in a masterful manner. He succeeded in overturning the entire European system of alliances, in uniting Germany, and in preparing the ground for his *Lebensraum* policy.

The initial situation was by no means favorable to his ambitions. The terroristic aspects of his coming to power, the beatings and killings, above all, the persecution of a single segment of society solely because of their origin, ran counter to all civilized views of political conduct and produced a grim image of what was going on in Germany. There was the famous Maundy Thursday debate in the House of Commons, when Sir Austen Chamberlain, the former Foreign Secretary, declared that this was not the time to consider any further revision of the Versailles Treaty. He spoke of brutality, racial arrogance, and the policy of the iron heel. The slogan "Hitler means war," so long dismissed as a piece of refugee hysteria, suddenly seemed credible. There were anti-German outbreaks here and there in Europe, and the Polish ambassador went so far as to ask whether France was prepared to wage a preventive war in order to eliminate the Hitler regime. In the summer of 1933 Germany was almost totally isolated in the sphere of foreign policy.

Given these circumstances, Hitler found it advisable to make placating gestures and to stress continuity with the moderate Weimar policy. Although he despised the personnel of the Foreign Office and occasionally spoke of "those Santa Clauses in the Wilhelmstrasse," he left both the

435

bureaucracy and the diplomatic corps almost untouched. For at least six years, he told one of his followers, he must maintain a kind of truce with the European powers; all the saber rattling of nationalistic circles was a mistake, he said.[26] Typical of his strategy was his grand "peace speech" of May 17, 1933, although he mingled his sincere-sounding offers of reconciliation with some strong words against the persisting distinction between victors and defeated and even threatened to withdraw from the Disarmament Conference and from the League of Nations altogether if the victors continued to deny equal rights to Germany. But in the present situation he could easily assume the role of an advocate of reason and fairness by taking the European powers at their word, invoking their own slogans of "self-determination" and a "just peace." So great was the general gratification at Hitler's moderation that no one detected the warning contained within his speech. Along with the London *Times* many influential voices throughout the world supported Hitler's demand that Germany be treated on a footing of equality with the other powers. President Roosevelt was actually delighted with Hitler's tone.[27]

The most visible success of this policy was the Four Power Pact between England, France, Germany, and Italy that was drawn up in the summer of 1933. Although never ratified, it signified a kind of moral acceptance of Germany into the society of great powers. But Germany's first partner in international negotiations was the Soviet Union, which hastened to renew the Berlin Treaty that had expired in 1931. Russia was followed closely by the Vatican, which in July concluded the arrangements for a concordat with the Reich. But even though things were going well, in the autumn Hitler swung the rudder around with an abruptness that seemed to spring from a blind emotion and managed thereby to perceptibly improve his whole position.

His field of operations was the Disarmament Conference in Geneva, which had been meeting since the beginning of 1932. Because of her military weakness, Germany exerted a particularly strong moral sway at this conference. The principle of equality compelled the other powers either to disarm or to accept the rearmament of Germany. In speech after speech, statement after statement, Hitler could stress Germany's readiness to disarm; the more France's anxieties came to the fore, the more simpleheartedly and persuasively Hitler could argue. France was watching events in Germany with deep uneasiness; she found these developments far more telling than Hitler's bland assurances, even though her persistent distrust— which blocked all negotiations—cast her in a bad light internationally. But by pointing to the system of repression inside the Reich, to the increasing militarization, the constant marching, the flags, uniforms and parades, the organizational vocabulary with its "storm troops," "brigades" and "headquarters guards," and the battle songs in which the whole human race trembled before a Germany that owned the world, France at last managed

436

to bring the other powers around. The equality conceded to Germany in principle was made dependent on a four-year period of probation, so that the others could observe whether their former enemy was sincerely ready for reconciliation and had abandoned all revanchist notions.

Hitler reacted by flaring up. On October 14, shortly after British Foreign Secretary Sir John Simon had presented the Allies' new views, Hitler announced his intention to quit the Disarmament Conference. Along with this, he proclaimed Germany's withdrawal from the League of Nations. His state of mind is indicated by his orders to the army—revealed at the Nuremberg Trials—to resist with armed force if an attempt were made to apply sanctions.[28]

This first coup, with which Hitler took the regime's foreign policy into his own hands, created stupefaction. It is true that he had not made the decision on his own—as has been widely thought. He was supported strongly by Foreign Minister von Neurath, who had previously advocated a deliberate sharpening of Germany's foreign policy. But the emotional posturing, the tone of grand indignation, unquestionably derived from Hitler himself. And it was also he who posed the alternatives as "withdrawal or dishonor." In a radio address delivered on the evening of October 14 he applied to foreign affairs the dual tactics which had proved of such value to him in domestic affairs: he masked his belligerence by a torrent of words and show of amicability. He called France "our ancient but glorious opponent" and stated that "anyone who can conceive of a war between our two countries is mad."

These tactics paralyzed the European powers, who in any case were hardly disposed to take decisive counteraction. None of their spokesmen had any idea what do do. Hitler was contemptuously tossing back in their faces the "honor" for which the Weimar regime had so long and patiently sued. His brashness stunned them. But some hid their surprise and embarrassment by congratulating the others on being rid of an inconvenient partner in negotiations. A few demanded military intervention; in the lobbies at Geneva angry exclamations of *"C'est la guerre!"* could be heard. But this was not meant to be taken seriously. Yet amid the tumult it seemed to dawn on people for the first time that this man was demanding of old Europe an admission of bankruptcy. Moreover, it was becoming apparent that he had delivered a fatal blow to a wounded League of Nations already undermined by fear, mistrust, and selfishness. At the same time, the idea of disarmament was killed off. If it is true, as has been remarked, that Hitler's conquest of power was actually a declaration of war upon the system of peace instituted at Versailles,[29] then the declaration was made on that October 14, 1933. But no one acknowledged it. General annoyance with the protracted Geneva palaver, with paradoxes and hypocrisies, was expressed above all in the British press. The conservative *Morning Post* declared that it would shed no tears over the League of

437

Nations and the Disarmament Conference; the proper feeling was relief that such "a humbug" had come to an end. When the newsreel in a London theater showed Hitler, the audience applauded.[30]

Fearing that the easy success of the surprise tactics would go to Hitler's head, Hermann Rauschning, coming from Geneva, called on him at the Berlin chancellery. He found Hitler "in the best of spirits; he was all keyed-up and eager to take action." With a contemptuous gesture he waved away what Rauschning had to say about the indignation at Geneva and the call for military sanctions. "You say they want war?" he asked. "They have no thought of it. . . . A sad crew is assembled there. They don't act, they only protest. And they'll always think of things too late. . . . These people will not stop Germany's rise."

For a time, Rauschning's report continues, Hitler paced back and forth in silence. He seemed to be aware that for the first time since January 30 he had entered a risky zone, which he must now cross, and that his forceful act could have the direst consequences for the country. Without looking up, Hitler justified his decision in a kind of monologue. In doing so he offered Rauschning a remarkable insight into the structure of his decision making:

I had to do that. A grand liberating act that everyone could understand was essential. I had to pull the German people out of this whole clinging network of dependencies, empty phrases and false ideas. I had to restore our freedom of action. I am not concerned here with the politics of the day. For the moment the difficulties may have mounted. So be it—that will be balanced out by the trust the German people will place in me as a result. It would have made no sense to us to go on debating the subject, as the Weimar parties did for ten long years. . . . [The people] want to see something being done, not the same fraud being continued. What was needed was not what the brooding intellect thinks is useful, but the dramatic act which demonstrates a resolute will to make a new beginning. Whether it was done wisely or not, the people at any rate understand only such acts, not the futile bargaining that leads to nothing. The people are sick of being led around by the nose.[31]

Shortly afterward it became apparent that he had reasoned rightly. For Hitler characteristically linked withdrawal from the League of Nations with another step that went considerably beyond the original pretext. He decided to hold a plebiscite on the issue, the first such plebiscite of his regime, and one staged with an enormous display of propaganda. This in turn was combined with new elections. For the Reichstag that had been elected on March 5 was to some extent still anachronistically divided on the pattern that had prevailed under the Weimar Republic.

The outcome of the voting could not be in doubt. Feelings of humiliation harbored for years, deep-seated resentment over the tricks by which Germany had been kept under since Versailles—all such emotions now

ON THE WAY TO THE FÜHRER STATE

broke forth, and even critics of the regime, who would soon be going over to active resistance, hailed Hitler's gesture. As the British ambassador reported to London, all Germans were united in the desire to avenge themselves upon the League of Nations for its manifold failures. Since Hitler had intertwined his policies as a whole with the resolution to withdraw from the League by framing his plebiscite question in general terms, there was no way for the voter to express approval of his position on the League of Nations and at the same time condemn his domestic policies. Thus the plebiscite was one of the most effective chess moves in the process of consolidating his power within Germany.

Hitler himself opened the campaign on October 24 with a major speech in the Berlin Sportpalast. He announced that the plebiscite was to take place on November 12, one day after the fifteenth anniversary of the 1918 Armistice. Once more facing an electoral challenge, Hitler worked himself up into a trancelike paroxysm. "For my part I declare," he cried out to the masses, "that I would sooner die than sign anything that in my most sacred conviction is not tolerable for the German people." He also asserted that "if ever I should be mistaken in this matter or if the people should ever believe that they can no longer support my actions . . . I wish them to have me executed. I will quietly await the blow!" As always, when he felt slighted, he ranted demagogically about the injustice that had been done to him. Speaking to the workers of the Siemens-Schuckert Works, dressed in boots, military trousers, and dark civilian jacket, standing on an enormous derrick, he stated:

We are gladly willing to co-operate in any international agreement. But we will do so only as equals. I have never, in private life, forced myself upon any distinguished company that did not want to have me or did not regard me as an equal. I don't need such people, and the German nation has just as much character. We are not taking part in anything as shoeshine boys, as inferiors. No, either we have equal rights or the world will no longer see us at any conferences.

Once again, as in earlier years, a frantic "poster war" was launched. "We want honor and equality!" In Berlin, Munich, and Frankfurt a procession of crippled veterans in wheelchairs was mounted. The veterans held signs: "Germany's Dead Demand Your Vote!" Considerable use was made of quotations from the wartime British Prime Minister, Lloyd George, who asserted that right was on Germany's side and that England would not have put up with such a humiliation for any length of time.[32] A wave of gigantic marches, protest festivals, and mass appeals once again rolled over the country. A few days before the election the nation was asked to observe two minutes of total silence in remembrance of its dead heroes. Hitler declared that the military tone of life in Germany was not for the sake of demonstrating against France "but to exemplify the political decision-making that is necessary for the conquest of Communism. . . . When the rest of the world barricades itself in indestructible fortresses, builds vast fleets of airplanes, constructs giant tanks, makes enormous cannon, it can scarcely talk about a menace when German National Socialists march entirely weaponless in columns of four and thus provide a visible expression of the German racial community and effective protection for it. . . . Germany has a right to security no less than other nations."

All the resentments of the people were expressed in the results of the plebiscite—but it also showed the effects of an intensification of propaganda. Ninety-five per cent of the voters approved the government's decision to withdraw from the League. And although this result was manipulated and accompanied by terroristic electioneering practices the outcome still more or less corresponded to public mood. In the simultaneous Reichstag election 39 million of the 45 million eligibles gave their vote to the Nazi "unity" candidates. The day was exuberantly hailed as "the miracle of the birth of the German nation."

During his coming to power Hitler had proved the value of a series of surprise actions on the domestic front; now he applied the same tactics to foreign affairs. The dismay at his break with Geneva was not yet over, and there was still indignation at his arrogant attempt to turn the democratic principle of the plebiscite against the democracies themselves, when he again seized the initiative. His purpose now was to arrange a dialogue on a new and more favorable plane with the powers he had just offended. In a memorandum issued in mid-December he rejected the idea of disarmament but declared himself willing to accept a general limitation of armaments to defensive weapons, provided Germany was allowed to raise a conscript army of 300,000 men.

This was the first of those offers, placed with such remarkable feeling for the situation, which for years prefaced each of his foreign-policy coups right up to the outbreak of the war. For the British the terms were just barely acceptable as a basis for negotiations, for the French unacceptable, just as Hitler had calculated in each case. And while the two Allies took council endlessly—the consultations protracted by French distrust—on how far each was willing to go in making concessions, Hitler could exploit their differences, and the fact that no binding agreements had yet been arranged, to push forward his own plans.

Again, about a month later—on January 26, 1934—a new move of Hitler's abruptly changed the picture: he concluded a ten-year nonaggression pact with Poland. To understand the startling effect of this move, we must call to mind the traditionally tense relations between Germany and Poland and the fund of old resentment between the two countries. Some of the bitterest points of the Versailles Treaty had been those concerned with territorial losses to the new Polish state, the creation of the Polish Corridor, which cut off East Prussia from the rest of the Reich, and the establishment of the Free City of Danzig. These areas became bones of contention between the two countries and the focuses of constant menaces. The Germans had been greatly disturbed by Polish border violations and injustices during the early years of the Weimar Republic, partly because they had pointed up Germany's general impotence, partly because of the offense to the old German sense of being able to lord it over the Slavic vassals. As France's ally, moreover, Poland fed the Germans' encirclement complex. Weimar foreign policy, including that of Gustav Stresemann, had stubbornly resisted any suggestions that Germany guarantee Poland's possession of her existing territory.

These anti-Polish feelings dominated the traditionally pro-Russian diplomatic and military circles and the old Prussian landowning class as well. Yet Hitler brushed them aside with hardly a qualm. On the other side Marshal Pilsudski displayed equal resolution: faced with France's halfhearted and nervous policy, he restructured Poland's entire pattern of alliances. Essentially he was acting on the premise that Hitler, as a South German, a Catholic and a "Hapsburger," could disassociate himself from the political traditions that Poland feared.

Here Hitler once more gave the lie to the popular view of him as an emotional politician, the victim of his whims and manias. Unquestionably he shared the national German enmity toward Poland. But he did not allow this to affect his policy. Although he had not yet defined what place Poland would occupy within his general concept of a vast eastward expansion, it may be assumed that there was no room for an independent Polish ministate within the framework of Hitler's continental visions. As recently as April, 1933, Hitler had made it plain to Ambassador François-Poncet that no one could expect Germany to accept in the long run the present state of her eastern border. But as long as Poland was independent, militarily strong, and protected by alliances, he acted on the basis of the situation he could not change and coolly tried to turn it to his advantage. "Germans and Poles will have to learn to accept the fact of each other's existence," he stated in his anniversary report to the Reichstag on January 30, 1934. "Hence it is more sensible to regulate this state of affairs which the last thousand years have not been able to remove, and the next thousand years will not be able to remove either, in such a way that the highest possible profit will accrue from it for both nations."

The profit Hitler derived from the treaty did in fact prove to be enormous. In Germany itself the pact was scarcely popular; but to the outside world Hitler could repeatedly adduce it as evidence of his conciliatory temper even with regard to notorious enemies. British Ambassador Sir Eric Phipps commented in a report to London that the German Chancellor had now proved that he was a statesman by sacrificing some of his popularity

441

to a rational foreign policy.[33] At the same time, Hitler had succeeded, by his Polish alliance, in discrediting the system of the League of Nations, which in all the preceding years had not managed to dampen the Polish-German tinderbox. Things had been left, as Hitler convincingly complained, so that the "tensions gradually . . . assumed the character of a hereditary political taint on both sides." And now, seemingly without effort, in the course of a few bilateral conversations, he eliminated the problem.

Finally, the pact proved that the barriers which had been erected around Germany were not nearly as stout as had been assumed. "With Poland, one of the strongest pillars of the Treaty of Versailles falls," General von Seeckt had once said, expressing one of the tenets of the Weimar Republic's foreign policy—and obviously suggesting that the problem could be solved by military action. Hitler was now demonstrating that imaginative political methods could achieve great effects. For the alliance not only freed Germany from the Franco-Polish threat on two fronts; it also knocked a sizable piece out of the system of collective guarantees of peace and left that system permanently irreparable. The Geneva experiment had, fundamentally speaking, already failed; Hitler had destroyed it with his first assault. Moreover, he had maneuvered France into the role of international troublemaker. The Foreign Ministers of the Weimar Republic had worn themselves out trying to wring concessions from an all-powerful and unyielding France. Hitler had simply turned his back on her temporarily. Henceforth he could devote himself to those bilateral negotiations, alliances, and intrigues that were central to his strategy of international relations. For he could win only if he confronted isolated opponents, never a united front. The game he had so skillfully staged in the domestic arena was now beginning again on the international plane. Already his fellow players were pressing forward. The first of them, in February, 1934, was the British Keeper of the Privy Seal, Anthony Eden.

The unpredictability of Hitler's manner must be counted among his prime tricks as a negotiator. Just as Hugenberg, Schleicher, Papen, and a vast entourage had once done, Eden, Sir John Simon, André François-Poncet, and Benito Mussolini thought they would be meeting a moody, limited, booted party boss who, to be sure, possessed a certain demagogic talent. The fellow who had obviously had to overcome his insignificance and borrow character for himself from a mustache, a forelock, and a uniform, who in an ordinary business suit looked rather like an imitation of the man he pretended to be, was for some time the favorite butt of European humor. He was pictured as a kind of "Gandhi in Prussian boots" or a feeble-minded Charlie Chaplin seated on a much too high chancellor's throne—at any rate "to the highest degree exotic," as a British observer, Arnold Toynbee, wrote ironically, "one of these political 'mad mullahs,'

442

non-smokers, non-drinkers of alcohol, non-eaters of meat, non-riders on horseback, and non-practisers of blood-sports in their cranky private lives."[34]

Negotiators and visitors who came to Hitler with such preconceptions were therefore all the more surprised. For years he astonished them by a schooled statesmanlike manner which he could easily put on and for which they were totally unprepared. Eden was amazed at Hitler's smart, almost elegant appearance, and wondered at finding him controlled and friendly. He listened readily to all objections, Eden wrote, and was by no means the melodramatic actor he had been described as being. Hitler knew what he was talking about, Eden commented in retrospect, and respect still rings in his remark that the German Chancellor had had complete command of the subject under discussion and had not once found it necessary to consult his experts even on questions of detail. Sir John Simon remarked to von Neurath on a later occasion that Hitler was "excellent and very convincing" in conversation, and that before meeting him he had had a completely false picture of him. Hitler also surprised his interlocutors by his quick-wittedness. When the British Foreign Minister hinted that the English liked people to abide by treaties, Hitler showed ironic surprise and replied: "That was not always the case. In 1813 the German Army was prohibited by treaty. Yet I do not recollect that at Waterloo Wellington said to Blücher: Your Army is illegal. Kindly leave the field."

When Hitler met Mussolini in Venice in June, 1934, he contrived to combine "dignity with friendliness and candor" in his manner, according to a diplomatic eyewitness, and left a "strong impression" behind among the initially skeptical Italians. Arnold Toynbee was surprised to hear him discourse on Germany's guardian role in the East; his remarks, moreover, made excellent sense. In his relations with foreign visitors Hitler showed himself quick-witted, well prepared, often charming; and as François-Poncet noted after one meeting with him, he also contrived to give the impression of "fullest sincerity."[35]

Like the Germans who had once come to gape at Hitler as if he were an acrobat in a circus, the foreigners came in growing numbers, and in so doing extended the aura of greatness and admiration that surrounded him. They listened all too eagerly to his words about the people's longing for order and work, to his assurances of his love of peace, which he was fond of connecting with his personal experiences as a soldier at the front. The foreigners showed understanding for his sensitive sense of honor. It was already beginning to be customary, especially within Germany itself, to distinguish between the fanatical partisan politician of the past and the responsible realist of the present. For the first time since the days of the Kaiser a majority of the German people had the feeling that they could identify with their own government without feelings of pity, anxiety, or shame. Papen, who otherwise was certainly no spokesman for the general mood, was probably expressing a widely held view when he paid tribute, at

443

a cabinet meeting of November 14, 1933, to the "genius of the Chancellor."

Meanwhile, the decibel level of propaganda was stepped up, and more was made of Hitler as the leader and savior than ever. On the morning of May 1 Goebbels prolonged his introductory speech until the sun, which had been battling with the clouds, began to break through and Hitler could step before the masses in a blaze of light. Such clever symbolism conferred upon the image of the Führer the sacredness of a supernatural principle. And the concept of the "leader" was made to permeate the entire social system down to the very smallest units. The rector was described as the "leader of the university," the businessman as the "factory leader." Everyone was fitted into some leader-follower relationship, and all these relationships culminated in the archleader Hitler. An ecstatic Thuringian churchwarden went so far as to declare: "Christ has come to us through Adolf Hitler."

The personality and the destiny of the great, lonely, chosen man, who had turned away the country's miseries or taken them upon himself, became the subject of a multitude of Führer poems, Führer films, Führer pictures, or Führer dramas. In Richard Euringer's *Thingspiel* Deutsche Passion (German Passion)*, performed with great success in the summer of 1933 and subsequently hailed as the model of National Socialist drama, Hitler appeared as a resurrected Unknown Soldier, a crown of thorns made of barbed wire upon his head, entering a world of profiteers, stockholders, intellectuals, and proletarians—the representatives of the "November Republic." He has come because, in the words of the play, which continually sounds Christian motifs, he "had mercy on the people." When the mob wants to scourge and crucify him, he checks them by a miracle and leads the nation "to warfare and workfare" (*zu Gewehr und Gewerk*). He reconciles the living with the war dead in the great people's community of the Third Reich. Then "a glory breaks" from his wounds and he ascends into heaven with the words: "It is finished!" The stage directions for the final scene read: "Organ tone from the skies. Nostalgia. Sacral. Rhythmically and harmoniously mingled with the secular marching song."

Closely akin to such literary rubbish was the broad and polluted stream of kitsch culture. Everyone jumped in, trying to cash in on the mood of the moment. A brand of canned herring was called "Good Adolf." Coin banks were made in the form of SA caps. Pictures of Hitler appeared on ties, handkerchiefs, hand mirrors, and the swastika decorated ash trays and beer mugs. Some Nazi officials warned that the Führer's picture was being exploited and profaned by a money-grubbing band of pseudoartists.

---

* *Thingspiele* pretended to be dramatic re-creations of the ancient Teutonic judicial assembly, the *Thing,* which had met outdoors. In practice they were potpourris of Nazi propaganda, Germanic mythology, and borrowings from Wagner and the Brothers Grimm.—TRANS.

444

It is clear that the excessive tributes had their effect upon Hitler himself. He was aware that the whole thing was artificially manufactured in line with his program: "The masses need an idol," he declared. Nevertheless, the lineaments of the "leader-pope" began coming to the fore again, after having been suppressed somewhat just after the seizure of power. Now, however, this kind of leadership was extended from the party to the entire nation. As early as February 25, 1934, Rudolf Hess, speaking at the Königsplatz in Munich amid the roar of cannon and addressing by radio nearly a million political bosses, leaders of the Hitler Youth and the Labor Service, had made them take the oath: "Adolf Hitler is Germany and Germany is Adolf Hitler. He who pledges himself to Hitler pledges himself to Germany."

Reinforced by his band of disciples, Hitler became more and more at home with this equation, which meanwhile was being given a theoretical foundation in an extensive literature on political science. Sample: "The new and decisive aspect of the Führer Constitution is that it goes beyond the democratic distinction between rulers and ruled to create a unity in which the Leader and the following have merged." All selfish interests and all social antagonisms were abolished within him; a total unity of the German people corresponded to the total enemy on the outside. The Führer had the power to bind and to loose; he knew the way, the mission, the law of history.

Hitler's speeches show him in full agreement with all this; he reckoned in centuries and occasionally suggested that he was on special terms with Providence. And just as he had overruled the many Old Fighters who had believed the party program, so he made his Danzig followers hew to the new line on Poland. He insisted on discipline, with no allowance made for local interests. "Everything in Germany begins with this man and ends with him," his adjutant Wilhelm Brückner wrote.

The surer Hitler felt in the possession of power, the more conspicuously his old bohemian traits came to the fore, his lapses into torpor, his moodiness. For the present he still kept regular office hours, entered his office punctually at ten o'clock in the morning, and to evening visitors displayed the mountains of documents he had worked through. But he had always hated routine. "A single idea of genius," he used to say, "is more valuable than a whole lifetime of conscientious office work." Scarcely, therefore, had the excitement of being a Chancellor faded, with the glamour of the historical decor and the thrill of sitting at Bismarck's desk, than he began discarding it all—just as in his youth he had dropped the piano, school, painting. Sooner or later, in fact, he would drop everything—at the end even the political game and his love of oratory. Ultimately, all he held on to were his obsessive ideas, those products of anxiety and ambition.

Significantly, his manner soon reverted to the Schwabing *condottiere* style of the twenties. Constantly trailing behind him a motley caravan of

445

demiartists, strong-arm men, and adjutants, he would always be traveling between the chancellery, the Brown House, Obersalzberg, Bayreuth, parade grounds, and meeting halls. As the years went on, his need to be in motion increased. On the morning of July 26, for example, he delivered an address in Munich to a delegation of 470 Italian Young Fascists; at 2 P.M. he attended the funeral of Admiral von Schroeder in Berlin; and by 5 P.M. he was at a concert in Bayreuth. On July 29, still in Bayreuth, he was the guest of honor at a reception given by Winifred Wagner, and the following day laid a wreath on the composer's grave. In the afternoon he spoke at the German Gymnastic Festival in Stuttgart, then went to Berlin, then to a meeting with high party officials at Obersalzberg. On August 12 he took part in a Richard Wagner Festival in Neuschwanstein, where in the course of his speech he referred to himself as completing the plans of King Ludwig II. From there he returned to Obersalzberg for a week. On August 18 he left for Nuremberg to see to preparations for the party rally, and a day later went to Bad Godesberg for a discussion with SA and SS leaders. It would appear that, now, having achieved success, he was once more prey to the fluctuating desires and interests of his earlier years. Often, he would let himself drift irresolutely for a long while, then he would suddenly display an explosive energy—especially in questions concerning power. In the political realm he manifested a peculiar and surely rare combination of indolence and genius. Soon he was shirking the many burdensome routine duties of his office and brazenly going to the opera or the movies instead. During those early months as Chancellor he once more read through all of Karl May's nearly seventy volumes of adventure stories—of which he later said that they had opened his eyes to the world. It was this unusual style of undisguised laziness that prompted Oswald Spengler to remark sarcastically that the Third Reich was "the organization of the jobless by the job-shirkers."[36] Rosenberg, for example, was highly indignant that Hitler preferred an ice revue to a demonstration Rosenberg had organized. In years past, Gottfried Feder had wanted to assign an army officer to Hitler to help him handle a proper day's agenda. But Goebbels explained his master's working methods in characteristically high-flown terms. "What we . . . are constantly endeavoring to bring to bear has become for him a system in world-wide dimensions. His creativity is that of the genuine artist, no matter in what field he may be working."

If we look at the matter in retrospect, Hitler accomplished an amazing amount in the first year of his chancellorship. He had eliminated the Weimar Republic, taken the decisive steps toward building a government dependent upon him personally as leader, had centralized the nation, politically regimented it, and had brought it to the point of becoming the weapon he considered it to be, as indeed he considered everything to be a weapon. He had initiated an economic turnaround, had thrown off the fetters of the League of Nations, and had won the respect of the outside world. Within a short time, a pluralistic free society with its many centers of power and influence had been burned down to "pure, uniform, obedient ashes." As he himself put it, he had "got rid of a world of opinions and institutions and installed another in its place." Only disorganized groups without political weight were left of the shattered opposition.

Granted, what Goebbels called the "process of resmelting the nation" had not taken place without the use of violence. But we should not overestimate the part played by brute force in the course of the seizure of power. Hitler spoke of the "least bloody revolution in world history." This soon became one of the rhetorical slogans of the regime. And it certainly contained a kernel of truth. And yet—consider a decree such as Göring's of June 22, 1933, "For Combating Griping and Defeatism." The mere expression of discontent was viewed as a "continuation of Marxist agitation," and hence a punishable offence. Such a decree made plain what methods were used to heat the smelting crucible.

Similarly, when we contemplate the "miracle" of the folk community, we cannot overlook its illusory character. It was an impressive façade, but for the most part it only covered over and did not eliminate social conflicts. One episode from the first few days of the regime throws light on the way the national "reconciliation" was compounded of coercion and deception. The episode is as grotesque as it is illuminating: on Hitler's order the notorious leader of "Killer Storm Troop 33," Hans ("Firebug") Maikowski, was honored with a state funeral. He had been assassinated on the night of January 30, 1933, returning from the historic torchlight parade. A policeman named Zauritz who had been killed that same night was likewise granted a state funeral. In the name of the "folk community" and over the protests of the church officials, the policeman, who had been a Catholic and a leftist, was without more ado placed on a bier in the Lutheran cathedral alongside the storm trooper, who had been a gangster and a freethinker. To complete the missing element in this forcible reconciliation, the former Crown Prince was sent to lay wreaths on these coffins.

Nevertheless, the second phase of the seizure of power had proceeded more swiftly and more smoothly than anticipated. The necessary measures to organize government and party into a leader state were taken in the course of that legalistic game, which simultaneously prepared the next steps even as it was sanctioning the present one. In the provinces Reichstatthalter—federal governors—acted as party bosses, deposing ministers, appointing officials, participating in cabinet meetings, and exercising virtually unlimited authority as soon as the autonomy of the states was abrogated by law and the Reichsrat, the upper house, abolished. The federal government also stripped the states of their judiciary independence. A new organizational scheme for the party divided the country into thirty-two gaus, the gaus into sections, local groups, cells and blocks.

A statute of December 1, 1933, proclaimed the unity of party and state, but in fact Hitler was bent on separating the two. He had his reasons for leaving the national headquarters of the NSDAP in Munich. It was evident that he meant to keep the party from directly affecting government affairs. Hence his appointment of feeble, submissive Rudolf Hess, who lacked any power base of his own, to the post of Führer's deputy. Certainly no political primacy of the National Socialist Party existed. Unity was present only in the person of Hitler, who continued to foster a multiplicity of divided authorities and who allowed the party only in a few special cases to assume governmental functions and carry through its totalitarian claims.

Almost all the powerful institutions in Germany were overwhelmed. Hindenburg no longer counted. He was, as his friend and Neudeck neighbor von Oldenburg-Januschau pungently remarked, "the President we no longer have." Significantly, the leadership of the party, in taking that mass oath of February 25, swore allegiance to Hitler, not to the President, as should have been the case under the statute promulgating the unity of party and state. The old man still figured in a good many schemes as the supposed embodiment of justice and tradition; but in the meantime he had not only capitulated to Hitler, but allowed Hitler to corrupt him. His willingness to support the Nazi conquest of all power in the state with his moral authority certainly contrasted remarkably with the dour reserve with which he had left the Weimar Republic to its fate. On the anniversary of the Battle of Tannenberg the new rulers made him a gift of the Domain of Langenau, which bordered on Neudeck Estate, and the woodlands of Preussenwald, free and clear. He reciprocated with a gesture almost unprecedented in German military history, conferring upon retired Captain Hermann Göring "in recognition of his preëminent services in war and peace" the honorary rank of an infantry general.

The army remained the single institution that had escaped "co-ordination." The SA was clearly seething with impatience to carry out that final *Gleichschaltung*. "The gray rock must be drowned by the brown tide," Ernst Röhm was in the habit of remarking. Röhm and Hitler were now increasingly at odds, with Röhm suspecting that Hitler might abandon the revolution for reasons of tactics and opportunism. From Hitler's point of view, the army and the SA constituted the only remaining still independent power factors whose self-assurance had not been shattered. The manner in which he used each to smash the other, thus solving the existential problem of every revolutionary leader is still another example of his tactical genius. He arranged for the revolution to devour first and foremost its most loyal children, and represented his perfidious act as a great service to history.

As always in the decisive situations of his life, he continued to hesitate, to answer those who pressed him to act with "We must let the situation ripen." But from the spring of 1934 on, forces entered into play that, operating along different paths, accelerated matters. On June 30, 1934, many different interests and impulses coincided, and all met before the rifle barrels of the execution squads.

Chapter 3

THE RÖHM AFFAIR

The tactics of legal revolution developed by Hitler made possible a relatively bloodless seizure of power, and avoided that deep rent in the body
politic with which every nation emerges from a revolutionary period. But
those same tactics had the drawback that the old leaders could infiltrate the
revolution by adaptation and thus could contantly threaten the existence
of the new regime, at least theoretically. Overrun and for the time being
carried along, the former ruling class was by no means eliminated, by no
means paralyzed. At the same time, the militant advance guard of the SA,
who had fought for the movement and cleared the obstacles from the path
to power, found themselves cheated of the wages of their wrath. Scornfully,
and with some bitterness, the brown pretorians watched the way "reaction"—the capitalists, generals, Junkers, conservative politicians and
others in the "cowardly bunch of philistines"—clambered onto the reviewing stands at the victory celebrations for the national revolution and
sedulously moved their black tailcoats in among the brown uniforms. If
everyone enrolled in the party, where would the revolutionaries find their
enemies?

An old-fashioned, straightforward roughneck like Röhm could not help
being furious at the way things were going. And he let his displeasure be
known quite early, in repeated public statements. By May, 1933, he had
thought it appropriate to issue an order warning the storm troopers against
all the false friends and false celebrations, and reminding them of unfulfilled goals: "We have celebrated enough. I wish that from now on the SA

449

and SS visibly withdraw from the endless succession of celebrations. . . .
Your task is to complete the National Socialist Revolution and to bring
about the National Socialist Reich. That still remains to be done." Hitler,
craftier than the clumsy Röhm, regarded the revolution as a pseudolegal
process of undermining the established order. It operated by demagoguery,
attrition, and deception; force was merely an auxiliary instrument handy
for purposes of intimidation. Röhm, on the other hand, could not conceive
of a revolution without an insurrectionary phase, a storming of the citadels
of the former powers, culminating in the classical "night of the long
knives." Nothing of the kind had taken place, and Röhm was deeply disappointed.

After a short period of tactical uncertainty he tried to keep his storm
troops out of the great national smelting process. He emphasized the need
for a martial posture and hailed the special mentality of the SA: "It alone
will win and preserve the victory of pure, unadulterated nationalism and
socialism." He warned his subleaders against taking posts and positions of
honor in the new government. While his rivals Göring, Goebbels, Himmler,
Ley, and countless followers of the third rank extended their influence by
acquiring bastions of political power, Röhm tried to go the opposite way.
By consistently building up his forces, which soon increased to between 3.5
million and 4 million men, he was preparing the way for the SA government, which one day would be superimposed right on top of the existing
order, crushing it.

Under these circumstances the old antagonisms between the SA and the
Political Organization inevitably flared once again. There was the natural
resentment of militant revolutionaries against the thick-necked, middle-
class egotists of the Political Organization, who were apt to win out in the
petty skirmishes for sinecures and jobs. The rancor increased after Hitler
demanded, with growing insistence, the end of revolutionary activities. As
early as June, 1933, the government had begun breaking up the many
unauthorized camps for protective custody set up by the SA. Soon afterward, the SA's auxiliary police squads were disbanded. In vain, Röhm's
followers pointed to the sacrifices they had made, the battles they had
endured; they felt that they had been passed over. They were the forgotten
revolutionaries of the unconsummated revolution. More and more often
word went out that the seizure of power was over, and the tasks of the SA
had been fulfilled. Röhm sharply retorted to such pronouncements in June,
1933. Those who were now calling for abatement of revolutionary fervor,
he declared, were betraying the revolution; the workers, peasants, and
soldiers who were marching under the banners of his storm troops would
finish their job without consideration for the "co-ordinated philistines and
gripers." He added, "Whether they like it or not, we shall continue our
struggle. Along with them, if they at last grasp what is at stake! Without
them, if they don't want to grasp it. And against them, if so it must be."

That was also the meaning of the slogan "The Second Revolution," which henceforth began to circulate through the barracks and headquarters of the SA. This slogan implied that the seizure of power in the spring of 1933 had bogged down in a thousand wretched halfway measures and compromises, had been altogether betrayed and must be pushed on to the point of total revolution, to a taking possession of the entire state. Many have pointed to this as proof that there was indeed some kind of constructive social concept, no matter how sketchy, within the brown formations. But no such definable concept ever arose out of the fog of phrases about the "sacred socialist seeking-the-whole," and no one attempted to describe how the SA state would be made up. This socialism never went beyond a crude, unconsidered soldier's communism—even more radicalized in Röhm's case by the cliquishness of homosexuals against a hostile world. The gist of it was that the SA state would be the kind of state that would solve the desperate social problem of so many unemployed storm troopers. There were also the cheated expectations of political adventurers who had masked their nihilism in the ideology of the Nazi movement and refused to understand why, now, after the victory had been won at last, they should bid adieu to excitement, fighting, and turmoil.

The very aimlessness of the SA's revolutionary fervor had in the meantime aroused anxieties in much of the public. No one knew against whom Röhm was planning to turn the enormous force that he flaunted in a furious series of parades, inspections, and spectacular demonstrations throughout Germany. Ostentatiously he set about reviving the old military tendencies within the SA, but he also sought connections and suppliers of funds in industry. He set up a task force of his own, the SA field police, and was likewise beginning to build up the SA's own judiciary. The latter set extremely severe penalties for unwarranted beatings, robbery, theft, or plundering by the SA; but it also ruled that "as retribution for the killing of an SA man the SA leader in charge of the case can require that up to twelve members of the enemy organization which prepared the murder may be condemned." The language was just sufficiently ambiguous to suggest that "condemned" meant "executed." At the same time, Röhm tried to secure a footing in the administration of the states, in academic and publishing fields, and in general to project the special claims of the SA everywhere. He was continually criticizing the regime, its foreign policy, its attacks on the unions, and its repression of freedom of opinion. He denounced Goebbels, Göring, Himmler, and Hess in the bitterest terms. As for his opinion of Hitler, he was personally outraged by the Führer's deviousness and would freely air his grievances when among friends:

Adolf is rotten. He's betraying all of us. He only goes around with reactionaries. His old comrades aren't good enough for him. So he brings in these East Prussian generals. They're the ones he pals around with now. . . . Adolf knows perfectly well what I want. I've told him often enough. Not a second pot

451

of the Kaiser's army, made with the same old grounds. Are we a revolution or aren't we? . . . Something new has to be brought in, understand? A new discipline. A new principle of organization. The generals are old fogies. They'll never have a new idea. . . .

But Adolf is and always will be a civilian, an "artist," a dreamer. Just leave me be, he thinks. Right now all he wants to do is sit up in the mountains and play God. And guys like us have to cool our heels, when we're burning for action. . . . The chance to do something really new and great, something that will turn the world upside down—it's a chance in a lifetime. But Hitler keeps putting me off. He wants to let things drift. Keeps counting on a miracle. That's Adolf for you. He wants to inherit a ready-made army all set to go. He wants to have it knocked together by "experts." When I hear that word I blow my top. He'll make it National Socialist later on, he says. But first he's turning it over to the Prussian generals. Where the hell is revolutionary spirit to come from afterwards? From a bunch of old fogies who certainly aren't going to win the new war? Don't try to kid me, the whole lot of you. You're letting the whole heart and soul of our movement go to pot.[37]

What Röhm most wanted was to absorb the numerically smaller Reichswehr into his brown mass army and thereby create a National Socialist militia. It seems that Hitler had no intention whatever of letting him do this. The disagreement on the purpose of the SA was old, and Hitler continued to hold that the brown formations should carry out a political, not a military function. They were to be an enormous "Hitler shock troop," not the cadres of a revolutionary army. Outwardly, however, he faked indecisiveness, obviously hoping to hit upon some compromise between Röhm's ambitions and the claims of the Reichswehr. Undoubtedly he shared with Röhm a profound aversion, reinforced by his experiences of 1923, for the arrogant, stiff, monocle-wearing "old fogies," and Himmler once heard him remark about the generals, "One day they'll take a shot at me."[38] But their backing was indispensable if he were to consolidate his power. He kept in mind the great lesson of the November putsch, never again to get involved in open conflict with the armed forces. He attributed his defeat at that time to the opposition of the army, just as he attributed his success in 1933 to the support or at least the benevolent neutrality of the army leadership. Moreover, he would need their technical expertise for the rearmament program which he had already launched in the summer of 1933. In view of his expansionist plans, he knew there was no time to lose. Moreover, only the regular army possessed the offensive power that he required—a militia such as Röhm had in mind was, strictly speaking, an instrument of defense.

Yet Hitler must have been pleasantly surprised by the way top army men behaved toward him. In Defense Minister von Blomberg and in the new chief of staff, Colonel Walther von Reichenau, he found two partners who, for different reasons, were entirely amenable to his wishes.

Blomberg was an enthusiast by temperament. He had in turn subscribed to democracy, anthroposophy, the idea of a Prussian socialism, then "something close to Communism"—this after a trip to Russia—and finally been drawn more and more to authoritarian ideas until he succumbed to Hitler's blandishments. In 1933, Blomberg later avowed, he had been vouchsafed things he no longer could have hoped for: faith, veneration for a man, and complete dedication to an idea. A friendly remark of Hitler's, a contemporary source tells us, could bring tears to his eyes; and Blomberg used to say that a cordial handshake of the Führer's could cure him of colds.[39]

Reichenau was of a different stamp: a sober man with a Machiavellian turn of mind who kept his ambitions free from emotion. He quickly decided that he could make use of Nazism to further his personal career and the power of the army. At the proper moment the Nazis could be tamed, he thought. As intelligent as he was coolheaded, by nature decisive, sometimes to a fault, he was the almost perfect embodiment of the modern, technically trained and socially unbiased army officer who unfortunately carried his lack of prejudices to moral categories also. At a meeting of army commanders in February, 1933, he opined that the general breakdown could be stemmed only by dictatorship. This thesis so well suited Hitler's purposes that he must have asked himself why he should turn down the proffered allegiance of the military experts in favor of the troublesome Röhm. Among his intimates he tended to make fun of these "bandylegged SA men who think they're the material for a military elite."

Hitler's usual way of handling his enemies was to play them off against each other and let them fight it out between them. But in this case he was fairly frank about which side he favored. It is true that he constantly whipped up the SA's militant activism and would, for example, exhort the storm troopers: "Your whole life will be nothing but struggle. From struggle you came; do not hope for peace today or tomorrow." His appointment of Röhm to the cabinet on December 1 and his remarkably cordial letter of thanks to the chief of staff at the end of the year were widely interpreted, within the SA, as an official blessing. Nevertheless, he repeatedly assured the army that it was and would remain the sole armed force in the nation. And his decision at the beginning of the new year to reintroduce compulsory military service within the framework of the army ran counter to all Röhm's plans for a vast militia. But Röhm continued to believe that Hitler was, as always, playing some deep game and secretly agreed with him now as he supposedly had in the past.

Consequently, Röhm decided that he was being blocked by some of Hitler's advisers. Accustomed to overcoming all difficulties by frontal assault, he resorted to noisy invective and heavy pressure. He called Hitler a "weakling" who had fallen into the hands of "stupid and dangerous creatures." But he, Röhm, was going to "free him from those fetters." And while the SA began posting armed guards around its headquarters, Röhm sent a memorandum to the Ministry of Defense declaring the defense of the country was the "domain of the SA" and leaving the army the sole task of military training. Incessantly speechmaking and fulminating, he thus gradually set the stage on which his destiny was to be played out. At the beginning of January, 1934, only a few days after Hitler had thanked his chief of staff and intimate friend in such warm words for his services, the Chancellor ordered Rudolf Diels, chief of the secret state police office (the incipient Gestapo) to gather incriminating documents on "Herr Röhm and his friendships" and also on the SA's terroristic activities. "This is the most important assignment you have ever received," he told Diels.

Meanwhile, the army had not been idle. Röhm's memorandum had made it plain to the Reichswehr leaders that there was no midcourse: Hitler would have to choose between themselves and the SA. Ostentatiously meeting the Nazis halfway, early in February Blomberg directed that the "Aryan clause" be applied to the officer corps and made the swastika the official symbol of the armed forces. Army Commander in Chief General von Fritsch justified this step on the grounds that it would "give the Chancellor the necessary impetus against the SA."[40]

In fact, Hitler now found himself forced to take an unambiguous position. On February 2 he delivered an address to the gauleiters assembled in Berlin. The speech both reflected his perplexities at the time and constituted a noteworthy statement of principles. The minutes of the meeting record:

The Führer stressed . . . that those who go on saying the Revolution isn't over yet are fools . . . and continued that in the movement we have people who by revolution mean nothing but a permanent state of chaos. . . .

The Führer said that the most crucial task at the moment was the selection of people who on the one hand are competent, on the other hand can carry out the measures of the administration in blind obedience. The party must act as a kind of monastic order, assuring the necessary stability for the entire future of Germany. . . . The first Leader had been chosen by Destiny; the second must from the start have a loyal, sworn community behind him. No one may be selected who has a private power base!

Only one man can be the Leader. . . . An organization with such a hard core and strength will endure forever; nothing can overthrow it. The community within the movement must be incredibly loyal. There must not be any internecine struggles; we must never allow differences to be bared to outsiders! The people cannot trust us with blind faith if we ourselves destroy this trust. Even if wrong decisions are made, the effects can be mitigated by our unconditionally sticking together. We must never allow one authority to be played off against the other.

Therefore: no superfluous discussions! Problems which the various headquarters have not yet clarified may under no circumstances be discussed in public, for that would entail involving the masses of the people in the decision-making process. That was the insanity of democracy, whereby the value of all leadership is lost.

We must never engage in more than a single fight at a time. Fights in single file. Not "Many enemies, much honor," but "Many enemies, much stupidity." Moreover, the people cannot wage or understand twelve struggles going on at once. Consequently we must always present the people with only a single idea, make them concentrate on one single idea. In questions of foreign policy it is crucial to have the entire people hypnotically behind one; the whole nation must be literally filled with a sporting spirit, be following this struggle with the passion of gamblers. This is essential. If the whole nation takes part in the struggle, the whole nation is the loser. If it is indifferent, only the leadership loses. In the one case the people are roused to fury against the opponent, in the second case only against the leader.[41]

These principles were in fact to obtain deep into the war years. The practical conclusions were not long in coming. As early as February 21, 1934, Hitler confided to Anthony Eden that he intended to reduce the SA by two thirds and insure that the remaining formations received neither weapons nor military training. A week later he summoned the commanders of the army and the leaders of the SA and SS, headed by Röhm and Himmler, to the Ministry of Defense, on Bendlerstrasse. In a speech that the army officers received with applause and the SA leaders heard with horror, he sketched the basic lines of an agreement between the Reichswehr and the SA. The duties of the brown-shirted storm troops would be limited to a few minor military functions; their chief assignment was to be the political education of the nation. Hitler begged the SA leadership not to obstruct him in such grave times—and added menacingly that he would crush anyone who tried to.

Röhm failed to note these warnings or regarded them as mere verbal maneuvers. For the time being he kept his composure and invited everyone present to a "reconciliation breakfast." But as soon as the generals had left, he freely vented his anger. He is said to have called Hitler an "ignorant corporal" and declared bluntly that he "had no intention of keeping the agreement." He is also alleged to have said that Hitler was "disloyal and badly in need of a vacation." Subsequently SA Obergruppenführer Lutze went to see Hitler at Obersalzberg and in a conversation lasting several hours reported Röhm's insults and veiled threats.

In all this Röhm was actuated not just by defiance and the arrogance of knowing that, as he declared, he had the power of thirty divisions behind him. Rather, he understood only too well that Hitler was confronting him with an unacceptable alternative. To tell him that he must either educate the nation or quit was the equivalent to giving him the sack. For no one could seriously imagine that those "bandylegged" SA men were the right people to instruct the Aryan master race.

Convinced of the hopelessness of his situation, Röhm seems to have called on Hitler early in March and proposed a "little solution": that the army take in several thousand SA leaders. This would at least provide for some of Röhm's people. But both Hindenburg and the army leadership would not hear of this. Röhm found himself driven by an outraged and increasingly impatient following, and by his own craving for status, to take once more the path of revolt.

From the spring of 1934 on, the slogans of the second revolution were again in currency. But although there was talk of putsch and rebellion, there is no indication of a specific plan of action. In keeping with the rough-and-tough stance of these blusterers, they were satisfied with bloodthirsty phrases. Röhm himself had spells of resignation, occasionally considered returning to Bolivia, and at one point told the French ambassador that he was sick. Nevertheless, he kept trying to break out of the ever more tightly closing ring of isolation and to make contact with Schleicher and probably with other oppositional circles. He organized a new wave of giant parades and, in general, tried by incessant triumphant marches to make a show of the SA's unbroken vigor. At the same time, he obtained sizable quantities of arms—partly by purchases abroad—and stepped up the military-training program of his units. Of course, all this may only have served to keep his disappointed and irritably loafing storm troopers occupied. But such activities were regarded by Hitler and the army leadership as a challenge. Certainly they provided a disquieting background to the rebellious bluster.

It appears that by the spring Hitler stopped trying to settle matters amicably with Röhm and instead steered toward a solution by violence. On April 17, at a spring concert given by the SS in the Berlin Sportpalast, Hitler appeared in public with Röhm for the last time. Extending the assignment given to Diels, he now directed several party bureaus—by his own later testimony—to look into the rumors about a second revolution and to track down their sources. It is tempting to associate the build-up of the Sicherheitsdienst (the security service of the SS, the notorious SD), which began simultaneously with this assignment, and likewise Heinrich Himmler's take-over of the Prussian Gestapo. Obviously there was a connection with the fact that the judicial authorities at this point began to prosecute SA crimes for the first time. Theodor Eicke, the commandant of Dachau concentration camp, supposedly received instructions to draw up a "Reich list" containing the names of "undesirable persons."

It was a veritable roundup that Röhm could scarcely misconstrue. Plainly they were out to get him. His principal enemies were the functionaries of the Political Organization (PO), above all Göring, Goebbels, and Hess, who envied the SA chief of staff his enormous power base and the position of second man in the state that went with it. Heinrich Himmler soon joined them; as commander of the SS, then still a subdivision of the SA, he stood to profit by Röhm's fall. Alongside these party people, cautiously operating in the background but more and more making its presence felt, was the army leadership. By skillfully peddling information about Röhm and by playing up its own docility, it hoped to draw Hitler over to its side. In February, 1934, the corps of army officers voluntarily set aside one of its dearest traditions, the principle of drawing its members from a special stratum of society. Instructions were issued to the effect that henceforth "origin in the old officer caste" was not to be the basic requirement for a military career, but rather "consonance with the new government." Shortly afterward, the Reichswehr introduced political education for the troops. On Hitler's birthday, April 20, Minister of Defense Blomberg published an extravagant article in praise of the Führer. Simultaneously, he renamed the Munich barracks that housed the List Regiment, in which Hitler had once served, the Adolf Hitler Barracks. The army's strategy was to stir up the ill-feeling between Hitler and Röhm until an open quarrel ensued from which the army generals would emerge the victors. They reasoned that Hitler would not realize that by stripping Röhm of power he was disarming himself and placing himself at the mercy of the army.

The rising tension was palpably communicated to the public mind. For a year Hitler had continued to keep the population breathless by fireworks, speeches, appeals, coups, and histrionics. Now both the public and the producer seemed equally exhausted. The pause for reflection offered the nation a first opportunity to take account of its real condition. Not yet completely overwhelmed and corrupted by propaganda, it noted coercion, pressure and regimentation, persecution of defenseless minorities, concentration camps, difficulties with the churches, the specter of inflation caused by reckless spending, terrorism and threats from the SA, and growing distrust on the part of the rest of the world. The result was a reversal of sentiment that even a noisy "campaign against gripers and criticasters," launched by Goebbels, was unable to stem. What emerged in the spring of 1934 was not a massive mood of dissatisfaction that found vent in any broadly based oppositional spirit; but unmistakably a sense of skepticism, of uneasiness, of suspicion, was spreading, and along with it an intimation that something was rotten in the state of Germany.

The spreading disenchantment suggests that we glance once more at the conservative stage managers of the events of January, 1933. And, in fact, although they now had forfeited all power to act, they seemed to feel that something should be done. In June, 1934, when Hindenburg was about to leave for his summer vacation at Neudeck, his parting words to his Vice-Chancellor were: "Things are going badly, Papen. Try to straighten them out." Since, however, there was no question of the President's intervening himself—the old man was visibly failing—the conservatives took up the idea of a monarchist restoration. Hitler had rejected this idea in no uncertain terms, the last time in his Reichstag speech of January 30, 1934. But Hindenburg now, on Papen's urging, promised to add a passage to his testament recommending a return to the monarchy. After all, the monarchist faction reasoned, under pressure of events Hitler would sooner or later have to accept a good many things he did not like.

In view of the reports of Hindenburg's condition, a rapid decision on Hitler's part was all the more urgent. His own plans assumed he would take over the office of President. This would assure him supreme command of the army and would thus form the concluding act in the seizure of power. On June 4, therefore, he once more met Röhm in order—as he explained in his later self-justifying speech—"to spare the Movement and my SA the shame of such a disagreement, and . . . to solve the problem without severe conflicts." In a discussion lasting for some five hours he pleaded with Röhm "of his own accord to oppose this madness" of a second revolution. But Röhm was far from ready to capitulate and gave him only the customary empty assurances.

The propaganda campaign against the gripers was screwed to a higher pitch of intensity. In addition to the SA, the conservative positions of the old bourgeoisie, of the nobility, of the churches, and above all of the monarchy came under the fire of Goebbels's Propaganda Ministry. But Röhm, evidently unsuspecting, went on vacation. In an order of the day he informed his followers that he was suffering from a rheumatic complaint and had to go to Bad Wiessee for a cure. To ease the tension somewhat, he sent the majority of the SA formations on leave for the month of July. His order warned "the enemies of the SA" against harboring any false hopes that the storm troopers would not return from their leaves, and in grimly ambiguous terms he threatened those enemies with an "appropriate answer." Interestingly enough, the order of the day did not mention Hitler's name.

Contrary to all his subsequent asseverations, it appears that Hitler could not have believed that Röhm, however recalcitrant, had plans for occupying the capital, seizing control of the government, and, in the course of a "conflict of the bloodiest kind, lasting several days," removing him personally.

Nine days later, Hitler went to Venice for his first trip abroad. He looked nervous, distracted and ill-humored as, wearing a light-colored raincoat, he walked forward to meet the Italian dictator. According to a political joke that went the rounds in Germany, Mussolini allegedly murmured, *"Ave, Imitator!"* Certainly there could not have been a less auspicious beginning for this curious relationship, filled with mutual admiration and no doubt blindness, soon to be dominated by Hitler with his conception of "brutal friendship."[42] At least during this period Hitler's mind was on other things than the threat of Röhm.

There were other threats, however. Concerned that the obviously impending death of Hindenburg would destroy the last chance to steer the regime onto a more moderate course, conservative backers of Franz von Papen urged him to take some sort of stand. On Sunday, June 17, while

Hitler was meeting with his assembled party leaders in Gera, the Vice-Chancellor delivered a speech at Marburg University. It had been ghosted for him by the conservative writer Edgar Jung and had far more bite than anything Papen himself might have produced. In a sensational fashion he came out strongly against the National Socialist revolution for its violence and unbridled radicalism. He condemned the roughshod methods of *Gleichschaltung*. He protested against the "unnatural claim to totality" and against the plebeian contempt for intellectual work. Then he continued:

No nation can afford an eternal revolt from below if that nation wishes to continue to exist as a historical entity. At some time the movement must come to an end; at some time a firm social structure must arise, and must be maintained by an incorruptible judiciary and an uncontested State authority. Permanent dynamism cannot shape anything lasting. We must not let Germany become a train tearing along to nowhere in particular. . . .

The government is well informed concerning the elements of selfishness, lack of character, mendacity, beastliness and arrogance that are spreading under the guise of the German Revolution. Nor is the government unaware that the treasure of confidence that the German people bestowed upon it is in jeopardy. Those who want closeness and intimate contact with the people must not underestimate the people's intelligence, must have confidence in them in return, not forever try to keep them in leading strings. . . . Not by whipping people up, especially whipping up the youth, and not by threats against helpless parts of the nation, but only by an honest dialogue with the people, can confidence and eager commitment be intensified. . . . Every word of criticism must not instantly be dubbed ill will, and despairing patriots must not be labeled enemies of the State.

The speech created a tremendous stir, even though it was heard by very few. Goebbels abruptly canceled the projected evening radio broadcast and kept the speech from appearing in the press. Hitler himself evidently took Papen's re-emergence as a personal challenge and went into a rage before his party leaders. He furiously denounced "all the little pygmies" and threatened that they would be "swept away by the force of our common ideal. . . . A while ago they had the power to prevent the rising of National Socialism; but never again will they be able to put the awakened people to sleep. . . . So long as they do nothing but gripe, we do not have to be concerned about them. But if they should ever try to move even in the slightest degree from criticism to a new act of treachery, they had better realize that what faces them today is not the cowardly and corrupt bourgeoisie of 1918, but the fist of the entire people." When Papen thereupon said that he would resign, Hitler backed off by proposing that they go together to call on Hindenburg in Neudeck.

It seems in fact that for a moment Hitler lost his grasp of the entire situation and misread the signs. He had no doubt been told occasionally that the President was not pleased by this or that. He was also aware of the

459

worries of the army leadership. With his knowledge of Herr von Papen, he assumed that the man would not have spoken as he had in Marburg if he had not had a whole coalition behind him: the entire power of the army leadership, the President, and the still influential conservative circles.

On June 21 Hitler went to Neudeck and once more slighted Papen by not asking him to come along—contrary to the agreement he had made only two days before. But the purpose of his visit was precisely to undermine the alliance between Hindenburg and Papen. He also wanted to ascertain the President's mood and capacity for making decisions. On such a mission, the Vice-Chancellor would only be a burden. Even before he called on the President, Hitler heard from Walther Funk, his Reich press chief, who was staying in Neudeck, about the old field marshal's typical military response: "If Papen cannot keep discipline, he has to take the consequences."

The talk with Hindenburg seems to have reassured Hitler. Nevertheless, the incident had taught him that he had no time to waste. Immediately after his return he withdrew to Obersalzberg for three days, in order to think the situation through. Everything points to the probability that the final decision to strike was taken then, and the date for action also determined. On June 26, back in Berlin, Hitler at once ordered the arrest of Edgar Jung. When Papen tried to remonstrate, Hitler refused to see him. To Alfred Rosenberg, who happened to be with him in the chancellery garden, Hitler said with a threatening gesture in the direction of the neighboring vice-chancellory. "Yes, it all comes from there. One of these days I'll have that whole office cleaned out."

As far back as the beginning of June the SS and SD had received orders for an intensified watch on the SA and been put on an active footing. SS Commandant Eicke, of Dachau, conducted "war games" with his staff in preparation for some strike in the region around Munich, Lechfeld, and Bad Wiessee. Rumors circulated about contacts Röhm was supposedly having with Schleicher and Gregor Strasser. Someone warned former Chancellor Brüning that his life was in danger; he secretly left Germany. Schleicher, who received many similar warnings, left Berlin for a while, but soon returned. Colonel Ott, a friend, proposed that they visit Japan together. Schleicher refused; he was not going to run out on the country, he said.

A so-called "Reich list" had been drawn up; it held the names of persons who at the proper moment were to be arrested or shot. This list circulated among Göring, Blomberg, Himmler, and Himmler's deputy Reinhard Heydrich, who was now beginning to emerge into prominence. Heydrich and SD Chief Werner Best could not agree about Obergruppenführer Schneidhuber of the Munich SA; the one man thought him "decent and loyal," the other regarded him as "just as dangerous" as the rest. Viktor Lutze discussed with Hitler whether only the very top leadership or a larger group of "chief culprits" should be liquidated. Lutze was later to bewail the wickedness of the SS, which to settle its own scores enlarged the original group of seven victims first to seventeen and finally to more than eighty persons.

On June 25 an alleged secret order from Röhm calling the storm troops to arms, came into the possession of the Abwehr (Conterintelligence) Department in the Defense Ministry. It should have been evident that the document was a forgery, if only because it included in its list of recipients Himmler and Heydrich, Röhm's worst enemies. Probably that same day Edmund Heines, SA Gruppenführer in Silesia, received word that the army was making preparations for some kind of action against the SA. Simultaneously, General von Kleist, the district commander of Breslau, received information that presented a "picture of feverish preparations on the part of the SA."[43] Day after day warnings were issued in radio speeches or at public demonstrations to the spokesmen of the second revolution, and other warnings to the conservative opposition.

On June 21 Goebbels, at a summer solstice festival in Berlin Stadium, declared: "Only force impresses this type, pride and strength. They're going to feel it. . . . They will not hold back the forward march of the century. We will pass over them." Four days later Hess, in a radio address, inveighed against the "players at revolution" who distrusted the "great strategist of the revolution," Adolf Hitler. "Woe to him who breaks faith!" On June 26 Göring, at a meeting in Hamburg, gave a firm no to all monarchist plans: "We the living have Adolf Hitler!" He uttered threats against the "reactionary clique with their selfish interests." As he put it: "If one of these days the cup should run over, then I'll strike! We have worked as no one ever worked before, because behind us stands a nation that trusts us. . . . Anyone who sins against this trust has forfeited his head." Hess made it clear that National Socialism was there to stay: "Any withdrawal of National Socialism from the political stage of the German people would . . . bring on chaos throughout Europe."

While the bluff storm troopers prepared for their leaves, Röhm and his closest associates had settled into the Hotel Hanslbauer in Wiessee. On June 25 the League of German Officers expelled Röhm.

In so doing, they were withdrawing their protection from him and consigning him to his fate. A day later Himmler informed all SS and SD top leaders of the "impending revolt of the SA under Röhm." Additional opposition groups would take part in it, Himmler said. Next day SS Gruppenführer Sepp Dietrich, commander of the SS Guard Battalion Berlin, asked the chief of the organization section of the army for additional weapons to carry out a secret assignment from the Führer. To help matters, Dietrich showed the men a "firing squad list," purportedly prepared by the SA, on which the name of the officer he was speaking to figured. To soothe any doubts that might arise, Colonel von Reichenau

461

employed, as did Himmler, deception, lies, and frightening fictions. Soon the rumor was going around that the SA had threatened to kill "all older army officers."

Meanwhile, the upper stratum of the Reichswehr leadership had been alerted to the SA putsch and had been told that the SS was on the side of the army and therefore should receive arms from it if necessary. An order issued by Lieutenant General Beck on June 29 warned all officers at army headquarters on Bendlerstrasse in Berlin to have their pistols at hand. That same day the *Völkische Beobachter* published an article by Defense Minister Blomberg that took the form of a declaration of total loyalty. It was also a request to Hitler, in the name of the army, to take measures to curb the SA.

Everything was now prepared. The SA had been kept in ignorance. The SS and SD, backed by the army, were ready to strike. The conservatives were intimidated, and the President, ill and relapsing into the vagueness of senility, was in distant Neudeck. One last attempt by several of Papen's associates to get to Hindenburg and have him impose a state of emergency was frustrated by Oskar von Hindenburg's fear and stupidity.

Hitler himself had left Berlin early in the morning on June 28 in order to, as he himself later explained, "present an outward impression of absolute calm and to give no warning to the traitors." A few hours later he was in Essen to attend the wedding of Gauleiter Terboven. But all around him frenzied activity was already developing, while he himself repeatedly dropped into sulky, absent-minded brooding. That evening he telephoned Röhm and ordered him to summon all the higher SA leaders to Bad Wiessee for a frank discussion on Saturday, June 30. Evidently the telephone conversation went amicably, if only because Hitler wished to lull any suspicions his chief of staff might have. At any rate, when Röhm rejoined his fellows at table in Bad Wiessee, he looked "very contented."

All that was needed now was the uprising. In fact, the SA had remained calm, and a good many of its members had dispersed. The weeks of investigation by the Sicherheitsdienst had produced no results that would have justified bloody proceedings. While Hitler went to Bad Godesberg on June 29 and Göring ordered his Berlin units on full alert, Himmler set about producing the SA "mutiny" provided for in the plans, which so far had failed to take place.[44] Summoned by handwritten, anonymous notes, units of the Munich SA suddenly appeared on the streets and marched about aimlessly. Their surprised leaders were called and promptly ordered their men to go home; but Gauleiter Wagner of Munich could now report to Bad Godesberg the appearance of allegedly rebellious SA formations. Hitler had just attended a Labor Service ceremony in front of the Hotel Dresden, overlooking the Rhine, an affair that culminated in 600 Labor Service workers bearing torches forming a glowing swastika on the slope of the hill across the river. The message from Gauleiter Wagner reached

Hitler shortly after midnight. Simultaneously, word arrived from Himmler that the Berlin SA was planning a sudden occupation of the government district next day. "In these circumstances I could make but one decision," Hitler later declared. . . . "Only a ruthless and bloody intervention might still perhaps halt the spread of the revolt."

It may be that Hitler was genuinely alarmed by the two messages; possibly he imagined that Röhm had seen what was up and was preparing a counterstroke. To this day no one has been able to establish to what extent Hitler himself was among the deceived, whether and how much he was misled by Himmler in particular. For, by eliminating the leadership of the SA, Himmler was indubitably furthering his own rise.

In any case, Hitler discarded his original plan of flying to Munich next morning and decided to leave at once. At dawn, which came around four o'clock, he arrived in Munich accompanied by Goebbels, Otto Dietrich, and Viktor Lutze. The action began. At the Bavarian Ministry of the Interior Hitler settled accounts with the "mutineers" of the previous day, Obergruppenführer Schneidhuber and Gruppenführer Schmidt. In a fit of fury he ripped the epaulets from their shoulders and ordered them taken to Stadelheim Prison.

Immediately afterward, he set out for Bad Wiessee in a long column of cars. "Whip in hand," as his chauffeur, Erich Kempka, described the events, Hitler entered "Röhm's bedroom, two police detectives with cocked pistols behind him. He blurted out: 'Röhm, you're under arrest!' Sleepily, Röhm raised his head from the pillows and stammered: *'Heil, mein Führer!'* 'You're under arrest!' Hitler bellowed for the second time, turned on his heel and left the room." The procedure was the same for the other SA leaders who had already arrived. Only a single one of them, Edmund Heines of Silesia, who was surprised in bed with a homosexual, put up any resistance. Those who were still on their way to Bad Wiessee were intercepted by Hitler on his way back to Munich. Like their comrades they were taken to Stadelheim—making a total of some 200 of the higher SA leaders from all parts of the country. Toward ten o'clock in the morning Goebbels telephoned Berlin and gave the agreed code word: "Hummingbird." Thereupon Göring, Himmler, and Heydrich also dispatched their squads. The SA leaders on the Reich list were picked up, taken to the Lichterfelde Cadet Academy, and in contrast to their fellows in Munich were lined up against a wall and shot without more ado.

Meanwhile, Hitler had gone to the Brown House, now heavily guarded by army troops. After a brief address to the party paladins who had been hastily convoked, he at once began drawing up the guidelines for the forthcoming propaganda on the purge. For several hours he dictated instructions, orders, and official explanations, in which he himself figured in the third person, as *"der Führer."* But in his haste to cover up and color the events he made a strange oversight. Contrary to the later official version, none of the many announcements made on June 30 mentioned a putsch or attempted putsch by Röhm. Instead there was talk of "gravest misconduct," "opposition," "pervert dispositions," and although occasionally something about a "plot" was thrown in, the overwhelming impression was that Hitler had acted as a guardian of morality. As Hitler put it in one of his less happy metaphors: "The Führer gave the order for the ruthless cleaning out of this pestilential sore." Now, however, the public was safe. "In the future he will no longer stand for millions of decent people being incriminated and compromised by a few persons with perverted dispositions."

Quite understandably, to the very end many SA leaders could not grasp what was going on. They had planned neither a putsch nor a plot, and Hitler had never before looked into their morality. Berlin SA Gruppenführer Ernst, for example, who, according to the messages from Himmler, had planned an attack on the government quarter for the afternoon of June 30, was actually in Bremen about to set out on his honeymoon. Shortly before he was to board the ship, he was arrested. Thinking this was a coarse wedding joke on the part of some of his fellows, he enjoyed the whole thing immensely. He was taken by plane to Berlin, where he was still laughing as he showed his handcuffs and joked with the SS squad that conducted him from the plane to the waiting police car. The extras that were being sold outside the airport building were already reporting his death, but Ernst still suspected nothing. Half an hour later he died at the wall in Lichterfelde, incredulous to the last, a perplexed *"Heil Hitler!"* on his lips.

Hitler flew back to Berlin that evening. Before leaving, he had ordered Sepp Dietrich to go to Stadelheim Prison, ask for the surrender of certain persons, and execute these persons at once. Hans Frank, the Bavarian Minister of Justice, intervened and succeeded—if we are to believe him— in reducing the number of victims. Reich Commissioner von Epp, on whose staff Röhm had long ago served as the friend and promoter of the rising demagogue, vainly tried to dissuade Hitler from his bloody course. It may be, however, that his intercession had some effect and induced Hitler to postpone the decision on Röhm.

In Berlin Hitler was received by a large delegation at cordoned-off Tempelhof airfield. One of those present set down his impression of the arrival shortly after the event:

The plane from Munich was announced. In a moment we saw it looming swiftly larger against the background of a blood-red sky, a piece of theatricality that no one had staged. The plane roared down to a landing and rolled toward us. Commands rang out. An honor guard presented arms. Göring, Himmler, Körner, Frick, Daluege and some twenty police officers went up to the plane. Then the door opened and Adolf Hitler was the first to step out.

His appearance was 'unique,' to use a favorite word of Nazi commentators. A

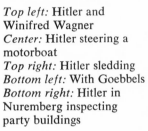

Top left: Hitler and
Winifred Wagner
Center: Hitler steering a
motorboat
Top right: Hitler sledding
Bottom left: With Goebbels
Bottom right: Hitler in
Nuremberg inspecting
party buildings

Hitler and Röhm, February, 1934

Hitler at the Nuremberg party rally, 1936

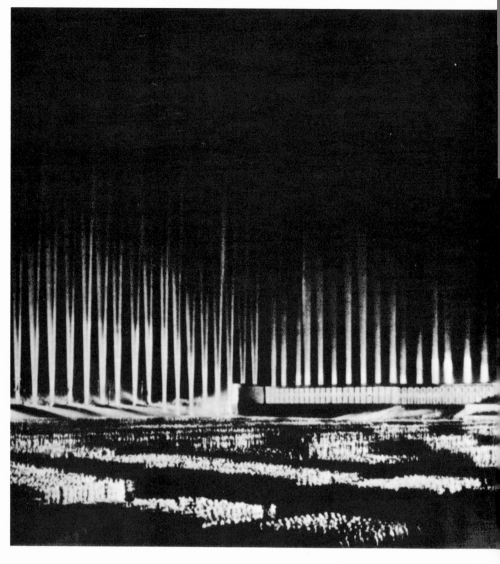

"Vaults of light" and memorial ceremonies climaxed the regime's mass meetings
Top: Vault of light
Bottom left and center: Memorial service in Nuremberg
Bottom right: Memorial procession in Munich, November 9, 1935

Top: Until 1936 Angelika
Raubal, Hitler's half-sister
and Geli Raubal's mother,
ran the Berghof household
Center: Hitler greeting Eva
Braun at Obersalzberg
Bottom: Hitler with his dog
at Obersalzberg

Plan for the rebuilding of Berlin: a splendid boulevard
more than three miles long was to become the new center
of the Reich

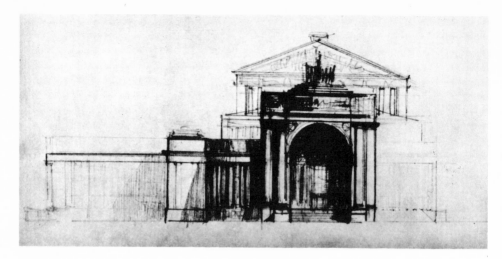

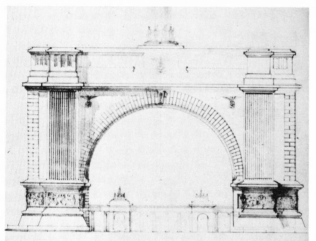

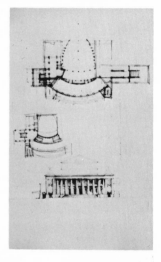

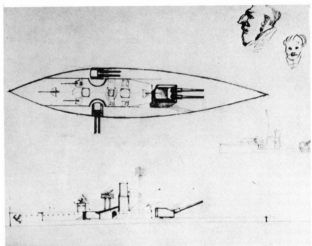

From Hitler's recently
found sketchbook of 1925:
public buildings, domed
halls, arches of triumph,
tanks, battleships, and a set
for Richard Wagner's
Tristan

Entry into Vienna, March,
1938
Left: Hitler speaking from
the balcony of the Hofburg
Top: Clusters of people on
the Prince Eugene
Monument
Bottom: SS forcing Jewish
citizens to clean the
sidewalks with their hands

Top: Hitler visiting
Mussolini in Florence, May,
1938
From left to right:
Mussolini, Himmler,
Ribbentrop, Ciano, Hitler,
Hess
Bottom: Prime Minister
Chamberlain at
Obersalzberg during the
Sudeten crisis, September,
1938

Top: German troops entering Prague, March, 1939
Bottom: Hitler at the window of the Hradschin

Ribbentrop reporting to Hitler after signature of the German-Soviet nonaggression pact, August 23, 1939

Top: Hitler and Ribbentrop in front of the command car
of the Führer's headquarters in Poland, 1939
Bottom: Hitler, Keitel, Himmler, Todt inspecting the
West Wall

brown shirt, black bow tie, dark-brown leather jacket, high black army boots—
all dark tones. He wore no hat; his face was pale, unshaven, sleepless, at once
gaunt and puffed. . . . Hitler silently shook hands with everyone within
reach. . . . I . . . heard amid the silence the repeated monotonous sound of
clicking heels.[45]

Impatient and nervous, Hitler asked to see the list of those liquidated
even before he left the airfield. Because of the "unique opportunity," as
one of the participants later stated, Göring and Himmler had extended the
killings far beyond the group of "Röhm putschists." Papen escaped death
solely because of his personal relationship with Hindenburg. Nevertheless,
his position as Vice-Chancellor was ignored, his protests disregarded, and
he was placed under house arrest. Two of his closest associates, his private
secretary, von Bose, and his ghost writer, Edgar Jung, were shot, and two
others arrested. A squad had killed Under-secretary Erich Klausener, the
head of Catholic Action, at his desk in the Ministry of Transportation.
Another squad had tracked down Gregor Strasser in a pharmaceutical
plant, brought him to Gestapo headquarters on Prinz-Albrecht-Strasse, and
shot him in the cellar of the building. Around noon a troop of killers had
broken into Schleicher's home in Neu-Babelsberg, asked the man sitting at
his desk whether he was General von Schleicher, and without waiting for a
reply fired. Frau von Schleicher was likewise killed.

Among the murdered were also one of General von Schleicher's associ-
ates, General von Bredow, and former General State Commissioner von
Kahr, whose "treachery" on November 9, 1923, Hitler had never forgiven.
Another victim was Father Stempfle, who had been one of the editorial
readers of *Mein Kampf* but had since moved far from the Nazi party.
Another was the engineer Otto Ballerstedt, who had crossed Hitler's path
during the period of the party's rise. An utterly innocent music critic, Dr.
Willi Schmid, was killed because of a confusion with SA Gruppenführer
Wilhelm Schmidt. The rage for murder seemed to have been most violent
in Silesia, where SS leader Udo von Woyrsch lost control over his units.
Significantly, the liquidations frequently took place wherever the victim
was found, in offices, in homes, on the street, with utterly brutal casualness.
Many corpses were not found until weeks later, in woods or rivers.

June 30 was not a good day for any of Röhm's followers, even if they
were engaged in praiseworthy actions against Jews. Three SA men who
happened to demolish a Jewish cemetery on that day were expelled from
the SA and given a year's prison term.[46]

At a press conference held that very day, Göring actually boasted that he
had stretched his assignment on his own initiative. We do not know how
many of these arbitrary executions Hitler approved of. The purge represented a break with his tactical imperative of strict legality, and every
additional victim made that break all the more obvious. For years Hitler
had practiced all the arts of dissimulation, had abstained from the old wild

465

poses and carefully built up the image of himself as a temperate, if also imperious, politician. Now, so close to his goal of total power, he was risking the loss of his painfully earned credit in a single act of self-unmasking. Suddenly he and his cronies had dropped their disguise and appeared in all the harshness of their nature. If Hitler intervened, as several accounts have claimed, to moderate the course of events, it must have been from such considerations.

Still, Hitler let the killing take on the miscellaneous quality that it did. By shooting in all directions he would deprive all sides of any hope of profiting from the crisis. Hence the barbarous insouciance of the killings anywhere and everywhere, the corpses left where they dropped, the ostentatious traces left by the murderers; and hence, also, the abandonment, for once, of any pretense of justice. There were no trials, no weighing of evidence, no verdicts; there was nothing but an atavistic slaughter. Later, Rudolf Hess tried to justify the indiscriminate killing: "During those hours when the very existence of the German nation was at stake, it was not permissible to judge the amount of guilt borne by individuals. Despite the harshness there is a profound meaning in the practice of the past, in which mutinies among soldiers were punished by a bullet for every tenth man, without the slightest inquiry into guilt or innocence."

Once again Hitler had acted wholly in terms of the ends of power. The contemporary polemicists were surely mistaken when they pictured him as a sadist decking out his blood lust by references to pitiless Renaissance princes.[47] The other view of him is equally mistaken: that he was emotionally indifferent, cold and unfeeling as he eliminated comrades, followers, and intimate friends of many years' standing. In fact, the first view applies more accurately to Göring, the second to Himmler; both went about their murderous business efficiently—with total lack of scruple. Unlike them, Hitler seemed to feel considerable inner pressure. All those who met him during this period noted his extraordinary agitation. The strain on his nerves was evident in all his movements. In his speech of justification to the Reichstag he himself spoke of the "bitterest decisions" of his life. And unless all indications are deceptive he was haunted for months afterward by memories of his murdered friends and followers—for example, in that highly secret conference of January 3, 1935, when he hastily summoned the heads of the party and the army and in a dramatic scene exhorted them to achieve unity. On this, as on many other occasions, it turned out that his nerves were not as armored as his conscience. In keeping with his maxim that one must always strike faster and harder than the enemy, the smooth course of the June 30 purge was based largely on a surprise assault. How conspicuous, therefore, is Hitler's hesitation before he ordered the first execution of seven SA leaders, and his hesitation again before the killing of Röhm. In both cases, Hitler's conduct can be adequately explained only on grounds of sentimentality. He was obeying the reflex of an emotional tie which at least for a few hours proved stronger than the cold rationale of power.

By Sunday, July 1, Hitler had overcome the previous day's uncertainties and was once more in firm control of his own reactions. Toward noon he appeared repeatedly at the historic window in the chancellery to greet a crowd rounded up by Goebbels, and in the afternoon he actually gave a garden party for the party bigwigs and members of the cabinet, to which their wives and children were also invited. While the firing squads were still at work in Lichterfelde, a few miles away, he moved about among his guests in excellent humor, chatting, drinking tea, showing affection for the children—all the while breathless and in flight from reality. There is an element of high drama in this scene; what comes to mind is the physiognomy of one of those Shakespearean villains who are not fully up to the requirements of evil. And from the midst of this sham that he had so hastily set up he evidently gave the order to kill Ernst Röhm, who was still waiting in his cell in Stadelheim. Rudolf Hess had for hours tried in vain to obtain instructions for the execution. Shortly before six o'clock, Theodor Eicke and SS Hauptsturmführer Michael Lippert entered Röhm's room. Together with the latest edition of the *Völkische Beobachter,* which carried a lengthy account under banner headlines of the events of the previous day, they laid a pistol on Röhm's table and told him he had ten minutes in which to use it. Nothing disturbed the quiet; prison guards were told to fetch the weapon. When Eicke and Lippert entered the cell, shooting, Röhm was standing in the middle of the room, his shirt histrionically ripped open exposing his chest.

Base and repellent as were the circumstances surrounding this murder of a friend, we must nevertheless ask whether Hitler had any alternative. No matter how far Röhm might have been willing to go in bringing about the SA state, his real goal was the primacy of the ideological soldier. In his proud sense that he had a following of millions pressing behind him, he was incapable of recognizing that he was being overambitious. For he would necessarily encounter bitter opposition from both the Political Organization and the army, and at least passive resistance on the part of the general public. It is true that he thought he was still being loyal to Hitler. But it was only a question of time before the objective contradictions would lead to personal antipathy. With his keen tactical sense, Hitler had instantly realized that Röhm's aims also threatened his own position. After the elimination of Gregor Strasser from the party, the SA chief was the only remaining individual who had preserved personal independence of Hitler and who resisted the hypnotic spell of Hitler's will. Hence he was Hitler's only serious rival, and it would have flouted all the principles of tactics to grant him as much power as he wanted. Certainly Röhm had not planned a putsch. But he embodied, for a suspicious Hitler, the permanent threat of a potential putsch.

467

On the other hand, Röhm could not simply be deposed or isolated. He was not just any lieutenant; he was a popular generalissimo. An attempt to strip the chief of staff of his powers would indeed have sparked some sort of uprising. And even if Röhm could have been deposed, he would have remained a permanent threat, for he had many connections and influential friends. A court trial was virtually out of the question. After the unsatisfactory outcome of the Reichstag fire trial, Hitler had little confidence in the judiciary. But above and beyond that, Hitler's own secrecy complex made it unthinkable to give an intimate friend, and one who was driven to the wall, the opportunity to defend himself in public. Too much would have come out. It was precisely their many years of friendship that made Röhm so strong, but also left Hitler no other way out. A bare three years later Hitler declared that to his "own sorrow" he had been forced "to destroy this man and his following." And on another occasion, speaking to a group of high-ranking party leaders, he remarked upon the decisive share that this greatly gifted organizer had had in the NSDAP's rise and conquest of power. When the time came to write the history of the National Socialist movement, he said, Röhm would always have to be remembered as the second man, right beside himself.[48]

In view of this situation, Hitler had no choice but a "vigilante killing on a grand scale."[49] Röhm, too, could not simply give up his position. He had obligations to the dynamism and the unsatisfied cravings of his millions of followers. Both rivals were governed by objective necessities. Perceiving this, we cannot fail to see in the bloody affair of June, 1934, a measure of tragedy—the only instance of tragedy in Hitler's career.

The consequences at home and abroad made June 30, 1934, the decisive date, after January 30, 1933, in the Nazi seizure of power. Hitler immediately set about concealing the importance of the event by a great show of restored normality. As early as July 2 Göring instructed all police stations: "All documents concerning the action of the past two days are to be burned. . . ." Word went out from the Propaganda Ministry forbidding the press to publish the death notices of those killed or "shot while trying to escape." And at the cabinet meeting of July 3 Hitler had the crimes sanctioned by slipping in among some twenty decrees of rather secondary importance one consisting of only a single paragraph: "The measures taken on June 30, July 1 and 2 to suppress treasonous assaults are legal as acts of self-defense by the State."

But Hitler seemed to realize quickly that all efforts to hush up the affair were a waste of time. For a while he seemed perplexed and was evidently haunted by the murders of Röhm and Strasser. Otherwise his ten days of silence, breaking all the rules of psychology and propaganda, can hardly be explained. On July 13 he at last delivered to the Reichstag his speech of self-justification. But its verboseness, its lapses in logic, the gaps in the

468

explanations, and its one imperious gesture mark it as one of his poorer oratorical achievements.

After a rambling introduction summing up his own cares and merits, and once more resorting to the most reliable theme in his rhetorical stock, the Communist peril—which, he promised, he would combat in a war of extermination if it took a hundred years—he heaped all the blame on Röhm. Röhm had repeatedly confronted him with unacceptable alternatives, had admitted corruption, homosexuality, and excesses into his circle, had encouraged all these vices. Hitler spoke of the destructive, rootless elements who had "completely lost sympathy with any ordered human society" and who "became revolutionaries who favored revolution for its own sake and desired to see revolution established as a permanent condition." But the revolution, Hitler continued, "is for us not a permanent condition. When a fatal check is imposed by force upon the natural development of a nation, this artificially interrupted evolution may be set free by an act of violence so that it can resume its free natural development. But periodically recurring revolts . . . cannot lead to salutary development."

Once again he rejected Röhm's concept of a National Socialist army, and, referring to a promise he had given the President, he reassured the Reichswehr: "In the State there is only one bearer of arms, and that is the army; there is only one bearer of the political will, and that is the National Socialist Party." It was only toward the end of his speech, which lasted several hours, that Hitler became aggressive.

Mutinies are suppressed in accordance with laws of iron which are immutable. If anyone reproaches me and asks why I did not turn to the regular courts of justice for conviction of the offenders, then all I can say to him is this: in this hour I was responsible for the fate of the German people, and thereby I became the supreme judge of the German people! . . . I gave the order to shoot the ringleaders in this treason, and I further gave the order to cauterize down to the raw flesh the ulcers of this poisoning of the wells in our domestic life. . . . Let the nation know that its existence—which depends on its internal order and security—cannot be threatened with impunity by anyone! And let it be known for all time to come that if anyone raises his hand to strike the state, then certain death is his lot.

Hitler's uncharacteristic wavering from justification to aggression reflected the profound shock that the events of June 30 had been to the public. Instinctively, the public seemed to sense that on this day a new phase had begun and that other frightening adventures, might lie ahead. Up to then, illusions about the nature of the regime had still been possible; it might have been argued that injustice and terrorism were the inevitable concomitants of a revolution, that they would cease with time, and that on the whole the new regime was aiming at orderliness. But no such belief in a happy ending could survive the massacre.

469

Hitler had openly claimed for himself the role of the "supreme judge," who could dispose over life and death without let or hindrance. Henceforth, there were no longer any legal or moral guarantees against arbitrary acts by Hitler or his cohorts. As if in explicit corroboration of these tendencies, all the accomplices in the crime, from Himmler and Sepp Dietrich down to the low-ranking SS bullies, were rewarded and praised. On July 4 at a ceremony in Berlin they were all presented with an "honorary dagger." It is by no means a fabrication of hindsight to see a direct connection between the killings of June 30 and the subsequent practice of mass murder in the camps of the East. In fact, Himmler himself in his famous Posen speech of October 4, 1943, established this link and thus confirmed that "continuity of crime" which permits of no distinctions between a purportedly constructive initial period of Nazi rule, inspired by passionate idealism, and a later period of self-destructive degeneration.

The public's uneasiness soon gave way to a certain relief that the SA's revolutionary activities—which had revived deep-seated fears of disorder and mob rule—had at last been brought to an end. Official propaganda tried to pretend that the public reaction had been one of "incredible enthusiasm." There was nothing of that kind, which explains Hitler's often-repeated charge against the middle class: that it was obsessed with constitutionality and always raised a loud outcry "when the government renders a noxious menace to the nation harmless, for example by killing him." But the public did tend to interpret the two-day orgy of killing in terms of its traditional antirevolutionary feelings. The movement was at last "overcoming its adolescence"; the moderate, order-oriented forces around Hitler were triumphing over the chaotic energies of Nazism. This notion was supported by the fact that among those liquidated were notorious murderers and sadistic ruffians. Actually, the whole operation against Röhm presents itself as a paradigm of Hitler's trick of striking in such a way that reaction would be split, so that those who were most outraged had reason to thank him. How well he had put it across can be seen in the telegram from President Hindenburg expressing his "profoundly felt gratitude." "You have saved the German people from a grave peril," the President wired. He also bestowed the ultimate accolade: "He who wishes to make history must also be able to shed blood."

The reaction of the army was perhaps even more decisive in alleviating the public's doubts and premonitions. Feeling itself the real victor of those three days, the army blatantly expressed its satisfaction at the elimination of the "brown trash." On July 1, while the killing was going on unabated, the Berlin Guards Company goose-stepped down the Wilhelmstrasse, past the chancellery, to the tune of Hitler's favorite Badenweiler March. Two days later Defense Minister von Blomberg congratulated Hitler for the successful completion of the "purge." And, contrary to his policy of earlier years, Hitler now made a point of reinforcing the Reichwehr's sense of triumph. In his Reichstag speech he not only named it the sole bearer of arms in the state but also declared that he would preserve "the army as an unpolitical instrument." He assured the officers and soldiers that he could not "demand from them that as individuals each should take up a clear-cut position towards our Movement."

By these unusual and never-to-be-repeated concessions Hitler expressed his gratitude to the army leadership for having remained loyal to him in the recent critical hours, when his fate lay in their hands. Once again, everything had hung in the balance after the SS squad had killed General von Schleicher, his wife, and General von Bredow. If at this moment the army had insisted on a legal investigation, the theory of a conspiracy would have been exploded and the blow against the conservatives exposed as the murderous coup it was. The bourgeois Right would not have been permanently paralyzed; it might possibly have emerged from the affair with increased confidence. It would have preserved moral standing. In any case, Göring would not have gone uncontradicted when he concluded the Reichstag session of July 13 by declaring that the entire German people, "man by man and woman by woman," was united in a single outcry: 'We always approve everything our Führer does.'"

Hitler, with his intuition for power relationships, had realized that if the army would stand for the murder of army men, he had achieved the breakthrough to unlimited control. An institution that accepted such a blow could never again effectively oppose him. At the moment the army leadership was still gloating, and Reichenau was commenting complacently that it had not been a simple matter to have the whole thing appear as a purely internal party dispute. But Hitler had not intended to give the army a large enough part in the elimination of Röhm to put him under obligation to it. He involved it just far enough to corrupt it. It was an unequal alliance that these dilettantes in uniform, who were dabbling in politics, struck up with Hitler. Defense Minister von Blomberg had made the unforgettable statement that henceforth the German officer's honor must consist in being cunning. But, as has been trenchantly pointed out,[50] the military were guided by political incompetence and arrogance.

If the public order was actually threatened by rebels and conspirators, as von Blomberg later represented the situation, then the army probably had the duty to intervene. If that were not the case, then it should have called a halt to the killing. Instead, it had waited, had made weapons available, and in the end its leaders had congratulated themselves on their acuteness at emerging with clean hands and nevertheless as victors. They succumbed not to the "nemesis of power," as the English historian John W. Wheeler-Bennett has asserted, but to their failure to recognize how short-lived this victory would be. At the height of the killing former State Secretary Planck urged General von Fritsch to intervene. The commander in chief of the army replied that he had no orders to do so. Planck warned him: "If you,

General, stand by idly watching, sooner or later you will suffer the same fate." Three and a half years later, Fritsch, together with Blomberg, was dismissed under a dishonoring cloud. The charge, as in the cases of Schleicher and Bredow, was based on forged documents, and now it was the turn of the SA to rejoice over the "revenge for June 30." *Les institutions périssent par leur victoires.*

This aphorism was totally borne out by subsequent events. It is true that June 30 dealt a fatal blow to the SA. Its formerly rebellious self-assertive profile henceforth almost vanished behind petty bourgeois features. Brass knuckles and rubber truncheons gave way to collection boxes. But the army did not assume the place vacated by the storm troopers. Three weeks later Hitler coolly took advantage of the manifest weakness of the army leadership. On July 20, 1934, he freed the SS "in view of its great services . . . especially in connection with the events of June 30" from its subordination to the SA and raised it to the rank of an independent organization directly subordinate to himself. At the same time, it was allowed to rival the army in maintaining armed fighting forces—at first of only one division.

Few acts so clearly reveal the core of Hitler's technique as this decision. No sooner was the SA eliminated than he was promoting the building of a new power center of the same kind, in order to be able to continue his game of protecting his own rule. All those who were intimately or remotely participants in the events of June 30 naïvely assumed that the purge had resolved a question of power. But Hitler secured his own personal power precisely by never really settling the power conflicts within his entourage. He merely shifted them to other planes and continued playing out the game with new pieces, in altered confrontations.

Politically, as well as tactically, the SS took over many of the functions of the SA. But it markedly avoided that claim to independence which Röhm's following had always so obtrusively made. For the SA had never wholly submitted to the principle of blind obedience; it had always emphasized its aloofness from the despised corps of party people. By contrast, the SS felt itself to be a totally loyal elite, serving as the sentinel and vanguard of the National Socialist idea, a pure instrument of the Führer's will. In this spirit it began, on June 30, its inexorable process of expansion in all directions. Soon the SA and then the party also vanished in its mighty shadow, so that there ceased to be any road to power that bypassed the SS.

The rise of the SS, which so crucially determined the history and features of the Third Reich and by no means ended with the downfall of the regime, incidentally revealed something else: that Röhm had rightfully considered himself as being, in the last analysis, of one mind with Hitler. Himmler, constantly prodded by Reinhard Heydrich restively operating in the background, tranformed the Reichsführung-SS* into a mighty, many-branched

---

* Himmler enjoyed the unique and personal title of Reichsführer-SS. The Reichsführung was the central office of the SS, his personal headquarters.

apparatus. Ultimately, it became a genuine subsidiary government that penetrated into all existing institutions, undermined their political power, and gradually began replacing them. What Himmler thus accomplished was nothing less than Ernst Röhm's impatient though ultimately vague vision. Röhm's ambitious lieutenants had dreamed of an SA state. Himmler brought into being, at least in its initial phases, an actual SS state. Röhm was liquidated because he wanted to achieve by immediate action what Hitler, as he explained to intimates, sought to arrive at "slowly and deliberately, by taking the tiniest steps at a time."

June 30 also signified the elimination of a type of personality that had been almost indispensable for the history of Hitler's rise: the rough daredevil, usually a onetime army officer, who had fought first in the Free Corps and then as one of Hitler's street-battle heroes, trying to carry over his wartime experiences into civilian reality and suddenly left without any assignment once the goal was reached. Machiavelli pointed out in a famous aphorism that power is not maintained with the same following that has helped to win it. Mussolini is said to have made this comment to Hitler when they met in Venice. In the course of the conquest of power a limited degree of revolution from below had been permitted. By destroying the top leadership of the SA, Hitler choked off that limited revolution. The Röhm affair concluded the so-called period of struggle and marked the turning point away from the vague, utopian phase of the movement to the sober reality of a disciplined state. The romantic barricade fighter was replaced by the more modern revolutionary types such as the SS produced: those passionless bureaucrats who supervised a revolution whose like had never been known. Thinking not in terms of the mob but in terms of structures, they placed their explosive charges deeper than perhaps any revolutionaries before them.

But Röhm's impatience would scarcely have been a mortal flaw had not Hitler had other things in mind besides eliminating the SA chief. As the propaganda campaign preceding the operation indicated, the events of June 30, 1934, were aimed at any opposition, at any independent position in general. For years to come there was no serious organized resistance. The dual thrust of the operation also disclosed an aspect of Hitler that one might have thought he had transcended. Strictly speaking, he charged the SA leaders only with premature haste and stupidity. But his boundless hatred, nourished by old resentments, erupted against those conservatives who had thought to "hire" and outwit him:

They're all mistaken. They underestimate me. Because I come from below, from the "lower depths," because I have no education, because my manners aren't what they with their sparrow brains think is right. If I were one of them they'd call me a great man—now, already. But I don't need them to confirm my historic greatness. The rebelliousness of my SA has cost me many trumps. But I still hold others. I'm not at a loss for resources when something goes wrong for me once in a while. . . .

I've spoiled their plans. They thought I wouldn't dare, that I'd be too cowardly. They could already see me thrashing in their nets. They thought I'd become their tool. And behind my back they made jokes about me, said I no longer had any power, that I'd thrown away my party. I saw through it all long ago. I've taught them a lesson they'll remember for a long time. What I lost in passing judgment on the SA I'll regain in bringing judgment down on these feudal gamblers and professional card-sharpers, the Schleichers and their crew.

If I call upon the people today, they'll follow me. If I appeal to the party, it will stand as solid as ever. . . . Come on, Messrs. Papen and Hugenberg—I'm ready for the next round.[51]

What he knew, and really meant, was that there would be no next round for these opponents.

To sum up, the challenge facing Hitler before June 30 required the simultaneous solution of no fewer than five problems. He had to quash Röhm and his rebellious band of SA permanent revolutionists definitively. He had to satisfy the demands of the army. He had to dispel public dissatisfaction with the rule of the streets and visible terrorism. He had to head off the conservatives' counterplans. All this had to be done without becoming the prisoner of one side or the other. He took care of it all by means of a single limited operation and at a cost of relatively few victims. With this behind him, he could move directly to his principal aim, which would complete the process of seizing power. That aim was to succeed Hindenburg as President.

From the middle of July on, the President's condition was visibly deteriorating. His death was expected any day. On July 31 the government for the first time issued an official bulletin on the state of his health. And although on the following day the news sounded somewhat more optimistic, Hitler irreverently anticipated the event by presenting to the cabinet a law concerning the succession. The new law was to take effect on Hindenburg's death. It provided for combining the office of President with that of the Führer and Chancellor, a measure that could be justified by evoking the law of January 30, 1934, which gave the administration powers to alter the Constitution. But since this authority derived from the Enabling Act, any action based on it should have taken into account the guarantees explicitly set forth in that act. Inviolability of the office of the President was one of the guarantees. But the "law concerning the head of state" boldly ignored that limitation—once more violating Hitler's principle of legality—and thus broke through the last barrier to Hitler's dictatorship. Hitler's exuberant highhandedness is further shown in his affixing the signature of Vice-Chancellor von Papen to the new law, though Papen was not even present at the cabinet session.

That same day Hitler went to Neudeck to visit Hindenburg on his death-bed. But the old man was only conscious for moments and addressed Hitler as "Your Majesty." In spite of his imposing stature he had always felt comfortable only in relationships of dependency or feudal homage. He died on the following day, in the morning hours of August 2. In a government proclamation he was hailed as a "monumental memorial of the distant past," whose "almost incalculable services" culminated in the fact that "on January 30, 1933 . . . he opened the gates of the Reich for the young National Socialist Movement," that he led the Germany of yesterday to "profound reconciliation" with the Germany of tomorrow and became in peace what he had been in war, "the national myth of the German people."

The death of Hindenburg made no tangible break. In the plethora of obituaries and testimonials of grief, the legal measures went almost unnoticed. But those carefully prepared measures sealed the new situation. A decree of Hitler's instructed the Minister of the Interior to prepare a plebiscite in order to give the union of chancellorship and presidency—which was presented as already "constitutionally valid"—the "explicit sanction of the German people." For Hitler declared, he was "firmly permeated with the conviction that every state power must proceed from the people and be confirmed by the people in free and secret elections." To disguise the absolute power that would now center in himself he announced that the "greatness of the departed" did not permit him to claim the title of President for himself. He therefore wished, "in official as well as in unofficial communication to continue to be addressed only as Führer and Chancellor."

On the day of Hindenburg's death the army leadership also felt called upon to offer its unconditional loyalty to Hitler. In an act of opportunistic overzealousness, for which legal authority was not created until three weeks later, Defense Minister von Blomberg had all the officers and enlisted men of the armed forces in all garrisons take an oath of allegiance to the new commander in chief. The old oath had been to "nation and fatherland"; now the men had to swear "by God" unconditional obedience to Hitler personally. It confirmed the totalitarian character of Hitler's leader state, which could never have been brought into being without the aid of the armed forces. Soon afterward, this personal oath of allegiance was required of government officials, including the cabinet ministers, and thus "something resembling monarchy" was restored.

The obsequies for the deceased President gave Hitler the opportunity for one of those great displays of theatrical veneration of the dead that the regime had brought to a high art. It was also an occasion for Hitler to flaunt his heightened sense of power. After the Reichstag's memorial session on August 6, the central feature of which was Hitler's tribute to the deceased and music from Wagner's *Götterdämmerung,* the army paraded past its new commander in chief outside the Kroll Opera House. But hard on the heels of the "only bearer of arms in the nation," in the same parade step, wearing the same steel helmets and in part with fixed bayonets, came

475

an honor shock troop of the SS Adolf Hitler Bodyguard Regiment, a special formation of the Hermann Göring Police Battalion, an honor unit of the SA, and other groups of paramilitary formation outside the Reichswehr. On the following day Hindenburg was interred at the site of his 1914 victory, in the court of the Tannenberg monument in East Prussia. In his funeral oration Hitler declared that the name of the deceased would remain immortal, "even when the last trace of this body has vanished." He concluded: "Dead warlord, now enter into Valhalla!"

The plebiscite on August 19 served the same purpose as these elaborate obsequies. In an interview with the British journalist Ward Price at this time Hitler stressed that the German public was thus being given the opportunity to confirm or reject the policies of its leaders. And with a touch of malicious irony he added: "We wild Germans are better democrats than other nations."[52] But in reality the plebiscite, noisily organized with all the tried-and-true methods of propaganda, once again served the purpose of mobilizing unpolitical feelings for political purposes. This sound and fury was meant to dispel the tangible and lasting uneasiness over the virtually "Oriental" solution in the Röhm affair. And once again Hitler was wooing the public, attempting to win back its momentarily lapsed affection. In his funeral oration to the Reichstag Hitler had implored the public to let bygones be bygones and henceforth "to look from the transitory moment into the future."

But the prestige of the new rulers had evidently been seriously damaged. Far from the 100 per cent elections of totalitarian regimes, the affirmative votes did not rise above 84.6 per cent. In some districts in Berlin, also in Aachen and Wesermünde, they did not even reach 70 per cent. And in Hamburg, Lübeck, Leipzig, and Breslau nearly a third of the population voted "no." For the last time some elements of the country were registering opposition, chiefly the socialist and Catholic groups.

Hitler's chagrin at the outcome of the plebiscite was clearly reflected in the following day's proclamation. It announced the conclusion of the fifteen-year struggle for power, since "starting with the highest leadership of the Reich and extending through the entire administration down to the officials of the smallest town . . . the German Reich is today in the hand of the National Socialist Party." But the struggle for the allegiance of "our dear people," Hitler declared, must continue with undiminished vigor until "even the last German wears the symbol of the Reich as a profession of faith in his heart."

Two weeks later Hitler struck a similar note, adding, however, a threat against all malcontents, in the proclamation with which he opened the sixth party rally at the Kongresshalle in Nuremberg. As usual he let Gauleiter Wagner of Munich, whose voice was almost identical to his own, read his message: "We all know whom the nation has entrusted with the leadership. Woe to those who do not know it or forget it! Revolutions have always been rare in the German nation. With us, the agitated age of the nineteenth century has at last come to an end. In the next thousand years there will not be another revolution in Germany."

At this same time the real revolution in Germany was beginning. To be sure the forces within the movement that had aimed at violent overturn were now eliminated. Their energies had been channeled chiefly into propaganda and keeping an eye on the populace. Insofar as Hitler had undertaken to control them in deference to Hindenburg and the army, the "lion-taming" concept of the spring of 1933 was celebrating its last belated victory. But Hitler's imperious statement in Nuremberg that on that day he had "the sole power in Germany in everything" went along with his resolve to try everything.

The barbarous aspects of the regime, its anti-Semitism, the German claims to hegemony, the sense of a special national mission—all these have focused attention upon the related ideological and political forces. But the social impulses that supported Nazism were no less strong, perhaps stronger. Many middle-class groups expected that after assuming power the Nazis would smash the frozen authoritarian structures and the social bonds that the revolution of 1918 had failed to budge—but would do so in the course of an orderly upheaval. For these groups Hitler meant above all a chance to complete the German revolution. After so many unsuccessful beginnings they no longer trusted the democratic forces to do it and had never wanted to trust the Communists.

Obviously, the new flood of proclamations about the end of the revolution aimed principally at soothing the emotions of a still distraught public. And by the autumn of 1934 signs of a return to more orderly conditions began to appear. Not that they in any way changed Hitler's long-range goals. These remained unalterable. In the midst of all the reassuring phraseology, he explicitly warned in his final speech at Nuremberg against the illusion that the party had lost its revolutionary impetus and abandoned its radical program: "In its teaching unalterable, in its organization hard as steel, in its tactics supple and adaptable, but in its over-all image an Order." Thus it would face the future. Among intimates he made similar remarks to the effect that he was putting an end to the revolution only to outward appearances and that he was now shifting it inward.

Because of these disguises, so deeply rooted in Hitler's character, the revolutionary nature of the regime is not immediately apparent. The social change it produced was accomplished within unusual forms. Among Hitler's remarkable achievements, which assure him a place in the history of great political upheavals, was the realization that insurrectionary revolutions were irrevocably things of the past. Hitler for the first time drew the logical conclusion from the insight—already formulated by Friedrich Engels in 1895—that revolutionaries of the old type were necessarily weaker than the established power. Consequently, it was Hitler who created the modern concept of revolution. For men like Röhm, revolution was always commotion and took place in the streets. Modern revolution, on the other hand, did not overcome power but "seized" it, and employed bureaucratic rather than bellicose methods. It was a quiet process. Shots hurt their ears, to generalize Malaparte's remark about Hitler.

For all that, this revolution reached deep and spared nothing. It gripped and changed the political institutions, shattered the class structures in the army, the bureaucracy, and to some extent in the economy. It broke up, corrupted, and enfeebled the still influential nobility and the old upper crust. In a Germany that owed its charm as well as its provinciality to the same backwardness, it introduced that degree of social mobility and egalitarianism indispensable to a modern industrial society. It would not be fair to object that such modernization was only incidental or even contrary to the declared intention of the brown revolutionaries. Hitler's admiration for technology was well known. Where methods were concerned, he thought entirely in modern terms—especially since he needed, for his expansionist aims, a rational and efficient industrial state.

The structural revolution that the regime brought in was distorted by an antiquarian perspective that made much of folklore and ancestral heritage. In other words, the sky over Germany was and remained romantically darkened. The peasantry, for example, became the object of widespread sentimentalizing, while its actual economic plight visibly accelerated, and the so-called "flight from the land" reached a new statistical high between 1933 and 1938. Similarly, by its industrialization programs (especially in central Germany with its militarily vital chemical plants) the regime furthered the very urbanization that it simultaneously denounced. Though for the first time it integrated women into the industrial process, it continued to condemn all the liberal and Marxist tendencies to defeminize women. It made a cult of tradition, but a "confidential report" circulated early in 1936 stated: "The link with tradition must be thoroughly destroyed. New, altogether unknown forms. No individual rights . . ."

In an attempt to grasp this two-faced character of the phenomenon some writers have spoken of a "double-revolution,"[53] a revolution against the bourgeois order in the name of bourgeois standards, against tradition in the name of tradition. The cozy romantic decor need not be considered as cynical masquerade; quite often it was an effort to fix in thought or in symbol something irrevocably lost in reality. The majority of Nazi fellow travelers, at any rate, interpreted the idyllic trimmings of National Socialist ideology in this way. Hitler himself in his secret speech to the officer class of 1938 spoke of the anguish and depressing conflicts caused by political and social progress whenever it clashed with those "sacred traditions" that rightly claimed men's loyalty and attachment: "There have always been catastrophes. . . . Those affected have always had to suffer. . . . Precious memories always had to be abandoned, traditions always had to be superseded. The past century, too, inflicted deep grief upon many. It is so easy to talk about ages, so easy to talk about, let us say, other Germans who in those days were pushed out. It was necessary! It had to be. . . . And then came the year eighteen and added a new great sorrow, and that too was necessary, and finally came our revolution, and it has drawn the ultimate conclusions, and it too is necessary. There is no other way."[54]

The dual nature of the National Socialist revolution to a high degree marked the regime as a whole and gave it its peculiar Janus-faced appearance. The foreign observers who poured into Germany in growing numbers, lured by the "Fascist experiment," and who reported on a peaceful Germany in which the trains ran on time as they had in the past, a country of bourgeois normality, of rule of law and administrative justice, were just as right as the exiles who bitterly lamented their misfortune and that of their persecuted and harried friends. The suppression of the SA undeniably put a halt to the dominion of violence and ushered in a phase of stabilization in which the authoritarian forces of political order braked the dynamism of totalitarian revolution. For a while it appeared as if normality once again replaced the state of emergency. At least, for the time being, there was an end of those conditions in which (in the words of a July 1, 1933, report to the Bavarian Prime Minister) everybody arrested everybody else, and everybody threatened everybody else with Dachau. It has been observed that in the Germany of 1934 to 1938, in the midst of coercion and flagrant injustice, there were idyllic enclaves that were sought out and cultivated as never before. Emigration abroad fell off considerably, and even the emigration of Jewish citizens continually diminished.[55] But many were emigrating inwardly, into the *cachettes du coeur*. The old German mistrust of politics, the aversion to its commitments and importunities, seemed confirmed and vindicated during those years.

A dual mentality corresponded to the "dual state." Political apathy went hand in hand with displays of jubilant approval. Again and again Hitler created pretexts for lashing the nation to enthusiasm: coups and sensations in foreign policy; spectacles, monumental building programs, and even social measures, all of which had the effect of stimulating the imagination and raising self-confidence. The essence of his art of government consisted largely in understanding how to manipulate popular need. The consequence was a curiously nervous, exceedingly artificial graph of popularity, marked by abrupt upswings amidst phases of disgruntlement. But Hitler's own charisma and the respect the nation accorded him for having succeeded in restoring order were the basis for his psychological power. Those who compared the horrors of the years past—the riots, the unemployment, the arbitrary brutality of the SA, and the humiliations in foreign policy—with the hypnotic counterimage of power-conscious order, as manifested in parades or party rallies, would seldom track down his errors. Moreover, the regime made a point of stressing its authoritarian-conservative features, representing itself as a more stringently organized version of government by militant German Nationalists. Papen's idea of the "new state" might have been conceived along similar lines.

And, for all its austerity and police-state sterility, the regime satisfied to a high degree the craving for adventure, heroic dedication, and that gambler's passion in which Hitler shared and for which modern social-welfare states leave so little room.

Behind this picture of order, however, a radical energy was at work. Very few of the contemporaries had any idea of how radical it was. The frightened bourgeois soon convinced themselves that Hitler had acted as a conservative, antirevolutionary force in defeating Röhm. But in fact he had been obeying the law of revolution, had been the more radical as against the merely radical revolutionary. "A second revolution was being prepared," Göring had accurately stated on the afternoon of June 30, "but it was made by us against those who have conjured it up."

Even then, anyone who looked closer should not have failed to see that a state consecrated to order, full employment, and equal rights on the international front could not possibly satisfy Hitler's ambition. In November, 1934, it is true, he assured a French visitor that he was not thinking of conquests. He was, he said, concerned with building a new social order that would earn him the gratitude of his people and consequently a more lasting monument than any dedicated to a victorious general. But such statements were empty rhetoric. His dynamism had never been nourished by the ideal of a totalitarian welfare state with its spic-and-span dreariness, its complacency, and all the common man's felicity he despised. The source of his inner drive was a fantastically overwrought, megalomaniacal vision leaping far beyond the horizon and claiming for itself a life span of at least a thousand years.

BOOK VI

The Years of Preparation

Chapter 1

It does not suffice to say, as the French do, that their nation was taken by surprise. Neither a nation nor a woman is forgiven for an unguarded hour in which the first adventurer who comes along can sweep them off their feet and possess them. We do not solve the mystery by such phrases, but merely formulate it differently.

Karl Marx

Woe to the weak!

Adolf Hitler

THE AGE OF
FAITS ACCOMPLIS

Historians have looked back upon the mid-thirties with some vexation. This was the period in which Hitler repeated, on the plane of foreign policy, those same practices of overwhelming his opponents that had yielded him such easy triumphs at home. And he applied them in the same effortless manner and with no less success. In accord with his thesis "that before foreign enemies are conquered the enemy within must be annihilated,"[1] he had behaved rather quietly in the preceding months. His only flamboyant gestures had been his withdrawal from the League of Nations and his treaty with Poland. Secretly, meanwhile, he had begun rearmament, since he was well aware that without military force a country could have only the most limited freedom of movement in the realm of foreign policy. He would have to get through the transitional phase from weakness to power without breaches of treaties and without provoking powerful neighbors. Once again, as at the beginning of his seizure of power, many observers predicted his impending fall. But by a series of foreign-policy coups he managed within a few months to throw off the restrictions imposed by the Versailles Treaty and to occupy vantage points for his intended expansionist movements.

The reaction of the European nations to Hitler's challenges is all the harder to understand because the process of seizing power, with its bloody finale in the Röhm affair, had provided some inkling of the man's nature and policies. In a speech of January, 1941, Hitler declared, peeved, but quite rightly: "My program from the first was to abolish the Treaty of Versailles. It is futile nonsense for the rest of the world to pretend today that I did not discover this program until 1933, or 1935, or 1937. . . . These gentlemen would have been wiser to read what I have written—and written thousands of times. No human being has declared or recorded what he wanted more often than I. Again and again I wrote these words: 'The abolition of the Treaty of Versailles.' "[2]

From the very start no one could be in doubt about this particular aim, at the very least. And since abrogation of the Treaty of Versailles represented a direct threat to almost all the nations of Europe, there must have been strong though possibly somewhat hidden factors that contributed to Hitler's effortless triumphs.

Once again Hitler's deep inner ambiguity, which governed all his behavior, all his tactical, political, and ideological conceptions, proved of crucial importance. It has been rightly pointed out that he would surely have roused the united opposition of the European nations, or of the whole civilized world, had he been merely an excitable nationalistic spokesman for German international equality, an anti-Communist, an aggressive prophet of *Lebensraum,* or even a fanatical anti-Semite of the Streicher type. But he was all of these together and, moreover, had the knack of countering every fear he aroused with a hope. By "letting the one quality emerge and the other recede, as opportunity offered, he divided his opponents without ever betraying himself. . . . It was an ingenious recipe."[3]

The basic anti-Communist mood of liberal-conservative bourgeois Europe served him as a vital means for fending off suspicions of himself and his policies. It is true that in the spring of 1933 the French writer Charles du Bos assured a German friend that an abyss had opened up between Germany and western Europe. But while this may have been true, morally, it was hardly so from the psychological view. Beyond all opposing interests, all crisscrossing enmities, Europe retained its common emotions, above all the dread of revolution, arbitrariness, and public chaos. And it was as the apostle of order that Hitler had so successfully presented himself inside Germany.

To be sure, the gospel of Communism had lost a good deal of its aggressive promise and intensity. But Europe was once more reminded of the famous specter in the Popular Front experiment in France, in the Spanish Civil War, and in the Moscow trials. Everywhere Communism had taken a severe beating, but it had nevertheless displayed sufficient energy to revive the old fears. With his keen instinct for the moods and secret motivations of his opponents, Hitler had exploited this fear factor. In countless speeches he had referred to "the undermining work of the

484

Bolshevist wirepullers," their "thousand channels for money and propaganda," their "revolutionization of this continent." He was heightening deliberately the psychosis of fear: "Then cities burn, villages collapse in ruin and rubble, and each man no longer knows his neighbor. Class fights against class, occupation against occupation, brother destroys brother. We have chosen a different plan." He described his own mission to Arnold Toynbee by saying that he had come into the world to lead mankind in the inevitable struggle against Bolshevism.

Thus this peculiarly alienated, atavistically reactionary Hitler Germany aroused profound anxieties in Europe but also encouraged many secret expectations: that Germany would somehow assume the ancient role of serving as a bulwark against evil, or a "breakwater," as Hitler himself said, in an age in which "the Fenris wolf seems once more to be raging over the earth." Within the framework of such far-reaching considerations on the part of Germany's western neighbors in particular, Hitler's contempt for justice, his extremism, his multifarious atrocities, scarcely seemed to matter—despite all the momentary indignation they aroused. Those were problems for the Germans to worry about. To the mind of conservative Europe, the man's sinister martial features—a good deal less strange, at any rate, than those of Stalin—were highly appropriate for a protector and the commander of a bulwark. Of course, nobody wanted or expected him to amount to anything more than that.

Here we have, down to incidentals, the same mixture of naïveté, stupidity, and vanity that all the conservative participants who collaborated with Hitler, from Kahr to Papen, had demonstrated. Of course, the statesmen felt some trepidations, but such feelings did not affect their politics. When Chamberlain heard Hermann Rauschning's report on Hitler's aims, he flatly refused to believe it. With a sharp sense for the repetitive nature of events and even the similarity of faces, Hitler called the appeasers in London and Paris "my Hugenbergers."[4]

The popularity of the authoritarian concept, both at home and abroad, played directly into Hitler's hands. He himself called the "crisis of democracy" the prevailing phenomenon of the age. And many a contemporary observer regarded "the idea of dictatorship as contagious at present . . . as in the last century the idea of freedom."[5] In spite of the shocking concomitants, regimented Germany emitted a seductive radiation that in eastern and southeastern Europe countered the hitherto dominant influence of France. It was not by chance that Foreign Minister Joseph Beck of Poland kept signed photographs of Hitler and Mussolini in his office. They and not their bourgeois counterparts in Paris or London, with their anachronistic impotence, seemed to be the true voices for the spirit of the age. The age was persuaded that reason would always be defeated in the free interplay of social and political interests; the new order's program was power through discipline. That order's dominant representative, whose

485

success would transform in a trice the political atmosphere of Europe and set entirely new standards, was Adolf Hitler.

And as he combined in his own self the tendencies or moods, all worked to his advantage. He derived considerable profit from European anti-Semitism, which had a large following in Poland, Hungary, Rumania, and the Baltic countries, but was also widespread in France, and which even in England in 1935 inspired the leader of a Fascist group to propose settling the Jewish problem radically and hygienically by "death chambers."[6]

Hitler wrung further profit from the contradictions within the existing peace settlements. The Treaty of Versailles had for the first time introduced moral factors into international relations, factors such as guilt, honor, equality, and self-determination. Hitler played upon these themes more and more loudly. For a time, as Ernst Nolte has trenchantly remarked, he must paradoxically have seemed the last faithful follower of Woodrow Wilson's long-since-faded principles. In his role of heavy creditor to the victorious Allies, clutching a bundle of unpaid promissory notes, he achieved lasting effects, particularly in England. For his appeals not only touched the nation's guilty conscience but also chanced to coincide with traditional English balance-of-power policy. British statesmen who believed in that policy had long been watching with uneasiness France's overpowering influence on the Continent. Hence Hitler constantly received encouragement from English voices. The London *Times* quoted Lord Lothian as saying that any order which did not concede to the Reich the most powerful position on the Continent was "artificial." A leading member of the Royal Air Force early in 1935 told a German that it would arouse "no indignation" in England if Germany were to announce that she was rearming in the air, contrary to the terms of the Treaty of Versailles.[7] But both, the British and the continental Europeans, the victors and the vanquished, the authoritarians and the democrats, sensed an impending change in the climate of the era. And this was another element Hitler made use of. In 1936 he declared:

We and all nations have a sense that we have come to the turning point of an age. Not only we, the former defeated, but the victors also have the inner conviction that something is wrong, that men seem to have taken leave of reason. . . . Everywhere the nations seem to feel that a new order must come, especially on the Continent where the people are so closely crowded together. The motto for this new order must read: reason and logic, understanding and mutual consideration! Those who think that the word "Versailles" could possibly stand at the entrance to this new order are sadly mistaken. That would not be the cornerstone of the new order, but its gravestone.[8]

Thus Europe offered Hitler as many gateways for invasion as Germany had. A belated opposition would hammer away at the antitheses between Hitler and Europe; this was a misconception, for there were a large number of shared feelings and interests. With some bitterness Thomas Mann, voicing the attitudes of a minority, spoke of the "painfully slow and reluctant way in which we Germans, those of us who are exiles at home or exiles abroad, who have believed in Europe and thought we had Europe morally behind us, were forced to realize that in fact we do not have it behind us."[9]

The many encouragements he received from English sources tended to support Hitler in his boldest expectations. He clung to the idea he had advanced at the beginning of 1923 of an alliance with England. That remained, in fact, the central concept of his foreign policy, for it was essentially the idea of partitioning the world. England, as the dominant sea power, would command the seas and overseas territories. Germany, as the unchallenged land power, would dominate the vast Eurasian continent. Thus England occupied a key place in Hitler's schemes in the early years of the regime, and the manner in which his actions were received across the Channel immensely fortified Hitler's sense that he was on the right path.

To be sure, not all his actions were equally well received. In May, 1933, Rosenberg had visited London and been sharply rebuffed. The spectacular withdrawal from the League of Nations had not exactly raised Hitler's stock in England. Another blot had been the murder, by Austrian Nazis, of Austrian Chancellor Engelbert Dollfuss in July, 1934—even though Hitler, as later became apparent, may not have been told of the planned assassination. But selfish interests proved, as always, stronger than moral outrage—especially since Hitler himself was quick to repudiate the affair. The assassins had fled to Germany; he turned them over to the Austrian government, abruptly dismissed Theo Habicht, the inspector of the Austrian National Socialist Party, and recalled Dr. Rieth, the German ambassador, who was implicated in the events. Franz von Papen, Catholic, conservative, and once again a reassuring figure to anxious bourgeois, was sent to take his place.

The unanimity of the foreign reaction to the assassination of Dollfuss had taught Hitler that he would have to proceed more carefully. The attempted coup in Vienna had been hastily organized and poorly co-ordinated. Beyond that, Hitler recognized that his position was not yet strong enough for major challenges; he would do better to wait for provocatory pretexts or imperceptibly to work his opponents into the position known in chess as a "forced move"—when a player has only one legal move open to him. Then his own carefully premeditated actions would be disguised as countermoves.

Circumstances arranged matters favorably. Soon afterward, Hitler obtained his hoped-for increase in prestige by winning the plebiscite held in the Saar on January 13, 1935. The region, which had been separated from the Reich under the Treaty of Versailles, voted by an overwhelming majority for reunion with Germany: there were only about 2,000 votes for union with France as against 445,000 for reunion with Germany and approximately 46,000 for continuance of the status quo, administration by the League of Nations. Although the result had never been in doubt, Hitler presented the vote as a personal triumph. One of the injustices of Versailles had at last been righted, he declared three days later in an interview at Obersalzberg with the American journalist Pierre Huss. Only a few weeks later the Western powers handed him the opportunity for one of those counterstrokes that from now on became his favorite device.

The tactical weakness of the leading European powers vis-à-vis Hitler stemmed from their desire for negotiations. They were forever coming forward with proposals that were supposed to fetter the unruly fellow, or at least put him in an uncomfortable position. Early in 1935 he had received offers from England and France, among others, to extend the Locarno Pact by an agreement limiting the threat of air attacks. There were likewise offers for similar pacts from eastern and central European countries. Far from considering these proposals seriously, Hitler merely used them as a springboard for his tactical maneuvers. They permitted him to spread uncertainty, to achieve easy effects by sham declarations, and to cover up the aims he was unerringly pursuing.

During 1934 he had already taken steps to reach an accord with England on air armaments. His purpose was to induce London, merely by entering into negotiations, to treat the armaments restrictions imposed on Germany by the Treaty of Versailles as nonexistent. At the same time, Hitler proceeded on the assumption that the talks in themselves, and the aura of intimacy they would inevitably create, would be excellent means of sowing distrust between England and France. For this reason he was quite ready to encourage the English side to undertake extensive rearmament. After the talks had been broken off in the aftermath of Dollfuss's assassination, Hitler approached the British government with a new offer at the end of 1934. Characteristically, he increased his demands, as he would always do after a defeat. Hitherto he had asked only that Germany be permitted half the British strength in the air. Now he mentioned, in a casual remark, that parity was "a matter of course"; it had ceased to be an object of negotiation, as far as he was concerned. Rather, the key offer was now for a naval agreement with England.

This proposal by Hitler has been called, with some exaggeration, his "crowning idea."[10] The negotiations on the air agreement had broken down only partly because of the Vienna events; the chief reason for their failure was that the British, though interested, were not ready for a bilateral pact. The offer for a naval agreement, on the other hand, struck them at a vulnerable spot.

Hitler's special envoy, Joachim von Ribbentrop, launched a trial balloon in the middle of November, 1934, when he met with the then Keeper of the Privy Seal Anthony Eden and Foreign Secretary Sir John Simon. Early in

1935 the contacts were continued. On January 25 Hitler "unofficially" received Lord Allen of Hurtwood, and four days later—again "unofficially"—the liberal politician Lord Lothian. The German Chancellor complained about the limping progress of the disarmament negotiations, stressed that both sides had parallel interests, then referred to Great Britain's uncontested dominion of the sea before he made his first specific proposal: he would be ready to conclude an agreement regulating naval strength between Germany and England in the ratio of 35 to 100. In return, Germany, in keeping with her national tradition, would be allowed the stronger land army. Such was the outline of the grand design. In his conversation with Lord Lothian Hitler gave the matter another original twist. If he might speak not as Chancellor of the Reich, he said, but as a "student of history," he would regard as the surest guarantee of peace a joint Anglo-German statement to the effect that henceforth any disturber of the peace would be called to account and punished jointly by these two countries.

The impending visit of the British Foreign Secretary to Berlin would provide the opportunity for discussions of substance. It was set for March 7, 1935. The talks show how closely he had measured the interests and psychology of the other side. For he skillfully implanted in the British those arguments for appeasement that would dominate the politics of the following years. The British came away from the talks with the belief that Hitler urgently desired a treaty in order to legalize his rearmament and at last make Germany eligible for alliances. This need was a trump card that must not go unplayed. Here was a way to end the armaments race, to keep German rearmament within controllable bounds, and to tie Hitler's hands after all. Of course, France would be alarmed by an Anglo-German treaty, but she would have to realize that "England has no permanent friends, but only permanent interests," as the *Naval Review* wrote. These interests would be served if a great power like Germany voluntarily acknowledged the British claim to dominion on the seas, especially under the moderate conditions that Hitler had set. The Versailles era, which meant so much to France, was in any case over, and, as a Foreign Office memo of March 21, 1934, quipped, if there had to be a funeral it might as well be arranged as long as Hitler was in a mood to pay the services of the gravediggers.[11]

The real meaning of all these considerations was simply that they spelled the end of the solidarity created during the World War and confirmed in the Treaty of Versailles. Once again Hitler had demonstrated his ability to blast apart the united front of his opponents. Even more astonishing was his faculty for spreading among the victors, as he had already done among the vanquished, the sense that the system of peace they themselves had proclaimed only fifteen years earlier was intolerable. In the election campaigns during the last years of the republic he had shown his ingenuity in taking a problematical situation and producing a stylized version of it as

489

an absurdity and cynical injustice. Now he successfully applied the same trick to foreign affairs. For a moment it seemed as though his antagonists would organize for resistance after all. But instead they produced only an empty defensive gesture, which Hitler saw through immediately. After that they gave him even freer scope.

As if it wished to strengthen the position of its Foreign Secretary the British government on March 4 published a White Paper that condemned Germany's rearmament as an open breach of treaty. Germany's bellicose tone was causing growing insecurity. Therefore the British government thought it proper to increase its air power. Instead of being cowed, Hitler went into a sulk, and canceled the visit from Sir John Simon on the grounds of a sudden "cold." Simultaneously, he exploited the alleged wrong inflicted upon him to launch a counterattack. On March 9 he made an official announcement that Germany had established an air force. The French government responded by extending the term of military service for the conscript classes from the years of low birth rate. The British Foreign Secretary, however, merely told the House of Commons that he and Mr. Eden still intended to go to Berlin.

Making the most of this disparate reaction, Hitler went a step further on the following weekend. He pointed to the measures taken by Germany's neighbors, in whom Germany had repeatedly and vainly put her trust ever since the days of Woodrow Wilson, until she found herself in the midst of a heavily armed world reduced to "a condition of impotent defenselessness as humiliating as it is ultimately dangerous." He was, therefore, reinstating universal military service and establishing a new army with a peacetime strength of thirty-six divisions and 550,000 men.

Hitler combined this proclamation with a brilliant military celebration. On March 17, the day of mourning that had now been renamed Heroes' Memorial Day, he organized a grand parade in which units of the new air force already participated. Alongside von Mackensen, the only living marshal of the old imperial army, and followed by the top-ranking generals, Hitler marched along Unter den Linden to the terrace of the Schloss, where he pinned honorary crosses to the flags and emblems of the army. Then, with tens of thousands cheering, he reviewed the parade. But although the reintroduction of universal military service was popular as a sign of defiance to the Versailles Treaty, Hitler did not dare link it with another plebiscite, as he had done with comparable actions in the past.

The crucial factor at the moment was the reaction of the Versailles signatory powers to this open breach of the treaty. But after only a few hours Hitler saw that his gamble had been successful. The British government did issue a protest, but in the very protest note inquired whether Hitler still wished to receive the Foreign Secretary. To the German side that was a "regular sensation,"[12] as one of the persons closely involved commented. France and Italy, on the other hand, were prepared to take some strong countermeasures, and in the middle of April arranged for a conference of the three powers in Stresa on Lake Maggiore. Mussolini took the lead in urging that Germany be stopped in her tracks. But the representatives of Great Britain made it clear from the start that they had no intention of imposing sanctions. The result was that the conference petered out in an exchange of ideas. Mussolini observed that consultations are the last refuge of indecisiveness when confronted with reality.

Hitler drew his conclusions, and when Simon and Eden arrived in Berlin at the end of March, they found him thoroughly self-confident. With patient courtesy he waited to hear their proposals, but he himself made no promises. After going on at great length about the Bolshevist menace he once again referred to the German nation's lack of living space and offered a global alliance, the first stage of which was to be the proposed naval pact. When the British statesmen said a firm no to the establishment of a special Anglo-German relationship, and above all refused to sacrifice Britain's close co-operation with France, Hitler found himself in a difficult negotiating position. For a moment the whole idea of the alliance, his grand design, seemed to have failed. But he remained impassive. When the following day's talks threw a new opportunity his way, he used it for a bold bluff. Sir John Simon responded to the German demand for parity in the air by asking what the present strength of the German air force was. Hitler, after a brief pause of seeming hesitation, answered that Germany had already attained parity with England. This information took the others' breath away. For a while no one said a word; the British negotiators' faces betrayed embarrassed surprise and doubt. Yet this was the turning point. Now it became evident why Hitler had postponed the talks until he could announce the building of the air force and the introduction of conscription. England could not be won by wooing alone; Hitler could lend weight to his proposals only by pressure and threats. Not fondness but weapons brought nations to the conference table. Immediately after this round of negotiations Hitler, together with Göring, Ribbentrop, and several cabinet members, went to the British Embassy for a breakfast. Sir Eric Phipps, the ambassador, had lined up his children in the reception room. They stretched out their little arms toward Hitler in the German greeting, and brought out a bashful *"Heil."*[13]

The British, at any rate, had been deeply impressed. Another opportunity to isolate Hitler soon arose when the League of Nations, on April 17, condemned Germany's violation of the Versailles Treaty. Shortly afterward, France concluded a treaty of alliance with the Soviet Union. Nevertheless, the British abided by the date for signing the naval pact that had been agreed on in Berlin. It seems clear that Hitler saw this as a telling admission of weakness and planned to exploit it. He therefore instructed his special envoy, Ribbentrop, to initiate the talks in the Foreign Office on

June 4 by putting the agreement in the form of an ultimatum. England must accept the proportion of naval strength of 35 to 100; that was not a German proposal but an unshakable decision on the Führer's part. Acceptance of it was the precondition for the beginning of negotiations. Flushed with anger, Sir John Simon reproved the head of the German delegation and walked out of the session. But Ribbentrop gruffly stuck to his terms. Arrogant and limited as he was, he obviously lacked any sense of how to handle the matter. For here right at the start of the negotiations he was pushing the other party to accept the very method they had recently condemned in their White Paper, then in their protest note after the reintroduction of universal military service, later in Stresa, and most recently in the Council of the League of Nations. He dismissed all the remonstrances "categorically," to use one of the favorite words in his subsequent report; he wanted the alliance to be no less than "eternal"; and when the British objected that he was reversing the order of business, he declared it .came to the same thing whether difficult matters were discussed at the beginning or the end. The negotiators parted with nothing accomplished.

Two days later, however, the British asked for another meeting; their opening statement declared that the British government had decided to accept the Chancellor's demand as the basis for further naval discussions between the two countries. And, as if the special relationship of trust that Hitler wanted of England had already been established, Sir John Simon remarked, with a discreet gesture of complicity, that they would have to let a few days pass in consideration of the situation in France, where governments were "unfortunately not so stable as in Germany and England."[14] A few days later the text of the treaty had been worked out. With some feeling for symbolism, the day for signing was fixed as June 18, the hundred and twentieth anniversary of the day the British and Prussians had defeated the French at Waterloo. Ribbentrop returned home to be hailed by Hitler as a great statesman, "greater than Bismarck." Hitler himself called this day "the happiest of [my] life."[15]

It was in fact an extraordinary success, and it granted Hitler everything he could hope for at the moment. British apologists have ever since pointed to Great Britain's security requirements and to the possibility that Hitler could have been tamed by concessions. But the question remains whether those requirements and vague hopes could justify an agreement that condoned a policy of brash violation of treaties, sabotaged Western solidarity, and set the political situation in Europe in motion in such a way that there was no knowing when and where it would come to a stop. The naval agreement has rightly been called an "epochal event whose symptomatic importance was greater than its actual content."[16] Above all, it proved to Hitler once again that the methods of blackmail could accomplish absolutely anything, and it nourished his hopes of ultimately concluding the grand alliance for the partition of the world. This pact, he exulted, was "the beginning of a new age." He firmly believed, he said, "that the British have sought the understanding with us in this area only as the initial step to very much broader co-operation. A German-British combination will be stronger than all other powers together." Given the seriousness of his historical pretensions, it was more than a gesture of empty ceremony when Hitler, in Nuremberg at the beginning of September, accepted the presentation of a reproduction of Charlemagne's sword.

The Anglo-German naval treaty had a further consequence that once and for all demolished all the existing political relationships in Europe. In the two and a half years since Hitler had been appointed Chancellor, Mussolini had pursued a policy of critical reserve toward Hitler in spite of their ideological fraternity. He had shown "a keener sense of the extraordinary and menacing character of National Socialism than most western statesmen."[17] Gratified though he was by the victory of the Fascist principle in Germany, he could not suppress his deep uneasiness about this neighbor to the north who was bursting with the dynamism, vitality, and discipline he had laboriously been trying to instill into his own people. The meeting in Venice had only served to confirm his mistrust of Hitler. But it seems also to have aroused that inferiority complex for which he thereafter tried to compensate more and more by posturings, imperial actions, or the invoking of a vanished past. Ultimately, it would drive him deeper and deeper into his fateful partnership with Hitler. In a speech shortly after the Venice meeting he had declared, with a glance at Hitler's racial ideas, that thirty centuries of history permitted Italians "to look with sublime indifference upon certain doctrines on the other side of the Alps which have been developed by the descendants of those who in the days of Caesar, Virgil and Augustus were still illiterates." According to another source he had called Hitler a "clown," denounced the race doctrine as "Jewish," and expressed sarcastic doubts about whether anyone would succeed in transforming the Germans into "a racially pure herd," adding: "According to the most favorable hypothesis . . . six centuries are needed." Unlike France, let alone England, he was prepared at various times to counter Hitler's breaches of treaties by military gestures: "The best way to check the Germans is by calling up the military class of 1911." At the time of Dollfuss's assassination he had ordered several Italian divisions to the northern border, telegraphed the Austrian government that he was prepared to offer it all support in defending the country's independence, and finally even permitted the Italian press to publish popular lampoons on Hitler and the Germans.

He now wished to cash in on all this good conduct. His glance fell upon Ethiopia, which had been occupying Italy's imperialistic fantasies ever since the end of the nineteenth century, when an attempt to extend the colonies of Eritrea and Somaliland had failed miserably. England and

493

France, he decided, would impose no obstacles to a conquest, since they would continue to need Italy in the defensive front against Hitler. Addis Ababa, situated in a kind of no man's land, could not really be more important to the two great powers than Berlin. Mussolini interpreted the half-promises that Laval had made in January, when he visited Rome, and the silence of the British at Stresa, as signs of discreet consent. The Duce also reasoned that the Anglo-German naval pact had increased the value of Italy to the Western powers, especially to France.

By means of deliberately provoked border incidents and oasis conflicts, he stirred up feeling for his colonial war, which had an oddly anachronistic air. While France assured him passive support, for fear that a further pillar of her system of alliances would collapse, he dismissed all attempts at mediation with one of those virile Caesarian gestures he had at his command. Surprisingly, it was England who then came forward. After having refused as recently as April to counter Hitler's troublemaking with sanctions, in September England demanded that sanctions be imposed on Mussolini, and to emphasize her resolve ostentatiously reinforced her Mediterranean fleet. Now, however, France objected; France found herself unwilling to risk her good relations with Italy for the sake of an England that had just demonstrated her unreliability as an ally by coming to an arrangement with Hitler. This refusal in turn angered the British. In Italy outrage was whipped up to the point of boastful talk about a preventive war against Great Britain (mockingly referred to as "Operation Madness"). In short, all understandings and time-tested loyalties now disintegrated. In France, influential partisans of Mussolini, including many intellectuals, openly came out in favor of the Italian expansionist policies. Charles Maurras, the spokesman of the French Right, publicly threatened with death all deputies who demanded sanctions against Italy. Ironic defeatists queried, *"Mourir pour le Négus?"* Soon the same question would be applied to Danzig.

There could be only one justification for the British gesture, especially in view of Hitler's stance: if the British government were prepared to counter Mussolini's act of aggression with all resolution, not shrinking from the risk of war. Obviously, British determination did not go quite that far, and thus it merely brought on the misfortune more speedily. Mussolini felt that the threat of sanctions had been such an insult to the pride and honor of Italy that he was bound to go ahead. On October 2, 1935, at a mass demonstration to which 20 million people, assembled in the streets and plazas throughout Italy, listened enthusiastically, he declared war on Ethiopia: "A great hour in the history of our country has struck. . . . Forty million Italians, a sworn community, will not let themselves be robbed of their place in the sun!" It would have taken only the closing of the Suez Canal or an oil embargo to render the Italian expeditionary army with its modern equipment incapable of battle. The Ethiopians would then

494

have inflicted upon the Italians a devastating defeat, as the Emperor Menelik had done on the same ground forty years earlier. Mussolini later admitted that this would have been "an inconceivable disaster" for him. But England and France shrank from such a course, as did the other members of the League of Nations. A few half-hearted measures were taken, their feebleness only diminishing what prestige the democracies and the League of Nations still had. There were many reasons for caution. President Beneš, for example, who emerged as a particularly vigorous advocate of economic sanctions, prudently excepted Czechoslovakia's own exports to Italy.

The internal contradictions and antagonisms of Europe afforded Mussolini almost unlimited freedom to maneuver. And with unprecedented brutality, which established a new style of inhumane warfare, the modern Italian army set about destroying an unprepared and nearly defenseless enemy. It even employed poison gas. No less unprecedented was the way in which prominent military officers, including Mussolini's sons Bruno and Vittorio, boasted of the sport they had had in their fighter planes harassing fleeing hordes of human beings and raining death upon them with incendiary bombs and machine guns.[18] On May 9, 1936, the Italian dictator stood on the balcony of the Palazzo Venezia announcing his "triumph over fifty nations" to an ecstatic mob, and proclaimed the "reappearance of the Empire upon the fated hills of Rome."

Hitler had at first observed strict neutrality in the conflict, and not only because he had sufficient reasons to be annoyed with Mussolini. This Ethiopian adventure disturbed his fundamental design in foreign policy. That design had always envisioned a partnership with England and Italy. But the crisis was setting his two prospective allies against one another and confronting Hitler with an unforeseen alternative.

Surprisingly, after prolonged hesitation he decided to take Italy's side, and supplied the Italians with raw materials, especially coal, although only a few months earlier he had hailed the Anglo-German treaty as the beginning of a new era. He was obviously not prompted by ideological sympathy. Economic factors did not seem to play a decisive part, either, although he was certainly influenced by such considerations. Much more important was the fact that he saw in the war another chance to create havoc within the established order of things. His trick for manipulating any crisis consisted in supporting the weaker opponent against the stronger. Thus, as late as the summer of 1935, in two highly secret transactions, Hitler had supplied the Emperor of Ethiopia with war materials valued at approximately 4 million marks. Included were thirty antitank guns that were clearly meant to serve against the Italian aggressor. Out of similar considerations he now supported Mussolini against the Western powers. The decision came all the easier for him because, as a secret speech he delivered in April, 1937, makes plain, he did not take England's commitment very seriously. The principles England was defending—the integrity of small nations, the protection of peace, the right of self-determination—meant nothing to him, whereas he saw Italy's imperialistic gamble as representing the true laws and logic of politics. He made the same grave mistake in August and September, 1939, caused, no doubt, by his inability to think in terms other than those of naked-power interests. Moreover, in the exultation of his rapid successes he felt sufficiently secure to test the newly concluded pact with England by a certain degree of strain, provided he could win over another potential ally who up to then had refused to march with him despite all his overtures.

In addition to using the Ethiopian War to break his isolation in the south, Hitler seized upon the obvious indecisiveness of the Western powers and the paralysis of the League of Nations to launch another of his surprise coups. On March 7, 1936, German troops occupied the Rhineland, which had been demilitarized since the conclusion of the Locarno Pact. By the logic of events, that would have had to be his next step, but to all appearances it came unexpectedly even to Hitler himself. If we may judge by the documents, the action had originally been planned for the spring of 1937. But in the middle of February he began to wonder whether he could not advance the date, in view of the international situation. Apparently he made up his mind only a few days later, when Mussolini twice in quick succession informed him that the spirit of Stresa was dead and Italy would not participate in any sanctions against Germany. Yet this time, too, Hitler waited for a pretext that would enable him to assume before the world's eyes his favorite role of one who had been abused. He wanted to be able to cry out against the shame that had been inflicted upon him.

This time he took his cue from the Franco-Soviet mutual assistance pact. The agreement had been negotiated some time before, but not yet ratified. It lent itself all the better to Hitler's purposes because it had been the subject of protracted domestic controversies within France and had stirred considerable concern internationally as well, especially in England. In order to disguise his intentions, on February 21 Hitler granted an interview to Bertrand de Jouvenel. He expressed his desire for rapprochement and in particular repudiated the intense anti-French bias of *Mein Kampf*. At the time he was writing the book, he explained, France and Germany had been enemies; but by now there were no longer any grounds for conflict. Jouvenel then asked why the book, widely regarded as a kind of political bible, was still being reprinted in unaltered form. Hitler replied that he was not a writer who revised his books, but a politician: "I make my corrections every day in my foreign policy, which is aimed entirely at rapprochement with France. . . . My corrections will be written in the great book of History." But when the interview was not published in *Paris-Midi* until a full week later, and in fact not until the day after the Chamber of Deputies had ratified the Franco-Soviet Pact, Hitler felt he had been hoodwinked.

When François-Poncet called on him on March 2, Hitler angrily told the ambassador that he had been made a fool of. Political intrigues had kept the interview from being published in time; all his statements had since been outstripped by events, and he would be making new proposals.

The directive that War Minister von Blomberg prepared for the occupation of the Rhineland was dated that same March 2. On March 7 his troops crossed the Rhine, with the population cheering and throwing flowers. But Hitler was well aware of the risk he had taken. Later he referred to the forty-eight hours after the occupation as the "most nerve-racking" period in his life. He did not want to go through another such strain for the next ten years, he said. The build-up of the army had only just begun. If it came to fighting, he had only a handful of divisions against the nearly 200 divisions of France and her East European allies, for in the meanwhile the forces of the Soviet Union had also to be added. And although Hitler himself did not appear to have suffered a nervous breakdown, as one of the participants later asserted, the nerves of the sanguine War Minister did give out. Shortly after the beginning of the operation, he was all for withdrawing the troops in view of the French intervention that could certainly be expected. "If the French had marched into the Rhineland," Hitler admitted, "we would have had to withdraw with our tails between our legs, for the military resources at our disposal would have been wholly inadequate for even a moderate resistance."[19]

Nevertheless, Hitler did not hesitate to take the risk, and his readiness to do so was undoubtedly connected with his increasingly contemptuous assessment of France. In his time-tested manner he made the operation as safe as possible. Once again he ordered it for a Saturday, knowing that the decision-making committees of the Western powers could not meet on weekends. Once again he accompanied his breach of a treaty, this time a double violation of the treaties of Versailles and Locarno, with pledges of good behavior and emphatic offers of alliances, even proposing a twenty-five-year nonaggression pact with France and a return of Germany to the League of Nations. Again he had his step legitimized by the democratic process, making it the issue of an election in which he for the first time achieved the "totalitarian dream figure"[20] of 99 per cent of the vote. "Abroad and domestically that always has enormous effect," he later said. How consciously he combined this plan of surprise blows with reassuring talk is evident from a remark in the table talk in which he criticized Mussolini's indulgence toward the Curia: "I would march into the Vatican and fetch out the whole crew. I would then say: 'Sorry, I made a mistake!'—But they would be gone!" Quite rightly he called this phase, which left the strongest imprint on his tactics, the "age of *faits accomplis.*"[21]

The Reichstag speech in which Hitler supported his action exploited to the hilt the contradictions, fears, and longings for peace in Germany and the rest of Europe. Again he drew a picture of the "horror of the Com-

497

munist international dictatorship of hate," the danger from the sinister East, which France was bringing into Europe. He pleaded for "raising the problem of the general antagonisms among European nations and states out of the sphere of irrationality and passion and placing it under the quiet light of higher insight." Specifically, he justified his action on the grounds that in the German legal view the Franco-Soviet Pact must be regarded as a violation of the Locarno Pact, since it was undeniably aimed against Germany. And although the French disagreed, Hitler's argument had a certain validity, even if his own policy of revisionism was what had prompted a France concerned for her security to enter the alliance with Russia.

His arguments and assurances did not fail to make an impression. The Paris government did consider a military counterblow for a moment—as we now know—but shrank from general mobilization in view of the prevailing pacifist mood. England, for her part, had difficulty understanding the French excitement; the British thought that the Germans were merely returning "to their own back garden." And when Eden advised Prime Minister Stanley Baldwin to respond to France's anxiety at least by having the military staffs make contact, he was told: "The boys won't have it."[22] Of all of France's allies, only Poland indicated any readiness to intervene. But, left dangling by the passive French government, it ended by falling into considerable embarrassment in its efforts to find even a reasonably plausible explanation vis-à-vis Berlin for its seeming aggressiveness.

Thus everything followed the model of the preceding crises. Hitler's abrupt action was followed by loud protests and threats, then serious consultations, finally conferences (with and without Germany), until the prolonged palavers had used up all the energy that might have been produced by injured righteousness. The Council of the League of Nations, which came hastily to London for a special session, unanimously declared Germany in violation of her treaties, but it also took grateful note of Hitler's repeatedly announced "desire for co-operation." And, as if to say that its own vote sprang from a rather absurd whim, it recommended negotiations with the treaty breaker. When the Council set up a neutral zone in the Rhineland about thirteen miles in width and demanded that Germany refrain from building fortifications in this area, Hitler merely replied that he would not bow to any dictates, that German sovereignty had not been restored in order to be restricted or eliminated immediately afterward. This was the last time the powers were to speak in the forceful tone of victors; in any case they had been using that tone less and less of late. That was certainly implied by the London *Times,* which saw in Hitler's conduct "a chance for reconstruction."

What all these reactions added up to was the admission that the Western powers were no longer able or no longer willing to defend the peace system they had established in and after Versailles. Only a year before, after the weak reaction to Germany's reintroduction of universal military service, François-Poncet noted anxiously that Hitler must now be convinced that he could "permit himself anything and prescribe the laws for Europe." Encouraged by the cheers of his own people and by the weakness and egotism of the other side, he continued to climb higher and higher. Returning from his triumphal ride through the reoccupied Rhineland, after a speech preceded by pealing bells at Cologne Cathedral and followed by fifteen minutes of radio silence, he turned to his cronies in the special train and once again expressed his relief at the limpness of the Western powers: "Am I glad! Good Lord, am I glad it's gone so smoothly. Sure enough, the world belongs to the brave man. He's the one God helps." Passing by glowing blast furnaces, slag heaps, and derricks in the nocturnal Ruhr district, he was overcome by one of those moods of euphoria that brought on in him a desire for music. He asked that a record of Wagner's music be played, and, listening to the prelude of *Parsifal,* meditated: "I have built up my religion out of *Parsifal.* Divine worship in solemn form . . . without pretenses of humility . . . One can serve God only in the garb of the hero." But even in such moments, spoiled by almost incomprehensible successes and virtually stunned by the cheers he had received, he was still very close to his early days with their dreary resentments. Even in good fortune he was incapable of summing up much serenity or magnanimity. That is clear from the remark he made at the next selection, the funeral march from *Götterdämmerung:* "I first heard it in Vienna. At the Opera. And I still remember as if it were today how madly excited I became on the way home over a few yammering Yids* I had to pass. I cannot think of a more incompatible contrast. This glorious mystery of the dying hero and this Jewish crap!"[23]

At first the occupation of the Rhineland scarcely affected the actual balance of forces among the European powers. But it gave Hitler that safety in his rear troops—in the West—which was essential to him if he were to realize his aims in the Southeast and East. And the time was now drawing nearer. No sooner had the excitement over his operation faded than he began building a strongly fortified line of defense along the German western frontier. Germany's face was now turning to the East.

An intensified sense of the Communist threat would have to be whipped up in order to prepare the people psychologically for the turn to the East. And as if he himself were pulling all the stops in the historical process, Hitler once more found circumstances meeting him halfway. The Communist International had resolved upon its new Popular Front tactics in the

---

* A typical Hitler formulation: *mauschelnde Kaftanjuden. Mauscheln* means "to talk with a Jewish accent" and also carries overtones of "to cheat." The caftan, which some Jews in Vienna still wore, seemed to excite a peculiar horror in Hitler, and became in itself a term of abuse. By comparison, the last word of the passage, *Judendreck,* is relatively mild.—TRANS.

summer of 1935. Those tactics met with spectacular success in the Spanish elections of February, 1936, and shortly afterward in France, where the electoral victory of the united French Left benefited chiefly the Communists, who increased their seats in the Chamber of Deputies from ten to seventy-two. On June 4, 1936, Léon Blum formed a Popular Front government. Six weeks later, on July 17, a military revolt in Morocco touched off the Spanish Civil War.

When the Spanish Popular Front government turned to France and the Soviet Union for aid, General Franco, the rebel leader, asked for similar backing from Germany and Italy. Together with a Spanish officer, two Nazi functionaries set out from Tetuan in Morocco for Berlin, to transmit personal letters from Franco to Hitler and Göring. Both the Foreign Office and the War Ministry declined to receive the delegation officially, but Rudolf Hess decided to take the matter straight to Hitler, who was in Bayreuth for the annual festival. On the evening of July 25 the three envoys met Hitler as he was returning from the Festspielhaus on its hill above the town and handed him the letters. Out of the euphoric mood of the moment, without consulting the ministers concerned, the decision was taken to lend active support to Franco. Göring, as commander in chief of the air force, and von Blomberg as War Minister, immediately received directives to this effect. The most important immediate measure, and perhaps the decisive one, consisted in the dispatch of several formations of Junkers 52's. With the help of these planes Franco was able to transport his troops across the Mediterranean and create a bridgehead on the Spanish mainland. During the following three years he received support in the form of war matériel, technicians, advisers, and the Condor Legion. Nevertheless, the German aid did not significantly affect the conduct of the war, and in any case lagged far behind the forces placed at Franco's disposal by Mussolini. Documents reveal the interesting fact that here again Hitler acted chiefly with tactical ends in view and showed a rational coolness entirely devoid of ideology.[24] For years he did virtually nothing to bring about a victory by Franco, but he did all in his power to keep the conflict going. He was always fully aware that crisis was useful to him. Every critical situation demands a frank admission of real interests, like a creditor's oath that he is concealing none of his assets. Every critical situation produces discord, ruptures and reorientations. And such troubles offer a springboard for the political imagination. The real profit Hitler was able to derive from the Spanish Civil War consisted in the turmoil it introduced into European conditions.

Compared with that, all other gains paled—even that of putting the German air force and tank troops to test in battle. One further gain that counted was the militant demonstration of superiority to all rival political systems. The cries of indignation arising from the entire civilized world at the bombardment of the port of Almería, or the air raid upon Guernica, were complemented by perverse respect for the inhuman brutality with which the Communist threat was challenged and ultimately smashed. On a vastly larger plane this matched the discovery Hitler had made in the beer-hall brawls: terrorism exerts an attraction upon the masses.

Soon, too, it became possible to discern the polarization to which the war was pushing things—and once again familiar lines appeared. Anti-Fascism created its legend on the battlefields of Spain, when the Left, split into numerous cliques and factions, rent by internal feuds, nevertheless united in the International Brigades as if for "the final conflict" and once more demonstrated the continuing force of the old myths. But the concept of the power and danger of the Left had never been much more than a legend. It had exerted its most significant function as legend: to bring together and mobilize the opposition.

This was the effect of the Left's commitment in Spain, despite all its defeats. It finally brought together the Fascist powers that had long been at odds and had only tentatively begun to approach one another. The result was the "Berlin-Rome Axis," presumably a new and triumphant element of strength around which the decadent democracies and the antihuman, terroristic systems with a leftist tinge rotated in jittery orbits. From this point on, there existed a Fascist International of sorts, its power center in Germany. And simultaneously the line-up of the Second World War first appeared in outline.

For all the inadvertent prodding from outside, this alliance did not come into being with ease. Several hurdles had to be taken. The reservations on the Italian side were matched by considerable reservations in Germany. Bismarck had remarked that it was impossible to engage in any political relationships with Italy because as friend and as foe she was equally untrustworthy. During the First World War that comment had become an axiom, and it was as difficult to make an alliance with Italy acceptable to the public as, for example, the one with Poland. The bias did not go quite so far as Mussolini presumed when in December, 1934, he remarked to Ulrich von Hassell, the German ambassador in Rome: "I have the feeling that no war would be so popular in Germany as a war with Italy." Still, the Germans were hardly convinced by Ciano's assurance that Fascist Italy had abandoned all intrigue and attempts to seek its own advantage and was no longer "the whore of the democracies."

What strengthened the tie in the end was the personal liking Hitler and Mussolini developed for one another, after their unpropitious first meeting in Venice. Despite obvious differences between them—Mussolini's extrovert nature, his practicality, spontaneity, and ebullience contrasted markedly with Hitler's solemn rigidity—both men had important traits in common. They shared a craving for power, a hunger for greatness, irritability, boastful cynicism and theatricality. Mussolini felt himself the elder and liked to take a patronizing tone, a kind of Fascist precedence, toward his

501

German partner. At any rate, a number of leading Nazi functionaries began reading Machiavelli. A heavy bronze bust of the Italian dictator stood in Hitler's study in the Brown House; and in a most unusual burst of veneration Hitler referred to Mussolini during a visit from the Italian Foreign Minister in Berchtesgaden in October, 1936, as "the leading statesman in the world, to whom none may be remotely compared."

Mussolini had been watching Hitler's obvious wooing with a good measure of skeptical reserve. His inveterate fear of "Germanism" recommended restraint. So did the interests of his country, which, strictly speaking, pointed in the opposite direction. To be sure, he had won his East African colonial empire partly because National Socialist Germany had provided a distraction. But Germany could do nothing to secure this empire. Rather, everything now depended on Italy's consolidating her new acquisitions by a policy of good behavior toward the West. That, however, was a political consideration, and, in the light of Hitler's rapid ascent, Mussolini no longer wanted to engage in mere politics. He wanted to make history, to participate in the march to greatness, to display dynamism, to arouse faith, to satisfy the old "yearning for war," and so on— there were many other phrases to express such fateful self-infatuation. Therefore, no matter what he might have felt originally about the German dictator, Mussolini was impressed by the boldness with which the strange fellow left the League of Nations, proclaimed universal military service, repeatedly defied the world, and broke up stultified European patterns. Mussolini was all the more provoked because it seemed as though Hitler, who had made such a poor showing at Venice, had taken over the original Fascist policy of éclat and was putting it across with remarkable energy. Concerned for his own standing, Mussolini began considering the rapprochement.

Hitler himself removed the most serious obstacle. Convinced that everything could be arranged later on among friends, he pretended to give way on the question of Austria. In July, 1936, he concluded a pact with Vienna whose main point was his recognition of Austrian sovereignty. He promised nonintervention in Austrian affairs, and in exchange for this received the concession that "decent" Nazis would no longer be barred from assuming political responsibility. Naturally, Mussolini interpreted this treaty as largely his own personal triumph. Even so, he might still have been wary of moving closer to Germany had not some curious circumstances favored such a tie at this very moment. For likewise in July the League of Nations powers revoked their not very effective edict of sanctions against Italy. Thus, with a confession of failure, they left Ethiopia to its conqueror. At the same time, Mussolini was able to satisfy his pride in Spain, where his commitment far exceeded Hitler's and where he appeared as the leading Fascist force.

In September Hans Frank called upon Mussolini to bring him a note from Hitler. It began by the most flattering tributes to Italian hegemony in the Mediterranean region before proposing close co-operation. Mussolini still hung back; but he was obviously only displaying a great man's majestic indolence. A month later he sent his son-in-law and Foreign Minister, Count Ciano, to Germany to reconnoiter. Shortly afterward the prominent Fascists Tullio Cianetti and Renato Ricci, Minister of Corporations, then a thousand Fascist *avanguardistas,* made similar trips. At last, in September, 1937, Mussolini went himself.

To honor his guest, Hitler put on a display of all the spectacle of which the regime was capable. The effects, as Munich Gauleiter Wagner attested, were of Hitler's own devising. On arrival Mussolini found that he was to pass down a lane of busts of the Roman Emperors, flanked by laurel trees. Thus the Duce, restorer of the Roman imperium, was placed in the line of the noblest ancestry in European political history. During their first conversation Hitler conferred the highest German decoration on his guest as well as a golden party badge, which he alone had hitherto worn. Meanwhile, designer Benno von Arent had created a mile-long triumphal avenue in Berlin between the Brandenburg Gate and the West End, lined with white pylons from which were festooned garlands, banners, and streamers, reiterating the symbols of fasces and swastika. On Unter den Linden hundreds of columns were set up, crowned with gold imperial eagles. For the night show the stage managers had conceived a play of lights featuring the green-white-red of Italy and the black-white-red of Hitler Germany.

Hitler had taken leave of his guest in Munich, before Mussolini was to be conducted to Berlin. But as the Italian dictator's special train reached the city limits of Berlin, Hitler's train surprisingly appeared on the adjacent track and accompanied the Duce's, their two cars side by side, for the last stretch of the way. At last it pulled a bit ahead, and when Mussolini arrived at the Heerstrasse station, his host was already waiting at the predetermined spot and holding out his hand in greeting. Standing beside Hitler in the open limousine, deeply impressed by the solemnity and the obvious sincerity of the tributes that were being paid him, Mussolini entered the capital of the Reich. Sightseeing, parades, banquets, and demonstrations followed one another in continual whirl. At a drill ground in Mecklenburg the Italian dictator was shown the newest weapons and the striking power of the new German army. At the Krupp plant in Essen he saw the capacity of German war industry. On the evening of September 28 at the Maifeld, close to the Olympic Stadium, Hitler held a "demonstration of the nations of the 115 millions," at which he again cleverly ministered to the pride of his guest. He hailed Mussolini as "one of those lonely men of the ages on whom history is not tested, but who themselves are the makers of history."

Obviously overwhelmed by the impressions of the past few days, the Duce delivered a speech in German in which he opposed to the "false and mendacious idols of Geneva and Moscow" the "radiant truth" that tomorrow all Europe would be Fascist. Before he had finished his speech a tremendous thunderstorm with torrents of rain scattered the audience in panic, and he found himself suddenly alone. At the Maifeld, Ciano noted ironically, there had been "beautiful choreography: lots of sentiment and lots of rain." Drenched, Mussolini had to find his way back to Berlin. Nevertheless, the impression of that visit to Germany remained with him for the rest of his life.

"I admire you, Führer!" he had exclaimed in Essen at the sight of a giant cannon until then kept a strict secret. But the feeling was mutual. Little as Hitler was capable of undivided feelings in other respects, he manifested toward the Italian dictator a rarely candid, seemingly almost naïve liking, and preserved it through the many disappointments of later years. Mussolini was one of the few persons toward whom he did not show pettiness, calculation, or envy. A contributing factor was that both had come from simple circumstances. With Mussolini he did not have that sense of constraint he felt almost everywhere else in Europe with representatives of the old bourgeois class. Their mutual understanding was spontaneous, at any rate after the unfortunate first meeting at Venice had been put behind. Trusting in this, Hitler had, in the agenda, reserved only a single hour for political discussion.

Mussolini was unquestionably a man of judgment and political acumen; but the style of personal foreign policy practiced by Hitler, the method of direct dialogue, handshakes, man-to-man talk, appealed to the stronger side of his nature. Under the influence of Hitler he yielded to it more and more, and the result was that ultimately he became curiously vulnerable, diminished, and finally drained, like so many of Hitler's other victims. Even then, when he allowed political rationale to be corrupted by flatteries and grandiose theatrical effects, he was basically lost; the inglorious end at the gasoline station on the Piazzale Loreto, not quite eight years later, could already have been foreseen. For, in spite of all his ideological community with Hitler, his own future depended on his not losing sight of their fundamental difference of interests: the difference between a weak, saturated power and a strong, expansionist power. Under the spell of the visit he had already veered far too widely from the categories of politics to the unpolitical category of blind shared destiny. That became clear in the course of his Berlin speech, when he referred to a precept of Fascist and personal morality; that precept held, he said, that when one has found a friend, one must "march together with him to the end."

Thus Hitler had succeeded with surprising rapidity in achieving one side of his design for alliances. For the first time in modern history two governments joined under ideological auspices to form a "community of action . . . and contrary to all the predictions of Lenin these were not two socialist but two Fascist governments." The question was whether Hitler, after entering upon an alliance that flaunted its ideological nature, could win over his other dreamed-of partner, England. Or had he not, in terms of his own premises and aims, already taken the first step which was to prove fatal for him?

Some time back, shortly after the reoccupation of the Rhineland, Hitler had made a fresh effort to bring England over to his side. Once again he did not employ the Foreign Office, by now relegated to a technical apparatus for routine tasks. Hitler was bent on carrying out his designs largely by himself, with the aid of special envoys. Since the happy conclusion of the naval pact, he considered Joachim von Ribbentrop a natural-born diplomatic genius and expert on the British mentality. Hitler now assigned him the task of bringing about the alliance with England.

His choice could hardly have been worse, but also hardly more characteristic. In the end none of the leading personalities of the Third Reich came in for such unanimous contempt as Ribbentrop. Friend and foe denied that there was anything in the least likable about him, or that he had the slightest practical competence. The favor and protection that this henchman enjoyed with Hitler from the summer of 1935 on indicates to what extent the Führer was already using mere instruments and seeking relationships whose chief element was servility. For Ribbentrop's bombast and pompousness toward the outside world were matched by an almost lunatic obsequiousness toward Hitler. Forever wearing the clouded brow of the statesman, he was the quintessence of the petty bourgeois type that had risen so rapidly with the class shifts after 1933. Now he was busily casting his resentments and catastrophic inclinations into demonic molds of historic grandeur. Soon he designed a fancy diplomatic uniform for himself; the epaulets were embroidered with a globe on which the German eagle perched proprietarily.

Ribbentrop now conveyed a message, via a mediator, to British Prime Minister Baldwin proposing a personal meeting between the Prime Minister and Hitler. Such a conversation would "determine the fate of generations," he said, and would represent the fulfillment of the German Chancellor's "greatest wish." Baldwin was a great procrastinator; he was phlegmatic and loved his comfort. As one of his intimates has described it, the go-between had great difficulty in getting the Prime Minister to look up from his evening game of patience and hear out the proposal. Still less was he interested in the enthusiastic feelings the proposal awoke in his entourage. Baldwin instinctively drew away from complications of this sort. He was no more concerned with this fellow Hitler than he was with the rest of Europe, of which, as Churchill bitingly commented, he knew little and disliked what he knew. But if there had to be a meeting, let Hitler come to see him; he did not like either planes or traveling by boat. The thing was not to make any great fuss about it. Perhaps, he conceded, the Chancellor could come in August; they could meet in the mountains or in the Lake District. That was about all he cared to say about the matter. "Then a drop of Malvern soda water and to bed," the report concludes. Later on, there was some talk of arranging the meeting on a ship off the English coast. Hitler himself, his adjutant of the time has related, "beamed with joy" at the thought of the impending meeting.[25]

In the meantime he had enlarged his scope to include Japan in his system of alliances. In the spring of 1933 he had first mentioned that Far Eastern country as a possible ally alongside of England and Italy. In spite of all the racial incompatibilities, Japan seemed like an Asiatic version of Germany: late on the scene, disciplined, and unsatiated; moreover she had a common border with Russia. According to Hitler's new plan, all England had to do was to keep quiet in Eastern Europe and the Far East. Germany and Japan together, each secure in her rear, could attack the Soviet Union from two sides and destroy it. They would thus be freeing the British Empire of an acute threat. At the same time, they would be extirpating the sworn enemy of the existing order, of Old Europe. And they would be securing themselves *Lebensraum*. Hitler pursued this concept of a world-embracing anti-Soviet alliance for two years, trying principally to make it attractive to the British. Early in 1936 he proposed it to Lord Londonderry and Arnold J. Toynbee.

The planned meeting with Baldwin fell through; why, we do not exactly know, but it would appear that Eden's vigorous objections were a significant factor. And although Hitler was "gravely disappointed" that the British had repulsed his fourth attempt at a rapprochement, he still did not give up. In the summer of 1936 he appointed Ribbentrop to succeed Leopold von Hoesch, the deceased German ambassador in London. Ribbentrop's assignment was to transmit to the British the offer of a "firm alliance," in which "England was merely to allow Germany a free hand in the East." That was, as Hitler told Lloyd George shortly afterward, "the last effort" to make Great Britain understand the aims and necessities of German policy.[26]

The effort was accompanied by a renewed campaign against Communism, "the ancient adversary and old enemy of mankind," as Hitler put it in a significantly theological-sounding phrase. The Spanish Civil War had provided him with a plethora of new arguments and images. Thus he evoked "the brutal mass slaughter of nationalist officers, pouring gasoline over the wives of nationalist officers and setting fire to them, slaughtering the children and babies of nationalist parents." And he predicted similar horrors for France, which had already completed the transition to the Popular Front: "Then Europe will drown in a sea of blood and tears," he prophesied. "European culture which—fertilized by classical antiquity—has a history that will soon reach two and a half millennia, will be replaced by the cruelest barbarism of all time." Along with this, in those apocalyptic images he so favored, he offered himself as the bulwark and refuge: "The whole world may begin to burn around us, but the National Socialist State will tower like platinum out of the Bolshevistic fire."

But although the campaign was extended over months, it did not pro-duce the expected result. The British, too, were certainly aware of the Communist menace, but their phlegmatic tempers, their soberness, and their distrust of Hitler were stronger than their fear. By November, 1936, however, Japan was prevailed upon to sign the Anti-Comintern Pact. The treaty provided for common defensive measures against Communist sub-version; both parties swore that they would make no political agreements with the U.S.S.R., while in case of an attack by the Soviet Union they would take no measures which might be helpful to the aggressor. For the rest, Hitler hoped that the weight of the German-Japanese-Italian triangle would soon add some additional pressure to his own wooing of England. But he seems also to have begun to think of other ways to force Britain to leave him free to march eastward. At any rate, there are indications that from the end of 1936 on, he no longer totally excluded from his considera-tions the idea of a war against the England which obstinately resisted all his blandishments.[27]

Psychologically, this change can undoubtedly be traced to the mounting self-confidence that followed from his series of successes. "Today we have once again become a world power!" he proclaimed in the Munich Hof-bräuhaus on February 24, 1937, at the annual celebration of the party's founding. A new tone of challenge and impatience can be detected in all his speeches of this period. In the impressive balance sheet of achievements with which he came before the Reichstag on January 30, 1937, after four years of his government, he "most solemnly" withdrew Germany's signature from the discriminatory clauses of the Versailles Treaty. Shortly afterward, he mocked at the "Esperanto languages of peace, of reconcilia-tion among nations" that weaponless Germany had spoken for years. "It would seem that this language is not so well understood internationally. Our language is being understood again only since we have had a large army." And, reverting to the old Lohengrin image, the idea of the White Knight with whom he usually identified, he declared: "We move through the world as a peace-loving angel, but one armed in iron and steel."

At any rate he was now secure enough to show considerable pique. In the course of the spring he did make still another attempt at approaching England by offering a guarantee for Belgium. But at the same time he offended the British government by abruptly canceling an announced visit of his Foreign Minister von Neurath to London. And when Lord Lothian called upon him on May 4, 1937, for a second conversation, he showed himself out of sorts and vehemently criticized British policy. The British were incapable of recognizing the Communist peril, he said, and in general did not understand their own interests. He added that he had always been pro-English, had been so during his time as a "writer." A second war between the German and the English peoples would be tantamount to the departure of both powers from the stage of history; it would be as useless as it was ruinous. Instead, he was offering collaboration on the basis of defined interests.[28] Once more he waited for a reaction from London. He waited half a year. When it did not come, he reshaped his design.

Although an essential premise of Hitler's ideal scheme had remained unfulfilled, he had nevertheless carried out his projects to an amazing extent. Italy and Japan were won over. England was wavering and had lost considerable prestige. France's weakness had been exposed. No less important was the fact that he had destroyed the principle of collective security and restored the *sacro egoismo* of nations as the prevailing political principle. Faced with the swift shifts in power relationships, the smaller countries grew visibly uneasy, thus accelerating the dissolution of the anti-German front. After Poland, Belgium now turned her back on her impotent French ally. Hungary, Bulgaria, and Yugoslavia also reoriented their policies. Along with the fatal blow Hitler had inflicted upon the Versailles system, innumerable sources of conflict reappeared, which the system had only suppressed but not eliminated. All of southeast Europe began to falter. Naturally, its statesmen admired the example of Hitler, who had overcome the weakness of his own country, put an end to Germany's humiliations, and taught the erstwhile victors "to shiver and shake." As "Europe's new Man of Destiny"[29] Hitler soon found himself the focus of a good deal of political pilgrimaging. His advice and his assistance counted for something. His stupendous achievements seemed to prove the superior capacity of totalitarian regimes to take action. Evidently the liberal democracies must lag hopelessly behind with their palavering, their judicial appeals, their sacred weekends and their Malvern soda water. French Ambassador François-Poncet, who had been in the habit of meeting diplomatic colleagues of friendly or allied countries for intimate dinners at Horcher's, Berlin's luxury restaurant, has reported that fewer and fewer people came, with each of Hitler's successes.[30]

Reactions in Germany itself extended to considerably greater depths. The shrinking number of skeptics had the wind knocked out of their sails. Ivone Kirkpatrick, first secretary at the British Embassy in Berlin, recorded the fact that Germans who had been calling for caution found all their warnings refuted. Kirkpatrick observed that Hitler was reinforced in his conviction that he could do anything and that many Germans now enlisted under the Nazi banners, having held off only because they thought Hitler was going to lead the country straight to disaster.[31] Instead he was piling up successes, winning prestige, international respect. A nation with pride still badly shaken at last found itself impressively represented, and derived a grim satisfaction from the surprise coups which left yesterday's powerful victors stupefied. An elemental craving for righting scores was being gratified.

The regime's achievements at home answered this craving in another way. The recently crushed country, which had seemed to incorporate all the crises and abuses of the age within its apparently hopeless national and social wretchedness, suddenly found itself admired as a model. Goebbels, characteristically self-congratulating, called this unexpected change "the greatest political miracle of the twentieth century." Delegations from all over the world came visiting to study German measures for economic revival, for the elimination of unemployment. They looked into the widely ramified system of social benefits: the improvement of labor conditions, the factory canteens and workers' housing, the newly established athletic fields, parks, kindergartens, the plant contests and professional competitions, the Strength-Through-Joy fleet of cruise ships and the people's vacation resorts. The model of a hotel for the masses, planned to extend for about 2½ miles on the island of Rügen, with its own special subway system to shuttle the tens of thousands of vacationers, received the Grand Prix at the Paris World's Fair of 1937. Even critical outsiders were impressed by the regime's accomplishments. In a letter to Hitler, Carl J. Burckhardt hailed the "Faustian achievement of the Autobahn and the Labor Service."[32]

In his major Reichstag speech on January 30, 1937, Hitler had declared that the "period of surprise actions" was over. His next steps followed with a good deal of logic from the initial position he had assumed with each of his actions. Just as the treaty with Poland had given him the principal key to the advance against Czechoslovakia, the reconciliation with Italy offered the lever for the annexation of Austria. German politicians began paying frequent visits to Poland. Polish politicians were invited to Germany. Hitler issued assurances of friendship and statements that Germany withdrew all claims on Polish territory. By such steps he tried to draw Poland closer, and while he had Göring, on a visit to Warsaw, emphasize again that Germany took no interest in the Polish Corridor, he himself told Josef Lipski, the Polish ambassador in Berlin, that Danzig, so long a point of contention, was really in the sphere of Poland. Simultaneously he reinforced the relatively new ties with Italy. Early in November, 1937, he persuaded Italy, again with Ribbentrop's aid, to join the Anti-Comintern Pact. Joseph C. Grew, the American ambassador in Tokyo, pointed out in an analysis of this triangle that the participating powers were not only anti-Communist but that their policy and their practices ran counter to those of the so-called democratic powers; they represented a coalition of have-nots who had made "overthrow of the status quo" their goal. Significantly, Mussolini let it be known in the conversations with Ribbentrop that preceded the signing ceremony that he was tired of playing the guardian of Austrian independence. In other words, the Italian dictator was preparing to abandon his old stand for the sake of his new friendship. He did not seem to sense that by so doing he was giving up his last card. "We cannot impose independence on Austria."

This conversation took place in the Palazzo Venezia on November 5, 1937, the same day Hitler in the Berlin chancellery gave the Polish

509

ambassador a guarantee for the integrity of Danzig; at 4 P.M. on the very same day Hitler met with the leaders of the armed forces. The Foreign Minister, von Neurath, was also present. In a four-hour-long, top-secret speech Hitler revealed to them his "fundamental ideas." These were the old obsessions of racial menace, existential anxiety, and geographic constriction, for which he saw the "only and perhaps seemingly visionary relief" in the winning of new *Lebensraum,* in the building of a vast unbroken empire. After the assumption of power and the years of preparation these "fundamental ideas" were now ushering in—with amazing consistency—the expansionist phase.

Chapter 2

VIEW OF AN UNPERSON

At this point the reader may question, both on moral and literary grounds,
the emphasis we have placed on Hitler's achievements and triumphs, and
wonder if the negative aspects of these years have not deliberately been
ignored. But this was indeed the period when he developed remarkable
control and energy, seemed to know intuitively when to push forward and
when to show restraint, threatened, cajoled, and took action so forcefully
that all resistance yielded before him. He managed to concentrate upon his
person all the attraction, the curiosity, and the fears of the age. This
capacity was further strengthened by his extraordinary gift to represent this
power with overwhelming effect.

This moment in history is typical for Hitler's peculiarly patchwork
career, a career marked by such sharp breaks that it is often difficult to find
the connecting links between the different phases. The fifty-six years of his
life are divided between the first thirty years with their dullness, their
obscure asocial circumstances, and the suddenly electrified political half.
The later period, however, falls into three distinct segments. At the beginning there are approximately ten years of preparation, of ideological
development, and of tactical experimentation. During this time Hitler
ranked as no more than a marginal radical figure, distinguished, it is true,
by an unusual talent for demagoguery and political organization. Then
followed the ten years in which he riveted the attention of the age, and in
retrospect seems to stand before a film of flashing scenes of mass jubilation
and crowd hysteria. He himself was fairly sensitive to the fairy-tale character of this phase of his life; indeed, he could not fail to feel that he had
been "elected" to his role and remarked that it "had not been the work of
men alone." And then followed six more years of grotesque errors, mistake
piled upon mistake, crimes, convulsions, destructive mania, and death.

Reviewing this, we are once again drawn to look at the person of Adolf Hitler. His individual outline is still blurred; at times it might seem as if he emerged more distinctly from the imprint he made upon political and social conditions than from any account of his personal biography; as if the statue into which he stylized himself reveals, amid all the pomp of his political self-display, more of his essence than the human being behind it.

Political events during these years of success were accompanied by incessant fireworks: grand spectacles, parades, dedications, torchlight processions, demonstrations, bonfires leaping from mountaintop to mountaintop. We have already made the point of the close connection in totalitarian regimes between foreign and domestic policy; but even closer was the connection of both with propaganda policy. Memorial days, deliberately created incidents, state visits, harvest festivals or the death of a party member, the conclusion or breach of treaties—all these served as the pretext for great spectacles, whose purpose was to integrate the nation more and more closely, preparing it for mobilization in every sense of the word.

In Hitler's government the connection between policy and propaganda was so intimate that sometimes the emphasis shifted, so that politics took second place to become merely the handmaiden of theatrical effects. In planning the grand boulevard of the future rebuilt Berlin, Hitler was even willing to conceive of a rebellion against his rule. Carried away, he described how the armored vehicles of the SS would come rolling invincibly up the 400-foot-wide avenue, advancing slowly upon his palace. His theatrical nature was never quite submerged and led him to subordinate political to histrionic categories. In this amalgam of aesthetic and political elements, Hitler's origins in late-bourgeois bohemia and his lasting connection with that sphere can clearly be recognized.

The style of National Socialist spectacles also points back to these origins. Some have perceived the influence of the showy, colorful ritual of the Catholic Church. But equally evident is—once again—the heritage of Richard Wagner, whose splendiferous theatrical liturgy was carried to its ultimate point in the operatic excesses of the party rallies. The hypnotic fascination of these spectacles, which still comes through in the cinematic records of them, is partly due to these origins. "I had spent six years in St. Petersburg before the war in the best days of the old Russian ballet," Sir Nevile Henderson wrote, "but for grandiose beauty I have never seen a ballet to compare with it."[33] The spectacles testify to a precise knowledge of the dramaturgy of grand scenes and of the psychology of the common man. The forest of flags and the flickering torches, the marching columns and the blaring bands combined to make a magic that the mentality of the age, haunted by images of anarchy, could scarcely resist. Each detail was tremendously important to Hitler. Even in the festivals with their vast blocks of humanity he personally checked seemingly trivial points. He

512

approved every scene, every movement, as he did the selection of flags or flowers, and even the seating order for guests of honor.

Significantly, Hitler's talents as stage manager reached their summit when the object of the celebration was death. Life seemed to paralyze his inspiration, and his attempts in that direction never went beyond a dreary nod to peasant folklore: hailing the joys of dancing about the Maypole or the rearing of large families. On the other hand, he could always invent impressive effects for funeral ceremonies. Though the form may vary, the message was always the same. As Adorno said of Richard Wagner's music: "Magnificence is used to sell death."[34]

He also had a distinct preference for nocturnal backdrops. Torches pyres, or flaming wheels were continually being kindled. Though such rituals were supposed to be highly positive and inspirational, in fact they struck another note, stirring apocalyptic associations and awakening a fear of universal conflagrations or dooms, including each individual's own.

The ceremony of November 9, 1935, commemorating the dead of the march to the Feldherrnhalle twelve years before, was a model for many other such solemnities. The architect Ludwig Troost had designed two classicistic temples for Munich's Königsplatz; these were to receive the exhumed bones, now deposited in sixteen bronze sarcophagi, of the first "martyrs" of the Nazi movement. The night before, during the traditional Hitler speech in the Bürgerbräukeller, the coffins had been placed on biers in the Feldherrnhalle, which was decorated with brown drapes and flaming braziers for the occasion. Shortly before midnight Hitler, standing in an open car, drove through the Siegestor into Ludwigstrasse, lit by flares set on masts, and on to the Odeonsplatz. SA and SS units formed a lane, their torches making two moving lines of fire down the length of the broad avenue. The audience was massed behind these lines. The car crawled slowly to the Feldherrnhalle. With raised arm, Hitler ascended the red-carpeted stair. He paused before each of the coffins for a "mute dialogue." Six thousand uniformed followers, carrying countless flags and all the standards of the party formations, then filed silently past the dead. On the following morning, in the subdued light of a November day, the memorial procession began. Hundreds of masts had been set up with dark red pennants bearing the names of the "fallen of the movement" inscribed in golden letters. Loudspeakers broadcast the Horst Wessel song, until the procession reached one of the offering bowls, at which the names of the dead were called out. Alongside Hitler at the head of the procession walked the former corps of leaders, in brown shirts or in the historic uniforms (gray windbreaker and "Model 23" ski cap, supplied by the "Bureau for November 8–9"). At the Feldherrnhalle, where the march had once ended before the blazing guns of the army, the representatives of the armed forces now joined the marchers—a piece of revisionist symbolism. Sixteen artillery salvos boomed over the city. Then solemn silence descended while

513

Hitler laid a gigantic wreath at the memorial tablet. While "Deutschland, Deutschland über Alles" was played at a mournful tempo, all began to move toward Königsplatz down a lane of thousands upon thousands of flags dipped in salute to the dead. United in the "March of Victory," the names of the fallen were read out in a "last roll call." The crowd answered, "Present!" in their behalf. Thus the dead took their places in the "eternal guard."

A tribute to the dead also took center stage at the Nuremberg party rally. But the reference to death was present in nearly every ceremonial and in the speeches and appeals throughout the several days of the annual party congress at Nuremberg. The Bodyguard Regiment stood saluting while Hitler drove, to the pealing of bells, into the flag-decked city. The regiment's black dress uniforms added an accent that was repeated in the ritual surrounding the "blood banner" and in the ceremonial in the Luitpoldhain: Hitler, with two leading paladins at a respectful distance behind him and to either side, walked up to the monument between more than 100,000 SA and SS men stationed in enormous squadrons along the broad ribbon of concrete, the "Street of the Führer." While the flags dipped, he stood meditating for a long time, the manifest embodiment of the concept "leader": in the midst of the mute soldiers of the party, but "surrounded by empty space, the insuperable gulf of Caesarian loneliness, which belongs to him alone and to the dead heroes who gave their lives because they believed in him and his mission."[35]

For maximum impressiveness, many spectacles were shifted to the evening or night hours. At the party rally in 1937 Hitler arrived to address the lined-up political leaders toward eight o'clock in the evening. As soon as Robert Ley had reported to him the presence of these subleaders, "the enveloping darkness was suddenly illuminated with a flood of whiteness. Like meteors," the official report read, "the beams of the one hundred and fifty giant searchlights shoot into the obscured, gray-black night sky. The tall columns of light join against the cloud ceiling to form a luminous halo. An overwhelming sight: caught by a faint breeze, the flags in the stands ringing the field quiver gently in the glittering light. . . . The grandstand is . . . bathed in dazzling brightness, crowned by the shining golden swastikas in the oak wreath. On the left and right terminal, pyres leap from great basins."

With fanfares blaring, Hitler entered the high central section of the grandstand, and at a command a torrent of more than 30,000 flags poured from the stands opposite into the arena. The silver tips and fringes of the flags sparkled in the beams of the searchlights. As always, Hitler himself was the first victim of this orchestration of masses, light, symmetry, and the tragic sense of life. Especially in speeches to old followers, after the period of silence in memory of the dead, he frequently fell into a tone of total rapture; in strange phrases he held a kind of mystic communion until the searchlights were lowered to strike the middle of the arena and flags, uniforms, and band instruments flashed red, silver, and gold. "I have always felt," he cried in 1937, "that man, as long as life is given to him, ought to yearn for those with whom he shaped his life. For what would my life be without all of you! That you found me long ago and that you believed in me has given your lives a new meaning, posed a new task. That I have found you is what has made my life and my struggle possible!"

A year before he had cried to the same assemblage:

At this hour do we not again feel the miracle that has brought us together! Long ago you heard the voice of a man, and it struck to your hearts, it awakened you, and you followed this voice. You followed it for years, without so much as having seen him whose voice it was; you heard only a voice, and you followed.

When we meet here we are all filled with the wondrousness of this coming together. Not every one of you can see me, and I cannot see every one of you. But I feel you and you feel me! It is faith in our nation that has made us small people great, that has made us poor people rich, that has made us vacillating, dispirited, anxious people brave and courageous; that has made us who had gone astray able to see, and that has joined us together.

In their pontifical displays of magnificence the party rallies were the public climax in the National Socialist calendar year. In addition, they were for Hitler personally the realization of his youth's monumental costume dreams. Members of his entourage have recorded the excitement that regularly gripped him during the week at Nuremberg. As might be expected, his displaced sexuality was released in an unquenchable torrent of speech. As a rule he delivered between fifteen and twenty speeches during those eight days, including the cultural speech devoted to basic principles, and the grand concluding address. In between he would speak as often as four times a day, speeches to the Hitler Youth, to the Women's Corps, to the Labor Service or the army, whatever the program of the party rally required.

Almost every year, moreover, he satisfied his passion for building by a series of new cornerstone layings for the temple city that was planned on an enormous scale. Then there were parades, drills, conferences, in a whirl of color. The Nuremberg party rallies also acquired importance as the occasion for political decisions: the Reich flag law or the Nuremberg racial laws were promulgated, though rather hastily improvised, within the framework of a party rally. It is even conceivable that the rally might eventually have evolved into a kind of general assembly of a totalitarian democracy. At the end hundreds of thousands would march, wave upon wave, for up to five hours, past Hitler in the medieval market place in front of the Frauenkirche. And Hitler stood as if frozen, arm held out horizontally, in the back of his open car. Around him a mood of romantic frenzy gripped the old city, "an almost mystical ecstasy, a kind of holy madness," as a foreign

515

observer noted. Many others lost their critical reserve during those days and were forced to confess, as did a French diplomat, that momentarily they themselves had become Nazis.[36]

The fixed calendar of festivals that filled the Nazi year began with January 30, the day of the seizure of power, and concluded with November 9, the anniversary of the Munich putsch.[37] That year was an endless succession of dedications, roll calls, processions, and memorials. A special Bureau for the Organization of Festivals, Leisure, and Celebrations saw to the creation of "model programs for celebrations of the National Socialist Movement and for organizing the setting of National Socialist demonstrations on the basis of the organizational tradition evolved during the period of struggle." This bureau published a magazine of its own.

Alongside the regular round there were many holidays prompted by special occasions. The outstanding one—which impressed on the world the deceptive picture of a Third Reich whose citizens enjoyed the austere felicity of a welfare state accompanied, regrettably, by a few drastic features—came with the Olympic games of 1936.

The games had already been scheduled for Berlin before Hitler's accession to power. The Nazis contrived to profit overwhelmingly by the opportunity of being hosts to the world. They did everything in their power to counter what they regarded as the distorted image of a hectically rearming Reich bent on war. Rather, they were determined to show the country in the most idyllic light. Weeks before the beginning of the games all ugly anti-Semitic tirades were stopped. No malicious caricatures were to be displayed. The district propaganda chiefs of the National Socialist Party were instructed to obliterate from building walls and fences any remaining traces of slogans hostile to the regime, even exhorted to make sure that "every home owner keep his front garden in irreproachable order." To the solemn ringing of the Olympic bell, in the midst of royal highnesses, princes, cabinet ministers and many guests of honor, Hitler opened the games on August 1. And, while an earlier marathon winner, the Greek Spyridon Louis, handed him an olive branch as the "symbol of love and peace," a chorus struck up the anthem composed by Richard Strauss, and swarms of doves of peace flew up. Hitler was offering a picture of a reconciled world. And, fittingly, some of the teams, including the French who had so recently been provoked, offered the Hitler salute as they marched past the grandstand. Later, in an impulse of tardy protest, they pretended that what they had given was the "Olympic salute."[38] All through the two weeks a series of brilliant spectacles kept the guests breathless and filled them with admiration. Goebbels invited a thousand persons to an Italian Night on Peacock Island. Ribbentrop hosted nearly as many in his garden villa in Dahlem. Göring gave a party in the Opera House, whose hall was draped in precious silk. And Hitler received the multitude of guests who had used the games as a pretext to see the man who seemed to hold in his hands the fate of Europe and perhaps of the world.

The purpose of all the ceremonies and mass celebrations was obviously to engage the popular imagination and rally the popular will into a unitary force. But beneath the surface it is possible to discern motives that throw light upon Hitler's personality and psychopathology. We are not referring only to his inability to endure routine, his naïve craving for circuses, for the roll of drums, the blare of trumpets, the grand entrance, for dazzling illusions and the cheap brilliance of Bengal lights. The vault of light was not merely the fit symbol of Hitler's craving to substitute illusion for reality. Albert Speer has told us how he happened to invent this device, which had the practical purpose of disguising a most prosaic reality: by a combination of darkness and glaring light effects he wanted to distract attention from the paunches of the middle and minor party functionaries who had grown fat in their prebends.[39]

In addition, the resort to ceremonials also reveals a strenuous desire to stylize, to represent the triumph of order over a shifting existence forever threatened by chaos. We might call these efforts techniques of exorcism undertaken by a terrified mind. When certain contemporaries likened all the to-do with marching columns, forests of banners and blocks of humanity to the rites of primitive tribes, the comparison was not so artificial as it sounded. From the psychological point of view, what was operative here was the same urge to stylize that had dominated Hitler's life from a very early period. Thus he had sought orientation and support against the world in a succession of new roles: from the early role of the son of good family and idling student, promenading in Linz with his cane and kid gloves, through the various roles of leader, genius, and savior, to the imitation Wagnerian end, where his aim was to enact an operatic finale. In every case he practiced autosuggestion, presenting himself in disguises and borrowed forms of existence. And when after one of his successful foreign-policy coups he called himself, with naïve boastfulness, "the greatest actor in Europe," he was expressing a need of his nature as well as an ability.

It was, in turn, a need that emerged from the fundamental Hitlerian motif of insecurity and anxiety. He was good at portraying feelings; he took pains not to show them. He repressed all spontaneity. But certain small peculiarities betrayed him—especially his eyes, which never stood still. They roamed restlessly even in moments of statutelike rigidity. So fearful was he of a frank emotion that he held his hand before his face whenever he laughed. He hated being surprised while playing with one of his dogs, and as soon as he knew he was being observed, one of his secretaries has reported, he would "roughly chase the dog away." He was constantly tormented by the fear of seeming ridiculous or of making a *faux pas* that would cause him to forfeit the respect of members of his entourage, down to his janitor. Before he ventured to appear in public in a new suit or a new hat, he would have himself photographed so that he could check the effect. He did not swim, never got into a rowboat ("After all, what business would I have in a rowboat!"), or mounted a horse, he said; altogether he was "not at all fond of show-off stunts. How easily they might go wrong; parades teach that time and again."[40] He regarded life as a kind of permanent parade before a gigantic audience. Thus he occasionally would try to dissuade Göring from smoking by offering the highly characteristic argument that one could not be represented on a monument "with a cigar in one's mouth." When Heinrich Hoffmann returned from Russia in the autumn of 1939 with photographs that showed Stalin holding a cigarette, Hitler forbade their publication; he was protecting a "colleague" in order not to detract from the constant dignity that should surround a dictator.

For similar reasons he was tormented by fears that his private life would be exposed. Significantly, not a single personal letter of his exists. Even Eva Braun received only terse, sober notes; yet he was so wary that he never entrusted even these to the mails. The comedy of aloofness from her, which he played out to the last with the less intimate members of his wider entourage, likewise testifies to his inability to lead a life without posing. The most personal letter he left is paradoxically a letter to authorities: that petition to the magistracy of the city of Linz which he wrote at the age of twenty-four in explanation of his draft evasion. On one occasion he remarked that it was "especially important" and "an old experience in the life of a political leader: One should never write down anything that one can discuss, never!" And elsewhere he stated: "Far too much is written; this begins with love letters and ends with political letters. There is always something incriminating about doing so." He constantly observed himself and literally never spoke an unconsidered word, as Hjalmar Schacht commented. His desires were secret, his feelings hidden, and the widespread notion of an emotionally ungoverned, wildly gesticulating Hitler actually reverses the proportion of rule and exception. In fact his was the most concentrated life imaginable, disciplined to the point of unnatural rigidity.

Even Hitler's famous outbursts of rage were apparently quite often deliberate instances of play-acting. One of the early gauleiters has described how Hitler raged so in the course of one of these fits that spittle literally ran out of the corners of his mouth and down his chin, so helplessly infuriated did he appear to be—but his consistent, intellectually controlled argumentation, which never ceased throughout the outburst, belied appearances. It would be too much to say that he deliberately tried to engender something like a "shudder of awe" at pathological frenzy. But we can assume that in such situations he did not lose control and that he was exploiting his own emotions just as purposefully as he did those of others. He usually had a reason for making such scenes and unleashed his temperament according to circumstances. He could be just as engaging and charming as he was brutal or ruthless. He was capable of shedding tears, pleading, or working himself up into one of his famous rages, which to the very end aroused the horror of all his interlocutors and often broke their resistance. He possessed "the most terrifying persuasiveness." Along with this he had the power of exerting a hypnotic effect upon his interlocutor. The leadership of the party, the gauleiters and Old Fighters who had shoved their way to the top alongside him, undoubtedly were "a band of eccentrics and egotists all going in different directions," and certainly were not servile in the traditional sense. The same is true for at least a part of the officers' corps. Nevertheless, Hitler imposed his will on them as he pleased. And he did so not only at the height of his power but equally well before, when he was a marginal figure on the political Right, and at the end, when he was only the burned-out husk of a once mighty man. Several diplomats, particularly those of Germany's allies, fell so completely under his spell that eventually they seemed to be rather his familiars than representatives of their governments.

Caricatures of Hitler long portrayed him as addressing individuals as if they were a mass meeting. But in fact he did nothing of the kind. He had a large scale of nuances at his disposal and was even more effective in personal conversations than on the platform. A public demonstration kindled in him a mood of shrill exaltation, particularly since his first use of the microphone, when he listened intoxicated to the amplification of his voice.

It has been rightly pointed out that Hitler's ability to exploit his own temperament for demagogic purposes was most clearly manifested in his attitudes toward the German minorities outside German borders.[41] Depending on his needs of the moment, he could lament or forget their fate. He did not worry about the Germans in South Tyrol, Poland, or the Baltic republics as long as they had no place in his grand design for foreign policy. But as soon as the situation changed, the "intolerable wrongs of these most loyal sons of the nation" threw him into raging indignation. His outbursts were obviously not just pretense. But the keener observer noted the element of artificial hysteria in them. Secretly, Hitler was exploiting the rage of which he seemed to be the defenseless victim. His remarkable capacity for empathy, his actor's gift for merging wholly with a role, stood him in good stead. In the course of a conversation he would quite often show the most variegated sides of his personality, for example, would shift with pantomimic transitions from a muted tone to an abrupt outburst, pounding on the table or drumming nervously on the arm of his chair. At intervals of a few minutes he would show himself detached, sincere, suffering or triumphant. Before he became Chancellor, he would occasionally play the mimic when he was with his intimates; once, according to a participant, he put on a performance—with masterly malice—of Mathilde Kemnitz, later Ludendorff's wife, vainly attempting to induce him, Hitler, "to marry her. . . . Hitler stripped the fine lady, as it were, of her priestly, philosophical, scholarly, erotic and other skins, until all that remained was a nasty, acrid onion."[42]

He regarded himself as a lover of music, but in actuality it meant little to him. He had, it is true, gone countless times to all of Wagner's operas and heard *Tristan* or *Die Weistersinger* more than a hundred times each. But symphonic works and chamber music he largely ignored. On the other hand, he could sit through endless performances of *Die Lustige Witwe* or *Die Fledermaus;* it was again the characteristic grouping of grandiose and silly preferences. He listened to records only when nothing better offered, for they cheated him of the visual setting; with records, he limited himself to grand bravura scenes. After his visits to the opera he spoke exclusively on questions of stage technique or the character of the production, virtually never mentioning problems of musical interpretation.[43] Music meant little more to him than an extremely effective acoustic means to heighten theatrical effects; as such, however, it was indispensable, for drama without music had not the slightest appeal to him. One of his secretaries has remarked that his library contained not a single literary classic, and even on his many visits to Weimar, with its theatrical tradition going back to Goethe, he never went to the theater but only to the opera. The supreme expression of opera to him was the finale of *Götterdämmerung*. In Bayreuth, whenever the citadel of the gods collapsed in flames amid musical uproar, he would reach out into the darkness of the box, take the hand of Frau Winifred Wagner, who was sitting behind him, and breathe a deeply moved *Handkuss* upon it.[44]

This craving for theater touches at the core of his being. He had the feeling that he was always acting on a stage and needed resounding alarums, explosive effects with lightnings and fanfares. Obsessed with the actor's immemorial fear of boring the audience, he thought in terms of catchy numbers, trying to surpass the preceding scene, whatever it was. The restiveness that marked his political activities and gave them that character of surprise which so confused his opponents was as much related to this fear of being boring as his fascination with catastrophes and universal conflagrations. Fundamentally he was a theatrical person, trusting dramatic effects more than ideological persuasion, and really himself only in those sham worlds that he opposed to reality. His lack of seriousness, the hypocritical, melodramatic and cheaply villainous quality that clung to him originated in the theatricality as much as in his contempt for the appearances of reality—an element of strength whenever it coincided with his peculiarly sharp perception of underlying real conditions.

One of the conservatives who smoothed Hitler's path to power commented that he never lost a sense of the disproportion between his lowly origins and the "successful leap to the heights." As he had done in his youth, he continued to think in terms of social status. Occasionally he tried to divert attention from his embarrassing petty bourgeois origins by ostentatiously calling himself a "worker," sometimes even a "proletarian."[45] But most of the time he strove to cover up his low status by a mythologizing aura. It is an ancient, tested recipe of political usurpation that the lowliest and the most inconspicuous are summoned to rule. In the introductory passages of his speeches he again and again evoked the "myth of the man from the people," the days when he had been an "unknown frontline soldier in the First World War," a "man without a name, without money, without influence, without a following," but summoned by Providence. He liked to introduce himself as the "lonely wanderer out of nothingness." Thus he liked to have resplendent uniforms around him, for they pointed up the simplicity of his own costume. His air of unassuming austerity and soberness, together with his unwedded state and his withdrawn life, could be splendidly fused in the public mind into the image of a great, solitary man bearing the burden of his election by destiny, marked by the mystery of self-sacrifice. When Frau von Dircksen once remarked to him that she often thought of his loneliness, he agreed: "Yes, I am very lonely, but children and music comfort me."

As such remarks reveal, he lacked cynicism in regard to his own person and role, and was rather inclined to consider himself in a deadly serious light. Looking out from the Berghof, he could see the blocklike massif of the Untersberg, where according to legend Charlemagne lay sleeping until the day when he would return to scatter Germany's enemies. With a good deal of sentimental feeling Hitler considered the fact that his home was situated opposite this mountain a significant sign. "That is no accident. I recognize a summons in it." More and more frequently he withdrew to his eyrie, especially when he wanted to escape the "corrosive" Berliners or the "crude" folk of Munich. He preferred the Rhineland temperament, and years later happily recalled how when he visited Cologne the crowd had begun to rock back and forth out of sheer enthusiasm. "The greatest ovation of my life."[46] The conviction that he was the instrument of some higher power prompted him regularly to apostrophize Providence whenever he was describing the nature of his historical mission:

I am well aware of what a man can do and where his limits lie, but I hold to the conviction that men who have been created by God ought also to live in accordance with the will of the Almighty. God did not create the races of this earth in order for them to give themselves up, to bastardize and ruin themselves. . . . Ultimately the individual man is weak in all his nature and actions when he goes contrary to almighty Providence and its will, but he becomes immeasurably strong the moment he acts in harmony with this Providence! Then there pours down upon him that force which has distinguished all the great men of the world.[47]

This conviction sustained his ideological notions and lent them the weight of a religious principle. It gave him hardness, resolution, and unmerciful drive. This conviction also kindled the cult surrounding his person, which amounted to pure idolatry. Robert Ley called him the only human being who never erred. Hans Frank declared that he was as solitary as the Lord God. And an SS group leader stated that he was even greater than that god who had had only twelve faithless disciples, whereas Hitler stood at the head of a great people vowed to loyalty to him. As long as Hitler coolly received such tributes and merely exploited the testimonials to his genius for psychological purposes, to increase his power, they were an important supplement to his energy. But when the sense of his historical mission was no longer held in check by Machiavellian calculations, when he himself succumbed to the notion that he was indeed superhuman, the descent began.

His lack of social contact was only the reverse of this mythologizing view of himself. The higher he rose, the more the area of emptiness around him widened. Increasingly, he shrank from the Old Fighters, who continued to press their unbearable claims to close personal contact. He had scarcely any but staged relationships, within the framework of which everyone was either an extra or an instrument. People had never really roused his interest and his concern. He made it a maxim that "one could not do enough to cultivate ties with the common people"; but the very phraseology betrayed the artificiality of this thought. Significantly, even his passion for architecture was limited to the building of gigantic backdrops; he would listen with utter boredom to plans for residential areas.

The fact that no conversation was possible in his presence was only another aspect of the same process of social impoverishment. Either Hitler himself talked, and all others listened, or all the others talked and Hitler sat lost in thought, apathetic, locked away from the world around him, not raising his eyes, "picking at his teeth in a frightful way," as one participant described it. "Or else he paced restlessly. He did not give one a chance to speak; he interrupted one constantly; he jumped with incredible flights of fancy from one subject to another."[48] His inability to listen went so far that he could not even follow the speeches of foreign statesmen on the radio; having lost the habit of being contradicted, he was either absent-minded or indulged in monologues. Since he scarcely read any longer and tolerated only yes men or admirers in his entourage, he plunged into an intellectual isolation that deepened steadily. Once and for all his mind became fixed on his early convictions, which had hardened into theses he neither expanded nor modified, but merely gave a sharper cutting edge.

He spoke incessantly of these, as if intoxicated by his own voice. The conversations recorded by Hermann Rauschning, from the early thirties, have preserved something of the self-important intonation of a man wonder-struck by his own tirades. There is a similar note, though with considerably diminished concentration, in the table talk recorded in the Führer's headquarters. "The word," Hitler declared, could build "bridges into unexplored regions." When Mussolini was in Germany on a state visit, Hitler regaled him with a one-and-a-half-hour monologue after a meal, without once giving his impatient guest the opportunity for a reply. Almost all visitors and associates had similar experiences, especially during the war, when the torrent of words stretched on into the depths of the night, growing more excessive as the hour advanced. The headquarters generals, desperately struggling with their sleepiness, found themselves exposed to "solemn cosmic blather" about art, philosophy, race, technology, or history, and had to listen with defenseless respect. He always needed listeners, although they, too, were only extras, so to speak, in whose presence he could whip up the excitement that fueled his thoughts. A keen observer commented that he would dismiss his visitors in the manner of "a person who has just given himself a morphine injection."[49] If his interlocutor managed an occasional objection, that served only as a stimulus to further, boundlessly wild associations, without limit, without order, without end.

The inability to relate, which isolated him humanly, benefited him politically, for he recognized only pieces in a game. No one could cross the belt of remoteness, and those who approached most closely to him were merely at a somewhat reduced distance. Characteristically, his strongest emotions were reserved for a few dead persons. In his private room at Obersalzberg there hung a portrait of his mother, and one of Julius Schreck, his chauffeur, who died in 1936. None of his father. Geli Raubal dead was apparently closer to him than the living girl had ever been. "In a sense Hitler is simply not human—unreachable and untouchable," Magda Goebbels had already said in the early thirties. While still at the peak of his power, the cynosure of millions, he yet had something about him that belonged to the forgotten young man of the Vienna or early Munich years; he was a stranger even to his closest relatives. Albert Speer, whom for a time he regarded with some sentimentality as the embodiment of his youthful dream of brilliance and distinction, told the Nuremberg tribunal: "If Hitler had had any friends, I would have been his friend." But he, too, did not cross the gulf. In spite of many days and nights of joint planning, when both men would lose themselves in their colossal projects, Speer was never more than Hitler's preferred architect. It is true that Hitler, in an unusual tribute, spoke of his "genius," but the dictator did not trust him in matters that went beyond technical problems.

What was lacking from this one relationship with traces of an erotic element was also lacking in the other: in contrast to Geli Raubal, Eva Braun was merely Hitler's mistress, with all the anxieties, secrecies, and humiliations involved in such a position. She related that at a dinner in the Hotel Vier Jahreszeiten in Munich Hitler sat beside her for three hours, not allowing her to address him; shortly before everyone rose from the table he thrust into her hand "an envelope with money." He had met her at the end of the twenties in Heinrich Hoffmann's photographic studio, and possibly this acquaintanceship was one of the factors that drove Geli Raubal to suicide. Some time after his niece's death Hitler made Eva his mistress. She was a simple, moderately attractive girl with unpretentious dreams and thoughts that were dominated by love, fashion, movies, and gossip, by the constant fear of being thrown over, and by Hitler's egocentric whims and his manner of a petty domestic tyrant. With his craving for regimentation he had forbidden her sun-bathing, dancing, and smoking. ("If I were ever to see Eva smoking, I'd break off at once.") He was quite jealous, and yet he neglected her in an offensive way. In order "not to be so alone" she had several times asked him for a dog ("that would be lovely"), but Hitler had simply passed over the request without comment. For a long time he kept her in almost insultingly mean circumstances. Her diary has been found, and the notes illuminate her unhappy situation. A characteristic passage runs:

There's only one thing I wish, to get very sick and know no more about him for at least a week. Why is nothing happening to me, why must I go through all this? If only I'd never seen him. I'm in despair. Now I'll buy sleeping powder again, then I'll be in a half trance and stop thinking so much about it.

Why doesn't the devil come and take me. It's certainly better with him than it is here.

For three hours I waited in front of the Carlton and had to watch him buying flowers for Ondra [Annie Ondra, a film actress] and inviting her to dinner. He needs me only for certain purposes, it isn't possible otherwise.

When he says he's fond of me he means it only at that moment. Just like his promises which he never keeps. Why does he torment me so and not put an end to it right away?

In the middle of 1935 Hitler said "not a kind word" to her for three months, and in addition she learned that recently a "Valkyrie" had been his constant female companion ("he's fond of such dimensions"). She obtained an overdose of sleeping pills and wrote a letter demanding some word from Hitler, even if it came through some outsider. "God, I'm afraid he won't answer today," the last entry of this period reads. "I've decided on 35 pills this time it's going to really be a 'dead certain' business. If only he would have somebody call."

Eva Braun made two attempts at suicide, the first as early as November, 1932, by shooting herself in the neck, the second on the night of May 28, 1935. Evidently Hitler was considerably irritated by these attempts, all the more so since he had not forgotten Geli's fate. In 1936 Hitler's half-sister, Frau Raubal (Geli's mother), at last left the Berghof, and Hitler let Eva Braun take her place. Only after that did the tension between the two relax. Eva continued to be kept in semiconcealment, stealing in by side entrances and using rear staircases, contenting herself with a photograph of Hitler when he left her alone at mealtimes. She was hardly ever permitted to appear in Berlin, and as soon as guests arrived, Hitler almost invariably banished her to her room. But as she felt more secure, Hitler also lost some of his apprehensions, and soon she became a member of that innermost circle of persons before whom he dropped the airs of the great man and at teatime fell asleep in his armchair, or in the evening, with unbuttoned coat, invited his guests to watch movies or chat by the fireplace. But this more relaxed atmosphere also brought out his crude, unfeeling traits. Thus he said to Albert Speer in his mistress's presence: "A highly intelligent man should take a primitive and stupid woman. Imagine if on top of everything else I had a woman who interfered with my work! In my leisure time I want to have peace."[50] There are some amateur 8-millimeter film shots showing Eva Braun in Hitler's company on the Berghof terrace, always in that mood of high spirits that is somewhat too ebullient to be believed.

The course of one of Hitler's ordinary days has been described by a number of persons. He would open the door of his bedroom, which he regularly locked, a crack in the morning, and his hand would mechanically reach out for the newspapers that were lying ready at hand on a hassock beside the door; then he vanished again. Walks, traveling, conferences on building, receptions, automobile rides did not give the day an exterior framework but merely split it up into a series of distractions. Though Hitler knew so well how to impose an unmistakable style upon public display, he could not shape the little actions and whims of a day into a personal style. He had no private life.

The entourage continued to consist of adjutants, secretaries, chauffeurs, and orderlies. "Part of his circle consisted of ephebes," one observer wrote, "men with curled hair, vulgar, square-set, with effeminate gestures." As in the past he preferred the uncritical, dull milieu of simple people to which he had been accustomed from childhood. Whenever he was at Obersalzberg he spent the long evenings in their company in an unchangingly monotonous pattern. One of the participants has declared: "What remains in my memory of social life at Obersalzberg is a curious vacuity."[51] The evening would begin with three or four hours of movies. Hitler preferred social comedies with insipid wit and sentimental endings. He also liked many foreign films, some of which were not allowed to be shown in the public cinema houses; Hitler saw a number of his favorites as many as ten times and even more frequently. Wearily, with leaden limbs, the circle then gathered in front of the fireplace. As at the big dining table, the huge pieces of furniture, set far apart for purposes of display, hindered any exchange of ideas. Hitler himself had a paralyzing effect upon the company. "Very few people ever felt comfortable in his presence," one of his old companions had remarked years before. For one or two hours the conversation dragged tediously along, repeatedly trickling away in banalities. Sometimes Hitler sat silently staring into space, or brooding into the fire, while the circle remained mute out of a mixture of respect and ennui. "It cost great self-control to attend these endless sessions in front of the unvarying setting of the leaping flames."[52]

Between two and three in the morning Hitler would literally dismiss Eva Braun, and shortly afterward leave the room. Only then did the company, as if liberated, revive to brief, hectic gaiety. The evenings in Berlin followed a similar course, except that the group was larger, the atmosphere less intimate. All efforts to introduce some variation in the routine broke down against Hitler's resistance. For in the trivial emptiness of these hours he tried to compensate for the pressure of the day, when he was prisoner of his own image.

How sharp the contrast of these evenings was with the classic totalitarian myth of the solitary lighted window. As Goebbels told it, "Every night, until six or seven in the morning, light can be seen streaming from his window." And a recitation for a youth-group program ran:

> Full many a night it is no novelty
> That we may sleep while you are full of cares.
> For many a night you wake untiringly,
> And there is no one who your brooding shares
> Until, clear-eyed at dawn, the light you see.

In the summer of 1935 Hitler had decided to enlarge his modest weekend house at Obersalzberg into a rather pretentious residence, and he himself had sketched to scale the ground plan, the renderings, and cross-sections of the new building. The sketches have been preserved and are clear evidence of Hitler's fixation on any idea he had once had; he was simply incapable of attacking a task from a new point of view. The original idea always remained preserved in his sketches, with only minor changes. No less striking, however, is the loss of proportion—as, for example, in the sketch of the oversized window with the view of Berchtesgaden, the Untersberg, and Salzburg, which Hitler later liked to show to his guests as the largest lowerable window in the world. Here was the "basic infantile trait in Hitler's nature," which Ernst Nolte attributed chiefly to his greed to appropriate, his obstinate and uncontrollable determination to possess.

This lifelong mania for record size, speed, and numbers was characteristic of a man who had never managed to overcome his youth with its dreams, injuries, and resentments. Even at sixteen he had wanted to extend the 360-foot-long frieze on the Linz museum by another 300 feet, so that the city would have the "biggest sculptural frieze on the Continent." And years later he wanted to provide Linz with a bridge 270 feet high above the river, a bridge "unequaled anywhere in the world." Later on, the same urge would make him compete on the highways, preferably against heavy American cars. And years afterward he would still gloat over these races, remembering how his supercharged Mercedes would outdistance every other car on the road. The biggest lowerable window had its counterpart in the biggest marble table top made of one piece (18 feet long), the biggest domes, the vastest grandstands, the most gigantic triumphal arches, in short, in an indiscriminate elevation of gigantic abnormality. Whenever one of his architects told him that in his sketch of a building he had "beaten" the size of a historically important edifice, he was filled with enthusiasm. The megalomaniacal architectural works of the Third Reich combined this infantile mania for beating records with the traditional pharaonic complex of ambitious dictators who were trying to offset the frailty of a dominion based exclusively on themselves as individuals by building on a grand scale. This ambition sounds repeatedly in Hitler's statements—as, for example, at the party rally of 1937:

Because we believe in the eternity of this Reich, its works must also be eternal ones, that is . . . not conceived for the year 1940 and not for the year 2000; rather, they must tower like the cathedrals of our past into the millennia of the future.

And if God perhaps makes the poets and singers of today into fighters, he has at any rate given to the fighters the architects who will see to it that the success of this struggle finds its imperishable corroboration in the documents of a great and unique art. This country must not be a power without culture and must not have strength without beauty.

Through these enormous architectural works Hitler was also trying to satisfy his onetime dreams of being an artist. In a speech of the same period he declared that if the First World War "had not come he would . . . perhaps, yes even probably, have become one of the foremost architects, if not the foremost architect of Germany." Now he became the foremost patron of architecture. Aided by a number of select architects, he conceived the reconstruction of many German cities with vast buildings and avenues, whose oppressive size, lack of grass, and archaizing elements of form added up to an impression of solemn and deadly vacuity. In 1936 he conceived the plan of converting Berlin into a world capital, "comparable only to ancient Egypt, Babylon, or Rome." Within some fifteen years he wanted to transform the entire inner city into a single showy monument of imperial grandeur, with vast boulevards, gleaming gigantic blocks of buildings, the whole dominated by a domed assembly hall that was to be the highest in the world, almost 900 feet, with a capacity of 180,000 people. From the Führer's platform in the interior, under a gilded eagle big as a house, he intended to address the nationalities of the Greater Germanic Reich, and to prescribe laws to a world prostrate before him. A grand avenue over three miles long was to link the building to a triumphal arch 240 feet high, the symbol of victories in battles and empire-building wars. And, year after year, Hitler raved at the height of the war, "a troop of Kirghizes will be led through the capital of the Reich so that they may fill their imaginations with the power and grandeur of its stone monuments."

The so-called Führer's Building was planned on a similar scale. It was to be a fortresslike palace in the heart of Berlin, covering 6 million square feet and containing, along with Hitler's residence and offices, many reception rooms, colonnades, roof gardens, fountains and a theater. It is hardly surprising that when his favorite architect in later life came upon the old sketches again, he "was struck by the resemblance to a Cecil B. De Mille set."[53] In conceiving such architecture Hitler was in accord with the spirit of the age, from which otherwise he seemed so distant.

In drawing up comprehensive plans for rebuilding almost all the larger German cities Hitler was realizing his ideal of the artist-politician. Even in the midst of urgent government business he always found time for prolonged discussions with architects. At night when unable to sleep he would make drawings of ground plans or renderings of buildings; he often went through the so-called ministerial gardens behind the chancellery to Speer's office, where he stood before a "model avenue" 90 feet long, illuminated by spotlights. Together with his younger associate he would wax enthusiastic over fantasy edifices that were destined never to be built. Among the buildings that were planned to give the city of Nuremberg "its future and therefore its eternal character" was a stadium for 400,000 spectators that was to be one of the most tremendous structures in history. There was to be an arena with stands seating 160,000 people, a processional avenue, and several convention halls—all clustered in a spacious "temple area." Following a suggestion of Speer's, Hitler devoted special attention to the materials used, so that even as ruins overgrown with ivy, the buildings would still testify to the greatness of his reign, as do the pyramids of Luxor to the power and glory of the pharaohs. At the cornerstone laying for the convention hall in Nuremberg he declared:

But if the Movement should ever fall silent, even after thousands of years this witness here will speak. In the midst of a sacred grove of age-old oaks the men of that time will admire in reverent astonishment this first giant among the buildings of the Third Reich.

But while architecture was his first love, he did not ignore the other arts. The youth enthralled by painting and music drama was still present in him. To be sure, he had decided that the artistic rank of an era was only the reflection of its political greatness. By this logic he regarded cultural productions as the real legitimation of his achievements as a statesman. The proud prophecies in the initial period of the Third Reich must be understood in this sense; the dawn of an "incredible blossoming of German art" or of a "new artistic renaissance of Aryan man" was predicted because it had to come. And Hitler was therefore all the more discountenanced when this Periclean dream of his refused to come true.[54] Shutting himself off more and more from the world, he developed a pseudoromantic cult of what he called "the basic elements of life": rich plowland, steel-helmeted heroism, peaks glistening with eternal snow, and vigorous laborers performing their work despite all obstacles. That this formula resulted in cultural atrophy was as obvious in literature as in the fine arts, even though the annual art shows, sometimes juried in part by Hitler himself, tried to cover up the prevailing dreariness by lavishly arranged celebrations. Hitler's vituperation of "November art," which took up a good deal of space in almost every one of his speeches on art, reveals the emphatic way in which he equated artistic and political standards. He would threaten the "cultural Neanderthalers" with custody in a mental hospital or prison; and he declared that he would annihilate those "international scribblings on art" which were nothing but "offscourings of brazen, shameless arrogance." The exhibition of "degenerate art" organized in 1937 was partly a fulfillment of this threat.

In Hitler's attitudes toward art we again encounter that phenomenon of early rigidity which characterizes all his mental and imaginative processes. His standards had remained unchanged since his days in Vienna, when he paid no heed to the artistic and intellectual upheavals of the period. Cool classicistic splendor on the one hand and pompous decadence on the other—Anselm von Feuerbach, for example, and Hans Makart—were his touchstones. With the resentments of the failed candidate for the academy, he raised his own taste into an absolute.

He also admired the Italian Renaissance and early baroque art; the majority of the pictures in the Berghof belonged to this period. His favorites were a half-length nude by Bordone, the pupil of Titian, and a large colored sketch by Tiepolo. On the other hand, he rejected the painters of the German Renaissance because of their austerity.[55] As the pedantic faithfulness of his own water colors might suggest, he always favored craftsmanlike precision. He liked the early Lovis Corinth but regarded Corinth's brilliant later work, created in a kind of ecstasy of old age, with pronounced irritation and banned him from the museums. Significantly, he also loved sentimental genre painting, like the winebibbing monks and fat tavernkeepers of Eduard Grützner. In his youth, he told his entourage, it had been his dream some day to be successful enough to be able to afford a genuine Grützner. Later, many works by this painter hung in his Munich apartment on Prinzregentenstrasse. Alongside them he put gentle, folksy idyls by Spitzweg, a portrait of Bismarck by Lenbach, a park scene by Anselm von Feuerbach, and one of the many variations of *Sin* by Franz von Stuck. In the "Plan for a German National Gallery," which he had sketched on the first page of his 1925 sketchbook, these same painters appear, together with names like Overbeck, Moritz von Schwind, Hans von Marées, Defregger, Böcklin, Piloty, Leibl, and, finally, Adolph von Menzel, to whom he assigned no fewer than five rooms in his gallery.[56] He early set special agents to buying up all the important works of these artists. He was bent on keeping them for the museum that some day, after the accomplishment of his goals, he intended to set up in Linz, with himself as director.

But just as everything he undertook began compulsively to shoot up into superdimensions, his plans for the Linz gallery rapidly expanded beyond all proportion. Originally, it was going to contain only a fine collection of German nineteenth-century art. But after his Italian trip in 1938, he obviously felt so overwhelmed and challenged by the riches of the Italian museums that he decided to erect a gigantic counterpart to them in Linz. His dream of "the greatest museum in the world" came to a final intensification at the beginning of the war, when it combined with a plan for redistributing the entire stock of European art. All works from so-called zones of Germanic influence would be transferred to Germany and assembled principally in Linz, which was to figure as a kind of German Rome.

In Dr. Hans Posse, director-general of the Dresden Gallery, Hitler found a respected specialist who would serve his ends. With a sizable staff of assistants, Posse scoured the European art market, buying, and later on mostly confiscating in the conquered countries, all important works of art, and cataloguing them in "Führer catalogues" running to many volumes. The paintings Hitler picked were assembled in Munich, and even during the war, whenever he came to that city he would first go to the Führerbau (the Führer's Building) to inspect the masterpieces and, escaping from reality, to lose himself in lengthy discussions of art. As late as 1943–44, 3,000 paintings were purchased for Linz, and in spite of all the financial burdens of the war 150 million Reichsmark were spent on them. When the space in Munich no longer sufficed, Hitler had the entire collection housed in castles such as Hohenschwangau or Neuschwanstein, in monasteries, and in caves. In the one repository of Alt-Aussee, a salt mine used since the fourteenth century, 6,755 Old Masters were stored by the end of the war, in addition to drawings, prints, tapestries, sculptures, and innumerable pieces of fine furniture—the ultimate expression of an infantile greed that had grown to monstrous dimensions. Among the paintings were works by Leonardo da Vinci and Michelangelo, as well as the Ghent Altar of the van Eyck brothers and canvases by Rubens, Rembrandt, Vermeer. Apparently considered on the same level was Hans Makart's *The Plague in Florence,* which Hitler had received as a gift from Mussolini after having insistently asked for it.

From the bunker of the Führer's headquarters during the last weeks of the war an order was issued to blow up the repository. The order was transmitted by August Eigruber, gauleiter of the Upper Danube region, on pain of execution if it were not obeyed. But it was never carried out.[57]

A curious note of inferiority, a sense of stuntedness always overlay the phenomenon of Hitler, and not even the many triumphs could dispel this. All his personal traits still did not add up to a real person. The reports and recollections we have from members of his entourage do not make him tangibly vivid as a man; he moves with masklike impersonality through a setting which he nevertheless dominated with uncontested sovereignty. Though one of the greatest orators of history, he coined not a single memorable phrase. And similarly there are no anecdotes about him, although while holding power he operated entirely by his own lights, more arbitrary and unrestricted than any other political actor since the end of absolutism.

Because of this bizarre personal element, a good many observers have called Hitler a dilettante. And, in fact, if we mean by this the prevalence of inclination over duty and of mood over regularity and permanence, then the advent of Hitler did indeed mean the entrance of the dilettante into politics. The circumstances of his early life were wholly marked by the dilettantism that ultimately brought him into politics, and the period during which he exercised power was one prolonged demonstration of personal idiosyncrasy at the helm of state. The audacity and radicality that made him so successful also came from the same source. A true *homo novus,* he was not hampered either by experience or by respect for the rules of the game. He did not feel the scruples of the specialists and shrank from nothing he conceived. Above all, he intuitively knew how to initiate great projects but was unaware of the practical difficulties in carrying them through; he always saw everything as child's play or dependent only on an act of will, not even realizing the extent of his boldness. With his "layman's delight in decision making"[58] he interfered, took over everywhere, formulated and carried out what others scarcely dared conceive. He had a dilettante's fear of admitting a mistake and the tyro's need to show off his knowledge of tonnages, calibers, and all kinds of statistical matters. His aesthetic preferences were also uninformed; they came down to his love of massiveness, his delight in tricks, surprises, and prestidigitator's effects. Significantly, he trusted inspiration more than he did thought and genius more than diligence.

He tried to cover up his dilettantism by utter lack of moderation, by making his amateurish projects so monumental that their amateurishness would be invisible. Magnitude justified everything, in buildings as well as in people. In this respect he was a man of the nineteenth century. He heavily concurred with Nietzsche's saying that a nation was nothing but nature's byway for producing a few important men. "Geniuses of the extraordinary type," he remarked, with a side glance at himself, "can show no consideration for normal humanity." Their superior insight, their higher mission, justified any harshness. Compared with the claims genius could make to greatness and historical fame, the sum of individuals amounted to no more than "planetary bacilli."

These muddled images of genius, greatness, fame, mission, and cosmic struggle reveal a characteristic element of the Hitlerian imagination. He thought mythologically, not socially, and his modernity was permeated by archaic traits. The world and humanity, the intricate weft of interests, temperament, and energies, were thus reduced to a few antitheses to be grasped instinctively: friend and foe, good and evil, pure and impure, poor and rich, the radiant white knight against the horrid dragon crouched over the treasure. It is true that Hitler had objected to the "perverted title" of Rosenberg's principal work; National Socialism, he said, did not constitute the myth of the twentieth century against reason, but "the faith and the knowledge of the twentieth century against the myth of the nineteenth century." But in fact Hitler was far closer to the party's philosopher than such comments would suggest. For Hitler's rationality was always limited to methodology and did not light up the gloomy corners of his anxieties and prejudices. His sober plans were based on a few mythological premises, and this close conjunction of coolness and wrongheadedness, Machiavellianism and black magic, rounds out the picture of the man.

A few crude assumptions, borrowed at random from the trashy tracts of whole generations of patriotic professors and pseudoprophets, had shaped the traditional German view of the country's history. It was all a matter of hereditary foes and enemies bent on encirclement. Hence the popularity of such notions as the stab in the back, Nibelungen loyalty, and the stark alternatives of victory or annihilation. National Socialism was not, it is true, quite so prone to the phenomenon of "seduction by history"[59] that characterized Italian or French Fascism, and which is in fact among the fundamental traits of Fascist thinking in general. Hitler had no ideal era he could invoke. His use of history was passionate rejection; he would operate by invoking a distorted image of past weakness and dissension. Hitler derived just as powerful a force from castigating the past as did Mussolini from singing the praises of the Roman Empire. Hitler played on national feeling by recalling concepts like "Versailles" or the "period of the Weimar System." Sure enough, a "language regulation" issued by Goebbels to local propaganda chiefs required that the period from 1918 to 1933 be always designated as "criminal." History, Paul Valéry once remarked, is the most dangerous product ever brewed by the chemistry of the human brain; it makes nations dream or suffer, impels them to become megalomaniacal, bitter, vain, insufferable. The hatreds and passions of the nations during the first half of this century have been stirred by false history far more than by all the racist ideologies or by envy or desire for expansion.

It was necessary for Hitler to reject the past because there was no era in German history that he admired. His ideal world was classical antiquity: Athens, Sparta ("the most pronounced racial state in history"), the Roman Empire. He always felt closer to Caesar or Augustus than to the Teutonic freedom fighter Arminius; they, and not the illiterate inhabitants of the Teutonic forests, were for him among the "most glorious minds of all history," whom he hoped to find again in the "Olympus . . . that I shall enter."[60] The downfall of those ancient dominions preoccupied him: "I often think about what destroyed the ancient world." He made open fun of Himmler's antediluvian primitivism and reacted sarcastically to all the potsherd cult and Teutonic herbalism: "At the same period that our forebears were presumably making the stone troughs and clay pitchers that our archaeologists fuss so much about, an Acropolis was being built in Greece."[61] And elsewhere: "The Germanic tribes who remained in Holstein were still boors after two thousand years . . . on no higher a level of culture than the Maori [today]." Only the tribes that had migrated to the south had risen culturally, he said. "Our country was a wallow. . . . If anybody asks about our ancestors, we always have to refer to the Greeks."[62]

In addition to the classical lands, England was the country he admired and wanted to emulate. It had known how to combine national coherence, a sense of masterfulness, and the ability to think in terms of vast areas. England was the opposite of German cosmopolitanism, German faintheartedness, German narrowness. And finally—again the object of reluctant wonder as well as of unnamable anxieties—he admired the Jews. Their racial exclusiveness and purity seemed to him no less admirable than their sense of being a chosen people, their implacability and intelligence. Basically, he regarded them as something akin to negative supermen. Even Germanic nations of relatively pure racial strains were, he declared in his table talk, inferior to the Jews: if 5,000 Jews were transported to Sweden, within a short time they would occupy all the leading positions.[63]

Muddled and heterogeneous these ideal images might be, but out of them he constructed the idea of the "new man": the type that combined Spartan hardness and simplicity, Roman ethos, British gentlemanly ways, and the racial morality of Jewry. Out of greed for power, patriotic devotion and fanaticism, out of persecutions and the miasma of the war, this racist phantasmagoria repeatedly arose: "Anyone who interprets National Socialism merely as a political movement knows almost nothing about it," Hitler declared. "It is more than religion; it is the determination to create a new man."

His sincerest and most solemn thought, the idea that compensated for all his anxieties and negations, his one positive concept, was this: to gather again the Aryan blood that had wasted itself on all the seductive Klingsor gardens of this world and to guard the precious grail for all time in the future, thus becoming invulnerable and master of the world. All the calculations of power tactics and all cynicism stopped short of this vision: "the new man." As early as the spring of 1933 Hitler had seen to the issuance of the first laws, which were soon extended into a comprehensive catalogue of purposeful legislation partly aimed at putting an end to what he called racial decadence, partly at bringing about "the rebirth of the nation . . . by the deliberate breeding of a new man." At the Nuremberg party rally of 1929 Hitler had declared in his concluding speech: "If Germany would have a million children annually and eliminate seven to eight hundred thousand of the weakest, the result in the end might be an increase in her energies." Now the intellectual pimps of the regime took up such suggestions and codified them into a world-wide campaign against the "degenerate and the infected." Racial philosopher Ernst Bergmann declared that he would gladly see "a million of the human sweepings of the big cities shoved aside."[64] Many actions to "safeguard the good blood" ran parallel to the anti-Semitic measures; they ranged from special laws regulating marriage and genetic hygiene to programs of sterilization and euthanasia.

Pedagogical measures supplemented the eugenic measures; for "an intellectual race is something more solid and more durable than a race itself," Hitler commented. He supported this remark on the grounds of the "superiority of the mind over the flesh." A novel educational system with National Political Educational Institutions, Adolf Hitler Schools, Order Castles (Ordensburgen), and special academies organized mainly by Rosenberg (which never got beyond their bare beginnings), were to school an elite selected on racial principles, and to prepare it for a variety of tasks. In one of his monologues to an intimate, Hitler described the new type of man, which was partly realized in the SS, with predatory, demonic features, "fearless and cruel"—so that he himself was frightened by the image he conjured up. Ideals of this sort can scarcely be called political. A totalitarian regime does not require demonism from its human tools but discipline. What is wanted is not the fearless man but the brutal one, a type whose aggression is trained and can be used for specific purposes. The ideal, then, is essentially a literary one, derived at some remove from Nietzsche's "blond beast." But Hitler was always prone to translate literature into reality. The model new man was terrifying in other ways also. Distinguished by rigid obedience and narrow idealism, he was not so much cruel as mechanically unmoved and perfectionistic, ready for anything, and upheld by that sense of superiority which is based on the "instinct to annihilate others," as Hitler put it in one of his last recorded monologues, that of February 13, 1945.

But only the outlines of this vision emerged. Aryan racial substance and superiority could not be recovered so rapidly from the racially muddied material. "All of us suffer from the sickness of mixed, corrupt blood," Hitler once admitted. And in fact his ideal betrays how much he suffered from his own impurity and frailty. He reckoned in long spans of time. In a speech of January, 1939, to a group of higher-ranking military men he spoke of a process lasting a hundred years. It would take that long before a majority of the German people possessed those characteristics with which the world could be conquered and ruled. He did not doubt that this project would succeed. "A State," he had long ago said in the concluding words of *Mein Kampf,* "which in the age of racial poisoning dedicates itself to the care of its best racial elements, must some day become lord of the earth."[65]

He himself did not have much time left. Both the desperate state of racial decadence and the consciousness of the shortness of a human life drove him forward. In spite of his fundamentally apathetic attitude, his life was marked by feverish unrest. A letter of his written in July, 1928, makes the point that he is now thirty-nine years old, so that "even at best" he has "barely twenty years available" for his "tremendous task." The thought of premature death incessantly tormented him. "Time is pressing," he said in February, 1934, and continued: "I do not have long enough to live. . . . I must lay the foundation on which others can build after me. I will not live long enough to see it completed." He also feared assassination; some "criminal, an idiot" might eliminate him and thus prevent the accomplishment of his mission.

Out of such anxiety complexes he developed a pedantic carefulness about himself. From the ever-widening security system built up by Himmler, which took in the entire country, to his vegetarian diet, which he adopted at the beginning of the thirties, he tried by elaborate precautions to preserve his life—odd though it might seem to safeguard the "tremendous task" by a police apparatus and gruel. He did not smoke, did not drink, avoided even coffee or black tea, and contented himself with thin infusions of herbs. In later years, with some assistance from his personal physician Dr. Morell, he became addicted to medication; he was incessantly taking some drug or other, or at least sucking on lozenges. He observed himself with hypochondriacal concern, regarding occasional stomach cramps as signs of impending cancer. In the course of the presidential campaign in the spring of 1932 one of his followers called on him in a Hamburg hotel and Hitler told him over a plate of vegetable soup that he had no time to waste, that he could not "lose a single year more. I must come to power shortly in order to be able to solve the gigantic tasks in the time remaining to me. I must! I must!" Many remarks of later years, and a number of speeches, contain similar references; in his private circle comments to the effect that he did not have "much time left," would "soon leave here," or would "live only a few years" became standing phrases.

Medical findings throw little light on the matter. In later years Hitler did suffer from gastric pains, and from 1935 on he occasionally complained of circulatory problems. But we now have the files of his medical examinations and these reflect no condition that would have justified his worry. We must be content with positing psychogenic causes, which are peculiar to the biographies of many historical figures with a similar sense of mission. This assumption is supported by his pathological mania for traveling, appearing as a continuous attempt at escape, and by his increasing nervous insomnia, which during the war led him to literally turn day and night upside down in the Führer's headquarters. His hectic temperament made him incapable of any regular activity or effort. Whatever he began had to be completed at once; and we may well believe the report that he scarcely ever read a book straight through to the end. He could spend days in what seemed like a narcotic trance, "dozing like a crocodile in the Nile mud," before he erupted without transition into impetuous activity. In his speech of April,

1937, at the Vogelsang Ordensburg, he spoke of his "damaged" nerves and declared almost imploringly: "I must restore my nerves. . . . That is self-evident. Worries, worries, worries, insane worries; it truly is a tremendous burden of worries." And, standing before the model of his capital, he exclaimed with tears in his eyes: "If only my health were good."[66] Many of his actions whose abruptness seemed to spring from cold-blooded calculation were apparently partly the expression of the unrest that came from his premonitions of death. "I will no longer see it completed!" In an address to the propaganda chiefs in October, 1937, he said, according to the notes of one of the participants,

> . . . that as far as man's knowledge could go, he did not have long to live. People did not grow old in his family. His parents had both died young.
> It was therefore necessary to solve the problems that had to be solved (*Lebensraum*) as quickly as possible, so that this could still be done in his lifetime. Later generations would no longer be able to do it. Only he himself was still in a position to.
> After grave inner struggles he had freed himself from what remained of his childhood religious notions. "I now feel fresh as a colt in pasture."

But a psychological consideration also underlay this increasing insistence on Hitler's part. From the end of 1937 on, he worried more and more that the revolution, braked by his seizure of power, might lose its dynamism and quietly fade away. The domestic moderation, the peace gestures, the everlasting holiday atmosphere, in short, the regime's whole masquerade, might be taken at its face value. If that happened, "the leap to the great final goals might be missed." With boundless faith in the power of propaganda, he counted on propaganda to transform the artificially constructed idyllic stage set into the idyl itself. In his important secret speech of November 10, 1938, to the top editors of the domestic press he keenly analyzed this dichotomy:

> Circumstances have forced me to talk almost exclusively of peace for decades. Only by constantly stressing Germany's desire for peace and peaceful intentions was it possible for me to win the German people their freedom bit by bit and to give the nation the arms which were always necessary as the prerequisite to the next step. It is obvious that such peace propaganda, carried on for decades, also has its dubious aspects; for it can easily lead to fixing in the brains of many persons the notion that the present regime is identical with the decision and the desire to preserve peace in all circumstances.
> That, however, would lead to a false idea of the aims of this system. Above all it would also lead to the German nation's . . . being imbued with a spirit which in the long run would amount to defeatism and would necessarily undo the achievements of the present regime.
> The reason I spoke only of peace for so many years was because I had to. It has now become necessary to psychologically change the German people's course in a gradual way and slowly make it realize that there are things that

536

must, if they cannot be carried through by peaceful means, be carried through by the methods of force and violence. . . .

This work has required months, it was begun systematically; it is being continued and reinforced.[67]

And in fact from the second half of 1937 on, the suppressed radical energies were once more released and the nation organized more consistently than ever to serve the violent intentions of the regime. Only now did the rise of the SS state begin. Its most visible expression was the increase in the number of concentration camps and the accelerated recruitment and equipping of armed SS formations. The Red Cross was instructed to prepare for possible mobilization. The Hitler Youth were ordered to be ready to step into the armaments plants, taking over for the labor force, who would be sent into the army. The regime launched massive attacks against the judiciary, the churches, and the bureaucracy, cowing those branches of society even more thoroughly. Hitler ranted more violently than ever against the skeptical intellectuals ("these impudent, shameless scribblers" who would be "useless as building blocks for a people's community"). The simple of heart, on the other hand, were forever being hailed. In November, 1937, the press received directives to keep silent about the preparations for "total war" being initiated in all the branches of the NSDAP.[68]

The economic field as well was being regeared. Once again, the businessmen, contrary to the theory that capitalist interests were the dominant force in the Third Reich, proved willing tools who "had no more influence upon the political decisions than their day laborers."[69] Should they fail to meet the demands set for them, "it is not Germany that would be ruined, but at most a few managers," Hitler had hinted as early as the autumn of 1936 in a memorandum concerning his economic program. As always, he was proceeding entirely from considerations of efficiency. We misread his matter-of-fact view of all practical problems if we view the regime's economic policy in ideological terms. Basically, the economic system remained capitalist; but it was in many ways overlaid by authoritarian command structures and atypically distorted.

In his memorandum Hitler explicitly admitted his expansionist intentions—for the first time since he had become Chancellor. He had had to speed up his plans, he indicated, because of the country's troubling situation in raw materials and foodstuffs, thus once more evoking the old terror of a hopelessly overpopulated country with the proverbial 140 inhabitants per square kilometer. A Four-Year Plan on the Soviet Russian model was to supply the sinews for the *Lebensraum* policy. Hermann Göring was put in charge. He promptly proceeded to bully the businessmen into carrying out the plans for autarchy and rearmament without regard to the costs or the economic consequences. At the ministerial session devoted to Hitler's memorandum, Göring insisted that the country must act "as if we were in

537

the stage of imminent peril of war." A few months later he told a meeting of big businessmen that producing economically no longer mattered; what counted was simply to produce at all. It was a plan for *Raubbau*—strip mining the economy, as it were—and its aim was a war of conquest, for only such a war could justify it. "We must always remember that if we lose, everything's shot anyhow," Hitler later commented, during the war itself.

When Hjalmar Schacht criticized these methods, there was a breach which soon forced him out of the cabinet. Hitler now felt that time was running out. His memorandum had ruled that economic rearmament must be conducted "in the same tempo, with the same resolution, and if necessary with the same ruthlessness" as the political and military preparations for war. The concluding sentences were similarly dramatic: "Herewith I am setting the following task: First. The German army must be ready for commitment within four years. Second. The German economy must be ready for war within four years."

Reports on morale during this period speak of "a certain fatigue and apathy."[70] The overorganization of people was becoming almost unbearable. The regime's policy toward the churches, the defamation of minorities, the racial cult, the pressure upon the arts and the sciences, and the excessive zeal of minor party functionaries engendered anxieties that could be expressed only in the most covert terms; such griping was totally ineffective. The majority tried, as far as possible, to go on living, ignoring both the regime and its injustices. The report cited above notes that "the German greeting [*Heil Hitler*]—which at any rate is a sensitive measure of shifts in political moods—has yielded almost entirely to the older customary salutations, or is only casually responded to, outside the circles of party members and officials."

Though such local reports were scarcely definitive, they fed Hitler's sense of urgency and showed him what had to be done: he must shake the populace out of its lethargy and create a situation in which anxiety, pride, and an offended sense of self-importance combined so that "the inner voice of the people itself slowly began to scream for violence."

"Where Hitler draws perspectives, war is always in sight," Konrad Heiden wrote around this time, and in the same passage asked whether the man could continue to exist "without disintegrating the world."[71]

Chapter 3

Give me a kiss, girls! This is the greatest day
of my life. I shall be known as the greatest
German in history.

Adolf Hitler on March 15, 1939,
to his secretaries.

THE "GREATEST GERMAN
IN HISTORY"

Hitler's real plans came to light in the secret conference of November 5,
1937, whose course we know from the record kept by one of the participants, Colonel Hossbach. To a restricted circle consisting of Foreign
Minister von Neurath, War Minister von Blomberg, Commander of the
Army von Fritsch, Commander in Chief of the Navy Admiral Raeder, and
Air Force Commander Göring, Hitler unveiled ideas that struck some of
those present as sensational at the time, and others later on when they were
disclosed at the Nuremberg trial.

The psychological importance of his statements evidently outweighs
their political weight. For what Hitler produced in an exalted mood, inspired by the favorable circumstances, in the course of more than four
hours of nonstop speech to the group assembled in the chancellery, was
nothing more than the design he had developed years before in *Mein
Kampf.* Now he presented it as the "result of detailed considerations and
the experiences of his four and a half years as head of government," but it
was the same old concept from which he had never strayed, which had
become the fixed point of all his steps and maneuvers. Only the tone of
impatience was new. He would ask those present, he added portentously
after his introductory words, "to regard the following statement as his
testamentary bequest in case of his decease."

If the goal of German policy, he began, were considered as the safe-
guarding, preservation, and increase of the body of the nation, the "problem of space" must immediately be confronted. All economic and social

539

difficulties, all racial dangers, could be mastered only by overcoming the scarcity of space; the future of Germany absolutely depended on that. The problem could no longer be solved by reaching out for overseas colonies, as had been possible for the powers of the liberalistic colonial age. Germany's living space was situated on the Continent. Granted, every expansion involved considerable risks, as the history of the Roman Empire or the British Empire demonstrated: "Neither earlier nor at the present time has there ever been space without a master; the aggressor always comes up against the possessor." But the gain, specifically a spatially coherent Greater Reich ruled by a solid "racial nucleus," justified a high stake. "For the solution of the German question all that remains is the way of force," he declared.

Once that resolve had been taken, he continued, all that remained was to decide on the most favorable time and circumstances for applying that force. Six to eight years later, conditions could develop only unfavorably for Germany. If, therefore, he was "still alive, it was his unalterable resolve to solve the question of German space between 1943–1945 at the latest." But he was also determined, if an earlier opportunity offered, to take advantage of it—whether the occasion were a severe domestic crisis in France or a military involvement of the Western powers. In any case, the subjection of Austria and of Czechoslovakia must come first, and he made it clear that he would not be content with the demand of the racial revisionists for annexation of the Sudetenland but had in mind the conquest of all Czechoslovakia as a springboard for far-reaching imperialist aims. By that conquest Germany would win not only twelve divisions but also the food supply for an additional 5 million to 6 million persons, this in the event "that a compulsory emigration of two million from Czechia, of one million persons from Austria, would be successfully carried out." For the rest, he considered it probable that England and France had "already written off Czechia." There was strong likelihood that some conflicts would erupt as early as the coming year, in the Mediterranean area, for example; these conflicts would involve a heavy drain on the Western powers. In that case he was determined to strike in 1938, without waiting. In view of these circumstances, from the German viewpoint a rapid and complete victory by Franco in the Spanish Civil War was undesirable. Rather, the interests of the Reich required continuance of the tensions in the Mediterranean area. In fact, it might be wise to encourage Mussolini to undertake additional expansionist moves, in order to create a *casus belli* between Italy and the Western powers. Anything of that sort would provide a magnificent opportunity for Germany to begin the "assault upon Czechoslovakia" with "lightning rapidity."

This exposition evidently stunned and disturbed some of the group, and in his description of the conference Colonel Hossbach notes that the subsequent discussion "at times took a very sharp tone." Neurath, Blomberg, and Fritsch, in particular, opposed Hitler's arguments and explicitly warned him against the risks of a war with the Western powers. Possibly Hitler had convoked the conference chiefly to communicate his impatience and, as he had explained to Göring before the beginning of the meeting, "to light a fire" under generals Blomberg and Fritsch "because he was by no means satisfied with the rearmament of the army." During the heated discussion Hitler suddenly became aware of a difference of opinion that came very close to being a matter of principle. Four days later Fritsch asked him for another meeting, and Foreign Minister Neurath—"shaken to the core," as he later declared—also tried to see him and dissuade him from his bellicose course. But Hitler had meanwhile decided to leave Berlin and had withdrawn to Berchtesgaden. Obviously ill-humored, he refused to receive the Foreign Minister before his return to Berlin in the middle of January.

It is surely more than accidental that the men who opposed him on November 5 all fell victim to the major shuffle by which Hitler, a short time later, removed the conservatives from their last remaining strongholds, especially in the army and the Foreign Office. The conference seems to have proved to him that his sweeping plans, which required steady nerves, a readiness to take risks, and a kind of brigand's courage could not be carried out by the inhibited, cautious representatives of the old bourgeois ruling class. Their sobriety and bristly stiffness antagonized him; his old antibourgeois resentments reawakened. He hated their arrogance and their class-conscious pretensions. The ideal Nazi diplomat was, to his mind, not a proper official but a revolutionary and secret agent, an "entertainment director" who would know how "to matchmake and to forge." A general, to his mind, should be like "a butcher's dog who has to be held fast by the collar because otherwise he threatens to attack anyone in sight." Neurath, Fritsch, and Blomberg scarcely fitted this conception. In this regime they were, as one of them commented, one and all "saurians."[72]

The November conference of 1937 marked a mutual disillusionment. The conservatives, especially the military leaders who had never learned to think beyond the narrow confines of their own goals and interests, found to their astonishment that Hitler meant what he had said. He was, as it were, actually being Hitler. And Hitler, for his part, found his contemptuous views of his conservative partners confirmed. For some years they had kept silent, obeyed, and served. Now they were manifesting their true pusillanimous nature. They wanted Germany's greatness, but without taking risks. They wanted rearmament but no war, Nazi order but not Nazi ideology.

From this angle, we can better understand the obstinate conservative efforts during the preceding years to retain a limited independence in diplomatic and military affairs. Hitler had partly outwitted such attempts on the part of the Foreign Office by instituting his system of special envoys. On the other hand he had not been able to pry open the far more coherent social bloc of the officer caste. He now saw that this was the next order of business. And as chance had come to his aid so often before, a number of developments now played into his hands. Three months later, he had ousted his top generals and totally reorganized both the diplomatic and the military structure in accord with his program for the future.

The seemingly innocent starting point was Blomberg's decision to remarry; his first wife had died years before. It was rather awkward that the bride, Fräulein Erna Gruhn, had "a past," as Blomberg himself admitted. Consequently, she did not meet the strict status requirements of the officer corps. Seeking advice, Blomberg took Göring into his confidence as a fellow officer. Göring strongly urged him to go ahead with the marriage, and even assisted him in getting rid of a rival by paying the man off and arranging his emigration. On January 12, 1938, the wedding took place, in an atmosphere of some secrecy. Hitler and Göring were the witnesses.

Only a few days later, rumors began circulating that the field marshal's marriage was a *mésalliance* of interest to the vice squad of the police. A police file soon provided evidence that Blomberg's newly wedded wife had spent some time as a prostitute and had once been convicted of serving as a model for lewd photographs. Twelve days after the wedding, when Blomberg returned from a brief honeymoon, Göring informed him that he had become unacceptable. The officer corps, too, saw no reason to come to the defense of the field marshal who for so long had been devoted to Hitler with boyish exuberance. Two days later, on the afternoon of January 26, Hitler received him for a farewell visit. "The embarrassment for me and for you was too great," he declared. "I could no longer wait it out. We must part."

In a brief discussion about a possible successor, Hitler rejected the presumptive candidate, Fritsch, and Göring as well. The latter, in his greed for posts, had desperately tried to secure the appointment. Apparently Blomberg, still abjectly loyal, proposed what Hitler in any case intended, that he take over the position himself. "When Germany's hour strikes," Hitler said at the end of the interview, "I will see you at my side and the whole past will be regarded as wiped out."

The decision had evidently been taken while Göring was still intriguing to exclude his rival, Fritsch. For now, instigated by Göring and Himmler jointly, a second police file was brought to light, this time on Fritsch, in which he was charged with homosexuality. In a scene out of a third-rate drama, the unsuspecting commander in chief of the army was confronted with a hired witness in the chancellery. The man's accusations soon proved untenable, but that did not matter. They had served their purpose: providing Hitler with the pretext for the thoroughgoing shakeup of personnel on February 4, 1938. Fritsch, too, found himself dismissed. Hitler took over the post of commander in chief of the armed forces. The War Ministry was dissolved, replaced by the High Command of the Armed Forces (Oberkommando der Wehrmacht, abbreviated OKW), headed by General Wilhelm Keitel. For a prize specimen of Hitlerian comedy, we may read General Jodl's diary note on Keitel's installation: "At 1 P.M. Keitel is ordered to the Führer in civilian dress. The latter pours out his heart on the difficulties which have descended upon him. He is growing more and more lonely. . . . He says to K: I am relying on you; you must stick it out with me. You are my confidant and only adviser on defense questions. Unified and coherent leadership of the Armed Forces is sacred and inviolable to me." Hitler then continued without transition and in the same tone of voice: "I shall take command of them myself with your help." As successor to Fritsch he appointed General von Brauchitsch, who, like Keitel, seemed the natural candidate for the post because of his servility and weakness of character; he had announced that he was "ready for anything" that was asked of him. In particular, he gave assurances that he would lead the army closer to National Socialism. In the course of these measures sixteen older generals were additionally retired, forty-four transferred. In order to alleviate Göring's disappointment, Hitler named him a field marshal.

With one blow, without a jot of opposition, Hitler had thus eliminated the last power factor of any significance. He had put across, as it were, a "bloodless June 30." Contemptuously, he declared that all generals were cowardly. His disdain was increased by the shameless eagerness many generals had shown to occupy the vacated positions. Such behavior made it plain that the unity of the officer corps had at last been shattered and caste solidarity—which had notably failed to put in an appearance in the case of the murders of von Schleicher and von Bredow—no longer existed. Speaking for the benefit of "later historians," General von Fritsch resignedly recorded his indignation at this "shameful treatment." To be sure, one group of army officers began to plot some action against the dictator and tried to make contact with Fritsch. Now, and once again six months later, he refused to support them, remarking fatalistically: "This man is Germany's fate and this fate will go its way to the end."

Meanwhile, the reshuffling was not limited to the armed forces. At the same cabinet session in which Hitler announced the changes in the top military leadership, he also informed Neurath of his dismissal from the post of Minister of Foreign Affairs. Ribbentrop replaced Neurath. Simultaneously, several important ambassadorships (Rome, Tokyo, Vienna) were changed. The careless way in which Hitler controlled the state is evident from the manner in which he appointed Walter Funk Minister of Economics. Hitler had met him at the opera one night, and during the intermission assigned him the post. Göring, he added, would give him further instructions. At the cabinet session of February 4 he was introduced as Schacht's successor. That was, incidentally, the last meeting of the cabinet in the history of the regime.

Throughout the crisis Hitler was worried that the events might be viewed abroad as symptoms of hidden struggles for power and therefore as a sign of weakness. He also feared new conflicts if the court-martial investigation of the Fritsch case—which he had had to concede to the generals—brought the intrigue to light and rehabilitated Fritsch. "If the troops find out about that, there'll be a revolution," one of the insiders had predicted. Consequently, Hitler decided to cover up the one crisis by another, far more comprehensive one. As early as January 31, Jodl had noted in his diary: "Führer wants to divert the spotlights from the Wehrmacht [the armed forces]. Keep Europe gasping and by replacements in various posts not awaken the impression of an element of weakness but of a concentration of forces. Schuschnigg is not to take heart, but to tremble."

Thus Hitler resolutely headed into another crisis. Since the July agreement of 1936 he had done nothing to improve German-Austrian relations. Rather, he had used the terms of the agreement solely to pick an endless series of new quarrels, bickering over clauses like a shyster lawyer. With growing concern the Vienna government had observed the ring gradually tightening. The obligations under the agreement, which it had assumed only under intense pressure, limited its freedom of action as much as did the ever closer ties between Rome and Berlin. In addition, the strong Nazi underground movement within Austria, encouraged and funded by the Reich, was stirring up trouble. It had a double basis for its passionate campaign for Anschluss: the ancient German dream of unification, feasible at last with the breakup of the Dual Monarchy in 1919; and Hitler's Austrian origin. The very idea of unity seemed to be incarnate in the person of Hitler. Nazi propaganda was operating upon a country that still remembered its days as a great power while at present living in a functionless rump state that meant nothing to most of the citizens. Humiliated, spurned by the new nations which had once been part of the shattered monarchy, impoverished, and insultingly kept in a dependent status, the population of Austria craved change. Existing conditions were so bad that few asked what would follow. With an acute sense of ethnic and historical ties, many Austrians turned their eyes more and more upon a self-assured Germany that seemed utterly transformed and was spreading panic among the arrogant victors of yesterday.

Desperately, Kurt von Schuschnigg, the successor to the assassinated Chancellor Dollfuss, looked around for help. In the spring of 1937 he vainly tried to secure a British declaration guaranteeing Austria's independence. When that was not forthcoming, his prolonged and tenacious opposition to the Nazis, which he had backed up by bans and persecution, gradually weakened. At the beginning of February, 1938, Papen proposed a meeting between him and the German Chancellor. Reluctantly, Schuschnigg agreed. On the morning of February 12 he arrived in Berchtesgaden. Hitler received him on the steps of the Berghof.

Immediately after the two men had exchanged greetings, the Austrian Chancellor found himself the victim of a tirade. When he remarked on the impressive panorama offered by the grand living room, Hitler brushed the remark aside: "Yes, my ideas mature here. But we haven't met to talk about the beautiful view and the weather." Then he worked himself up. Austria's whole history, he said, was "a continuous betrayal of the people. In the past it was the same as it is today. But this historical contradiction must at last come to its long overdue end. And let me tell you this, Herr Schuschnigg: I am firmly determined to put an end to all of it. . . . I have a historic mission and I am going to fulfill it because Providence has appointed me to do so. . . . I have traveled the hardest road that ever a German had to travel, and I have accomplished the greatest things in German history that ever a German was destined to accomplish. . . . You certainly aren't going to believe that you can delay me by so much as half an hour? Who knows—perhaps I'll suddenly turn up in Vienna overnight, like the spring storm. Then you'll see something!" His patience was exhausted, he continued. Austria had no friends; neither England nor France nor Italy would lift a finger for her sake. He demanded the right for the Austrian National Socialists to agitate freely, the appointment of his follower, Seyss-Inquart, as Austrian Minister of Security and of the Interior, a general amnesty, and accommodation of Austrian foreign and economic policy to that of the Reich.

According to Schuschnigg's account, when the time came to go to dinner, the man who a moment before had been gesticulating excitedly was transformed into an amiable host. But in the subsequent conversation, when the Austrian Chancellor remarked that because of his country's constitution he could not give any conclusive assurances, Hitler wrenched open the door, gestured for Schuschnigg to leave, and shouted in an intimidating tone for General Keitel. After Keitel came in, closed the door behind him, and asked for his orders, Hitler said: "None at all. Have a seat." Shortly afterward, Schuschnigg signed. He refused Hitler's invitation to sup with him. Accompanied by Papen, he crossed the border to Salzburg. During the entire ride he did not say a word. But Papen chattered on easily: "Yes, that's the way the Führer can be; now you've seen it for yourself. But next time you'll find a meeting with him a great deal easier. The Führer can be distinctly charming." The next time Schuschnigg came under guard and on his way to Dachau concentration camp.

The Berchtesgaden conference gave a great boost to the Austrian Nazis. They heralded their impending victory by a series of boastful acts of violence, and all of Schuschnigg's efforts to stem the tide came too late. In order to offer last-minute opposition to the open disintegration of state power, he decided on the evening of March 8 to call a plebiscite for the following Sunday, March 13. In this way he hoped to refute, before the eyes of the whole world, Hitler's claim that he had the majority of the Austrian people behind him. But Berlin immediately objected, and he was forced to drop his plan. Urged on by Göring, Hitler decided to take military action against Austria if necessary; for Ribbentrop had reported from

London that England was not in the least disposed to fight for this trouble-some leftover of the Versailles Treaty. Without England, Hitler knew, France would not intervene.

For a time it seemed that the German grab for Austria was stirring old allergies in Mussolini and forcing Italy toward a rapprochement with England. On March 10, therefore, Hitler sent Prince Philip of Hesse to Rome with a handwritten letter in which he spoke of the Austrian conspiracy against the Reich, the suppression of the nationalistic majority, and the prospect of civil war. As a "son of the Austrian soil" he had finally been unable to look on, inactive, he continued, but had decided to restore law and order in his homeland. "You, too, Your Excellency, could not act differently if the fate of Italy were at stake." He assured Mussolini of his steadfast sympathy and once again pledged the inviolability of the Brenner Pass as the boundary between Germany and Italy: "This decision will never be amended or altered." After hours of excited preparation, shortly after midnight he issued Directive No. 1 for Operation Otto:

If other measures do not succeed, I intend to march into Austria with armed forces in order to restore constitutional conditions there and to prevent further outrages against the nationalistic German population. I personally shall command the entire operation. . . . It is to our interest that the entire operation proceed without the use of force, with our troops marching in peacefully and being hailed by the populace. Therefore every provocation is to be avoided. But if resistance is offered, it must be smashed by force of arms with greatest ruthlessness. . . .

For the time being no security measures are to be taken on the German frontiers with other countries.

The terse, self-assured tone of this document almost entirely concealed the mood of hysteria and indecision in which it had come into being. All reports from members of Hitler's entourage speak of the extraordinary chaos surrounding the decision, the panicky confusion that overtook Hitler on the verge of this first expansionist action of his career. A multitude of overhasty mistaken decisions, choleric outbursts, senseless telephone calls, orders and cancellations of orders, followed in quick succession during the few hours between Schuschnigg's call for a plebiscite and March 12. Once again, to all appearances, those "damaged nerves" were giving trouble. First, the military leadership was told in great excitement to prepare an operational plan within a few hours. Hitler flared up at Beck and later Brauchitsch for their remonstrances. Then he canceled his marching order, then issued it again. In between came pleas, threats, misunderstandings. Keitel later spoke of the period as a "martyrdom."

If Göring had not taken the initiative at the moment he did, the public and thus the world would presumably have realized how much psychotic uncertainty and irritation Hitler showed in situations of great pressure. But Göring, who because of his part in the Fritsch affair had every interest in the operation and its obscuring effects, vigorously pressed the vacillating

Hitler forward. Years later, Hitler remarked, almost stammering, with the admiration of a high-strung man for another's phlegmatic, cold-blooded temperament:

The Reich Marshal has gone through a great many crises with me. He's ice-cold in crises. In times of crisis you cannot have a better adviser than the Reich Marshal. The Reich Marshal is brutal and ice-cold in crises. I've always noticed that when it's a question of facing up to a decision he is ruthless and hard as iron. You'll get nobody better than him, you couldn't find anybody better. He's gone through all the crises with me, the toughest crises, and was ice-cold. Whenever the going was really hard, he turned ice-cold. . . .

On March 11 Göring issued an ultimatum demanding the resignation of Schuschnigg and the appointment of Seyss-Inquart as Austrian Chancellor. Upon instructions from Berlin, the Nazis all over Austria poured into the streets that afternoon. In Vienna they thronged into the chancellery, filled the stairways and corridors, and settled down in the offices until, toward evening, Schuschnigg announced his resignation over the radio and ordered the Austrian army to retreat without offering resistance to the invading German troops. When President Miklas stubbornly refused to appoint Seyss-Inquart as the new Chancellor, Göring, in one of his many telephone conversations with Vienna, gave one of his go-betweens characteristic instructions:

Now listen closely: The important thing now is for Inquart to take possession of the entire government, keep the radio and everything else occupied. . . . Seyss-Inquart is to send the following telegram. Write this down:
"The provisional Austrian Government, which after the resignation of the Schuschnigg Government regards its task as the restoration of peace and order in Austria, addresses to the German Government an urgent appeal to support it in its task and to help it to prevent bloodshed. For this purpose it requests the German Government to dispatch German troops as soon as possible."

After a brief dialogue, Göring said in conclusion: "Now then, our troops are crossing the frontier today. . . . And see to it that he sends the telegram as soon as possible. . . . Present the telegram to him and tell him we are asking—he doesn't even have to send the telegram, you know; all he needs to say is: Agreed." And while the Nazis throughout the country began to occupy the public buildings, Hitler at last issued the marching order at 8:45 P.M.—even before Seyss-Inquart had been informed of his own appeal for help. Hitler rejected a later request from Seyss-Inquart to stop the German troops. A bare two hours later, the impatiently awaited word from Rome arrived: at half-past ten Philip of Hesse telephoned, and Hitler's reaction revealed how much tension he had been under:

Hesse: I have just come back from the Palazzo Venezia. The Duce accepted the whole affair in a very, very friendly manner. He sends you his cordial regards.
Hitler: Then please tell Mussolini I shall never forget him for this.

Hesse: Very well, sir.

Hitler: Never, never, never, whatever happens. . . . As soon as the Austrian affair is settled, I shall be ready to go through thick and thin with him, no matter what happens. . . . You may tell him that I thank him ever so much; never, never shall I forget.

Hesse: Yes, my Führer.

Hitler: I will never forget, whatever may happen. If he should ever need any help or be in any danger, he can be convinced that I shall stick to him, whatever may happen, even if the whole world were against him.[73]

On the afternoon of March 12, to the peal of bells, Hitler crossed the border at his birthplace, Braunau. Four hours later, he passed flower-decked villages and hundreds of thousands of persons lining the streets to enter Linz. Just outside the city line the Austrian ministers Seyss-Inquart and Glaise-Horstenau awaited him; with them was Heinrich Himmler, who had gone to Vienna the previous night to begin purging the country of "traitors to the people and other enemies of the State." With palpable emotion Hitler delivered a brief address from the balcony of the town hall to a crowd waiting in the darkness below him. In the speech he evoked once more the idea of his special mission:

If Providence once called me from this city to assume the leadership of the Reich, it must have charged me with a mission, and that mission can only have been to restore my dear homeland to the German Reich. I have believed in this mission, have lived and fought for it, and I believe I have now fulfilled it.

Next morning he laid a wreath on the grave of his parents in Leonding.

Everything seems to indicate that up to this time Hitler had as yet made no specific decisions about the future of Austria. Presumably he wanted to wait to the last to see what the foreign reaction would be, to test out the chances, repercussions, and accidents of the new situation, confident that he could exploit them more rapidly than his antagonists. It would appear that he decided upon immediate Anschluss only under the impact of the triumphal ride from Braunau to Linz, the cheers, the flowers and the flags. This elemental delirium seemed to permit no alternatives. Late on the evening of March 13, in the Hotel Weinzinger in Linz, he signed the "law concerning the reunion of Austria with the German Reich." One of those present reports that he was deeply moved. For a long time he remained quiet and motionless. Tears trickled down his cheeks. Finally he said, "Yes, the right political action saves blood."[74]

On this and the following day, when Hitler entered Vienna from the direction of Schönbrunn Palace amid cheering and the tolling of bells, he was enjoying the realization of his earliest dream. The two cities that had witnessed his failures, had disdained and humiliated him, at last lay at his feet in admiration, shame, and fear. All the aimlessness and impotence of those years were now vindicated, all his furious craving for compensation at last satisfied, when he stood on the balcony of the Hofburg and announced to hundreds of thousands in the Heldenplatz the "greatest report of a mission accomplished" in his life: "As Führer and Chancellor of the German Nation and of the Reich I hereupon report to History the entrance of my homeland into the German Reich."

The scenes of enthusiasm amid which this "reunion" took place "mocked all description," a Swiss newspaper wrote.[75] And although it is hard to determine how much of this clamor, how much of the flowers, the screaming and the tears, sprang from organized or spontaneous passion, there can be no doubt that the event stirred the deepest emotions of the nation. For the people who lined the streets for hours in Linz, Vienna, or Salzburg, this was the consummation of a longing for unity that had outlasted, as an elemental need, all the ancient dissensions, divisions and fraternal wars of the Germans. And it was out of this feeling that the people hailed Hitler as the man who had superseded Bismarck and brought his work to completion. The cry of "One People, One Reich, One Leader" was more than a clever slogan. That alone explains how not only the churches but also socialists like Karl Renner could let themselves be carried along by the euphoria of union.[76] The hope for an end of domestic political strife arose out of the same state of mind, though also from the existential anxiety of a nonviable republic. Added to such longings was the desire to have the powerful united Reich regain something of that brilliance that had dimmed since the end of the monarchy. Old Austria seemed to be returning in this prodigal son of Austria, however illegitimate and vulgar he might be.

In this aura of consummation and bliss the physical force that accompanied the event went unnoticed. "The Army was joined by standards of the SS detached units, 40,000 men of the police, and Death's Head Formation Upper Bavaria as second wave," the official journal of the High Command of the armed forces noted. These units instantly set up a system of rigorous repression. It would be mistaking Hitler's psychology to imagine that his resentments were forgotten for any length of time in the euphoria of triumph. And in fact the uninhibited savagery with which his squads now openly fell upon opponents and so-called racial enemies betrays something of his unforgotten hatred for Vienna. The sometimes ferocious excesses, particularly of the Austrian Legion, which had just returned from Germany, nakedly revealed what might be called the "Oriental" element that Hitler had introduced into German anti-Semitism; now he was unleashing it in followers of his own origin and his own emotional structure. "With bare hands," Stefan Zweig wrote, "university professors were compelled to scrub the streets. Devout, white-bearded Jews were dragged into the temple and forced by yowling youths to do knee bends and shout 'Heil Hitler' in chorus. Innocent persons were caught en masse in the streets like rabbits and dragged off to sweep out the latrines of the

SA barracks. All the morbidly filthy hate fantasies orgiastically conceived in the course of many nights were released in broad daylight."[77] A wave of refugees poured into non-German Europe. Stefan Zweig, Sigmund Freud, Walter Mehring, Carl Zuckmayer, and many others fled from Austria. The writer Egon Friedell threw himself out of his window. Nazi terror manifested itself in all openness. But these circumstances did not weigh heavily in the outside world. The impression of rejoicing was too strong, the German reference to the Wilsonian principle of self-determination too irrefutable. That principle was confirmed triumphantly with the predictable 99 per cent of the votes in the regime's fifth and last plebiscite on March 16. The Western powers indicated that they were disturbed; but France was deeply embroiled in her domestic problems, and England refused to give France or Czechoslovakia any guarantees. England also rejected a proposal by the Soviet Union for a conference to prevent further aggression on the part of Hitler. Chamberlain and the European conservatives continued to regard Hitler as the commandant of their anti-Communist bulwark, who must be won over by generosity and simultaneously tamed. The Left, meanwhile, reassured itself with the thought that Schuschnigg was nothing but the representative of a clerico-Fascist regime ripe for overthrow, and one that had formerly fired upon workers. The League of Nations did not even hold a meeting on the question; the world by now was not bothering about mere gestures of indignation. Its conscience, as Stefan Zweig wrote bitterly, "only growled a little before it forgot and forgave."[78]

Hitler stayed in Vienna less than twenty-four hours; it is hard to say whether his bias against the hated "sybaritic city" or his impatience prompted him to return so hurriedly. In any case, the effortlessness with which he had achieved this major victory encouraged him to push at once toward the next goal. Only two weeks after the annexation of Austria he met with Konrad Henlein, the leader of the Sudeten Germans, and declared his readiness to solve the Czechoslovakian question within the foreseeable future. Another four weeks later, on April 21, he discussed with General Keitel the plan for a military attack upon Czechoslovakia. Out of regard for world opinion he rejected an "attack out of a clear sky, without any pretext or possibility of justification." He would prefer a "lightning-like action on the basis of an incident," for example an "assassination of the German Ambassador in conjunction with an anti-German demonstration."

As with Austria, Hitler was again able to utilize the inherent contradictions of the Versailles system. For Czechoslovakia was one grand negation of the principle upon which it was supposedly based. Its creation had been far less connected with the right of self-determination than with France's strategical interests. For Czechoslovakia was a small multinational state in which one minority was pitted against the majority of all the other minorities, who were all manifesting that egotistic nationalism it had itself shown during its own struggle for independence. Chamberlain had once denigratingly called it not a state but "scraps and patches." The comparatively high degree of freedom and political participation that the government granted its citizenry did not suffice to control the centrifugal forces operating within it. The Polish ambassador in Paris spoke bluntly of a "country condemned to death."[79]

By all the laws of politics there was bound to be a clash with Czechoslovakia as German strength grew. The 3.5 million Sudeten Germans had felt oppressed ever since the foundation of the republic, and they attributed their economic distress, which was in fact very serious, less to structural causes than to the "alien rule" of Prague. Both Hitler's seizure of power and the elections of May, 1935, when Konrad Henlein's Sudeten German party had become the strongest political party in the country, enormously swelled their self-assurance, and the annexation of Austria had inspired massive demonstrations under the slogan of "Home to the Reich." As early as 1936 an anonymous letter writer from the Sudetenland has assured Hitler that he looked upon him "as a Messiah"; and such hysterical expectations were now stirred up by wild speeches, provocations, and clashes. Hitler had coached Henlein to constantly present Prague with such high demands that they would "be unacceptable to the Czech government." He encouraged him to adopt a challenging attitude. He thus laid the grounds for that crisis which would require him to intervene. In the meantime, he let events take their course. Early in May he traveled with a large retinue of ministers, generals, and party functionaries on a state visit to Italy, where Mussolini now had to try to surpass Hitler's hospitality. The backdrop of the Eternal City was festively decorated with flags, fasces, and swastikas. The houses along the railroad line were freshly painted, and near San Paolo Outside the Walls a special station had been erected, at which the King and Mussolini received Hitler. Hitler noticed, however, with some irritation that protocol required Mussolini to keep in the background. Hitler himself, as head of state, was the guest of Victor Emmanuel III, whom he contemptuously called "King Nutcracker." Right from the start he offended the King by small rudenesses, such as entering the royal carriage before him. He also objected to the reactionary and arrogant manners of the court. Long afterward, he justified his later acts of suspicion against his Axis partner on these grounds.

On the other hand, the reception and the tributes paid him by Mussolini deeply impressed him. In resplendent parades the new *passo romano*—the Roman parade steps—was displayed. At a naval show in Naples one hundred submarines simultaneously vanished beneath the waves, to reappear a few minutes later with ghostly precision. Extensive tours enabled Hitler to satisfy his aesthetic inclinations, and years later he tended to extol the "magic of Florence and Rome." How beautiful Tuscany and Umbria were, he would exclaim. In contrast to Moscow, Berlin, or even Paris, where the architectonic proportions lacked harmony both in details and overall impression, and everything had just bypassed him, Rome had "really moved" him.

Politically, too, the trip proved a success. Since Mussolini's visit to Germany the Axis had been subjected to considerable strains. The annexation of Austria had reawakened the old anxieties about South Tyrol. But Hitler now succeeded in allaying these. In particular, his speech during the state banquet in the Palazzo Venezia, a display both of style and psychological instinct, brought about a shift. Ciano, who mentioned an initial mood of "universal hostility," noted with amazement the sympathy Hitler was able to win by speeches and personal contacts. The city of Florence, Ciano commented, had "welcomed the Führer with heart and head."[80] When Hitler boarded the train for Germany on May 10, concord appeared restored, and Mussolini shook his hand vigorously, saying, "Henceforth no force will be able to separate us."

In the few political conversations held during those days Hitler had gathered that Italy would grant Germany a free hand toward Czechoslovakia. The Western powers, too, had meanwhile called upon Prague to meet the Sudeten Germans halfway. And Hitler informed those powers that the Czechoslovakian question was soluble. The British ambassador in Berlin had told Ribbentrop that Germany would win all along the line.[81] Hitler was therefore all the more surprised when the Prague government, troubled by rumors about German preparations for an attack, ordered partial mobilization on May 20, and England and France explicitly came out with references to their obligations to aid Czechoslovakia. They were, moreover, supported by the Soviet Union.

A conference was hastily called at the Berghof on May 22. Hitler felt forced to halt his preparations. He had occasionally mentioned the fall of 1938 as the moment for his action against Czechoslovakia; now it appeared that his timetable was being upset. His indignation mounted when the international press hailed the "May crisis" as finally an effective check to Germany. As had happened during the comparable humiliation of August, 1932, he remained hidden in his mountain retreat for several days, and quite probably the same cravings for revenge, the same wild fantasies of destruction, moved him now. In later years he repeatedly referred to the "grave loss of prestige" he had suffered during those days. Finally, in his neurotic fear of showing signs of weakness, he thought it appropriate to inform both Mussolini and the British Foreign Secretary in special messages that nothing could be achieved with him "by threats, pressure or force," that in fact these "would certainly only accomplish the opposite and make him hard and unyielding." On May 28 he came to Berlin for a conference with his top people in military and foreign affairs. With a map before him, he expatiated with growing fury on how he intended to wipe out Czechoslovakia. His former military directive for "Operation Green" had begun with the sentence: "It is not my intention to smash Czechoslovakia by military means in the immediate future without provocation. . . ." The new version ran: "It is my unalterable decision to smash Czechoslovakia by military action in the near future."[82] In a defiant reaction he set the date for precisely October 1.

He now bent every effort to increase the tensions. At the end of June maneuvers were held near the Czech border, while work on the west wall at the French border was pushed at an accelerated pace. With Henlein carrying out instructions to seek confrontation, Hitler cautiously stirred the greed of Czechoslovakia's other neighbors, especially the Hungarians and the Poles. The Western powers pressed the Prague government for more and more concessions. As if the one gesture of resolution had consumed all their strength, they returned to their former compliance, and the policy of appeasement now moved toward its climax. Honorable or understandable though their motives might be, that policy suffered equally from ignorance of Hitler and ignorance of the special problems of Central Europe. The appeasers had a deep distaste for the complex animosities in Central Europe, and they capitulated before the impossibility of threading their way through the labyrinth of ethnic, religious, national, racial, cultural, and historical grievances. For Nevile Henderson the Czechs were "the damned Czechs." Lord Rothermere stated in the *Daily Mail* that the Czechs were of no concern to Englishmen. Chamberlain summed up the fundamental mood when he spoke of "a quarrel in a faraway country between people of whom we know nothing!" The mission of inquiry in Czechoslovakia on which the British government had dispatched Lord Runciman in August was an admission of indifference.[83]

It is against this background that we must see the fateful editorial in the London *Times* of September 7, which proposed ceding the Sudetenland to the Reich. For after many weeks in which the crisis continued to worsen of its own accord, while Hitler seemingly restrained himself, the whole world was awaiting the speech with which he would wind up the Nuremberg party rally on September 12. It is quite possible that the many evidences of the spirit of appeasement contributed to the exceptionally violent and challenging tenor of that speech. But the unforgotten humiliation of May, to which he repeatedly reverted at length, was also a factor. He spoke of "infamous deception," of "terroristic blackmail" and the "criminal aims" of the Prague government. He once more worked himself up over the imputation that he had retreated in the face of his opponents' resolute posture, and he denounced their preparations for war. He had now drawn the necessary conclusions, he continued, which would permit him to strike back at once in the future. "In no circumstances shall I be willing any longer to regard with endless tranquillity a continuation of the oppression of German compatriots in Czechoslovakia. . . . The Germans of Czechoslovakia are neither defenseless nor deserted. Let this be noted."

The speech was the signal for an uprising in the Sudetenland that cost many lives. In Germany a period of hectic military activity began. Blackout drills were held and automobiles requisitioned. For a moment war seemed inevitable. Then events took a surprising turn. Prime Minister Chamberlain, in a message dispatched on the night of September 13, declared his willingness to come to any desired place, without consideration of questions of prestige, for a personal discussion with Hitler. "I propose to come across by air and am ready to start tomorrow," Chamberlain wrote.

Hitler felt exceedingly flattered, although the proposal involved slowing down on the collision course on which he had been hurtling. "I was thunderstruck," he later declared. But the insecurity that all his life had made him incapable of gestures of magnanimity continued to govern his behavior. His guest was almost seventy and about to enter a plane for the first time in his life. But Hitler was incapable of meeting Chamberlain halfway. He proposed Berchtesgaden as the place for the conference. When the British Prime Minister arrived at the Berghof on the afternoon of September 15, after having traveled for nearly seven hours, Hitler went no farther to meet him than the top step of the large outside staircase. Once again he had placed General Keitel intimidatingly among the members of his entourage. When Chamberlain expressed the desire for a private conversation, Hitler agreed, but with the probable intention of further tiring the old man poured out upon him a rambling review of the European situation, Anglo-German relations, his own degree of resolution, and his successes. Despite his stoic equanimity, Chamberlain undoubtedly saw through Hitler's tricks and maneuvers, and in his report to the cabinet two days later he referred to him as "the commonest little dog" he had ever seen.[84]

When Hitler at last came round to talking about the current crisis, he demanded nothing less than the annexation of the Sudeten territory. Chamberlain interrupted to ask whether he would be content with that or whether he wanted to dismember Czechoslovakia entirely. Hitler replied by referring to Polish and Hungarian demands. But all that did not interest him, Hitler declared, nor was the present the time to discuss the technical arrangements: "Three hundred Sudeten Germans have been killed, and that cannot go on, that has to be settled at once. I am determined to settle it; I don't care whether or not there is a world war."

Chamberlain responded testily that he did not see why it had been necessary for him to take so long a journey if Hitler had nothing to say to him except that he had decided on force anyhow. Hitler then became somewhat more conciliatory. He would "today or tomorrow look into the question of whether a peaceful solution of the question was still possible." The decisive factor, he continued, would be "whether England is now ready to consent to a detachment of the Sudeten German region on the basis of the right of peoples to self-determination; with regard to which he [the Führer] must remark that this right of self-determination had not recently been invented by him in 1938 especially for the Czechoslovakian question, but had been created in 1918 in order to establish a moral basis for the changes resulting from the Versailles Treaty." They agreed that Chamberlain would fly back to England for a cabinet session to discuss this question; in the meantime, Hitler promised, he would take no military measures.

As soon as Chamberlain had departed, Hitler propelled the crisis and his own preparations further. The obliging attitude of the British Prime Minister had thrown him into consternation, for it threatened to frustrate his further plans for annexing the whole of Czechia. But in the hope that Chamberlain would be overruled by his own cabinet, by the French, or by the Czechs, Hitler continued his arrangements. While the German press unleashed a savage campaign of atrocity stories, he set up a Sudeten German Free Corps "for the protection of the Sudeten Germans and the continuance of disturbances and clashes." It was placed under the leadership of Konrad Henlein, who had fled to Germany. Hitler also urged Hungary and Poland to make territorial demands upon Prague, while also encouraging the Slovaks in their efforts to secure autonomy. Finally, in order to stir clashes on a larger scale, he had members of the Sudeten German Free Corps occupy the cities of Eger and Asch.

He was consequently stunned when Chamberlain, at their second meeting in the Hotel Dreesen in Godesberg on September 22, brought word that England, France, and even Czechoslovakia acquiesced to the cession of the Sudeten territory. Moreover, in order to remove Germany's fears that Czechoslovakia might be used as the "tip of a lance" against the flank of the Reich, the British Prime Minister proposed that the existing treaties of alliance between France, the Soviet Union, and Czechoslovakia be dissolved. Instead, an international guarantee would assure the country's independence. All this was so astonishing that Hitler asked once more whether this offer had the approval of the Prague government. Chamberlain replied that it had. There was a brief, embarrassed pause before Hitler answered quietly: "I am very sorry, Mr. Chamberlain, that I can now no longer enter into these matters. After the developments of the past few days this solution will no longer do."

Chamberlain showed his vexation. He asked angrily what circumstances had meanwhile changed the situation. Hitler once more evaded an answer by referring to the demands of the Hungarians and the Poles, then indulged in denunciations of the Czechs, lamented the sufferings of the Sudeten Germans, until at last he found the saving obstacle and immediately seized upon it: "It is vital to act quickly. The decision must be made in a few days. . . . The problem must be settled once and for all by October 1, completely settled."

After three hours of fruitless bargaining, Chamberlain returned to the

Hotel Petersberg across the Rhine. When an exchange of letters likewise proved fruitless, he asked for a written memorandum on the German demands, and announced that he was leaving. Hitler, State Secretary von Weizsäcker has related, "clapped his hands as if he had witnessed a successful entertainment" when these events were described to him. The news of the Czechoslovak mobilization, which exploded right in the middle of the chaotic, highly emotional concluding conversations, intensified the sense of approaching disaster. Nevertheless, Hitler now seemed ready to make a few trivial concessions, while Chamberlain showed signs of giving up and made it plain that he would no longer permit himself to be used by Hitler as a mediator.

The British cabinet met on Sunday, September 25, to discuss Hitler's memorandum. It flatly rejected the new demands and promised the French government British support in case of a military involvement with Germany. Prague, too, which had accepted the Berchtesgaden conditions only under the utmost pressure, now regained its freedom of action and rejected Hitler's proposals. Preparations for war began in England and France.

In the face of this unexpected intransigence by the opposing side, Hitler once more adopted the role of a man enraged beyond all bearing. "There's no point at all in going on with negotiations," he shouted at Sir Horace Wilson on September 26. "The Germans are being treated like niggers; nobody dares to treat even Turkey this way. On October 1 I'll have Czechoslovakia where I want her."[85] Then he set a deadline for Wilson: he would hold back his divisions only if the Godesberg memorandum were accepted by the Prague government by 2 P.M. on September 28. In the past several days he had vacillated constantly between a safe partial success and a risky total triumph that far better suited his radical temperament. He would sooner conquer Prague than receive Karlsbad and Eger as a gift. The tensions racking him during these days were discharged in the famous speech in the Berlin Sportpalast, by which he once again aggravated the crisis, while at the same time contrasting it with the tempting idyl of a continent at last entering a period of tranquillity:

And now before us stands the last problem that must be solved and will be solved. It is the last territorial claim which I have to make in Europe, but it is the claim from which I will not recede and which, God willing, I will make good.

Scornfully, he pointed out the contradictions between the principle of self-determination and the reality of the multinational State of Czechoslovakia. In describing the course of the crisis he again put himself into the dramatic role of the offended party, cried out against the terror in the Sudetenland, and in giving refugee figures allowed himself to be carried far beyond facts:

We see the appalling figures: on one day 10,000 fugitives, on the next 20,000, a day later, already 37,000, again two days later 41,000, then 62,000, then

78,000: now 90,000, 107,000, 137,000, and today 214,000. Whole stretches of country have been depopulated, villages are burned down, attempts are made to smoke out the Germans with hand grenades and gas. Mr. Beneš, however, sits in Prague and is convinced: "Nothing can happen to me: in the end England and France stand behind me."

And now, my fellow-countrymen, I believe that the time has come when one must mince matters no longer. . . . He will have to hand this territory over to us on October 1. . . . The decision now lies in his hands: Peace or War!

Once again he gave assurances that he was not interested in wiping out or annexing Czechoslovakia: "We want no Czechs!" he shouted, and as he came to his peroration worked himself up into a state of ecstasy. Eyes raised to the roof of the hall, fired by the greatness of the hour, the cheering of the masses, and his own paroxysm, he ended on a rapturous note:

Now I go before my people as its first soldier and behind me—let the world know this—there marches a people, and a different people from that of 1918. . . . It will feel my will to be its will. Just as in my eyes it is its future and its fate which gave me the commission for my action. And we wish now to make our will as strong as it was in the time of our struggle, the time when I, as a simple unknown soldier, went forth to conquer a Reich. . . . And so I ask you, my German people, take your stand behind me, man by man, and woman by woman. . . . We are determined!

Now let Mr. Beneš make his choice!

Storms of applause followed, and while Hitler, bathed in sweat, glassy-eyed, sat down, Goebbels sprang up. "One thing is sure: 1918 will never be repeated!" he shouted. William Shirer observed from the balcony the way Hitler looked up at Goebbels "as if those were the words which he had been searching for all evening and hadn't quite found. He leaped to his feet and with a fanatical fire in his eyes that I shall never forget brought his right hand, after a grand sweep, pounding down on the table, and yelled with all the power of his mighty lungs: 'Ja!' Then he slumped into his chair exhausted."[86] That evening Goebbels coined the slogan: *Führer befiehl, wir folgen!* ("Führer command, we obey!") The masses went on chanting it long after the end of the meeting. As Hitler departed, they began to sing *Der Gott, der Eisen wachsen liess,* a combat song repudiating subjection.

Still inspired by the heat and the hysteria of the previous night, Hitler once again received Sir Horace Wilson next day at noon. If his demands were rejected he would destroy Czechoslovakia, he threatened; and when Wilson replied that England would intervene militarily if France found herself compelled to hasten to the aid of Czechoslovakia, Hitler declared he could merely note the fact: "If France and England strike, let them do so. It is a matter of complete indifference to me. I am prepared for every eventuality. It is Tuesday today, and by next Monday we shall all be at war."[87] That same day he ordered additional mobilization measures.

But the afternoon of September 27 again dampened his euphoria. In order to test and increase the populace's enthusiasm for war, Hitler had ordered the second motorized division to pass through the capital on its way from Stettin to the Czechoslovak border and to roll down the broad East-West axis, through Wilhelmstrasse past the chancellery. Perhaps he hoped the military spectacle would bring people pouring into the streets and awaken a fighting spirit which, whipped up by a last appeal from the chancellery balcony, could be converted into a general "cry for violence." What actually happened has been recorded by the American journalist William Shirer in his diary:

I went out to the corner of the Linden where the column was turning down the Wilhelmstrasse, expecting to see a tremendous demonstration. I pictured the scenes I had read of in 1914 when the cheering throngs on this same street tossed flowers at the marching soldiers, and the girls ran up and kissed them. . . . But today they ducked into the subways, refused to look on, and the handful that did stood at the curb in utter silence. . . . It has been the most striking demonstration against war I've ever seen.

. . . I walked down the Wilhelmstrasse to the Reichskanzlerplatz, where Hitler stood on a balcony of the Chancellery reviewing the troops. . . . There weren't two hundred people there. Hitler looked grim, then angry, and soon went inside, leaving his troops to parade by unreviewed.[88]

The sobering effect of this incident was reinforced by a flood of bad news indicating that France's, England's, and Czechoslovakia's preparations for war were going further than expected and the strength of these Allies evidently surpassed by a good deal Germany's potentialities. Prague alone had mobilized a million men and together with France would be able to commit three times as many troops as Germany. In London air raid shelters were being dug and hospitals evacuated. The population of Paris was leaving the city in droves. War seemed inevitable. In the course of the day Yugoslavia, Rumania, Sweden, and the United States issued warnings declaring in favor of Germany's adversaries. And since the deadline Hitler had set expired in a few hours, the either-or mood in the chancellery began to swing around. During the late evening hours of September 27 Hitler started to dictate a letter to Chamberlain that struck a definitely conciliatory tone, offering a formal guarantee for the continued existence of Czechoslovakia and ending with an appeal to reason. But in the meantime other things had been happening which promised to give developments an unexpected twist at the last moment.

A plot had been forming and had made considerable progress in the course of the preceding year. The conspirators were a small but influential group, for the first time people from all political camps. Their joint initial purpose had been to prevent war; but the boldness with which Hitler was heading toward a conflict caused them to raise their own sights, until they arrived at plans for assassination and rebellion. The motive force and the middleman for all the groups was the head of the Central Section of the Abwehr (Army Counterintelligence), Lieutenant Colonel Hans Oster. If it is true that German military tradition has always been entirely divorced from political opposition, and that the German character, too—as Bernardo Attolico, the Italian ambassador in Berlin, remarked at the time— lacks all conspiratorial qualities such as patience, knowledge of human nature, psychology, tact, or the capacity for hypocrisy, then Oster was one of the exceptions. A curious mixture of morality and cunning, ingenuity, psychological calculation and loyalty to principles, he had early taken a critical attitude toward Hitler and Nazism. For some time he had tried vainly to persuade his fellow soldiers to share his views. The officer corps was a group of narrow specialists wedded to inaction. But they finally began to stir when they could no longer blink at the fact that Hitler was headed toward war, and when the Fritsch affair had roused their caste pride. Other groups, too, began to be mobilized; and Oster consistently drew them in. Covered by the apparatus of the Abwehr and its chief, Admiral Canaris, he succeeded in forming a widely ramified resistance group.

The resistance had realized that a totalitarian regime, once entrenched, could be overturned only by the combined action of internal and external enemies. On this principle, representatives of the German opposition made virtual pilgrimages to Paris and London, trying to contact influential figures. Early in March, 1938, Carl Goerdeler was in Paris urging the French government to take an uncompromising position on the Czechoslovakian question. A month later he set out once more, but both times he received only noncommittal replies. His visit to London brought similar results. It throws significant light upon the complex of problems involved in this and subsequent missions that Sir Robert Vansittart, chief diplomatic advisor to the British Foreign Secretary, exclaimed in consternation to his German visitor that what he was saying was actual treason to his country.[89]

Much the same reception was accorded Ewald von Kleist-Schwenzin, a conservative politician who had long ago retreated in disgust to his Pomeranian estates, but now used his connections with England to urge the British government to stiffen its resistance to Hitler's expansionist plans. Hitler would not be content with the Anschluss of Austria, he warned; there was reliable information that his plans aimed far beyond the annexation of Czechoslovakia and that he was striving for nothing less than world dominion. In the summer of 1938 von Kleist himself went to London. Chief of Staff Ludwig Beck had given him a kind of assignment: "Bring me certain proof that England will fight if Czechoslovakia is attacked, and I will put an end to this regime."[90]

Two weeks after von Kleist, the industrialist Hans Böhm-Tettelbach went to London on the same mission; and no sooner was he back from his trip than several new efforts were undertaken on the part of a resistance group in the Foreign Office headed by State Secretary von Weizsäcker, who used Embassy Councillor Theo Kordt in London as his intermediary. On September 1 Weizsäcker himself asked Danzig High Commissioner Carl Jacob Burckhardt to urge the British government to use "unambiguous language" toward Hitler. Probably the most effective step, he told Burckhardt, would be to send a "blunt, plainspoken Englishman, a general with a riding crop, for instance." That might make Hitler sit up and listen. "At the time Weizsäcker spoke with the candor of a desperate man who is risking everything on the last card!" Burckhardt wrote at the time.

Meanwhile, Oster was pressing Theo Kordt's brother Erich, who worked in the Foreign Ministry as chief of the Ministeramt, to somehow produce threats of intervention from London. The problem was to make London use the kind of language that would impress a "half-educated and ruffianly dictator." A flood of information and warnings about Hitler's intentions poured into London and Paris. All to no avail. Although such envoys as von Kleist had told Vansittart that they were coming with, as it were, "a rope around their necks," all pleas were ignored. The appeasers were too eager to make concessions, or too suspicious, or crassly uncomprehending. A high-echelon British intelligence service officer responded to the initiative of a German staff officer, who had come to London as "a damned impudence," and Vansittart's astonished remark about treason demonstrated how hard it was for these people of fixed ideas to grasp the conspirators' motives.

To be sure, some of these emissaries did not exactly make a good case for themselves. Some showed monarchist tendencies or made revisionist demands not unlike Hitler's. The German conservatives and the army circles, for whom almost all the emissaries were speaking, were also under suspicion of having kept their traditional openness toward the East. For England and France, there was an odor of faint unsavoriness about that lot: there had, after all, been the Rapallo treaty (of rapprochement between Russia and Germany in 1922) and all those years of co-operation between the Reichswehr and the Red Army, which had persisted up to the time Hitler put an end to it. It was therefore inevitable that a good many of the foreign diplomats should think that the reactionary monarchist forces of old Germany, the Junkers and the militarists, were reforming in the resistance movement. Thus the choice looked like "Hitler or the Prussians," and few were prepared to opt for the spirit of yesterday as against the crude but at least uncompromisingly Western-oriented dictator. "Who will guarantee that Germany will not become Bolshevistic afterwards?" Chamberlain retorted when French Chief of Staff Gamelin spoke to him on that dramatic September 26 of the plans of the German resistance movement. What Chamberlain meant was that Hitler's guarantees were more reliable than those of the German conservatives. Once again it was the old anti-Russian bias, the nightmare of the West, which Napoleon on St.

Helena had evoked more than a century earlier and which French Premier Daladier now quoted anxiously: "The Cossacks will rule Europe."

Oppositionist activities at home ran parallel to the efforts abroad. In the nature of things these activities were conducted primarily by the military. In a series of memoranda of increasing sharpness, Ludwig Beck tried to oppose Hitler's determination for war. He was most emphatic in his memorandum of July 16, which once again warned against the perils of a major conflict, referred to the persistent weariness of the German population, and underlined Germany's meager defensive strength to the West. Beck summed up all the political, military, and economic objections in the conclusion that Germany would in no way be able to survive the "life and death" struggle which was bound to follow from Hitler's challenging behavior. Simultaneously Beck urged Field Marshal Brauchitsch to persuade the higher officers to act collectively. He wanted them to stage a kind of "general strike of the generals" and force an end to the preparations for war by threatening to resign in a body.

Brauchitsch at last seemed to yield to Beck's expostulations. He convoked a conference of generals on August 4, at which he had Beck's July memorandum read aloud and called on General Adam to report on the weakness of the west wall. By the end of the conference almost everyone present had been brought around to Beck's point of view. Only Generals Reichenau and Busch raised a few objections. Brauchitsch himself, on the other hand, declared his complete agreement. But to Beck's astonishment he did not make the speech that had been drafted by Beck and was to culminate in a call for a joint protest. Instead, he had Beck's memorandum presented to Hitler, thus exposing his chief of staff. When on August 18 Hitler, at a conference in Jüterbog, announced that during the next few weeks he would solve the Sudeten question by force, Beck resigned.

Like Brauchitsch's perfidy, this resignation was a product of the characteristic timidities of the German military leadership. But it was also a reaction, and perhaps an understandable one, to the success Hitler was having with his aggressive foreign policy. Beck gave up his struggle partly because it had proved impossible to extract more resolute language from the Western powers. Unless the British Prime Minister or the French Premier were ready to stand up to Hitler, the German resistance was bound to be halfhearted.

Nevertheless, under Beck's successor, General Halder, the conspirators did not suspend their efforts. Even as he assumed office, Halder told Brauchitsch that he rejected Hitler's war plans just as firmly as his predecessor and was determined "to utilize every opportunity for the struggle against Hitler." Halder was no *frondeur;* rather, he was the typical meticulous, sober General Staff officer. But Hitler, whom he hated in a rather special way, denouncing him as a "criminal," "madman," and "bloodsucker," left him no choice. He himself spoke of the "compulsion to opposition," and called it a "terrible and agonizing experience." More coolheaded than Beck, and more consistent, he immediately expanded the ratiocinations of the conspirators into a plan for a *coup d'état*. On Oster's suggestion he negotiated with Hjalmar Schacht and had concluded all the preparations before September 15.[91]

The plan was keyed to the outbreak of war. At the moment war was declared a sudden coup would be led by General von Witzleben, commander of the Berlin defense district. Hitler and a number of leading functionaries of the regime would be arrested and subsequently brought to trial in order to expose to the whole world the Nazis' aggressive aims. In this way the participants hoped to avoid creating a new stab-in-the-back legend and to win support for their undertaking against an enormously popular Hitler, whose popularity was at this moment further swelled by nationalistic fervor. Thus they hoped to avert the danger of civil war. What counted was not the ideas and moral categories of a small elite, Halder thought, but the assent in principle of the population. Reichsgerichtsrat Hans von Dohnanyi, a high official in the judiciary, had been keeping a secret file since 1933 in preparation for a trial of Hitler. Oster had also drawn the police commissioner of Berlin, Count Helldorf, into the plot, and the vice-commissioner, Count Fritz-Dietlof von der Schulenburg. He had established close contact with various commanders in Potsdam, Landsberg an der Warthe, and Thuringia, with such leading Socialists as Wilhelm Leuschner and Julius Leber, and with Dr. Karl Bonhoeffer, psychiatric director of Berlin's Charité Hospital, who in one variant of the putsch plan was to function as chairman of a committee of doctors who would declare Hitler mentally ill. Meanwhile, Friedrich Wilhelm Heinz, former leader of the Stahlhelm, was planning a kind of "conspiracy within the conspiracy." He had been assigned the task of recruiting young army officers, workers, and students to reinforce the shock troop of the army corps staff headquarters, which at the proper moment was to invade the chancellery. But Heinz considered the idea of trying Hitler and the plan of incarcerating him in a mental hospital completely unrealistic. Hitler alone, he told Oster, was stronger than Witzleben with his entire army corps. Consequently, he gave his men secret instructions not to arrest Hitler but to shoot him down at close quarters without more ado.[92]

Thus everything was prepared, more thoroughly and with seemingly greater chances of success than ever again. Heinz's shock troop, well provided with arms and explosives, was in readiness in private houses in Berlin. All military and police measures had been arranged for. Plans for the smooth take-over of the radio were ready, and proclamations to the populace drafted. Halder had announced that the signal to strike would be given the moment Hitler issued the marching order against Czechoslovakia. Everyone was waiting.

With the London declaration of September 26 that in case of an attack on Czechoslovakia England would take her place at France's side, the other side at last seemed to have taken that resolute posture that was so essential to the conspirators' plans. In the course of September 27 they even succeeded in drawing the hesitating Brauchitsch into the operation. At noon Hitler issued readiness orders for the first wave of attacks and a few hours later ordered the mobilization of nineteen divisions. General mobilization was expected for the following day at 2 P.M. Erich Kordt was going to insure that the big double door behind the guard at the entrance to the chancellery was opened. Toward noon Brauchitsch went to hear Hitler's decision. Witzleben's group waited impatiently in the defense district headquarters on Hohenzollerndamm; the general himself was visiting Halder at army High Command headquarters. Heinz's shock troop awaited orders in its quarters. At this point, with all in readiness, a courier brought word to Chief of Staff Halder that Hitler had, on Mussolini's mediation, consented to a softer line and had agreed to a conference in Munich.

The news was a bombshell. Each of the participants in the plot instantly realized that the basis for the whole plan of action had been removed. Confusion and numbness gripped them all. Only Gisevius, one of the civilian conspirators, tried in a desperate torrent of words to persuade Witzleben to strike anyhow. The whole undertaking had been based too exclusively upon a single pivot in foreign policy; now, any chance for action was lost. This, strictly speaking, had been the crucial though perhaps inevitable dilemma of the project for a coup all along: it depended on certain moves of Hitler, on certain reactions of the Western powers. The conspirators were not mistaken about Hitler's nature; their plan failed because they had not realized that England's intentions had always been to give Hitler the chance, by concessions, "to be a good boy," as Henderson put it. "We could not be as candid with you as you were with us," Halifax regretfully told Theo Kordt after the Munich Conference.[93]

The shock had reverberations that extended far beyond the moment. Merely the news of Chamberlain's flight to Berchtesgaden had had a paralyzing effect on the conspirators; now the resistance as a whole suffered a collapse from which it never again really recovered. Granted that it had all along been burdened by scruples, conflicts of loyalty and problems with the oath of allegiance. Granted, too, that the participants, in their protracted nocturnal discussions and private soul-searchings, had repeatedly come up against the limits forged by upbringing and reinforced by habit: the limits where the call of conscience ended and overthrow of Hitler seemed like betrayal. The entire history of the German resistance displays this conflict, which robbed the actors of that ultimate resolution without which they could not succeed. But now, in addition, the conspirators were forced to the belief that Hitler could master any situation, that fortune was with him, that history was on his side.

"It would have been the end of Hitler," Goerdeler wrote to an American friend at this time. And though this statement leaves open a number of questions, the prediction that immediately followed was fulfilled to the letter: "In shrinking from a small risk, Mr. Chamberlain made war inevitable. The English and the French people will now have to defend their freedom with arms, unless they prefer a slave's existence."[94]

On the following day, toward 12:45 P.M. on September 29, the conference of the heads of government of England, France, Italy, and Germany began in Munich. Hitler had insisted on an immediate meeting because he was firmly determined to march into the Sudetenland on October 1. In order to synchronize policy with Mussolini, he went to Kufstein to meet Il Duce; and there is every indication that at this time he was still half determined to wreck the conference so that he could after all force through a total triumph. At any rate, over a map he explained to Mussolini his plans for a blitzkrieg against Czechoslovakia and the subsequent campaign against France. He let himself be persuaded, much against his will, to postpone these plans for the present, but left no doubt about his intentions: "Either the conference is successful in a short time, or the solution will take place by force of arms."[95]

However, there was no need for such sharp alternatives. The game of the Western powers, especially England, was to let Hitler know that he could have the Sudetenland without war; all four powers had long since conceded the justice of his claim, and the meeting served solely to draw up the text of this agreement.[96] The absence of any differences of opinion, as well as the sudden convocation of the conference, were the reasons for its unusually smooth course. After the exchange of greetings Hitler preceded the other participants into the meeting hall of the newly built Führerbau on Munich's Königsplatz. He dropped into one of the heavy armchairs around the low round table and invited his guests with a nervous gesture to take seats also. He was pale and excited, and initially copied Mussolini's self-assured manner, talking, laughing, or looking grim when Mussolini did. Chamberlain seemed careworn and aristocratic, Daladier quiet and uncomfortable.

Right at the start Hitler categorically rejected the request that representatives of Czechoslovakia participate. The powers remained among themselves, and soon Daladier, to whom Hitler turned in particular, was complaining about "the pigheadedness of Beneš" and the influence of the "warmongers in France."[97] Gradually ambassadors and advisers entered the room and took up positions around the negotiating table as auditors. There was a constant coming and going as the conference repeatedly dissolved into a number of individual conversations. Early in the afternoon Mussolini had presented the draft of an agreement that in reality had been worked out the night before by Göring, Neurath, and Weizsäcker in order to anticipate Ribbentrop, who was pushing for military action. That draft was the basis for the Munich Agreement, which was signed that night, between 2:00 and 3:00 A.M. It provided for occupation of the Sudeten region between October 1 and 10; a commission consisting of representatives of the four powers and Czechoslovakia were to work out the details. England and France undertook to guarantee the integrity of the diminished republic. All the participants seemed content for a moment; only French Ambassador François-Poncet exclaimed with a touch of uneasiness: *"Voilà comme la France traite les seuls alliés qui lui étaient restés fidèles."*[98] While secretaries and aides were busy making copies, the heads of state sat and stood around indecisively. Daladier had slumped exhausted into one of the armchairs; Mussolini chatted with Chamberlain. But Hitler, as one of the participants reported, stood motionless to one side, arms folded, staring into space.

His glumness continued throughout the next day. When Chamberlain called on him during the noon hours in his apartment on Prinzregentenstrasse, he was unusually monosyllabic and far from responding enthusiastically to Chamberlain's proposal for a further agreement that they henceforth settle problems by consultation. His irritation increased when he learned that the populace had hailed the British Prime Minister with loud ovations as he drove through Munich. Clearly, the experience of two days before in Berlin was being repeated: the people were not yet ready for the "first-class tasks" Hitler meant to set them. Chamberlain seemed to be the man of the hour.

But Hitler was upset not only by jealousy and the all too apparent apathy of the people toward the prospect of war. Under closer study his annoyance can be traced to far more complex causes. To be sure, the Munich Agreement was a personal triumph for him. Without the application of open force he had won an extensive area from a superior coalition. He had divested Czechoslovakia of its famous system of fortifications, dramatically improved his own strategic position, acquired new industries, and forced the hated President Beneš into exile. In fact "in the history of Europe there had not been for centuries . . . such profound changes without war."[99] To top it all, Hitler had won the approval of the selfsame great powers who were paying the piper. Once again he had created the classical Fascist constellation, the league between revolutionary force and established power. Significantly, shortly after the signing of the Munich Agreement, Czechoslovakia repudiated her pact with the Soviet Union and banned the Communist Party.

But all these triumphs seemed to Hitler too dearly bought. For he had been forced to set his signature to an agreement that could bind him, if not for the long run, yet long enough to upset his timetable and thus his grand design. He had wanted to march into Prague in the fall, just as he had marched into Vienna six months ago; and now he felt that he had been cheated out of both his timetable and the conqueror's glory. Schacht heard

565

him say: "That damned Chamberlain has spoiled my parade into Prague." And in January, 1939, shaking his head in astonishment, he told the Hungarian Foreign Minister that he had not thought it possible "that Czechoslovakia would be served up to me by her friends." As late as February, 1945, in those ruminations in the bunker, he discharged his rage against the "big capitalist philistines": "We should have started the war in 1938. That was our last chance to keep it localized. But they yielded to us everywhere. Like cowards they gave in to all our demands. That actually made it difficult to seize the initiative for hostilities. We missed a unique opportunity at Munich."[100]

Back of all this there was also his old tendency to drive matters to the extreme, to try the great gamble with his back to the wall. The Munich Agreement had been too facile to satisfy his nerves. He despised quick solutions and found, as he put it, "the prospect of being able to buy oneself off cheaply . . . dangerous." Again and again, his peculiar notions of fate overlaid his political sagacity. And apparently, from Munich on, he had determined how to deal with this refractory nation, which still resisted him in spite of all its cheering: he would bind it irrevocably to him by an extreme challenge sealed in blood.

Against this triple background of cool scheduling, the requirements of his nerves, and mythologizing conceptions of politics, Hitler became more and more bent on war. Chamberlain's complaisance had taken him "in a sense by surprise," he later almost apologized. He now felt nothing but comtempt for his opponents. Speaking to his generals he mocked the enemy as "little worms." In a speech in Weimar on November 6 he alluded, with unmistakable reference to Chamberlain, to the "umbrella types of our former bourgeois party world," and called the French Maginot Line the *limes* of a nation preparing to die.[101]

Hitler's bellicosity scarcely accorded with the real relations of forces and can be viewed as a first sign of his incipient loss of contact with reality. For today it is generally accepted that in the fall of 1938 he would have survived an armed conflict for only a few days. The opinion of Allied and German military experts, the documents and statistics, permit no room for doubt. General Jodl declared at the Nuremberg trial: "It was entirely out of the question, with five fighting divisions and seven armored divisions in the western fortification, which was nothing but a large construction site, to keep 100 French divisions at bay. From a military point of view that was impossible."[102] The softness of the Western powers therefore seems all the more incomprehensible. Beyond all the practical reasons for the policy of appeasement, their conduct seems most convincingly explained as Hitler explained it, as a form of political resignation. The peculiar compound of agreement with Hitler, submission to blackmail and sheer bewilderment, might possibly explain their betrayal of solemn obligations to their allies. But they were also betraying traditional European values, inasmuch as

Hitler proclaimed his hostility to those values in almost every one of his speeches, his decrees, and his actions. Oddly enough, the Western powers did not seem to have considered the long-range political repercussions, in particular, the devastating loss of prestige that Munich would inevitably produce. England and France lost almost all credibility. Henceforth their word, their pacts, seemed to be written in water; and soon other countries, especially those of Eastern Europe, began making their own deals with Hitler. But above all the Soviet Union did not forget that the Western powers had excluded it from Munich; and only four days after the conference the German ambassador in Moscow indicated that Stalin was "drawing conclusions" and would be reviewing his foreign policy.

Meanwhile, Chamberlain and Daladier had returned to their capitals. But instead of the outraged demonstrations they had expected, they were lustily cheered as though, a Foreign Office official commented, the people were "celebrating a great victory over an enemy, instead of the betrayal of a small ally." Depressed, Daladier pointed to the cheering thousands and whispered: "The idiots!" Chamberlain, more naïve and more optimistic than his French colleague, waved a sheet of paper in the air on his arrival in London and announced "peace in our time." It is difficult in retrospect to empathize with the spontaneous feeling of relief that once more united Europe; it is difficult to summon up respect for the illusions of the time. In London the crowd in front of 10 Downing Street began singing "For He's a Jolly Good Fellow." *Paris Soir* offered Chamberlain "a patch of French soil" for fishing, and commented that it would be impossible "to imagine a more fruitful symbol of peace."[103] When, in the subsequent House of Commons debate, Winston Churchill began his speech with the words, "We have sustained a total unmitigated defeat," there was a great outcry.

The German troops, in consonance with the agreement, moved into the Sudetenland. On October 3 Hitler crossed the former German frontier in a four-wheel-drive type of Mercedes. At the same time, Wenzel Jaksch, leader of the Sudeten German Social Democrats, flew to London. As was to be the practice in later years, the army units had been followed promptly by the Security Service and Gestapo squads in order to "begin at once with purging the liberated territories of Marxist traitors to the people and other enemies of the State." Jaksch asked for visas and all kinds of aid for his threatened friends. Lord Runciman assured him the mayor of London was setting up a fund for the persecuted and that he personally would contribute. The London *Times* published photographs of the German troops marching into the Sudetenland amid a cascade of flowers and greeted by cheering crowds. But Editor in Chief Geoffrey Dawson refused to publish shots of those who were fleeing from these troops. Wenzel Jaksch was given no visas. The Poles and Hungarians now snatched sizable portions of the abandoned, mutilated country. The history of that autumn is replete with acts of blindness, egotism, weakness, and treachery. Those of Wenzel

567

Jaksch's friends who managed to hide out within the country were shortly thereafter handed over to Germany by the new Prague government.

Hitler's vexation at the outcome of the Munich conference sharpened his impatience. Only ten days later he was after Keitel with a top secret list of questions about the military potentialities of the Reich. On October 21 he gave orders for the military "liquidation of the remainder of Czechoslovakia" and for "taking possession of the Memel region." In a postscript dated November 24 he also ordered preparations for the occupation of Danzig. Simultaneously, he encouraged the Slovak nationalists to adopt the role of the Sudeten Germans in the new Czech republic and thus speed the further disintegration of Czechoslovakia from within.

He also embarked on a campaign for intensified psychological mobilization of the nation, for he had recently been given reason to doubt the public's will. To be sure, there was great enthusiasm in Germany for the bloodless conquests. Hitler's prestige had once again risen to dizzying heights. But he himself realized that the rejoicing held a considerable degree of relief that war had been avoided. He found the pretext he needed when, early in November, a Jewish exile shot down Legation Secretary Ernst vom Rath in the German Embassy in Paris. Out of an assassination prompted by personal motives Hitler quickly constructed one of those "assaults of world Jewry" which he still counted on to rouse and unite the public. Solemn memorial services, complete with music by Beethoven and statements by all and sundry, were held even in schools and factories. For the last time the SA came forth in its once usual but long since abandoned role of exponent of blind popular fury. On the night of November 9, 1938, synagogues went up in flames all over Germany, Jewish homes were devastated, stores pillaged, nearly a hundred persons killed, and some 20,000 arrested. *Das Schwarze Korps,* the SS newspaper, was already advocating extermination "with fire and sword" as the "actual and final end of Jewry in Germany."

But the inveterate bourgeois instincts of the populace could only take alarm at excesses supposedly produced by street mobs; this sort of thing revived memories of the years of disorder and lawlessness.[104] It was a further symptom of Hitler's galloping loss of contact with reality that he could believe his own most powerful emotions would necessarily yield the most powerful psychological effect upon the people. The contrast between his own "Balkan" mania about the Jews and lukewarm German anti-Semitism was now growing more and more patent. Significantly, the campaign was successful only in Vienna.

The apathy of the masses drove him to increase his efforts. The period after the Munich conference was marked by an intensified propaganda drive, in which Hitler himself soon took part with mounting vehemence. An irritable speech at Saarbrücken on October 9, a Weimar speech on

November 6, a speech in Munich on November 8, even the major summing up of 1938, compounding pride, hate, nervousness, and self-assurance, formed part of this campaign. In the latter he called for the "coherence of the racial body politic" and once more attacked Jewry, prophesying the "annihilation of the Jewish race in Europe."

His secret addresses of the same period to German newspaper editors were motivated by the need to swing the press away from his tactics of pledging peace and appealing for reconciliation—whose bad effects he had observed in Berlin and Munich—to a tone of aggressive resolution. The speech was practically an order for psychological mobilization. Again and again, Hitler stressed the necessity of having behind him "a German people strong in faith, united, self-assured, confident." At the same time he vented his wrath upon his critics and the seditious intellectuals:

When I look at the intellectual classes among us, well, unfortunately we need them, you know; otherwise we might some day, I don't know, exterminate them or something. But unfortunately we need them. Now then, when I look at these intellectual classes and call to mind their behavior and consider it, the way they've behaved toward me, toward our work, I become almost fearful. For ever since I have been politically active and especially since I have led the Reich, I have had nothing but successes. And nevertheless this crowd floats around in an abominable, disgusting way. What would happen if we had a failure for once? Because that too is possible, gentlemen. Then how would this flock of chickens act up? . . . In the past it was my greatest pride to have built up a party which stood pigheadedly and fanatically behind me even in times of setbacks, stood fanatically especially in such times. That was my greatest pride and . . . we must educate the whole nation to that attitude. It must be trained to absolute, pigheaded, unquestioning, confident faith that in the end we will achieve everything that is necessary. We can do that, we can succeed in doing that, only by a continuous appeal to the vigor of the nation, by emphasizing the affirmative values of a people and as far as possible omitting the so-called negative sides.

To that end it is also necessary that the press in particular blindly adhere to the principle: What the leadership does is right! . . . Only in that way will we free the people from, I would put it this way, from a doubt that can only make the people unhappy. The masses do not want to be burdened with problems. The masses desire only one thing: to be well led and to be able to trust the leadership, and they want the leaders not to quarrel among themselves, but to appear before them unified. Believe me, I know precisely what I am talking about, the German people will regard nothing with greater joy than when I, for example, let's say on a day like November 9 [anniversary of the Beer Hall Putsch] go out on the street and all my associates are standing beside me, and the people say: "That's so-and-so and that's so-and-so and that's so-and-so and that's so-and-so." And these people all feel so secure at the idea that everyone sticks together, all follow the Führer, and the Führer sticks to all these men; these are our idols. Maybe some intellectuals won't understand this at all. But these ordinary people out there . . . that's what they want! That has been so in past German history too. The people are always glad whenever a few stick together up on top; it makes it easier for the people to stick together down at the bottom.[105]

The pace of events themselves, which Hitler deliberately accelerated after the Munich conference, also formed part of the process of psychological mobilization. At times the observer had to ask himself whether this was breathless politics or whether breathlessness was assuming political form. Week after week the pressures against defenseless Czechoslovakia increased from within and from without. On March 13 Hitler summoned the Slovak nationalist leader Tiso to Berlin and pressed him to defect from Prague. A day later, at a Parliament session in Bratislava, the Slovak Declaration of Independence was read aloud; it had been drafted by Ribbentrop and handed to Tiso already translated into Slovak. The evening of that same day Czech President Hácha, accompanied by Foreign Minister Chvalkovsky, arrived in Berlin. There he was put through a special ordeal which Hitler later gloatingly called "Háchaizing." The guests were received with all the honors required by protocol; but only after a nerve-wracking waiting period, in the course of which they vainly tried to discover the subject to be negotiated, were they admitted to the chancellery. It was by then between one and two o'clock in the morning. Hácha, old and sickly, had to tramp wearily through the endless corridors and halls of the newly built chancellery before he reached Hitler, who sat at his desk in the semidarkness of a gigantic study illuminated only by a few bronze floor lamps. Beside him were the pompous Göring and once more Hitler's bogeyman, General Keitel. The President's opening remarks were steeped in the servility of a country fully aware of her own haplessness. The minutes of the meeting note:

President Hácha greets the Führer and expresses his gratitude for being received by him. He said he had long desired to meet the man whose wonderful ideas he had frequently read and followed. He himself had until recently been an unknown. He had never dealt with politics, but had been merely a judicial official in the Viennese administrative apparatus and . . . had been summoned to Prague in 1918 and in 1925 had become Chief Justice of the Supreme Court. As such he had had no relations with the politicians, or as he preferred to call them, the "politicos". . . . He had never been persona grata. He'd met President Masaryk only once a year at a dinner for judges, and Beneš even more rarely. The one time he had had a meeting with Beneš, they had quarreled. Moreover, the whole regime had been alien to him, so that immediately after the great change he had asked himself whether independence had even been at all good for Czechoslovakia. This past autumn the task had fallen to him to head the State. He was an old man . . . and he believed that the fate of Czechoslovakia was well safeguarded in the Führer's hands.[106]

When Hácha concluded this astonishing speech with the request that his people nevertheless be accorded the right to their own national existence, Hitler launched into one of his rambling monologues. He complained about

570

the oft-demonstrated hostility of the Czechs, the impotence of the present government to control domestic conditions. He referred to the continuing Beneš spirit, and finally heaped reproach on reproach upon his guests, who sat there silent and "as if turned to stone," with "only their eyes . . . showing they were alive." His patience was now exhausted, he continued.

At six o'clock the German army would be advancing into Czechia from all sides, and the German air force would occupy the airfields. There were two possibilities. The first was that the advance of the German troops would develop into a battle. In that case this resistance would be broken by force of arms, using all means. The other possibility was that the entry of the German troops would take place in a tolerable manner; in that case the Führer would find it easy, when reshaping Czech conditions, to permit Czechoslovakia a generous life of her own, autonomy and a degree of national freedom. . . .

This was the reason he had asked Hácha to come here. This invitation was the last kindness he would be able to show the Czech people. . . . The hours were passing. At six o'clock the troops would march in. He was almost ashamed to say that there was a German division to match every Czech division. The fact was that the military operation was no small one; it had been organized on a very liberal scale.

Hácha, in a virtually extinct voice, asked how with four hours at his disposal he could arrange to restrain the entire Czech nation from offering resistance. Hitler replied haughtily:

The military machine that was now rolling could not be stopped. Let him get in touch with his officials in Prague. It was a major decision, but he saw dawning the possibility of a long period of peace between the two peoples. If the decision were otherwise, he saw the annihilation of Czechoslovakia. . . . His own decision was irrevocable. Everyone knew what a decision of the Führer meant.

Dismissed from Hitler's study shortly after two o'clock, Hácha and Chvalkovsky tried to get through to Prague by telephone. Göring pointed out that time was running out and his planes would soon be bombing the Czech capital. With rough good humor he began describing the destruction, when the President suffered a heart attack. For a moment the group standing around him feared the worst. "Tomorrow the whole world will be saying he was murdered during the night in the chancellery," one of those present noted. But Dr. Morell, held in readiness by a careful stage manager, helped to revive the broken man. Thus the authorities in Prague were given their instructions not to resist the German invasion, and shortly before four o'clock in the morning Hácha signed the document of submission, by which he "placed the fate of the Czech people and country in the hands of the Führer of the German Reich."

As soon as Hácha had left, Hitler lost all his customary control. Exuberantly he rushed into the room where his secretaries were sitting and

571

invited them to kiss him. "Girls," he cried, "Hácha has signed. This is the greatest day of my life. I shall be known as the greatest German in history."[107] Two hours later his troops crossed the border. The first formations arrived in Prague, in a snowstorm, by nine o'clock. Once more cheering people were waiting on the sidewalks, but they were only a minority; the majority turned away or stood mute, tears of helplessness and rage in their eyes. That same evening Hitler himself entered the city and spent the night in Hradschin Palace. "Czechoslovakia," he announced, drunk with victory, "has herewith ceased to exist." It had all been the work of two days. When on March 18 the British and French ambassadors submitted protest notes in Berlin, Hitler had already set up the Protectorate of Bohemia and Moravia. As a placatory gesture he placed at its head Konstantin von Neurath, then Minister of Foreign Affairs, now "protector" of Bohemia and Moravia, who was regarded as a moderate. He had arranged a protective treaty with Slovakia and was already on his way back to Berlin. It seemed as if Mussolini's remark shortly before Munich was once again proving true: "The democracies exist to swallow toads."

Nevertheless, the seizure of Prague ushered in the turning point. The Western powers were too deeply disillusioned; they felt hoodwinked, their good will and patience abused. As late as March 10, Chamberlain had told some journalists that the danger of war was abating and a new era of *détente* dawning. Now, on March 17, he spoke in Birmingham of a shock more severe than any before, referred to the many breaches of pledges inherent in the action against Prague, and finally asked: "Is this the end of an old adventure or is it the beginning of a new?" On the same day he recalled Ambassador Henderson from Berlin for an indefinite time. Lord Halifax, for his part, declared that he could well understand Hitler's preference for bloodless triumphs, but the next time blood would have to be spilled.[108]

But the occupation of Prague was a turning point only for Western policy. In the apologias of the appeasers, and in the attempts at self-exoneration by German accomplices of the regime, the argument constantly recurs that it was Hitler who changed with his entry into Prague; that only then had he set out on the road of injustice and radically expanded his valid revisionist aims; that after Prague it was no longer the right of self-determination but the glory of a conqueror that became his goal. We have since learned, however, how such considerations miss Hitler's motives and intentions, and in fact the very core of his nature. He had long ago decided on his course. Prague was only a tactical problem for him, and the Moldau was certainly not his Rubicon.

And yet, the undertaking was an act of self-revelation. Colonel Jodl had once smugly noted, in the days of continuous triumphs in foreign policy: "This kind of politics is new for Europe." In fact, the dynamic conjunction

572

of threats, flatteries, pledges of peacefulness and acts of violence applied by Hitler was an unfamiliar, numbing experience; and the Western statesmen might well have been deceived for a while about Hitler's true intentions. Lord Halifax confessed his own confusion when he compared trying to make out what Hitler was up to, to the groping of a blind man seeking a way across a swamp while everyone on the shores was shouting different warnings about the next danger zone. Hitler's operation against Prague, however, had finally dispelled the fog. For the first time Chamberlain and his French counterparts seemed to begin to perceive what Hugenberg had had to realize: this man could not be controlled and tamed—except, perhaps, by force.

Prague signified another kind of turning point in Hitler's career: it was, after almost fifteen years, his first grave mistake. Tactically, he had achieved his victories by his ability to give all situations an ambiguous character, so that his opponents' front and their will to resist was splintered. Now for the first time he was acting in an unequivocal manner. Whereas until then he had always assumed dual roles and had played, as an antagonist, the part of a secret ally, or provoked conditions while alleging that he was opposing them, he now revealed his innermost nature without ambiguity. In Munich he had once more, although reluctantly, set up the "Fascist constellation," that is to say, achieved a victory over one enemy with the help of the other. The assault on the Jews in November, 1938, seemed to be his first break with this formula. Prague wiped out any doubt that he was the universal enemy.

It was inherent in his tactics that the very first mistake was irreparable. Hitler himself later recognized the fateful significance of his seizing Prague. But his impatience, his arrogance, and his far-flung plans left him no choice. On the day after the occupation of Prague he ordered Goebbels to give the following instructions to the press: "The employment of the term 'Greater German Empire' is undesirable . . . (and) reserved for later occasions." And, in April, when he was preparing to celebrate his fiftieth birthday, he ordered Ribbentrop "to invite a number of foreign guests, among them as many cowardly civilians and democrats as possible, and I will show them a parade of the most modern of all armed forces."[109]

573

Chapter 4

The thought of striking was always in me.

Adolf Hitler

UNLEASHING THE WAR

From the spring of 1939 Hitler exhibited a noteworthy inability to break his own momentum. The infallible sense of tempo he had shown only a few years before, in the course of taking power, now began to desert him and to give way to a neurasthenic craving for sheer movement. Faced with the weakness and disunity of his antagonists on the European scene, he undoubtedly could have won all his revisionist demands and probably some of his more far-reaching *Lebensraum* plans by means of his tactic of enlisting the co-operation of the conservative powers. Now he abandoned the tactic. The regime's propaganda announced that the Führer's genius consisted in his ability to wait. But now, whether out of arrogance, whether corrupted by the effectiveness of "non-negotiable demands," or whether out of frantic restiveness—Hitler no longer waited.

Only a week after the occupation of Prague he boarded the cruiser *Deutschland* in Swinemünde and sailed toward Memel. This small seaport on the northern frontier of East Prussia had been annexed by Lithuania in 1919, in the confusion of the immediate postwar period. A demand for its return was only a matter of time. But in order to lend dramatic verve and proof of his imperiousness to the process of recovering the city, Hitler informed the Lithuanian government in Vilna on March 21 that its envoys were to arrive in Berlin "tomorrow by special plane" to sign the protocol of cession. Meanwhile, he himself, with the reply still in doubt, set out for Memel. And while Ribbentrop "Háchaed" the Lithuanian delegation, Hitler—seasick and in ill humor—held two impatient radio conversations from on board the *Deutschland*. He demanded to know whether he would be able to enter the city peaceably or would have to force his way in with the ship's guns. On March 23, toward half past one in the morning, Lithuania consented to the cession, and at noon Hitler once again held one of his loudly cheered entries into Memel.

Two days earlier Ribbentrop had summoned Josef Lipski, the Polish ambassador in Berlin, to meet with him, and had proposed negotiations on a comprehensive German-Polish settlement. Ribbentrop returned with some emphasis to demands he had made several times before, including the return of the Free City of Danzig and the building of an extraterritorial road and rail link across the Polish Corridor. In return he offered to extend the 1934 Nonaggression Pact for twenty-five years and to guarantee formally Poland's borders. How seriously the offer was meant is evident from the simultaneous attempt to enlist Poland in the Anti-Comintern Pact. In general Ribbentrop's overtures were aimed at striking a bargain with a "distinctly anti-Soviet tendency." One draft of a Foreign Office note, for example, rather brazenly offered Warsaw, as its reward for increased cooperation, the prospect of receiving possession of the Ukraine. Following this line, Hitler, in a conversation with Brauchitsch on March 25 rejected a violent solution of the Danzig question but thought a military action against Poland under "specially favorable political preconditions" worth considering.

There was a reason for the curious indifference with which Hitler left open the question of conquest or alliance. Actually it was not Danzig he was really concerned about. The city served him as the pretext for arranging a dialogue and, as he hoped, a deal with Poland. With some justice he considered his offer generous; it gave Poland the prospect of a gigantic acquisition in return for a meager concession. For Danzig was indeed a German city; its separation from the Reich had been imposed by the Treaty of Versailles in order to satisfy a Polish need for prestige that had steadily ebbed with the passing years. In the long run, Poland could have hardly held on to the city. The demand for a connecting link to East Prussia was likewise a relatively fair effort to amend the decision that had separated East Prussia from the Reich. What Hitler really wanted was related to the ultimate grand goal of all his policies: the winning of new living space.

Among the essentials of his planned march of conquest was a common boundary with the Soviet Union. Until that was attained, Germany was cut off from the Russian steppes by a belt of countries extending from the Baltic to the Black Sea. One or several of these must place at his disposal the area for military deployment so that he could get at Russia. Otherwise the war could not be begun.

Theoretically, Hitler could meet this condition in three possible ways. He could win the intervening states by alliances; he could annex some of them; or he could let the Soviet Union annex some, thus moving her border up to Germany. In the course of the following months Hitler made use of all these options. The alertness and iciness with which he switched, while a speechless world looked on, from one to the other, showed him for the last time at the height of his tactical intelligence.

After the occupation of Prague, which had so patently put the patience of the Western powers to a hard test, he appeared determined to evoke no new tensions for the time being and to return to the first method: finding an ally against the Soviet Union. For a serious conflict with the West was bound to endanger all his expansionist goals. Among the intervening countries, Poland seemed best suited to his plans. Poland was a country with an authoritarian government and strong anti-Communist, anti-Russian, and even anti-Semitic tendencies. Thus there were "solid common factors"[110] on which an expansionist partnership under German leadership might be founded. Moreover, Hitler himself was partly responsible for Poland's recent good relationship with Germany, additionally secured by a non-aggression pact.

Consequently, far more than an ordinary swap, far more than satisfaction of the regime's desire to revise the terms of the Versailles Treaty depended on the Polish government's reply to Ribbentrop's proposals. For Hitler, his whole *Lebensraum* idea was at stake. It is this aspect which explains the obstinacy and the consistent radical spirit that he manifested on this question. He saw this as a question of all or nothing.

Poland, however, was extremely vexed by the German proposals. For they endangered the foundations of her whole previous policy and made her critical situation even more critical. The country had hitherto found safety by maintaining the strictest equilibrium between her two neighboring giants, Germany and Russia. Their temporary impotence in 1919 had made possible the establishment of a Polish state, and subsequently Poland had enlarged her territory at the expense of these two countries. And if the Poles had learned in the course of their long history that they had as much reason to fear the friendship of these two neighbors as their hostility—the lesson was now more important than ever. The German offer ran strictly counter to this fundament of Polish policy.

It was an exceedingly perilous situation that demanded more prudence and adaptability than a romantic people, which for centuries had felt abused, could possibly summon up. Faced with a choice between its two neighbors, Poland on the whole inclined slightly more toward Germany. But the new Germany was also more restive and greedy than a Soviet Union involved in internal power struggles, purges, and doctrinaire disputes. Polish Foreign Minister Josef Beck, a man given to intrigues and engaged in reckless juggling, complicated the situation still further by pressing ambitious plans for a "third Europe." His idea was to establish a neutral block of powers, under Polish leadership, extending from the Baltic to the Hellespont. And he thought that he could derive advantages for Poland from Hitler's aggressive policy. His ostensibly pro-German policy secretly aimed at "methodically reinforcing the Germans in their errors," and he hoped "not only for the unconditional integration of Danzig into Polish territory, but, also, far beyond that, for all of East Prussia, Silesia, even Pomerania . . . our Pomerania," as Poland's propagandists now began saying more and more frequently and more openly.[111]

These secret Polish dreams of becoming a great power underlay the unexpectedly sharp refusal with which Beck finally rebuffed Hitler's proposal. Simultaneously, he mobilized a few divisions in the border area. In strictly objective terms he might not even have considered the German demands unjustified. Danzig, he admitted, was merely a kind of symbol for Poland.[112] But every concession must seem like a reversal of the basic aims of Polish policy, the effort to attain both equilibrium of power in Europe and a limited degree of hegemony for Poland herself. For this reason, too, the only tactical way out of the situation—gaining time by partial concessions—was barred. Moreover, Beck and the Warsaw government feared that Hitler's first demands would be followed by an endless succession of new ones, so that only an unequivocal refusal could preserve the integrity of Poland. To sum up, Poland found herself confronted with her typical situation: she had no choice.

This impasse was fully exposed when Beck, on March 23, 1939, rejected the British proposal of consultative agreement between Great Britain, France, the Soviet Union, and Poland. He did not want to enter any group to which the Soviet Union belonged. He had rejected an anti-Soviet alliance with Germany and was still less prepared to accept an anti-German alliance with the Soviet Union. What he failed to see was that given the acuteness of the situation Hitler had created, he had to choose. From now on his only protection against the Soviet Union was the dread protection of Germany; and only the aid of the Soviet Union could save him from the German demands. He knew quite well—and the Soviet Union confirmed his knowledge in a Tass communiqué of March 22—that such aid meant the equivalent of suicide for Poland. But Beck was prepared to face destruction rather than to accept protection from Poland's old oppressor to the East. Politically, he based his attitude on the dogma of the insurmountable antagonism between Germany and the Soviet Union. But by rejecting both his neighbors with equal vehemence he unwittingly created the conditions for a rapprochement between them. The front for the outbreak of the war was beginning to take shape.

Simultaneously, Beck was reassured by the attitude of the British government. Still indignant at Hitler's occupation of Prague, Chamberlain at the end of March decided upon a desperate step. Acting on the basis of several unconfirmed reports of an impending German *coup de main* against Danzig, he asked Warsaw whether Poland had any objections to a British declaration guaranteeing her integrity. Despite the warnings of some of his more perspicacious fellow countrymen, who regarded it as "childish, naïve and at the same time unfair to propose to a country in Poland's situation that it compromise its relations with so strong a neighbor as Germany,"[113] Beck promptly consented. He later declared that he needed less time to

577

make his decision than was needed to flip the ash from a cigarette. On March 31 Chamberlain made his famous statement in the House of Commons: England and France "in the event of any action which clearly threatened Polish independence . . . would feel themselves bound at once to lend the Polish Government all support in their power."[114]

This promise of assistance was the great turning point in the policies of that phase. England had decided unconditionally to oppose Hitler's expansionist ambitions wherever and whenever it encountered them. It was an extraordinary and impressive decision, though one as deficient in wisdom as it was superabundant in dramatic consequences. Its origins in the emotions of a disappointed man were all too apparent, and critics quickly pointed to the inherent flaws of such a guarantee: it required no counterguarantee from the Poles if Hitler attacked some other European country, and did not oblige the Poles to conduct negotiations for aid with the Soviet Union, whose partnership would necessarily be of crucial importance. Moreover, the grave question of war or peace for Europe was being given into the keeping of a handful of stubborn, nationalistic men in Warsaw who a short while ago had made common cause with Hitler against Czechoslovakia, betraying the very principles of independence they were now so anxiously appealing to.

Chamberlain's decision of March 31 forced Hitler to reassess his position. He considered the British guarantee a warrant for the eccentric Poles to involve Germany in military undertakings whenever it pleased them. But far more crucial in his eyes was that England had now at last revealed herself as an enemy. She would not allow him to move freely against the East and was evidently resolved to push matters to the ultimate confrontation. He could not obtain the grand mandate of the bourgeois powers to proceed against the Soviet Union. Consequently, his whole strategic concept was threatened. It seems clear that this last day of March gave him the final impetus to that radical turn which had been hinted at in various remarks since the end of 1936, but which had been repeatedly postponed. Now he actually proceeded "to the liquidation of the work of his youth," as he had phrased it a short while before. He abandoned his courtship of England, which had rejected him. He concluded correctly that whenever he set out to conquer new *Lebensraum* in the East he would clash with England. Consequently, to achieve his central idea he would first have to defeat Great Britain. If he wished to avoid a two-front war, one more thing followed: he would have to come to a temporary arrangement with the future enemy. It so happened that the conduct of Poland provided him with an opening. An alliance with the Soviet Union was now within reach.

Hitler's policy during the following months was one grand, large-scale maneuver to bring about this swing and so shape the antagonistic fronts in Europe to accord with his purposes. Admiral Canaris, who happened to be present when news of the British guaranty to Poland arrived, reported Hitler's furious outburst: "I'll cook them a stew that they'll choke on."[115]

The following day he utilized the launching of the *Tirpitz* in Wilhelms-haven for a violent speech against the British "encirclement policy." He issued a dire warning to the "satellite states whose task is to be set against Germany" and indicated that he was about to terminate the Anglo-German Naval Treaty:

I once made an agreement with England—namely, the Naval Treaty. It is based on the earnest desire which we all share never to have to go to war against England. But this wish can only be a mutual one.

If this wish no longer exists in England, then the practical preconditions for this agreement are removed and Germany also would accept this very calmly. We are self-assured because we are strong, and we are strong because we are united. . . . Those who are powerless lose the right to live![116]

Everyone who met Hitler during this period has reported him flaring up furiously against England.[117] Early in April the Propaganda Minister issued a directive whose tenor was that England must be represented as Germany's most dangerous adversary. Simultaneously Hitler broke off his negotiations with Poland. He ordered State Secretary von Weizsäcker to inform the Poles that the offer had been unique and would not be repeated. At the same time new demands, as yet unspecified, were hinted at. And, as if to stress the gravity of the situation, Hitler suddenly once more expressed interest in the German minorities in Poland, whom he had overlooked for years during which they, together with the Jews, had been the favorite victims of the Poles' resentments and outbreaks of chauvinistic arrogance.

But even more can be read from the secret message Hitler issued to the armed forces on April 3, setting up a new operation with the code name "Case White":

The present attitude of Poland requires . . . the initiation of military prepa-rations to remove, if necessary, any threat from this direction for all future time.

The German relationship to Poland continues to be governed by the principle of avoiding trouble. Poland's policy toward Germany hitherto has been based upon the same principle, but if she should change it and adopt an attitude threatening to the Reich, a final reckoning may become requisite without regard to the existing treaty.

The aim then will be to shatter the Polish forces and create in the East a situation in keeping with the requirements of national defense. The Free State of Danzig will be declared territory of the German Reich by the beginning of the conflict at the latest. . . .

The major goals in the build-up of the German Armed Forces will continue to be determined by the hostility of the western democracies. "Case White" merely forms a precautionary supplement to the preparations.[118]

A note appended to the document referred to a directive from Hitler to "make the preparations in such a way that execution will be possible at any time from September 1, 1939, on."

Although outwardly everything remained unchanged, Europe now

579

seemed to be gripped by a nervous tension. In Germany a propaganda campaign translated Hitler's aggressive remarks into screeching agitation. In Poland, and for the first time in England also, there were more or less violent anti-German demonstrations. And, as if Italian pride forbade that country's keeping out of the bickerings and brawls of Europe, Mussolini now reminded the world of his existence by a great show of Italy's strength and courage. On April 7, 1939, he sent his troops to attack little Albania, and in imitation of his envied German model set up a protectorate over the country. Shortly before in Berlin he had let it be known that he felt called upon "to acquire something" also.

The result was that the Western powers now issued guarantees of aid to Greece and Rumania also. Germany then warned the smaller European countries against "English lures," thus generating more nervousness. Whereupon the United States, after years of disillusioned retreat into isolation from international affairs, let its voice be heard once more. On April 14 President Roosevelt addressed a letter to Hitler and Mussolini calling upon them to give a ten-year guarantee of nonaggression to thirty-one countries, which he mentioned by name.

Mussolini at first refused to acknowledge receipt of the message. Hitler, however, was delighted at this unexpected challenge. Ever since he had first come forth as a speaker, his oratorical temperament had always responded best in argument. The naïve demagoguery of Roosevelt's appeal, with its listing of countries with which neither Germany nor Italy had common borders or differences of opinion (among them Eire, Spain, Turkey, Iraq, Syria, Palestine, Egypt, and Persia), offered Hitler an easy target. He announced through DNB, the German News Agency, that he would deliver his reply in a speech to the Reichstag.

Hitler's speech of April 28 was one of the recognizable milestones along the course of the European crisis. It marked the destination as war. Following Hitler's tried-and-true pattern, it was full of avowals of peace, loud in asseverations of innocence, and silent about all his real intentions. Once again Hitler tried to commend himself as the spokesman for a program of limited and moderate revisions in the East; but attacks upon the Soviet Union as evil incarnate were noticeably absent. Simultaneously he displayed all his sarcasm, all his apparent logic and hypnotic persuasiveness, so that many a listener called the speech "probably the most brilliant oration he ever gave."[119] He combined his attacks upon England with expressions of admiration and friendly feelings for her. He assured Poland that despite all his disappointments with her he was ready to continue negotiations. And he ranted against the "international warmongers," the "provocateurs," and "enemies of peace" whose aim was to recruit "mercenaries of the European democracies against Germany." He denounced the "jugglers of Versailles who, either in their maliciousness or their thoughtlessness, placed 100 powder barrels all over Europe."

580

Finally he came to the climax, his answer to the American President, which was greeted by the deputies with tempestuous enthusiasm and roars of laughter. Hitler divided Roosevelt's letter into twenty-one points, which he answered in sections. The American President, he said, had pointed out to him the general fear of war; but Germany had participated in none of the fourteen wars that had been waged since 1919—"but in which the States of the 'Western Hemisphere,' in whose name President Roosevelt speaks, were indeed concerned." Germany also had nothing to do with the twenty-six "violent interventions and sanctions carried through by means of bloodshed and force" during that period, whereas the United States, for example, had carried out military interventions in six cases. Furthermore, the President had pleaded for the solution of all problems at the conference table, but America herself had given sharpest expression to her mistrust in the effectiveness of conferences by leaving the League of Nations, "the greatest conference of all time"—from which Germany, in violation of Wilson's pledge, was for a long time excluded. In spite of this "most bitter experience," Germany had not followed the example of the United States until his, Hitler's, administration.

The President was also making himself the advocate of disarmament. But Germany had, for all times, learned her lesson, ever since she had appeared unarmed at the conference table in Versailles and been "subjected to even greater degradation than can ever have been inflicted on the chieftains of the Sioux tribes." Roosevelt was taking so great an interest in Germany's intentions in Europe that the question necessarily arose what aims American foreign policy was pursuing, for example, toward Central or South American countries. The President would surely regard such a question as tactless and refer to the Monroe Doctrine. And although it was surely tempting for the German government to behave in the same way, it had nevertheless addressed all the countries mentioned by Roosevelt and asked whether they felt threatened by Germany. "The reply was in all cases negative, in some instances strongly so." However, Hitler continued, "it is true that I could not cause inquiries to be made of certain of the States and nations mentioned because they themselves—as, for example, Syria—are at present not in possession of their freedom, but are occupied and consequently deprived of their rights by the military agents of the democratic States." Then he continued:

Mr. Roosevelt! I fully understand that the vastness of your nation and the immense wealth of your country allow you to feel responsible for the history of the whole world and for the history of all nations. I, sir, am placed in a much more modest and smaller sphere. . . . I cannot feel myself responsible for the fate of the world, as this world took no interest in the pitiful state of my own people.

I have regarded myself as called upon by Providence to serve my own people alone and to deliver them from their frightful misery. . . .

581

I have conquered chaos in Germany, re-established order and enormously increased production in all branches of our national economy by strenuous efforts. . . . I have succeeded in finding useful work once more for the whole of 7,000,000 unemployed, who so appeal to the hearts of us all. . . . I [have] united the German people politically, but I have also re-armed them; I have also endeavored to destroy sheet by sheet that Treaty which in its 448 articles contains the vilest oppression which peoples and human beings have ever been expected to put up with.

I have brought back to the Reich provinces stolen from us in 1919; I have led back to their native country millions of Germans who were torn away from us and were in misery; I have re-established the historic unity of German living space and, Mr. Roosevelt, I have endeavored to attain all this without spilling blood and without bringing to my people, and consequently to others, the misery of war.

I, who twenty-one years ago was an unknown worker and soldier of my people, have attained this, Mr. Roosevelt, by my own energy. . . . You, Mr. Roosevelt, have a much easier task in comparison. You became President of the United States in 1933 when I became Chancellor of the Reich. In other words, from the very outset you stepped to the head of one of the largest and wealthiest States in the world. . . . Conditions prevailing in your country are on such a large scale that you can find time and leisure to give your attention to universal problems. . . . My world, Mr. Roosevelt . . . is unfortunately much smaller . . . for it is limited to my people.

I believe, however, that this is the way in which I can be of the most service to that for which we are all concerned, namely, the justice, well-being, progress and peace of the whole human community.[120]

This speech contained more than mere rhetorical effects. Implicit in it was a remarkable political decision. Two days earlier England had introduced conscription; and in reply Hitler now abrogated the Anglo-German Naval Treaty and the Nonaggression Pact with Poland. Dramatic though they seemed, these declarations had no immediate consequences; they were only a gesture. But with that gesture Hitler liquidated the pledge contained in all such agreements, the pledge to settle disputes peaceably. In fact the speech as a whole might best be compared with the Western powers' guarantee of Poland, or with Roosevelt's intervention. It was a moral declaration of war. The adversaries were taking up their positions.

Hitler had delivered his speech on April 28. On April 30 the British ambassador in Paris asked French Foreign Minister Georges Bonnet what he thought about Hitler's somewhat uncanny silence in regard to Russia. And in fact from this moment on the Soviet Union, hitherto merely a mighty shadow on the periphery, began to move into the center of events. Hitler's reticence was as much a symptom of the changing situation as the sudden activity of the Western powers toward Russia. A secret race for alliances was beginning, heightened on all sides by distrust, fear, and jealousy. Upon the outcome of that race the question of war or peace would be decided.

The initial move had come on April 15, with an offer by France to the Soviet Union to adjust the treaty of 1935 to the changed world situation. For the system of collective security, which the appeasers had allowed Hitler to wrest from them during the period of lovely illusions and which they were now hurriedly trying to reinstate, could have a deterrent effect only if Moscow participated, thus convincing Hitler of the hopelessness of resorting to force. From the start the negotiations, into which England too soon entered, suffered from the mutual distrust of the participants. With reason, Stalin doubted the Western powers' determination to resist, while the Western powers in their turn, and above all Chamberlain, could never overcome the deeply rooted suspicion that the bourgeois world felt for the land of world revolution. Nor were their advances of any great interest to Moscow, since clumsy diplomacy had obligated the West to defend the entire girdle outside the Soviet Union from the Baltic to the Black Sea.

In addition, the negotiating position of the Western powers was hampered by the constant efforts of the Eastern European nations to interfere. They passionately opposed any alliance with the Soviet Union and regarded any guarantees by her as sealing their own doom. In fact the Western diplomats were soon forced to realize that Moscow could be won over only by considerable territorial, strategic, and political concessions that did not look so very dissimilar to the ones they wanted to refuse, with the Soviet Union's aid, to grant Hitler. If the efforts of the Western powers were inspired by the principle of protecting the small and weak nations against the expansionist greed of the great nations, they could not help falling into an insoluble dilemma. "On the basis of these principles," the French Foreign Minister formulated this impasse, "a treaty with the Kremlin cannot be arranged, for these are not the Kremlin's principles. Where community of principles is lacking, there can be no negotiating on the basis of principles. In that case only the primitive form of human conduct can obtain: force and exchange. Interests can be bartered, advantages that are hoped for and disadvantages which one wishes to avoid, booty that one would like to seize, violence that one will not put up with. All these factors can be weighed against one another, move for move, cash for cash. . . . Western diplomacy, on the other hand, provides a spectacle of well-meaning and dreamlike impotence."[121]

The course of the negotiations of the following months must be seen in this light, especially the still controversial question of whether the Soviet side seriously sought an agreement or was not merely bent on keeping out of the obviously approaching conflict, even of furthering it, in order later to carry the doctrine of revolution into an exhausted, shattered Europe with better chances for success than ever before. Even while the protracted negotiations were in progress, constantly interrupted by fresh scruples on the part of the West, the Soviet Union began its bold double game with Hitler. After a speech by Stalin on March 10 had dropped the first hint, the Soviet Union several times approached the German government and made plain its interest in a rearrangement of relations. Ideological differences, the Russians indicated, "need . . . not disturb." The Soviet Union replaced her Foreign Minister of many years' standing, Maxim Litvinov—a man of Western orientation and Jewish descent who figured invariably in Nazi polemics as "the Jew Finkelstein"—by Vyacheslav Molotov, and inquired in Berlin whether this shift might favorably influence the German attitude.[122]

We have no reason to think that the leaders of the Soviet Union were unaware of Hitler's changeless aim: the great war to the East, the conquest of an empire at Russia's expense. But they were, unless all indications are deceptive, prepared for the moment to take into the bargain a tremendous increase in power for Hitler's Reich, and even its first expansive step toward the East. Chief among their motives was the fear that the capitalist and Fascist powers might come to an arrangement after all, in spite of their momentary hostility, and divert German dynamism against the common Communist enemy in the East. Since the end of the World War, in which Russia had lost her western provinces and the Baltic countries, the Soviet Union had regarded itself as also a "revisionist power." And Stalin evidently expected that Hitler would be more inclined to understand and treat generously the Soviet Union's determination to reconquer the lost territories than would the slow-moving statesmen of the West with their scruples, principles, and moralistic pettiness. Fear and the determination to expand: these two fundamental motivations of Hitler were also Stalin's.

Tactically, Moscow's initiatives could not have come more conveniently for Hitler. To be sure, anti-Bolshevism had been one of the great themes of his political career. The Communist Revolution had repeatedly provided him with compelling images of horror. Thousands of times he had conjured up the "human slaughterhouses" in the interior of Russia, the "burning villages" and "deserted cities" with their destroyed churches, raped women, and GPU executioners. National Socialism and Communism were "worlds apart," he had declared; the gulf between them could never be bridged. Unlike the ideologically indifferent Ribbentrop, who soon after Stalin's speech of March 10 had recommended an approach to the Soviet Union, Hitler was uncertain, the captive of his own ideology. And during the months of negotiations he repeatedly wavered. Several times he ordered the contacts to be broken off. Only his profound disappointment at the conduct of England and the vast profit to be had from avoiding the nightmare of fighting on two fronts during the planned attack on Poland finally persuaded him to set aside all his scruples. And just as Stalin entered upon the desperate gamble with the "Fascist world plague" in the expectation of ultimately triumphing, so Hitler reassured himself that later on he would be able to make up for his "betrayal," since he had not abandoned his intention of bringing about a later confrontation with the Soviet Union. In fact, he was preparing for that by establishing a common border. What was involved, he shortly afterward told his intimates, was a "pact with Satan to drive out the devil." And, on August 11, only a few days before Ribbentrop's sensational trip to Moscow, Hitler informed a foreign visitor with almost incomprehensible candor: "Everything I am doing is directed against Russia; if the West is too stupid and too blind to grasp this, I shall be forced to come to an understanding with the Russians, strike at the West, and then after its defeat turn against the Soviet Union with my assembled forces."[123] Despite all his cynicism, his lack of scruple where tactics were concerned, Hitler was too much of an ideologist to follow the logic of his plans without uneasiness. He was never able to forget completely that the pact with Moscow was only the second-best solution.

As if circumstances were playing into his hands, a new improvement in his position came to him around this same time. Disturbed by the rumors of an impending conflict, Mussolini's son-in-law and Foreign Minister, Count Galeazzo Ciano, invited Ribbentrop to Milan early in May and urged him to postpone the outbreak of the war for at least three years, in view of Italy's inadequate preparations. The German Foreign Minister informed Ciano that the great conflict was planned only "after a long period of peace of from four to five years." When the vague exchange of ideas produced a few other points of agreement, Mussolini abruptly took a hand personally in the negotiations. For years, out of an obscure feeling of anxiety, he had refused to define Italy's relationship to Germany in a treaty of alliance specifying mutual obligations. Now he had Ciano announce without more ado that Germany and Italy had agreed on a military alliance.

Although Hitler might feel that this pact would strengthen his position vis-à-vis the Western powers, the alliance could only bring misfortune to Mussolini. The elementary rules of diplomacy should have taught him better: since he owed to the backing of Germany whatever conquests the world would ever permit him to make, his next move should have been to secure what he had acquired by coming to an agreement with the Western powers. Instead he now tied his country's destiny unconditionally to a stronger power that was bent on war, and thus reduced himself to the status of a vassal. Henceforth he must, as he had once said in a moment of exuberance in Berlin, "march to the end" with Hitler.

The so-called Pact of Steel obligated each of the partners to provide military support to the other upon the outbreak of hostilities. It drew no distinction between attacker and attacked, between offensive and defensive arms. It was an unconditional pledge of military aid. Later, when Ciano first saw the German draft that was subsequently incorporated almost unchanged into the wording of the pact, he said: "I have never read a treaty like it. It is real dynamite."

The pact was signed in a grand ceremony in the Berlin chancellery on

May 22, 1939. "I found Hitler very well, quite serene, less aggressive, slightly aged," the Italian Foreign Minister noted. "There are somewhat darker rings around his eyes. He sleeps little. Less and less." Mussolini himself seems to have received the reports from his Berlin delegation with some anxiety. A week later he sent a personal memorandum to Hitler in which he once again emphasized Italy's desire for a period of several years of peace. He recommended using this interlude for "loosening the inner cohesion of our enemies by favoring the anti-Semitic movements, support- ing . . . the pacifistic movements, promoting aspirations for autonomy (Alsace, Brittany, Corsica, Ireland), accelerating the breakdown of morals, and inciting the colonial peoples to rebellion."[124]

The day after the signing of the Pact of Steel Hitler had summoned the commanders in chief of the army, navy, and air force to his office in the chancellery and outlined his ideas and intentions. According to the minutes kept by his chief adjutant, Lieutenant Colonel Rudolf Schmundt, he pre- dicted with extraordinary acuteness the course of the first phase of the war: the overwhelming thrust into Holland and Belgium and subsequently— contrary to the strategy of the First World War—an advance not upon Paris but on the Channel ports, as launching places for the bombing and blockade of England. For in this speech England appeared as the chief antagonist. Hitler said:

The mass of eighty millions [Germans] has solved the ideational problems. The economic problems must also be solved. . . . Courage is needed to solve the problems. The principle of circumventing a solution of problems by adapt- ing to circumstances must not be allowed to obtain. Rather, what is necessary is to adjust circumstances to requirements. Without invasion of foreign countries or attacking the property of others, this is not possible. . . .

Danzig is not the object at stake. We are concerned with expanding our living space in the East and securing our food supplies. . . . In Europe no other possibility is open. . . .

The question of sparing Poland can therefore no longer be considered and we are left with the decision to attack Poland at the first suitable opportunity.

We cannot expect a repetition of the Czech solution. This time there will be fighting. Our task is to isolate Poland. Success in this isolation is decisive. . . . It must not come to a simultaneous conflict with the West. . . .

Basic principle: Conflict with Poland—beginning with the attack on Poland —will succeed only if the West stays out of it. If that isn't possible, then it is better to attack the West and in doing so simultaneously finish off Poland. . . .

The war with England and France will be a life-and-death struggle. . . . We will not be forced into a war, but we cannot get around it.[125]

From this point on, the signs of the war to come increased. On June 14 General Blaskowitz, commander in chief of Army Group 3, ordered his units to complete all preparations for marching against Poland by August

20. A week later the Oberkommando of the Wehrmacht (OKW) (High Command of the Armed Forces) presented the timetable for the offensive, and another two days later Hitler gave orders to work out precise plans for seizing the bridges over the lower Vistula. On July 27, finally, the directive for the conquest of Danzig was formulated. Only the date was left open.

Meanwhile, the German press, after a longish silence, resumed its anti-Polish campaign, extending the demands of Germany to the entire Corridor, Posen, and parts of Upper Silesia. An incident in Danzig, in the course of which an SA man was killed, provided fresh material for the propaganda campaign. The Polish government reacted with increasing toughness and decreasing moderation. It insisted on conducting its dialogue with the Reich in the icy tone of an outraged great power. Various signs indicated that it was gradually adjusting to the idea that war was inevitable. It tightened the Danzig customs regulations, thus initiating a crisis which led to an angry exchange of notes between Warsaw and Berlin. Provocations, warnings, and ultimatums followed in quick succession; the various white and blue books are filled with them. In Danzig itself camp followers began to arrive, "harbingers of evil and stormy petrels," who by their actions or exaggerated reports worsened the crisis. "Everywhere they want the catastrophe," Italian Ambassador Attolico wrote resignedly. When the German ambassador in Paris called on the French Foreign Minister Georges Bonnet on August 8, before going on vacation, both men were in a pessimistic mood. "As I listened to him," Bonnet later wrote, "I had the feeling that everything had already been decided. And when he took his leave I realized that I would not see him again."

Three days later Carl Jacob Burckhardt, the League of Nations high commissioner for Danzig, arrived at Obersalzberg for a conversation. Hitler seemed "much older and grayer," as Burckhardt later described him. "He gave the impression of fear and seemed nervous." He was also much exercised over the Poles' arrogant determination, which in reality suited his plans. He complained, he threatened that if there were the slightest incident he would smash the Poles without warning, wipe Poland off the map. "I will strike them like lightning with the full power of a mechanized army." When his visitor suggested that this would lead to a general war, Hitler declared excitedly: "Then so be it. If I have to wage war, I would rather do so today than tomorrow." He said he could only laugh at the military strength of England and France; nobody was going to scare him with the Russians; the plans of the Polish General Staff exceeded "all the visions of Alexander and Napoleon by far." Once again he tried, through Burckhardt, to launch his idea of a permanent balance of power with the West:

This eternal talk about war is foolishness and is driving the nations insane. What is the real question?

Only that we need grain and lumber. I need room in the East because of the grain; I need a colony for lumber, only one. We can manage. Our crops have

587

been excellent in 1938 and this year. But one of these days the soil will have enough and will go on strike like a body that has been doped. What then? I cannot have my people suffering hunger. Wouldn't I be better off leaving two millions on the battlefield than losing even more from hunger? We know what it's like to die of hunger. . . .

I have no romantic goals. I have no desire to dominate. Above all, I want nothing of the West, not today and not tomorrow. I desire nothing from the thickly settled regions of the world. There I am seeking nothing; once and for all, absolutely nothing. All the ideas that people ascribe to me are inventions. But I must have a free hand in the East.[126]

Next day Ciano called at the Berghof. He came to sound out the chances for a conference on a peaceful settlement of the looming conflict. But he found Hitler at a table spread with strategic maps, wholly absorbed in military problems. Germany, Hitler said, was virtually unassailable in the West. Poland would be crushed within a few days, and since Poland in the later confrontation with the Western powers would be on their side, he would be eliminating one enemy at once. In any case he was determined to utilize the next Polish provocation as the pretext for an attack, and he gave the deadline as "end of August at the latest." If he waited too long, autumn rains would make the roads in the East too muddy for motorized forces. Ciano, who on the previous day had heard from Ribbentrop that Germany wanted neither Danzig nor the Corridor, but war with Poland, "soon realized that there is nothing more to be done. He has decided to strike and he will strike."

By chance, an Anglo-French commission of military men had just begun negotiations in Moscow. The commission had arrived in the Soviet capital the previous day in order to conduct staff conferences exploring the military aspects of the alliance that had been under discussion for months. This group had set out for Moscow on August 5. A plane would have taken them there in a day. But with provoking casualness they had sailed to Leningrad aboard a freighter whose speed, as a later Soviet account noted with some bitterness, "was limited to thirteen knots."

When the delegation finally arrived, it was too late. Hitler had forestalled them.

In the middle of July Moscow had once again taken the initiative and revived the German-Soviet trade negotiations broken off by Hitler three weeks earlier. This time Hitler did not hesitate, although he may have been merely counting on the discouraging effect the negotiations would have on England and Poland. Both in Moscow and in Berlin he saw to it that the thread was taken up and spun further. On the evening of July 26 Julius Schnurre, an official of the Economic Department of the German Foreign Office, had dinner with two Russian diplomats. While dining these men explored the possibilities of a political rapprochement. The Soviet chargé d'affaires, Georgi Astakhov, declared that in Moscow they had never quite been able to understand why National Socialist Germany had taken so hostile an attitude toward the Soviet Union. Schnurre replied that "there could be no question of our being any threat to the Soviet Union. . . . German policy is aimed at England." In any case a "far-reaching compromise of mutual interests" was quite conceivable to him, all the more so since antagonisms between their two countries did not exist "along the entire line from the Baltic to the Black Sea and to the Far East." England could offer the Soviet Union "at best participation in a European war and the hostility of Germany," whereas Germany could guarantee that she could continue her development unmolested. In addition, the German diplomat concluded, "in spite of all the differences in their views there is one common element in the ideology of Germany, Italy and the Soviet Union: opposition to the capitalist democracies of the West."[127]

These were the crucial phrases which for three weeks dominated a German-Soviet exchange of views conducted with growing intensiveness. And from now on it was Germany that pressed forward with undisguised eagerness, while the Russians dragged their feet. On August 14 Ribbentrop sent Count Friedrich von der Schulenburg, the German Ambassador in Moscow, telegraphic instructions containing the great bid of delimiting spheres of interest between the Baltic and the Black Sea. He referred again to the two countries' shared opposition to the "capitalistic western democracies," dangled the prospect of quick booty, and in order to accelerate the "historic turning point" offered to come promptly to Moscow. In excellent spirits, expecting an affirmative answer from Moscow, Hitler told his military commanders the same evening that now "the great drama is approaching its climax."

But Molotov, who had instantly perceived the advantage that German impatience offered him, maneuvered elaborately on questions of timing and agenda. He asked about German readiness to conclude a nonaggression pact, worked out a plan for phased rapprochement, and finally proposed a "special protocol" which, as he remarked with sibylline obscurity, would define "the interests of the contracting parties in various questions of foreign policy." By that he actually meant preparations for the partition of Poland and the liquidation of the Baltic states. He finally suggested, as the date for Ribbentrop's trip to Moscow, August 26 or 27, and though the Germans twice nervously pressed for an earlier date, would not be budged.

Ribbentrop had asked his ambassador to explain that "German-Polish relations are growing more acute from day to day. The Führer does not wish to have our efforts to clarify German-Russian relations suddenly disturbed by the outbreak of a German-Polish conflict. He considers previous clarification necessary in order to be able to take account of Russian interests in case of such a conflict."

Hitler, fearing that he would be unable to keep his military timetable, finally took an unconventional step to break the deadlock. In a telegram dispatched on the evening of August 20 and addressed to "Herr J. V. Stalin, Moscow," he asked the leader of the Soviet Union to receive Ribbentrop as early as August 22 or 23. His Foreign Minister, he said, had "plenipotentiary authority to draw up and sign the nonaggression pact as well as the protocol."

Hitler waited for the answer in a state of extreme tension. Since he could not sleep, he telephoned Göring in the middle of the night, spoke of his worries, and expressed his annoyance at Russian stolidity. Since the beginning of the second half of August he had pushed forward the preparations for war without letup. He had called up 250,000 men, concentrated rolling stock, ordered two battleships and part of the submarine fleet to prepare to sail, and in a secret instruction canceled the party rally intended for the first week in September, the so-called "Reich Party Day of Peace." For twenty-four hours, war or peace, the success or failure of his plans, depended on Stalin. At last, at 9:35 P.M. on August 21, the reply arrived: The Soviet government "agrees to Herr von Ribbentrop's arriving in Moscow on August 23."

Freed from unbearable suspense, Hitler summoned the top military command for a conference at Obersalzberg next day at noon, in order, as he said, to acquaint them with his "irrevocable decision to act."

Once again a desperate race against the impending doom began. The Western powers had not remained unaware of the lively exchanges between Moscow and Berlin. The British cabinet, moreover, had early been informed by von Weizsäcker of the far-ranging German-Soviet contacts.[128] Everything now depended on the immediate conclusion of the Anglo-French military consultations that had begun so belatedly in Moscow.

These negotiations, which on the Soviet side had been conducted by Marshal Voroshilov, had soon come to a halt because of a seemingly insoluble problem: Poland's determined opposition to granting any passage rights to the Red Army. While the Soviet negotiators stubbornly demanded to know how they were to make contact with the enemy, if Warsaw took this position, and while the Western delegates tried to protract the negotiations, Poland recklessly disavowed her guarantor powers and flatly declared that she absolutely refused to allow the Soviet Union to enter territory that had been hers as recently as 1921. Increasingly disturbed by news of a German-Soviet rapprochement, the West pressed Warsaw to yield. Bonnet and Halifax implored the Polish Foreign Minister, urging that the entire system of alliances would collapse if Poland persisted in her refusal. But Beck remained haughtily negative. Poland, he said on August 19, could not even permit "discussion in any form of the use of part of our territory by foreign troops. For us that is a question of principle. We have no military agreement with the U.S.S.R. We do not want one."

Another appeal on the following day also failed. Even when faced with doom, Poland stuck to her principles with a kind of magnificent obstinacy. When the French ambassador passionately protested, Marshal Rydz-Smigly replied coldly: "With the Germans we run the risk of losing our freedom. With the Russians we lose our soul."[129] Even on the night of August 22, when the dramatic news of Ribbentrop's impending journey to Russia arrived, Poland remained unimpressed. The world order had been virtually turned upside down, the country was as good as lost, but Poland's politicians commented that the visit merely showed how desperate Hitler's situation was.

Distraught by the way things were going, France at last decided to wait no longer for Warsaw's consent but to act on her own initiative. On the evening of August 22 General Doumenc informed Marshal Voroshilov that he had received full powers from his government to conclude a military convention granting the Red Army passage through Poland and Rumania. But when Voroshilov insistently demanded proof of Poland's and Rumania's consent, Doumenc had to be evasive and could only repeat that he had come to conclude the agreement. At last, alluding to Ribbentrop's impending visit, he said: "But time is passing." Marshal Voroshilov replied ironically: "Undoubtedly time is passing." They parted with nothing accomplished.

Next day, in spite of strenuous efforts by Georges Bonnet to change Beck's mind, Polish consent had still not been obtained. Toward noon Ribbentrop arrived in the Soviet capital and almost immediately went to the Kremlin. And as though the participants wanted to show the world a spectacle of uncomplicated totalitarian diplomacy, the Nonaggression Pact and the delimitation of spheres of interest was agreed upon with the first conference of three hours' duration. A query from Ribbentrop about an unforeseen Soviet demand was answered by Hitler with a terse wire: "Yes, agreed."

Only now was Poland ready to consent, in an involuted announcement, to the French demand. General Doumenc had permission to declare, Beck conceded, that he had "obtained assurance that in case of a joint action against a German aggression a collaboration between Poland and the U.S.S.R. under technical conditions that are to be settled later is not excluded." The Western powers noted with satisfaction that Poland had yielded. But while Hitler, with his "Yes, agreed," had offered the Soviet Union half of Eastern Europe, including Finland and Bessarabia, "the Western powers promised that the Poles would promise to allow the Russians to use the desired area under certain circumstances in limited fashion for a limited time as a base of operations under Polish control."[130]

During the night hours of August 23 Ribbentrop and Molotov signed the Nonaggression Pact and the secret supplementary protocol, which became known only after the war when it played into the hands of the German defense lawyers at the Nuremberg trial.[131] In the protocol the contracting parties agreed that "in the event of a territorial and political transformation" Eastern Europe would be divided into spheres of interest along a line running from the northern border of Lithuania south along the rivers Narew, Vistula, and San. The question was explicitly left open "whether the interests of both parties make the maintenance of an independent Polish State appear desirable and how the frontiers of this State should be delimited." These dry formulas exposed the fundamentally imperialistic character of the agreement, and bluntly made plain the connection with the planned war.

That connection has proved to be the rock on which all the elaborate Soviet attempts at self-exoneration have foundered. Of course Stalin could offer numerous sound reasons for the Nonaggression Pact. It let him have the famous "breathing space," gave the country a buffer zone of possibly vital importance toward the West, and above all insured that the vacillating Western powers would be irrevocably engaged in conflict with Germany if Hitler returned to his real aim and attacked the Soviet Union. Stalin's apologists have also asserted that on that August 23, 1939, he had done only what Chamberlain had done the previous year in Munich. Chamberlain had sacrificed Czechoslovakia, as Stalin was now abandoning Poland, in order to buy time. None of these arguments, however, allow us to forget the secret protocol which, as it were, converted the Nonaggression Pact into an Aggression Pact. Chamberlain, after all, despite Hitler's repeated offers, had never carved out spheres of interest with the German dictator. Rather, he had scotched Hitler's great dream of unhindered attack upon the Soviet Union, whose leaders now were proving far less scrupulous. Whatever validity we may grant the Soviet justifications on the grounds of *Realpolitik,* the supplementary agreement was "unworthy of an ideological movement which claimed to have the deepest insight into the historical process,"[132] a movement that had never represented world revolution as an act of naked expansionism, but had championed and upheld it as the moral necessity of the human race.

Significantly, the evening in Moscow took an almost comradely turn. Ribbentrop later reported that Stalin and Molotov had been "very nice," that being with them "felt like being among old party comrades."[133] Although he was somewhat embarrassed when, in the course of the night the conversation turned to the Anti-Comintern Pact, of which Ribbentrop was the author, Stalin's geniality encouraged him to scoff at the pact. According to the account of a German participant, he declared that the agreement had "basically not been directed against the Soviet Union, but against the Western democracies. . . . Mr. Stalin interjected that the Anti-Comintern Pact in fact had alarmed chiefly the City of London and the English shopkeepers. The Reich Foreign Minister agreed and remarked jokingly that Mr. Stalin was surely less alarmed by the Anti-Comintern

Top: German tank units entering Poland
Bottom: Warsaw, SS operation

Left: Hitler looking at burning Warsaw through a battery commander's telescope
Top: Warsaw in flames
Bottom: Polish cavalry attack

Left: Movie stills of Hitler's
reaction to the French
request for an armistice,
June, 1940
Right: Hitler in Paris,
leaving the Invalides, July
23, 1940

Top: German advance in the East, 1943
Bottom Left: Sketch for a memorial pyramid for the war dead—in the Dnieper region
Bottom right: Himmler, Reich Commissioner for the Consolidation of German Racial Stock

In the Führer's headquarters: Ribbentrop, Hitler, Bormann

Pogroms and liquidations in
the East, 1942

The disastrous winter of 1942-43
Top: Infantrymen digging dugouts south of Vitebsk
Center: Interrogation of German generals and officers after the defeat at Stalingrad, February, 1943, in the bunker of Soviet General Chuikov
Bottom: Dead German soldiers in the snow at Stalingrad

Top: In the Führer's headquarters: Hitler with the heads
of the Wehrmacht listening to a report by Keitel, 1944
Bottom right: Hitler and his physician, Dr. Morell
Bottom left: Large dining room in the Wolf's Lair

July, 1944
Top left: Stauffenberg being welcomed by Hitler to the
Führer's headquarters
The conspirators facing the People's Tribunal:
Bottom left: von Hase and von Witzleben
Right row: Julius Leber, General Helmuth Stieff, Major
General von Moltke, Carl Goerdeler

Afternoon of July 20, 1944
Center: Hitler with Mussolini, Bormann, Göring, and
Ribbentrop
The conspirators:
Top row: Werner von Haeften, Ludwig Beck, Yorck von
Wartenburg
Bottom row: von Tresckow, Admiral Canaris, von Oster

Hitler shortly after the
bombing of July 20, 1944

Hitler's physical
deterioration, 1944
Top: The last time at the
Berghof
Bottom: At headquarters

Hitler's bunker extended
under the chancellery
garden and ended there in a
round concrete tower that
served as an emergency exit

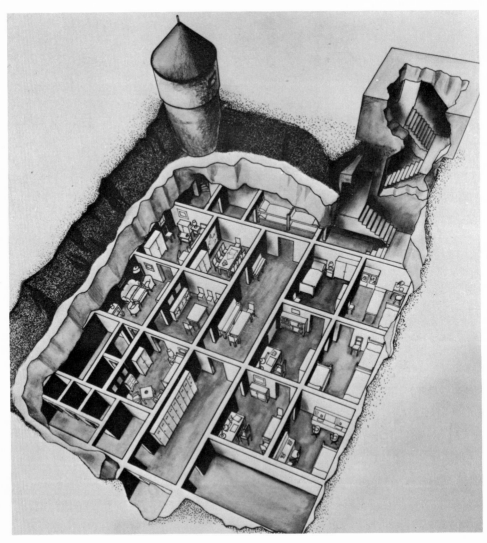

Top: On April 20, 1945, his last birthday, Hitler received a group of Hitler Youths and gave them military decorations
Bottom: The last photograph of Hitler in the ruins of the chancellery

Soviet soldiers sight-seeing among the ruins of the Berlin chancellery

Pact than the City of London and the English shopkeepers." The report continues:

In the course of the conversation Mr. Stalin spontaneously proposed a toast to the Führer in the following words: "I know how much the German people love their Führer and I therefore should like to drink to his health."

Mr. Molotov drank to the health of the Reich Foreign Minister and Ambassador Count von der Schulenburg. Furthermore, Mr. Molotov toasted Mr. Stalin, remarking that it had been Stalin who by his speech of March this year, which was well understood in Germany, had initiated the reversal of relations. Messrs. Molotov and Stalin drank repeatedly to the Nonaggression Pact, the new era in German-Russian relations, and to the German people. . . .

In parting Mr. Stalin addressed the following words to the Reich Foreign Minister: The Soviet Union takes the new Pact very seriously; he could guarantee on his word of honor that the Soviet Union would not betray her partner.[134]

It truly seemed as if, amid toasts and clinking glasses, the deceptive veil of old hostility had been parted and that only now, in the fateful intimacy of that night, the closeness between the two regimes was revealed to themselves and the world. In fact August 23, 1939, has been repeatedly cited by those who wish to prove a conformity in nature between the two regimes. In truth, it was much more a conformity in methods and, as now became evident, in the men. Stalin's toast to Hitler was no empty phrase; he kept his promise with pedant loyalty. In spite of all the omens and warnings from experts, in June, 1941, barely two years later, he refused to the last to believe that Hitler was going to attack the Soviet Union. Even as the German troops advanced, the freight cars rolled westward with the supplies the Russians were obligated to deliver under the economic accord. The astonishing gullibility of the crafty Soviet ruler rested to a considerable degree upon the admiration he felt for a man who, like himself, had risen from low estate to historic importance. In Hitler he respected the only man of the period whom he regarded as his equal; and as we know, Hitler reciprocated this feeling. All "deadly enmity" could never diminish the two men's mutual sense of the other's greatness; and beyond ideologies they felt themselves linked by the rank that history confers. In his memoirs, Rumanian Foreign Minister Grigore Gafencu has cited the observations of the French historian Albert Sorel on the first partition of Poland: "Everything that increased Russia's distance from other powers brought it closer to Prussia. Like Russia, Prussia was a parvenu on the great stage of the world. It had to clear the way for its own future, and Catherine saw that it had every intention of doing so with great methods, great possibilities and great aims."

These sentences apply as neatly both to the situation and the psychology of Hitler and Stalin: their restive desire for change, their gigantic dreams, and the bold stroke that brought them together in one of the most dramatic coups in history. The ideologies of both were marked by an acute sense of power politics. Hitler once said that "he was not among those who let historic moments pass by unused," and the same was true of Stalin. Neither man was in the least disturbed by the expostulations of uncomprehending followers. The Moscow Pact threw the Communist parties of the world into one of those crises that consumed what was left of their influence. Similarly, on the morning of August 25 indignant followers of Hitler threw hundreds of swastika armbands over the fence of the Brown House in Munich.[135]

On the same day the Western military missions left Moscow. Subordinate Soviet generals saw them off. The day before, they had asked Marshal Voroshilov for a meeting, but Voroshilov later apologized, saying that he had been duck hunting.

From Hitler's point of view, the conclusion of the Moscow Pact had paved the way for a quick, stunning victory over Poland. What followed was merely a mechanical procedure, "as when a fuse burns to the end." In the interval he was concerned entirely with the effort to strengthen his alibi, to fend off any mediation, and to separate the Western powers from Poland even further than he had done so far so successfully. All the initiatives and final offers of the remaining week, all those sham negotiations to which so many vain hopes were attached, sprang from this triple aim.

Hitler's address to the High Command on August 22 at Obersalzberg had already been dominated by these considerations. In the best of spirits, fully confident of success in Moscow, he reported on the situation and once more justified his unshakable determination to go to war. His own standing and authority, as well as the economic situation, required the conflict. "There is no other choice left to us; we must act." Political considerations and the alliances also argued for a rapid decision: "In two or three years all these fortunate circumstances will no longer exist. No one knows how long I may live. Therefore conflict better now," one of the jottings taken by a participant reads.[136] Once more Hitler outlined why the Western powers would not seriously intervene:

The opponent still had the hope that Russia would come forth as an adversary after the conquest of Poland. The opponents have not reckoned with my great resoluteness. Our opponents are little worms. I saw them in Munich.

I was convinced that Stalin would never accept the English offer. Russia has no interest in the preservation of Poland. In connection with the trade treaty we arrived at the political dialogue. Proposal of a Nonaggression Pact. Then came a comprehensive proposal from Russia. . . . Now Poland is in the situation I wanted to have her.

We need have no fear of blockade. The East will supply us with grain, cattle, coal, lead, zinc. It is a great goal that demands a great commitment. My only fear is that at the last moment some *Schweinehund* will present me with a mediation plan.

594

In the second part of his address, held after a simple meal, Hitler seemed somewhat less certain about the attitude of the Western powers. "There can be no other outcome." Consequently, "the most iron resolution" was requisite. "Shrink from nothing . . . life-and-death struggle." This formula promptly transported him into one of his mythologizing moods in which history appeared before him as a bloody panorama filled with battles, victories, and downfalls. In the earlier part of his address he had referred to the "founding of Greater Germany" as "a great achievement," but commented that it was "regrettable that it was achieved by a bluff on the part of the political leadership." Now he declared:

A long period of peace would not be good for us. . . . Manly bearing. Not machines struggling with one another, but human beings. The qualitatively better man on our side. Spiritual factors decisive.

Annihilation of Poland in foreground. Goal is elimination of the vital forces, not the attainment of a specific line. . . .

I shall provide the propagandistic pretext for launching the war, no matter whether it is credible. The victor is not asked afterward whether or not he has told the truth. What matters in beginning and waging the war is not righteousness, but victory.

Close heart to pity. Proceed brutally. Eighty million people must obtain what they have a right to. Their existence must be guaranteed. The stronger is in the right. Supreme hardness.

Hitler dismissed his generals by remarking that the order for commencing hostilities would be issued later, probably for Saturday morning, August 26. On the following day General Halder noted in his diary: "Y [Day] = Aug. 26 (Saturday) final—no further orders."

This timetable, however, was once again upset. For although practically the entire framework of Western policy had collapsed as soon as the pact was signed, England led the way in demonstrating a stoic equanimity. Poland was as good as doomed, but the British cabinet dryly announced that the latest events had changed nothing. Military preparations were ostentatiously continued and increased. In a letter to Hitler Chamberlain warned against any doubts of the British determination to fight:

No greater mistake could be made. . . . It has been alleged that, if His Majesty's Government had made their position more clear in 1914, the great catastrophe would have been avoided. . . . His Majesty's Government are resolved that on this occasion there shall be no such tragic misunderstanding.[137]

The Prime Minister also made a statement to the House of Commons pitched in the same tone. England would not retreat an inch—unlike France, which kept up an air of resolution with considerable difficulty and whose press expressed its defeatist attitude in the question, *"Mourir pour Dantzig?"* Danzig was no more the issue for Chamberlain than for Hitler. For him, as for the French, it was "a far-away city in a foreign land." No one was going to have to die for it. But now, when the Moscow Pact had shattered her whole policy, England recognized the things her people would have to fight and die for. The policy of appeasement had been partly based on and sustained by the bourgeois world's fear of Communist revolution. In the script of English statesmen, Hitler was assigned the role of a militant defender of the bourgeois world. That was why they had endured all his slaps in the face, his provocations and outrages. But this was the only reason. By coming to an agreement with the Soviet Union, he indicated that he was not the opponent of revolution that he had pretended to be; he was no protector of the bourgeois order, no "General Wrangel of the world bourgeoisie." Although the pact with Stalin was a masterpiece of diplomacy, it contained an inconspicuous flaw: it abrogated the premises on which Hitler and the West had carried on their dealings. Here was something that could not be glossed over, and with rare unanimity the British, including the stoutest spokesmen for appeasement, now showed their resolve to oppose him. Although Hitler had a deserved reputation for psychological acuity, it became clear in this decisive moment that, after all, he was the psychologist only of the exhausted, the resigned, the doomed. And he was far better able to estimate the moves of victims than of adversaries.

Consequently, Hitler reacted with extreme ire to the many evidences of British determination. When Ambassador Henderson delivered his Prime Minister's letter at Obersalzberg, he had to listen to a tirade which ended with Hitler's saying he was now finally convinced that Germany and England would never be able to come to an agreement. Nevertheless, two days later, in the early afternoon of August 25, he repeated his "great bid" to divide the world. He offered a German guarantee for the existence of the British Empire, a limit on armaments, and a formal acknowledgment of the German western border in return for the right of Germany to move to the East without restriction. And as he had done so often before, he linked his outrageous demand with one of those ploys with which he tried to prove his essential harmlessness. "He said he was an artist by nature and not a politician and once the Polish question was settled he would conclude his life as an artist and not as a warmaker; he did not want to transform Germany into a great military barracks; and he would do so only if he were forced to. Once the Polish question was settled, he would retire."

Ambassador Henderson was implored to pass the offer on at once. But no sooner had he left the room, at 3:02 P.M. on August 25, than Hitler sent for General Keitel and confirmed his order to attack Poland at dawn the next day.

A few hours later, he was once more deep in doubt. Two messages had arrived at the chancellery in the course of the afternoon. One came from London and made it plain that Hitler's last attempt to drive a wedge between England and Poland had failed. After months of protracted negotiations, the British government now transformed the temporary guarantee of aid to Poland into a treaty of assistance. Hitler could not fail to see in this the most resolute rejection of his great offer. Nor could there any longer be doubt that England was determined to intervene. One of those present saw Hitler after receiving the news "sitting at the table for a considerable time, brooding."

He was harder hit by the other message, which roused him from his brooding. It came from Rome and made it clear that Italy was trying to creep out of the alliance so recently and pompously concluded. For weeks, as the conflict seemed to be coming closer, Mussolini had alternated abruptly between sanguine exultation and moods of despair. Ciano's diary notes with some irony the way the Duce rocked back and forth on his "emotional seesaw." At one time he appeared determined to keep out of Hitler's war; "then he says that honor compels him to march with Germany. Finally he states that he wants his part of the booty in Croatia and Dalmatia." Two days later "he wants time to prepare the break with Germany"; then again "he still thinks it possible that the democracies will not march and that Germany might do good business cheaply, from which business he does not want to be excluded. Then, too, he fears Hitler's rage."

Amid this confusion of crisscrossing impulses, at 3:30 P.M. on August 25, Mussolini assured the German ambassador of unconditional assistance, only to send a telegram to Hitler two hours later taking it all back, or at any rate making his assistance dependent on a vast amount of material aid that Germany could not possibly deliver—"enough to kill a bull," Ciano commented. Reminding Hitler that they had not envisaged the war's coming so soon and that Italy's army was not equipped, Mussolini tried to wriggle out of the alternative between doom and betrayal.

Strictly speaking, Hitler had no reason to be upset. The Italians might well feel miffed; they had been offended countless times by contemptuous treatment; and even the belated letter in which Hitler had informed Mussolini of the pact with Moscow had been a model of diplomatic slighting. It had dismissed an ally's claim to consultation with trivial phrases and an allusion to newspaper atrocity propaganda, but had said not a word about the ideological and political consequences resulting from Hitler's reversal of his previous positions. Nevertheless, Hitler dismissed Italian Ambassador Attolico "with an icy face" and "the chancellery echoed with unkind words about 'the disloyal Axis partner.'" A few minutes later Hitler canceled the order to advance. "Führer rather shaken," Halder noted in his diary.

Once again events seemed to undergo a dramatic slowdown. Three days passed before Hitler, sleepless, his voice cracking, appeared before an assemblage of high party and military leaders and attempted to justify

597

Mussolini's conduct. He was in a bleak mood and commented that the impending war would be "very difficult, perhaps hopeless." But he did not change his mind; rather, as always, opposition seemed to reinforce his determination: "As long as I live there will be no talk of capitulation." The new date he set for launching the attack was September 1.

As a result, the events of the last few days—the passionate efforts to preserve peace, the messages, travels and exchanges between the capitals, all have an unreal air. To the observer with hindsight much of it seems a kind of late-night show, full of sham dialogue, transparent confusion, and grotesque intermezzos. Daladier's moving personal appeal was futile. The French ambassador Coulondre, who told Hitler everything "that my heart as a man and a Frenchman could inspire me to say," wasted his words. England's conciliatory gesture was answered by Hitler with a torrent of fresh reproaches, so that even the patient Henderson lost his self-control and began to outshout Hitler, telling him he did not want "to hear such language from him or anyone else. . . . If he wanted war, he could have it." In vain, finally, was Mussolini's imploring letter; he had tried to persuade Hitler to settle for a solution by conference so that "the rhythm of your magnificent creations will not be interrupted."

Only two antagonists seemed to know that they had reached a dead end: Hitler and Beck. They alone thought exclusively of war, the former urgently, impatiently fixated upon his self-appointed timetable, the other fatalistically, wearily, facing an ineluctable fate. Hitler was so obsessed with the employment of his military power that he did not even see the political opportunities the moment offered. We have private notes from British diplomats from which we can deduce the maneuvers London expected and the concessions it was preparing. Merely for renouncing war Hitler probably could have obtained not only Danzig and the road and rail link through the Polish Corridor, but also an assurance by Great Britain of restitution of Germany's colonies and negotiations for a grand new settlement.[138]

But Hitler was no longer thinking of alternatives. Here was the first sign of his inability to think beyond military goals or to examine the military situation for its political potentialities. That inability was to grow worse in the course of the following years. Thus he took up the British proposal for direct negotiations with Poland but promptly twisted it into an ultimatum, demanding that a Polish plenipotentiary negotiator come to Berlin within twenty-four hours. The intention behind this particular chess move was all too obvious. He meant to force the Poles either to capitulate or, as had happened to the Czechoslovaks, to appear as the troublemakers. The list of demands the Germans had prepared for the negotiations was studded with sham concessions. There was still the insistence on the return of Danzig, but otherwise there was a play for world opinion: the proposal of a series of plebiscites, offers of compensation, international controls, guarantees of

598

minority rights, and plans for demobilization. After a conversation with Hitler on the afternoon of August 29, Halder noted: "Führer has hope of driving a wedge between England, French and Poles. Underlying idea: Bombard with demographic and democratic demands. Then came the actual timetable: August 30: Poles in Berlin. August 31: Blow up. Sept. 1: Use of force."

But the Poles did not come to Berlin; Schuschnigg's and Hácha's shadows loomed too large before Colonel Beck. To the steady urgings of the British and French, to which the Italians soon lent their voice, he responded that there was nothing to negotiate. On the morning of August 31 Henderson was informed that Hitler would issue the order to attack unless the Polish government consented by twelve o'clock to send a negotiator. Once again, as recently in Moscow, a struggle against the clock was waged with Polish indolence. Henderson tried, through two envoys, to change the minds of his Polish colleagues in Berlin. Ambassador Lipski received the visitors, as one of them reported, in his already partly evacuated office. He was "white as a sheet," with trembling hands took the document offered him, stared absently at the German demands, and finally murmured that he could not understand what was written there; all he knew was that they must remain firm and that "even a Poland abandoned by her Allies is ready to fight and to die alone."[139] Death was Poland's only idea. Nor was the content of the telegram that Beck sent to his ambassador in Berlin at 12:40 P.M. any different. It was a document of perplexity, and remarkable only for the coincidence in time. For at the very same minute Hitler signed "Directive Number 1 for the Conduct of the War." A short while later he told the Italian ambassador that it was all over.[140] The directive began:

Since all political possibilities have been exhausted of eliminating by peaceful means a situation on the eastern frontier which has become intolerable for Germany, I have decided on the solution by force.

The attack on Poland is to be conducted in consonance with the preparations made for Case White. . . . Day of Attack: September 1, 1939. Time of Attack: 4:45 A.M. . . .

In the West it is essential to let the responsibility for initiating hostilities be placed unequivocally upon England and France. For the time being trivial border violations are to be opposed on a purely local basis. The neutrality of Holland, Belgium, Luxemburg and Switzerland, which we have guaranteed, is to be scrupulously observed. . . .

At nine o'clock that night all radio stations broadcast the list of the German proposals to Poland, which had never been submitted to Poland herself. Approximately at the same time SS Sturmbannführer (Major) Alfred Naujocks staged a sham Polish attack on the German radio station at Gleiwitz, broadcast a brief proclamation, fired some pistol shots, and left behind the corpses of several concentration camp inmates. A few hours later, at dawn on September 1, the Polish commander of the fortress on the peninsula Westerplatte, near the harbor of Danzig, a Major Sucharski, reported: "At 4:45 A.M. the cruiser Schleswig Holstein opened fire upon the Westerplatte with all her guns. The bombardment is continuing." Simultaneously, the troops emerged from their prepared positions all along the German-Polish border. No declaration of war was issued. The Second World War had begun.

Hitler, it is true, was still hoping to limit the conflict. Shortly before ten o'clock he drove to a session of the Reichstag at the Kroll Opera House. The streets were almost deserted; the few pedestrians watched silently as the car passed in which Hitler sat in a field-gray uniform. His speech to the Reichstag was brief, serious, and peculiarly flat. Once again he asseverated his love of peace and "endless patience." Again he tried to arouse hopes in the West, evoked the new friendship with the Soviet Union, made some embarrassed remarks about his Italian ally, and finally heaped charge upon charge on the Polish government. After a wild flight of fancy about the number of border incidents in the preceding days, he declared that "tonight for the first time Polish regular soldiers fired on our own territory. Since 5:45 A.M. we have been returning the fire, and from now on bombs will be met with bombs." Henceforth, he wanted simply to be the first soldier of the Reich. "I have once more put on that coat that was most sacred and dear to me. I will not take it off again until victory is secured, or I will not survive the outcome."

Hitler's persistent hope of limiting the conflict to Poland was nourished chiefly by the hesitation of the Western powers. Contrary to their obligation under their alliance, they did not answer the German attack with an immediate declaration of war. The French government in particular resorted to a series of evasions: advice of the General Staff, a renewed attempt at mediation by Mussolini, the uncompleted evacuation of the big cities; and finally it tried to delay the beginning of the dreaded war by at least another few hours.[141] Although England's attitude was more determined, the gravity of the situation was fully realized. In Parliament Chamberlain declared on September 1: "Eighteen months ago I prayed that the responsibility would not fall upon me to ask this country to accept the awful arbitrament of war." Now, he continued, he was on the point of demanding assurances from the German government that it would cease its aggressive action against Poland and withdraw its troops. When an MP angrily called out to ask whether a time limit had been set, the Prime Minister replied: "If the reply to this last warning is unfavorable—and I do not suggest it is likely to be otherwise—His Majesty's Ambassador is instructed to ask for his passport. In that case we are ready."[142]

But Hitler failed to hear the warning, or understood only that England, in spite of the clear terms of the alliance, was still ready to temporize. Initially, therefore, he did not even answer the British note of September 1.

And while England and France engaged in complicated negotiations in order to arrive at a joint procedure, the German troops advanced tempestuously in Poland. It seems probable that these signs of weakness on the opposing side encouraged Hitler to rebuff Mussolini, who on September 2 enumerated the advantages of the situation and tried to persuade him to accept a solution by conference. "Danzig is already German," he informed Hitler, "and Germany has in her hands pledges which guarantee her the greater part of her claims. Moreover, Germany has already had her 'moral satisfaction.' If she accepted the proposal for a conference she would achieve all her aims and at the same time avoid a war, which even now looks like becoming general and of extremely long duration."

During the night hours of September 2 England at last decided to forgo joint action with France. Ambassador Henderson was told to deliver to the German Foreign Minister at 9 A.M. Sunday an ultimatum that would expire at 11 A.M. Ribbentrop did not receive Henderson personally; in his place he sent his chief interpreter, Dr. Paul Schmidt. Schmidt has described the scene when he brought the British note to the chancellery. Hitler's antechamber was so crowded with members of the cabinet and party leaders that he had difficulty making his way through the throng. When he entered Hitler's office, he saw Hitler sitting at his desk, while Ribbentrop stood by the window.

Both looked up tensely when they caught sight of me. I stopped some distance from Hitler's desk and slowly translated the British government's ultimatum. When I finished there was dead silence. . . .

Hitler sat immobile, staring into space. He was not stunned, as was later asserted, nor did he rant, as others claimed. He sat absolutely silent and unmoving. After an interval, which seemed an eternity to me, he turned to Ribbentrop, who had remained standing frozen by the window. "What now?" Hitler asked his Foreign Minister with a furious glare, as if to say that Ribbentrop had misinformed him about the probable reaction of the British. Ribbentrop replied in a muted voice: "I assume that within the hour the French will hand us a similar ultimatum."[143]

When Ambassador Coulondre called on the German Foreign Minister toward noon, England was already at war with the Reich. The French ultimatum corresponded to the British one with the exception of one significant detail. As though even now the government in Paris shrank from using the word "war," it threatened, if Germany refused to withdraw her troops from Poland at once, to fulfill those "contractual obligations which France has undertaken toward Poland and which are known to the German government." When Coulondre returned to his embassy, he burst into tears in the presence of his associates.[144]

But England, too, had difficulty adjusting to the reality of war. In desperation Poland waited for military aid, or at least some relief; when she realized that she was without actual assistance, it was far too late. The ponderousness of the British responses was, however, not simply a matter of temperament or of inadequate military preparation. The guarantee for Poland had never been popular in England. There was no traditional friendship between the two countries, and Poland was regarded as one of those dictatorial regimes that merely showed up the constriction and oppressiveness of authoritarian government, but not the glamour and allure of power.[145] When in the early days of September an opposition conservative urged a member of the cabinet to provide help for Poland and mentioned the plan then being discussed, of setting fire to the Black Forest with incendiary bombs, he was answered: "Oh, we can't do that, that's private property. Next you'll be insisting that we bomb the Ruhr region."

France, for her part, had pledged to launch an offensive with from thirty-five to thirty-eight divisions by the sixteenth day of the war. But the country was psychologically fixed on defense and incapable of planning an offensive. General Jodl declared at Nuremberg: "If we did not collapse in 1939, that was only because the approximately one hundred and ten French and English divisions in the West, which during the campaign in Poland were facing twenty-five German divisions, remained completely inactive."[146]

Under these circumstances the modernized German armies were able to overrun Poland in a single victorious onslaught. To their perfection and smoothly functioning impetus the opposing side would offer, as was later admitted, mere gestures of "touching absurdity." The co-operation of hitherto unknown swarms of armored formations with motorized infantry units and the dominant air force, whose Stuks plummeted with deafening screams upon their targets, the precision of the intelligence and supply system—all the might of this advancing, mechanized colossus—left the Poles little more than their courage. Beck had declared with assurance that his country's forces were "organized for a flexible, delaying war of movement. There will be great surprises." But the real significance of this campaign was that the Second World War was, so to speak, fighting against the First. Nowhere was the disproportion so evident as in the cavalry attack on Tuchel Heath, when a Polish mounted unit rode its horses against German tanks.

As early as the morning of September 5 General Halder noted after a military conference: "Enemy as good as beaten." On September 6 Cracow fell; a day later the Warsaw government fled to Lublin; and in still another day the German advance units reached the Polish capital. All organized resistance began to collapse. In two great pincer movements initiated on September 9 the remnants of the Polish forces were encircled and slowly crushed. Eight days later, when the campaign was nearly ended, the Soviet Union fell upon the already overwhelmed country from the East—having first prepared an elaborate legalistic and diplomatic smoke screen to shield her from the charge of aggression. On September 18 the German and

Soviet troops met in Brest-Litovsk. The first blitzkrieg was over. When Warsaw fell a few days later, Hitler ordered all the bells in Germany to be rung for a week, every day between noon and one o'clock.

The question nevertheless remains whether he felt unclouded satisfaction at the rapid military triumph or whether, through all the cheering and all the pealing of bells, he had not recognized that victory was already eluding him. His grand design was turned upside down. He was fighting on the wrong front, not against the East, as he might have been able to persuade himself during the far too brief Polish campaign, but henceforth against the West. For nearly twenty years all this thinking and talking had been determined by a diametrically opposite idea. Now his nervous restiveness, his arrogance, and the corrupting effect of great successes had overriden all rational considerations and finally destroyed the "Fascist" constellation. He was "at war with the conservatives before he had defeated the revolutionaries."[147] There are some indications that he was already aware of this most fatal of errors during those early days of victory. His entourage has spoken of fits of pessimism and sudden attacks of anxiety: "He would have been glad to draw his head out of the noose."[148] Shortly after the war with England became a certainty, he remarked to Rudolf Hess: "All my work is now disintegrating. My book was written for nothing." Occasionally he compared himself to Martin Luther, who had no more wanted to fight against Rome than he himself against England. Then again, he would muster all the casual knowledge about England he had picked up to persuade himself of England's weakness and democratic decadence. Or he would try to quiet his apprehensions by speaking of a "sham war," by which the British government was formally satisfying an unpopular duty to an ally. As soon as Poland was finished, he had declared at the end of August: "We'll hold a great peace conference with the Western powers." Now Poland was finished and he was hoping for just that.

It is within this context that we must see Hitler's attempts, immediately after the Polish campaign and later, in conjunction with the defeat of France, to wage the war against England lackadaisically and halfheartedly. The propaganda threats were louder than the actual blows; it was for this that the British coined the phrase "phony war." For almost two years Hitler's conduct of the war was partly governed by the effort to set the topsy-turvy constellation back on its feet again, to return to the design that he had frivolously abandoned. He tried repeatedly, but in vain.

A few weeks before the outbreak of the war—on July 22, 1939—he had said to Admiral Dönitz that on no account must a war with England be allowed to develop; a war with England would mean nothing less than "finis Germaniae."[149]

Now he was at war with England.

INTERPOLATION III

The Wrong War

> The horoscope of the times does
> not point to peace but to war.
>
> Adolf Hitler

In regard to the Second World War there can be no question about whose was the guilt. Hitler's conduct throughout the crisis, his highhandedness, his urge to bring things to a head and plunge into catastrophe, so shaped events that any wish to compromise on the part of the Western powers was bound to come to nothing. Who caused the war is a question that cannot be seriously raised. Hitler's policy during the preceding years, in the strict sense his entire career, was oriented toward war. Without war his actions would have lacked goal and consistency, and Hitler would not have been the man he was.

He had said that war was "the ultimate goal of politics." That sentence must be taken as one of the key premises of his world view. In many passages in his writings, speeches, and conversations he repeatedly developed the underlying train of thought: the aim of politics was to guarantee a people's *Lebensraum;* the requisite living space had from time immemorial been conquered and held only by struggle; consequently, politics was a kind of permanent warfare, and armed conflict was only its actualization and maximum intensification. War was, as Hitler formulated it, the "strongest and most classic manifestation" of politics and indeed of life itself. In pacifism, on the other hand, human beings would necessarily fade away and "be replaced by animals" who more obediently conformed to the law of nature. "As long as the earth turns around the sun," he declared in solemn, half-poetic accents to Bulgarian Ambassador Dragonoff, "as long as there are cold and warmth, fertility and infertility, storm and sunshine, so long will struggle continue, among men and among nations. . . . If people lived in the Garden of Eden they would rot. What mankind has become, it has become through struggle." And during the war he maintained to his table companions that a peace of more than twenty-five years would do great harm to a nation.[1]

In these mythologizing realms of his thought, the lust for conquest, the desire for fame, or revolutionary beliefs were not sufficient reason for unleashing a war. Hitler actually called it "a crime" to wage war for the acquisition of raw materials. Only the issue of living space permitted resort

607

to arms. But in its purest form war was independent even of this factor, and sprang solely from the almighty primal law of death and life, of gain at the expense of others. War was an ineradicable atavism: "War is the most natural, the most ordinary thing. War is a constant; war is everywhere. There is no beginning, there is no conclusion of peace. War is life. All struggle is war. War is the primal condition."[2] Unmoved by friendships, ideologies, and present alliances, he occasionally told his table companions that some distant day, when Mussolini's reforestation program had taken effect, it might be necessary to wage war against Italy, too.

These ideas also make it clear why National Socialism had no utopian concept, but only a vision. Hitler called the notion of a grand, comprehensive order of peace "ridiculous." Even his dreams of empire did not culminate in the panorama of a harmonious age; they were filled with the clash of arms, riot, and tumult. No matter how far Germany's power might one day stretch, somewhere sooner or later it would come upon a bleeding, fought-over frontier where the race would have been hardened and a constant selection of the best would be taking place. This cranky fixation on the idea of war once again showed, far beyond the Social-Darwinist starting point, the degree to which Hitler and National Socialism were a product of the First World War. It had molded their sentiments, their practical handling of power, and their ideology. The World War, Hitler repeated incessantly, had never stopped for him. To him, as to that whole generation, the idea of peace seemed curiously stale and unpleasant. It was certainly not a theme to arouse their imaginations, which were fascinated rather by struggle and hostility. Soon after the end of the struggle for power, shortly after the domestic opponents had been eliminated, Goebbels told a foreign diplomat that "he often thought back full of longing to those earlier times when there were always opportunities for combat." A member of Hitler's most intimate entourage spoke of his "pathologically militant nature." So dominant was this urge that ultimately it crushed and devoured everything else, including Hitler's long demonstrated political genius.

But if all his thoughts were bent on war, the one that began on September 3, 1939, with the declarations of war by the Western powers, the one marked by absurdly reversed fronts, was not the war he had sought. Shortly before he became Chancellor, he had told his entourage that he would begin the war that had to come free of all romantic emotions, guided only by tactical considerations. He would not play at war and would not be tricked into a trial at arms. "*I* shall wage the war. *I* shall determine the suitable time for attack. There is only one most favorable moment. I will wait for it. With iron resolution. And I will not miss it. I will employ all my energy to compelling it to come. That is my task. If I succeed in forcing that, I have the right to send the young to their deaths."[3]

Apparently he had failed in this self-imposed task. But had he really failed? The question cannot be why or even whether Hitler began the

Second World War of his own free will. It can only be why he, who up to this point had almost alone determined the course of events, stumbled into war at this time contrary to all his plans.

Certainly he misread England's attitude and once more gambled in defiance to all common sense. He had too frequently emerged triumphant from similar situations not to have been misled; he had come to think of the possibility of the impossible as a kind of law of his life. Hence, too, the many vain hopes he harbored in the following months. First he told himself that England would come around after the rapid subjugation of Poland. Then he expected the intervention of the Soviet Union on the German side. For a while he counted on the effects of reduced military activity against Great Britain, later on the effects of heavy bombing, and then expected the turning point to come from victory over England's continental vassal: "The war will be decided in France," he told Mussolini in March, 1940. "If France were finished . . . England would have to make peace."[4] After all, he argued, England had entered the war without any strong motive, chiefly because of Italy's indecisive attitude. Any of these factors, he thought, might prompt England to withdraw from the conflict. He simply did not see what else might actuate the enemy. So sure was he of his reasoning that in the so-called Z Plan he treated the U-boat building program, which had already been cut back, with noticeable neglect; instead of twenty-nine monthly launchings the plan called for only two.

But illusions about England's determination to fight cannot sufficiently explain Hitler's decision to go to war. He was after all conscious of the high degree of risk. When the British government made its intentions clearer by signing the pact of assistance with the Poles on August 25, Hitler rescinded an order to attack already issued. Nor did the following week give him any reason to reassess the situation. When, therefore, he renewed the order to attack on August 31, there must have been some special feeling that overrode his sense of risk.

One of the striking aspects of his behavior is the stubborn, peculiarly blind impatience with which he pressed forward into the conflict. That impatience was curiously at odds with the hesitancy and vacillations that had preceded earlier decisions of his. When, in the last days of August, Göring pleaded with him not to push the gamble too far, he replied heatedly that throughout his life he had always played vabanque. And though this metaphor was accurate for the matter at hand, it hardly described the wary, circumspect style with which he had proceeded in the past. We must go further back, almost to the early, prepolitical phase of his career, to find the link with the abruptness of his conduct during the summer of 1939, with its reminders of old provocations and daredevil risks.

There is, in fact, every indication that during these months Hitler was throwing aside more than tried and tested tactics, that he was giving up a policy in which he had excelled for fifteen years and in which for a while he had outstripped all antagonists. It was as if he were at last tired of having to adapt himself to circumstances, tired of the eternal talking, dissimulation, and diplomatic wirepulling, and were again seeking "a great, universally understandable, liberating action."

The November putsch of 1923, one of the great caesuras that so strikingly divide up his life, was also an example of such a liberating action. As we have noted earlier, it marked Hitler's specific entry into politics. Until that point, he had made a name for himself by the boldness of his agitation, by the radical alternatives of either/or that he announced the night before the march to the Feldherrnhalle: "When the decisive struggle for to be or not to be calls us, then all we want to know is this: heaven above us, the ground under us, the enemy before us." Until that time he had recognized only frontal relationships, both inwardly and outwardly. His thrusting, offensive style as an orator was matched by his rude tone of command as party chairman. Orders were issued in a brusque, categorical tone. Only after the collapse of November 9, 1923, did Hitler realize the possibilities of the political game, the use that might be made of tactical devices, coalitions, and sham compromises. That insight had transformed the rude putschist into a politician who played his cards with deliberation. But even though he had learned to play his new part with sovereign skill, he had never been able entirely to conceal how much it had gone against the grain and that his innate tendency continued to be against detours, rules of the game, legality, and in fact against politics in general.

Now he was returning to his earlier self. He was going to slash through the web of dependencies and false concessions, to recover the putschist's freedom to call any politician a swine for presenting him with a proposal for mediation. Hitler had behaved "like a force of nature," Rumanian Foreign Minister Gafencu reported in April, 1939, after a visit to Berlin. That phrase would also describe the demagogue and rebel of the early twenties. Significantly, along with his decision for war, his old apolitical alternatives about victory or annihilation, world power or doom, cropped up once more. In his heart of hearts he had always preferred them; now they regularly recurred, sometimes several times in the same speech. "All hope for compromise is childish: victory or defeat," he told his generals on November 23, 1939. And later: "I have led the German people to a great height even though the world now hates us. I am risking this war. I have to choose between victory or annihilation. I choose victory." And then a few sentences further: "It is not a single problem that is at stake, but whether the nation is to be or not to be."

It was wholly in keeping with this retreat from the game of politics that he increasingly lapsed, in terminology and in the tenor of his statements, back into the plane of irrationality. "Only he who struggles with fate can have Providence on his side," he remarked in the above-mentioned speech.

A member of his entourage noted, during the last days in August, a striking "tendency toward a *Nibelungentod.*" Hitler again defined the war as a "fateful struggle which cannot be dispensed with or negotiated away by any clever political or tactical skill, but really represents a kind of struggle with the Huns [as in the *Nibelungenlied*] . . . in which one either stands or falls and dies; either/or."[5]

The following years were to show that Hitler's defection from politics did not spring from a passing mood. Strictly speaking, he never again returned to politics. All efforts on the part of his entourage, the urgent pleas of Goebbels, the proposals of Ribbentrop or Rosenberg, even the occasional recommendations of such foreign statesmen as Mussolini, Horthy, and Laval, were in vain. His consultations with chiefs of the satellite states (which took place more and more rarely as the war went on) finally became the last vestige of former maneuverings. But they had nothing to do with political activity. Hitler himself accurately called them "hypnotic treatments." His attitude may be summed up in the reply he gave to Ambassador Havel, the Foreign Office's liaison man at headquarters, when in the spring of 1945 Havel urged him to seize the last opportunity for a political initiative: "Politics? I don't engage in politics any more. All that disgusts me so." In a totally contradictory way, he justified his political inaction on grounds of changing circumstances. While the war was going well, he held that time was working for him; in periods of setbacks he feared that his negotiating position would be unfavorable. "I see myself as a sort of spider," he declared during the second phase of the war, "lying in wait for a run of luck. The thing is only to be alert and ready to pounce at the right moment." In fact, such images concealed his continuing distaste for politics, whose stakes seemed to him too small, whose points too insipid, and which offered none of the excitement that transformed successes into triumphs. Many a time during the war years he commented that one must oneself "cut off possible lines of retreat . . . for then one fights more easily and resolutely."[6] Politics, according to his later viewpoint, was merely a possible line of retreat.

In renouncing politics, Hitler also returned to the principled ideological positions he had formerly held. The intellectual rigidity that had so long been hidden by his boundless tactical and methodical adroitness emerged again, becoming increasingly marked as time went on. The war brought on a process of petrifaction which soon gripped his whole personality. An alarming sign of the dehumanizing process came right at the start in Hitler's casual order of September 1, 1939, the day the war began, that incurably ill persons be granted a "mercy death."[7] The phenomenon assumed most tangible form in Hitler's insanely mounting anti-Semitism, which itself was a form of mythologizing atrophy of consciousness. Early in 1943 he told a foreign chief of state: "The Jews are the natural allies of Bolshevism and the candidates for the positions now held by those intellec-

611

tuals who would be assassinated in case of Bolshevization. Therefore . . .
the more radically one proceeds against the Jews, the better." He said he
preferred a naval battle like Salamis to an ambiguous skirmish and would
rather smash all bridges behind him, since Jewish hatred was in any case
gigantic. In Germany there was "no turning back on the course once
taken." His sense of entering upon the final conflict was obviously deepening. And the figure of the diplomat had no place in eschatology, he
thought.

In our search for the specific impulse that set these processes in motion
we cannot pretend that Hitler's boredom with politics and his impatience
are the whole explanation. Some writers have posited a shattering of his
personality structure caused by illness. But evidence is lacking for this
thesis. And often this sort of argument represents the effort of a disillusioned partisan of the regime to explain the difference between the successful and the unsuccessful phases in Hitler's life. What comes to the fore
during this second phase is the totally unchanged, rigid character of his
ideas and ideologies. What stands revealed is not so much a break as the
immutable core in Hitler's nature.

But certainly his impatience was operative in all of it: the craving for
dramatic intensifications, the rapid satiation with successes, the dynamism,
whose author he was and whose victim he now became, and, finally, the
phenomenon of temporal anxiety, which from 1937 on stamped his style of
action, and was now reinforced by a sense that time was not only running
out on him but working against him. Through sleepless nights, he told
Mussolini, he had brooded over the advisability of postponing the war for
two years. But then, considering the inevitability of the conflict and the
growing strength of the enemy, he had "abruptly attacked Poland in the
autumn." On September 27, 1939, he said something similar to von
Brauchitsch and Halder, and in a memorandum composed two weeks later
he affirmed: "Given the situation . . . time can more probably be regarded as an ally of the Western powers than as our ally." He was forever
rationalizing his decision, speaking of "the good fortune of being permitted
to lead this war in person" and even of his jealousy at the idea that
someone after him might begin this war. Again, with a withering glance at
any possible successor, he declared that he did not want "stupid wars"
coming after his death. His address to his generals on November 23, 1939,
sums up his reasons for timing the war when he did. After an analysis of
the situation he commented:

As the final factor I must in all modesty mention my own person as irreplaceable. Neither a military nor a civilian personality could replace me. The
attempts at assassination [like that of Nobember 8, 1939, in the Bürgerbräu-
keller] may be repeated. I am convinced of the strength of my brain and of my
resolution. Wars will always be ended only by the annihilation of the opponent.
Anyone who thinks differently is irresponsible. Time is working for the enemy.

The present balance of forces can no longer improve for us; it can only deteriorate. If the enemy will not make peace, then our own position worsens. No
compromises. Hardness toward ourselves. I shall attack and not capitulate. The
fate of the Reich depends upon me alone. I shall act accordingly.

It is clear that Hitler was no longer speaking in political terms. The
mood is visionary. And he found his new approach vindicated by his
sensational successes in the initial phase of the war. Against Poland he had
played the role of generalissimo* with some restraint. But he fell more and
more in love with the part; and something of the infantilism that made him
seek to perpetuate all pleasant experiences could be recognized in his total
devotion to the map table at the Führer's headquarters. Playing general
brought new stimuli, new excitements to his nerves, but also posed a
dangerous challenge. Here was the supreme test of his "strength of brain,"
of his hardness and resolution, and of his theatrical temperament. He faced
decisions of the "most gigantic sort" and of the most deadly seriousness.
His remark that only artistic people have the qualities for great generalship
underlines this aspect. The effortless victories of the early period strengthened his conviction that after the fame of demagogue and politician he
would also win glory as the supreme commander. And when, as the war
went on and on, this glory failed to come his way, he began to pursue
it—breathlessly, defiantly, until he attained doom.

Hitler's urge for war was so compelling that he not only conceded to
reverse his fundamental design but went into the conflict in spite of inadequate preparation. The downcast mood in the streets, the ostentatious
refusals to cheer on various occasions in the preceding months, testified to
inadequate psychological preparation of the people; and in his impatience
Hitler did little to improve it. After the Reichstag speech of April 28,
1938, he avoided going before the masses. Presumably he acted on the
assumption that the drama of events would in itself generate sufficient
mobilizing energies. But the satisfaction the people had obviously felt upon
the reoccupation of the Rhineland, the annexation of Austria, and the entry
into the Sudetenland had evaporated by the time Prague was occupied.
Such gratifications were no longer to be had. Neither Danzig nor the Polish
Corridor seemed of great importance to the prestige of the nation that had
recovered from its long humiliation. Granted, the war against Poland was
more popular than any of the other engagements of the Second World War;
but it lacked the magnetic element. Neither the atrocity stories about
murdered, tortured, or raped Germans nor the actual number of some

* The melodramatic translation "warlord" for *Feldherr* has already become traditional in books about Hitler. Strictly speaking, *Feldherr* means no more than
"commanding general" or "supreme commander"; its slightly bombastic connotation
is exaggerated by "warlord." But a one-for-one translation of *Feldherr* is sometimes
useful. We have therefore adopted "generalissimo," although that word, too, has a
misleading "Chinese" connotation.—TRANS.

7,000 victims of Polish persecution could fire the popular mind. A few months after the beginning of the war expressions of discontent increased; the SD noted that the mood of the population was "that's what comes when a war is started without sufficient preparation." Between Christmas and New Year's Day police power had to be used for the first time against crowds of discontented people.[8]

Hitler had obviously hastened the war for fear that the population's preparedness might sink to a still lower level. He must have thought that it would be wise to begin the struggle while he could still draw on the abating momentum of former years. "Those who avoid battles," he had once remarked, "will never acquire the strength to fight battles." And in one of his last speeches, in which he justified his timing of the war ("there could not have been . . . a more fortunate moment than that of 1939"), he acknowledged that his decision had also been influenced by the psychological consideration that "enthusiasm and readiness to sacrifice . . . cannot be bottled and preserved. Such spirit arises *once* in the course of a revolution and will gradually fade away. Dull routine and the comforts of life will once more exert their spell on people and make them philistines again. It would have been wrong to let slip away all we had been able to achieve by National Socialist education, by the tremendous wave of enthusiasm that lifted our people." On the contrary, he continued, war offered the chance to kindle that spirit anew.[9]

In the psychological realm, then, the war was supposed to partly create the spirit necessary to wage it. And in a certin sense this was Hitler's basic idea for the entire conflict—which once again revealed his gambler's temperament. In a speech delivered at the beginning of July, 1944, he publicly admitted this principle when he conceded that the war was "a prefinancing of the future achievements, the future work, the future raw materials, the future nutritional base; but it is also tremendous training for mastering the tasks which will face us in the future."

Preparations in the fields of economics and armaments were actually far sketchier than the psychological preparations. To be sure, official propaganda repeatedly referred to enormous defensive efforts; and the whole world believed this, as it believed the speeches of leading members of the regime who boasted that the German economy had been geared for war for years. Thus Göring, when appointed commissioner of the Four-Year Plan, averred that Germany was already at war, though not yet a shooting war. The reality, however, was quite different. The country was, it is true, ahead of its enemies in steel production. Its coal supplies were also larger and its industries in many cases capable of greater production than those of the Allies. But in spite of all the efforts at autarchy Germany was still heavily dependent on foreign sources for crucial war materials. For example, she imported 90 per cent of her tin, 70 per cent of her copper, 80 per cent of her rubber, 75 per cent of her oil, and 99 per cent of her bauxite. She had stockpiled sufficient raw materials for approximately a year; but supplies of copper, rubber, and tin had been almost consumed by the spring of 1939. Without the vigorous economic support of the Soviet Union Germany would probably have succumbed to a British economic blockade within a short time. Molotov himself pointed this out in a conversation with Hitler.

The situation with regard to military equipment was not much different. In his Reichstag speech of September 1, 1939, Hitler declared that he had expended 90 billion marks on armaments. But this was one of those high-flying fictions he regularly indulged in when he cited figures.[10] In spite of all expenditures in the preceding years Germany was armed only for the war that Hitler launched on September 1, not for the war of September 3. The army did consist of 102 divisions, but only half of these were active and battle-ready. The state of its training left much to be desired. The navy was distinctly inferior to the British and even to the French fleets; not even the strength permissible under the Anglo-German Naval Treaty of 1935 had been attained. Shortly after the Western declarations of war reached Berlin, Grand Admiral Raeder declared tersely that the German fleet, or rather "the little that is finished or will be finished in time, can only go down fighting honorably." The air force alone was stronger than the forces of the enemy; it had 3,298 planes at its disposal. On the other hand, the ammunition supply had been half consumed by the end of the Polish campaign, so that the war could not have been actively continued for even three or four weeks. At Nuremberg, General Jodl called the existing reserves at the outbreak of the war "literally ridiculous." Troop equipment also amounted to considerably less than the four-month stock that the High Command of the army had demanded. Even a small-scale attack from the West in the fall of 1939 would probably have brought about Germany's defeat and the end of the war, military experts have concluded.[11]

There is no doubt that Hitler saw these difficulties and risks. In his memorandum of October 9, 1939, "on the waging of the war in the West" he discussed these matters and devoted a special section to analyzing "the dangers of the German situation." His chief concern was a protracted war, for which he considered Germany not sufficiently armed politically, materially, or psychologically. But he thought such weaknesses were intrinsic to Germany's general plight, and thus believed that "by no matter what efforts they cannot be essentially improved within a short time." Essentially, this meant that as things stood Germany was in no position to wage a world war.

Hitler reacted to this dilemma with an enormously significant twist that revealed all his shrewdness and all his cunning—cunning even toward himself. If Germany was incapable of waging a major, protracted war against an enemy coalition, she must bring her power to bear as events demanded, in spaced, short and concentrated blows against selected individual opponents, thus step by step enlarging her economic base until she finally reached the position to wage world war. This was the strategic concept of blitzkrieg.[12]

For a long time the idea of blitzkrieg was understood merely as a tactical or operative method of annihilating the enemy's military forces by surprise attack. But in fact it was a prescription for total warfare, which took account of the specific weaknesses and strengths of the German situation and ingeniously combined them in a novel method of conquest. By using the interval between successive campaigns for a fresh build-up of armaments, the material burden on the economy and the public could be kept relatively low. Moreover, the preparations could be attuned directly to the next enemy. Each time a triumph was celebrated, the fanfares provided psychological stimulation for the next thrust. In the final analysis, it was an attempt to get around that discouraging saying of the days of the First World War, that Germany won her battles but lost her wars, by breaking up the war into a series of victorious engagements. But though the plan corresponded so well to the nature of the regime and to Hitler's improvising style, which depended so largely on momentary inspirations, it had a serious flaw. It was bound to fail as soon as a strong enemy coalition came into being, committed to fight a protracted war.

Hitler had such faith in the blitzkrieg concept that he was in no way prepared for the alternative of large-scale warfare. In the summer of 1939 the armed forces operations staff suggested that it would be wise to draw up contingency plans and undertake war games in view of a full-scale conflict. Hitler ruled against this, emphasizing that the war against Poland would be localized. His memorandum of October 9 was the first concrete attempt to define the situation and the goals of a conflict with the West. He also repeatedly rejected proposals to retool the economy for the needs of a protracted total war; industrial production in 1940 went down slightly from the previous year. And shortly before the winter of 1941–42 production of military goods was actually cut back in anticipation of the impending blitz victory over the Soviet Union. Here, too, the experience of the First World War was influencing Hitler. He wanted to avoid the psychologically wearing effects of a rigorously restricted economy that for years scanted the wants of the people.

The continuity between the First and the Second World War is tangibly present on a variety of planes, and not only as a matter of interpretation. Hitler himself would often say that behind him lay only an armistice, whereas before him was "the victory we threw away in 1918." In his speech of November 23, 1939, referring to the First World War, he wrote: "Today the second act of this drama is being written." In the light of this continuity, Hitler appears as the specifically radical representative of a concept of German world hegemony that can be traced back to the late Bismarck period. As early as the turn of the century, it had condensed into specific war aims, and after the failed attempt of 1914–18 a fresh attempt was made to carry it out, with new and greater resolution, in the Second

616

World War. An imperialistic drive nearly a century old culminated in Hitler.[13]

This view can be upheld on many grounds. The general connection between Hitler and the prewar world, his origins in its complexes, ideologies, and defensive reactions, in itself represents a weighty argument. For in spite of all his modernity Hitler was a profoundly anachronistic phenomenon. In his naïve imperialism, in his magnitude complex, in his conviction of the inescapable choice between ascent to world power or doom, he was a leftover of the nineteenth century. In principle the biased young man of the Vienna days repeated the typical and fundamental movement of the conservative ruling classes of the period: flight from their fears of the socialist menace into expansionist ideas. Hitler merely extended and radicalized that tendency. Whereas the conservatives expected war and conquest to bring about a "general clean-up" that would bolster the social and political status ("strengthening of the patriarchal order and principles" was the way they phrased it), Hitler always thought in gigantically expanded categories, regarding war and expansion as something that went far beyond class interests, as the nation's and even the race's sole chance for survival. In Hitler's thinking social imperialism of the traditional variety was peculiarly mixed with biologizing elements.

The direction of Hitler's expansionist plans also corresponded to tradition reaching into the past. It had long been a part of German ideology that the East was the natural *Lebensraum* for the Reich. The fact that Hitler had come from the Dual Monarchy reinforced his tendency to look in this direction. As far back as 1894 a statement by the strident Pan-German Association had guided the nation's interest toward the East and Southeast, "in order to assure the Germanic race those living conditions which it needs for the full development of its energies." At the notorious "council of war" held on December 8, 1912, Chief of Staff von Moltke insisted that "the press should be used to build up sentiment for a war against Russia." Hence some papers were soon calling for the inevitable decisive struggle with the East. The question, according to the press, was whether the hegemony over Europe would fall to Teutons or Slavs. A few days after the outbreak of the First World War the Foreign Office put forth a plan for the "formation of several buffer states" in the East, all of which were to stand in military dependence on Germany. A memorandum by the president of the Pan-Germans, Heinrich Class, "On the German War Aim," which was distributed as a leaflet in 1917, went even further. It demanded extensive provinces in the East and suggested a "racial clean-up" by exchange of Russians for Volga Germans, transference of the Jews to Palestine, and a relocation to the East of Germany's Polish population. Hitler's design for an Eastern policy surely derived from such grandiose wartime proposals. When we add to this the influence of Russian exile circles in Munich and his own bent for intellectual extremism, we have the full-blown Hitlerian plan.

617

Similarly, Hitler's ideas about alliances were by no means without precedent. That Germany must obtain England's neutrality in order to join with Austria-Hungary in a war of conquest to the East, with possibly a simultaneous war against France, was not wholly alien to the foreign policy of the Wilhelminian Empire. Shortly after the outbreak of the 1914 war, the German Chancellor Bethmann-Hollweg discussed the very same idea, even thinking, by means of a blitzkreig in the West, to arrive at an alliance with England in order to proceed jointly with England against Russia. Toward the end of the war he declared that the conflict "could have been avoided only by an understanding with England." Here was the original sketch for Hitler's ideal plan as formulated in *Mein Kampf;* and when he came to power, Hitler did in fact promptly seek an understanding with England and British neutrality. The Weimar Republic, especially under the guidance of Gustav Stresemann, had given precedence to rapprochement with France.

But beyond these matters of ideology, geopolitics, and alliances, the continuity of German military ambitions can also be seen embodied in the attitudes of social groups. It was chiefly the conservative ruling class whose spokesmen drafted the expansive projects of the period of the monarchy and in whom the collapse of 1918 had bred an exacerbated status complex. Ever since, they had been bent on restoring Germany's shaken self-confidence and winning back the lost territories (especially from Poland). Throughout the Weimar period even the most temperate representatives of that class had always been averse to offering a guarantee of the Eastern borders. A 1926 memorandum for the Foreign Office from the army chiefs, for example, set forth in highly characteristic fashion the following guidelines for German foreign policy: liberation of the Rhineland and the Saar, elimination of the Polish Corridor and repossession of Polish Upper Silesia, Anschluss of German Austria, and finally elimination of the demilitarized zone. Here we have, in somewhat different order, the foreign-policy schedule followed by Hitler during the thirties.

The members of the former ruling class looked to the Führer of the National Socialist Party to carry out their revisionist aims. He seemed well qualified for this mission since he was supremely skillful in manipulating the Versailles Treaty and the widespread feelings of humiliation it evoked as integrating factors for the mobilization of the nation. Significantly, at the beginning of his chancellorship, they actually encouraged him to take a still bolder course. In the matter of withdrawal from the Disarmament Conference, or from the League of Nations, the conservative members of the cabinet pressed the hesitating Hitler to take the plunge. The same applied to the question of disarmament. Up to the occupation of Prague they approved entirely of his objectives, even though they questioned his gambler's methods.

At this point the continuity ends. For what the revisionistic conserva-

tives of the type of von Neurath, von Blomberg, von Papen, or von Weizsäcker regarded as the goal was to Hitler not even a stage, but merely a
preliminary step. He despised his halfhearted partners because they
stopped short of reaching out for world power as he did. His fixed aim
continued to be not new (or even old) borders, but vast new areas, over
half a million square miles, indeed all the land as far as the Urals and
eventually beyond. "We shall impose our laws upon the East. We shall
break through and gradually smash forward to the Urals. I hope that our
generation will live to accomplish that. . . . Then we shall have a healthy
selection [of the fittest] for the entire future. In this way we will create the
preconditions allowing the whole of Europe—directed, ordered and led by
us, the Germanic race—to survive for generations its destined battles with
an Asia that will undoubtedly flare up again. We do not know when that
will be. But if the mass of humanity amounting to one to one and a half
billions surges forward, then the Germanic race with its, as I hope, 250 to
300 millions, together with other European races totaling from 600 to 700
million people, and with a deployment area extending to the Urals or in a
century beyond the Urals, will pass the test of its struggle for survival
against Asia."[14]

What made this kind of imperialism qualitatively different from that
under the kaisers, what shattered the continuity, was less the enormous
hunger for sheer space (for that had been already suggested among the Pan-
Germans and in more specific terms of power politics in Ludendorff's 1918
plans for handling the East) than the ideological additives that lent it
coherence and impetus: the notions of selection, racial bloc, and eschatological mission. Something of the sudden insight into this difference—
which as a rule came much too late—breaks through in the assessment of
Hitler's character by a conservative at the time: "This man doesn't even
belong to our race. There is something utterly alien about him, as if he
belonged to an otherwise extinct primitive race."[15]

Hitler's statement that the Second World War was the continuation of
the First was also not the imperialistic commonplace for which it has
generally been taken. He himself knew better. For the last time he wanted
the generals and his conservative partners to believe that he was the trustee
of their unrealized dreams of power, who would deliver to them their
rightful victory of 1918. But he had far more sweeping victories in mind.
The revisionist sentiments merely served him as useful links with the past.
Once more we have the peculiar duality of proximity and distance that
characterized all his relationships. Against the background of an undia-
lectic concept of continuity it is easy to overlook the nature of the phenomenon. Hitler was not Wilhelm III!

Long ago, in *Mein Kampf,* he had written that his program represented a
declaration of war against the existing order, against the known state of

affairs, in short, against the established view of life in general. In September, 1939, he began waging that struggle by armed force and beyond the frontiers. The First World War had already been in part a clash of ideologies and systems of rule; the Second became such a clash in an incomparably more acute and doctrinaire fashion, a kind of world-wide civil war to decide not so much the kind of power that would henceforth rule the world as the kind of morality.

The enemies who faced one another after the unexpectedly rapid subjugation of Poland had no avowed territorial object of dispute, no aims of conquest; and for a time, during the "phony war" of that autumn, it seemed as if the war had lost its rationale. Might this mean that peace could be restored again? On October 5 Hitler had gone to Warsaw for the victory parade and had announced an important "appeal for peace" for the following day. Hardly anyone suspected how pointless the announcement of these vague hopes was. Two weeks earlier Stalin had informed Hitler that he had little use for an independent rump Poland. With his newly arisen antipathy for cautious politics, Hitler promptly agreed to the proposed negotiations. When they ended on October 4, Poland had once more been partitioned by her overpowering neighbors. But along with that act, all chance was lost of ending the war with the Western powers by a political solution. A foreign diplomat remarked after Hitler's Reichstag address that he had threatened peace with the punishment of forced labor.

Within the framework of his larger design, Hitler had acted with total consistency. Although he would have welcomed a once more neutralized West, Stalin's offer at last provided him with a common border with the Soviet Union. And, after all, he had begun the war against Poland to achieve just that. As early as October 17 he had issued a significant order to General Keitel, chief of the High Command of the armed forces. Keitel had been instructed to consider, in future planning, that the occupied Polish region "has military importance for us as an advanced glacis and can be utilized for deployment. To that end the railroads, road and communications must be kept in order and exploited for our purpose. Any signs of consolidation of conditions in Poland must be stamped out."

Morally, too, he now crossed the boundary that made the war irrevocable. In the same conversation he demanded the repression of any sign "that a Polish intelligentsia is coming forward as a class of leaders. The country is to continue under a low standard of living; we want to draw only labor forces from it." Territory that went far beyond the borders of 1914 was incorporated into the Reich. The remainder was set up as a general government under the administration of Hans Frank; one part was subjected to a ruthless process of Germanization, the other to an unprecedented campaign of enslavement and annihilation. And while the commandos, the *Einsatzgruppen,* commenced their reign of terror, arresting, resettling, expelling, and liquidating—so that one German army officer

620

wrote in a horrified letter of a "band of murderers, robbers and plunderers" —Hans Frank extolled the "epoch of the East" that was now beginning for Germany, a period, as he described it in his own peculiar brand of bombastic jargon, "of the most tremendous reshaping of colonizing and resettlement implementation."

With the intensified stress on ideology, Heinrich Himmler was now visibly gaining more power. Hitler had occasionally remarked in private that Himmler did not shrink from proceeding "with reprehensible methods" and by doing so not only established order but also created accomplices. It would seem that this motive, quite aside from all expansionist plans, contributed to the more and more undisguised criminalization of the system. The idea was to bind the entire nation to the regime by complicity in an enormous crime, to engender the feeling that all the ships had been burned, that Salamis feeling of which Hitler had spoken. This, too, like his relinquishing the means of politics, was an attempt to cut off all avenues of retreat. In nearly every speech Hitler delivered after the beginning of the war the formula recurs: a November, 1918, will not be repeated. No doubt he sensed what General Ritter von Leeb wrote in his diary on October 3, 1939: "Poor mood of the population, no enthusiasm at all, no flags flying from the houses. Everyone waiting for peace. The people sense the needlessness of the war." The annihilation policy in the East, which began immediately, was one of the ways of making the war irrevocable.

Now Hitler again no longer had a way out; once more, reliving old excitements, he stood with his back to the wall. The conflict would have to be, as he habitually phrased it, "fought out to the end." To United States Undersecretary of State Sumner Welles, who called on him on March 2, 1940, he said that it was "not a question of whether Germany would be annihilated." Germany would defend herself to the utmost; "at the very worst, all will be annihilated."

BOOK VII

Victors
and Vanquished

Chapter 1

Only a genius can do that!

Wilhelm Keitel

Since last September I have thought
of Hitler as a dead man.

Georges Bernanos

THE GENERALISSIMO

Well before the end of October, 1939, Hitler began moving his victorious divisions to the West and deploying them in new positions. As always, whenever he had arrived at a decision, a feverish urge for action had gripped him. Certainly the concept of sitzkrieg, as the phony war was called in contrast to blitzkrieg, did not apply to Hitler's behavior. Even before the Western powers had reacted to his "peace appeal" of October 6, he summoned the three commanders of the services, together with Keitel and Halder, and read them a memorandum on the military situation. It began with a historical review of France's hostility toward Germany, going back as far as the Peace of Westphalia in 1648, on which grounds he justified his determination to attack at once in the West. His aim, he declared, was "annihilation of the strength and ability of the Western powers to once more oppose the . . . further development of the German nation in Europe."[1] Yet the war in the West, he went on, was only the requisite detour to eliminate the menace in the rear before the great march of conquest to the East began. He next went into a detailed discussion of the methods of mobile warfare that had been applied in Poland, and recommended these for the campaign in the West. The crucial thing, he declared, was the massive commitment of tanks to keep the operative forward movement of the army in flux and to avoid trench warfare like that of 1914–18. This was the approach that proved so strikingly successful in May and June of the following year.

Like Directive Number 6 on the conduct of the war, which was presented at the same time, the memorandum was meant to overcome the halfheartedness of the top-ranking officers. "The main thing is the will to

625

defeat the enemy," Hitler exhorted his audience. In fact a number of the generals considered Hitler's plan to "bring the French and British to the battlefield and to rout them," both wrong and risky, and instead recommended putting the war "to sleep" by assuming a consistent defensive posture. One of the generals spoke of the "insanity of an attack." Generals von Brauchitsch and Halder, and above all General Thomas, chief of the Armaments Office, and General von Stülpnagel, Quartermaster General, offered specific objections. They pointed to the scanty stocks of raw materials, the exhausted reserves of ammunition, the dangers of a winter campaign, and the enemy's strength. In fact the accumulation of political, military, and sometimes even moral scruples was once more impelling the officers into active resistance. General Jodl told Halder that the intrigues of the military officers indicated "a crisis of the worst sort" and that Hitler was "embittered that the soldiers are not following him."[2]

The more reluctance the generals showed, the more impatiently Hitler pressed for the beginning of the offensive. He had originally set the date between November 15 and 20, then advanced it to November 12 and thus forced the military to make a decision. As in September, 1938, they confronted the choice of either preparing a war they regarded as fatal or overthrowing Hitler; again, von Brauchitsch was half ready to go over to the opposition, while in the background the same actors operated: Colonel Oster, General Beck, now retired, Admiral Canaris, Carl Goerdeler, Ulrich von Hassell, the former ambassador in Rome, and others. The center of their activities was army general headquarters in Zossen, and early in November the conspirators decided on a *coup d'état* if Hitler continued to insist on his order for an offensive. Von Brauchitsch offered to make a last attempt to change Hitler's mind in a conference already scheduled for November 5. That was the day on which the German contingents were to occupy their starting positions for the advance upon Holland, Belgium, and Luxembourg.

The conference in the Berlin chancellery led to a dramatic clash. At first Hitler listened with seeming calm to the objections that the commander in chief had summed up in a kind of "countermemorandum." Hitler disposed of the reference to unfavorable weather conditions by remarking that the weather would also be bad for the enemy. As for the generals' concern about inadequate training, he answered that this could hardly be amended in four weeks. When von Brauchitsch finally criticized the conduct of the troops in the Polish campaign and spoke of breaches of discipline, Hitler leaped at the chance for one of his great outbursts. Raging—as Halder put it in his notes of the episode—he demanded documents. He wanted to know where, in what units, the alleged events had occurred, what had been done about them, whether death sentences had been imposed. He declared that he personally would look into the matter on the spot and went on to say that in reality it was only the army leadership that had not wanted to

626

fight and therefore had for so long retarded the tempo of rearmament. But now he was going to "eliminate the spirit of Zossen," that is, the slackness of the army General Staff. Bluntly, he forbade von Brauchitsch to go on with his report. Stunned, his face pale, the commander in chief left the chancellery. "Br[auchitsch] has completely collapsed," one of the participants noted. That same evening Hitler once more explicitly confirmed the order for attack on November 12.

Although this meant that the condition for a *coup d'état* was met, the conspirators did nothing. The mere threat against the "spirit of Zossen" had sufficed to reveal their weakness and indecisiveness. "Everything is too late and gone totally awry," one of Oster's confidants, Colonel Groscurth, wrote in his diary. With self-betraying haste Halder burned all incriminating material and called an immediate halt to the preparations for a coup. Three days later in the Bürgerbräukeller in Munich Hitler barely escaped an attempted assassination that was obviously the work of a lone individual. Thereafter, fear of a large-scale probe by the Gestapo smothered the last remaining plans for a coup.

Moreover, chance was kind to the conspirators and saved them from their own resolutions; for on November 7 the date for the offensive had to be postponed because of weather conditions. Hitler, however, granted a postponement of only a few days. How set he was against the long-term postponement the military men demanded is evident from the fact that up to May, 1940, when the attack finally began, the process of on-again-off-again was repeated a total of twenty-nine times. During the second half of November the commanders were called to Berlin for ideological morale building. Göring and Goebbels delivered bracing speeches; then Hitler himself appeared before them on November 23, and in three speeches given within the course of seven hours tried at once to convince and to intimidate the officers.[3] Looking back upon the preceding years, he charged them with lack of faith. He professed to be profoundly offended. "I cannot endure anyone's telling me the troops are not all right." Threateningly, he added: "A revolution at home is not possible, either with you or without you." His determination to launch an immediate assault upon the West was irrevocable, he said, and answered the objections of several officers to the violation of Dutch and Belgian neutrality by declaring it inconsequential. ("Nobody will question it when we have won.") Balefully he told them: "I shall shrink from nothing and destroy everyone who is against me," and ended his speech with the following ringing words:

I am determined to lead my life in such a way that I can meet death with equanimity when my time comes. Behind me stands the German people, whose morale can only deteriorate. . . . If we meet the test of this struggle successfully—and we will meet it—our times will go down in the history of our people. In this struggle I shall stand or fall. I will not survive the defeat of my people. Abroad, no capitulation; at home, no revolution.

The crisis among the officers in the fall of 1939 had far-reaching consequences. Insisting as he did on total commitments, Hitler henceforth distrusted not only his generals' loyalty but also their professional advice. The peremptory way in which he himself now assumed the role of generalissimo had its origins in these events. On the other hand, the renewed evidence of the weakness and compliance of the generals, especially of the OKH (Army High Command), suited his desire to reduce the organs of military leadership to purely instrumental functions. In preparing the strike against Denmark and Norway, which was meant to assure him Swedish iron ore and win an operational base for the struggle against England, he completely excluded the OKH. Instead, he transferred the planning to a special staff within the OKW (High Command of the Armed Forces). Thus he managed to install within the military hierarchy the system of rival authorities so fundamental to his practice of government. He thought his decision brilliantly confirmed when the risky enterprise begun in April, 1940, which ran counter to all the principles of naval warfare and had been regarded by the Allied staffs as almost inconceivable, proved a total success. Thereafter he no longer met with open opposition from the generals. The full weakness of those generals had already been exposed during the autumn crisis when Halder approached State Secretary von Weizsäcker and asked whether bringing in a soothsayer might not have some influence on Hitler; he could obtain a million marks for the purpose, he said. Commander in Chief von Brauchitsch, on the other hand, gave a visitor the impression that he was "completely done for, isolated."

At dawn on May 10, 1940, the long-awaited offensive in the West began at last. The night before, Colonel Oster, through his friend Colonel G. J. Sas, the Dutch military attaché in Berlin, had informed the other side. But when the din of artillery and the drone of bombers began in the morning, the skeptical Allied general staffs were taken completely by surprise. They had thought the warning a trap. By committing large British and French forces hastily brought up from northern France, they finally managed to check the German advance through Belgium east of Brussels. They gave no thought to the fact that their counteraction was scarcely opposed by the German air force. For this was the real trap. Walking into it had already cost them the victory.

The original German plan of campaign, a variant of the old Schlieffen Plan, called for bypassing the French lines of fortifications by a massed assault through Belgium and a descent upon northwestern France. The German leadership was well aware of what was wrong with this plan: it lacked the element of surprise, so that the offensive was liable to be brought to a standstill and freeze into trench warfare even sooner than in the First World War. Moreover, it required the commitment of large tank formations in terrain cut up by many rivers and canals. All this would seem to imperil the rapid decision upon which Hitler's whole strategy was based. But there appeared to be no alternative. Another plan presented in October, 1939, by General von Manstein, chief of staff of Army Group A, had been rejected by Brauchitsch and Halder, and ultimately Manstein had been relieved of his command. He had argued for shifting the main weight of the German advance from the right wing to the center, thus regaining the element of surprise, since it was generally held that the Ardennes would not permit extensive tank operations. The French leadership had therefore placed relatively weak forces on this sector of its front, and Manstein's plan was founded on this fact. Once the German tanks had overcome the problems of the mountainous and wooded terrain, he argued, they could roll almost unhindered across the plains of northern France to the sea, and cut off the Allied armies that had been marched into Belgium.

What had vexed the army High Command was precisely what instantly fascinated Hitler: the bold and unexpected character of this plan. It is said that he had already been occupied with similar notions at the time he learned of Manstein's proposal. By mid-February, 1940, therefore, after a talk with the general, he ordered a reformulation of the plan of campaign. That decision was to prove crucial.

It was by no means numerical advantage or technological superiority that made the war in the West such a breath-taking victory. The forces that confronted one another on May 10 were nearly equal in strength; in fact the Allied side had a slight edge in numbers. Besides the 137 divisions of the Western powers, there were 34 Dutch and Belgian divisions. These confronted 136 German divisions. The Allied air forces had some 2,800 planes, the German air force barely 1,000 more than that. On the Allied side approximately 3,000 tanks and armored vehicles faced 2,500 on the German side, although most of the latter were organized in special armored divisions. But the decisive factor was the remarkable German plan of operations, which Churchill aptly called the strategy of the "scythe-cut"[4] and forced the opponent to a "battle with reversed fronts."

The German attack once again began with an onslaught against Holland, Belgium, and Luxembourg. No declaration of war was made, and the enemy air forces were destroyed on the ground. "Fortress Holland" fell in five days. Hitler himself had developed the idea of dropping small, highly trained units of parachute troops at strategically important points behind the front; this proved a decisive factor in the rapid victory. Similarly, the center of the Belgian system of defense collapsed when Fort Eben Emael, the key to the system of fortifications guarding Liège, was eliminated by one such unit, which landed inside the fort area in gliders. Meanwhile, the advance through Luxembourg and the Ardennes, again a complete surprise to the enemy, made rapid progress. By May 13 the tank formations were able to cross the Meuse at Dinant and Sedan. On May 16 Laon fell, on May 20 Amiens; and that same night the first formations reached the

629

Channel coast. At times the advance proceeded so rapidly that the main units lost contact with the vanguard, and Hitler, suspicious as always, distrusted his own triumph. "The Führer is frightfully nervous," Halder noted on May 17. "He is alarmed by his own success, doesn't want to risk anything, and consequently would prefer to stop us." And on the following day: "The Führer is unaccountably fearful about the southern flank. He rages and shouts that we are on the point of ruining the whole operation and exposing ourselves to the dangers of defeat."[5]

In fact there was no danger. When Britain's new Prime Minister, Winston Churchill, alarmed by the situation at the front, flew to Paris, General Gamelin admitted to him that the majority of his mobile forces had already fallen into the German trap. Gamelin, commander in chief of the Allied armies, tried to conjure up memories of past glories. In an Order of the Day for May 17 he repeated word for word General Joffre's proclamation before the first Battle of the Marne in September, 1914, calling upon the soldiers not to yield a foot of soil. But the Allied leaders did not succeed in collecting their retreating armies, building new lines, and organizing a counterattack. The Allied defeat would have been complete if General Guderian's tank spearhead had not received the order, on May 24, to stop in its tracks. It was at this time only a few miles south of Dunkirk and not in contact with the enemy. The German slowdown for forty-eight hours left the Allies a port and thus the chance to escape. Within a week, in one of the most daring improvisations of the war, with the aid of some 900 largely small ships, fishing boats, excursion steamers, and private yachts, nearly 340,000 men—the greater part of the Allied formations—were ferried to England.

The responsibility for the order to halt before Dunkirk has since been the object of extensive investigation. Some have held that Hitler himself deliberately let the majority of the British Expeditionary Corps escape in order to keep open the way for the compromise with England that he continued to hope for. But such a decision would have contradicted the war aim formulated in his memorandum. It would also have contradicted Directive Number 13 of May 24, which began: "Next goal of operations is the annihilation of the French, British and Belgian forces encircled in Artois and in Flanders by the concentric attack of our northern wing. . . . During this operation the task of the Air Force is to break all enemy resistance in the encircled parts and to prevent the escape of the British forces across the Channel." Hitler's order to halt met with vehement opposition within the army High Command, but was approved by General von Rundstedt, the commander of Army Group A. Its underlying intention was rather to give a respite to the tank formations, exhausted by two weeks of fighting, and enable them to recoup their strength for the impending battle for France. Göring's boasts that his Luftwaffe would transform the port of Dunkirk into a sea of flames and sink every ship that tried to

630

dock there reinforced Hitler in his decision. When the city, which had been undefended and within Guderian's reach ten days earlier, at last fell into German hands on June 4, Halder noted tersely: "Dunkirk taken, coast reached. Even the French are gone."

Yet the superior operational plan was not alone responsible for the German successes. When Hitler's armies turned south, after completing the encirclement maneuver at the Channel coast, they encountered a discouraged, broken enemy whose defeatism had been only magnified by the debacle in the north. The French command was operating with formations that had already been beaten, with divisions that had been dispersed, had deserted, or had simply passed into dissolution. As early as the end of May a British general called the French army a rabble without the slightest discipline.[6] Millions of refugees aimlessly tramped the roads, dragging carts heaped high with possessions, blocking the movements of their own troops, carrying them along into the confusion, overtaken by German tanks, driven into panic by the bombs and the screams of the Stukas. Every step toward organized military resistance was submerged in the indescribable chaos. The country had been prepared for defeat but not for collapse. From the French headquarters in Briare there was only a single telephone link to the troops and to the outside world, and that was not in operation between twelve and two o'clock in the afternoon because the postmistress went to lunch at this time. When General Brooke, commander in chief of the British Expeditionary Force, asked about the divisions assigned for the defense of "Fortress Brittany," General Weygand, the newly appointed supreme commander, shrugged resignedly: "I know they're a pure figment of the imagination." Many commanding generals stared at their maps as if these were a blank wall. It was in fact as if the sky were falling down upon France.

Although the German planning for the Battle of France had provided for scarcely any reactions on the enemy's part, and although the directives seemed to suggest extensive marching drills rather than a campaign, Hitler was nevertheless surprised by the speed of the advance. On June 14 his troops marched through the Porte Maillot into Paris and lowered the tricolor from the Eiffel Tower. Three days later Rommel covered 150 miles in a single day. And when Guderian on the same day reported that he had reached Pontarlier with his tanks, Hitler wired back to ask whether it was not a mistake: "You probably mean Pontailler-sur-Saône." But Guderian reported back: "No mistake. I am myself in Pontarlier on the Swiss border." From there he advanced northeast and broke into the Maginot Line from the rear. The defensive line that had dominated France's strategy and all her thinking fell almost without a fight.

With the German victory now tangible, Italy rushed in to help. Mussolini hated, as he was wont to say, the reputation of unreliability that clung to his country, and he wanted to banish it by "a policy as straight as a sword

631

blade." But the matter was not so simple. His decision to stay out of the war for the present had started to waver in October, in view of the German triumphs in Poland. In November he had regarded the idea that Hitler might win the war as "utterly intolerable." In December he had said to Ciano that he "openly wished for a German defeat." He had informed the Dutch and the Belgians of the date set for the German attack. Early in January, 1940, he wrote to Hitler, advising him against his present course. As the "dean of dictators" Mussolini tried to turn Hitler's momentum toward the East:[7]

Nobody knows better than I, who possess nearly forty years of political experience, that politics makes its own tactical demands. This also applies to revolutionary politics. . . . Therefore I understand your . . . having avoided the second front. In Poland and the Baltic region, therefore, Russia has become the great gainer from the war, without risking anything. But I, who am a revolutionary by birth and have never changed my views, tell you that you cannot constantly sacrifice the principles of your revolution in favor of the tactical requirements of a momentary political situation. I am convinced that you may not lower the anti-Semitic and anti-Bolshevistic banner that you held high for twenty years . . . and I am only doing my absolute duty when I add that a single further step to extend your relations with Moscow would have devastating consequences in Italy. . . .

But at a conference at the Brenner Pass on March 18, 1940, Hitler succeeded without any special effort in dispelling Mussolini's disgruntlement and in rekindling his partner's old admiration and lust for loot. "Neither can it be denied that the Duce is fascinated by Hitler," Ciano wrote, "a fascination which involves something deeply rooted in his makeup."

From that point on, Mussolini's determination to take part in the war grew steadily. It would be humiliating, he said, "to remain with our hands folded while others write history. It matters little who wins. To make a people great it is necessary to send them to battle even if you have to kick them in the pants."[8] Against the will of the King, of industry, of the army, even against the will of some of his influential fellow Fascists in the Grand Council, he began working toward Italy's entry into the war. Early in June, 1940, Marshal Badoglio opposed the order to begin offensive operations. His soldiers, he said, "did not even have a sufficient number of shirts." Mussolini dismissed the argument: "I assure you that it will all be over with by September. I need several thousand casualties to be able to take my place at the peace table as a belligerent." On June 10 the Italian army launched its attack but quickly ground to a halt on the outskirts of the border town of Menton. Indignantly, the Italian dictator declared: "It is the material I lack. Even Michelangelo had need of marble to make statues. If he had had only clay, he would have become a potter."[9] Only a week later events overtook his ambitions, when President Lebrun entrusted Marshal

Pétain with the formation of a new French government. As his first official act, Pétain transmitted to the German High Command, through the Spanish government, his request for an armistice.

Hitler received the news in the small Belgian village of Bruly-le-Pêche, near the French border, where he had set up his headquarters. A famous photograph has preserved his reaction: his right foot raised as he danced a joyful jig, laughing, slapping his thigh. And it was here, in the context of an exuberant toast, that Keitel for the first time hailed him as the "greatest generalissimo of all times."

There is no denying that the successes were unprecedented. In three weeks the Wehrmacht had overrun Poland; in something more than two months it had overwhelmed Norway, Denmark, Holland, Belgium, Luxembourg, and France, driven the British back to their island, and effectively challenged the British fleet. And all this was accomplished with comparatively small casualties. The campaign in the West had cost the German side 27,000 lives, compared with 135,000 dead on the enemy side.

The successes of the campaign cannot be attributed solely to Hitler's personal merits as a commander; but they were also not entirely the product of luck, shrewd counsel, or the enemy's failures. The importance of armored formations had been recognized in France and elsewhere during the thirties, but only Hitler had drawn the necessary conclusion and equipped the Wehrmacht with ten armored divisions—against some resistance. He had recognized France's weakness and demoralized impotence far more acutely than his generals, who were still caught up in outmoded notions. And no matter how small his personal contribution to Manstein's plan of campaign may have been, he immediately grasped its importance and changed the whole concept of German operations accordingly. He showed that he had an eye for unconventional possibilities, all the keener because of his lack of background and hence of bias. He had studied military literature long and intensively; his bedside reading throughout almost the whole of the war consisted of naval records and manuals of military science. He used his stupendous memory of matters military for purposes of self-display. The almost lunatic sureness with which he could rattle off tonnages, calibers, ranges, or specifications of various weapons systems frequently staggered and irritated his entourage.

At the same time, he was also able to apply such knowledge imaginatively. He had a keen sense of the potentialities of modern weapons, he knew where to commit them and where they would be most effective. This was coupled with remarkable insight into the psychology of the enemy. All these qualities found expression in the accurately placed surprise strokes, in the correct predictions of tactical countermeasures, and in the lightning grasp of favorable opportunities. The plan for the coup against Fort Eben

Emael came from Hitler, as did the idea of equipping dive bombers with sirens whose scream was devastating.[10] Similarly, in defiance of the views of many experts, he insisted on providing tanks with long cannon. With some justice he has been called the "most informed and versatile specialist in military technology of his age."[11] Unquestionably, he was not just the "commanding corporal" that some of the haughty apologists for the German generals have depicted.

Ultimately his weaknesses began to cancel out his strengths, when operative boldness became absurd self-inflation, energy became rigidity, and courage the gambler's love of risks. But that time was still some distance in the future. In the meantime, he had conquered his own generals. In the light of his brilliant success over the feared enemy, France, even the reluctant generals acknowledged his "genius" and admitted that he had analyzed the situation far better than they. He had obviously considered not only the military factor but also matters beyond the limited horizon of their expertise. This was one of the reasons for the sometimes almost incomprehensible trust, the misguided confidence in victory, of the later years. Those early victories encouraged the repeated rebuilding of new houses of cards, the cherishing of ever-new deceptive hopes. For Hitler himself the triumphant conclusion of the campaign in France brought a magnification of his already unbridled arrogance. It provided the maximum corroboration of his sense that he was a man of destiny.

On June 21 the Franco-German armistice negotiations began. Three days before, Hitler had gone to Munich to see Mussolini. During that meeting his major aim was to repress his Italian ally's craving for laurels. For in return for his extra's role on the battlefield the Duce was demanding nothing less than Nice, Corsica, Tunisia, and Jibuti, also Syria, bases in Algeria, Italian occupation of France as far as the Rhone, surrender to him of the entire French fleet, and, when the time came, Malta and transfer to Italy of British rights in Egypt and the Sudan. But Hitler, his mind already busy with the next stage of the war, contrived to make it clear to Mussolini that Italy's ambitions would only delay the victory over England. The terms of the armistice were bound to have a considerable psychological influence on England's determination to continue the struggle, he said. Hitler also feared that the completely updated French fleet, which had escaped his grasp and now lay at anchor in various parts in North Africa and England, might be prompted by excessively hard terms to go over to the enemy or even to continue the fight from the colonies in the name of France. Finally, it may be that he was stirred by a fleeting emotion of magnanimity. At any rate, he convinced Mussolini that it was crucially important to entice a French government into accepting the armistice. The Italians were acutely disappointed by the result of the negotiations; but Hitler's manner as well as his arguments did not fail to make their impression. The cynical Ciano noted: "He speaks today with a moderation and clearsightedness that are really surprising after such a victory as he has had. I cannot be said to hold especially tender feelings for him, but at this moment I really admire him."[12]

However, Hitler showed far less magnanimity in his arrangements for the armistice ceremony. To drive the humiliating lesson home, he had the signing held in the forest of Compiègne, northeast of Paris, where on November 11, 1918, the armistice terms were presented to the German delegation. The railroad car in which the historic meeting had taken place was removed from its museum and installed in the clearing in which it had stood in 1918. Flags were draped over the monument with its fallen German eagle. The French text of the draft treaty had been prepared by candlelight only the night before in the small village church of Bruly-le-Pêche; from time to time Hitler had gone over to the church in person and asked the translators how the work was progressing.

The meeting itself also underlined the elements of symbolic compensation. When Hitler, followed by a large retinue, got out of his car shortly before 3 P.M., he walked straight up to the granite block in the middle of the clearing. The inscription spoke of the "criminal pride of the German Empire" that had been vanquished at this spot. Feet planted wide apart, he placed his hands on his hips in a gesture of defiance and contempt for this place and all it signified.[13] After he had given the order to raze the monument, he entered the railroad car and took the chair in which Marshal Foch had sat in 1918. Shortly afterward, the French delegation entered.

General Keitel then read the preamble of the treaty to the French. It once more evoked history: the breach of solemn promises, "the German people's period of suffering," its "dishonoring and humiliation," which had begun in this place. Now, on this same spot, the "profoundest disgrace of all times" was being wiped out. Even before the text of the treaty itself was handed over, Hitler rose, saluted with outstretched arm, and left the car. Outside, a military band played the German national anthem and the Horst Wessel song. Then he walked to his car, parked in one of the lanes of beech that radiated starlike from the clearing.

On that day, June 21, 1940, he had reached the peak of his career. Once, in the days of its beginning, he had vowed not to rest until the injustice of November, 1918, was rectified. With that vow, he had won a hearing and a following. Now he had reached the goal. The old resentment once more proved its force. The Germans themselves, pointless though they had felt the war to be at first, regarded the scene at Compiègne as an act of metapolitical justice and celebrated with considerable emotion the moment of "restored right."[14] During this period many doubts evaporated or swung around to respect and devotion. Those who hated him were isolated. Seldom in the preceding years had the nation emotionally subscribed to a regime with such complete lack of reservations. Even the liberal historian Friedrich Meinecke wrote: "I intend . . . to relearn

635

many though not all things."[15] Something of this deep emotion surrounding the events was also expressed in Hitler's own conduct. On the night of June 24–25, shortly before the armistice took effect, he ordered the lights to be put out and the windows opened in his farmhouse in Bruly-le-Pêche. Then for several minutes he stared into the night.

Three days later he went to Paris. He had summoned a retinue of art experts, including Albert Speer, Arno Breker, and the architect Hermann Giessler. From the airfield he went directly to the Opera. Knowledgeably rhapsodizing, he took it upon himself to guide the party. He then drove down the Champs-Elysées, stopped at the Eiffel Tower, lingered for a long time at the tomb of Napoleon in the Invalides, and waxed enthusiastic about the majestic backdrop of the Place de la Concorde. Finally he drove to Montmartre, where he found Sacré Coeur dreadful. After three hours he was done, but he declared that the "dream of his life" had been fulfilled. Afterward, accompanied by two old cronies, he went on a tour of several days over the battlefields of the First World War and visited Alsace. At the beginning of July, amid cheers, torrents of flowers, and the pealing of bells, he entered Berlin. That was the last triumphal entry of his life.

The grand military parade, with which he had wanted literally to take possession of the French capital, was canceled, partly to spare the feelings of the French, partly because Göring was unable to guarantee safety from British air raids. In fact Hitler was still uncertain about the reaction of the British and was closely watching each of their steps. He had smuggled into the Franco-German armistice agreement a clause that was intended as a quiet offer to London.[16] And when Ciano came to Berlin at the beginning of July and again presented the Italian demands, Hitler put him off on the grounds that they must avoid anything that might strengthen the will to resist across the Channel. The Foreign Office was already drafting detailed proposals for a peace treaty, and Hitler himself was preparing for an appearance in the Reichstag, at which he was going to make a "generous offer." But he also spoke of his determination, in case of rejection, "to loose a storm of fire and iron upon the English."

Meanwhile, the expected countersignal once again did not come. On May 10, when the Wehrmacht launched its attack in the West, Great Britain had replaced Prime Minister Chamberlain with the man who for many years had been his fiercest opponent, Winston Churchill. The new chief of state declared in his inaugural speech that he had nothing to offer the nation "but blood, toil, tears and sweat."[17] It was as if a deeply defeatist Europe enmeshed in its complicated concessions to Hitler regained in Winston Churchill its standards, its language, and its will to self-preservation. Beyond all political issues, Churchill gave to the conflict its grand moral element, the simple and instantly appealing meaning of a storybook legend. If it is true that no match for Hitler had appeared in the thirties, it is also true that one must know the measure of an era in order to take the measure of the man who dominated it. In Churchill Hitler found something more than an antagonist. To a panic-stricken Europe the German dictator had appeared almost like invincible fate. Churchill reduced him to a conquerable power.

As early as June 18, a day after the French government had taken what Churchill called its "melancholy decision" to surrender, Churchill had come before the Lower House and reasserted his resolve to go on fighting. "If the British Empire and its Commonwealth last for a thousand years, men will say: 'This was their finest hour.' " Feverishly, he organized the defense of the British Isles against the feared invasion. On July 3, while Hitler was still waiting for a signal of compromise, he demonstrated his refusal to yield by ordering the navy to open fire upon yesterday's allies, the French fleet in the port of Oran. Surprised and disappointed, Hitler postponed indefinitely the speech to the Reichstag that he had announced for July 8. In the exultation of victory he had firmly counted on the British to abandon the hopeless struggle, all the more so since he still had no intention of damaging their Empire. But once again Churchill ostentatiously made it plain that there would be no negotiations. Over London radio he declared on July 14:

Here in this strong City of Refuge which enshrines the title-deeds of human progress . . . here, girt about by the seas and oceans where the Navy reigns . . . we await undismayed the impending assault. Perhaps it will come tonight. Perhaps it will come next week. Perhaps it will never come. . . . But be the ordeal sharp or long, or both, we shall seek no terms, we shall tolerate no parley we may show mercy—we shall ask for none.[18]

Thereupon Hitler summoned the Reichstag to meet in the Kroll Opera House at 7 P.M. on July 19. In a speech of several hours he answered Churchill and the British government:

It almost causes me pain to think that I should have been selected by Fate to deal the final blow to the structure which these men have already set tottering. It never has been my intention to wage wars, but rather to build up a state with a new social order and the finest possible standard of culture. Every year that this war drags on is keeping me away from this work, and the causes of this are nothing but ridiculous nonentities, as it were "Nature's political misfits. . . ." Only a few days ago Mr. Churchill reiterated his declaration that he wants war. . . . Mr. Churchill ought, perhaps, for once, to believe me when I prophesy that a great Empire will be destroyed—an Empire which it was never my intention to destroy or even to harm. I do, however, realize that this struggle, if it continues, can end only with the complete annihilation of one or the other of the two adversaries. Mr. Churchill may believe that this will be Germany. I know that it will be England.[19]

Contrary to general expectations, Hitler's speech did not contain his grand offer of peace but merely a highly general "appeal to reason." This change was a first manifestation of his loss of hope, in the face of Churchill's intransigence, of ever making peace with England. In order not to betray any sign of weakness, Hitler combined his appearance with a display of military power by appointing Göring Reichsmarshal and twelve generals field marshals. He also announced a large number of other promotions. But the principal indication of his real state of mind was the order he had already given three days before his address to the Reichstag: "Directive Number 16 on the preparation of a landing operation in England." The code name Sea Lion was selected for this project.

Significantly, up to this point he had developed no ideas on the continuation of the war against England because this war did not fit into his design, and the changed situation had not prompted him to revise his strategy. Spoiled by luck and by the weakness of his enemies hitherto, he trusted in his genius, in fortune, in those fleeting opportunities he had learned to utilize so instantaneously. Directive Number 16 was rather evidence of chagrin than of definite operational intentions. The introductory sentence pointed clearly to that: "Since England, in spite of her militarily hopeless situation, as yet shows no signs of readiness for a rapprochement, I have decided to prepare a landing operation against England, and if necessary to carry it out."

It remains a possibility, therefore, that Hitler never seriously considered the landing in England but employed the project merely as a weapon in the war of nerves. From the autumn of 1939 on, the military authorities, especially the commander in chief of the navy, Admiral Raeder, had repeatedly but vainly tried to interest him in the problems of a landing operation. And, in fact, as soon as Hitler assented to the plan he began introducing reservations and mentioning difficulties of the sort he had never previously recognized. Only five days after he had launched Sea Lion he spoke of the difficulties of the operation in extremely pessimistic terms. He demanded forty army divisions, a solution of the supply problem, complete mastery of the air, the establishment of an extensive system of heavy artillery along the Channel, and a large-scale mining operation; all this was to be accomplished in no more than six weeks. "If it is not certain that preparations can be completed by the beginning of September, other plans must be considered."

Hitler's qualms were not connected solely with his complexes about England. Rather, he well understood the type of resistance Churchill had alluded to. A world power with remote overseas bases had all sorts of ways of holding out. Invasion or conquest of the motherland was not necessarily defeat. For example, England could go on fighting from Canada, could draw him deeper and deeper into the conflict in the wrong area, and finally involve him in the dreaded war with the United States. Even if he succeeded in destroying the British Empire, Germany would not gain from that, as he commented in a conference on July 13, 1940, but "only Japan, America and others." Consequently, with every step he took to intensify the war against England he was undermining his own position. Not only sentimental but also political reasons argued for his seeking England's assistance rather than her defeat.

Out of such considerations Hitler, though with signs of embarrassment, developed his strategy of the following months: gradually to force England, by political maneuvering and by restricted military action, to make peace. Then he would after all be able, with his rear position secured, to undertake his march to the East. It was the old dream on which he was still fixated, the ideal constellation that he had pursued for so long by political means and which he now, undeterred, sought in open conflict.

The military means of applying pressure included the "siege" of the British Isles by the German submarine fleet and, above all, the air war against England. The paradoxes of his design emerged in the curiously halfhearted manner with which Hitler waged the struggle. Disregarding all the arguments of his military advisers, he refused to go over to the concept of "total" air or naval warfare. The Battle of Britain, the by now legendary air battle over England that began on August 13, 1940 ("Eagle Day"), with the first major raids on airfields and radar stations in the south of England, had to be broken off on September 16 after heavy losses because of bad weather conditions. The Luftwaffe had failed to achieve any one of its goals. British industrial potential had not been struck a really heavy blow, nor had the populace been psychologically crushed, nor had the Luftwaffe won air superiority. And although Admiral Raeder had reported a few days before that the navy was ready for the landing operation, Hitler postponed the project "for the present." A directive from the High Command of the armed forces dated October 12 specified "that the preparations for the landing in England are from now until spring to be maintained solely as a means of political and military pressure upon England."[20] Operation Sea Lion had been abandoned.

The military actions were accompanied by an attempt to force England by political means to yield—by forming a "continental bloc" embracing all of Europe. This project seemed easily realizable. Part of Europe was already Fascist, another part allied to the Reich by sympathy or treaties, still another part conquered or vanquished; and the defeats had for the most part brought to the fore an imitative Fascism which so far had scarcely any following but still held power and the lure that went with power. His military triumphs had magnified the hypnotic aura emanating from Hitler and his regime. He was not only the awe-inspiring dictator of the Continent; he also seemed to embody power itself, the current of history and the wave of the future. The defeat of France, on the other hand, was felt to be proof of the impotence and approaching end of the democratic system. Pétain expressed the prevailing disenchantment with democracy after the collapse of France by saying that his country "had been morally corrupted by politics."[21]

The great continental coalition was to embrace all of Europe, including the Soviet Union, Spain, Portugal, and the remnant of unoccupied France that was ruled from Vichy. Alongside this project there were plans for attacking Great Britain on the periphery: taking up the conflict in the Mediterranean by conquering the two gateways to that area: Gibraltar and the Suez Canal. In this way England's imperial position in North Africa and the Near East would be cracked open. There were other contingency plans hinging upon the occupation of Portugal's Cape Verde and the Canary Islands, also the Azores and Madeira. Contacts were made with the government in Dublin; the Irish might well be interested in an alliance, and air bases there would be highly useful for the attack on England.

Beyond the military possibilities, a grand political perspective opened before Hitler one more time in this summer of 1940. Never had a Fascist Europe been closer, never German hegemony more within reach. For a while is almost seemed that he was grasping the opportunity being offered to him. At any rate, in the autumn of 1940 Hitler once more plunged into intense activity in the realm of foreign policy. He negotiated several times with the Spanish Foreign Minister, and in the second half of October went to Hendaye to meet Franco. Then he met Pétain and his deputy, Laval, in Montoire. But aside from the Tripartite Pact, which was concluded on September 27 with Japan and Italy, his diplomatic efforts came to naught. A notable failure was the attempt made in the middle of November during a visit by Molotov in Berlin to include the Soviet Union within the Tripartite Pact and, by steering her to the British-dominated areas on the Indian Ocean, make her a partner in fresh plans for partitioning the world.

That all these overtures were without effect was no doubt because of that contempt for political action now dominating Hitler and which his new sense of triumphant achievement had only strengthened. As most of the preserved minutes demonstrate, his onetime skill at negotiation had yielded to conceited imperiousness, his former circumspect groping had given way to crude dishonesty; and instead of the finespun reasons with their persuasive half-truths of earlier years, his interlocutors more and more encountered the transparent egotism of one whose only argument was his superior power. But in the negotiations as in the parallel military plans such as Operation Felix (Gibraltar), Attila (preventive occupation of the remainder of France), and others, the impression remains that he took up such matters in a singularly distracted fashion and with divided interest. Sometimes he actually seemed inclined to abate all military activities against Great Britain and rest content with the purely chimerical effect of the continental bloc. For this seemed the only way to keep the United States from entering the war. Given his unswerving goal of eastward expansion, that possibility appeared an ever-growing threat which would wipe out all efforts, sacrifices, and designs.[22]

The fear of American intervention lent a new and menacing color to all considerations in the summer of 1940 and, above all, reinforced Hitler's fear of the passing of time. Since the subjugation of France he had squandered his energy in curiously indecisive diplomatic and military actions. German troops were garrisoned from Narvik to Sicily, and from the beginning of 1941 on, called upon for help by a hapless Italian partner, they were also stationed in North Africa. But there was no guiding idea behind all the activity; the war was running away in undesired directions. This was what came of the war's having been begun with reversed fronts, virtually for its own sake, and with no general plan. "Führer is obviously depressed," his army adjutant noted about this time after a comprehensive situation report given by Hitler. "Impression that at the moment he does not know how the war ought to continue."[23]

In the autumn, while the war was thus threatening to slip from his grasp, Hitler began to think it out afresh and to bring it back to a scheme. He had two alternatives. He might attempt after all to build a mighty bloc of powers which, by including the Soviet Union and Japan, might at the eleventh hour force a reversal of the United States' position. That would involve considerable concessions in several directions and would also postpone for years the planned eastward expansion. On the other hand, he might seize the first possible moment to strike eastward, defeat the Soviet Union in a blitzkrieg, and form the bloc of powers not with a partner, but with a vassal.

For several months Hitler wavered. In the summer of 1940 he had been full of impatience to get the senseless and bothersome Western war over with. As early as June 2, during the assault upon Dunkirk, he had predicted that England would now be ready for a "reasonable conclusion of peace" so that he would have his "hands free at last" for his "great and proper task: the conflict with Bolshevism."[24] A few weeks later, on July 21, he called upon Brauchitsch to make "mental preparations" for the war against Russia. In the intoxication of victory during this period he had even considered making his assault on Russia in the autumn of that same year. It took a memorandum from the OKW and the Wehrmachtführungsstab to convince him of the unfeasibility of the plan. Nevertheless, since that time he had clearly abandoned his original idea of two confrontations at separate times. He was now of a mind to combine the war in the West with eastward expansion: the concept had widened to that of a single world war. On July 31 he explained this conception to General Halder:

England's hope is Russia and America. If the hope of Russia is eliminated, America is eliminated also, because elimination of Russia will be followed by an enormous increase in the importance of Japan in the Far East. . . . Russia need tell England no more than that she does not want to have Germany great, and England will hope like a drowning man that in six or eight months the whole situation will be changed. But if Russia is smashed, England's last hope is wiped out. Then Germany is the master of Europe and of the Balkans.

Decision: In the course of this war Russia must be finished off. Spring 1941.

In September, however, and once again early in November, Hitler appeared to waver another time and to prefer the idea of alliance. "Führer hopes to be able to incorporate Russia into the front against England," Halder noted on November 1. But another entry only three days later pointed to the opposite: Hitler had said that Russia was going to remain "the whole problem of Europe. Everything must be done in order to prepare for the great reckoning."

These vacillations appear to have come to a stop in the course of December, when Hitler seems to have made the decision that so thoroughly accorded with his nature, with his lifelong design, and with his present overestimation of himself: to begin the war with the Soviet Union as soon as possible. The re-election of Franklin Delano Roosevelt as President of the United States, and his conversation with Molotov, had evidently speeded the decision. At any rate, only a day after the Soviet Foreign Minister's departure he commented that this would "not even remain a marriage of convenience." He thereupon issued the order to scout out suitable terrain for a Führer's headquarters in the East and for three command posts in the North, the Center and the South, and to build these "with maximum haste." On December 17 he expatiated to General Jodl on his operational ideas for the campaign, and concluded with the remark that "we must solve all Continental European problems in 1941, since from 1942 on the United States would be in a position to intervene."[25]

The decision to attack the Soviet Union even before the war in the West was decided has often been viewed as one of Hitler's "blind," "puzzling," or "hardly comprehensible" resolves. Yet it contained more rationality, and at the same time more desperation, than is evident at first glance. Hitler himself ranked this order to attack as one of the many "most difficult decisions" he had to make. In the reflections that he dictated early in 1945 to Martin Bormann in the bunker beneath the chancellery, he declared:

During the war I had no more difficult decision to make than the attack upon Russia. I had always said that we must avoid a two-front war at all costs, and moreover no one will doubt that I more than anyone else had reflected upon Napoleon's Russian experience. Then why this war against Russia, and why at the time I chose?

We had lost hope of being able to end the war by a successful invasion on English soil. For this country, ruled by stupid leaders, had refused to grant our hegemony in Europe and would not conclude a peace without victory with us as long as there was a Great Power on the Continent which in principle confronted the Reich as an adversary. Consequently the war would have to go on forever, with moreover increasingly active participation of the Americans. The importance of the American potential, the ceaseless rearmament . . . the closeness of the English coasts—all that meant that we rationally should not allow ourselves to be drawn into a war of long duration. For time—it is always a matter of time!—would necessarily be working more and more against us. In order to persuade the English to surrender, in order to compel them to make peace, we consequently had to dispel their hope of confronting us on the Continent with an enemy of our own class, that is, the Red Army. We had no choice; for us it was an inescapable compulsion to remove the Russian piece from the European chessboard. But there was also a second, equally cogent reason which would have been sufficient: the tremendous danger that Russia meant for us by the mere fact of her existence. It would necessarily be fatal for us if some day she attacked us.

Our sole chance to defeat Russia consisted in anticipating her. . . . We must not offer the Red Army any advantage of terrain, place our Autobahnen at her disposal for the deployment of her motorized formations, allow her the use of our railroad network to move men and materials. If we seized the initiative we could defeat her in her own country, in her swamps and moors, but not on the soil of so civilized a country as ours. That would have given them a springboard for the onslaught upon Europe.

Why 1941? . . . Because we could allow ourselves as little delay as possible, since our enemies in the West were steadily increasing their fighting power. Moreover, Stalin himself was by no means remaining inactive. Consequently, time was working against us on both fronts. The question therefore is not: "Why as early as June 22, 1941?" but "Why not earlier?" . . . In the course of the last weeks I was obsessed with the fear that Stalin might forestall me.[26]

All of Hitler's cogitations in the summer and fall of 1940 were linked by the secret hope of remedying the stalled and misdirected military situation by a sudden, surprising sally of the sort that had often saved him from his various plights in the past. At the same time, such a sally might help him achieve his larger victory. In his fantasies the campaign against Russia was transformed into the unexpected turning point which like a touch from a magic wand would solve all difficulties and open the way to world dominion. Germany, he raved to his generals on January 9, 1941, would be "invulnerable. The gigantic spaces of Russia conceal immeasurable riches. Germany must dominate them economically and politically, but not annex them." In that way she would have at her disposal all the potentialities for waging war against whole continents in the future. Then she could never again be defeated by anyone.

The rapid collapse of the Soviet Union, as he imagined it, would give Japan the signal for her long-envisaged "southern expansion," which she had hitherto postponed chiefly because of the Soviet threat to her rear. That expansion in turn would tie down the United States in the Pacific area and consequently draw the Americans away from Europe, so that Great Britain would be forced to surrender. By a far-flung threefold pincers movement over North Africa, the Near East, and the Caucasus, in conjunction with the conquest of Russia, he would push forward to Afghanistan. That country would then be used as a base from which to strike the stubborn British Empire at its heart, in India. Rule of the world was, as he saw it, within his grasp.

The weaknesses in this conception were vast, and Hitler must have recognized at least some of them. Hitherto he had always made security in the West a prerequisite for the attack upon the Soviet Union and had viewed avoidance of a two-front conflict as a kind of fundamental law for German foreign policy. Now he was trying to obtain this security by a preventive blow and plunging into the adventure of a two-front war in order to anticipate having to fight a war on two fronts. He also underestimated the enemy just as he overestimated himself. "In three weeks we shall be in Petersburg," he declared at the beginning of December. He told Bulgarian Ambassador Dragonoff that the Soviet Army was "no more than a joke."

But above all, what once more emerged was his inability to think a thought through to the end while retaining his hold on reality. Once he had conceived the first steps, he invariably at some point soared off into fantasy and brought his speculations to a visionary rather than a rational conclusion. A prime instance of this was the carelessness with which he considered the developments in the East that might follow the expected victory. It was the same mistake he had made in attacking Poland and then after the campaign in France. Even if he succeeded in another blitz campaign, in advancing to Moscow or even the Urals before the descent of winter, the war was by no means over, as he ought to have told himself. For beyond Moscow, beyond the Urals, lay vast spaces, where Russia's remaining forces could be mustered and organized.

At any rate, powerful German contingents would necessarily be tied down on the more or less open frontier where he planned to stop, and this factor would surely have some bearing on England's and America's determination to fight. But Hitler never thought things through in this way. He contented himself euphorically with such vague formulas as "collapse" or "reduction to rubble." When Field Marshal von Bock, who was to receive the appointment of commander in chief of the Army Group Center, told him early in February that he thought a military victory over the Red Army possible but could not conceive of "how the Soviets are to be forced to make peace," Hitler answered vaguely that "after the conquest of the Ukraine, Moscow and Leningrad . . . the Soviets will certainly consent to a compromise." The remark revealed the whole shallowness of his ideas.

However, he would now no longer hear of any objections. Undeterred by arguments or opposition, he prepared the attack. In October, 1940, on the night after his meeting with Pétain, he received a letter from Mussolini informing him of Italy's intention to invade Greece. Foreseeing the complications that this unexpected step was bound to have for the German flank in the Balkans, Hitler changed his travel plans and went to Florence for a hastily arranged meeting. But Mussolini, eager to pay the Germans back for the many similar surprises they had inflicted on him, as well as for their many victories, had hurried through the operation a few hours before

Hitler's arrival. But the necessity of sending German contingents to Greece when the Italian ally blundered into the expected trouble, did not keep Hitler from continuing the planning and the deployment for the campaign in the East. The same was true when Mussolini ran into trouble in Albania and in December, 1940, finally saw the North African front collapse. In every case Hitler met the disasters with equanimity and dispatched more and more fresh divisions to the threatened scenes without for a moment being distracted from his principal goal.

On February 28, 1941, he considered himself forced to anticipate the Russians by marching into Bulgaria from the territory of his ally Rumania. A month or so later he had to conquer Yugoslavia, which under a group of rebellious officers had attempted to withdraw from German influence. But in spite of these new engagements he did not lose sight of the campaign against the Soviet Union. He merely postponed it by four possibly fateful weeks. On April 17 he received the capitulation of the Yugoslav army; six days later the Greeks surrendered, after having so long and so effectively resisted Mussolini's soldiers. The German corps sent to North Africa under General Rommel needed only twelve days to recover all the territory the Italians had lost. Shortly afterward, between May 20 and 27, 1941, German parachute troops captured the island of Crete, and for a moment the entire British position in the Mediterranean seemed in deadly peril. With growing emphasis Raeder and the heads of the navy called for a grand offensive against the British Near Eastern positions by the autumn of 1941. That would, they promised, strike the Empire "a deadlier blow than the taking of London." The anxieties of the Allied side, which were published after the war, largely confirmed this view. But Hitler once more refused to deviate from the obsession of eastward expansion. Some members of his entourage tried to change his mind, but in vain.[27] In the West, the material weight of the United States was making itself felt more and more. The air war was already lost, and the U-boat war threatening to be lost. But not even this increasingly acute situation could check Hitler's plans.

There can be no doubt that Hitler saw and considered the many drawbacks of his new design: the risk of the two fronts, the experience of Napoleon with the insuperable spaces of Russia, the weakness of his Italian ally, and the squandering of his own forces in a manner that completely belied the whole idea of blitzkrieg. The obstinacy with which he ignored the counterarguments was not principally due to fixation on his central idea. Rather, he was becoming more and more aware that this summer of 1941 offered him the last remaining chance to carry out that concept. He was, as he himself said, in the situation of a man who has only one bullet left in his gun. And the special nature of his situation was that the effectiveness of the charge was steadily diminishing. For, as he knew, the war could not be won if it assumed the character of a war of matériel and attrition. Such a war would necessarily put Germany into a position of increasing dependence on the Soviet Union, while in the end inevitably confirming the superiority of the United States.

It is conceivable that in the background of his thoughts the vague hope still lurked that such a strike might regain the neutrality of the conservative powers whose assistance he had had and gambled away. For he would be restoring the onetime enemy to his proper place as an enemy. This, at any rate, was the hope that prompted his old admirer Rudolf Hess to fly to England on May 10, 1941, on a self-appointed mission to put an end at last to the "wrong war." The disdain with which he was received made it plain that this opportunity, too, had been squandered and that Hitler really had no choice. His decision to launch the war in the East at this particular time resembled an act of desperation.

A great many of Hitler's remarks from the autumn of 1940 on indicate how clearly he grasped his dilemma. His talks with diplomats, generals, and politicians, quite aside from their function in the given instance, constitute in toto a document showing a continual process of self-persuasion. His belittling of the enemy served the same purpose as his excoriation of that same enemy. The Soviet Union was on the one hand a "clay colossus without a head," and on the other hand a "bolshevized wasteland," "simple gruesome," "a mighty national and ideological onslaught that threatens all of Europe"; and the pact he had concluded with that country not so long ago had suddenly become "very painful." Then again he tried to pretend that he was not waging a two-front war: "Now the possibility exists," he told his generals on March 30, 1941, "to strike Russia with our rear safe; that chance will not soon come again. I would be committing a crime against the future of the German people if I did not seize it!"

His contentions were sustained by the certainty, which he claimed with ever-increasing impatience, that Providence presided over all his decisions. This growing effort to invoke irrational support strikingly reflected his state of uneasiness. Quite often his gestures of magical self-reassurance occurred as abrupt interjections in matter-of-fact conversations. For example, in a conversation with a Hungarian diplomat in March, 1941, after making a comparison between the armaments of Germany and the United States, he declared: "Thinking over my courses and proposals of the past, I have arrived at the conviction that Providence has arranged all this. For what I originally sought would have been, if I had attained it by peaceful means, merely a partial solution which sooner or later would have given rise to new conflict. My only special wish is for an improvement in our relationship with Turkey."

Ever since the summer of 1940 there had been a number of diplomatic contretemps between Germany and the Soviet Union. Some had arisen through Moscow's ruthless attempts to secure her own perimeter against the by now formidable power of the Reich. With this aim the Soviet Union annexed the Baltic countries and parts of Rumania, and tenaciously opposed German efforts to obtain greater influence in the Balkans. Nevertheless, Sir Stafford Cripps, the British ambassador in Moscow, predicted in the spring of 1941 that the Soviet Union would "with absolute certainty" resist all efforts to involve her in the war against Germany unless Hitler himself decided to attack the Soviet Union; but he was afraid that Hitler would not do his enemies this favor.

And then he did that very thing. It was the last and most serious example of his suicidal impulse to double his stake once the game was going against him. The significant aspect of his present reckoning was that it balanced only on the negative side. If he lost the campaign against the Soviet Union, the war as a whole was lost. But if he won in the East, the whole war was by no means won, however he might delude himself about that.

But in still another respect Hitler's decision to attack revealed a significant consistency. The Moscow Pact dated back to what had still been the "political" phase of his life. It had been a tactically motivated act of betrayal of his own ideological principles. Consequently, since he had now gone beyond his political phase, the pact had become an anachronism. "The Pact never was honestly intended," Hitler now confessed to one of his adjutants. "For the ideological abysses are too deep." What counted now was the honesty of his radical philosophy.

Shortly after three o'clock in the morning of June 22, 1941, Mussolini was roused from sleep by a message from Hitler. "At night I don't even disturb my servants, but the Germans make me jump out of bed without the slightest consideration," he grumbled. The message began with a reference to "months of anxious pondering" and then informed Mussolini of the impending attack. "Since I have won through to this decision," Hitler assured him, "I again feel inwardly free. Despite all the sincerity of my efforts to bring about a final *détente,* collaboration with the Soviet Union has nevertheless often been a heavy burden for me; for somehow it seemed to me a breach with my whole background, my views and my former obligations. I am happy to be rid of these spiritual torments."[28]

The feeling of relief was undoubtedly there but accompanied by a note of anxiety. Granted that the entourage, and especially the top military leaders, expressed extraordinary optimism. "For the German soldier nothing is impossible," the Wehrmacht communiqué of June 11, 1941, had concluded, summing up the fighting in the Balkans and in North Africa. Only Hitler himself showed signs of depression and nervousness. But he was not the man to be deterred from realizing his life's dream when only a few weeks' fighting separated him from it. Then vast spaces in the East would be won, England would bow, and America yield. The world would pay homage to him. The risk increased the allure of the goal. On the night before the assault, in the midst of the bustle of preparations all around him, he said: "I feel as if I am pushing open the door to a dark room never seen before, without knowing what lies behind the door."[29]

Chapter 2

> When "Barbarossa" starts, the world
> will hold its breath and keep still.
>
> Adolf Hitler

THE THIRD WORLD WAR

Before dawn, about 3:15 A.M. on June 22, 1941, Hitler launched the offensive against the Soviet Union with 153 divisions, 600,000 motorized vehicles, 3,580 tanks, 7,184 artillery pieces, and 2,740 airplanes. It was the mightiest military force concentrated on a single theater of war in history. Alongside the German formations there were twelve divisions and ten brigades of Rumanian troops, eighteen Finnish divisions, three Hungarian divisions, and two and one-half Slovak divisions. Later this force was joined by three Italian divisions and the Spanish "Blue Division." True to the pattern of most of the preceding campaigns, the attack started without a declaration of war. Once again the Luftwaffe took the lead with a massed surprise assault, which at one blow wiped out half of the approximately 10,000 Soviet Russian military planes. And, as had already been done in Poland and in the West, the attackers pushed massed wedges of tanks deep into the enemy territory, then closed the pincers thus formed to yield vast battles of encirclement. In the preceding years Hitler had steadily maintained that he was not planning any "Argonauts' expedition" to Russia;[30] now he set out on one.

A second wave, following hard upon the military formations, consisted of the notorious *Einsatzgruppen:* special squads to whom Hitler had issued the assignment—as early as March 3—to exterminate "the Jewish-Bolshevistic intelligentsia" in the field of operations.[31] From the outset these commandos gave the conflict its frightful, totally unexampled character. And for all that the campaign was strategically linked with the war as a whole, in its nature and in its morality it signified something else entirely. It was, so to speak, the Third World War.

At any rate, it dropped out of the framework of the "normal" European war, the rules of which had hitherto governed the conflict, although in Poland there had been glimmerings of a new and more radical practice. But

648

the SS's reign of terror in the conquered Polish territories had evoked opposition among the local military commanders. It was his experience with this reaction on the part of the regular army that now prompted Hitler to introduce his ideologically motivated extermination campaigns in the very zone of active operations. For after so many complications, detours, and reversed fronts, this war in Russia was in every sense *his* war. He waged it mercilessly, obsessively, and became increasingly neglectful of all other theaters. He made no tactical concessions. In particular, he abandoned his previous practice of seeking the military decision first, with the aid of seductive slogans of liberation, only to begin the work of enslavement and destruction after the military victory had been won. Here in Russia he was seeking nothing but "final solutions." On March 30, 1941, he had summoned to the Berlin chancellery nearly 250 high-ranking officers of all branches of the service. He lectured them for two and a half hours on the novel nature of the impending war. Halder's diary recorded the following statements:

Our tasks in Russia: smash the armed forces, break up the State. . . . Struggle of two ideologies. Annihilating verdict upon Bolshevism, is equivalent to asocial criminality. Communism tremendous danger for the future. We must abandon the viewpoint of soldierly comradeship. The Communist is no comrade before and no comrade afterwards. What is involved is a struggle of annihilation. . . .

The struggle must be waged against the poison of sedition. That is no question of courts-martial. The commanders of the troops must know what is at stake. They must lead the way into the struggle. . . . Commissars and GPU men are criminals and must be treated as such. . . . The fight will be very different from the fight in the West. In the East harshness is kindness toward the future.

The leaders must demand of themselves the sacrifice of overcoming their scruples.[32]

Although none of those present took issue with what he was telling them, Hitler distrusted his generals. He thought them biased in favor of the traditional standards of their class and therefore did not content himself with mere slogans calling for harshness. Rather, his whole effort was bent toward abolishing the distinction of his special commandos; he wanted to fuse these elements into a totality that would make criminals of all by having all participate in waging his war of annihilation. In a succession of preparatory directives, administration of the rear areas was detached from the army and assigned to special Reich commissioners. Heinrich Himmler in his capacity of Reichsführer-SS was assigned to take over "special tasks" in the theater of operations. He had at his disposal four *Einsatzgruppen* (task forces) of security police and SD men, a total strength of 3,000 men, to carry out the tasks "arising from the conflict of two opposed political systems which is to be carried out on a basis of finality."

In May, 1941, at a meeting in Pretzsch, Reinhard Heydrich orally gave

the leaders of these groups the order to murder all Jews, "Asiatic inferiors," Communist functionaries, and gypsies.[33] A "Führer's decree" of
the same period made members of the armed forces immune to prosecution
for crimes against enemy civilians. Another directive, the so-called Commissar Order of June 6, 1941, specified that the political commissars of the
Red Army, being "the authors of barbarously Asiatic methods of fighting
. . . when captured in battle or in resistance are on principle to be disposed of by gunshot immediately." And a "guideline" of the High Command of the armed forces, which was issued to the more than 3 million
soldiers of the Eastern armies immediately before the beginning of the
attack, called for "ruthless and energetic measures against Bolshevistic
agitators, guerrillas, saboteurs, Jews, and total elimination of all active and
passive resistance."[34] A strident campaign against the "Slavic subhumans"
supplemented these measures. It conjured up images of the "Mongol
onslaught" and defined Bolshevism as the contemporary form of the
Asiatic scourge represented by Attila and Genghis Khan.

These elements gave the war in the East its unusual dual character. It
was undoubtedly an ideological war against Communism, and the offensive
was sustained by a crusading mood. But simultaneously, and to a considerably greater degree, it was a colonial war of conquest in the style of the
nineteenth century, though directed against one of the old European great
powers and aimed at wiping out that Power. Hitler himself exposed the lie
of the ideological justifications whose strident propaganda dominated the
foreground. In the middle of July, speaking to a group of the topmost
leaders, he irritably rejected the formula of a "war of Europe against
Bolshevism." He clarified his view as follows: "Fundamentally, therefore,
what matters is conveniently dividing up the gigantic cake so that we can
first control it, secondly administer it, and thirdly exploit it." But such
annexation plans were to be kept secret for the present. "Nevertheless we
can and will carry out all necessary measures—shooting, resettlement, and
so on."[35]

While the army plunged tempestuously ahead, reaching the Dnieper in
two weeks and a week later thrusting to Smolensk, the *Einsatzgruppen* set
up their reign of terror in the occupied territories. They combed cities and
towns, herded together Jews, Communist functionaries, intellectuals, and
in general all potential leaders of society, and liquidated them. Otto
Ohlendorf, one of the task-force commanders, testified in Nuremberg that
in the course of the first year his unit murdered approximately 90,000 men,
women, and children. The Jewish population of western Russia was especially affected; during this same period it is conservatively estimated that
about half a million Jews were killed.[36] Unmoved, Hitler pushed the
extermination program forward. Over and beyond all the aims of conquest
and exploitation, his statements of that period manifest the old, deep
ideological hatred, once more as extreme as in his early years. "The Jews

650

are the scourge of humanity," he told Croatian Foreign Minister Kvaternik on July 21, 1941. "If the Jews were given their way, as they are in the Soviet paradise, they would carry out the maddest plans. That is how Russia has become a plague center for humanity. . . . If only one country for whatever reasons tolerates a Jewish family in it, that family will become the germ center for fresh sedition. If there were no longer any Jews in Europe, the unity of the countries of Europe would no longer be disturbed."

In spite of their rapid advance, the German armies were able to start their pincers movement only in the central sector. On the other fronts they merely managed to roll the enemy back. "No enemy in front of us and no supplies behind us": that was the quip for the special problems of this campaign. Nevertheless, by July 11 nearly 600,000 Russian prisoners were in German hands, including more than 70,000 deserters. Both Hitler and the army High Command thought the collapse of the Red Army was near. As early as July 3 Halder had noted: "It is probably not saying too much if I assert that the campaign against Russia was won within two weeks." But he recognized that stubborn resistance based on the vastness of the area would occupy the German forces for many weeks to come.

Hitler himself declared several days later that he did not believe resistance in European Russia would last much longer than six weeks. He did not know where the Russians would go then. "Perhaps the Urals or beyond the Urals. But we will follow them." He would not shrink from pushing even beyond the Urals. He would pursue Stalin wherever he fled. But he did not think he would have to be fighting after the middle of September; in six weeks or so it would be pretty much all over.[37] In the middle of July the emphasis in the armaments program was shifted to submarines and aircraft, and planning was begun for the return march of the German divisions, since this was expected to take place in two weeks. When General Köstring, the last military attaché in Moscow, appeared at the Führer's headquarters at this time to report, Hitler led him to a military map, gestured at the conquered territories, and declared: "No pig will ever eject me from here."[38]

The relapse into the coarseness of his early years corresponded to the satisfaction Hitler evidently felt in showing what he was capable of. He described the battles in the East to Spanish Ambassador Espinosa as sheer "massacres of human beings." Sometimes, he said, the enemy had attacked in waves twelve or thirteen rows deep and had simply been cut down, "the people reduced to chopped meat." The Russian soldiers, he said, were "partly in a state of torpor, partly of sighs and groans. The commissars are devils and . . . were being shot down." Simultaneously, he indulged in long hate-filled fantasies. He conceived of starving out Moscow and Leningrad and thus bringing about an "ethnic catastrophe" that would "deprive not only Bolshevism of its centers, but wipe out the Moscovites." Then he wanted to raze both cities to the ground. A gigantic reservoir would be created on the spot where Moscow had once stood, to extinguish all memory of the city and everything it had been. As a precautionary measure, he ordered that the expected offers of surrender be turned down, and justified this measure to his intimates: "Probably some people will clap their hands to their heads and ask: How can the Führer destroy a city like St. Petersburg? By nature I belong to an entirely different genus. But when I see that the species is in danger, my feelings give way to ice-cold resolution."[39]

In the course of August the German armies, after breaking through the "Stalin Line," succeeded after all in impressive pincers movements on all the sectors of the front. Nevertheless, it became apparent that the optimistic reckonings of the previous month had been deceptive. However great the number of prisoners, the hordes of reserves that the enemy continually brought up to the front seemed even greater. Moreover, the Russians fought far more bitterly than had the Poles or Allied troops; and their determination to resist increased, after initial crises, as they recognized the annihilating nature of the war Hitler was waging. Moreover, the attrition of matériel in the dust and mud of the Russian steppes was greater than had been expected, and every victory drew the army more deeply into the endless spaces. In addition, the German war machine for the first time seemed to be reaching the limits of its capacity. Industry, for example, was producing only a third of the required 600 tanks a month. The infantry was obviously inadequately motorized for a campaign involving distances vaster than any hitherto conceived. The Luftwaffe could not handle a two-front war. And supplies of fuel at times shrank to the demand for a single month. In the face of all this, the question of where the remaining reserves could most effectively be applied became paramount. On what sector of the front could a blow be delivered that might decide the war?

The army High Command and the commanders of the Army Group Center unanimously demanded that they be allowed to concentrate all formations for the attack on Moscow. The enemy, they assumed, would assemble all available forces outside the capital for the great decisive battle. Thus the campaign could be concluded within the schedule, and the rules of blitzkrieg could be abided by. Hitler, on the contrary, called for attacking in the north, in order to cut the Russians off from access to the Baltic. Simultaneously, he wanted an advance on a broad front in the south, with the aim of seizing the rich agricultural and industrial regions of the Ukraine and the Donetz Basin and the oil supplies of the Caucasus. This plan was a prime sample both of his arrogance and his dilemma. Although he pretended that in his certainty of victory he could afford to ignore the capital, he was actually trying to relieve the economic strain, which was becoming more and more evident. "My generals know nothing about a war economy," he repeatedly declared. The obstinate dispute, which once again revealed the divisions between Hitler and the generals, was finally ended by a directive ordering the Army Group Center to place its motorized formations at the disposal of the commanders in the north and south. "Unacceptable," "outrageous," Halder noted, and proposed to Brauchitsch that they hand in a joint resignation. But the commander in chief refused.

The great victory in the Battle of Kiev, which netted the German side approximately 665,000 prisoners and enormous quantities of matériel, seemed once again to confirm Hitler's military genius—especially since this success also ended the flank threat to the central sector and thus truly opened the way to Moscow. In fact Hitler now consented to the offensive against the capital. But blinded by the unbroken succession of triumphs, spoiled by fortune in war, he thought he could simultaneously continue to pursue his far-flung aims in the north and in the south as well: cutting the Murmansk railroad line, capturing Rostov and the oil region of Maikop, and advancing the more than 375 miles to Stalingrad. As if he had forgotten the old rule about concentrating all forces at one place at a time, he thus made his troops draw farther and farther apart. On October 2, 1941, Field Marshal von Bock, with reduced forces, at last opened the offensive against Moscow, after a delay of nearly two months. On the following day Hitler made a speech in the Berlin Sportpalast, in which he surpassed himself in vulgar boasting. He described Germany's enemies as "democratic nonentities," "louts," "animals and beasts," and announced that "this enemy is already broken and will never rise again."

Four days later the autumnal rains began. Fighting superior enemy forces, the German armies opened their offensive on a hopeful note, achieving two great encirclements near Vyasma and Bryansk. But then the deepening morass crippled all operations. The movement of supplies slowed; fuel in particular grew short; more and more vehicles and guns became stuck in the mud. The halted offensive did not begin moving forward again until the middle of November, when mild frost ensued. The tank troops assigned to complete the northern encirclement at last came within almost twenty miles of the Soviet capital near Krasnaya Polyana, while the units attacking from the west approached to within more than thirty miles of the city's center. Then the Russian winter descended abruptly. The temperature dropped to twenty degrees below and later sometimes even to sixty below zero.

The onset of intense cold found the German armies completely unprepared. Certain that the campaign would be over in three to four months, Hitler in one of his characteristic gestures had again placed his back against the wall and ordered no winter equipment for the troops. "For there will be no winter campaign," he had rebuked General Paulus when the commander recommended precautionary measures for the coming winter. At the front thousands died of cold. Vehicles and automatic weapons failed. The wounded froze to death in the hospitals, and soon the casualties from cold exceeded those lost in the fighting. "There was panic here," Guderian declared, and at the end of November he reported that his troops were "done for." A few days later, in temperatures of twenty below zero, the formations outside Moscow made a last desperate attempt to break through the Russian lines. A few units penetrated as far as the suburbs of the capital. Through their field glasses they could see the towers of the Kremlin and observe movements in the streets. Then the offensive ground to a halt.

Meanwhile, altogether unexpectedly, a Soviet counteroffensive began with freshly introduced Siberian elite divisions. The German troops were thrown back with heavy losses. For a few days the front appeared to waver and be on the point of vanishing into the Russian snow. Hitler unyieldingly rejected all appeals by the generals to avoid the disaster by tactical withdrawals. He feared the loss of weapons and gear, and dreaded the enormous psychological effects that would necessarily follow the shattering of his image of personal invincibility.[40] On December 16 he issued an order demanding of every soldier "fanatical resistance" in their present positions, "without regard for enemy breakthroughs on the flank and rear." When Guderian remonstrated against the senseless sacrifices this order entailed, Hitler asked whether the general believed that Frederick the Great's grenadiers had died gladly. "You stand too close to the events," he charged Guderian. "You have too much pity for the soldiers. You ought to disengage yourself more."

To this day it is widely believed that the "stand" order outside Moscow, and Hitler's obstinate determination, stabilized the crumbling front. But the armies' loss of substance and the longer supply lines canceled out all conceivable advantages. Moreover, the decision also suggested Hitler's growing incapacity to react flexibly. The process of stylizing himself into a monument, which he had undergone for so many years, was now obviously affecting his temperament and locking him into a sort of monumental rigidity. But no matter what he decided in the face of this crisis, there could no longer be any doubt that much more than his projected blitzkrieg, Operation Barbarossa, ground to a halt before the Soviet capital. Clearly, his entire plan for the war had foundered.

This was his first severe setback after nearly twenty years of unremitting political and military triumphs. His decision to hold the positions outside Moscow at all costs sprang from his consciousness of being at a turning point. His gamble had been carried to such a pitch that it had to collapse at the first defeat, and all its premises went down with it. By the middle of November, at any rate, he seems to have been filled with forebodings. He spoke to a small group about the idea of a "negotiated peace" and once again voiced vague hopes that the conservative ruling class of England would see the light.[41] It was as though he wanted to forget that it was he who had betrayed the principle of his successes and would never again be in a position to fight one main enemy with the aid of the other. Ten days later, when the disastrous cold descended, he seemed for the first time to have an intimation that he was facing more than an isolated failure. In a military conference held toward the end of the war General Jodl stated that already then, in view of the calamity of the Russian winter, Hitler as well as he realized that "victory could no longer be achieved."[42] On November 27 Quartermaster General Wagner tendered a report at the Führer's headquarters whose gist Halder summed up in one sentence: "We have reached the end of our human and material forces." And that same evening, in one of those bleak, misanthropic moods that so often assailed him during the crises of his life, Hitler told a foreign visitor: "If the German people are no longer so strong and ready for sacrifice that they will stake their own blood on their existence, they deserve to pass away and be annihilated by another, stronger power." In a second conversation, later that night and again with a foreign visitor, he voiced the same idea and added the remark: "If that is the case I would not shed a tear for the German people."[43]

Recognition that his design for the war as a whole had failed also lurked behind Hitler's decision, on December 11, 1941, to declare war on the United States—the war he had dreaded all along. Four days before, 350 Japanese carrier planes had attacked the American fleet at Pearl Harbor and the airfields on Oahu with a hail of bombs, thus initiating the conflict in the Far East. In Berlin Ambassador Oshima requested that the Reich immediately enter the war on his country's side. And although Hitler had repeatedly pressed his Far Eastern ally to attack the Soviet Union or the British Empire in Southeast Asia and had made it plain how inopportune a war against the United States would be for Germany, he instantly acted on the Japanese request. He did not even blame the Japanese for their insulting secrecy—though at bottom he thought he alone had the right to such secrecy. And he brushed aside Ribbentrop's objection that, according to the letter of the Tripartite Pact, Germany was by no means obligated to give aid. The spectacular surprise attack with which Japan had begun the war had deeply impressed him, and by now he had reached the point of being carried away by such dramatics. "My heart swelled when I heard of the first Japanese operations," he said to Oshima.

There were some advantages in beginning the war with the United States immediately. The German naval forces were now free to conduct the war at sea without restriction, whereas they had previously had to put up with all provocations by the American side. Moreover, the Japanese strikes came at the right moment to veil the crisis in Russia. And, finally, defiance also played a part in Hitler's decision, bitterness at the way the war had gone off the rails, so that in mockery of all his plans he had not been able to win it in a series of lightning blows.

All these arguments, however, were not very convincing and could not conceal the fact that Hitler was entering the new conflict with America without a major motive. In little more than two years he had gambled away a dominant political position and united the most powerful countries in the world, despite all their previous enmities, in an "unnatural alliance." The decision to go to war against the United States was even less free, even more coerced, than the decision to attack the Soviet Union. In fact, it was really no longer an act of his own volition but a gesture governed by a sudden awareness of his own impotence. That gesture was Hitler's last strategic initiative of any importance.

The effect of American participation in the war instantly became apparent in a stiffening and extension of Allied efforts. On the day of the German attack upon the Soviet Union, Winston Churchill had declared in a radio address that he would not retract anything he had said against Communism for twenty-five years, but that in the face of the drama beginning in the East "the past with its crimes, it follies and tragedies" faded. Churchill always tried to preserve an awareness of the distance that separated him from his new ally, but President Roosevelt threw himself into the support of the Soviet Union with the total commitment that the moment and the enemy required. Some time before the American entry into the war, he had included the Soviet Union along with Britain in the Lend-Lease program of material support. But now he mobilized the entire potential of the country. Within a single year he increased the number of tanks built to 24,000, the production of planes to 48,000. By 1943 he had twice doubled the strength of the American army to a total of 7 million men, and by the end of the first year of the war had raised American armaments production to the same level as that of the three Axis powers taken together. By 1944 he had doubled it once more.

On American initiative the Allies now began co-ordinating their strategy. Unlike the Tripartite Pact powers, which were never able to develop unified military planning, the Allied commissions and staffs that were immediately established held more than 200 conferences and consistently arranged for joint measures. They were aided by the fact that they agreed on a distinct goal—to defeat the enemy—whereas Germany, Italy, and Japan were pursuing extremely vague and at the same time excessive aims, each by itself in different parts of the world. The three great have-not powers were as fascinated as they were driven by their own dynamism. Mussolini commented on their vast appetite for territory in a remark he made at the end of August, 1941, when he joined Hitler in inspecting the ruins of the fortress of Brest-Litowsk. The German dictator was going on in his usual way about his plans for carving up the world. Utilizing a pause, Mussolini, the story goes, interjected with ironic mildness that when the partitioning was over there would be "nothing left but the moon."

Otherwise that meeting was chiefly intended as a reply to the enemy alliance, whose outlines could already be discerned. Some two weeks before, Roosevelt and Churchill, after meeting off the coast of Newfoundland, had formulated their war aims in the Atlantic Charter. The Axis partners now countered with Hitler's slogans of a "New Order for Europe" and "European solidarity." Taking up the watchword of a "Pan-European crusade against Bolshevism," they tried to rouse that type of internationalism (an unexamined inner contradiction) that was peculiar to all the Fascist movements. But in this matter, too, the consequences of Hitler's renunciation of politics soon made themselves felt. It was exactly as if he had not been the man who had used the principle of tactical duality to supreme advantage—that form of courtship which inextricably combined intimidation with promises. For now he seemed to count only the principle of crude domination. "If I conquer a free country only to give it back its freedom, what's the point?" he asked early in 1942. "One who has spilled blood has the right to exercise rule." And he said he could only smile when "the blabbermouths claim that union can be brought about by talking. . . . Union can only be created and preserved by force." Even later, under the impact of continual defeats, he rejected all the proposals by members of his entourage that would have relaxed the stupid pattern of crushing the rest of Europe and instituted relations more akin to partnerships. It drove him "mad," he declared, when people kept coming at him all the time about the alleged honor of these "stinking little countries" that existed only because "a few European powers could not agree on devouring them." Nowadays all he could think of was the stark and uninspired concept of mustering all one's force and stubbornly holding out.

The same tendency, sharpened by moods of panic, meanwhile led at the front to his first serious disagreement with the generals. As long as the German armies had been successful, differences of opinions could be covered over and recurrent mistrust drowned out in ringing toasts to victory. But when the tide began to turn, the long repressed resentment came to the fore with redoubled force. Hitler now intervened more and more frequently in operations; he issued direct instructions to army groups and sector staffs, and quite often even interfered in the tactical decisions on the divisional and regimental levels. The commander in chief of the army was "hardly more than a letter-carrier," Halder noted on December 7, 1941. Twelve days later, in conjunction with the disputes over the "hold-the-line" order, Brauchitsch was allowed to resign—in disfavor. In keeping with the prime solution he had found for all previous crises in the leadership, Hitler himself assumed the role of commander in chief of the army. It was only one more proof of the totally chaotic organization on all planes that he thus became his own subordinate twice over. For, in 1934, after Hindenburg's death, he had assumed the (predominantly ceremonial) office of supreme commander of the armed forces. And, in 1938, after Blomberg's resignation, he had taken over the (actual) High Command of the armed

657

forces. Now he justified his decision in a remark that, along with expressing his deep distrust of the army people, announced his intention to heighten the role of ideology: "Anybody can handle operational leadership—that's easy," he declared. "The task of the commander in chief of the army is to give the army National Socialist training. I know no general of the army who could perform this task the way I would have it. Therefore I have decided to take over the command of the army myself."

Along with von Brauchitsch, the commander in chief of Army Group Center, von Bock, was relieved and replaced by Field Marshal von Kluge; von Rundstedt, commander in chief of Army Group South, was replaced by Field Marshal von Reichenau. General Guderian was relieved of his command for infractions of the "hold-the-line" order; General Hoepner was actually cashiered and General von Sponeck condemned to death. Field Marshal von Leeb, commander in chief of Army Group North, voluntarily resigned. Many other generals and divisional commanders were recalled. The "expressions of contempt" Hitler had applied to von Brauchitsch since the end of 1941 now represented his opinion of the high-ranking officers as a whole: "A vain, cowardly scoundrel—who has completely ruined the whole campaign plan in the East by his continual interference and his continual disobedience." Half a year earlier, in the jubilant days of the Battle of Smolensk, he had said that he had "marshals of historic stature and a unique corps of officers."[44]

During the early months of 1942 the grim defensive battles on all sectors of the front continued. Again and again war diaries note "undesirable developments," "awful mess," "day of savage fighting," "deep penetrations," or "dramatic scene with the Führer." At the end of February Moscow was once again more than sixty-two miles from the front. At this time total German casualties came to something over 1 million, or 31.4 per cent of the Eastern army. The heavy fighting did not ebb until the spring, with the beginning of the thaw; by then both sides were exhausted. Visibly scarred by what had happened, Hitler admitted to his table companions that the winter disaster had virtually stunned him for a moment; no one could imagine what energy these three months had cost him and what a terrible toll they had taken of his nerves. Goebbels, visiting him at the Führer's headquarters, was shocked by his appearance. He found him "very much aged"; he did not recall ever having seen him "so serious and so subdued." Hitler complained of spells of dizziness and declared that the mere sight of snow gave him physical pain. When he went to Berchtesgaden for a few days at the end of April and was caught by a belated snowstorm there, he hurriedly departed again. "It's a kind of flight from the snow," Goebbels noted.

But when "this winter of our discontent," as Guderian called it, was over and the German advance began moving once more with the coming of spring, Hitler regained his confidence. Sometimes, in moods of elation, he would even grumble that fate was letting him wage war only against second-class enemies. But his self-confidence was brittle and his nerves unstable. One of Chief of Staff von Halder's diary entries makes that clear: "His underestimation of the enemy potentialities, always his shortcoming, is now gradually assuming grotesque forms. There is no longer any question of serious work. Morbid reaction to momentary impressions and complete incomprehension of the apparatus of leadership and its possibilities are characteristic of this so-called 'leadership.' "

From the plan of operations for the summer of 1942 it might appear that Hitler had learned from the experiences of the preceding year. Instead of being distributed among three spearheads as heretofore, all offensive forces were to be massed in the south in order "finally to annihilate what vital defensive strength the Soviets have left and to remove from their grasp as far as possible the principal sources of energy for their war economy." It was also planned to cease operations in good time, prepare winter quarters, and, if need be, build a defensive line corresponding to the west wall (*Ostwall*), which in itself would allow Germany to wage a hundred years' war. "But in that case it would no longer cause us any special concern."[45]

But when the German troops reached the Don, during the second half of July, 1942, and had not yet been able to throw the projected pincers around the enemy forces, Hitler once more fell victim to his impatience and his nerves and forgot all the lessons of the past summer. On July 23 he gave orders to divide the offensive into two simultaneous, separating operations. Army Group B was to advance through Stalingrad to Astrakhan on the Caspian Sea. Army Group A was to annihilate the enemy armies near Rostov, then reach the eastern coast of the Black Sea and march toward Baku. The forces that at the beginning of the offensive had occupied a front of about 500 miles would, at the end of the operations, have to cover a line more than 2,500 miles long against an enemy whom they had been unable to engage in battle, let alone defeat.

Hitler's euphoric judgment of what the German army could do was presumably based on the illusory look of the map. In the late summer of 1942 his power had reached the point of its greatest extension. German troops stood on the North Cape and along the Atlantic Coast, in Finland, and throughout the Balkans. In North Africa General Rommel, whom the Allies had thought already beaten, had with inferior forces thrown the British back across the Egyptian border as far as El Alamein. In the East Wehrmacht soldiers crossed the border into Asia at the end of July. In the south they reached the burning, shattered refineries of Maikop at the beginning of August. But Hitler obtained hardly any of the oil that had served, during the cruel struggles of the preceding weeks, as the reason for the offensive. On August 21 German soldiers raised the swastika flag on the Elbrus, the highest mountain in the Caucasus. Two days later the Sixth Army reached the Volga at Stalingrad.

But appearances were misleading. For the rapidly spreading war on three continents, on the seas and in the air, the men, the armaments, the transport, the raw materials and the leadership were lacking. By the time Hitler reached his zenith, he had long been a defeated man. The abrupt succession of crises and setbacks that now descended, their effects worsened by his rigidity, revealed the unreal nature of this enormously expanded power.

The first symptoms of crisis appeared in the East. Since the beginning of the 1942 summer offensive Hitler had transferred his headquarters from Rastenburg to Vinnitsa in the Ukraine; and here, in the daily strategy conferences, he defended his decision to conquer both the Caucasus and Stalingrad. His defense grew increasingly vehement, although possession of the city on the Volga had meanwhile become virtually meaningless so long as the German armies could check traffic on the river. On August 21 there was an angry dispute when Halder argued that German effective strength was not sufficient for two such wearing offensives. The chief of staff implied that Hitler's military decisions ignored the limits of what was possible and, as he later put it, gave "full power to wishful thinking." When in the course of the argument he pointed out that the Russians were producing 1,200 tanks monthly, Hitler, almost beside himself, forbade him to utter "such idiotic nonsense."[46]

Approximately two weeks later the slowing of the advance on the Caucasus front gave rise to another clash in the Führer's headquarters. This time the submissive General Jodl dared to defend Field Marshal List, commander of Army Group A. Moreover, Jodl quoted Hitler's own words to prove that List was only obeying the instructions he had received. In a rage, Hitler broke off the conversation. On September 9 he demanded that the field marshal resign, and that same evening he himself took over the command of Army Group A. From this point on he suspended almost all contact with the generals attached to the Führer's headquarters. For several months he even refused to shake hands with Jodl; he avoided the conference room. Conferences took place in very restricted groups, the atmosphere permanently icy, in his own small blockhouse, and precise minutes were taken. Hitler left his blockhouse only after dark, and by concealed paths. Henceforth he also took his meals alone, only his Alsatian dog keeping him company; he rarely asked visitors to join him. Thus the evening gathering at table dropped out of his life, and with it ended all that petty bourgeois sociability and cozy social intercourse in the Führer's headquarters. At the end of September Hitler finally relieved Halder of his duties also. For some time he had been impressed by the reports from General Zeitzler, chief of staff to the commander in chief, West. They were distinguished by a wealth of tactical ideas and an optimistic attitude. Hitler said he now wanted "a man like this Zeitzler" at his side, and he appointed him the new army chief of staff.

Meanwhile, with increasing casualties, more and more units of the Sixth Army had reached Stalingrad and occupied positions in the north and the south of the city. To all appearances the Russians were determined this time not to evade but to give battle. An order of the day from Stalin had fallen into German hands. In it he informed his people in the tone of a concerned father of his country that from now on the Soviet Union could no longer surrender territory. Every foot of soil must be defended to the utmost. As though he felt personally challenged by this order, Hitler now demanded, against the advice both of Zeitzler and of General Paulus, the commander of the Sixth Army, the capture of Stalingrad. The city became a prestige item, its capture "urgently necessary for psychological reasons," as Hitler declared on October 2. A week later he added that Communism must be "deprived of its shrine." The bloody struggle for houses, residential areas, and factories which then began caused high casualties on both sides. Yet everyone momentarily expected news of the fall of Stalingrad.

Since the winter disaster, when the specter of defeat had first appeared to him, Hitler had been giving all his energy to the Russian campaign. It became more and more obvious that he was neglecting all the other theaters of war. He still preferred thinking in terms of vast spans of time and distances, in eons and continents; but North Africa, for example, was too remote for him. In any case, he never adequately recognized the strategic importance of the Mediterranean area and thus once again demonstrated how nonpolitical and abstract, how essentially "literary" his thinking was. Lacking supplies and reserves, the Afrika Korps wasted its offensive strength. Submarine warfare, too, suffered from Hitler's bias. Up to the end of 1941 no more than sixty U-boats were available for assignment. A year later the complement of approximately one hundred units, which had been called for at the beginning of the war, was at last attained. But by then the enemy, having felt the brunt of the U-boat warfare, had devised defensive measures that swung the balance the other way.

In the air war, too, the whole picture now changed. At the beginning of January, 1941, the British cabinet had issued a strategic plan for the air war that aimed at eliminating Germany's synthetic fuel industry in a series of purposeful air raids and thus, by "paralyzing vital segments of industry" numb the entire war-making ability of the Reich.[47] But the concept, which undoubtedly would have given the events of the war a very different course if it had been implemented immediately, was not carried out until more than three years later. In the meantime, other views prevailed, principally the idea of area bombing, terror bombing of the civilian population. The new phase was initiated on the night of March 28, 1942, with a major raid by the Royal Air Force on Lübeck. The historic city of patricians "burned like kindling," according to the official report. In response Hitler called in two bomber groups of approximately one hundred planes from Sicily. In the following weeks they carried out reprisal attacks, so-called Baedeker raids, against the artistic treasures of old English cities. The vast proportional difference in strength that had meanwhile developed became apparent when the British on May 30, 1942, responded with the first 1,000-bomber raid of the war. During the second half of the year the Americans joined them, and from 1943 on, Germany was exposed to an incessant air offensive, "round-the-clock" bombing. Taking account of the changed situation, Churchill declared in a speech in London's Mansion House: "Now this is not the end. It is not even the beginning of the end. But it is, perhaps, the end of the beginning."[48]

Events on the fronts confirmed this dictum. On November 2 General Montgomery, after preparatory massed artillery fire lasting for ten days, broke through the German-Italian positions at El Alamein with overwhelmingly superior forces. Shortly afterward, in the early morning hours of November 8, British and American troops landed on the coasts of Morocco and Algeria and occupied French North Africa as far as the Tunisian border. Some ten days later, on November 19, two Soviet army groups launched—in a raging snowstorm—the counteroffensive at Stalingrad. After successfully breaking through the Rumanian sector of the front they encircled some 220,000 men with 100 tanks, 1,800 guns and 10,000 vehicles between the Volga and the Don. When General Paulus reported the encirclement, Hitler ordered him to move his headquarters into the city and form a defense perimeter, a so-called hedgehog position. Only a few days before, Hitler had telegraphed to Rommel, in response to his request for permission to retreat: "In your present situation there can be no other thought but to persevere, to yield not a step, and to throw into the battle every weapon and every soldier that can still be freed for service. . . . It would not be the first time in history that a stronger will triumphed over the enemy's stronger battalions. But you can show your troops no other way but the one that leads to victory or to death."

The three November offensives of 1942 marked the turning point of the war. The initiative had finally passed to the opposite side. As if he wanted one more stab at playing generalissimo, Hitler on November 11 ordered his troops to march into the unoccupied part of France. And in his annual speech delivered in commemoration of the putsch of November, 1923, he struck one of those rigid poses whose basis can only be the willingness to let the worst happen. "There will no longer be any peace offers coming from us," he cried. In contrast to imperial Germany, he continued, there now stood at the head of the Reich a man who "has always known nothing but struggle and with it only one principle: Strike, strike, and strike again!"

In me they . . . are facing an opponent who does not even think of the word capitulate. It was always my habit, even as a boy—perhaps it was naughtiness then, but on the whole it must have been a virtue after all—to have the last word. And let all our enemies take note: The Germany of the past laid down its arms before the clock struck twelve. I make it a principle not to stop until the clock strikes thirteen![49]

This principle now became his new strategy, replacing all other concepts: Hold out! When the defeat of the Afrika Korps was already sealed, in his fixation on holding out he ordered several units, which he had hitherto withheld from Rommel, sent to the by now lost cause in Tunis. He curtly rejected Mussolini's pleas that he try for another understanding with Stalin. He rejected all proposals to shorten the Eastern front by drawing in the lines. He wanted to stay in North Africa, hold Tunis, advance in Algeria, defend Crete, keep twenty-four European countries occupied, defeat the Soviet Union plus England and the United States. And with all that, his basic emotion intruding more and more frequently upon all rational thought, he wanted to guarantee that now at last—as he put it in the midst of retreat, flight, and nemesis—"international Jewry is recognized in all its diabolic dangerousness."[50]

The symptoms of his intellectual decay were accompanied by a process of organizational dissolution that could be felt everywhere. The night after the beginning of the Allied landing in North Africa Hitler delivered the above-mentioned speech in Munich. Then, accompanied by his adjutants and personal intimates, he went to the Berghof in Berchtesgaden. Keitel and Jodl stayed in a building on the edge of town. The armed forces operations staff (*Wehrmachtsführungsstab*) was quartered in a special train at the Salzburg railroad station, while the General Staff of the army, which was really in charge of things, was far away in its headquarters near Angerburg in East Prussia. During the following days Hitler remained in Berchtesgaden. Instead of consulting and organizing defensive measures, he merely took satisfaction in the fact that it was he against whom all this gigantic armada had been assembled. He became intoxicated with the far-reaching operations of the kind he could no longer mount and criticized the enemy's deliberate procedures. He himself, he said, would have acted more directly, and psychologically more effectively, by landing just outside Rome, in this way cutting off the Axis troops in North Africa and southern Italy.[51]

Meanwhile, the ring around Stalingrad was closing ever more tightly. Hitler did not return to Rastenburg until the evening of November 23, and it cannot be definitely ascertained whether he underestimated the seriousness of the situation or was attempting by a display of composure to conceal it from himself and his entourage. At any rate, when General Zeitzler asked to see him in connection with several overdue decisions, Hitler attempted to put him off until the following day. The chief of staff insisted on a meeting and proposed that immediate orders go to the Sixth Army to break out of the pocket. The result was one of those disputes that flared up repeatedly until the early part of February, when Hitler's hold-the-line strategy ended in a debacle. By about two o'clock in the morning Zeitzler apparently thought he had convinced Hitler. At any rate, he informed the headquarters of Army Group B that he expected to obtain the signature to the break-out order early in the morning. The truth was that Hitler had evidently made one of his pseudoconcessions. But the quarrel went on into the following weeks. It took a wealth of variant forms. Hitler mustered all his arts of persuasion: long, seemingly reasonable silences, endless talking about trivialities, yielding on other points, firing an overwhelming barrage of figures. But through it all, with growing obstinacy, Hitler held to his resolve. Contrary to his usual habit, he even tried on occasion to strengthen it by enlisting the support of others. With psychological adroitness he had Göring—whose prestige had taken such a beating and who now seemed only to be waiting for a chance to exude optimism once more—issue an assurance that the Luftwaffe would be able to supply the encircled army. In the course of an argument with Zeitzler he summoned Generals Keitel and Jodl; at this time these three held the posts of chief of staff, chief of the High Command of the armed forces, and chief of the armed forces operations staff. Standing, his expression solemn, Hitler formally asked them their views: "I have a very grave decision to make. Before I make it, I should like to hear your opinions. Should I abandon Stalingrad or not?"

As always, Keitel abjectly confirmed his wishes: "With flashing eyes he exclaimed: 'Mein Führer, stand at the Volga!'" And Jodl recommended waiting and seeing. Zeitzler alone once again pleaded for a break-out. Hitler was thus able to sum up the results of the conference: "You see, Herr General, I am not alone in my opinion. It is shared by both of these officers, whose rank is higher than yours. I will therefore abide by my previous decisions." Sometimes one has the impression that Hitler, after so many partial, inadequate successes, had come to an ultimate decision that in Stalingrad he would challenge not only Stalin, not only his enemies in this sprawling, multifront war, but fate itself. The ever more patent crisis did not deter him; rather, in a curious way he put his trust in it. For his oldest recipe for success, repeatedly confirmed ever since the party conflict of the summer of 1921, had been to seek out crises in order to derive new impetus and confidence in victory from overcoming them. From the military point of view the Battle of Stalingrad was not really the turning point of the entire war; but it was that for Hitler. "If we abandon it—Stalingrad—we are really abandoning the whole meaning of the campaign," he declared. With his passion for mythologizing, he surely felt it as a sign that this city bore the name of one of his great symbolic enemies. Here he wanted to win or go down to his doom.

By the end of January, the Sixth Army was in a hopeless position, the soldiers totally exhausted and demoralized by cold, epidemics, and hunger.

But when General Paulus asked permission to surrender on the ground that the collapse was inescapable, Hitler telegraphed back: "Forbid surrender. The army will hold its position to the last soldier and the last cartridge, and by its heroic endurance will make an unforgettable contribution to the building of the defensive front and the salvation of Western civilization." Speaking to the Italian ambassador, he compared the Sixth Army to the 300 Greeks at Thermopylae. And Göring made a similar comparison in a speech on January 30, when resistance died in the ruins of Stalingrad and only a few desperate and isolated remnants continued to defend themselves: "In future days this will be said of the heroic battle on the Volga: If thou comest to Germany, say thou sawest us lying at Stalingrad, as the law of honor and warfare hath commanded for Germany."

Three days later, on February 2, the last remnants of the Sixth Army surrendered. A few days before, Hitler had appointed General Paulus a field marshal and promoted 117 other officers to the next higher rank. Shortly before 3 P.M. a German reconnaissance plane flying high above the city radioed that "no more fighting" could be observed in Stalingrad. Ninety-one thousand German soldiers were taken prisoner; 5,000 of them returned home years later.

Hitler's indignation at Paulus for not having the greatness to cope with disaster and for capitulating prematurely was discharged at the military conference in the Führer's headquarters:

How easy he has made it for himself! . . . The man should shoot himself as generals used to fall upon their swords when they saw that their cause was lost. That's to be taken for granted. Even a Varus commanded the slave: Kill me now! . . . what does 'life' mean? Life is the nation; the individual must die. What remains alive beyond the individual is the nation. But how can a man be afraid of it, afraid of this second in which he can free himself from misery, if duty does not hold him in this vale of wretchedness. Paulus . . . will be speaking on the radio in no time—you'll see. [Generals] Seydlitz and Schmidt will speak on the radio. They'll lock those men in their rat-infested cellars, and two days later they'll have them so worn down they'll talk at once. . . . How can anyone be so cowardly? I don't understand it. . . . What are we to do about it? What hurts me most personally is that I promoted him to field marshal. I wanted to give him that last pleasure. That's the last field marshal I appoint in this war. Best not to count your chickens before they're hatched. . . . That's as ridiculous as anything can be. So many people have to die, and then one man like that comes along and at the last minute defiles the heroism of so many others. He could free himself from all misery and enter into eternity, into national immortality, and he prefers to go to Moscow. How can there be any choice. There's something crazy about it.[52]

In its psychological though not its military aspect Stalingrad was in fact one of the great turning points of the war. Both in the Soviet Union and among the Allies the victory produced a tangible change of mood and awoke hopes that afterward were often disappointed. At the same time, among Germany's allies and in the neutral countries, faith in Hitler's superiority suffered a distinct blow. In Germany, too, confidence in Hitler's skill as a leader, already weakened, visibly faded. At his daily conference with his associates Goebbels issued instructions to exploit the defeat "psychologically for strengthening our people." He declared that "every word about this heroic struggle would go down in history" and required that the armed forces communiqué in particular be "so phrased . . . that down the centuries it will continue to stir hearts." As models he recommended Caesar's addresses to his soldiers, Frederick the Great's appeal to his soldiers before the Battle of Leuthen, and Napoleon's proclamations to his Guard. "Only now, perhaps," a special message from the office of the Reich propaganda chief read, "have we entered the Frederician era of this mighty and decisive conflict. The Battles of Kolin, Hochkirch, Kunersdorf, all three names signify grave defeats for Frederick the Great, veritable catastrophes, far worse in their effects than anything that has taken place in recent weeks on the Eastern front. But Kolin was followed by a Leuthen, Hochkirch and Kunersdorf by a Liegnitz, a Torgau and a Burkersdorf— and at last by ultimate victory. . . ." Yet despite such inspiring parallels, which henceforth right down to the end of the war were repeatedly cited in ever more hortatory terms, a *Sicherheitsdienst* report stated: "The conviction is general that Stalingrad means a turning point in the war. . . . Our fickle racial comrades are inclined to regard Stalingrad as the beginning of the end."

For Hitler the debacle of Stalingrad meant a fresh thrust into mythological realms. From that time on, his imagination was captivated by images of catastrophic collapse. The Casablanca Conference, at which Churchill and Roosevelt at the end of January proclaimed the principle of unconditional surrender, and thus on their part burned all bridges behind them, reinforced these fantasies. Starting with the strategy of holding firm at any price, which dominated all of 1943, as the end drew nearer Hitler more and more categorically developed the strategy of a flamboyant downfall.

Chapter 3

We must turn the newly won Eastern territories into a Garden of Eden.

Adolf Hitler

It is a great evil when men who determine the destiny of the earth deceive themselves concerning what is possible. . . . Their obstinacy or, if you will, their genius lends a temporary success to their endeavors. But since these come into conflict with the plans, the interest, the entire moral existence of their contemporaries, forces of opposition turn against them. After a certain time, which for their victims is very long but in the historical view is very short, nothing remains of all their enterprises but the crimes they have committed and the sufferings they have caused.

Benjamin Constant

LOST REALITY

From the beginning of the Russian campaign on, Hitler led a retired life. His headquarters, which also housed the High Command of the armed forces, was once again located in the extensive woods beyond Rastenburg in East Prussia. A system of walls, barbed wire, and mines protected the grouping of bunkers and buildings. The prevailing atmosphere was peculiarly gloomy and monotonous. Visitors have described the place as a blending of monastery and concentration camp. The small, unadorned rooms with their plain deal furniture formed a striking contrast to the pomp of past years, the spacious halls, the grand perspectives and all the theatrical lavishness of Berlin, Munich, and Berchtesgaden. Sometimes it seemed as if Hitler had retreated back to the cave. Italian Foreign Minister Ciano compared the inhabitants of the headquarters with troglodytes, and found the atmosphere depressing: "One does not see a single colorful spot, not a single lively touch. The anterooms are full of people smoking, eating and chatting. Smell of kitchens, uniforms, heavy boots."[53]

During the early months of the war Hitler had taken occasional trips to the front, and visited battlefields, headquarters, or military hospitals. But after the first failures he began to shun reality and withdraw into the abstract world of map tables and military conferences. From that time on, his experience of the war was almost exclusively as lines and figures on paper landscapes. He faced the public less and less often; he shrank from the onetime grand appearances. With the defeats he lost the energy he needed for striking poses. Once he had dropped his monumental attitudes, the changes in him showed all too plainly: he moved through the scenery of headquarters wearily, with hunched shoulders, one foot dragging, eyes staring dully out of a pasty face. His left hand had a slight tremble. Here was a man obviously on the physical downgrade, a bitter man, who admitted that he was plagued by melancholia. And he plunged ever deeper into the complexes and hatreds of his early years. To be sure, Hitler's personality had always been marked by rigid, static features. But with this phase it is clear we are witnessing a galloping process of regression. At the same time it seems as if this regression were once more revealing his true, unvarnished nature.

The isolation into which Hitler had retreated after the quarrel with the generals increased after Stalingrad. He often sat brooding, sunk in deep depression. Or else, with inward turned gaze, he would take a few aimless steps at the side of his Alsatian through the headquarters terrain. A tense awkwardness hung over all relationships: "Faces froze into masks," one of the participants wrote. "Often we stood about in silence." Goebbels noted in his diary:

> It is tragic that the Führer has so cut himself off from life and is leading an excessively unhealthy life. He no longer gets out in the fresh air, no longer has any relaxation; he sits in his bunker, acts, and broods. . . . The solitude in the Führer's headquarters and the whole method of work there naturally have a depressing effect on the Führer.[54]

In fact Hitler began more and more palpably to suffer from his self-chosen isolation. In contrast to his youth, he complained, he could "no longer stand being alone." His life style, already marked by a spartan note during the first years of the war, became plainer and plainer. The meals at the Führer's table were notorious for their simplicity. Only once more did he attend a performance of *Götterdämmerung* in Bayreuth, and after the second Russian winter he no longer wanted even to hear music. From 1941 on, it had been his task, he later declared, "in all circumstances not to lose my nerve, but where there is a breakdown anywhere constantly to find escapes and remedies in order somehow to fix matters up. . . . For five years I have been cut off from the outer world; I have not gone to the theater, not heard a concert, no longer see any movies. I live solely for the task of leading this struggle because I know that unless a person of iron will stands in the background, the struggle cannot be won." The question remains, however, whether the very sacrifices he imposed on himself in his maniacal insistence on the exercise of will, whether this single-minded concentration upon the war, did not constrict his mind and rob him of all inner freedom.

The tensions he underwent were discharged, more powerfully than ever before, in an unquenchable urge to launch into tirades. He found a new audience in his secretaries, for whom he tried in vain to provide a "congenial atmosphere" by offerings of cake and a fireplace fire. Sometimes he had his adjutants, his doctors, Bormann, or some chance guest join them. As his insomnia grew worse, he steadily extended his monologues. By 1944 the members of the circle would be desperately forcing their eyes to stay open until the graying dawn. Only then, as Guderian reports, would Hitler "lie down for a brief slumber, from which the pushing brooms of the scrubwomen at his bedroom door would awaken him by nine o'clock at the latest."

He continued to stick to the themes which had been part of the repertory of earlier years, and which are recorded in the table talk: his youth in Vienna, the First World War and the years of struggle, history, prehistory, nutrition, women, art, the fight for survival. He grew exercised over the "hopping around" of the dancer Gret Palucca, over the "stunted smears" of modern art, over Conductor Knappertsbusch's fortissimi, which forced opera singers to shriek so that they "looked like tadpoles." He spoke of his disgust with the "idiotic bourgeoisie," with the "herd of swine" in the Vatican or with the "insipid Christian heaven." Along with ruminations about the imperial racial state, Hannibal's elephants, Ice Age catastrophes, Caesar's wife, or "the gang of jurists" came recommendations for a vegetarian diet, a prospectus for a popular Sunday newspaper that would carry "lots of pictures," and serialized fiction "so that the gals can get something out of it."[55] Stunned by the unending torrent of words, the Italian Foreign Minister commented that Hitler was probably very happy to be Hitler because it permitted him to talk eternally.

More striking than the endless flow of his monologues was, at least in the recorded material, the crudity of expression, in which he unmistakably relapsed back to his origins. The ideas themselves, the anxieties, wishes and aims, were unchanged from his early days. What is more, he now laid aside all the disguises and statesmanlike poses, and fell back on the vehement and vulgar phrases of the beer-hall demagogue, not to say the denizen of the flophouse. With a good deal of zest he discussed cannibalism among the partisans or in besieged Leningrad. He called Roosevelt a "cracked fool," Churchill's speeches "a souse's bullshit," and irritably denounced von Manstein as a "pisspot strategist." He praised the Soviet system for forgoing all the "humanitarian blather," and imagined how he would meet a mutiny in Germany by "shooting a batch of a few hundred thousand

669

people." One of his favorite, "constantly repeated" maxims was the sentence: "A dead man can no longer put up a fight."[56]

Among those symptoms of decline must be included the intellectual narrowing that threw him back to the viewpoint of a local party leader. From the third winter on, he could see the war in no other light than that of a "seizure of power" expanded to global dimensions. In the "period of struggle," too, he comforted himself, he had faced overwhelmingly superior forces—"a single man with a small band of followers." The war was nothing but a "gigantic repetition" of earlier experiences. The record of one of the table talks reads: "At lunch . . . the chief pointed out that this war was a faithful copy of the conditions of the period of struggle. What took place among us then as a struggle of parties in the domestic realm is taking place today as the struggle of nations in the foreign realm."[57]

In keeping with the precipitate aging of his appearance, he occasionally complained that the years were robbing him of all his gambler's pleasure in taking risks. Intellectually, too, he more and more lived in the past. The garrulous reviews of matters long past, with which he filled his nocturnal monologues, had the sound of an old man's nostalgias. In his military decisions he frequently referred to the experiences of the First World War, while his interest in armaments became more and more restricted to the traditional weapons systems. He neither grasped the crucial importance of radar and the splitting of the atom nor the value of a heat-seeking ground-to-air rocket or a sound-guided torpedo. He also blocked the large-scale production of the first jet plane, the Messerschmitt 262. With senile obstinacy he insisted on far-fetched objections, reversed or changed decisions, confounded his entourage with hastily reeled-off statistics, or took refuge in broad psychological generalizations. When on the basis of a newspaper report of British experiments with jet planes he was at last persuaded early in 1944 to permit the manufacture of the Me 262, he tried to hedge by ordering that the plane not be built as a fighter against the Allied air raiders. Instead, contrary to the advice of the experts, it was to be employed as a fast bomber. The physical strain on the pilots would be intolerable, he decided, and also argued that the faster planes were really slower in air combat. In fact, he snatched at anything for an argument; and while Germany's cities were reduced to rubble, he refused even to permit a few experimental uses of the plane as a fighter. Finally he banned any further discussion of the subject.

Naturally these struggles with his own people increased his usual abnormal suspiciousness. Often he obtained information from staff headquarters over the heads of his closest military advisers, and occasionally he sent his army adjutant, Major Engel, to the front by plane to check the actual situation. Officers who came from the battle areas were not allowed to speak on military matters with anyone, especially not with the chief of staff, before they had been received in the Führer's bunker. With his obsession for checking up, Hitler praised his organization for one of its crucial defects. On the whole vast Eastern front, he declared, there was "not a regiment and not a battalion whose position was not followed up three times a day in the Führer's headquarters here." One major reason so many officers came to grief was this paralyzing paranoia, which undermined every relationship. Eventually he quarreled with all the commanders in chief of the army, all the chiefs of staff, eleven of the eighteen field marshals, twenty-one of nearly forty full generals, and nearly all the commanders of the three sectors of the Eastern front. The space around him grew increasingly emptier. As long as Hitler remained in headquarters, Goebbels declared, his dog Blondi was closer to him than any human being.

After Stalingrad his nerves were plainly giving out. Up to then Hitler had rarely lost his stoic bearing which, he believed, was among the attributes of great commanders. Even in critical situations he had maintained an ostentatious calm. But now that pose was accompanied by signs of fatigue, and his violent fits of rage revealed the price that years of overtaxing his strength had cost. When General Staff officers delivered their situation reports, he railed at them as "idiots," "cowards," and "liars." Guderian, who at this time saw him again after a long interval, noted in astonishment Hitler's "irascibility, and the unpredictability of his words and decisions." He was also subject to unwonted sentimental lapses. When Bormann told him of his wife's confinement, Hitler reacted with tears in his eyes. More often than ever, he spoke of his retirement and how he would give himself up to meditating, reading, and running a museum.

There is some evidence that from the end of 1942 on, the entire stabilization system of his nerves gave way. He concealed this only by a tremendous act of desperate self-discipline. The generals attached to the Führer's headquarters felt the symptoms of the crisis, although the later descriptions of a Hitler continually raging, totally subject to the explosions of an unrestrained temperament, belong in the category of apologetic exaggeration. The minutes of the military conferences, some of which have been preserved, indicate instead that he made strong efforts to fit the image he had chosen for himself. On the whole, he succeeded.

The very stringency of the daily schedule at headquarters helped. Immediately after awakening, Hitler studied the news. Toward noon the grand conference was held. Then followed more conferences, dictation, reception of guests, and discussions until the evening conference, which usually took place during the night. All this regular attention to duties did violence to his nature and was in deliberate opposition to his inveterate yearning for passivity and indolence. As late as December, 1944, he sketched, in a casual remark, the image of a genius saved by steady purpose; with difficulty and occasional deviations he was trying to conform to that image:

Genius is something will-o-the-wispy if it is not sustained by perseverance and fanatical tenacity. That is the most important thing there is in human life. People who have only inspirations, ideas, and so on, but who do not have firmness of character, who lack tenacity and perseverance, will amount to nothing in spite of all. They are adventurers. If things go well, they climb; when things go badly, they immediately slump down and give up everything. But you can't make world history with that kind of attitude.[58]

In its functionalism and gloom the Führer's headquarters was not unlike that "state cage" into which his father had once led him and where the people, according to young Hitler, had "sat crouching on one another close as monkeys." The mechanism into which he forced his life was so anti-pathetic to his nature that it could only be maintained artificially. Medica-tion and druglike preparations enabled him to meet the unaccustomed demands upon his nature. Until the end of 1940 the drugs do not seem to have influenced his health significantly. Ribbentrop, it is true, reported a heated dispute in the summer of 1940, in the course of which Hitler dropped into a chair and began groaning that he had a feeling of dissolu-tion and sensed he was on the verge of a stroke.[59] But the description suggests that this scene should be reckoned among those half-hysterical, half-histrionic displays that Hitler used as a method of coercive argumenta-tion. His medical checkups at the beginning and the end of the year merely showed slightly increased blood pressure and those gastric and intestinal disturbances from which he had always suffered.[60]

With hypochondriacal pedantry Hitler noted every deviation in the findings of his checkups. He was constantly observing himself, taking his pulse, reading medical books, and taking medicines "literally in quantity": sleeping and kola pills, digestives, cold pills, vitamins. Even the eucalyptus candies that were always on hand gave him the sense of looking after his health. If a medicine were prescribed for him without an exact dosage, he took it from morning to night almost incessantly. Professor Morell, the onetime fashionable Berlin doctor for skin and venereal diseases, had advanced through the good offices of Heinrich Hoffmann to the rank of one of Hitler's personal physicians. For all his devotion to medicine, Professor Morell was not without traces of quackery. He gave Hitler injections almost daily: sulfanilamide, glandular preparations, glucose, or hormones that were suppcsed to improve or regenerate his circulation, his intestinal flora, or the state of his nerves. Göring sarcastically called him "Reich Injection Master."

As time went on, Morell naturally had to resort to stronger drugs and shorter intervals in order to maintain Hitler's performance. On top of this, he had to prescribe sedatives to calm the jangled nerves, so that Hitler was exposed to a permanent process of physiological stress. The consequences of this constant interference with his body processes by at times as many as twenty-eight different drugs became evident during the war, when the strain of events, the loss of sleep, the monotony of the vegetarian diet, and his troglodyte's existence in the bunker world of headquarters, intensified the effects of the medicines. In August, 1941, Hitler complained of bouts of weakness, nausea and chills and fever. Swellings formed on his leg, quite possibly a reaction against the years of artificial regulation of his body. From this time on, at any rate, spells of exhaustion appeared with greater frequency. After Stalingrad he took a drug against depressive moods every other day.[61] Thereafter, he could no longer endure bright light, and for this reason had a cap with a greatly enlarged vizor made for his walks outdoors. Sometimes he complained about disturbed balance: "I always have the feeling of tipping to the right."[62]

In spite of the visible changes in his exterior, his bowed back, his rapidly graying hair, he retained to the end an unusual capacity for work. Quite rightly, he himself attributed his remarkable energy to Morell's efforts, overlooking the extent to which he was consuming his physical reserves. After the war, Professor Karl Brandt, who was a member of Hitler's medical staff, said that the effect of Morell's treatment was to "draw on what one might call life for years in advance" and that it had seemed as if Hitler "every year aged not a year but four or five years." Hence the sudden and premature graying and his shattered appearance. In the euphorias produced by his drugs he seemed to glow like a wraith.

It would therefore be a mistake to attribute the symptoms of degeneration, the crises and fitful outbursts on Hitler's part, to structural changes in his personality. The abuse of his physical potential and the consumption of his reserves partly covered over and partly intensified the existing elements, but did not cause—as has sometimes been asserted—the destruction of a hitherto intact personality.[63] This is the qualification that must be placed on all the disputes over the effects of the strychnine contained in some of Morell's drugs, or whether Hitler suffered from Parkinson's disease (*paralysis agitans*), or whether the trembling of his left arm, the stooped posture, and his locomotive difficulties were of psychosomatic origin. However shadowy he looked outwardly, masklike in his rigidity, leaning on a cane as he moved about headquarters, he was still the man he had once been. What is so staggering in his appearance during those last years is not so much his rapid aging as the consistency—bordering on paralysis—with which he took up and carried out his early obsessions.

He was a person who continually needed artificial charging. In a sense Morell's drugs and medicines replaced the old stimulus of mass ovations. As noted above, Hitler shrank from the public after Stalingrad and in fact delivered only two more major speeches. Soon after the beginning of the war, he had begun this withdrawal, and all the propaganda efforts to create a mythology out of his remoteness was a poor substitute for the former sense of his omnipresence, by which the regime had been able to tap a vein of energy, spontaneity, and spirit of sacrifice in the German people. Now this potential for affecting the masses was gone. For fear of losing his aura of invincibility, Hitler would not set foot in the shattered cities; for the same reason he would not face the masses after the defeats, although he presumably sensed that this shrinking could lose him not only power over men's minds but also the source of his own energies. "Everything I am, I am through you alone," he occasionally had cried to the masses. Beyond all the aspects of techniques of power, he had thereby been affirming a constitutional, almost a physiological dependency. For the rhetorical excesses in which he had indulged from the first, uncertain appearances in Munich beer halls all the way to the painful, determined efforts of the last two years, never had as their sole purpose the rousing of the energies of others. They served also to rally his own forces and were, beyond all political occasions and ends, a means of self-preservation. In one of his last great speeches he prepared the country for his coming silence by pointing to the momentousness of the events at the front: "What need is there for me to do much talking now?" But among his intimates he later complained that he no longer trusted himself to speak before 10,000 persons and declared that he probably would never again be able to deliver a major speech. The conception of the end of his career as an orator was associated with the idea of the end in general, of death.[64]

Along with this retreat from the public, Hitler's peculiar weakness as a leader became apparent for the first time. Ever since the days of his rise he had always maintained his superiority by the charisma of the demagogue and by tactical ingenuity. But in this stage of the war he had to meet other demands on leadership. The principle of rival authorities—the domestic intrigues and struggles, this whole chaos of powers that he had constructed around him in preceding years and manipulated with Machiavellian skill—was scarcely appropriate for the struggle against a resolute enemy. It turned out to be one of the fateful weaknesses of the regime. For it consumed the energies that the fight against the outside antagonist required and finally led to a condition approaching total anarchy. In the military field alone there were the theaters of war under the parallel authority of the High Command of the armed forces (OKW) and High Command of the army (OKH), the undefined special position of Göring, the authority of Hitler and the SS, which cut across all other channels of command, the confusion of all kinds of army divisions, grenadier units, air force infantry formations, the SS-in-arms, and the militia, each accessible to various official channels. On top of all this, finally, there was the relationship to the troops of allied countries, a relationship undermined by mutual distrust. The administrative structure in occupied Europe was similarly confused; new forms of domination were constantly being developed, from outright annexation through protectorate, government general, and civil administration. Hardly ever has a centering of all power in a single person ended in such total and blatant disorganization.

It is by no means clear, however, whether Hitler ever really recognized the ruinous effects of his style of leadership. Rational classifications, structural arrangements, any kind of quiet authority, were fundamentally so alien to him that until literally the last days of the war he repeatedly encouraged his entourage to feud over positions, competences, and ridiculous questions of rank. There are indications that he had more confidence in the hunger for power and the egotism manifested in such quarrels than in all possible unselfish attitudes, because they comported with his view of the world. The very objectivity of specialists made him suspicious of them. And so he tried to wage the war as far as possible without their help, without consultation, without the relevant documentation, without logistical calculations; he tried to wage the war in the anachronistic style of the solitary commanders of antiquity—and lost it.

Hitler's weakness in leadership emerged most sharply in the course of 1943, when he had as yet developed no strategic conception of the further course of the war. He was uncertain, reluctant to make decisions, vacillating; and Goebbels spoke unequivocally of a "Leader crisis." The propaganda chief repeatedly urged the hesitant Hitler to regain the initiative in the war by rigorously mobilizing all reserves. In conjunction with Albert Speer, who had been appointed Armaments Minister the previous year, and with Robert Ley and Walther Funk, Goebbels elaborated plans for an overall simplification of the administration, a drastic cutback in consumption for the privileged classes, an increase in armament production, and other similar measures. He was to notice, however, that the gauleiters and the top SA and party officials had long since lost their sacrificial devotion and veered toward becoming a parasitical ruling class. On February 18, 1943, Goebbels addressed a band of invited followers in the Sportpalast and posed his famous ten rhetorical questions. "In an uproar of wild enthusiasm," as he put it, he obtained their consent to "total war." This speech was aimed chiefly at breaking resistance among the higher functionaries, whose luxurious living would be affected. But it was intended also to overcome Hitler's indecisiveness by a radicalizing appeal to the masses.[65]

Hitler's reluctance to impose the austerities of total war on the nation was partly the result of another memory, the shock of the November revolution of 1918. But it was also colored by his deep distrust of the inert and fickle masses. It is almost as if he realized how brittle and temporary his rule was and knew how much stood in the way of his intention of "compelling to greatness," as he once put it, a shrinking and unwilling German people. England, in its war effort, was able to lower the level of private comfort far more drastically than the Reich, and England also employed far more women in the armaments industries than did Germany.[66]

But there was still another factor in Hitler's holding back from total war: the intrigues of Martin Bormann, who scented in the effort by Goebbels and Speer all sorts of dangers to his own position. By adaptability, diligence, and craftiness Bormann had worked his way upward in the preceding years to the post of "Führer's secretary." And behind that unassuming title he had established one of the strongest power bases within the regime. His short, stocky figure in the ill-fitting party functionary's uniform was a fixed feature in all pictures of the Führer's headquarters. He was always there, keeping watch, pondering, a cunning expression on his peasant face. The undetermined sphere of his authority, which he steadily enlarged by referring to the Führer's alleged desires, assured him powers that in fact raised him to the status of the man who "secretly ran Germany." Hitler, for his part, seemed happy to be freed of the burden of routine administrative work by this seemingly unassertive secretary. It was soon Bormann who granted or withdrew both authority and the Führer's favor, who pushed through appointments and promotions, who praised, pestered, or eliminated people in government, but who all the while kept well in the background and could always come up with one slander or one flattery more than even his most powerful adversaries. By means of the visitor lists he controlled Hitler's contacts with the outside world, and according to the testimony of one observer erected "a veritable Chinese wall" around Hitler.

He was helped in this by a growing desire for isolation from reality on Hitler's part. Just as the onetime flophouse inmate had in imagination lived in palaces, the generalissimo who was having to retreat on all fronts constructed more and more magnificent imaginary worlds that he rapturously inhabited. Hitler's tendency to reject reality took an increasingly pathological form after the turning point of the war. This is evidenced in much of his behavior, such as his habit of traveling across the country in a curtained parlor car, and if possible by night. He would keep the windows of the conference room at the Führer's headquarters closed, and sometimes even blacked out, even in the most beautiful weather. Significantly, he began the day by looking over the prepared excerpts from the press; only then would he examine the latest data. His entourage has reported that he accepted the event itself more calmly than its echo in the press; reality irked him less than its image.

Hitler's conversational style, constantly degenerating into monologue, his inability to listen or to register objections, and his growing insistence on columns of figures, his *rage du nombre,* must be reckoned a part of this syndrome. As late as the end of 1943 he was still speaking with total scorn of a study by General Thomas that presented the Russian potential as a serious danger. He bluntly declared that he wanted to see no more memoranda of this sort. At the same time he refused to visit the front or the staff headquarters behind the front. His last visit to the headquarters of an army group took place on September 8, 1943.[67] Many disastrous decisions resulted from this ignorance of the reality, for marks on maps told nothing about the climate, the degree of exhaustion of the soldiers, or the extent of their psychological reserves. And in the curiously abstract atmosphere of the conference room, realistic data on the state of equipment or supplies were hard to come by. The preserved minutes of conferences, moreover, have recorded the truckling attitude of the military chiefs, their undignified flatteries. Once Halder had departed, this tone took over completely, so that ultimately all military conferences became no more than "show sits" as the jargon of the Führer's headquarters described those fraudulent lectures to the statesmen of Germany's allies. An attempt by Speer to have Hitler meet some of the younger front-line officers came to nothing; neither did the effort to persuade him to visit bombed cities. Goebbels jealously pointed to the much more impressive example of Churchill. Once, when the Führer's special train on its way to Berchtesgaden with blinds raised by mistake stopped beside a hospital train full of wounded men, Hitler became very agitated and ordered the blinds to be drawn at once.[68]

It is true that in the preceding years contempt for reality had been his strength. How else could he have risen out of nothingness and put across his bold triumphs in statesmanship? His early military successes may also have been partly based on that. But now that the tide had turned, disregard of reality drastically multiplied the effects of every defeat. On those occasions when reality forced itself all too painfully on him, he once more raised his old laments that he had become a politician against his will and was sorely burdened by the necessities of office which kept him from immortalizing himself with his cultural projects. "It's a pity," he would say, "that I have to wage war on account of a drunken fellow [Churchill], instead of serving the works of peace, like art." He said he was longing to go to the theater or the Wintergarten in Berlin and "be human again." Or he spoke bitterly of deception and treachery all around him, of the way the generals were always misleading him, and gave way more and more to an unwonted tone of lachrymose misanthropy: "I meet nothing but betrayal!"

From comparable observations during the twenties one of his early followers had drawn the conclusion that Hitler needed self-deception in order to be able to act at all.[69] He craved vastly overblown sham worlds, against whose background all obstacles became insignificant and all problems trivial. He was capable of acting only on the basis of false pretenses. That note of fantastical overexcitement associated with his personality derived from this disturbed relationship to reality. We might say: only unreality made him real. In his comments to his entourage, even in those weary, toneless monologues in the last phase of the war, his voice became animated only when he spoke of the "gigantic tasks," the "enormous plans" for the future. Those were his real reality.

It was a monstrous prospect that opened before the favored group who sat deep into the night about the Führer's table whenever he vouchsafed it "insights through the side door into paradise." An entire continent was to

677

be transformed by mass annihilation, extensive resettlements, assimilations and redistribution of the vacated areas. The program called for the conscious destruction of the past and the reshaping of all structures according to a plan without regard for historical tradition. True to his intellectual tendency, Hitler moved in spheres of vast proportions. Centuries shrank before his eyes, which saw only eternity; the world was reduced, and nothing was left of the Mediterranean but a mere, as he put it, "briny puddle." The innocent age was approaching its end, and the millennium of a new way of thinking was dawning, a way founded upon science and artistic prophecy, and demanding gigantic projects. Its central idea was the salvation of the world from centuries-old infection in an eschatological struggle between pure and inferior blood.

His mission was to provide the good blood with an imperial basis: an empire dominated by Germany, comprising the greater part of Europe as well as vast areas in Asia, which a century hence would be "the most compact and the most colossal power bloc" that had ever existed. Unlike Himmler and the SS, Hitler was free of all romanticism about the East. "I'd rather tramp on foot to Flanders," he commented, and bewailed the need to conquer territory in an easterly direction. Russia, he said, was "a dreadful country . . . the end of the world." He associated Russia with images of Dante's inferno. "Only reason bids us go to the East."

Presiding over this power bloc would be a racially homogeneous master race described by Hitler as "creatively Aryan humanity of the Atalantine-Aryan-Nordic type." It would be divided into a social hierarchy of three strata: the National Socialist "high nobility," veterans of the struggle; the party members, who would form a kind of "new middle class"; and "the great anonymous masses . . . the collective of those who serve, those who never come of age," as Hitler explained it. But these would still be called to rule over the "class of subject alien nationals . . . let us not flinch at calling them the modern slave class." And however repellent this picture may seem to us, it had the sound of an ideal order, at least for the ideological vanguard of National Socialism. As Communism preached the utopia of a consistently egalitarian society, this was the utopia of a consistently hierarchic society. The difference was that the historically determined destiny of a class to rule was replaced by the "natural" destiny of a race to rule.

The prewar years had seen a host of measures to purify the race, such as the SS marriage regulations and the genetic point system introduced by the Race and Settlement Bureau of the SS. Now, in the conquered regions of the East, a new, far more comprehensive and radical campaign was launched. Once again Hitler and the executives of the new order proceeded with a combination of positive and negative measures, linking endeavors to select good blood with extermination of those of inferior race. "They will fall like flies," the SS announced in one of its widely disseminated propaganda releases. And from Hitler's monologues there emerged a picture of, as he phrased it, a biological "process of mucking out" all contaminants of alien races, with subsequent Germanization.

As always he displayed extraordinary energy for destruction. On October 7, 1939, in a secret decree he had appointed the Reichsführer-SS Heinrich Himmler to the new post of Reich Commissioner for Consolidation of German Racialism, commissioned to undertake a racial "clean-up" in the East and prepare the region for an extensive resettlement program. Nevertheless, in this field, too, there soon developed that confusion of authorities and intentions that the regime engendered wherever it took action. The conquered Eastern territories became the testing ground for a multiplicity of genetic theories, which never progressed beyond their amateurish beginnings; and similarly, no more than a few confused outlines of the new order ever came into being.

In annihilation, on the other hand, the regime displayed the greatest effectiveness. The special vocabulary surrounding the extermination program was a good indication of how closely the regime identified its nature and its destiny with these activities. For this was the "world-historical task," the "glorious page in our history," the "supreme stress test," in the course of which the followers were being trained to a new kind of heroism and toughness. "It is considerably easier in many cases," Himmler declared, "to go into battle with a company than with the same company in some area to hold down an antagonistic population of culturally lower type, to carry out executions, transport people out of the area, take away howling and weeping women . . . this quiet compulsion to act, this quiet activity, this standing guard over our Weltanschauung, this need to be consistent, to be uncompromising—in many ways that is much, much harder."[70] He defined his task: What was above all involved was "a perfectly clear solution" of the Jewish question. What was involved was the decision "to make this race disappear from the earth." But since the majority of the German people were still not sufficiently enlightened about racial matters, the SS "has borne that for our people; we have taken the responsibility upon ourselves . . . and will then take the secret with us to our graves."[71]

We still do not know when Hitler made the decision on the "final solution" of the Jewish question, for no document on the matter exists. Much earlier than his closest followers, evidently, he understood such words as "elimination" or "extermination" not merely metaphorically, but as acts of physical annihilation, because such thoughts held no terrors for him. "Here too," Goebbels wrote with an undertone of admiration, "the Führer has been the fearless vanguard and spokesman of a radical solution." Even at the beginning of the thirties Hitler had, among his intimates, called for the development of a "technique of depopulation" and explicitly added that by that he meant the elimination of entire races. "Nature is cruel; therefore we also are entitled to be cruel. When I send the flower of German youth into the steel hail of the coming war without feeling the slightest regret over the precious German blood that is being spilled, should I not also have the right to eliminate millions of an inferior race that multiplies like vermin."[72]

Even the procedure of killing the victims by poison gas, first applied in an old, remote castle in the forest near Kulmhof, in December, 1941, can be traced back to Hitler's own experiences in the First World War. At any rate, a passage in *Mein Kampf* expresses the wish that "twelve or fifteen thousand of these Hebrew corrupters of the people had been held under poison gas" as happened to hundreds of thousands of German soldiers at the front.[73] In any case, whenever the decision for the final solution was made, it had nothing to do with the deteriorating military situation. It would be a crude misunderstanding of Hitler's fundamental intentions to represent the massacre in the East as the expression of growing bitterness at the development of the war, as an act of revenge upon the ancient symbolic enemy. Rather, that act was fully consistent with Hitler's thinking and was, given his premises, absolutely inevitable. On the other hand, the plan, temporarily considered in the Race and Settlement Bureau of the SS and in the Foreign Office as well, to establish the island of Madagascar as a kind of great ghetto for some 15 million Jews, negated Hitler's intentions on a crucial point. For if Jewry really was, as he had repeatedly stated and written, the infectious agent of the great world disease, then to his apocalyptic mind there could be no thought of providing a homeland for that agent, no course but to destroy its biological substance.

As early as the end of 1939 the first deportations to the ghettos of the Government General (Poland) began. But Hitler's specific decision for mass extermination apparently was made during the period of active preparation for the Russian campaign. The speech of March 31, 1941, which informed a sizable group of higher-ranking officers about Himmler's "special tasks" in the rear area, represents the first concrete reference to plans for mass killings. Two days later Alfred Rosenberg, after a two-hour talk with Hitler, confided with a shudder to his diary: "Which I do not want to write down today, but will never forget." Finally, on July 31, 1941, Göring issued to SD Chief Reinhard Heydrich the directive concerning the "desired final solution of the Jewish question."[74]

Efforts at concealment characterized the operation from the start. Beginning in January, 1942, the Jews were systematically rounded up throughout Europe, but the endless stream of trains that transported them started off toward unknown destinations. Deliberately spread rumors spoke of newly built, beautiful cities in the conquered East. The killer squads were given ever-changing reasons as justifications for their activities, the Jews being alternately presented as ringleaders of resistance and carriers of plagues. Even the ideological vanguards of National Socialism seemed to be unable to face the consequences of their own doctrines.

680

Hitler's own striking silence lends some support to this conjecture. For in the table talk, the speeches, the documents or the recollections of participants from all those years not a single concrete reference of his to the practice of annihilation has come down to us. No one can say how Hitler reacted to the reports of the *Einsatzgruppen,* whether he asked for or saw films or photos of their work, and whether he intervened with suggestions, praise, or blame. When we consider that he ordinarily transformed everything that preoccupied him into rampant speechmaking, that he never concealed his radicalism, his vulgarity, his readiness to go to extremes, this silence about the central concern of his life—involving, as it did in his mind, the salvation of the world—seems all the stranger. We can only guess about his motives: his characteristic mania for secrecy, a remnant of bourgeois morality, the desire to keep what was happening abstract and not weaken his own passion by letting himself see what it led to. Nevertheless, we are left with the disturbing picture of a savior who buries his great redeeming act deep in the charnel house of his heart. Of the entire top leadership, only Heinrich Himmler once attended a mass execution, at the end of August, 1942. He nearly fainted, and subsequently suffered a hysterical fit.[75]

The SS bureaucracy ultimately invented a special terminology, full of words like "emigration," "special treatment," "sanitary measures," "change of residence," or "natural diminution." Translated back into reality, such terms meant the following:

Moennikes and I went directly to the pits. We were not stopped. Then I heard rifle shots in quick succession behind a mound of earth. The people who had got off the trucks, men, women and children of every age, had to undress on orders from an SS man who held a riding whip or dog whip in his hand. They had to deposit their clothing, shoes, upper and underclothes separately, at certain places. I saw a heap of shoes containing at a guess eight hundred to a thousand shoes, and huge piles of underclothing and clothing. Without an outcry or weeping these people undressed, stood together in family groups, kissed and said goodbye to each other, and waited for the beckoning gesture of another SS man who stood at the pit and likewise held a whip in his hand. During a quarter of an hour that I stood by the pits I heard no laments or pleas for mercy. I observed a family of some eight persons. . . . An old woman with snow-white hair held a year-old baby in her arms and sang something to it and tickled it. The child crowed with pleasure. The couple looked on with tears in their eyes. The father held a boy of about ten by the hand, and spoke comfortingly to him in a low voice. The boy was fighting back his tears. The father pointed his finger up at the sky, caressed his head, and seemed to be explaining something to him. At this point the SS man by the pit called out something to his fellow. The other man divided off about twenty persons and instructed them to go behind the mound of earth. The family I have been speaking of was among them. I still remember very clearly how a girl, black-haired and slender, as she passed close by me gestured at herself and said: "Twenty-three years!" I

681

walked around the mound of earth and stood in front of the huge grave. The people lay pressed so closely together on top of one another that only the heads could be seen. Blood was running from almost all the heads down over the shoulders. Some of those who had been shot were still moving. A few raised their arms and turned their heads to show they were still alive. . . . I looked around to see who was doing the shooting. It was an SS man, sitting on the ground at the rim of the narrow side of the pit, a submachine gun on his knees, and smoking a cigarette. The completely naked people walked down a flight of steps that had been cut into the earthen wall of the pit, stumbled over the heads of those who were already lying there, to the place that the SS man indicated. They lay down in front of the dead or wounded; some stroked those who were still living and murmured what seemed to be words of comfort. Then I heard a series of shots. I looked into the pit and saw the bodies twitching, or the heads already lying still on the bodies in front. Blood ran from the back of their necks.[76]

That was the reality. Gradually, however, by the establishment of a string of highly organized murder factories the work of annihilation was removed from the eyes of the populace, rationalized, and changed over to poison gas. On March 17, 1942, the camp of Belzec, with a daily kill capacity of 15,000 persons, began functioning. It was followed in April by Sobinor, close to the Ukrainian border, capacity 20,000; then Treblinka and Maidanek, with approximately 25,000, and above all Auschwitz, which became "the greatest institution for human annihilation of all times," as its commandant, Rudolf Höss, boasted at his trial with a note of crazed pride. Here the entire killing process, from the selection of the new arrivals and the gassing of them to the elimination of the corpses and the exploitation of whatever remained, had been elaborated into a smooth system of interlocking procedures. The annihilation was carried out hastily, with increasing acceleration "so that we don't find ourselves stuck in the middle of it some day," as the SS chief of Lublin, Odilo Globocnik, explained. Many eyewitnesses have described the resignation with which people went to their deaths: in Kulmhof more than 152,000 Jews; in Belzec 600,000; in Sobinor 250,000; in Treblinka 700,000; in Maidanek 200,000; and in Auschwitz more than 1 million. And the shootings continued alongside the mass gassings. According to the exaggerated estimate of the Reichssicherheitshauptamt,* annihilation was to be extended to approximately 11 million Jews.[77] More than 5 million were murdered.

Hitler and his *Lebensraum* commissioners regarded the Eastern part of Europe as vacant territory without a history. Its Slavic inhabitants were to be in part exterminated, in part retained to serve the German master race as a helot population. One hundred million persons were eventually to be

* The main office for security, founded by Heydrich and after his death run by Ernst Kaltenbrunner; ultimately all the police forces of the Reich were made subordinate to it.

transplanted to the Eastern plains; millions must be brought there, Hitler explained, until "our settlers are numerically far superior to the natives." European emigration must no longer go to America, but only to the East. "In ten years at the latest," he wanted to receive a report of "at least twenty million Germans living in the Eastern territories."[78]

The "gigantic cake" was to be divided into four Reich commissariats (Eastland, Ukraine, Caucasia, and Moscovia). Alfred Rosenberg, the former leading ideologue of the party, who in recent years had been repeatedly outmaneuvered and who had been knocking around without employment before his significant appointment as Reich Minister for the Occupied Eastern Territories, vainly urged partitioning of the Soviet Union into politically autonomous nationalities. Hitler rejected the concept because he considered it dangerous to shape new political units on an ethnic or historical basis. Everything depended, he said, on "avoiding any political organization and thus keeping the members of these nationalities on the lowest possible cultural level." He was even prepared, he declared, to grant these peoples a certain degree of individual liberty, because all liberty had a reactionary effect, since it negated the supreme form of human organization, the state.

With unflagging enthusiasm, he drafted the details of his imperial daydream: Germanic masters and Slavic serfs together filling the vast Eastern spaces with bustling activity, though with the racially based class distinctions emphasized vividly in every conceivable way. Before his mind's eye arose German cities with gleaming governors' palaces, towering cultural and administrative structures, while the settlements of the native population would deliberately be kept inconspicuous. These were by no means to be "in any way refurbished let alone embellished." Even the "mud stucco" or the thatched roofs would not be permitted to show uniformity, he said.

He insisted on a low educational standard for the Slavic populace. They would be allowed to learn the meaning of traffic signs, the name of the capital of the Reich, and a few words of German, but no arithmetic, for example. General Jodl, he added on one occasion, had quite rightly objected to a poster in Ukrainian forbidding crossing of a railroad embankment, for "it can well be a matter of indifference to us whether a native more or less is run over." In that facetious Machiavellianism that he fell into in relaxed moments, he added that it would be best to teach the Slavic nationals "nothing but a sign language" and use the radio to present them with "what they can digest: music without limit. . . . For gay music promotes joy in labor." He regarded all concern for the health of the subject populations, all hygiene, as "sheer madness," and recommended spreading the superstition "that inoculation and so on is a very dangerous business." When he discovered in a memorandum a proposal to ban the sale and use of abortifacients in the occupied eastern territories, he became wildly excited and declared that he would "personally shoot down . . . the idiots" responsible for this idea. On the contrary, he went on, it seemed to him essential to promote a "vigorous business in contraceptives." And becoming facetious once more: "But I supposed we'd have to get the help of the Jews to get such things into lively circulation."[79]

A system of broad roads and lines of communication ("the beginning of all civilization") was to make the territory governable and help to open up its natural resources. One of Hitler's favorite ideas was a railroad to the Donetz Basin with a track width of twelve feet, on which two-story trains would travel back and forth at a speed of 125 miles per hour. At the intersections of the principal arteries of communication there would arise cities conceived as great military bases. These would hold sizable units of mobile military forces, and would be secured at a radius of twenty or twenty-five miles by a "circuit of beautiful villages" with a well-armed rural population. In a memorandum dated November 26, 1940, Himmler had already issued guidelines for rural reconstruction in the conquered Polish territories; he fixed the social hierarchy among the German settlers, from hired man to the representative of an "autochthonous leadership," with just as much pendantry as the layout of the villages and farms ("wall thick-nesses . . . less than 38 centimeters will not be permitted"). Above all the "provision for greenery" was to help express the German tribes' in-herited love of trees, shrubs, and flowers and give the landscape as a whole a German imprint. The planting of village oaks and village lindens was therefore just as important as bringing "the electric lines . . . as incon-spicuously as possible up to the buildings." The same romantic idyl was also planned for the rural defense areas of Russia: small, well-garrisoned settlements in the midst of hostile surroundings would preserve the primal situation of the permanent fight for survival, and would thus prove their viability.

Meanwhile, however, it soon became apparent that the vastness of the area presented something of a problem. Those who had been primarily designated as new settlers were the *Volksdeutsche,* the Germans living in the countries of southeastern Europe and overseas, and also decorated soldiers, sailors, or airmen, and members of the SS. The East belonged to the SS, declared Otto Hofmann, chief of the Race and Settlement Office of the SS. According to the calculations of the planners, however, there were no more than 5 million of such settlers. Assuming extremely favorable circumstances, according to a memorandum dated April 27, 1942, "we can count on a figure of eight million Germans in these areas in about thirty years."[80] For the first time a certain degree of agorphobia seemed to be current.

A whole list of measures was devised to overcome this unexpected dilemma. Thus someone thought of "reawakening in the German people the urge toward settlement in the East" and also allowing the racially

684

valuable neighboring peoples to participate in the colonization. A memorandum of Rosenberg's considered not only the settlement of Danes, Norwegians, and Dutch, but "after the victorious termination of the war also Englishmen." All would be "members of the Reich," Hitler declared, and boasted that this procedure would have a significance similar to the inclusion of several German states in the Customs Union a hundred years earlier. Simultaneously, according to the recommendations of a memorandum issued by Rosenberg's Ministry for the Occupied Eastern Territories, 31 million of the 45 million inhabitants of western Russia were to be expatriated or killed. Furthermore, it was intended to introduce rival sects and, if this measure should prove insufficient, it would be only necessary, Hitler suggested, "to drop a few bombs on their cities and the job will be done."

The greatest hopes were placed in the measures for recovery of good blood. Hitler compared his activity during the so-called time of struggle with the effect of a magnet that had drawn all the metallic element, all the iron content, of the German people. "Now we must also proceed in this way in building the new Reich," he declared at the beginning of February, 1942, speaking in the Führer's headquarters. "Wherever Germanic blood is to be found anywhere in the world, we will take what is good to ourselves. With what the others have left they will be unable to oppose the Germanic Empire." In Poland "race commissions" had investigated the "Germanism" of large numbers of selected persons and in some cases brought them back to Germany for *Umvolkung* (restoration to the race), whether they wished it or not. Minors in particular were taken. Henceforth, Himmler declared at the evening meal in Rastenburg, they would institute annual "fishing parties for bloodlines," throughout France, and he proposed that the children taken should be removed to German boarding schools in order to teach them the accidental nature of their French nationality and make them conscious of their Germanic blood. "For we will recuperate the good blood, which we can make use of, and incorporate it among us, or else, gentlemen—you may call this cruel, but nature is cruel—we will destroy this blood."[81]

Behind these proposals for "broadening the blood base" there once again cropped up that old fear of the extinction of the Aryan, of the second "expulsion from paradise" that Hitler had conjured up in *Mein Kampf*.[82] But if it should prove possible, he ranted, to keep the Reich "racially high and pure, it would gain a crystalline hardness and be unassailable." Then the Germans' greater force, boldness, and barbaric vitality would once again come into their own, all false religions of reason and humanity would go down to destruction, and natural order would triumph. As the "most gluttonous predator in world history" National Socialism had Nature and her promises on its side. And with that strangely distorted sense of reality he had, so that his own visions always seemed already within his grasp, he

685

saw growing up in a few years, within those Eastern "nurseries of Germanic blood," the longed-for type of human being, "regular master personalities," as he enthusiastically described them, "viceroys."

Simultaneously, he backed the efforts sponsored chiefly by Himmler and Bormann to establish new legislation concerning marriage. Their argument ran that the population shortage after the war would tend to get more serious, since 3 or 4 million women would necessarily have to remain unmarried. As Hitler remarked, such losses translated into divisions "are intolerable for our people." In order to make it possible for these women to have children, and at the same time to provide "decent, physically and psychically healthy men of strong character" with the opportunity for increased reproduction, special arrangements would have to be made. A procedure for application and selection would enable such men "to enter a firm marital relationship not only with one woman, but with an additional one."

These ideas were set forth in a memorandum by Bormann. Himmler supplemented them, suggesting, for example, that the privileged position of the first wife be secured by conferring upon her the title *Domina,* and that the right to enter a second marriage be reserved for the time being "as a high distinction for the heroes of the war, the bearers of the German Cross in gold, and the bearers of the Knight's Cross." Later, he explained, "it could be extended to the bearers of the Iron Cross First Class and to those who wear the silver and gold bar for close-quarters combat." For, as Hitler was wont to say, "The greatest fighter deserves the most beautiful woman. . . . If the German man is to be unreservedly ready to die as a soldier, he must have the freedom to love unreservedly. For struggle and love belong together. The philistine should be glad if he gets whatever is left."[83]

Such speculations were carried even further within the top leadership of the SS. There was strong sentiment, for instance, in favor of mandatory divorce for marriages that remained childless for five years. Moreover, "all single and married women who do not yet have four children shall be obliged up to the age of thirty-five years to have four children begotten upon them by racially unexceptionable German men. Whether these men are married is of no consequence. Every family which already has four children must release the husband for this operation."[84]

The Eastern settlement program was, however, also intended to provide a solution for Europe's national and ethnic disputes. The Crimea, for example, which was the favorite target of the settlement plans, was to be "completely cleansed," as Hitler put it, and under the ancient Greek name of Tauria, or even Gotenland (Gothland), was to be incorporated directly into the Reich. Simferopol would be renamed Gotenburg and Sevastopol Theoderichhafen.[85] According to one of the projects, that attractive peninsula, which over the millennia had attracted Scythians and Huns, Goths and Tatars, was to be transformed into a "great German spa." Others envisioned a "German Gibraltar" to dominate the Black Sea. As prospective settlers, the 140,000 persons of German blood living in Rumanian Transnistria were considered, and for a while some 2,000 Palestine Germans also haunted memoranda and files. But above all it was the population of South Tyrol on whom the new-order fanatics who were doing the planning for the Crimea lighted. Gauleiter Frauenfeld, who had been appointed commissioner general for the Crimea, suggested transporting the South Tyrolese to the peninsula in a body. Hitler termed that idea "extraordinarily good." He thought "the Crimea extremely well suited in respect to climate and landscape to South Tyrolean nationals." Besides, it was "a land of milk and honey compared with the present region settled by the South Tyrolese." Transportation of the South Tyrolese to the Crimea would not impose any special difficulties physically or psychologically. "They need only sail down a German river, the Danube, and they're already there." Frauenfeld also had the idea of building a new metropolis for the peninsula in the Yaila Mountains.

Although a Führer's directive had been issued as early as the beginning of July, 1942, to evacuate the Russian populace from the Crimea, all the resettlement plans became entangled in the confusion of authorities and the additional chaos produced by the events of the war. Extensive resettlement took place only in Ingria (Ingermanland), the country between Lake Peipus and Lake Onega, which had been designated as the first resettlement area because, according to the *Lebensraum* specialists, it had preserved a comparatively strong component of Germanic blood in the population. Early in 1942 the Finnish government was informed that it could have "its" Ingers back. And in fact up to the spring of 1944, when the area was lost again, some 65,000 persons were moved to Finland. From this single example we can see in what manner the regime would have carried out its vision of a new order. For it solved a nonexistent minorities problem and created a new one in Finland.[86]

Hitler's lust for expansion, however, was not directed solely toward the East. He had repeatedly averred, even after the war broke out, that he desired no conquests in the West. But this highmindedness soon came into collision with his inability to give back anything he had once obtained. No one could blame him, he observed during the period when victory seemed very near, if he took the position: he who has, keeps! "For anyone who gives away what he has is committing a sin, since he is alienating that part of this earth that he as the stronger has conquered with effort. For the earth is like a trophy cup and therefore tends always to fall into the hands of the strongest. For tens of thousands of years there has been a tugging back and forth on this earth."[87]

Soon his ambitions went far beyond all the war aims conceived by *völkisch* and Pan-German circles. His "Great Germanic Empire of the German Nation" embraced nearly the entire continent of Europe in one unitary, totalitarian, and economically independent imperium. The individual members were to be reduced to vassals whose one purpose was to serve his aspirations for world power. "Old Europe has outlived its usefulness," Hitler is reported to have said in a conversation with Slovak President Tiso. He saw Germany in the position of Rome poised for the overpowering of the other city-states of Latium. Occasionally he spoke of Europe's "rubbish heap of small countries" that he intended to clean out. Alongside America, the British Empire, and the Greater East Asian bloc to be formed by Japan, Europe—under the leadership of Germany—would constitute the fourth of those economic empires into which he envisioned the world of the future as divided. For centuries, in his view, the old Continent had been able to solve its overpopulation problems, or at least to cover them up, with the aid of overseas possessions. But with the colonial age coming to its end, only the thinly populated East could offer a way out. "If the Ukraine were administered by European methods," he declared, "it would be possible to get three times its present production out of it. We could supply Europe without limit with what can be produced there. The East has everything in unlimited quantities: iron, coal, oil, and a soil that can grow everything Europe needs: grain, linseed, rubber, cotton, and so on."

In his so-called second book, the sequel to *Mein Kampf,* written in 1928, Hitler had already developed the idea that this Europe was not to arise as the result of federation, but by the racially strongest nation's subjugating the others. This early view of his determined his style of ruling over both conquered and allied countries. Occasionally he received offers of collaboration within the framework of a Fascist federated Europe; one such offer, for example, came from certain elements in France. But Hitler regarded such offers merely as arrogance and did not even deign to reply. Sometimes, it is true, he was apt to reject the idea of the nation in the name of the "higher concept of race": "It [race] breaks up the old and affords the possibility of new combinations," he declared. "Employing the concept of the nation, France carried her great revolution beyond her borders. Employing the concept of race, National Socialism will extend its revolution until the New Order has been achieved all through the world."

Immediately after the campaign in France, a draft defining the border in the West was worked out under his personal supervision. It provided for the territory of the Reich to include Holland, Belgium, and Luxembourg, thus extending to the coast of Flanders. "Nothing in the world can prompt us to . . . give up again the Channel position won by the Western campaign," he is quoted as saying. From the Channel the new boundary would run "about from the mouth of the Somme eastward to the northern rim of the Paris basin and along Champagne to the Argonnes, there turning southward and passing farther across Burgundy and west of the Franche-Comté to the Lake of Geneva."[88] Historical treatises, and measures for

Germanization, were to provide a historical base for these annexations. Nancy was henceforth to be known as Nanzig; Besançon would be called Bisanz.

Hitler also declared that he would "never again leave Norway." He intended to make Trondheim a German city of 250,000 inhabitants and build it up into a great naval base. Early in 1941 he issued orders to this effect to Albert Speer and the heads of the navy. Similar bases to guard the sea routes were to be established along the French Atlantic coast as well as in northwestern Africa. Rotterdam was to become the "largest port in the Germanic area." There were also plans for organizing the economy in the conquered countries on the pattern and in harmony with the interests of German industry, to accommodate wages and cost of living to the conditions in Germany, to regulate problems of employment and production on a continental scale, and to redistribute markets. The internal frontiers of Europe would soon lose their importance, one of the ideologues of the new order wrote, "except for the Alpine frontier where the Germanic Empire of the North and the Roman Empire of the South" meet.

The wider panorama was of such grandeur that the regime itself was awestricken. At the center of the stage there would be the world capital of Germania, which Hitler meant to transform into a metropolis that would stand comparison with the capitals of ancient empires, "with ancient Egypt, Babylon or Rome . . . what is London, what is Paris by comparison?" And radiating from it would extend, from the North Cape to the Black Sea, a dense network of garrisons, party citadels, temples of art, camps, and watchtowers, in whose shadow a generation of master personalities would pursue the Aryan blood cult and the breeding of the new godman. SS formations would be stationed in the regions with inferior blood, such as the Bavarian Forest or Alsace-Lorraine. "Through them a refreshening of the blood of the population would be provided." Following old, deeply incised psychic tracks, Hitler combined his vision of the new Europe with the mythology of death. After the end of the war, when the great reckonings with the churches had begun and the pope in tiara and full pontificals had been hanged in St. Peter's Square, Strassburg Cathedral would be converted into a monument to the Unknown Soldier, while on the borders of the empire, from the rocky capes of the Atlantic to the steppes of Russia, a chain of monumental towers would be built as memorials to the dead.[89]

Projects such as these reveal an unbridled mania for planning, an elemental drive, blind to all obstacles as well as to the rights and claims of others, dictating destinies, trampling down "bastard races," resettling peoples, or, as the above-mentioned memorandum of the East Ministry curtly put it, "scrapping" them. Yet to Hitler himself the building of the new order was "something wonderfully beautiful." Here we see once again the strange incongruities of National Socialist philosophy, the combination of stoic objectivity and irrationality, of "ice-coldness" and belief in magic, of modernity and medievalism. Through the supercities of the future would march an ideological vanguard. They would revive the "Cimbrian art of knitting" and plant exotic root. They would propagate themselves, breeding for blond and blue-eyed issue, and begetting largely male children through the practice of abstinence, long hikes and proper nutrition. For along with the sweeping, ruthless dictates of National Socialism there was an element of trivial fantasy play. With "holy earnestness" Nazi philosophers considered the question of oatmeal porridge and organic manure, the possibility of developing a perennial rye, of steatopygia in the women of primitive tribes, and ravings about the flylike witch of epidemics, Nasav.[90] They were great at the institutionalization of nonsense; there was a "Special Commissioner of the Reichsführer-SS for the Care of Dogs" and an "Assistant Secretary for Defense against Gnats and Insects." Even as Hitler made fun of all superstition, he was always extremely subject to it. He inclined toward all sorts of crude theories about falling heavens and moons, saw the Mongoloid origin of the Czechs in their drooping mustaches, and planned—in the empire of the future—to forbid smoking and introduce vegetarianism.[91]

The same incongruities pervade his great dream of 200 million racially conscious persons established as masters of the Continent, secure in their rule because monopolizing the military and technological power, planning on a vast scale but personally abstinent, eager soldiers, and bearers of many children while all the other peoples of Europe would have been reduced to slavery, leading "their modest and contented existences beyond good and evil." The masters themselves fulfilled their historic mission and danced around fires on Midsummer's Night, honoring the laws of nature, art, and the idea of greatness, and seeking relaxation from the burdens of history in the Strength-Through-Joy mass hotels on the Channel Islands, on the fjords of Norway, or in the Crimea, to the accompaniment of jolly folklore and operetta music. In moments of depression, Hitler would speak of how far off the realization of his visions was, 100 or 200 years; "like Moses" he would see "the Promised Land only in the distance."

The series of setbacks from the summer of 1943 on pushed the dream even further off. After the failure of the great offensive against the Russian lines near Kursk, the Russians surprisingly went over to the attack in the middle of July, and with apparently inexhaustible reserves threw back the desperately fighting German troops. In the southern sector the ratio of the forces was one to seven, in the north and center army groups about one to four. In addition an army of partisans supported the Soviet offensive by carefully co-ordinated actions. In the course of August alone, for example, they destroyed the railroad tracks in the German rear area in 12,000 places. Early in August the Red Army retook Orel, some three weeks later

Kharkov, on September 25 Smolensk, and then the Donets Basin. By mid-October they were at the gates of Kiev.

Meanwhile, the situation in the Mediterranean was also deteriorating. Despite all the encouragements and concessions by the Germans, by the beginning of the spring it had become all too clear that Italy was on the verge of collapse. Mussolini, a tired and sick man, had lost more and more of his power and had become a gesticulating marionette, totally lacking in conviction, tugged from all sides by the contesting parties. In the middle of April he had met Hitler in Salzburg. His entourage had been pressing him to speak up boldly and tell his Axis partner that Italy would continue the war only under certain conditions. In particular, he was to repeat his demand that peace be concluded in the East—a stipulation he had vainly made several weeks before. But once again he succumbed to Hitler's torrent of words. On arrival the Duce had seemed "like a broken old man," Hitler summed up the conference. But four days later, when leaving for home again, he had seemed "in fine fettle, eager for action."

Three months later, on July 19, 1943, the increasingly critical situation brought the two men together in Feltre in northern Italy. For meanwhile the Allies had conquered Tunis and Bizerte. They had taken captive the African forces, which against Rommel's advice had been reinforced to 250,000 men, and in mid-July had launched their blow against the "soft-underbelly" of the Axis by opening a second front in Sicily. Mussolini now hoped to be released from the alliance and to make Hitler see that it was also in the German interest for Italy to drop out of the war so that the Wehrmacht could concentrate on defending the line of the Alps. But again Hitler would not even listen to arguments. Instead, he tried to convince Mussolini, who had come to the meeting with his generals, that Italy must hold out. For three hours he talked away in German at Mussolini, without calling upon the interpreter at all. The Duce looked pale and seemed not to be concentrating. In fact he was far more concerned with the reports of the first sizable air raid on Rome than with Hitler's portentous perspectives. Hitler's one idea, persistently varied but recurring in every phrase and every sentence, was that the only choice was to fight and win or go down to doom. "If anyone tells me that our tasks can be left to another generation, I reply that this is not the case. No one can say that the future generation will be a generation of giants. Germany took thirty years to recover; Rome never rose again. This is the voice of History."[92]

But Mussolini merely kept silent. The call of history to which he had been so susceptible all his life, seemed no more able to rouse him out of his apathy than the instinct for self-preservation. He remained passive in the following days also, after his return to Rome, although, like everyone else, he sensed that the ground was shaking underfoot and that his fall was impending. Although he knew there was a scheme afoot to strip him of his powers and replace him by a triumvirate of prominent Fascists, he did not prevent the meeting of the Grand Council on the night of July 24. At the last moment one of his followers called upon him to smash the plot; he told the man to shut up. Mutely, with an air of astonishment, he listened to the passionate ten-hour arraignment of himself. The following evening he was arrested. Not a hand was lifted to help him. Noiselessly, after so many paroxysms and theatrical excitements, he and Fascism vanished from public life. Marshal Badoglio, appointed head of government, dissolved the Fascist party and relieved the functionaries of their position.

Although Hitler was not unprepared for the fall of Mussolini, he nevertheless was deeply affected. The Italian dictator was the only statesman for whom he had felt a measure of personal attachment. He was even more disturbed by the political consequences of the event, especially the all too obvious "parallels with Germany," which according to the reports of the political police the public was well aware of. Significantly, he refused to make a speech, but he ordered massive measures to prevent disturbances. Then he whipped up a plan for the freeing of Mussolini (Operation Oak), the military occupation of Italy (Operation Black), and the arrest of Badoglio and the King, with the aim of restoring the Fascist regime (Operation Student). At the evening conference of July 25 he rejected Jodl's proposal that they wait for more exact reports:

There can be no doubt about one thing: in their treachery they will announce that they are going to stick with us; that is perfectly obvious. But that is an act of treachery, for they won't stick with us. . . . Sure that what's-his-name [Badoglio] declared right away that the war would be continued, but that changes nothing. They have to do that, it's what treachery does. But we'll go on playing the same game, with everything prepared to take possession of that whole crew like a flash, to clean up the whole riff-raff. Tomorrow I'm going to send a man down there who'll give the commander of the Third Armored Grenadiers Division orders to drive straight into Rome with a special group and immediately arrest the whole government, the King, the whole lot, especially the Crown Prince, get our hands on that rabble, especially Badoglio and the rest of the crew. Then you'll see they'll turn limp as a rag, and in two or three days there'll be another overthrow of the government.[93]

Later that evening, while he was redistributing the troops in the Italian theater and arranging for reinforcements, Hitler felt an impulse to occupy the Vatican also: "Especially the whole Diplomatic Corps in there," he commented. He thrust aside all objections: "I don't give a hang. That rabble is there; we'll get all those swine out. Later we can apologize." He finally dropped the idea. Nevertheless, he managed to send in enough additional troops so that when Badoglio shortly afterward arranged an armistice with the Allies the Germans were able to overwhelm the numerically superior Italian forces and occupy all the key positions in the country.

The arrested dictator was moved about for a few days, until a German commando squad liberated him from a mountain hotel on the Gran Sasso.

Spiritlessly he let himself be reinstalled in power; he saw that it only meant a different form of imprisonment. In October he had to cede Trieste, Istria, South Tyrol, Trient, and Laibach to Germany; he put up with it without emotion. All he really wanted was to return to the Romagna, his native soil. His thoughts revolved around death. For a woman admirer who asked him for his autograph during this period, he wrote on a picture: *"Mussolini defunto."*

These events did not weaken Hitler's determination; on the contrary. The personal weaknesses, halfway measures, and treacheries he encountered only fed his sense of distance from humankind and produced that grand tragic aura he associated with historical importance. During the years of his rise he had derived his greatest certainties from the periods of crisis. Now, too, his faith in himself increased with every setback; it was part of his fundamentally pessimistic sense of life that he drew strength and vindication from the disasters. "Hitherto every worsening of the situation has ultimately meant an improvement for us," he told his generals. Part of the effect he went on having upon his entourage, upon the skeptical military men and the wavering functionaries, undoubtedly sprang from this conviction that flew in the face of all reality. Eyewitnesses have described how from the autumn of 1943 on he moved through the dark backdrop of the bunker at the Führer's headquarters surrounded by a wall of silence and misanthropy, and more than one person who saw him had the impression "of a man whose life was slowly ebbing away."[94] But all have emphasized his undiminished magnetism, which he still possessed in strangest contrast to his outward appearance. We may have to discount this account to some extent: those who report it, after all, have to justify their own passivity at a time when there was less and less excuse for it. But no matter how much we subtract, there remains the remarkable phenomenon of energy multiplied by disaster.

The arguments he could still muster were comparatively weak. He preferred to point back to the period of struggle, which he now stylized into the great parable of the triumph of will and tenacity. Then he would speak of the miraculous "secret weapons" with which he was going to retaliate for the Allied terror raids on Germany. He also made much of the rift that was bound to occur in the enemy's "unnatural coalition." But, characteristically, he was not prepared even to consider the possibilities of a separate peace with one side or the other. In December, 1942, and once again in the summer of 1943, the Soviet Union had indicated through its representatives in Stockholm that it was willing to negotiate with Hitler over a separate peace. By fall of that year, in growing fear that the Western powers were playing for a war of exhaustion between Germany and Soviet Russia, the U.S.S.R. cautiously mentioned terms. She offered restoration of the Russo-German borders of 1914, a free hand in the Straits question, and extensive economic ties. The Russians kept their deputy Foreign Minister and former ambassador to Berlin, Vladimir Dekanozov, in Stockholm for an exchange of views from September 12 to 16. But Hitler rejected all negotiations. He regarded the Soviet contact as a mere tactical maneuver; and in fact to this day it has remained unclear how serious Moscow's intentions were. But Hitler's intentions remained obsessively and rigidly determined by the decision once taken. With a shrug Hitler told his Foreign Minister, who was for responding to the peace feelers: "You know, Ribbentrop, if I came to an agreement with Russia today, I'd attack her again tomorrow—I just can't help myself." To Goebbels he remarked in the middle of September that the time for such contacts was "totally un-suitable"; he could negotiate with some prospect of success only after a decisive military victory.[95]

Up to this point decisive military victories had only whetted his appetite for ever more decisive military victories. But a turning point was no longer conceivable. By this time the god of war, as Jodl remarked, had long ago turned away from the German side and moved into the enemy camp. In 1938, at the time the great architectural projects were being conceived, Albert Speer had set up an account to finance the vast buildings for the world capital of Germania. Now, at the end of 1943, he quietly liquidated the account, without mentioning it to Hitler.

BOOK VIII

Catastrophe

Chapter 1

Kill him!

Claus Schenk von Stauffenberg at the
end of 1942, in answer to the question
of what should be done with Hitler

OPPOSITIONS

At the beginning of 1944 the assault upon Fortress Europe began in earnest, forging Hitler to the defensive on all fronts. In the south the Western powers pressed forward as far as Central Italy. Their technological advantage, based for the most part on superior radar, enabled them to wage almost total air warfare, while the German side was forced temporarily to cease submarine attacks. In the East, meanwhile, the Russians were racing toward the battlefields on which the German armies had won their first great victories in the summer of 1941. Though his defensive lines were wavering and breaking everywhere, Hitler merely continued to repeat his formula of resistance to the last man, thus once again revealing that his talents as a generalissimo covered only offensive situations. The speed of the retreat kept him from carrying out his aim of leaving the enemy nothing but "a totally scorched and destroyed land."[1] But the landscape itself was the scene of a ghostly drama. Oil-soaked iron grids had been set up above gigantic fires, and members of "Squad 1005" worked feverishly and silently around these. Their assignment was to locate the innumerable mass graves of nearly three years of rule, to exhume the corpses, and to eliminate all traces of the massacres. Gigantic clouds of black smoke rose up from these cremation sites. The regime was abjuring its visions and reducing them to an *idée fixe*.

Ever since it had become apparent that strength was departing from Hitler's colossus, resistance had been stirring everywhere in Europe. In many cases it was centered in the Communist parties, but it also sprang from leagues of military officers, from the Catholic Church, or from groups of intellectuals. In some countries, such as Yugoslavia, Poland, and even France, it became organized in paramilitary formations, calling themselves

697

the Home Army or the Fighting Forces of the Interior, to wage an embittered and bloody war against the occupation troops. The Germans answered the growing number of assassinations and acts of sabotage with summary executions of hostages, in which the death of a single guard might often be paid for by twenty, thirty, or even more victims. The revenge of SS Division Das Reich upon the French village of Oradour-sur-Glane and its 600 innocent inhabitants marked the climax of this merciless guerrilla war. Tito's famous breakthrough operation on the Neretva, or the Warsaw uprising of the summer of 1944, were battlelike actions that became legends of the European Resistance.

Simultaneously, oppositional forces reappeared also inside Germany. In the past years they had been undone first by Hitler's diplomatic, then his military successes, and after the victory over France had reached the nadir of discouragement. But now the changing fortunes of the war brought out all the repressed doubts that had been present since the beginning of the Hitler regime, alongside of the cheering and jubilation. After Stalingrad, and once more after the defeats of the winter of 1943–44, the prevalent mood in Germany for considerable spells of time was compounded of fear, war weariness, and apathy. It was a mood that spurred the efforts of the opposition, since there was at last some hope of a response. After the many disappointments of earlier years the oppositionists were afraid that the rapidly approaching military defeat would once more, and forever, rob them of their chance to act. This concern enormously strengthened their resolution. But it also provides grounds for the charge, which has been repeatedly voiced, that the German opposition opportunistically resolved to topple the regime only when it was already falling. All that happened, it has been argued, is that a few nationalists roused themselves to act because they were more eager to save the country's power than its morality.

We cannot judge this matter without taking into account the difficulties the opposition faced in 1944. Some time before, the Gestapo had blown the cover of the "Central Bureau," Oster's office, and arrested its chief members. Admiral Canaris had been largely frozen out, and General Beck temporarily incapacitated by a severe illness. Moreover, Mussolini's fall had given Hitler a good scare and prompted him to still greater wariness. He tried more than ever before to keep his movements secret. His staff had instructions to conceal scheduled appointments even from the highest persons in the leadership, such as Göring and Himmler. On the rare occasions that he did appear in public he usually changed the program at short notice, sometimes only minutes before he was due to appear. Even in his own headquarters he used to wear the heavy, armored cap that came down over his ears. In his radio address of September 10, 1943, dealing with the events in Italy, there was a distinctly threatening note in the way he called upon his "field marshals, admirals, and generals" to show their loyalty to him and dash the enemy's hopes of finding in the German officers corps "traitors like those in Italy today."

The dilemma faced by the active opponents of the regime in Germany was computed of a complicated complex of inhibitions of a traditional order. While throughout the European Resistance, national and moral duty coincided almost completely, in Germany these norms clashed sharply, and for a good many of those who opposed the regime the contradiction was insoluble. Throughout all their years of plotting and planning, many leading members of the opposition, particularly the military men, were unable to overcome entirely that last emotional barrier. What they were projecting still seemed to them treason, a renewed "stab in the back." Unlike the European Resistance, what they could initially expect from their liberating act was not liberty but defeat and surrender to an implacable enemy. And it would take an arrogant moralist to belittle the conflict of those who, despite their hatred of Hitler and their horror of the crimes he instigated, nevertheless could not forget the crimes of Stalin, the atrocities of the "Red Terror," or the great purges, as well as the victims of the Katyn Forest massacre.

Such scruples also marked the unending discussions whose gravity can be appreciated today only by an act of historical empathy. How binding was an oath taken to one who had committed perjury? How far did the duty of obedience extend? Above all, there was the question of assassination, which some saw as essential and as the only consistent, grand act of resistance, whereas others, whose moral integrity cannot be called into question,[2] rejected the idea to the very end. But both groups were isolated within their own country, surrounded by a gigantic intelligence apparatus and always vulnerable to denunciation. In addition, the dependence of all their plans upon the course of events was a perpetual brake upon action. Every victory of Hitler's diminished the chances for an internal coup; every defeat weakened the opposition's stance with regard to the Allies, whose support was indispensable.

Given these circumstances, the history of the German opposition is a saga of scruples, contradictions, and mix-up. The sources sometimes lead one to think that a good many of the doubts that plagued the opposition were inspired by a mania for creating problems, thus dodging the obligation to act. Other scruples served one group among the higher officers as an excuse for their own moral rigidity. But even considering all this, there remains in all the statements and activities of the German opposition an unmistakable note of deep despair. This evidently sprang not so much from the feeling of powerlessness in the face of the brutal regime as from the inner impotence of people who had recognized the anachronistic, crippling nature of their values, but were nevertheless unable to give those values up. Significantly, such men as Generals Beck, Halder, and von Witzleben, or Admiral Canaris, much as they despised Hitler, had to conquer a thousand resistances within themselves before they could resolve to act, and after the first failure in the autumn of 1938 they never again summoned up the momentum. It took the entry of a number of young officers, less hampered by preconvictions, to supply new energy to an enterprise that had run down from the weight of its arguments and counterarguments. One of them, Colonel von Gersdorff, recognized this contrast. He has described how carefully Field Marshal von Manstein, in the course of a talk, excluded himself from the circle of the conspirators. At last, after a pause for reflection, he broke the silence by asking: "Then you want to kill him?!" And received the terse reply: *"Jawohl, Herr Feldmarschall,* like a mad dog!"

From the spring of 1943 on, there was a series of attempts at assassination. Not one came off, either because of technical failure, or Hitler's knack for scenting danger, or because some seemingly incredible chance intervened. Two explosives that Henning von Tresckow and Fabian von Schlabrendorff had placed in the Führer's plane in the middle of March, 1943, after Hitler had visited the headquarters of Army Group Center, failed to explode. A week later von Gersdorff planned to blow himself up, together with Hitler and all the leaders of the regime, during a tour of the Berlin Arsenal. This project came to nothing because Hitler suddenly cut the visit to ten minutes, so that the time fuse could not be set off. Colonel Stieff planned to set off a bomb during a military conference in the Führer's headquarters; this failed because the bomb exploded prematurely. A young infantry captain named Axel von dem Bussche volunteered in November to sacrifice himself: while showing new army uniforms, he would leap upon Hitler, seize him, and at the same time set off the explosion. But on the day before this plan was to be carried out, an Allied bomb destroyed the uniforms. When in December von dem Bussche appeared with a new set of samples, Hitler suddenly decided to go to Berchtesgaden. By so doing he frustrated both this attempt and another planned for December 26 by a colonel who wanted to carry a time bomb into the Führer's headquarters in his briefcase. This was the first appearance on the scene of Colonel Claus Schenk von Stauffenberg. Shortly afterward von dem Bussche was severely wounded, whereupon another officer put himself at the disposal of the conspirators: Ewald Heinrich von Kleist. For reasons never explained Hitler did not appear at the presentation planned for February 11. An attempt by Cavalry Captain von Breitenbuch to shoot Hitler down during a conference at the Berghof failed because the SS guard, allegedly on orders from Hitler himself, refused the captain admittance to the great hall. A number of other projected assassinations ended similarly.

The conspirators were no more successful in their efforts to gain foreign backing for their operation and to obtain certain assurances from the Western powers in case of a successful *coup d'état.* Their repeated tries to make contact by all sorts of routes invariably went wrong. Granted, the reluctance of the Allied statesmen was far from incomprehensible. Why should they tie their own hands when victory was at last within sight? Moreover, they were justifiably concerned about affronting the Soviet Union, and with the elation that sprang from certainty of victory they were incapable of grasping the involved politico-moral conflicts of the German conspirators. Moreover, there was in Roosevelt, Churchill, and several of their advisers an unmistakable hostility toward the very type of person who now came forward to offer himself as the pillar of a new system, but who seemed only to represent the system of the day before yesterday: "militarists," "Prussian Junkers," "the General Staff."

Nor was this feeling on the part of the Western powers mollified when in 1943 none other than Heinrich Himmler for a moment bobbed up on the periphery of the opposition. Disturbed by Hitler's seemingly morbid obstinacy and urged on by several of his own followers, he had obtained a medical affidavit that apparently described Hitler's general condition as pathological. Thereupon, though constantly vacillating, he had allowed Walter Schellenberg, chief of the foreign service of the SD, to utilize go-betweens in Spain, Sweden, and America to sound out the possibilities of a compromise peace without and against Hitler.[3]

Meanwhile several conservative plotters were attempting to play off the key figures of the regime against one another and simultaneously extend the opposition's connections into the realms of the SS, the police forces, and the Gestapo. On August 26, 1943, a meeting between Johannes Popitz, Prussian Secretary of the Treasury, and Heinrich Himmler provided the opposition with information on the acute qualms even among the regime's top leaders. But then the threads broke, almost simultaneously in all directions. Among the foreign countries, England in particular took a strong stand against all efforts at a premature peace settlement. Domestically, the leading members of the opposition themselves became involved in fierce controversy. Undoubtedly Popitz and the advocates of the resistance by intrigue who were playing along with Himmler and the SS intended to outwit their partners after the success of the planned coup, and re-establish legal conditions. This was nothing but a stupid revival of the conservatives' old illusions in the spring of 1933 that they would be able to "tame" Hitler. But in addition it was a failure to realize that even the most temporary alliance with one of the infamous members of the regime would utterly compromise the meaning and ethics of the opposition. In the course of one dispute in the headquarters of Army Group Center several of the younger officers indignantly told Admiral Canaris that in the future they would refuse to shake hands with him if a planned contact with Himmler were actually undertaken.

Such differences of opinion, and in general the peculiar babble of voices presumably speaking for the German opposition, should make it clear that it was not a bloc. To treat it as if it were a single concept is inaccurate; it was a loose assemblage of many groups objectively and personally antagonistic and united only in antipathy for the regime. Three of these groups emerge with somewhat sharper contours: (1) The Kreisau Circle, called after Count Helmuth James von Moltke's Silesian estate. This was chiefly a discussion group of high-minded friends imbued with ideas of both Christian and socialist reform. As a civilian group its opportunities were limited, and it practiced revolt only in the sense of intellectual encouragement. "We are being hanged because we thought together," von Moltke wrote in one of his last letters from prison, with a note of almost happy pride at the power of the spirit thus attested by his death sentence.[4] (2) Then there was the group of conservative and nationalist notables gathered around Carl Goerdeler, the former mayor of Leipzig, and General Ludwig Beck, the former army chief of staff. These men, not yet cognizant of the meaning of Hitler's policies, were still claiming a leading role for a Greater Germany within Europe. It has seriously been questioned whether they even offered any real alternative to Hitler's imperialistic expansionism. So strong was their leaning toward an authoritarian state that they have been called a continuation of the antidemocratic opposition in the Weimar Republic. Moltke spoke tersely of the "Goerdeler trash."[5] (3) Finally there was the group of younger military men such as von Stauffenberg, von Tresckow, and Olbricht, with no pronounced ideological affiliations, although for the most part they sought ties with the Left and in contrast to Beck and Goerdeler did not look to a rapprochement with the Western powers, but with the Soviet Union.

In terms of background, a strikingly large number of the conspirators belonged to the Old Prussian nobility. There were also members of the clergy, the academic professions, and high-ranking civil servants. On the whole, those oppositionists who were now beginning to urge action were people originally from the conservative or liberal camp, with a sprinkling of Social Democrats. The Left was still suffering from the effects of the persecution, but it, too, with characteristic ideological rigidity, feared any alliance with army officers as a "pact with the devil." Among the many participants in the opposition there was, significantly, not a single representative of the Weimar Republic; that republic did not survive even in the Resistance. But members of the lower middle class were also conspicuously absent, and also businessmen. The former showed the "little man's" dull constancy to a course once taken and his inability to enter into any commitments beyond the personal realm. The latter remained fixated upon the traditional German alliance between industrial interests and power politics. Business always came to heel when the state whistled. That meant an economy capable of unusual performance; but it also led by many involved paths all the way to the defendants' benches in the Nuremberg trials of industrialists. Finally, there were scarcely any workers in the Resistance. Their opposition was greater than historians have so far noted, but it was still far less than their role of grand historic antagonists to Fascism called for. Fundamentally, they offered no real resistance on a realistic basis at all but, rather, a series of demonstrations, mute and planless, as if they were stunned from their defeat of 1933 and from the fading of all dreams about the power and importance of the proletariat.[6] All these groups, moreover, were intimidated by the events of the war; they were exhausted and had experienced a failure of nerve. What can really be called opposition came "from above."

It remained isolated. In February, moreover, von Moltke was arrested and the Kreisau Circle broken up. Shortly afterward, the Abwehr was subjected to a merciless investigation, so that discovery of the conspiracy had to be daily reckoned with. Goerdeler and Beck, repeatedly wavering, made a last attempt in April, 1944, to act before time ran out. They sent an offer to the United States to throw open the Western front after the *coup d'état* and permit Allied parachute units to land in the territory of the Reich. But once again they received no reply. Their only course now was to place the elimination of the regime on the plane of moral argument, independent of all strategic and political considerations. Several of the conspirators seem to have taken the view that the top leadership should see the disaster through to the end and experience their just retribution.

It was chiefly Stauffenberg who now took over. He established new connections and recruited new conspirators. In spite of the Allied formula of unconditional surrender, in spite of the danger of a new stab-in-the-back legend, in spite of the possible charges of tardiness and opportunism, he pushed straight through all inhibitions and steered toward assassination and a coup. The scion of an old family of South German nobility, related to the Yorck and Gneisenau families, he had in his youth associated with the Stefan George circle. Legend has it that on January 30, 1933, he placed himself at the head of an enthusiastic crowd in Bamberg, to hail the beginning of the new regime. That happens not to be true, but he certainly watched with moderate approval the regime's revolutionary tendencies and Hitler's early successes.

He made a distinguished career as an officer attached to the General Staff. The 1938 pogroms against the Jews first aroused doubts in him; and in the course of the war, as he observed the occupation in the East and what was being done to the Jews there, he developed into a principled opponent of the Nazi government. He was thirty-seven years old and had lost his right hand, two fingers of his left hand, and an eye in the North African theater. Stauffenberg provided an organizational frame for an undertaking that had bogged down in mental maneuverings. He replaced obsolete notions, which trapped many military men in an inextricable tangle of clashing principles, with something akin to revolutionary resolve. "Let's get to the essence," he once began a conversation with a new conspirator. "With all the means at my disposal I am practicing treason."[7]

Time was pressing. In the spring the conspirators had succeeded in winning over none other than Rommel, the field marshal, who enjoyed great popularity. Around the same time Himmler remarked to Admiral Canaris that he had definite knowledge that a revolt was being planned by certain groups in the Wehrmacht; he, Himmler, would strike at the proper moment. Moreover, the Allied invasion was expected at any time, and it could be assumed that this would scotch all the conspirators' subsidiary political aims. It would also provide the tradition-bound older officers with a new alibi.

On July 4, 1944, the Gestapo arrested Julius Leber and Adolf Reichwein as they were attempting to extend the network of Resistance cells by making contact with the Communist group that had formed around Anton Saefkow. In thus striking, the Gestapo itself propelled events toward a decision. Even Stauffenberg seems to have wavered for a moment at this time. A message from Tresckow, which incidentally revealed the innermost motivations of the conspirators, implored Stauffenberg to put aside all considerations of success or failure and wait no longer: "The assassination must be attempted, *coûte que coûte*. Even if it does not succeed, they must act in Berlin as if it did. The practical purpose no longer matters; what matters is that the German resistance movement should have taken the plunge before the eyes of the world and of history. Compared to that, anything else is of no consequence."[8]

On June 6, 1944, the invasion forces began moving out of the ports of southern England. An armada of 5,000 vessels headed for the coast of Normandy, while British and American parachute units dropped on the flanks of the intended landing zone. Toward three o'clock in the morning the first landing craft entered the water several miles off the coast, and, in rough seas, moved out of the shadow of the transport fleet.

As they approached shore toward dawn some three hours later, thousands of planes flew over the coastal strip and dropped a hail of bombs on the German positions. Simultaneously, the entire landing area was bombarded by heavy naval guns. At some points, especially at the foot of the Cotentin Peninsula and near the mouth of the Orne, the landing operation succeeded against unexpectedly meager German resistance. But in the central part of the landing area, near Vierville, the Americans ran into a German division that by chance had been alerted for an invasion exercise, and encountered withering fire (Omaha Beach). The defenders fired at a "carpet of people," one report put it; the entire beach was covered with burning armored vehicles, ships, and dead and wounded men. By evening the Americans had taken two small bridgeheads, and the British and Canadians had seized an expanse of beach amounting to nearly 200 square miles. Above all, the Allies possessed numerical superiority in the landing area.

The quick success of the landing operation once again exposed German inferiority in matériel and military forces. Even the time and place of the invasion had taken the Germans by surprise. Because of German weakness in the air, the Allied troops and fleets had assembled undiscovered in

704

the deployment area of southern England. German military counterintelligence had, it is true, precisely predicted the time of the landing, but the Abwehr was in bad odor and no attention had been paid to this information. Field Marshal von Rundstedt, the commander in chief in the West, had informed Hitler as recently as May 30 that no signs of an impending landing could be observed. Field Marshal Rommel, inspector of the coastal defenses, had left his headquarters on June 5 and gone to Berchtesgaden for a talk with Hitler. Moreover, the German leadership was convinced that the enemy attack would come at the narrowest point of the Channel, in the Pas de Calais, and had therefore placed the main force there. Hitler, on the other hand, guided by his peculiar "intuition," had expressed the view that Normandy was just as likely an invasion area; but he had finally bowed to the opinion of his military experts, all the more so since that opinion seemed to be confirmed by various movements on the enemy's part.

The invasion exposed a disastrous failure of leadership on the German side. The crisis had been foreshadowed when Hitler could not manage to forge the divergent views of his generals into a coherent plan for fending off a landing. The result was a series of muddled compromises, aggravated by the prevailing confusion of authority. On June 6 various command centers were scattered all over Berchtesgaden, not one of them able to function wholly independently, communicating with one another solely by telephone throughout the morning, and arguing chiefly over the release of the four reserve divisions in the West. Hitler himself, meanwhile, after one of his long, empty nights of palaver had gone to bed toward morning, with orders not to be awakened for the present. A first military conference took place at last early in the afternoon; but Hitler had asked the participants to meet in Castle Klessheim, about an hour's drive by car from Berchtesgaden, for he was expecting Hungarian Premier Sztójay there on that day. After his arrival he went up to the map table; from his look one could not tell whether he suspected the Allies of a feint or was himself trying to deceive his entourage. In Austrian dialect he said the equivalent of: "So this is it!" A few minutes later, after being briefed on the latest developments, he went to the upper rooms for the "show sit." Shortly before five o'clock in the afternoon he finally issued the order "that the enemy is to be annihilated at the bridgehead by evening of June 6."

Almost throughout the initial phase of the invasion Hitler retained that somnambulistic calm, seemingly divorced from reality, that he had displayed on the first day. Again and again in the preceding months he had declared that the offensive in the West would decide victory or defeat: "If the invasion is not repulsed, the war is lost for us." Now, with his faith in his infallibility, he was unwilling to realize that the landing operation was indeed the invasion. Instead, he held considerable forces in the area between the Seine and the Scheldt, where they waited in vain for the landing of those phantom divisions that the enemy by a stratagem had conjured up for him ("Operation Fortitude"). Meanwhile, in his usual manner, he interfered in the fighting even on the lower planes of command and made decisions rationally incompatible with the situation at the front.

On June 17 Hitler at last yielded to Rundstedt's and Rommel's impatient urging and came to the rear area of the invasion front for a personal briefing. The talks took place in the Wolfsschlucht II Führer's headquarters in Margival, north of Soissons, which had been set up in 1940 for the invasion of England. Hitler "looked pale and sleepless," Rommel's chief of staff, General Speidel, wrote. "He played nervously with his glasses and with pencils of all colors, which he held in his hand. He was the only one seated, hunched on a stool, while the field marshals were kept standing. His earlier magnetic force seemed gone. After a brief, frosty greeting he started shouting, bitterly expressing his displeasure at the successful landing of the Allies and trying to find fault with the local commanders."

Rommel pointed out the enormous enemy superiority. Hitler rejected that excuse, as he rejected, too, the request for permission to withdraw the threatened German forces from the Cotentin Peninsula and to bring up the reserves from the Pas de Calais. Instead, Hitler expatiated with increasing emphasis upon the "decisive" effect of the secret "V" weapons, and promised "masses of turbo fighters" that would drive the enemy from the skies and at last force England to her knees. When Rommel attempted to turn the discussion to political questions and to insist, in view of the grave situation, on steps toward ending the war, Hitler brusquely interrupted him. "Don't you worry about the continuance of the war, but about your invasion front," he said.[9]

The antipathies that emerged in the course of this meeting intensified Hitler's already strong distrust of the officer corps. Significantly, shortly before his arrival he had had the area ringed by SS units, and during the one-dish meal with von Rundstedt and Rommel he started to eat only after the food had been tasted. Throughout the meal two SS men were posted behind his chair. Before they parted the generals tried to persuade Hitler to come to Rommel's headquarters and listen to the reports of several front-line commanders. Reluctantly, Hitler agreed to come on June 19. But shortly after Rundstedt and Rommel had left Margival, he himself returned to Berchtesgaden.[10]

Within ten days the Allies had landed nearly a million men and 500,000 tons of matériel. But even now, after calling on Hitler in Berchtesgaden, the field marshals could not persuade him to yield them so much as freedom of decision in operational matters. Icily, he listened to their representations and ignored their request for a talk in a small group. Instead, he abruptly relieved von Rundstedt of his post. He appointed Field Marshal von Kluge to succeed him.

Kluge's first appearance at the front made it plain how deceptive and distorted the image of reality had become in Hitler's entourage. Kluge had just spent two weeks as a guest at the Berghof, and in spite of his critical if vacillating attitude toward Hitler, he had become imbued with the view that the leadership of the troops in the West was suffering from a failure of nerve and defeatism. On his arrival at the invasion front, he reproached Rommel in a heated argument with being unduly impressed by the enemy's material superiority and therefore blocking Hitler's justified orders. Furious at the commander in chief's "Berchtesgaden style," Rommel challenged him to go to the front and see for himself. As could be expected, two days later Kluge returned from his visit to the front considerably sobered. On July 15 Rommel, by way of Kluge, addressed a teletype message to Hitler: "The unequal struggle is nearing its end," he wrote, and concluded with a demand: "I must ask you immediately to draw the necessary conclusions from this situation." To General Speidel he remarked: "If he [Hitler] draws no conclusions, we shall act."[11]

Stauffenberg was also bent on taking action—all the more so since it appeared that the entire Eastern front was also breaking under the impact of the Soviet summer offensive. A fortunate circumstance had arisen: on June 20 Stauffenberg had been appointed chief of staff to General Friedrich Fromm, commander of the army reserve (sometimes called the home army), and thus had admission to the military conferences in the Führer's headquarters. Upon taking office on July 1 he had told Fromm that he must in fairness inform him he was planning a *coup d'état*. Fromm had listened silently and asked his new chief of staff to assume his duties.

On July 6 and 11 Stauffenberg had been summoned to conferences in the Führer's headquarters at the Berghof. After so many fiascos he had now resolved to undertake both the assassination and the leadership of the coup personally. On both occasions he had taken a package of explosives with him and had arranged for his immediate return to Berlin. But he had both times given up his plan since neither Göring nor Himmler, whom he intended to eliminate simultaneously, was present in the conference room. Another attempt on July 15 miscarried because Stauffenberg found no opportunity to set the ignition mechanism before the beginning of the conference. On July 11 and July 15 the troops that were to occupy Berlin had been placed on emergency footing; both times the undertaking had to be called off and all elements of suspicion eliminated.

On July 17, two days after the last attempt, the conspirators learned that an order for Goerdeler's arrest was pending. Unlike the cases of Leber, Reichwein, Moltke, and Bonhoeffer, they felt that Goerdeler was not the sort of person who would be able to keep silent under Gestapo interrogation. Stauffenberg took this information as the final mandate for action; the Rubicon had now been crossed, he remarked. That same day Rommel was severely wounded, thus putting one of the key figures in Stauffenberg's game out of commission. For the field marshal enjoyed great prestige among the Allies, and the latest idea had been to have him obtain an armistice in the West, evacuate the occupied areas, and use the returning armies to support the coup. Nevertheless, Stauffenberg refused to be deterred at this point. He would now act no matter what the circumstances, he declared, but added that this would be his last attempt.

A few days earlier the Führer's headquarters had again been transferred from Berchtesgaden back to Rastenburg. The convoy stood ready to depart and everyone had already gone to their cars when Hitler turned back once more and re-entered the Berghof. He stepped into the salon, stood a while in front of the big window, and then walked about the room with slow, uncertain steps. For a few moments he lingered in front of Anselm Feuerbach's *Nana*. He indicated to one of the bystanders that he probably would not be returning to this place.[12]

Stauffenberg had an appointment to report in Rastenburg on July 20.

The assassination attempt and the dramatic events of that day have been frequently described: the sudden shift of the conference to a barrack whose thin walls did not confine the explosion; Stauffenberg's belated arrival, after he had been surprised in an adjacent building while he was setting the time fuse with a pair of pliers; the search for Stauffenberg immediately after he had placed the bomb under the heavy map table and left the room; the explosion as Hitler, leaning over the table and propping his chin in his hand followed General Heusinger's report on the map. Stauffenberg stood beside his readied car some distance away and observed a huge cloud of smoke rise up over the barrack, wood and paper whirl through the air, and people rushing out of the shattered building. Then, certain that Hitler was dead, he made his escape and flew to Berlin, while much precious time passed.

Like everyone else in the room, Hitler had experienced the explosion as an "infernally bright darting flame" and a deafening crash. When he got up out of the burning, smoking debris with blackened face and the back of his head singed, Keitel came running toward him, shouting, "Where is the Führer?" and helped him get out of the room. Hitler's trousers hung in shreds; he was covered with dust, but only lightly injured. He had escaped with slight bleeding at his right elbow, and a few trivial bruises on the back of his left hand; and although both his eardrums had been ruptured, he suffered some loss of hearing only for a short time. The injuries to his legs were the worst; many splinters of wood had been driven into the flesh. But at the same time he discovered to his surprise that the trembling in his left leg had largely ceased. Of the twenty-four persons who had been in the room at the time of the explosion, only four were severely injured. A prime factor in protecting Hitler had been the heavy table top he was leaning over at the moment of detonation. He was excited, but at the same time

708

seemed curiously relieved. Repeatedly, and with some satisfaction, he told his retinue that he had long known of a conspiracy and now at last he could unmask the traitors. He displayed his tattered trousers like a trophy and did the same with his jacket, which had a square hole ripped out of the back.[13]

His calm derived principally from the sense of a "miraculous rescue." It was as if he owed to this treacherous act his reinforced sense of his own mission. That, at any rate, was his interpretation of the event when Mussolini arrived in Rastenburg in the afternoon for a previously announced visit. As they looked at the devastated conference room, Hitler said: "When I call it all to mind again, I conclude . . . that nothing is fated to happen to me, all the more so since this isn't the first time I've miraculously escaped death. . . . After my rescue from the peril of death today I am more than ever convinced that I am destined to carry on our great common cause to a happy conclusion."

Obviously impressed, Mussolini added: "This was a sign from heaven."[14]

In the course of the afternoon, however, his self-mastery was to give way. Toward five o'clock Hitler and Mussolini were back at the Führer's bunker where Göring, Ribbentrop, Dönitz, Keitel, and Jodl were assembled. The conversation once again centered around Hitler's salvation, but soon passed into mutual and increasingly ugly reproaches. Admiral Dönitz inveighed against the treacherous army, and Göring joined him; but then Dönitz also attacked the air force and its inadequate performance. Whereupon Göring attacked Ribbentrop for the failure of his foreign policy and, if the account of the incident is correct, finally raised his marshal's baton and waved it threateningly. Ribbentrop, addressed without the preposition denoting nobility, rapped back at Göring that he was the Foreign Minister and that his name was *von* Ribbentrop. For a while Hitler seemed lost in thought; he sat dully brooding, sucking on the various colored lozenges prescribed by Dr. Morell. But when one of the disputants spoke of the purge of Röhm, he sprang to his feet and began without the least preamble to rage. The punishment he had inflicted on the traitors then was nothing in comparison to the retaliation he would practice now, he screamed; he would annihilate the guilty together with their wives and children; no one who had opposed the workings of Providence would be spared. While he was shrieking, white-clad SS servants moved silently through the rows of chairs, accompanying the murderous tirade by serving tea.

The events in Berlin, with their crises, climaxes, and debacle, have also been described many times over: the incomprehensibly delayed launching of "Operation Valkyrie"; the failure to cut off news from the Führer's headquarters; Remer's telephone conversation with Hitler ("Major Remer, do you hear my voice?"); the arrest of Fromm; Stauffenberg's persistent pleading and propelling the slow-moving mechanism into action; Field Marshal von Witzleben's angry scene at the headquarters of the High

Command of the armed forces; the radio announcement around nine o'clock that Hitler would speak to the German people that very evening; the first signs of helpless perplexity on the part of the conspirators; the arrest of City Commandant von Hase; then again Stauffenberg still passionately urging but meeting no response, and finally reappearing late in the evening, resigned, his eyeflap removed, passing through the rooms of the OKW; and finally Fromm's theatrical reappearance on the scene, suddenly reasserting control over the seemingly paralyzed military apparatus on which the conspirators had placed their hopes. All this followed by the arrests, by Beck's several unsuccessful attempts at suicide, by the hastily arranged executions in front of the sandpile in the inner courtyard, illuminated by the headlights of a few trucks; and finally Fromm's "Hurrah!" for the Führer.

Toward one o'clock in the morning Hitler's voice spoke over all German radio stations:

German racial comrades! I do not know how many times an assassination attempt against me has been planned and carried out. If I speak to you today, I do so for two reasons: first, so that you may hear my voice and know that I myself am uninjured and well. Secondly, so that you may also learn the details about a crime that has not its like in German history.

A very small clique of ambitious, wicked and stupidly criminal officers forged a plot to eliminate me and along with me virtually the entire staff of the German leadership of the armed forces. The bomb which was planted by Colonel Count von Stauffenberg burst two meters to the right of me. It very seriously injured a number of associates dear to me; one of them has died. I myself am completely uninjured except for some very small scrapes, bruises or burns. I regard it as a confirmation of my assignment from Providence to continue to pursue my life's goal as I have done hitherto. . . .

The group represented by these usurpers is ridiculously small. It has nothing to do with the German armed forces, and above all with the German army. It is a very small coterie of criminal elements which is now being mercilessly extirpated. . . . We will settle accounts the way we National Socialists are accustomed to settle them.[15]

That same night a wave of arrests began, directed against all suspects whether or not they had anything to do with the coup. A second wave about a month later ("Operation Thunderstorm") again rounded up several thousand suspected oppositionists, chiefly members of former political parties.[16] A "July 20th Special Commission," staffed by 400 investigators, continued until the last days of the regime, tracking down every clue and issuing a steady series of bulletins about its success, thus demonstrating the extent of the resistance. Crushing pressure, torture and blackmail soon uncovered the outlines of an opposition that had functioned for years, had been extremely thorough theoretically but incapable of action. It had produced a plethora of letters and diaries, which gave it the character of a permanent monologue. The way the persecutors went about their task is illustrated by the fate of Henning von Tresckow, who had shot himself on July 21. He was mentioned in the armed forces communiqué with praise as one of the army's outstanding generals. But as soon as his part in the abortive coup came to light, his corpse was dragged from the family vault, to the accompaniment of savage abuse of his relatives, and taken to Berlin, where it was used in the interrogation of his stubbornly denying friends as a means of breaking their morale.

In general, the regime, contrary to its ideal of dispassionate sternness, displayed a remarkable cruelty, for which Hitler himself repeatedly gave the cues. Even in his periods of utmost control, he had shown a need to avenge himself in the most excessive fashion for every snub, every rejection. The savage extermination policy practiced upon the Poles, for instance, was not primarily the application of a theory concerning the treatment of the peoples of the East. Rather, it was Hitler's personal revenge upon the one country in the East whose alliance he had vainly sought in order to realize his main vision, the grand march against the Soviet Union. And when Yugoslavia attempted, as a result of an army officers' coup, to withdraw from the Tripartite Pact into which she had been forced, Hitler was so beside himself with fury that he had the defenseless capital of the country systematically bombed from a low altitude for three full days. That was "Operation Punishment." Now, in 1944, a few days after the attempted assassination, he commented after a military conference: "This has to stop. It won't do. These are the basest creatures that ever in history wore the soldier's tunic. We must repel and expel the offscourings from a dead past who have found refuge among us."

On the legal measures to be taken, he declared:

This time I'm making short work of it. These criminals are not to be brought before a court-martial, where their accomplices are sitting and where the trials are dragged out interminably. They're going to be expelled from the armed forces and face the People's Court. And they're not to receive the honorable bullet, but are to hang like common traitors! We'll have a court of honor expel them from the service; then they can be tried as civilians and they won't be soiling the prestige of the services. They must be tried at lightning speed, not be given a chance to make any grand speeches. And within two hours after the announcement of the verdict it has to be carried out! They must hang at once without the slightest mercy. And the most important thing is that they're given no time for any long speeches. But Freisler [the president of the People's Court] will take care of things all right. He is our Vishinsky.[17]

Such in fact was the procedure. A "court of honor" with Field Marshal von Rundstedt presiding and Field Marshal Keitel, General Guderian, and Generals Schroth, Specht, Kriebel, Burgdorf, and Maisel as associates, on August 4 meted out dishonorable discharges to twenty-two officers, among them one field marshal and eight generals. For the first time in the history

711

of the German army this was done without giving the persons involved a chance to plead. Hitler received daily reports on the interrogations. He also insisted on being kept abreast of arrests and executions, and "greedily devoured the information." He received Roland Freisler, the president of the People's Court and the chief executioner, in the Führer's headquarters, and ruled that the condemned were to be denied the consolations of religion or, in fact, any consolations of any kind. His instructions were: "I want them to be hanged, strung up like butchered cattle."[18]

On August 8 the first eight conspirators were executed in Plötzensee Prison. One by one they entered the execution room in prison garb and wooden shoes. Passing by the guillotine, they were led to the hooks fastened to a rail running across the ceiling. The executioners took off their manacles, passed a rope around their necks and bared the bodies to the hips. Then they raised the condemned, dropping them into the noose, and pulled off their trousers while they were slowly strangled. The records as a rule noted the duration of the execution as up to twenty seconds, but the orders were to protract the process of dying. After each execution the executioner and his aides braced themselves with a drink held ready on a table. Movies were taken of the proceedings, and that same evening Hitler had these films shown down to the last twitches of the condemned.

Hitler's savagery expressed itself not only in the intensity but also in the extent of the persecution. *Sippenhaft*—responsibility of the conspirators' next of kin—was justified on an ideological basis. Two weeks after the failed coup, Heinrich Himmler declared in a speech at the gauleiters' meeting of August 3, 1944, held in Posen:

> For we shall introduce here absolute responsibility of kin. We have already acted on that basis and . . . let no one come to us and say: what you are doing is Bolshevistic. No, don't take this amiss, it isn't Bolshevistic at all, but a very old custom practiced among our forefathers. You can read up about it in the Teutonic sagas. When they placed a family under the ban and declared it outlawed, or when there was a blood feud in a family, they were utterly consistent. When the family was outlawed and banned, they said: This man has committed treason; the blood is bad; there is traitor's blood in him; that must be wiped out. And in the blood feud the entire clan was wiped out down to the last member. The family of Count Stauffenberg will be wiped out down to the last member.[19]

Following this principle, all relatives of the Stauffenberg brothers ranging from a three-year-old child to a cousin's eighty-five-year-old father were arrested. Members of the families of Goerdeler, von Tresckow, von Seydlitz, von Lehndorff, Schwerin von Schwanenfeld, Yorck von Wartenburg, von Moltke, Oster, Leber, von Kleist, and von Haeften, as well as many others, suffered a similar fate. Field Marshal Rommel was threatened with both the arrest of his family and a public trial unless he committed suicide. Generals Burgdorf and Maisel, who carried that message of

Hitler's to him, also brought him an ampoule of poison. Half an hour later they took the corpse to an Ulm hospital and forbade any autopsy: "Do not touch the corpse," Burgdorf informed the medical head of the hospital. "Everything has already been arranged from Berlin."

The executions continued until April, 1945.

Thus the trail of the attempted coup of July 20 trickled out in execution barracks and morgues. The plot had failed primarily because of the psychological obstacles in the way of an act that ran counter to far too many habits of thought and reflexes sanctified by the traditional values of the military class. The resolute core among the conspirators was desperately frustrated by this problem.

One handicap that burdened "Operation Valkyrie" from the start was the fact that it had been planned to fit into the fiction of the "legal coup," respecting the officers' complex about violating their oath, and their horror of mutiny. On the crucial day of July 20, one of the chief rebels, General Hoepner, had refused to take command of the army reserve until he received a written order explicitly empowering him to do so. Pedantry of this sort gave the coup, in spite of all its moral high-mindedness, a peculiarly clumsy and almost farcical character. In retrospect, many of the episodes and details have some of that unforgettable quixotic quality displayed by General von Fritsch in 1938: after Himmler's schemes had brought about his resignation, he wanted to challenge the Reichsführer-SS to a duel. Here, an ancestral world, imbued with rigid values, was encountering a group of unprincipled revolutionaries; and those among the conservatives who did not succumb to the new spirit reacted, almost without exception, awkwardly and oddly. Goerdeler, for example, thought he could bring Hitler around and induce a change of heart in verbal confrontation. Consequently, he had all along opposed the idea of an assassination, and a few days after July 20, while in flight, he greeted a woman co-conspirator with the admonishment: "Thou shalt not kill." Stauffenberg and other conspirators intended, after the restoration of legality, to surrender voluntarily to a court of law.

Most of the group demonstrated the same kind of inveterate rectitude, even after the failure of the coup. Incapable of fleeing and hiding, they waited for their arrest. "One mustn't run—one must endure," Captain Klausing, one of the leading plotters in the High Command of the armed forces, explained. Theodor Steltzer even returned from Norway. General Fellgiebel, immediately before his arrest, rejected a proffered pistol; that just wasn't done, he remarked. The old-fashioned, touching nature of all this behavior was exemplified by the way Carl Goerdeler strapped the knapsack to his back, picked up a staff, and set out on foot to escape his pursuers. In the interrogations, too, some of the participants were obviously more intent on proving the seriousness and resoluteness of the opposition than on defending themselves. Others for moral reasons refused to lie, though their pride was only playing into the hands of the investigators. One of the heads of the July 20 special commission commented that "because of the manly attitude of the idealists we were instantly on the right track."

The highly moral basis of the undertaking led to another curious fact: the attempted putsch was started without a shot being fired—which necessarily reduced its chances of success. The initial decision to utilize military channels of command was justified on the ground that the idea was to issue orders, not engage in shooting. Hans Bernd Gisevius, one of the conspirators, quite rightly asked why the SS leader and the pro-Hitler general who blocked the way of the rebels at the Bendlerstrasse headquarters of the OKW had not been arrested and "immediately stood up against the wall." Shooting the two, he said, would have sparked the coup and given it credibility by imparting to it the nature of an extreme challenge. At this point it became apparent that July 20 was an officers' coup in another respect: it lacked the enlisted men who could shoot, make arrests and occupy positions. In the accounts of that day we repeatedly come upon mentions of the small squad of officers who held themselves in readiness for special assignments. Late in the evening not even the High Command of the armed forces had a detachment of guards at its disposal; Colonel Jäger vainly asked General von Hase for the shock-troop platoon with which he was to arrest Goebbels. Basically, the plot had no striking power; and even the officers at its head were mostly intellectual types, staff officers rather than tough-minded soldiers like Major Remer. Beck's two failures in his effort to commit suicide at the end of the day can be taken as a symbol of the conspirators' utter ineffectuality when it came to acting.

Finally, however, the coup also lacked popular support. On the evening of July 20, as Hitler was accompanying Mussolini back to the railroad station at headquarters, he paused by a group of railroad workers and said: "I knew from the first that men of your sort were not involved. It's my deep conviction that my enemies are the 'vons' who call themselves aristocrats."[20] He had always felt almost insultingly sure of the common man, as though he had a sure grasp of the peoples' wishes, behavior, and limits even now. And, in fact, the public, with a kind of mechanical reaction, first viewed the coup as a crime against the state that evoked a mixture of indifference and repugnance. One of the reasons for this reaction, to be sure, was the still considerable coherence of the state and, above all, Hitler's continuing prestige.

He still exerted psychological power, although its basis had meanwhile changed. What the public now felt was not so much its onetime admiration as a dull, fatalistic sense of an indissoluble reciprocal bond. That feeling was reinforced by both domestic and Allied propaganda, by the threatening advance of the Red Army and the intimidating pressures of the Gestapo, the system of informers, and the SS. All this was blanketed by a vague hope that this man would know the way to avert disaster, as he had done so often in the past. The failure of the assassination and the premature end of the coup spared the German public that decisive question with which the conspirators wanted to confront it by revealing the moral baseness of the regime, the conditions in the concentration camps, Hitler's deliberate war policy, and the practice of extermination. Goerdeler was convinced that the public would cry out with indignation and that a popular uprising would erupt. But the question was not posed.

Thus July 20 was confined to the decision and the act of a few individuals. The social make-up of the conspiracy, however, meant that when it was crushed, more than a number of rebels died. The doomed Prussian nobles who formed the core of the uprising constituted a class rich in tradition, "perhaps the only and certainly the strongest force capable of governance that Germany has produced in modern times." It alone possessed "what a ruling class needs and what neither the German high aristocracy nor the German bourgeoisie nor, so it seems, the German working class had or have: coherence, style, desire to rule, forcefulness, self-assurance, self-discipline, morality."[21]

Granted, Hitler had corrupted this class, had stripped its members of their powers and exposed their parasitical aspects. But only now did he liquidate them. Along with the bearers of many resounding names, old Germany stepped off the stage. Granted, their eminence had long since been squandered, gambled away in opportunistic and shortsighted collaboration with Hitler. Nevertheless, it must also be granted that the decision to break the onetime alliance came from these men. Hitler's savage reaction sprang from his never-abandoned resentment toward this old world, his hatred for its gravity, its ethics, its discipline. He had the same ambivalence toward it that he had always felt toward the bourgeois world. "I have often bitterly regretted that I did not purge my officer corps the way Stalin did," he remarked.[22] Taken in this light, July 20 and the executions that followed it constituted the consummation of the National Socialist revolution.

Seldom has a social class managed to carry out its "exodus from history" more nobly than did these Prussian Junkers. But it is also true they made the sacrifice only for their own sakes. Ostensibly they acted in the name of that "sacred Germany" which Stauffenberg once more invoked in his pathetic outcry before the execution squad. But behind that slogan was the conviction of acting as a class, of being subject as a class to a special moral imperative that gave them the right to resistance and made it their duty to overthrow a tyrant. "We are purifying ourselves," General Stieff replied when asked why they were going ahead with an act whose success was so uncertain.

This desire for self-purification governed all their actions. Hence they could overlook the possible charges of treason, perjury, or stab in the back.

It rendered them immune to the misinterpretations and calumnies they saw coming. "Now the whole world will descend upon us and berate us," Henning von Tresckow said to one of his friends shortly before his death. "But I still hold firmly to the conviction that we acted rightly."[23] In fact both Nazi and Allied propaganda, in one of those dreadful harmonies they exhibited more and more frequently at this stage of the war, denounced the conspirators. Both sides were committed to the thesis of the monolithic character of the regime, of the identity between Führer and people—the Allies even well beyond the war's end. The occupation authorities, for instance, prohibited publication about the German Resistance. The rather reluctant respect that is nowadays accorded the conspirators preserves elements of this earlier unease. None of their ideas and values have come down to the present day. They left scarcely a trace; and the accidents of history curiously underlined their total disappearance. The bodies of the executed men were turned over to the Anatomical Institute of Berlin University. The head of the Institute had close friends among the conspirators, and therefore blocked their use as cadavers. He had them cremated intact and the ashes buried in a nearby village cemetery. There an Allied air raid destroyed most of the urns.

The events of July 20 once more gave the regime a vigorous radicalizing impulse. If it ever approached the abstract concept of totalitarian rule, it did so in those last months, during which greater devastation was wreaked on the country than in all the preceding years of the war. On the very day of the assassination Hitler appointed Reichsführer-SS Heinrich Himmler as commander of the army reserve, thus deliberately humiliating the Wehrmacht. Five days later, Goebbels, who had been incessantly urging Hitler to tighten up the domestic front, was assigned the new post of Reich commissioner for Total War Commitment. Under the slogan "The people want it!" he instantly issued indexes of restrictions, embargos, and shutdowns. Almost all theaters and revues were closed, all academies, all schools of domestic science and commerce. All furloughs were canceled. Obligatory labor for women up to fifty was introduced, and many similar measures taken. On August 24 Goebbels announced total mobilization. Soon all remotely fit men between the ages of fifteen and sixty were drafted into the *Volkssturm* (militia). "It takes a bomb under his backside to make Hitler see reason," Goebbels commented.[24]

Simultaneously, the production of armaments once again reached the highest figures since the beginning of the war. The retreats and incessant air raids constantly caused new difficulties, but Albert Speer repeatedly succeeded in overcoming these by vigorous and ingenious improvisations. The production of artillery pieces was increased from 27,000 in 1943 to more than 40,000, the number of tanks from 20,000 to 27,000, of planes from 25,000 to nearly 38,000. But these extreme increases ruthlessly used up all reserves of strength, as if in preparation for the last battle. There was no way of replacing the resources consumed by such production; the feat could not be maintained, let alone repeated. Consequently, it only accelerated the collapse—all the more so when the Allies began those systematic attacks on refineries that they had once before planned and then rejected. The production of airplane fuel, for example, dropped from 156,000 metric tons in May, 1944, to 52,000 metric tons in June to 10,000 tons in September, 1944, and finally to 1,000 tons in February, 1945.

Thus the means for continuing the war were beginning to cancel one another out. The retreats and bombings resulted in serious losses of raw materials; these in turn reduced the production of weapons and the ability to use the weapons produced, so that new losses of territory followed, which in turn enabled the enemy to base its air forces closer and closer to German territory. From this point on, almost every operational decision was influenced by considerations of armaments; every military conference revolved around reserves of raw materials, transportation difficulties, shortages. From August, 1944, explosives had to be stretched by the use of up to 20 per cent salt. On the airfields readied fighter planes stood with empty tanks. And in a memorandum of that same period Speer came to the conclusion: "Considering the time needed by the processing industries, the production dependent on chromium, which means the entire production of armaments, will cease on January 1, 1946."[25]

Meanwhile, the Russians had advanced through the shattered front in the central sector as far as the Vistula. Thanks to Hitler's obstinate refusal to yield ground, they had been able to cut off and encircle more and more German divisions. The situation in the West developed in similar fashion, a series of breakthroughs and encirclements, once the Allies initiated the war of movement at the end of July. Hitler, who in the past had so successfully employed this very operational method, found himself increasingly incapable of responding to it. He continued to reject all proposals for a mobile defense, such as the newly appointed Chief of Staff Guderian was constantly making. Instead, as if compulsively fixated upon his offensive ideas, he continually developed new plans for attack that prescribed to the local commanders the sectors and even the details of the villages, bridges, and roads over which they were to advance.

The Wehrmacht at this time still comprised more than 9 million men. But these forces were deployed over half the continent, from Scandinavia to the Balkans. Hitler's determination to hold lost positions for the sake of prestige, and the necessity of protecting the vanishing base of raw materials, strangled all operational freedom. In August, 1944, Rumania with her oil fields was lost to the Red Army, in September, Bulgaria; and while the German position in the Balkans was cracked open almost without opposition, exhausted Finland withdrew from the war. About the same time the British landed in Greece and captured Athens. By the end of August the Allies had also taken northern France, sweeping up gigantic

717

quantities of material and armaments as well as an army of prisoners. In the early days of September their tank forces reached the Moselle, and a week later, on September 11, an American patrol for the first time crossed the western boundary of Germany. Shortly afterward, a Russian thrust into East Prussia was beaten off. But there could now be no doubt about it: the war was coming home to Germany.

Nevertheless Hitler did not even think of surrender. He met the first signs of disintegration in the Wehrmacht with drastic measures; at the beginning of September, for example, he had Himmler threaten deserters with arrest of kin. He was counting on dissension among the Allies, on the intervention of "Providence," which he saw confirmed again by the events of July 20, and on a sudden turn of affairs. "They are stumbling into their ruin," he declared in the course of a conversation in the Führer's headquarters, and made clear his resolve to continue the war under all circumstances:

I think I can say this, that it is impossible to imagine a greater crisis than the one we have already experienced in the East this year. When Field Marshal Model went there, Army Group Center was actually nothing but a hole. There was more hole than front, but then at last there was more front than hole. . . . We will fight even on the Rhine if need be. That doesn't matter in the least. Come what may we will continue this struggle until, as Frederick the Great said, one of our accursed enemies tires of continuing to fight, and until we obtain a peace which will guarantee the life of the German nation for the next fifty or a hundred years, and which above all does not sully our honor a second time, as happened in 1918. . . . If my life had been ended [on July 20], that would have been for me personally—I believe I may say this—only a liberation from anxieties, sleepless nights, and a severe nervous disease. It is only a fraction of a second; then one is released from all that and has one's rest and eternal peace. Nevertheless I am grateful to Providence that I was left alive.[26]

All the same his body seemed to be reacting violently to the incessant overstrain. After July 20 Hitler hardly left the bunker. He avoided the open air, fearing infections and assassins. His doctors urged him to leave the musty, confined rooms with their depressing atmosphere, but he refused. Instead, disillusioned and bitterly misanthropic, he buried himself more and more deeply in the world of the bunker. In August he began complaining about constant headaches; in September he suffered an attack of jaundice. Along with this, he was tormented by dental troubles. And in the middle of the month, shortly after the Allied troops had penetrated the territory of the Reich in force, he collapsed with a heart attack.

For some time he lay torpid on his cot, his voice low and quivering, and at times all desire to live seemed to have ebbed out of him. Attacks of dizziness, sudden sweating, and stomach cramps followed in quick succession, all connected, with a severe infection. That this bout of illness was of hysterical origin, or at any rate psychosomatic, seems all too likely; and the hypothesis is reinforced by the fact that just now, as had happened in the autumn of 1935, an operation on his vocal chords was necessary. On October 1, while being treated by one of his doctors, Hitler briefly fainted. Shortly afterward, the illnesses began to diminish; only the trembling in the limbs persisted, stronger than ever now. He also had spells of disturbed equilibrium, and, occasionally, during one of his rare walks, when he finally let himself be persuaded to take one, he would suddenly veer to one side as if directed by an alien hand. But his recuperation was on the whole quite surprising. Possibly he was pulling himself together for those fundamental decisions that had to be made in view of the impending final phase of the war.

Strategically, he was left with only two options. Returning to the old theory of the bulwark, he could gather the greater part of Germany's remaining forces in the East and thus reinforce the long defensive front. Or else he could once more muster his forces for a blow against the West. Ever since the summer of 1943 the question had been asked whether it would be better to look for the way out of the quandary in the East or in the West. Now this question was being put in military terms—weak and fundamentally untenable though it was. Early in 1944 Hitler, in a radio address, had tried to revamp his old claim to being Europe's rescuer from "Bolshevist chaos." Comparing his mission to that of ancient Greece and Rome, he declared that this war would achieve its higher meaning when it was seen as a decisive struggle between Germany and the Soviet Union, that it was fending off a new invasion by the Huns, which menaced all of Western Europe and America. If Soviet Russia were to win, "within ten years the continent of the most ancient culture will have lost the essential features of its life. The scene so dear to all of us of millennial artistic and material evolution would be wiped out. The peoples who stand as the representatives of this culture . . . would die wretchedly somewhere in the forests or marshes of Siberia, those of them who had not been finished off by a shot in the nape of the neck."[27] But now, only a few months later, he decided on an offensive against the West, at the cost of weakening the hard-pressed Eastern front.

This decision has frequently been viewed as a last great unmasking, as the self-revelation of an unprincipled cynic. And it does almost seem to rend a veil and expose him as the nihilistic revolutionary Hermann Rauschning had pictured: a man without a concept, a program, a goal, who merely used concepts, goals, and programs for the accumulation of power and the cranking up of actions. Undeniably, the predicament in which he found himself at this time brought to light some basic elements of this character: his faithlessness toward ideas and convictions, his contempt for principles. And certainly the decision casts a peculiar light upon the already tattered banner of "struggle against Bolshevism." It was, strictly speaking, more compromising than the Moscow Pact, which Hitler in any case could justify as a detour and tactical maneuver. For now there were no more detours left.

And yet the decision to attack in the West does not contradict Hitler's lifelong fixation. Close scrutiny reveals its inherent consistency. Naturally defiance and despair influenced it—for he now hated the West, which had destroyed his grand design. And presumably in the radical moods of the last year he discovered once again his greater closeness to Stalin, that "fellow of genius," as he had often called him, for whom one had to have "unreserved respect."[28] All in all, Hitler was prompted by a higher degree of calculation than we might expect of him on the verge of doom, at the end of his power and his life.

He believed that his admiration for Stalin gave him certain clues to the Russian's behavior. Greatness, he knew, was by its nature inexorable; it would have no truck with those shifts that were the business of bourgeois statesmen. A new offensive against the East, therefore, could possibly delay the end, but certainly could not avert it. An offensive in the West, on the other hand, might produce a shock of surprise among the Americans and British, who he believed were easily shaken. Thus he would recapture the initiative and so secure that gain in time which might yet bring about the hoped-for split in the enemy coalition. In this sense the offensive was a kind of last desperate offer to the Western Allies to make common cause with him.

Above all, however, an offensive seemed possible only in the West; and this consideration virtually decided the matter. There he could advance once again, once again bring to bear his genius as a commander, which had been proved in offensive operations. The vast expanses of the Eastern front, with its gigantic rear areas, where he himself had gone astray even in the days of optimum force, offered far less of an operational base or goal than the West. In the West, moreover, the offensive could take off from the west wall's system of fortifications. And since it would have shorter distances to cover, less fuel would be needed. Moreover, Hitler also thought that his armies in the East would put up a bitter resistance in any case. In the East fear was on his side, whereas in the West he had to reckon with a growing defeatism. The Morgenthau Plan (so-called after Roosevelt's Secretary of the Treasury, Henry Morgenthau, Jr.) for the dismemberment and agrarianization of Germany had just become known, and was being exploited by the propaganda specialists to build up anxiety. Though not entirely unsuccessful in this, they did not manage to create anything like the wild terror they had counted on. Consequently, the offensive was to confer upon the war in the West some of the grimness it already had in the East.

On December 11 and 12, a few days before the attack was started, Hitler summoned the troop commanders of the Western front in two separate groups to meetings in the headquarters of Field Marshal von Rundstedt. Having first been relieved of weapons and briefcases, they were driven about haphazardly to confuse their sense of orientation until the column of cars at last stopped at the entrance to an extensive system of bunkers that proved to be the Adlerhorst (the Eagle's Nest) Führer's headquarters near Bad Nauheim. They were led down a lane formed by SS men to Hitler. One of the participants was stunned to discover "a stooped figure with a pale and puffy face, hunched in his chair, his hands trembling, his left arm subject to a violent twitching which he did his best to conceal." An armed bodyguard stood behind every chair, and one of the participants later declared: "None of us would have dared so much as to pull out his handkerchief."[29]

In a two-hour speech combining justifications with encouragements, Hitler informed the assembled commanders of Operation Autumn Mists. The attack was to advance through the Ardennes toward Antwerp, the Allies' most important supply port, and subsequently to annihilate all enemy forces to the north. Hitler admitted that his plan was a gamble and seemed to stand "in a certain disproportion to the forces and their condition." But the risk acted as a challenge to him; for the last time he was staking everything on a single card. He pointed out the advantages of an offensive strategy, especially within an overall defensive framework. He implored the officers "to make it plain to the enemy that no matter what he does he can never count on a surrender, never, never." And then he came back to his ever-growing hope:

Never in the history of the world have there been coalitions like that of our enemies, composed of so many heterogeneous elements with such totally divergent aims. . . . These are countries that are already bickering with one another over their aims every day. And he who sits like a spider in his web, so to speak, watching this development, can see these antagonisms blowing up more and more with every passing hour. If they are hit by a few more very heavy blows, at any moment this artificially sustained common front may suddenly collapse with a tremendous clap of thunder . . . provided always that this battle in no circumstances leads to a further weakening of Germany. . . .

Gentlemen, on other fronts I have accepted sacrifices beyond the call of necessity in order to create here the preconditions for another offensive.[30]

On December 16, with low-hanging clouds grounding the enemy air force, the offensive began on a front of seventy-five miles. Hitler had withdrawn several battle-hardened divisions from the Eastern front. The enemy was hoodwinked by deceptive radio messages. To avoid attracting attention, some of the heavy equipment was pulled into position by horses. Low-flying planes were assigned the task of drowning out with their motors the noises and clanging in the German positions. The surprise actually succeeded, and enabled the German divisions to break through at many points. But after only a few days it became apparent that the offensive would have been condemned to failure even without the fierce American

721

defense, simply because the German side quickly ran out of energy and reserves. One tank group stopped a mile from an American supply dump containing 3 million gallons of gasoline. Another unit waited in vain on the ridge near Dinant for fuel and reinforcements, so that it could roll on the short distance to the Meuse. Just before Christmas, moreover, the weather changed; dense swarms of Allied planes reappeared in the blue skies and within a few days flew 15,000 sorties, literally smashing to pieces the German supply lines. On December 28 Hitler once more summoned the division commanders to his headquarters to implore and bully them:

Never in my life have I accepted the idea of surrender, and I am one of those men who have worked their way up from nothing. Our present situation, therefore, is nothing new to me. Once upon a time my own situation was entirely different, and far worse. I say this only so that you can grasp why I pursue my goal with such fanaticism and why nothing can wear me down. No matter how much I might be tormented by worries, even if my health were shaken by them—that would still have not the slightest effect on my decision to fight on. . . ."[31]

In the East, meanwhile, the Red Army had begun its preparations for an offensive on a broad front, and on January 9, 1945, Guderian once more called on Hitler to alert him to the threatening danger. But Hitler would not hear of it; he was thinking only of his own offensive, which had once more restored the possibility of planning and operating. He called all warnings to the contrary "completely idiotic" and ordered the chief of Foreign Armies Intelligence, East, who had furnished Guderian with his information, to be "locked up in a lunatic asylum at once." The Eastern front had never been buttressed by so many reserves as it was at the moment, Hitler stated. The chief of staff retorted: "The Eastern front is a house of cards. If the front is penetrated at a single point, it will collapse."

Early in January the troops in the Ardennes made two further attempts to advance to the south. They were thrown back to their starting positions by January 16. But in the meanwhile, on January 12, the first blow of the Russian offensive under Marshal Konev struck at the bridgehead of Baranov and effortlessly crashed through the German lines. A day later the armies of Marshal Zhukov crossed the Vistula on both sides of the Polish capital, while farther north two armies pushed toward East Prussia and the Gulf of Danzig. The entire front between the Baltic and the Carpathians was in motion. A tremendous war machine with infantry superiority of eleven to one, tanks seven to one, and artillery twenty to one, pushing an enormous avalanche of human beings before it, rolled over the scattered German efforts at resistance. By the end of the month Silesia was lost, and the Russians had reached the Oder. The Red Army was only a hundred miles from Berlin. On some nights the inhabitants of the German capital could hear the rumble of heavy artillery.

On January 30, 1945, twelve years after his appointment as Chancellor of the Reich, Hitler delivered his last speech over the radio. Once again he tried to conjure up the peril of the "Asian tidal wave" and appealed in curiously weary and unconvincing phrases to every individual's spirit of resistance. "However grave the crisis may be at the moment," he concluded, "in the end it will be mastered by our unalterable will, by our readiness for sacrifice, and by our abilities. We will overcome this emergency also."[32]

On that same day Albert Speer addressed a memorandum to Hitler informing him that the war was lost.

Chapter 2

To put the matter briefly, someone
who has no heir for his house would
do best to have himself burned with
everything that is in it—as if on a
magnificent pyre.

Adolf Hitler

GÖTTERDÄMMERUNG

On January 16, after receiving news of the beginning of the great Soviet
offensive, Hitler returned to the chancellery. The vast gray pile, once intended to be the starting point for the reconstruction of the capital, had
meanwhile become surrounded by a landscape of craters, ruins, and
mountains of rubble. Bombs had damaged many of the wings, blown loose
porphyry and marble, and blasted out windows, whose empty frames were
boarded up. Only the section in which Hitler's apartments and offices were
located had remained undamaged; in this wing even the windows were
scarcely shattered.

Soon the almost continual air raids had forced Hitler to retire so often to
the shelter installed twenty-four feet beneath the garden of the chancellery
that after a while he decided to move in there. In any case, this withdrawal
to the cave fitted in with the traits that were emerging with ever-increasing
force: the fear, the suspicion, and the denial of reality. For a few weeks he
continued taking his meals in the upper rooms, but in these, too, the
curtains were always drawn. Meanwhile, outside, with the fronts cracking
everywhere, against a background of burning cities and roads choked with
refugees, of ruins and collapsing supplies, unprecedented chaos broke out.

But through it all some guiding energy seemed to be at work, arranging
matters, as it were, so that the Third Reich did not just end but went down
to destruction. Hitler had repeatedly posed the alternative of world power
or doom. A flat, undramatic end would have disavowed his entire previous
life and his operatic temperament, his fascination with stunning effects.
Early in the thirties, in one of his fantasies about the impending war, he

724

had declared that if the National Socialists did not win, "even as we go down to destruction we will carry half the world into destruction with us."[33]

But there was more than defiance and despair, more than histrionics, in his craving for catastrophe. In fact, Hitler saw disaster as his ultimate chance for survival. The study of history had taught him that only grand downfalls lent themselves to the process of mythmaking. Consequently, he was staking all his remaining strength on staging his departure. When Otto Ernst Remer, the officer who had suppressed the July 20 coup and had been rewarded by being promoted to a general's rank, asked him at the end of January why he wanted to continue the struggle in spite of admitted defeat, Hitler replied darkly: "From total defeat springs the seed of the new." He made a similar remark to Bormann about a week later: "A desperate fight retains its eternal value as an example. Think of Leonidas and his three hundred Spartans. In any case it does not suit our style to let ourselves be slaughtered like sheep. They may exterminate us, but they will not be able to lead us to the slaughter."[34]

This determination lent an obstinate consistency to Hitler's behavior through the entire final phase and shaped his last conception of how to wage the war: the strategy of grandiose doom. As early as the autumn of 1944, when the Allied armies had advanced to the German border, he had ordered the practice of "scorched earth" for the territory of the Reich and insisted that nothing but a desert should be left to the enemy. But the policy, which at first seemed justified by operational considerations, soon developed into an abstract mania for destruction, totally without any discernible purpose. Not only industrial plants and supplies were to be demolished, but all facilities essential for the maintenance of life: supplies of food and sewerage systems, amplifying stations, long-distance cables and radio towers, telephone centrals, switching diagrams and stocks of spare parts, municipal registries, and bank-account records. Even those artistic monuments that had survived the air raids were consigned to destruction: the historic buildings, castles, churches, theaters, and opera houses. Hitler's vandal nature was still there beneath the veneer of cultural respectability. Now that barbarian syndrome emerged undisguised. In one of the last military conferences he joined with Goebbels in regretting that they had not unleashed a revolution in the classical style. Both the seizure of power in 1933 and the annexation of Austria had been marred by the "flaw" of insufficient opposition. Goebbels, who now reverted to his radical beginnings and during these weeks with good reason moved closer to Hitler than ever before, eagerly chimed in that if there had been such opposition they "could have smashed everything to pieces." Hitler, for his part, regretted his numerous concessions: "Afterwards you rue the fact that you've been so kind."[35]

In a similar spirit, at the very beginning of the war—according to an account by General Halder—he opposed the opinions of the generals, insisting on the bombing and bombardment of Warsaw when the city was ready for surrender, and extracted aesthetic thrills from the images of destruction: the apocalyptically darkened sky, the walls pulverized by a million tons of bombs, people panic-stricken and wiped out.[36] During the campaign in Russia he waited impatiently for the annihilation of Moscow and Leningrad, similarly in the summer of 1944 for the doom of London and Paris, and later he voluptuously pictured the effects an air raid would have upon the canyons of Manhattan. But he had been thwarted in all of this.[37] Now he could once again, and almost without check, pursue his primal bent for destruction. That emotional bias matched effortlessly with his special strategy of doom and with his revolutionary hatred for the old world. It provided the slogans of the final phase in an act of extreme self-revelation. "Under the ruins of our devastated cities the last so-called achievements of the bourgeois nineteenth century have finally been buried," Goebbels raved. "Together with the monuments of culture, the last obstacles to the fulfillment of our revolutionary task are likewise falling. Now, when everything lies in ruins, we are forced to reconstruct Europe. In the past private ownership imposed bourgeois restraint upon us. Now the bombs, instead of killing all Europeans, have only razed the walls of the prisons that had incarcerated them. . . . The enemy who strove to annihilate Europe's future has succeeded only in annihilating the past, and consequently everything old and worn out is gone."[38]

The air raid shelter into which Hitler had withdrawn extended beneath the chancellery garden and ended in a round concrete tower that also served as an emergency exit. In the twelve rooms of the bunker's upper level, called the "ante-bunker," some of the staff, Hitler's diet kitchen, and several service rooms were located. A spiral staircase led into the lower Führer bunker, which consisted of twenty rooms. A wide corridor gave access to it. A door on the right led to the rooms occupied by Bormann, Goebbels, the SS physician Dr. Stumpfegger, and several offices. On the left was a wing of six rooms occupied by Hitler. At the front the corridor opened into the large conference room. During the day Hitler mostly stayed in his living room, which was dominated by a portrait of Frederick the Great and contained only a small desk, a narrow sofa, a table, and three armchairs. The bareness and closeness of the windowless room made for a depressing atmosphere. Many visitors complained of this. But undoubtedly this last refuge of concrete, stillness and electric light expressed something of Hitler's true nature, the isolation and artificiality of his existence.

All witnesses to the events of those weeks agree in their description of Hitler. Above all they noted his hunched posture, his gray and somber face, his progressively feebler voice. The once hypnotic eyes were now glazed with weariness and exhaustion. More and more he let himself go; it seemed as if the many years of maintaining a stylized image were at last exacting their price. His jacket was frequently soiled by driblets of food; crumbs of cake clung to his sunken, old man's lips. Whenever, during the daily report, he took his glasses into his left hand, they clinked lightly against the desk top. Sometimes he would lay them aside as if caught napping. He was kept on his feet by will alone, and the trembling of his limbs tormented him partly because it belied his view that an iron will could achieve anything. An elderly General Staff officer described his impression as follows:

Physically he presented a dreadful sight. He dragged himself about painfully and clumsily, throwing his torso forward and dragging his legs after him from his living room to the conference room of the bunker. He had lost his sense of balance; if he were detained on the brief journey (seventy-five to a hundred feet), he had to sit down on one of the benches that had been placed along either wall for this purpose, or else cling to the person he was talking to. . . . His eyes were bloodshot; although all documents intended for him were typed out in letters three times ordinary size, on special "Führer typewriters," he could read them only with strong glasses. Saliva frequently dripped from the corners of his mouth.[39]

By now his postponement of sleep had literally reversed day and night; the last military conference usually ended toward six o'clock in the morning. Then, lying on the sofa totally drained, Hitler waited for his secretaries to give them their instructions for the coming day. As soon as these women entered the room, he rose heavily. "With shaking legs and quivering hand," one of them subsequently reported, "he stood facing us for a while and then dropped exhausted down on the sofa again. His servant would prop up his feet. He lay there completely torpid, filled with only one thought . . . chocolate and cake. His ferocious appetite for cake had become actually morbid. Whereas in the past he had eaten at most three pieces of cake, he now had the platter handed to him three times, and heaped his own plate each time. . . . He virtually did not talk at all."[40]

In spite of this precipitate decline, even now Hitler refused to let the conduct of operations out of his hand. A mixture of obstinacy, suspicion, sense of mission, and will power repeatedly lent him new impetus. One of his doctors who had not seen him since the beginning of October, 1944, was stunned by the impression he made in mid-February, 1945. He particularly noted Hitler's weakening memory, his inability to concentrate, and his frequent spells of absent-mindedness. Early in February Guderian offered a plan for building a defensive position in the East that ran completely counter to Hitler's concept. Hitler did not say a word; he merely stared at the map. Then he rose slowly, took a few staggering steps and paused, staring into space, then tersely dismissed the participants in the conference. Yet there is no saying how much play-acting went into such scenes. A few days later an objection by the chief of staff provoked one of his major outbursts: "Cheeks flushed with rage, with raised fists, he stood before me with his whole body shaking, beside himself with fury and altogether out of control. After each eruption of wrath Hitler paced back and forth on the edge of the rug, then paused right in front of me and hurled the next reproach at me. He choked up with shouting; his eyes bulged from their sockets and the veins in his temples swelled."[41]

Such shifts of mood were characteristic of his state during those weeks. He abruptly dropped people who had been close to him for years, and just as abruptly drew others to himself. When his doctor of many years, Karl Brandt, together with his associate von Hasselbach, attempted to check Morell's influence and free Hitler from his fatal dependence on drugs, Hitler abruptly dismissed Brandt and shortly afterward condemned him to death. With similar brusqueness, Guderian, Ribbentrop, Göring, and many others were shunted aside. Frequently Hitler lapsed into that dull brooding that had been characteristic of his early formative years. Absently, he would sit on his sofa, a male pup of Blondi's latest litter on his lap. He called the pup Wolf and was training it himself. In every obstacle, every retreat, he saw treachery. Humanity was too wicked, he occasionally complained, "for it to be worthwhile going on living."[42]

The already noted need to vent his misanthropy by tasteless teasing of his entourage once again grew stronger. Thus he might tell a group of women that "lipstick is manufactured from Paris sewage." Or during meals he would speak of Morell's drawing blood from him and would banter with his nonvegetarian guests: "I'll have blood-sausages made for you from my surplus blood. Why not? After all, you're so fond of eating meat." One of his secretaries had reported how one day, after the usual grand lament over treachery, he spoke mournfully of the time after his death: "If anything happens to me, Germany will be leaderless; for I don't have a successor. The first went mad [Hess], the second has thrown away the attachment of the people [Göring], and the third is rejected by the party membership [Himmler] . . . and is a totally unartistic person."[43]

Nevertheless, he managed repeatedly to throw off these depressions. Frequently he took his stimulus from the chance mention of an admired troop leader, or some other resounding triviality. It is possible to trace in the minutes of the last conferences the way he habitually seized upon a word, a reference, reshaping it, magnifying it, and finally deriving a euphoric certainty of victory from it. Sometimes he manufactured illusions by the skin of his teeth. From the autumn of 1944 on he had had many so-called people's grenadier divisions levied—infantry divisions stiffened by experienced front-line cadres. At the same time he directed that the remnants of defeated traditional divisions should not be dissolved; they should continue as entities and be allowed gradually to "bleed to death," because he considered the demoralizing effect of a severe defeat something from which a division never recovered.[44] The result of this order, however, was that in spite of increasing casualties he could cherish the illusion of a tremendously growing armed force. One of the features of that mad world of the bunker was his dealing in ghost divisions, which he repeatedly deployed for new offensive operations and finally for decisive battles that would never take place.

Even now his entourage followed him almost without a murmur into the more and more transparent fantasies fabricated from self-deception, distortion of reality, and delusion. Shaking, with bowed torso, he sat in front of the map table and swept his hand jerkily over the maps. Whenever a bomb struck some distance away and the ceiling light began to flicker, his eyes wandered restively over the unmoving faces of the officers who stood erect and straight before him: "That was close!" But frail and feeble though he was, he still preserved something of his magnetic powers.

It is true that certain signs of dissolution seeped into the bunker. There were breaches of protocol and revealing informality on the part of the staff. It became a rarity for anyone to stand up when Hitler entered the main conference room; hardly a conversation stopped. But these were revocable laxities; the predominant note remained the unreal climate of court societies, if anything, intensified by the unreality of the cave dweller's world. One of the participants in the military conferences has reported that everyone was "psychically almost suffocated by this atmosphere of servility, nervousness and prevarication. You felt it to the point of physical illness. Nothing was authentic there except fear."

Yet Hitler still succeeded in transmitting confidence and in awakening the most preposterous hopes. In spite of all the mistakes, lies, and misconceptions, his authority remained entirely unchallenged until literally the last hour, when he no longer had the power to punish or reward and could no longer enforce his will. Sometimes it seems as if he had the faculty for shattering, in ways hard to understand, the relationship to reality of all those who entered his presence. In the middle of March Gauleiter Forster appeared in the bunker in despair. Eleven hundred Russian tanks were at the gates of Danzig, he reported; the Wehrmacht had only four Tiger tanks. He was determined, he announced in the anterooms, to present "the whole frightful reality of the situation" to Hitler with all candor and "to force a clear decision." But after only a brief conversation he returned "completely transformed." The Führer had promised him "new divisions," he said; he would save Danzig, "and there's positively no doubt about it."[45]

Such incidents also permit another conclusion: of how artificial the system of loyalties in Hitler's entourage was, how dependent upon the Führer's continual commitment of his own person. His excessive suspiciousness, which assumed morbid and grotesque forms during the last months, was not without grounds. Even before the Ardennes offensive he had tightened the existing strict rules of secrecy by an unusual measure: the army commanders had to give him a written pledge of silence. On

729

January 1, 1945, the Luftwaffe fighter-plane force, briefly revived by summoning up its last reserves, fell victim to this suspicion. On that day a grand armada of approximately 800 planes launched a surprise low-level attack upon the Allied airfields in Northern France, Belgium, and Holland. Within a few hours, with a loss of approximately one hundred of their own planes, they put close to 1,000 enemy aircraft out of action. But on the return flight, thanks to the exaggerated rules of secrecy, they ran into their own antiaircraft fire and lost nearly 200 additional planes.

When Warsaw was lost by mid-January, Hitler ordered the officers in the sector to be arrested at gunpoint, and had his acting chief of staff subjected to hours of interrogation by Kaltenbrunner and Gestapo Chief Müller.

As he came to distrust everyone with whom he now had dealings, he once again reached out to his old fellow fighters, as though they could give him back the daredevil spirit, the radicalism and the faith of the past. His appointment of the gauleiters to the newly created posts of Reich defense commissioners was one such way of reviving old intimacies. Now he also remembered Hermann Esser, the party comrade of his early ventures into politics, pushed into the background some fifteen years before. On February 24, the twenty-fifth anniversary of the proclamation of the party program, he had Esser read a proclamation in Munich, while he himself received a deputation of high party functionaries in Berlin. In his address to them he tried to inspire the group with the idea of a heroic Teutonic struggle to the last man: "Even though my hand trembles," he assured the group, who had been visibly shocked by the sight of him, "and even if my head should tremble—my heart will never tremble."[46]

Two days later the Russians in Pomerania broke through to the Baltic, thus giving the signal for the conquest of Germany. In the West the Allies at the beginning of March overran the west wall along its full extent from Aachen to the Palatinate. On March 6 they captured Cologne and established a bridgehead on the right bank of the Rhine at Remagen. Then the Russians opened another grand offensive in Hungary and put Sepp Dietrich's elite SS units to flight. Almost simultaneously Tito's partisan armies went over to the attack, while the Western Allies crossed the Rhine at several additional points and advanced tempestuously into the interior of Germany. The war was entering its concluding phase.

Hitler reacted to the general collapse with renewed orders to hold out, with fits of rage and itinerant courts-martial. For the third time he relieved Field Marshal von Rundstedt of his post, had Sepp Dietrich's units stripped of their armbands with the embroidered divisional name, and on March 28 tersely dismissed his chief of staff, ordering him to take a six-month recuperation leave at once. As the minutes of the conferences demonstrate, he had lost any over-all view and squandered his time in useless bickerings, recriminations, and reminiscences. Nervous and inconsistent meddling only made matters worse. At the end of March, for example, he gave the order to send a reserve unit of twenty-two light tanks to the vicinity of Pirmasens. Then, in response to alarming reports from the Moselle he directed them "to the vicinity of Trier," then changed the order to "in the direction of Koblenz," and finally, in response to changing reports from the front, ordered so many changes of direction that no one could possibly make out where the tanks were in actuality.

Now the strategy of doom reached the stage of realization. Rather than a calculated scheme of self-destruction, it was a chain reaction of reckless responses, outbursts of rage, and fits of hysterical weeping. Hitler's heart was trembling after all. And yet at almost every juncture we can detect a craving for catastrophe. In order to create an atmosphere of maximum intransigence, Hitler had as early as February issued instructions to the Propaganda Ministry to attack the Allied statesmen in such a way and to insult them so personally "that they will no longer have any possibility of making an offer to the German people."[47] With nothing but burned bridges behind him, he entered the last stage of the fight. A series of commands, the first of which was issued on March 19 (the "Nero Command"), ordered that "all military, transportation, communications, industrial and food-supply facilities, as well as all other resources within the Reich which the enemy might use either immediately or in the foreseeable future for continuing the war, are to be destroyed."

Preparations were at once made in the Ruhr for demolition of the mines and pitheads, for blocking canals by the sinking of cement-laden barges and for evacuation of the population into the interior, Thuringia, and the vicinity of the central Elbe. The abandoned cities, as Gauleiter Florian of Düsseldorf was slated to proclaim, were to be set afire. A so-called flag order made it clear that surrender was not to be thought of: all male persons were to be taken from houses showing a white flag and shot at once. An order to the commanders dated the end of March called for "the most fanatical struggle against the now mobile enemy. No consideration for the population can be taken."[48] In curious contrast were the efforts to safeguard the art treasures that had been looted from all over the continent, or Hitler's preoccupation with the model of the city of Linz. These were last, futile stirrings of the lost dream of a state dedicated to beauty.

With the end drawing near, the mythologizing tendencies became increasingly dominant. Germany, embattled on all sides, was stylized into the image of the solitary hero. Idealized contempt for life and glorification of death by violence had long been deeply impressed upon the German mentality. Now that spirit was once again invoked. The fortresses and defense perimeters that Hitler had ordered to be established throughout the country and inflexibly held, symbolizing in miniature the idea of the forlorn hope that Germany as a whole represented. "There is only one thing I still want: the end, the end!" It was surely not accidental that Martin Bormann, in his last preserved letter from the chancellery written in early April, 1945, should have reminded his wife of the doom of "those old boys the Nibelungs in King Etzel's [Attila's] hall." We may surmise that the assiduous secretary had also taken over this notion from his master.[49]

Goebbels, on his part, could exult once more when Würzburg, Dresden, and Potsdam were leveled to the ground. For these acts of senseless barbarism sustained Hitler's prediction that the democracies would ultimately be the losers, since they would have to betray their principles. Nor was that the only gratification. For these air raids were entirely in tune with Hitler's own passion for destruction. In his proclamation of February 24 Hitler had actually voiced his regret that the Berghof on Obersalzberg had hitherto been spared by bombs. Not long after, the attack came. Three hundred and eighteen four-motored Lancaster bombers transformed the site, according to the report of an eyewitness, into a "moon landscape."

The surmise that Hitler wanted to keep himself secure from the processes of doom he was so zealously sponsoring is probably mistaken. It is much more likely that despite all the shipwreck those weeks and days were irradiated by complex feelings of fulfillment. The suicidal impulse that had accompanied him throughout his life and predisposed him to take maximum risks, was at last reaching its goal. Once again he stood with his back to the wall, but now the game was up; there were no stakes left to double. In this end there was an element of excited onanism that alone explains the still considerable power of will summoned up by this "cake-gobbling human wreck," as one member of his intimate entourage called the Hitler of the final weeks.

But the program for doom now encountered an unexpected block. Albert Speer, who had come close to being Hitler's friend and had been his partner in past architectural enthusiasms, in the fall of 1944 began using his authority as Armaments Minister to counter Hitler's destructive orders. Speer made his opposition felt in the occupied countries and in the German border areas as well. In taking this course, he was by no means free of scruples. Increasingly disenchanted though he had become, he was still conscious of owing a great deal to Hitler, whose personal liking for him had determined his whole career, and given him generous opportunities to develop his art, influence, fame, power. But when Speer was put in charge of the destruction of industries, his sense of responsibility, peculiarly colored by objective as well as romantic motivations, ultimately proved stronger than feelings of personal loyalty. In a series of memorandums he had tried by means of realistic situation analyses to persuade Hitler that from a military point of view the war was hopeless. All he gained, however, was Hitler's disfavor, though modified by Hitler's sentimentality. In February he had, in his "despair," finally conceived the plan of killing the inmates of the Führer's bunker by introducing poison gas into the underground ventilation system. But a last-minute reconstruction of the air shaft balked the plan and once again saved Hitler from assassination. On March 18 Speer handed him another memorandum predicting the impending "final collapse of the German economy with certainty" and reminding him of the leadership's obligation "in a lost war to preserve a nation from a heroic end." Speer later reproduced the gist of the conversation in a letter to Hitler:

From the statements you made that evening the following was unequivocally apparent—if I did not misunderstand you: If the war is lost, the people will be lost also. It is not necessary to worry about what the German people will need for elemental survival. On the contrary, it is best for us to destroy even these things. For the nation has proved to be the weaker, and the future belongs solely to the stronger eastern nation. In any case, only those who are inferior will remain after this struggle, for the good have already been killed.

These words shook me to the core. And a day later when I read the demolition order and, shortly afterward, the stringent evacuation order, I saw these as the first steps toward carrying out these intentions.[50]

Although the demolition order stripped Speer of power and overrode all his instructions, he traveled to the regions close to the front and convinced the local authorities of the senselessness of the order. He had explosives disposed of under water and issued submachine guns to the heads of plants vital for the civilian economy so they could defend themselves against the appointed demolition squads. Called to account by Hitler, he insisted that the war was lost, and refused to go on vacation, as Hitler required. Later, in a dramatic scene, Hitler demanded that he take back what he had said about the war's being lost, and then, when Speer remained obstinate, that he declare his faith in ultimate victory. Finally, as an almost piteous compromise, he asked Speer for an expression of hope in nothing more than "a successful continuance of the war": "If you could at least hope that we have not lost! You must certainly be able to hope. . . . that would be enough to satisfy me." But Speer still did not answer. Abruptly dismissed and given twenty-four hours to think it over, he finally escaped the threatened consequences by making a personal declaration of loyalty. Hitler was so moved that he actually restored part of Speer's former powers.[51]

During these days Hitler left the bunker for the last time in order to visit the Oder front. He drove in a Volkswagen to the castle at Freienwalde, where generals and staff officers of the Ninth Army were waiting for him: a stooped old man with gray hair and sunken face who occasionally, with an effort, ventured a confident smile. Over the map table he pleaded with the officers standing around it: the Russian onslaught upon Berlin must be broken; every day and every hour gained was precious; he was fabricating the most frightful weapons and these would bring about the turning point; that was why he begged them to make a final effort. One of the officers commented that Hitler looked like a man who had risen from the grave.

But while in fact it proved possible to check the Soviet advance in the East for a short while, the Western front now fell apart. On April 1 General Model's army group in the Ruhr area was encircled, and by April 11 the Americans reached the Elbe. Two days earlier Königsberg had fallen. At the Oder, meanwhile, the Russians were preparing their offensive against Berlin.

In those hopeless days Goebbels, according to his own account, consoled the despondent Führer by reading aloud to him from Carlyle's *History of Frederick the Great,* choosing the chapter that describes the difficulties the King encountered in the winter of 1761–62:

> How the great king himself did not see any way out and did not know what to do; how all his generals and ministers were convinced that he was finished; how the enemy already looked upon Prussia as vanquished; how the future appeared entirely dark, and how in his last letter to the Minister Graf Fincken-stein he set himself a time limit: if there was no change by February 15 he would give up and take poison. "Brave king!" Carlyle writes, "wait but a little while, and the days of your suffering will be over. Behind the clouds the sun of your good fortune is already rising and soon will show itself to you." On February 12 the Czarina died; the Miracle of the House of Brandenburg had come to pass. The Führer, Goebbels said, had tears in his eyes.[52]

The tendency to seek signs and portents outside reality extended far beyond books as the end came closer; here once again the irrationality of Nazism was revealed, which had been somewhat masked by its seeming modernity. In the early part of April Robert Ley became all excited over an inventor of "death rays." Goebbels sought predictions in two horoscopes; and while American troops had already reached the foothills of the Alps, while Schleswig-Holstein was cut off and Vienna lost, out of planetary conjunctions, ascendants, and transits in the quadrant, hopes once more flickered up of a great turning point in the second half of April. Still full of these parallels and prognoses, Goebbels learned on April 13—he was returning from a front-line visit to Berlin during a heavy air raid and was sprinting up the steps of the Propaganda Ministry in the glare of fires and exploding bombs—that President Roosevelt had died. "He was in ecstasy," one witness has described the scene, and immediately telephoned the Führer's bunker. "My Führer, I congratulate you!" he shouted into the telephone. "It is written in the stars that the second half of April will be the turning point for us. Today is Friday, April 13. It is the turning point!"[53]

In the bunker itself Hitler had meanwhile summoned cabinet ministers, generals, and functionaries, all the skeptics and men of little faith whom he had had to receive repeatedly during the past months in order to "hypnotize" them again and again. In a rush of words, with an old man's excitability, he showed them the report: "Here! You never wanted to believe it. . . ."[54] Once more Providence seemed to be trying to show it was on his side, to corroborate all the many miraculous dispensations of his life in one last overwhelming intervention. For a few hours a mood of noisy exhilaration prevailed in the bunker, a mingling of relief, gratitude, confidence, and something approaching certainty of victory. But nowadays no feeling could last. Later, Speer recalled, "Hitler sat exhausted, looking both liberated and dazed as he slumped in his armchair. But I sensed that he was still without hope."

Roosevelt's death had no effect upon military events. Three days later the Russians, with 2.5 million soldiers, 41,600 artillery pieces, 6,250 tanks, and 7,560 airplanes, opened the offensive against Berlin.

On April 20, Hitler's fifty-sixth birthday, the leadership of the regime met for the last time: Göring, Goebbels, Himmler, Bormann, Speer, Ley, Ribbentrop, and the top leaders of the Wehrmacht. A few days earlier Eva Braun had unexpectedly arrived, and everyone knew what her coming signified. Nevertheless, the artificial optimism of the bunker persisted; Hitler himself tried, during the birthday congratulations, to revive it once more. He delivered a few brief speeches, praised, encouraged, exchanged reminiscenses. In the garden he received a number of Hitler Youths who had proved their courage in the struggle against the rapidly advancing Soviet armies; he patted and decorated them. About the same time, the last death penalties arising out of the July 20, 1944, plot were carried out—as though sacrifices were being offered to some pagan demigod.

Originally Hitler had expressed the intention of leaving Berlin on his birthday and withdrawing to Obersalzberg, there to continue the fight from the "Alpine redoubt" within sight of the legend-haunted Untersberg. Some of the staff had already been sent ahead to prepare the Berghof. But on the eve of his birthday he had begun to waver. Goebbels in particular had passionately urged him to take up his post at the gates of Berlin for the struggle that would decide the war and, if need be, to seek death amid the ruins of the city as the only end appropriate to one of his historic rank. In Berlin, Goebbels argued, it was still possible to achieve a "moral world's record." Everyone else, however, now besought him to abandon the lost city and use the still remaining narrow corridor to the south for escape. In a few days or even hours the ring around Berlin would be closed. But Hitler remained uncertain, consenting only to the establishment of a northern and a southern command, in case Germany should be divided in the course of the enemy advance. "How am I to call on the troops to undertake the battle for Berlin," he declared, "if at the same moment I withdraw myself to safety!" Finally he said that he would leave the decision to fate.[55]

On the evening of that same day the exodus began. Himmler, Ribbentrop, Speer, and nearly the entire top command of the Luftwaffe joined the long columns of trucks that had been readied for departure. Pale and sweating, Göring took his leave of Hitler. He spoke of "extremely urgent tasks in South Germany." But Hitler merely stared vacantly at Göring's still massive figure;[56] and there is some indication that his contempt for the weaknesses and opportunistic calculations that he now discovered all around him was already predetermining his decision.

At any rate, he gave orders that the Russians, who had advanced as far as the city line, were to be thrown back in a major attack by all available forces. Every man, every tank, every plane, was to be committed, and any unauthorized actions were to be punished with maximum severity. He entrusted SS Obergruppenführer Felix Steiner with the leadership of the offensive. But he himself started the units marching, determined their initial positions, and set up divisions that had long ago ceased to exist. One of the participants later expressed the suspicion that the new chief of staff, General Krebs, unlike Guderian did not bother giving Hitler accurate information, but instead let him occupy himself with "war games" that bore no relationship to reality but that took account of his illusions as well as the nerves of everyone involved.[57] A vivid impression of the confusion of those days can be gathered from the notes of Karl Koller, chief of staff of the Luftwaffe:

April 21. Early in the morning Hitler telephones. "Do you know that Berlin is under artillery fire? The center of the city!" "No." "Don't you hear that?" "No! I am in the Werder game park."

Hitler: "Intense excitement in the city over distant artillery fire. It is said to be a heavy caliber railroad battery. The Russians are said to have seized a railroad bridge across the Oder. The Air Force is to locate and attack the battery at once."

I: "The enemy has no railroad bridge across the Oder. Maybe he has been able to capture a heavy German battery and turn it around. But probably what you are hearing are medium cannon of the Russian field army; by now the enemy should be able to reach the center of the city with them." Prolonged debate over whether or not the firing comes from a railroad bridge over the Oder and whether artillery of the Russian field army can reach the center of Berlin. . . .

Soon afterwards Hitler in person is again on the phone. He wants exact figures on the current air strikes south of Berlin. I reply that such questions cannot be answered out of hand because communications with the forces no longer function reliably. We have to be content, I say, with the current morning and evening reports, which are automatically sent in; he is most enraged about this.

Afterwards he telephones again and complains that jets did not come yesterday from their fields near Prague. I explain that the airfields are constantly covered by enemy fighters so that our own planes . . . cannot get away from the fields. Hitler rails. "Then we don't need the jets any more. The Air Force is superfluous."

In his vexation Hitler mentions a letter from the industrialist Röchling, and screams: "What that man has written is enough for me! The whole leadership of the Air Force ought to be strung up at once!"

In the evening between eight-thirty and nine he is again on the telephone.

"The Reich Marshal is maintaining a private army in Karinhall. Dissolve it at once and . . . place it under SS Obergruppenführer Steiner"—and he hangs up. While I am still considering what this is supposed to mean, Hitler calls again. "Every available Air Force man in the area between Berlin and the coast as far as Stettin and Hamburg is to be thrown into the attack I have ordered in the northeast of Berlin." . . . And there is no answer to my question of where the attack is to take place; he has already hung up. . . .

In a series of telephone calls I try to find out what is going on. Thus I learn from Major Freigang of General Konrad's staff that he has heard Obergruppen-führer Steiner is supposed to lead an attack from the Eberswalde area in a southward direction. But so far only Steiner and one officer have arrived in Schönwalde. Army units for the attack unknown.

I telephone the Führer bunker, finally reaching General Krebs at 10:30 p.m., and ask for more precise information about the planned attack. . . . Hitler breaks into the conversation. Suddenly his excited voice sounds on the phone: "Do you still have doubts about my order? I think I expressed myself clearly enough." At 11:30 p.m. another call from Hitler. He asks about the Air Force's measures for Steiner's attack. I report on this, emphasizing that the troops are altogether unused to battle, and have neither been trained nor equipped for ground fighting, moreover lack heavy arms. He gives me a brief lecture on the situation. . . ."[58]

It is necessary to know this background to grasp the fictitious nature of the Steiner offensive, on which Hitler was placing such far-reaching hopes. "You will see," he retorted to Koller, "the Russians will suffer the greatest defeat, the bloodiest defeat in their history at the gates of the city of Berlin." During the entire following morning he waited nervously, and in increasing despair, for a report on the course of operations. At three o'clock, at the beginning of the conference, no report from Steiner had yet arrived, but it now became apparent that his orders of the previous day had so confused and opened the front that the Red Army was able to break through the outer defensive ring in the northern part of Berlin and pene-trate the city with its tank spearheads. The Steiner offensive never took place.

In the afternoon the storm burst that made the conference of April 22 memorable. After a brief, brooding silence, as if still dazed by his utter disappointment, Hitler began to rage. He embarked on what amounted to a general denunciation of the cowardice, baseness, and faithlessness of the world. His voice, which in past weeks had dropped almost to a whisper, once more regained some of its former strength. Alerted by his screams, those living in the bunker crowded into the stairways and hallways while Hitler shouted that he had been betrayed. He cursed the army and spoke of corruption, weakness, lies. For years he had been surrounded by traitors and failures. He shook his fists furiously while he spoke; tears ran down his cheeks; and as always in the disastrous disenchantments of his life, every-thing collapsed along with the one hysterically magnified expectation. This was the end, he said. He could no longer go on. Death alone remained. He would meet death here in the city. Those who wanted to could go south; he himself would stick it out in Berlin. He rejected the protests and pleas of those around him, who regained their capacity for speech only after Hitler fell silent in exhaustion. He would not permit them to drag him around any farther; he should never have left the Wolf's Lair. Telephoned attempts at persuasion by Himmler and Dönitz had no effect. He refused to listen to Ribbentrop. Instead, he declared once more that he would remain in Berlin and meet his death on the steps of the chancellery. According to one of the witnesses he repeated that phrase ten or twenty times. After he had dictated a radio message announcing (and thus making irrevocable) his decision that he personally had taken over the defense of the city, he ended the conference. It was eight o'clock in the evening. All the participants were shaken and exhausted.[59]

Subsequently, in Hitler's private rooms, the arguments were revived in a smaller circle. Hitler had sent for Goebbels and proposed that he and his family move into the Führer's bunker. Then he began gathering his personal papers and ordered the documents to be burned. Next, he commanded Generals Keitel and Jodl to go to Berchtesgaden. He refused their request for operational orders. When they renewed their objections, he declared emphatically: "I shall never leave Berlin—never!" For a moment each of the generals, independently of one another, considered whether they should forcibly remove Hitler from the bunker and take him to the "Alpine redoubt," but quickly realized that the idea was impracticable. Keitel thereupon left for the headquarters of General Wenck's army, thirty-seven miles south of Berlin, an army that once more was to be the focus of exaggerated hopes in the few remaining days; Jodl, only a few hours later, gave the following account:

Hitler has . . . made the decision to stay in Berlin, lead the defense, and shoot himself at the last moment. He said he could not fight for physical reasons, and in any case would not personally fight because he could not risk being wounded and falling into the enemy's hands. We all emphatically tried to dissuade him, and proposed that the troops be shifted from the west to the fighting in the East. He answered that everything was falling apart anyhow, he couldn't do it; the Reich Marshal could try. Someone remarked that none of the soldiers would fight for the Reich Marshal. To that Hitler said: "What do you mean, fight? There isn't much fighting left to do."[60]

At last he seemed to be bowing to the inevitable. The tremendous consciousness of mission that had accompanied him from early on, and had only occasionally been obscured but never shaken, now yielded to resignation. "He has lost his faith," Eva Braun wrote to a woman friend. Only once in the course of the evening, when SS Obergruppenführer Berger mentioned the people that had "endured so loyally and so long," did Hitler relapse into the agitation of the afternoon. "With face flushed purple," he shouted something about lies and treachery.[61] But, later, as he was bidding good-bye to his adjutant Julius Schaub, two of his secretaries, the stenographers, and many other persons of his entourage, he seemed calm again. And when Speer, filled with "conflicting feelings" once more flew into encircled, burning Berlin next day to bid him good-bye, he likewise displayed an almost unnatural composure and spoke of his impending death as a release: "It is easy for me." Hitler remained calm even when Speer confessed that for months he had worked against the orders given him; he seemed rather impressed by Speer's initiative.[62]

But the next fit of fury was already in the offing. Indeed, the remaining hours of this life were marked by more and more abrupt changes of mood, from euphoria directly to profoundest depression. The symptoms suggest that these leaps were reflections of a final breakdown, produced by years of abuse of Morell's mind-distorting drugs. That evening, it is true, Hitler had dismissed his doctor with the words: "I don't need drugs to see me through."[63] But after Morell's departure he continued to take the medicines. The equanimity he now achieved was surely, viewed as a whole, not philosophical in origin. Far from submission to his fate, there was always, in his resignation, an undertone of careless contemptuousness. He could be vacant, but not calm. The stenographic minutes of one of the last conferences has preserved the characteristic combination of illusionary exuberance, depression, and contempt:

For me there is no doubt about this: the battle has reached a climax here. If it is really true that differences have arisen among the Allies in San Francisco—and they will arise—then a turning point can come about only if I deliver a blow to the Bolshevistic colossus at one place. Then the others may after all realize that there is only one force that can check the Bolshevistic colossus, and that is I and the party and the present German State.

If fate decides differently, then I would vanish from the stage of world history as an inglorious fugitive. But I would think it a thousand times more cowardly to commit suicide at Obersalzberg than to stand and fall here. I don't want anyone saying: You as the Leader . . .

I am the Leader as long as I can really lead. I cannot lead by sitting down somewhere on a mountain. . . . I did not come into the world solely in order to defend my Berghof.

He then referred with gratification to the enemy's casualties, which, he said, had "consumed a great part of his strength." In the house-to-house fighting for Berlin the enemy would be "forced to bleed to death." He added: "Today I shall lie down slightly reassured, and wish to be awakened only when a Russian tank stands before my sleeping nook." Then he grieved over all the memories he would be losing in death, and stood up shrugging: "But what does all that matter! Sooner or later everyone has to leave all such nonsense behind."

On the evening of April 23 Göring wired from Berchtesgaden to ask whether Hitler's decision to remain in Berlin brought into force the law of June 29, 1941, which appointed him, the Reich Marshal, as successor. The telegram was couched in loyal terms, and Hitler had received it calmly. But

Göring's old antagonist, Martin Bormann, succeeded in representing the matter as a kind of *coup d'état*. With a few whispered words, he incited Hitler to one of his grand outbursts. Hitler denounced Göring for laziness and failure, accused him of having "made corruption in our state possible" by his example, called him a drug addict, and finally—in a radio message written by Bormann—stripped him of all his offices and privileges. Then, exhausted and with an expression of dull satisfaction, he slumped back into his apathetic state and added contemptuously: "Well, all right, Let Göring negotiate the surrender. If the war is lost anyhow, it doesn't matter who does it."[64]

He now had no reserves left. The feelings of impotence, anxiety, and self-pity demanded expression. The pathetic camouflages of the past would no longer serve. All his life he had needed and sought roles to play. Now he was at a loss: the role of the beaten man had never entered his repertory, while the panache of the Wagnerian hero put too great a strain upon his remaining energies. The lack of control that was expressed in the fits, bursts of rage, and spells of uncontrolled sobbing was partly caused by this loss of his roles.

That was once more revealed on the evening of April 26, when General Ritter von Greim, whom he had appointed Göring's successor as commander in chief of the air force, flew into the encircled city with the pilot Hanna Reitsch. They came because Hitler had insisted on making the appointment in person. He had tears in his eyes, as Hanna Reitsch described it. His head drooped and his face was deathly pale when he spoke of Göring's "ultimatum." "Now nothing remains," he said. "Nothing is spared to me. No loyalty, no honor is left; no disappointment, no treachery has been spared me—and now this on top of it all. Everything is over. Every possible wrong has been inflicted upon me."

Nevertheless, he still had one hope, a small one, but he elaborated it in interminable soliloquies into one of his phantasmagorical certainties. During the night he summoned Hanna Reitsch and told her that the great cause for which he had lived and fought now seemed lost—unless the army of General Wenck, which was approaching, managed to break through the ring of the besiegers and relieve the city. He gave her a vial of poison. "But I still have hope, dear Hanna. General Wenck's army is moving up from the south. He must and will drive the Russians back far enough to save our people."

That same night the first Soviet shells struck the chancellery, and the bunker vibrated under the impact of tumbling walls. In some areas the conquerors had moved to within a half a mile of the chancellery.

The following day, SS Gruppenführer Fegelein, Himmler's personal representative in the Führer's headquarters, was picked up in civilian dress, and within the bunker new laments at the steadily spreading treachery were heard. Hitler's suspicions now turned against everyone. Eva Braun, who was related to the arrested man, since Fegelein had married her sister Gretl, exclaimed: "Poor, poor Adolf, they've all deserted you, all betrayed you." Aside from Eva, only Goebbels and Bormann remained beyond suspicion. They formed that "phalanx of the last" which Goebbels had hailed years before, in one of his paeans to doom. The more Hitler succumbed to his fits of melancholia and his misanthropies, the more closely he drew these few loyal souls around him. Since his return to the chancellery he had spent most of his evenings with them, although occasionally Ley was included. There was evidence of something secret going on, which soon aroused the curiosity of the other bunker inmates.

Years later it became known that Hitler, in meetings between the beginning of February and the middle of April, had embarked on a kind of general retrospective, summing up his life, as it were. In a series of lengthy monologues he once more examined the course he had taken, the premises and goals of his policies, and their prospects and errors. As always, he elaborated his reflections verbosely and chaotically. But on the whole the pages as they stand constitute one of the fundamental documents of his life. They reveal his intellectual energy, though somewhat diminished, and also the old obsessional ideas.

The starting point of his reflections was the still rankling failure of an Anglo-German alliance. Up to early 1941, this senseless mistaken war could have been ended, especially since England had "proved her will to resist in the sky above London" and moreover "had on the credit side of her ledger the shameful defeats of the Italians in North Africa." Had the war been thus ended, America would have been kept out of European affairs. The "phony" world powers, France and Italy, would have been compelled to renounce their "anachronistic politics of greatness" and instead could have undertaken a "bold policy of friendship with Islam." England, still the heart of his grand design, would have been able to devote herself "entirely to the welfare of the Empire," while Germany, secure in the rear, could turn to her true task, "the goal of my life and the reason for the genesis of National Socialism: the extirpation of Bolshevism."[65]

Probing for the causes that had ruined this design, he once again encountered the enemy who from the very beginning had blocked his way and whose power he had nevertheless failed to appraise correctly. This was, as he now saw it in retrospect, his most serious mistake: "I had underestimated the overpowering influence of the Jews upon the British under Churchill." And he complained: "If only fate had sent an aging and calcified England a new Pitt instead of this Yid-ridden half American souse!" Now he hated the arrogant islanders, whom he had courted in vain more than any other of his enemies, and did not conceal his satisfaction that in the days to come they would be departing from history and, in keeping with the law of life, would go to their doom. "The English people will die of hunger or tuberculosis on their damned island."[66]

The war against the Soviet Union, he insisted once again, stood above all arbitrary considerations. It had been the principal goal of all his endeavors. Granted, it was possible that it might fail and end in defeat. But not to have undertaken it would have been worse than any defeat, equivalent to an act of treason. "We were condemned to wage war, and our concern could only be to choose the most favorable moment for its start. At the same time it was beyond question that we could never give up once we had become involved in it."

As to what the most favorable moment might have been, Hitler manifested far less certainty. The excitement with which he returned to this theme on several evenings, examining its tactical and strategic aspects and finding justifying arguments, indicates that he considered his choice of the moment his gravest error. Characteristically, he presented the situation as one without alternatives:

It is the nemesis of this war that it began for Germany too soon on the one hand, somewhat too late on the other hand. From the military point of view it was to our interest to begin it a year earlier. In 1938 I ought to have seized the initiative, instead of letting it be thrust upon me in 1939, since it was inevitable in any case. But I couldn't do anything since the British and French accepted all my demands at Munich.

To that extent, then, the war came some time too late. In regard to the preparation of our morale, however, it came far too soon. I had not yet had time to shape the people to the measure of my policies. I would have needed twenty years to bring a new elite to maturity, an elite which so to speak had imbibed the National Socialist way of thinking with its mother's milk. It is the Germans' tragedy never to have enough time. Circumstances are always forcing us. And if we lack time, that is chiefly due to our lack of space. The Russians, in their tremendous plains, can afford the luxury of not being hurried. Time is working for them. It is working against us. . . .

Fatefully, I have to complete everything during the brief span of one human life. . . . Where the others have an eternity at their disposal, I have only a few miserable years. The others know that they will have successors who will take up their work just where they have left it, who will make the same furrows with the same plow. I ask myself whether the man will be found among my immediate successors who is destined to take up the torch that is slipping from my hand.

It is my other nemesis that I have been serving a nation with a tragic past, a nation so inconstant, so fickle as the Germans, falling with a strange calm according to circumstances from one extreme to the other.[67]

These were the premises whose prisoner he was, the fundamental obstacles in situation and material that he had been forced to accept as he found them. But he had also made mistakes, he concluded, fateful acts of thoughtlessness. He had made all sorts of unnecessary concessions. And it is exceedingly illuminating that now, in his searching retrospect, he disavowed one of the few intact human relationships of his life:

When I regard events soberly and stripped of all sentimentality, I must admit that my immutable friendship with Italy and with the Duce can be placed on the debit side of the ledger, as one of my errors. One might even say that the Italian alliance proved more useful to our enemies than to ourselves . . . and in the end it will contribute to our—if the victory proves not to be ours after all—our losing the war. . . .

Our Italian ally hampered us almost everywhere. For example, he prevented us from employing revolutionary policies in North Africa . . . for our Islamic friends suddenly saw in us voluntary or involuntary accomplices of their oppressors. The memory of the barbarous reprisals against the Senoussis is still very much alive among them. Moreover, the Duce's ridiculous claim to be regarded as the "sword of Islam" arouses just as much laughter today as it did before the war. This title belongs by rights to Mohammed and to a great conqueror like Omar. Mussolini had it conferred on himself by a few poor devils whom he paid or terrorized. There was a chance for us to pursue a grand policy toward Islam. But we missed that opportunity, like so much else, because of our loyalty to the Italian alliance. . . .

From the military point of view it is hardly any better. Italy's entry into the war almost immediately enabled our enemies to have their first victories, and made it possible for Churchill to inspire his countrymen with fresh courage and the Anglophiles all over the world with new hope. Although the Italians had already shown themselves incapable of holding Abyssinia and Cyrenaica, they had the nerve to plunge into the totally senseless campaign against Greece without asking us, without even informing us. . . . That forced us, contrary to all our plans, to intervene in the Balkans, which in turn resulted in a catastrophic delay for the beginning of the war against Russia. . . . We should have been able to attack Russia starting with May 15, 1941 and . . . end the campaign before the winter. Then everything would have turned out differently!

Out of gratitude, because I could not forget the Duce's attitude during the Anschluss, I always refrained from criticizing and condemning Italy. On the contrary, I tried to treat her as our equal. Unfortunately the laws of life show that it is a mistake to treat as equals those who are not really equal. . . . I regret that I did not follow the dictates of reason, which prescribed to me a brutal friendship in regard to Italy.[68]

On the whole, to his mind it was his soft-heartedness, his lack of toughness and implacability, which led to his failure after he had been so close to triumph. In this last document, too, he revealed his own unmistakable brand of radicalism. "I fought against the Jews with open vizard; before the war started, I gave them fair warning. . . ."[69] He regretted not having ruthlessly eliminated the German conservatives from public life, of having supported Franco, the nobility, and the church in Spain rather than the Communists, and, in France, of having failed to liberate the working class from the hands of a "bourgeoisie of fossils." Everywhere, he now thought, he should have fostered the uprising of the colonial peoples, the awakening of the oppressed and exploited nations. The Arabs, the Iraqis, the entire Near East, which had hailed the German victories, should have been incited to revolt. The German Reich was now collapsing not because of its bellicosity and sins against moderation, but because of its incapacity for radicalism, its fixation on morality. "What might we have done!" he grieved. Hugh R. Trevor-Roper has commented on the remarkable lucidity with which Hitler in these soliloquies analyzed the strengths and weaknesses of his concept of world power. He was in no doubt about the principle. He realized that Europe could be dominated by a continental power that controlled western Russia, drew upon the reserves of Asia, and simultaneously presented itself as the advocate of the colonial nations by linking political revolution with slogans of social liberation. He also knew that he had gone to war with the Soviet Union over the question of who would assume this part. The issue had gone against him, he believed, because he had not been able to fight on consistently revolutionary principles. He had entered the war with the fuss-and-feathers diplomats and generals of the old school, additionally hampered by his friendship with Mussolini, and had not been able to free himself from these burdens. His radicalism had not been sufficient; he had revealed too many bourgeois sentiments, too much bourgeois halfheartedness. He, too, had been split—this was the conclusion of his meditations. "Life forgives no weakness!"[70]

His decision to call it quits came on the night of April 28 and in the early hours of the morning of April 29. Shortly before 10 P.M., in the midst of a conversation with Ritter von Greim, Hitler was interrupted by his valet, Heinz Linge. Linge handed him a Reuter's report that Reichsführer-SS Heinrich Himmler had made contact with the Swedish diplomat Count Bernadotte in order to negotiate a surrender in the West.

The shock that followed this report was more violent than all the emotions of the past week. Hitler had always regarded Göring as opportunistic and corrupt; thus the Reich Marshal's betrayal came as no surprise. But Himmler had always made loyalty his watchword and prided himself on his incorruptibility. His conduct now signified the breach of a principle. For Hitler it was the gravest imaginable blow. "He raged like a madman," Hanna Reitsch described the ensuing scene. "He turned purple, and his face was almost unrecognizable." In contrast to the preceding outbursts, however, this time his strength gave out after a short time, and he withdrew with Goebbels and Bormann for a conversation behind closed doors.

Once more, his single decision brought all the others in its wake. As part of his revenge Hitler had Hermann Fegelein, Himmler's liaison man, subjected to a short, sharp interrogation, then shot in the chancellery by members of his escort squad. He then sought out Greim and ordered him to attempt to get out of Berlin in order to arrest Himmler. He would not hear of any objections. "A traitor must never be my successor as Führer," he said. "See to it that he does not!"

Hastily, he had the small conference room prepared for a civil wedding ceremony. A district magistrate named Walter Wagner, who was serving in a nearby militia unit, was fetched and asked to marry the Führer and Eva Braun. Goebbels and Bormann were the witnesses. Because of the special circumstances both parties requested a war wedding, which could be performed without delay. They attested that they were of pure Aryan descent and free of hereditary diseases. The record noted that the applications had been accepted, the banns "examined and found in order." Then Wagner, according to the record, turned to the parties:

> I come herewith to the solemn act of matrimony. In the presence of the above-mentioned witnesses . . . I ask you, My Leader Adolf Hitler, whether you are willing to enter into matrimony with Miss Eva Braun. If such is the case, I ask you to reply, "Yes."
> Herewith I ask you, Miss Eva Braun, whether you are willing to enter into matrimony with My Leader Adolf Hitler. If such is the case, I ask you too to reply, "Yes."
> Now, since both these engaged persons have stated their willingness to enter into matrimony, I herewith declare the marriage valid before the law.

The participants then signed the document. Hitler's new wife was so agitated by the circumstances that she began signing her maiden name. Then she crossed out the initial letter B and wrote, "Eva Hitler, née Braun." The entire party then went together to the private rooms, where the secretaries, Hitler's diet cook, Fräulein Manzialy, and several of the adjutants had gathered for drinks and melancholy reminiscences of times past.

From this point on, it seems, the direction of events finally slipped from Hitler's hands. It is likely that he would have wished to stage the concluding act more grandiosely, more disastrously, with a greater display of lofty emotion, style, and terror. Instead, what now took place seemed oddly hapless, improvised, as though in view of the many seemingly miraculous reversals in his life he had up to this very moment never really considered the possibility of an irrevocable end. At any rate, the gruesome idea of having this wedding on the verge of a double suicide, as if he feared nothing so much as "illegitimacy" on his deathbed, marked the beginning of a trivial departure. It demonstrated how spent he was, drained of even his histrionic effects, even though the Wagnerian reminiscence of joining his beloved in death might in his eyes give the procedure a saving note of tragedy. But, henceforth, whatever else might remain associated with his name, his death contributed nothing to mythology. Possibly he was now giving up more than the right to direct the life he had always regarded as a role to be played.

For all its casual character, this marriage represented a significant step. It was not only a gesture of gratitude toward the one living being aside from the dog Blondi who, as Hitler once remarked, remained faithful to him to the last. It was also a definitive act of abdication. As the Führer, he had repeatedly declared, he must not be married. The mythological conception he had of his status could not be reconciled with ordinary human ties. Now he was abandoning this stand, with the implication that he no longer believed in the survival of National Socialism. In fact he did remark to his guests that the cause was done for and would not spring to life again.[71] Then he left the group and went into one of the adjacent rooms to dictate his last will.

He produced a political and a private testament. The former was dominated by violent polemics against the Jews, by asseverations of his own innocence, and appeals to the spirit of resistance: "Centuries will pass, but the ruins of our cities and monuments will repeatedly kindle hatred for the race ultimately responsible, who have brought everything down upon us: international Jewry and its accomplices!"

Twenty-five years had passed. He had experienced an unprecedented rise, undreamed-of triumphs and defeats, despairs and downfall, and he himself had remained unchanged. Down to the very phrasing, the ideological passages of the testament might have been taken from the first document of his political career, the letter to Adolf Gemlich in 1919, or from one of his speeches as a young local agitator. The phenomenon of early and total rigidity, of the rejection of all experience, which was so typical of Hitler, was confirmed for the last time in this document.

In a special section he expelled Göring and Himmler from the party and from all of their offices. He named Admiral Dönitz as his successor in the posts of President, Minister of War, and supreme commander of the armed forces. His comment that in the navy the sense of honor still survived, that any thought of surrender was alien to it, was obviously intended to be understood as an injunction to continue the struggle even beyond his death, to ultimate doom. At the same time, he appointed a new government, headed by Goebbels. The document concluded: "Above all I call upon the leaders of the nation and all followers to observe the racial laws scrupulously and to implacably oppose the universal poisoner of all races, international Jewry."[72]

His personal testament was considerably shorter. Whereas the political document asserted his claims on history, the personal one expressed the custom's official's son who had remained behind all the disguises. It read:

During the years of struggle I did not think I could responsibly undertake to establish a marriage. But now, before the completion of this earthly course, I have decided to take as my wife the girl who after long years of faithful friendship entered this city, already almost besieged, of her own free will, in order to share my fate with me. At her request she is joining me in death as my wife. Death will compensate us for what my work in the service of my people robbed from us both.

All that I own—in so far as it had any value—belongs to the party. If this ceases to exist, to the state; and if the state also is annihilated, no further decision on my part is necessary.

My paintings in the collections I bought over the years were never collected for private purposes, but always only for the expansion of a gallery in my hometown of Linz on the Danube. It would be my heartfelt wish if this bequest could be duly carried out. I appoint as executor of my will my most faithful party comrade, Martin Bormann. He is legally entitled to make all final decisions. He may transfer any personal mementos, or whatever is needed for the maintenance of a modest middle-class standard of living, to my brother and sisters, and particularly to my wife's mother, and to my faithful associates who are well known to him—principally my old secretaries, Frau Winter, etc., who for many years have sustained me by their work.

I myself and my wife choose death to escape the disgrace of removal or surrender. It is our desire to be burned at once at the place in which I have performed the greater part of my daily work in the course of twelve years of service to my people.

The two documents were signed at four o'clock in the morning on April 29. Three copies were prepared, and in the course of the day arrangements were made to have them taken out of the bunker by different routes. One of the people selected for this messenger service was Colonel von Below, Hitler's Luftwaffe adjutant, who took with him a postscript directed to General Keitel. That was Hitler's last message and ended with the characteristic sentences:

The people and the armed forces have given their all in this long and hard struggle. The sacrifice has been enormous. But my trust has been misused by many people. Disloyalty and betrayal have undermined resistance throughout the war. It was therefore not granted to me to lead the people to victory. The Army General Staff cannot be compared with the General Staff in the First World War. Its achievements were far behind those of the fighting front.

The efforts and sacrifices of the German people in this war have been so great that I cannot believe that they have been in vain. The aim must still be to win territory in the East for the German people.[73]

At various times during the past weeks Hitler had expressed anxiety that he might have to appear as an "exhibit in the Moscow zoo" or as the principal actor in a "show trial staged by Jews."[74] These fears were intensified when, in the course of April 29, the news of Mussolini's death reached him. The Duce and his mistress, Clara Petacci, who had hastily joined him that same day, had been caught by partisans and on the afternoon of April 28 shot without formalities in the small north Italian hamlet of Mezzagra. The bodies were taken to Milan and suspended by the heels from the roof of a garage on the Piazzale Loreto, where a screaming mob beat, spat upon, and stoned the corpses.

Under the impact of this news, Hitler began making the arrangements for his own death. He charged many members of his entourage, including

747

his servant Heinz Linge, his chauffeur Erich Kempka, and his pilot Hans Baur, with the task of seeing that his remains did not fall into the enemy's hands. The preparations he made seemed like a last manifestation of his lifelong efforts to conceal his real self. It is difficult to imagine a greater contrast than that between Hitler's crawling into a hole to die, as it were, and the end of Mussolini, who called upon his remaining adherents to go together to the Valtellina and there "die with the sun in our faces."

But Hitler also feared that the poison he had provided might not bring about death fast enough or reliably enough. Consequently, he ordered the effect of the poison to be tried out on his Alsatian dog. At midnight Blondi was coaxed to the toilet in the bunker. Sergeant Tornow, who was in charge of Hitler's dogs, forced the animal's mouth open while Professor Haase, one of the medical staff, reached into the dog's gullet and with forceps crushed an ampoule of poison inside. Shortly afterward Hitler entered the room and glanced expressionlessly at the corpse. He then invited the occupants of the two adjacent bunkers to come to the conference room for farewells. With a faraway expression, he went down the row, silently shaking hands with each person. Several said a few words to him, but he did not answer, or only moved his lips inaudibly. Shortly after three o'clock in the morning he had a telegram sent to Dönitz complaining about inadequate military measures, and in a kind of stale, repetitive gesture he once more commanded the admiral to proceed "instantly and unsparingly against all traitors."

Late in the forenoon the military conference took place as usual. With no sign of emotion, Hitler received the information that the Soviet troops had by now occupied the Tiergarten, Potsdamer Platz, and the subway on Vosstrasse, in the immediate vicinity of the chancellery. Then he ordered delivery of 200 liters of gasoline. At two o'clock he had his lunch in company with his secretaries and his cook; at the same moment, two Soviet sergeants raised the Red flag on the dome of the nearby Reichstag. After the meal he summoned his most intimate associates, including Goebbels, Bormann, Generals Burgdorf and Krebs, his secretaries, Frau Christian and Frau Junge, and several orderlies. Together with his wife, he shook hands with all of them and then, mute and stooped, he vanished inside his room. And as though this life, which had so largely been governed by staged happenings and had always aimed at glaringly dramatic effects, could only end with a preposterous climax, at this time a dance began in the chancellery canteen (if we are to believe the accounts of the participants), a dance in which the weeks of strained nerves sought violent release. Even repeated remonstrances that the Führer was about to die could not bring it to a halt.[75] It was April 30, 1945, shortly before 4 P.M.

What happened thereafter has never been completely and unequivocally clarified. According to the statements of most of the survivors of the bunker, a single shot sounded. Shortly afterward, Rattenhuber, the commander of the SS guards, entered the room. Hitler was sitting hunched over, face smeared with blood, on the sofa. Beside him was his wife, an unused revolver in her lap; she had taken poison. In contrast to this version of things, most Soviet accounts have held that Hitler also ended his life by poison. But there are contradictions in the Soviet story. On the one hand, it denies that any traces of a bullet were detectable in the fragments of a skull that were found later. On the other hand, the story attempts to say who in Hitler's entourage had been assigned to deliver the "mercy shot" to make sure of his death. These contradictions tend to indicate that the Soviet version of Hitler's suicide has a political coloration. It sounds like a last echo of the attempts constantly made during Hitler's lifetime to refute him by belittling him, as though a certain mentality could not bear to concede abilities and strength to the morally reprehensible. It was the story of the Iron Cross or his gifts as political tactician or statesman all over again: he was now begrudged the courage required for the obviously sterner death by a bullet.[76]

Rattenhuber ordered the bodies to be taken into the courtyard. There he had the gasoline poured over them and invited the mourners to come up. No sooner had they assembled than Russian shelling drove them back to the bunker entrance. Hitler's SS adjutant Otto Günsche thereupon tossed a burning rag upon both corpses, and when the leaping flames swathed the bodies, everyone stood at attention and gave the Nazi salute. A member of the guards detachment who passed by the spot half an hour after this ceremony could "no longer recognize Hitler because he was pretty well charred." And when he visited the spot again toward eight o'clock "a few flakes were flying up in the wind," as he put it. Shortly before 11 P.M. the remains of the almost totally consumed bodies were swept onto a canvas shelter half, according to Günsche's account, "let down into a shell hole outside the exit from the bunker, covered over with earth, and the earth pounded firm with a wooden rammer."[77]

Long ago, in the days of struggle, Hitler had let himself be represented grandiloquently as "the man who would rather be a dead Achilles than a living dog." Later on, he had begun to elaborate the scenario for his obsequies. His burial place was to be a mighty crypt in the bell tower of the gigantic structure he had planned to build on the bank of the Danube at Linz. But in fact he was hastily shoveled into a shell hole among mountains of rubble, fragments of wall, cement mixers, and scattered rubbish.

This was not yet the end of the story. Goebbels tried to coax the Russians into separate negotiations by references to their "common holiday of May 1." When these efforts failed, Goebbels and his family committed suicide. Bormann, together with the other inhabitants of the bunker, made an attempt to break out. Then Soviet troops occupied the abandoned bunker and immediately set about searching for the remains of Hitler's body. A medical report dated May 8, 1945, of an autopsy of a severely charred male body came to the conclusion that this was "presumably Hitler's corpse." Other statements shortly afterward cast doubt on this assertion. Then again Soviet sources maintained that Hitler had after all been identified on the basis of dental studies; but this statement, too, was questioned, and rumors arose that the British authorities were hiding Hitler in their zone of occupation. At the Potsdam Conference in July, 1945, Stalin assured his Western colleagues that the Russians had not found the corpse and that Hitler was hiding in Spain or South America.[78] In the end the Russians managed to swathe the whole question in such obscurity that the wildest versions concerning the end of Hitler circulated. Some said he had been shot in the Berlin Tiergarten by a German squad of officers. Others had him fleeing in a submarine to a remote island. Still other stories maintained that he was living in a Spanish monastery or on a South American hacienda. All his life Hitler had owed his successes largely to one or the other of his enemies. Now, once more, his ill-wishers—as if in a last display of all the mistakes of the era—made it possible for him to live a mythical posthumous life.

For all that the event had no consequences, it was a symbol. It once again forcibly suggested that the appearance of Hitler, the conditions of his rise and his triumphs, were founded upon premises that point far beyond the narrow framework of merely German conditions. Granted, every nation bears the responsibility for its own history. But only a mind that has learned nothing from the misfortunes of these times will call him the man of a single nation and refuse to recognize that a powerful tendency of the age culminated in him, a tendency that dominated the entire first half of this century.

Thus Hitler not only destroyed Germany. He also put an end to old Europe with its nationalisms, its conflicts, its hereditary foes, and its insincere imperatives—as well as with its brilliance, its grandeur, and the magic of its *douceur de vivre*. Possibly he was deceiving himself when he called that Europe "outmoded." His unique radicality, his visions, his missionary fever, and, as the outcome of these, an unprecedented explosion of energy, were needed to destroy it. But ultimately it must be granted that he could not have destroyed Europe without the help of Europe.

CONCLUSION

The Dead End

A man once said to me: "Listen, if you do that, Germany will fall apart in six weeks."

I said: "What do you mean by that?"

"Germany will just collapse."

I said: "What do you mean by that?"

"Germany will just cease to exist."

I answered: "Once upon a time the German people survived the wars with the Romans. The German people survived the Great Migrations. The German people survived the later great battles of the Early and Late Middle Ages. The German people survived the wars of religion at the dawn of modern times. The German people survived the Thirty Years' War. The German people later survived the Napoleonic Wars, the Wars of Liberation; it even survived a World War, even the Revolution—it will survive even me!"

Adolf Hitler, 1938

Almost without transition, virtually from one moment to the next, Nazism vanished after the death of Hitler and the surrender. It was as if National Socialism had been nothing but the motion, the state of intoxication and the catastrophe it had caused. It is not accidental that in the contemporary accounts dating from the spring of 1945 certain phrases crop up repeatedly—to the effect that a "spell" had been broken, a "phantasmagoria" shattered. Such language borrowed from the sphere of magic conveys the peculiarly unreal nature of the regime and the abruptness of its end.

Hitler's propaganda specialists had talked constantly of invincible alpine redoubts, nests of resistance, and swelling werewolf units, and had predicted a war beyond the war—but there was no sign of this. Once again it became plain that National Socialism, like Fascism in general, was dependent to the core on superior force, arrogance, triumph, and by its nature had no resources in the moment of defeat. The cogent point has been made that Germany was the only defeated country in the Second World War that failed to produce a resistance movement.[1]

This impermanence also showed up in the conduct of the regime's leaders and functionaries. It was especially apparent in the course of their efforts during the Nuremberg trials to exculpate themselves ideologically. They denied or belittled the crimes that shortly before had had eschatological portent, so that in the end everything—the violence, the war, the genocide—assumed the character of a ghastly, stupid misunderstanding. That behavior, too, contributed to the impression that Nazism had not been a phenomenon spanning and characterizing the era, but a superficial movement sprung from an individual's urge for power combined with the resentments of a restive nation with a craving for conquest. For had it been deeply rooted in the times, had it been one of the age's elemental movements, a military defeat could not have consigned it so abruptly to oblivion.

Nevertheless, after only twelve years it had given the world a different aspect; and it is patent that such tremendous processes cannot be adequately explained solely as resulting from the whims of an individual in power. Such events become possible only if this individual embodies the emotions, anxieties, or interests of a multitude, and if powerful forces of the age are impelling him onward. Here we see once more Hitler's role and importance in relation to the energies that surrounded him. An enormous, chaotic potential of aggressiveness, anxiety, devotion, and egotism lay ready to hand; but it needed to be called forth, concentrated, and applied by an imperious figure. To that figure it owed its impetus and legitimacy, with that figure it celebrated its imposing victories, and with that figure it went down to destruction.

But Hitler was more than the unifying figure for many of the tendencies of the age. He also imposed direction, extension, and radicalness upon the course of events. In this he was aided by his habit of thinking in absolutes and subordinating everything, principles, opponents, allies, nations, and ideas, icily or maniacally to his own monstrous goals. His extremism corresponded to his inward remoteness. August Kubizek had noted his friend's tendency "to overturn the millennia." And although we should not lay undue emphasis on such recollections, Hitler's later way of dealing with the world did have something of the infantile radicalness that this phrase suggests. His own remark, that he confronted "everything with a tremendous, ice-cold absence of bias,"[2] points in the same direction. We might even contend that contrary to his claim, which he dated back to his youth, he never grasped the true nature of history. He thought of it as a kind of hall of fame with doors wide open to ambitious men. He knew nothing of the meaning and the justification of tradition. In spite of the aura of bourgeois decline that surrounded him, he was a *homo novus*. And in that spirit, with an unconcern that seems abstract, he went about realizing his intentions. He changed the map of Europe, destroyed empires, and promoted the rise of new powers, evoked revolutions, and brought the colonial age to an end. Finally, he enormously widened the horizon of mankind's experience. To paraphrase a saying of Schopenhauer, whom he revered after his fashion, it might be said that he taught the world some things it will never forget.

Dominant among his motivations—and here he was borne along on the powerful current of his era—was an inescapable sense of being threatened—the fear of annihilation that had seized many political entities and nations in the course of centuries. But only now, at this crossroads in history, did this annihilation become a universal force threatening all mankind. One of the photos from the new chancellery shows Hitler's desk, on which lies a folio-sized book titled *The Salvation of the World*.[3] And at various junctures in his life it became evident that he took his role of savior with the utmost seriousness. That was not only his mission and "cyclopean task," but also—in this life dominated by histrionic concepts—the great exemplary part that he connected with memories of his early favorite opera, *Lohengrin,* and with the myths of a good many liberating heroes and white knights.

For him the idea of salvation was indissolubly linked with European pride. Aside from Europe no other continent counted, no other culture of significance existed. All other continents were only geography, areas for slaves and exploitation, unhistorical empty spaces: *hic sunt leones.* Thus Hitler's attitude was also a last exaggerated expression of Europe's claim to remain master of its own history, and thus of history in general. By the time he was done, Europe played the same part in his view of the world that Germanism had in his early years: it was the supreme value, but so threatened that it was already almost lost. He was extremely alert to the pressure of dissoluton to which the Continent was exposed on all sides, to the dangers to its nature that came both from outside and from inside, to the vastly multiplying "lesser breeds" of Asia, Africa, and America that were swarming over the globe and virtually suffocating it, and to the democratic ideologies within Europe itself that denied its history and its greatness.

He himself, it is true, was a figure of the democratic era, but he represented only its antiliberal variant, which flourished on rigged elections and the charisma of a leader. One of the things he learned from the November, 1918, revolution, and was never to forget, was an insight into the obscure connection between democracy and anarchy. He had seen, he thought, that chaotic conditions were the real, unfalsified expression of true popular rule and that the law of such rule was arbitrariness. Thus Hitler's dictatorship may be regarded as a last desperate effort to hold old Europe to the conditions that had made for her onetime greatness, to defend the sense of style, order, and authority against the dawning era of democracy with its consultation of the masses, its egalitarian encouragement of everything plebeian, its emancipation, and its concomitant decline of national and racial identity. He saw the Continent subject to a mighty dual assault by two alien forces, devoured by "soulless" American capitalism, on the

CONCLUSION

one hand, and by "inhuman" Russian Bolshevism on the other hand. Rightly, the nature of his commitment has been defined as a "death agony."

Expand these ideas to a global plane, and we see the parallel to the state of mind of the early Fascist followings, those middle-class masses who saw themselves being slowly crushed by the unions on the one hand and the department stores on the other, by Communists and anonymous corporations—all this against a general background of panic. In these terms Hitler can also be understood as an effort to maintain a kind of third-force position between the two dominant powers of the times, between Left and Right, East and West. This may account for his appearance of dualism, so that none of the unequivocal definitions, none of the attempts to classify him as conservative, reactionary, capitalistic, or petty bourgeois, really comprehend him. By standing between all positions he shared in all of them and usurped crucial elements of them; but he combined them into his own unique, unmistakable phenomenon. His accession to power brought to an end the conflict that Wilson and Lenin had initiated over Germany after the First World War. The former had tried to win Germany over to parliamentary democracy and the idea of international peace, the latter to the cause of world revolution. Twelve years later, the struggle was renewed and settled in Solomonic fashion by the partition of the country.

The third position that Hitler sought to occupy was intended to embrace the entire continent, with Germany as its vital nucleus. He held that the contemporary mission of the Reich was to reinvigorate tired Europe and rouse her to a consciousness of her grandeur. He wanted to make up for the missed imperialistic phase in Germany's development, and though coming late on the historical scene win the highest imaginable prize: hegemony over Europe secured by vast expansion of power in the East, and through Europe domination of the world. With some justification he assumed that under developing patterns of power, the chances for conquering an empire were growing slimmer, and since he always thought in sharp alternatives, he saw Germany condemned either to found an-empire or "to close her existence . . . as a second Holland and a second Switzerland," if not worse, "to vanish from the earth or serve others as a slave nation."[4] That the country lacked the energies and resources to meet this aim did not much worry him. What really was at stake, he argued, was "to force the German people, who are hesitating to confront their destiny, to take the road to greatness." When someone pointed out the risk of ruining Germany by setting her such goals, he merely answered that in that case everything would be "in a mess."[5]

Hitler's nationalism, consequently, was also not without its equivocations and rode roughshod over the interests of the nation. Still, it was vehement enough to be taken as a challenge and aroused widespread resistance. This must be said even though Hitler formulated the defensive emotions of an age and a continent, and even though his messianic slogans proved effec-

756

tive far beyond the borders of Germany, so that through him Germany was the object of respect and even envy.[6] In spite of such "internationalism," Hitler never managed to give his own defensive intentions more than a harsh and narrow nationalistic profile. In the bunker mediations of the spring of 1945 he referred to himself as "Europe's last chance," and in light of that idea tried to justify his application of force against the whole Continent: "It [the Continent] could not be conquered by charm and persuasiveness. I had to rape it in order to have it."[7] But Europe's chance was precisely what Hitler was not, not even prospectively, not even as an illusion or a possible way. At no time was he able to convince people beyond his own borders that he offered them a viable political alternative. During the war, when the campaign against the Soviet Union could have been presented as a European crusade, he revealed himself as the sworn enemy of "imposed internationalism" that he had been from the start. He remained profoundly a European provincial with his gaze irretrievably fixated on the antagonisms of a vanished era.

We are thus once again compelled to confront Hitler's oddly fractured position in time. Despite his fundamentally defensive posture, he was long regarded as the really progressive, modern figure of the age. To most of his contemporaries it was clear that he was striding toward the future. Yet to our present-day sensibility, what is most striking is the anachronistic quality he displays. During the twenties and thirties the mélange of elements that were regarded as modern and in keeping with the spirit of the age were technology and collectivist ideas, monumental proportions, bellicose attitudes, the pride of the mass man, and the aura of stardom. One of the reasons for Nazism's success was that Hitler ingeniously appropriated all these elements. Another of these "modern" elements was the imperious manner of great individuals. Hitler's rise and sovereignty took place within a pattern of Caesaristic tendencies stretching all the way from the totalitarian cult of personality in Stalin's Soviet Union to the autocratic style of President Roosevelt. Against such a background Hitler, who blatantly proclaimed himself a ruler of this type, seemed the perfect representative of the new age. He himself also consistently stressed the optimistic, future-oriented character of Nazism. Its reactionary features, its pessimistic nostalgia with regard to civilization, were largely given voice by Himmler, Darré, and a sizable band of the SS leadership.

In reality the prospect of the future horrified him. He was glad, he commented at the dinner table in the Führer's headquarters, that he was experiencing only the beginnings of the technological age. Later generations would no longer know "how beautiful the world once was."[8] In spite of all his deliberately progressivist gestures, he was profoundly retarded, a captive of the images, standards, and impulses of the nineteenth century—which in fact he considered to be, alongside classical antiquity, the most important era in history. Even his death, trivial and botched though it may seem, reflected both aspects of the era that he admired and once again represented: something of its sonorous splendor, as expressed in the *Götter-dämmerung* motifs of the staging, but also something of its trashiness, when he lay dead on the bunker sofa like a ruined gambler of the opera-hat era beside his newly wedded mistress. It was a finale in which he dropped out of the period and once again revealed the antiquated basis of his nature.

The rigidity we have noted so often in the course of his life can be seen in its real significance only against this background: he wanted to cling fast to the unique moment in which the world had presented itself to him during his formative years. Unlike the Fascist type in general, he was not seduced by history but by his own educational experience, the shudders of happiness and terror that had been his in puberty. The salvation he wanted to bring about was therefore always aimed at restoring something of the great nineteenth century. Hitler's entire vision of the world, his manias about the fight for survival, race, space, his never-questioned admiration for the idols and great men of his youth, and in fact for great men in general (so that history seemed a mere reflection of their will, as was shown by his absurd hopes at the death of Roosevelt)—all this and much else may serve to define the extent of his fixation. All sorts of mental blocks restricted him to the horizon of the nineteenth century. For example, the supposedly dire figure of 140 inhabitants per square kilometer, which continually recurs in his speeches to justify his claims to *Lebensraum,* reveals his inability to grasp the modern solutions for exploiting what land is available and unmasks his modernism as mere rhetoric. The world was standing on the threshold of the atomic age, but he could still say, as he did in February, 1942, that he was grateful to the author of boys' fiction, Karl May, for having opened his eyes to the nature of the world.

He understood the nature of greatness itself in picture-book terms, in the vein of old adventure novels, embodied in the figure of the solitary superman. Among the constants of his thought was the desire to be not only great in himself, but also great in the manner, style, and temperament of an artist. When, in one of his speeches, he proclaimed the "dictatorship of genius," he was obviously thinking of the artist's claim to dominion. Significantly, he chose as his examples the persons of Frederick the Great and Richard Wagner, who both bestraddled the artistic and the political realms. Theirs was what he called "heroism"—and the gravest charge he hurled at his early opponent, Gustav von Kahr, was that Kahr was "not a heroic figure." To us the psychopathic nature of this attitude is only too apparent; we are repelled by the naïve, puerile nature it betrays, and its strained, artificial quality. The imperious pose he had adopted was also only a sham; and we will recall how much apathy and nervous weakness were concealed behind his posturings, what artificial stimulants he required for those grand

758

gestures of energy he practiced—in which, however, the mechanical twitching of galvanized muscles can always be detected. His amorality was similarly artificial and forced. He liked to put on the manner of a temperamental, violent autocrat in order to conceal the petty malevolence with which he was filled. In spite of all his highhanded crimes, he was much more the type of the pallid murderer, and certainly not free from the naggings of a morality that he scorned as a "chimaera." A glacial temperament and digestive troubles; such a constitutional type also belongs to the nineteenth century. Nervous weakness compensated for by superman poses: in this, too, Hitler revealed his link with the late-bourgeois age, with the period of Gobineau, Wagner, and Nietzsche.

Yet even this link was not a strong and firm one but marred by brittleness and alienation. Hitler has rightly been called "detached." Despite his many petty bourgeois inclinations, he did not really belong to that class, either; or at any rate was never rooted in it deeply enough to share its limitations. For this reason his defensiveness was so full of resentments, and for this reason he defended the world he allegedly wanted to protect until he succeeded in destroying it.

So it was that this reactionary man, unmistakably molded by the nineteenth century, propelled both Germany and large parts of the world into the twentieth century. Hitler's place in history is much closer to that of the great revolutionaries than to that of the conservative, preserving autocrats. Granted, he drew his crucial impulses from the desire to prevent the dawn of modern times and to return, by means of a grand, world-historical correction, to the starting point of all errors and mistaken developments. As he himself phrased it, he had come forth as a revolutionary against revolution.[9] But the mobilization of forces and the sense of commitment this rescue mission of his required enormously accelerated the emancipatory process. And the excessive stress on authority, style, and order, which were associated with his conduct, actually weakened the binding force of these social cements and ushered in those democratic ideologies that he had opposed with the energy of desperation. Abhorring revolution, he became in reality the German form of revolution.

Certainly Germany had been engaged since 1918 at the latest in an acute process of transformation. But this had been pushed forward halfheartedly and with great indecisiveness. It remained for Hitler to confer upon it the radicalness that made it properly revolutionary, thus profoundly changing a country that had become petrified in a good many authoritarian social structures. Under the demands of the totalitarian leader state, venerable institutions collapsed, people were wrenched out of their traditional slots, privileges were done away with, and all authorities that were not derived from or protected by Hitler were smashed. At the same time, Hitler succeeded in muting those anxieties and fears of uprooting that generally accompany any breach with the past. Or else he turned these emotions into socially useful energy, since he knew how to make himself credible to the masses as an all-embracing substitute authority. But above all he eliminated the one most obvious revolutionary phenomenon of which people were most afraid: the Marxist Left.

Certainly force and violence were involved. But Hitler's real feat consisted in pitting his own rival ideology against the mythology of world revolution and the historical destiny of the proletariat. Clara Zetkin had seen the Fascist followings composed principally of the disappointed of all groups, the "ablest, strongest, toughest and boldest elements of all classes."[10] None other than Hitler succeeded in fusing them all in a novel, vigorous mass movement. It was not destined to last. Nevertheless, for one alarming moment the slogan "Adolf Hitler Devours Karl Marx!"—with which Joseph Goebbels had taken up the struggle for "Red" Berlin—proved to be not quite so arrogant as it had seemed at first. At any rate, his utopia of class reconciliation boldly challenged the utopia of the dictatorship of the proletariat; the idea proved so effective that Hitler was able to draw into his own ranks sizable segments of the working class and incorporate them into his own motley following. To that extent he actually justified his claim to be the "smasher of Marxism." At any rate, he was not the last desperate gasp of dying capitalism, as a good many ideologists have described him.

As a figure in the German social revolution, consequently, Hitler represents an ambivalent phenomenon; the "duality" we have frequently noted is nowhere more evident than in this matter. For we cannot say that the revolution that was his work happened contrary to his intentions. The revolutionary idea of "renewal," of tranformation of the state and society into a militantly coherent *Volksgemeinschaft* ("people's community") free of internal conflicts, remained predominant. Hitler also had the desire for change and a conception of his goal, and he was prepared to connect the two. If we compare him with the political personalities of the Weimar period, with Hugenberg, Brüning, Papen, Breitscheid, and unquestionably with the Communist leader Thälmann, as well, he indubitably emerges as the more modern. Nor can the concomitants of the National Socialist revolution, its blunt radicalness, instinctuality, and seemingly unpolitical avarice, prevent us from calling its author and director a revolutionary. For seen in close-up, almost all violent changes look like "oversentimental and bloody charlatanism."[11] Possibly, then, Hitler's rule should not be regarded in isolation, but viewed as the terroristic or Jacobin phase of a widespread social revolution that propelled Germany into the twentieth century and that has not reached its end to this day.

And yet certain stubborn doubts return. Was not this revolution far more chancy, far blinder and more aimless, than it looks in retrospect to the interpreting mind? Did the changes spring not from long-term considerations but from Hitler's arbitrariness and lack of premises, his inadequate understanding of the special social, historical, and psychic nature of Germany? When he conjured up glowing pictures of the past, was this not a ploy with which he wanted to conceal the horror of the future he was hatching?

Such doubts arise partly because Nazism tended to wear extremely "conservative" ideological costumery. The question is whether in so doing it merely resembled the Communard who poured a few drops of holy water into his petroleum. But Hitler had not the slightest intention of reviving preindustrial forms of government. All the masquerades should not obscure the perception that—contrary to his claim of restoring Germany's past with its dignity, its pastoral charms, and its aristocratic values—he thrust the country into the present day with radical brutality. Once and for all he cut off the retreat back to the authoritarian state of the past; until Hitler came along, the Germans with their conservative temperament had managed to keep open that line of retreat through all social changes. Paradoxically, it was only after his arrival that the nineteenth century in Germany came to an end. No matter how anachronistic Hitler seemed, he was more modern, or at any rate more determined to represent modernity, than all his rivals on the domestic political scene. The whole tragedy of the conservative resistance movement was that its moral insight was so much greater than its political intelligence. Within the hearts of the conservatives, authoritarian Germany, deeply entangled in its romantic retardations, fought a hopeless struggle with the present. Hitler's advantage over all his rivals, including the Social Democrats, rested upon his having grasped the necessity for changes more keenly and decisively than they had done. To the extent that he negated the modern world, he did so in modern terms; and he managed to confer the features of the Zeitgeist upon his emotional bias. He distinctly felt the ambivalence into which he as a revolutionary was necessarily driven. On the one hand, for example, he praised the German Social Democrats for having swept away the monarchy in 1918, but on the other hand he spoke of the "grave pangs" that every social change caused.[12] In the final analysis, if we are reluctant to call him a revolutionary, it may be because the idea of revolution seems for most of us to be linked closely with the idea of progress. But Hitler's rule has also affected terminology; and one of its significant consequences surely is that the concept of revolution was stripped of the moral connotations it had had for so many years.

The National Socialist revolution did not merely shatter outmoded social structures. Its psychological effects went very deep, and possibly this was in fact its most significant aspect. For it totally transformed the entire relationship of Germans to politics. On many pages of this book we have mentioned the extent to which Germans were alienated from politics and oriented toward private concerns, virtues, and goals; Hitler's success was partly due to that state of affairs. For on the whole the people, restricted to marching, raising hands, or applauding, felt that Hitler had not so much excluded them from politics as liberated them from politics. The whole

761

catalogue of values, such as Third Reich, people's community, leader principle, destiny, or greatness, enjoyed such widespread approval in part because it stood for a renunciation of politics, a farewell to the world of parties and parliaments, of subterfuges and compromises. Hitler's tendency to think heroically rather than politically, tragically rather than socially, to put overwhelming mythical surrogates in place of the general welfare, was spontaneously accepted and understood by the Germans. Adorno said of Richard Wagner that he made music for the unmusical. We might add, and Hitler politics for the unpolitical.

Hitler undercut the German alienation from politics in two ways. First, by incessant totalitarian mobilization he inevitably drew people into the public realm; and although this was done chiefly on the occasion of stupefying mass festivities whose true purpose was to consume all political interest, he could not prevent the inadvertent result: the opening of a new area of experience. That is, for the first time in its history the nation was consistently forced out of its private world. Granted, the regime permitted only ritual forms of participation in the public realm. But still, the consciousness of such participation changed people. The whole of German inner life was gradually destroyed by the undermining effects of the social revolution, the whole realm of personal gratification with its dreams, its secluded felicity, and its yearning for nonpolitical politics.

In addition, the political and moral catastrophe that Hitler brought upon the country also served to change attitudes. Auschwitz might be said to represent the fiasco of the private German universe and its autistic narcissism. It is incontestably true that the majority of Germans knew nothing of the practices in the death camps, and at any rate knew far less about them than the world public whose attention had been called, in repeated cries of alarm from the end of 1941 on, to the mass crimes that were taking place.[13] The apathy and lack of reaction to the circulating rumors derived to some extent from the feeling that the events in the camps belonged to that political sphere that had always been alien and uninteresting to them.

This, too, helps explain why the Germans after 1945 tended to repress their recent experience. For putting Hitler behind them also meant to some extent putting a whole way of life behind them, taking leave of the private world and the cultural type they had been for so long. It remained for the younger generation to complete the break, to cut the ties to the past and achieve freedom from sentiment, prejudices, and memories. Paradoxically, in doing so, in a sense it actually completed Hitler's revolution. This younger generation thinks politically, socially, and pragmatically to an extent hitherto uncommon in Germany. It has, aside from some marginal individuals, renounced all intellectual radicalness, all asocial passion for grand theories, and it has shed the qualities that for so long had been peculiar to German thinking: the systematic approach, profundity, and contempt for reality. It argues soberly, objectively, and, to use a famous phrase of

Bertolt Brecht's, it no longer conducts conversations about trees.[14] Its mentality is highly contemporary; it has abandoned the realms of a past that never existed and an imaginary future. For the first time Germany is busy making her peace with reality. But along with this, German thought has lost something of its identity; it practices empiricism, is willing to compromise, and is concerned about the general welfare. The German sphinx, of which Carlo Sforza spoke shortly before Hitler came to power,[15] has yielded up its secret. And the world can feel the better for this.

Nevertheless, Fascist or related tendencies have survived in Germany, as they have elsewhere. What have survived above all are certain psychological hypotheses, though these may have no obvious connection with Nazism or may turn up under unusual, often leftist auspices. Similarly, certain social and economic concomitants of Nazism have survived. The ideological premises have had the shortest span of survival, for example, the nationalism of the period between the wars, the eagerness for great-power status, or the dread of Communism. A certain bias toward Fascist solutions may be seen as a reaction to the transition from stable conditions to the uncertain future of modern societies and will continue as long as the crisis of adjustment lasts. No one yet knows the most effective way to counter this trend. For the experience of Nazism did not promote rational analysis of the causes of the crisis; rather, it prevented it for a long time. The vast shadow cast by the death camps acted as a check upon our even thinking of the way in which the Nazi phenomenon might have been related to determinative factors of the era or to the more universal needs of men, to anxieties about the future, impulses to opposition, to the emotional transfiguration of simple things, to the awakening of nostalgic atavisms, to the desire to believe "that everything could be different, with different truths and different gods of very remote times, with dragons engraved upon very ancient stones."

These aspects of what had happened remained repressed for many years. Moral indignation beclouded the realization that the people who formed Hitler's following, who had perpetrated the cheering and the barbarities, had not been monsters. The world-wide unrest of the late sixties once again brought to the fore many of the elements that have repeatedly recurred in descriptions of pre-Fascist conditions: the cultural pessimism, the craving for spontaneity, intoxication, and a dramatic quality of life, the vehemence of youth and the aestheticizing of force. Of course, these are still a far cry from true pre-Fascist phenomena; all the comparisons between the recent and the earlier movements break on one reef: the question of the weak and the oppressed, for which Fascism had no answer.[16] When Hitler called himself "the greatest liberator of humanity," he significantly alluded to the "saving doctrine of the unimportance of the individual human being."[17]

But it is also well to remember that the Fascist syndrome has so far rarely ever appeared in pure form embracing all its elements and is always threatening to veer over into new variants.

To the extent that Fascism is rooted in the age's sense of crisis, it remains latent and will end only with the age itself. Since it is so much a reaction and a desperate defensive reflex, it lacks a positive shape of its own. This means that Fascist movements are more in need of a towering leader than other political groups. He absorbs the resentments, identifies the enemies, transforms despondency into intoxication, and makes weakness aware of its strength. The broad perspectives Hitler was able to extract from sheer anxiety must be held among his remarkable achievements. As no one else did, he overdrew the ideological and dynamic potentialities of the years between the wars. But upon his death everything collapsed, as it was bound to do; the whipped-up, concentrated, and deliberately manipulated emotions at once fell back into the diffuse, disorderly state in which they had originated.

This dead end was manifested on all planes. For all that Hitler had stressed the suprapersonal aspects of his work, had flaunted his mission and presented himself as the instrument of Providence, he did not last beyond his time. Since he could not offer any persuasive picture of the future state of the world, any hope, any encouraging goal, nothing of his thought survived him. He had always used ideas merely as instruments; when at death he abandoned them, they were compromised and used up. This great demagogue left behind him not so much as a memorable phrase, an impressive formula. Similarly, he who had wanted to be the greatest builder of all time left not a single building to the present. Nothing survived even of those grandiose structures that were completed. Shortly after the seizure of power radical zealots within the Nazi party were saying that "Hitler dead . . . will be more useful to the Movement than Hitler alive." It was argued that he would have to disappear into the darkness of legend, that even his corpse must vanish beyond recovery so that he would "end in a mystery for the credulous masses."[18] The postwar era proved that this had been a vast romantic misconception. What had been apparent by, at the latest, the turning point of the war was once again driven home: Hitler's catalyzing powers were indispensable and that everything, the will, the goal, the cohesiveness, instantly disappeared without the visible presence of the great "leader." Hitler had no secret that extended beyond his immediate presence. The people whose loyalty and admiration he had won never followed a vision, but only a force. In retrospect his life seems like a steady unfolding of tremendous energy. Its effects were vast, the terror it spread enormous; but when it was over there was little left for memory to hold.

NOTES
BIBLIOGRAPHY
INDEX

Notes

On the whole, German language material has been newly translated for the purposes of this book, even when the reference is to an original English publication (such as Alan Bullock's *Hitler*). *Mein Kampf,* however, is uniformly quoted in Ralph Manheim's translation (with some emendations approved by him), currently available in paperback (Sentry Edition), published by Houghton Mifflin Company, Boston. Short references, consisting of author's name and page number only, are fully listed in the bibliography.

The notes are not restricted solely to sources but frequently develop various subjects discussed in the text; therefore, proper names of people appearing in expository sections of the notes will be found in the index.

Where English translations of foreign works have been published, they are mentioned in the bibliography following the entry for the original work.

For this edition the author has cut the notes by about half; readers interested in the full apparatus are referred to the German edition.

PROLOGUE

1. This Ranke quotation is cited in one of Konrad Heiden's books. The author is aware of his indebtedness to Heiden in many respects. His was the earliest historical study of the phenomena of Hitler and National Socialism, and in the boldness of its inquiry and the freedom of its judgment it remains exemplary to the present day.
2. Speech of February 24, 1937, in the Munich Hofbräuhaus; see Kotze and Krausnick, p. 107.
3. Trevor-Roper, ed., Foreword to *Le Testament politique de Hitler,* p. 13.
4. Speech of May 20, 1937; see Kotze and Krausnick, p. 223.
5. Jacob Burckhardt, *Force and Freedom: Reflections on History,* pp. 313 ff. With Hitler in mind, Gottfried Benn in a famous letter to Klaus Mann specifically referred to Burckhardt's observation. Benn wrote: "But here and now you may constantly hear the question: did Hitler create the Movement or did the Movement create him? This question is significant; the two cannot be distinguished because they are both identical. What is really in-

volved here is that mysterious coincidence of the individual and the communal that Burckhardt speaks of in his *Reflections on History,* when he describes the great men who have moved history. Great men—it is all there: the dangers of the beginning, their appearance almost always in times of terror, the enormous perseverance, the abnormal facility in all things, especially in organic functions; but then also the premonition of all thinking persons that he is the one to accomplish things that are essential and that only he can accomplish." Gottfried Benn, *Gesammelte Werke* IV, pp. 246 f.

6. Jacob Burckhardt, p. 339.
7. Thomas Mann, "Bruder Hitler," in: *Gesammelte Werke* XII, p. 778.
8. Kühnl, "Der deutsche Faschismus," in: *Neue politische Literatur,* 1970:1, p. 13.
9. Jacob Burckhardt, p. 325.
10. Hitler speaking to the chiefs of the Wehrmacht in the chancellery on May 23, 1939; see Domarus, p. 1197.
11. *Mein Kampf,* p. 353.
12. Jacob Burckhardt, p. 325.

BOOK I

1. Cf. Dietrich, *Zwölf Jahre,* p. 149. See also Heiden, *Geschichte,* p. 75.
2. Ribbentrop, p. 45.
3. Maser, *Hitler,* p. 34. For Frank's story see Frank, *Im Angesicht des Galgens,* pp. 320 f.; also Maser, *Hitler,* pp. 26 f. Maser cannot, of course, prove his thesis. Nevertheless, he advances his argument as if it were conclusive. Even the fact that Hüttler waited until after his wife's death to legitimize Alois is, to Maser, in favor of his argument, although that fact suggests just the opposite of his conclusion. It is reasonable to assume that Hüttler would have been prompted to such an act of consideration only if he wished to admit that he himself was the father and had legitimized Alois as his own son. All the other arguments are equally dubious. In general, Maser cannot suggest any plausible motive for Hüttler's conduct. It is a very old assumption that Hüttler insisted on the change of name as a condition for appointing Alois Schicklgruber his heir; cf., for instance, Kubizek, p. 59. We must add that the question of who Hitler's grandfather was is really of secondary importance. Only Hans Frank's version could have given it a new psychological dimension; aside from that, it is merely a matter of minor interest.
4. *Mein Kampf,* p. 6.
5. *Mein Kampf,* pp. 8, 10.
6. *Mein Kampf,* p. 10.
7. *Mein Kampf,* p. 18. Hitler alleged a "serious lung ailment," but the assertion will not hold water. Cf. Jetzinger, p. 148; also Heiden, *Hitler* I, p. 28. The episode is also reported in Zoller, p. 49, where Hitler traces his dislike for alcohol back to it. On the incident of the discarded report card cf. Maser, *Hitler,* pp. 68 ff.
8. Kubizek repeatedly stresses Hitler's striking tendency to confound dream

and reality. See, for example, pp. 100 f. For the episode of the lottery ticket (which follows here), see pp. 127 ff.

9. Kubizek, p. 79.

10. *Ibid.*, pp. 140 ff. However, the scene appears to have been exaggerated and retouched. On the whole, Kubizek's credibility is suspect. His memoirs were conceived with the intention of glorifying Hitler. The value of the book consists less in demonstrable facts than in the descriptions and character judgments that quite often emerge against the author's will.

11. *Mein Kampf*, p. 5. Hitler speaks of the "lovely dream" on p. 18. Cf. the letter to Kubizek dated August 4, 1933, in which Hitler speaks of the "best years of my life"; facsimile in Kubizek, p. 32.

12. Oral communication from Albert Speer. On Hitler's fantasy of withdrawing from politics see *Tischgespräche*, pp. 167 f.

13. Cf. Andics, p. 192. Also, for this and the previously mentioned facts and statistics: Jenks, pp. 113 ff. In 1913, 29 per cent of the students in the Faculty of Medicine were Jews, 20.5 per cent in the Faculty of Law, and 16.3 per cent in the Faculty of Philosophy. By contrast, the Jewish proportion among criminals was 6.3 per cent, considerably lower than the Jewish proportion in the population at large. Cf. Jenks, pp. 121 f.

14. *Mein Kampf*, p. 19. The following "classification list" is printed in Heiden, *Hitler* I, p. 30 (*Der Führer*, p. 52).

15. *Mein Kampf*, p. 20.

16. *Ibid.*, p. 20.

17. Quoted in Maser, *Hitler*, pp. 82 ff. Cf. also the report of the Vienna Gestapo dated December 30, 1941, quoted in Smith, p. 113.

18. *Mein Kampf*, pp. 21 f.

19. We owe the precise calculation of Hitler's monthly income to Franz Jetzinger, who with pedantic ingenuity has tracked down all the sources of such income. The comparison to the earnings of a junior magistrate is also his. It is interesting to note, incidentally, that at this time Mussolini was employed in Austrian Trent as editor-in-chief of *L'Avvenire del Lavoratore* and secretary of the socialist Labor Bureau. For these two jobs he received a total income of 120 crowns—not much more than Hitler's income as one of the unemployed. See Kirkpatrick, *Mussolini*.

20. Kubizek, pp. 126, 210–20, 256 f., 307. Also Jetzinger, pp. 194 ff. For Hitler's remark that he heard *Tristan* in Vienna thirty or forty times, see Cameron and Stevens, *Hitler's Secret Conversations*, pp. 270 f. Jenks, p. 202, has shown that during Hitler's years in Vienna Richard Wagner was incontestably the most popular operatic composer; at the Hofoper alone Wagner operas were given on at least 426 evenings during that period.

21. *Tischgespräche*, pp. 275, 323, 422. Also Kubizek, p. 199, describes Hitler venting his anger upon the Academy. This must refer to his first rejection, since Kubizek was not in Vienna at the time of the second rejection and saw nothing of Hitler again after he returned.

22. *Mein Kampf*, p. 23. In much the same sense Stefan Zweig notes in *Die Welt von gestern*, p. 50, "the worst threat that existed in the bourgeois world was falling back into the proletariat." See also Heiden, *Geschichte*, p. 16.

23. Greiner, p. 25. Greiner's memories of Hitler raise many questions. In contrast to Kubizek he has no proof of the close acquaintanceship that he claims to have had with Hitler. Nevertheless, his work does contain a number of hints that increase our knowledge. His evidence can be used, however, only to the extent that it is supported by other accounts, or by other examples of similar behavior on Hitler's part.

24. *Mein Kampf*, p. 40.

25. Cf. Wilfried Daim, *Der Mann, der Hitler die Ideen gab.* Lanz considered Hitler his disciple; he named, among other disciples who had early seen the importance of his doctrines, Lord Kitchener and Lenin! This fact sheds considerable light on Lanz himself and the pathological structure of his thought. His principal work, published in 1905, bore the illuminating title: *Theozoologie oder die Kunde von den Sodoms-Äfflingen und dem Götter-Elektron. Eine Einführung in die älteste und neueste Weltanschauung und eine Rechtfertigung des Fürstentumes und des Adels* ("Theo-zoology or the Lore of the Sodom-Apelings and the Electron of the Gods. An Introduction into the Oldest and Newest Philosophy and a Justification of Royalty and Nobility"). The blue-blond "Arioheroicans" were in his view "masterpieces of the gods," equipped with electric organs and even transmitters. By eugenic concentration and breeding for purity the Arioheroic race was to be redeveloped and once again provided with the divine electromagnetic-radiological organs and powers it had lost. The age's anxiety feelings, elitist leanings toward secret societies, fashionable idolization of Science by dabblers in the sciences, all tied together by a considerable dose of intellectual and personal fraud, combined to shape this doctrine.

    Daim surely overestimates Lanz's influence on Hitler; it seems certain that this influence did not extend beyond the limits described in the text. The situation is obviously different in regard to several other Nazi leaders, such as Darré and above all Heinrich Himmler. Directly or indirectly, in both the breeding catalogues of the SS Race and Settlement Bureau and in the practice of exterminating "unfit" lives, or Jews, Slavs, and gypsies, the weird and murderous notions of Lanz von Liebenfels in a way persisted.

26. *Mein Kampf*, pp. 56 ff.

27. Greiner, p. 110. Cf. Bullock, *Hitler*, p. 39; but see also Shirer, *Rise and Fall*, p. 26.

28. *Mein Kampf*, p. 325. The assurance, urged as "a certainty," that Hitler had no relations with women in Linz or Vienna, comes from Kubizek and of course applies only to the time Kubizek spent with Hitler (Kubizek, p. 276).

29. *Mein Kampf*, pp. 55, 69.

30. *Ibid.*, p. 122.

31. Maser, *Frühgeschichte*, p. 92, has a different opinion; he maintains that Kubizek was in the right as against Hitler, but adduces no evidence to justify his view. For the cited phrases from Hitler see *Mein Kampf*, pp. 39 f., where Hitler also admits that his knowledge of union organization at the time he began work at the building site was still "practically non-existent." There is no reason to doubt this assertion. Hitler's anti-Semitism

at this time was not yet thoroughgoing or consistent. As late as 1936 Hanisch, his companion from the home for men, insisted that Hitler in Vienna had not been an anti-Semite. Hanisch presented an extensive list of Jews with whom Hitler had allegedly maintained cordial relations. Cf. Smith, p. 149.

32. Cf. *Jahrbuch der KK Zentralanstalt für Meteorologie*, 1909, pp. A 108, A 118, cited in Smith, p. 127. Werner Maser (*Frühgeschichte*, p. 77) has challenged Konrad Heiden and the historians deriving from him. Making downright assertions on a flimsy foundation, Maser argues that financial reasons would "with certainty" not have forced Hitler to seek shelter in a doss-house. But in calculating Hitler's financial situation Maser has assumed that Hitler's inheritance from his father was available to him as a permanent annuity. In reality it amounted to about 700 crowns and, depending on how quickly Hitler spent it, was bound to be used up sooner or later. Maser is so bent on showing that Hitler had financial security that he even suggests the possibility (and in a later passage terms it a probability) that Hitler lived in the doss-house "because he wanted to study the conditions there."

33. Heiden, *Hitler* I, p. 43. Some interesting details on the home for men are to be found in Jenks, pp. 26 ff. According to Jenks, the home was restricted to persons with an income of under 1,500 crowns per year. It had 544 beds and was the fourth project of this type built by a foundation committed to alleviating the housing shortage. From 1860 to 1900 the population of Vienna had risen by 259 per cent; after Berlin (281 per cent) this was the steepest increase in Europe. Paris, for example, showed a population increase of only 60 per cent during the same period. The statistics obtained by Jenks show that in the eight predominantly proletarian districts of Vienna there was an average of 4.0 to 5.2 persons per room.

34. *Mein Kampf*, p. 34.

35. Thomas Mann, "Sufferings and Greatness of Richard Wagner," in: *Essays of Three Decades*.

36. Rauschning, *Gespräche*, pp. 215 f. Also Albert Speer in a note to the author dated September 15, 1969.

37. Thomas Mann, *Gesammelte Werke* 12, pp. 775 f.

38. Friedrich Percyval Reck-Malleczewen, *Diary of a Man in Despair*, p. 24.

39. *Mein Kampf*, p. 41; also Kubizek, p. 220.

40. *Mein Kampf*, pp. 42 ff.

41. Houston Stewart Chamberlain, *Die Grundlagen des 19. Jahrhunderts*, I, p. 352.

42. Bullock, p. 36; for this whole context cf. also Hans-Günter Zmarzlik, "Social Darwinism as a Historical Problem," in: Hajo Holborn, ed., *Republic to Reich*.

43. *Tischgespräche*, pp. 179, 226, 245, 361, 447; many other similar phrases may be found in the table talk and in the wartime speeches.

44. Robert W. Gutman, *Richard Wagner*, p. 309.

45. *Mein Kampf*, p. 128.

46. Thomas Mann, *Gesammelte Werke* 9, p. 176.

47. *Mein Kampf,* pp. 123 f.
48. For the complex of motives governing his departure from Vienna cf. *Mein Kampf,* p. 123.
49. The description of this affair of the call-up follows the conclusions of Jetzinger, pp. 253 ff. He also deserves the credit for having uncovered the circumstances.
50. *Mein Kampf,* p. 158.
51. Thomas Mann, *Betrachtungen eines Unpolitischen,* p. 461.
52. Around the turn of the century Georges Sorel popularized this remark of Proudhon's. The quotation reads in full: "War is the orgasm of universal life which fructifies and moves chaos, the prelude for all creations, and which like Christ the Saviour triumphs beyond death through death itself." Quoted in Freund, *Abendglanz Europas,* p. 9. "Sacred Hymns" was the title Gabriele d'Annunzio gave to the collection of his poems pleading for Italy's entry into the war (*Gli inni sacri della guerra giusta*).
53. *Mein Kampf,* p. 163.
54. *Mein Kampf,* p. 164.
55. Hitler's letter to Justizassessor Hepp in February, 1915; photocopy in the Institut für Zeitgeschichte, Munich. The previous remark is quoted from Fritz Wiedemann, *Der Mann der Feldherr werden wollte,* p. 29. The cited letter indicates that it deserves credence even in this somewhat deprecatory phrasing; it is the more credible because it trenchantly characterizes Hitler's general manner of expressing his ideas, right down to the table talk of later years. Cf. also Wiedemann, p. 24, and *Mein Kampf,* pp. 166 f.
56. *Mein Kampf,* p. 190.
57. *Ibid.,* p. 169.
58. All these quotations *ibid.,* pp. 182 ff.
59. *Ibid.,* p. 172.
60. Regrettably, Hitler's medical file disappeared even before 1933, and has not been recovered. Hitler's military papers merely note tersely that he was "gassed." The chemical in question was mustard gas, the effects of which generally did not blind, but greatly reduced sight and sometimes occasioned temporary blindness.
61. *Mein Kampf,* pp. 202 f.
62. *Ibid.,* p. 204.
63. Communication from Speer to the author. The remark was made on the occasion of Hitler's visit to Speer's sickbed in Klessheim Palace. See Albert Speer, *Inside the Third Reich,* p. 335. The above-mentioned speech is that of February 15, 1942. In context the passage reads: "How important is a world that I myself can see if it is repressive, if my own people are enslaved? In that case, what can I see worth seeing?" The text is cited from Kotze and Krausnick, p. 322. See also Maser, *Frühgeschichte,* p. 127. Maser quotes a personal communication from General Vincenz Müller, who allegedly informed General von Bredow, on orders from Schleicher, that Hitler's blindness had been solely "hysterical in nature." But on the wartime personnel roster Hitler was recorded as wounded, "gassed."
64. *Mein Kampf,* p. 293.

65. *Ibid.*, pp. 204 f.
66. Kessler, *Tagebücher 1918–1937*, p. 173.
67. Preiss, p. 38 (speech of March 23, 1927).
68. Kessler, p. 206.
69. Winston Churchill, as quoted in Deuerlein, *Aufstieg*, p. 23 (without source).
70. *Mein Kampf*, p. 207. On the question of the red armband see Maser, *Frühgeschichte*, p. 132. Ernst Deuerlein has even argued that in the winter of 1918–19 Hitler entertained the notion of joining the Social Democratic Party. See Deuerlein, *Aufstieg*, p. 80.
71. *Mein Kampf*, p. 208.
72. *Mein Kampf*, p. 206.

INTERPOLATION I

1. Ernest Niekisch in: *Widerstand* III, 11, issue of November, 1928. See also Hitler in the special issue of the *VB* (*Völkischer Beobachter*) of January 3, 1921, and in the speech of September 22, 1920, also of April 12, 1922, which show broad variations on the same theme. The *VB* of July 19, 1922, for example, called Germany the "ideological training ground for international finance," a "colony" of the victorious powers. Hitler sometimes denounced the Reich government as a "bailiff for the Allies" and the Weimar Constitution as the "law for enforcing the Treaty of Versailles"; cf. also Hitler's speech of November 30, 1922 (this speech, as well as those mentioned in the following notes for which no other source is given, will be found in the corresponding issue of the *VB*).
2. *Münchener Beobachter*, October 4, 1919. This is the sheet from which the *Völkische Beobachter* later emerged; the quoted article purports to be a missive from an unnamed Catholic clergyman of Basel.
3. "Krasnij Terror," October 1, 1918, quoted by Nolte, *Faschismus*, p. 24.
4. Hitler's memorandum on the expansion of the NSDAP of October 22, 1922, Bayerisches Hauptstaatsarchiv, Abt. I, 1509. The proclamation of the National Socialist Party headquarters cited earlier is printed in *VB*, July 19, 1922.
5. See the speech of April 12, 1922. For Hitler's other assertions see the speeches of July 28, 1922; April 27, 1920; September 22, 1920; April 21, 1922; and the article in *VB* for January 1, 1921. Rosenberg, who obviously helped to shape the notions about atrocities in Russia, wrote in the *VB* of April 15, 1922, that Russia had "during Lenin's 'government' become a battlefield strewn with corpses, an inferno in which millions upon millions of persons wander about famished, where millions are diseased, starved, and have died a miserable death on deserted roads." The following quotation is taken from Hitler's Reichstag speech of March 7, 1936. See Domarus, p. 587.
6. Karl Jaspers, *Man in the Modern Age*, p. 10.
7. *Ibid.*, p. 63.
8. Bertolt Brecht, *Gesammelte Werke*, vol. 2, Frankfurt am Main, 1967, pp. 561 ff.

9. Thorstein Veblen, *Imperial Germany and the Industrial Revolution*, p. 86.
10. Julien Benda, *The Betrayal of the Intellectuals*, p. 135.
11. Friedrich Nietzsche, "The Dawn," in: Walter Kaufmann, ed. and trans., *The Portable Nietzsche*, p. 84.
12. Hermann Bahr, *Der Antisemitismus. Ein internationales Interview.* Bahr's publication was based on conversations with many German and European writers and people in public life.
13. Werner Sombart, *Die Juden und das Wirtschaftsleben*, pp. 140 f. See also the thoughtful comments on it in Eva G. Reichmann, *Flucht in den Hass,* pp. 82 ff. But cf. also Franz Neumann, *Behemoth*, p. 121. Neumann argued that anti-Semitism in Germany was extremely feeble and that the German people were "the least anti-Semitic"; this very fact, he held, was what made anti-Semitism a suitable weapon for Hitler.
14. *VB,* April 6, 1920. Arthur Moeller van den Bruck spoke of the "German mania for taking over all the ideas of the Westerners," as though it were an honor to be received into the circle of the liberal nations.
15. *Libres propos,* p. 225. After eating, Hitler regularly rinsed his mouth; out of doors he almost always wore gloves, at least in his later years. Cf. also Kubizek, p. 286. The fear of venereal infection was, it is true, the prevailing anxiety of that whole generation. Zweig, *Die Welt von gestern,* pp. 105 ff., speaks of the extent to which it dominated people's minds in Vienna.
16. The quotations and references are taken from, in order, *VB* of March 3, 1920, September 12, 1920, January 10, 1923, *Mein Kampf,* pp. 233 ff. and 257 ff. For this whole context cf. Nolte, *Epoche,* pp. 480 ff., where the central importance of anxiety as a factor in Hitler's conduct as a whole is discussed. Similarly, Franz Neumann in his "Notizen zur Theorie der Diktatur" has pointed out the function of anxiety in the totalitarian state. See his *Demokratischer und autoritärer Staat,* pp. 242 ff. and 261 ff., where the verdict is rendered that Germany in that phase of its history was "the land of alienation and anxiety."
17. *Tischgespräche,* p. 471.
18. Preiss, p. 152; also *VB* of January 1, 1921, and March 10, 1920—which, incidentally, appeared under the banner headline of: "Clean Out the Jews!" The article demanded immediate expulsion of all Jews who had immigrated after August 1, 1914, and the removal of all others from "all government posts, newspapers, theaters, and motion picture houses." Special "collection camps" were to be set up to receive them.
19. *Mein Kampf,* pp. 65, 247, 249.
20. Stefan George, "Das Neue Reich," in: *Gesamtausgabe,* vol. 9.
21. George L. Mosse, "Die Entstehung des Faschismus," in: *Internationaler Faschismus 1920–1945,* p. 29.

BOOK II

1. In the proclamations of the Bavarian People's Party (April 9, 1919), of the Bavarian Landtag (April 19), and in a report of the Bavarian

Gruppenkommando on "The Bolshevist Danger and Ways of Fighting It" (July 15, 1919), the new men were indiscriminately equated with "elements alien to country and race," "foreign, politicizing Jews," "unscrupulous alien scoundrels" from the prisons and penitentiaries, "Jewish rascals," and "misleaders of labor." See Franz-Willing, *Die Hitlerbewegung*, pp. 32 ff. This crude propaganda always put Eisner on a par with the Communist leaders Lewien, Leviné, and Axelrod, all of whom were in fact Russian *emigrés*. The influence of that association has persisted to this day.

2. Josef Hofmiller, "Revolutionstagebuch 1918/1919," in *Schriften* 2, Leipzig, 1938, p. 211. As for the number of victims, the extremely bitter fighting between April 30 and May 8, 1919, took a total of 557 lives, according to the police inquiry. In a report of the army's Military History Research Institute on "The Repression of Soviet Rule in Bavaria in 1919," published in 1939, the total is subjected to analysis. Of these 557 persons "38 White and 93 Red soldiers, 7 citizens and 7 Russians, fell in battle. In summary executions under martial law 42 members of the Red Army and 144 civilians were shot. No fewer than 184 innocent persons were killed either because of their own foolishness or unfortunate mischance. In forty-two cases the cause of death could not be ascertained. Three hundred and three wounded persons were reported." Different figures are given by Maser, *Frühgeschichte*, pp. 40 f. Cf. also Emil Gumbel, *Verräter verfallen der Feme*, p. 36 passim.

3. *Mein Kampf*, p. 208. The reference is to Feder's crackpot idea of "smashing interest slavery"; as one of the lecturers he was trying to popularize this notion in his talks.

4. See Ernst Deuerlein, "Hitlers Eintritt in die Politik und die Reichswehr," in VJHfZ 1959: 2, p. 179. Incidentally, Hitler was not, as he puts it in *Mein Kampf*, p. 215, appointed as an "educational officer," but was carried on the roster as a "liaison man." It is a moot question whether his motive in covering up his real activity was a desire to share in the prestige of bourgeois education or in that of officer's rank, or whether he merely wanted to avoid the dubious repute of liaison man, which implied "informer."

5. The full text of Hitler's letter, which is dated September 16, 1919, is printed by Deuerlein, "Hitlers Eintritt in die Politik und die Reichswehr," pp. 201 ff.

6. In order to lessen Drexler's importance, Hitler does not give his name ("I had not quite understood his name"). Instead, he repeatedly speaks of him as "that worker," or uses similar phrases. When at last he has to mention Drexler as the chairman, he does so without indicating that it was Drexler who pressed the pamphlet on him. See *Mein Kampf*, pp. 219 ff.

7. *Mein Kampf*, p. 224. Also Adolf Hitler, "10 Jahre Kampf," in: *Illustrierter Beobachter*, IV:31 (August 3, 1929).

8. *Mein Kampf*, p. 355.

9. *Mein Kampf*, pp. 293, 353.

10. Cf. the record of the Munich Political Intelligence Service in Reginald

NOTES FOR PAGES 123 TO 137

H. Phelps, "Hitler als Parteiredner im Jahre 1920," in: VJHfZ 1963:3, pp. 292 ff. Phelps also relates the story of the finding of the documents he reproduces. Hitler's romanticizing, exaggerated account of the meeting may be found in *Mein Kampf*, pp. 365 ff.

11. The importance of the program was long underestimated, and it was often dismissed as a mere opportunistic propaganda trick. That opinion over-looks the seriousness and the anxious sincerity of those who drafted the program. Hitler himself, moreover, was at that time not playing the kind of part that this interpretation assumes. Recently, more balanced evaluations of the party program have begun to appear; cf., for example, Jacobsen and Jochmann, *Ausgewählte Dokumente*, p. 24, or Nolte, *Epoche*, p. 392. A different view is taken by Bracher, *Diktatur*, p. 98.

12. On the "Protocols" see Günter Schubert, *Anfänge nationalsozialistischer Aussenpolitik*, pp. 33 ff. In the first Hitler speech for which the full text is available, the speech of August 13, 1920, Hitler used many themes from the "Protocols." Cf. Phelps, "Hitlers grundlegende Rede über den Anti-semitismus," VJHfZ, 1968:4, p. 398.

13. Cf. *Mein Kampf*, p. 170, where Hitler states that "movements with a definite spiritual foundation . . . can . . . only be broken with tech-nical instruments of power if these physical weapons are at the same time the support of a new thought, idea or philosophy." Two pages further on he writes: "Any attempt to combat a philosophy with methods of violence will fail in the end, unless the fight takes the form of attack for a new spiritual attitude." Similar statements may be found in Hitler's speech of August 13, 1920, VJHfZ, 1968:4, pp. 415, 417.

14. Rauschning, *Gespräche*, pp. 174 f.

15. *Mein Kampf*, p. 485.

16. Deuerlein, "Eintritt," p. 211 (Doc. 19) and p. 215 (Doc. 24).

17. Dietrich Eckart admitted in *VB*, July 15, 1922, that he had personally received 60,000 marks from General von Epp. The newspaper cost 120,000 marks, and in addition had debts amounting to 250,000 marks. This liability was also assumed by the NSDAP. Hitler himself declared that he "paid a heavy price" for his foolishness at the time; and it appears that the party had to bear the burden of these debts until 1933. As one method of supporting the newspaper, every party member undertook to subscribe to the *VB;* from January, 1921, on the membership dues of .50 mark were supplemented by an equal sum for the support of the party newspaper. The circulation remained static at first, then dropped to almost 8,000 before rising, in the spring of 1922, to 17,500 subscribers. Cf. Dietrich Orlow, *The History of the Nazi Party 1919–1933*, p. 22.

18. Report by Heinrich Derbacher of a meeting with Dietrich Eckart in January, 1920. From the posthumous papers of Anton Drexler, quoted in Deuerlein, *Aufstieg*, p. 104; also, with further quotations, Nolte, *Epoche*, p. 403.

19. Konrad Heiden, *Hitler, a Biography*, cited by Bullock, p. 81.

20. Karl Alexander von Müller, *Im Wandel einer Welt*, p. 129.

21. *Libres propos*, p. 151.

22. Cf. especially the speeches in VJHfZ 1963:3, pp. 289 ff. and VJHfZ 1968:4, pp. 412 ff.

23. *Ibid.,* pp. 107 ff. The party committee's reply is also printed here.

24. Quoted in: *Rudolf Hess, der Stellvertreter des Führers,* no author indicated; published in the series *Zeitgeschichte,* Berlin, 1933, pp. 9 ff.

25. Rauschning, *Gespräche,* p. 81.

26. *Mein Kampf,* pp. 504–06.

27. Speech of August 1, 1923, quoted in Boepple, p. 72.

28. Hitler in *VB,* August 30, 1922; also *Mein Kampf,* p. 100. In the party of the early period small craftsmen and small businessmen were distinctly overrepresented—187 per cent in proportion to their numbers in the general population. On this subject cf. Iring Fetcher, "Faschismus und Nationalsozialismus," p. 53.

29. *Mein Kampf,* p. 470.

30. *Tischgespräche,* pp. 261 f.; here Hitler mentions a whole list of his tactics and tricks; cf. also *Mein Kampf,* pp. 504 f., and Heiden, *Geschichte,* p. 28.

31. K. A. v. Müller, pp. 144 f.

32. Norman H. Baynes, *The Speeches of Adolf Hitler,* vol. I, p. 107; also R. H. Phelps in: VJFfZ 1963:3, p. 299.

33. *Tischgespräche,* p. 451; also Heiden, *Geschichte,* p. 109. For the following remark of Hitler, see *Mein Kampf,* p. 467.

34. Kurt G. W. Luedecke, *I Knew Hitler,* pp. 22 f.; also Ernst Hanfstaengl, *Zwischen Weissem und Braunem Haus,* p. 43.

35. Cf. *Tischgespräche,* p. 224.

36. Communicated to the author by Albert Speer. Speer was present at this scene; "Wolfsburg" was the name of an estate in the vicinity.

37. According to Hitler's statement; cf. Görlitz and Quint, *Adolf Hitler,* p. 185.

38. Boepple, p. 118.

39. Cf. Maser, *Hitler,* p. 405, for many details. Further references in Heiden, *Geschichte,* pp. 143 ff.; Franz-Willing, p. 177, and Bullock, pp. 84 f. Bullock underestimates the importance of foreign financial backers, probably because the sources of support have been only recently uncovered.

40. Franz-Willing, p. 182. Cf. also Luedecke, p. 99. Luedecke speaks of a woman of some fifty-odd years who called at the business office after a Hitler speech and spontaneously gave the party an inheritance she had just received. On this and related matters see also Orlow, pp. 108 ff., which contains further references.

41. According to a speech in the Reichstag by Helmut von Mücke, a former naval officer who originally counted among the leaders of the NSDAP. In July, 1929, he had discussed the party's methods of financing itself in an open letter. See *Verhandlungen des Reichstags,* vol. 444, pp. 138 f.

42. Cf. Maser, *Frühgeschichte,* pp. 410 f.; also Heiden, *Geschichte,* p. 46, and Walter Laqueur, *Deutschland und Russland,* pp. 76 f.

43. Heiden, *Hitler* I, p. 162.

44. Boepple, p. 87.

45. Hitler spoke these words as early as September 12, 1923; see Boepple, p. 91.
46. Quoted in Heiden, *Geschichte*, p. 143.
47. The letter is printed in *Illustrierter Beobachter*, 1926:2, p. 6.
48. As the meeting was breaking up, Interior Minister Schweyer stepped up to Hitler, who was feeling himself the victor of the evening, tapped him on the chest "like an angry schoolmaster," and said that this victory had been "nothing but a breach of faith." This is the incident referred to in the quoted remark by Heiden in *Hitler* I, p. 181.
49. Statement by Julius Streicher at the Nuremberg trial, IMT VII, p. 340.
50. Cf., for example, Maser, *Frühgeschichte*, pp. 453 f.; Maser even charges Hitler with having sued for the favor of the monarchist generals. See also Heiden, *Geschichte*, pp. 162 f. Bullock, pp. 113 f., straddles the fence; on the one hand he charges Hitler with incompetence as a revolutionary and on the other hand denies that Hitler intended a revolutionary uprising.
51. *Der Hitlerprozess*, p. 28. The previous quotation, in which Hitler contrasts his conduct with that of the Kapp putschists, is taken from his speech of November 8, 1934. Hans von Hülsen characterized the trial as a "political carnival"; quoted in Deuerlein, *Aufstieg*, p. 205.
52. This reprimand to the court was pronounced by Minister of State von Meinel; cf. Deuerlein, *Hitler-Putsch*, p. 216; *ibid.*, pp. 221 f. for the remarks of Pöhner.

BOOK III

1. Bracher, *Diktatur*, p. 139. Hitler's assertion that he first developed the idea of the autobahnen and of a cheap "people's car" is reported by Frank, p. 47. Hanfstaengl, p. 114, declares that Hitler's cell looked like a delicatessen store. He says that Hitler found the surplus useful for inducing the guards to be even more favorably inclined to him than they already were. On the horde of visitors, their requests, concerns, and intentions, cf. the report of the prison director dated September 18, 1924, BHStA I, p. 1501.
2. Hitler on February 3, 1942, to a group of Old Fighters; cf. Shirer, *Rise and Fall*, p. 90n.
3. *Mein Kampf*, p. 36.
4. *Ibid.*, pp. 212 f.
5. *Ibid.*, pp. 154 f.
6. Olden, *Hitler*, p. 140, and *Mein Kampf*, pp. 24, 31, 493. According to various sources, among those who worked on correcting and editing the manuscript were Stolzing-Cerny, the music critic of the *Völkische Beobachter;* Bernhard Stempfle, the former monk and priest as well as editor of the anti-Semitic *Miesbacher Anzeiger;* and, though with limited success, Ernst Hanfstaengl. However, Ilse Hess, Rudolf Hess's wife, has disputed all allegations of editorial assistance by others and also denied that Hitler dictated the book to her husband. Instead, she maintained, Hitler "himself typed the manuscript with two fingers on an ancient typewriter during his imprisonment in Landsberg." Cf. Maser, *Hitlers "Mein Kampf,"* p. 20; also Frank, p. 39.

7. *Mein Kampf,* pp. 325, 412, 562; also *Hitlers Zweites Buch,* p. 221.
8. Rauschning, *Gespräche,* p. 5; also his *Revolution des Nihilismus,* p. 53.
9. Trevor-Roper, "The Mind of Adolf Hitler." Preface to *Hitler's Table Talk,* p. xxxv. Heiden, *Geschichte,* p. 11, spoke of Hitler's having a "distinct talent for combination." Cf. also R. H. Phelps, "Hitlers grundlegende Rede über den Antisemitismus," in: VJHfZ, 1968:4, pp. 395 ff.
10. Preiss, pp. 39 f. It may be pointed out here that this attempt to present Hitler's *Weltanschauung* coherently cannot be based exclusively upon *Mein Kampf;* earlier and later utterances must be taken into account. There is all the more justification for this approach because Hitler's ideology in essentials did not change after 1924.
11. *Mein Kampf,* p. 662.
12. *Tischgespräche,* p. 346; also p. 321 and Domarus, p. 647.
13. *Mein Kampf,* p. 296.
14. *Ibid.,* pp. 383, 290.
15. Cf. Ernst Nolte, *Eine frühe Quelle,* p. 590. Nolte deserves much credit for having unearthed this half-forgotten and at any rate largely ignored publication, *Der Bolschewismus von Moses bis Lenin. Zwiegespräche zwischen Adolf Hitler und mir,* and subjecting it to analysis. Cf. also Nolte, *Epoche,* pp. 404 ff. The identity of Christianity and Bolshevism, he comments, was also "the central thesis of the table talk," although Hitler even at the height of his power would never have dared to say so bluntly. On the 30 million victims, cf. Hitler's speech of July 28, 1922, quoted in Boepple, p. 30.
16. Printed in: *Der Nationalsozialist,* I:29 (August 17, 1924), quoted from Eberhard Jäckel, *Hitlers Weltanschauung,* p. 73.
17. Trevor-Roper, *op. cit.,* p. xxv, *n.* 9.
18. *Ibid.;* for the preceding quotation cf. *Libres propos,* p. 321.
19. *Mein Kampf,* pp. 138 ff.
20. Our approach here owes a good deal to the summing-up presented by H. R. Trevor-Roper in his fundamental lecture on "Hitler's War Aims," given at the 1959 congress of historians in Munich; cf. VJHfZ 1960:2, pp. 121 ff.
21. *Mein Kampf,* p. 649, 652.
22. *Ibid.,* p. 654.
23. *Ibid.,* pp. 654 f.
24. Nolte, *Faschismus,* pp. 135 f.
25. Albert Speer, *Inside the Third Reich,* p. 440: Speer's letter to Hitler of March 29, 1945. Also IMT XLI, pp. 425 ff. Hitler's speech at Erlangen is printed in Preiss, p. 171.
26. *VB* of March 7, 1925; also Heiden, *Geschichte,* p. 190.
27. Luedecke, p. 234.
28. Otto Strasser, *Hitler und Ich,* p. 113. According to this account, Goebbels made the demand in a speech that he delivered standing on a chair. With good reason doubts have been expressed about this scene; all the same, Gregor Strasser, who is more credible than his brother, confirmed it. Helmut Heiber may therefore be right in his conjecture that Goebbels actually uttered the words in dispute, but not under the dramatic cir-

NOTES FOR PAGES 237 TO 256

cumstances described by Otto Strasser; rather, that he spoke in these terms to a small group, in conversation. Cf. *Goebbels-Tagebuch 1925–26,* p. 56*n.*

29. These drawings cannot be definitely dated. According to Albert Speer, who bases his opinion on remarks by Hitler, the sketches date from this period. On the other hand, Speer's office manager, Apel, who drew up a list of the Hitler sketches in the architect's possession, assigns the date "about 1924" to the drawing of the "Grand Triumphal Arch," the "Great Hall," the "Berlin South Station," and the "Berlin State Library." Some of the sketches are reproduced in Speer's *Inside the Third Reich.*

30. Cf. *Goebbels-Tagebuch 1925–26,* p. 60; also Hinrich Lohse, *Der Fall Strasser,* p. 5.

31. Sir Nevile Henderson, *The Failure of a Mission, Berlin 1937–1939,* p. 282.

32. *Goebbels-Tagebuch,* pp. 92 ff.

33. The report also states: "Violently firing their revolvers and employing iron flagpoles like lances, the National Socialists penetrated the ranks of the Communists. Nine lightly injured and five gravely injured persons were removed from the scene of the battle." A month before, a battle in the Pharus Halls in Berlin's North End had ended with ninety-eight serious casualties. After it Goebbels wrote triumphantly: "Since this day they know us in Berlin. We are not so naïve as to believe that now everything has been done. Pharus is only a beginning." See *Goebbels-Tagebuch,* p. 119*n.*

34. Quoted in Heiden, *Hitler,* I, p. 242; see also Goebbels, "Der Führer als Staatsmann," p. 51.

35. Sales began to rise significantly only after the NSDAP made its breakthrough and became a mass party. Wider distribution was helped by the issuance of a cheap edition costing eight marks for both volumes. In 1930, 54,086 copies were sold, in 1931, 50,808, and in 1932, 90,351; the following year the annual sale passed the 200,000 mark, and thereafter repeatedly exceeded it. In 1943, total sales of the book were alleged to be 9,840,000; cf. Hermann Hammer, "Die deutschen Ausgaben von Hitlers 'Mein Kampf,' " in: VJHfZ 1956:2, pp. 161 ff.

36. Shirer, *Rise and Fall,* p. 134; Shirer refers to a study by Professor Oron James Hale in *The American Historical Review,* July, 1955.

37. Geheimes Staatsarchiv, Munich, quoted in Tyrell, *Führer befiehl . . . ,* pp. 269 ff. In this speech, also, Hitler referred, by way of comparison, to primitive Christianity.

38. Quoted in Tyrell, pp. 211 ff., also p. 196; see also Heinrich Hoffmann, *Hitler Was My Friend,* pp. 151 ff.

39. Preiss, p. 81.

BOOK IV

1. Bracher, *Auflösung,* p. 291.
2. Heiden, *Hitler* I, p. 268.

3. Quoted from Shirer, *Rise and Fall*, p. 136.
4. A study by S. M. Lipset defines the typical Nazi voter as follows: "An independent Protestant member of the middle class who lived either on a farm or in a very small town and who formerly had voted for a centrist party or a regional party that opposed the power and influence of big industry and the unions"; cf. Nolte, *Theorien*, p. 463.
5. Frank, p. 58.
6. Quoted in Heiden, *Hitler* I, p. 275, and in Kühnl, *Die nationalsozialistische Linke*, p. 374.
7. Cf. Albert Krebs, *Tendenzen und Gestalten der NSDAP*, pp. 138 f.
8. The *Daily Mail* of September 24, 1930, quoted according to the *VB* of September 25. Lord Rothermere's article began significantly by calling on Englishmen to change their conception of Germany which, he said, they remembered chiefly as prisoners of war. He pointed out that Germany was not free as other nations were; that the Allies had made the regaining of her full national freedom dependent upon payments and conditions imposed upon her against her will. And he asked whether it was wise to insist upon the ultimate letter of the law. It would be best for the welfare of Western civilization, he concluded, if there came to the helm in Germany a government permeated by the same healthy principles with which Mussolini had renewed Italy in the last eight years.
9. Quoted from Bullock, p. 163, and *Frankfurter Zeitung*, September 26, 1930. Cf. also *Mein Kampf*, p. 345: "The movement is anti-parliamentarian, and even its participation in a parliamentary institution can only imply activity for its destruction, for eliminating an institution in which we must see one of the gravest symptoms of mankind's decay."
10. Hitler's statement is not complete and not recorded in the transcript of the trial; the quotations given here sum up the substance of different texts. See the attempt to reconstruct the exact wording on the basis of press reports in Peter Bucher, *Der Reichswehrprozess*, pp. 237 ff.
11. Willi Veller's letter of August 16, 1930, abridged, quoted from Tyrell, pp. 297 f.
12. A. François-Poncet, *The Fateful Years*, pp. 5 ff.
13. J. Curtius, *Sechs Jahre Minister der deutschen Republik*, p. 217.
14. Report of the British ambassador for July 16, 1931, cited from Bullock, pp. 177 f.
15. The meeting was continued in Berlin shortly afterward. According to the testimony of Ernst Poensgen, Hitler pleaded with the captains of industry to withdraw their support for Brüning, but without success. See Poensgen's *Erinnerungen*, p. 4; also Dietrich, *Mit Hitler in die Macht*, p. 45.
16. Ernst von Weizsäcker, *Erinnerungen*, p. 103, adds to the remark on the postmaster generalship the anecdotal phrase: "Then he can lick my ass on the stamps." Hindenburg habitually called Hitler the "Bohemian corporal" because he mistakenly assumed that Hitler came from Braunau in Bohemia. But it is also possible that he intended simultaneously to stress a certain foreignness and un-Germanness in Hitler, who struck him as "bohemian" in both senses of the word.

17. Carl J. Burckhardt, *Meine Danziger Mission,* pp. 340, 346. Hitler made it clear that he could not be considered bourgeois in an interview with Hanns Johst published in *Frankfurter Volksblatt,* January 26, 1934. Cf. also *Tischgespräche,* p. 170.

18. Cf. G. W. F. Hallgarten, *Hitler, Reichswehr und Industrie,* p. 120. Hallgarten gives details on the expenses of the NSDAP and the amount of support contributed by industry. See also Heiden, *Hitler,* vol. I, pp. 313 f. Some emendations may be found in Henry A. Turner, "Fritz Thyssen und 'I Paid Hitler'" in: *Faschismus und Kapitalismus in Deutschland,* pp. 87 ff. The magnitude of the sums and the difficulties involved are illuminated by Thyssen's unsuccessful attempt to withdraw 100,000 marks for the benefit of the NSDAP from the strike fund of the Northwest Group of the Association of German Iron and Steel Industrialists. When Ludwig Grauert, then business manager of the association, undertook the transaction without obtaining Chairman Ernst Poensgen's consent, Poensgen rebuked him sharply. Krupp actually demanded Grauert's dismissal, and Grauert was saved only when Thyssen came forward asserting that the 100,000 marks had merely been a loan—which he promptly paid back out of his own pocket. Cf. Turner, "Thyssen," pp. 101 ff.

According to partially supported testimony given in court by Friedrich Flick, the Nazis received only 2.8 per cent of the money he spent for political purposes; cf. *ibid.,* p. 20. Partly because of the altogether inadequate source materials, the question of how much financial support Hitler received from industry has become a broad field for speculation colored by ideology. Franz Xaver Schwarz, treasurer of the NSDAP, by his own testimony burned in the spring of 1945 all the documents in the Brown House in order to save them from confiscation by the advancing American troops. In addition, the source most frequently cited—Fritz Thyssen's *I Paid Hitler*—has proved to be highly unreliable. Thyssen himself has contested the book's authenticity. In Monte Carlo, where he was living in exile, he had granted several interviews to the editor, Emery Reves, in the spring of 1940. These interviews were to provide material for a volume of memoirs. The rapid advance of the German armies in France put an abrupt end to the undertaking. Reves fled to England with the documents and later published the interviews, considerably expanded. Reves tells another story which, however, seems a good deal less credible since it was not even accepted by the denazification tribunal in Königstein/Taunus.

In the above-mentioned study H. A. Turner has demonstrated that the very passages historians have hitherto regarded as especially relevant are among those parts of the book that Fritz Thyssen, the putative author, never saw, a fact Reves himself has confirmed. It further reduces the book's value as a source that, for example, the passage in which Thyssen speaks of the "deep impression" Hitler's Düsseldorf speech made upon the industrialists present does not appear in the stenographic record of the interview; thus it is obviously a later addition; moreover, Thyssen explicitly objected to it after the war. The other so frequently cited passage, in which

Thyssen gives a figure of 2 million marks as the size of the Nazi party's annual subsidy, was likewise more or less pulled out of a hat, as Turner convincingly demonstrates. Concerning the size of the actual payments, cf. Turner's conclusions: "After weighing all the facts we must recognize that the financial subsidies from industry were overwhelmingly directed *against* the Nazis" (p. 25). We are still justified in assuming that the greater part of the funds available to the NSDAP came from membership dues. According to a police report, these were so high that they kept a good many persons from joining the party; see F. J. Heyen, *Nationalsozialismus im Alltag*, pp. 22 and 63.

19. Thus Eberhard Czichon, *Wer verhalf Hitler zur Macht?* as one example among many similar writers on the subject; see also the review by Eike Henning, "Industrie und Faschismus," in: *Neue politische Literatur*, 1970:4, pp. 432 ff., with many other citations and references. Czichon tends to prefer general references and unpublished documents, so that his sources in many cases can scarcely be checked. Frequently, too, he indulges in apparently deliberate deceptions, inaccuracies, and faulty references. Ernst Nolte has shown that Czichon reports a payment from IG Farben to the NSDAP in such a way that the reader would think the payment had been made before the seizure of power, whereas the document itself shows that the money was paid in 1944 (Ernst Nolte, *Der Nationalsozialismus*, p. 190). Czichon also asserts, referring to Bracher, *Auflösung*, p. 695, that after talking with Papen in Cologne on January 4, 1933, Hitler met with Kirdorf and Thyssen; but this passage is not to be found in Bracher. There is a similar misleading reference on Czichon's part to *Die Machtergreifung* by H. O. Meissner and H. Wilde. More examples are given by Eike Henning, *op. cit.*, p. 439.

20. The speech was given on January 26, not, as is usually stated, on January 27. Cf. Otto Dietrich, *Mit Hitler in die Macht*, pp. 44, 46. G. W. F. Hallgarten also stresses the differing attitudes among various branches of industry; see his *Hitler;* also his *Dämonen oder Retter*, pp. 215 f.; also Fetcher, "Faschismus und Nationalsozialismus: Zur Kritik des sowjet-marxistischen Faschismusbegriffs," *Politische Vierteljahresschrift*, 1962:1, p. 55.

21. R. Dahrendorf, *Gesellschaft und Demokratie in Deutschland*, p. 424. Dahrendorf argues—and he is surely right about the motives—that the big businessmen supported Hitler in the same way that they granted financial aid to every right-wing party that had prospects of coming to power, not at all as part of a plot. Their attitude, that is, was largely defensive; they were thinking only of reinsurance or, to quote a famous remark by Hugo Stinnes in 1919, they were paying "a social-insurance premium against uprisings." Hallgarten, too, concludes that although Hitler was vigorously supported by industry's funds, this by no means signified that he was "made" by industry; Hallgarten, cf. *Dämonen*, p. 113. We might say, then, that although "industry" did not put Hitler in power, he would scarcely have attained power against its declared will.

22. The full text of the speech is given in Domarus, pp. 68 ff.

23. Speech to the Hamburg Nationalist Club in the ballroom of the Hotel Atlantic, February 28, 1926. The transcript notes at this point "tempestuous applause"; cf. Werner Jochmann, *Im Kampf um die Macht,* pp. 103, 114.

24. Documents on British Foreign Policy 1919–1939, 2nd series, vol. I, p. 512, *n.* 2.

25. Arnold Brecht, *Vorspiel zum Schweigen,* p. 180, points out that the authors of the Constitution deliberately renounced taking over the provision in the American Constitution that only native-born citizens can become candidates for the highest office in the land. Ironically, they did so in order not to exclude their Austrian brothers. Incidentally, the efforts to obtain citizenship for Hitler began as early as the autumn of 1929. At that time Frick unsuccessfully attempted to have him naturalized in Munich. Six months later, by which time Frick had advanced to the position of a Minister in Thuringia, Frick tried to obtain German citizenship for Hitler by appointing him to a civil-service post. The post Frick had in mind was that of a police inspector in Hildburghausen, which happened to be vacant. But the situation seemed a bit ludicrous, and Hitler called off the effort. Next Klagges tried to have Hitler appointed to a teaching post at the technical college in Brunswick, but this too failed. A solution was finally found: Hitler was appointed Regierungsrat with the Berlin delegation from Brunswick.

26. Goebbels, *Kaiserhof,* pp. 22 ff.

27. *Ibid.,* pp. 120 f.

28. On this whole subject cf. Frank, pp. 90 f.; Hanfstaengl, pp. 231 ff. The reference to the unwritten law that no one must mention his niece's name in Hitler's presence is based on information from Albert Speer.

29. For the different versions cf. Hansfstaengl, pp. 231 ff.; Heiden, *Hitler* I, p. 371; Görlitz and Quint, pp. 322 ff: Frank, p. 90. The complaints by Gauleiter Munder of Württemberg that Hitler was being excessively diverted by the company of his niece from his political duties were certainly a significant factor in Munder's removal.

30. Cf. on this and what followed: Frank, p. 90. Ernst Hanfstaengl (p. 242) relates a story that he alleges was bandied about in the Hitler family, to the effect that Geli had been made pregnant by a Jewish drawing master from Linz. Hanfstaengl also reports that Geli's body was found with a broken nose, but he gives no supporting evidence. In response to an inquiry Hanfstaengl informed the author that this had been generally known at the time, but so far as I know the fact appears nowhere in the scholarly literature.

31. *The Dual State* is the title of a study by Ernst Fraenkel (London and New York, 1941).

32. *Mein Kampf,* pp. 474 ff.

33. *Ibid.,* pp. 478 f.

34. Krebs, *Tendenzen,* p. 154; also Preiss, pp. 45 f.

35. *Mein Kampf,* p. 473.

36. H. R. Knickerbocker, *The German Crisis,* p. 227.

37. Heinrich Brüning, *Memoiren 1918–1934,* p. 195.
38. Harry Graf Kessler, *In the Twenties,* p. 426; also Werner Jochmann, *Nationalsozialismus und Revolution,* p. 405; and Helmut Heiber, *Joseph Goebbels,* p. 65.
39. Preiss, p. 179 (speech of March 7, 1932).
40. Harold Nicolson, *Diaries and Letters 1930–1939,* English ed., entry for January 24, 1932.
41. Goebbels, *Kaiserhof,* p. 87. The make-up of the Nazi Reichstag faction after the July elections is quite interesting. There were 230 Nazi deputies altogether. Of these, fifty-five were blue-collar and white-collar workers, fifty peasants, forty-three independent representatives of commerce, the crafts and industry, twenty-nine functionaries, twenty civil servants, twelve teachers, and nine former army officers. Cf. *Reichstags-Handbuch,* 6. Wahlperiode, Berlin 1932, p. 270.
42. For details cf. Bracher, *Auflösung,* pp. 522 ff.; also W. Conze, "Zum Sturz Brünings," in VJHfZ 1952:3, pp. 261 ff.; also H. Brüning, *Memoiren,* pp. 273 and 597 ff. The importance of the information on the favorable turn in the disarmament negotiations has been challenged by historians; there are indications that Brüning overestimated it. For a characterization of the pressures on Hindenburg at Gut Neudeck cf. Theodor Eschenburg, "The Role of the Personality in the Crisis of the German Republic" in Holborn, ed., *Republic to Reich,* pp. 43 f.
43. The statistics on the dead and wounded in the bloody weeks after the lifting of the ban on the SA differ greatly. Cf., for example, Wilhelm Hoegner, *Die verratene Republik,* pp. 312 f.; also Friedrich Stampfer, *Die vierzehn Jahre der ersten deutschen Republik,* p. 629, and Bullock, pp. 213 f., who refers to the account given by Albert Grzesinski. Reliable figures on the victims have not been drawn up to this day. The "Roll of Honor of Those Killed for the Movement," which was later published by H. Volz, gives the following figures for the Nazis: 1929, eleven dead; 1930, seventeen; 1931, forty-three; 1932, eighty-seven.
44. Preiss, p. 194.
45. *Völkischer Beobachter,* August 21–22, 1932. Hitler's scornful reference to Hindenburg's age was made in the speech of September 4, 1932. In context it went: "When today the President of the Reich is presented to me as an opponent, it makes me laugh. I will endure the struggle longer than the President." Preiss, p. 189.
46. Cf. the statistics in Bracher, *Auflösung,* pp. 645 ff.; also the evidence bearing chiefly on the social situation (unemployment) in H. Bennecke, *Wirtschaftliche Depression,* pp. 158 ff. Bennecke's statistics likewise bring to light the remarkable fact that there was no direct, at best an indirect connection between unemployment and voting for the NSDAP. The percentage of votes netted by Hitler's party was much greater in the rural areas, which did not suffer nearly so severely from the effects of the Depression, than in, say, the Ruhr district or even Berlin, where the Nazi percentage of the vote did not reach as much as 25 per cent—approximately half that of the NSDAP vote in Schleswig-Holstein.

NOTES FOR PAGES 349 TO 361

47. According to Wheeler-Bennett, *The Nemesis of Power*, p. 256. For the provisions of the planned constitutional reform, cf. Bracher, *Auflösung*, pp. 537 ff. and 658 f.

48. Cited in Bernhard Schwertfeger, *Rätsel um Deutschland*, p. 173. Hitler's letter, mentioned in the next paragraph, was called a "masterpiece" by Goebbels and is in fact a good example of Hitler's tactics, psychology, and faculty for hair-splitting; it is printed in Domarus, pp. 154 ff. According to Brüning, *Memoiren*, p. 634, however, the letter was ghosted in the Hotel Kaiserhof by Hjalmar Schacht.

49. Franz von Papen, *Der Wahrheit eine Gasse*, p. 250. Here, too, on page 249, are details about the war-games study as given by then Lieutenant Colonel Ott.

50. Rauschning, *Gespräche*, p. 254. The following remark of Hitler's may be found in the *Tischgespräche*, p. 364. On the resigned attitude of his antagonists, see also Eschenburg, in Holborn, *Republic to Reich*, pp. 47 ff.

51. Harold Laski, in the *Daily Herald*, November 21, 1931, as quoted in Viscount Templewood, *Nine Troubled Years*, p. 121.

52. Bullock, p. 243.

53. Bracher, *Auflösung*, p. 691. Hitler himself conceded that the Cologne meeting had been a turning point; at the time, he commented, he had "gathered the impression that his affairs stood very well." Cf. *Tischgespräche*, p. 365.

The version of the meeting presented here has, incidentally, not gone unchallenged. Papen, in particular, has vigorously denounced it (see his letter to *Das Parlament*, III:14, April 8, 1953). However, the account given in his self-justificatory *Memoirs* makes considerable demands upon the reader's credulity. Among other things, he tries to make the meeting appear quite accidental and casual; he repeatedly stresses that its sole purpose was to obtain information. This version contradicts Schroeder's declaration, in a sworn affidavit, that only a few weeks before Hitler had refused to negotiate with Papen. Even if Papen's later assertion is correct, that no offer was made, the fact remains that Hitler felt himself to have been directly addressed by Hindenburg through Papen. At the very least the offer existed in the person of Papen; as a diplomat he should have known this, and undoubtedly did know it. Furthermore, Papen alleges that he conducted the conversation in the interests of Schleicher, and for the sake of supporting Schleicher. Moreover, Papen further alleges, the plan for a duumvirate referred not to Hitler and himself, but to Hitler and Schleicher. If nothing else, then, the anxious secrecy surrounding the meeting reveals the absurdity of this version.

54. The estate, purchased principally with funds supplied by industry, was not given formally to Hindenburg, but to his son, in order to evade the inheritance tax. Hindenburg also worried a good deal about Papen's coup of July 20, 1932. Brüning has recorded: "Erwin Planck, who visited me in the hospital one evening four days before Schleicher's resignation from the chancellorship, told me about the difficulties the administration was encountering because of Hindenburg's fear of indictment, and I have been

told that this was one reason for Hindenburg's finally consenting to appoint Hitler Chancellor." Cf. H. Brüning, "Ein Brief," in: *Deutsche Rundschau,* 1947, p. 15. In the summer of 1935 Brüning added, in conversation with Count Kessler, that Oskar von Hindenburg "slithered into all sorts of murky stock exchange dealings and consequently found himself in a position where he was constantly afraid of 'revelations.' " Count Kessler, *In the Twenties,* p. 469.

55. According to Brüning, *Memoiren,* p. 645, who had his information from Schleicher, Hindenburg allegedly said: "Thank you, Herr General, for everything you have done for the Fatherland. Now, with God's help, let us see how the cat jumps."

56. Kessler, *In the Twenties,* p. 443.

57. Thomas Mann, "Bruder Hitler," in: *Gesammelte Werke* 12, p. 774.

58. Report of Police Detective Feil, HStA Munich, Allgemeine Sonderausgabe I, No. 1475.

59. Hitler to Schleicher, beginning of February, 1933. Cf. Brüning, *Memoiren,* p. 648.

60. Cf. Frank, pp. 121 f. In the published version of his book, however, Frank does not quote the eschatological passage cited here; cf. on this Görlitz and Quint, p. 367.

INTERPOLATION II

1. Gottfried Benn, "Doppelleben," *Gesammelte Werke* IV, p. 89.

2. G. A. Borgese, *Goliath: The March of Fascism,* p. 361.

3. Friedrich Franz von Unruh in a series of articles, "Nationalsozialismus," which was published in the *Frankfurter Zeitung* between February 22 and March 3, 1931.

4. E. Vermeil, "The Origin, Nature and Development of German Nationalist Ideology in the 19th and 20th Centuries," in: *The Third Reich,* p. 6. Cf. also Rohan D'O. Butler, *The Roots of National Socialism,* W. M. Govern, *From Luther to Hitler,* and W. Steed, "From Frederick the Great to Hitler. The Consistency of German Aims," in: *International Affairs,* 1938:17.

5. Friedrich Meinecke, *The German Catastrophe.*

In spite of many accurate observations on single items, all historians who have tried to assess Hitler as the focal point of centuries of history run one great risk: they come dangerously close to the Nazis' own interpretations of their movement. For that is what the Nazis were claiming when they usurped the Hansa, mysticism, Prussianism and Romanticism, and hailed their Third Reich as the fulfillment of German history. But there is something equally dubious about the opposing school, which seeks to represent National Socialism, and totalitarianism in general, as aspects of the crisis of the democratic era, flowing out of its rebellion against tradition and its petrified systems, its social antagonisms and economic weaknesses. For this school Nazism is the consequence of the modern rather than the German character; it is the negative utopia of the total state, such as was evoked in many pessimistic prophecies of the nineteenth century. For National Socialism viewed itself precisely as the world-historical corrective of that crisis. In the German accounts that posit this interpretation, Hitler frequently appears as an overwhelming foreign influence, a "counterpoise to tradition, especially to the Prusso-German and Bismarckian tradition," as Gerhard Ritter puts it in his contribution to the collection of essays in *The Third Reich* (pp. 381 ff.), in which he consistently takes a stand diametrically opposite to that of E. Vermeil. Ritter argues that even the wrongheaded attitudes of which the Germans have been accused were on the whole characteristic of the age: "It is astonishing how many expressions of nationalistic ambition, militaristic principles, racist pride and anti-democratic criticism can be found in the intellectual and political literature of all European countries."

None of these excessively one-sided interpretations can possibly grasp the nature of the phenomenon; the standard Marxist interpretation makes that crystal clear. Constantly hampered by their own actions and by piety toward their comrades who went down to defeat, the Marxist spokesmen have basically never been able to free themselves from the well-known, officially proclaimed definition of National Socialism as a manifestation of the "open terroristic dictatorship of the most reactionary, chauvinistic and imperialistic elements of finance capital." Consequently, if this thought is followed to its logical conclusion, the key personalities of National Socialism must have been not Hitler, Goebbels, and Streicher, but Hugenberg, Krupp, and Thyssen. Such a view is in fact actually taken by, for example, Czichon, in *Wer verhalf Hitler zur Macht?* and by many others. Cf. for this whole subject the instructive survey in Bracher, *Diktatur,* pp. 6 ff.

6. Cf. Note 13 to Interpolation I. During a stay in Germany in the early twenties the Rumanian Fascist leader Codreanu complained, significantly, that there was no visceral, consistent anti-Semitism in that country; cf. Nolte, *Krise,* p. 263.
7. Rudolf Höss, at one time commandant of Auschwitz; see Gustave Mark Gilbert, *The Psychology of Dictatorship,* p. 250.
8. Harold J. Laski, "The Meaning of Fascism" in: *Reflections on the Revolution of Our Time,* p. 106.
9. *Die Herrschaft der Minderwertigen* was the title of an embittered criticism of democracy by Edgar J. Jung, who later became Papen's assistant and was killed during the purge of June 30, 1934.
10. Thomas Mann, *Betrachtungen eines Unpolitischen,* p. 113.
11. Pierre Viénot, *Is Germany Finished?,* p. 97.
12. Domarus, p. 226.
13. Albert Speer, in a memo to the author; for Hitler's rejection of Hess or Himmler as his successor, cf. Speer, *Inside the Third Reich,* pp. 137, 276.
14. G. Ritter asserts in *Carl Goerdeler,* p. 109, that the idea of having fallen into the hands of an unscrupulous adventurer would have seemed absolutely grotesque to the majority of the German bourgeoisie. Rudolf Breitscheid's reaction is reported by Fabian von Schlabrendorff, *Offiziere gegen Hitler,* p.

788

12; Julius Leber's comment on the lack of an intellectual foundation comes from a diary entry; see his *Ein Mann geht seinen Weg,* pp. 123 f. Many Social Democrats secretly expected that Hitler would quickly tangle with Papen and Hugenberg, and they would reap the benefit. "Then there will be a settlement of accounts, and very different it will be from 1918," Prussian ex-State Secretary Abegg threatened in conversation with Count Kessler; see Kessler, *In the Twenties,* p. 447.

15. Kessler, p. 428.

BOOK V

1. What went on at this meeting and how important it proved to be was first revealed during the Nuremberg trial; see IMT XXXV, pp. 42 ff.; also IMT V, pp. 177 ff., XII, pp. 497 ff., and XXXVI, pp. 520 ff.
2. See Domarus, pp. 207, 209, 211, 214; also Baynes, I, pp. 238, 252.
3. Hans Mommsen, "The Reichstag Fire and Its Political Consequences," in Holborn, ed., *Republic to Reich,* pp. 129 ff.
4. Cf. IMT IX, pp. 481 f. and PS-3593. To the very end, incidentally, Göring vigorously denied having participated in any way in setting the fire. He remarked—quite believably—he would not have needed any pretexts to strike against the Communists. "Their debt was so heavy, their crime so tremendous, that without any further prompting I was determined to begin the most ruthless war of extermination with all the instruments of power at my command against this plague. On the contrary, as I testified at the Reichstag Fire trial, the fire which forced me to take measures so rapidly was actually extremely awkward for me, since it forced me to act faster than I intended and to strike before I had made all my thorough preparations." Hermann Göring, *Aufbau einer Nation,* pp. 93 f.
5. Brecht, *Vorspiel,* pp. 125 f. The emergency decree of February 28, 1933, read: "Articles 114, 115, 117, 118, 123, 124 and 153 of the Constitution of the German Reich are for the time being nullified. Consequently, curbs on personal liberty, on the right of free expression of opinion, including freedom of the press, of association, and of assembly, surveillance over letters, telegrams and telephone communications, searches of homes and confiscations of as well as restrictions on property, are hereby permissible beyond the limits hitherto established by law."
6. Goebbels, *Kaiserhof,* p. 271, and Bullock, p. 264.
7. Proclamation by Hitler of March 10, 1933, cited in Domarus, p. 219. On the other hand cf. Hitler's anger when faced with a complaint by von Winterfeld, Deputy Chairman of the German National People's Party, of March 10, 1933, in: BAK Reel 43 II, 1263. Concerning Hitler's letter to Papen, copies of which were sent to Hindenburg and to the Defense Minister, see Martin Broszat, *Der Staat Hitlers,* p. 111. From January 31 to August 23, 1933, the German newspapers reported the following violent deaths: 196 enemies of National Socialism and 24 followers of Hitler. During the period up to the March elections 51 opponents and 18 Nazis were killed.

8. Bracher, Sauer, Schulz, *Machtergreifung*, p. 158. As early as March 17, the *VB* triumphantly calculated that merely by excluding the eighty-one Communist deputies the NSDAP would have ten seats over an absolute majority.

9. *Berliner Börsenzeitung* of March 22, 1933, quoted from Horkenbach, p. 127.

10. The speech is printed in Domarus, pp. 229 ff.

11. Quoted from Philipp W. Fabry, *Mutmassungen über Hitler*, p. 91; for the following quotation, which evidently reproduces the sense of remarks made in the President's entourage, see Brüning, *Memoiren*, p. 650.

12. Rauschning, *Gespräche*, pp. 78 ff. For Carl Goerdeler's assertion see Edouard Calic, *Ohne Maske*, p. 171.

13. Speech to the Reichsstatthalters of July 6; cf. *VB* of July 8, 1933.

14. *Ibid.*

15. Rauschning, *Gespräche*, p. 96; also Luedecke, *I Knew Hitler*, p. 518.

16. Thus in the above-mentioned speech to the Reichsstatthalters on July 6.

17. Heyen, *Alltag*, p. 134; report of the district magistrate of Bad Kreuznach.

18. François-Poncet, *The Fateful Years*, pp. 67 f.

19. Golo Mann, *Deutsche Geschichte*, p. 804.

20. Gottfried Benn, "Antwort an die literarischen Emigranten," *Gesammelte Werke* IV, p. 245.

21. Bracher, *Diktatur*, p. 271.

22. Edgar J. Jung, "Neubelebung von Weimar?" in: *Deutsche Rundschau*, June, 1932. For the remark of Paul Valéry, see Thomas Mann, *Nachlese. Prosa 1951–55*, p. 196.

23. Gottfried Benn, in the letter mentioned in note 20.

24. Rauschning, *Gespräche*, pp. 151, 179 f.

25. David Schoenbaum, *Die braune Revolution*, p. 150; also T. Eschenburg, "Dokumentation," in: VJHfZ 1955:3, pp. 314 ff; also Historikus, *Der Faschismus als Massenbewegung*, p. 7.

26. Thus to Mayor Krogmann of Hamburg on March 15, 1933; cf. Jacobsen, *Aussenpolitik*, p. 395; here, too, on p. 25, illuminating information on the shifts in personnel that took place in the course of the seizure of power. In the Foreign Service, for example, "at most six per cent were replaced for political reasons," and only a single diplomat, von Prittwitz-Gaffron, the German ambassador to Washington, quit the service because he had political reservations. For Hitler's opinion of the Foreign Office see Rauschning, *Gespräche*, p. 250.

27. See Shirer, *Rise and Fall*, p. 210, for the foreign reaction.

28. IMT XXXIV, C-140.

29. Nolte, *Krise*, p. 138.

30. Thus the British journalist G. Ward Price in the course of an interview with Hitler on October 18, 1933. See *VB* of October 20, 1933; also Horkenbach, p. 479.

31. Hermann Rauschning, *Gespräche*, pp. 101 ff.

32. Cf. report of the British ambassador of November 15, 1933, in *Documents on British Foreign Policy 1919–1939*, 2nd Series, vol. VI (1933–34),

London, 1957, pp. 38 ff. Cf. also the telegram that Martin Niemöller and other clergymen addressed to Hitler on this occasion: "In this hour of decision for the people and the Fatherland we salute our Führer. We thank him for the valiant action and the clear speech that have preserved Germany's honor. In the name of more than 2,500 Protestant pastors who do not belong to the German Christian religious movement we pledge loyal obedience and intercessory remembrances." Quoted from Fabry, *Mutmassungen*, p. 123.

33. *Documents on British Foreign Policy*, 2nd series, vol. IV, report of January 30, 1934.

34. Thus Arnold Toynbee in 1937; quoted in M. Gilbert and R. Gott, *The Appeasers*, p. 82. See also Karl Lange, *Hitlers unbeachtete Maximen*, pp. 113 f. Similarly, Sumner Welles remarked that American attention concentrated chiefly on Hitler's idiosyncrasies and on the resemblance of his mustache to Charlie Chaplin's; Gilbert and Gott, pp. 125 f.

35. Many further references in Jacobsen, *Aussenpolitik*, pp. 369 ff. The episode with Sir John Simon is reported by Ivone Kirkpatrick, *The Inner Circle*, p. 68.

36. Cf. Anton M. Koktanek, *Oswald Spengler in seiner Zeit*, p. 458. On Hitler's reading of Karl May, see *Libres propos*, p. 306; also Otto Dietrich, *Zwölf Jahre*, p. 164.

37. Rauschning, *Gespräche*, pp. 143 f. There are, however, two differing versions of Röhm's intentions. According to one, he wanted to organize the SA as a kind of militia alongside the army; according to the other, he wanted to see the SA declared the official armed force, and the army incorporated into it. The documents, and a number of different indications, suggest strongly that Röhm advocated both ideas, depending on whom he was talking to, and conceived of the first version as a transition to the second.

38. Görlitz and Quint, p. 440.

39. Rudolf Diels, *Lucifer ante portas*, p. 278. On von Blomberg's and von Reichenau's personalities see also Hermann Foertsch, *Schuld und Verhängnis*, pp. 30 ff.; also Friedrich Hossbach, *Zwischen Wehrmacht und Hitler 1934–1938*, p. 76, and VJHfZ 1959:4, pp. 429 ff.

40. Conference of commanders of February 2–3, 1934, quoted from the notes of General Liebmann in the IfZ, Munich, Blatt 76 ff. The "Aryan clause" was a provision in the law for the restoration of the civil service dated April 7, 1933; it stated that all Jews who had not been employed in the civil service before the First World War, or who could not prove that they had fought at the front, must be dismissed from the civil service.

41. NSDAP principal archives, Hoover Institute, Reel 54, Folder 1290; cf. also Jacobsen and Jochmann, under date of February 2, 1934.

42. *The Brutal Friendship* is the title of F. W. Deakin's book on Mussolini, Hitler, and the fall of Italian Fascism, taken from a remark made by Hitler in April, 1945.

43. Cf. Helmut Krausnick, *Der 30. Juni 1934. Bedeutung, Hintergründe, Verlauf*, supplement to *Das Parlament*, June 30, 1954, p. 321. In this case

the managers in the background fumbled the ball and for a moment permitted a glimpse of what the strategy really was. For Kleist and Heines met to have a candid confrontation, in the course of which, as Kleist later remarked, they came to the joint suspicion "that we . . . were being incited against one another by a third party—I thought of Himmler—and that many of the reports came from him." Kleist made this statement before the International Military Tribunal in Nuremberg; it is quoted here from Heinrich Bennecke, *Die Reichswehr und der "Röhm-Putsch,"* p. 85.

44. The question of the individual who initiated the Munich "mutiny" remains somewhat obscure to this day. In addition to Himmler some evidence points to Gauleiter Wagner of Munich, who, however, probably would not have taken any action without prompting from Himmler.

45. Hans Bernd Gisevius, *To the Bitter End,* p. 160.

46. Heyen, *Alltag,* p. 129. The total number of victims during those two days has not been established to this day. The official figures spoke of seventy-seven, but probably twice that number would be more realistic. The estimates that ranged from 400 to as many as 1,000 dead were unquestionably exaggerated. In this connection cf. the "Official List of the Dead of June 30, 1934," IfZ, Munich, Sign. MA-131, Bl. 103458-64.

47. Cf., for example, Otto Strasser, *Mein Kampf,* p. 98; according to this account Hitler waxed enthusiastic over Cesare Borgia and occasionally related with pleasure how Cesare had invited his *condottieri* to a reconciliation feast: "They all arrived, those lords of the leading noble families, and sat down at the table to celebrate their reconciliation. At twelve Cesare Borgia rose and declared that now all contention was over. Whereupon two black-clad men stepped behind each of the guests and tied the *condottieri* leaders to their chairs. Then Borgia, going from one of the bound men to the next, killed them all one by one." Thus Strasser concludes his account of Hitler's remarks; but this bit of sensationalism scarcely deserves credence. At best it may be imagined as a tale told in a particular mood, on a special occasion. But in that case it would not have the value as characterization that Strasser wishes to ascribe to it.

48. Cf. Hermann Mau, "The Second Revolution," in: Holborn, ed., *Republic to Reich,* pp. 223 ff.

49. W. Sauer, in: Bracher, Sauer, Schulz, *Machtergreifung,* pp. 934 f.; Sauer also argues that Hitler, given his premises, had no choice but to kill Röhm.

50. Bracher, *Diktatur,* p. 268. In context von Blomberg's ghastly remark was to the effect that the Prussian officer's honor had consisted in being stringently proper; henceforth the German officer's honor must consist in being cunning. Cf. Görlitz, ed., *Der deutsche Generalstab,* p. 348.

51. Rauschning, *Gespräche,* pp. 161 ff.

52. Domarus, p. 433.

53. Thus David Schoenbaum, *op. cit.,* who has contributed a mass of evidence to support this thesis; see especially pp. 196 ff. and 226 ff. On the revolutionary nature of National Socialism and of the Third Reich as a whole cf. also Dahrendorf, *Gesellschaft und Demokratie,* pp. 431 ff. and

H. A. Turner, Jr., "Faschismus und Antimodernismus in Deutschland," in: *Faschismus und Kapitalismus in Deutschland,* pp. 157 ff.

54. Jacobsen and Jochmann, under date of January 25, 1939, p. 9. Cf. also Hitler's speech of June 27, 1937, in Würzburg, in which he said that never in history had "this painful process been completed more prudently, sensibly, cautiously and with greater sensitivity than in Germany"; see Domarus, p. 703.

55. The Jewish emigration from Germany amounted to:

1933	63,400
1934	45,000
1935	35,500
1936	34,000
1937	25,000
1938	49,000
1939	68,000

Cf. the documents of the Reichsvereinigung der Juden in Deutschland, Deutsches Zentralarchiv Potsdam, Rep. 97.

BOOK VI

1. *Mein Kampf,* p. 682; similarly, pp. 334 f.
2. Speech of January 30, 1941; see *My New Order,* pp. 912 f.
3. Nolte, *Faschismus,* pp. 189 f.
4. Rauschning, *Gespräche,* p. 255.
5. Paul Valéry, cited in Ignazio Silone, *The School for Dictators.* For Hitler's statements on the "crisis of democracy" cf. the speech (remarkable in other respects also) at the Vogelsang Ordensburg of April 29, 1937, in Kotze and Krausnick, pp. 111 ff.
6. Arnold Spencer Leese, quoted in Nolte, *Krise,* p. 332.
7. Wing Commander Archie Boyle to Navy Lieutenant Obermüller; cf. letter from Rosenberg to Hitler dated March 15, 1935, quoted in Jacobsen, *Aussenpolitik,* p. 78. For the *Times* quotation from Lord Lothian cf. Robert Ingrim, *Von Talleyrand zu Molotov,* p. 153.
8. Speech of March 22, 1936, quoted in Domarus, p. 610.
9. Thomas Mann, "Dieser Friede."
10. Robert Ingrim, *Hitlers glücklichster Tag,* p. 107.
11. *Ibid.,* p. 143.
12. Paul Schmidt, *Statist,* p. 292.
13. *Ibid.,* p. 301. However, Phipps changed his view of Hitler during his spell of duty. Soon afterward, he told the American ambassador in Paris that he regarded Hitler as a fanatic who would be content with nothing less than ruling all Europe. He informed his American colleague in Berlin that Germany would not wage war before 1938 but that war was the goal; cf. Gilbert and Gott, pp. 26 ff.

14. Quoted in Ingrim, *Hitlers glücklichster Tag,* p. 133; see also Erich Raeder, *Mein Leben,* I, pp. 298 ff.

15. Joachim von Ribbentrop, *Zwischen London und Moskau,* p. 64.

16. Bracher, *Diktatur,* p. 323. The following remark of Hitler's is quoted in Erich Kordt, *Nicht aus den Akten,* p. 109.

   For the British justification of appeasement, cf., for example, the speech in the House of Commons given by Sir Samuel Hoare on July 11, 1935, quoted in Winston Churchill, *The Second World War,* I, p. 141. At the time Churchill objected to the government's policy, but voted for it with the majority of 247 to 44.

17. Nolte, *Epoche,* p. 288.

18. Nolte, *Krise,* p. 162.

19. Schmidt, *Statist,* p. 320. The probably exaggerated statement that Hitler was for a time close to a nervous breakdown comes from Kordt, *Nicht aus den Akten,* p. 134; it is supported by no other source.

20. Bracher, *Diktatur,* p. 325. In the *Tischgespräche,* p. 169, Hitler admitted that he had "called an election after every coup; that is enormously effective at home and abroad."

21. Heinrich Hoffmann, *Hitler Was My Friend,* p. 82; also *Tischgespräche,* pp. 155, 169. Ciano spoke in the same sense of the "fascistic rule" of accomplished facts: *Cosa fatta capo ha.* See *Ciano's Hidden Diary 1937–1938,* p. 9.

22. Anthony Eden, *Facing the Dictators,* p. 407.

23. Frank, *Im Angesicht des Galgens,* pp. 204 f.

24. Cf. ADAP, Series D, vol. III. The Italian fighting forces in Spain amounted to more than 50,000 men, whereas the Germans had approximately 6,000— who, however, were constantly rotated. Hitler forbade official recruiting of volunteers for Spain. In keeping with this policy, the German commitment was not publicized, but kept strictly secret.

25. Fritz Wiedemann, *Der Mann, der Feldherr werden wollte,* p. 150. For the episode of the nocturnal conversation with Baldwin, see *Gilbert and Gott,* p. 34.

26. T. Jones, *A Diary with Letters 1931–1950,* p. 251. On Ribbentrop's assignment cf. his remark to Premier Kiosseiwanoff of Bulgaria on July 5, 1939, in ADAP VI, p. 714; see also C. J. Burckhardt, pp. 285, 295.

27. Cf. on this Axel Kuhn, *Hitlers aussenpolitisches Programm,* pp. 198 ff. But remarkably, for the time being, military planning remained largely uninfluenced by the new attitude.

28. Cf. James R. M. Butler, *Lord Lothian,* p. 337.

29. Bullock, p. 355.

30. François-Poncet, p. 114.

31. Kirkpatrick, *The Inner Circle,* p. 81.

32. Letter of May 23, 1936, BAK, Reel 43 II, 1495.

33. Quoted in Bullock, p. 379.

34. Theodor W. Adorno, *Versuch über Wagner,* p. 155. This cult of death can be found in all Fascist movements; it was most elaborated in the Rumanian Iron Guard and would surely be worth a detailed study.

35. Karlheinz Schmeer, *Die Regie des öffentlichen Lebens im Dritten Reich,* p. 113; here, too, are to be found elaborate descriptions and analyses of the staging of party rallies.

36. Cf. Robert Coulondre, *De Staline à Hitler,* p. 246, and Paul Stehlin, *Auftrag in Berlin,* p. 56. The remark about "mystical ecstasy" was made by François-Poncet, Coulondre's predecessor in Berlin, who continues: "Seven days yearly Nuremberg was a city devoted to revelry and madness, almost a city of convulsionaries, Holy Rollers, and the like. The surroundings, the beauty of the spectacles presented, and the luxury of the hospitality offered exerted a strong influence upon the foreigners whom the Nazi Government was careful to invite annually. Many visitors, dazzled by Nazi display, were infected by the virus of Nazism. They returned home convinced by the doctrine and filled with admiration for the performance." (*The Fateful Years,* p. 209.)

37. January 30 was followed in the year's calendar of ceremonies by Memorial Day (middle of March), then the Führer's Birthday (April 20), Labor Day (May 1), Mother's Day (beginning of May), Reich Party Day (beginning of September), Harvest Thanksgiving (end of September, beginning of October), and finally November 9.

38. Thus, for example, Paul Stehlin, p. 53, and François-Poncet, p. 205, who even provides a description of this salute (which had never been used before and was never used again). Incidentally, most of the teams offered this salute as they marched in; the British and Japanese were the exceptions that attracted the most attention.

39. Albert Speer, *Inside the Third Reich,* p. 58.

40. *Tischgespräche,* p. 433 f.; also Heinrich Hoffmann, pp. 196 f. On Hitler's constant fear of a *faux pas,* cf. Albert Zoller, *Hitler privat,* p. 126. Hitler once expressed his dismay that Mussolini let himself be photographed in bathing trunks: "A really great statesman would not do that."

41. Bullock, p. 376.

42. Krebs, *Tendenzen,* pp. 128 f.

43. Cf. for example Hans Severus Ziegler, *Hitler aus dem Erleben dargestellt,* pp. 54, 57, 58, 64, 67, 70, etc. All the remarks and behavior noted in these pages have also been heard or observed by Albert Speer, as he has informed the author.

44. Communication from Albert Speer, who usually sat on the other side of Frau Wagner and so could not miss observing this little scene.

45. C. J. Burckhardt, p. 340.

46. *Tischgespräche,* p. 227. The reference to the symbolic meaning of the Untersberg for Hitler is based on information from Speer; cf. also *Inside the Third Reich,* p. 86.

47. Domarus, p. 704 (speech of June 27, 1937, in Würzburg).

48. Hermann Rauschning, *The Voice of Destruction,* p. 255. Chapter XVIII ("Hitler Himself") from which this passage is taken was omitted in the German edition of the *Gespräche;* it has now been printed in Theodor Schieder, *Hermann Rauschnings "Gespräche mit Hitler" als Geschichtsquelle,* p. 80. The passage is here retranslated from the original German text.

795

49. Rauschning, *Gespräche*, p. 162. Elsewhere (p. 104) Rauschning comments that Hitler's eloquence seemed like a "physical excess."

50. Speer, p. 92; there, too, further references to the relationship between Hitler and Eva Braun. See also p. 130.

51. Speer, p. 94; similarly, Zoller, p. 21. The characterizations of the entourage come from Hitler's personal physician, Professor Karl Brandt; cf. *Tischgespräche*, p. 47.

52. Zoller, p. 21; for the remark cited above see Luedecke, p. 459. The reference to the films Hitler preferred I owe to Regierungsrat Barkhausen, Bundesarchiv Koblenz, who was charged with providing the films for Hitler during the thirties. The catalogue containing some 2,000 titles which could not be shown publicly in Germany can be seen at the Bundesarchiv.

53. Speer, p. 159.

54. Speer in a communication to the author; Hitler, Speer says, considered Pericles "a kind of parallel" to himself.

55. Speer in a communication to the author; Speer adds that Hitler's rejection of the works of Lucas Cranach, for example, was due to the fact that Cranach's female figures did not correspond to his own plumper ideal. Cranach's women were "unaesthetic," Hitler said to Speer.

56. See the illustration between pages 144 and 145.

57. For this whole subject see Hildegard Brenner, *Die Kunstpolitik des Nationalsozialismus*, especially the chapter headed "Der Führerauftrag Linz," pp. 154 ff.

58. Speer, p. 230.

59. Cf. Nolte, *Epoche*, p. 500.

60. *Tischgespräche*, p. 186; the following remark *ibid.*, p. 171.

61. *Ibid.*, p. 446.

62. *Ibid.*, pp. 159, 173; see also Speer, pp. 94 ff.

63. *Libres propos*, p. 253. In *Mein Kampf* he commented: Blood purity "is a thing that the Jew preserves better than any other people on earth. And so he advances on his fatal road until another force comes forth to oppose him, and in a mighty struggle hurls the heaven-stormer back to Lucifer." *Mein Kampf*, p. 662.

64. Klaus Dörner, "Nationalsozialismus und Lebensvernichtung," in: VJHfZ 1967:2, p. 131; also Domarus, p. 717, where Hitler declares in the course of a party rally proclamation: "But Germany has experienced her greatest revolution as a consequence of the first policy of racial hygiene ever systematically undertaken in this country. The results of this German racial policy will be more decisive for the future of our nation than the effects of all other laws. For they create the new man."

65. *Mein Kampf*, p. 688. The speech to the officers is printed in Jacobsen and Jochmann, under the date of January 25, 1939.

66. Speer, p. 138.

67. Domarus, p. 974.

68. Cf. Jacobsen, *Aussenpolitik*, p. 435. For Hitler's attacks on the intellectuals cf. the speeches of April 29, 1937, and May 20, 1937, printed in Kotze and Krausnick, pp. 149 f. and 241 f.

69. Nolte, *Faschismus,* p. 325.
70. Situation report by the district magistrate of Bad Kreuznach, quoted in Heyen, pp. 290 f., with further such references.
71. Heiden, *Hitler* II, pp. 215, 251.
72. Italian Ambassador Attolico in conversation with Carl Jacob Burckhardt. See C. J. Burckhardt, p. 307. Cf. also Hitler's remark in *Tischgespräche,* p. 341, that the Foreign Office was "a hodgepodge of nobodies." For the remark on the generals cf. Fabian von Schlabrendorff, *Offiziere gegen Hitler,* p. 60; for the remark on the diplomats, H. Rauschning, *Gespräche,* pp. 249 ff.
73. IMT XXXI, 2949-PS, pp. 368 ff.
74. Seyss-Inquart's memorandum of September 9, 1945, IMT XXXII, 3254-PS, p. 70.
75. *Neue Basler Zeitung,* March 16, 1938, quoted in M. Domarus, p. 822.
76. Cf. Bracher, *Diktatur,* p. 338.
77. Stefan Zweig, *Die Welt von gestern,* pp. 446 f.
78. *Ibid.,* p. 448.
79. C. J. Burckhardt, p. 157; for Chamberlain's remark see Bernd-Jürgen Wandt, *München 1938,* p. 26.
80. *Ciano's Hidden Diary 1937–1938,* p. 114. See also Kirkpatrick, *Mussolini.*
81. Henderson to Ribbentrop on May 21, 1938, ADAP II, No. 184. Similarly, on April 22, Undersecretary Butler told a representative of the German Embassy in London that England was aware that Germany would reach her next goal (he mentioned the Czechoslovak question); *ibid.,* I, No. 750.
82. IMT XXV, 388-PS, pp. 422, 434.
83. Cf. Gilbert and Gott, p. 99, also p. 89. Chamberlain made his remark in his radio address of September 27, 1938; London *Times* of September 28, 1938. At this time the Czech ambassador in Rome, F. K. Chvalkovsky, commented to Mussolini that "Bohemia is completely unknown in England. Once, when he was a student in London, he was given a violin to play at a party, simply because it was known that he was a Czech. There was a confusion of thought between Bohemians and gypsies." *Ciano's Hidden Diary 1937–1938,* p. 174.
84. Duff Cooper, *Old Men Forget,* p. 229. The account of the meeting is based upon Paul Schmidt, *Statist,* pp. 395 ff., on the minutes of the meeting, and on a letter of Chamberlain's, both reprinted in Freund, *Weltgeschichte* I, pp. 133 ff.
85. Notes by Ivone Kirkpatrick, quoted in Bullock, p. 461.
86. Cf. Shirer, *Rise and Fall,* p. 398. Hitler's speech is printed in *My New Order,* pp. 517 ff.
87. Kirkpatrick's notes, quoted by Bullock, p. 461; see also Paul Schmidt, *Statist,* p. 409.
88. Shirer, *Rise and Fall,* p. 399. The same behavior has been recorded by many other observers; cf., for example, P. Schmidt, *Statist,* p. 410; Fritz Wiedemann, pp. 176 f.; Kordt, *Nicht aus den Akten,* pp. 259 f., 265 ff. C. J. Burckhardt wrote to a friend at the end of August that it was impossible to imagine "the horror, the despair of the masses when the talk of war

797

began again. . . . Never have I so keenly felt that the peoples are not responsible for the crimes of their leaders." *Meine Danziger Mission*, p. 155.

89. Cf. Peter Hoffmann, *Widerstand, Staatsstreich, Attentat*, p. 79. In Paris, in the course of his visits there that spring, Goerdeler met chiefly with Pierre Bertaux and Alexis Léger (who as a poet uses the pseudonym of St.-John Perse), then the highest-ranking official at the Quai d'Orsay.

90. *Ibid.*, p. 83. Beck would have considered a public statement of readiness to aid Czechoslovakia and a demonstration of military firmness "certain proof."

91. On Halder's relationship to Hitler cf. Helmut Krausnick, "Vorgeschichte und Beginn des militärischen Widerstandes gegen Hitler," in: *Die Vollmacht des Gewissens*, p. 338, and H. B. Gisevius, *To the Bitter End*, pp. 288 f. Gisevius's account carries special weight since he was among the sharpest critics of Halder. Also Gerhard Ritter, *Carl Goerdeler*, p. 184.

92. It appears that Canaris and Oster were informed of this plan and approved it—in large part on the grounds that only in this way could the problem of the oath of loyalty to Hitler personally be abruptly eliminated—that problem which had so fateful an effect right up to the twentieth of July.

93. Hans Rothfels, *Opposition gegen Hitler*, p. 68; also Helmuth K. G. Rönnefarth, *Die Sudetenkrise* I, p. 506.

94. Ritter, *Goerdeler*, pp. 198 f. Shortly after the Munich conference Nevile Henderson wrote to the same effect: "As things stand, by preserving peace we have saved Hitler and his regime." Klaus-Jürgen Müller, *Das Heer und Hitler*, p. 378. Here once again, incidentally, Hitler followed up on his success by promptly dismissing a number of army officers, such as General Adam, who had emerged as oppositionists, thus snatching important key positions from the Opposition.

95. *Ciano's Hidden Diary 1937–1938*, p. 166.

96. *Ibid.*, pp. 166–68. All the concomitant circumstances make it plain that the only question at issue was how to set forth in a treaty the actual existing agreement. Of course, in the eyes of the two Western government heads, the conference also aimed at pinning Hitler down and thus making further expansion more difficult for him; but it is significant that all guarantees were merely set forth in supplementary agreements not signed by all the participants.

97. *Ibid.*, p. 167. For the course of the Munich conference cf. Stehlin, pp. 125 f.; Schmidt, *Statist*, pp. 415 f.; and François-Poncet, pp. 269 ff.

98. *Ciano's Hidden Diary 1937–1938*, p. 168.

99. Nolte, *Faschismus*, p. 281.

100. *Le Testament politique de Hitler*, pp. 118 f. The original text of the notes (the "Bormann Vermerke") published in this book have not yet been made available. This, in part, may be the reason that the language and thought have a pithiness hardly characteristic of Hitler. We must also consider that the manuscript undoubtedly was revised and that the passages cited here represent a concentrate from a long-winded text full of outbursts and digressions. Albert Speer, in conversation with the author,

has argued that Goebbels must have edited the text extensively, and perhaps written some of it himself; the diction on the whole, Speer points out, is much more in keeping with the Propaganda Minister's style than with Hitler's. For Schacht's testimony cf. IMT XIII, p. 4. A similar remark of Hitler's is recorded for September, 1938, in the diaries of Helmuth Groscurth: "He [Hitler] said he had been forced to draw back in September and had not reached his goal. He would have to wage war during his lifetime, he went on, for never again would a German enjoy such unlimited trust; he alone could do it. War aims: a) Dominion in Europe b) Domination of the world for centuries to come. The war would have to be launched soon because the others were rearming." Helmuth Groscurth, *Tagebücher eines Abwehroffiziers 1938–1940,* p. 166.

101. Cf. the speech of August 22, 1939, Domarus, pp. 1234 f.
102. IMT XX, p. 397. Keitel declared in Nuremberg that the German offensive capacity would not even have sufficed to break through Czechoslovakia's border fortifications; IMT X, p. 582.
103. Cf. Gilbert and Gott, pp. 144 ff.
104. See, for example, the report of the British chargé d'affaires in Berlin, *Documents on British Foreign Policy,* 2nd Series III, p. 277. For the quotation from *Das Schwarze Korps,* see Bracher, *Diktatur,* p. 399. Details on reactions to the pogrom in various parts of the Reich in Marlis Steinert, *Hitlers Krieg,* p. 75.
105. The speech, a key document to the understanding of Hitler's mentality, is printed in: VJHfZ 1958:2, pp. 181 ff.
106. Notes by Legation Councillor Hewel, ADAP IV, No. 228.
107. Zoller, p. 84; the following quotation is taken from the Proclamation to the German People of March 15, which had evidently been framed before the conversation with Hácha; cf. Domarus, p. 1095.
108. Quoted in Nolte, *Faschismus,* p. 330; on Chamberlain's speech in Birmingham cf. Michaelis and Schraepler, XIII, pp. 95 ff.; also Gilbert and Gott, p. 164; and Shirer, p. 454.
109. Erich Kordt, *Wahn und Wirklichkeit,* p. 153. For Hitler's later criticism of the operation against Prague, cf. *Le Testament politique de Hitler,* pp. 119 f. For the instructions to the press of March 16, 1939, cf. Hillgruber, *Strategie,* p. 15.
110. Sebastian Haffner, *Der Teufelspakt* (p. 92), a very stimulating, sharply expressed study, which also contains the reference to the three possible courses open to Hitler.
111. C. J. Burckhardt, p. 157.
112. Thus the record of the conversation among Beck, Chamberlain, and Halifax on April 4, 1939, quoted in Freund, *Weltgeschichte* II, p. 122.
113. *Ibid.,* p. 97.
114. Shirer, p. 454.
115. Gisevius, p. 363.
116. Domarus, pp. 1119 ff.
117. Cf., for example, François-Poncet, p. 282; also Grigore Gafencu, *Derniers Jours de l'Europe,* pp. 98 ff. For the following cf. Michaelis and Schraepler, XIII, pp. 211 f., 214 f.

118. IMT XXXIV, pp. 380 ff. (120-C).

119. Shirer, p. 471; Bullock (p. 504) expresses a similar opinion.

120. *My New Order,* 674 ff.

121. Quoted in Freund, *Weltgeschichte* II, pp. 373 f.

122. Notes of Embassy secretary Julius Schnurre on a conversation with Georgi Astachov, the Soviet chargé d'affaires in Berlin, on May 5, 1939; cf. ADAP VI, p. 355; also notes of von Weizsäcker on a conversation with Soviet Ambassador Merekalov on April 17, 1939; *ibid.,* No. 215.

123. C. J. Burckhardt, p. 348. On Hitler's hesitation and his wavering attitude, cf. p. 325 f.; also Bullock, pp. 515 f. The remark on the "pact with Satan" was made in a conference on August 28; cf. Halder, *Kriegstagebuch* I, p. 38.

124. ADAP VI, pp. 514 ff.

125. IMT XXXVII, pp. 546 ff.

126. C. J. Burckhardt, pp. 341 ff.

127. ADAP VI, No. 729.

128. Ernst von Weizsäcker, *Erinnerungen,* p. 235.

129. Georges Bonnet, *Avant la catastrophe.*

130. Freund, Weltgeschichte III, p. 124; here, too, p. 123, the Polish Foreign Minister's declaration of August 23, 1939, and, p. 165, the exchange of telegrams between Ribbentrop and Hitler.

131. The Soviet judges succeeded, however, in preventing the admission of the supplementary protocol as evidence, so that it played no further part in the trial.

132. Nolte, *Krise,* p. 204.

133. Hans-Günther Seraphim, ed., *Das politische Tagebuch Alfred Rosenbergs,* p. 82. "That is," Rosenberg commented indignantly, "about the most brazen insult that can be inflicted upon National Socialism."

134. Report of the secretary, Hencke, dated August 24, 1939, cited in Freund, *Weltgeschichte* III, pp. 166 ff.

135. Hoffmann, *Hitler Was My Friend,* p. 103. For the remark on unused historic moments cf. Hillgruber, *Staatsmänner* I, p. 122.

136. Six separate versions of this address have been preserved, each differing from the others in its stresses. Cf. the comparative analysis by Winfried Baumgart in VJHfZ 1968:2, pp. 120 ff. The version cited here is to be found in: IMT XXVI, 798-PS (first part) and 1014-PS (second part). Concerning the impression the speech made on its audience cf. Erich Raeder, *Mein Leben* II, pp. 165 ff. and Erich von Manstein, *Verlorene Siege,* pp. 19 f.

137. W. L. Shirer, *Rise and Fall,* p. 545.

138. From notes by Sir Ivone Kirkpatrick, Sir Orme Sargent, and Lord Halifax, cited in Gilbert and Gott, pp. 320 ff.

139. Birger Dahlerus, *The Last Attempt,* pp. 104–05; also notes by Sir Nevile Henderson dated August 31, 1939, quoted in Freund, *Weltgeschichte* III, pp. 372 f.

140. Note by Paul Schmidt concerning a conversation between Hitler and Attolico on August 31, 1939, 7 P.M., cited in Freund, *Weltgeschichte* III, p. 391. For Directive Number 1 see ADAP VII, pp. 397 ff.

141. In the negotiations with England France expressed the desire not to begin military operations until September 4: to be precise, as Bonnet stressed to Halifax, on Monday evening; cf. M. Freund, *Weltgeschichte* III, pp. 412 f.
142. Speech of September 1, 1939, The New York *Times*, September 3, 1939, p. 3.
143. Schmidt, *Statist*, pp. 463 f.
144. Stehlin, *Auftrag*, p. 234; also ADAP VII, p. 445. Shirer, *Rise and Fall*, p. 617, points out this noteworthy difference.
145. Gilbert and Gott, pp. 284 f.; see also p. 274 for the following episode.
146. IMT XV, pp. 385 f.
147. Nolte, *Krise*, p. 205.
148. C. J. Burckhardt, p. 351.
149. Karl Dönitz, *Zehn Jahre und zwanzig Tage*, p. 45.

INTERPOLATION III

1. *Hitler's Table Talk*, p. 661; also Hillgruber, *Staatsmänner* I, p. 388.
2. Rauschning, *Gespräche*, p. 12; also *Tischgespräche*, p. 172.
3. Rauschning, *Gespräche*, p. 16.
4. Hillgruber, *Staatsmänner* I, pp. 102 f. In the same conversation Hitler remarked that he would wait until the fall of 1940 before committing the U-boats "with full energy," but that he hoped "by then to have finished with his enemies" (pp. 92 f.).
5. Thus in a strategy conference of July 31, 1944; cf. Heiber, *Lagebesprechungen*, p. 587; also Ernst von Weizsäcker, *Erinnerungen*, p. 258.
6. Thus to the members of the Bulgarian regency council during a conversation at Klessheim Palace on March 16, 1944, cited by Hillgruber, *Staatsmänner* II, p. 377. In the same conversation Hitler remarked that "this war can be waged all the more resolutely the less we imagine that there are any other ways to end it"; *ibid.*, p. 376.
7. The order was couched in the form of a letter that read as follows: "Reichsleiter Bouhler and Dr. Brandt are charged with the responsibility of extending the authorization of physicians to be specified by name so that patients reasonably considered to be incurably ill may, after the most serious consideration of the state of their sickness, be granted a mercy death. Adolf Hitler." Cf. IMT XXVI, p. 169. However, the euthanasia program could not be carried out to the extent intended, chiefly because of the protests from the churches that soon began.
8. Report of the Security Service (SD) for Domestic Questions dated January 8, 1940, cited in Heinz Boberach, ed., *Meldungen aus dem Reich*, pp. 34 f.
9. Address to the divisional commanders, December 12, 1944; cf. Heiber, *Lagebesprechungen*, p. 718. Also *Hitlers zweites Buch*, p. 138. Hitler's various efforts before the outbreak of the war to provide himself with an alibi against the charge of war guilt were so transparent that they proved worthless. Later, explaining his offers for a solution to the questions of Danzig and the Polish Corridor during the last days of August, Hitler

himself said bluntly: "I needed an alibi, especially for the German people, to show them that I had done everything possible to preserve peace." Cf. Schmidt, *Statist*, p. 469.

10. According to *Statistisches Handbuch des Deutschen Reiches* the expenditures for armaments during the years of Nazi rule in peacetime were as follows:

Fiscal Year	Arms Budget (billions of marks)	Total Budget (billions of marks)
1933–34	1.9	8.1
1934–35	1.9	10.4
1935–36	4.0	12.8
1936–37	5.8	15.8
1937–38	8.2	20.1
1938–39	18.4	31.8

11. Cf. IMT XV, pp. 385 f. (General Jodl's testimony, with the remark about the "ridiculous" reserves; in the same context Jodl also stated that "actual rearmament had to be carried out after the war began.") Also Hans-Adolf Jacobsen, *Fall Gelb*, pp. 4 ff. On the munitions situation cf. i.a. Halder, *Kriegstagebuch* I, p. 99. On September 1, 1939, the strength of the Luftwaffe was: 1,180 bomber planes, 771 single-engine fighter planes, 336 dive bombers, 408 twin-engine fighters, 40 ground attack planes, 552 transport planes, 379 reconnaissance planes, and 240 naval aircraft. By the end of 1939 an additional 2,518 aircraft were built; in 1940, 10,392; in 1941, 12,392; in 1942, 15,497; in 1943, 24,795; in 1944, 40,953; and even in 1945, 7,541 planes were produced. See Hillgruber, *Strategie*, p. 38n.

12. Alan S. Milward, in his *German Economy at War*, was the first to show that the concept of blitzkrieg arose out of more than merely tactical considerations, that it was a method of waging modern war that took account of Germany's specific situation. Cf. also *Le Testament politique de Hitler*, pp. 106 ff.

13. This is the explicit or implicit thesis of Fritz Fischer and his school; see particularly Fischer, *Griff nach der Weltmacht* and *Krieg der Illusionen;* Helmut Böhme, *Deutschlands Weg zur Grossmacht;* Klaus Wernecke, *Der Wille zur Weltgeltung.* But see also, for in some cases highly controversial views: Egmont Zechlin, "Die Illusion vom begrenzten Krieg," in: *Die Zeit,* September 17, 1965; Fritz Stern, "Bethmann Hollweg und der Krieg," in: *Recht und Staat,* Heft 351/352; Wolfgang J. Mommsen, "Die deutsche Kriegszielpolitik 1914–1918," in *Juli 1914,* the German edition of the *Journal of Contemporary History,* Munich, 1967; and, above all, Karl Dietrich Erdmann in the introduction to: Kurt Riezler, *Tagebücher, Aufsätze, Dokumente,* pp. 17 ff.

14. Heinrich Himmler in one of his speeches in Posen (October 4, 1943); Himmler was unquestionably reflecting Hitler's view as it emerged around this time in, for example, the table talk, and was expressing it in concentrated form; IMT XXIX, p. 172 (1919-PS).

15. Otto Hintze to Friedrich Meinecke; cf. *Die deutsche Katastrophe,* p. 89.

BOOK VII

1. IMT XXXVII, pp. 466 ff. (052-L).
2. Franz Halder, *Kriegstagebuch* I, p. 98; cf. also pp. 93 ff. General von Leeb, commander of an army group, spoke of the "insanity of an attack." See Jacobsen, *Fall Gelb,* pp. 50 f. Von Leeb also commented on Hitler's "appeal for peace": "So the Führer's speech in the Reichstag was only lying to the German people." For the alternative of "putting the war to sleep," cf. the sketch that General Jodl wrote in Nuremberg on "Hitler as a Strategist," printed in: *Kriegstagebuch des OKW* (KTB/OKW) IV, 2, p. 1717. For the officers' opposition during this period as a whole cf. Harold C. Deutsch, *Verschwörung gegen den Krieg,* pp. 71 ff.
3. Heinz Guderian, *Erinnerungen eines Soldaten,* p. 76. The Hitler speech cited here has been preserved in several largely consonant versions. One of the two versions used here is Nuremberg Document PS-789 (IMT XXVI, pp. 327 ff.); the other is N 104/3 in the Freiburg im Breisgau military archives; its probable author is Helmuth Groscurth.
4. Churchill, *The Second World War* II, p. 74.
5. F. Halder, *Kriegstagebuch* I, p. 302.
6. Lieutenant General Alan Brooke, quoted in Arthur Bryant, *The Turn of the Tide,* p. 147.
7. Cf. Gibson, *The Ciano Diaries,* pp. 191, 192, 225, 332. For the following letter from Mussolini to Hitler see *Hitler e Mussolini, Lettere e Documenti,* p. 35.
8. Gibson, *The Ciano Diaries,* pp. 235–36.
9. *Ibid.,* p. 267. The preceding remark is cited in Raymond Cartier, *La seconde guerre mondiale* I, p. 137; cf. also Michaelis and Schraepler, XV, p. 150.
10. So Albert Speer has informed the author; cf. also the above-mentioned sketch by Jodl in KTB/OKW IV, 2, pp. 1718 f., who also, incidentally, credits Hitler with the timely development of a 7.5-centimeter antitank gun.
11. Heiber, *Lagebesprechungen,* p. 30.
12. Gibson, *The Ciano Diaries,* p. 266.
13. Cf. the description in Shirer, *Berlin Diary,* p. 331.
14. Nolte, *Epoche,* p. 435.
15. Meinecke, *Briefwechsel,* pp. 363 f. The Opposition went into a deep depression. Ulrich von Hassell's diary (*Vom anderen Deutschland,* pp. 156 ff.) speaks of "badly shaken minds" among Oster, Dohnanyi, Guttenberg, and also Goerdeler. Von Kessel, he says, was "wholly resigned and would like to study archaeology." An anonymous acquaintance in the Opposition camp proved to be representative of a widespread mood: he was "inclined to believe that a man who achieved such successes must be walking with God." Von Hassell himself summed up the inner conflict of many conservative Oppositionists in the phrase: "One might feel desperate under the tragic burden of being unable to rejoice in such successes." For the following episode at Bruly-le-Pêche see Speer, *Inside the Third Reich,* pp. 170 f.

16. This was Article 8 of the agreement, stating: "The German government solemnly declares to the French government that it does not intend to employ for its purposes those vessels of the French navy now in ports under German control."
17. Winston Churchill, speech in House of Commons, May 13, 1940.
18. Winston Churchill, *Blood, Sweat and Tears,* p. 334 (speech of July 14, 1940).
19. Hitler, *My New Order,* pp. 836 ff.
20. Karl Klee, *Dokumente zum Unternehmen 'Seelöwe,'* pp. 441 f. For Admiral Raeder's report—which, however, gave the navy a chance for a successful landing "only on the assumption that command of the air is achieved"— see KTB/OKW I, p. 63.
21. Speaking on June 6, 1940, to Sir Edward Spears; quoted in Michaelis and Schraepler XV, p. 261. On November 28, 1940, in a speech to the French Chamber of Deputies, Alfred Rosenberg attempted to interpret what had happened in the same light: "The decadent successors of the French Revolution have clashed with the first troops of the great German Revolution. With that . . . this era of 1789 is now approaching its end. In a triumphal victory it has been . . . crushed when, already rotten, it still arrogantly attempted to go on dominating the destiny of Europe in the twentieth century as well." Rosenberg, *Gold und Blut,* p. 7.
22. This fear of American intervention, always present, had been given renewed impetus by Roosevelt's tough speech of July 19, 1940, which could only be interpreted as a resolute challenge; cf. the notes of Dieckhoff, the German ambassador in Washington, of July 21, 1940, in: ADAP X, pp. 213 f.; also Halder, KTB II, p. 30 (July 22, 1940). From that moment on this fear affected almost all discussions on strategy; cf., for example, Raeder, *Mein Leben* II, pp. 246 f.; also KTB/OKW I, pp. 88 ff. For an overall view see Friedländer, *Prelude to Downfall.*
23. Tagebuch Engel, November 4, 1940, quoted in Hillgruber, *Strategie,* p. 354*n.*
24. Thus at the headquarters of Army Group A (von Rundstedt's) in Charleville; cf. Klee, *Das Unternehmen "Seelöwe,"* pp. 189 f.
25. KTB/OKW I, p. 996. There is a great deal of controversy on the question of when Hitler definitively decided to attack the Soviet Union; cf. particularly Gerhard L. Weinberg, "Der deutsche Entschluss zum Angriff auf die Sovjetunion," in: VJHfZ 1953:2, pp. 301 ff., and the replies of H. G. Seraphim and A. Hillgruber, *ibid.,* 1954:2, pp. 240 ff.
26. *Le Testament politique de Hitler,* pp. 93 ff. In conclusion Hitler also cited Germany's dependence on deliveries of Russian goods, which Stalin could at any time use for purposes of blackmail, especially in regard to Finland, Rumania, Bulgaria, and Turkey. Hitler then continued: "It would not have been fitting for the Third Reich, as the representative and protector of Europe, to sacrifice these friendly countries on the altar of Communism. That would have dishonored us, and moreover we would have been punished for it. From the moral as well as from the strategic point of view it would therefore have been a wrong decision." *Ibid.,* p. 96. On June 12,

1941, Hitler gave a similar justification in speaking to Marshal Antonescu, the Rumanian Chief of State; cf. Hillgruber, *Staatsmänner* I, pp. 588 ff. Another indication that the war against the Soviet Union was Hitler's "real" war may be found in his remark of July, 1940, that he must fight the war in the East before finishing the war in the West because he could "hardly ask the people to undertake a new war against Russia, given the mood that would prevail after a victory over England." Cf. Bernhard von Lossberg, *Im Wehrmachtsführungsstab.*

27. The men involved were chiefly Admiral Raeder, General Rommel, Baron von Weizsäcker, Count von der Schulenburg, the German Ambassador in Moscow, and General Köstring, the military attaché at the Embassy in Moscow. On the idea of the offensive in the Near East cf. Bullock, p. 639. Bullock believes that barely a fourth of the forces provided for the attack on the Soviet Union would probably have sufficed to deliver a fateful blow to British rule in the Near East.

28. ADAP XII, 2, p. 892.

29. Gisevius, *Adolf Hitler,* p. 471. On Hitler's depressed mood during the period before the beginning of the campaign, which was in such striking contrast to the optimism of the military leaders, see, for example, Walter Schellenberg, *Memoiren,* pp. 179 f.

30. Thus to the British ambassador, cited in Jacobsen, *Aussenpolitik,* p. 377.

31. KTB/OKW I, p. 341.

32. Halder, *Kriegstagebuch* II, pp. 335 ff.

33. Cf. Krausnick, "Judenverfolgung," in: *Anatomie des SS-Staates* II, pp. 363 ff., with further references to sources. Hitler personally edited the text of the assignment for Himmler and ordered it included in the High Command of the armed forces directive for March 13, 1941; cf. KTB/ OKW I, pp. 340 ff. Further to that assignment see Walter Warlimont, *Im Hauptquartier der Wehrmacht,* pp. 167 ff.

34. Cf. Nuremberg Document NOKW-1692, reprinted in Hans-Adolf Jacobsen, "Kommissarbefehl und Massenexekutionen sowjetischer Kriegsgefangener," in: *Anatomie des SS-Staates* II, pp. 223 f. The "commissar order" is printed *ibid.,* pp. 225 ff. See also the testimonies of the generals at Nuremberg, IMT XX, pp. 635, 663; IMT XXVI, pp. 406 ff., and XXXIV, pp. 252 ff., 191 ff.

35. IMT XXXVIII, pp. 86 ff. (221-L). Along the same lines Rosenberg informed the "most intimate participants in the Eastern problem" on June 20, 1941: "From today on we are not waging a crusade against Bolshevism solely to save the poor Russians from this Bolshevism for all time to come, but rather we are doing so in order to further German world policy and to secure the German Reich." Cf. IMT XXVI, p. 614 (1058-PS).

36. Affidavit of Otto Ohlendorf, Nuremberg Documents IV, pp. 312 ff.; further data in Helmut Krausnick, "Judenverfolgung," pp. 367 f.

37. Thus to Japanese Ambassador Oshima on July 15, 1941; cited in Hillgruber, *Staatsmänner* I, pp. 600 ff. For Halder's note see his *Kriegstagebuch* III, p. 38.

38. See Alexander Dallin, *German Rule in Russia 1941–1945,* p. 62. For the

shift in emphasis in the armaments program and for the planning of the return march from the Soviet Union, cf. Directive 32 b of July 14, 1941, printed in Walther Hubatsch, *Hitlers Weisungen,* pp. 136 ff., and KTB/ OKW I, pp. 1022 ff.

39. *Hitler's Table Talk,* p. 44. For the intended fate of Leningrad and Moscow, see Halder, *Kriegstagebuch* III, p. 53; *Tischgespräche,* p. 251; Hillgruber, *Staatsmänner* I, p. 643; KTB/OKW I, pp. 1021, 1070; Zoller, *Hitler privat,* p. 143. In his speech of November 8, 1941, Hitler also declared that Leningrad would not be captured, but starved out; see Domarus, p. 1775. A detailed prognosis for the annihilation of the city was elaborated in an order issued by Admiral Kurt Fricke, naval chief of staff, dated September 29, 1941: "It is planned to surround the city in a close encirclement and level it to the ground by bombardment with artillery of all calibers and by continual bombing from the air. Pleas for surrender resulting from the city's predicament will be rejected, since the problem of sheltering and feeding the population cannot and should not be solved by us. In this war for our existence we can have no interest in preserving even a part of this urban population." Cited in: Michaelis and Schraepler XVII, pp. 380 ff.

40. Cf., for example, the references in various conversations in Hillgruber, *Staatsmänner* I, pp. 64, 594, 619, 628. According to Halder, Marshal Coulaincourt's memoirs of the campaign of 1812 were withdrawn from circulation in the winter of 1941–42. See Dallin, *German Rule in Russia, 1941–1945.*

41. Halder, *Kriegstagebuch* III, p. 295; also Hillgruber, *Strategie,* pp. 551 f. The following spring Hitler once more declared that he would have "gladly waged this war against Bolshevism with the British navy and air force as partners." See *Tischgespräche,* p. 244.

42. KTB/OKW IV, 2, p. 1503.

43. In conversations with Swedish Foreign Minister Scavenius and with Croatian Foreign Minister Lorkovič. Cited in Hillgruber, *Staatsmänner* I, pp. 657, 661.

44. To Ambassador Oshima on July 15, 1941, cited in *ibid.,* p. 605. For the opinion of Brauchitsch see Goebbels, *Tagebücher 1942–43,* p. 132. Hitler did commute General von Sponeck's death sentence to imprisonment, but two and a half years later, after the attempted assassination of July 20, 1944, the Gestapo turned up at Germersheim Fortress and made short work of shooting the general.

45. Goebbels, *Tagebücher 1942–43,* p. 133.

46. Franz Halder, *Hitler als Feldherr,* pp. 50, 52. As Speer (p. 239) reports, the ascent of Mount Elbrus was one cause of Hitler's vexation. He took a characteristically exaggerated view: "For hours he raged as if his entire plan of campaign had been ruined by this bit of sport."

47. See Speer, p. 287. In a personal communication Speer has informed the author: "As I have now learned from a member of the RAF staff, there were technical obstacles to carrying out the concept of paralyzing vital segments of industry. There was, for example, the impossibility of finding the target at night, over great distances, by electronic means, and of course

there was the inadequate range of the fighter escorts for the American daylight bombers. These bombers had tried to attack Schweinfurt by day without escort, but had to take excessively heavy losses. All that changed in 1944." About one-third of the German capacity to wage war was dependent on the production of synthetic gasoline; the air force relied on that source for all its fuel. See Hillgruber, *Strategie*, pp. 420 f.

48. Churchill, speech at the Mansion House, November 10, 1942.
49. See Domarus, pp. 1935, 1937 f., 1941.
50. *Ibid.*, p. 1937.
51. Speer, pp. 245 f.; also Warlimont, pp. 284 f.
52. Heiber, *Lagebesprechungen*, pp. 126 ff.
53. Gibson, *The Ciano Diaries*, p. 556; also Goebbels, *Tagebücher 1942–43*, p. 126, and Speer, p. 302.
54. Goebbels, *Tagebücher 1942–43*, p. 241. For the preceding remark see Speer, p. 249.
55. These phrases may be found, in the order given, in *Tischgespräche*, pp. 210, 212, 303, 348, 171, 181.
56. See, in the order given, *Tischgespräche*, pp. 355, 351, 361, 468, 258, and Zoller, p. 174.
57. *Tischgespräche*, p. 465. The parallel to the "period of struggle" first comes up in the speech of November 8, 1942, where it is promptly used several times; see Domarus, pp. 1935, 1936, 1937, 1941, 1943, 2085; also *Tischgespräche*, p. 364, i.a.
58. Heiber, *Lagebesprechungen*, pp. 779 f.; cf. also Henry Picker in: *Tischgespräche*, pp. 128, 130; also Speer, p. 243.
59. Ribbentrop to the Nuremberg tribunal psychiatrist Douglas M. Kelley, cited from Hans-Dietrich Röhrs, *Hitler. Die Zerstörung einer Persönlichkeit*, pp. 53 f.
60. See the extensive references to Hitler's health in Maser, *Hitler*, pp. 332 f.
61. Morell log, cited *ibid*, p. 339; the drug was prostacrinum, an extract of seminal vesicles and prostate glands. On Morell and his methods of treatment, cf. Trevor-Roper, *The Last Days of Hitler*, pp. 59 ff.
62. Report of Dr. Erwin Giesing of June 12, 1945, cited in Maser, *Hitler*, p. 429.
63. This is Röhrs's (*Hitler*, p. 121) wholly erroneous view. On the question of whether Hitler was suffering from one of the forms of Parkinson's disease, or only from what is called the Parkinson syndrome, see *ibid.*, pp. 43 ff. and 101 f.; also the study by Johann Recktenwald, *Woran hat Adolf Hitler gelitten?* which assumes a Parkinson syndrome caused by encephalitis. See also Maser, *Hitler*, pp. 326 ff. and Bullock, pp. 717 f. Probably the exact nature of Hitler's illness can no longer be determined, since no examination with a specific investigatory aim was ever undertaken. Because of the extremely inadequate documentation, none of the various diagnoses can be persuasively supported or rejected; the principal symptom of both Parkinson's disease and the Parkinson syndrome, namely the shaking arm or leg, can also be caused by many other diseases.

64. See Heiber, *Lagebesprechungen*, p. 608, and the speech of November 8, 1942, Domarus, p. 1944.

65. A variety of interpretations has been offered for the motives and the background of this speech. Some see it in connection with the demand for "unconditional surrender" formulated in Casablanca a good three weeks earlier (see, for example, Werner Stephan, *Joseph Goebbels*, pp. 256 f.), some as an attempt by the Propaganda Minister to enhance his personal position and announce his claims to the position of second in command, for with the disintegration of Hitler's personality and Göring's simultaneous loss of prestige, that position had become crucial. Cf. Rudolf Semler, *Goebbels—the Man Next to Hitler*, pp. 68 f., also Roger Manvell and Heinrich Fraenkel, *Doctor Goebbels*, pp. 245 f., Heiber, *Joseph Goebbels*, pp. 328 ff., and the balanced summing-up by Günter Moltmann, "Goebbels' Speech on Total War, Feb. 18, 1943," *Republic to Reich*, pp. 298 ff. On the initiative of the Goebbels-Speer-Ley-Funk combination see also Speer, pp. 254 ff.

66. In England, for example, the number of servants in private households was reduced to one-third of what it had been before the war, whereas in Germany the figure actually increased; cf. Speer, pp. 220, 540. The number of women employed in industry rose only slightly during the war, from 2,620,000 on July 31, 1939, to 2,808,000 on July 31, 1943; a year later it had dropped again to 2,678,000. See USSBS, *The Effects of Strategic Bombing on the German Economy*. Also confidential report of the Economic Conference of February 26, 1943, BAK 115/1942; see also BAK NS 19/1963. For the preceding remark of Hitler, see Rauschning, *Gespräche*, p. 22.

67. This was a visit to Army Group South (von Manstein). Earlier that year there had been a total of two visits to front-line headquarters: on February 17 to Army Group South and on March 13 to Army Group Center (von Kluge). A visit was planned for June 19, 1944, to the invasion front, that is, to Rommel's headquarters in Roche-Guyon Palace, but this plan was canceled at short notice. See Hans Speidel, *Invasion 1944*, pp. 112 ff.

68. Speer, pp. 245, 295 f., 299 f.

69. Krebs, *Tendenzen und Gestalten*, pp. 124 ff.

70. Hans Buchheim, "Befehl und Gehorsam," in: *Anatomie des SS-Staates* I, pp. 338 f.

71. *Ibid.*, p. 329.

72. Rauschning, *Gespräche*, p. 129. For the remark of Goebbels see *Tagebücher 1942–43*, date of March 27, 1942.

73. *Mein Kampf*, p. 679.

74. IMT XXVI, p. 266 (710-PS). Rosenberg's remark is cited from Robert M. W. Kempner, *Eichmann und Komplicen*, p. 97. On the question of the specific decision for the "final solution" see Krausnick, "Judenverfolgung," pp. 360 ff. The concept "final solution" first appeared around the same time, in a decree of the *Reichssicherheitshauptamt* dated May 20, 1941; see IMT NG-3104.

75. See the report of SS Obergruppenführer Erich v.d. Bach-Zelewski, ND, NO-2653.
76. Part of the statement of the engineer Hermann Friedrich Gräbe on the mass shooting of some 5,000 Jews in Dubno (Ukraine) on October 5, 1942, by SS and Ukrainian militiamen; see IMT XXXI, pp. 446 ff. (2992-PS).
77. Cited from Bracher, *Diktatur*, p. 463. On the number of Jews killed in the big extermination camps of the East, see Heinz Höhne, *Der Orden unter dem Totenkopf*, p. 349. The remark of Rudolf Höss is quoted in his autobiographical account, *Kommandant in Auschwitz*, p. 120—where, incidentally, in a curious perversion of ambition he claims some 3 million victims for Auschwitz alone.
78. *Hitler's Table Talk*, p. 426.
79. *Tischgespräche*, pp. 190, 271 f., 469. In the same spirit Himmler, in a memorandum on the General Plan for the East dated April 27, 1942, suggested retraining the midwives in the Eastern territories as abortionists. See Heiber, "Der Generalplan Ost," in: VJHfZ 1958:3, p. 292.
80. Cf. the document in VJHfZ 1958:3, p. 299. For Otto Hofmann's statement see ND, NO-4113.
81. IMT XXXVII, p. 517; also *Tischgespräche*, p. 253.
82. *Mein Kampf*, p. 383.
83. *Tischgespräche*, p. 288, and Zoller, p. 105.
84. A statement by Kaltenbrunner, who was echoing similar ideas in the top leadership of the SS; cf. IMT XXXII, p. 297 (3462-PS). For this context cf. Martin Bormann's memorandum of January 29, 1944, cited in Jacobsen and Jochmann, *Ausgewählte Dokumente*, under that date.
85. *Hitler's Table Talk*, pp. 110, 621. See also the note on Rosenberg's conversation with Hitler of December 14, 1941, in: IMT XXVII, p. 272 (1517-PS). The name "Tauria" was Rosenberg's idea; Hitler preferred "Gotenland."
86. Dallin, pp. 281 f.
87. *Tischgespräche*, p. 320. The metaphor of the "trophy cup" bobbed up elsewhere, for example, in the course of Hitler's nocturnal monologue on January 30, 1933. See Görlitz and Quint, *Adolf Hitler*, p. 367.
88. From the draft by State Secretary Stuckart; see the records of the interrogation of Stuckart's associate H. Globke on September 25, 1945, RF-602, IMT IV, pp. 472 ff.; also ND, NG-3572, NG-3455, and the file notation on the predatory discussion in Göring's headquarters on June 19, 1940, printed in IMT XXVII, pp. 29 ff. (1155-PS). According to Erich Kordt, *Nicht aus den Akten*, p. 393, Calais and Boulogne were to remain in German possession as bases. For Hitler's comment on the Channel positions see *Tischgespräche*, p. 336.
89. Ever since 1940 a National Planning Commission for the Design of German Soldiers' Cemeteries had been at work under the direction of Professor Wilhelm Kreis. The Commission's assignment was defined as follows: "Facing westward on the cliffs of the Atlantic coast magnificent structures will rise as an eternal memorial to the liberation of the Continent from dependency on the British and to the unification of Europe

under the leadership of her German heartland nation. The austere, noble beauty of the soldiers' cemetery at Thermopylae serves as symbol for the German inheritance of the spirit of Hellas's classical culture. Towers soaring massively over the plains of the East will rise as symbols of the taming of the chaotic powers of the eastern steppes by the disciplined might of Teutonic forces for order—surrounded by the graves of the warrior generation of German blood who, as so often for the past two thousand years, saved the existence of Occidental civilization from the destructive tidal waves out of Central Asia." Cited in Brenner, *Die Kunstpolitik des Nationalsozialismus*, pp. 128 f.

90. These examples are taken from the collection of Himmler's letters by Helmut Heiber, *Reichsführer!* . . . and in order of quotation may be found on pp. 194, 222 f., 251, 145, 95. See also Heiber's foreword, especially pp. 22 f.

91. Zoller, p. 73, and *Libres propos*, p. 123. On Hitler's superstitiousness see *Tischgespräche*, pp. 166 f. and 333.

92. *Hitler e Mussolini*, pp. 165 f., cited from Bullock, p. 706. Schmidt, *Statist*, relates that Hitler gave Mussolini "a regular tongue-lashing." Mussolini, Schmidt wrote, had been "so excited by the news of the air raid on Rome that after his return from Rome he urgently requested my notes on the conversations. He had not been able to follow them, we were told."

93. Heiber, *Lagebesprechungen*, p. 231 (on May 20, 1943).

94. Speer, p. 301.

95. Goebbels, *Tagebücher 1942–43*, pp. 392 ff. For Hitler's remark to Ribbentrop see *Zwischen London und Moskau*, p. 265.

BOOK VIII

1. Himmler, referring to Hitler's orders. What must be achieved, he stated in a letter to SS leader and Police Chief Prützmann dated September 7, 1943, was a situation in which "no human being, no cattle, not a bag of grain, not a railroad track remains behind; not a house remains standing, not a mine exists that has not been wrecked for years to come, not a well that has not been poisoned. The enemy must really find a totally scorched and destroyed country. . . . Do everything that is humanly possible." Quoted from Heiber, *Reichsführer!* . . . , p. 233.

2. For example, Helmuth James Graf von Moltke and the majority of his friends belonging to the Kreisau Circle. George F. Kennan called Count von Moltke "the greatest person, morally, and the largest and most enlightened in his concepts, that I met on either side of the battle lines"; George F. Kennan, *Memoirs 1925–1950*, p. 121.

3. See Schellenberg, pp. 279 ff. On Himmler's affidavit, see Felix Kersten, *Totenkopf und Treue*, pp. 209 ff. After reading this medical report (which, however, was prepared without an examination of the patient), Kersten concluded that Hitler belonged in a mental hospital, not in the Führer's

headquarters. For the entire subject of the "resistance" within the SS, its motives and its various initiatives, see Höhne, pp. 448 ff.

4. Cited in Dietrich Ehlers, *Technik und Moral einer Verschwörung*, p. 102. It is a common misunderstanding, probably first voiced by Bullock, p. 736 f., that the Kreisau Circle consisted merely of thinkers and that its members were even proud of their contempt for all action; cf. especially Ger van Roon, *Neuordnung im Widerstand*, where ample evidence is presented to refute this notion.

5. See Ehlers, p. 93. For the principle arguments against the German nationalist conspirators see Hannah Arendt, *Eichmann in Jerusalem*, pp. 98 ff.

6. Inquiries among the workers, inspired by the Jesuit priest Alfred Delp, who belonged to the Kreisau Circle, yielded rather discouraging results. Von Trott's memoranda also speak of widespread passivity in the working class; cf. Hans Mommsen, "Gesellschaftsbild und Verfassungspläne des deutschen Widerstands," in Schmitthenner and Buchheim, ed., *Der Deutsche Widerstand gegen Hitler*, p. 75. A Social Democratic opinion poll taken in 1942 came to the conclusion: "We will not be able to bring the masses out into the streets"; see Emil Henk, *Die Tragödie des 20. Juli 1944*, pp. 21 ff., and Allen Welsh Dulles, *Germany's Underground*, p. 108. During the war significant resistance by the radical Left existed only after the beginning of the attack on the Soviet Union. That resistance came to a focus in the "Rote Kapelle" headed by Lieutenant Harro Schulze-Boysen and Administrative Secretary (Oberregierungsrat) Arvid Harnack; some of the members engaged in espionage for the Soviet Union. In August, 1942, some one hundred persons were arrested in connection with these activities; many of them were executed shortly afterward. Another group around Anton Saefkow was caught early in July, 1944; its fate, as we shall see below, played a part in precipitating Stauffenberg's decision to act.

7. Ehlers, p. 143. For the biography of Stauffenberg see now Christian Müller, *Oberst i.G. Stauffenberg*. Incidentally, when Stefan George died in Minusio near Locarno on December 4, 1933, Stauffenberg with his two brothers and eight other friends of George were at his bedside.

8. Fabian von Schlabrendorff, *Offiziere gegen Hitler*, p. 138.

9. Speidel, pp. 113 ff. Characteristically, Hitler had waited until a few hours before the meeting to inform the two field marshals that it would take place, and where.

10. A specific motive for Hitler's sudden departure has been occasionally mentioned. It is said that shortly after Rundstedt and Rommel left, a V-1 that had veered off course struck in the vicinity of the Führer's headquarters. Actually, we can regard this only as the pretext that Hitler used to avoid the confrontation; for why should a rocket accidentally striking in Margival have made a meeting in distant Roche-Guyon any more dangerous. On the incident itself see Speidel, p. 119.

11. Speidel, pp. 155 ff.

12. Communication to the author from Baroness von Below.

13. Zoller, p. 184. Hitler requested that the clothes "be sent to Fräulein Braun at the Berghof with instructions that she is to preserve them carefully."

14. Schmidt, *Statist,* p. 582.
15. Domarus, p. 2127 f.
16. Operation Thunderstorm was initiated abruptly on August 22, 1944, and resulted in the arrest of some 5,000 deputies and functionaries of the former political parties, including such persons as Konrad Adenauer and Kurt Schumacher. See Walter Hammer, "Die Gewitteraktion vom 22. 8. 1944," in *Freiheit und Recht,* 1959:8–9, pp. 15 ff.
17. W. Scheidt, *Gespräche mit Hitler,* cited from Eberhard Zeller, *Geist der Freiheit,* p. 538; also Heiber, *Lagebesprechungen,* p. 588.
18. Quoted in Ehlers, p. 113; see also Zeller, p. 461.
19. The speech is printed in: VJHfZ 1953:4, pp. 357 ff.; the passage quoted is on pp. 384 f.
20. Domarus, p. 2127.
21. Sebastian Haffner in a review in the magazine *Konkret,* 1964:2 of Kunrat von Hammerstein's book *Spähtrupp.*
22. Adolf Heusinger, *Befehl im Widerstreit,* p. 367.
23. Schlabrendorff, p. 154.
24. Cited in Bullock, p. 757, *n.* 1.
25. Speer, p. 406.
26. Heiber, *Lagebesprechungen,* pp. 615, 620 (August 31, 1944).
27. Radio address of January 30, cited in Domarus, p. 2083.
28. *Tischgespräche,* p. 468; see also p. 376.
29. General Bayerlein, cited in Cartier, Vol. II, p. 274. The description of Hitler is General von Manteuffel's, cited from Shirer, p. 1091.
30. Heiber, *Lagebesprechungen,* pp. 721 ff.
31. *Ibid.,* p. 740.
32. Domarus, p. 2198.
33. Rauschning, *Gespräche,* p. 115.
34. *Le Testament politique de Hitler,* p. 67. The preceding quotation is based on a memo to the author from Otto Remer. Remer, in conversation, had reminded Hitler that a few weeks earlier he had called the Ardennes offensive the last chance in this war, and had said that if it failed the whole war was lost.
35. "Lagebesprechung" of April 27, 1945, printed in *Der Spiegel* 1966:3, p. 42. On planning destruction see Speer, p. 403.
36. Cited in Trevor-Roper, *The Last Days of Hitler,* p. 72.
37. Cf. Speer, p. 425. On July 20, 1944, Hitler had told Mussolini that he was "determined to level London completely" by bombardment with V-2 rockets. They would "keep firing at London until the entire city is destroyed." See Hillgruber, *Staatsmänner* II, pp. 470 f. The order to defend Paris or reduce it to ashes was issued on August 23, 1944, but was disobeyed by General von Choltitz; see the account by Larry Collins and Dominique Lapierre, *Is Paris Burning?* The order itself is printed in Jacobsen, *1939–1945,* pp. 587 f.
38. Goebbels, cited in Trevor-Roper, *The Last Days of Hitler,* p. 51.
39. Printed in KTB/OKW IV, 2, pp. 1701 ff. Cf. the description in Gerhard Boldt, *Die letzten Tage,* p. 15.

40. Zoller, p. 150.
41. Guderian, p. 376; also Boldt, pp. 26 f. The doctor mentioned was Dr. Giesing; cf. the account in Maser, *Hitler,* pp. 350 f.
42. Zoller, p. 230. "From time to time," the report continues, "he raised his eyes to the portrait of Frederick the Great that hung above his desk and repeated his saying: 'Ever since I have come to know men, I love dogs.' "
43. *Ibid.,* pp. 204, 232.
44. Speer, p. 399.
45. Zoller, pp. 29 f. During a military conference in January Hitler wondered "whether a new shell ought not to be made now, after all" (Heiber, *Lagebesprechungen,* p. 867), and when General Karl Wolff visited him on April 18, Hitler elaborated on his "plans for the near future." See Eugen Dollmann, *Dolmetscher der Diktatoren,* p. 235.
46. Cited in Görlitz and Quint, p. 616; see also Domarus, pp. 2202 ff.
47. Speer, p. 426.
48. The "flag order" is printed in Jacobsen, *1939–1945,* pp. 591 f. The so-called Nero Command is printed in KTB/OKW IV, 2, pp. 1580 f.
49. Trevor-Roper, ed., *The Bormann Letters,* p. 198.
50. Speer, p. 440.
51. *Ibid.,* p. 453.
52. Bullock, pp. 780 f.
53. Statement by Frau Inge Haberzettel, one of the Propaganda Minister's secretaries. Cf. the description in Trevor-Roper, *Last Days,* p. 100. For Ley's death rays see Speer, p. 464.
54. Speer, p. 463. For the following description of Hitler, see p. 464.
55. *Ibid.,* p. 474. There are many witnesses to the attitude of Goebbels; the remark quoted here is taken from the "Lagebesprechung" of April 23, 1945; see *Der Spiegel,* 1966:3, p. 34.
56. Speer, p. 475.
57. *Ibid.,* p. 459.
58. Karl Koller, *Der letzte Monat,* pp. 19 ff.
59. The witnesses to the course of events are chiefly: Keitel, Jodl, General Christian, Colonel von Freytag-Loringhoven, Lorenz, Colonel von Below, and Fräulein Krüger, who was Bormann's secretary. Our account largely follows that of Trevor-Roper, who checked the statements of these witnesses and extracted the points of essential agreement; see *Last Days,* pp. 118 f.; also the statement of Gerhard Herrgesell, one of the stenographers, in: KTB/OKW IV, 2, pp. 1696 f.
60. See the transcript of this account in Koller, p. 31.
61. Quoted by Trevor-Roper, *Last Days,* p. 127.
62. Speer, p. 480; but see also p. 485.
63. Quoted in Trevor-Roper, *Last Days,* p. 128.
64. Speer, p. 483.
65. *Le Testament politique de Hitler,* p. 61 (February 4, 1945).
66. *Ibid.,* pp. 57 ff. (February 4, 1945).
67. *Ibid.,* pp. 87 ff.; 129 ff. (February 14 and 25, 1945). Hitler made very similar remarks in a military conference of March 5, 1943; see Heiber,

Lagebesprechungen, p. 171; see also the comparable early comment in Rauschning, *Gespräche,* p. 115.

68. *Ibid.,* pp. 101 ff. (February 17, 1945). The opening of the campaign in the East actually was postponed for a few weeks, but this decision was not due solely to Mussolini's invasion of Greece. Questions of weather, of time for the deployment of allies, and so on, played a part. Cf. the study "Hat das britische Eingreifen in Griechenland den deutschen Angriff auf Russland verzögert oder nicht?" (on file at the Militärgeschichtliche Forschungsamt Freiburg im Breisgau). See also Hillgruber, *Strategie,* p. 506. Hitler himself, moreover, sometimes said just the opposite, at least to Mussolini; cf. the reference in Nolte, *Epoche,* p. 586.

69. *Le Testament politique de Hitler,* p. 78.

70. *Ibid.,* p. 108 (February 17, 1945). For Trevor-Roper's comment see pp. 46 f. Hitler's opinion agrees amazingly with a remark of the French writer Drieu la Rochelle, who toward the end of 1944, shortly before his suicide, explained the defeat as follows: "The reason for the collapse of German policy lies not in its lack of moderation, but in its lack of decisiveness. In no field was the German revolution pushed ahead far enough. . . . The German revolution dealt far too circumspectly with the old men in business and in the army; it spared too much of the old bureaucracy. This double mistake was exposed on July 20. Hitler should have struck harshly at the disloyal Left, but also shown no mercy to the disloyal Right. Because he did not strike, or did not strike hard enough, the irreparable consequences emerged, with an increasingly dire effect, in the course of the war. In all the occupied countries of Europe German policy proved to be burdened by all the prejudices of superannuated rules of warfare and outmoded diplomacy; it was unable to exploit the novelty and breadth of the magnificent mission that had been offered to it; it proved incapable of transforming an old-fashioned war of conquest into a revolutionary war. It believed it would be able to reduce the violence of warfare to a minimum in order to win over European public opinion—and was forced to see this opinion turning against itself because it was offering the European public nothing new and compelling." Cited in Nolte, *Faschismus,* p. 380.

71. Cf. Trevor-Roper, *Last Days,* p. 175.

72. Hitler's political and personal testaments are both printed in: N.B. 3569-PS.

73. The original text of this document was destroyed; it is given here in von Below's reconstruction as cited by Trevor-Roper, *Last Days,* pp. 194 f.

74. See Lev Bezymenski, *The Death of Adolf Hitler,* p. 72; cf. also Trevor-Roper, *Last Days,* p. 196.

75. Trevor-Roper, *Last Days,* p. 198.

76. The Russian commission's autopsy report, Document 12, claims that remains of a crushed ampoule of poison were found in the mouth of the corpse, which it believed to be Hitler. But the report does not mention the distinct odor of bitter almonds given off by cyanide compounds, which was observed in the other bodies. German participants have denied that any

fragments of skull could have been found, given the degree to which the flames consumed the body; cf. Maser, *Hitler,* pp. 432 f. Given Hitler's fear that his suicide might be unsuccessful, it is not out of the question that he may have bitten a poison capsule and simultaneously pressed the trigger of his gun. Bezymenski's effort (p. 72) to exclude this possibility by referring to the "foremost Soviet forensic scientist" is not convincing, not even in the manner of presentation. For the statements of eyewitnesses see Trevor-Roper, *Last Days,* p. 201.

77. Statement of Otto Günsche, cited in Maser, *Hitler,* p. 432. The previous statement was made by the guard Hermann Karnau; see the detailed quotation in Fest, *The Face of the Third Reich,* p. 324, *n.* 40.

78. Bezymenski alleges (pp. 66 f.) as the motive for Soviet secrecy that the results of the medical investigation were being withheld in case "someone might try to slip into the role of the Führer saved by a miracle." Also, the aim was to exclude all possibility of error. There is no need to comment on the first argument, since silence could only give support to the claim that the Führer was still alive, and in fact did. The second argument is also scarcely convincing, since the credibility of the autopsy record could not increase in the course of years. For the various rumors see Trevor-Roper, *Last Days,* Preface; he also gives an illuminating account of his vain efforts to obtain information or co-operation from the Russians.

CONCLUSION

1. Trevor-Roper, *Last Days,* p. 45.
2. Rauschning, *Gespräche,* p. 212.
3. Photo in the author's possession.
4. *Hitlers Zweites Buch,* p. 174, and *Mein Kampf,* p. 646. Cf. also *Le Testament politique de Hitler,* pp. 62 f. (February 4, 1945): "Germany had no choice. . . . We could not rest content with a sham independence. That might be enough for Swedes or the Swiss, who are always willing to be put off with empty promises so long as their pockets are filled. The Weimar Republic asked for nothing more. But the Third Reich could not be content with such a modest claim. We were condemned to wage war."
5. *Tischgespräche,* p. 273; also Rauschning, *Gespräche,* p. 105.
6. Best known, and frequently cited in German apologetic works, is Winston Churchill's statement in *Great Contemporaries,* p. 226: "Whatever else may be thought about these exploits, they are certainly among the most remarkable in the whole history of the world."
7. *Le Testament politique de Hitler,* p. 139 (February 26, 1945).
8. *Tischgespräche,* p. 489.
9. Hitler to the Munich court during his trial, February 26, 1924. See Boepple, p. 110.
10. Cf. Minutes of the Conference of the Expanded Executive Committee of the Communist International, Moscow, June 12–13, 1923, cited in Nolte,

Theorien, p. 92. The speech is highly interesting because, contrary to all the conspiratorial theories that circulated later, it takes seriously the idea of Fascism as a catch-all for the masses disappointed with socialism.

11. Nietzsche, *The Dawn* (Morgenröte), aphorism 534.
12. Speech of January 25, 1939, cited in Jacobsen and Jochmann, *Ausgewählte Dokumente,* p. 9. For the remark on German Social Democracy, cf. *Libres propos,* p. 36. American social scientists, in order to avoid the peculiar moral problems of terminology, have introduced the concept of "modernization" into the discussion. The Fascist systems in Italy or Germany, it is argued, represent above all stages in the process of repressing traditional social structures. Much of this argument fails to consider adequately that "modernization" can be only one interpretative aspect and that Fascism cannot be defined exclusively by its attitude toward the process of industrialization, urbanization, and rationalization. A detailed and satisfying study remains to be published. Cf. David Apter, *The Politics of Modernization;* H. A. Turner, Jr., "Faschismus und Anti-Modernismus," in: *Faschismus und Kapitalismus in Deutschland,* pp. 157 ff., with further references.
13. At the beginning was the celebrated article in the New York *Post* of December 20, 1941, on the gassing of a thousand Warsaw Jews.
14. Bertolt Brecht, "An die Nachgeborenen" ("To Posterity"), in: *Selected Poems,* trans. H. R. Hays, New York, 1947, p. 173.
15. Carlo Sforza, *European Dictatorships,* pp. 138 f.
16. Cf. Nolte, *Theorien,* p. 71.
17. Rauschning, *Gespräche,* p. 212.
18. *Ibid.,* pp. 150, 262, 264.

Bibliography

(with Abbreviations)

ADAP = *Akten zur Deutschen Auswärtigen Politik 1918–1945*, Serie D: 1937–1945, Baden-Baden, 1950 ff.

Adorno, Theodor W., *Versuch über Wagner*, Munich, 1964.

Anatomie des SS-Staates, Olten and Freiburg i. Br., 1965.

Andics, Hellmuth, *Der ewige Jude: Ursachen und Geschichte des Antisemitismus*, Vienna, 1965.

Anonymous, *Rudolf Hess, der Stellvertreter des Führers* (in the series *Zeitgeschichte*), Berlin, 1933.

Apter, David, *The Politics of Modernization*, Chicago, 1965.

Arendt, Hannah, *Eichmann in Jerusalem*, New York, 1963.

Bahr, Hermann, *Der Antisemitismus: Ein internationales Interview*, Berlin, 1894.

BAK = Bundesarchiv Koblenz.

Baumgart, Winfried, "Zur Ansprache Hitlers vor den Führern der Wehrmacht am 22. August 1939," VJHfZ, 1968:2.

Baynes, Norman H., *The Speeches of Adolf Hitler, April 1922–August 1939*, 2 vols., London, 1942; New York, 1943.

Benda, Julien, *The Betrayal of the Intellectuals*, trans. Richard Aldington, Boston, 1955 (Beacon paperback).

Benn, Gottfried, *Doppelleben*, Wiesbaden, 1950.

———, *Gesammelte Werke*, Wiesbaden, 1958–61.

Bennecke, Heinrich, *Die Reichswehr und der "Röhm-Putsch,"* Vienna, 1964.

———, *Wirtschaftliche Depression und politischer Radikalismus*, Munich, 1968.

Bezymenski, Lev, *The Death of Adolf Hitler: Unknown Documents from Soviet Archives*, New York and London, 1968.

BHStA = Bayerisches Hauptstaatsarchiv.

Boberach, Heinz, ed., *Meldungen aus dem Reich: Auswahl aus den geheimen Lageberichten des Sicherheitsdienstes der SS 1939–1944*, Neuwied, 1965.

Boepple, Ernst, ed., *Adolf Hitlers Reden*, 3rd ed., Munich, 1933.

Böhme, Helmut, *Deutschlands Weg zur Grossmacht*, Cologne and Berlin, 1966.

Boldt, Gerhard, *Die letzten Tage der Reichskanzlei*, Hamburg, 1947 (*In the Shelter with Hitler*, London, 1948).

817

BIBLIOGRAPHY

Borgese, Giuseppe A., *Goliath: The March of Fascism,* New York, 1937.
Bormann Letters, The, see Trevor-Roper, H. R., ed.
Bracher, Karl Dietrich, *Auflösung = Die Auflösung der Weimarer Republik: Eine Studie zum Problem des Machtverfalls in der Demokratie,* Stuttgart and Düsseldorf, 1955.
————, *Diktatur = Die deutsche Diktatur: Entstehung, Struktur, Folgen des Nationalsozialismus,* Cologne and Berlin, 1969 (*The German Dictatorship: The Origins, Structure, and Effects of National Socialism,* New York, 1970).
Bracher, Karl Dietrich; Sauer, Wolfgang; Schulz, Gerhard; *Machtergreifung = Die nationalsozialistische Machtergreifung: Studien zur Errichtung des totalitären Herrschaftssystems in Deutschland 1933/34,* Cologne and Opladen, 1960.
Brecht, Arnold, *Vorspiel zum Schweigen: Das Ende der deutschen Republik,* Vienna, 1948 (*Prelude to Silence: The End of the German Republic,* New York, 1944; London, 1945).
Brenner, Hildegard, *Die Kunstpolitik des Nationalsozialismus,* Reinbek, 1963.
Broszat, Martin, *Der Staat Hitlers,* Munich, 1969.
Brüning, Heinrich, "Ein Brief," *Deutsche Rundschau* (July, 1947).
————, *Memoiren 1918–1934,* Stuttgart, 1970.
Bryant, Arthur, *The Turn of the Tide, 1939–1943,* London, 1957.
Bucher, Peter, *Der Reichswehrprozess: Der Hochverrat der Ulmer Reichswehroffiziere 1929/30,* Boppard, 1967.
Buchheim, Hans, "Die SS—das Herrschaftsinstrument. Befehl und Gehorsam," in: *Anatomie des SS-Staates.*
Bullock, Alan, *Hitler: A Study in Tyranny,* rev. ed., New York and Evanston, 1964 (Harper Torchbook ed.).
Burckhardt, Carl Jacob, *Meine Danziger Mission 1937–1939,* Zurich and Munich, 1960.
Burckhardt, Jacob, *Force and Freedom: Reflections on History,* New York, 1943.
Butler, James R. M., *Lord Lothian "Philip Kerr" 1882–1940,* London and New York, 1960.
Butler, Rohan D. O., *The Roots of National Socialism,* New York, 1942.
Calic, Edouard, *Ohne Maske: Hitler-Breiting Geheimgespräche 1931,* Frankfurt a. M., 1968 (*Secret Conversations with Hitler,* New York, 1971).
Cartier, Raymond, *La seconde guerre mondiale,* 2 vols., Paris, 1965.
Chamberlain, Houston Stewart, *Die Grundlagen des 19. Jahrhunderts,* 6th ed., Munich, 1906 (*The Foundations of the 19th Century,* London and New York, 1911).
Churchill, Winston, *Blood, Sweat and Tears,* New York, 1941 (English title: *Into Battle,* London, 1941).
————, *Great Contemporaries,* New York, 1937.
————, *The Second World War,* Vol. 1, *The Gathering Storm,* 1948; Vol. 2, *Their Finest Hour,* 1959–61.
Ciano, Count Galeazzo, see: Gibson, Hugh, ed.
Ciano's Hidden Diary 1937–1938, trans. Andreas Mayor, New York, 1953.
Collins, Larry, and Lapierre, Dominique, *Is Paris Burning?,* New York, 1965.

Conze, W., "Zum Sturz Brünings," VJHfZ, 1952:3.

Cooper, Duff, *Old Men Forget: The Autobiography of Duff Cooper*, London, 1953.

Coulondre, Robert, *De Staline à Hitler*, Paris, 1950.

Curtius, Julius, *Sechs Jahre Minister der deutschen Republik*, Heidelberg, 1938.

Czichon, Eberhard, *Wer verhalf Hitler zur Macht?*, Cologne, 1967.

Dahlerus, Birger, *The Last Attempt*, London, 1948.

Dahrendorf, Ralf, *Gesellschaft und Demokratie in Deutschland*, Munich, 1965.

Daim, Wilfried, *Der Mann, der Hitler die Ideen gab*, Munich, 1958.

Dallin, Alexander, *German Rule in Russia 1941–1945*, London and New York, 1957.

Deakin, F. W., *The Brutal Friendship: Mussolini, Hitler and the Fall of Italian Fascism*, London, 1962; New York, 1963.

Delmer, Sefton, *Die Deutschen und ich*, Hamburg, 1963.

Deuerlein, Ernst, ed., *Aufstieg = Der Aufstieg der NSDAP 1919–1933 in Augenzeugenberichten*, Düsseldorf, 1968.

Deuerlein, Ernst, "Eintritt" = "Hitlers Eintritt in die Politik und die Reichswehr," VJHfZ, 1959:2.

————, *Der Hitler-Putsch*, Stuttgart, 1962.

Deutsch, Harold C., *The Conspiracy Against Hitler in the Twilight War*, Minneapolis, 1968.

Diels, Rudolf, *Lucifer ante portas . . . Es spricht der erste Chef der Gestapo . . .*, Stuttgart, 1950.

Dietrich, Otto, *Mit Hitler in die Macht*, Munich, 1934.

————, *Zwölf Jahre = Zwölf Jahre mit Hitler*, Munich, 1955 (*Hitler*, Chicago, 1955; British title: *The Hitler I Knew*, London, 1957).

Documents on British Foreign Policy 1919–1939, Second Series (1930 ff.), London, 1950 ff.

Dönitz, Karl, *Zehn Jahre und Zwanzig Tage*, Frankfurt a. M. & Bonn, 1964 (*Memoirs: Ten Years and Twenty Days*, Cleveland, 1959).

Dollmann, Eugen, *Dolmetscher der Diktatoren*, Bayreuth, 1963.

Domarus = Domarus, Max, *Hitler: Reden und Proklamationen 1932–1945, kommentiert von einem deutschen Zeitgenossen*, 2 vols., Würzburg, 1962–63.

Dörner, Klaus, "Nationalsozialismus und Lebensvernichtung," VJHfZ, 1967:2.

Dulles, Allen Welsh, *Germany's Underground*, New York and London, 1947.

Eden, Anthony, *Facing the Dictators: The Eden Memoirs*, London and Boston, 1962.

Ehlers, Dietrich, *Technik und Moral einer Verschwörung*, Frankfurt a. M. & Bonn, 1964.

Erdmann, Karl Dietrich, ed., see: Riezler, Kurt.

Eschenburg, Theodor, "The Role of the Personality in the Crisis of the Weimar Republic," in: H. Holborn, ed., *Republic to Reich*.

Fabry, Philipp W., *Mutmassungen über Hitler*, Düsseldorf, 1969.

Faschismus und Kapitalismus in Deutschland, Göttingen, 1972.

Fest, Joachim C., *The Face of the Third Reich*, New York and London, 1972.

Fetcher, Iring, "Faschismus und Nationalsozialismus: Zur Kritik des sowjetmarxistischen Faschismusbegriffs," *Politische Vierteljahresschrift*, 1962:1.

819

Fischer, Fritz, *Griff nach der Weltmacht: Die Kriegszielpolitik des kaiserlichen Deutschland 1914–18*, Düsseldorf, 1961.

――――, *Krieg der Illusionen: Die deutsche Politik von 1911 bis 1914*, Düsseldorf, 1969.

Foertsch, Hermann, *Schuld und Verhängnis: Die Fritschkrise im Frühjahr 1938 als Wendepunkt in der Geschichte der nationalsozialistischen Zeit*, Stuttgart, 1951.

Fraenkel, Ernst, *The Dual State*, London and New York, 1941.

François-Poncet, André, *The Fateful Years: Memoirs of a French Ambassador in Berlin 1931–1938*, New York, 1949.

Frank, Hans, *Im Angesicht des Galgens: Deutung Hitlers und seiner Zeit auf Grund eigener Erlebnisse und Erkenntnisse*, 2nd ed., Neuhaus, 1955.

Franz-Willing, Georg, *Die Hitlerbewegung: Der Ursprung 1919–1922*, Hamburg and Berlin, 1962.

Freund, Michael, *Abendglanz Europas*, Stuttgart, 1967.

――――, *Weltgeschichte der Gegenwart in Dokumenten*, 3 vols., Freiburg i. Br., 1954–56.

Friedländer, Saul, *Prelude to Downfall: Hitler and the United States 1939–1941*, New York, 1967.

Gafencu, Grigore, *The Last Days of Europe: A Diplomatic Journey in 1939*, London, 1947; New Haven, Conn., 1948.

George, Stefan, *Gesamtausgabe*, Düsseldorf, 1964.

Gibson, Hugh, ed., *The Ciano Diaries 1939–1943*, London and New York, 1947.

Gilbert, Gustave Mark, *The Psychology of Dictatorship*, New York, 1950.

Gilbert, Martin, and Gott, Richard, *The Appeasers*, London, 1963.

Gisevius, Hans Bernd, *Adolf Hitler: Versuch einer Deutung*, Munich, 1963.

――――, *To the Bitter End*, trans. Richard and Clara Winston, Boston, 1947.

Goebbels, Joseph, "Der Führer als Staatsmann," in: *Adolf Hitler*, Cigaretten-Bilderdienst, Altona, n. d.

――――, *Kaiserhof = Vom Kaiserhof zur Reichskanzlei: Eine historische Darstellung in Tagebuchblättern*, Munich, 1934.

――――, *Tagebuch 1925–26*, see: Heiber, Helmut, ed.

――――, *Tagebücher 1942–43*, see: Lochner, Louis P., ed.

Göring, Hermann, *Aufbau einer Nation*, Berlin, 1934 (*Germany Reborn*, London, 1934).

Görlitz, Walter, ed., *Der deutsche Generalstab: Geschichte und Gestalt*, Frankfurt a. M., 1953 (*History of the German General Staff 1657–1945*, New York and London, 1953; British title: *The German General Staff: Its History and Structure*).

Görlitz, Walter, and Quint, Herbert A., *Adolf Hitler: Eine Biographie*, Stuttgart, 1952.

Govern, W. M., *From Luther to Hitler*, London, 1946.

Greiner, Josef, *Das Ende des Hitler-Mythos*, Zurich, Leipzig, Vienna, 1947.

Groscurth, Helmuth, *Tagebücher eines Abwehroffiziers 1938–1940*, ed. Helmut Krausnick and Harold C. Deutsch, Stuttgart, 1970.

Guderian, Heinz, *Erinnerungen eines Soldaten*, Heidelberg, 1951 (*Panzer Leader*, New York and London, 1952).

Gumbel, Emil Julius, *Verräter verfallen der Feme: Opfer, Mörder, Richter 1919–1929*, Berlin, 1929.

Gutman, Robert W., *Richard Wagner: The Man, His Mind, and His Music*, New York, 1968.

Haffner, Sebastian, *Der Teufelspakt: 50 Jahre deutschrussische Beziehungen*, Reinbek, 1968.

Halder, Franz, *Hitler als Feldherr*, Munich, 1949 (*Hitler as Warlord*, London, 1950).

————, *Kriegstagebuch: Tägliche Aufzeichnungen des Chefs des Generalstabs des Heeres 1939–1942*, 3 vols., Stuttgart, 1962–64.

Hale, Oron James, "Adolf Hitler, Taxpayer," *American Historical Review*, LX:4 (July 1955).

Hallgarten, George W. F., *Dämonen oder Retter*, Munich, 1966.

————, *Hitler, Reichswehr und Industrie*, Frankfurt a. M., 1955.

Hammer, Hermann, "Die deutschen Ausgaben von Hitlers *Mein Kampf*," VJHfZ, 1956:2.

Hammer, Walter, "Die Gewitteraktion vom 22. 8. 1944," *Freiheit und Recht*, 1959:8–9.

Hammerstein, Kunrat von, *Spähtrupp*, Stuttgart, 1963.

Hanfstaengl, Ernst, *Zwischen Weissem und Braunem Haus*, Munich, 1970.

Hassell, Ulrich von, *Vom anderen Deutschland*, Zurich and Freiburg i. Br., 1946 (*The Von Hassell Diaries 1938–1944*, New York, 1947; London, 1948).

Heiber, Helmut, "Der Generalplan Ost," VJHfZ, 1958:3.

————, ed., *Hitlers Lagebesprechungen*, Stuttgart, 1962 (much of this material is to be found in: Felix Gilbert, *Hitler Directs His War*, London, 1950; New York, 1951).

————, *Joseph Goebbels*, Berlin, 1962.

————, ed., *Reichsführer!* . . . *Briefe an und von Himmler*, Stuttgart, 1968.

————, ed., *Das Tagebuch von Joseph Goebbels 1925–26*, Stuttgart, n. d. (*The Early Goebbels Diaries*, ed. Alan Bullock and Helmut Heiber, London, 1962; New York, 1963).

Heiden, Konrad, *Geschichte des Nationalsozialismus: Die Karriere einer Idee*, Berlin, 1932 (*A History of National Socialism*, London, 1934; New York, 1935).

————, *Adolf Hitler: Das Zeitalter der Verantwortungslosigkeit. Eine Biographie*, 2 vols., Zurich, 1936–37 (*Der Führer: Hitler's Rise to Power*, trans. Ralph Manheim, Boston, 1944; new ed., New York, 1968).

————, *Hitler, a Biography*, New York and London, 1936 (vol. 1 of *Adolf Hitler*).

Henderson, Sir Nevile, *Failure of a Mission, Berlin 1937–1939*, London and New York, 1940.

Henk, Emil, *Die Tragödie des 20. Juli 1944*, Heidelberg, 1946.

Hennig, Eike, "Industrie und Faschismus," *Neue Politische Literatur*, 1970:4.

BIBLIOGRAPHY

Heusinger, Adolf, *Befehl im Widerstreit: Schicksalsstunden der deutschen Armee 1923–1945,* Tübingen and Stuttgart, 1950.

Heyen, Franz Josef, *Alltag = Nationalsozialismus im Alltag,* Boppard, 1967.

Hillgruber, Andreas, ed., *Staatsmänner = Staatsmänner und Diplomaten bei Hitler,* 2 vols., Frankfurt a. M., 1967–70.

Hillgruber, Andreas, *Strategie = Hitlers Strategie: Politik und Kriegführung 1940 bis 1941,* Frankfurt a. M., 1965.

Historikus (= Arthur Rosenberg), *Der Faschismus als Massenbewegung,* Karlsbad, 1934.

Hitler, Adolf, *Libres propos sur la guerre et la paix,* version française de François Genoud, Paris, 1952.

————, *Mein Kampf,* trans. Ralph Manheim, Boston, 1943 (Sentry paperback ed.).

————, *My New Order,* ed. Raoul de Roussy de Sales, New York, 1941.

————, *Hitler's Secret Conversations,* trans. Norman Cameron and R. H. Stevens, New York, 1953.

————, *Hitler's Table Talk 1941–44,* trans. Norman Cameron and R. H. Stevens, London, 1953.

————, *Hitlers Tischgespräche im Führerhauptquartier 1941–42,* ed. Henry Picker, Bonn, 1951.

————, *Hitlers Zweites Buch: Ein Dokument aus dem Jahre 1928,* Stuttgart, 1961 (*Hitler's Secret Book,* New York, 1962).

————, *Le testament politique de Hitler,* Notes recueillies par Martin Bormann (Bormann Vermerke), with a preface by Hugh R. Trevor-Roper, Paris, 1959.

————, "Zehn Jahre Kampf," *Illustrierter Beobachter,* IV:31 (August 3, 1929).

See also: Baynes, Norman H.; Boepple, Ernst; Domarus, Max; Heiber, Helmut.

Hitler e Mussolini: Lettere e Documenti, Milan, 1946.

Hitlerprozess, Der, Munich, 1924.

Hoare, Sir Samuel; see: Templewood, Viscount.

Hoegner, Wilhelm, *Die verratene Republik,* Munich, 1958.

Hoffmann, Heinrich, *Hitler Was My Friend,* London, 1955.

Hoffmann, Peter, *Widerstand, Staatsstreich, Attentat: Der Kampf der Opposition gegen Hitler,* Munich, 1969.

Hofmiller, Josef, "Revolutionstagebuch 1918/19," *Schriften* II, Leipzig, 1938.

Höhne, Heinz, *Der Orden unter dem Totenkopf: Die Geschichte der SS,* Gütersloh, 1967 (*The Order of the Death's Head,* New York, 1971).

Holborn, Hajo, ed., *Republic to Reich: The Making of the Nazi Revolution,* New York, 1972.

Horkenbach, Cuno, *Das Deutsche Reich von 1918 bis Heute* (volume covering the year 1933), Berlin, 1935.

Horn, Wolfgang, *Führerideologie und Parteiorganisation in der NSDAP 1919–1933,* Düsseldorf, 1972.

Höss, Rudolf, *Kommandant in Auschwitz,* Stuttgart, 1958 (*Commandant of Auschwitz,* London, 1959; New York, 1960).

Hossbach, Friedrich, *Zwischen Wehrmacht und Hitler 1934–1938,* Wolfenbüttel and Hanover, 1949.

HStA = Hauptstaatsarchiv.

Hubatsch, Walther, ed., *Hitlers Weisungen für die Kriegsführung*, Frankfurt a. M., 1962.

IfZ = Institut für Zeitgeschichte.

IMT, see *Trial of the Major War Criminals Before the International Military Tribunal*.

Ingrim, Robert, *Hitlers glücklichster Tag*, Stuttgart, 1962.

———, *Von Talleyrand zu Molotov*, Stuttgart, 1951.

Jäckel, Eberhard, *Hitlers Weltanschauung: Entwurf einer Herrschaft*, Tübingen, 1969.

Jacobsen, Hans-Adolf, *Aussenpolitik = Nationalsozialistische Aussenpolitik 1933–1938*, Frankfurt a. M. & Berlin, 1968.

———, *Fall Gelb: Der Kampf um den deutschen Operationsplan zur Westoffensive 1940*, Wiesbaden, 1957.

———, "Kommissarbefehl und Massenexekutionen sowjetischer Kriegsgefangener," in: *Anatomie des SS-Staates*, Olten and Freiburg i. Br., 1965.

———, *1939–1945: Der Zweite Weltkrieg in Chronik und Dokumenten*, 5th ed., Darmstadt, 1961.

———, and Jochmann, Werner, *Ausgewählte Dokumente zur Geschichte des Nationalsozialismus 1933–1945*, Bielefeld, 1961.

Jaspers, Karl, *Man in the Modern Age*, London and New York, 1951.

Jenks, William Alexander, *Vienna and the Young Hitler*, New York, 1960.

Jetzinger, Franz, *Hitlers Jugend*, Vienna, 1956 (*Hitler's Youth*, London, 1958).

Jochmann, Werner, *Im Kampf um die Macht: Hitlers Rede vor dem Hamburger Nationalklub von 1926*, Frankfurt a. M., 1960.

———, *Nationalsozialismus und Revolution: Ursprung und Geschichte der NSDAP in Hamburg 1922–1933*, Frankfurt a. M., 1963.

Jones, T., *A Diary with Letters 1931–1950*, London, 1954.

Jung, Edgar J., *Die Herrschaft der Minderwertigen—ihr Zerfall und ihre Ablösung durch ein neues Reich*, Berlin, 1930.

———, "Neubelebung von Weimar?", *Deutsche Rundschau*, June, 1932.

Kempner, Robert M. W., *Eichmann und Komplicen*, Zurich, Stuttgart, Vienna, 1961.

Kennan, George F., *Memoirs 1925–1950*, Boston, 1967.

Kersten, Felix, *Totenkopf und Treue: Heinrich Himmler ohne Uniform. Aus den Tagebuchblättern des finnischen Medizinalrats Felix Kersten*, Hamburg, n. d. (*The Kersten Memoirs 1940–1945*, London, 1956; New York, 1957).

Kessler, Harry Graf, *Tagebücher 1918–1937*, Frankfurt a. M., 1961 (*In the Twenties: The Diaries of Harry Kessler*, New York, 1971).

Kirkpatrick, Sir Ivone, *The Inner Circle*, London and New York, 1959.

———, *Mussolini: Study of a Demagogue*, London, 1964.

Klee, Karl, *Das Unternehmen "Seelöwe,"* Göttingen, Berlin, Frankfurt a. M., 1958.

———, *Dokumente zum Unternehmen "Seelöwe,"* Göttingen, Berlin, Frankfurt a. M. 1959.

Knickerbocker, H. R., *The German Crisis*, New York, 1932.

Koktanek, Anton Mirko, *Oswald Spengler in seiner Zeit*, Munich, 1968.

Koller, Karl, *Der letzte Monat,* Mannheim, 1948.

Kordt, Erich, *Nicht aus den Akten: Die Wilhelmstrasse in Frieden und Krieg. Erlebnisse, Begegnungen und Eindrücke 1928–1945,* Stuttgart, 1950.

——, *Wahn und Wirklichkeit: Die Aussenpolitik des Dritten Reiches. Versuch einer Darstellung,* Stuttgart, 1948.

Kotze und Krausnick = Kotze, Hildegard von, and Krausnick, Helmut, *Es spricht der Führer: Sieben exemplarische Hitler-Reden,* Gütersloh, 1966.

Krausnick, Helmut, *Der 30. Juni 1934: Bedeutung, Hintergründe, Verlauf,* supplement to *Das Parlament,* June 30, 1954.

——, "Judenverfolgung," in: *Anatomie des SS-Staates* II, Olten and Freiburg i. Br., 1965.

——, "Vorgeschichte und Beginn des militärischen Widerstandes gegen Hitler," in: *Die Vollmacht des Gewissens,* Munich, 1956.

Krebs, Albert, *Tendenzen und Gestalten der NSDAP: Erinnerungen an die Frühzeit der Partei,* Stuttgart, 1948.

KTB/OKW, see: Schramm, Percy Ernst, ed.

Kubizek, August, *Adolf Hitler, mein Jugendfreund,* Graz and Göttingen, 1953 (*The Young Hitler I Knew,* Boston, 1955; British title: *Young Hitler: The Story of Our Friendship,* London, 1954).

Kuhn, Axel, *Hitlers aussenpolitisches Programm,* Stuttgart, 1970.

Kühnl, Reinhard, "Der deutsche Faschismus," in: *Neue Politische Literatur,* 1970:1.

——, *Die nationalsozialistische Linke 1925–1930,* Meisenheim an der Glan, 1966.

Lange, Karl, *Hitlers unbeachtete Maximen: "Mein Kampf" und die Öffentlichkeit,* Stuttgart, 1968.

Laqueur, Walter, *Deutschland und Russland,* Berlin, 1965 (*Russia and Germany: A Century of Conflict,* Boston and London, 1965).

——, and Mosse, George L., ed., *Internationaler Faschismus 1920–1945,* Munich, 1966.

Laski, Harold J., *Reflections on the Revolution of Our Time,* London, 1943.

Leber, Julius, *Ein Mann geht seinen Weg,* Berlin, 1952.

Libres propos, see: Hitler.

Lochner, Louis P., ed. *Goebbels, Tagebücher aus den Jahren 1942–1943,* Zurich, 1948 (*The Goebbels Diaries,* New York and London, 1948).

Lossberg, Bernhard von, *Im Wehrmachtsführungsstab,* Hamburg, 1947.

Luedecke, Kurt G. W., *I Knew Hitler,* New York, 1937; London, 1938.

Mann, Golo, *Deutsche Geschichte des neunzehnten und zwanzigsten Jahrhunderts,* Frankfurt a. M., 1958 (*The History of Germany Since 1789,* New York, 1968).

Mann, Thomas, *Betrachtungen eines Unpolitischen,* Frankfurt a. M., 1956 (orig. 1918).

——, "Bruder Hitler," in: *Gesammelte Werke,* vol. 12 ("This Man Is My Brother," *Esquire,* XI:3).

——, *Dieser Friede,* New York and Toronto, 1938.

——, *Essays of Three Decades,* New York, 1965.

——, *Nachlese: Prosa 1951–1955,* Berlin and Frankfurt a. M., 1956.

Manstein, Erich von, *Verlorene Siege,* Bonn, 1960.

Manvell, Roger, and Fraenkel, Heinrich, *Doctor Goebbels: His Life and Death,* New York and London, 1960.

Maser, Werner, *Frühgeschichte* = *Die Frühgeschichte der NSDAP: Hitlers Weg bis 1924,* Frankfurt a. M. and Bonn, 1965.

————, *Hitler* = *Adolf Hitler: Legende, Mythos, Wirklichkeit,* Munich and Esslingen, 1971 (*Hitler: Legend, Myth & Reality,* New York, 1973).

————, *Hitlers "Mein Kampf,"* Munich and Esslingen, 1966 (*Hitler's "Mein Kampf": An Analysis,* London, 1970).

Mau, Hermann, "The 'Second Revolution'—June 30, 1934," in: Holborn, ed., *Republic to Reich.*

Meinecke, Friedrich, *Ausgewählter Briefwechsel,* ed. Ludwig Dehio and Peter Classen, Stuttgart, 1962.

————, *Die deutsche Katastrophe: Betrachtungen und Erinnerungen,* 5th ed., Wiesbaden, 1955 (*The German Catastrophe: Reflections and Recollections,* Cambridge, Mass., and London, 1950; repr. Boston, 1964).

Meissner, Hans Otto, and Wilde, Harry, *Die Machtergreifung,* Stuttgart, 1958.

Michaelis, Herbert, and Schraepler, Ernst, ed., *Ursachen und Folgen: Vom deutschen Zusammenbruch 1918 und 1945 bis zur staatlichen Neuordnung Deutschlands in der Gegenwart,* Berlin, 1958 ff.

Milward, A. S., *The German Economy at War,* London, 1965.

Moltmann, Günter, "Goebbels' Speech on Total War, February 18, 1943," in: Holborn, ed., *Republic to Reich.*

Mommsen, Hans, "Gesellschaftsbild und Verfassungspläne des deutschen Widerstands," in: Schmitthenner, Walter, and Buchheim, Hans, ed., *Der deutsche Widerstand gegen Hitler.*

————, "The Reichstag Fire and Its Political Consequences," in: Holborn, ed., *Republic to Reich.*

Mommsen, Wolfgang J., "Die deutsche Kriegszielpolitik 1914–1918," in *Juli 1914* (German ed. of *Journal of Contemporary History*), Munich, 1967.

Müller, Christian, *Oberst i. G. Stauffenberg: Eine Biographie,* Düsseldorf, 1970.

Müller, Karl Alexander von, *Im Wandel einer Welt: Erinnerungen 1919–1932,* Munich, 1966.

Müller, Klaus-Jürgen, *Das Heer und Hitler: Armee und nationalsozialistisches Regime, 1933–1940,* Stuttgart, 1969.

N.B. = *Nuernberger Beweise.*

ND = Nuremberg Document.

Neumann, Franz Leopold, *Behemoth: The Structure and Practice of National Socialism,* New York and London, 1942; rev. ed., New York, 1944.

————, *The Democratic and the Authoritarian State,* ed. Herbert Marcuse, Glencoe, Ill., 1957.

Nicolson, Harold, *Diaries and Letters 1930–1939,* London and New York, 1966.

Nietzsche, Friedrich, *The Portable Nietzsche,* ed. Walter Kaufmann, New York, 1954.

Nolte, Ernst, *Epoche* = *Der Faschismus in seiner Epoche,* Munich, 1963 (*The Three Faces of Fascism: Action Française, Italian Fascism, National Socialism,* London, 1965; New York, 1966).

————, *Faschismus* = *Der Faschismus von Mussolini zu Hitler,* Munich, 1968.

————, *Krise* = *Die Krise des liberalen Systems und die faschistischen Bewegungen,* Munich, 1968.

————, *Der Nationalsozialismus,* Berlin, 1970.

————, ed., *Theorien* = *Theorien über den Faschismus,* Cologne and Berlin, 1967.

Olden, Rudolf, *Hitler,* Amsterdam, 1936 (*Hitler,* New York, 1936; *Hitler the Pawn,* London, 1936).

Orlow, Dietrich, *The History of the Nazi Party 1919–1933,* Pittsburgh, 1969.

Papen, Franz von, *Der Wahrheit eine Gasse,* Munich, 1952 (*Memoirs,* New York and London, 1953).

Phelps, Reginald H., "Hitler als Parteiredner im Jahre 1920," VJHfZ, 1963:3.

————, "Hitlers grundlegende Rede über den Antisemitismus," VJHfZ, 1968:4.

Preiss, Hans, ed., *Adolf Hitler in Franken: Reden aus der Kampfzeit,* Munich, n.d.

Price, Ward, see: Ward Price, G.

Raeder, Erich, *Mein Leben,* 2 vols., Tübingen, 1956–57.

Rauschning, Hermann, *Gespräche mit Hitler,* Zurich, New York, 1940 (*Voice of Destruction,* New York, 1940; *Hitler Speaks,* London, 1939).

————, *Die Revolution des Nihilismus: Kulisse und Wirklichkeit im Dritten Reich,* 5th ed., Zurich and New York, 1938 (*The Revolution of Nihilism,* New York and London, 1939; British title: *Germany's Revolution of Destruction*).

Reck-Malleczewen, Friedrich P., *Diary of a Man in Despair,* New York, 1970.

Recktenwald, Johann, *Woran hat Adolf Hitler gelitten?,* Munich and Basel, 1963.

Reichmann, Eva Gabriele, *Flucht in den Hass: Die Ursachen der deutschen Judenkatastrophe,* Frankfurt a. M., n. d. (*Hostages of Civilization,* London, 1950).

Ribbentrop, Joachim von, *Zwischen London und Moskau,* Leoni, 1953 (*The Ribbentrop Memoirs,* London, 1954).

Riezler, Kurt, *Tagebücher, Aufsätze, Dokumente,* ed. Karl Dietrich Erdmann, Göttingen, 1972.

Ritter, Gerhard, *Carl Goerdeler und die deutsche Widerstandsbewegung,* Stuttgart, 1954.

Röhrs, Hans-Dietrich, *Hitler: Die Zerstörung einer Persönlichkeit,* Neckargemünd, 1965.

Rönnefahrt, Helmuth K. G., *Die Sudetenkrise in der internationalen Politik 1938,* 2 vols., Wiesbaden, 1961.

Roon, Ger van, *Neuordnung im Widerstand: Der Kreisauer Kreis innerhalb der Widerstandsbewegung,* Munich, 1967.

Rosenberg, Alfred, *Gold und Blut,* Munich, 1941. See also: Seraphim, Hans-Günther, ed.

Rosenberg, Arthur, see: Historikus.

Rothfels, Hans, *Opposition gegen Hitler: Eine Würdigung,* Frankfurt a. M., 1958 (*The German Opposition to Hitler: An Appraisal,* Chicago, 1962).

Roussy de Sales, Raoul de, see: *Hitler, Adolf, My New Order.*

Schellenberg, Walter, *Memoiren,* Cologne, 1956 (*The Labyrinth,* New York and London, 1956; British title: *The Schellenberg Memoirs*).

Schieder, Theodor, *Hermann Rauschnings "Gespräche mit Hitler" als Geschichtsquelle,* Opladen, 1972.

Schlabrendorff, Fabian von, *Offiziere gegen Hitler,* Frankfurt a. M. and Hamburg, 1959 (*The Secret War Against Hitler,* New York, 1965; London, 1966).

Schmeer, Karlheinz, *Die Regie des öffentlichen Lebens im Dritten Reich,* Munich, 1956.

Schmidt, Paul, *Statist auf diplomatischer Bühne 1923–1945: Erlebnisse eines Chefdolmetschers im Auswärtigen Amt mit den Staatsmännern Europas,* Bonn, 1950 (*Hitler's Interpreter,* New York and London, 1951).

Schmitthenner, Walter, and Buchheim, Hans, ed., *Der deutsche Widerstand gegen Hitler: Vier historisch-kritische Studien,* Cologne and Berlin, 1966.

Schoenbaum, David, *Die braune Revolution: Eine Sozialgeschichte des Dritten Reiches,* Cologne and Berlin, 1968.

Schramm, Percy Ernst, ed., *Kriegstagebuch des Oberkommandos der Wehrmacht,* 7 vols., Frankfurt a. M., 1961 ff. (cited as KTB/OKW).

Schubert, Günter, *Anfänge nationalsozialistischer Aussenpolitik,* Cologne, 1963.

Schwertfeger, Bernhard, *Rätsel um Deutschland,* Heidelberg, 1948.

Semler, Rudolf, *Goebbels—the Man Next to Hitler,* London, 1947.

Seraphim, Hans-Günther, ed., *Das politische Tagebuch Alfred Rosenbergs aus den Jahren 1934–35 und 1939–40,* Göttingen, 1956.

Sforza, Count Carlo, *European Dictatorships,* New York, 1931.

Shirer, William L., *A Berlin Diary,* New York and London, 1941.

———, *The Rise and Fall of the Third Reich,* New York and London, 1960.

Silone, Ignazio, *The School for Dictators,* New York and London, 1938.

Smith, Bradley F., *Adolf Hitler, His Family, Childhood and Youth,* Stanford, 1967.

Sombart, Werner, *Die Juden und das Wirtschaftsleben,* Munich and Leipzig, 1920.

Speer, Albert, *Inside the Third Reich,* New York and London, 1970.

Speidel, Hans, *Invasion 1944,* Tübingen & Stuttgart, 1961 (*We Defended Normandy,* London, 1951).

Stampfer, Friedrich, *Die vierzehn Jahre der ersten deutschen Republik,* Offenbach, 1947.

Steed, Wickham, "From Frederick the Great to Hitler: The Consistency of German Aims," in: *International Affairs,* 1938:17.

Stehlin, Paul, *Auftrag in Berlin,* Berlin, 1966.

Steinert, Marlis G., *Hitlers Krieg und die Deutschen,* Düsseldorf and Vienna, 1970.

Stephan, Werner, *Joseph Goebbels, Dämon einer Diktatur,* Stuttgart, 1949.

Stern, Fritz, "Bethmann Hollweg und der Krieg," *Recht und Staat,* no. 351/2.

Strasser, Otto, *Hitler und Ich,* Konstanz, 1948 (*Hitler and I,* Boston and London, 1940).

———, *Mein Kampf,* Frankfurt a. M., 1969.

Templewood, Viscount (Sir Samuel Hoare), *Nine Troubled Years,* London, 1954.

827

The Third Reich (published under the auspices of the International Council for Philosophy and Humanistic Studies and with the assistance of UNESCO), London, 1955.

Thyssen, Fritz, *I Paid Hitler*, London, 1941; repr. Port Washington, N.Y., 1971.

Tobias, Fritz, *Der Reichstagsbrand, Legende und Wirklichkeit*, Rastatt, 1962 (*The Reichstag Fire*, New York, 1964).

Trevor-Roper, Hugh R., *Blitzkrieg to Defeat: Hitler's War Directives 1939–1945*, New York, 1971.

———, ed., *The Bormann Letters*, London, 1954.

———, *The Last Days of Hitler*, New York, 3d ed., 1962.

———, ed., *Le Testament politique de Hitler*, Paris, 1959.

———, "The Mind of Adolf Hitler" = preface to *Hitler's Table Talk 1941–1944;* see under Hitler.

Trial of Major War Criminals Before the International Military Tribunal, 42 vols., Nuremberg, 1947–49 (cited as IMT).

Turner, Henry Ashby, "Faschismus und Antimodernismus in Deutschland," in: *Faschismus und Kapitalismus in Deutschland.*

———, "Fritz Thyssen und *I Paid Hitler,*" in: *Faschimus und Kapitalismus in Deutschland.*

Tyrell, Albrecht, *Führer befiehl . . . Selbstzeugnisse aus der Kampfzeit der NSDAP*, Düsseldorf, 1969.

Unruh, Friedrich Franz von, "Nationalsozialismus," series of articles in: *Frankfurter Zeitung*, February 22–March 3, 1931.

USSBS = United States Strategic Bombing Survey.

VB = *Völkischer Beobachter.*

Veblen, Thorstein, *Imperial Germany and the Industrial Revolution*, New York, 1954.

Vermeil, E., "The Origin, Nature and Development of German Nationalist Ideology in the 19th and 20th Centuries," in: *The Third Reich.*

Viénot, Pierre, *Is Germany Finished?*, London, 1931; New York, 1932.

VJHfZ = *Vierteljahreshefte für Zeitgeschichte.*

Ward Price, G., *I Knew These Dictators*, London, 1937.

Warlimont, Walter, *Im Hauptquartier der Wehrmacht 1939–1945*, Bonn, 1964 (*Inside Hitler's Headquarters 1939–45*, New York, 1964).

Weinberg, Gerhard L., "Der deutsche Entschluss zum Angriff auf die Sowjetunion," VJHfZ, 1953:2.

Weizsäcker, Ernst von, *Erinnerungen*, Munich, Leipzig, Freiburg i. Br., 1950 (*The Memoirs of Ernst von Weizsäcker*, Chicago and London, 1951).

Wendt, Bernd-Jürgen, *München 1938: England zwischen Hitler und Preussen*, Stuttgart, 1965.

Wernecke, Klaus, *Der Wille zur Weltgeltung*, Düsseldorf, 1969.

Wheeler-Bennett, John W., *The Nemesis of Power: The German Army in Politics 1918–1945*, London and New York, 1954; 2nd ed., 1964.

Wiedemann, Fritz, *Der Mann, der Feldherr werden wollte*, Velbert, 1964.

Zechlin, Egmont, "Die Illusion vom begrenzten Krieg," *Die Zeit*, Sept. 17, 1965.

828